GRAFFITI 365

BY Jay "J.SON" Edlin

FOREWORD BY
Andrew "Zephyr" Witten

ABRAMS, New York

FOREWORD

"Somewhere, a portion of contemporary art has to exist as an example of what the art and its context were meant to be."

—Donald Judd

"It's a small world, but I wouldn't want to paint it."

—Steven Wright

I spotted my first baby on Canal Street.

It was 1979, and Futura and I were employed by the City of New York, painting signs for a Morningside Heights beautification program [read: Gentrification Program]. Every Monday morning, we'd hop the turnstiles at 110th Street and Broadway and subway ourselves downtown to Canal Street to pilfer supplies at Pearl Paint. We were probably nice guys, and friendly with Alan, Pearl's manager, but with a paycheck calculated at $50 a sign . . . Well, you know. Sorry, Alan. We owe you.

The Mudd Club, downtown's *extremely* downtown answer to Studio 54, was the epicenter of the neo-punk No Wave scene. Because it was located on White Street, a block south of Pearl Paint, Canal Street was common territory for punk-band postering and occasional one-off acts of avant-garde street decoration. But these babies were different . . .

The babies, quickly hand-rendered yet remarkably exact, were drawn onto the concrete edge around the exit of the subway station. They were sweet and fresh, and Futura and I immediately knew we were looking at something special.

The babies were rendered with *our* tool, a black Niji marker. In 1979, the black Niji magic marker was *the* staple for all self-respecting vandals. And had the babies not been so damn cute, they could have easily made us mad. Graffiti writers are, if nothing else, territorial, pathologically possessive, and bombastic. We consider even our magic markers sacred. We don't want *you* using them.

The babies multiplied like Chinese wisteria. Within weeks they were everywhere, and then it was all about "Who?"

The "Who?," we soon discovered, was a low-talking, mousy kid from Pennsylvania Dutch Country named Keith. He looked as square as Mr. Rogers, but was not. He was, as it turned out, an ambitious student at SVA, the local art college for kids whose parents had a few dollars they were willing to risk. Like us, Keith loved rock music, drawing pictures, and smoking strong marijuana. Unlike us, he possessed extraordinary focus, a tireless work ethic, and a grasp of art history. Keith's relentless, image-based visual assault on Manhattan had already begun. When it was over, New York, and the world, would never be the same.

And so it was that New York Street Art—and the international street art movement—was born. Thank you, Keith Haring. We miss you terribly. You should have grown old with us, if for no other reason than to have witnessed your own legacy. Guess what? Your babies had babies. A lot of babies.

Now, let's talk about the book. The idea of Terror 161 creating the volume you are holding in your hands is a great one, and I'll tell you why. However, in the interest of full transparency, I did, at first, wonder why a publisher chose Bluebeard to write about sculling.

Terror (aka "J.SON") is a veteran of several particularly impassioned graffiti wars, and a guy whom I have (lovingly) nicknamed "The Bad Cop." Terror hands out accolades grudgingly, if at all. He knows what he likes, and he knows what he hates. He is an "old school" aesthetic curmudgeon. "Art" is not something he rhapsodizes about. He would put a dirty boot on an original Matisse to get to a dog-eared photo of a Billy 167 piece, and that's why I love him so. We need Terror, because, as this book loudly proclaims, he looks at the burger, and he couldn't give a rat's ass about the china it's served on.

The litany of writing on the topic of street art, and urban graffiti, almost makes it compulsory to defend the presence of more. But while the work by some of the artists within these pages may be familiar, this book is a big first. Because it is penned by a Bronx graffiti writer who began his own illegal wall-application process in 1972 (Year 2 on the graffiti calendar), there is an exclusive uniqueness to these pages. Welcome to what happens when a set of veteran eyes scans and accesses the continuum of illegally applied, or mass (and massive) public art. Imagine The History of Rock as explained by Jimi Hendrix, if that helps.

According to Terror, writing this book has opened his eyes. He now views the work of Swoon and Banksy with a different set of eyes altogether. The respect he once reserved exclusively for the likes of Chain and Seen is no longer thus reserved. With eyes widened by the excitement of pure revelation, Terror conveyed to me that street art, by abandoning the name as the centerpiece, has moved into a different space altogether—a place of "limitless possibilities."

The terrain around these artists, "street" and "graffiti," has shifted dramatically since Terror and I roamed the train yards with cans in hands. As the stadium, the ticket prices, the rules, the goal posts—and the goals—have moved, so have we. With the term "millionaire street artist" now a part of the cultural lexicon, the aspiration of getting your tag onto the D train's lead car can be dismissed as laughably quaint—so distant it is from the sweet lure of capitalist opportunism. Fortunately, through it all, Terror still appreciates the D train's front panel as the appropriate frame for an ambitious, upcoming artist.

—Zephyr

Andrew "Zephyr" Witten has been painting graffiti for more than thirty years, with the New York Times *dubbing him "the elder statesman of graffiti." He is the author of* Dondi White: Style Master General *and has written for* Vibe, The

INTRODUCTION

Growing up against the backdrop of the civil rights movement, gangs, hippies, and Vietnam War protests gave me a feeling of powerlessness.

The stories of San Francisco's flower children, communal living, free love, and a Utopian ideal never seemed closer than the images I saw in *Life* and *Look* magazines. But while my young age prevented me from participating in any forms of organized rebellion, it occurred to me that revolution begins at home. Tired of letting my parents make all my decisions for me, I saw juvenile delinquency as a very attractive alternative.

I remember first noticing the name "Taki 183" appearing all over the city, crudely scrawled with a skinny-tipped marker, in late '69 or early '70. My daily commute took me through the South Bronx and Harlem. While the adults on the Riverdale Express bus read their morning papers, I read the city's walls outside my window. Messages of protest adorning ghetto walls and boarded-up storefronts—Viva el Puerto Rico Libre, Buy Black, Off the Pig—started to disappear. Taki 183 spurred followers with a different message: We exist! Along with Taki 183, Snake 1, Joe 136, Junior 161, and Cay 161 became some of the earliest settlers in an unclaimed territory.

I wondered when these phantom celebrities did their dirty work, how they got away with it, and, most of all, who they were. My insular, alabaster neighborhood offered no clues. My existence as a scrawny, prep-school attending, parent-controlled robot sickened me. Graffiti, like some dysfunctional foreign legion, offered the promise of a more exciting life.

I bought a black Dri Mark marker and walked to the back seat of the Riverdale Express bus each morning. I had no idea how to become a graffiti artist, but I began scrawling my first tag, the ridiculously long and corny "The Amazing Kid 235." I had no style, but had staked my claim as king of the rear of the Riverdale buses by the end of 1971. There was no place to go but up.

By 1972, graffiti moved from walls and buses to the outsides of subway trains, first on the #1 Broadway line and, within a few months, on the lines running through the Bronx. I shortened my name to Tarantula 235 and added a crude little spider under my tag—my attempt to emulate Stay High 149's icon approach.

I began to hit the streets with my little Dri Mark, targeting anything with a smooth metal surface, but soon grew bored with my marker's limitations. Real writers used Uni-Wides and Mini-Wides filled with every color of Flo-master ink in the rainbow, but nobody I knew could tell me where to get them. And I had begun to watch the trains and witness the first masterpieces: A T. Rex 131 top-to-bottom on the #1 line mesmerized me. Its neatness and grandiosity exuded an elegance I couldn't even imagine aspiring to.

I began shoplifting spray paint from my local hardware store. Blessed with a cherubic, Kosher countenance, clerks never suspected me. In 1973, I began a nocturnal weekend spray-paint campaign that made me king of Riverdale within a year. Other local writers had popped up by this time, but nobody knew my identity. Kids asked if anyone knew who Tarantula was—that combination of fame and anonymity has always been graffiti's essence to me. By the end of the year, I had all the tools of the trade at my disposal, so I began to plot my train debut. I had also come out of the graff closet and networked with other local luminaries: Zap 231 (aka . . . Trail), Cheetah 2, Neon 2, and Blaze 235.

On a mild winter afternoon in 1973, we popped our subway cherries and ventured into the 242nd Street train yard: fourteen lanes of #1 trains on elevated tracks. Armed with two or three cans of paint apiece, we crossed over into the big time. I pulled out a can of white, stood on the wood covering the third rail, and reached as high as I could on the train to start my "T," but could barely reach above the blue line. My resulting piece, rendered at about 60 percent of respectable size, made me feel as if I had walked on the moon and planted my flag. Our group returned the following weekend, with similarly successful results. I got to see my first piece run across the Broadway elevation. I thought I had arrived. Stalking the trains for weeks in search of my second piece, I was in for a rude awakening: A Laz piece appeared smack in the middle of my name. Laz, a respected writer who hit trains with Moses 147 and B.One, the kings of Broadway, gave me the respect due someone of my stature—none.

By 1974, coming up with an original, unused name was almost impossible—thousands of kids wrote graffiti by then, and all the good ones were taken—but I longed for a name change. I racked my brain for a shorter, cooler name than Tarantula 235, but kept coming up empty. Finally, inspiration struck—in history class. I usually zoned out, but when I heard the phrase "reign of terror," I knew I had found my new moniker. I changed my number to 161, because Junior 161 and Cay 161 were the earliest kings of graffiti I remembered and idolized. Terror 161: the perfect Superman fantasy with which to escape my Clark Kent reality.

For the next two years, the #1 yard would be my second home. Local writers Tanx 2, Trail, Cheetah 2, and I would form the nucleus of The Masters of Broadway, aka The MOB, the crew I founded in 1975. The crew grew into one of the most dominant of its time, peaking in 1977, when Use 2 became king of Broadway.

I quit writing in 1976, having done about a hundred pieces on my home line and lots of insides. But I never stopped watching the #1 trains, sadly observing the last remnants of The MOB's work disappear. I also watched the work of the guys who stayed in the game, wishing that my name still mattered.

By 1979, my life approached normality. I attended college and manned the deli counter in the local supermarket for minimum wage. That same year, an old graffiti partner of mine got a job in my supermarket as a stock boy. Now in our twenties, our train days were nothing more than a youthful memory. We began to hang out and drink together after work. One night, after a few too many beers, we grabbed a few cans of spray paint and drove to the #1 yard. I did a horrible Terror piece, while he caught some Ammo tags in the parking lot above the yard. We never thought of it as anything serious or entertained any notion of doing it again—until we did it again. It still felt good, and it occurred to us how simple it would be to get away with it as grown men, with cars, in our twenties. Cops didn't suspect anyone over sixteen of writing graffiti. And certainly, no graffiti writers drove cars!

Soon, a few laughs became a serious undertaking, and Ammo and I came back to our beloved Broadway line, grown men playing a children's game. We made our presence known with alacrity. Almost nobody remembered us. The few people we ran into at the train yard averaged five to eight years younger than us. Writers often mistook us for cops. Paint stores didn't give us a second look as we cleaned out their racks. Our cars allowed us newfound freedom and a mobility we never dreamed of in the '70s. Ammo and I branched out to other lines and did ten times more damage than we had in our previous incarnations.

In the early '80s, things began to change. Crack and angel dust became the drugs of choice, and with them, a new wave of street violence spilled over into the graffiti world. A writer getting shot or stabbed became a real possibility. Graffiti territoriality meant that certain crews controlled specific yards and lay-ups. To venture into hostile turf was akin to suicide.

But galleries began to take an interest in graffiti, and the pioneers of street art began putting their own stamp on things. A few months earlier, I had begun to notice a new form of public writing. Icon-based, with imagery instead of letters, it bore no resemblance to the graffiti I practiced. The most ominous of this early group was Richard Hambleton, who drew eerie black paint-brushed silhouettes in alleys and parking lots. Kenny Scharf began plastering the city with cartoon imagery borrowed from the Jetsons and Flintstones.

I met Keith Haring at the "Beyond Words" show he co-curated with Futura 2000 at the Mudd Club in 1981. Keith had already begun hitting the streets and subway stations with markers and chalk, introducing the world to his whimsical hieroglyphics. An out-of-towner, art-school type, Keith lacked any of the criminality and machismo exhibited by most graffiti artists. Keith attended SVA and was a staple of the club scene. I let him sign my blackbook the night of the "Beyond Worlds" opening as a courtesy, but had no interest in him or his art.

Graffiti was changing. I grew up in the Classic Rock Era and didn't love the new music. Fictionalized media accounts of the Subway Culture that packaged graffiti as an element of hip-hip didn't resemble the reality I lived. Watching guys who I looked up to on the trains sign autographs and party with rock stars seemed against the grain of the illegality and rebelliousness that made graffiti exciting. Unlike many of my friends, I lacked the talent and desire to pursue an art career.

I didn't have much time left. I was getting older—ancient by graffiti standards. In 1973, we refused to believe the rumors that Stay High 149 was twenty-three years old. The entire graff universe knew that sixteen marked retirement age; I quit, for the second and final time, in 1984, at twenty-six.

When the subway graffiti movement ended in 1989, a lot of the paint previously designated for underground pursuits found its way into the light. I noticed street art proliferating. Stencils of rats began appearing around rat-infested tenements; stencils of street kids in hoodies began appearing in crack spots.

In the mid-1990s, Cost and Revs blurred the lines between graffiti and street art with a multimedia campaign that saw the city plastered with thousands of wheat-paste adverts offering a variety of pronouncements such as: COST FUCKED MADONNA, REVSUICIDE, and even a phone number where they could be reached. Shepard Fairey launched his OBEY GIANT campaign, putting in massive work worldwide and enlisting legions of acolytes to put his work up for him. UK stencilist Banksy caught fire, placing anti-establishment, humor-driven conceptual work in the most populated corners of Bristol. The trains had died, but a new generation, with a closer connection to art school and skateboarding than subway trains, was waiting in the wings.

I sat by, growing more bitter as these art-school kids set auction-house records. I didn't respect these "street artists," who spent days constructing a large portion of their art in the safety of a studio before slapping it up on a wall, facing little risk—even if apprehended.

When I set out to write this book, something Zephyr said resonated in my thick skull: "Every graffiti artist thinks graffiti ended the day after they quit." I realized that my notions of street art were myopic and set out to immerse myself in a world I had dismissed without experiencing. In sourcing street-art images for this project, culminating in a trip with Martha Cooper and Lady Aiko to Art Basel 2010, I can honestly say that style masters and toys exist in the factions of both genres. Street art has an unlimited range of media and looks. A layperson could never mistake a Judith Supine collage for a Banksy stencil, while a perception that all graffiti looks the same persists within the art world's highbrow set. I was pleasantly surprised when Lady Aiko, a founding member of the street art collective Faile, asked to do a collaborative wall with me.

For now, the term "street-art millionaire" has no graffiti correlative. But in my purist, time-warped eyes, the work of Haring, Basquiat, Banksy, and Fairey will always be like learning a second language. There are some tricks an old dog just can't learn. My heart lies with the moving monuments of Riff 170, Phase 2, Tracy 168, the late, great Billy 167, and their ilk. I yearn for the days when train yards were easy pickings and pieces ran untouched for years, but were I to mount a comeback, I could see myself wheatpasting a train-size poster of one of my whole cars onto the outside of a #1 train.

—JAY "J.SON" EDLIN

Born and raised in the Riverdale section of the Bronx, Tarantula 235 was arrested for tagging the door of PS 141 in January 1974; his parents grounded him, hoping graffiti was just a rebellious phase he'd soon outgrow. Today, his own children wonder the same thing about him. Tarantula 235 became Terror 161 in late 1974 and then J.SON in 1980. Founder of The Masters of Broadway crew on the #1 Broadway line, he would become one of the few remnants of the '70s to flourish in the violent, media-crazed '80s era of graffiti culture. He has written extensively on the culture from an "in the trenches" perspective.

001

11 Spring Street

Since the 1980s, a building in the SoHo section of Manhattan served as ground zero for urban artists from around the world. The hulking brick structure sported a facade caked in innumerable layers of wheatpaste and paint, left intact by the building's eccentric owner. When the property was sold to condo developers in 2006, the new owner, Caroline Cummings, became fascinated with the building's history. She reached out to Marc and Sara Schiller, leading street-art experts, and began a discussion on how to give the street artists one last hurrah before the famous facade was wiped clean.

In the final weeks of 2006, the Schillers invited street artists from all over the planet to come and leave their last marks on 11 Spring Street, but with a twist: This time, the work would be featured on the *inside* of the building. And come they did. More than fifty artists flocked to the site from as nearby as Brooklyn and as far away as Australia; they worked tirelessly over several weeks, eventually covering every inch of the interior of the building with works in countless media. Finally, the weekend before Christmas, the doors were thrown open to the public, and almost six thousand people poured through them to celebrate street art at its peak and to witness one of the last triumphs of public art over gentrification.

Today, 11 Spring Street stands clean as a whistle—divided into three condominiums and on the market for an estimated $35 million.

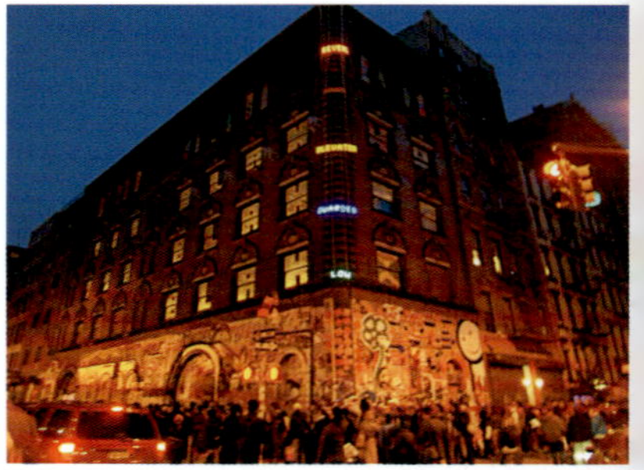

Photograph by Jake Dobkin (streetsy.com). New York City, 2008.
Detail: Photograph by Ray Mock. New York City, 2008.

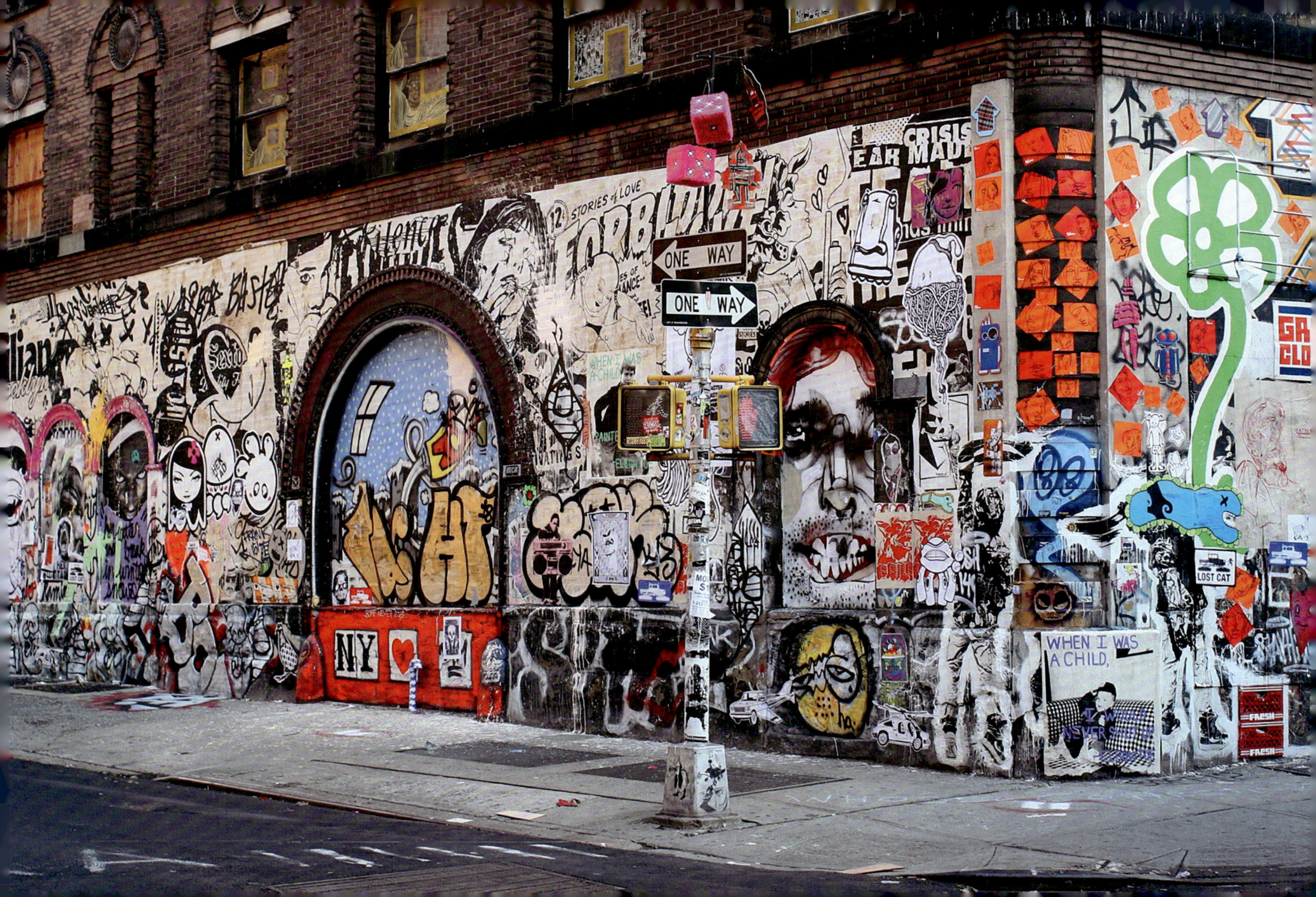
CRISIS
STORIES of LOVE
ONE WAY
ONE WAY
WHEN I WAS A CHILD,
NY
LOST CAT
FRESH
FRESH

002

3YB

The Three Yard Boys (or 3YB) began in 1973 as a crew of Harlem writers that included Stan 153, Piper 1, Jace 2, Rome 150, Boogie 150, and others. Many in the group had attended the same elementary school and started writing at the same time. When Stan 153 quit writing in 1974, he turned the crew over to Cliff 159 (see 071), who transformed it from a footnote in graffiti history to the biggest crew ever.

In 1975, Cliff 159 went all-city with his writing partner, In (see 171), at his side. The two hit up 3YB everywhere on the IRT subway lines and then did the unthinkable: They started recruiting writers from the lesser-known BMT and IND lines. This gave the pair access to almost any yard in the city and a large amount of paint with which to go bombing. Cliff gave the BMT writers his racking spots and then taxed them for the paint they stole, usually taking 20 percent off the top.

3YB was unstoppable in 1975, with Cliff, In, Jester (see 183), Diablo, Stim 1, Tee, Peace 108, Be 3, and others getting up with whole-cars, burners, and throw-ups. That same year, tragedy struck the crew when Stim 1 died while trying to jump from a moving train during a police chase in Brooklyn.

In 1976, 3YB was the largest crew out there—and that was a problem. If practically anyone could be in it, then what was its status? New crews, like the Death Squad (see 086), TMT, and the Fab 5 (see 120), were forming that kept their membership limited, and that's where the real writers wanted to be. By 1977, 3YB's domination had ended, and Cliff 159 entered the U.S. Army.

Piece by Ben 167 3YB; throw-ups (left to right) by In and Dye 167 (aka Jester). Photograph by Keith Baugh. New York City, 1975.

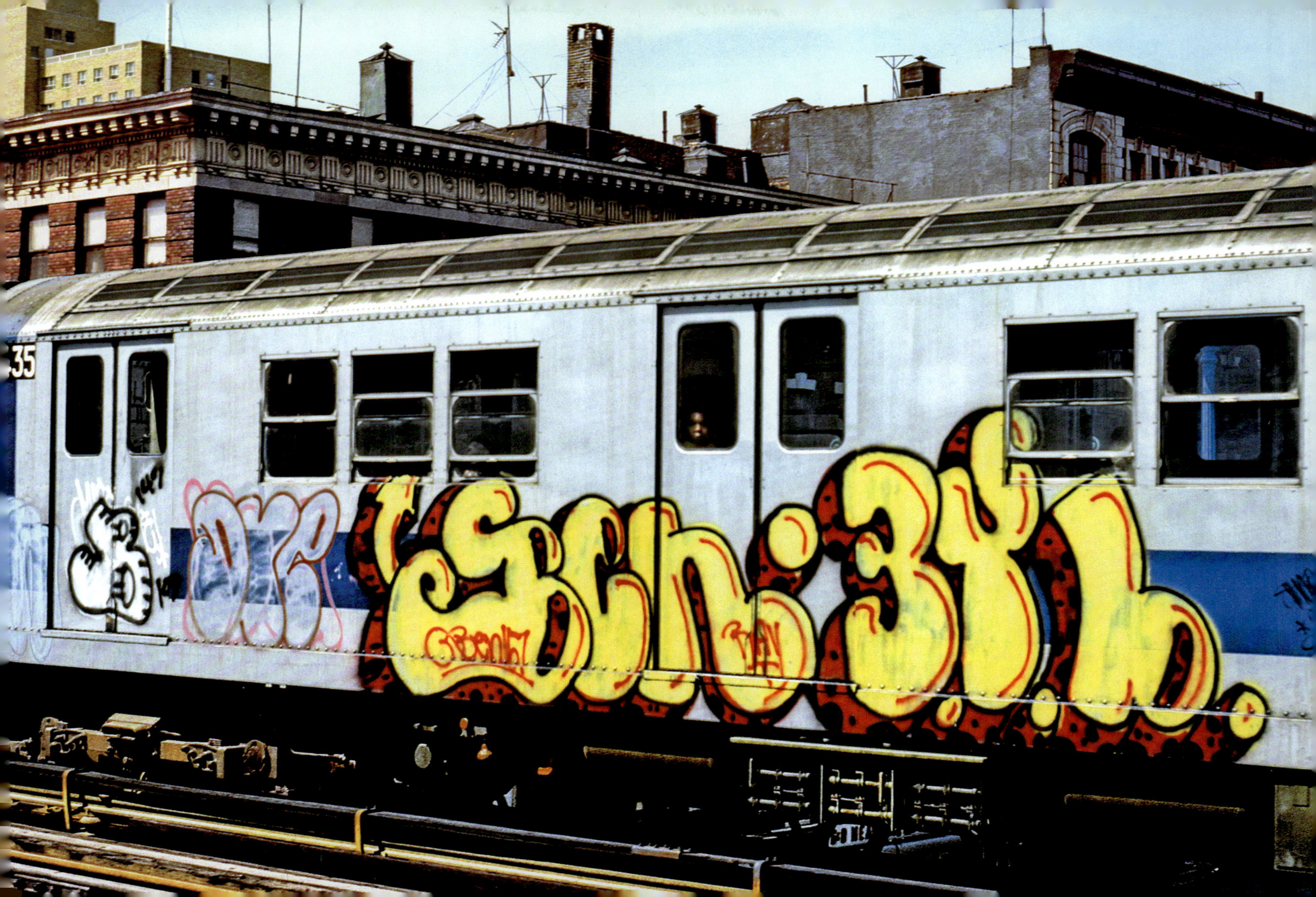
35

5 Pointz

Five Pointz is an industrial factory in Long Island City, just ten minutes by subway from midtown Manhattan. When you first view the building, it resembles the monolith at the beginning of *2001: A Space Odyssey*, but as you move toward the five-story structure, different colors appear to dot the facade, as in a pointillist painting. Upon closer examination, colors break apart and turn into names, and you realize that you're staring at an entire city block of graffiti.

The crew 5 Pointz originated as the Phun Factory, which was created in 1973 by Pat DiLillo; the crew used the factory as an alternative place for kids to paint graffiti murals. Pat recruited Iz the Wiz (see 177) to run the place, and Iz became the ambassador to a new generation of European writers, who were thrilled to meet a New York legend.

In 2002, after some battles with the landlord, the Phun Factory morphed into 5 Pointz, and Meres took over the helm. The factory's large production walls became a model for graffiti crews from all over the world, and writers began calling it "The Institute of Higher Burnin'." Those who seemed to benefit the most from 5 Pointz were the old-school writers who celebrated "Old Timer's Day" with a barbecue twice a year, painting and trading stories from their subway days while signing autographs for hundreds of fans.

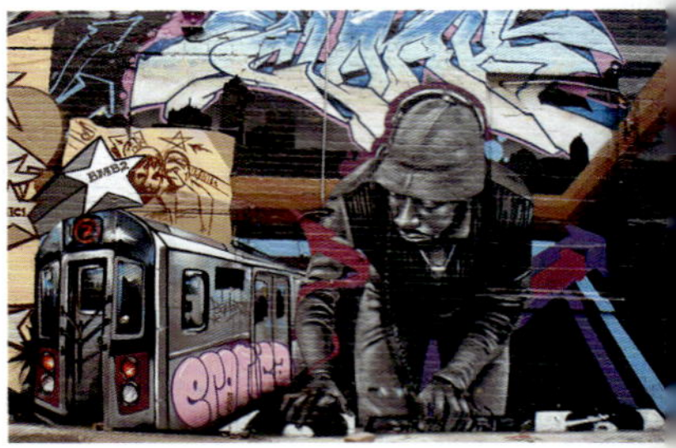

Photographs by Ernie Paniccoli. Queens, New York City, 2002.

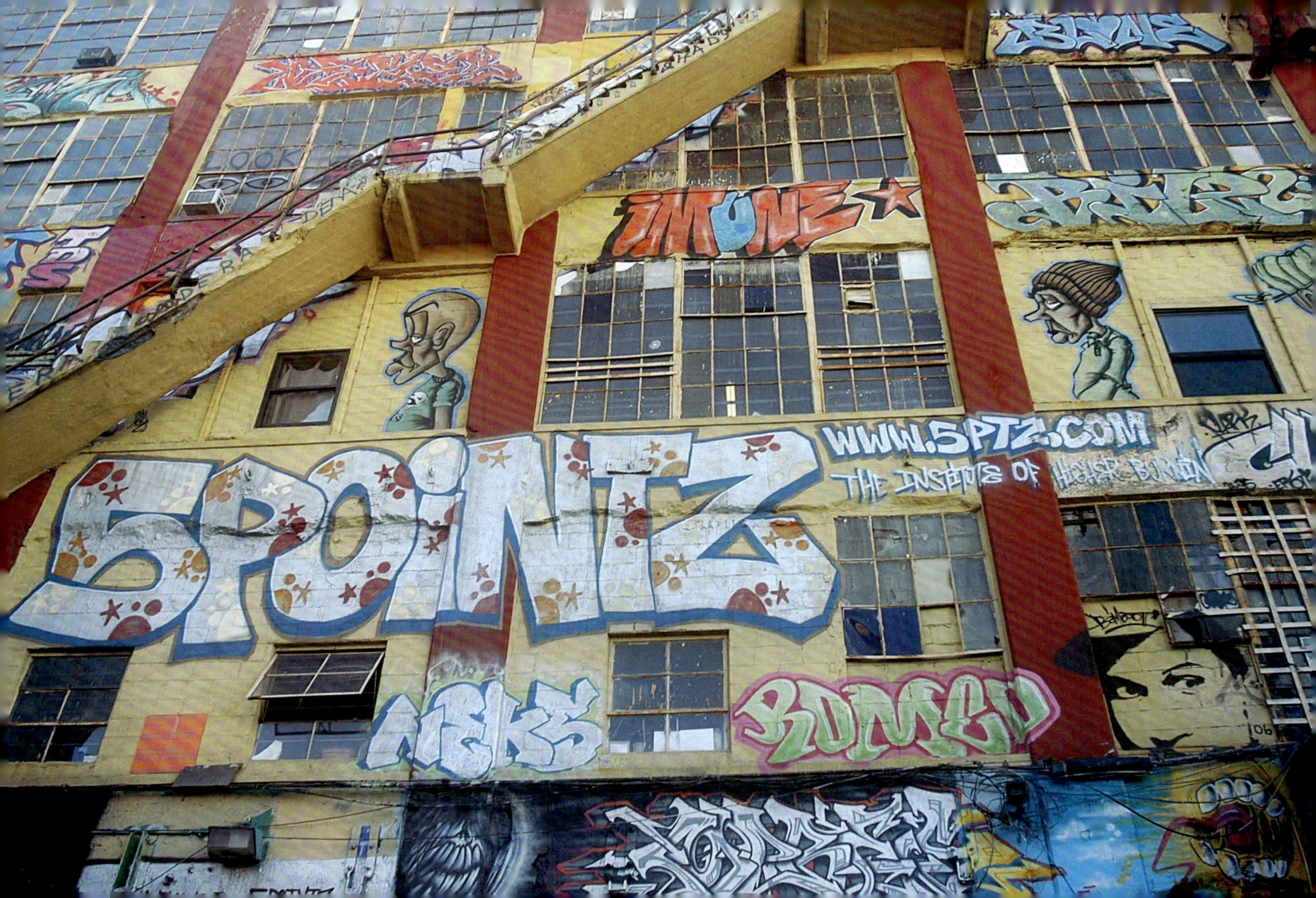
IMUNE
LOOK
WWW.5PTZ.COM
THE INSTITUTE OF HIGHER BURNIN
5POINTZ

A1one

Born and based in Tehran, Iran, A1one has altered the landscape of his city. The first artist to make his mark on the walls of Iran's capital, A1one created a unique visual language by fusing Iranian folk art, Farsi calligraphy, and Western graffiti.

Introduced to street art in 1998 by Nima, an Iranian rapper living in Germany, A1one continued his exploration of it on the Internet. He first hit the streets of Tehran in 2003 with a stencil inspired by Munch's painting *The Scream*. As a personal response to the pressures of the University of Tehran, A1one sprayed the image on the university's walls.

The authorities in Tehran were uncertain how to respond to this new art form and have not yet taken a legal stand against it, so the atmosphere has remained receptive to A1one and the new generation of Iranian street artists whose work A1one has inspired. In the past few years, A1one's murals, stencils, wheatpastes, and stickers have traveled throughout the world. His work has been exhibited in major European capitals, at the Melbourne Stencil Festival, and in New York City. A1one is also the founder of Kolah Studio, the center of a fervent Iranian underground art movement.

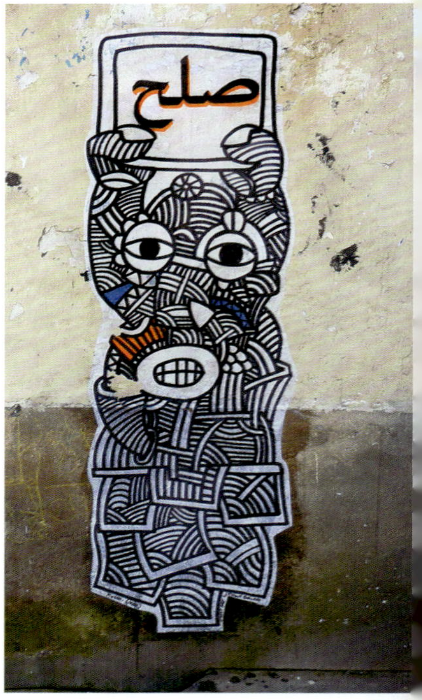

Photograph courtesy of A1one.
Tehran, Iran, c. 2008.
Detail: Photograph by Eric Marechal.
Paris, 2010.

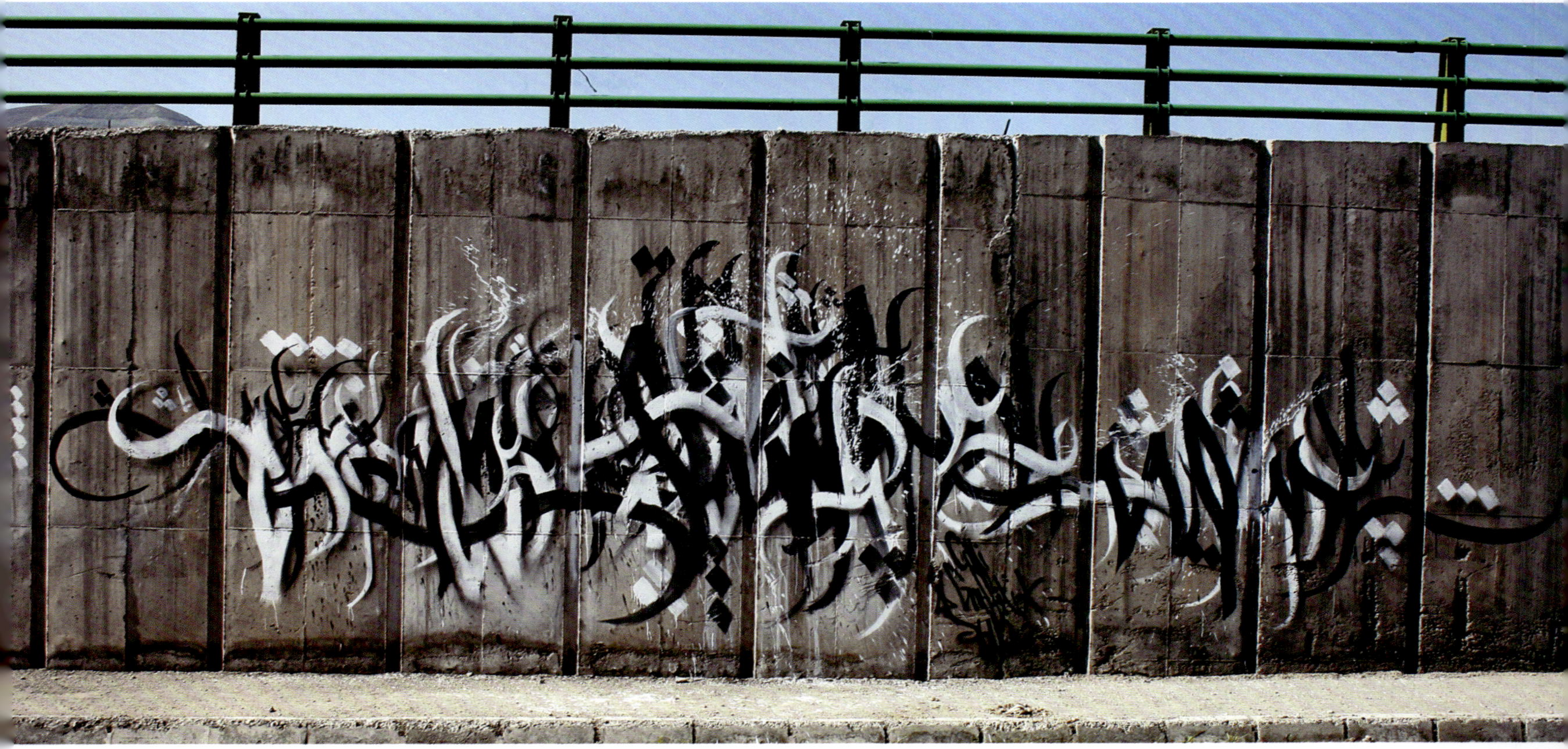

abandoned stations

During the course of its history, the MTA has rendered a handful of train stations obsolete, due to decreasing passenger usage or the expansion of other stations. There are over a dozen "ghost stations" scattered throughout the system, visible to subway riders for a few fleeting seconds as trains roar by their former stopovers.

Graffiti writers have been attracted to these forgotten outposts like moths to a flame. The stations remain illuminated after their discontinuance, and storage closets within them are still used by maintenance workers—easy prey for fame-craving kids willing to brave a long walk along dark tracks to the distant light. One of the system's most popular targets was the station at Broadway and 91st Street on the #1 line. Its vast tiled surfaces lent themselves to pieces on a grand scale.

If a writer entered and left the station undetected and hid every time a train passed by, his mission could be accomplished with ease. The next step would be getting on the train, pressing his face against the window, and peering into the darkened tunnel. Then, like a bolt of lightning, the self-styled billboard announcing his existence would appear for a glorious five seconds. Nobody else on the train would notice, but he'd know he was famous.

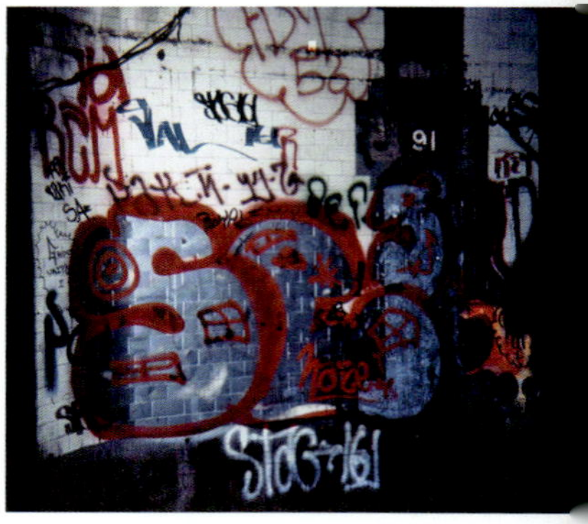

Photograph by Logan Hicks.
Croix Rouge Station, Paris, 2010.
Detail: Piece by SE-3/Haze; tags by Stag 161 and FDT 56.
Photograph by Matt Weber.
91st Street Station, New York City, 1973.

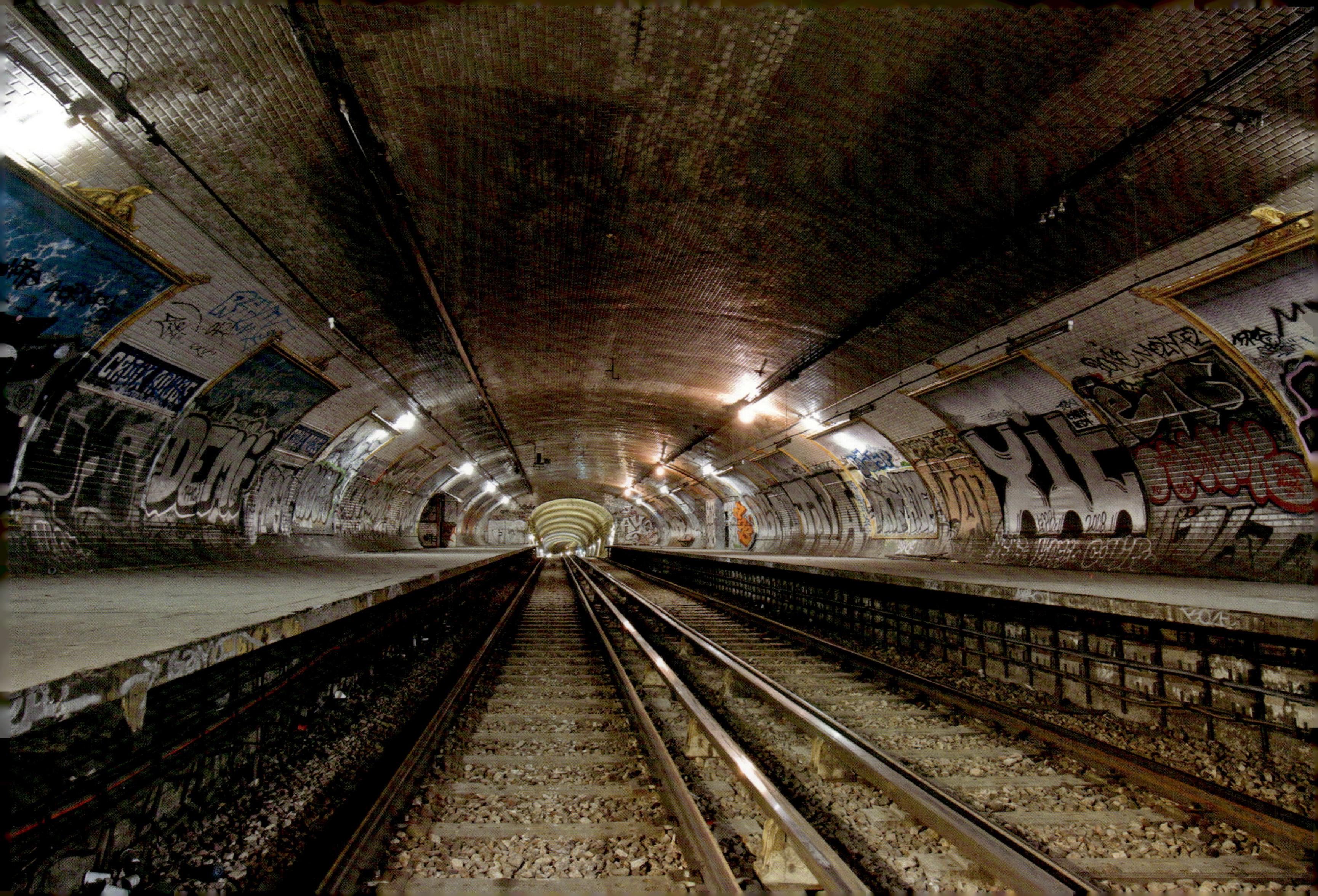

Above

When street art hit its stride in the first years of the new millennium, artists began exploring mediums beyond traditional painting, often moving as far as installation and conceptual sculpture. Above is just such an experimental artist. A mysterious character, rumored to be from Alaska, Above has been pathologically paranoid about his identity being revealed, but is equally obsessed with proliferating his moniker and getting press coverage for his campaigns and projects. Above traveled the world extensively from 2002 onward, depositing simple, two-dimensional arrows cut from cardboard or thin wood, stenciled with a solid-color arrow and shadow, and a word. Most often, each side of the board would carry an oppositional or complementary word, for example "Rise" written on one side and "Above" on the other.

Later in the decade, Above embarked on several epic voyages, eventually traveling to more than sixty cities in forty-five countries across the world. Along the way, Above would create large-scale murals in downtrodden communities, using his clever take on typography and wordplay. In 2006, Above created a large-scale installation in the Wooster Collective's [see 359] landmark 11 Spring Street show [see 001] in New York City.

One of Above's most notable collaborative trips, in 2007, was through Central and South America with noted street artist and wordsmith Ripo [see 279], during which they traveled and painted in Brazil, Mexico, Argentina, Peru, Chile, and other locales.

Photograph by Steve Rhodes.
Los Angeles, 2009.

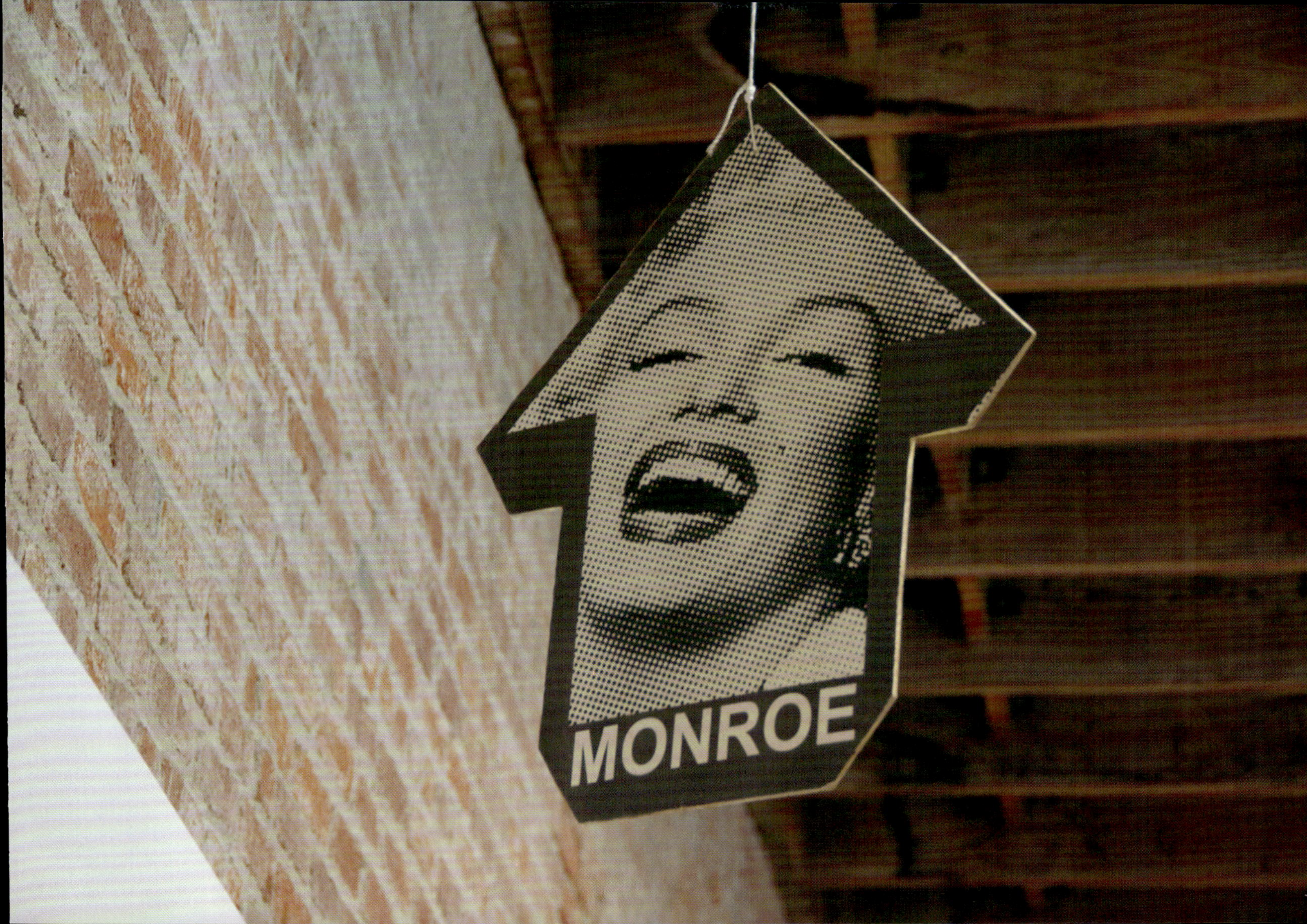
MONROE

acid etching

Staking a claim to public spaces motivates graffiti artists to risk life and liberty in pursuit of an insular form of fame that's difficult for the "straight" world to comprehend.

Once, the New York City subways served as the most visible outlet for graffiti artists to showcase their skills—this is no longer the case. Highway writing is removed within days. Desperate times call for desperate measures, and graffiti writers, like cockroaches, are resilient creatures. Scratchiti—using a box cutter or rock to carve your name onto transparent surfaces such as subway windows and bus shelters—became the last resort of a once proud culture. These markings were pure vandalism and offered nothing artful. Permanent? Yes. Stylish? No. Not possible with such primitive tools.

Acid etch and etch bath, products designed to make pretty designs on glass, inadvertently handed graffiti artists the most effective weapons to date in the war on their art. Homemade markers filled with formerly benign decorative chemicals could permanently melt their monikers into any glass or metal surface without sacrificing style. The acid markers took some getting used to, as the image, like a Polaroid picture, develops gradually before your eyes. But the loss of instant visual gratification was a small price to pay for permanency—once a window or bus shelter receives an acid bath, it's a wrap. Windows hit with etch markers must wear their ugly scars or be replaced. Metal surfaces, such as shiny subway-car exteriors, can never regain their original luster. Graffiti is not always pretty.

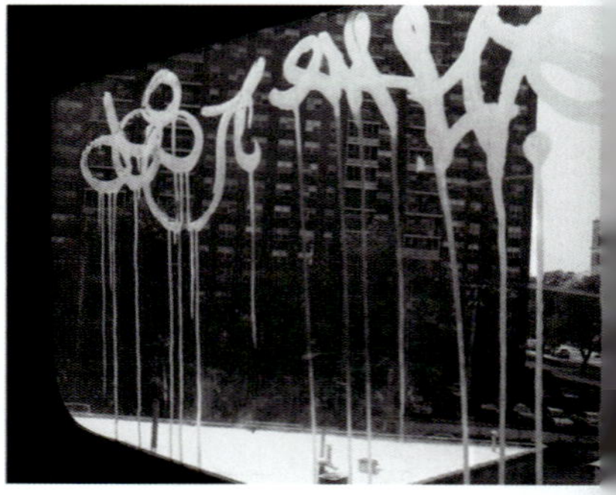

Photographs by Matt Weber. New York City, 2006.

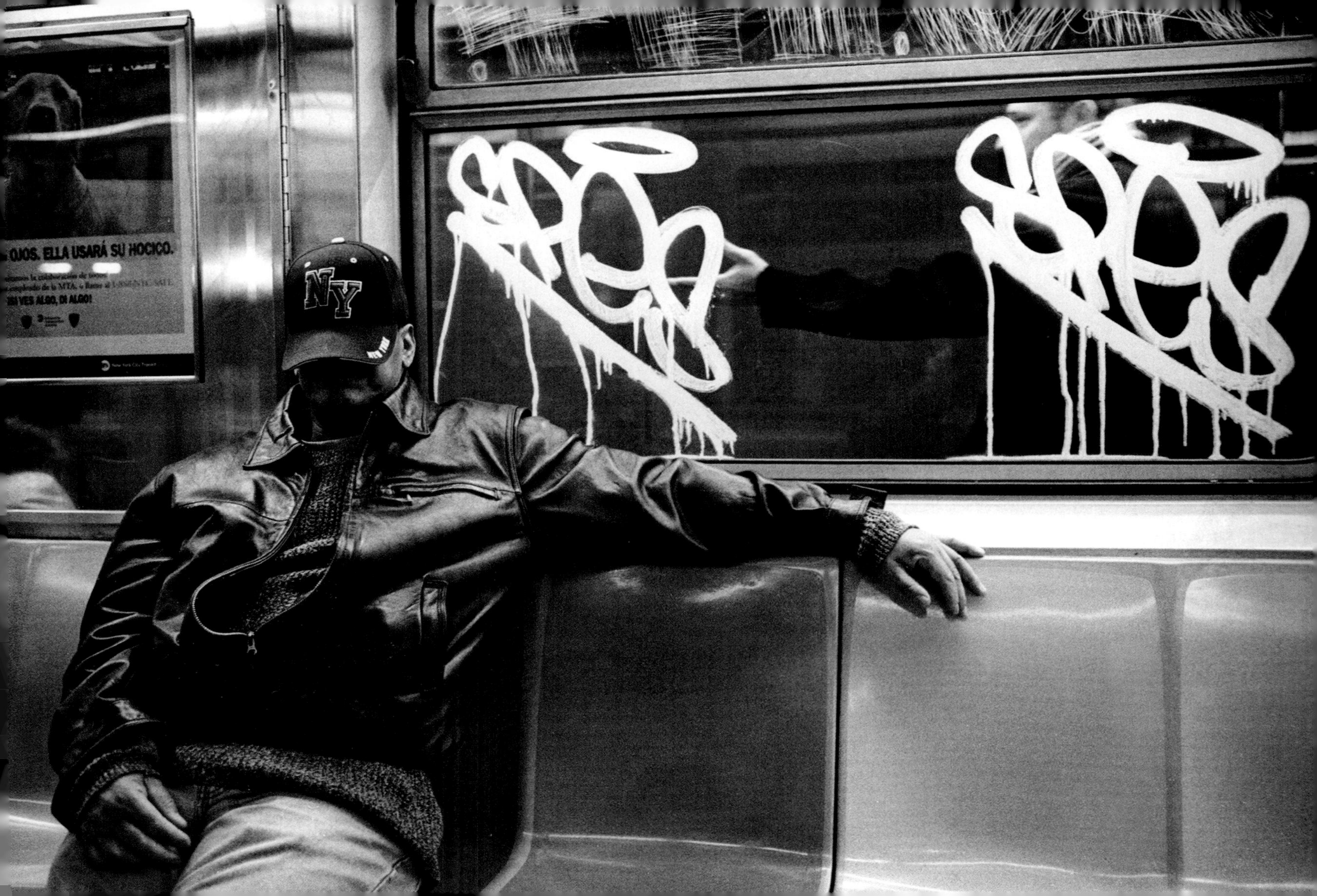
OJOS. ELLA USARÁ SU HOCICO.
SI VES ALGO, DI ALGO!
NY

Adek

Adek moved to New York City several years ago from the West Coast. His San Francisco bombing partner, New York expatriate MQ, must have forgotten to warn him that graffiti writers in New York had been reduced to permission-wall painters or wheatpaste and stencil applicators. Hardly the place for a man using the old-school method of bombing illegally for infamy's sake.

Since his arrival, Adek has destroyed the Big Apple as if he had a permit. He has claimed the city's streets with marker tags, giant throw-ups in the most populated areas, and super-wide fat cap tags on those roll-down steel gates that are scheduled to be legislated out of existence. Recently, Adek and a few of his boys blasted a Shepard Fairey [see 124] mural on Houston Street with a barrage of silver and black throw-ups. When Adek's work was removed from the wall, he came back and reclaimed the spot. Adek has undoubtedly reached the top of the Vandal Squad's most-wanted list. His outdated approach to graffiti may be unsettling to the Wooster Collective [see 359] set, but the streets don't come with a rule book.

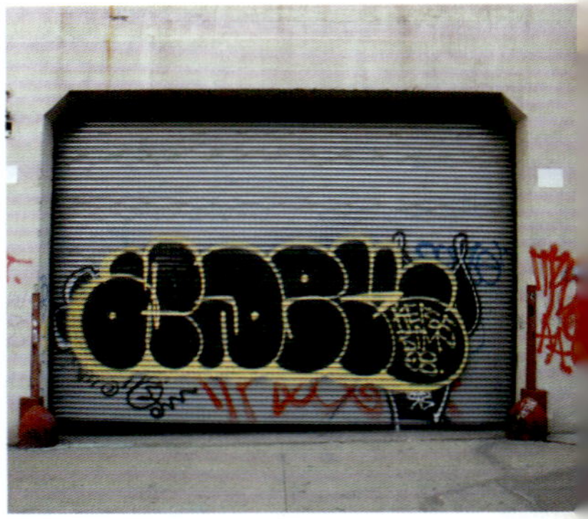

Throw-up by Adek on artwork by Shepard Fairey.
Photograph by Martha Cooper.
Houston and Bowery wall, New York City, 2010.
Detail: Photograph by Ray Mock.
Brooklyn, New York, 2009.

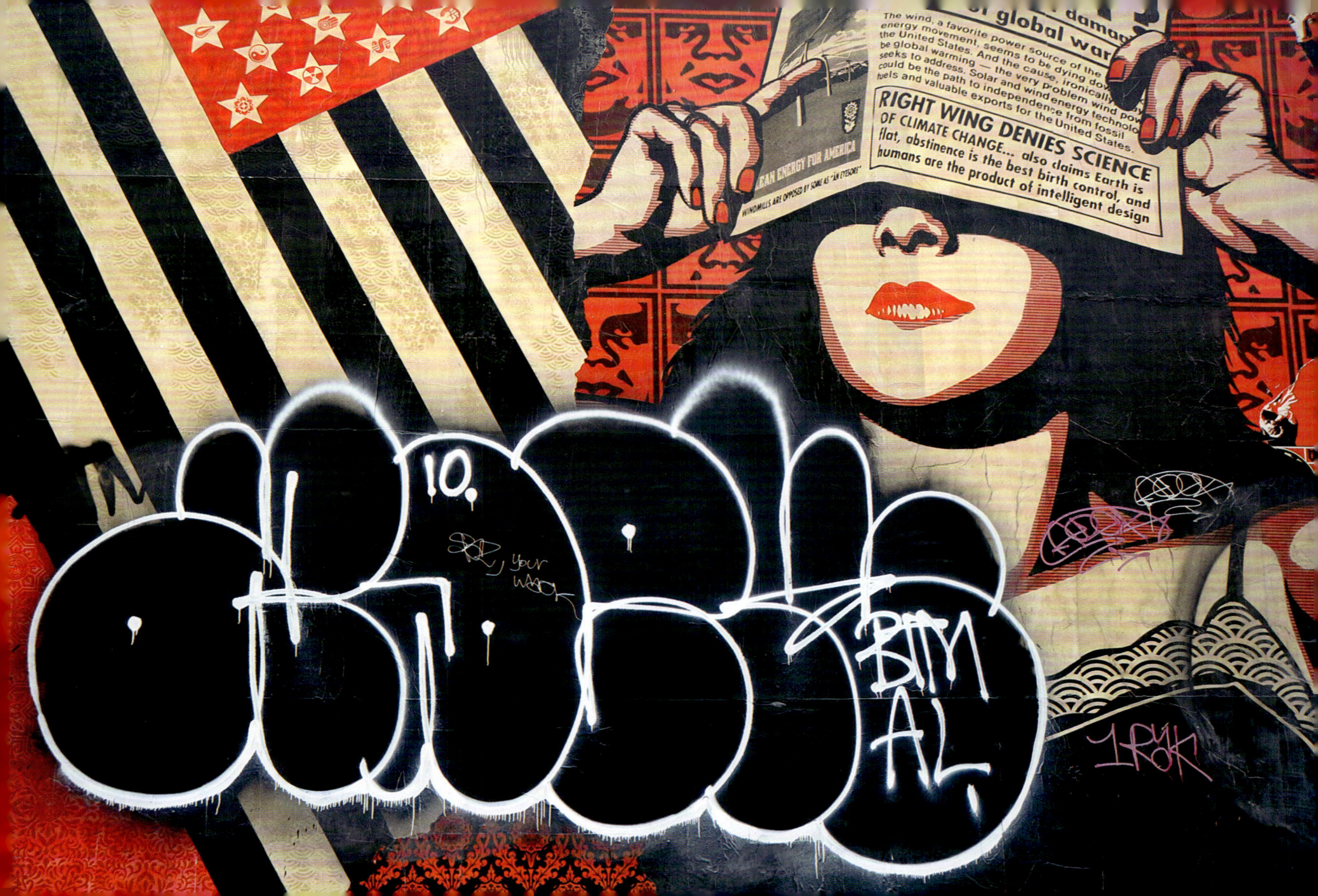
global war
The wind, a favorite power source of the energy movement, seems to be dying do the United States. And the cause, ironically be global warming — the very problem wind pow seeks to address. Solar and wind energy technolo could be the path to independence from fossil fuels and valuable exports for the United States.
RIGHT WING DENIES SCIENCE
OF CLIMATE CHANGE... also claims Earth is flat, abstinence is the best birth control, and humans are the product of intelligent design
WINDMILLS ARE OPPOSED BY SOME AS "AN EYESORE"
BTM
AL

Aiko

Aiko Nakagawa, better known as Lady Aiko, was born in Tokyo, Japan, and has lived in New York since the mid-1990s. One of street art's most consistent contributors, Aiko began her career as a founding member of the street-art crew known as Faile. Eventually splitting from the crew in the mid-2000s, Aiko embarked on a highly successful solo career, utilizing hand-cut stencils, spray paint, collage, and silkscreen printing, carrying forth a more delicate touch on female sexuality within Japanese, Americana, and pop-art–based works. After an intensely prolific period of working on the streets in the late 1990s and early 2000s, Aiko has all but moved into the private sector, creating works for exhibitions at countless galleries and museums, including the Brooklyn Museum, MoMA PS1, and MOCA Shanghai. Tapped into the ultra-hip set, Aiko has seen her work grace the walls of the Standard Hotels in New York and Hollywood, as well as projects for apparel brands like Diesel and DKNY.

Aiko is still known to create large-scale wall installations for her international exhibitions, and her fine art pieces are highly sought after.

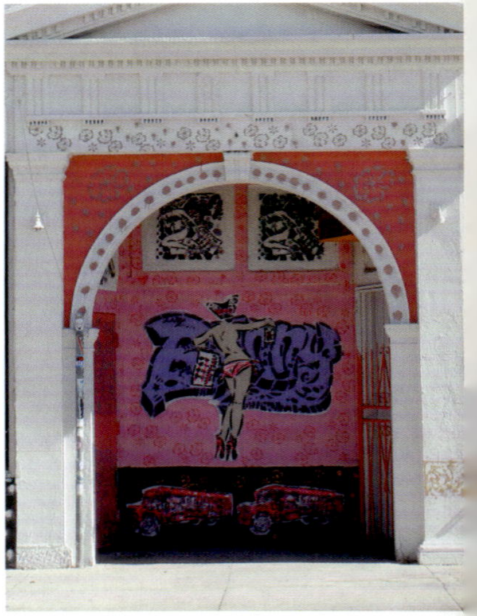

Photographs courtesy of Aiko.
Brooklyn, New York, 2010.
Detail: Miami, Florida, 2010.

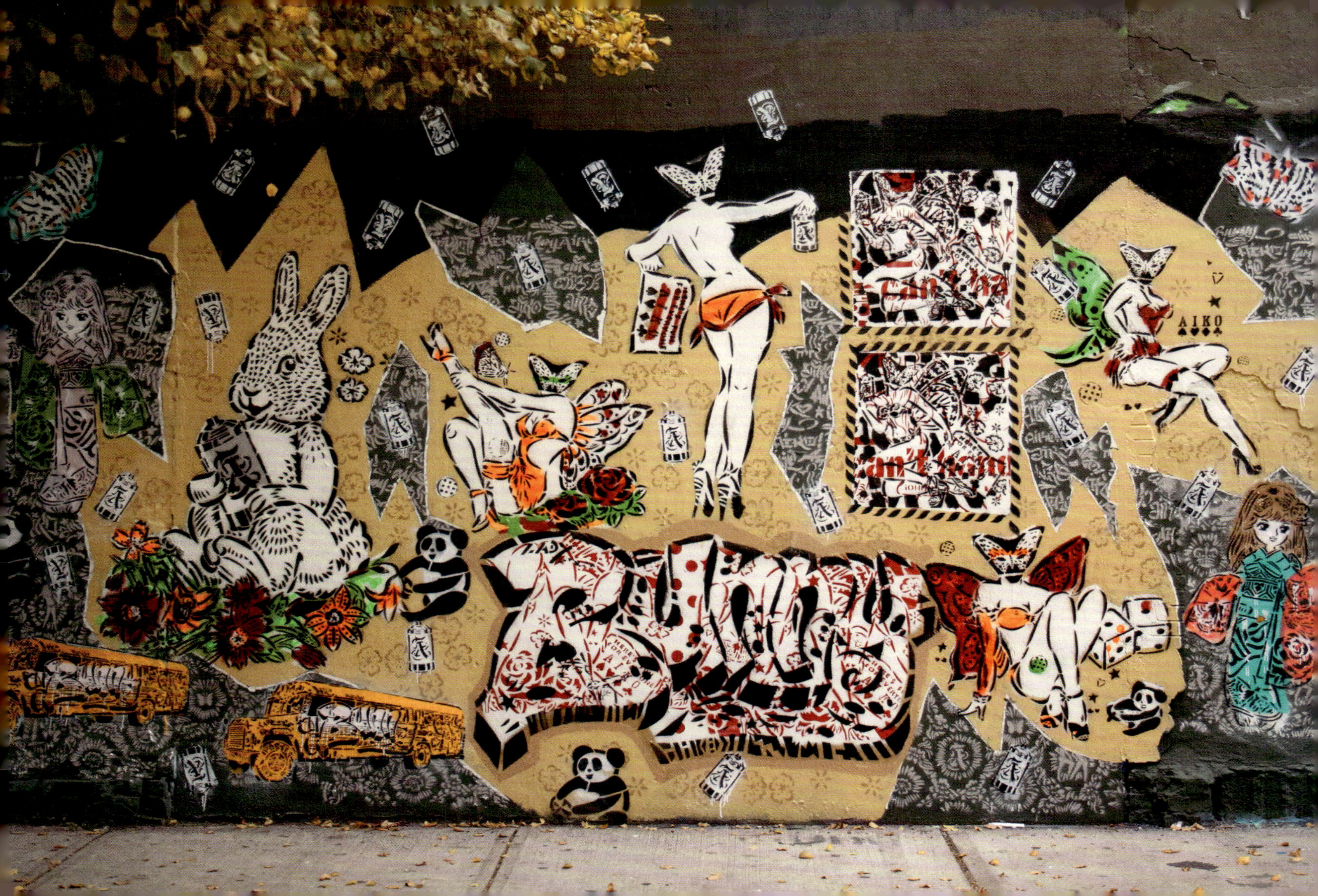
AIKO

Ajax

In the beginning, a name was the only arrow a writer held in his quiver. A writer's name needed to be original and chic to give him a chance to stand out in an ever-growing crowd, and graffiti writers mined many sources to choose an alias. Kids of the earliest era wanted to represent themselves as cool, rebellious, and tough. Formal titles, like Mr., Sir, and Dr., appeared before a multitude of noms de plume, as did prefixes like Kool, Ultra, Bad, and Super. But household cleaning products? In 1971, a Bronx kid named Joey decided to use Ajax as his alias, and when he told his friend John of his plan, John said, "You're Ajax? OK, I'll be Comet." They weren't alone: All 1, Wisk 5, and Mr. Bubble 174 also borrowed their names from cleaning products. From the early to mid-1970s, Ajax would distinguish himself by painting his name neatly, with a simple color scheme and, most important, a solid fill-in covering any trace of the train's surface underneath it. Writing first for the South Bronx–based Ebony Dukes [see TED Inc., 332] and later with the Crazy 5 [see 079], he became one of the best writers during a very competitive era. Ajax had a very simple outline away from which he rarely veered, but he would do whole cars with slogans, such as "Elect Ajax" or "Ajaxxafied," or he would simply add a few extra Xs at the end of his name for good measure.

The #2 and #5 trains showcased his talents for several of graffiti's golden years. Painting with Comet [see 071], Silver Tips [see 300], and his partner, Shake, Ajax unleashed a slew of top-to-bottoms, window-down pieces, and even a giant backward piece on a station. He also executed countless pieces for his girlfriend, Z-73, an early female pioneer. Ajax retired his cans in 1976 and never looked back. But Comet persevered, becoming king of the cleansers.

**Photograph by Jack Stewart.
New York City, 1974.**

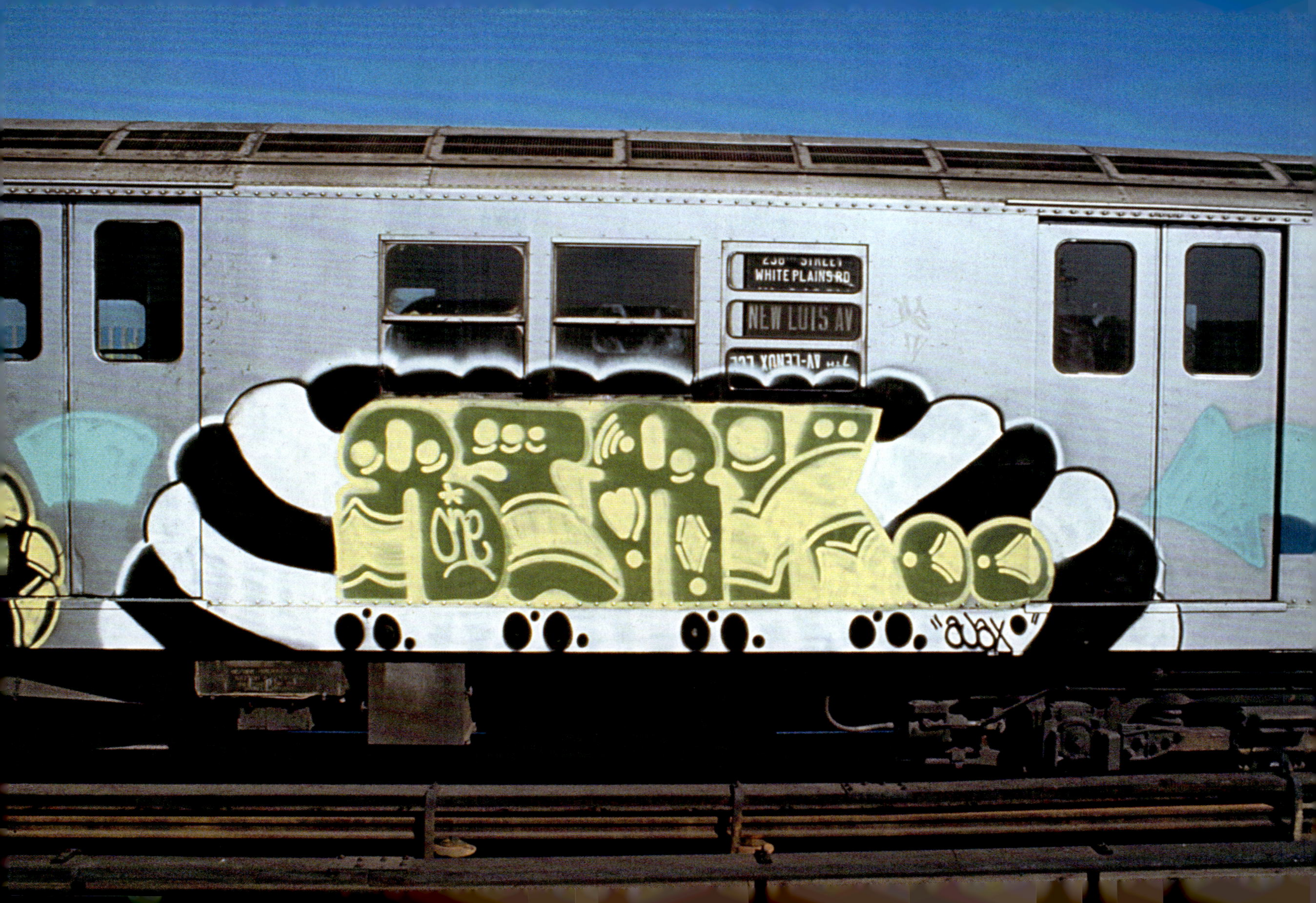
WHITE PLAINS RD
NEW LOTS AV

Ale 1

Ale 1 began writing in 1972 in the Bronx. He grew up in Co-op City, close to the #5 train, a line dominated by Hondo and Fresco at the time. Ale's first partner, MS 18 (aka Roach), accompanied him on his first bombing missions to the Esplanade lay-ups. Ale soon discovered the Baychester lay-up, a place he would make his own over the next several years. Ale became one of the major players in the golden era of graffiti in the Bronx, executing hundreds of pieces, including window-down whole-cars and top-to-bottoms. The list of his contemporaries reads like a ballot for the Graffiti Hall of Fame (see 151): Billy 167, Blade, John 150, Ajax, Silver Tips (see 300), Mike 170, Tav, and his most famous partner, Doo 2.

Together, Doo 2 and Ale pulled off some of the greatest whole-cars of their era. Ale believed in neatness. Influenced by the perfectly solid fill-ins and plain, neat letters of Ajax 1, Ale applied the same qualities to his work. Though not known for characters, Ale decided to show the graffiti world he could do them. In 1975, he executed a piece featuring a top-to-bottom Mickey Mouse, an image that was subsequently used by Lee (see 267) and Seen UA.

In addition to Ale, his primary name, he used the name Law as a backup. Ale enjoyed membership in many crews during his tenure, most notably Phase 2's INDs (see 255, 172). Ale quit in 1977, finding cars and women preferable to dirty hands, paint-covered clothing, and police raids. Now a successful family man, Ale continues to paint on canvas and has written a book on 1970s Bronx graffiti, a subject he knows all too well.

Photograph by Bryan Mechutan (Uni).
New York City, 1975.

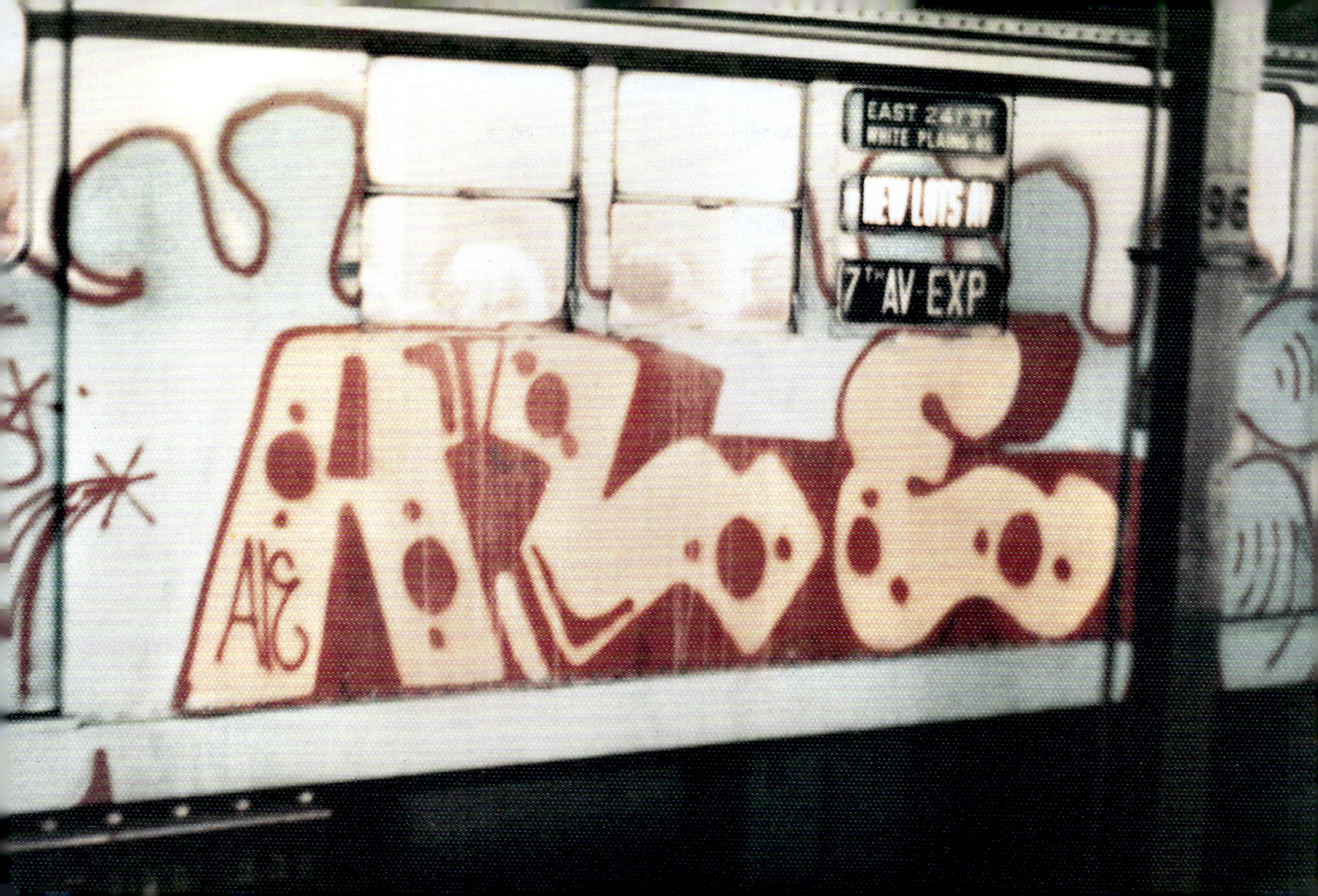
NEW LOTS AV
7TH AV EXP

012

Alexone

Born in 1976, Alexone is a legendary Parisian street artist. He discovered the graffiti movement at age twelve, and under the name Oedipe he developed a distinctly innovative calligraphic style that made its mark on walls throughout Europe. In 2000, he adopted the name Alexone and began to design colorful, fanciful characters to complement his writing.

Since then, Alexone has established a worldwide reputation; he has exhibited in countless cities, including Hamburg, Milan, Berlin, London, Amsterdam, Brussels, and Los Angeles. He has also participated in festivals, both in France and abroad, and his artwork has been featured in museums in Paris. In 2009, he was selected to create a monumental mural for the Cartier Foundation's landmark tribute to graffiti, "Born in the Streets."

Alexone creates an astonishing amount of work on his own, but he has also collaborated with a number of crews, including the GM crew and the 9e Concept group. A member of the elite Parisian crew Mac, he is known for his highly detailed aerosol portraits; his subjects have included fellow artists T.Kid 170 (see 335) and the late Dare from Switzerland, as well as fallen hip-hop icons.

Alexone also works as a graphic designer and illustrator; his products include sneakers, toys, posters, and a motley range of three-dimensional objects featuring his vibrant, constantly evolving aesthetic. Among the tools he uses to create his intriguing, occasionally unsettling surrealistic world are homemade pigments, glaze, resin, spray paint, fluorescent ink, assorted fabrics, and pasted papers.

Character at right by Alexone; lettering by T.Kid 170.
Photograph courtesy of T.Kid 170.
Paris, 2010.

Amanda Lynn

A prolific artist who designs murals, restores sculptures, and custom-paints motorcycles, Amanda Lynn has attained recognition for her fantasy paintings and imaginative illustrations, which appear on an eclectic array of surfaces.

After moving to San Francisco from a small town in Pennsylvania, Amanda Lynn studied at the San Francisco Academy of Art, where she became interested in portraying the details of the human figure. Not certain what direction her art career would take, she began painting with the legendary graffiti crew the 7th Letter. While working with Prairie Prince Studios on a set for a Bette Midler production, she learned how to use an airbrush and became involved with Underground Colors, a motorcycle and metal sculpture–restoration facility.

When not honing her skills at Underground Colors, Amanda Lynn paints. She credits her former teacher Robin Grass for introducing her to the realm of fantasy and for teaching her how to paint with acrylics. Amanda Lynn's paintings have been shown in galleries throughout the United States, as well as in Canada and Australia. Her work has also been featured in the 7th Letter's first traveling show in Tokyo, Taipei, and Barcelona, as well as in several exhibits of tattoo art. Her stylishly surreal portraits can be viewed on the walls of San Francisco's streets.

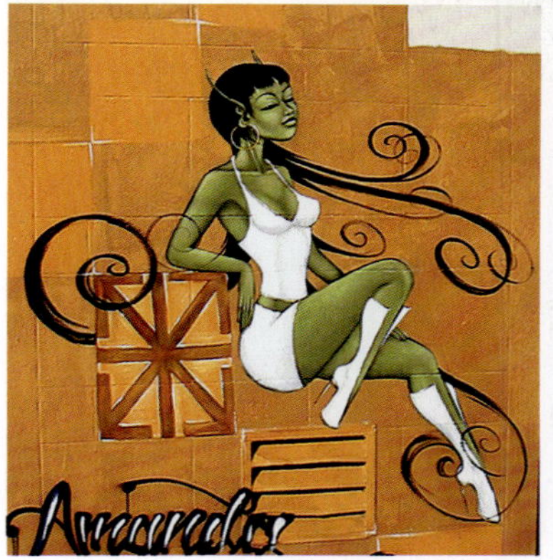

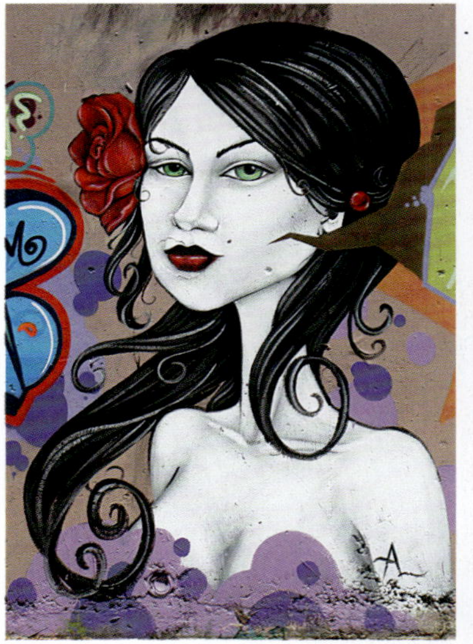

Photographs courtesy of Amanda Lynn.
San Francisco, 2008.
Detail top: San Francisco, 2007.
Detail bottom: San Francisco, 2009.

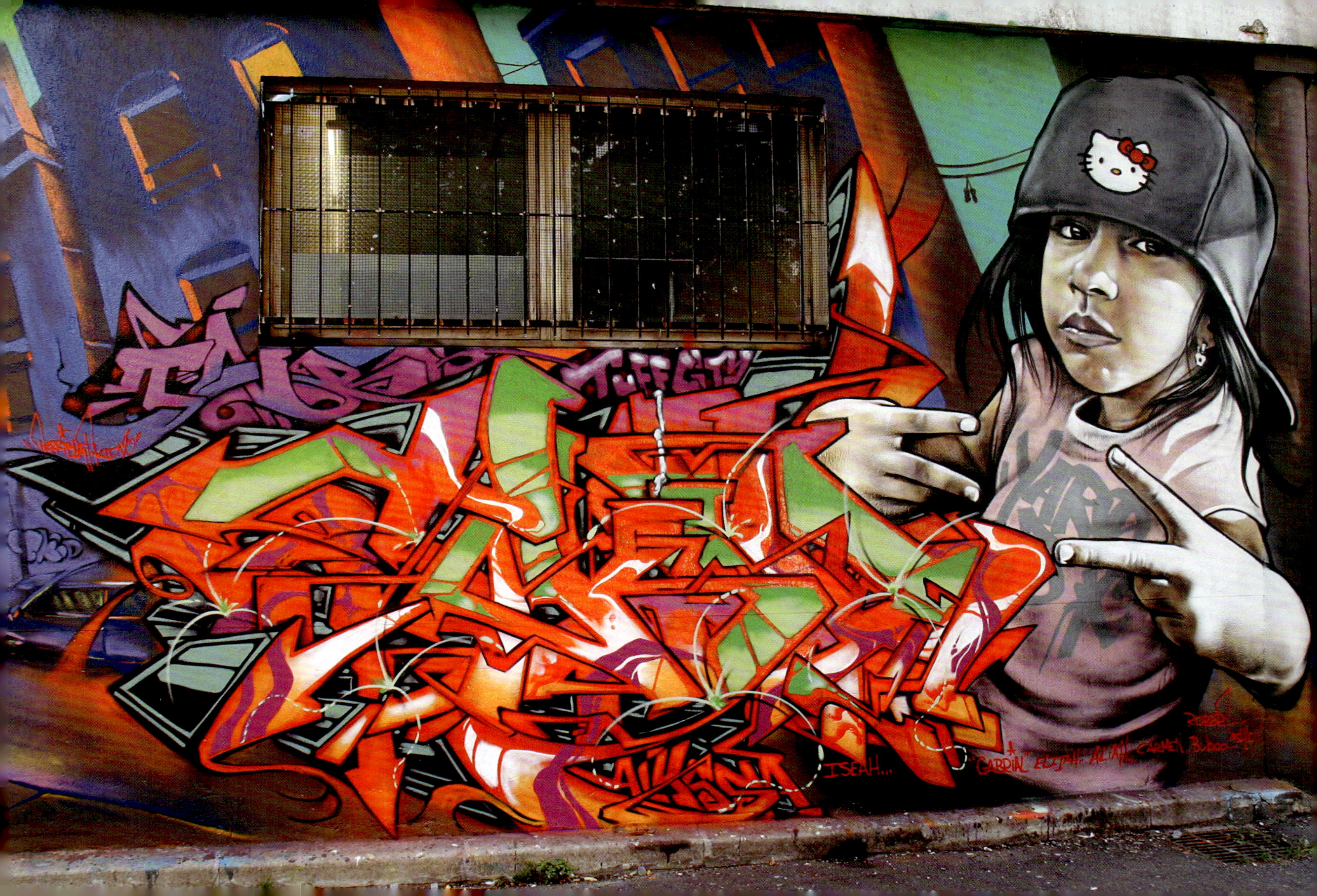
ISEAH...

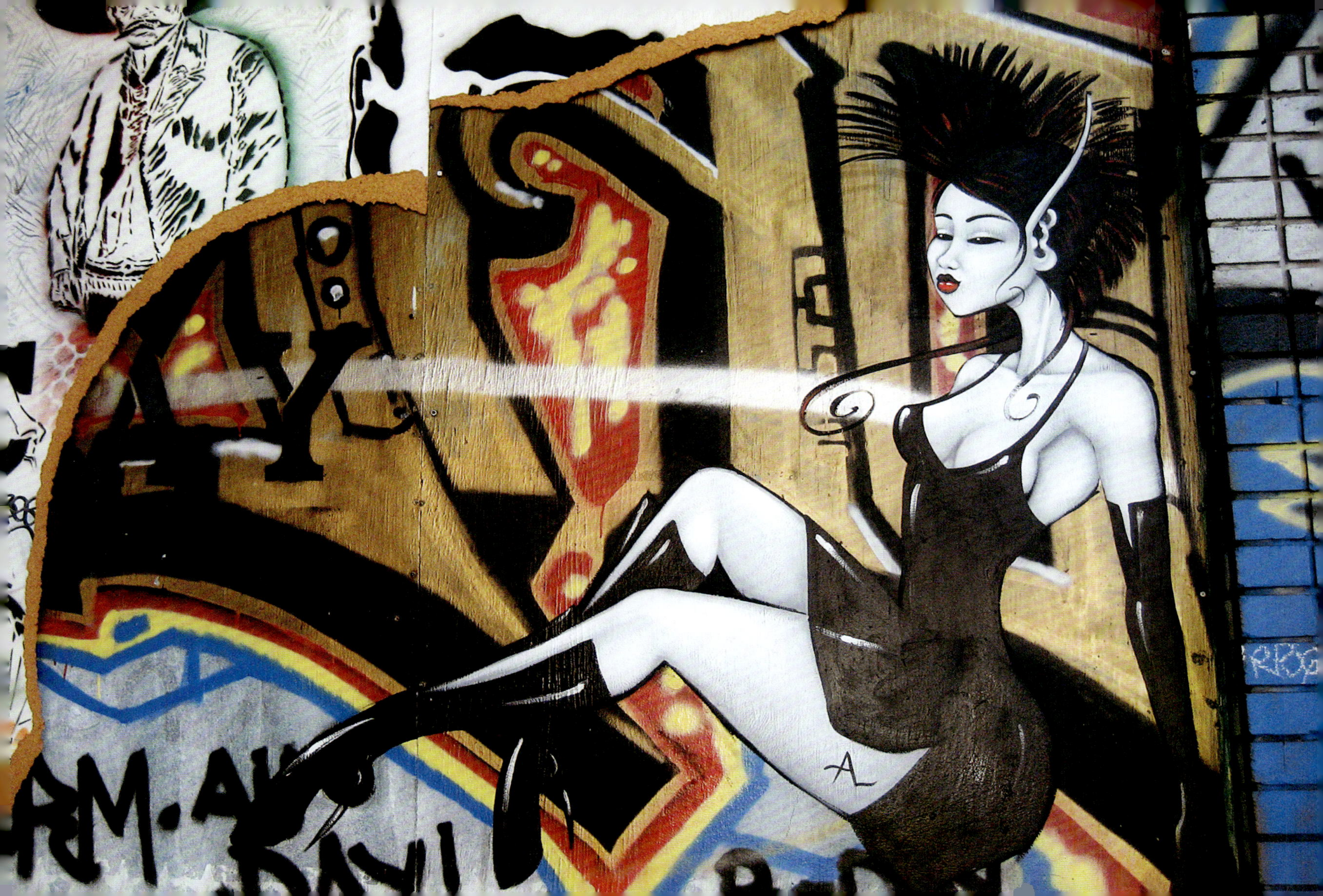

Ame72

Jamie Ame (aka Ame72) was born in Sheffield, England, in 1972, and he began creating street art in 1985, soon after watching the classic hip-hop film *Beat Street*. His early pieces consisted mostly of graffiti letters and characters modeled after those that that graced New York City subways and South Bronx walls back in the 1980s. His first canvas consisted of empty train carriages in Manchester, England.

Currently living in Tel Aviv, Israel, Ame72 is best known for his creative use of Lego stencils with bold images, which often satirize contemporary society's skewed values and misplaced priorities. Lego Guy, as he has come to be known, particularly targets consumerism and hypocrisy, highlighting issues such as homelessness and the futility of warfare.

Ame72's preferred medium has long been spray paint, but more and more frequently he fashions intricate sculptures from sand, snow, and metal. A full-time artist, Ame72 has created and exhibited artwork in England, the United States, Israel, Egypt, Australia, Belgium, Spain, and Thailand. His work has also been featured in the Animamix Biennial at MOCA Shanghai.

Notable pieces include "Where's the Missing Peace?" on the Israeli security wall in Bethlehem and "Rooms for Rent" outside Buckingham Palace in London.

**Photograph by Lois Stavsky.
Tel Aviv, Israel, 2009.**

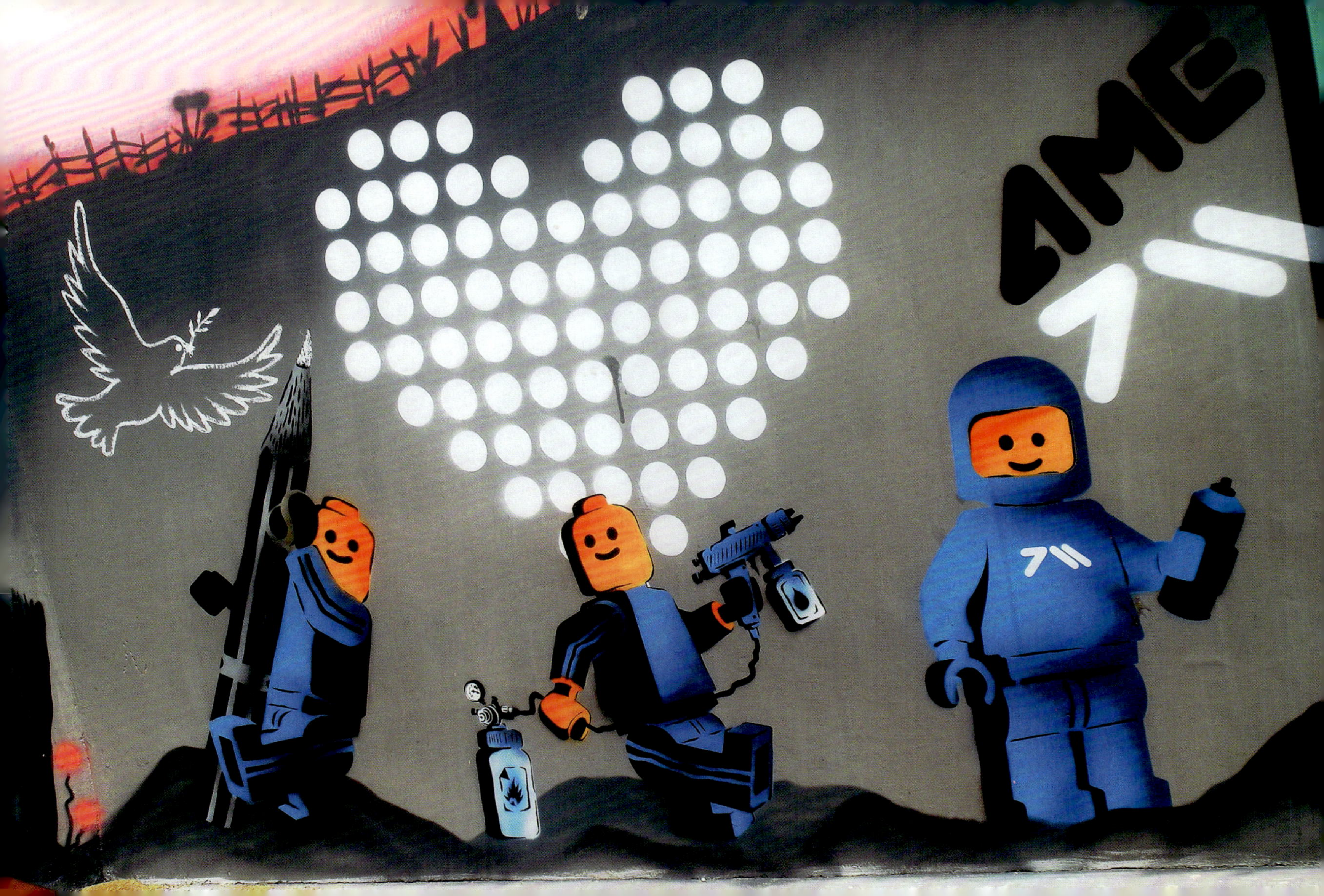

Andre

In the 1990s, graffiti experienced a boom in Paris, and at the forefront of the trend was a goofy character with extra-long skinny legs, a circular head, and an X and an O for eyes, who sometimes wore a top hat. When the world got its first glimpse of the romantic gentleman behind the gangly lad proliferating all over the cobblestoned streets of Paris, he exceeded all notions of the quintessential Frenchman. Dapper and coiffed like a French rockabilly—sporting tailored suits, leather jackets, and shades at all times—Andre challenged the common perception of graffiti artists.

Ever the charmer, Andre created the immensely popular "Love Graffiti" project, through which, for a fee, he could be hired to spray-paint a lover's name somewhere in Paris. Tied in with Space Invader (see 311) and Banksy (see 024) for his street credentials, Andre owns the uber-chic Parisian nightclub Le Baron. He is also a hired branding gun, injecting cool into commercial campaigns, hotel chains, and restaurants around the world.

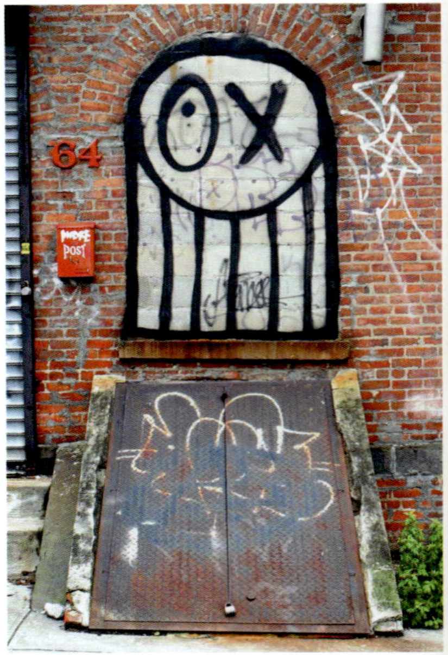

Photographs by Jake Dobkin (streetsy.com).
Los Angeles, 2008.
Detail: New York City, 2005.

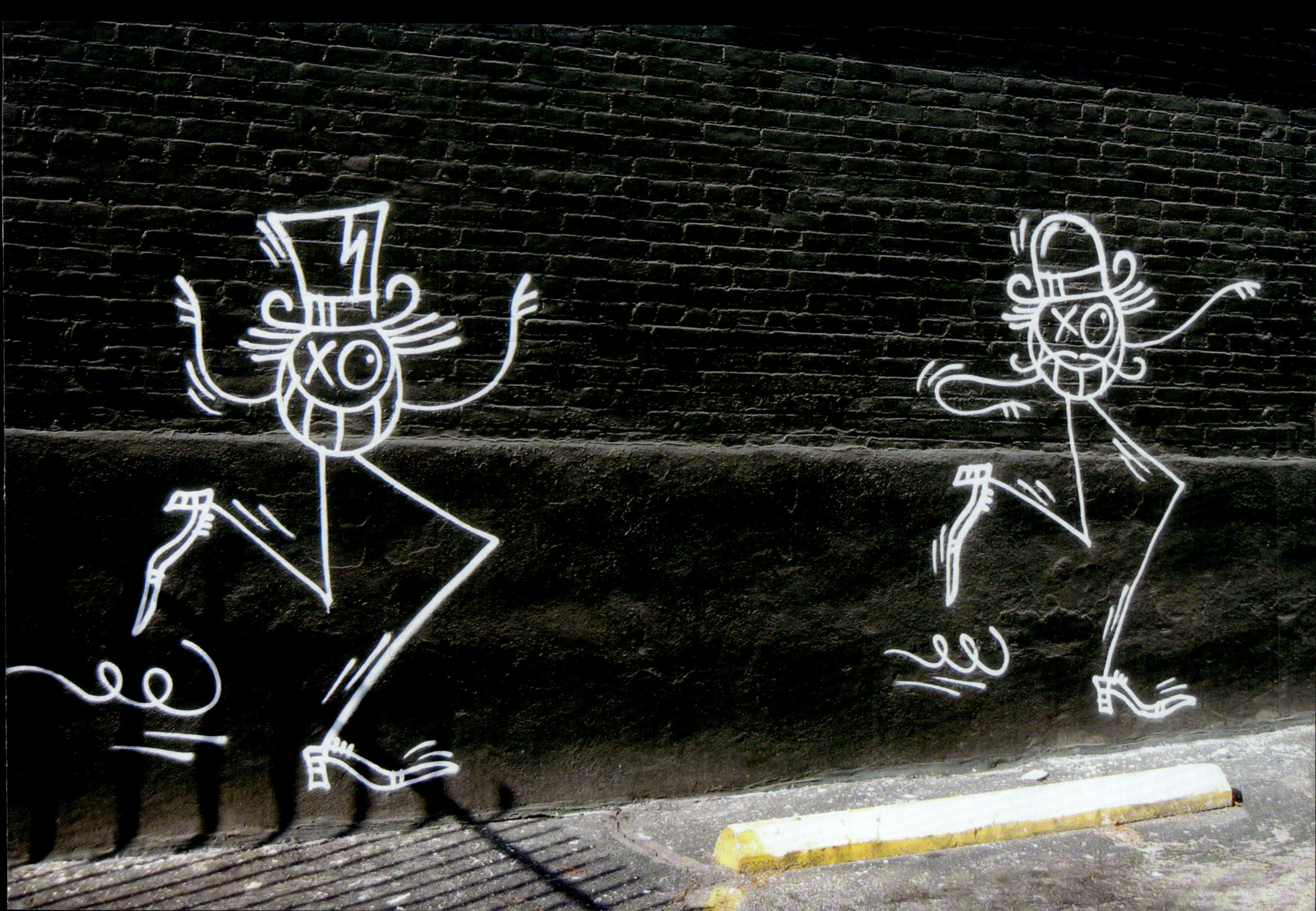

Apex One

Growing up in San Francisco, Apex One developed an interest in graffiti at a young age by observing the murals and pieces on the streets of his city. With a unique style that synthesizes everything from the burners he created as a young teen to the architecture he studied as an art student, he is one of San Francisco's most respected urban artists.

Vibrantly colored in elegantly designed patterns, his expertly fashioned letters have evolved into what the artist has labeled as "super burners." Celebrated for being layered with at least five hundred colors, these artworks are often created with various kinds and brands of paint from different continents that are rarely blended. Their purpose, suggests Apex, is to "capture a higher emotion" in the viewer.

Although Apex's work has also been executed on huge canvases and exhibited in galleries, the street remains his favorite milieu. He is always eager to chat with passersby while he paints in outdoor spaces, as he enjoys their comments and observations of his works in progress.

Along with fellow San Francisco–based graffiti artists Vulcan and Neonski, Apex One has lectured on the evolution of super burners and their impact on the art world. His work is featured in the noted anthology *Street Art San Francisco: Mission Muralismo*.

Photograph by Matt Isles.
San Francisco, 2007.

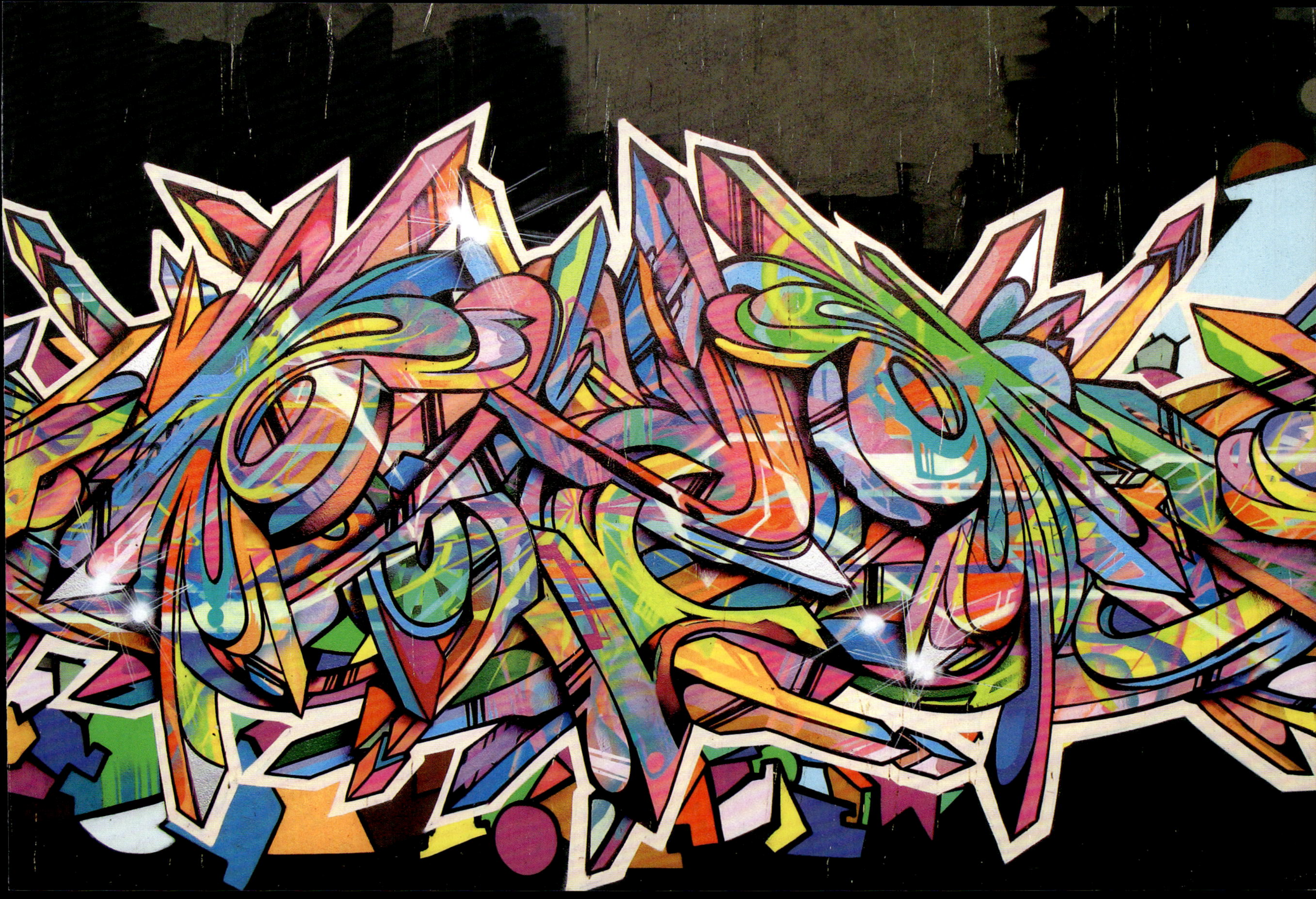

Armsrock

Born in 1984 in Copenhagen, Armsrock is one of street art's more mysterious characters. The young artist is known for his pencil-and-charcoal drawings of characters in everyday life—a grandmother knitting, a fruit seller hawking his wares, or children playing in the street. Armsrock sketches these out on large-format paper, then wheatpastes them to walls. The lack of ostentation in the characters he chooses reveals a certain tender appreciation for the underdog, as well as a sensitivity that counters the bravado more typically associated with urban artists.

Armsrock was in his early twenties when he gained recognition for his street work. He was taken under the wing of such street-art demigods as Marc and Sara Schiller and Swoon when he was still in art school, and he soon began to show in galleries internationally.

An inherently shy person, Armsrock was revealed to be a slight, blond young man with facial piercings, whose brain bubbles over with political frustrations and art theory—a boy who is loath to give an interview or pose for a camera. He works and resides in Bremen, Germany, and is relatively removed from the public spectacle that street art has become.

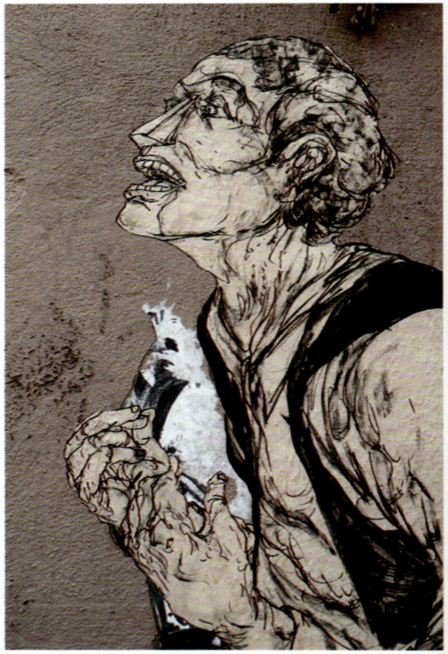

Photographs by Sam Horine. Brooklyn, New York, 2006.

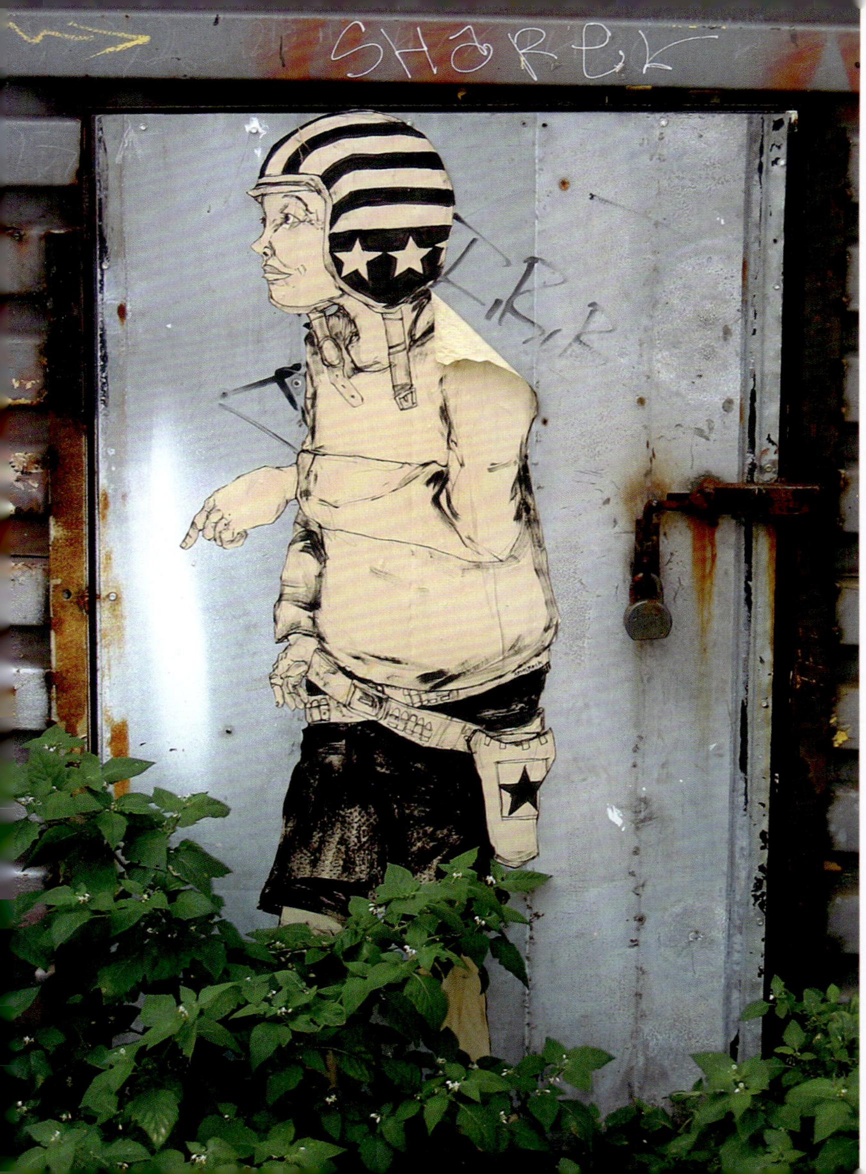

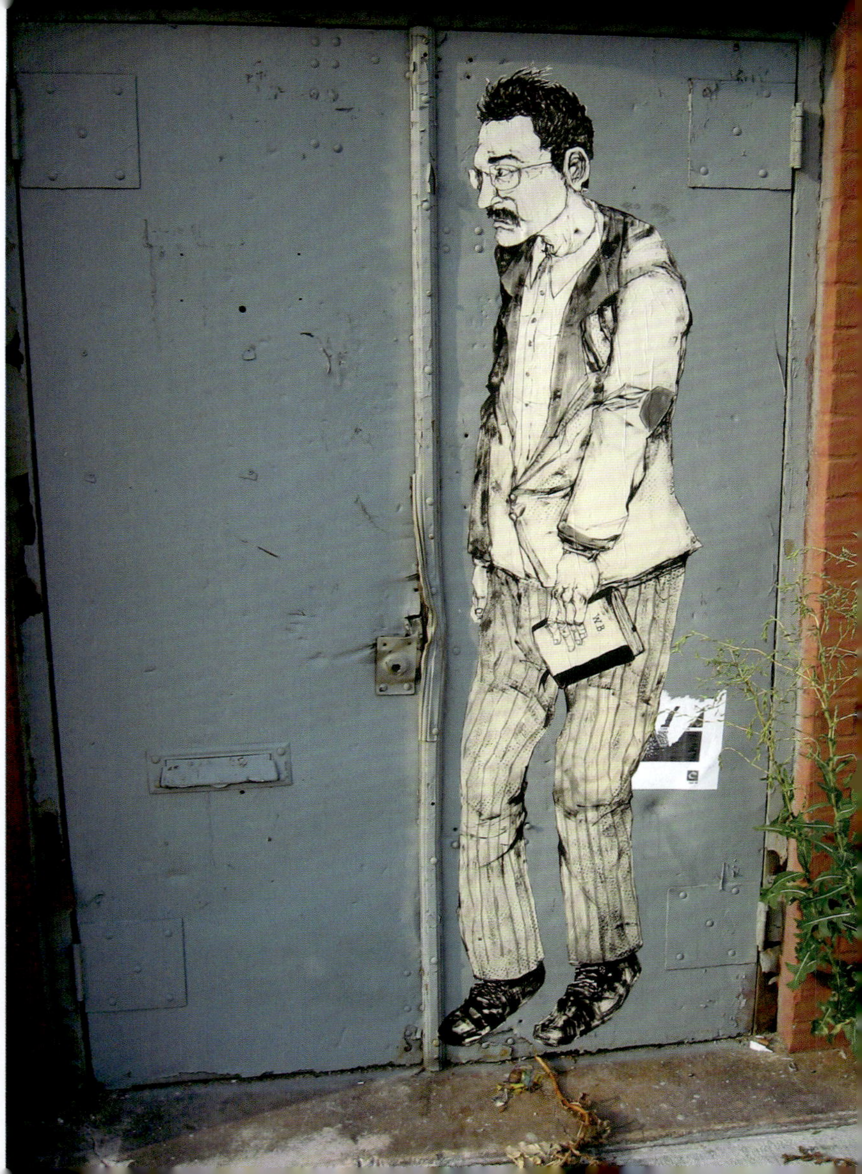

Aroe

Everything changed overnight after the fourteen-year-old Aroe watched a "Buffalo Gals" video on TV. Aroe was fascinated by what he saw and felt he had to do it. Shortly afterward, he opened the pages of *Subway Art* [see 323] for the first time, and this gave him a better understanding of the culture he knew little about yet instinctively hungered to be a part of.

The years that followed were filled with basic piecing and heavy illegal bombing, which led Aroe through school, the courts, his teens, and so on.

In the late 1990s, he took a brief hiatus, but still thought and talked about graffiti constantly. He often felt that among his friends and fellow writers, he was a small-time nobody headed for permanent obscurity. Aroe wasn't going to allow his often undisciplined graffiti to remain that way, and he became determined make a name for himself that would be impossible to ignore. Nowadays, as the leader of the hottest crew in the U.K., he is on a short list of the world's elite writers. He was a founding member of Britain's version of AWR/MSK, the Heavy Artillery crew [see 164], who paint all over the world, representing state of the art graffiti in the form of high-concept production walls. It would appear this Aroe is pointed in the right direction.

Photograph courtesy of Heavy Artillery.
United Kingdom, c. 2008.

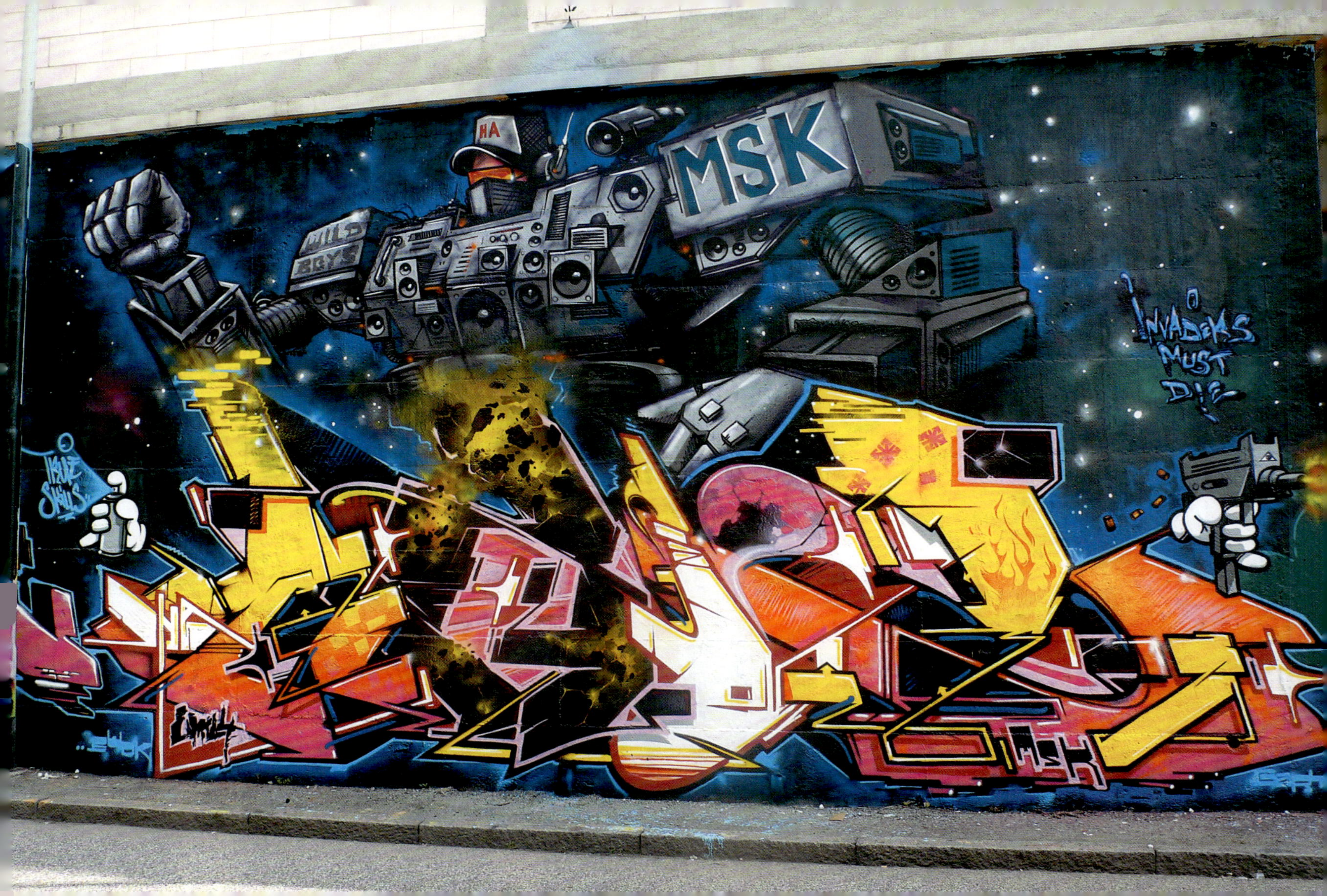
MSK
WILD BOYS

"art express"

In 1982, graffiti artists tried to convince MTA authorities to hire them to paint a New York City subway train; they were rebuffed. In contrast, Thalys, a manufacturer of high-speed European trains, rolled out the red carpet (literally) in 2009 for four of Europe's most accomplished graffiti and street artists. Each artist hailed from one of the four destinations serviced by a new lightning-fast model the company was introducing. The train blazes from Paris to Amsterdam or Cologne in three hours and fifteen minutes. What better way to promote this new wonder of transport than to hire artists whose art originated on trains?

The artists: Jon One (see 184), a Parisian expatriate who honed his craft in Harlem's 145th Street subway tunnel; Seak, an urban expressionist from Cologne, Germany; Sozyone, a street artist and master colorist from Brussels; and representing Amsterdam, Zedz, who blends letters with architecture, creating pieces resembling futuristic cities. The artists were given their own train cars to paint and three hours and fifteen minutes to get the job done—just like the train.

The artistically enhanced train embarked on its maiden voyage on December 13, 2009, a moving (in all senses) affirmation that a practice that was once thought to be malignant is now benign.

***Train Thalys TGV* by Jon One, Pro, Nunca, Opak, Seak, Sozyone, and Zedz.**
Photographs by Thalys (PGC).
Gare du Nord, Paris, 2009.

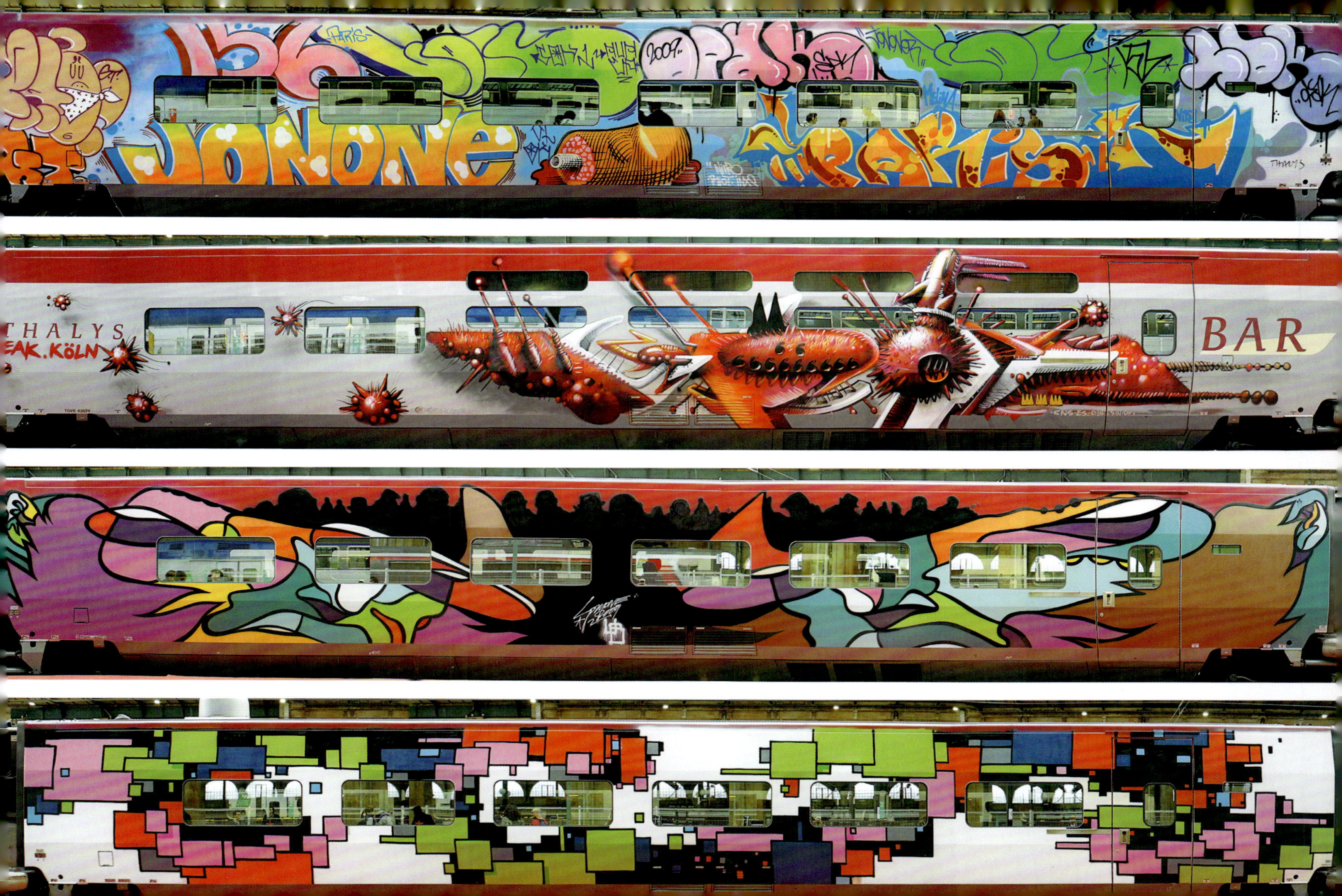
THALYS
BAR

Aryz

Toward the middle of the first decade of the 2000s, street art had hit such an apex of international popularity that it was becoming difficult to imagine where new stylistic innovation would come from. Stencils had been pushed to their multilayered limits, traditional graffiti had all but divorced the street art movement, and wheatpasting was being powerfully managed by a family of fine artists devoted to intricate woodcuts and oil paintings that they donated to the public.

It was in this climate that a new voice emerged, from the heavily painted streets of Barcelona—that voice belonged to a young artist who went by the name of Aryz. Using spray paint and rollers laden with industrial house paint, Aryz creates massive murals of characters in a highly distinctive style. He skyrocketed to international fame when an image of a roller piece he had created, which used several colors to create gradients, was widely circulated on the Internet. Depicting one of his signature fantasy characters, the piece demonstrated a wealth of understanding of color and a mastery of a typically crude technique that set the street-art and graffiti worlds on their heads.

Since his early recognition, Aryz has continued to earn his stripes within the community, painting murals in the spray-paint cafe Montana in Barcelona and creating large-scale mural works internationally, alongside the likes of the legendary Tats Cru.

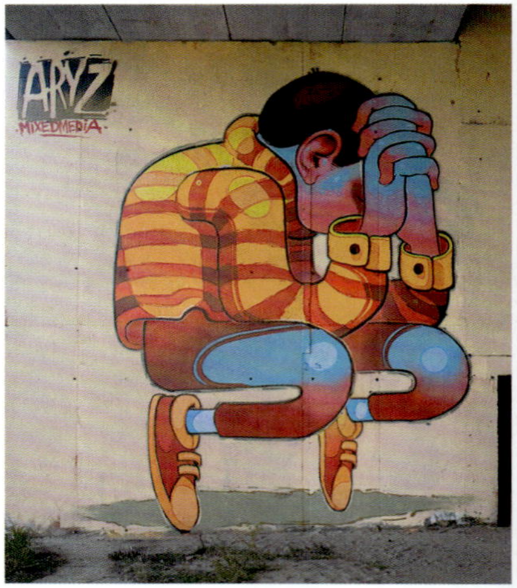

Photographs courtesy of Aryz. Barcelona, Spain, 2010.

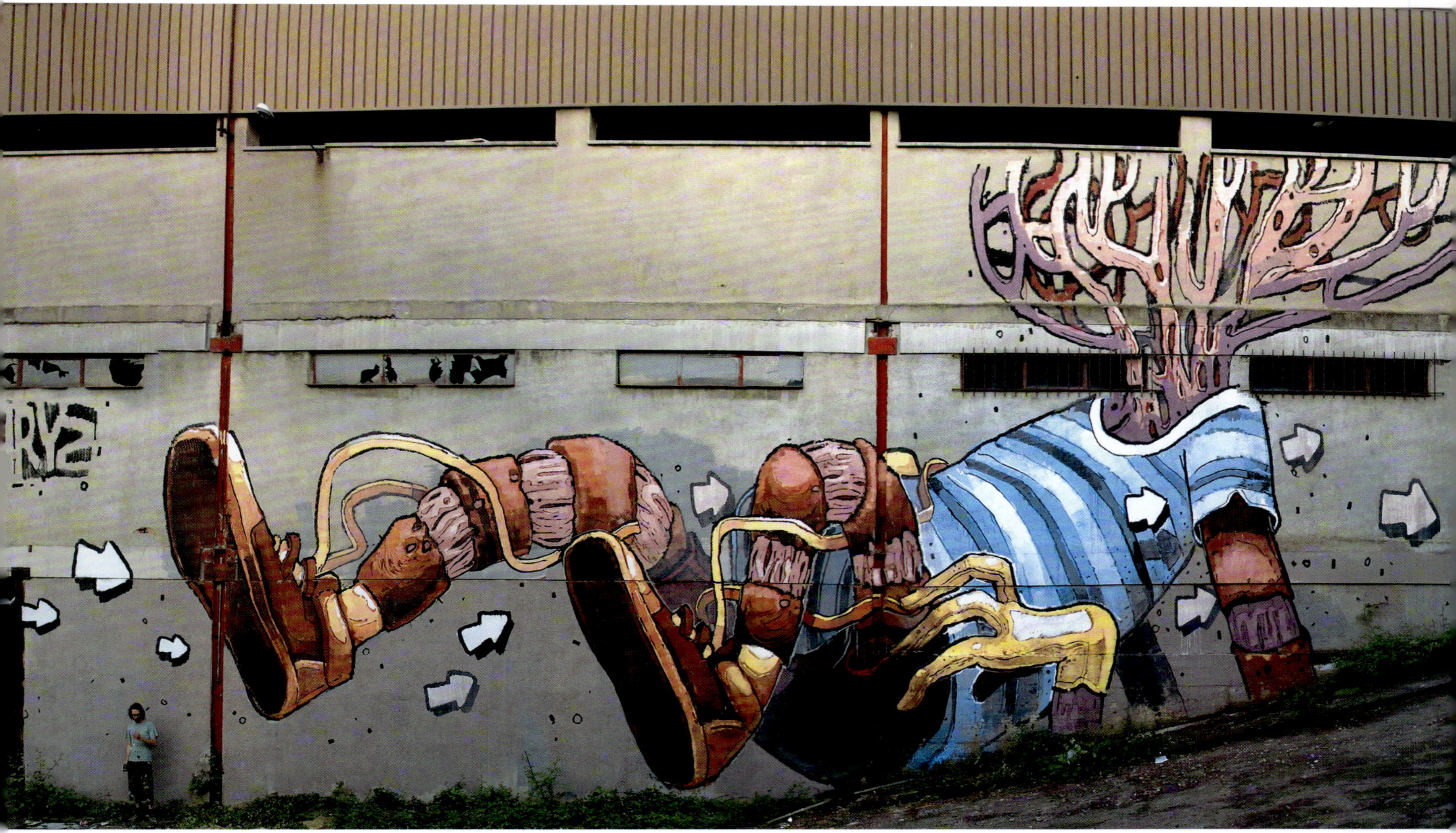

Askew One

When one thinks of international graffiti hot spots, New Zealand doesn't necessarily come to mind—but perhaps it should. New Zealand is home to Askew One, and he's hit just about everything there is to hit; his diverse résumé includes trains, highways, and large-scale productions.

Askew started writing in 1995, at the age of sixteen, in the graffiti purgatory of Auckland, New Zealand. He was isolated and searched for images from books, television, and the Internet to inform himself about the culture. Askew's talent came to him naturally, and by the year 2000 he had established himself as one of the best writers in New Zealand. But that's not enough for kids who write internationally, and Askew wanted to be known outside his country. To his surprise, other writers had already begun to notice him and started making the trek to New Zealand to seek him out.

Askew's work is deceptively simple, and it has its roots in the New York City subway movement. He has become the antithesis of what the graffiti mural movement is about, choosing to freestyle his pieces the way the old-timers did, rather than working from labored sketches. His work possesses a looseness that allows for mistakes, which lets him go in directions that others might not follow. Sometimes working in obscurity has its benefits.

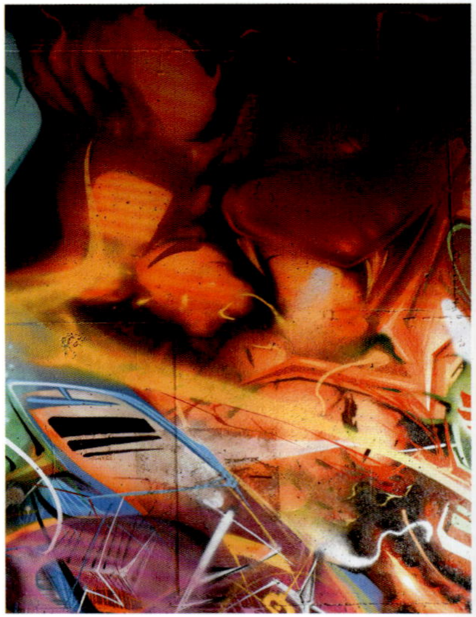

Photographs courtesy of Askew One.
New Zealand, 2010.

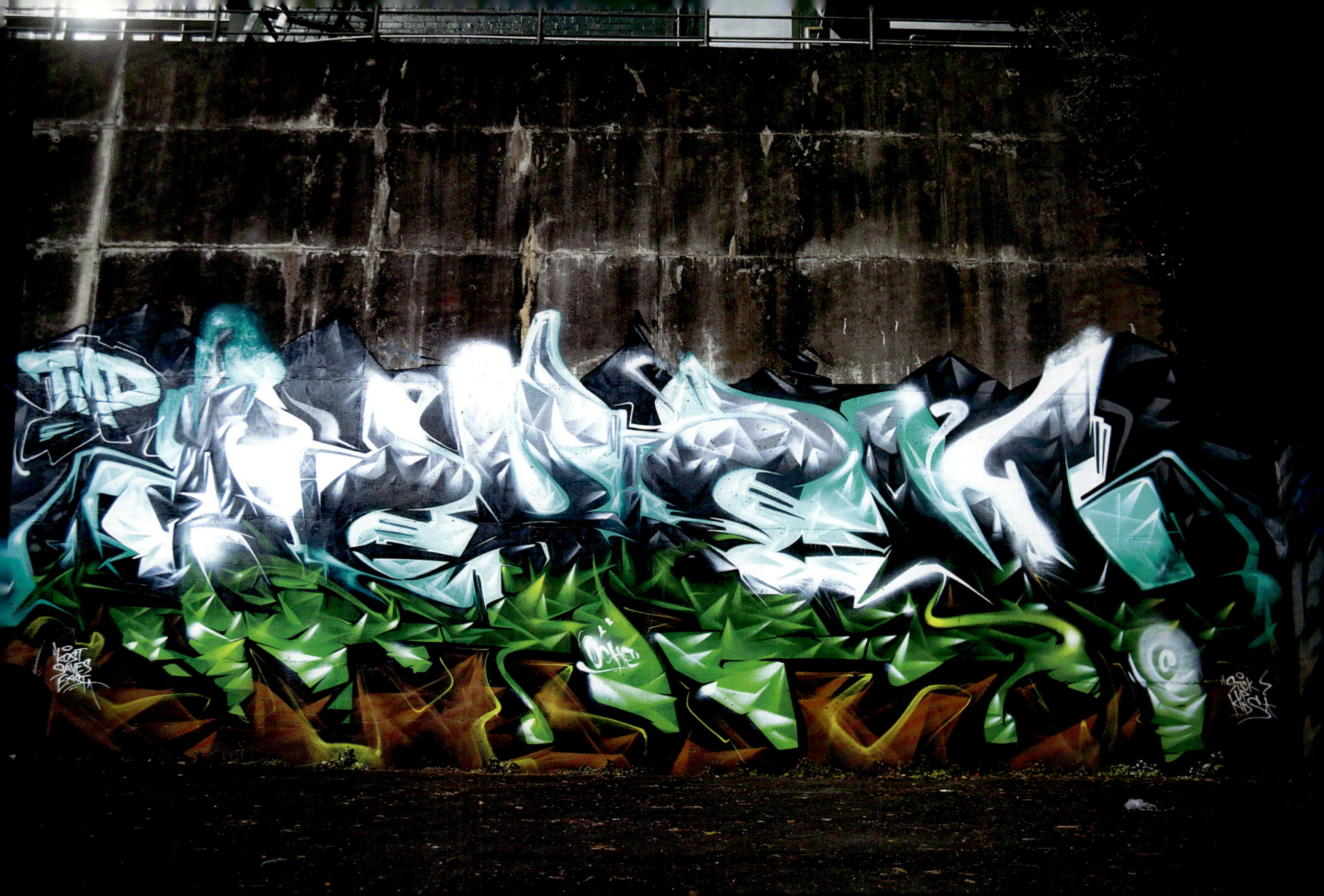

AWR/MSK/ The 7th Letter

The 7th Letter crew was formed in 2000 as an umbrella company for writers from AWR/MSK to work on projects other than walls, such as apparel and art shows. The roots of the crew go back to 1988, when AWR was one of the first major crews to be formed in California. AWR had quickly gelled as a tight band of brothers, including Eklips, Risk [see 280], and Saber [see 287]; this posed the question of what to do with newer writers who wanted to join. The solution was to form another crew called Mad Society Kings (MSK). The two crews hung out, and there was some cross-pollination.

At the time, there was no bigger crew in California—possibly the world—than MSK. Its members painted everywhere, including Europe. Saber morphed from talented writer to media celebrity in 1997 by painting the largest piece ever on the cement slope of the Los Angeles River, a painting that could be seen from satellites.

After eleven years of hard work, AWR and MSK merged into the 7th Letter. It continues to expand, and the 7th Letter now has footholds in areas as diverse as tattoo design, art direction, sculpture, photography, and graphic design.

Photographs by Paul "Krush" Meriaz, courtesy of Ewok.
Top: *Ewok* by Krush, *Krush* by Ewok. Los Angeles, 2010.
Bottom: Artwork by Krush, Tyke, and Ewok.
Los Angeles, 2008.

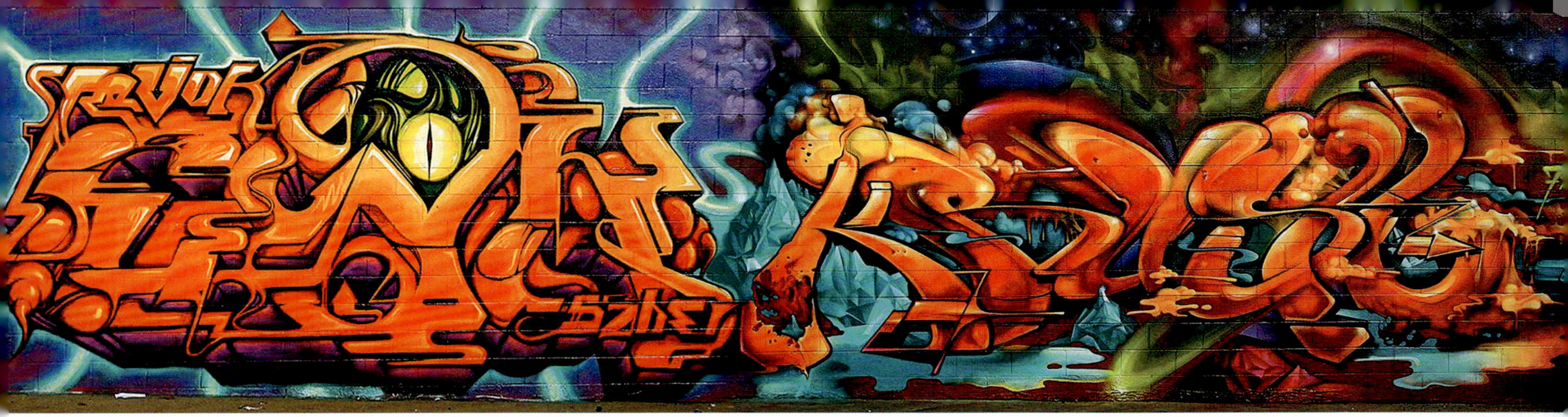

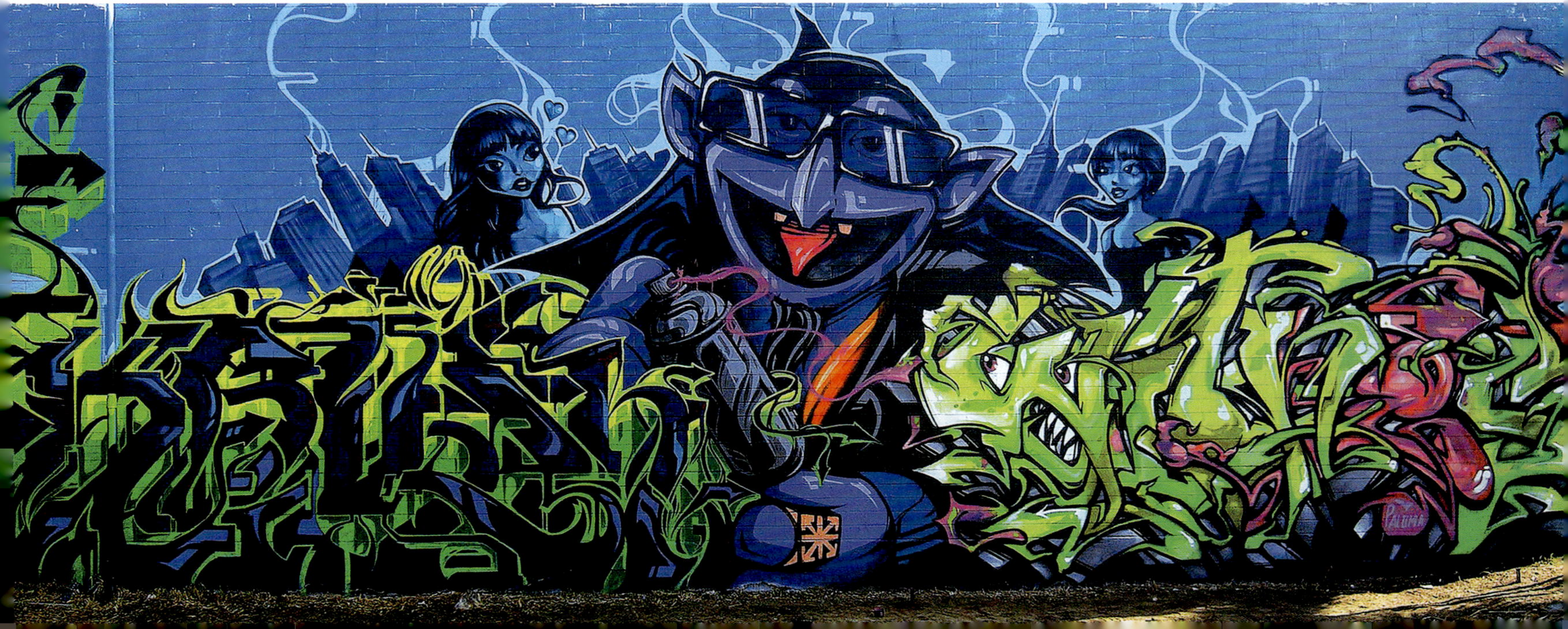

The Bandshell

During the 1970s, prep-school kids, famous graffiti artists, hippies, and hardened drug dealers all hung together at the Central Park Bandshell. Early subway legend Steve 161 played the role of graffiti mentor to his younger followers from the Upper West Side. Many original members of the Soul Artists [see 310], such as Malta, Coca 82, and Ali, were staples of the scene. By 1974, up-and-coming local writers such as ME1 [the original Pax], SE 3 [Haze], SIE 1, and War 1 were holding court there, rubbing elbows with legendary hippie graffiti god LSD Om.

For almost a decade, the Bandshell remained an epicenter for hanging out, copping drugs, getting high, and meeting famous writers. The later generation of "parkies," as Bandshell regulars were known, included Zephyr, Revolt, Bilrock, Crunch, and Rasta [see 270].

A psychedelic writer's bench without trains, a recreational pharmacy, and the high altar for a dysfunctional rite of passage—the Bandshell left an indelible imprint on those lucky enough to have survived the experience.

Photograph by Flint Gennari.
Central Park, New York City, 1975.

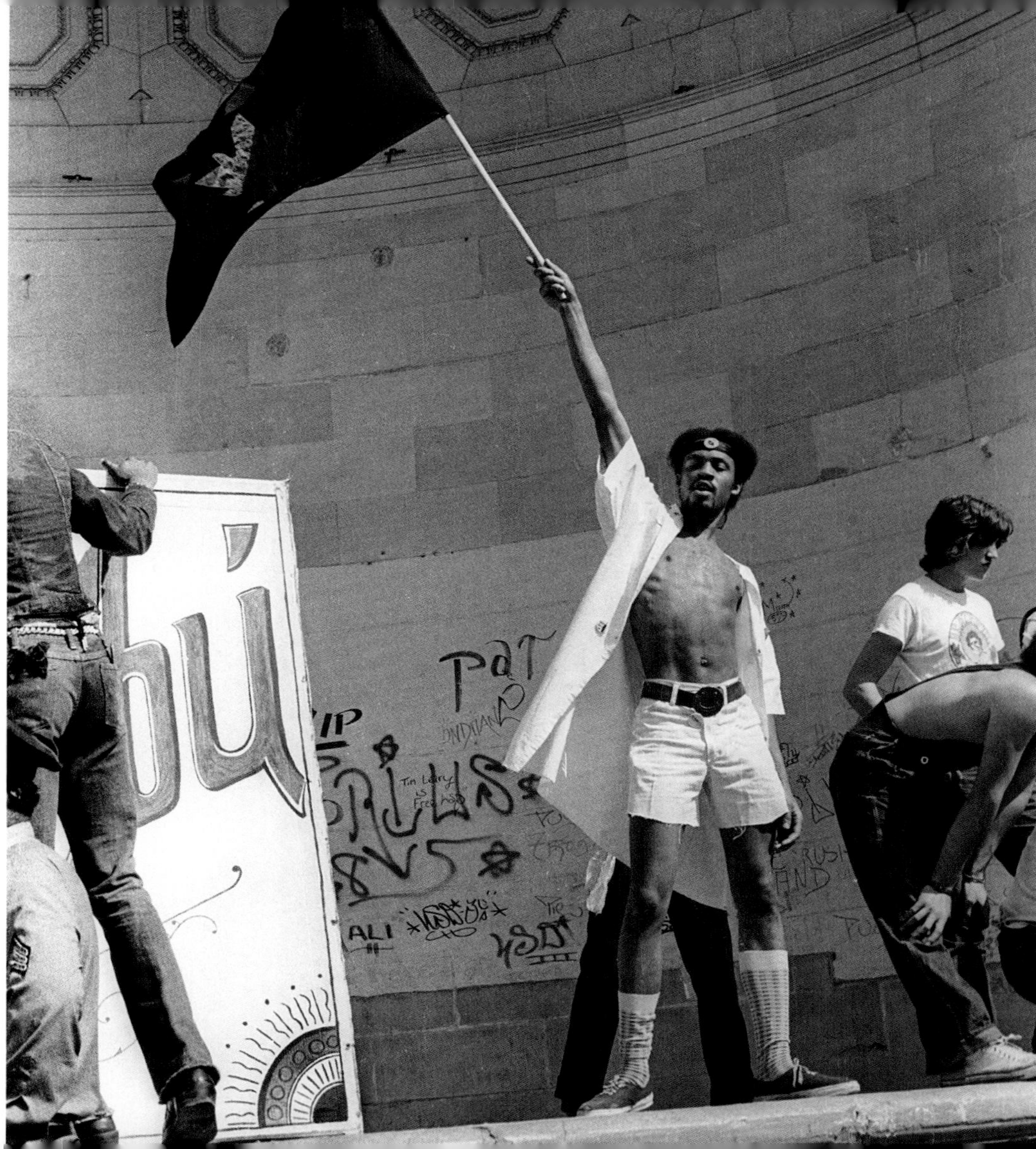
Pat
ALI

Banksy

British artist Banksy, whose real identity is alleged—but still unconfirmed—to be Bristol's Robin Gunningham, is in a class by himself. His provocative stenciling has made him the world's best-known, and best-paid, street artist. Folks inside and outside the art world's inner circles took note when Angelina Jolie plunked down $400,000 for three Banksy pieces at a 2006 Los Angeles exhibit. Her purchases suggested to some that Banksy had more in common with Damien Hirst than Taki 183 [see 331]. Banksy fans who were concerned that his outlaw pose was being corrupted by the dollar were undoubtedly pleased by his comments to Shepard Fairey [see 124] in a 2006 interview: "I love graffiti. . . . Graffiti equals amazing to me. Every other type of art compared to graffiti is a step down—no two ways about it. If you operate outside of graffiti, you operate at a lower level. Other art has less to offer people, it means less, and it's weaker. I make normal paintings if I have ideas that are too complex or offensive to go out on the street, but if I ever stopped being a graffiti writer I would be gutted."

Although Banksy's secret identity may no longer be secret, to lovers of his work—and there are many—he will always be Superman, and the 200,000-pound guerrilla.

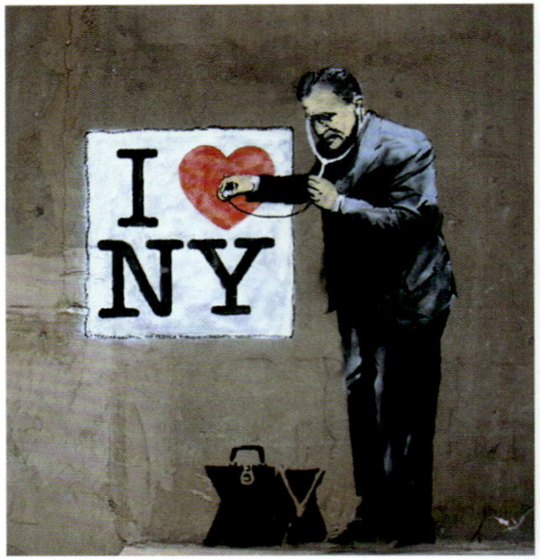

Photographs by Luna Park. New York City, 2010.

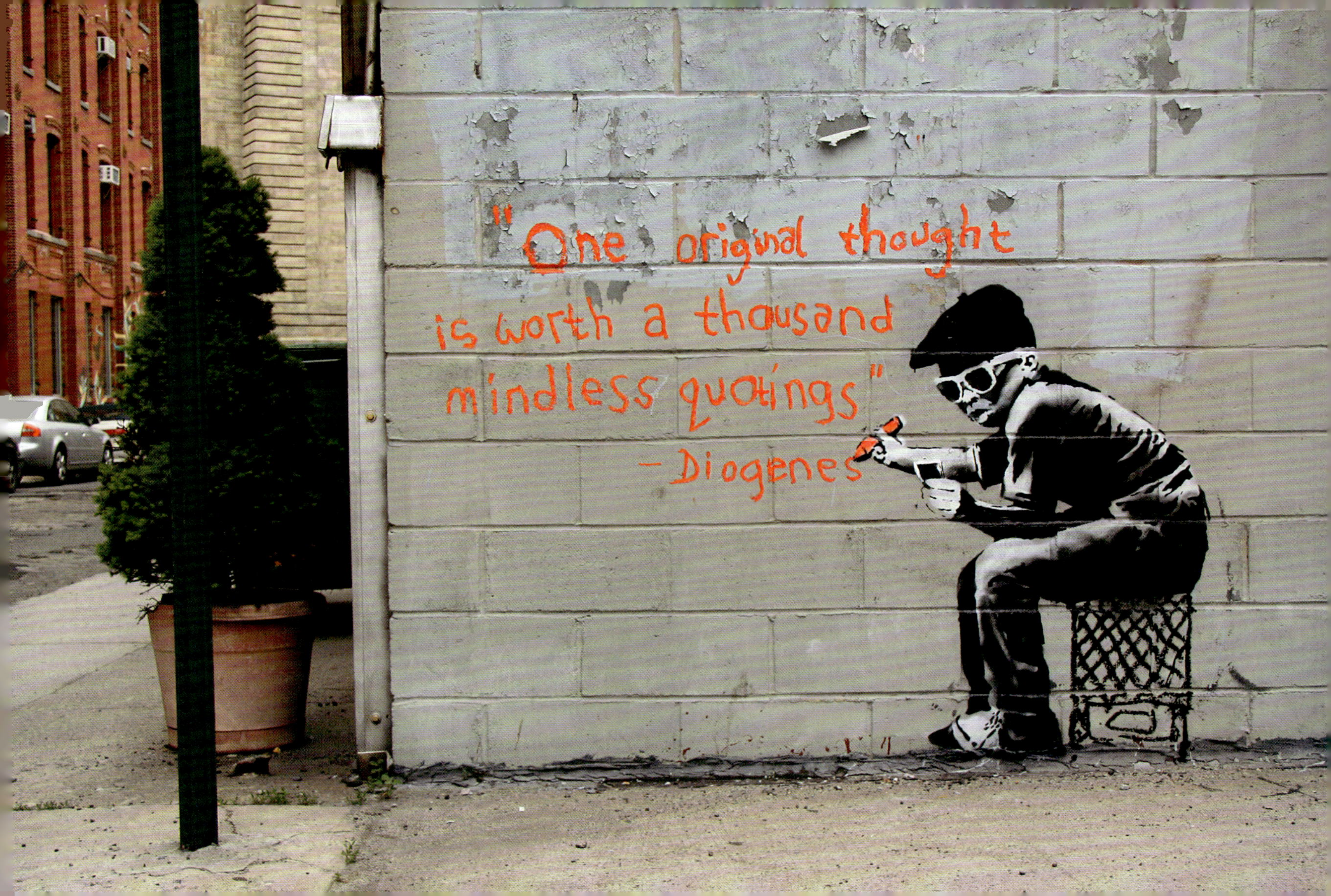
"One original thought
is worth a thousand
mindless quotings"
– Diogenes

Barnstormers

Amid the tobacco fields of North Carolina, innumerable barns stand abandoned. In 1999, the first of what would become countless collaborative painting projects began in a rural town called Cameron. A group of twenty-five artists, spearheaded by the elusive David Ellis [see 109], came together and began painting large-scale murals in and on dozens of barns, tractor trailers, shacks, and pieces of farm equipment. During the pilgrimage, a concept evolved, on the floor of a barn, that would become a component of a groundbreaking video project. An artist painted a mural the size of the entire floor, which was then covered over by the next artist painting directly on top of it, interacting with the work the previous artist had created. This process was filmed with a camera floating above the floor and pointed straight down at it. Shown later in time-lapse video form, the video became a piece of art in and of itself, blasting apart perceptions of what public art was and could be. Borrowing many of its artists from the Beautiful Losers school, the group became known as the Barnstormers and began to call itself a loose collective. The lineup included Ellis, Jose Parla, Swoon [see 329], Kami and Sasu [see 187], Doze Green [see 098], Kenji Hiarata, Maya Hayuk [see 162], Rostarr, and Stephen "ESPO" Powers. Over the ensuing decade, the Barnstormers would continue to make almost yearly trips to the South, inadvertently turning the sleepy rural town of Cameron into an urban-art mecca. They created performative installations of their large-scale works and have exhibited them internationally, including at several museums.

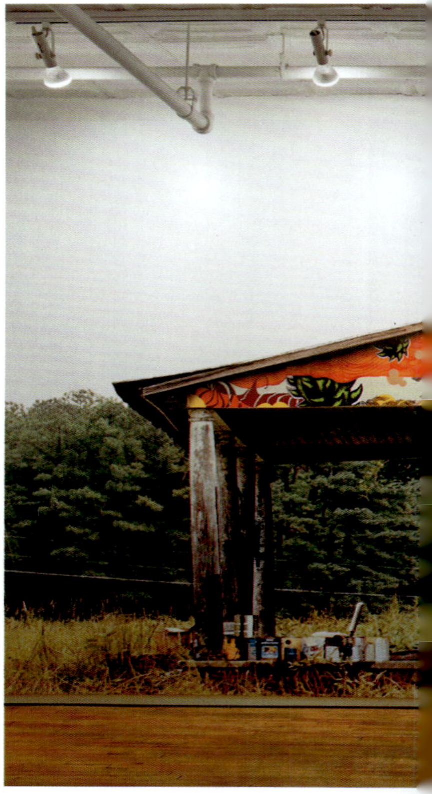

The Barn Painted by David Ellis/Barnstormers.
Photograph by GION.
Cameron, North Carolina, c. 1999–2002.

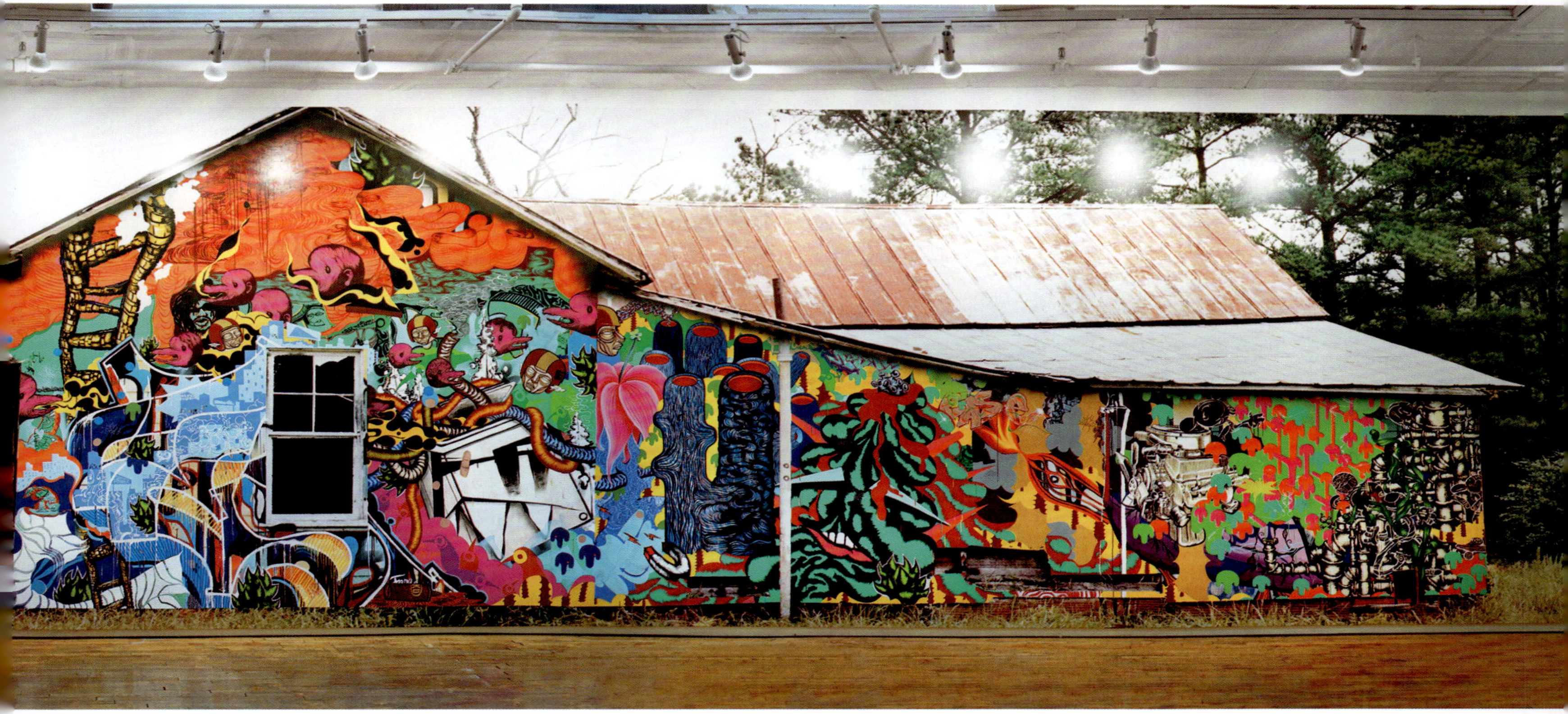

Jean-Michel Basquiat

Jean-Michel Basquiat was born in Brooklyn to middle-class parents, and at the age of seventeen he did what a lot of rebellious kids did—he wrote graffiti. He adopted the name SAMO and wrote with his friend Al Diaz (the graffiti writer formerly known as Bomb 1) on the trains and throughout the Lower East Side. By his own admission, Jean-Michel was not truly a subway graffiti writer; he was in fact a painter, and his graffiti had none of the characteristics of the New York writing movement. Basquiat wrote long, mind-bending messages like "SAMO as an escape clause." There was a certain grandeur to the messages, and the burgeoning underground art scene quickly adopted SAMO as an antihero.

In 1980, at the age of twenty, he appeared in the Times Square Show. By 1981, he had joined the Annina Nosei gallery and was becoming a professional painter. He used oil stick as his medium and painted spontaneously, allowing one image to inform the next. He put a crown over certain images, one of a number of references to graffiti. His bible was *Gray's Anatomy*, a book he had discovered after a childhood accident.

As great as Basquiat was becoming, the downtown scene wanted him to remain SAMO. Never one to be contained by galleries, critics, or fans, Basquiat put an end to SAMO for good with one exhaustive walk through the Lower East Side, during which he wrote "SAMO is dead" until he ran out of paint. Basquiat would go on to reap the mixed benefits of a booming economy, with investors looking to gamble on the next hot artist. His celebrity made him rich but also proved to be his undoing; in 1988, he died of a drug overdose at the age of twenty-eight.

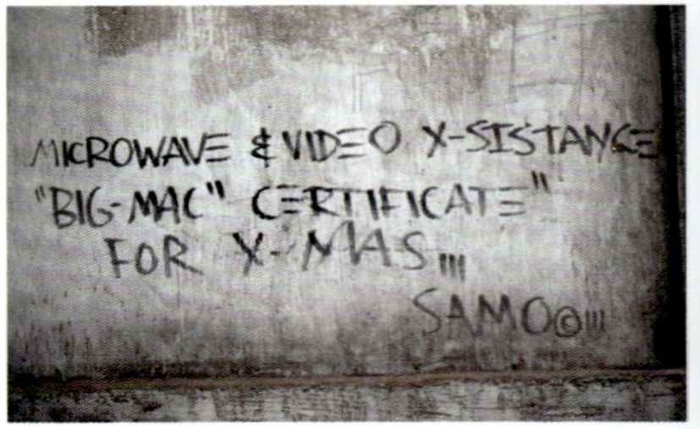

Photographs by Martha Cooper. New York City, 1982.

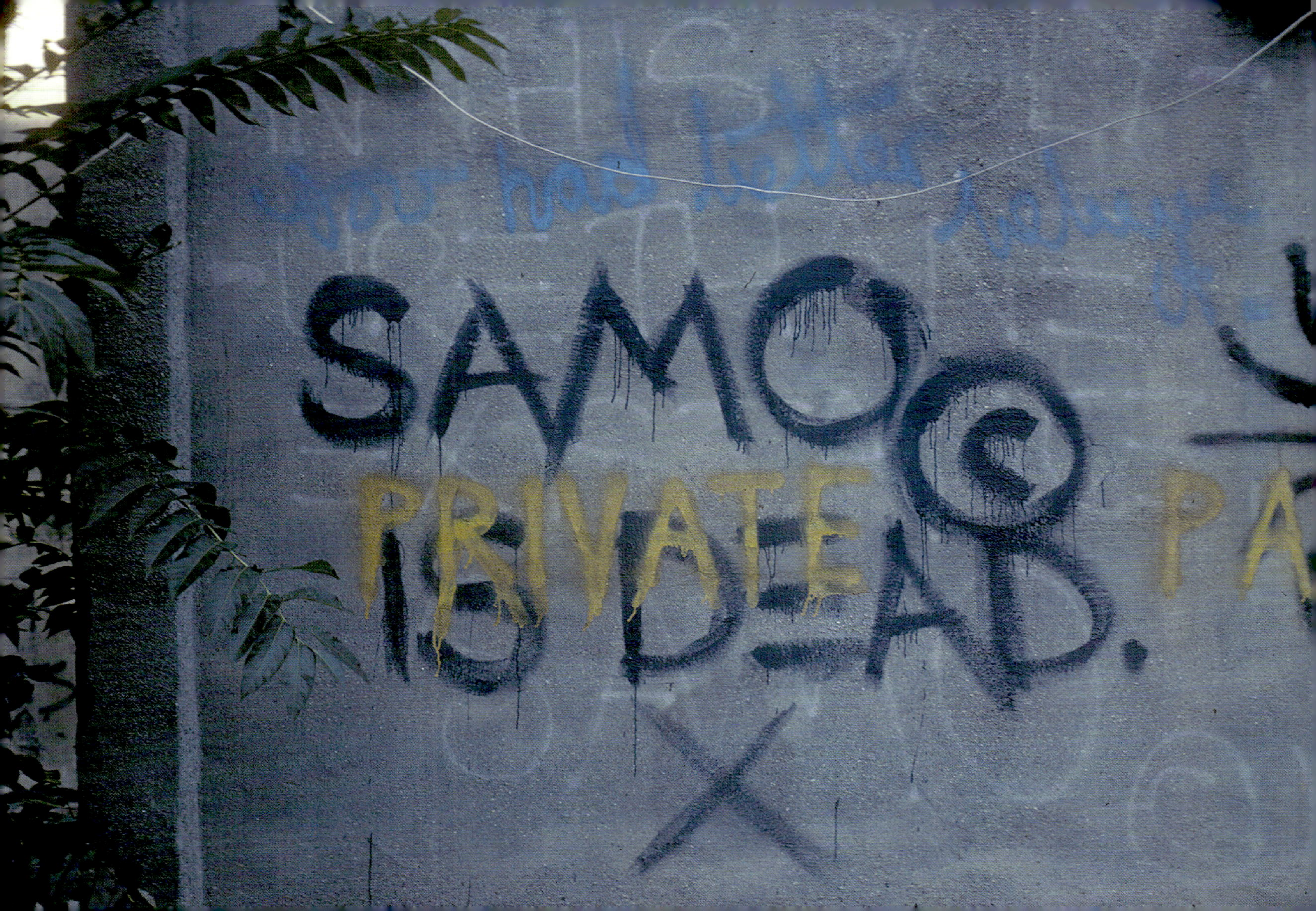
SAMO©
PRIVATE
IS DEAD.

Bast

If you have called New York City home anytime in the last ten years, you have seen the work of the Brooklyn-bred artist Bast. Immensely prolific with his wheatpasted silkscreens and stencils, Bast has permeated the urban landscape of the city for more than a decade. The artist himself, however, remains entirely elusive; like a street-art elephant in the city's cultural room, he is mysterious, talked about, but never revealed.

A longtime collagist, Bast draws inspiration from early punk-rock imagery, using cut-and-paste techniques to make mash-up imagery in a style that has become highly influential in both the street- and commercial-art worlds. Those who are inspired by Bast and have gone on to successful careers include Lady Aiko, Faile, and Judith Supine [see 326]. In fact, Bast was one of the earliest collaborators of legendary street-art powerhouse Faile [see 123]. Their styles were so similar that for many years, viewers would mistake one's work for the other's.

Unwilling to be interviewed, and not eager to offer his work up to the highest commercial bidder, Bast, alongside graffiti legend Revs [see 275], remains one of the most sought-after characters within the graffiti scene.

Bast exhibits his fine-art work internationally, including with New Image Art Gallery in Los Angeles.

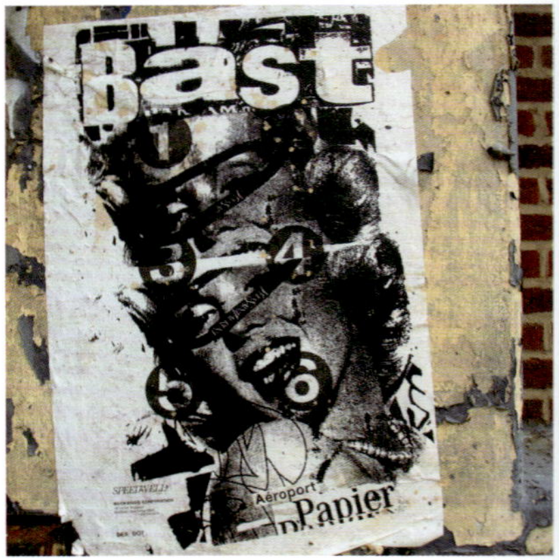

Artwork by Bast [far right] and Pan Am [camera wheatpaste].
Photograph by Becki Fuller.
Brooklyn, New York, 2010.
Detail: Photograph by Luna Park.
Brooklyn, New York, 2009.

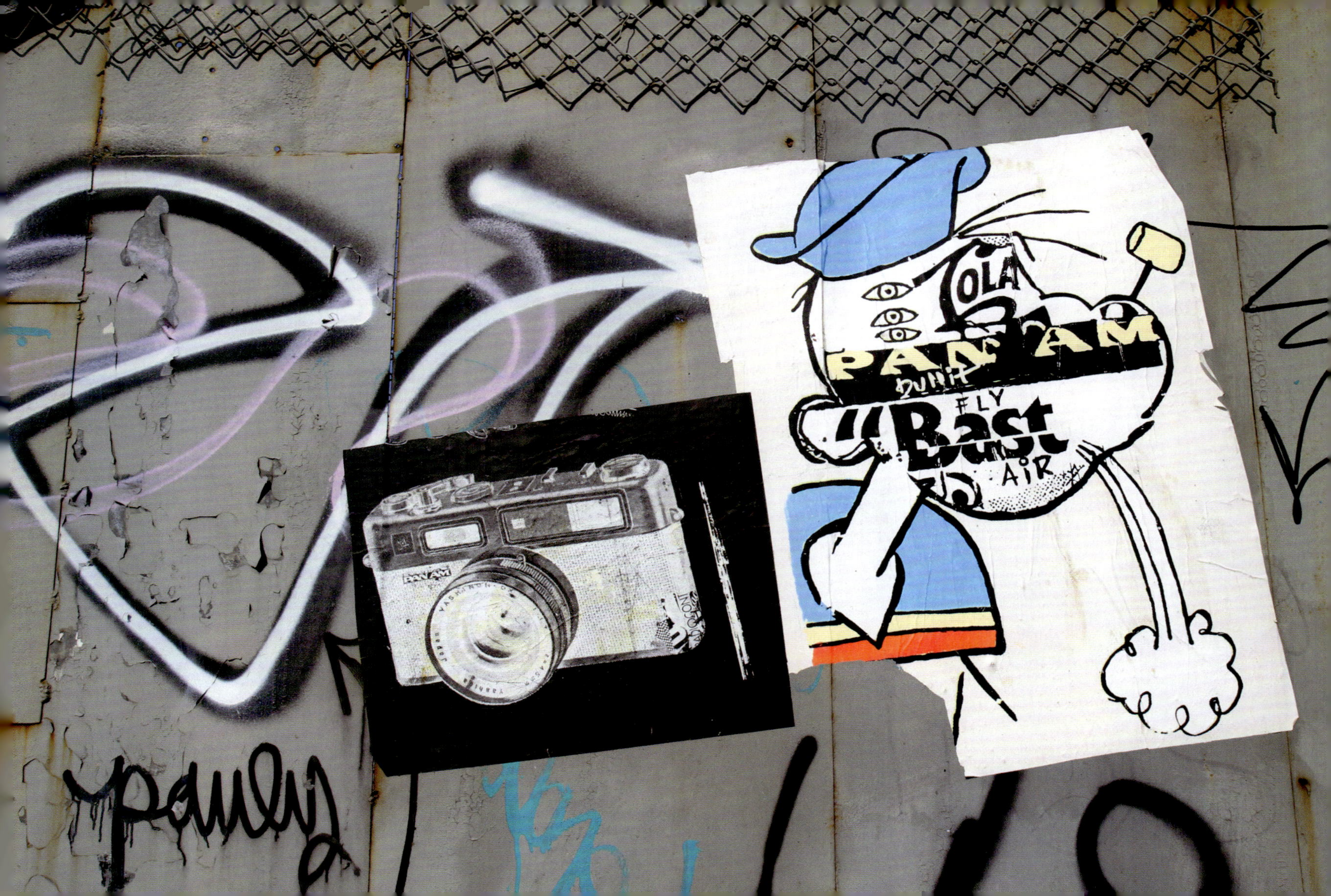
PAN AM
FLY
Bast
AIR
PAN AM

Bastardilla

Bastardilla, one of Colombia's most beloved street artists, is as alluring as her intriguing images. Based in downtown Bogotá, Bastardilla prefers to share her talents with those who live on the outskirts. Her huge, swirling images—sometimes sprinkled with glitter—grace the streets and alleyways of her country's most forlorn districts. Her paintings of mysterious women and fantastical creatures adorn the walls of indigent neighborhoods, such as Los Lachas, on Bogotá's hillside. Her iconic hummingbirds have come to represent Bastardilla's free soul and independent spirit.

Spurred by inequality and social injustice, Bastardilla exudes an almost mystical aura in her devotion to those less fortunate than herself. Inspired by their "modesty and authenticity," she began painting in the streets at age twelve. Although her work has been featured in galleries at home and abroad, Bastardilla is intent on maintaining her privacy and focusing on her passion. She is determined not to become distracted from creating artwork on the streets for the people she most admires.

Along with Stinkfish [see 321], Bastardilla was one of the organizers of "Memoria Canalla," a 2009 exhibit and lecture series that highlighted the history of Bogotá's street art, while also celebrating the genre as a global phenomenon.

Photographs courtesy of Bastardilla.
Bogotá, Colombia, c. 2010.

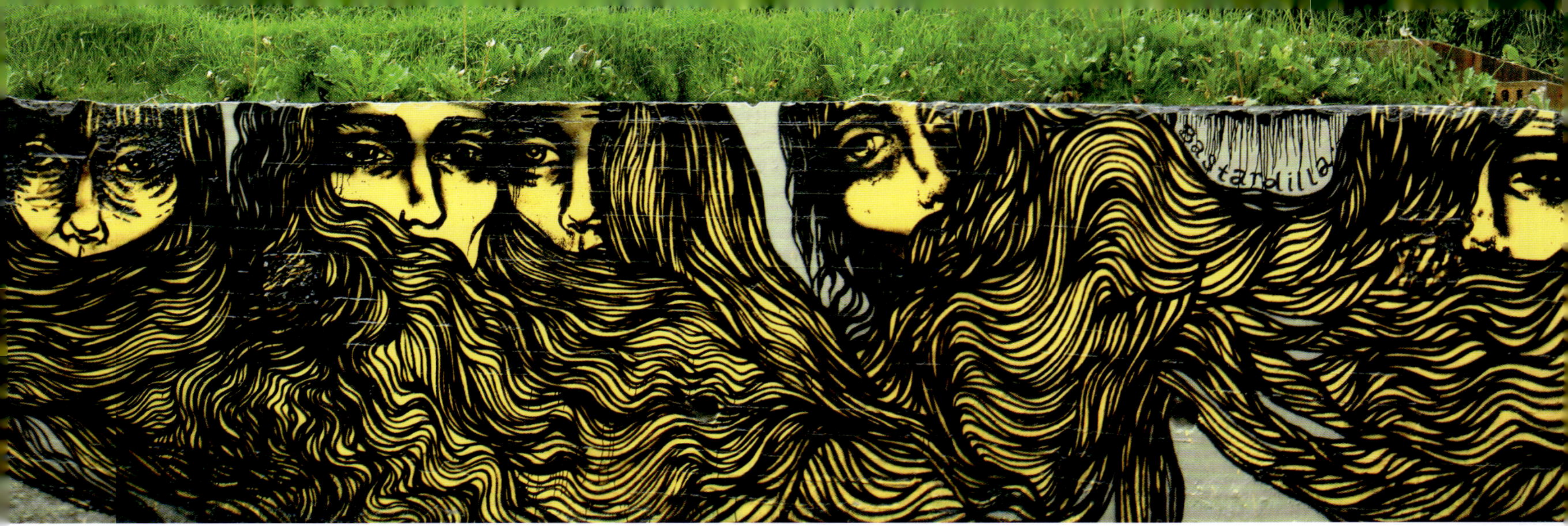
Bastardilla

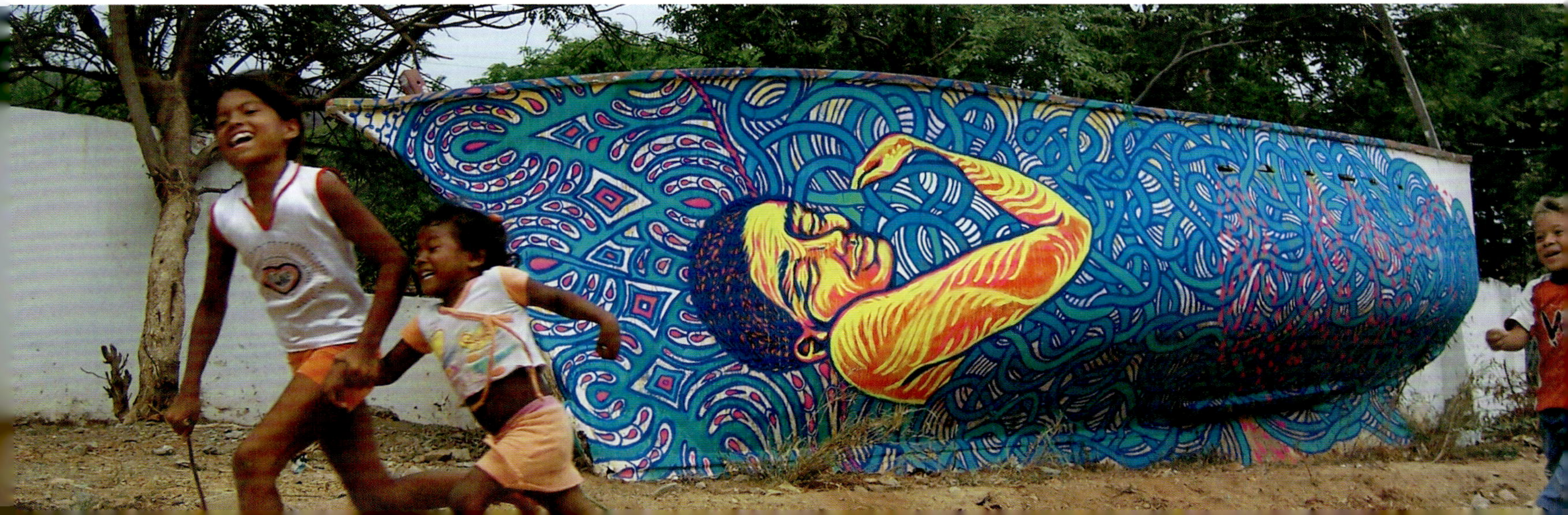

Bates

Bates has been one of the leading stylists in the global graffiti movement for almost a quarter of a century. He began writing in Copenhagen in 1984, inspired by the New York movement. His early pieces emulated several works and styles from *Subway Art* [see 323], a book that became the bible for Bates and his longtime partner, Great.

To describe Bates's style is almost impossible; he simply refuses to be pigeonholed. Every piece is new and different, and because of that, he has legions of fans—and a few detractors. The fans love the professional quality of his work; Bates is, among other things, an astonishing craftsman, and because of this he has represented three different paint companies. The detractors would ask where the authenticity is—who is the real Bates? His response always comes in the form of a piece, one of the thousand technicolor gems that have appeared around the world.

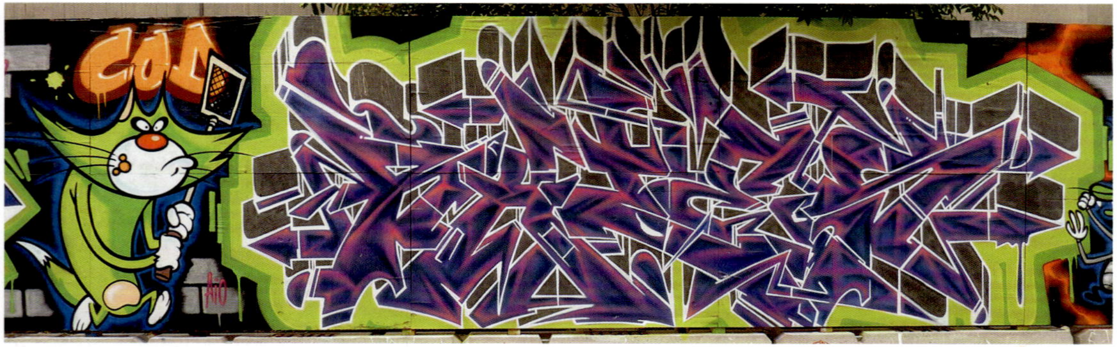

Photographs courtesy of Bates. Copenhagen, Denmark, 2010.

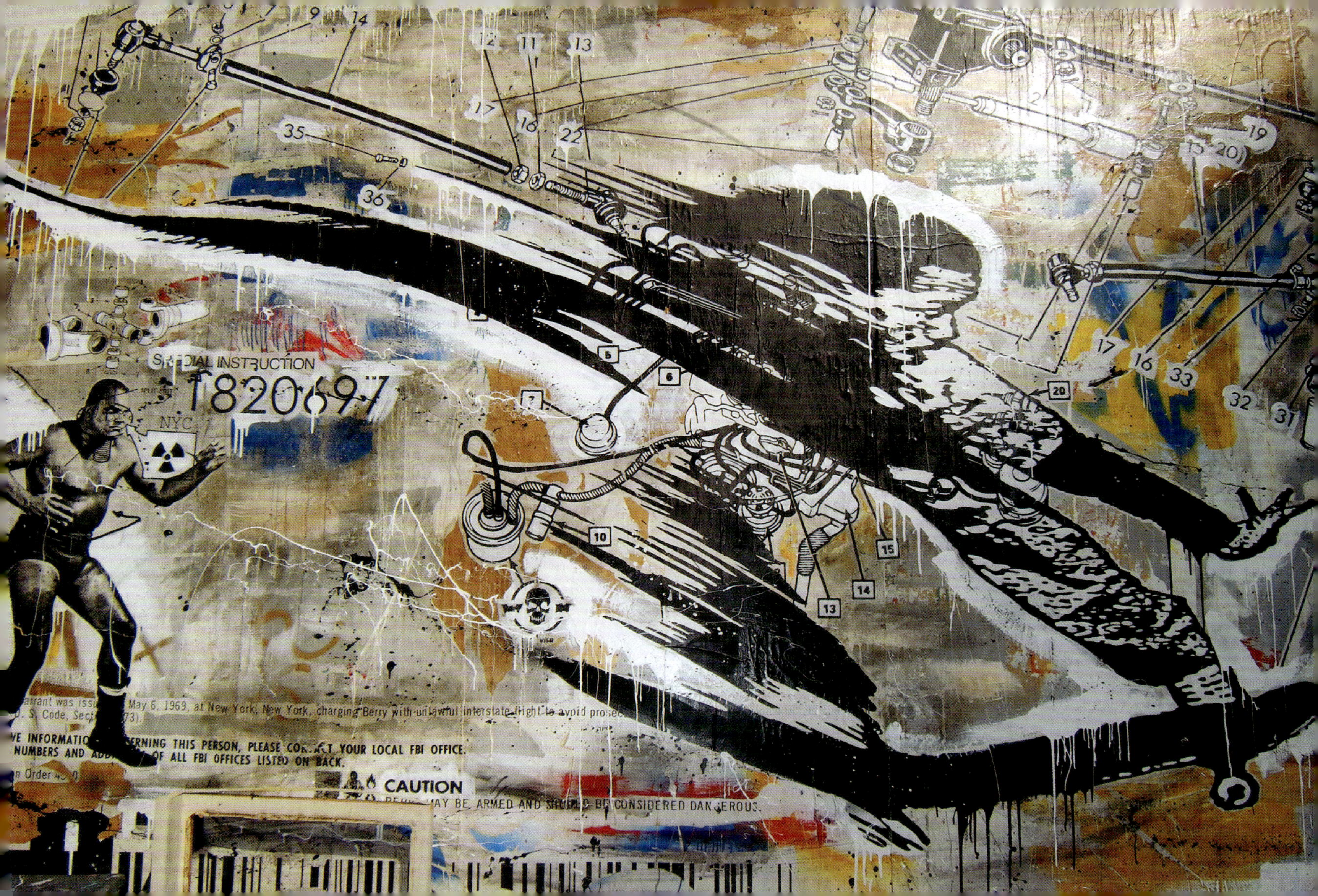

SPECIAL INSTRUCTION
T820697
NYC
May 6, 1969, at New York, New York, charging Berry with unlawful interstate flight to avoid prose
S. Code, Sect
THIS PERSON, PLEASE CO T YOUR LOCAL FBI OFFICE.
NUMBERS AND ADD OF ALL FBI OFFICES LISTED ON BACK.
CAUTION
MAY BE ARMED AND SHOULD BE CONSIDERED DANGEROUS.

Won ABC

Won ABC (Art Bombing Clan) is—in no particular order—an illustrator, an artist, a muralist, and a social commentator. His roots are in the German train-painting scene of the mid-1980s, where one of his most iconic images was a train painted as a dragon. He continued to bomb through the '90s, painting walls around the world.

Won ABC decided very early on that he would refuse to be co-opted by advertisers or galleries, and most of his public paintings have been for communities of people he enjoys. He's painted in Thailand, Sri Lanka, Jamaica, Belize, and Cuba; when he's happy and turned on by people, he leaves a painting behind, done with paint that he's happily paid for. He subscribes to the philosophy that "what you give is yours forever, what you keep is lost forever."

As technically adept as Won is, his concepts are what truly set him apart. In one of his recent paintings, the face of Tupac Shakur is seen staring out from the side of an American dollar bill that's filled with hip-hop iconography from guns to microphones. Many other writers with Won's technical ability would have done the portrait with a nicely lettered name, that's not enough for Won. If a work doesn't push the envelope, it's not worth his time.

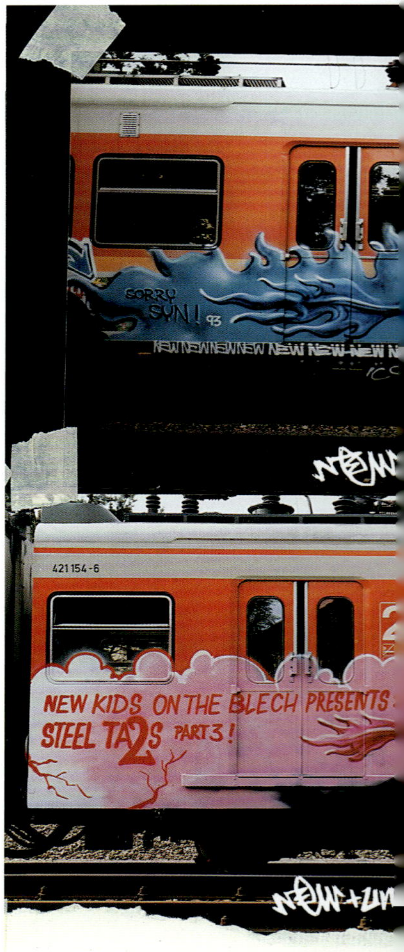

Photograph courtesy of Won ABC. Germany.

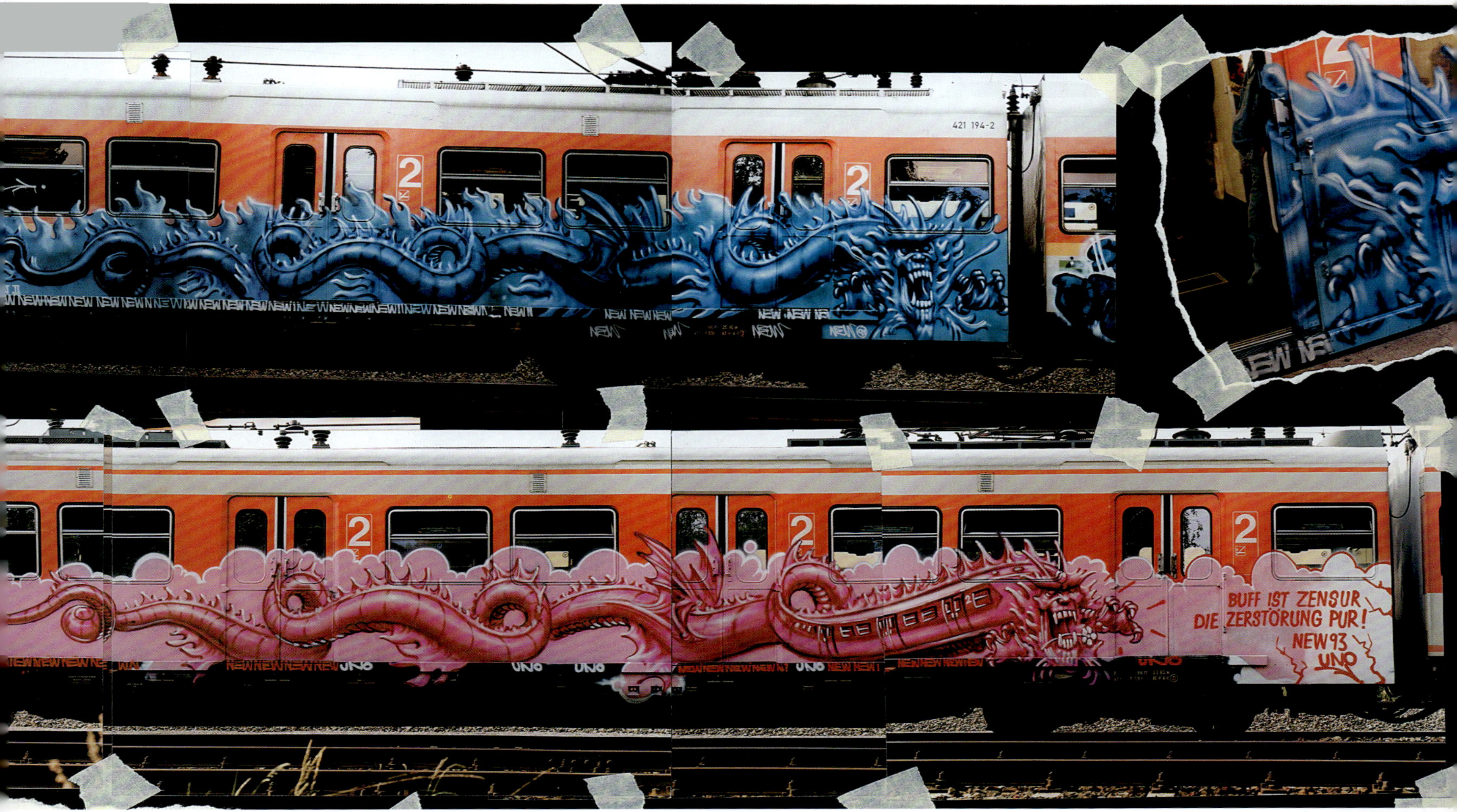
421 194-2
BUFF IST ZENSUR
DIE ZERSTÖRUNG PUR!
NEW93
UNO

The Wooster Collective

In 2003, SoHo residents Marc and Sara Schiller began noticing an abundance of stickers appearing on the streets of their downtown New York neighborhood. Using a small digital camera, they started to document the unusual work they were seeing. The Schillers gradually discovered an entire world of wheatpastes and stencils that defied the boundaries of traditional graffiti. Enthralled, they started a blog, woostercollective.com.

Between 2003 and 2006, through daily posts submitted by readers, the Wooster Collective blog became the premier online portal for street-art enthusiasts, showcasing emerging artists who would go on to become street art's figureheads, such as Swoon (see 329), Faile (see 123), Banksy (see 024), JR (see 185), and many others. In 2006, the Schillers collaborated with Caroline Cummings and curated the world-renowned 11 Spring Street show (see 001), which drew six thousand visitors.

Weathering the boom in the popularity of street art, woostercollective.com is alive and thriving today, free of advertising or endorsement. The Schillers receive more than two hundred e-mails a day, and are most often credited as the world's foremost street-art experts.

Photograph by Alexander Wagner.

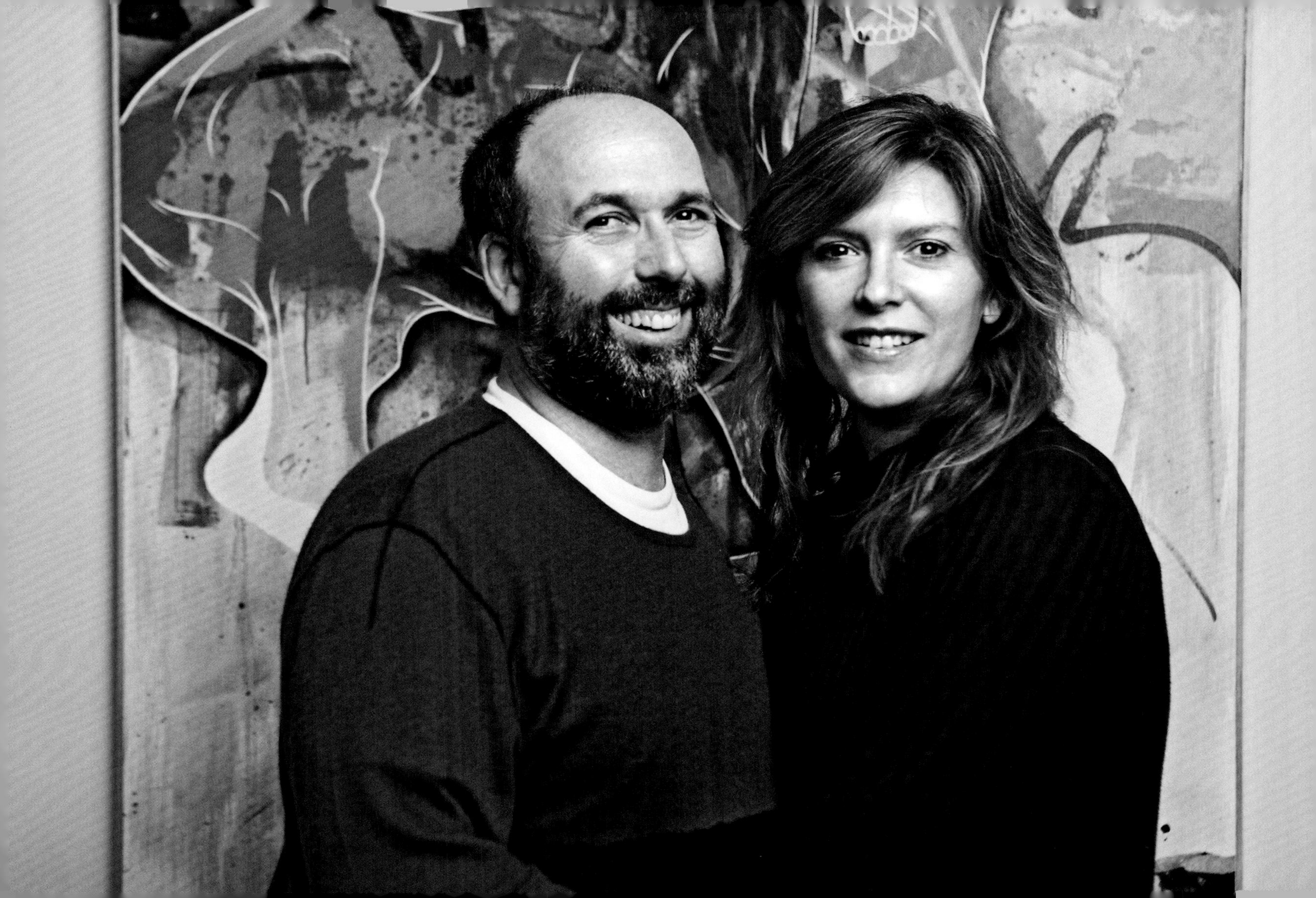

Word to Mother Nature

Word to Mother Nature was the name chosen by a young artist born and raised in a small English seaside town. Nature and the coastal setting of his childhood are echoed throughout his work, with subtle references to Sailor Jerry tattoos painted directly onto weather-worn timber.

Now living and working in London, Word to Mother Nature can often be found sketching away in a café or a park, or scavenging for interesting surfaces to paint and old printed matter to cut up and use for collage. He likes to use objects with past lives, seen as useless and discarded by someone. He takes these objects in and—while retaining as much of their original texture and color as possible—turns them into jaw-dropping pieces of handmade art. His work feels so organic that it's as though all these items have somehow made their way especially to him.

Word to Mother Nature has become well known for the looseness of his lines and his edgy, raw style. And, true to his name, he often includes words in his pieces, embedded among his colorful, Klimt-esque patterns and instantly recognizable, somber-eyed characters.

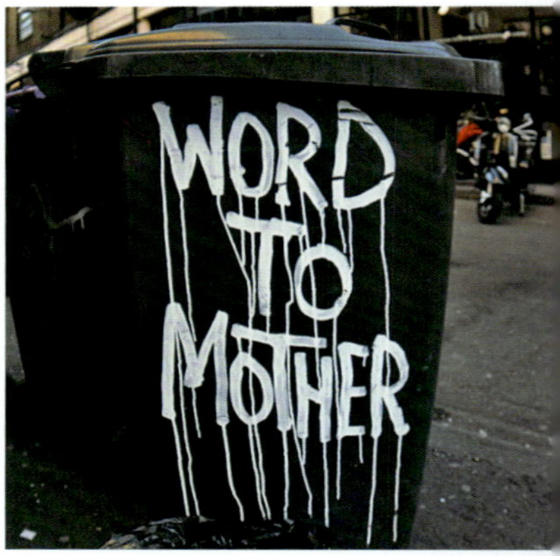

Photographs by George Macdonald.
Hackney, London, 2008.
Detail top: Brick Lane, London, 2009.
Detail bottom: Brick Lane, London, 2009.

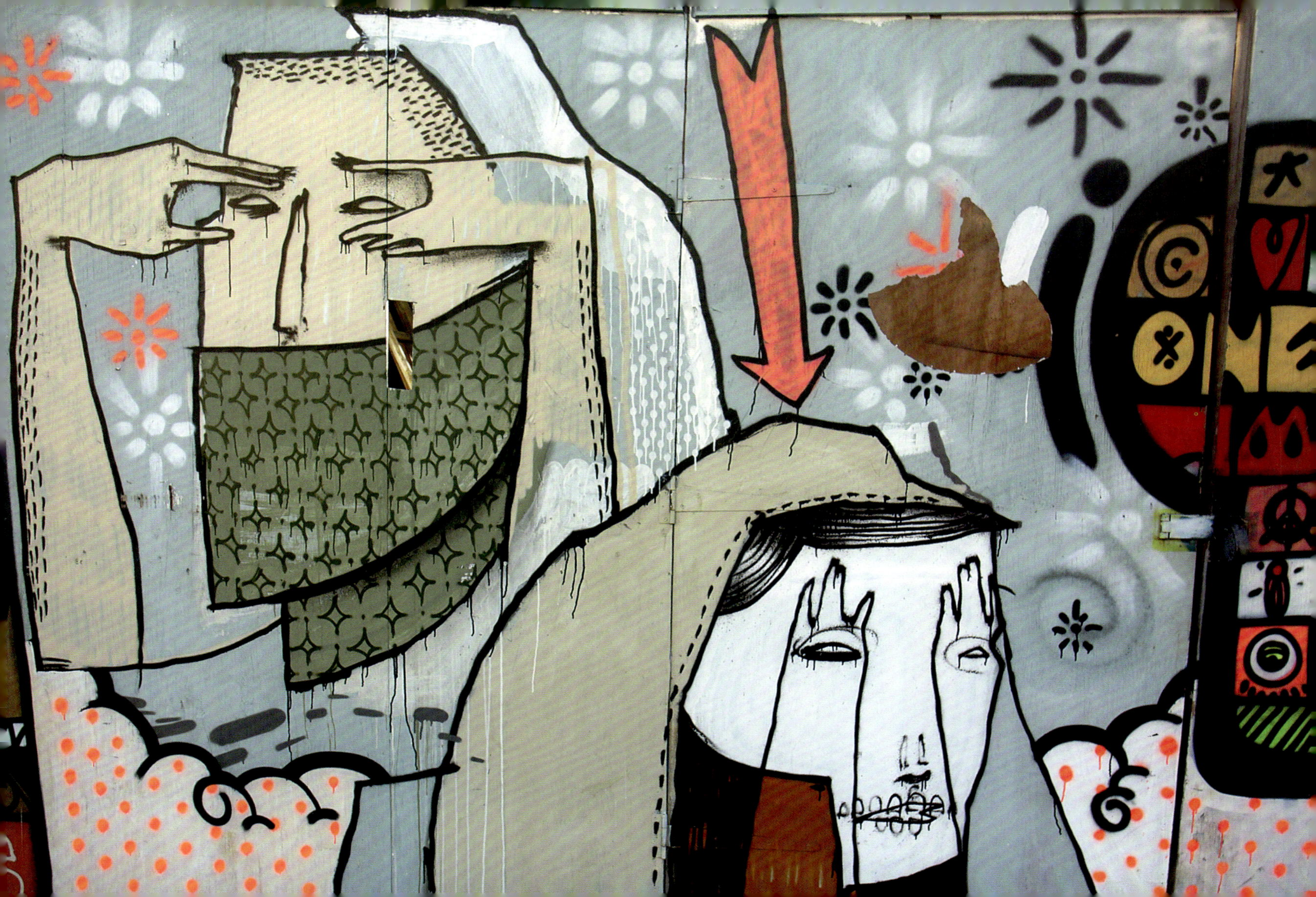

Wow 123

Wow 123 began writing in Bremen, Germany, in 1988, at the age of fourteen. He began refining his style on trains and walls around the Bremen area; he stuck mostly with lettering until 1995, when he took a trip to New York and was blown away by the murals of renowned artists like Ces, T-Kid, Bio, and the Tats Cru. When he arrived back in Germany, characters began to appear in his new works.

One thing remained constant in Wow 123's pieces: The characters never distracted from the overall piece. For him, the piece was the litmus test of a writer's skill, and he felt his pieces worked only if he stripped away all the camouflage and 3-D devices that other writers hid behind. If the outline held up, then the piece was solid.

Wow's style comes from a number of sources, including his mood at the time and the location he's painting in. He plays with soft letters, mechanical letters, wide 3-Ds, and Wild Style—which he feels comes straight out of the Bronx (and he enjoys that connection). Another distinct aspect of his work is the amount of effort he puts into keeping the paintings clean; he sometimes chides other artists for their sloppiness. Wow 123 will go down in history as one of Europe's greatest stylists.

Photograph courtesy of Wow 123.
Germany, 2010.

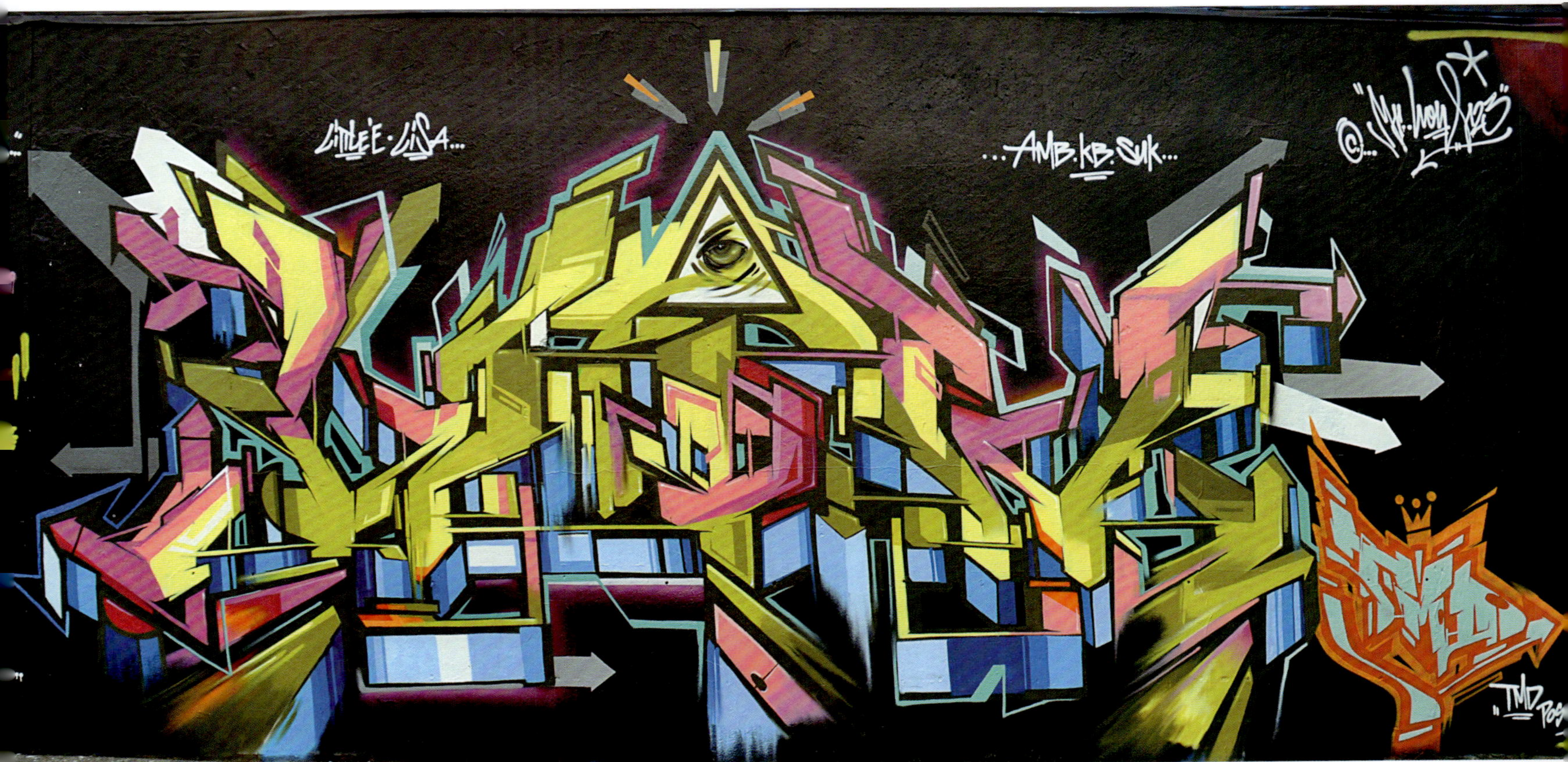

The Writer's Bench

During the 1970s, writer's benches existed all over New York. Brooklyn had one at Atlantic Avenue; Queens had two, one at Parsons Boulevard (for black writers), the other at Continental Avenue (for white writers). However, when someone referred to "the Bench," everyone knew this meant 149th Street and Grand Concourse in the Bronx. Technically, the Bench on the uptown side of that subway station belonged to the transit authority, but graffiti writers had laid claim to it and turned it into a clubhouse without walls.

Phase 2 (see 255) started hanging out at the Bench, giving style lessons while watching and critiquing the work on the trains as they rolled by. The regulars at the Bench included the most talented writers, as well as the most thuggish; a writer making the pilgrimage to 149th Street in hopes of meeting his idol ran the risk of being assaulted and robbed.

On a good day, Phase 2 or Riff 170 might let you see his latest blackbook masterpiece. On a bad day, you could get raided by the cops. Kids would wait for hours, hoping one of their pieces would roll by. Competition raged, and the chances of getting a compliment from your peers was remote. The Bench was a style lab, a proving ground, a place that separated the men from the boys—the benchmark of graffiti chic.

Photograph by Henry Chalfant. New York City, 1982.

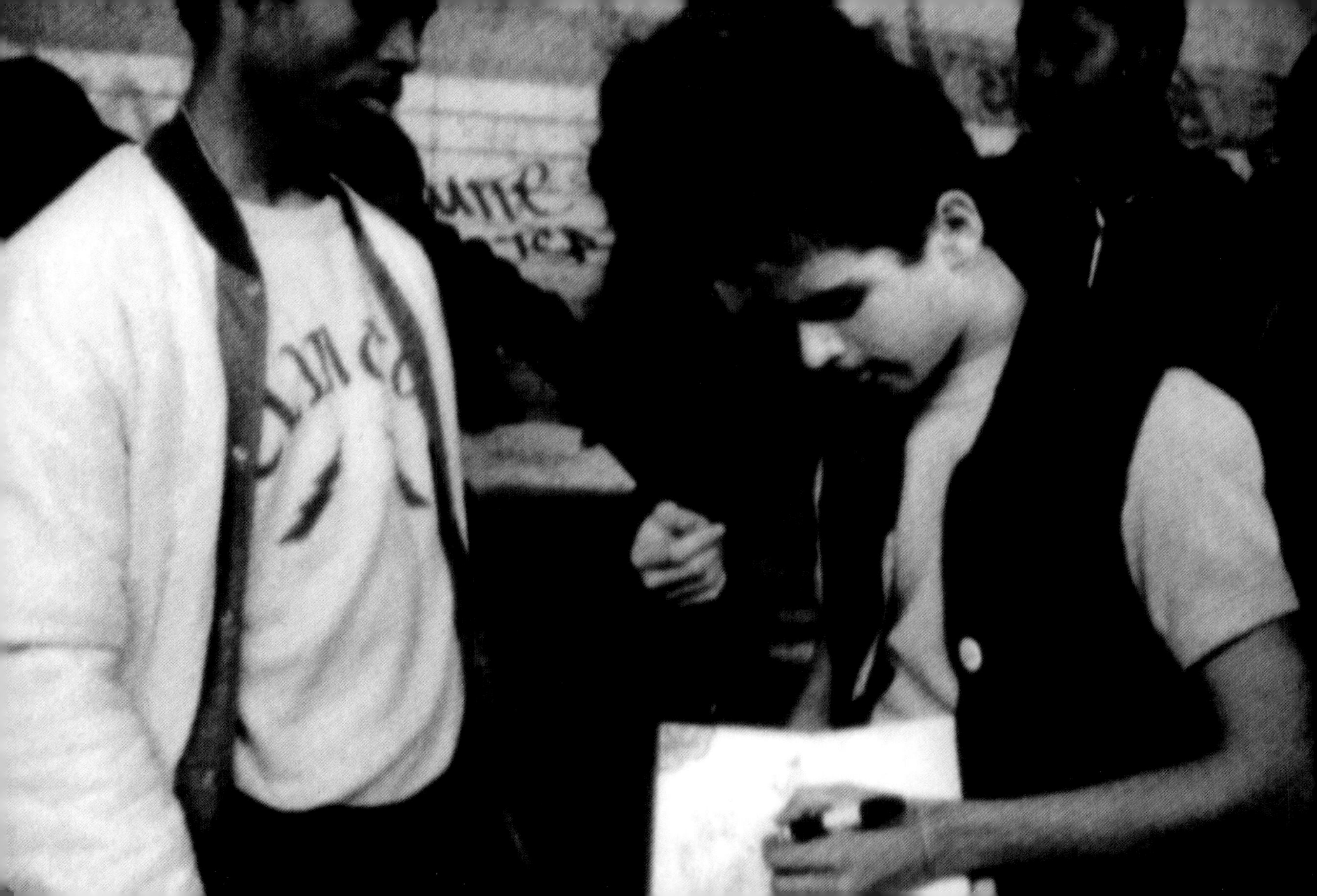

Zephyr

Zephyr began his writing career in the mid-1970s, and in 1979 he made the leap from tagger to piecer. His novel piecing style had great appeal; it didn't follow the script style of the day, which relied heavily on Death Squad [see 086] and TMT components. Zephyr particularly admired Rick Griffin's work, and its influence could be seen throughout his piece books from that era.

In 1980, his work matured, as he started mixing in design components from other artists he had written with, a list that included Futura 2000 [see 141], Seen [see 294], Dondi [see 097], Kel, and Noc 167. Perhaps no one had more of an impact on Zephyr than Dondi, but Zephyr was no acolyte, and he always retained his individuality.

Zephyr's impact on the culture was not only through his subway works; he was the driving force behind a number of graffiti projects that helped solidify the movement, among them the Sam Esses Studio, in 1980, and the Soul Artists [see 310] workshop, where writers learned to paint on canvas and network with each other. He floated in and out of the art world and was a mainstay at the Fun Gallery [see 140]. The logo he did for the film *Wild Style* has been seen throughout the world. In the 1990s he began writing about the movement, and his book *Dondi: Stylemaster General* is considered a must-have in any writer's collection. Not content to simply chronicle the movement, Zephyr returned to his roots in the late 1990s, choosing freights as his new medium and often painting with kids twenty-five years his junior.

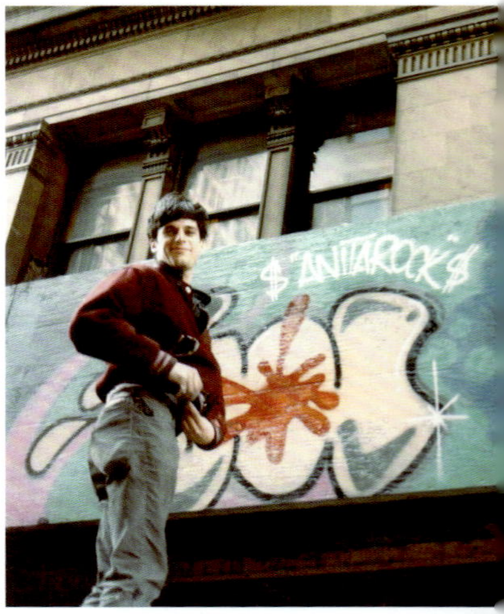

Photograph by Pjay One.
New York City 1980.
Detail: Photograph by Anita Rosenberg.
New York City, 1982.

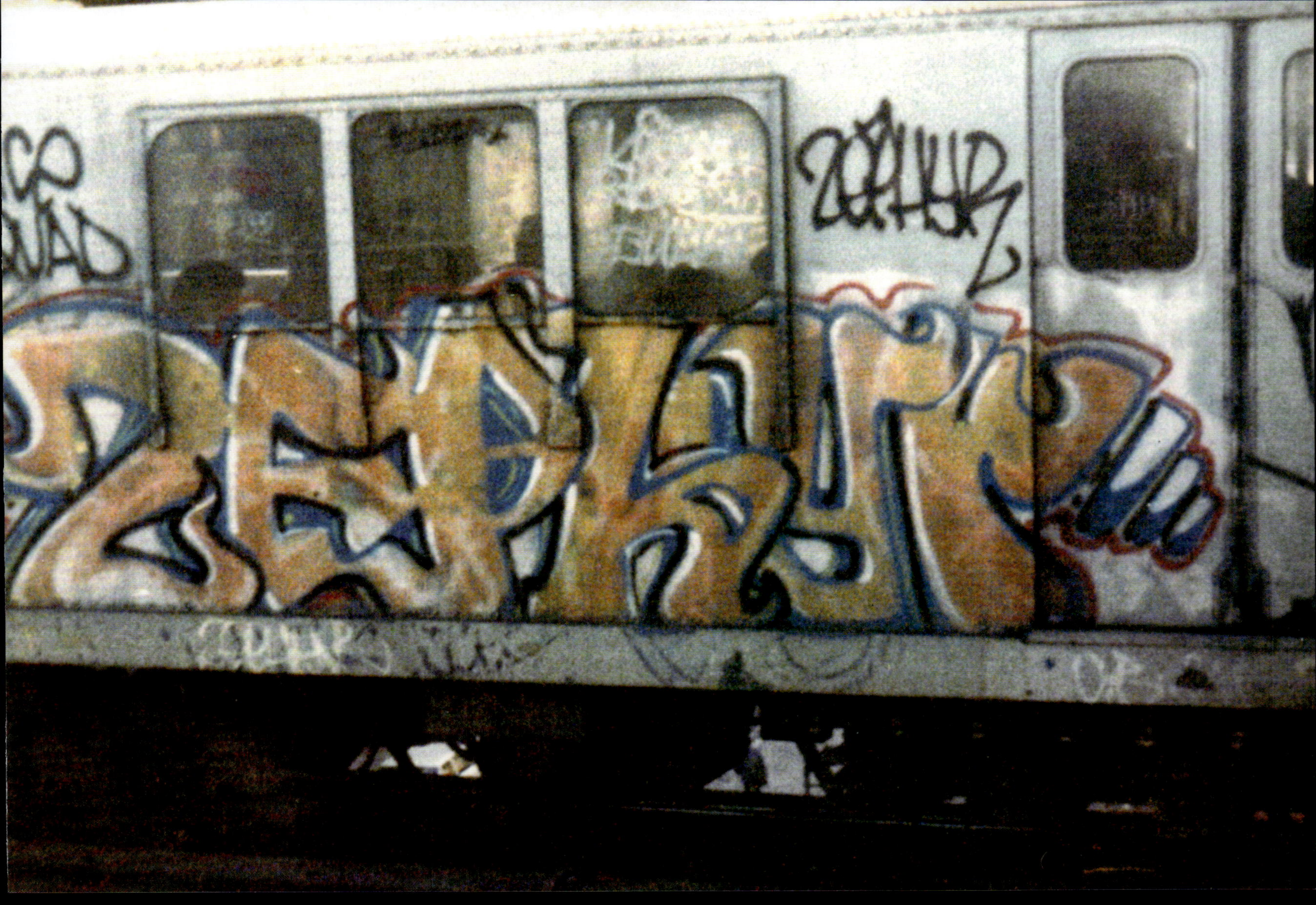

Zezao

In one of the grimiest, most overpopulated, and most dangerous cities in the world, it takes a special affinity for darkness and filth for a writer to descend into the sewage system and paint graffiti that, more than likely, no one will ever see. Zezao's hometown of São Paulo, Brazil, is precious to him, and the impulse behind his often-subterranean work is a wish to offer a healing energy to the city's pain and squalor. Zezao says that the color blue represents the life force for him, and that color dominates most of his work.

Zezao's abstracted, squiggly arabesques draw inspiration from a background in *pixação* (see 257), the unique lettering style born in São Paulo. He paints mostly in the poorest neighborhoods in the city, often offering to paint the homes of the destitute at no charge.

Now almost forty, Zezao is one of Brazil's best-known abstract-graffiti artists, and he has begun to exhibit in gallery settings, spreading his wings as far as the Jonathan LeVine gallery in New York City.

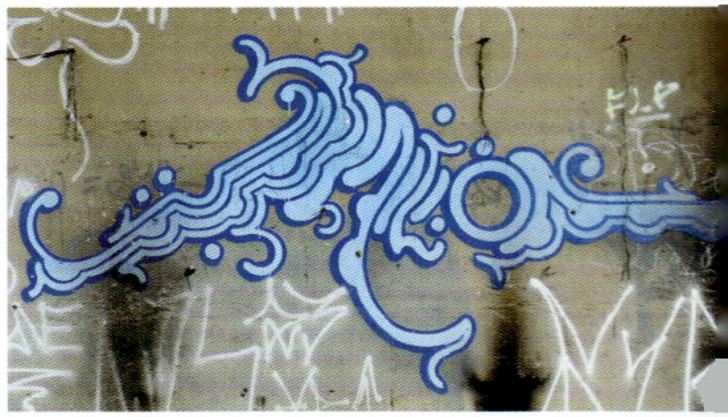

Photographs by Eric Marechal.
São Paulo, Brazil, 2010.

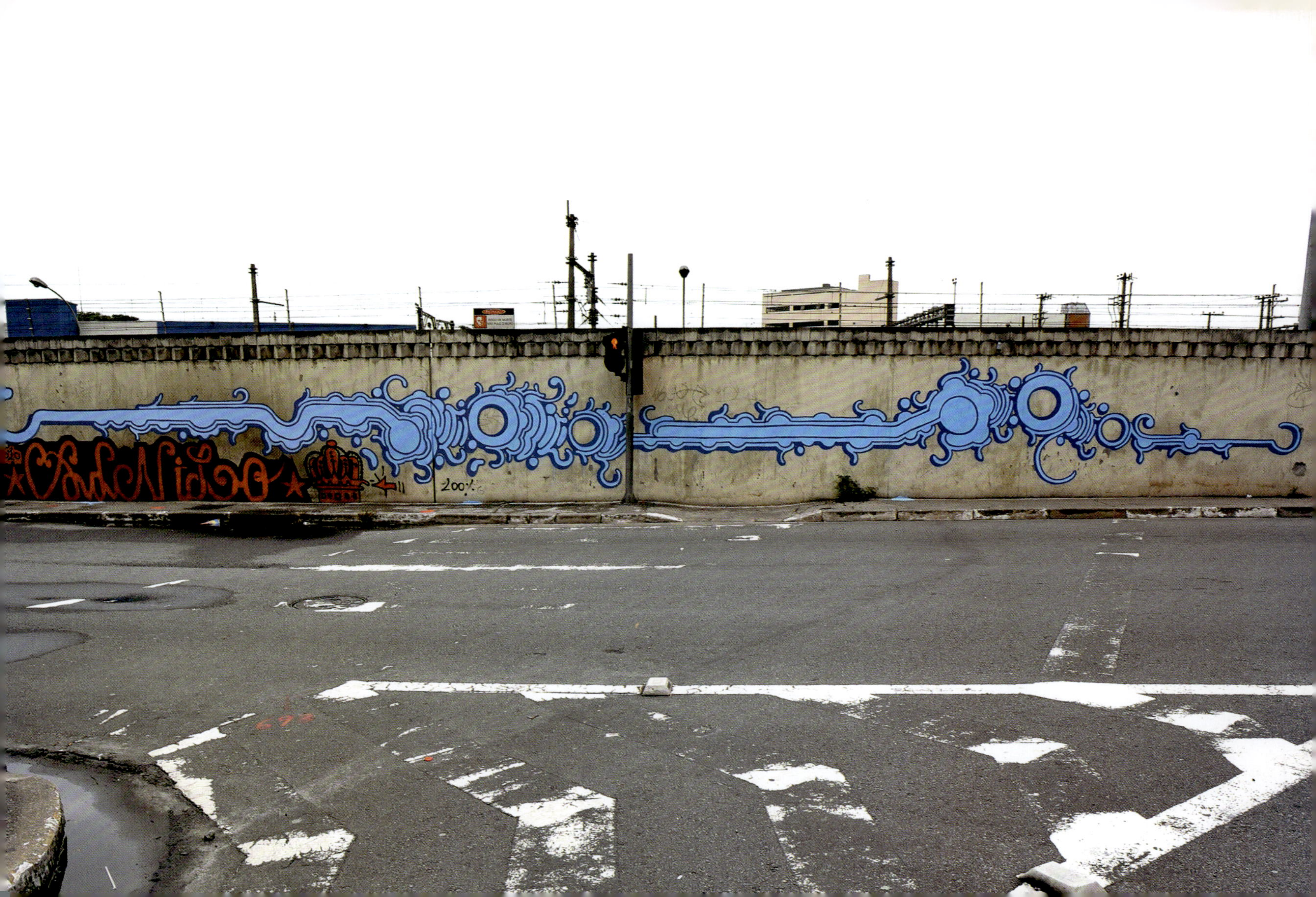

Zilda

Along with the broadening of acceptable mediums in graffiti came a vast widening of inspiration for urban art. Some artists, like Faile [see 123], Shepard Fairey [see 124], and Bast [see 027], were influenced by the cut-and-paste imagery of punk rock. Others, like Armsrock [see 017] and Swoon [see 329], sketched from what they saw on the street. Some went completely into their own worlds of fantastical animals and characters, like the Italian street artist Blu [see 040]. What street art had yet to see, however, was a classicist—someone with a deep affinity for Renaissance painting and drawing techniques. Enter Zilda.

In what looked like classical figure-drawing studies, the mysterious French artist [originally from the city of Rennes] used paintbrushes and drawing tools to create lifelike depictions of characters from another age, often nude—like an army of statues brought to life and wheatpasted to walls.

One notable Zilda project was titled "*Io sono una forza del passato*," which is Italian for "I am a force of the past." In this work, the artist wheatpasted numerous highly detailed stencil renderings of characters from classic Italian movies from the 1950s and 1960s around the streets of Rome. The title of the project could not have been a more apt description of Zilda's work.

Photographs courtesy of Zilda.
Right: Lisbon, Portugal, 2010.
Far right, top: Paris, 2009.
Far right, bottom: Paris, 2010.

ACKNOWLEDGMENTS

I would like to thank my wife, Claudia, my sons Dillon and Marlon, and my daughter, Raquel, for their patience and understanding as they lost me to a computer screen for the past two years. Everything I do is for them.

I would like to thank Andrew "Zephyr" Witten for his guidance and belief in my vision.

I would also like to thank my right hand throughout this project, Monica LoCascio, who signed on as a photo editor, but provided entrée into the world of street art, enabling me to connect with artists and writers whose passion and knowledge inspired and enlightened me.

I would like to thank iO Tillet Wright, one of the most creative and driven women I've ever met, without whose monumental literary contributions, this book would not have been possible. I would like to thank Martha Cooper, who became my consigliere on this project, granting me unlimited access to her formidable archives and her technical expertise. I would like to thank Luna Park and Becki Fuller for my visual introduction into the world of street art. Their images of public art will define their generation. I would like to thank Chris "Freedom" Pape, who answered the call when it came. I would like to thank Henry Chalfant, who has been a loyal friend for many years. I would like to thank Regina Stewart for granting me access to the Jack Stewart archives. I would like to thank Flint [Flint . . .] Gennari, whose breathtaking black-and-white photos from graffiti's early years capture the feeling of a long-forgotten era. I would also like to thank Ernie Paniccioli, who granted me unlimited access to his home and voluminous files.

I would like to thank my editor, Eric Klopfer, for his unwavering support and belief in me, and for having my back throughout the whole process. I would like to thank Eric Himmel for having faith in me and allowing this book to happen.

I would also like to thank my brother Andrew for his unwavering support throughout my life and his invaluable art world expertise. Finally, I thank: Frank Malt and aerosolplanet; Keith Baugh, whose book *Early New York Graffiti 1973–1975* amazed and inspired me; Med and Ces One at Tuff City Tattoos in the Bronx, for constant support over many years; Lois Stavsky, who delivered photos and big-time writing like clockwork; my boy Harley "Mr. Softy" Spiller, for his formidable linguistics and photos; Sever, who connected me with the MSK/AWR/7th Letter boys; Smith and Cycle, who generously opened their archives to me; and the incomparable Pjay One, who blessed me with some killer images.

Contributing writers: iO Tillet Wright, Jay "J.SON" Edlin, Andrew "Zephyr" Witten, Chris Pape, Lois Stavsky, Manuel Bello, Madeleine Moulton, Zang Greiner, Harlan Levey, R. J. Rushmore, Harley Spiller, Lil' Bryant Crenshaw, Carlo McCormick, and Nicholas Platz.

Photo Editor and Project Manager: Monica LoCascio
Editor: Eric Klopfer
Managing Editor: Ivy McFadden
Designer: Shawn Dahl, dahlimama inc
Production Manager: Anet Sirna-Bruder

Library of Congress Cataloging-in-Publication Data

Edlin, Jay (J.SON)
Graffiti 365 / by Jay "J.SON" Edlin ; foreword by Andrew "Zephyr" Witten.
p. cm.
ISBN 978-0-8109-9744-8 (alk. paper)
1. Street art. 2. Mural painting and decoration—21st century. 3. Graffiti. I. Title. II. Title: Graffiti three hundred sixty five.
ND2590.E35 2011
751.7'3—dc22
2011006934

Printed and bound in China
10 9 8 7 6 5 4 3 2 1

Abrams books are available at special discounts when purchased in quantity for premiums and promotions as well as fundraising or educational use. Special editions can also be created to specification. For details, contact specialsales@abramsbooks.com or the address below.

ABRAMS
THE ART OF BOOKS SINCE 1949
115 West 18th Street
New York, NY 10011
www.abramsbooks.com

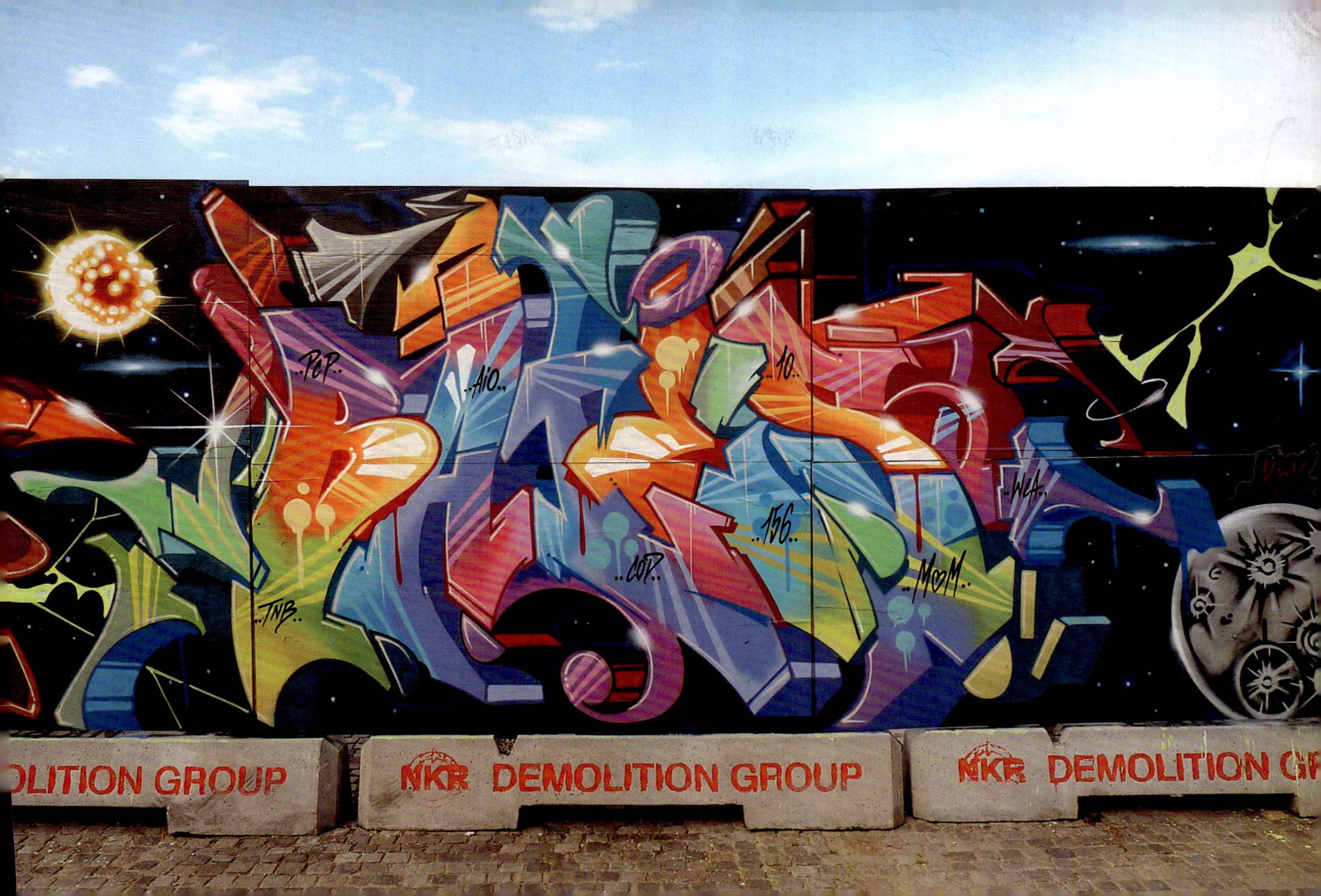
OLITION GROUP
NKR DEMOLITION GROUP
NKR DEMOLITION

Beautiful Losers

In 2007, curator, artist, and director Aaron Rose brought out a widely publicized film titled *Beautiful Losers*. This feature-length documentary tells the story of Rose's clan, a haphazard group of artists, filmmakers, and skateboarders who shot to prominence in the 1990s, tied together by their mutual sense of being outsiders, as well as a love for DIY art. The film—starring Rose, Barry McGee (see 214), ESPO, Mike Mills, Ed Templeton, Harmony Korine, and Shepard Fairey (see 124), among others—traces the tale of Rose's legendary Alleged gallery, where he exhibited the work of these young artists, alongside shock photographer Terry Richardson's early photography. It explores how the space created a nexus for the burgeoning skate culture, out of which the 1995 movie *Kids* emerged, and what many consider the original progression of graffiti into street art. As it delves into the writers' eventual art-world successes and the commercial opportunities that followed, the film essentially looks at the inherent outsiderness of the artists depicted and of the culture they come from.

Rose later closed the gallery and hit the road with the traveling "Beautiful Losers" exhibition, a large-scale group show of his Alleged artists, which has visited museums from Ohio to Europe to Tokyo.

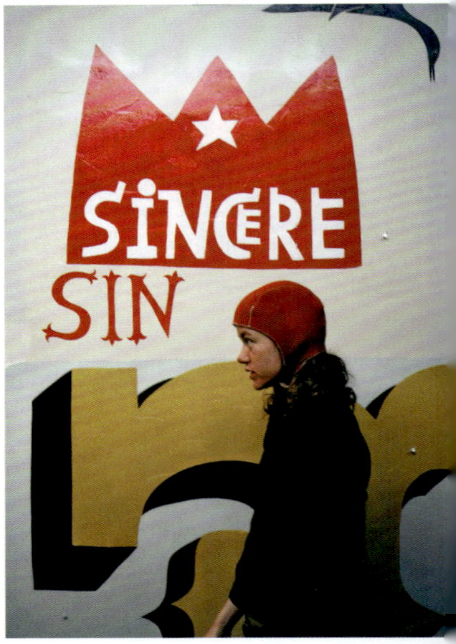

Photographs by Cheryl Dunn.
Tokyo, Shibuya, 2000.
Detail: Margaret Kilgallen in her studio.
San Francisco, 1998.

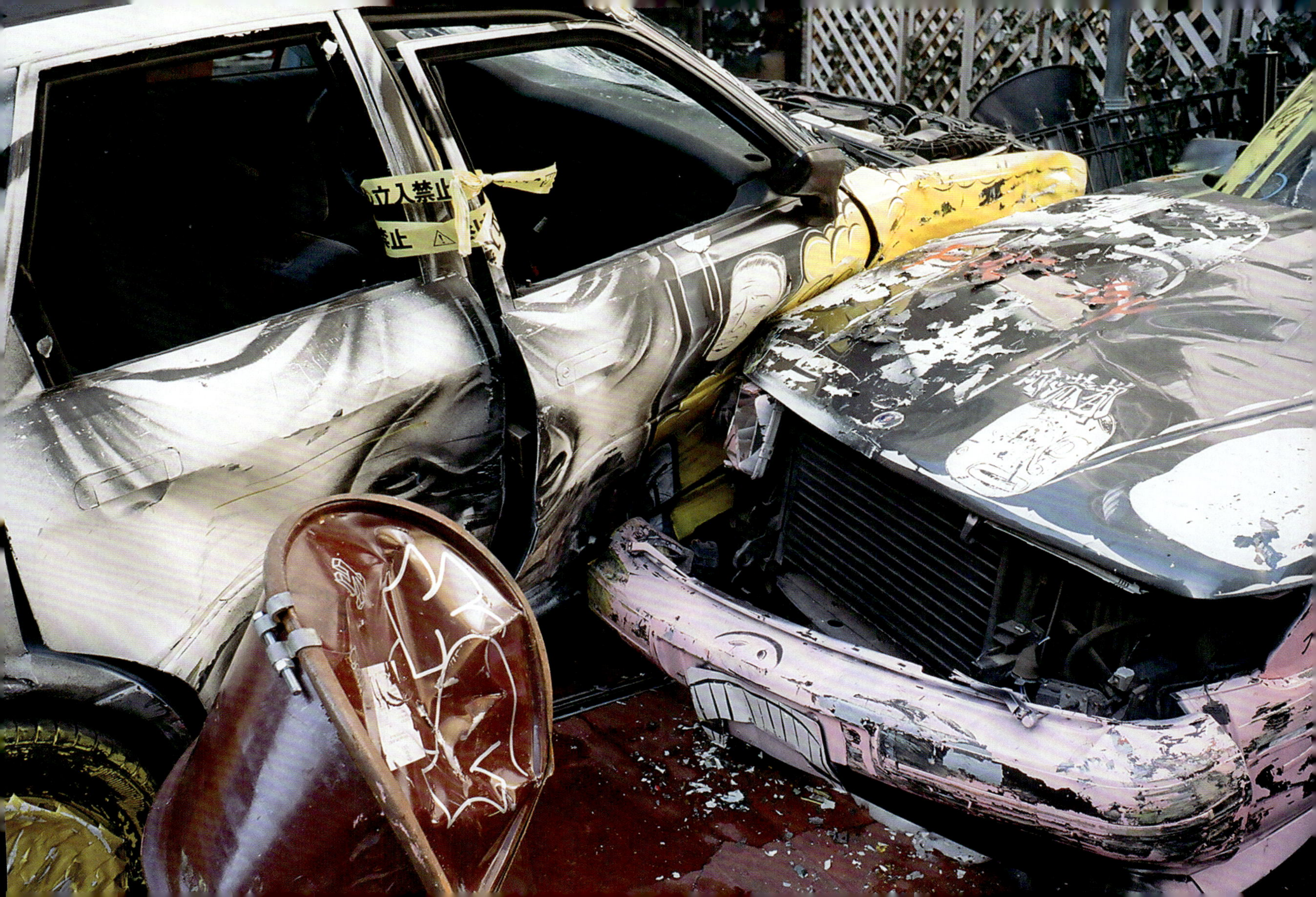
立入禁止
禁止

beef

There's only one thing graffiti artists hate more than the system: each other. Beef, or war, has always been a part of the fame game. In the subway days, some feuds were territorial [Bronx versus Brooklyn artists] and some were crew-related [MPC versus RTW [see 286]]. Throughout the 1970s, most disputes were settled with either fistfights or conciliatory measures, such as giving a writer paint if you had shown disrespect for his work. By the early '80s, the stakes had grown higher. Shootings and stabbings became real possibilities, as armed crews sought to augment their paint supplies at their competitors' expense. Most of the warfare occurred on the outsides of trains, where a beautifully executed, labor-intensive whole-car could be laid to waste in a matter of minutes with an enemy's throw-up plastered in the center of a masterpiece.

Nowadays, street artists compete for space with their aerosol predecessors, who consider street artists to be soft. While permission walls and gallery inclusion has somewhat thinned, the outlaw herd battles still rage. Currently there's anarchy in the U.K. Street-art king Banksy dissed a sleeping giant by placing a cheeky stencil over the remnants of a twenty-five-year-old piece by the retired old-school graffiti legend Robbo. Now, the two destroy each other's work daily. Both have enlisted their minions' aid in a battle of paint and wit that is wildly entertaining—and perhaps a bit suspect: smart money has Robbo, the six-foot-seven former soccer hooligan, becoming the protagonist of Banksy's next film.

Artwork by Robbo and Banksy.
Photographs by David Stuart [NoLionsInEngland].
London, 2009.

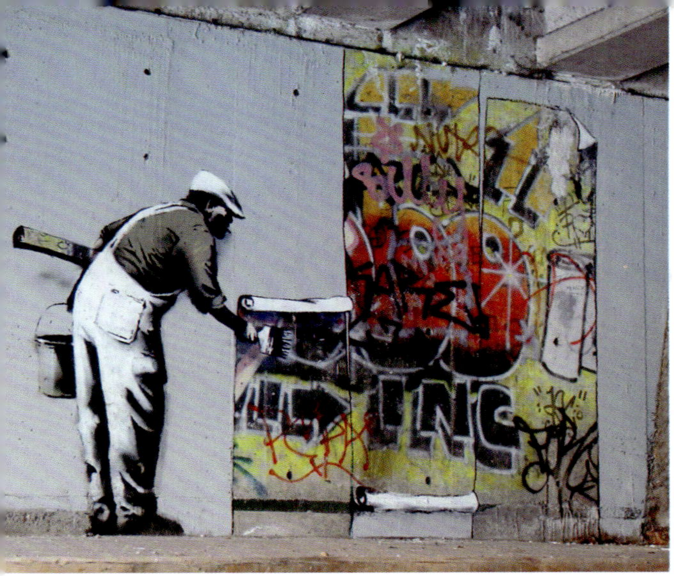

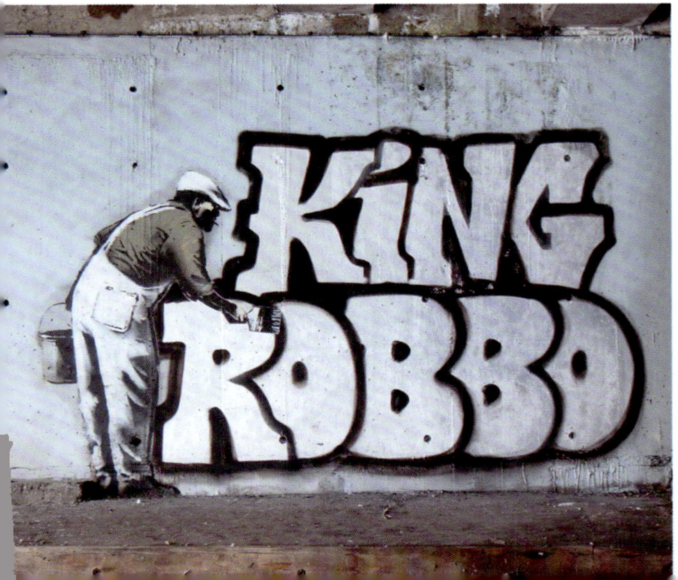
KING
ROBBO

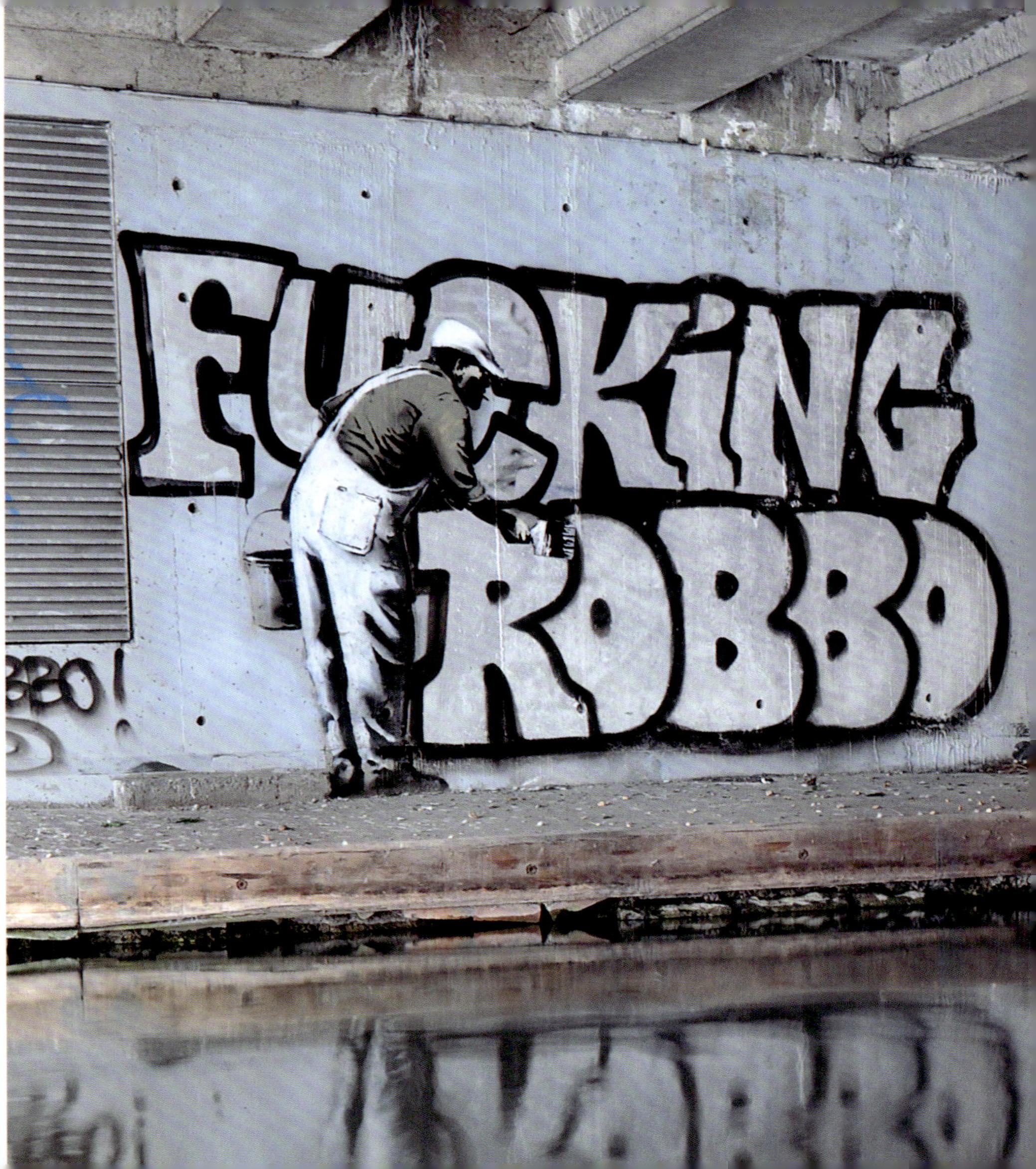
ROBBO

Belin

Born in 1979 in Linares, a town in southern Spain, Miguel Angel Belinchon, aka Belin, was a portrait painter before he was introduced to graffiti. He discovered graffiti in magazines and was spurred to experiment with it in the mid-1990s, when artists from other cities in Spain began to paint on the walls of Linares. By the late '90s, Belin had already begun to attain recognition for his lifelike characters, often infused with elements of caricature and surrealism, and noted for their strong visual impact.

Representing the crew OGT (Original Gay Team)—made up of writers from all over the world—Belin loves the camaraderie of painting with others. Intent on traveling and bringing his art to others, he has painted in Italy, Germany, England, the United States, Puerto Rico, and many cities throughout Spain. He has participated in graffiti festivals worldwide and has won numerous awards for his innovative, spirited pieces.

Belin's favorite artists range from the classical Spanish painter Velázquez to modern painters such as Picasso and Dalí. Among the graffiti artists whose works inspire him are Barcelona-based Suso33 and Ske from Puerto Rico. Continually breaking boundaries among different styles and genres, Belin also works as a graphic designer. Recent projects include collaborations with Ed Hardy, Dockers, Carhartt, and Montana Colors.

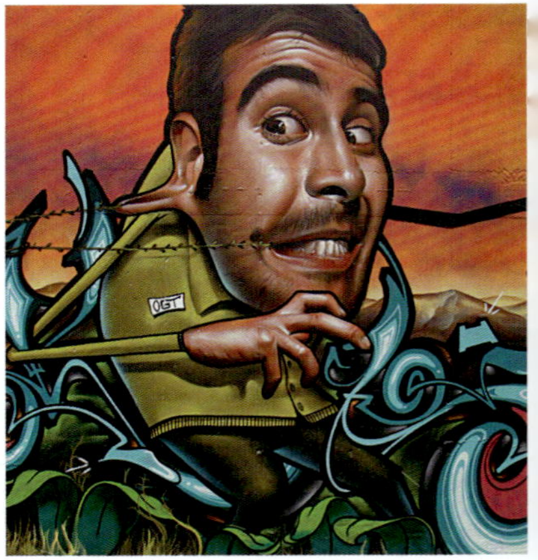

Photographs courtesy of Belin.
***Linares* by Belin and Myrhwan.**
Spain, 2009.
Detail: Bronx, New York, 2009.

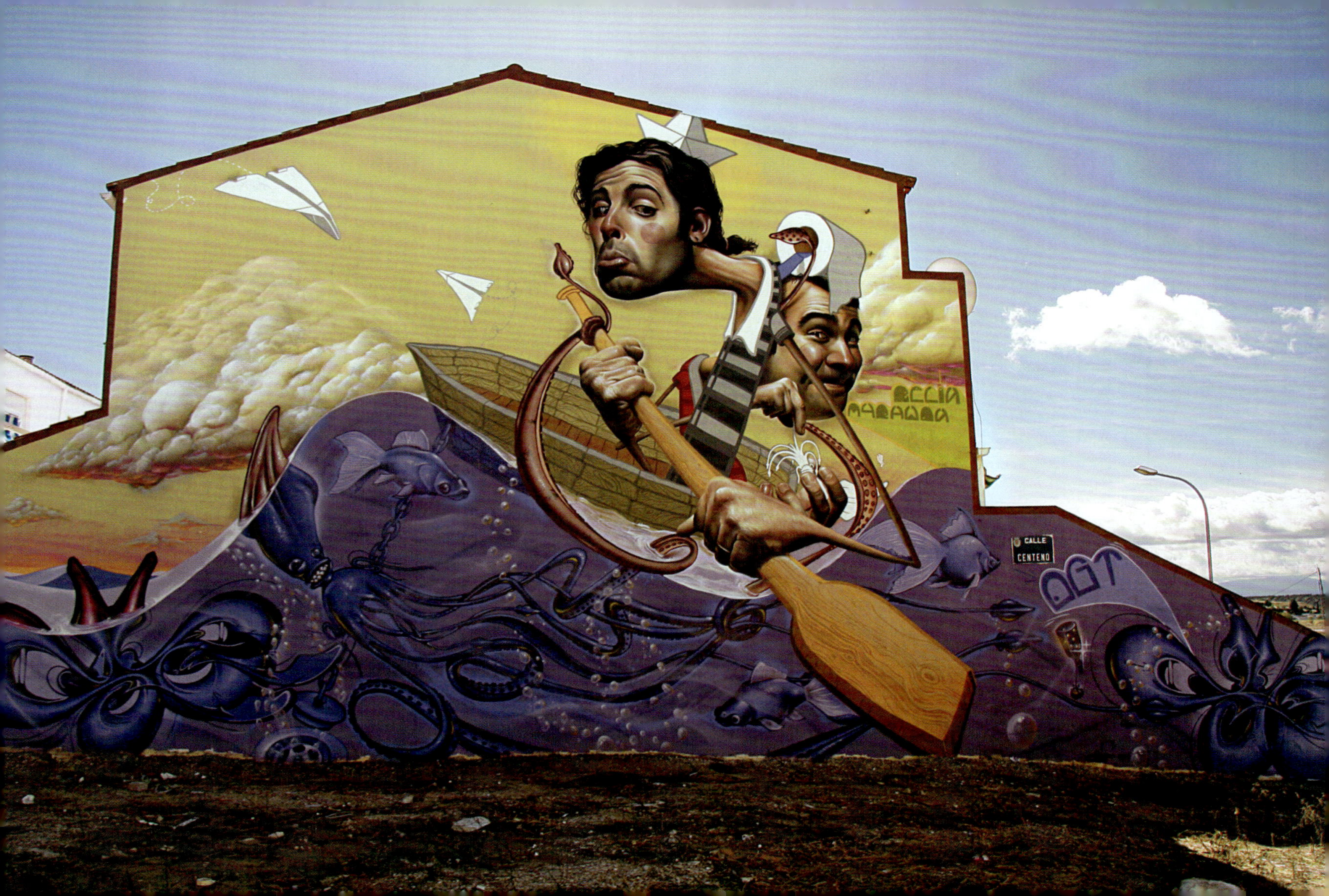
CALLE
CENTENO

Billboard Liberation Front

For well over two decades, the Billboard Liberation Front has been modifying the dreary advertisements littering highways and the urban environment. What began with a couple of friends altering a Max Factor billboard in the late 1970s soon emerged as an organization spearheading the anti-advertising movement. Though it wages war against the annexation of public space, the BLF insists that it has nothing against the actual advertisers. According to the group's website and spokesman Jack Napier, the BLF merely believes wealthy corporations should not be the only ones with access to a billboard.

The BLF is careful to cause no damage and has been known to leave a bottle of Scotch for the worker responsible for repairing their modifications. The BLF website boasts a how-to manifesto on altering outdoor advertisements that reads like a legal brief. Notable alterations turned Charles Manson into a Levi's spokesman and celebrated McDonald's fiftieth anniversary with a life-size figure of Ronald McDonald himself feeding a rotund child burgers on animatronics replay. One favorite from 1977 modified a Camel cigarette billboard to read Am I Dead Yet?

Those involved in the clandestine activities remain anonymous but claim to work day jobs in the advertising field. Is this, then, a way for them to expunge their guilt? Perhaps—but who can blame them?

Photograph by Steve Rhodes. San Francisco, 2010.

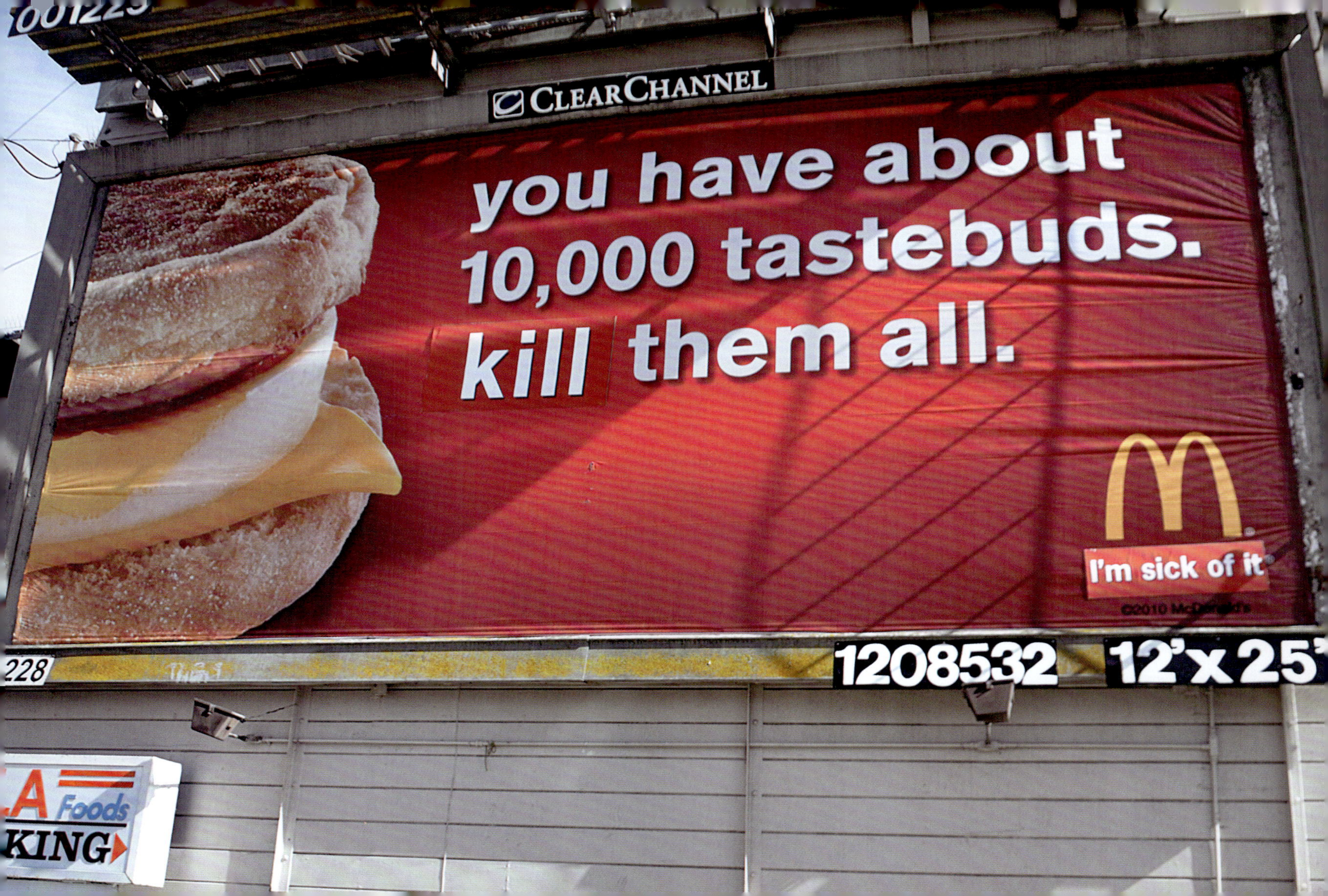
CLEAR CHANNEL
you have about
10,000 tastebuds.
kill them all.
I'm sick of it
1208532
228
Foods
KING

Billy 167

During the mid-1970s, the writing on the #2 and #5 subway lines reached a style zenith that eclipsed all others. Comet [see 071], Blade, John 150, Silver Tips [see 300], Ajax, Ale 1 [see 011], and Doo 2 experimented with colors and styles, bringing never-before-seen letterforms and color combinations to the trains. Billy 167, a timid white boy from the Bronx, lived a block from the elevated tracks of the storied lines and within striking distance of the Esplanade lay-up and the 180th Street train yard—a good thing for Billy and for graffiti. He began writing as a toy in 1973, with the unheralded moniker Bloodshed 216. In 1974, he became Billy 167 and entered into a partnership with the prolific Comet. The two unleashed a flurry of bubble-letter pieces that enhanced Comet's reputation and established Billy 167's.

Billy's apartment became graffiti central. Billy would sit in his kitchen and sketch outlines for hours, becoming a stylemaster. He re-created the alphabet, making it his own. Characters and backgrounds never factored in. Established writers and local toys would stop by to compete stylistically or in hopes of having Billy bless them with an outline of their name. From 1974 to 1978, Billy unleashed a barrage of pieces that raised the stylistic bar for generations to come. He collaborated with Tracy 168 [see 340], P'Nut 2, Blade, Checker 170, Ale 1, John 150, Repel, Don 1 [see 096], and Lee [see 267]. Crew memberships included INDs [see 172], MG Boys [see 221], Wild Style, 3YB [see 002], and his own crew, Slick Inc. Billy 167 did not survive the '80s. However, his lettering survived and remains one of the culture's foundations.

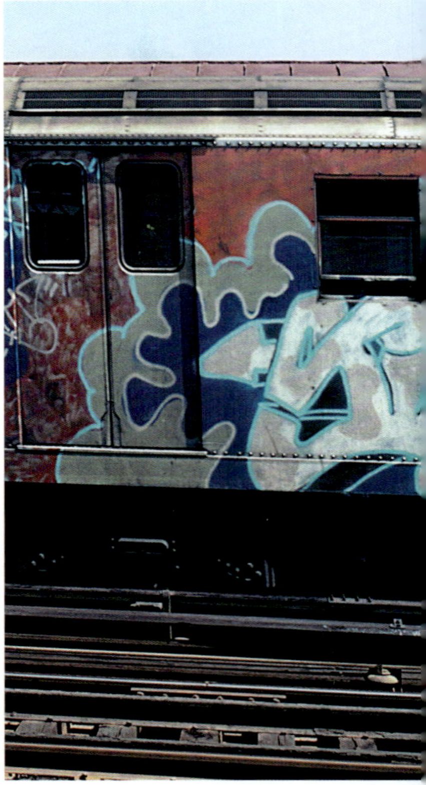

Photograph by Jack Stewart. New York City, c. 1976.

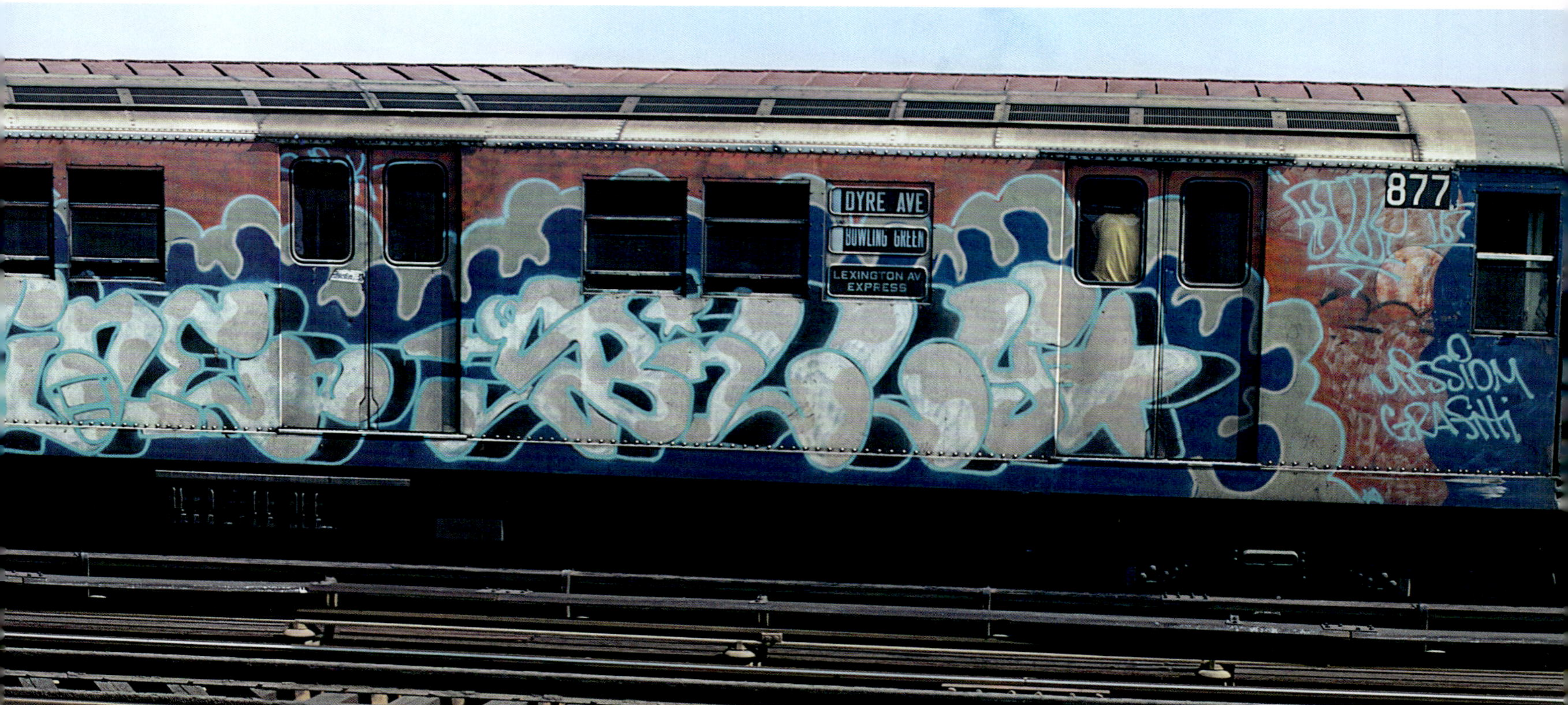
DYRE AVE
BOWLING GREEN
LEXINGTON AV EXPRESS
877

Binho

Binho was quoted recently as saying, "My hands have never been fully clean in twenty-five years—my brain as well." And that's pretty accurate. He began writing in 1984 in Brazil, just as the hip-hop movement circled the globe, and he quickly established himself as a major player in South America.

The lettering style that dominated his earlier works eventually gave way to the characters that kept popping into his head. While other writers did characters that acted as bookends or centerpieces, Binho's figures seemed to roam all over the place. In one of his pieces, a character skis right through the letters; in another, more complex work, he placed large lettering in the center of the piece, while his characters are shown watching television.

In the late '90s, Binho began branching out by printing magazines and books, designing works for major companies, and painting backgrounds for movies. He's painted with some of the best writers in the world, including Os Gemeos [see 248], Loomit [see 205], How, Nosm, and a host of others, and after a quarter of a century, his hands aren't getting any cleaner.

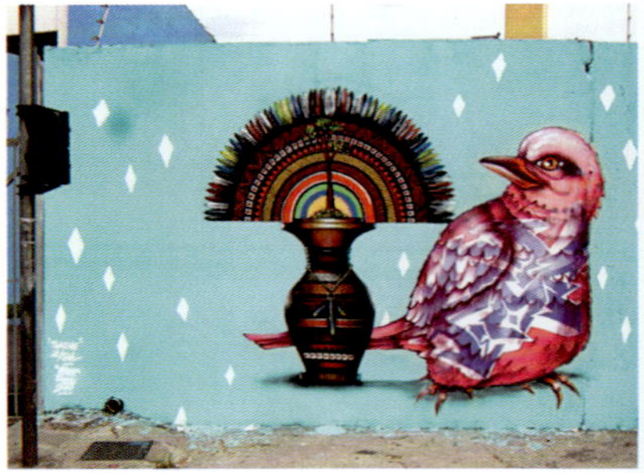

Photographs courtesy of Binho.
São Paulo, Brazil, 2009.
Detail: São Paulo, Brazil, 2010.

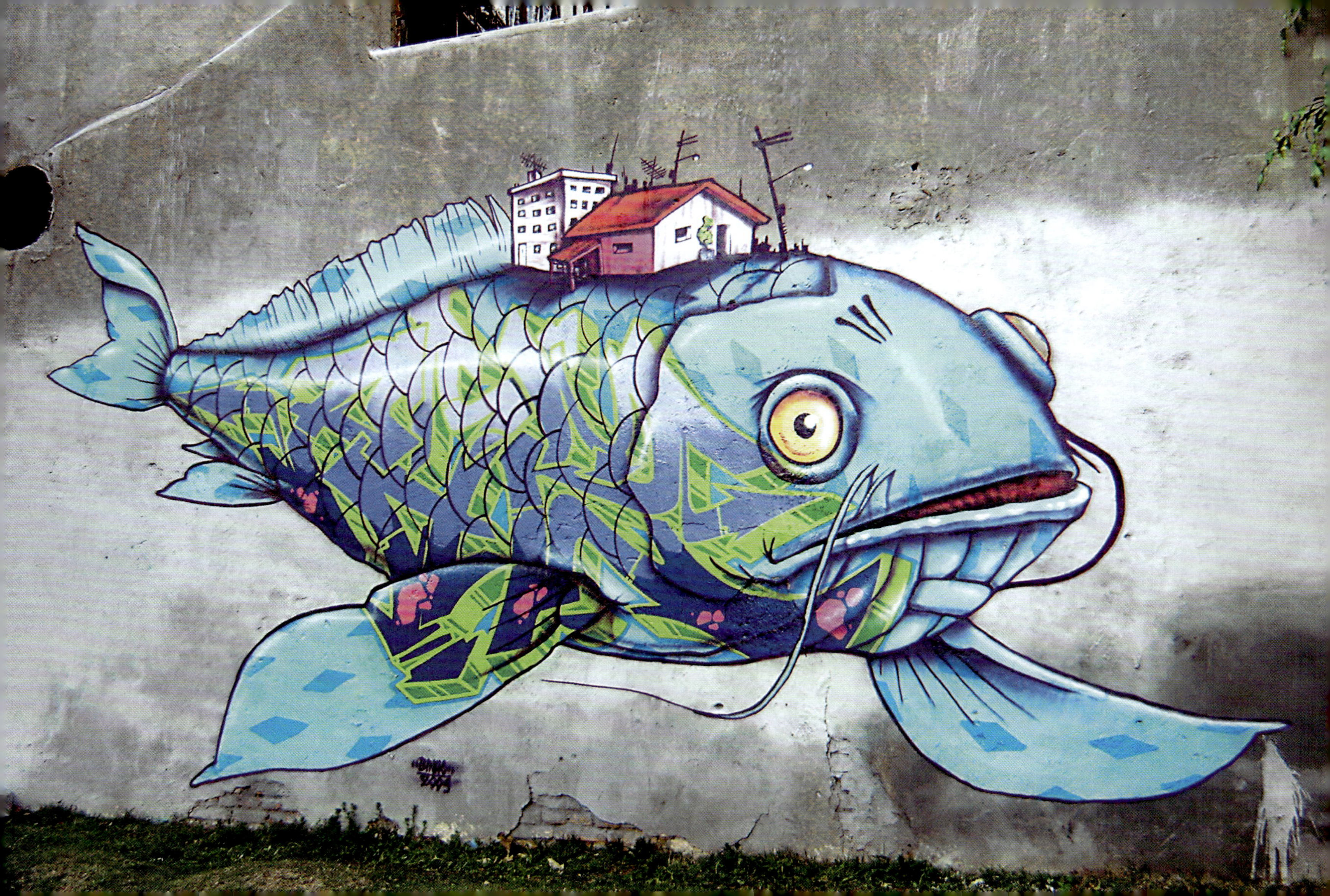

blackbooks

Small, medium, and large; pristine, tattered, and taped; prized, discarded, often robbed; thrown out by parents; and easily concealable: The black-covered sketchbooks that graffiti writers have used to collect the work of their peers and practice their own remain the most important link to graffiti's past. These books, containing works by the founders of the graffiti movement executed when they were teenagers in the early '70s, are highly prized—and extremely scarce. The combination of blackbook pages and alcohol-based markers lend the images to fading—a fitting parallel to the fleeting lifespan of aerosol pieces on the subways.

Many iconic graffiti masterpieces began as sketches inside an artist's blackbook. A blackbook drawing allows the viewer a more personal look into an artist's mind, as pencil lines, erasures, and fill-in techniques become apparent in a way photography doesn't reveal. Finding an original outline in a blackbook and matching it to the piece it became on a train remains a collector's most coveted prize. Blackbook art has become highly collectible of late, and several books containing sketches culled from various artists have been published. The formidable blackbook collection of graffiti collector and artist Martin Wong resides in the permanent collection of The Museum of the City of New York.

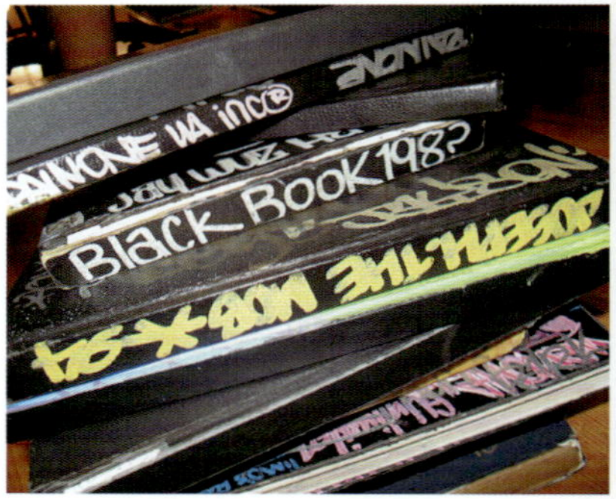

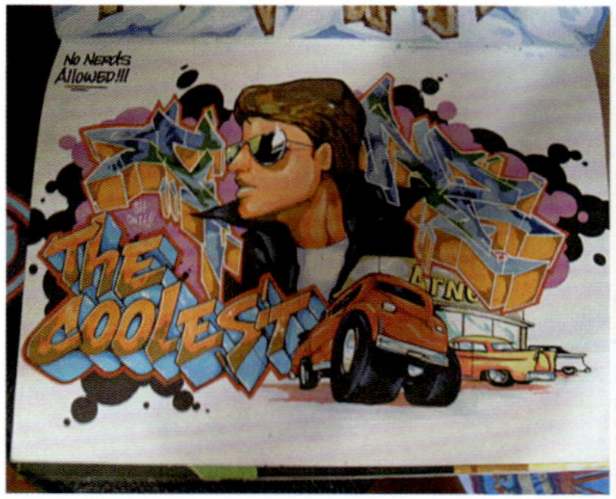

Photographs by Monica LoCascio.
Assorted pieces and tags by Lee 163'd, Serve, Skeme, Part, Tarantula 235, Zephyr, and Keith Haring.
Bottom detail: Artwork by Serve.
Private collection, 2010.

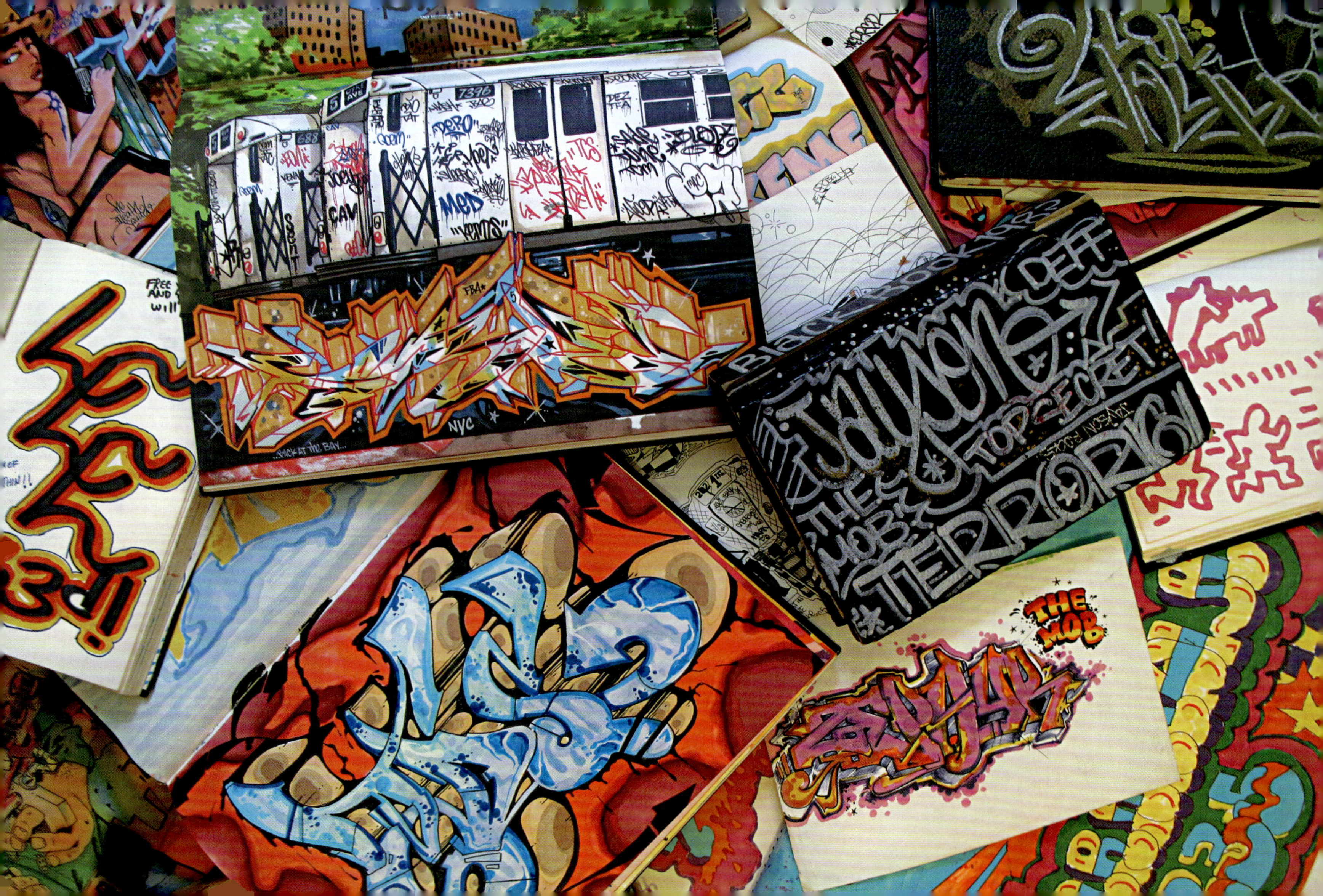
NYC
TOP SECRET!
THE MOB
TERROR
THE MOB

Blade

Even Blade (the most prolific writer to come out of the subway movement) started out small. He began writing in 1972, hitting his neighborhood walls and buses, but quickly moved to the subways, hitting the #2 and #5 lines at the Esplanade lay-up. Before the year was out, he had started to do pieces on the trains, stick-letter pieces featuring stars that mirrored the style of the day. In 1974, Blade did his first character piece: a simple snowman everyone enjoyed. Characters on trains in 1974 and 1975 were almost always culled from the funny papers or copied from other pop-culture reference points, but Blade's characters—gangsters, hookers, swamis, walking easels—were uniquely his own; these characters defined Blade as much as he defined them—after all, only Blade knew what they meant. The Crazy 5 (see 079) were all but over by 1975, with just Comet (see 071) and Blade moving forward. The two were an unstoppable force, and Comet and Blade would go down as one of the greatest writing partnerships in history.

In 1980, Blade did some of his greatest whole cars, competing with a crop of talented newer writers that included Lee, Dondi, and Seen. These cars were as much about concept as they were characters. His walking-letter car (one of the most iconic trains ever painted) had nicely rendered clouds in the background; when viewed from the streets, the painted clouds merged with the real ones, and his letters seemed to walk through the air. In the early 1980s, he quit the trains after beef with other writers resulted in the destruction of many of his pieces, but also after having executed more than five thousand pieces. Today, his canvases hang in museums and are widely sought after by international collectors.

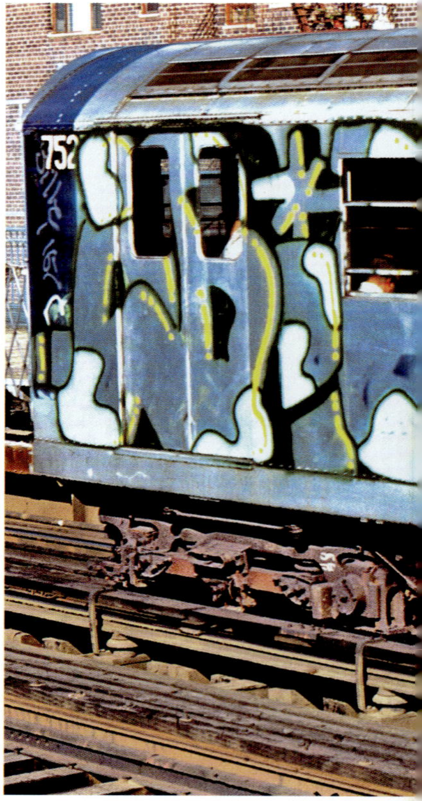

Pieces by Billy 167 (left) and Blade. Photograph by Keith Baugh. New York City, 1975.

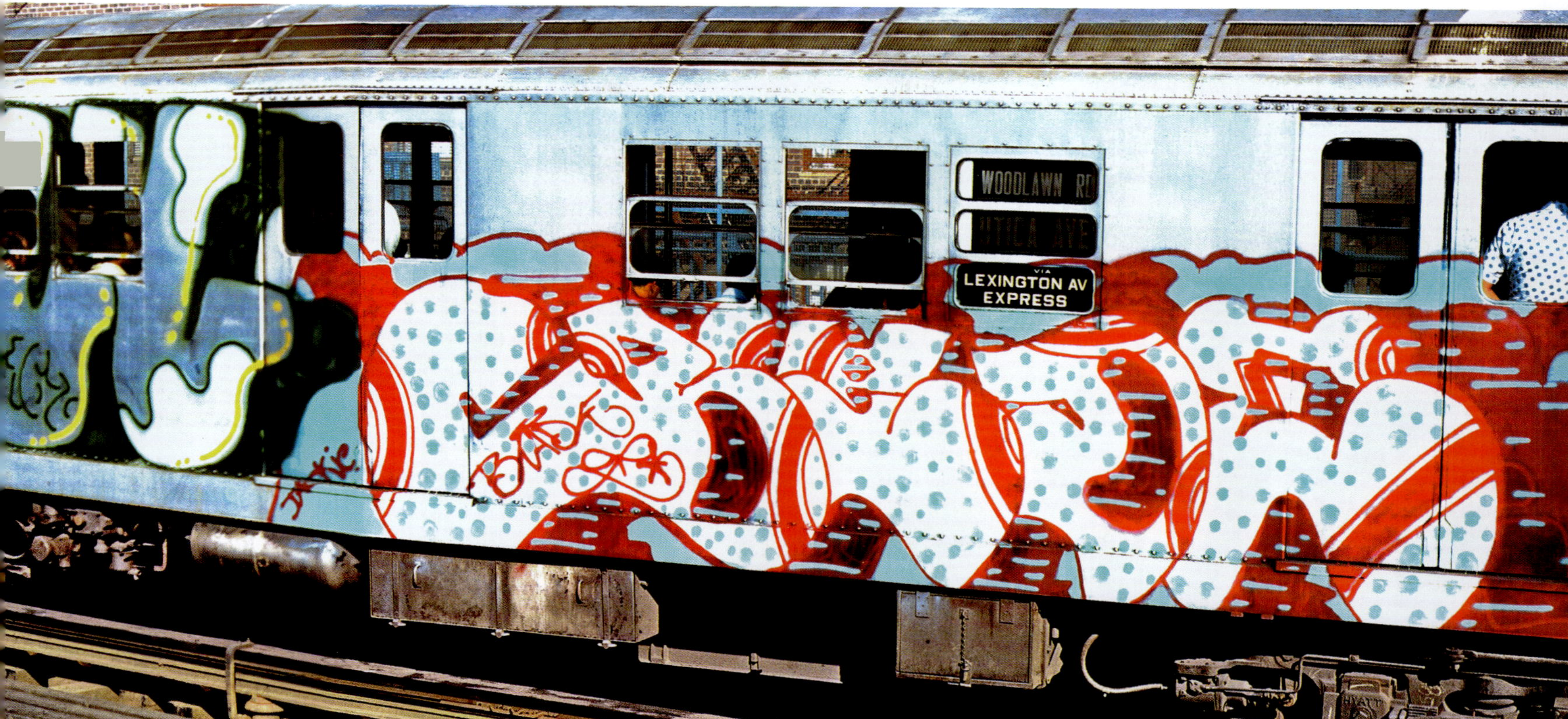
WOODLAWN RD
UTICA AVE
VIA
LEXINGTON AV
EXPRESS

Blek le Rat

Xavier Prou was born in Paris in 1951 to a Chinese mother and French father of Jewish descent. As a boy, he traveled with his father to Italy, where he witnessed propaganda artwork in the streets, primarily stencils depicting Mussolini. In 1971, as France was still struggling to rebuild and recover from the fallout of World War II, Prou traveled to New York City, where he got his first taste of what we now know as graffiti. He spent the next ten years of his life studying architecture in Paris. In 1981, he revisited New York City and came to the realization that the writing on the walls and subways had more significance than he'd ever imagined. Xavier christened himself Blek le Rat and began cutting crude stencils of a rat that he would use to mark the streets of Paris. Before long, his once simplistic stencils grew more complex, including portraits of fallen angels, more socially influenced pieces, and various images of himself. The now infamous Banksy speaks with reverence and humility of his predecessor: "Every time I think I've painted something slightly original, I find out that Blek le Rat has done it as well, only twenty years earlier. . . ." Blek le Rat now lives with his wife and son in the South of France, where he works in an abandoned castle.

Photographs by Lionel Belluteau.
Right: Cans Festival, London, 2008.
Far right: Paris, 2005.

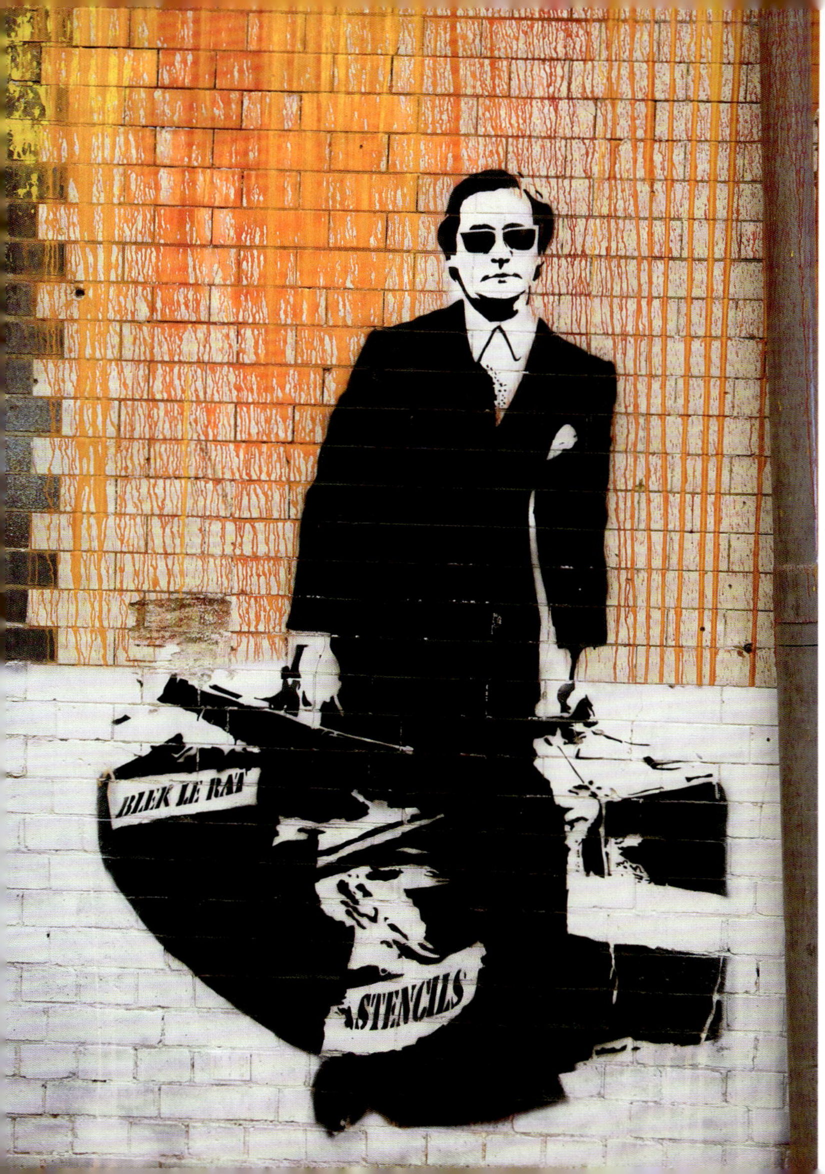
BLEK LE RAT
STENCILS

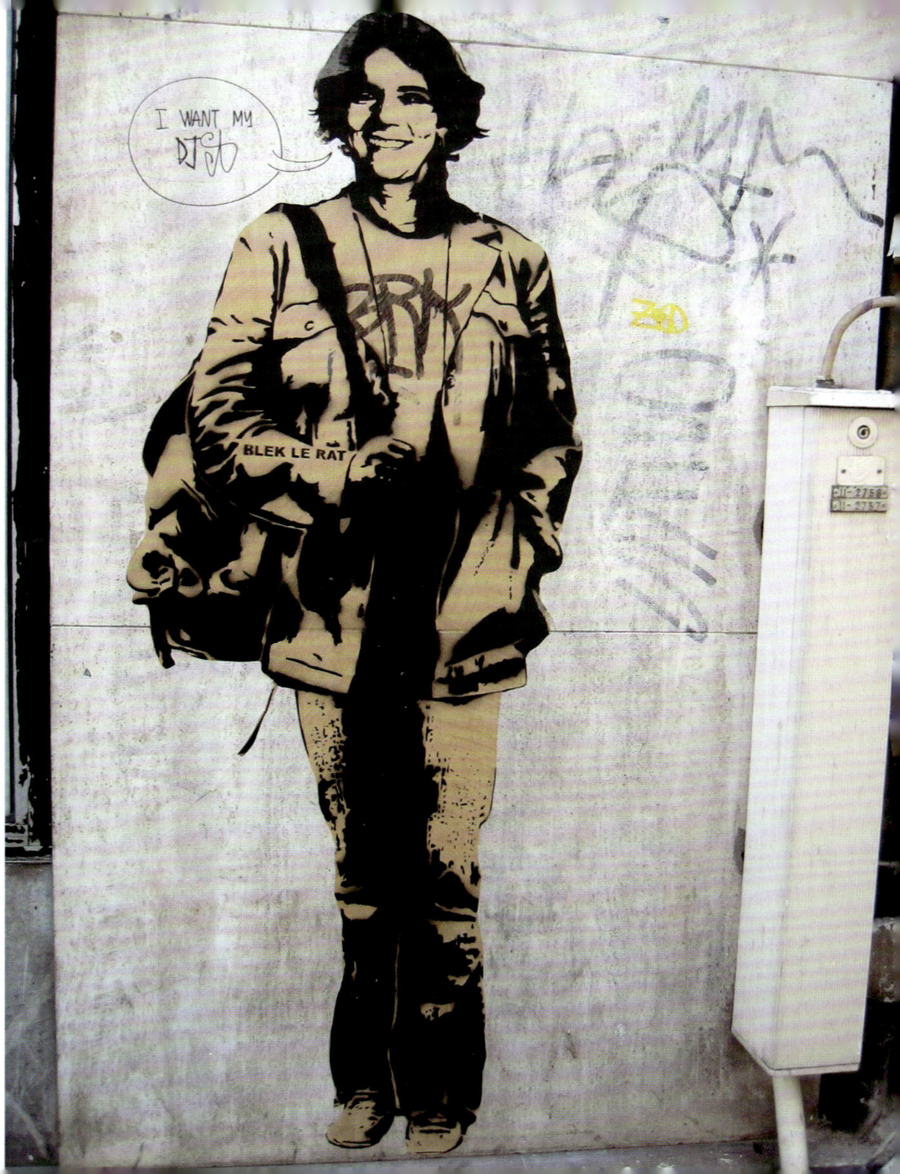
I WANT MY DJ
BLEK LE RAT

blockbuster

Graffiti artists have historically taken varied visual paths en route to their common goal: fame. Art versus ubiquity has always been a topic of debate. Beauty or the beast? While Cap and In saturated trains with throw-ups, Blade and Lee chose to transform entire subway cars into paintings. Both techniques were effective means to a similar end. Graffiti lettering styles also vary widely, from Wild Style, unreadable but intended to impress writing peers, to civilian or plain style, designed to communicate with the masses. The blockbuster is a gigantic rendition of a name in symmetrical block lettering, and it remains the most powerful communicative and aesthetic tool. Size matters, and blockbusters look best when executed on a grand scale. Blade made great use of this technique in the 1980s, often writing ANOTHER BLOCKBUSTER PRODUCTION on pieces that stretched the entire length of a subway car.

In 2008, the Los Angeles–based Metro Transit Assassins crew created the world's largest blockbuster, spelling out its initials along the Los Angeles River. It stretched over two thousand feet, and the Army Corps of Engineers was brought in to remove it at an alleged cost of $3.7 million. Members of the MTA crew were rounded up and charged with conspiracy, a charge usually reserved for organized crime members. The MTA blockbuster could be seen from office buildings and airplanes and made world headlines. A $3.7 million expenditure from a bankrupt city? Now *that's* fame!

Photograph by Luna Park. Los Angeles, 2009.

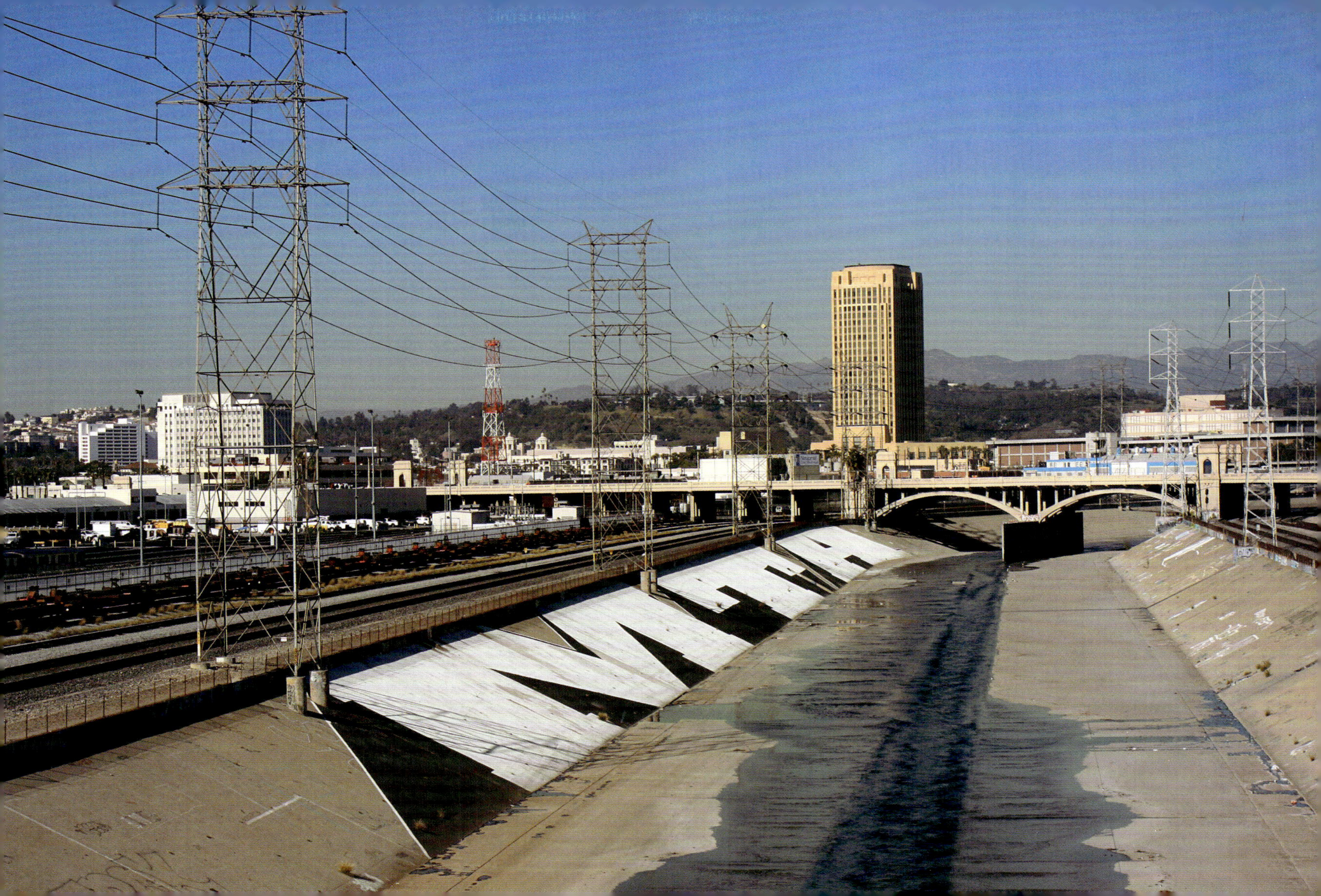

Blu

At the tender age of twenty-two, Blu turned the street-art world on its head with the 2008 release of his hand-animated video *Muto*. Capturing several thousand charcoal images on walls in Buenos Aires—painstakingly drawn, photographed, and then erased—the video employs stop-motion techniques to show the evolution of an ever-mutating cast of creatures that morph and dissolve into a surreal smattering of shapes and characters. The video also features a custom soundtrack that highlights what the characters do in the paintings. Revered for his exceptional technical ability, as well as the immense creativity in both the content and the form of the video, Blu became an instant star, turning the spotlight on his already vast and evolved body of outdoor work.

Based in illustration, the Italian artist is known for his large-scale public murals and is reluctant to enter the gallery world. He continues to travel the world, creating his large, intensely intricate works and collaborating with the likes of urban-art superstar Os Gemeos (see 248).

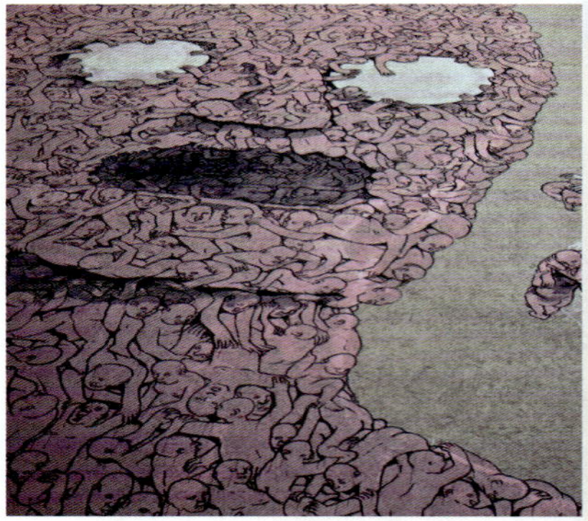

Main: Photograph by Ray Mock. Berlin, 2009.
Detail: Photograph by Vincent Cornelli. Berlin, 2009.

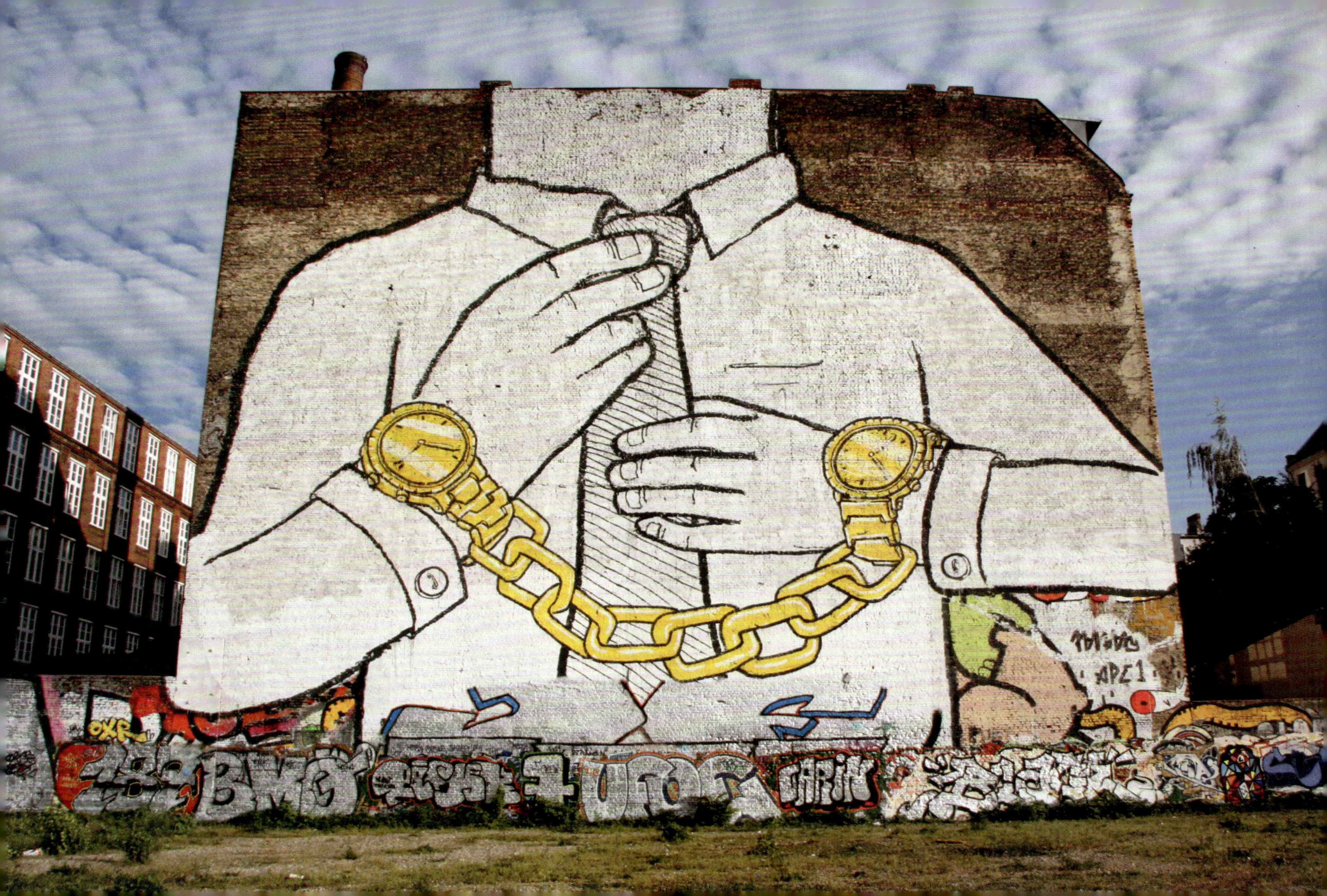

BNE

BNE is the abbreviated form of the San Francisco–based graffitist Benet. Although he has done throw-ups and blockbusters all over the globe, he is best known for his relentless, ubiquitous sticker campaign.

The black-and-white BNE stickers he has placed on parking meters, walls, doorways, newspaper machines, and all other things stationary and unguarded prompted the mayor of San Francisco to offer a reward for his capture. BNE has also done so much damage in Japan that he has been the subject of TV news stories in that country.

Stickers have long been ridiculed by the more hardcore spray paint–oriented segment of the graff community, but BNE's efforts are not lost on advertisers who track things like name recognition. It seems his name was more widely known than several brands whose names were tested against his in a marketing survey.

Perhaps the fame has gone to his head. In a recent interview he boasted, "I don't really see other graffiti artists as my competition. I'm going up against companies like Pepsi and McDonald's, who force their unwanted messages on the public every day. I love putting my stickers over their ads." The good news is that BNE contains no trans-fats or high-fructose corn syrup.

Photograph by Jake Dobkin (streetsy.com). New York City, 2010.

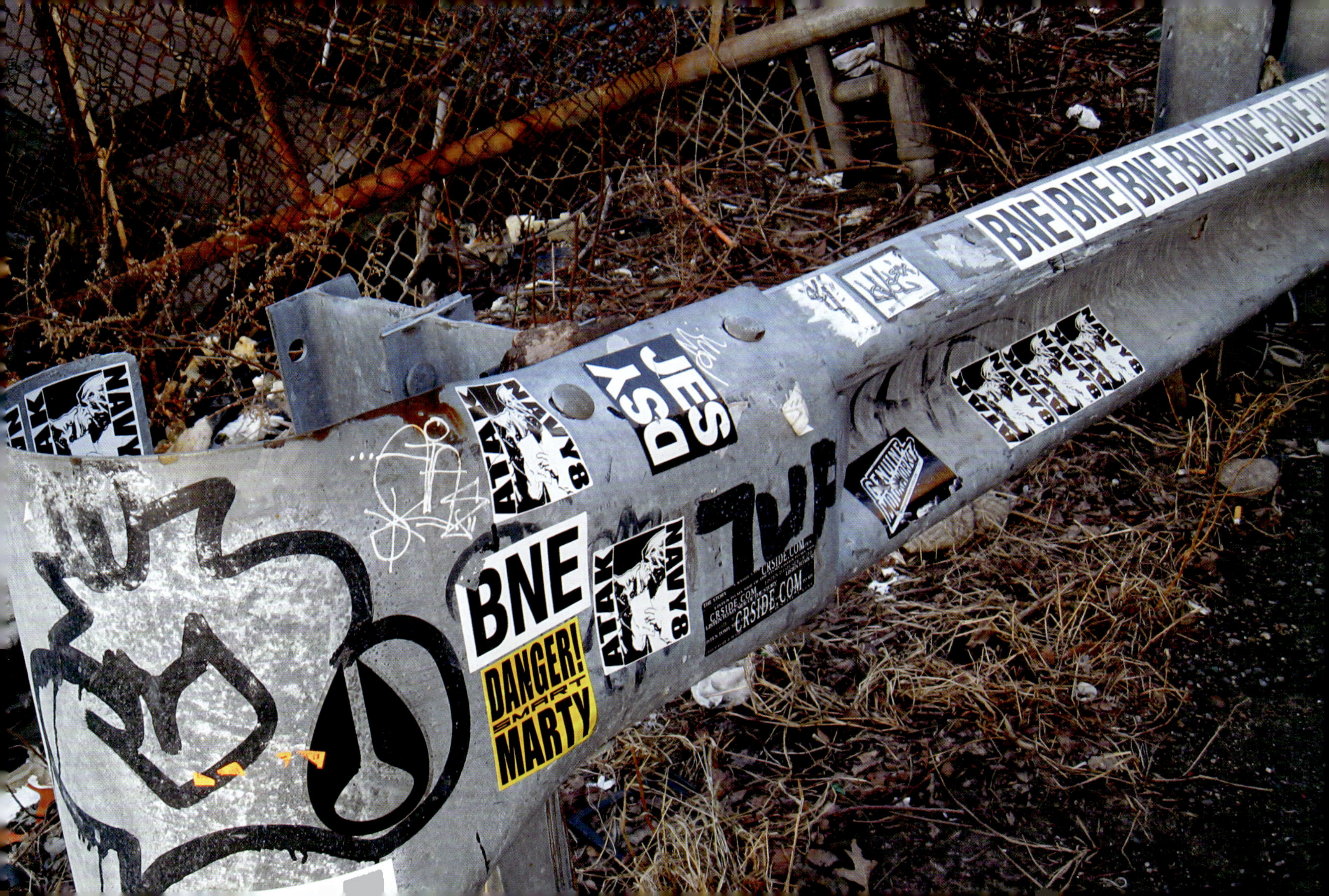
BNE
ATAK
NAVY8
JES
DSY
BNE
DANGER!
SMART
MARTY
CRSIDE.COM

Bo130 and Microbo

Italy is known for its luxurious landscapes and laid-back culture. Born and bred within this culture, the artists known as Bo130 and Microbo, a male-and-female artist team who have been a couple for more than a decade, developed into a multi-faceted entity: one part illustrator, one part designer, and eventually, three parts street artist. In Milano, they are now legends in the graffiti and street-art scenes, as much for their prolific work on the streets as for their generous, relaxed style.

Microbo, a pint-size ball of energy, channels an otherworldly vision of alien life on distant planets into her hyper-intricate work. Imagined creatures float within her squiggled lines, which then double as the eyes and noses of Bo130's characters.

Old fans of hip-hop culture, Bo and Microbo are heavily involved in street culture, and they have curated numerous graffiti/street-art exhibitions, including the massive "Urban Edge" show in Milan, in 2005. The artists were also the brains and brawn behind "*Izastickup*," one of the first seminal books on modern sticker graffiti, released in 2006. That same year, they created one of their uniquely intertwined large-scale murals for the Wooster Collective's (see 359) 11 Spring Street show (see 001) in New York.

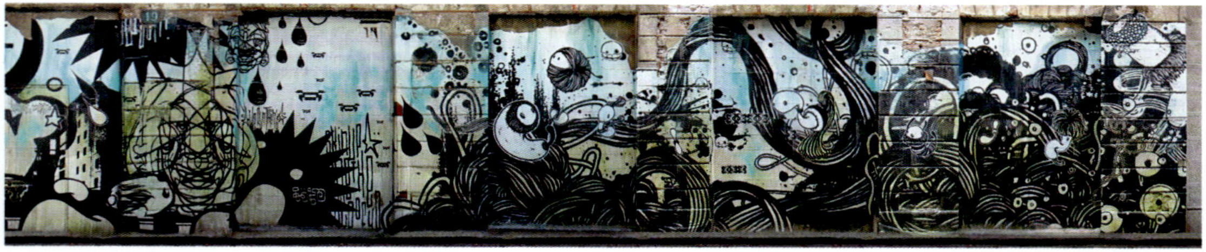

Photographs courtesy of Bo130 and Microbo.
Right: Artwork by Bo130. Milan, Italy, 2006.
Far Right: Artwork by Microbo. Milan, Italy, 2007.
Detail: Artwork by Bo130 and Microbo. Milan, Italy, 2009.

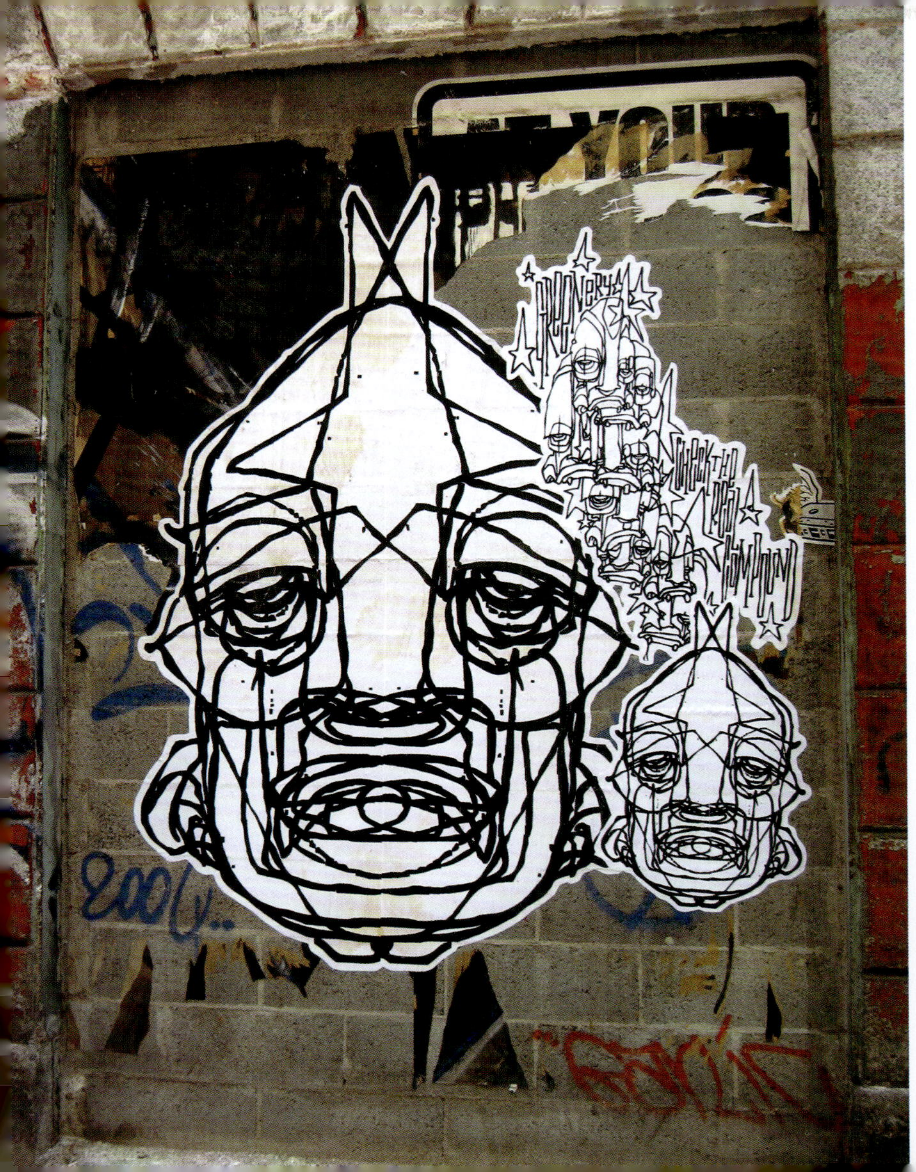
2004..

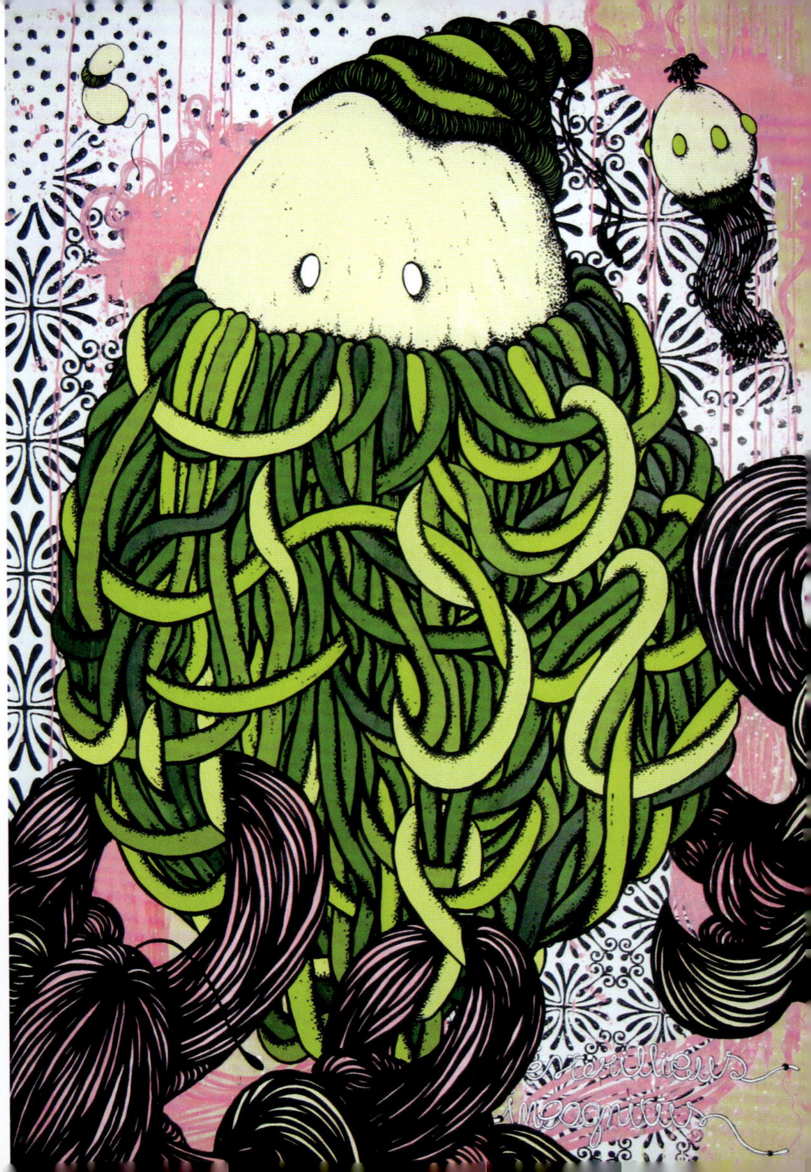
Incognitus

Chaz Bojorquez

In 1969, few people were thinking about graffiti outside of gang culture, and tagging as we now know it was virtually nonexistent. Inspired by the Mexican gang scribblings he was seeing in East Los Angeles, Chaz Bojorquez created his symbol that year: a stylized skull known as Señor Suerte. With its unique fusion of international calligraphic and lettering styles, Bojorquez's work showed some of the first known examples of stencils used in graffiti as we see it today.

After completing one year of state college, Bojorquez enrolled at the California Institute of the Arts, where he studied Asian calligraphy. He later combined this with the cholo graffiti influence to create the unique lettering style he used to bomb the streets of Los Angeles. During graffiti's popularity boom in the 1970s and 1980s, Bojorquez was often interviewed and considered by many to be the most influential figure within Los Angeles graffiti culture. In 1979, Bojorquez traveled the world, visiting and painting in thirty-five countries, and became one of the earliest foreign emissaries of the graffiti movement.

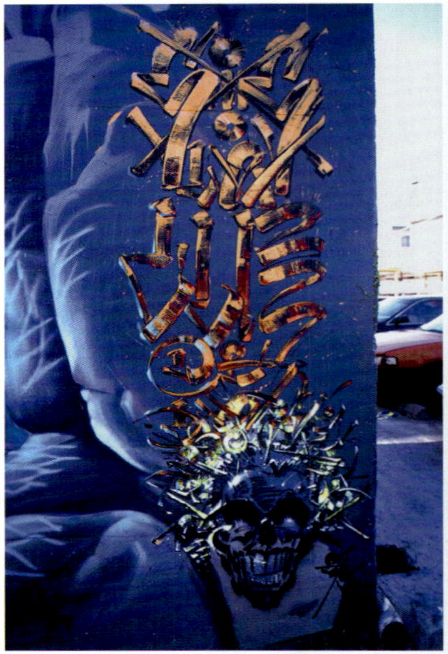

Photographs courtesy of Chaz Bohorquez.
Arroyo Seco River, Los Angeles, 1975.
Detail: Hollywood, California, 1999.

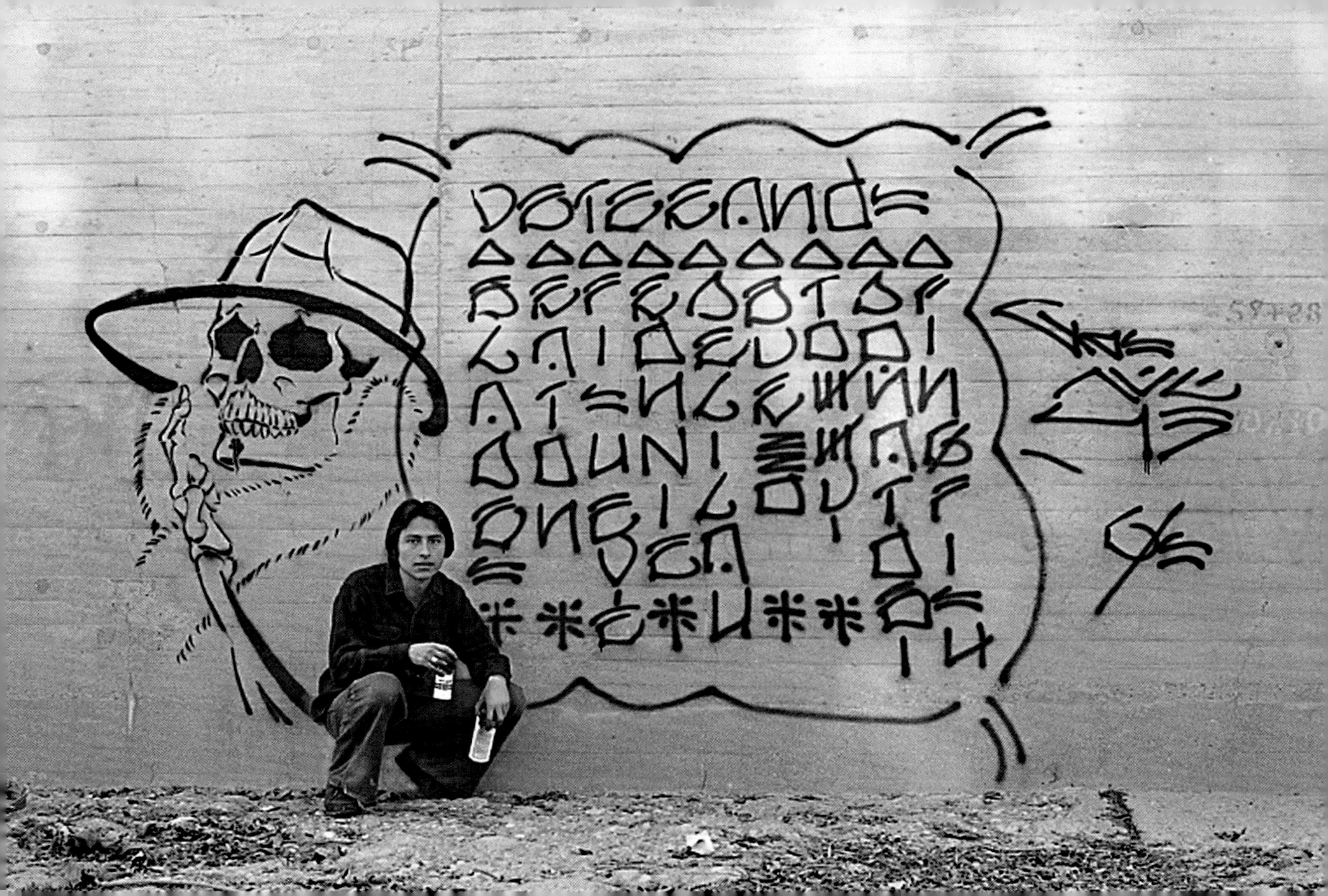

Konstantin Bokov

Konstantin Bokov is a seventy-year-old Ukrainian who lives in Manhattan. As a teenager in the 1940s, he herded sheep and played the accordion until one day, in his early twenties, he saw a van Gogh painting, and immediately put down his accordion and began to paint. He studied at Moscow's Surikov Art Institute, but in 1975 he was expelled from the Soviet Union for being "ideologically unreliable." He moved to New York City, where, by the 1980s, his lanky figure, draped in hand-painted caps and coats, had become a fixture on the SoHo and East Village art scenes. Bokov's beguiling output, created almost exclusively from inventively recycled materials such as film canisters, toothpaste boxes, and cottage-cheese containers, is both a scathing critique of wastefulness and a declaration of his love for art, simplicity, and people of every stripe. The artist happily places his sculptures, collages, drawings, and paintings out in the open, hanging them from streetlights, trees, and fences. Sometimes he leaves a single work; at other times he installs a dozen pieces, creating impromptu outdoor galleries. Although he has exhibited in galleries and museums, Bokov ultimately believes art should be free, and he grins widely when people take his creations home.

Photograph by Harley Spiller.
New York City, 1984.

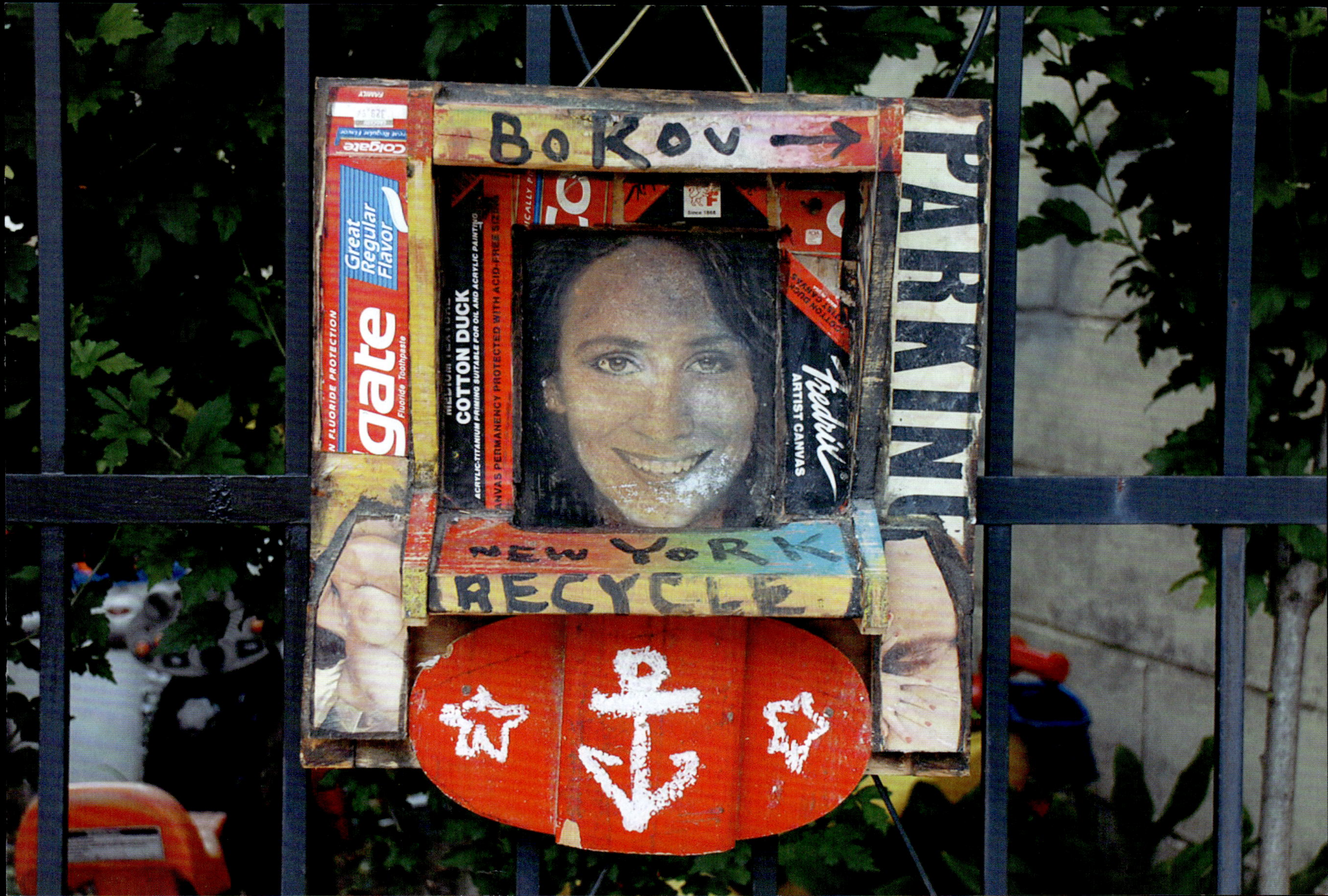
BoKov
PARKIN
Great Regular Flavor
gate
Fluoride Toothpaste
COTTON DUCK
ARTIST CANVAS
NEW YORK
RECYCLE

Bonom

If you walk around Brussels or Paris, chances are you will cross a piece or two from the young French artist Bonom. If it's night, there's an equally good chance you won't notice it. Bonom is a climber who jumps at challenges most people would avoid at all costs. He hits spots where he knows the work won't be touched until the building comes down. Cleanup crews and other artists aren't likely to follow his Spider-Man act. He also has a knack for measuring his risk, and his most difficult climbs result in work that is also the most visible to the public.

The subject matter of his work is mixture of real animals and mythical creatures (many of which he invents), placed in unexpected and often humorous situations. His work often elicts two distinct feelings: "Man, that is good," followed by "How the hell did he *do* that?"

In Paris, his work has often been seen as somewhat aggressive and difficult to digest, whereas in Brussels, he is the Belgian version of Banksy—his work has sparked broad discussion over the benefits of public art and the preservation of "good" vandalism.

Photograph courtesy of Bonom.

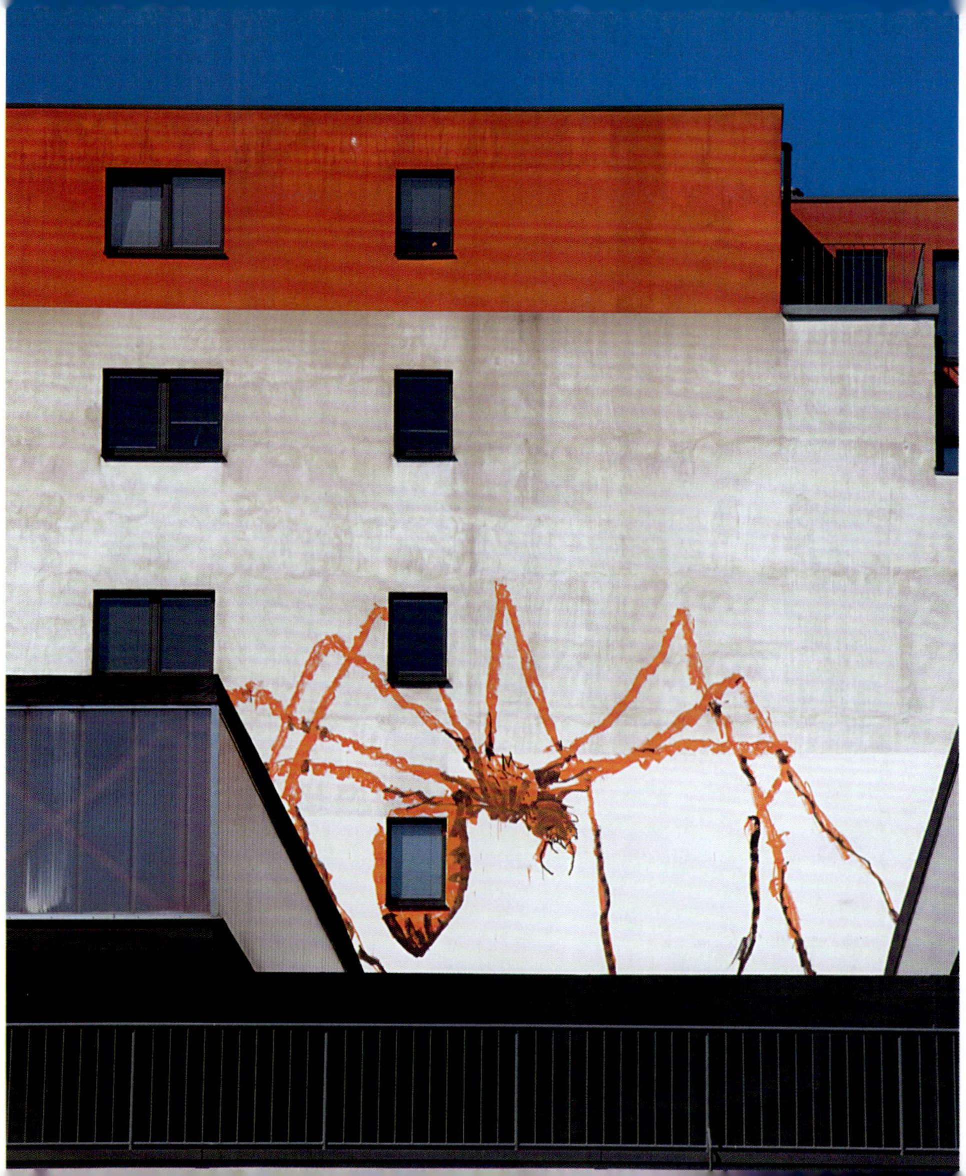

Borf

In 2004 and 2005, a single mysterious tagger had the city of Washington, D.C., in an uproar. Still shrouded in anonymity at the time, rebellious art student John Tsombikos was dusting the city with stencils of a young man's face and the perplexing word "Borf." The artist branched out into multicolored stencils and a large defacement of a high-traffic overpass in the city. With their anarchistic undertones, his mischievous antics got so far under the skin of D.C. residents that local news networks began to report on the story; eventually it even attracted the national attention of Fox News.

On July 13, 2005, Tsombikos was caught in the act, arrested, and charged with vandalism. Once his identity was made public, his mother made a statement that the young man featured in Borf's stencils was in fact Tsombikos's childhood best friend Bobby Fisher, who had committed suicide at the tender age of sixteen. Tsombikos pled guilty to one felony charge of destruction of property, whereupon he was sentenced to community service and fined $12,000 in restitution to the district. At a resentencing on February 9, 2006, a judge sentenced Tsombikos to thirty days in jail, in addition to a suspended seventeen-month sentence. Since his stint in the slammer, the airwaves have been carrying very few reports of Borf sightings.

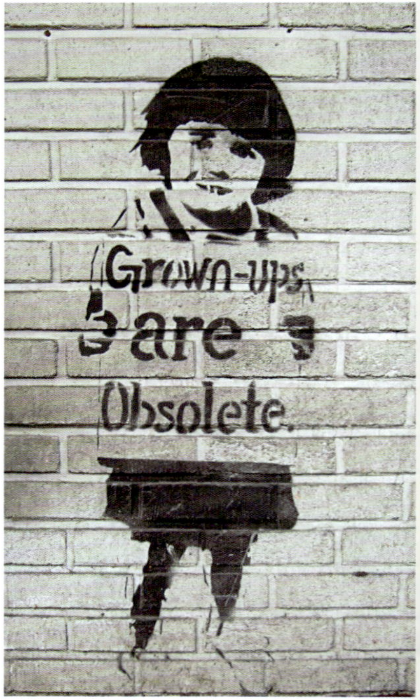

Photographs by Becki Fuller.
Brooklyn, New York, 2007.
Detail: New York City, 2007.

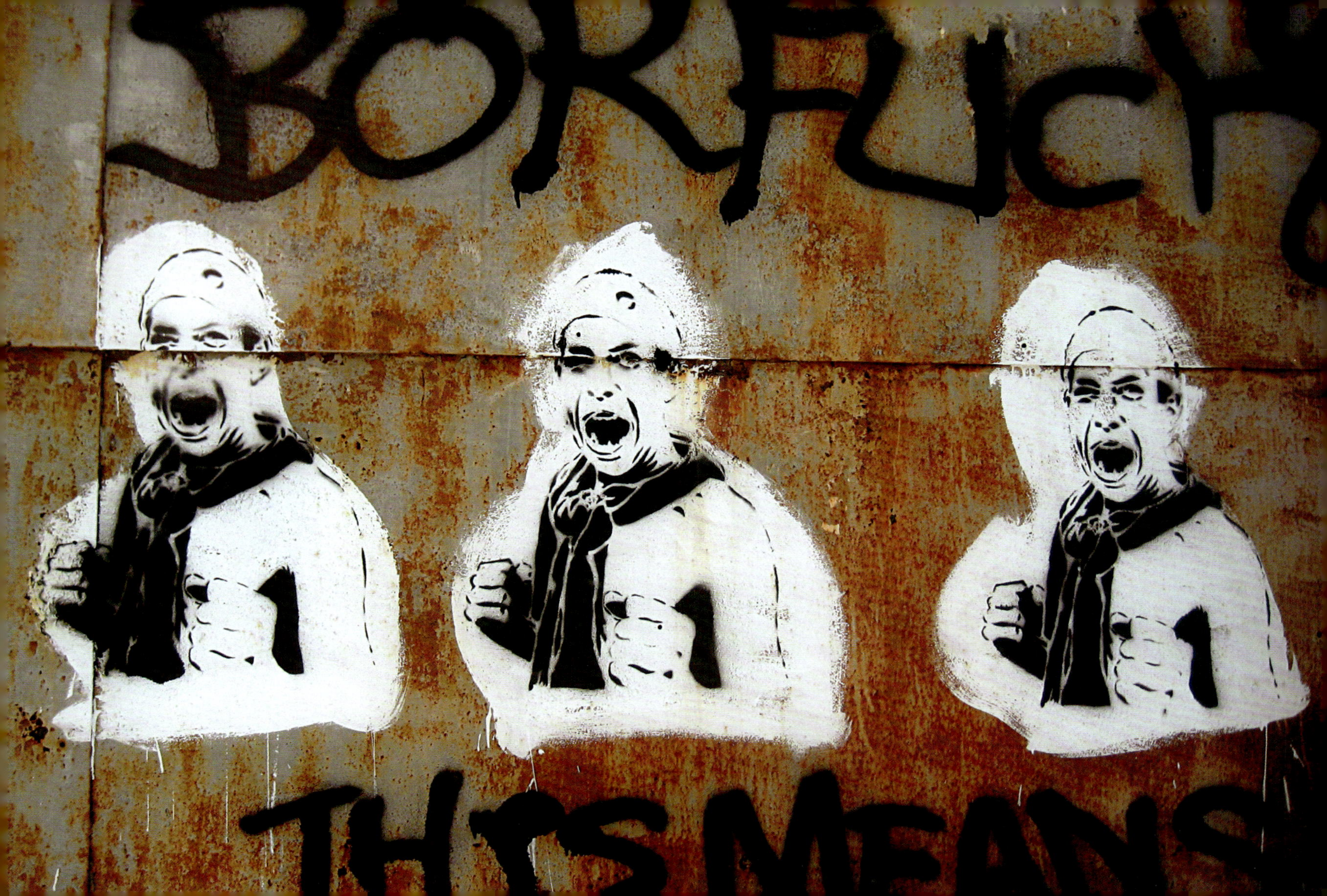
THIS MEANS

Boxi

With several layers of stencils and a palette in a range of grays, Boxi creates haunting, lifelike figures that meld into the space around them. He describes his somewhat unsettling compositions as "post-apocalyptic gray romanticism."

Born in Kent, England, in 1974, Boxi spent several years studying painting and fine arts at the prestigious London-based Central Saint Martins College of Art and Design. In 2000, he moved with his family to Berlin and has since made the fashionable Friedrichshain district home. It was the vibrant, creative Berlin youth culture that inspired him to create art in the streets. Had he remained in London, he quips, he'd still be painting in oils in his studio.

He credits two Berlin-based street artists, Evol and Pisa73, with introducing him to stenciling. And like Evol and Pisa73, Boxi uses photography as one of the tools to generate his lifelike images. He is particularly interested in how humans interact with one another and their environment.

Boxi has participated in exhibits throughout Germany, as well as in Denmark, Australia, and the United States. He has had several solo exhibits in Berlin, and his first U.S. solo exhibit took place in 2009 at the Carmichael Gallery of Contemporary Art.

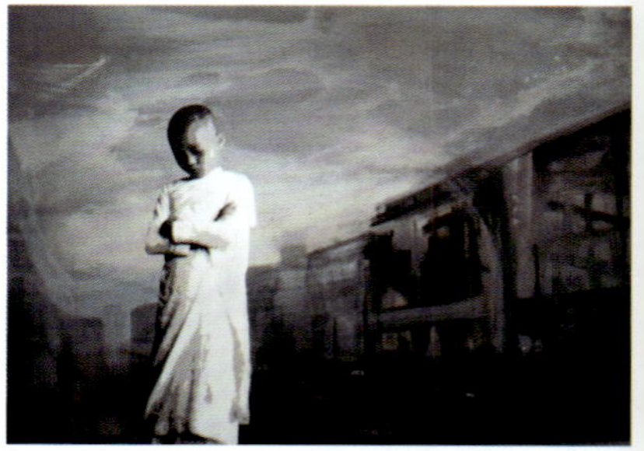

Photographs by Lois Stavsky. New York City, 2010.

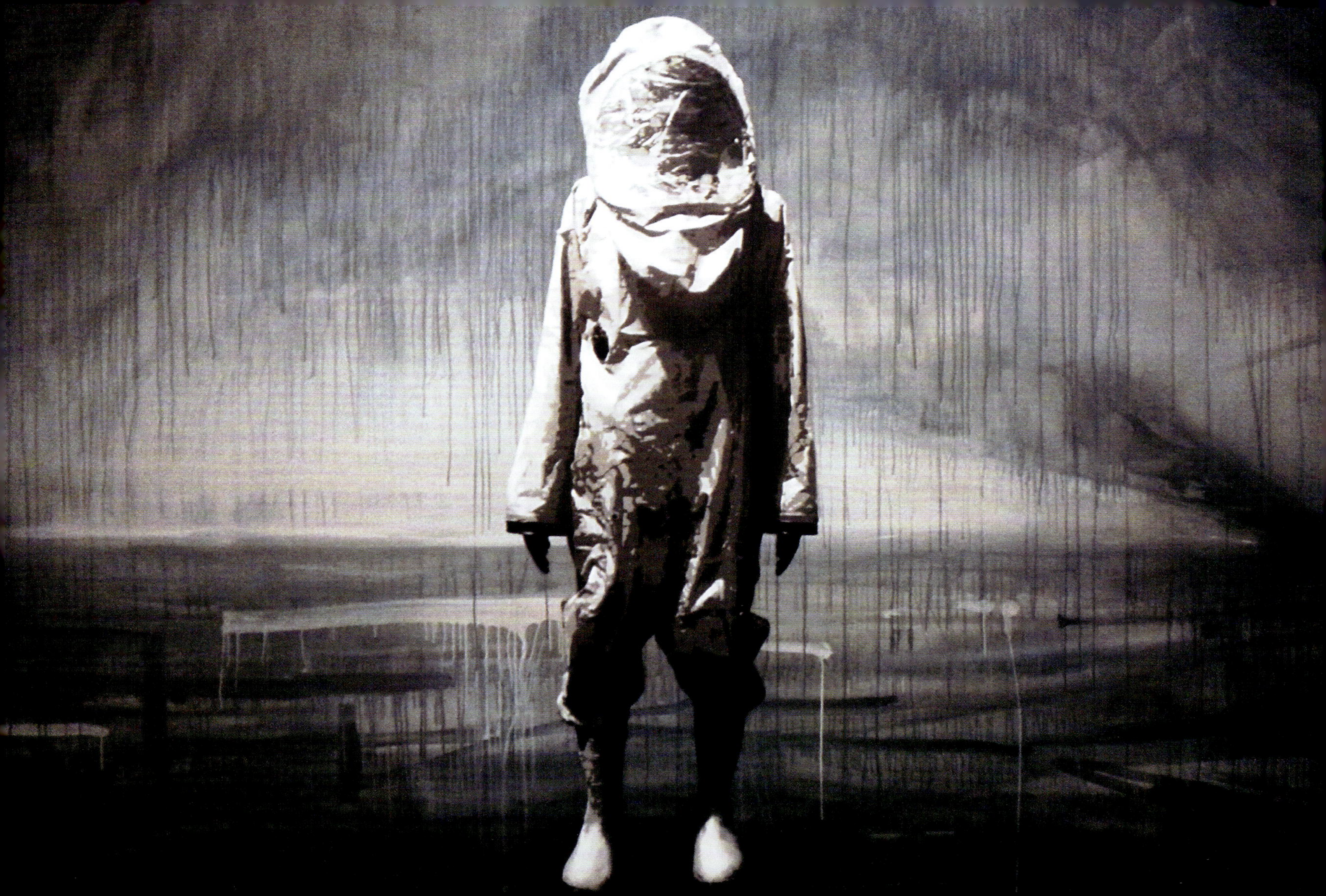

Broken Crow

Toward the end of the first decade of the twenty-first century, when street art's mainstream popularity craze was nearing its end, the art of the stencil was a less high-profile medium choice for public artists. Most had made the switch to fine art or had gone back to their graffiti core, and few were thinking about how to push stenciling to the next level.

Enter John Grider and Mike Fitzsimmons, collectively known under the melancholy moniker Broken Crow. A self-professed art collective, Broken Crow was born out of necessity—the need for another set of hands!

In 2005, having set out to create the largest-scale stencils possible, the duo soon realized that painting alone through stencils that large was physically impossible, and they formed a fast partnership out of their reliance on each other to create work. Based in Minneapolis, Minnesota, the duo took several years to break into public prominence, but through extensive travel and massive-scale public artworks, they eventually came into their own spotlight at the end of the decade, showing their works in a gallery space alongside legendary stencil artists like Logan Hicks [see 166].

Broken Crow's work touches on a melancholy happiness, almost childlike in its sweetness, that attempts to bring the creatures of the wild into the concrete jungles of urban sprawl. The duo continues to travel and paint wherever a wall and a floor to crash on present themselves.

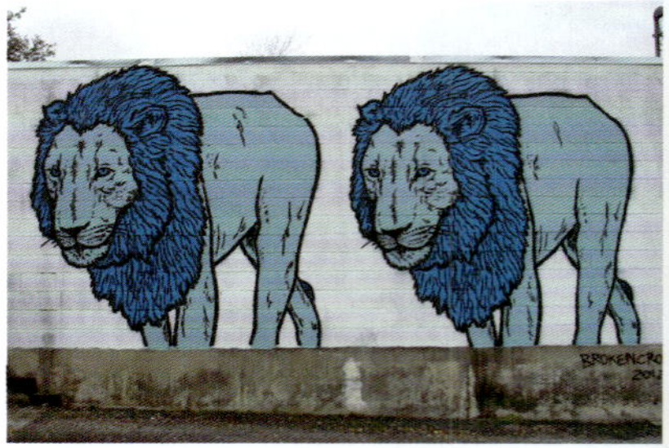

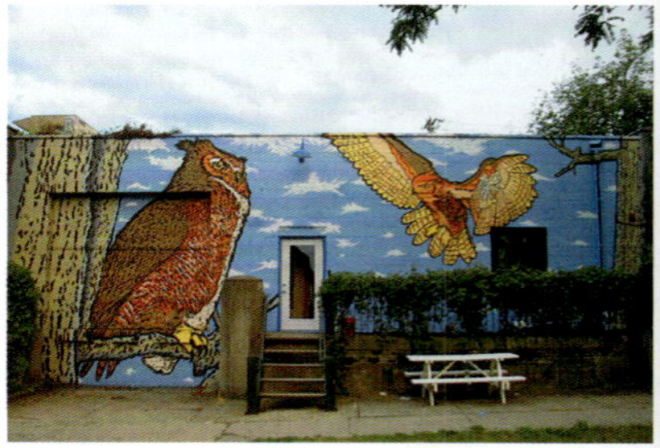

Collaboration with OverUnder and Paint Goggles. Photograph by Vincent Cornelli. Brooklyn, New York, 2009.
Detail photographs courtesy of Broken Crow.
Detail top: Austin, Texas, 2010.
Detail bottom: Minneapolis, Minnesota, 2010.

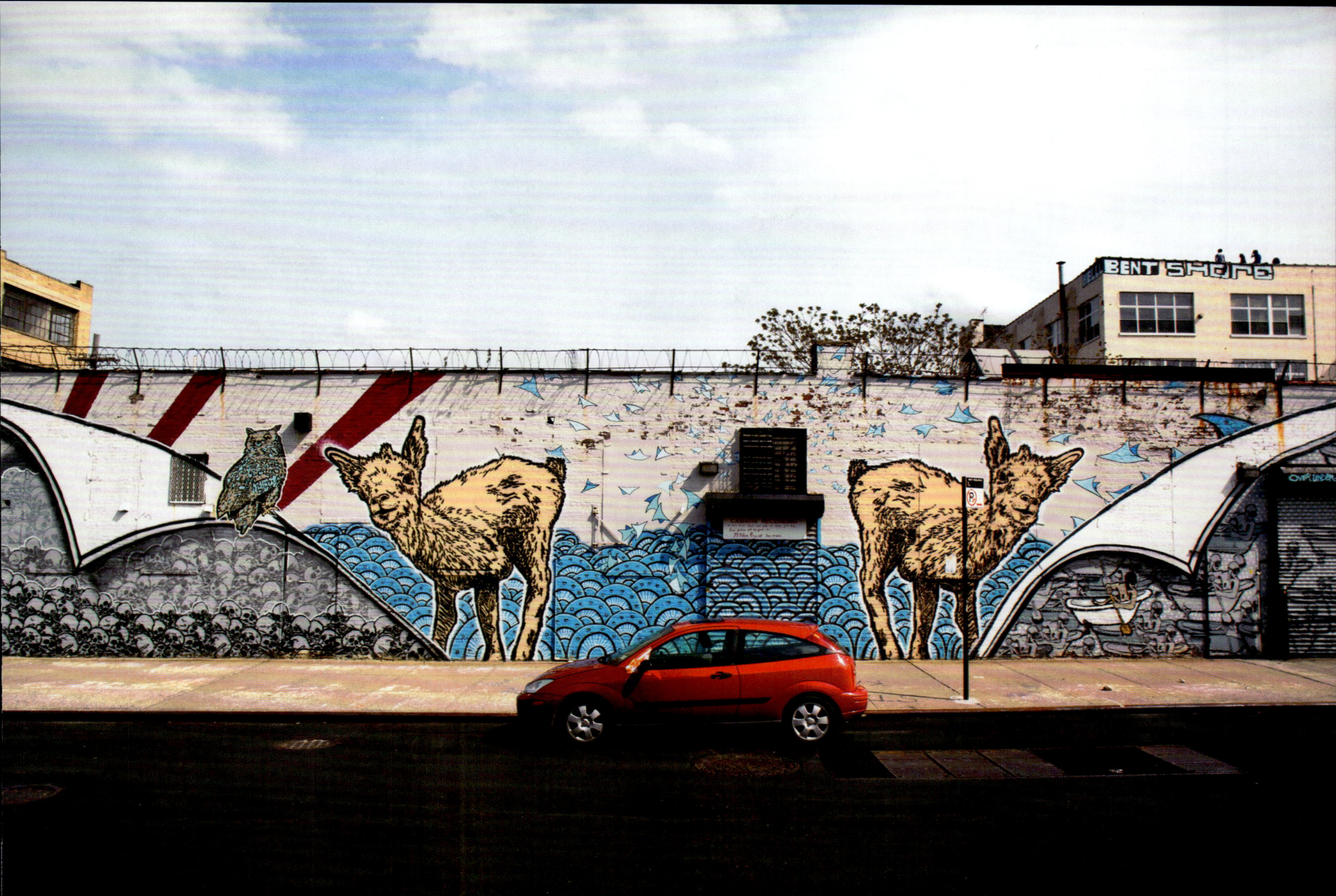
BENT SHORE

Brooklyn

Brooklyn has its own graffiti history, separate from that of the Bronx-Manhattan movement. Part of the problem in defining this history is the borough's vastness.

The upper tip of Manhattan is usually credited as the birthplace of the New York graffiti movement, partly because the narrowness of the geography there made the graffiti seem dense and concentrated. Brooklyn, however, is a vast, wide-open expanse, and to cover it was a Herculean task. A few writers did: Undertaker, Ash, Friendly Freddie, and Goldy all made a dent in the 1960s.

The first Brooklyn graffiti crew, however, wasn't formed until 1971; led by Dino Nod and Wicked Gary, it was based at Erasmus High School and called itself the Ex Vandals [see 118]. Less than one year after the Ex Vandals formed, graffiti moved on to piecing, but Brooklyn shone there as well; writers like Mico, Pistol 1, Spin 1, Flint 707 [see 135], and Super Strut quickly made the transition from taggers to piecing artists. Then, as the mid-1970s came around, throw-ups became more popular than piecing, and the Brooklyn writers helped dominate that scene, too, with two brothers, Tee and Stim 1, leading the way. By the close of the decade, style came back to the forefront again, as Dondi [protégé of the Brooklyn-based Top crew] created the new, style-based crew CIA. Dondi [see 097] began as a BMT writer, but saved his best efforts for the IRT lines.

Brooklyn writers remained influential through the end of graffiti's golden days: Ven represented Brooklyn well in the mid-1980s, often dragging old-school writers out of retirement for one last shot at glory. He continued his all-out bombing campaign into the '90s, and helped to form the clean-train movement.

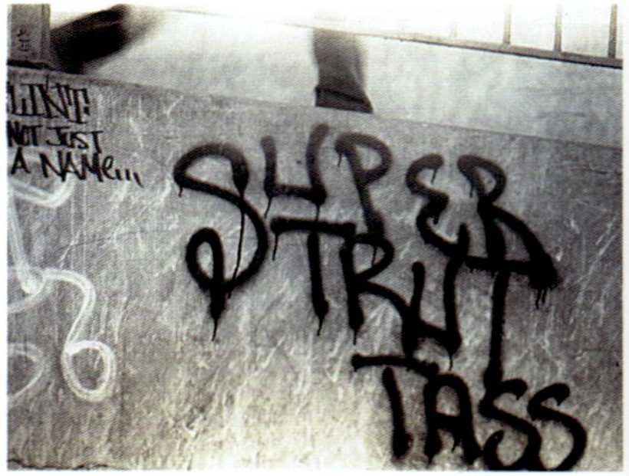

Piece by Spin.
Photograph by Jack Stewart.
New York City, 1973.
Detail: Tag by Superstrut.
Photograph by Flint Gennari. New York City, 1974.

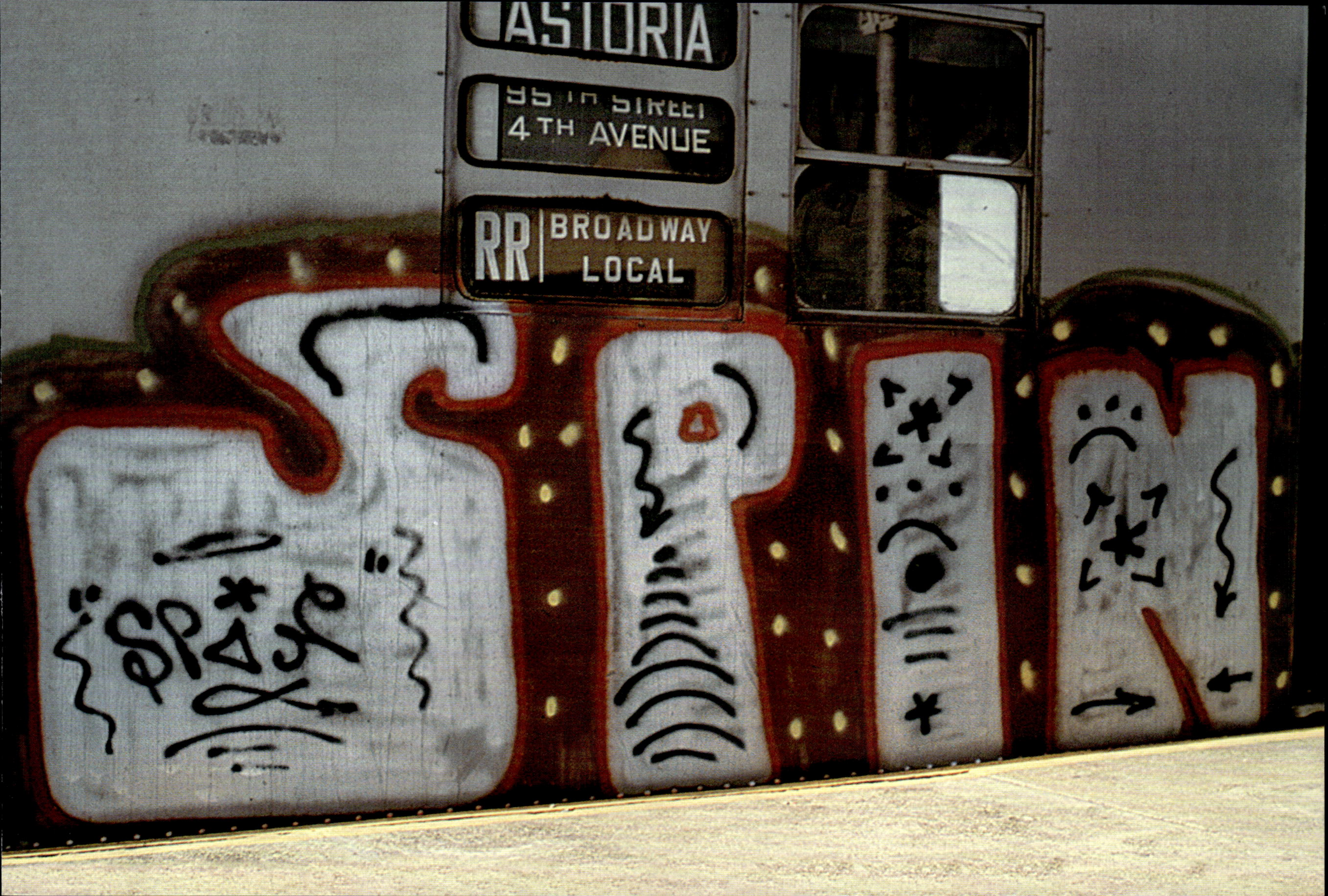
ASTORIA
4TH AVENUE
RR
BROADWAY
LOCAL

Buff Monster

The artist known as Buff Monster claims that he sees the color pink as a symbol of confidence, happiness, and individuality, thus explaining its presence in everything he does. The Hollywood-based artist is known for his very graphic painting, print, and installation work, but he came to prominence in Los Angeles via the wheatpasting, throughout the first decade of the 2000s, of several thousand hand-screened posters that showcased his signature character, a frilled bloblike creature with Xs for eyes.

A self-professed metal-head, Buff Monster is pictured with a heavily gelled, pencil-thin Mohawk and a pink shirt on his website, where he names his main influences as ice cream, metal, and Japanese pop culture.

Branching out from single- or two-tone poster images, Buff Monster moved into elaborate painted works on wood, which he has exhibited in galleries inside and outside Los Angeles. He has also embarked on a successful design career, which highlights his extensive work with designer vinyl toys. His instantly recognizable imagery, heavy on the nipple and cupcake references, can be seen internationally in magazines, on T-shirts, and even still, occasionally, on walls.

Photograph by Becky Snyder.
Venice, California, 2006.

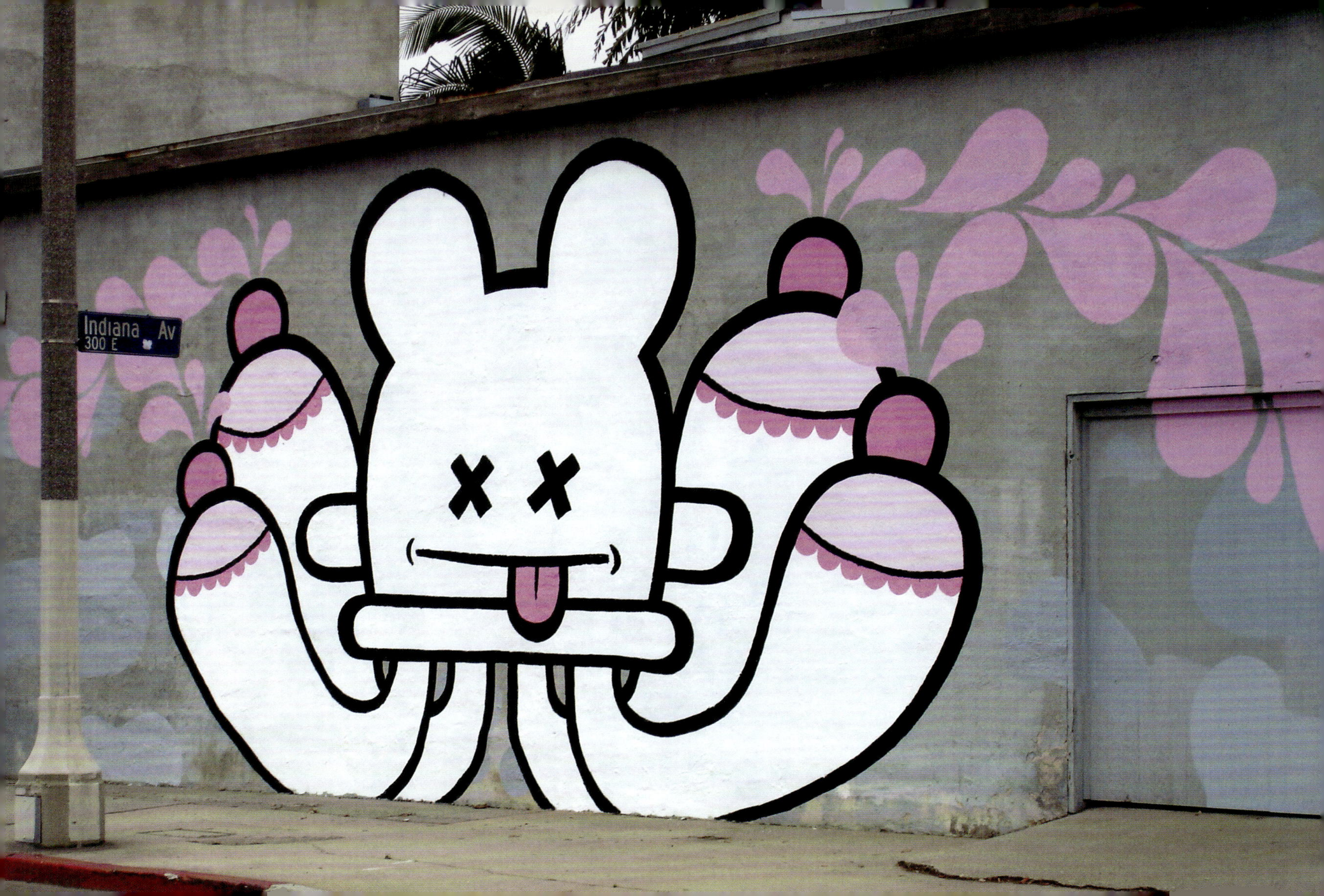
Indiana Av
300 E

Burning Candy

Do the men and women behind Burning Candy make street art or graffiti? It probably doesn't matter what box one might try to put them in; what matters is that this crew gets up indoors and outdoors, and that they have, in a few short years, transformed the London and Bristol landscapes with everything from tags and pieces to posters and massive commissioned murals. The London- and Bristol-based writers Tek 33, Cyclops, Sweet Toof (see 328), Rowdy, Mighty Mo, Gold Peg, Dscreet, Cept, and LL Brainwashed have all belonged to Burning Candy at some point.

The members of Burning Candy, even the older ones, belong to a new generation of writers, a generation that values lettering as much as characters. They admire the great writers, like Blade, as much as the old masters of the fine arts, like Michelangelo. They also recognize that graffiti is advertising, and so they use logos in their work. For example: Ask people from London if they've ever seen a name like Panik on a wall around town, and they'll probably look confused, even though Panik is one of London's greatest young writers. But if you ask a Londoner if he's ever seen a monkey head or a crocodile or a one-eyed Charlie Brown, you'll get a smile.

Not only do the members of Burning Candy get up, but their logos also strengthen the recognition of their names inside and outside of the graffiti community. It seems as if almost everyone in London and Bristol knows Burning Candy, even if they don't know that they know.

Photograph by Martha Cooper.
Miami, Florida, 2010.

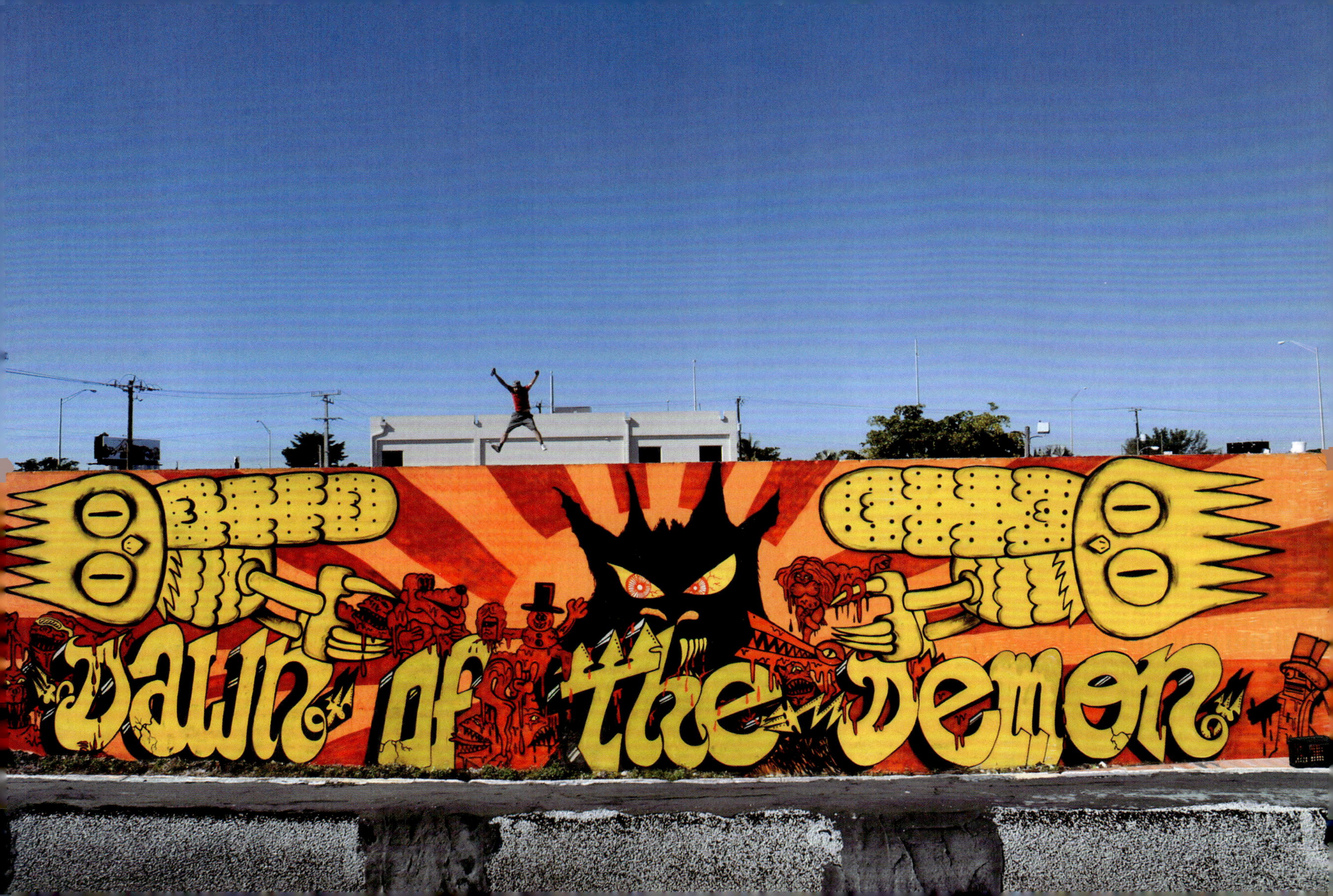
Dawn of the Demon

buses

Graffiti's first appearance on public transit (1969–1970) did not occur on the subways. Buses packed with school kids became a natural and easy target for the pioneers of the graffiti movement, who wanted to spread the message "we exist."

The inside of a bus proved easy prey for kids who outnumbered the driver fifty to one. Writers often lay in ambush at highly trafficked bus stops, converging with spray cans and hitting the backs of the buses, out of the driver's view. Clyde, a Bronx writer known for his script-style tag, rose to prominence as king of the buses. Buses began to look like the pictures of the earliest graffiti on trains, with multicolored signatures competing for real estate on both sides.

In Harlem, the bus yard by the Harlem River Drive made a perfect target for local writers such as Cool Cliff 120, Clancy 120, Topcat 126, Cop 5, Spade 130, Snake 131, and Sentry 120. In Upper Manhattan, the Washington Heights boys, Snake 1, Stitch 1, Web 2, Agee 170, and Jockey 1, became famous for blasting buses that ran throughout the city.

Once graffiti exploded and thousands joined the ranks, trains became the favored medium, with buses taking second place. Size mattered, and a train offered a bigger and smoother canvas. Train lines also covered more territory than bus routes. In the 1980s, Ban 2 became one of the last bus kings, plastering Bronx buses with drippy ink tags and witty sayings. Unfortunately, buses remain one of the least documented part of graffiti's history.

Tags by Stitch I, Mafia, Snake I–II, and Malo 125.
Photograph by Jon Naar.
New York City, 1973.

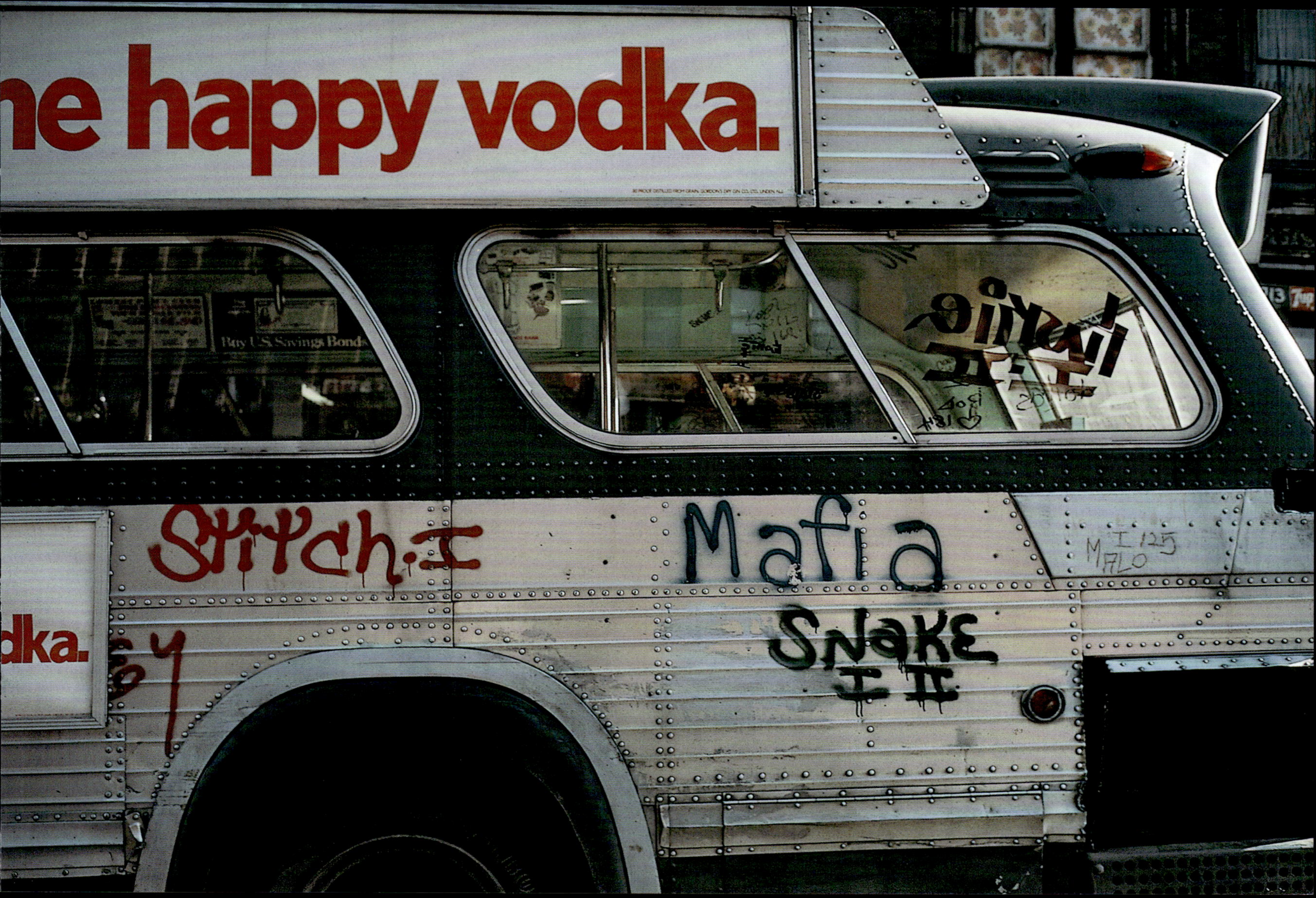

he happy vodka.
Buy U.S. Savings Bonds
Stitch I
Mafia
Snake II
dka.

C215

In the early 2000s, a rash of simplistic spray-painted images spread across the globe. Everyone savvy enough to wield an X-Acto blade was googling up an image of Che Guevara, cutting out his most recognizable facial elements, and spray-painting him on their garage. Among graffiti purists, stencils were being cast out as an art-school answer to graffiti; too great a departure from the tough, dangerous reputation illegal art had garnered for itself.

Then, in the middle of that decade, a smattering of hyper-detailed, seemingly cracked faces of old men sprayed in simple white popped up, signed "C215." They were a rare example of an artist using the pieces of card that hold a stencil's empty elements together (referred to as "bridges") to enhance the aesthetic of his pieces.

It was eventually revealed that C215 was in fact a Frenchman in his thirties, visiting New York from Paris.

C215 is quoted as saying, "I don't think life is funny. So when I go paint on the street, I don't want to joke." That spirit is embodied in his melancholy works. He claims to paint "mostly homeless people, refugees, street kids . . . people who really belong to the streets." Calling his work "contextual art," he intends to draw attention to the darkness of life for people living on the streets. Although C215 doesn't reveal whether he himself was ever homeless, his work leaves the viewer wondering what it was that made this particular subject so close to his heart.

Photograph by Remo Camerota. Paris, 2009.

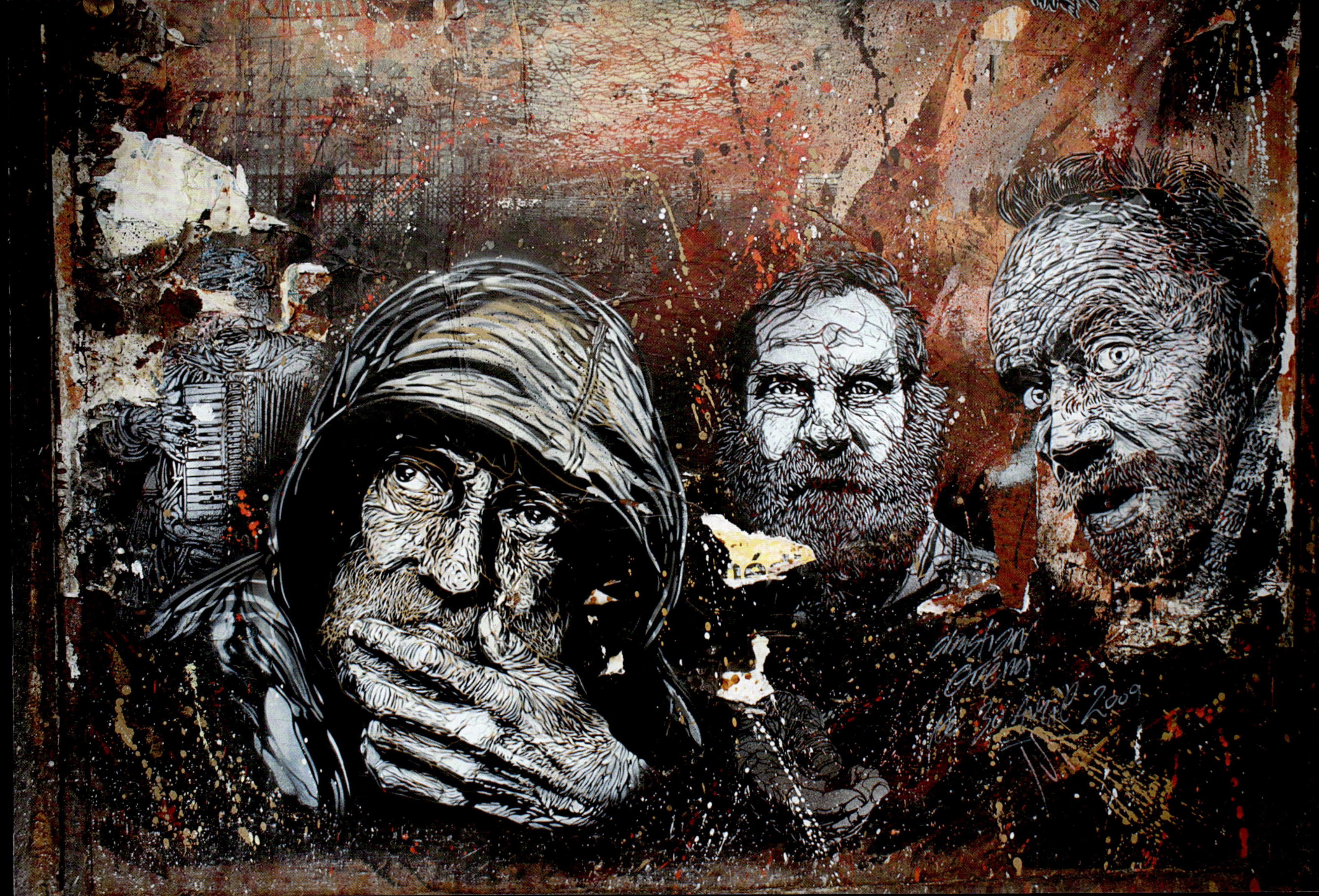

Caine 1

During his brief life, Ed Glowaski became the most important graffiti artist ever to come out of Queens. Known as Caine 1, he began writing in 1973. Light-years ahead of his peers artistically, Caine 1 soon became bored with simply painting his name. Caine was the first Queens writer to create thematic whole-cars with detailed character renderings, transforming subway cars into paintings.

By 1975, Caine had become the graffiti artist most watched by writers from other parts of the city. Word spread to the Bronx, and soon such stylemasters as Tracy 168 [see 340] and Riff 170 trucked out to the remote #7 yard in an attempt to show up Caine. In 1976, Caine 1, Mad 102, Chino 174, Roger, Dime 139, and some lesser-known Queens writers painted an entire ten-car train for the first time in history. Known as "The Freedom Train," in commemoration of America's bicentennial, it was immediately broken up by the embarrassed transit authorities.

Some of his most famous train paintings are "Welcome to Hell," which featured a top-to-bottom rendition of Alice Cooper's *Welcome to My Nightmare* character, and "Spellbound," featuring a dark wizard and drawing on occult themes.

In 1977, Caine 1, an alleged Satanist, made the headlines for selling human skulls he had robbed from graves. In the early 1980s, he became renowned for painting the backs of denim jackets and had begun selling canvases through the Manhattan gallery Graffiti Productions Inc. Caine was killed by an elderly neighbor in Queens who, assuming he was a burglar, shot him as he tried to break through a window in their apartment building.

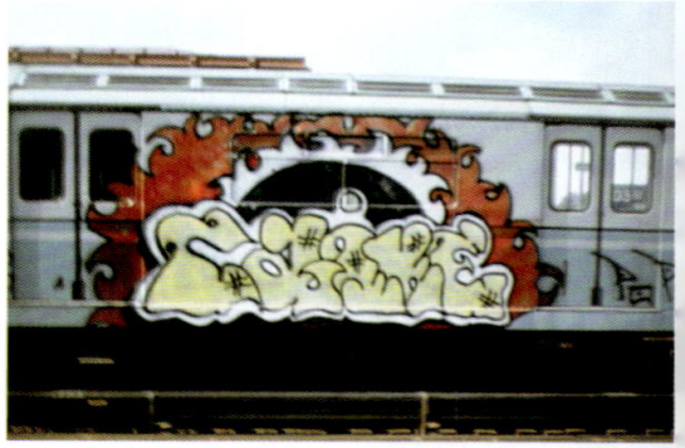

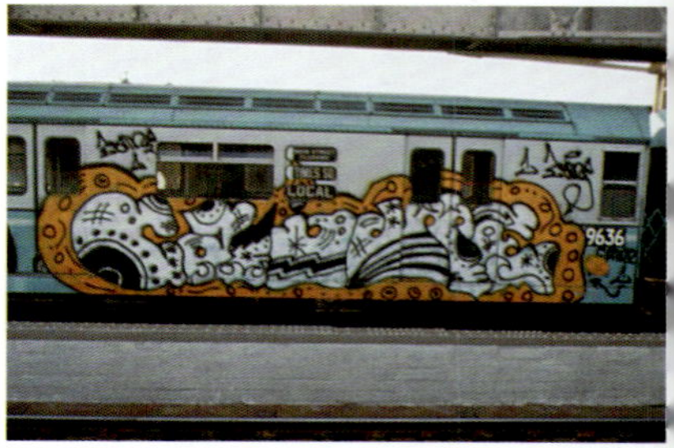

Photograph by Joseph Palletella.
New York City, 1975.
Detail top: Photograph by Jack Stewart.
New York City, 1974.
Detail bottom: Photograph by Jack Stewart.
New York City, 1974.

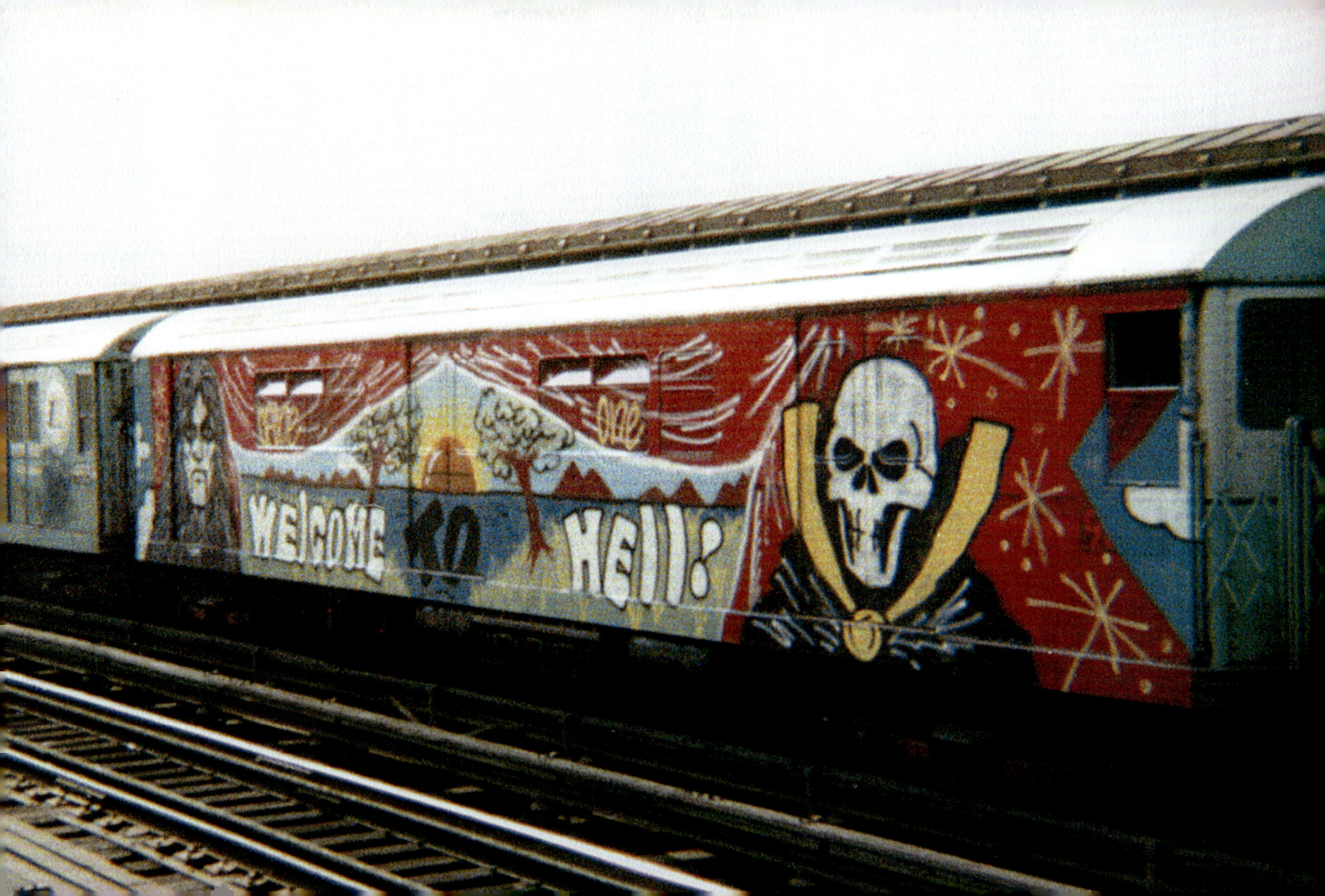
WELCOME TO HELL!
one
one

Can 2

Like most European writers, Germany's Can 2 discovered graffiti and hip-hop in one neat package in 1983, when, as he says, "The media brought break dance over here [Mainz , Germany], and of course, graff." Movies of the early 1980s, such as *Beat Street*, *Wild Style*, and *Style Wars* [see 322], as well as the book *Subway Art* [see 323], became his instructional manual.

That same year, at the age of thirteen. Can 2 began break dancing. Around the same period, his friend Zebster showed him a graffiti sketch, and the artistically inclined Can 2 decided to become a writer.

Early in his career, Can 2 practiced painting on the walls of his hometown, Mainz, just outside of Frankfurt, Germany. But by 1987, hip-hop jams had become big in Europe, and Can 2 began traveling throughout Europe and, shortly after, around the world. He developed a B-boy style of characters and a very clean NYC-based letter style; his mastery of lettering and character rendering has made him an old-school legend among European writers, but his style has never lost its subway-art edge. Often called "the German Seen," he readily admits that Richard "Seen" Mirando [see 294] is his idol.

Can 2 formed his own crew, SUK [Stick Up Kids], which includes members from around the globe. For the past several years, he and his good friend Atom have been repping the Montana team out of Germany, executing production walls globally. Now a family man, Can 2 paints—mostly legally—and has made his living art directing and executing graphic designs for some of the biggest companies in Europe.

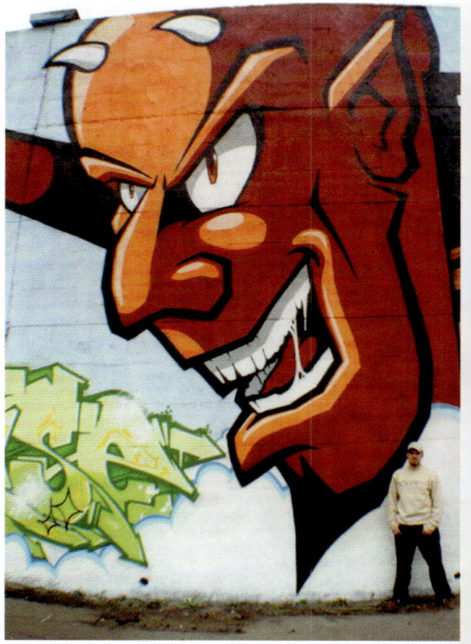

Photographs courtesy of Can 2.

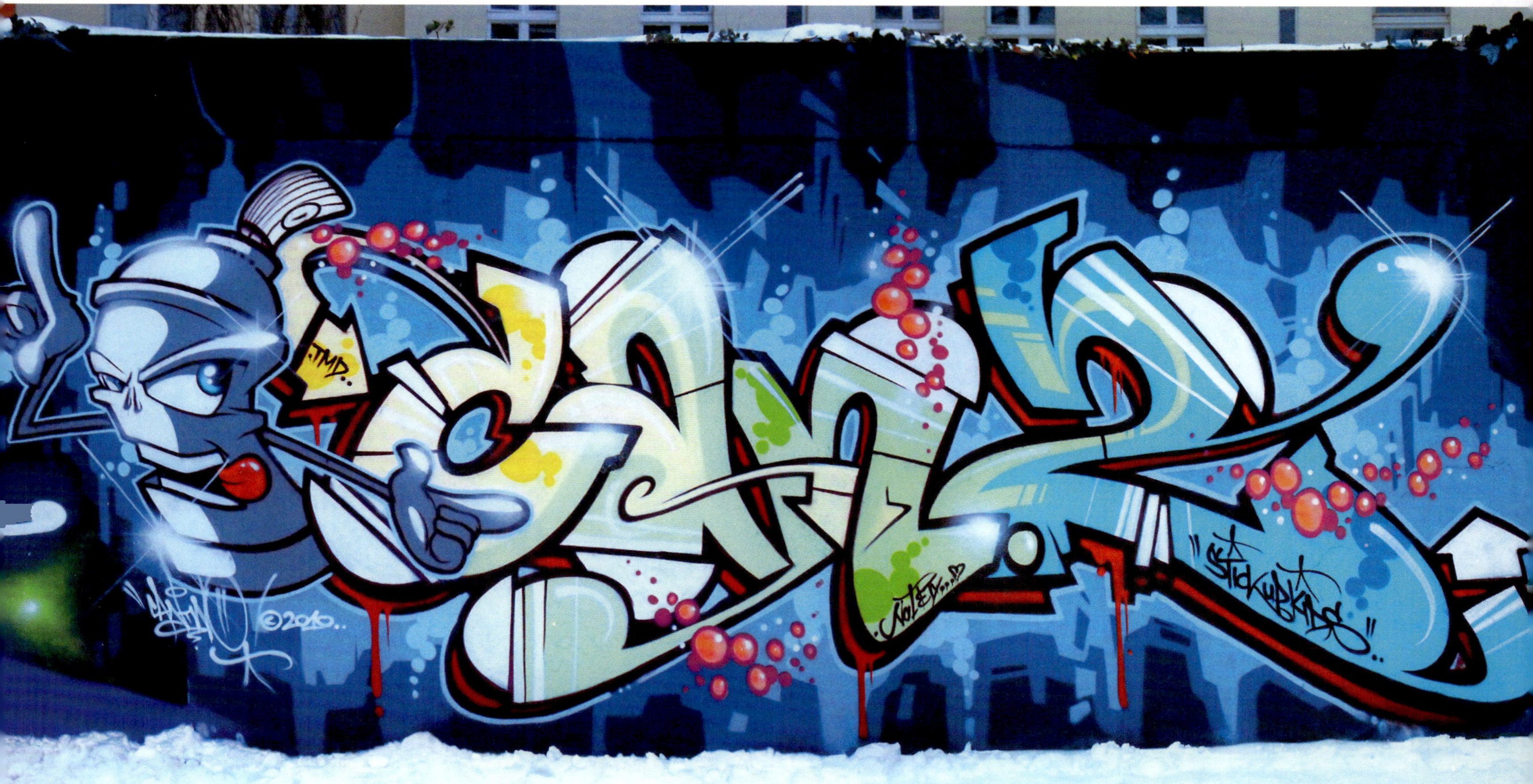
©2010..

The Cans Festival

In May 2008, London's Leake Street road tunnel was transformed into an extraordinary global showcase of stencil art called the Cans Festival, curated by famed British street artist Banksy (see 024). For about half a mile, the walls of the tunnel were stenciled with countless images by dozens of talented and inventive street artists from all over the world.

Among the artists invited by Banksy to join him in creating work for this landmark outdoor exhibit were Ame72 (see 014), Blek le Rat (see 038), C215 (see 053), Daniel Meli, Dolk (see 095), Faile (see 123), Logan Hicks (see 166), M-City (see 215), Orticanooodles, Sam3, and Vexta (see 350). The works that they created in a span of just a few hours ranged from starkly crafted, witty statements to intricate portraits done with multiple layers of stencils.

Thirty thousand people lined up for hours prior to the Cans Festival's opening, and for the following few months, hundreds of thousands of visitors—from local schoolchildren to elderly tourists—visited the tunnel. Throughout the summer of 2008, Banksy encouraged visitors to add their own stencil artwork. "I've always felt that anyone with a paint can should have as much say in how our cities look as architects or ad men," he said. "So getting to cover an entire street with graffiti is a dream come true, or—as some might call it—a complete nightmare."

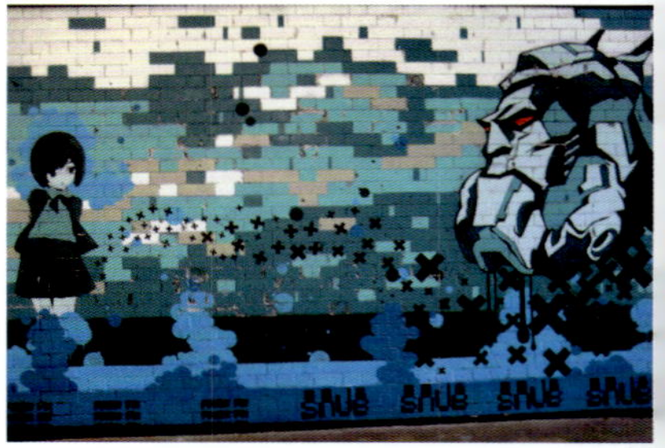

Artwork by Banksy (right), Hutch (far right), and Snub (detail).
Photographs by Lois Stavsky.
London, 2008.

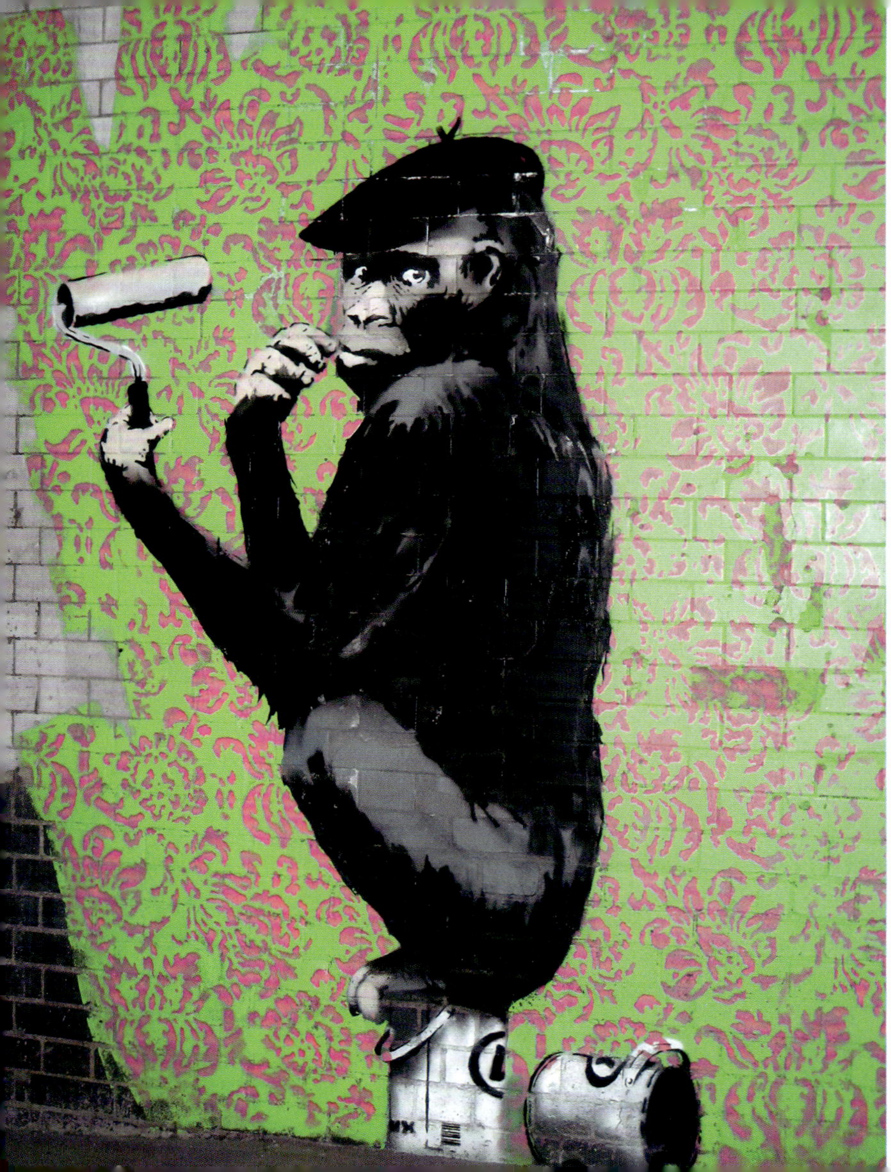

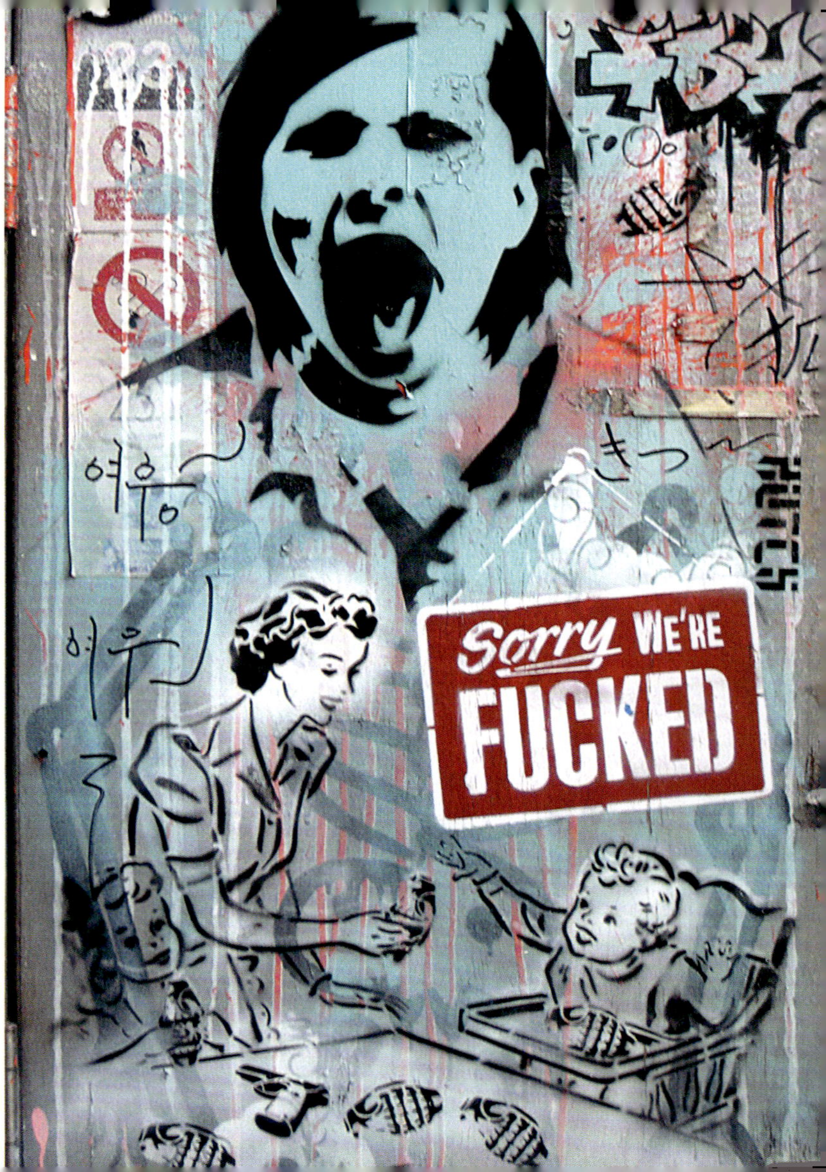
Sorry WE'RE
FUCKED

Cap One Da Bronx

Much has been written about Cap One. He has been one of the most polarizing figures in graffiti history, and for many, his name can evoke an immediate visceral response. Hero or villain? Here's Cap's insight on Cap: "I started writing in mid-1976. There was much bicentennial painting going on in my neighborhood; things were painted red, white, and blue. I noticed a spirit piece done for Independence Day and thought to myself: 'Wow, that's cool—I gotta do some of that.' I was thirteen years old, and the coolest things in the world to me were girls, rock and roll, and checking out the motorcycles that some guys in the neighborhood rode. These aspects of my life came together in 1979, when I joined a Bronx motorcycle club. I was still hitting trains as crews started battling to take over lines and yards. Being an outlaw, I jumped right into the action, taking over the #5 and #2 lines by 1982, and when I spoke up in *Style Wars* (see 322), Henry Chalfant played me as a villain. . . . By 1983, I had three thousand pieces, mostly throw-ups on trains, but also top-to-bottoms, color pieces, and blockbusters, as well as highway spots, rooftops, trackies, and buses. That was what graffiti meant to me—getting up—and I did it like no one else. I earned my crown the hard way, battling many crews, and not always just with paint. Nowadays, graffiti has evolved as the largest art movement of all time. I have been busy for over thirty years painting in many countries with companies and brother artists. Thanks to all true to our culture."

Throw-ups by Cap One, writing over Shy 147 (left) and Duro (right); BO throw-up (left corner) by Kado 7. Photograph by Martha Cooper. New York City, 1982.

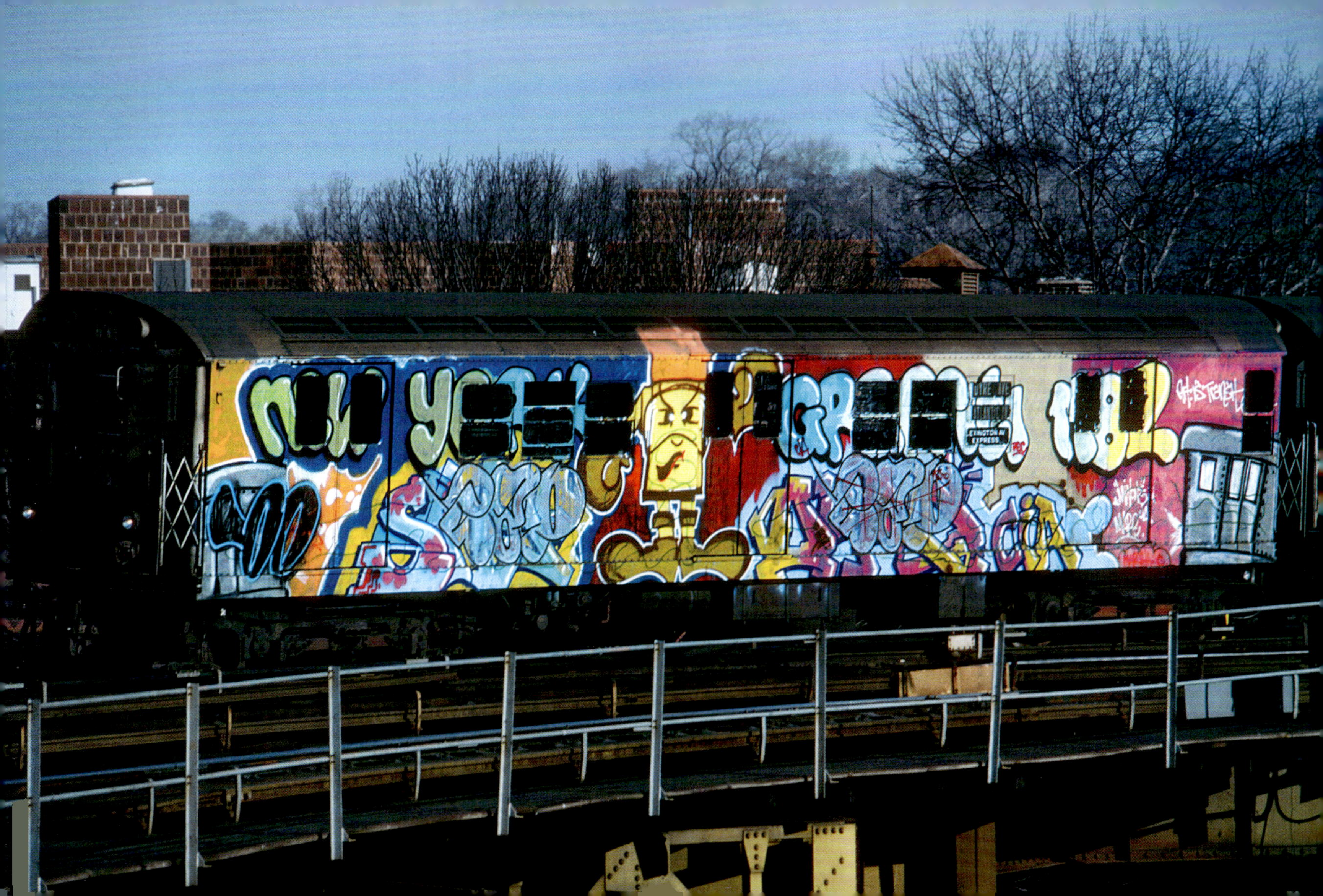

Cekis

Born in Santiago, Chile, in 1976, Nelson Rivas, aka Cekis, is one of the pioneers of the Latin American street-art movement. Inspired by the posters that were part of his city's landscape during the politically turbulent 1980s, he began painting on the streets of his city when he was fourteen years old. Since then, he has created murals in Buenos Aires, São Paulo, Valparaiso, Seville, Zurich, Hamburg, Baltimore, and New York.

A member of the first generation of postdictatorship urban artists in Chile, Cekis is renowned for his distinctive multilayered, multicolored portraits of the common man. As his compositions attest with their abstract forms and distinct typography, Cekis is particularly interested in the juxtaposition of diverse styles and global trends.

Since moving to New York City in 2003, Cekis has conducted mural workshops in a range of venues including the Bronx Museum of the Arts and The Point, a community-based organization dedicated to the cultural revitalization of the South Bronx. He has also been awarded several residencies, including the Keyholder Artist in Residence at Lower East Side Print Shop.

Cekis's work has been featured in exhibits in both private and public spaces, including the Rotunda Gallery in Brooklyn Heights, NYU, and the Abrons Arts Center. In 2009, he participated in the landmark "Chile Style" exhibit at the Carmichael Gallery in Los Angeles.

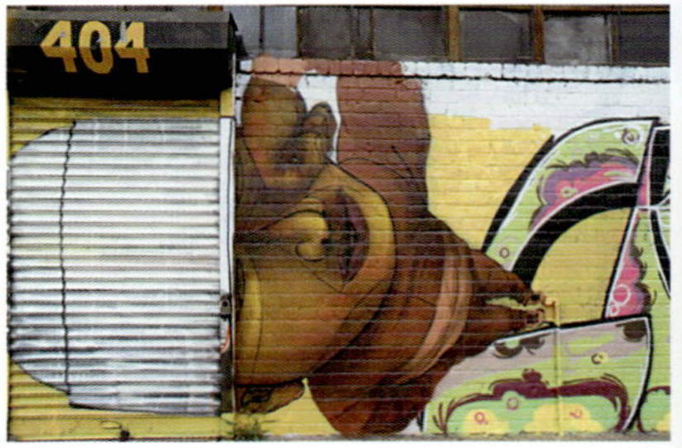

Photographs by Becki Fuller. Brooklyn, New York, 2010.

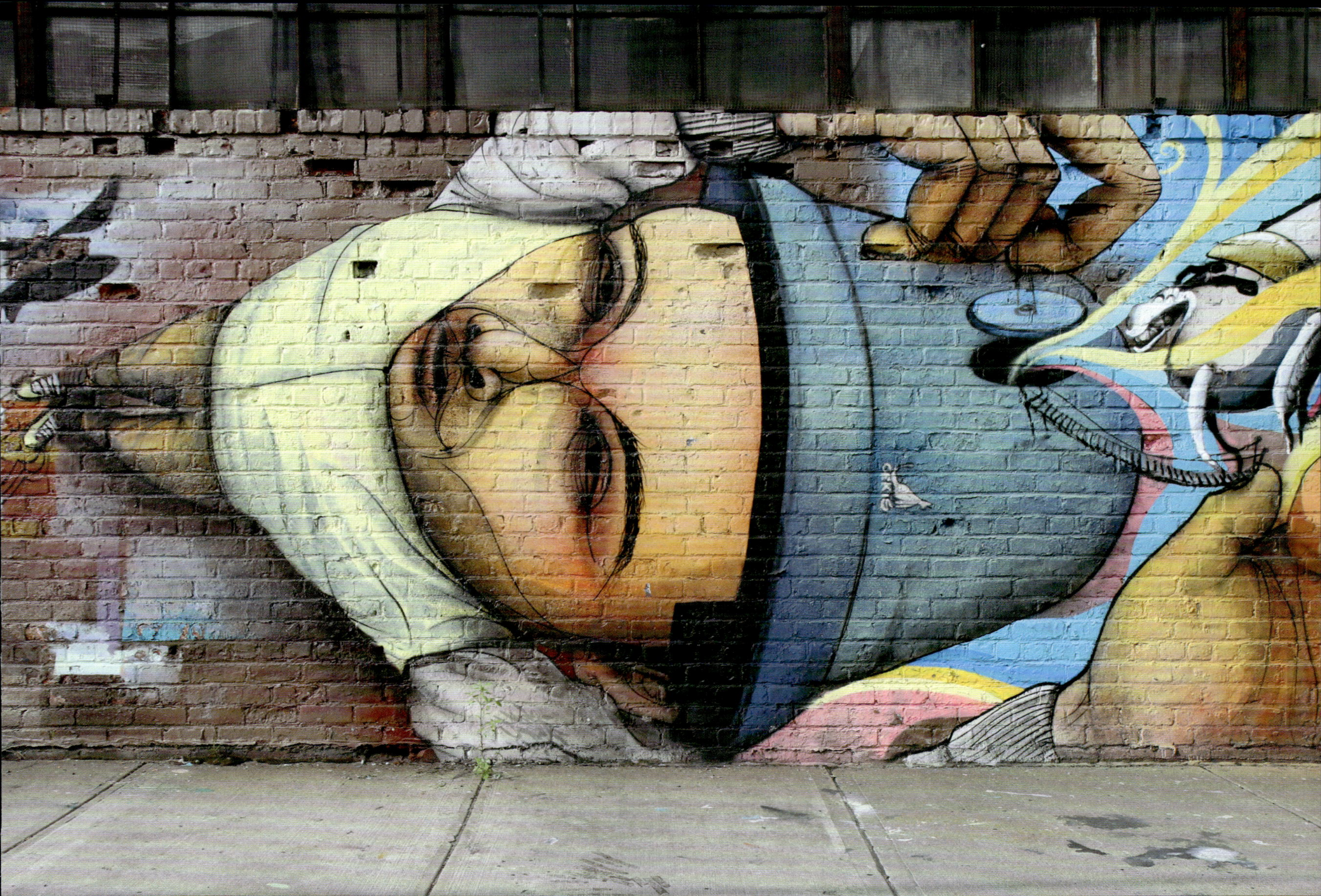

Cept

Mike Ballard started writing as Cept in 1986, a time when graffiti was still widely reviled and misunderstood by the public. His impressive pieces adorned large walls across East London for nearly a decade, the renowned Sclater Street being a favorite haunt of his. Associated with several crews, including Rolling People and Burning Candy in the U.K. and Justice n Crime in Belgium, he also painted with Eine and Tase in the mid-1990s.

He once described himself as approaching his artwork like a hip-hop producer approaches music, appropriating different styles and mixing them to create a new aesthetic. His psychedelic baroque style is indeed eclectic, but the influence of individual artists like Roy Lichtenstein is still plain to see. Although self-taught, Ballard went on to complete a master's degree in fine art in 2007, to help put into practice his increasingly ambitious plans.

Despite most of his work now appearing in galleries and under his real name, many will remember Ballard most fondly as Cept, and for the key role he played in forming the U.K. graff scene.

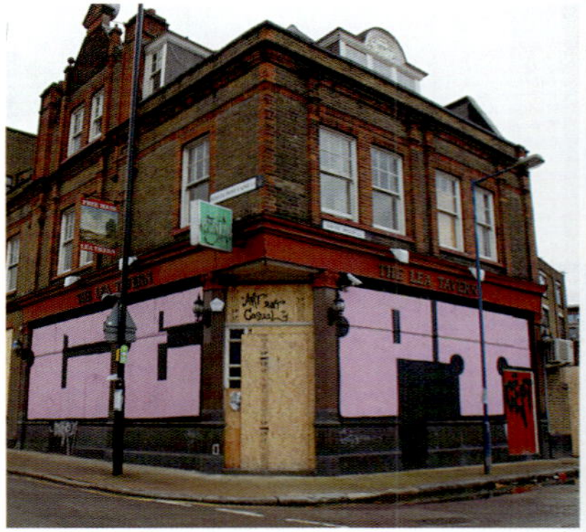

Photograph by David Stuart (NoLionsInEngland). Shoreditch, London, 2010.
Detail: Photograph by George Macdonald. Hackney Wick, London, 2008.

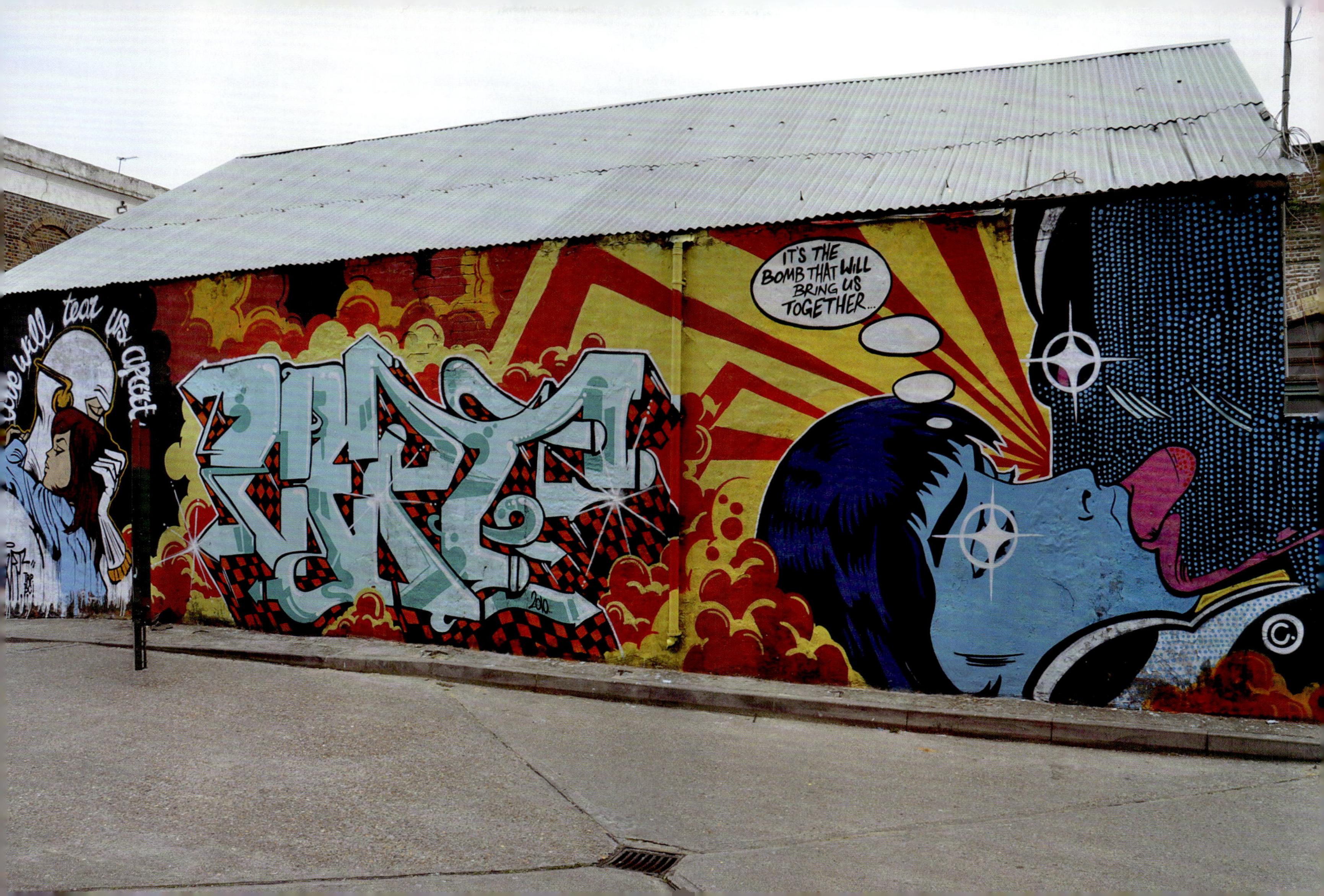
IT'S THE
BOMB THAT WILL
BRING US
TOGETHER...
we will tear us apart
2010

Cern

Among the expansive industrial sprawl in the outer reaches of Brooklyn, Manhattan's bigger sister, drab gray factory buildings spread across the low horizon in a monotonous architectural line. This neighborhood is called Bushwick. It is just beginning to feel gentrification's touch, but its primary occupants are still trucks and metal mills. Wide streets sprinkled with gravel cut through the landscape, occasionally traversed by a hipster on a bicycle. It is here that a group of graffiti artists, collectively known as Robots Will Kill (see 283)—and originally from another of New York's boroughs, Staten Island—optioned to paint an entire building, from the sidewalk to the rooftop.

As one drives down Johnson Street, the story-high faces created by one particular artist are enough to stop you in your tracks. They are hyper-detailed, yet abstracted at the same time, and the technical ability apparent in the artist's work is breathtaking. That artist goes by the name of Cern.

Cern started writing graffiti in the 1990s, expanding his style beyond the boundaries of typical lettering and into the fantastical, surrealistic character work he does today. He was included in the graffiti books *Burning New York* and *Graffiti World*. Cern is well known for his street work in New York City, and he also exhibits his canvases and watercolor work at galleries internationally.

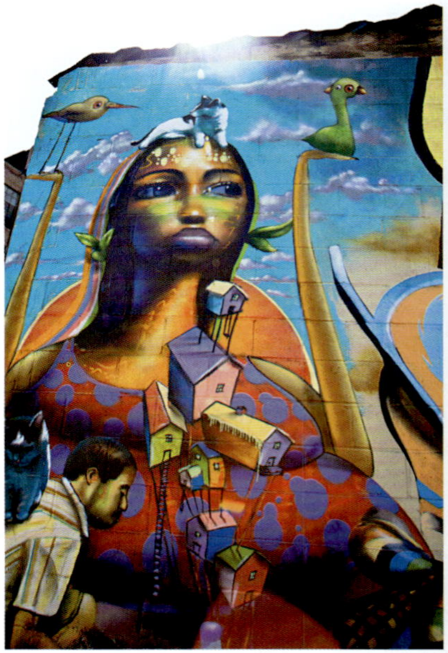

Photographs by Vincent Cornelli.
Brooklyn, New York, 2010.
Detail: Brooklyn, New York, 2009.

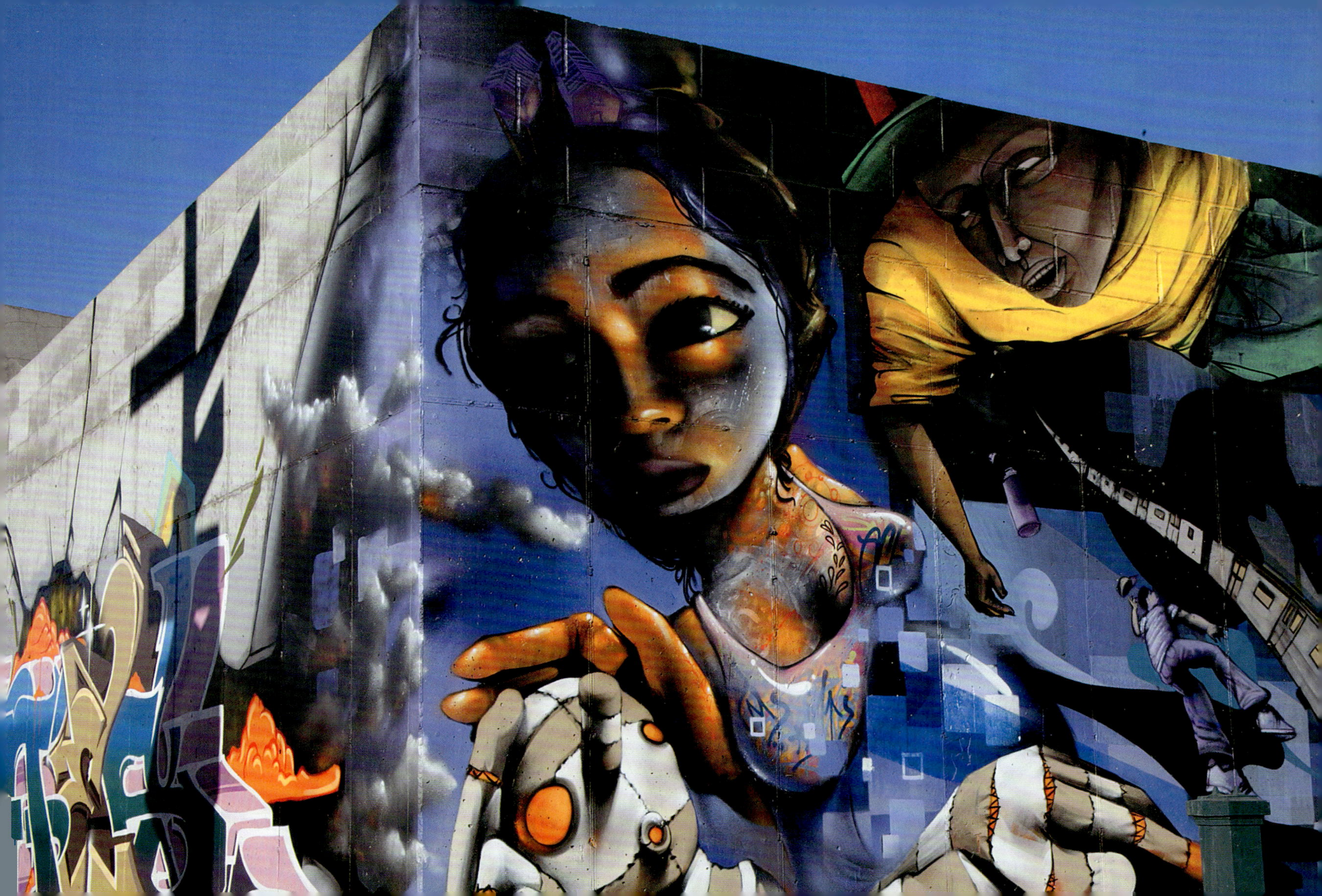

Ces

Ces's story began in 1983 in New Rochelle, where, as a pot-smoking teen, he painted alongside railroad tracks and warehouse facades with other graffiti-loving youths. Ces possessed innate artistic ability, and graffiti allowed him to share it with the public. Vet TMC, the king of Westchester and an early stylemaster, proved a great partner for Ces in his formative years. Although he painted a few trains in the early 1980s, Ces's fame reached a zenith in the early '90s, as he became one of the driving creative forces (along with Per One) of the FX crew. FX would be among the first American crews to collaborate with Europe's top talents, who would spread the word about Ces's skills upon their return to the Continent.

Soon, Ces became the most sought-after invitee to the myriad of graffiti events taking place all over the world. A seven-year partnership with Seen (see 294) ensued, which resulted in collaborations on canvases, tractor trailer paintings, and even some live trains.

For more than a decade, Ces has curated a rooftop Mecca in the Bronx that has drawn graffiti's royalty and been featured in the *New York Times*. Ces currently paints and sells canvases all over the world and, for the past dozen years, has been one of New York's most in-demand tattoo artists. He likes wearing shades indoors and wearing sneakers that match his T-shirts.

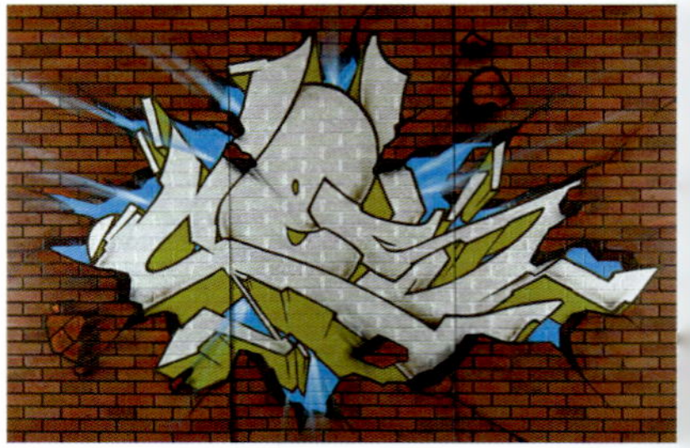

Photographs courtesy of Ces.
Photograph by Ces.
Hamburg, Germany, 1996.
Detail: Photograph by Adam Reich.
Bronx, New York, 2007.

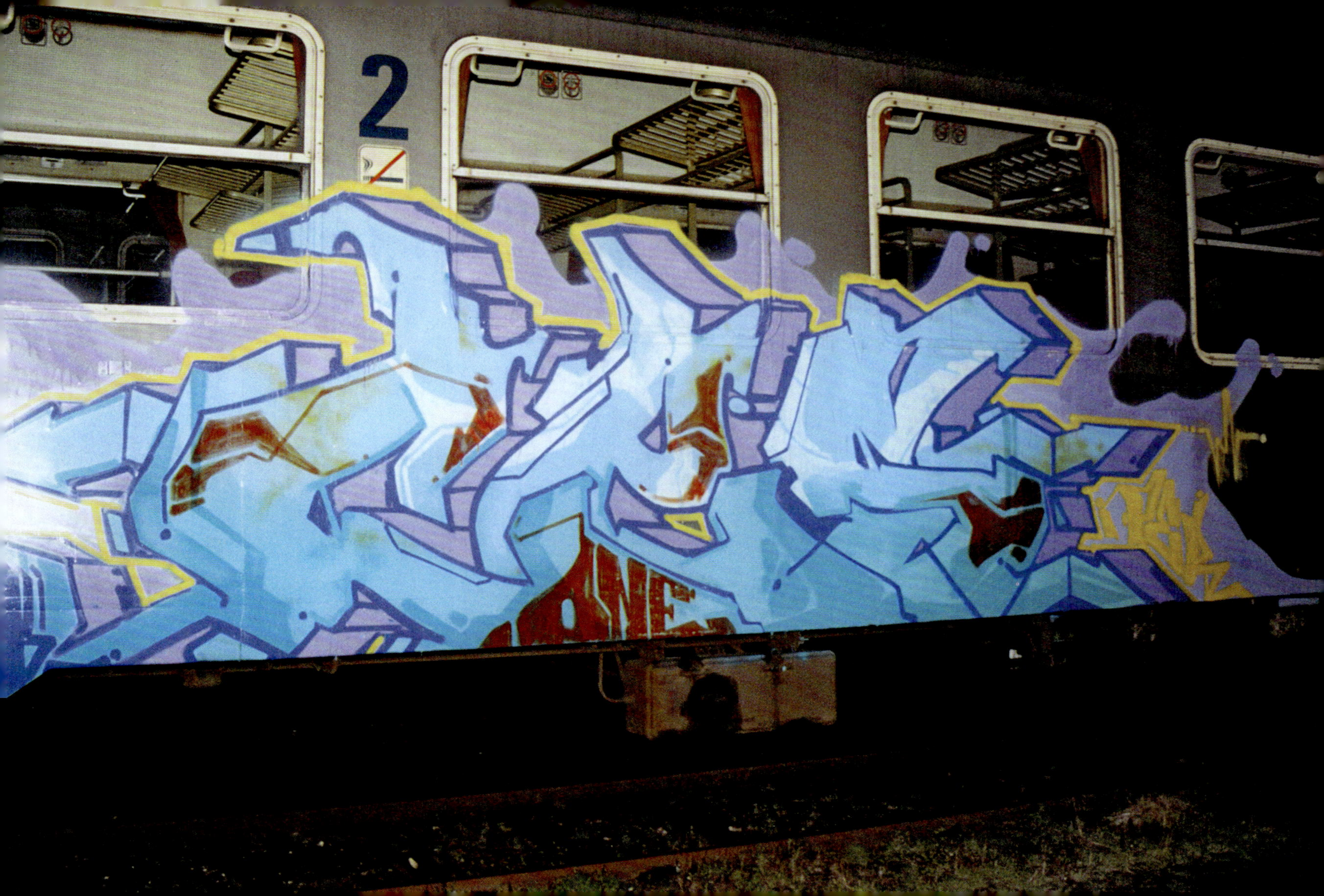
2

Chain 3

Chain 3, aka T.Bag 170, is one of the all-time great stylemasters. He began writing in 1974, after studying the work of Phase 2 [see 255], Riff 170, and Pel. As Chain met and befriended the next generation of writers at the Writer's Bench, he, Kool 131, and Mr. Jinx 174 started making a mental list of the best of the best. When the group formed the Death Squad in 1976, they went from one high school to the next, making an *actual* list of who the best writers were and adding them to their crew. The Death Squad would soon become the greatest style crew ever, formed with core members including Chain 3, Kool 131, Part [see 251], Magoo, Noc 167, Peso 131, Padre 2, Bear 167, and others.

In 1977, the Death Squad was the talk of the graffiti world, but members started moving in different directions. Mr. Jinx moved to Queens, Kool 131 concentrated on the Broadway line, and Chain 3 parted company with TDS, hooking up with a different crew, TMT [the Magnificent Team]. As part of the TMT crew, Chain 3 joined forces with brothers Tean and Kade 198, Teen, Fed 2, Best 149, and others to form a tight style unit of their own.

The years 1977 and 1978 saw some of the greatest style battles ever, as the TMT writers began to mature, and Chain 3 was right in the thick of it. TMT would also battle Dondi [see 097] and Kel from CIA, with all three crews adopting backup names that were similar. By 1979, the battles had lessened as the buff washed away the masterworks, and in 1980, Chain 3 gave way to the next generation. He remains active today, whether he's mentoring the latest members of TMT or painting with the original lineup of the crew.

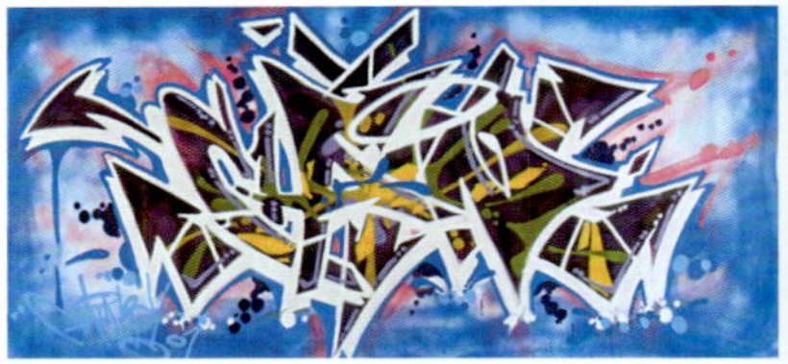

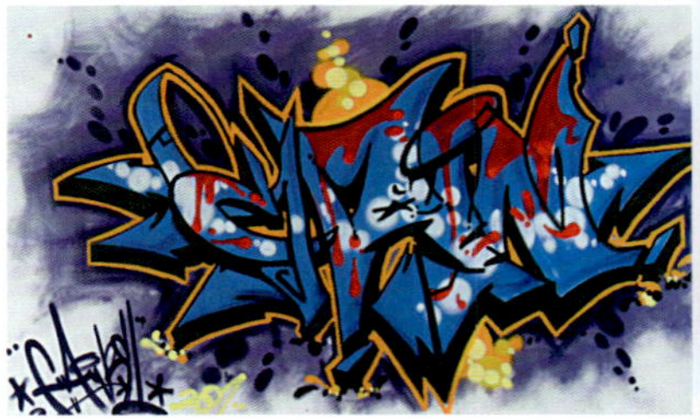

Photograph by Ces.
Bronx, New York, 2007.
Details: Photographs by Adam Reich.
Bronx, New York, 2007.

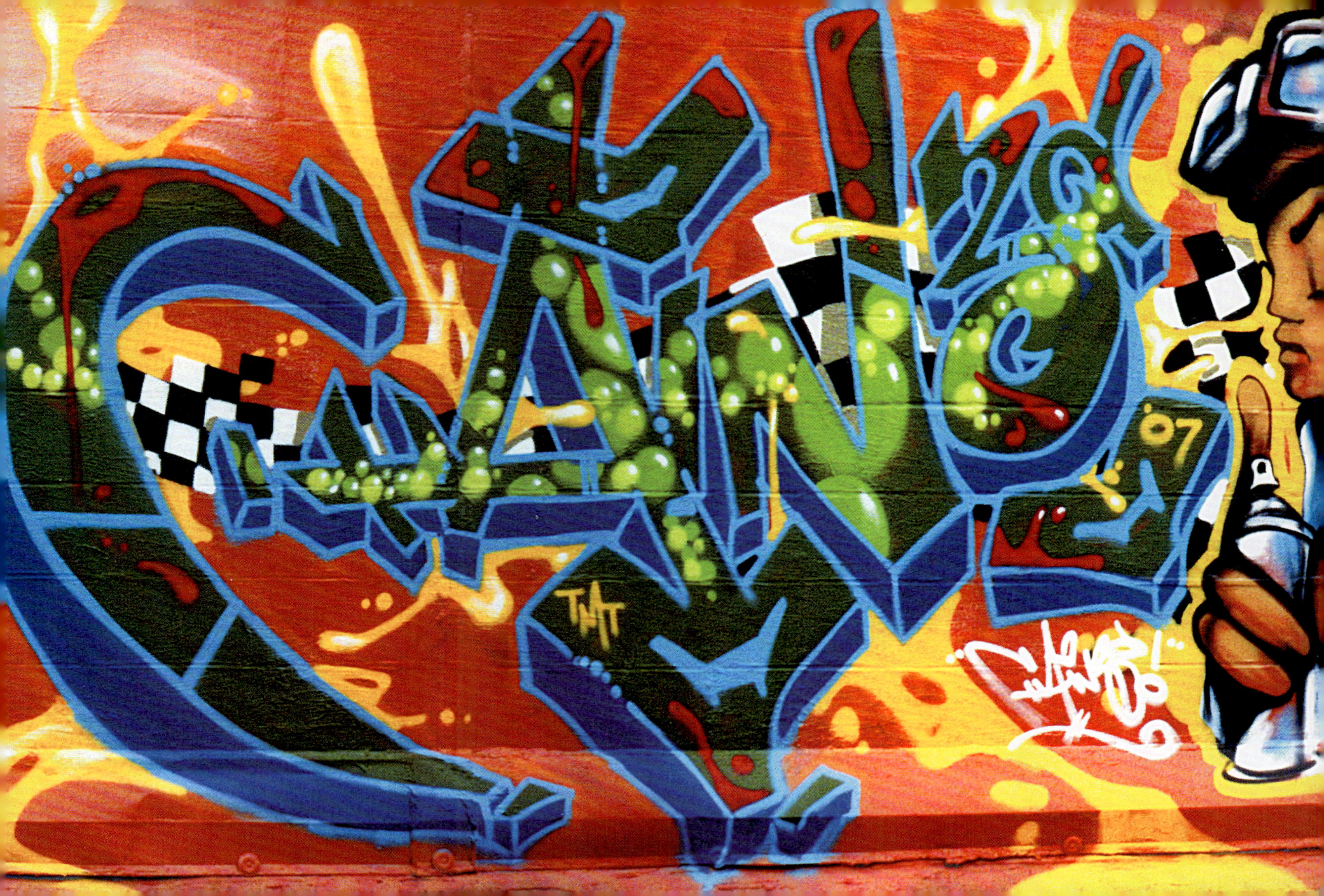
TMT

Henry Chalfant

Henry Chalfant stands alone as graffiti's most significant documentarian. A promising sculptor with a proclivity for outside-the-box thinking, he became mesmerized in 1976 by the art movement exploding across New York City's transit system. The visually powerful expressions of anonymous artists captivated Chalfant on two fronts: historical and anthropological.

Chalfant, a forty-year-old intellectual from Pennsylvania with an extensive art background, could not have been further outside the norm of the community he befriended. But by the time he had his first showing of photographs at New York's OK Harris Gallery in 1980, many graffiti writers, some of whom he met on subway platforms while photographing their work, considered him an ally. Chalfant treated the artists with respect, and his Grand Street studio became a meeting ground for writers.

Chalfant tried to remain neutral during the turbulent subway wars of the 1980s. He watched helplessly as beautiful whole-cars routinely got destroyed before he could snap his photographs. The answering machine in his studio remained perpetually full with writers' requests for him to photograph the work they had done the night before. More often than not, Chalfant got the shot.

Photograph by Ernie Paniccioli. New York City, 1992.

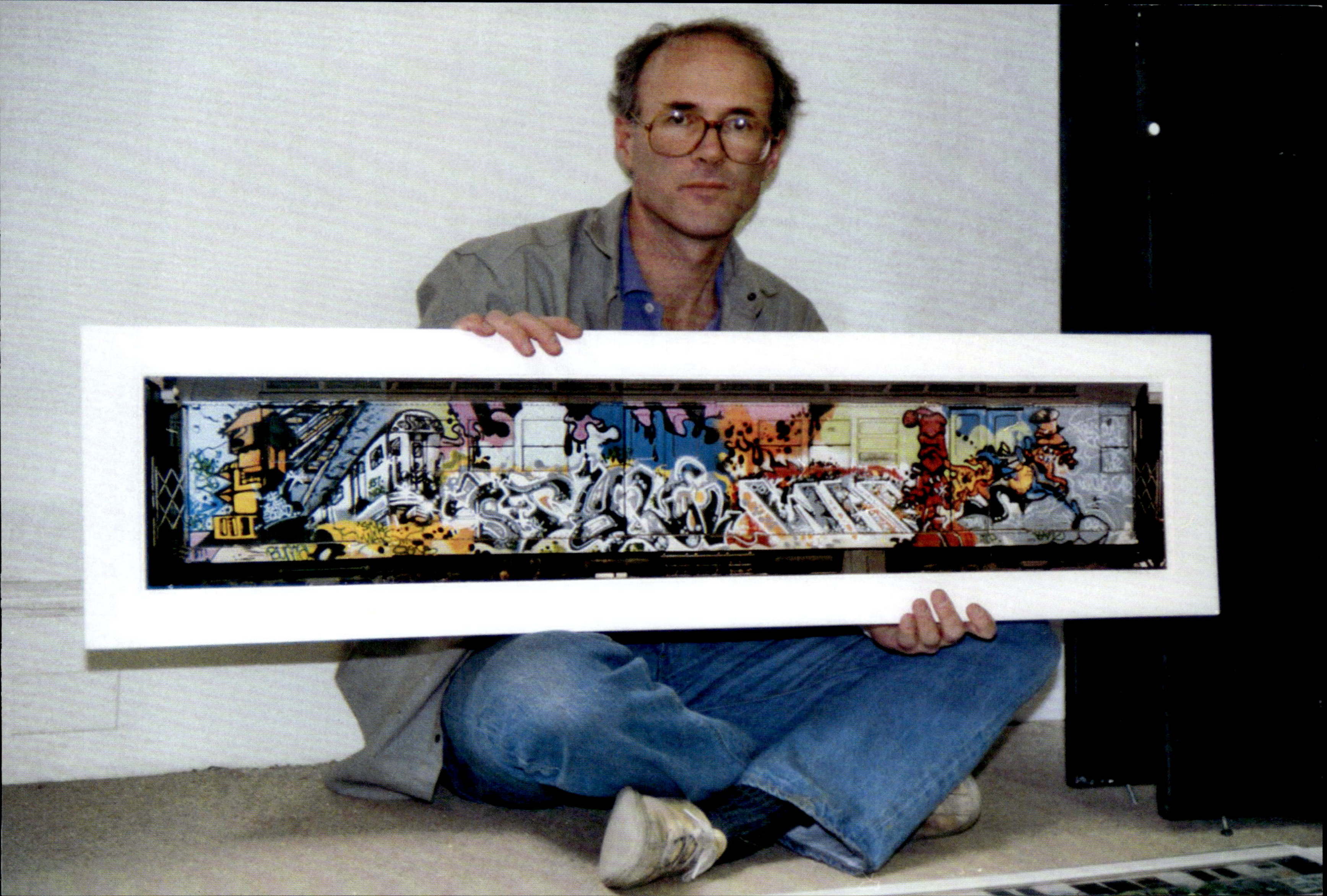

Chico

Since the 1970s, the East Village and the Lower East Side ("Loisaida," in Latino slang) have served as the epicenter of New York's "downtown" culture. Significant artists, from Jean-Michel Basquiat (see 026) to Keith Haring (see 160), have made this stretch of the city their home base, despite the neighborhood's reputation for roughness. As synonymous with the neighborhood as the artists who lived there was a certain series of murals that appeared on storefronts, walls, and pull-down gates on virtually every block. These murals featured the faces of local legends and three-times-life-size renderings of animals, and they were all the handiwork of one artist: Chico.

A native of the neighborhood and strongly influenced by the subway culture, Chico developed a passionate desire to uplift and better his community by painting public murals. In an area beleaguered with drugs and crime, his paintings often carried a message of warmth and sweetness. Clearly the work of one artist, his murals began to attract attention, and soon local business owners began hiring Chico to paint the gates or the facades of their buildings. As his local legend grew, Chico accepted employment offers from mainstream companies such as Coca-Cola. After more than two decades of gifting his art to his community, Chico and his work are permanent staples of the downtown landscape—a true Loisaida legend.

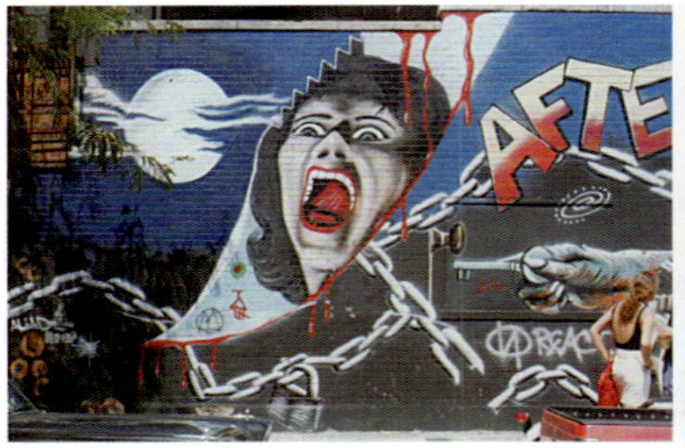

Photograph by Ernie Paniccioli.
New York City.
Detail: Photograph by Steam 156.

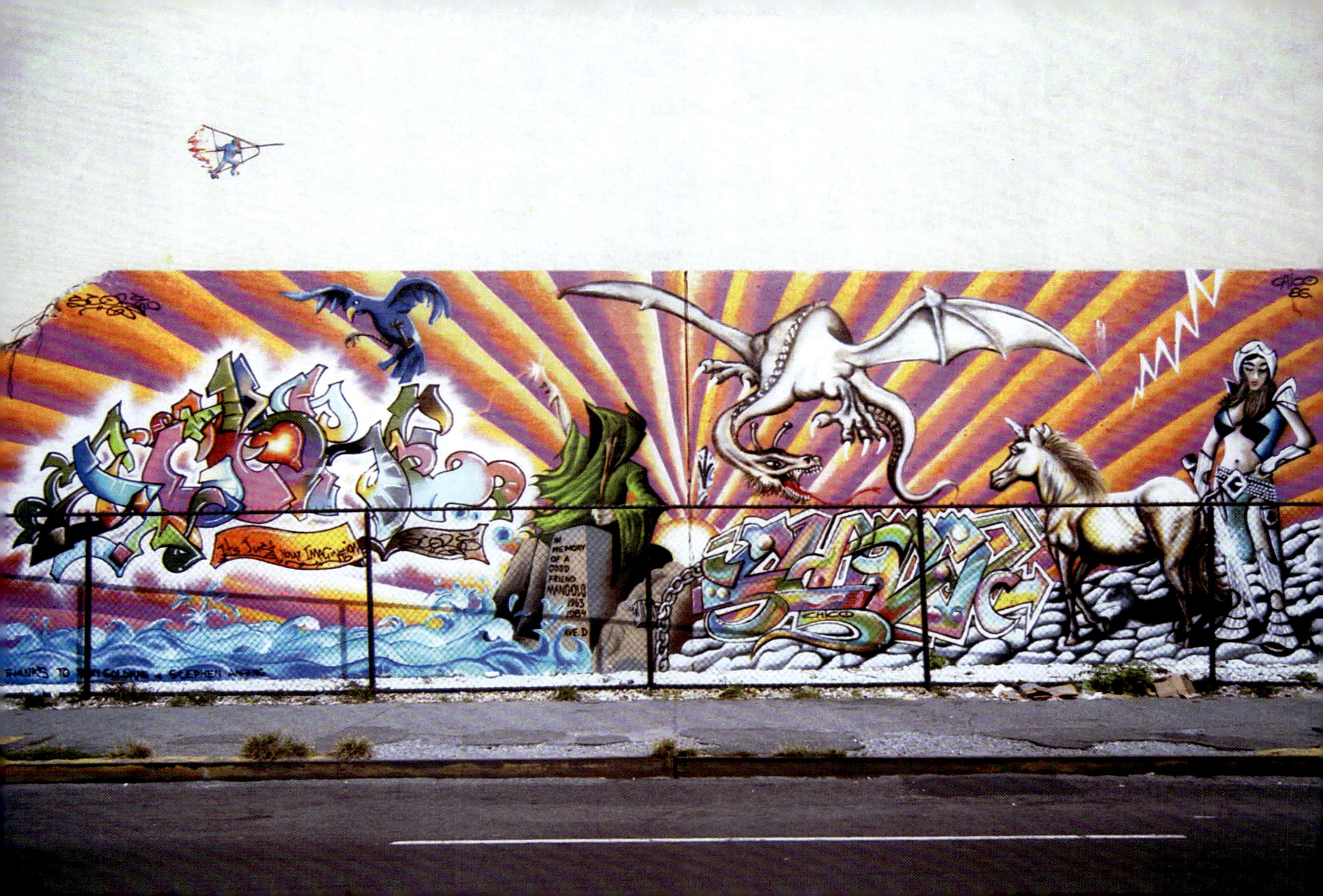
IN MEMORY OF A GOOD FRIEND MANGOLO 1963 1984
AVE. D

David Choe

The undisputed bad boy of street art, David Choe is as known for his wild ways as he is for his explosive work. Born in Southern California, Choe dropped out of art school to become a wandering artist and vagabond, stealing and painting his way to his next meal for a number of years. His work, filled with graphic imagery of sex and violence, is most often described as "dirty," and he is known for his alternative methods and materials.

In 2005, after a misunderstanding with a security guard, Choe was arrested and charged with violent assault, and he spent three months in a Japanese prison. Behind bars and deprived of art materials, Choe taught himself to be ultra-resourceful, creating blue ink from the dye leaking from his jeans, yellow from his urine, and red from his blood. In a new documentary titled *Dirty Hands*, he is seen punching himself in the face until his nose bleeds and then dripping the blood onto the canvas.

After his prison stint, Choe professed to having found God and referred to himself as a born-again Christian. He tamed his behavior and his public image, delivering whopping solo shows at the Jonathan LeVine Gallery in New York and an exhibition at the Lazarides Gallery in London, which was rumored to have sold out, to the tune of several million dollars.

Photograph by David Stuart (NoLionsInEngland). Regents Canal, London, 2009.

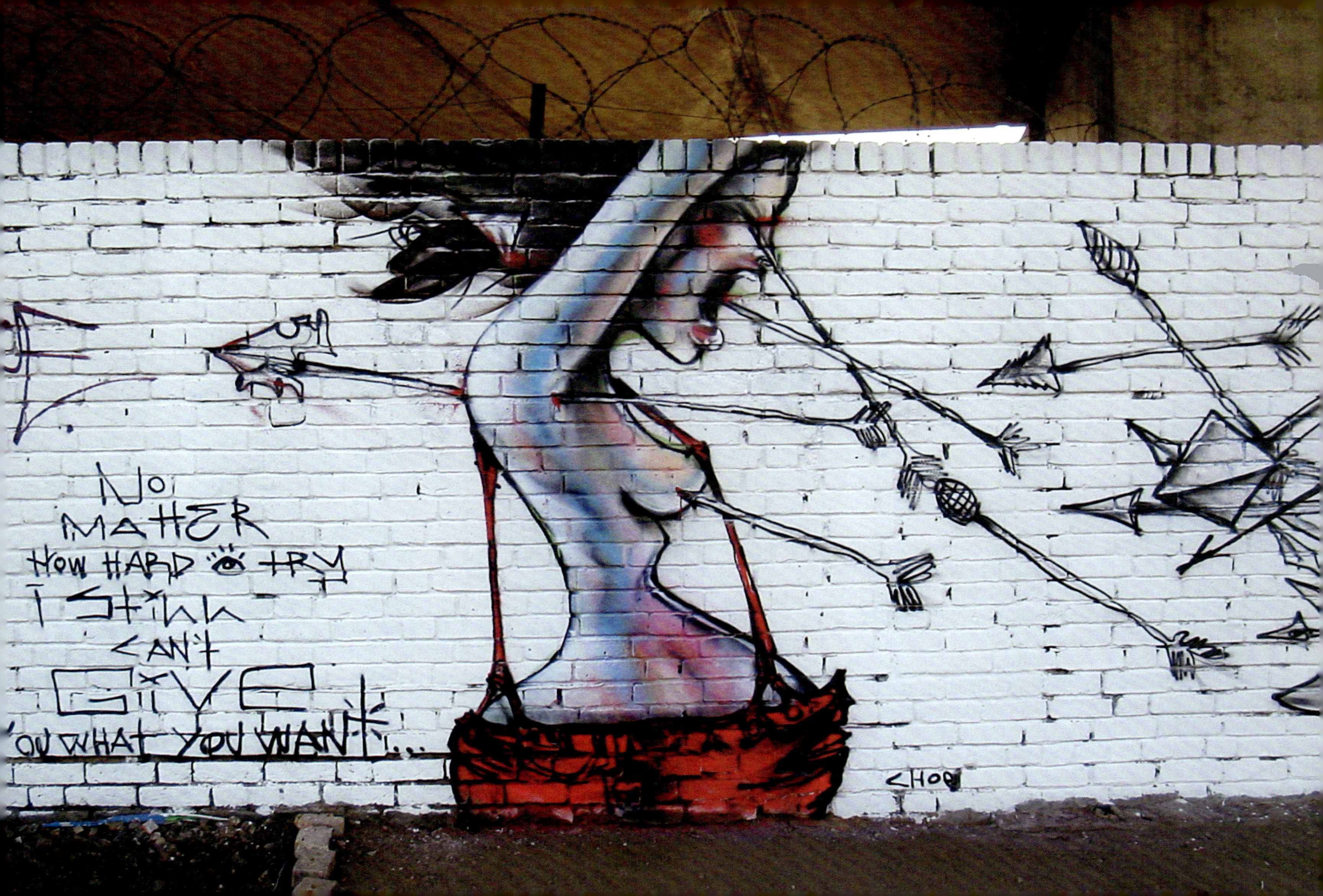
No
MATTER
HOW HARD TRY
I STILL
CAN'T
GIVE
OU WHAT YOU WANT...

Chor Boogie

Born Jason Haily in 1979, Chor Boogie grew up in a small coastal town near San Diego. Self-taught, he was creating imaginative and vibrant art from age five and loving the process; when he discovered graffiti at age ten, he was most inspired by its characters. His mature work reflects the influence of a range of artists from Leonardo da Vinci to Salvador Dalí, along with the impact of such diverse graffiti mentors as Phase 2 (see 255), Vulcan, and Pose 2.

With the streets as his principal canvas, Chor Boogie's intent is to create timeless, dynamic artworks that balance elements of line, light, space, and composition. As a recovering addict, Chor Boogie perceives the flow of colors, shapes, and movement as healing; he makes use of an inverted can technique that enables him to produce kinetic images with detailed, metallic effects.

Chor Boogie has created and exhibited murals throughout the United States and in a range of countries including Mexico, Australia, China, and Dubai. His artwork is displayed in the collection of San Diego's Museum of Contemporary Art. In 2007, he was granted the "Best Public Mural" award for a hundred-foot-long exterior wall he created in Minneapolis.

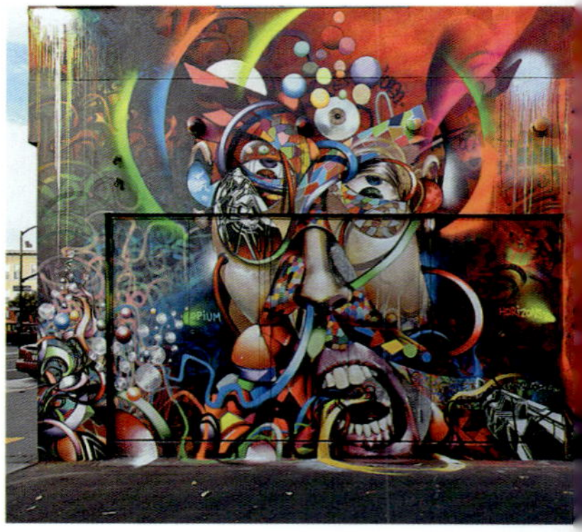

Purgatory, The Geisha.
Photograph courtesy of Chor Boogie.
San Francisco, 2009.
Detail: *Purgatory, 6 Opium Horizons.*
Photograph by Derek Chamberlain.
San Francisco, 2010.

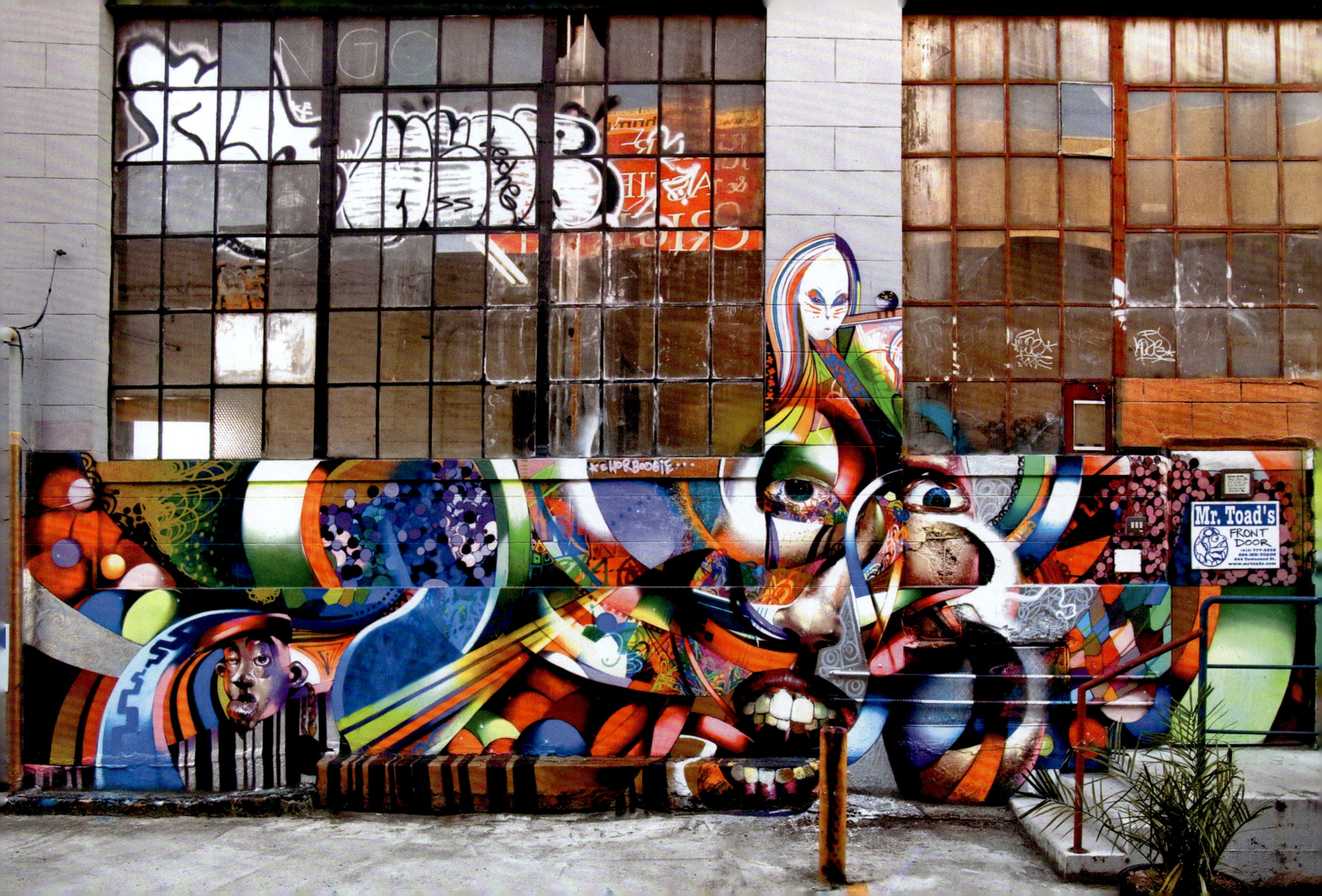
Mr. Toad's
FRONT DOOR

Chris 217

There was no mistaking it. It was a gritty, streaky black scrawl, and it was appearing all over the city at a time when graffiti was supposed to be beautiful. It was the name Chris 217. Graffiti had been around for a decade and had consistently tried to become better and more refined—and then there was Chris 217. He had no desire to write his name in a stylized way; he wanted to bomb. Graffiti was not a social thing for him, and he couldn't care less what other writers thought of his work.

Chris 217's assault on trains began after his older brother was struck by one, leaving him paralyzed for life; the young Chris began riding trains and kicking out their windows. That same energy would eventually channel its way into his graffiti.

By 1979, the adult Chris 217 had hundreds of cans of paint and as many pints of ink, and carried at least four markers with him at all times. He memorized the schedule of the sweepers in the #1 tunnels, often shadowing their movements through the trains. It was not uncommon for him to bring cleanser with him to wipe off names he didn't like and make room for his own.

If a tunnel was hot, he might bomb stations instead. The most outrageous example of this was the writing of his name 2,017 times in one evening at the 103rd Street station.

Photograph by Martha Cooper.
New York City, 1982.

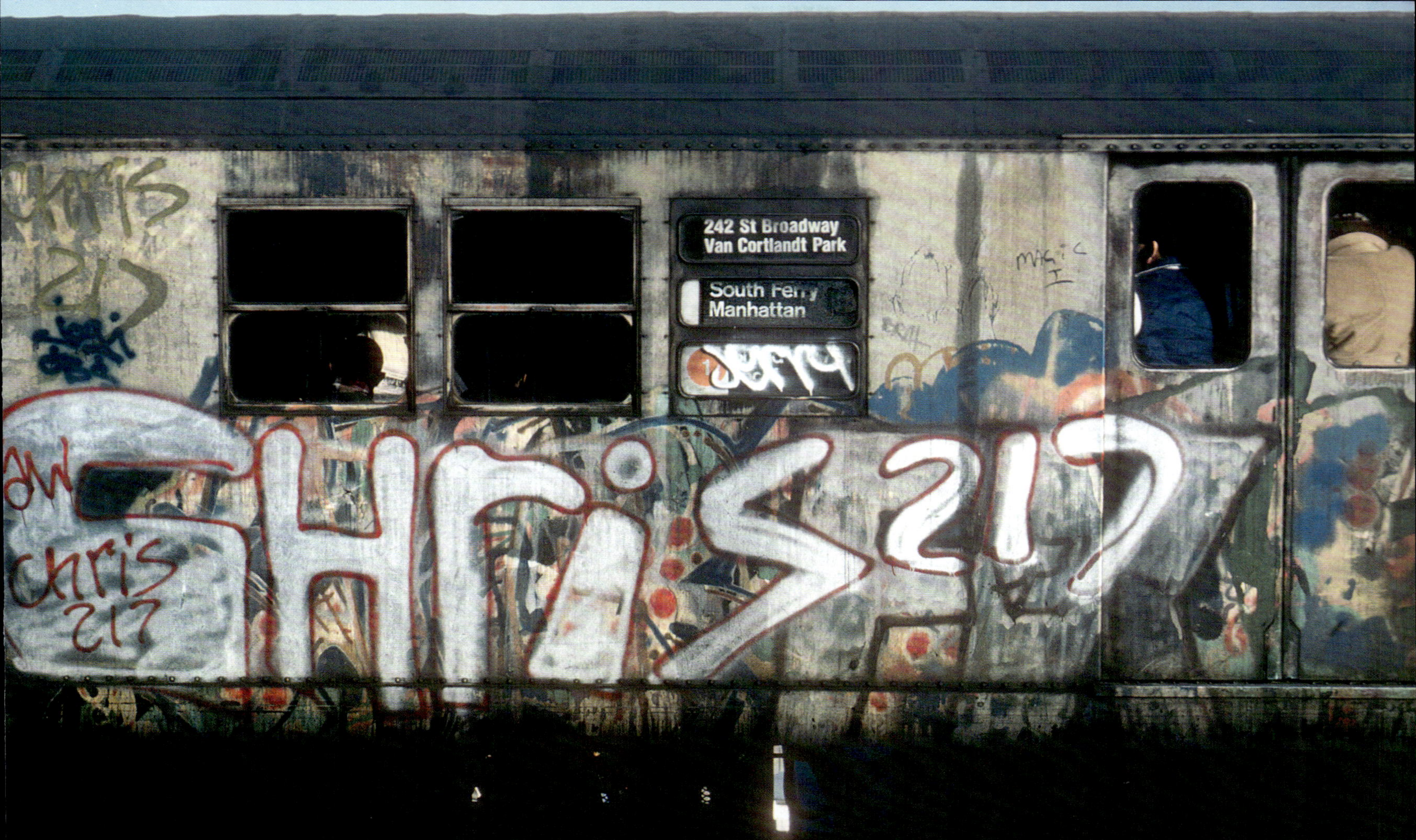
242 St Broadway
Van Cortlandt Park
South Ferry
Manhattan
chris
217

The Chrome Angelz

The young Mauritian known as Mode 2 had already been living in London for eight years by the time he met fellow graff writer Scribla at the Capital Radio Venture Day in London's Battersea Park in the summer of 1984. They hit it off straightaway and began painting and drawing together. Later that summer, they spotted Zaki Dee—rocking a graffed-up jacket—Eskimo, and Zerox walking toward the Covent Garden tube station.

At the time, Zaki Dee, Eskimo, and Zerox were known as the Trailblazers, and Scribla and Mode 2 joined their crew. But it wasn't until April 1985, at the Rap Attack gig at the Shaw Theatre, that Pride, a writer they had befriended, finally joined their gang. They then became known as The Chrome Angelz, or TCA.

TCA soon began painting with Parisian artist Bando, forming the Crime Time Kings together. TCA were already establishing themselves as one of Europe's finest graffiti crews when their work was heavily featured in Henry Chalfant and James Prigoff's influential 1987 book *Spraycan Art*. Over the next two decades, they would continue to work, both individually and as a crew, to create some of the finest graffiti in the world. Influenced by hip-hop, as well as the work of Dondi White and Futura 2000, Bando would visit NYC, where he would often paint with style master T.Kid 170. T.Kid's style pointers would then be exported back to Europe, where Bando became legendary.

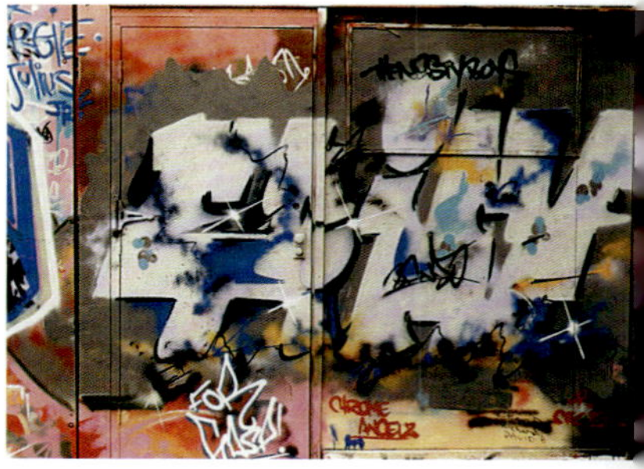

Photographs by Peter Pedrero.

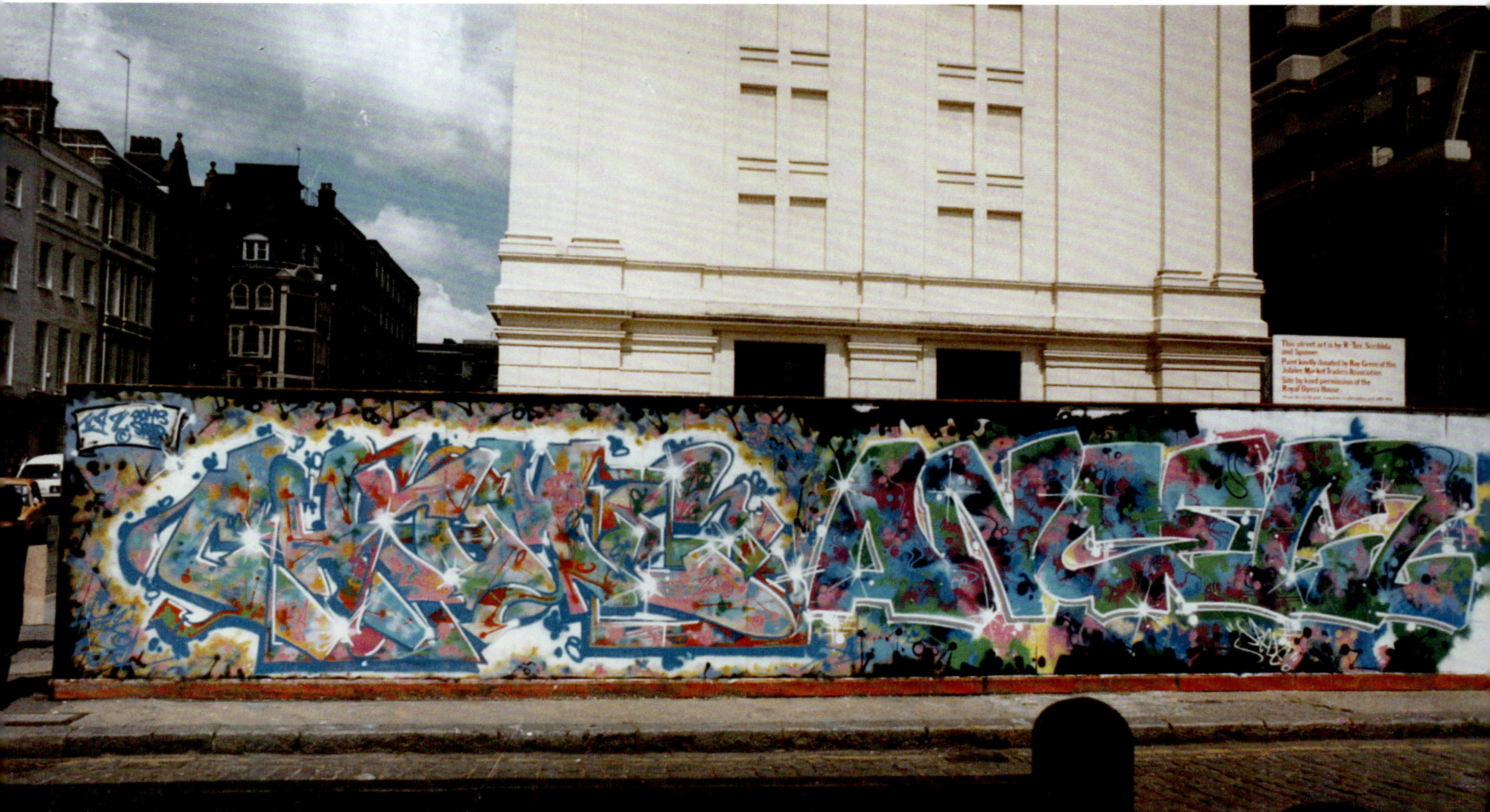
This street art is by R-Tez, Scribbla and Spooner
Paint kindly donated by Roy Green of the Jubilee Market Traders Association
Site by kind permission of the Royal Opera House

clean-train movement

On May 19, 1989, the Metropolitan Transit Authority announced it would pull any train with visible graffiti on its exterior out of service. The MTA declared a public victory—but the enemy hadn't raised the white flag. A die-hard group of graffiti artists continued painting trains, knowing that their work would be held back in the train yards and scrubbed clean, and the clean-train movement was born.

In the beginning, American writers painted clean trains to prove a point about public space, urban marginalization, and individual identity (and for the chance to place a photo of their work in one of the many emerging graffiti magazines documenting the scene). Today, with the passage of time and the increased criminalization of subway graffiti, the concentration of clean-train bombers has shifted to foreigners; especially since the advent of the Internet, the clean-train art movement, once localized in New York City, has become a global village. Networking with American "tour guides" is easy enough for an NYC-bound graffiti tourist, and plenty of Americans are granted the same courtesy when they go on foreign missions. Some clean-train bombers have hundreds of trains to their credit, although this work has not been seen by the general public.

The Vandal Squad, however, has made clean-train artists its number one priority for arrest and prosecution. Apartments of suspected artists are routinely raided by cops with search warrants, and the risks—computer and photo-collection seizures, heavy fines, and long jail sentences—come with very little reward. But graffiti has always been a "Never Say Die" kind of culture.

Piece by Sane.
Photograph by Smith.
New York City, 1988.

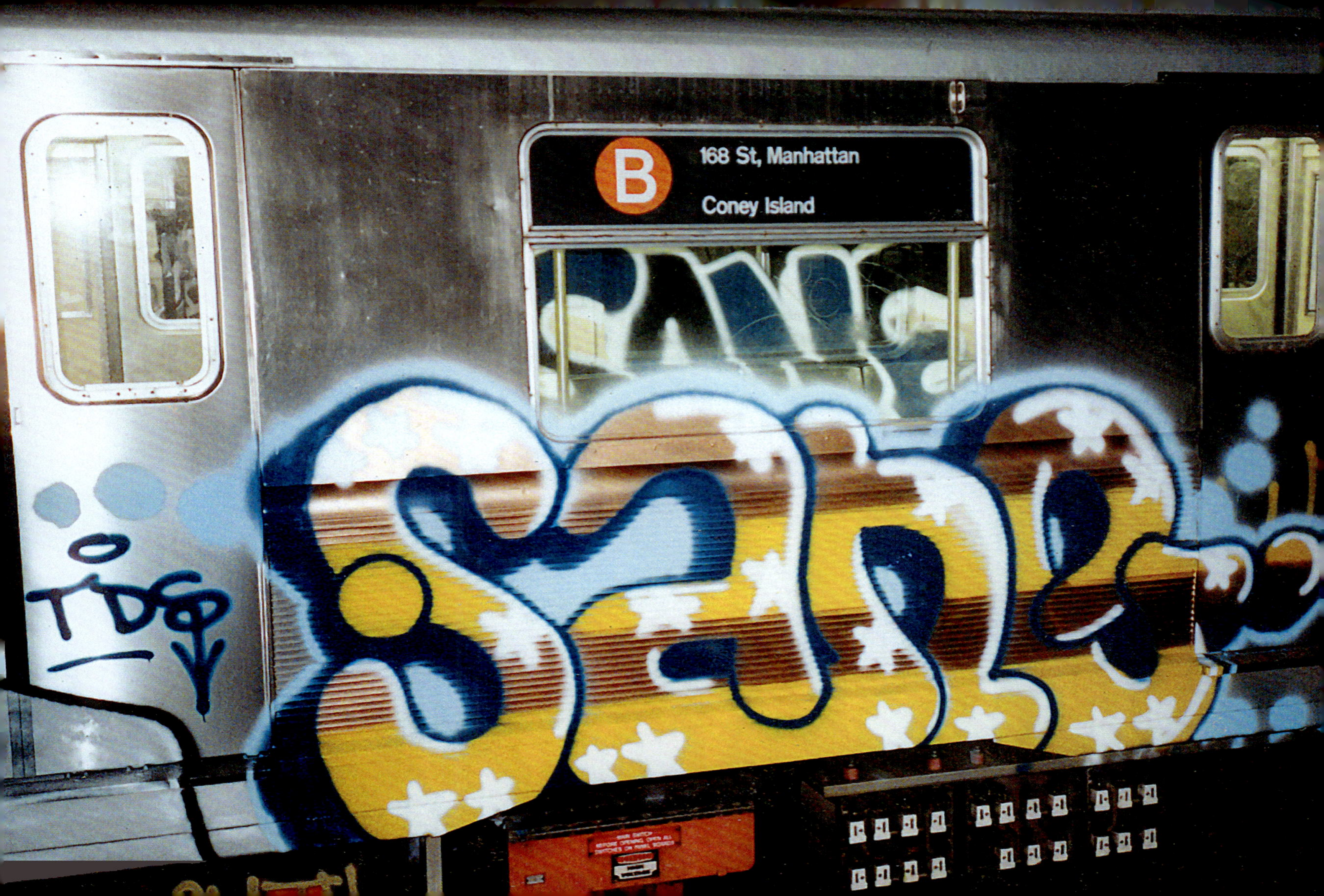
B
168 St, Manhattan
Coney Island

Cliff 159

Clifford Goodman is the ultimate graffiti success story. In 1972, he reinvented himself as Cliff 159 (later painting under the alias Paz 2), and his earliest tags, block letter outlines of his name, garnered immediate attention. He initiated the concept of going all-city during an era when writers were usually content to stay on their home turf. Though he spent his first few years as a quantity-over-quality bomber, he evolved along with the art form itself, adding whole-cars with characters to his already formidable repertoire. He became president of the Three Yard Boys, the most prolific crew ever to hit trains. Notable whole-cars depicting comic book icons Beetle Bailey, Dick Tracy, Snoopy, Charlie Brown, and The Thing from the Fantastic Four set Cliff 159 apart from other all-city bombers such as In and Vinny. A list of his collaborators includes Comet (see 071), Blade (see 031), Tracy 168 (see 340), Peace 108, Sin 158, True Too, Stim, Tee, and Be 3. Before enlisting in the army in 1977, Cliff 159 passed the torch to his last partner, Dean BYB, who went on to earn his own crown. Clifford Goodman died in the late 1980s from HIV-related illness, but Cliff 159's legacy transcends mortality.

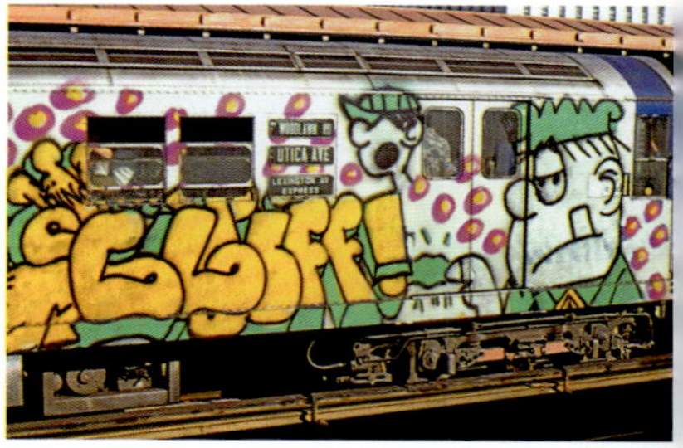

Photographs by Keith Baugh.
New York City, 1975.

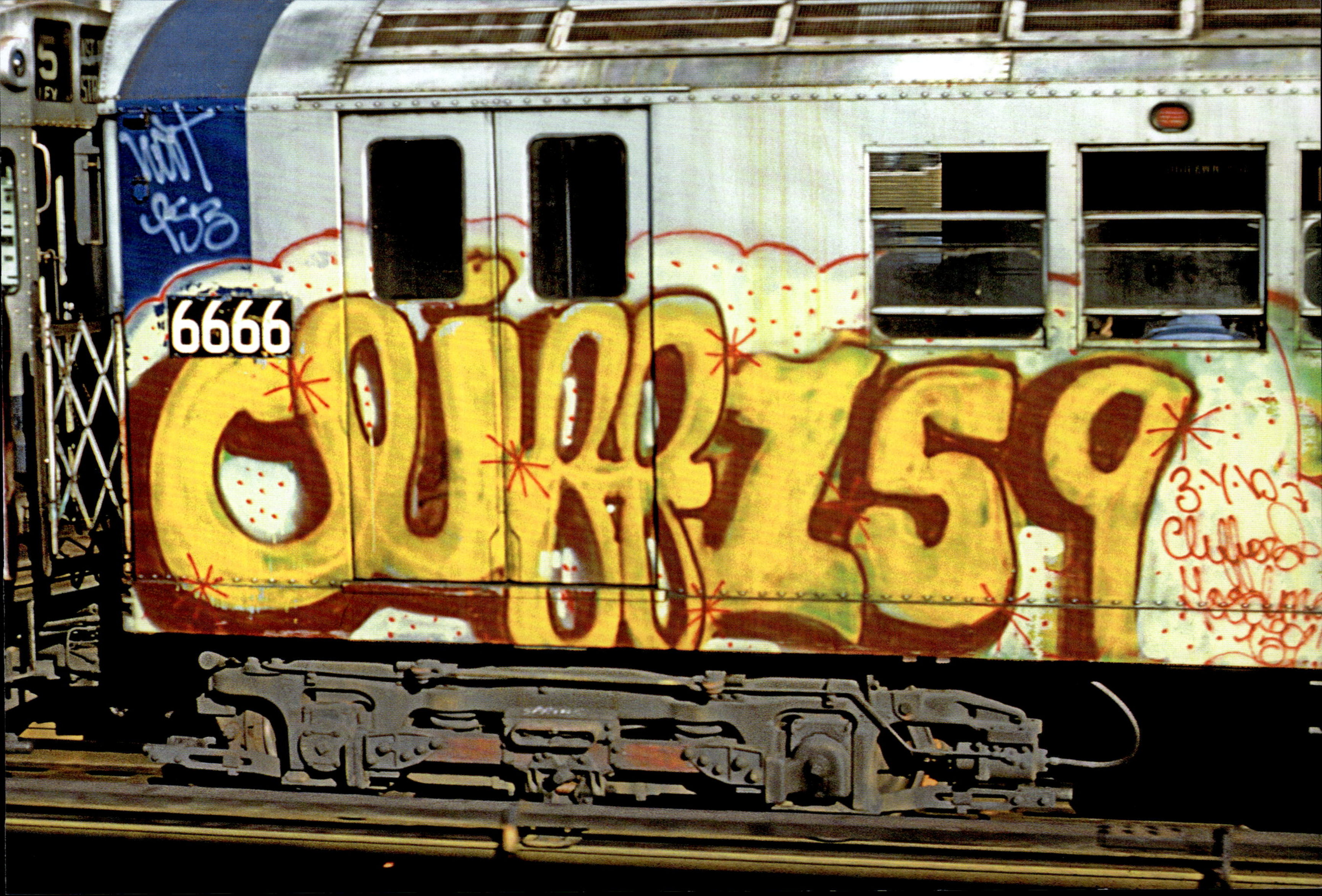
6666

Comet

Comet grew up on the famed #2 subway line and dreamed of becoming its king, but in 1973, Hondo 1 stood in his way, so he began hitting the Third Avenue #l and the #4 line with Priest 167 and Christ 167, making a name for himself while he patiently awaited Hondo's retirement. "As a kid, I was rebellious and had bad self-esteem," Comet recalls. "I got into graffiti to become somebody, and—sure enough—after a while people would say, 'There goes Comet,' like it meant something."

Comet's list of cohorts includes Silver Tips (aka UPS; see 300), Cliff 159 (an all-city king), Billy 167 (one of the greatest stylemasters ever to wield a can), and finally, Blade (see 037), his most enduring and prolific partner. This dynamic duo dominated the #2 and #5 lines from 1974 to 1981, producing such a great volume of whole-cars, blockbusters, and throw-ups that they were forced to paint over their own work (not to mention the work of countless other unfortunates).

While Blade's ambition was to transform entire train cars into thematic paintings, Comet's mind-set was better expressed by the words often written in his ubiquitous throw-ups: More, Again, Next, and Over!

Private collection.
New York City, 1974.

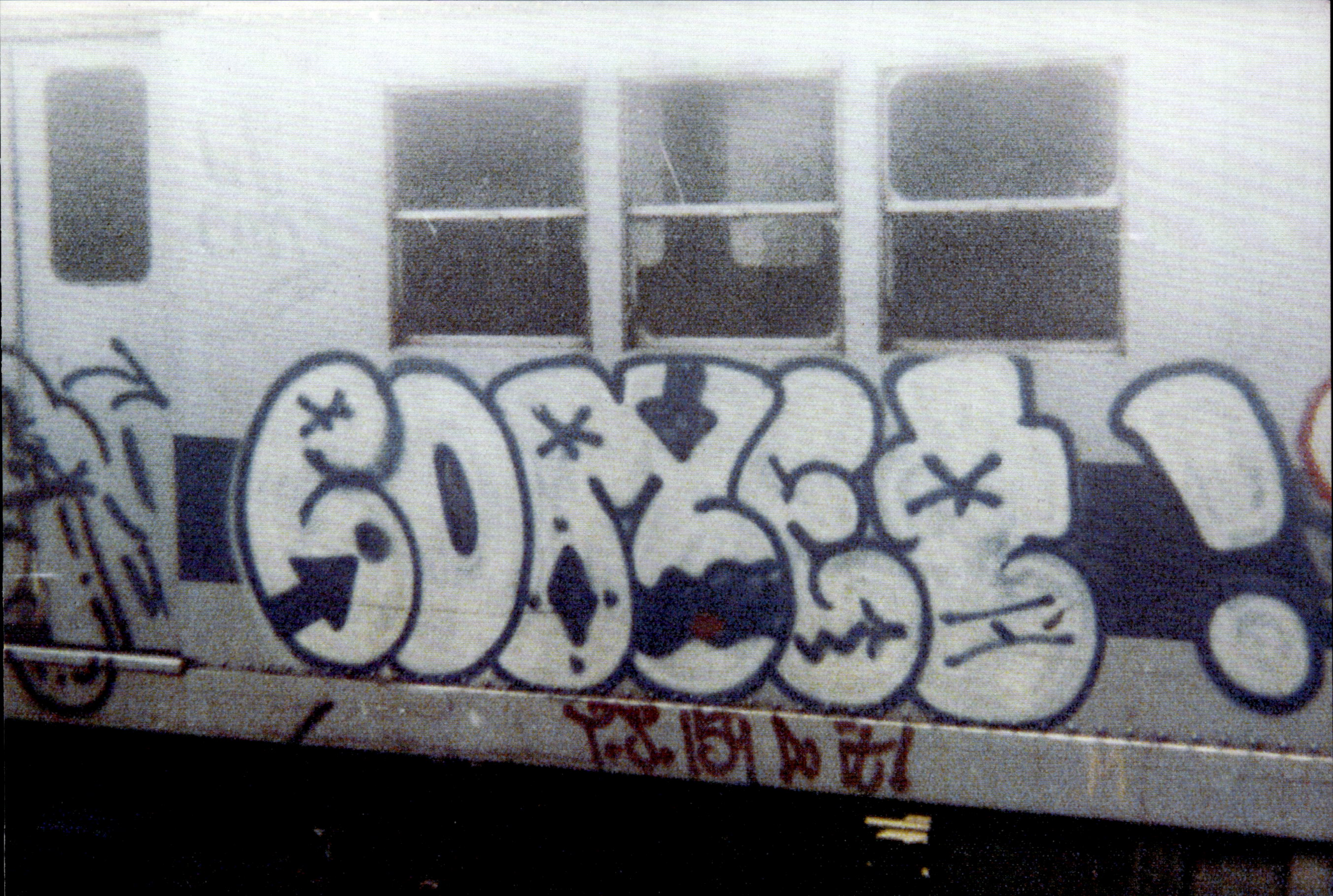

Joe Connolly

Many citizens don't appreciate graffiti's presence in their city, and governments are often criticized for not doing enough to curb what some see as a blight on a city's public face. Rarely, however, does an everyday citizen take the matter into his own hands. Meet Joe Connolly, better known as "the graffiti guerilla," a Los Angeles resident who has spent at least fifteen years doing graffiti removal and "educating" other citizens on how they, too, can be graffiti-removal specialists. Videos of him explaining the power of solvents and how to climb defaced rooftops with buckets of paint date as far back as 1995.

A former (very successful) Oriental rug salesman, Connolly witnessed a decline in the appearance of his Los Angeles neighborhood in the mid-1990s and started to become obsessed with graffiti, its meanings, its artists' methods, and even the gang cultures associated with it. Soon Connolly, a husband and father of two children, left his business to devote himself full-time to his vigilante project.

An obsessive and hyperactive person by nature, Connolly has familiarized himself intensively with the hieroglyphics of tagging and has funded his own mission for the last fifteen years; he has devised strategic methods to paint over sprayed graffiti while wasting a minimum of paint and has concocted his own chemical solvents to eat at marker tags.

Photograph by Marcin Wichary. Los Angeles, 1993.

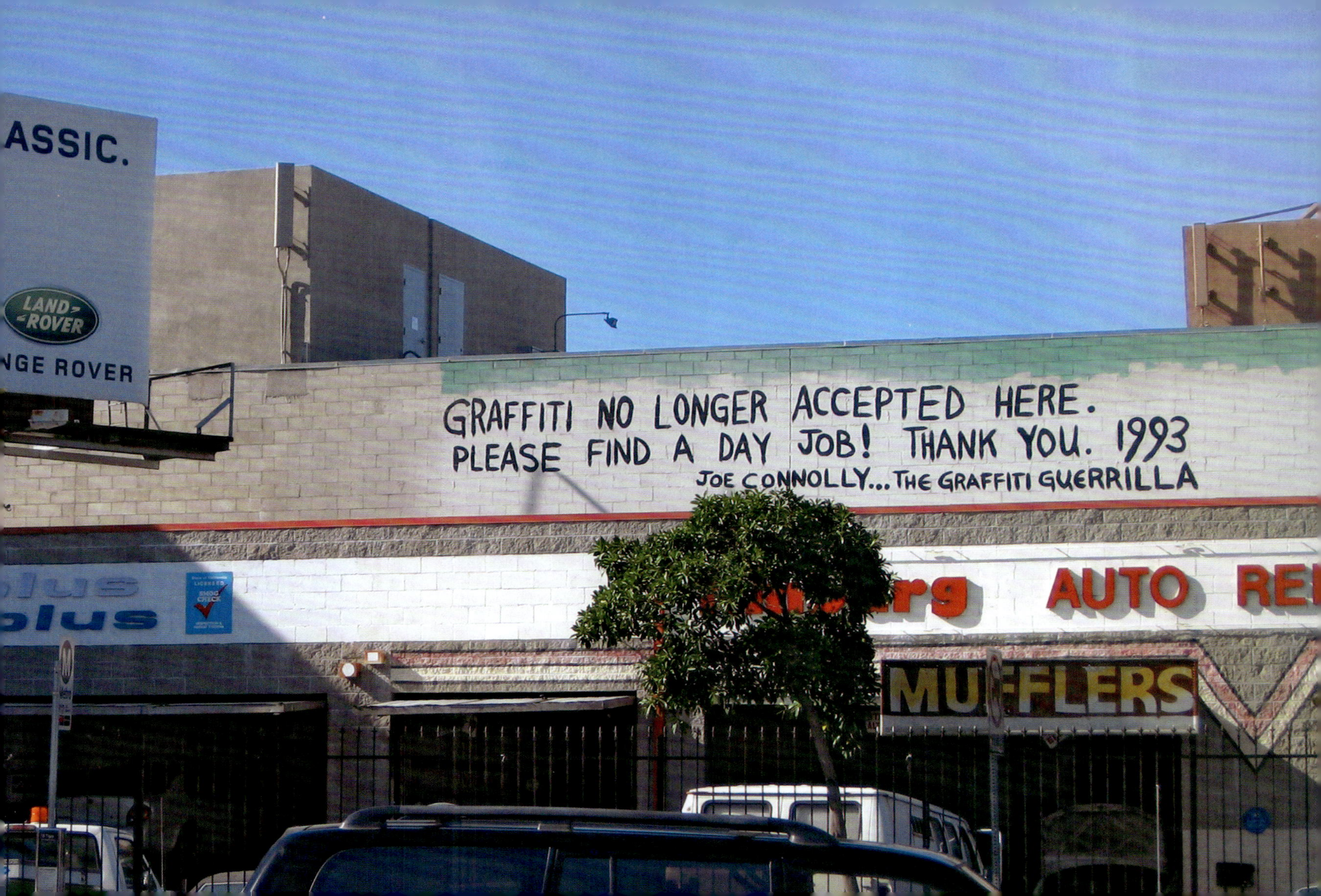
ASSIC.
LAND ROVER
NGE ROVER
GRAFFITI NO LONGER ACCEPTED HERE.
PLEASE FIND A DAY JOB! THANK YOU. 1993
JOE CONNOLLY... THE GRAFFITI GUERRILLA
AUTO
MUFFLERS

Martha Cooper

In the 1970s, Martha Cooper landed an assignment at the *New York Post* doing the weather page, which described the weather and featured accompanying photographs of New Yorkers basking in it. Marty, as she is known to friends, had a fascination with kids at play, and they became a staple of her weather shots. In 1979, one kid spoke up and said he was a graffiti writer; he promised Marty he could introduce her to the legendary Dondi [see 097], and her curiosity was piqued. The next week, they piled into her Volkswagen and made the trek out to New Lots, where Dondi lived. The meeting went well, and Marty became fascinated with graffiti.

Over the next four years, she befriended many writers and hip-hop kids, shooting thousands of rolls of film. She immersed herself fearlessly in the subculture, going in and out of train yards like a writer—and facing the same penalties if she were caught. She documented Dondi as he did one of his most iconic cars, shooting throughout the entire night. She traveled to the yards with other writers as diverse as Seen [see 294], J.SON, Cap, Skeme [see 304], Min [see 223], and Pink.

In the early 1980s, she teamed up with Henry Chalfant to produce *Subway Art* [see 323], a book that was turned down by every New York publisher. Investing their own money, the two photographers went to the Hamburg Book Fair in Germany and finally found a publisher in Thames & Hudson. *Subway Art* is now on its seventeenth printing and is credited as being the cornerstone for the European graffiti explosion. Marty continues to shoot graffiti worldwide.

**Artwork in window by Futura 2000.
Photograph by Henry Chalfant.
London, 1984.**

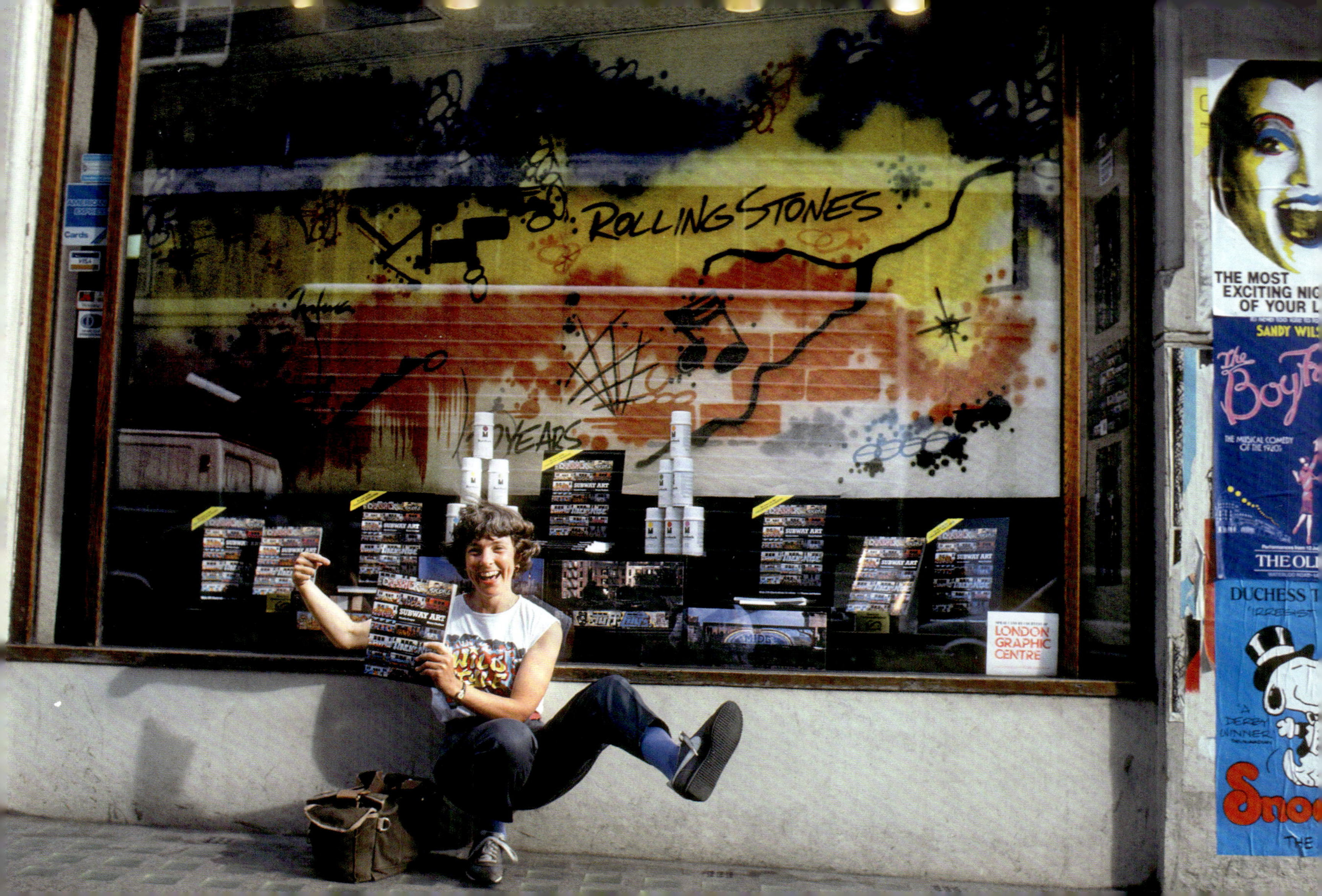
ROLLING STONES
SUBWAY ART
LONDON GRAPHIC CENTRE
THE MOST

Cope 2

Cope 2 walks in many worlds and makes a lot of friends and enemies in all of them. Cope's career on trains began on the #4 line in 1980. He knew his history, having had a front-row seat for the work of Tracy 168 [see 340], the MG Boys [see 221], Mitch 77 [see 227], and Ban 2, and he got his now-famous throw-up from bombing machine Cap One Da Bronx [see 057]. Cope waited his turn and proceeded to dominate every area of graffiti he undertook—he made graffiti his career even before street cred became a marketable asset. The Bronx bomber has, at one time or another, kinged the #4 line, taken over streets and rooftops in the Bronx, organized countless production walls, and painted trains all over the globe.

The most ambitious self-promoter in graff history, Cope 2 began sending pictures of his work to graff mags before the advent of the Internet made the graffiti community a global village. His video, *Kings Destroy*, and his book, *True Legend*, continue to sell well, and he is rarely in the country for more than a week at a time.

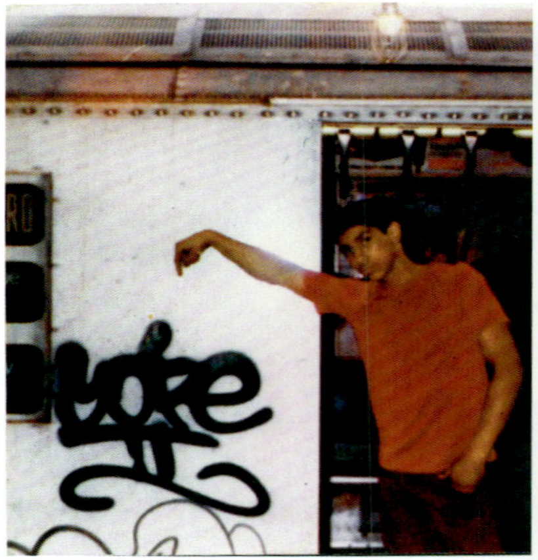

Photographs courtesy of Cope 2.
New York City, c. 2010.
Detail: New York City, c. 1982.

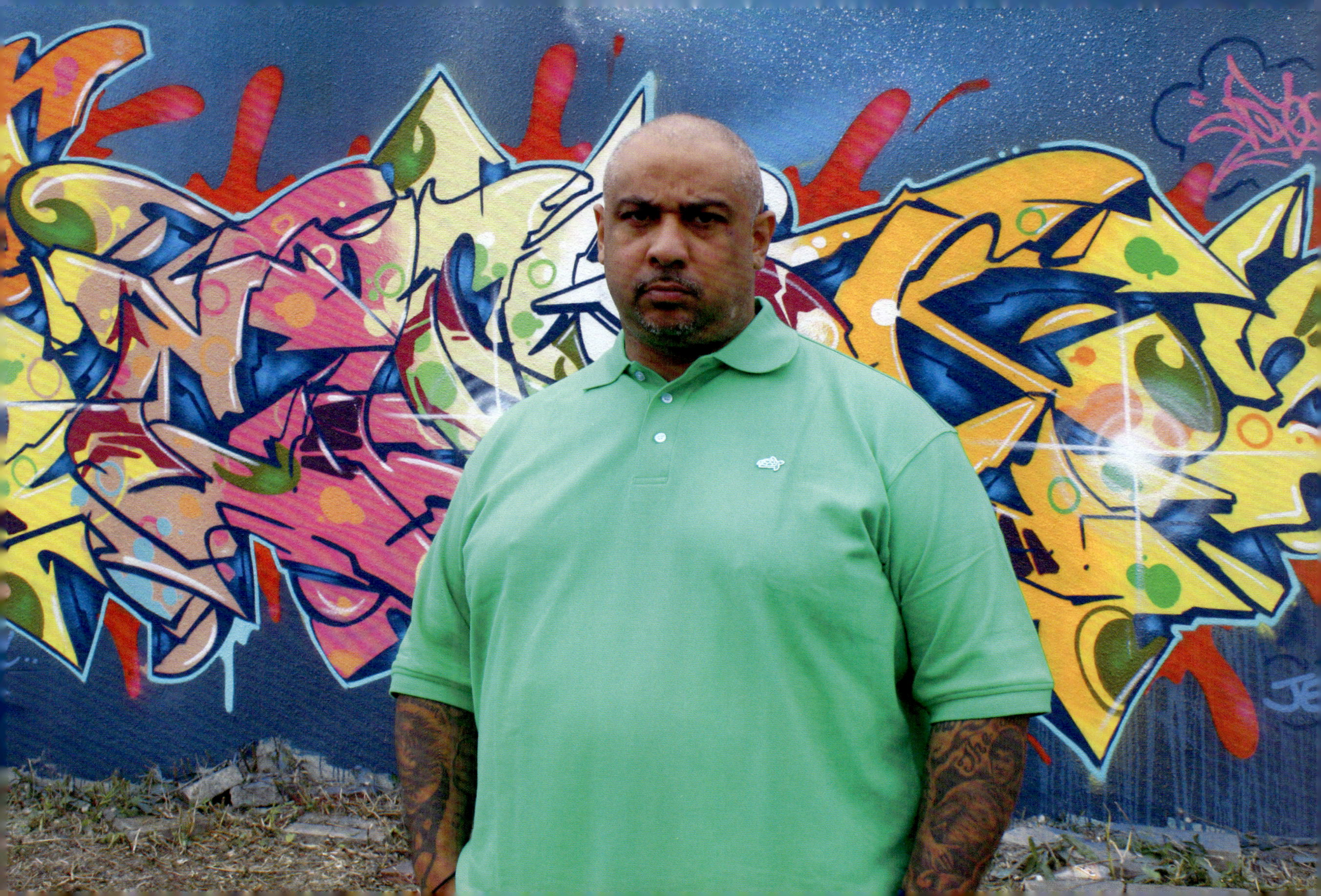

Cornbread

Cornbread became a graffiti legend at a time when graffiti didn't exist. In his early teens, he was sent to a juvenile detention center, where he observed gang graffiti on the walls. Missing his aunt's cornbread, he soon adopted the word as his name. The story would have ended upon his release in 1966, but then Cornbread fell in love, and love makes a person do funny things. Cornbread had it in his mind that if he wrote his name everywhere his beloved went, it would give him a step up when they finally met. In the end he did get the girl, but more important, he found his passion: writing graffiti.

He continued to write on the walls of Philadelphia and looked on in amusement as other writers joined in. They had funky names like Cool Earl, Tity, and Kool Klepto Kid, and they belonged to gangs that took their names from fraternity houses, like Delta Phi Soul. The black press in Philly adored Cornbread and egged him on to more daring feats, including hitting the side of the Jackson Five's tour jet. In the early 1970s, it was front-page news when a dead teenager was identified as Cornbread, and the eulogies rolled in. Of course, it wasn't Cornbread who had died, and after some thinking, he picked his biggest target to date—hitting the side of an elephant at the zoo with the slogan CORNBREAD LIVES!

After years of retirement, Cornbread recently went to work for the mayor of Philadelphia, who was desperate to stop the graffiti plague.

Photograph by Adam Wallacavage. Philadelphia, 2008.

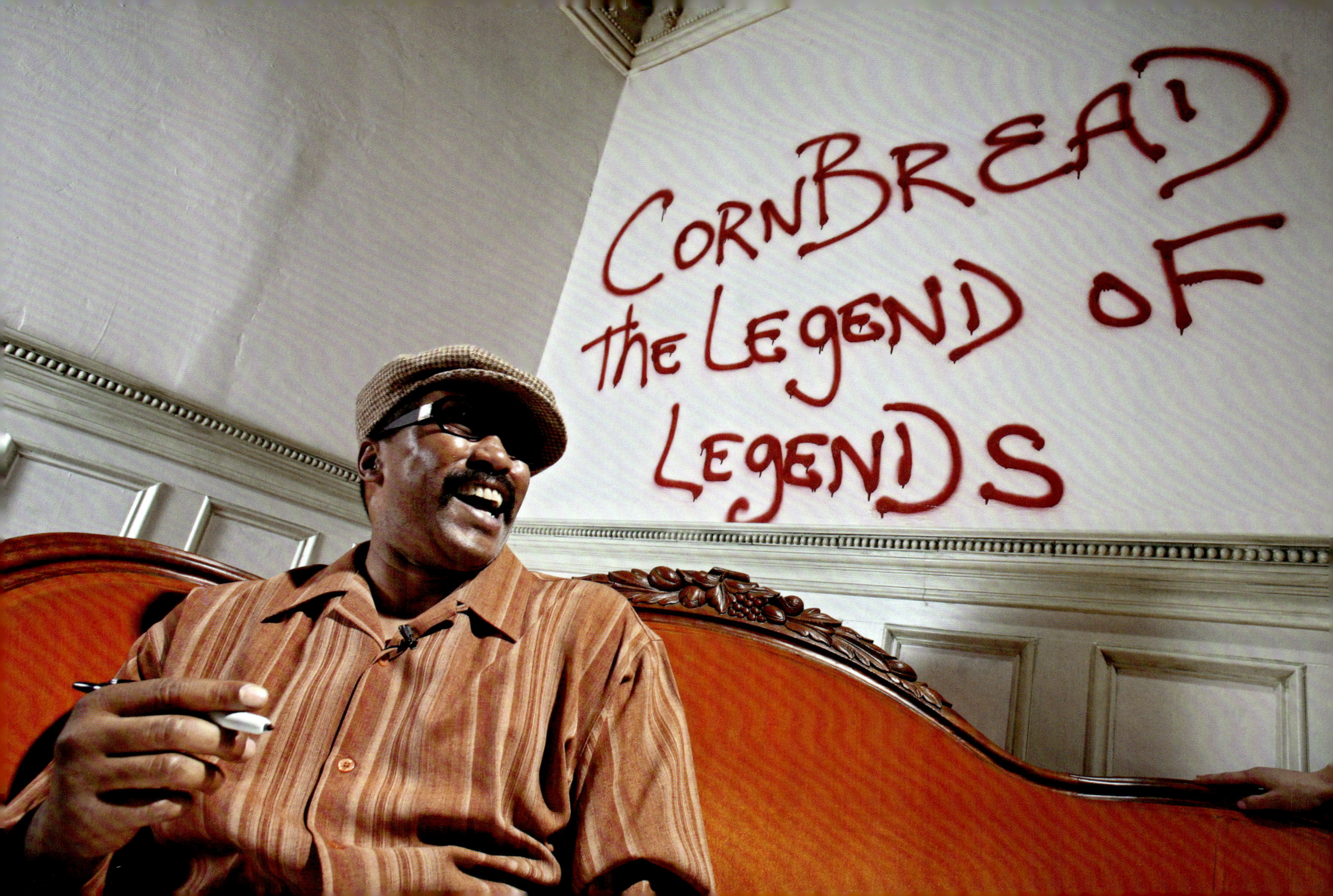
CORNBREAD
the LEGEND OF
LEGENDS

Cost and Revs

Godfathers of what would come to be known as street art, Cost and Revs were early visionaries who pushed the boundaries of "traditional" graffiti. Through a steadfast partnership, the duo created a proliferation of posters printed in simple black type on white paper, which they sprinkled across the walls of New York City, bearing messages as simple as COST/REVS, and as cryptic as WHO'S O.C.? ASK COST AND REVS.

The pair was also credited with the popularization of a technique known as "roller letters," in which the artist uses a paint roller to create oversize, simplistic line lettering, focusing on impact and size rather than the colorful intricacies afforded by spray paint. Sometimes these tags stretched an enormous fifteen or twenty feet in length.

Revs (see 275), the more mysterious of the two, has never revealed his name and refuses to sell his work. Devoted to the danger of graffiti, he was quoted as saying, "Once money changes hands for art, it becomes a fraudulent activity."

Beginning in 1995, Revs took to the subway tunnels, creating his most infamous work: a series of diary entries and personal ruminations, painstakingly written out in black spray paint deep within the dark catacombs under the city. Seemingly created never to be seen, many of these pieces still survive today.

Photograph by Cheryl Dunn.
Brooklyn, New York, 1996.

LIVIN
12/11/94
1 OF MANY
TO JOE PUBLIC... YOU MIGHT BE ASKIN YOURSELF RIGHT NOW, WHAT IS THIS SHIT... WHAT IS THIS ALL ABOUT? ... ITS ABOUT A KID WHO IS JUST LIVIN HIS LIFE AND TELLIN HIS STORY THE ONLY WAY HE KNOWS HOW. THE THING IS HIS STORY AINT NO DIFF THAN YOURS — WE ALL END UP BEING PIECES TO A PUZZLE FROM WHICH THERE IS ONLY ONE ALMIGHTY CREATOR. GOD
REVSUICIDE
WHO IS REVS
COST
PMER
FROST

Craola

Greg Simkins, a native of Torrance, California, has never been short on artistic talent or imagination. As a kid, he loved animals and at one point even spoke of becoming a veterinarian. Growing up in the Los Angeles area, he was heavily influenced by Disneyland, as well as a variety of books and movies. As a withdrawn adolescent, he would lie low in the back of the classroom, quietly doodling in his notebook. Eventually, Simkins began toying around with a can of aerosol using the moniker Craola, and the results caught the attention of the legendary Los Angeles graffiti crews CBS and WAI, who recruited him in a heartbeat. They blessed him with a couple of *Can Control* magazines and unwittingly created one of the most ripping styles in graffiti history.

In the late 1990s, Simkins earned a degree in studio arts from California State University, Long Beach. He soon began working as a commercial illustrator and eventually went digital, working on video games for Treyarch, a division of Activision. During this period, he began to delve deeper into his fine-art work. Eventually, Simkins fled the mainstream, preferring to work full-time as a painter. Focusing his energies on canvas yielded big results: one sold-out gallery show after another, which earned Simkins a solid place in pop-surrealism history. Now a husband and father, Craola can occasionally be found burning a graffiti piece along the sunny streets of Los Angeles.

Photograph by Dan Matusmoto. 2010.

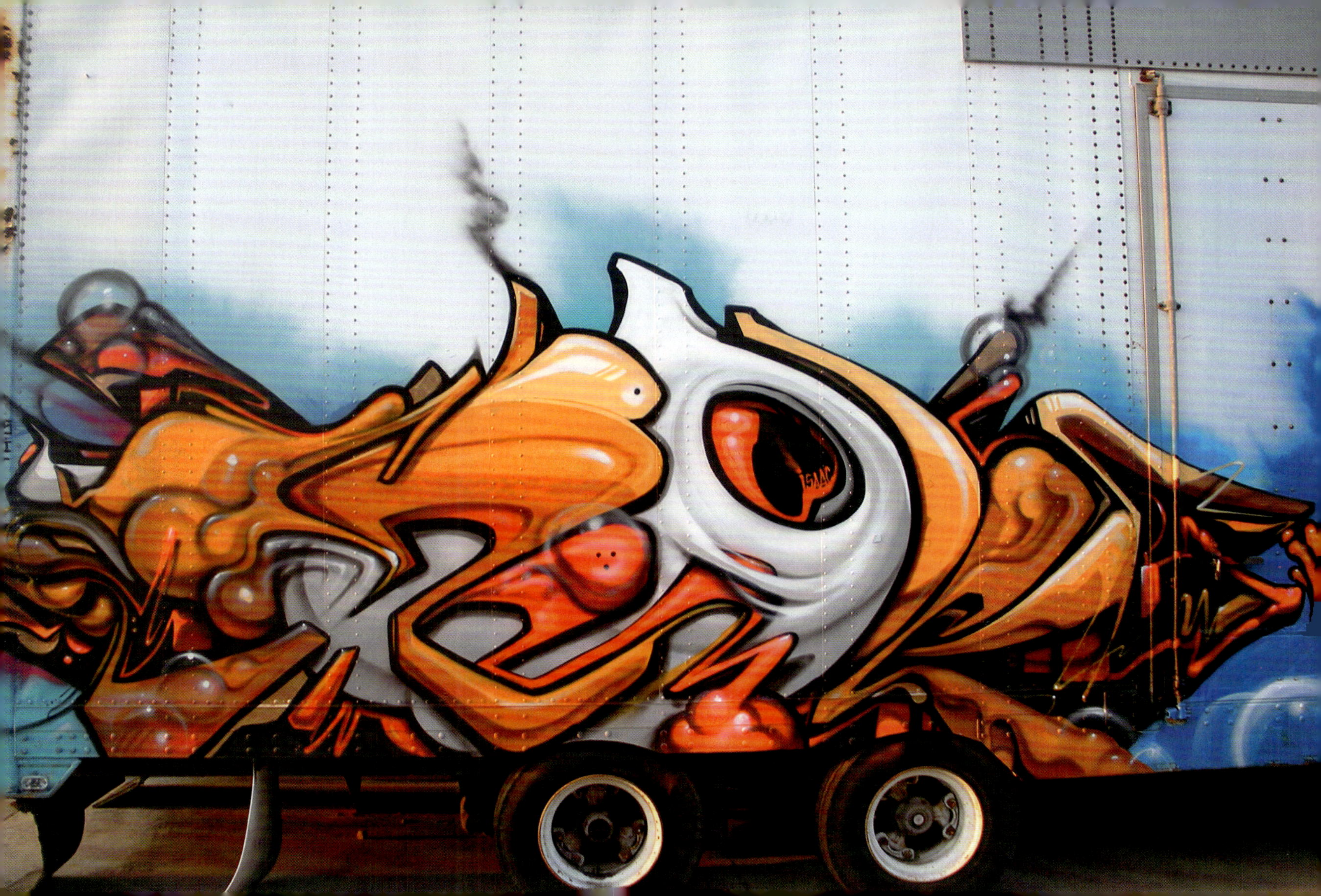
ISAAC

Crateman

As traditional spray-paint graffiti has become less trendy and less gallery-friendly than street art, artists are finding alternative ways to leave their mark. Early in the new millennium, the street-art–heavy city of Melbourne, Australia, was besieged by an army of giant creatures, multicolored men made of nothing other than milk crates. An artist known as Crateman began littering the city's rooftops, streets, and byways with his brigade of oversize buddies. They climbed up buildings in teams, sat reading atop houses, and even took breaks to go fishing.

The artist(s) behind this onslaught remain anonymous, but he (or they) proliferated the creatures furiously for a number of years, taking the Internet by storm and becoming a darling of the renowned street-art blog Wooster Collective (see 359).

Crateman never made the transition into the fine-art world, and the recent disappearance of his pieces suggests that the brief spate we had from him may be the last the world will see.

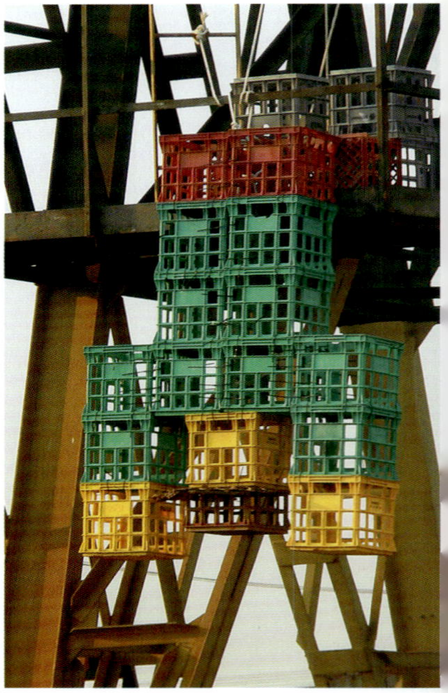

Photographs courtesy of Crateman. c. 2008.

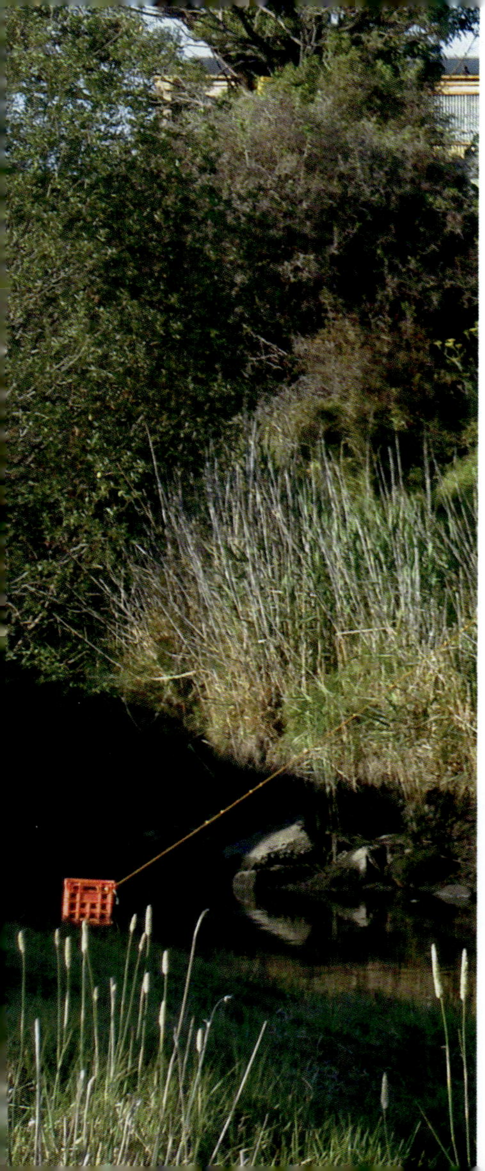
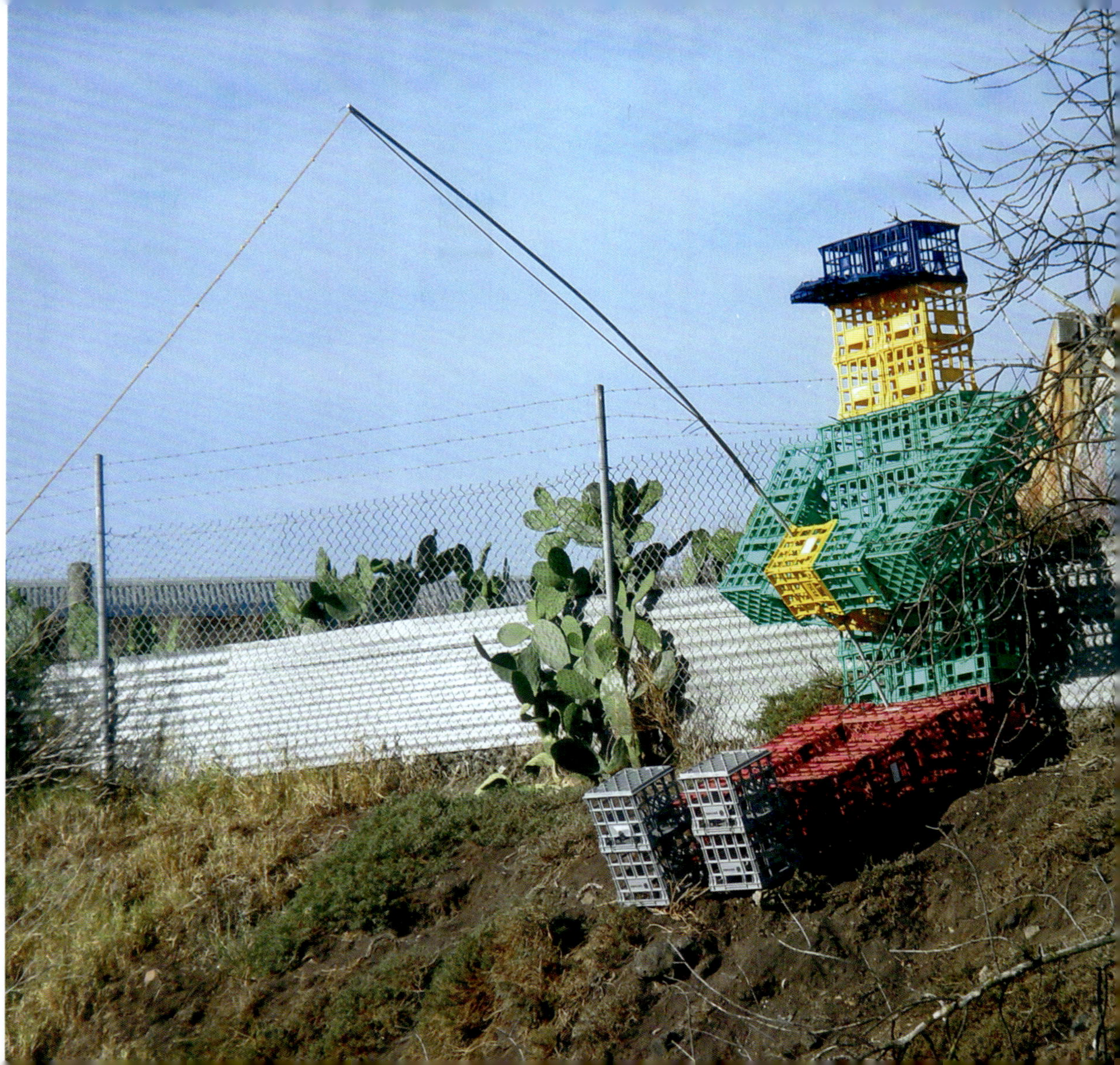

The Crazy 5

In 1972, a small group of teenagers began writing in the northern part of the Bronx; they had names like Crachee, Vamm, Blade [see 037], Death, and Tull 13. By 1973, they had established a name for themselves on the trains. The five writers decided to form their own crew and adopted the name The Crazy 5 [TC5].

TC5 would wind up putting more aerosol onto the sides of trains than any other crew. Initially, they took over the #2 and #5 lines in the early 1970s. As time went on, their style began to evolve, with Blade emerging as one of the most distinctive voices in graffiti history. The group wrote primarily in aboveground lay-ups, trying to distance themselves from the chaos of the train yards, where writers were arrested daily. Other writers soon joined TC5, including Comet, Ajax [see 010], Silver Tips [see 300], Shorty 5, and Fritz.

By 1974, the core of the group had retired. Blade found himself partnering with Comet; the two wrote together for seven years, and at one point, they had to begin going over their own work in order to do new pieces. Comet was a bomber who could also throw down with style; Blade became a famed whole-car specialist. Comet and Blade, the last stalwarts of the crew, finally quit in the early 1980s, and TC5 ended with them.

***Submarine* by Vamm.**
Photograph by Keith Baugh.
New York City, 1973.

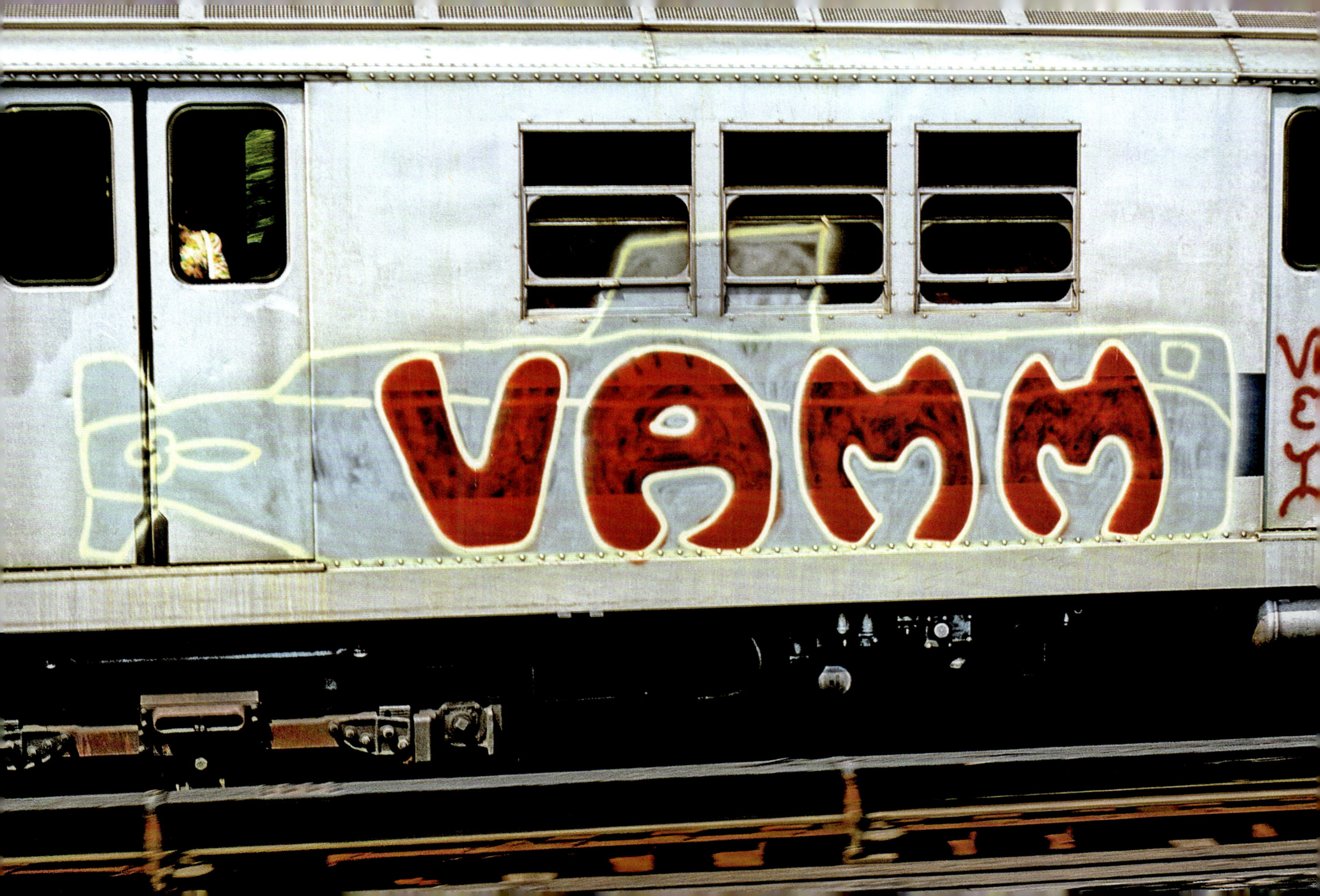

CT'Ink

A brotherly pair of men in their thirties are the backbone behind the work of CT'Ink, the powerhouse stencil and design collaborative. Based in Berlin, Pisa73 and Evol Taste together have redefined the level of photorealism one can expect from stencils and spray-painted street work. Both men painted for many years with various graffiti crews, including Berlin's infamous Fuck Your Crew, where Pisa73 primarily flexed his freehand character muscles.

Widely considered great masters of the craft of stencil art, the partners have come under fire from stencil purists and skeptics, who claim that CT'Ink uses laser cutters to attain the high level of detail in their work. (Laser cutters are generally seen as cheating in the arduous process of hand cutting a multilayered stencil.) Pisa73 and Evol Taste claim that they do not use laser cutters, but rather cut every single element of their imagery themselves.

Their work, sometimes involving as many as twenty different stenciled layers (each layer is a separate color of paint or element of detail), generally derives from photos they have manipulated or pieced together. Their images often make social commentary—one famous piece shows American soldiers huddled around a tank painted with the stripes associated with the Adidas brand.

Photographs by Lionel Belluteau.
Paris, 2008.

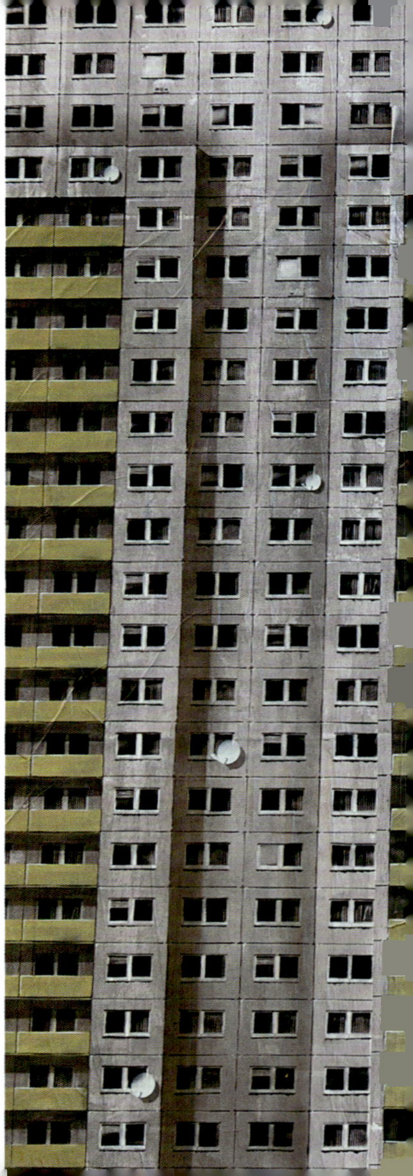

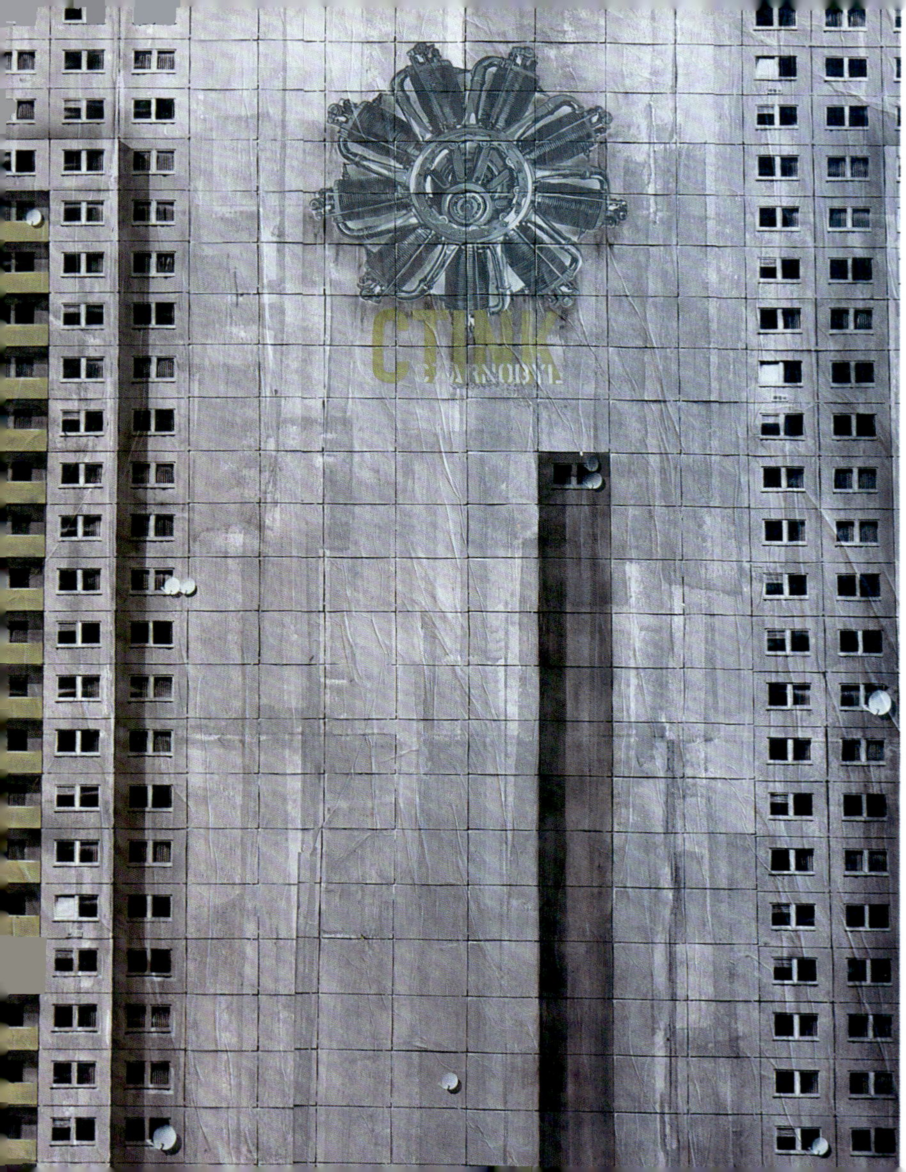

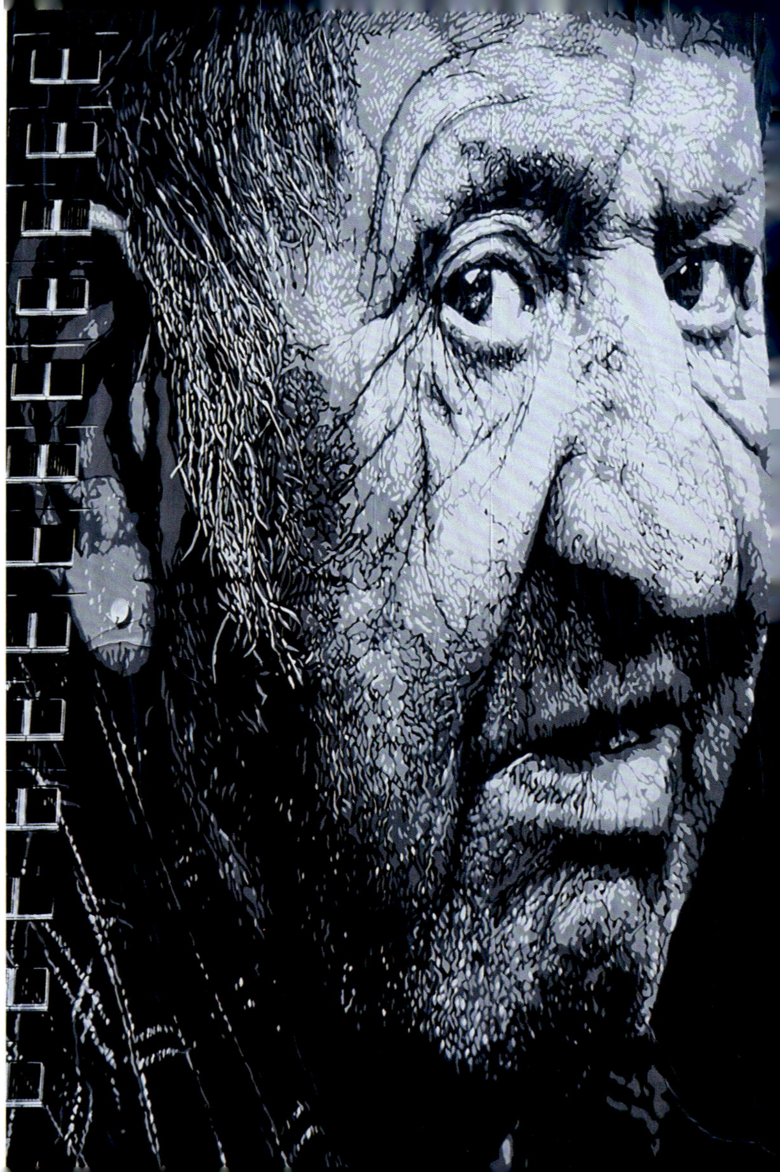

Cycle

Born in 1971, Cycle grew up along the Connecticut–New York border and made frequent trips to New York City in the 1980s. Floored by the graffiti he saw on the walls and subway trains as his father drove him through the Bronx, Cycle began to visit New York City himself as a teenager, skateboard in hand. While earning his BFA from George Washington University, Cycle used the city of Washington, D.C., as his canvas, spray-painting freights, walls, and streets with a bombing complement ranging from simple tags and throw-ups to elaborate pieces. He loved the creativity that graffiti spurred within him, as well as the sense of adventure that went along with it. A few years later, as a graduate student at the Academy of Art in San Francisco, Cycle began to fuse his graffiti with fine art.

These days, he is more likely to paint with a brush than with a spray can, as he is intent on bringing his diversely styled, graffiti-infused paintings into galleries. When he does paint outside, it is within legal venues, often in collaboration with Lady Pink, her husband, Smith, and the members of the second-generation TC5 crew. Among his early inspirations he cites Bio, T-Kid, Sane and Smith (see 289), Sento (see 295), and the skateboard graphic designers Jim Phillips, VC Johnson, and Pushead.

In the spring of 2010, he was one of twenty-five international urban artists to visit Israel as members of the Artists 4 Israel's "Murality Project," bringing his artistic vision to the bomb shelters in the southern town of Sderot.

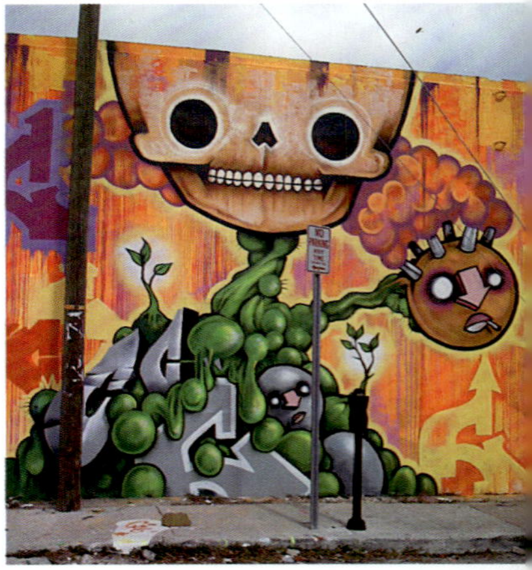

Photograph by Cycle Double Freight.
New York City, 2002.
Detail: Photograph courtesy of Cycle Double Freight.
Miami, Florida, 2007.

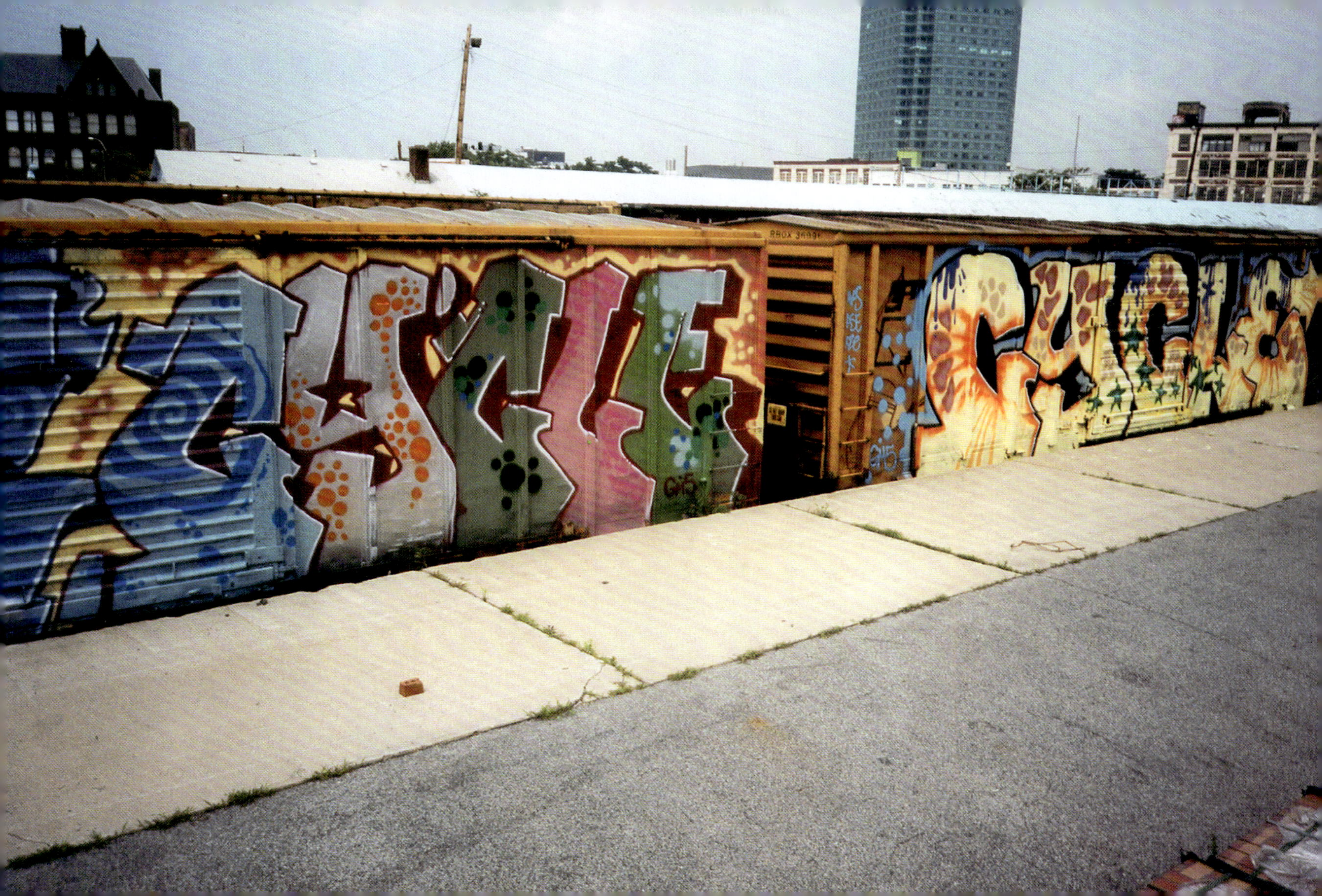

D*face

At the turn of the twenty-first century, one boxy face was smattered all over the streets of London—impossible to miss, the helmeted little creature with rectangular eyes was stuck to every lamppost and flat surface imaginable. Eventually, wheatpastes of the creatures began to crop up as well.

Behind the campaign of winged faces was a weary young graphic designer who had adopted the moniker D*face. Designing on a computer from 9 A.M. to 8 P.M., he would come home and screen-print his stickers until 1 A.M. before passing out—a hopeless devotee of illegal art. In 2003, D*face went out on a limb and founded the Outside Institute, which was London's first street-art-centric gallery space. Forced to shut its doors in 2005, the space rebranded and reopened in a new venue called StolenSpace. Run by D*face and a partner, StolenSpace is at the forefront of European galleries exhibiting urban art.

D*face himself made the leap from outdoor to indoor work with his first solo exhibition, "Death and Glory," at the StolenSpace Gallery in 2006, which promptly sold out. He has exhibited internationally, including at the Jonathan LeVine Gallery in New York. D*face still does design work, including numerous magazine covers, and he recently collaborated with pop star Christina Aguilera for the cover of her album *Bionic*.

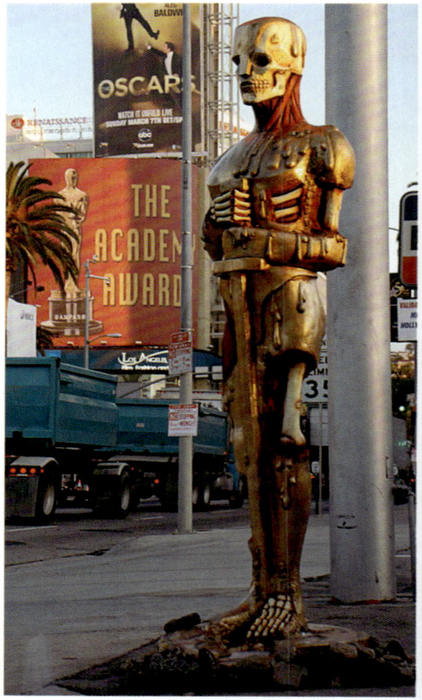

Photograph by Jake Dobkin (streetsy.com). New York City, 2009.
Detail: Courtesy of Camp D*Face. Los Angeles, 2010.

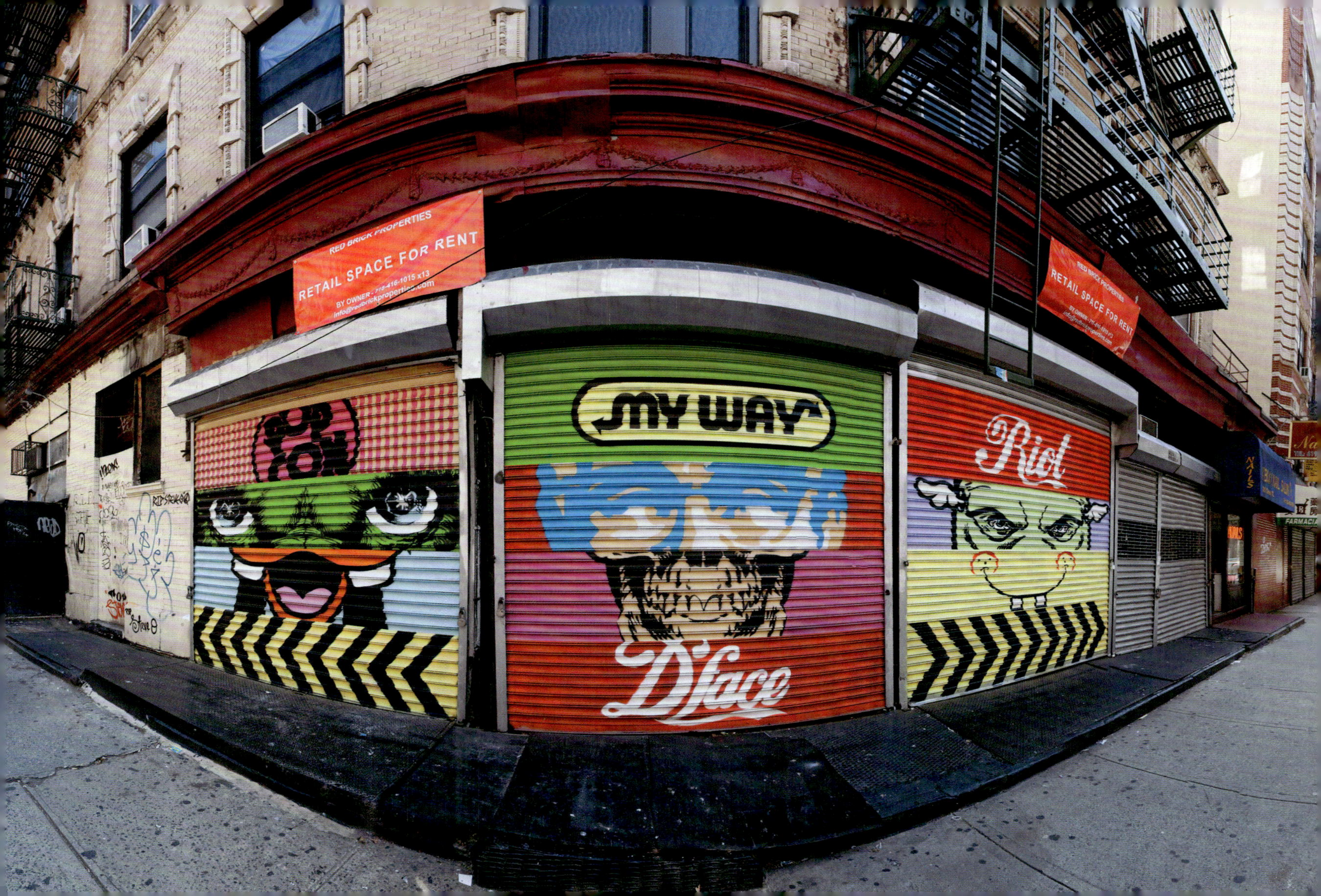
RED BRICK PROPERTIES
RETAIL SPACE FOR RENT
MY WAY
D*face
FARMACIA

Daim

If Mirko Reisser, aka Daim, didn't invent 3-D lettering, he certainly perfected it. Influenced by hip-hop and the works of his predecessors, Daim began painting traditional letter-based graffiti in Hamburg, Germany, in 1989. He began to hone his skills by painting constantly and traveling to jams all over Europe. Like many Europeans, he experimented with the popular 3-D lettering style. His process involves making a preliminary sketch in pencil and then using a computer to flesh it out.

He attended art school in Switzerland, where he partnered up with Mate, Tasek, and Neck, and formed the Trash Can Design crew. Daim mastered the art of twisting letters into positions that made them seem like sculptures. By altering perspective, he makes his pieces appear to be popping out of the walls he paints them on. The precision and perfection of a Daim's work caused one of his colleagues to exclaim, "It looks more like the work of a robot than a human."

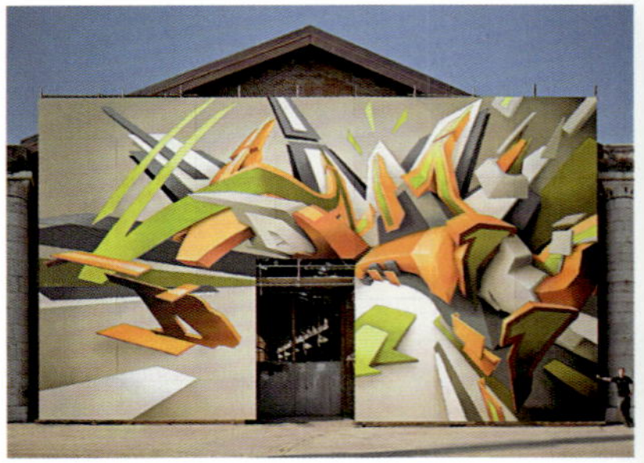

Photographs by MRpro.
Hamburg, Germany, 2006.
Detail: Venice, Italy, 2007.

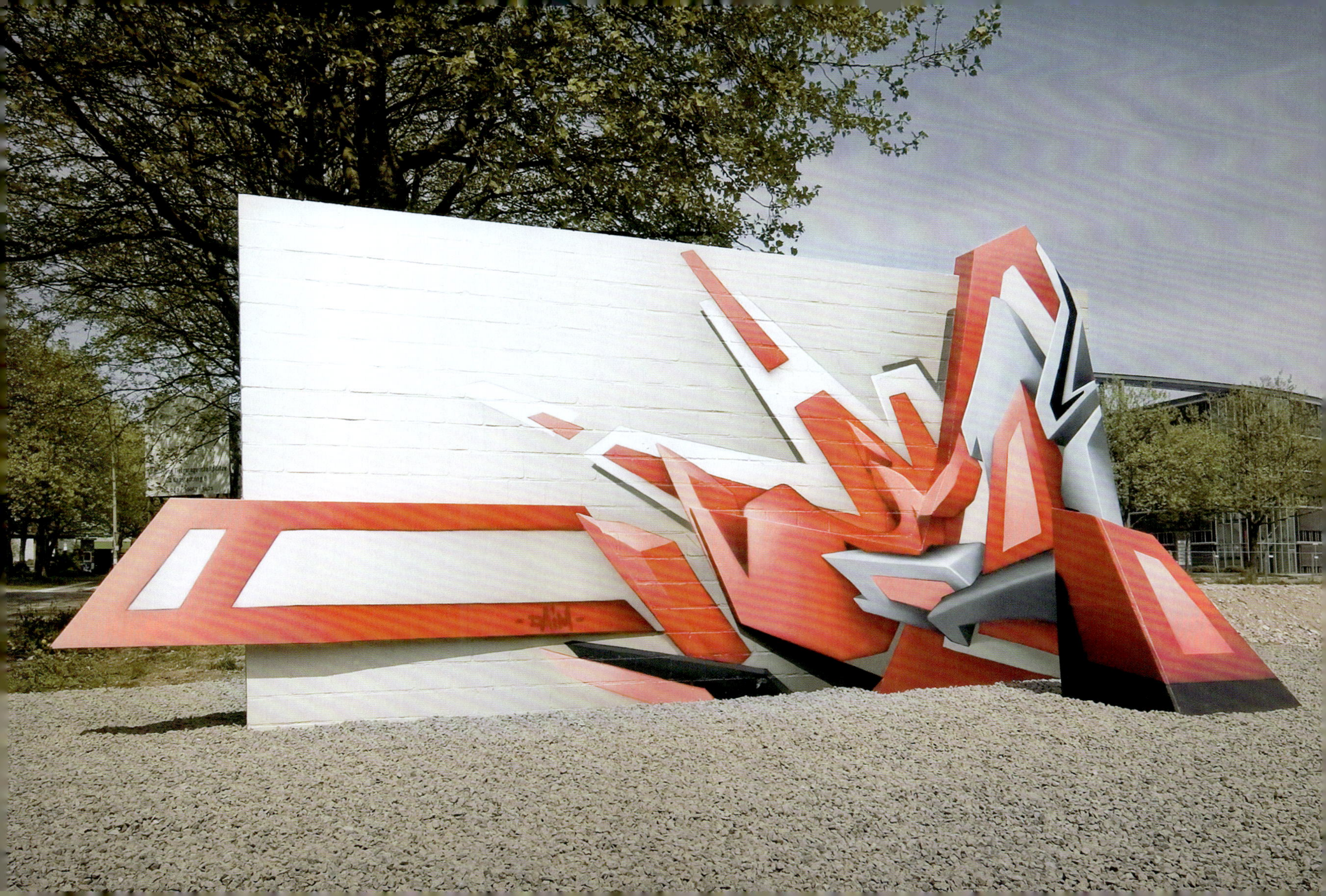

Dare TWS

For more than twenty years, Swiss-born Sigi von Koeding, aka Dare TWS (The Wild Side), evolved his style into one of the graffiti world's greatest, by incorporating readable letters with three-dimensional outlines and usually no more than two or three colors. Dare's humble and positive approach to art and life easily earned the respect of everyone he met. The scope of Dare's lifework was global; he attributed much of his success and inspiration to traveling, meeting new people, and the crew he collected and regarded as his second family. Everywhere he went, he left in his wake new friendships and fresh pieces to mark them with.

Dare painted his first canvas in 1992, and the nonephemeral quality of it, both literally and figuratively, left a lasting impression; he sometimes spent weeks on one canvas. His gallery exhibits allowed him to witness a viewer's reaction to his work—something graffiti artists rarely get to see. Dare was one of those few street artists who was able to enter the gallery world and not once compromise his style.

Sadly, in March 2010, the street-art world lost Dare to a swift battle with cancer, but as hundreds of tribute pieces and commemorations will attest, he won't be forgotten.

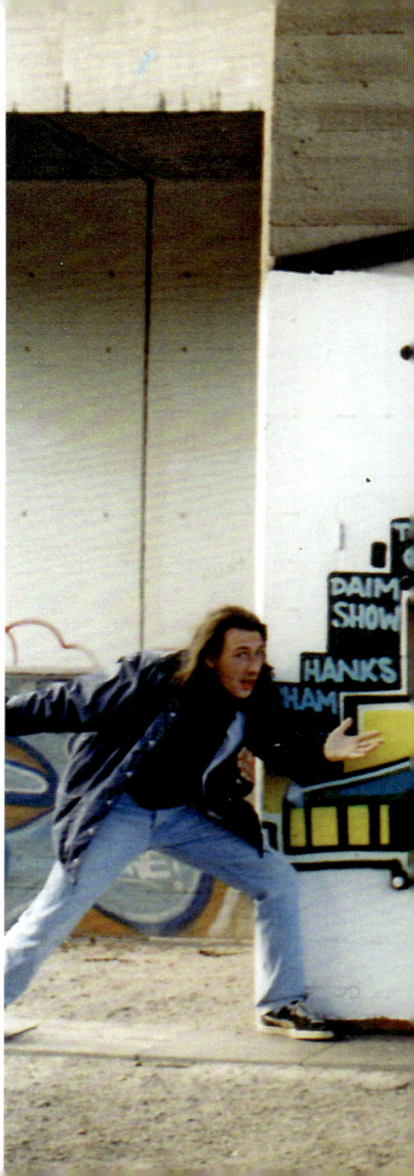

Photograph by Ces One. Basel, Switzerland, 1996.

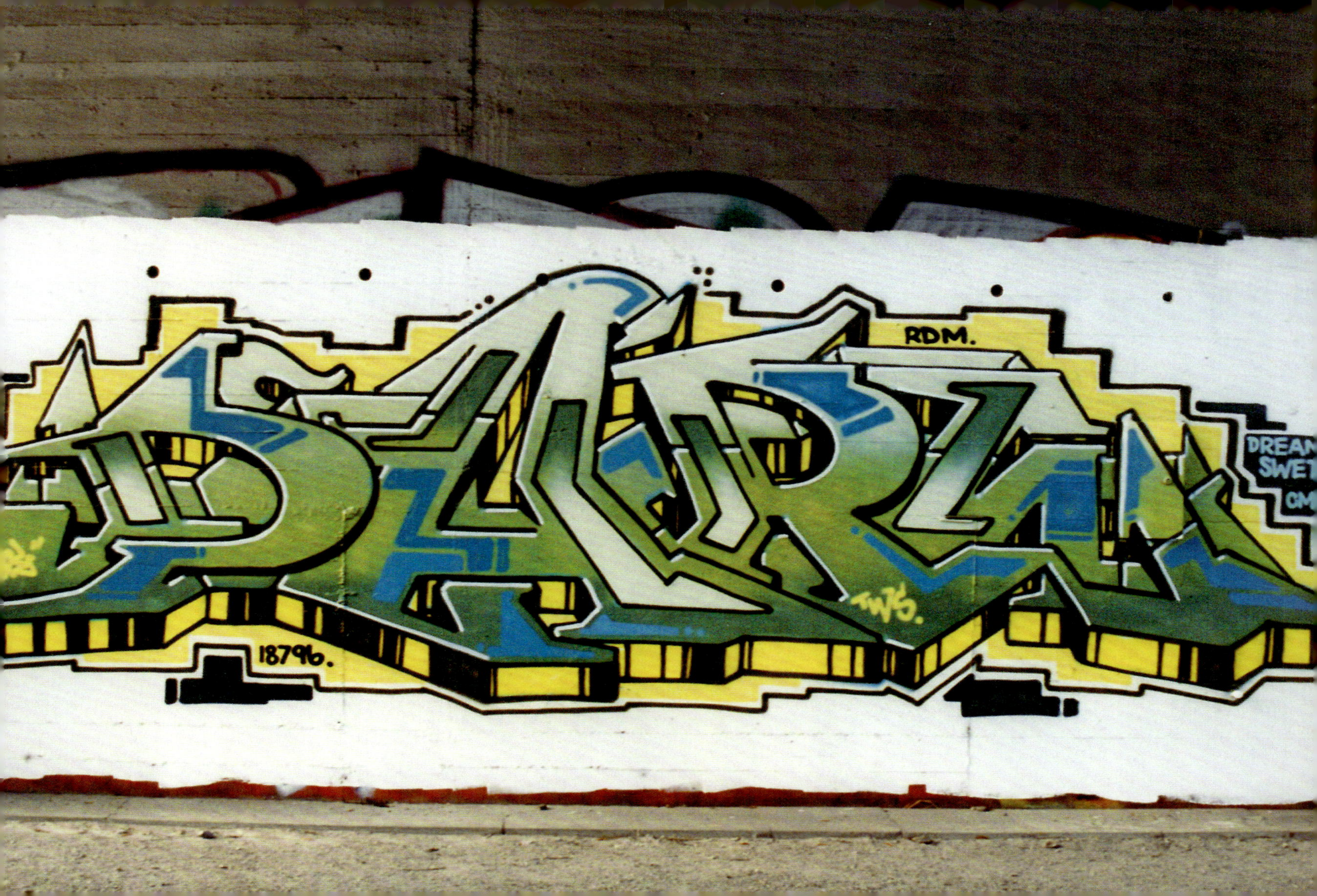
RDM.
18796.

Daze

Chris "Daze" Ellis spent the early part of his childhood in Brooklyn, but then grew up on Roosevelt Island in the early 1970s. As a teenager, Daze spent a lot of his spare time reading *MAD* magazine and comic books and watching Blaxploitation movies. He attended the High School of Art and Design [see 167], where he met a talented crop of graffiti writers with whom he would exchange styles and ideas in the school cafeteria.

With a head full of influences ranging from Don Martin to Don 1, Daze began painting graffiti on walls and trains in the late '70s. He approached graffiti with a definite sense of purpose and executed colorful pieces often augmented with early versions of his signature characters; these instantly recognizable characters occupied a middle ground between caricature and realism. By the time Daze quit graffiti, he had managed to paint with a who's-who list of the greatest writers of his era.

When the galleries opened their doors to graffiti artists in the early 1980s, Daze was at the forefront of the aboveground migration. His work continues to fetch high prices in galleries from Switzerland to Singapore. Although he makes his living selling paintings, Daze still puts in work on the streets. Whether he's painting with the OGs of the subway movement in Harlem's Hall of Fame or bringing New York City flavor to the streets of São Paulo, Daze keeps his bases covered.

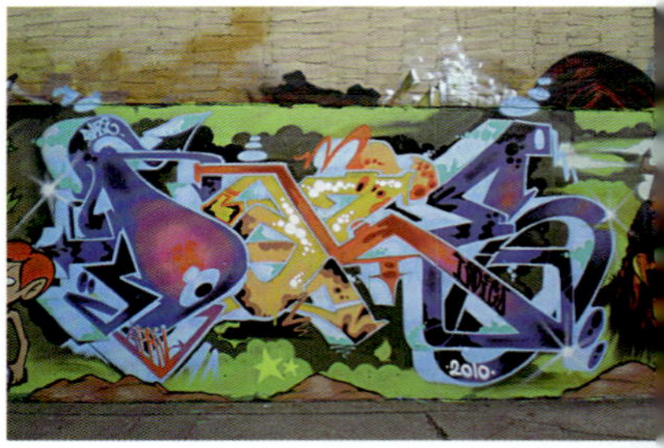

Photographs courtesy of Daze.
Bronx, New York, 2010.

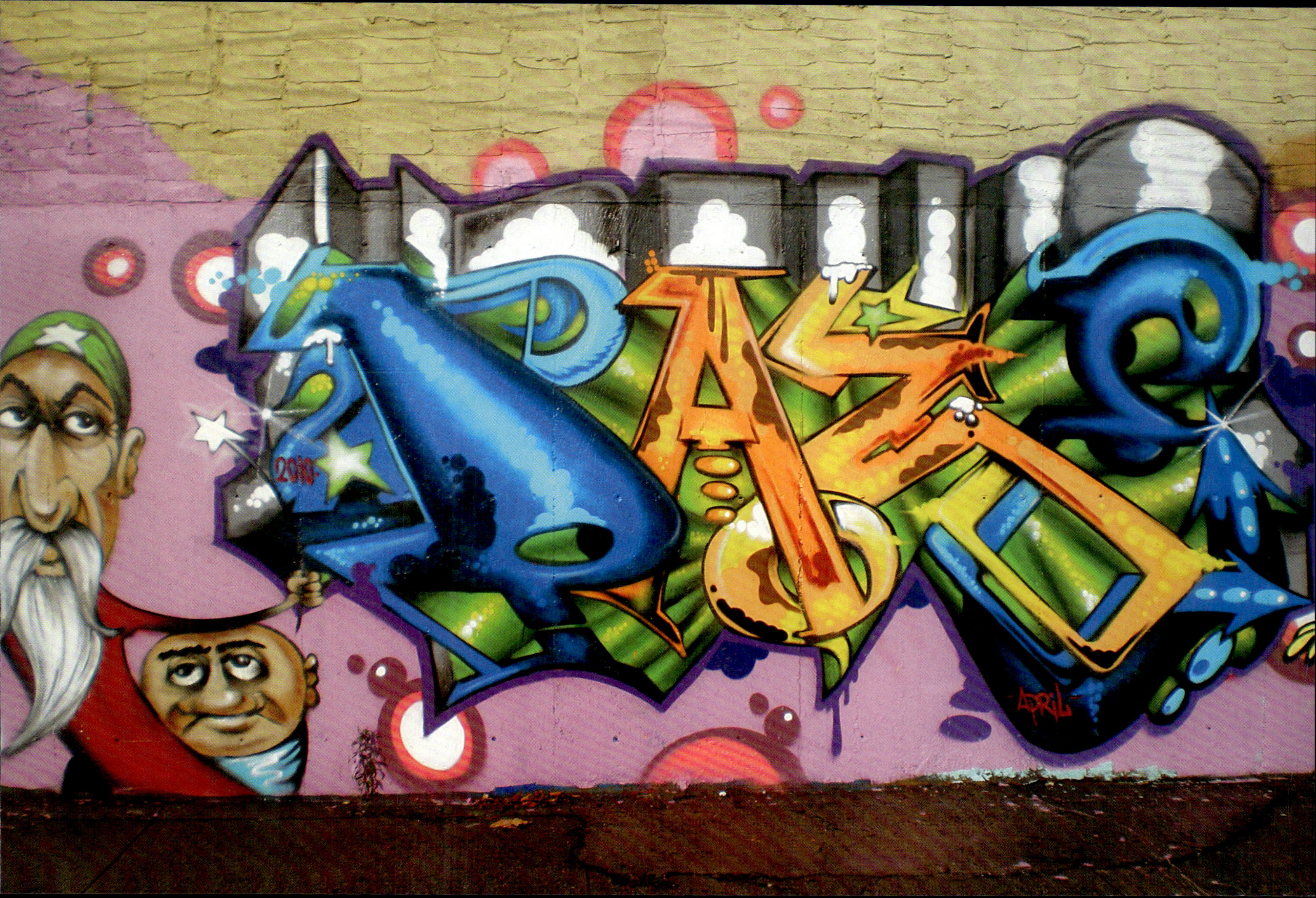
2010
APRIL

The Death Squad

The Death Squad (TDS) was created in the fall of 1976 by Chain 3, Kool 131, and Mr. Jinx 174. The mission statement of the founders was to get the best stylemasters of the day and unify them under one name. The day they started, they recruited Part (see 251) and Peso 131 by going to their high schools; from there, they continued to go to other schools, adding writers like NOC 167, Magoo 2, and Bear 167.

They did their first trains as TDS in October 1976, then were slightly derailed after an untimely raid spooked them for a while. In 1977, at the height of his career, Chain 3 announced his retirement, and Mr. Jinx moved to Queens; this allowed room for a partnership to develop between Kool and Part, who were pulling off some of the greatest cars ever seen in their home base of the #1 subway tunnel. It seemed like no one could top them, until Chain came out of retirement to hand out styles to a new crew called TMT. It's at this point in graffiti history that the term "style wars" is accurately ascribed by Best 149.

The two crews fed off each other and even occasionally painted together. The heyday of TDS ended when the crew was mugged in the #1 tunnel in 1980; its home turf had become a place where random violence could happen to anyone. Part and Kool moved around to other lines for a few more years, just to get things out of their system; then Padre 2 and Bear 167 died in the 1980s, and the crew all but faded away. The style innovations of Part, Kool, Chain, and Noc are still in use by writers around the world, and Part, Noc, and Chain continue to paint today on canvas, as well as walls.

***Inch/Worm* car by Kool 131 and Part TDS.**
Private collection.
New York City, 1976.

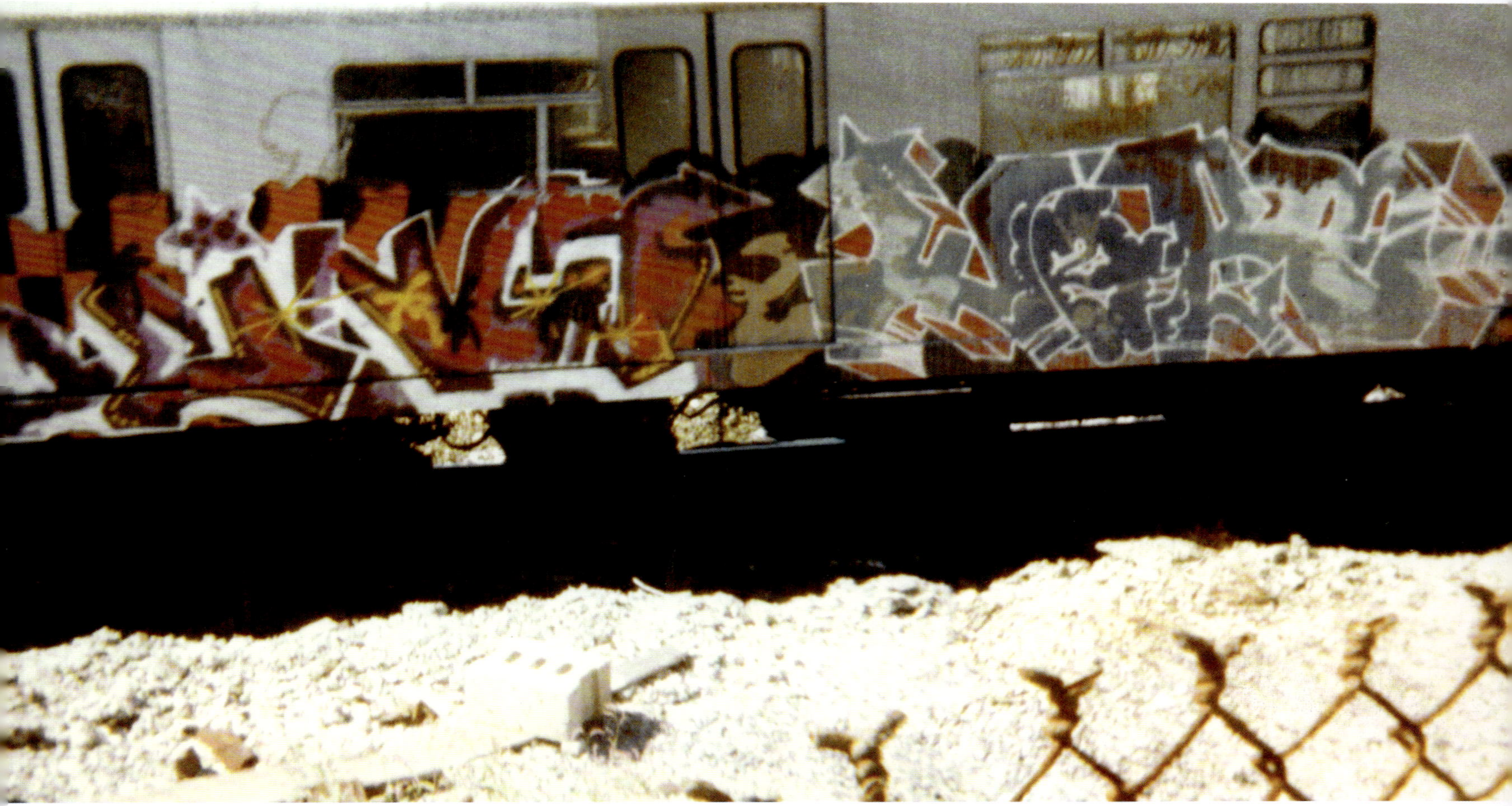

Michael DeFeo

Fifteen years and fifteen thousand flowers in Manhattan have established Michael DeFeo, aka the Flowerguy, as one of street art's most prolific and highly recognizable artists. His dopey, seemingly wilting flower, painted with a broad brush and screen printed, has become an iconic image on walls from Hong Kong to Paris. An upbeat symbol of childlike optimism amid urban chaos, DeFeo's flower reminds city dwellers around the world that positive growth can take root in the city.

His work has been featured on the cover of the "Reasons to Love New York" issue of *New York Magazine* three times—yes, three times—and one might think this commercial attention would diminish DeFeo's authority on the streets. But aside from his signature flower, Flowerguy is also highly regarded in art circles for his self-portraiture work. When he puts himself up on the walls outside, viewers realize that what he's got on his insides is more than just the fluffy stuff.

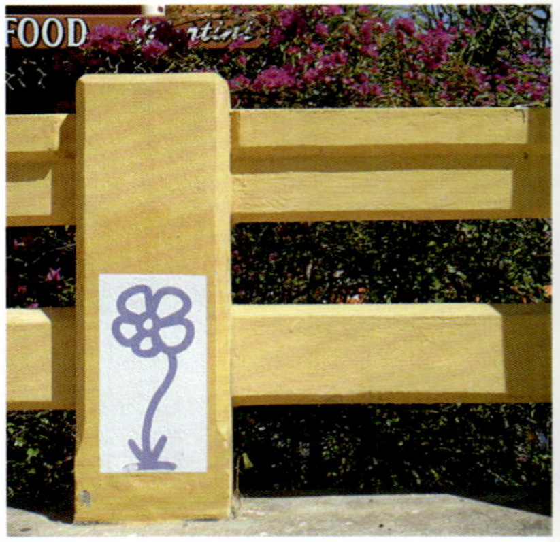

Photograph by Gavin Thomas.
New York City, 2007.
Detail: Photograph courtesy of Michael DeFeo.
Fort Lauderdale, Florida, 2010.

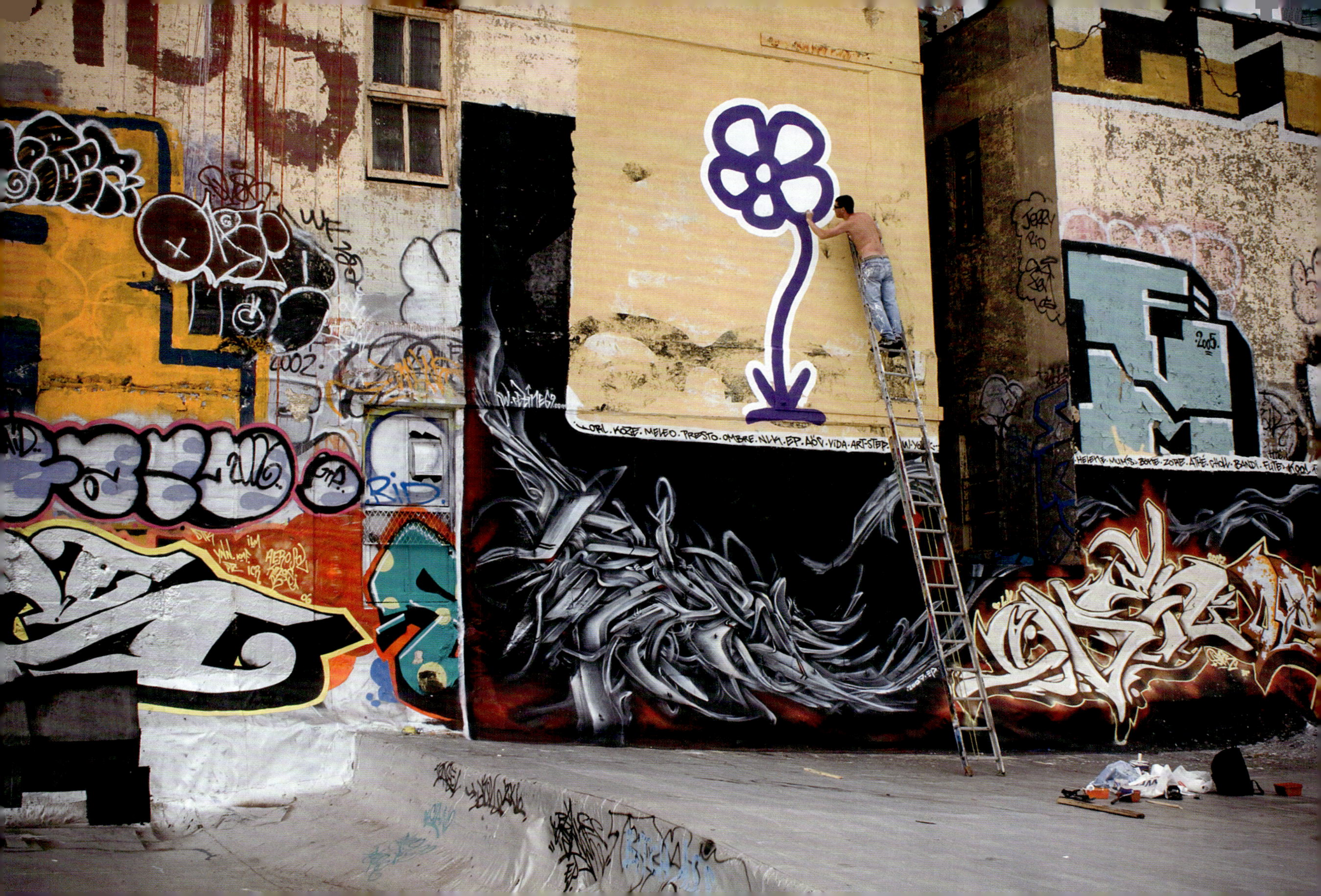

De La Vega

Born and raised in East Harlem, James De La Vega is best known for his chalk drawings and clever sayings that appear on a range of public spaces throughout New York City. De La Vega began drawing as a young child, emulating older family members. He studied fine arts at Cornell University and continued his studies abroad at the Sorbonne and at Oxford. A main inspiration and role model is his mom, Elsie Matos.

Following run-ins with the law in 2003, when he was charged with vandalism for painting a fish leaping out of a bowl on a blank wall in the Bronx, De La Vega has striven to work solely within legal venues. Identified with his slogan, Become Your Dream, De La Vega is intent on serving as a role model for those young New Yorkers whose dreams are often not realized.

His store in the East Village, fittingly called De La Vega Museum, is a showcase and retail outlet for his paintings, prints, and fashioned merchandise. An expanded version of his original space in East Harlem, it allows De La Vega to connect to a far larger range of folks than he could possibly have reached on East 104th Street.

**Photograph by Ernie Paniccioli.
New York City, 2006.**

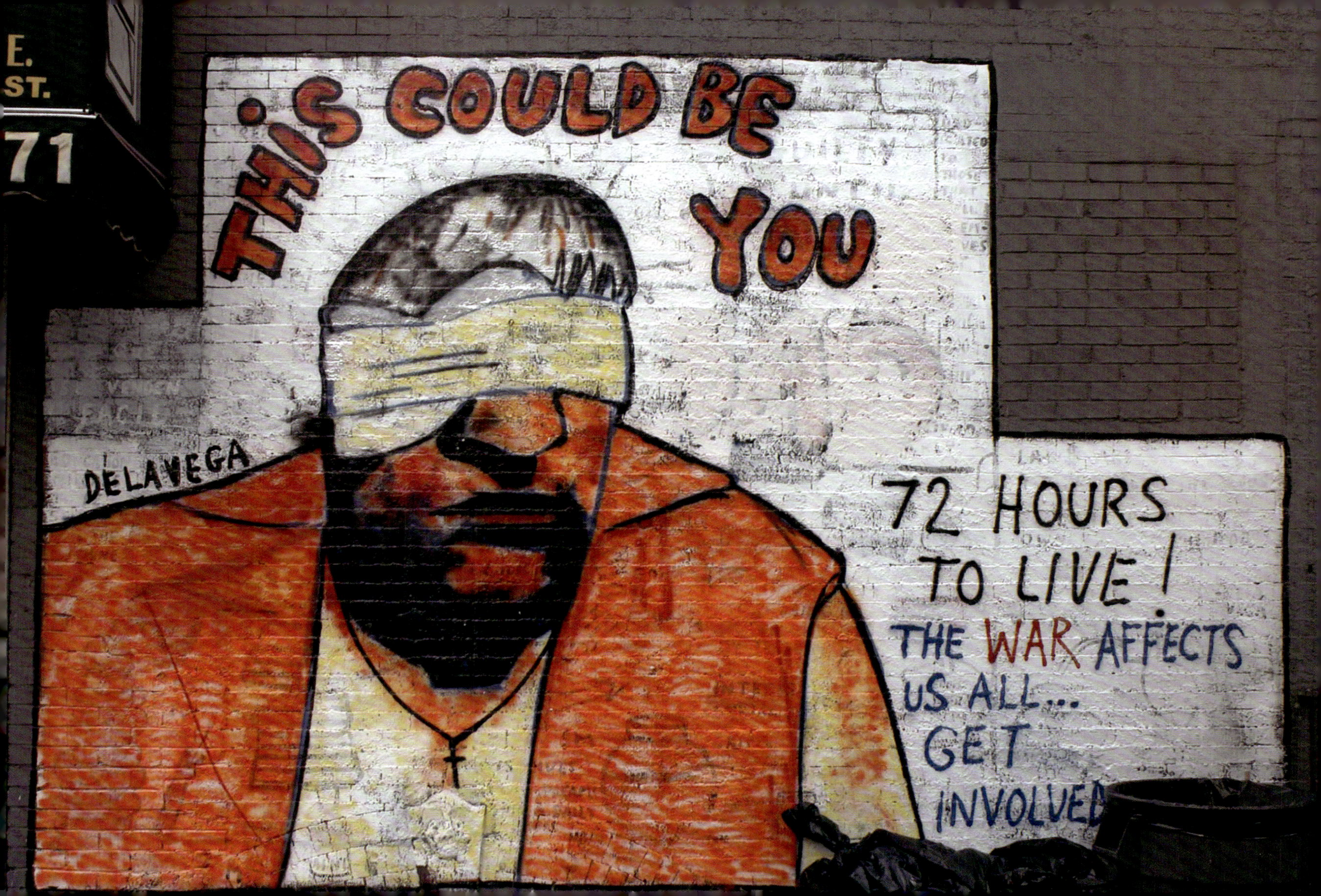
THIS COULD BE YOU
DELAVEGA
72 HOURS TO LIVE!
THE WAR AFFECTS US ALL... GET INVOLVED
E. ST.
71

Delta

If you were to look at a Delta sculpture in a gallery space today, you'd find little resemblance to his street work of the 1980s and '90s. Delta began his career in the Netherlands in the mid-1980s as a blue-collar writer with a hip-hop pedigree. In the early '90s, he became one of a group of writers who were fascinated with the impact a twisting 3-D effect could achieve. He painted walls and trains in Amsterdam under his own name and his alias, Mess, and he is known as an old-school legend in his homeland. He, Germany's Daim, and New York's Erni are considered the masters of modern 3-D lettering.

In 1994, Delta graduated from the Delft University of Technology with a degree in industrial design engineering. During the '90s, Delta stripped his letters bare and painted them as geometric shapes, rejecting in his style the blend-and-camouflage look that had been handed down by the New York writers. He began showing in galleries soon after, which led to further exploration of the structure of his name; his canvases began resembling blueprints more than graffiti.

Today, he has turned his attention to sculpture inspired partly by graffiti and partly by the Transformers toys of his youth. Some of the sculptures are as tall as three feet and resemble walking letters.

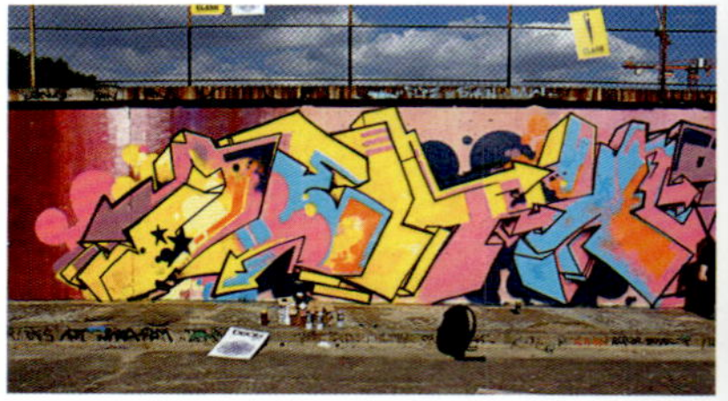

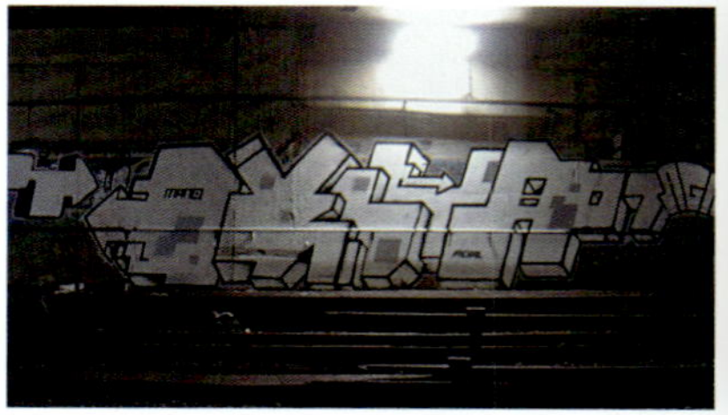

Photographs courtesy of Delta.
Amsterdam, the Netherlands, 1995.

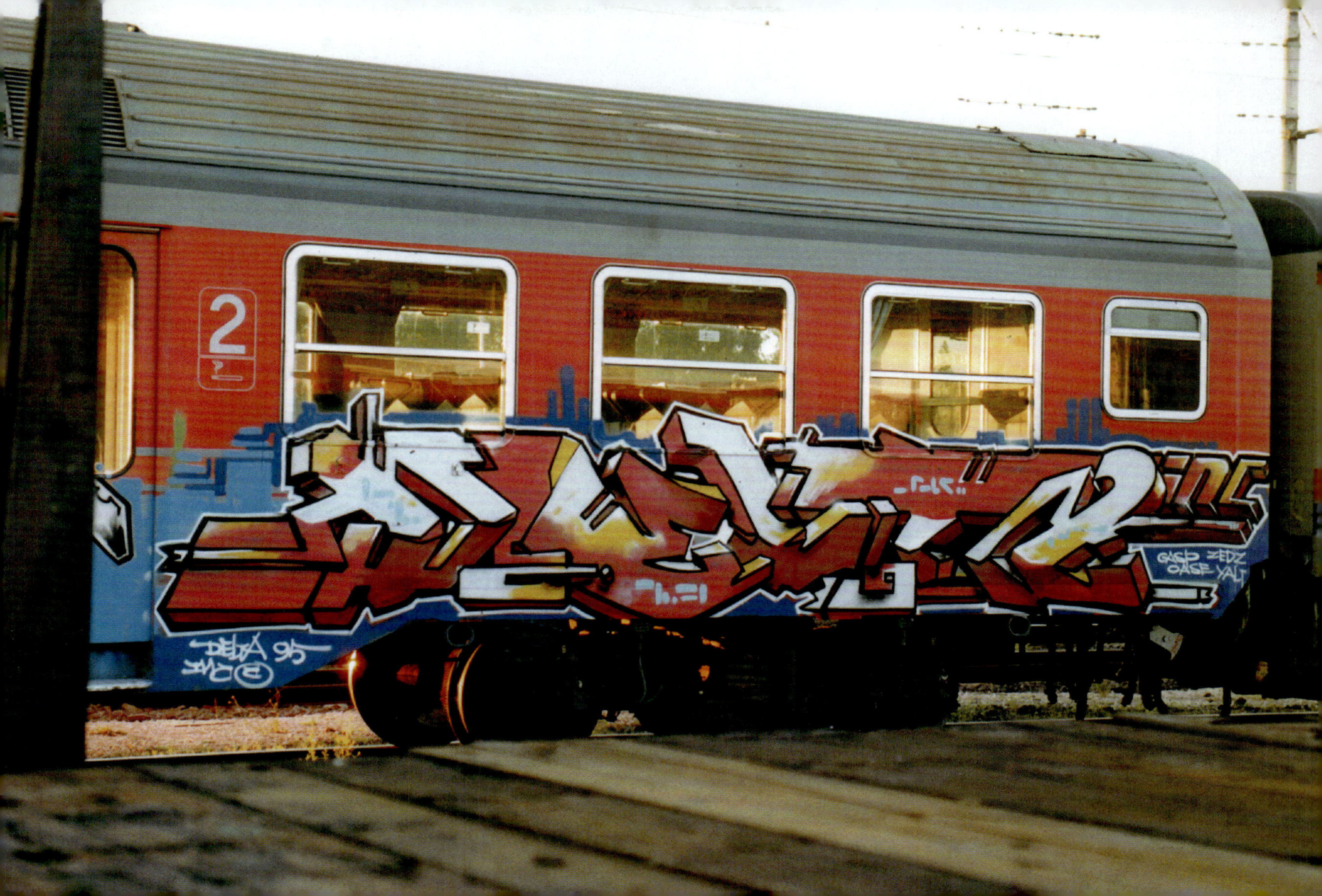
2
DELTA 95
GASP ZEDZ
OASE YALT

090

Dero

Perhaps his parents foresaw Dero's artistic future when they christened him "Blue." In 1979, when Dero began to pay attention to graffiti, daily exposure to Blade (see 037), Lee, and Slave's whole-cars running through his Bronx neighborhood inspired him to begin drawing on paper. Sketching led to painting and, eventually, a graduation to walls and rooftops around his neighborhood.

In 1983, Dero caught a lucky break when his cousin brought home a blackbook, loaned to him by a famous writer from his school. The book belonged to Dez, king of the #1 and #3 lines. Dero befriended Dez, who took him under his wing, bringing him to lay-ups and introducing him to a network of established writers. Dero recalls: "Dez called me up in 1984 and told me to meet him on a lay-up on the #4 line that night to go painting. I got lucky. Dez brought Duster UA, and we rocked a three-man car together."

Dero and Dez were close, but moving in different directions. Dero wanted to earn his own crown, and Dez had gotten caught up in the Harlem street game. Dero began painting with a newer crop of local writers, most notably Poem and Wane. Dero and his new partners dominated the lay-ups in the East Bronx, and from 1985 through 1987 Dero became king of the prestigious #2 and #5 lines. A graffiti purist, he didn't rely on fancy backgrounds or characters, but developed a crisp, symmetrical style of mechanical lettering at a time when writers put more emphasis on throw-ups and ink tags than style.

To this day, he remains a writer's writer, respected by those who know their style and history—one of the last true kings of the line.

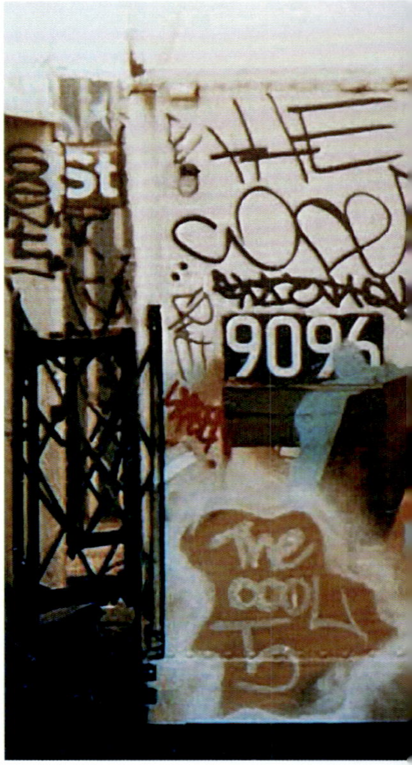

Photograph courtesy of Laser Burner. New York City, 1985.

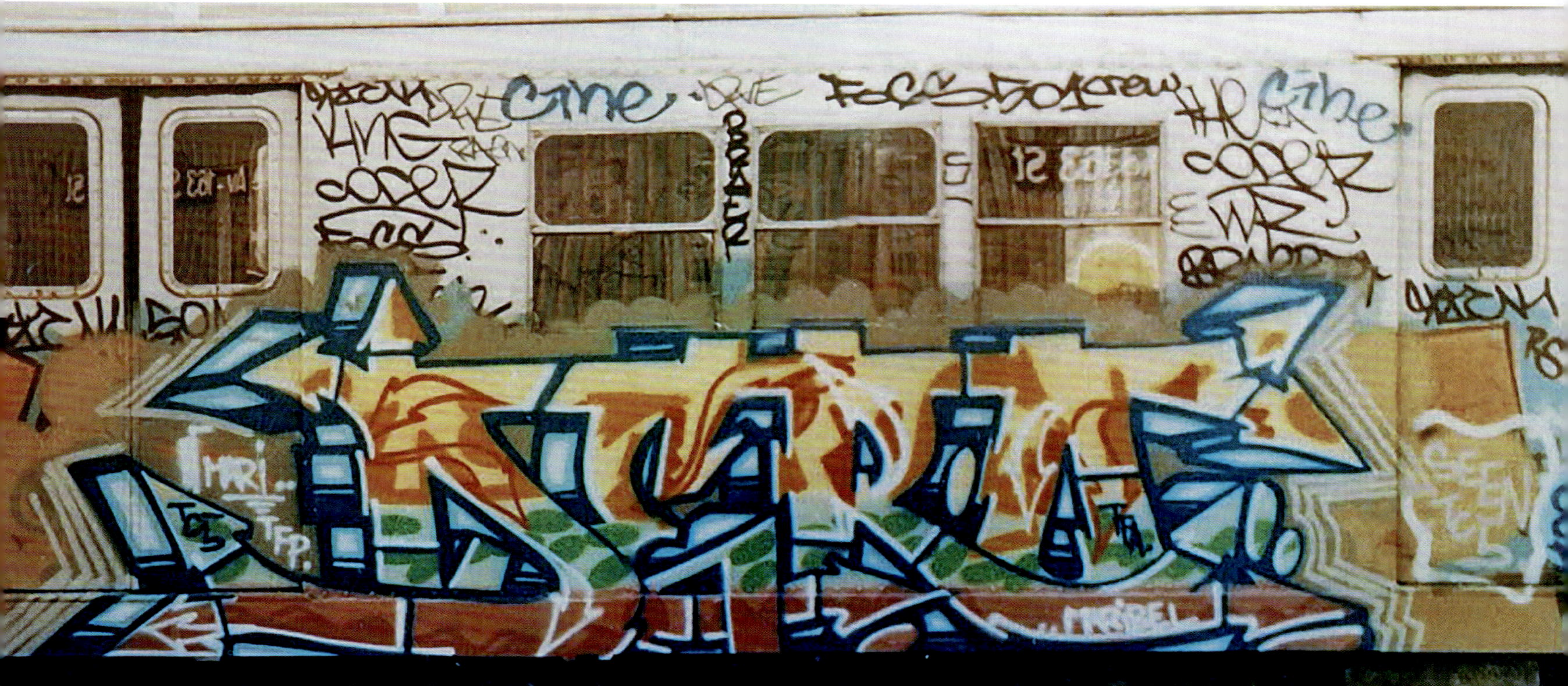

091

Deuce 7

In the middle of the first decade of the 2000s, street art went through an intense popularity boom. Some might assert that the sudden influx of attention, commercial job offers, and the cash that comes with both killed the renegade spirit of the art form. Around 2008, illegal street art in New York was going through a dry spell, in a state of withdrawal from the bouts of work that artists such as Gaia [see 142], Elbow Toe, and Judith Supine [see 326] had blessed the city with. There was a prevalent feeling that street art was dying—or selling out—when a new character appeared on the scene. Mysterious and ominously psychedelic, a series of brightly colored creatures—hybrids of spiders and grasshoppers, seemingly on acid—began appearing around the city, signed simply with the numbers 27.

It took months to discover that the artist behind the psychedelia was a native of Minneapolis, Minnesota, going by the name Deuce 7, who had hopped freight trains around the country to spread his work beyond his home state. Freights were, in fact, the first place the rest of the country had seen his work before his big splash in New York.

Using mostly spray paint and oil sticks in his work, Deuce 7 has crossed over into fine art through his exhibitions in numerous galleries in the United States and Europe.

Photograph by Luna Park.
Brooklyn, New York, 2009.
Details: Photographs by Vincent Cornelli.
New York City, 2007.

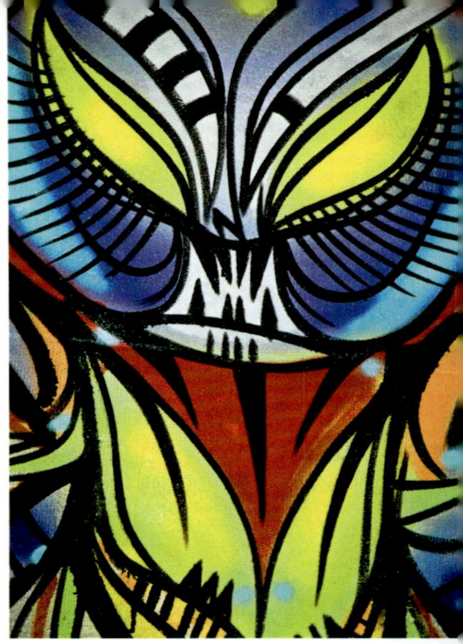

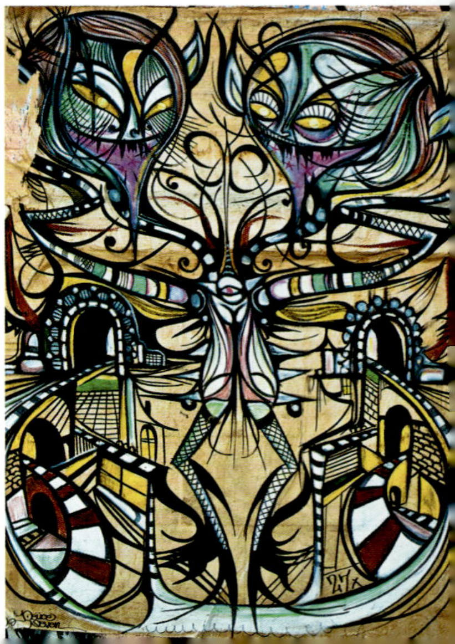

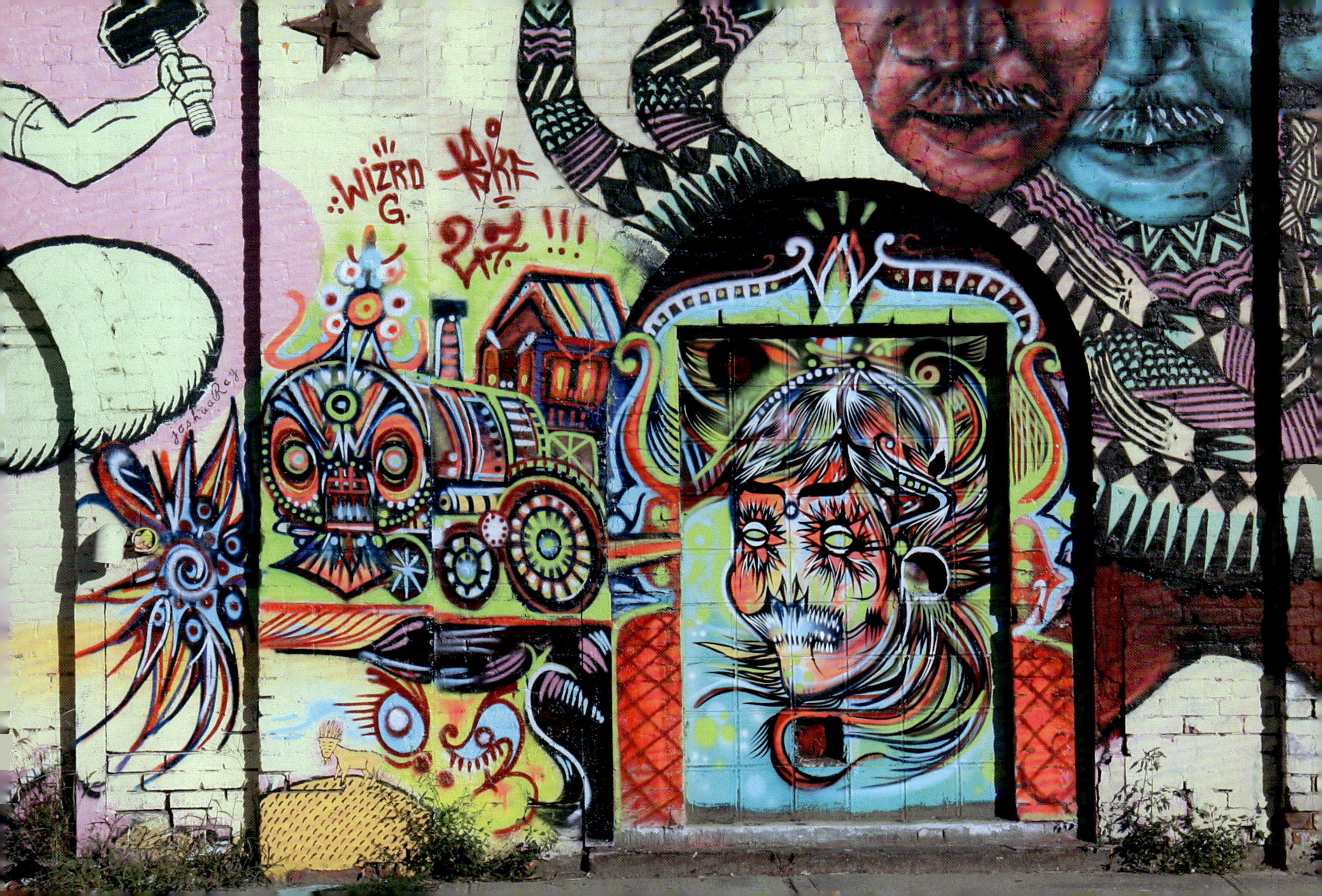
WIZRD G.
27 !!!

Dez

Dez (aka Spade 429, aka Kay Gee 103) hailed from Harlem's East River Houses, a public housing project in NYC. He grew up going to house parties and hip-hop jams in the parks around his neighborhood, learning to DJ at the ripe old age of twelve. Dez also was a part of the hip-hop organization "Zulu Nation" Chapter 13, and he DJ'd events throughout the city under the moniker Dj Kay Gee.

Dez began drawing graffiti in his notebooks at school, and his cohorts encouraged him to hit the streets. In 1980, Dez would turn the #3 yard into his personal studio, churning out a slew of plain-style pieces that would become his visual signature. Frequent accomplices included Pore, Mean 3, Due 2, Trap, Elkay and, most notably, Skeme (see 304). Although he was a few years younger, Dez painted with stylemasters such as Kase 2, Part TDS, and the TMT crew, in addition to forming his own group, the Famous Artists (TFA), in which he was versatile and could hold his own with his older peers.

When the crack scene hit New York City in the early 1980s, Dez was in the thick of it, and bad habits landed him in jail. After his first and only experience serving time, Dez got his life together and focused on his music, hustling mix tapes under a new name, DJ Kay Slay. He released four albums, two with Major Sony/Columbia Records and two on Koch/e1 records Independent. Dez currently hosts two radio shows on Hot97 NYC and Shade45 Sirius Satellite radio, produces albums, and designs and publishes *Straight Stuntin* magazine. His take on his success is "Even in my darkest hour, I always knew I was meant for something better."

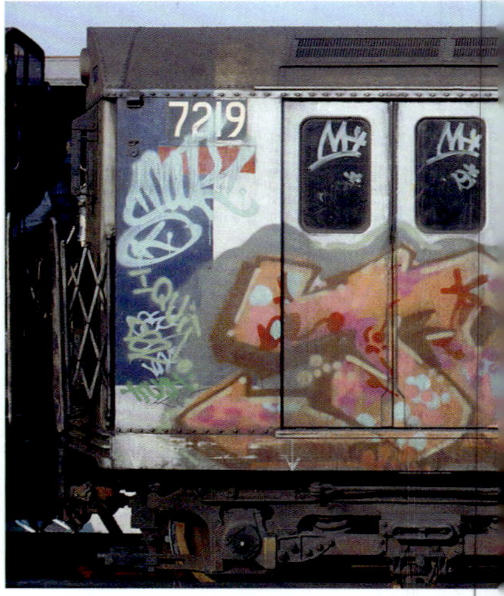

Photograph by Henry Chalfant. New York City, 1982.

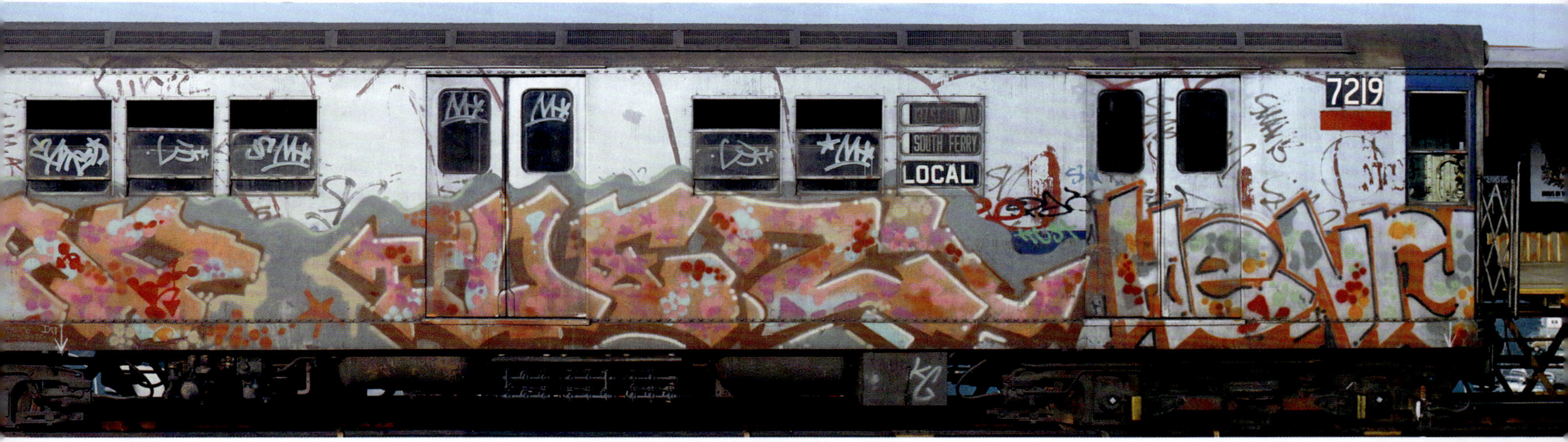
7219
SOUTH FERRY
LOCAL

Owen Dippie

Raised in Kawerau, in the Bay of Plenty region of New Zealand, Owen Dippie began drawing when he entered elementary school. Almost entirely self-taught, he has never stopped creating artwork. In the past several years, he has established a reputation for his exquisite photorealistic portraits of pop icons such as Michael Jackson, KRS-One, Tupac, Elvis Presley, and Brandon Lee.

Recently, Owen Dippie has been attracting considerable attention and garnering many fans for the enormous portraits of Biggie Smalls that he paints in public spaces, such as Long Island City's famed aerosol art Mecca, 5 Pointz [see 003]. A big fan of Biggie's music, Owen Dippie cites the late rapper's albums *Ready to Die* and *Life After Death* as the inspiration for these portraits.

Owen Dippie's work also moved inside gallery walls with his first exhibit in 2009. In the summer of 2010, he participated, alongside such artists as Shepard Fairey [see 124] and Swoon [see 329], in the New York City exhibit "Artefacts," an exploration of the work of twelve artists with a history in public art who are currently making their mark in the contemporary art world. His portraits of Andy Warhol, Jean-Michel Basquiat [see 026], and Keith Haring [see 160] were among the show's standouts.

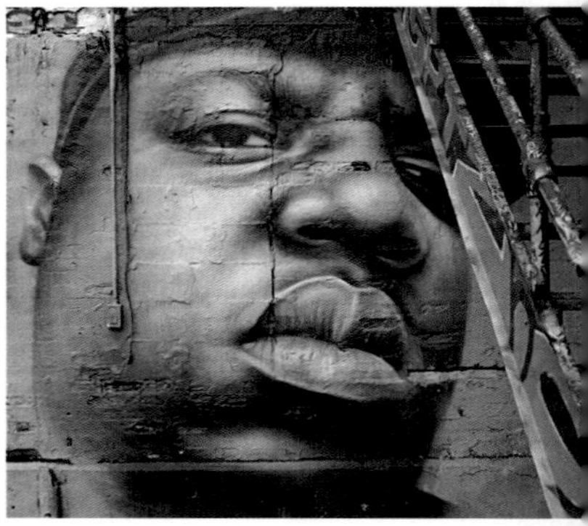

Photographs by Becki Fuller.
Bronx, New York, 2008.
Detail: Brooklyn, New York, 2009.

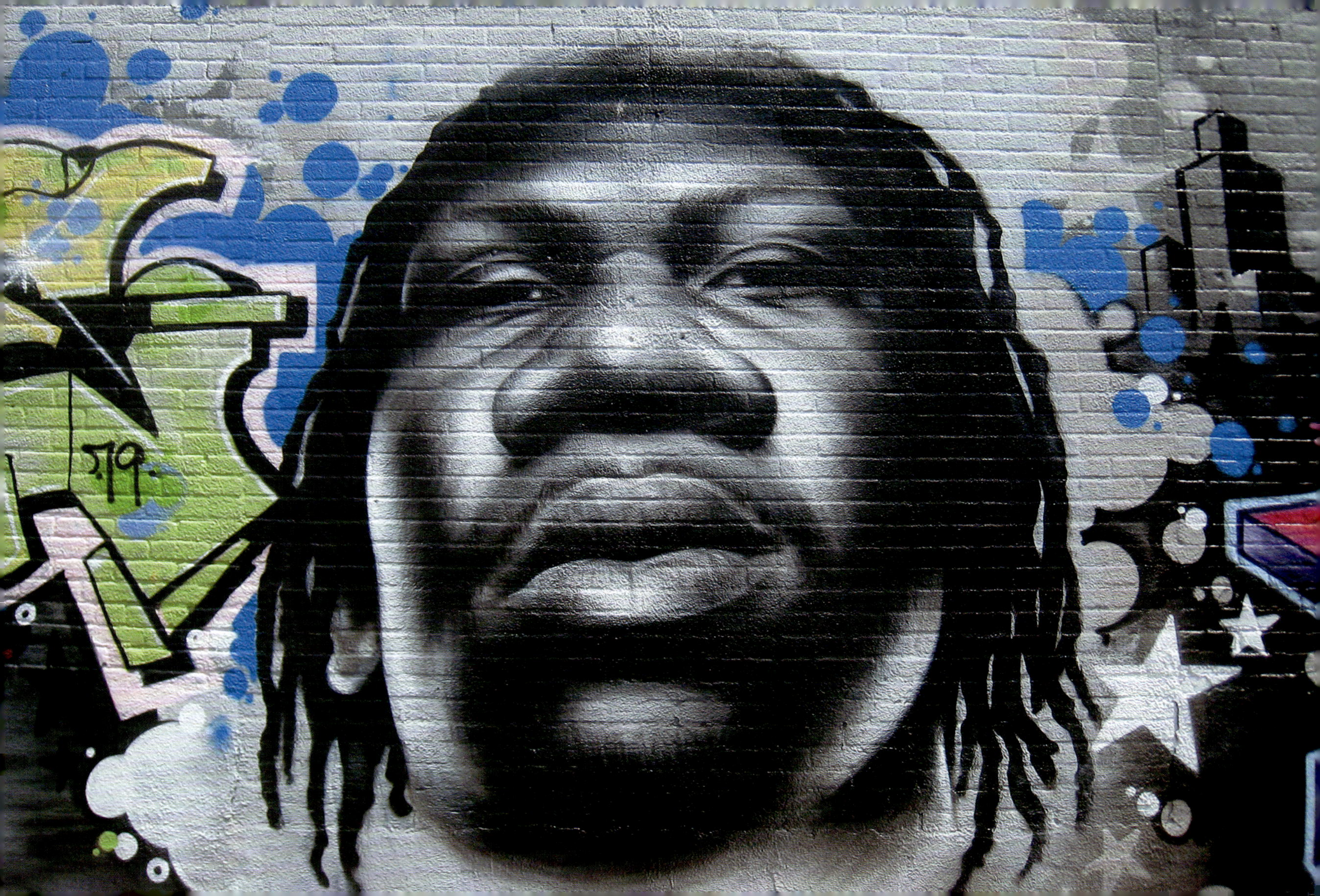

Dmote

Dmote started writing in Sydney, Australia, in 1985. At this time, young graffiti writers around the world were trying to emulate their heroes, and Dmote drew inspiration from Bronx writers such as Seen (see 294), Duster, Bio, Mack, Wane, and Dero, as well as Harlem artists like Skeme (see 304) and Shame. In Dmote's opinion, these writers represented the best of the best. He studied their work and strove to push the form, eventually making it his own through technique, use of color, and knowledge of letter structure.

Graffiti has taken him to subways, streets, and galleries in myriad cities around the world, including New York, Tokyo, São Paulo, London, and Sarajevo. His work has been featured in numerous magazines and videos. Although he is navigating a seamless transition into fine art, Dmote has retained the strong graphic visual vocabulary and bold design aesthetic that made him an internationally recognized name in underground culture.

What does Dmote have to prove after twenty-five years in the game? "Today competition is what drives me. Nothing makes me want to paint more than when I see my peers really rocking it," he explains.

Photograph courtesy of Dmote.
Bronx, New York, 2010.

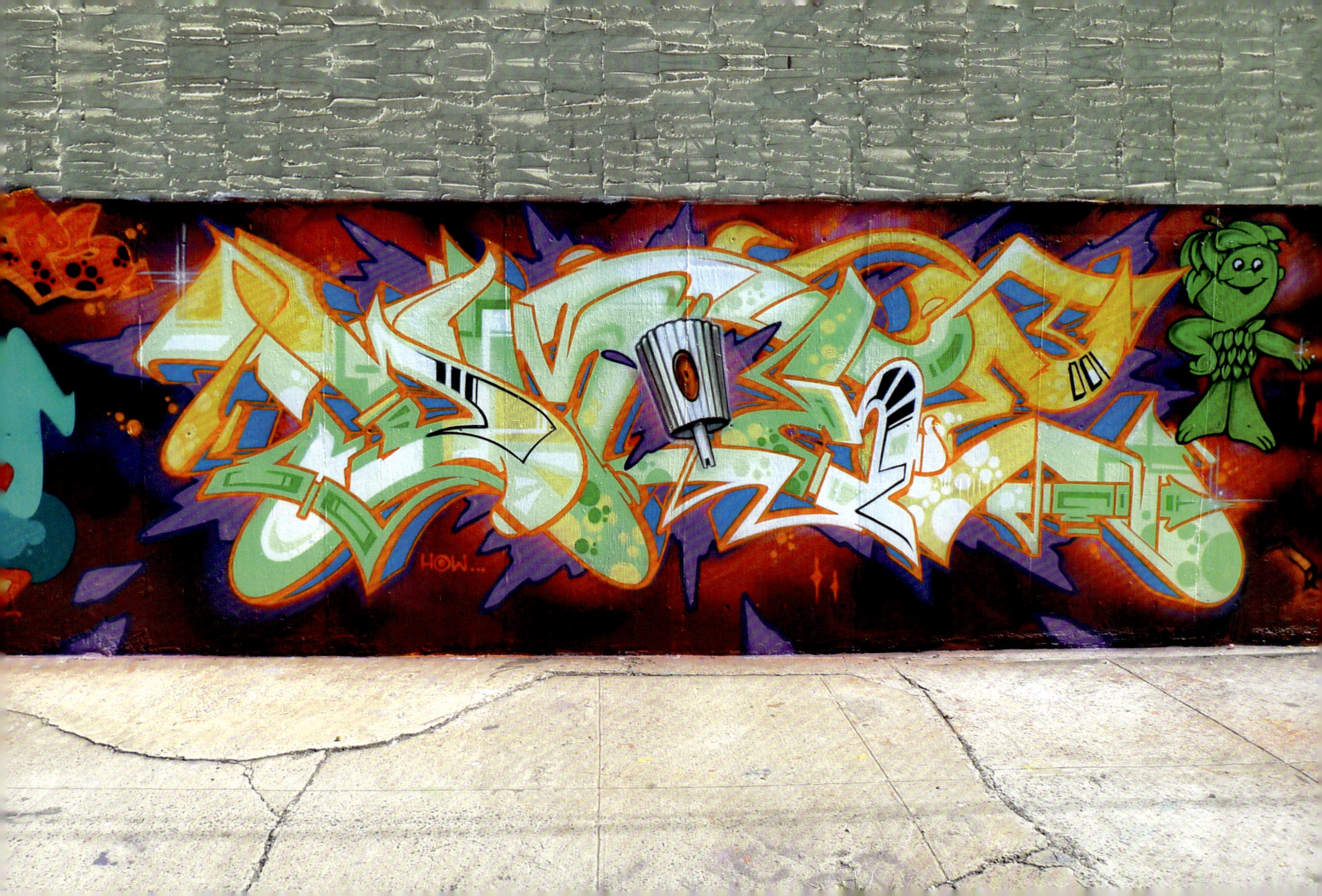
HOW...

Dolk

Dolk Lundgren, known simply as Dolk, is a popular Norwegian artist acclaimed for his satirical, striking stencil work. Stylistically similar to Banksy [see 024], Dolk gained instant popularity in 2006 with his image of Che Guevara sporting a Che T-shirt. That same year, he participated in the Nu-art Festival in Stavanger, Norway, alongside such internationally acclaimed street artists as D*face [see 082], Pobel, Eelus, Nick Walker [see 354], and Word to Mother Nature [see 360].

Dolk, who is self-taught, is particularly attracted to stencils for their accessibility. "They reach a large audience that understands what you are trying to convey," he says. "I have seen children and old people laugh at my stencil work. It is well worth every single cut." His goal is to create provocative work that passersby will look at and remember.

Dolk cites Banksy as his hero and notes among other inspirations Evola and Pisa from Germany and Sync of Australia, as well as the website Stencil Revolution (stencilrevolution.com). Devoted to creating life-size stencils in public places, Dolk sees his artwork as a gift to his city. His work has appeared on urban walls throughout the world, and in 2010 he was featured, along with M-City [see 215], in the exhibit "Eurotrash" at Brooklynite Gallery in New York City.

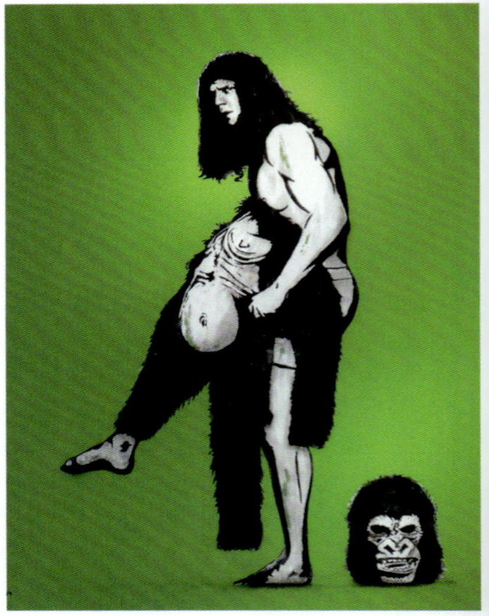

Photographs by Lois Stavsky. Brooklyn, New York, 2010.

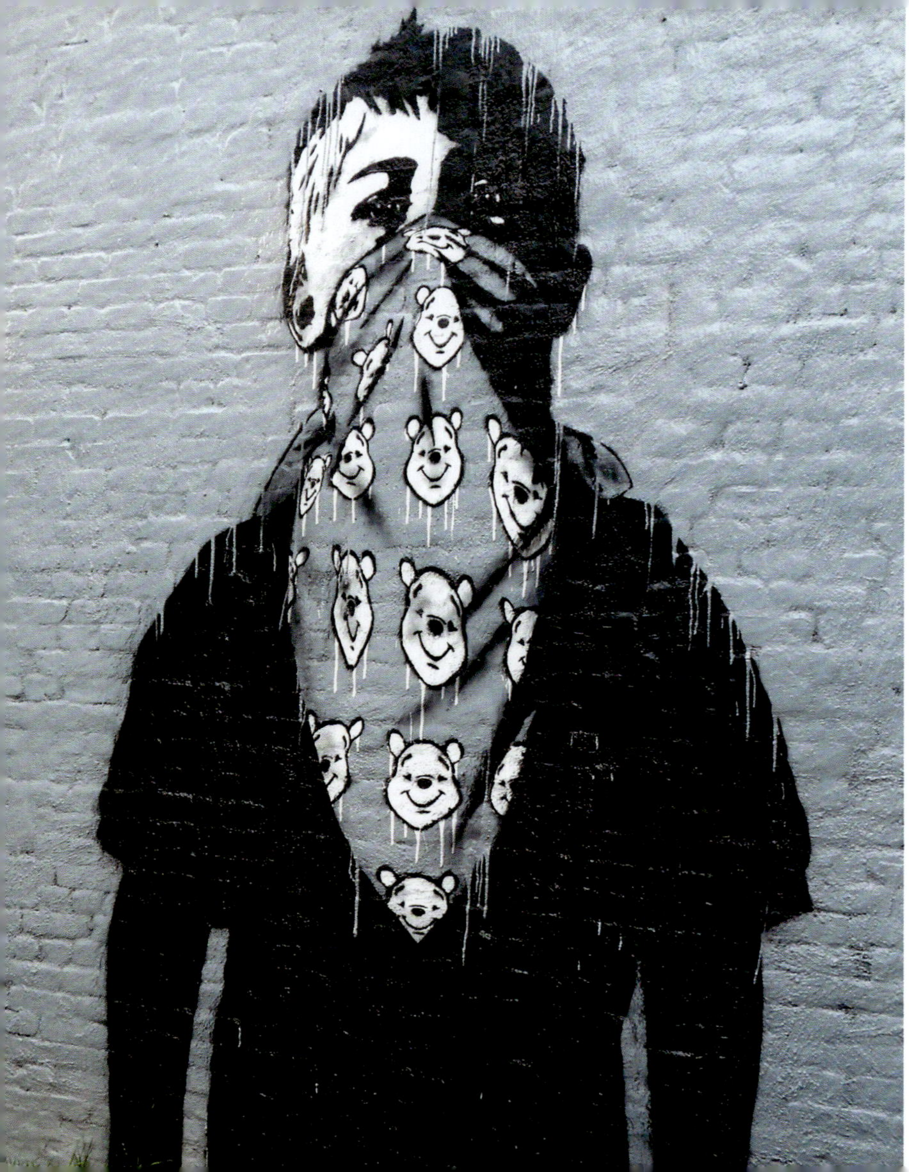

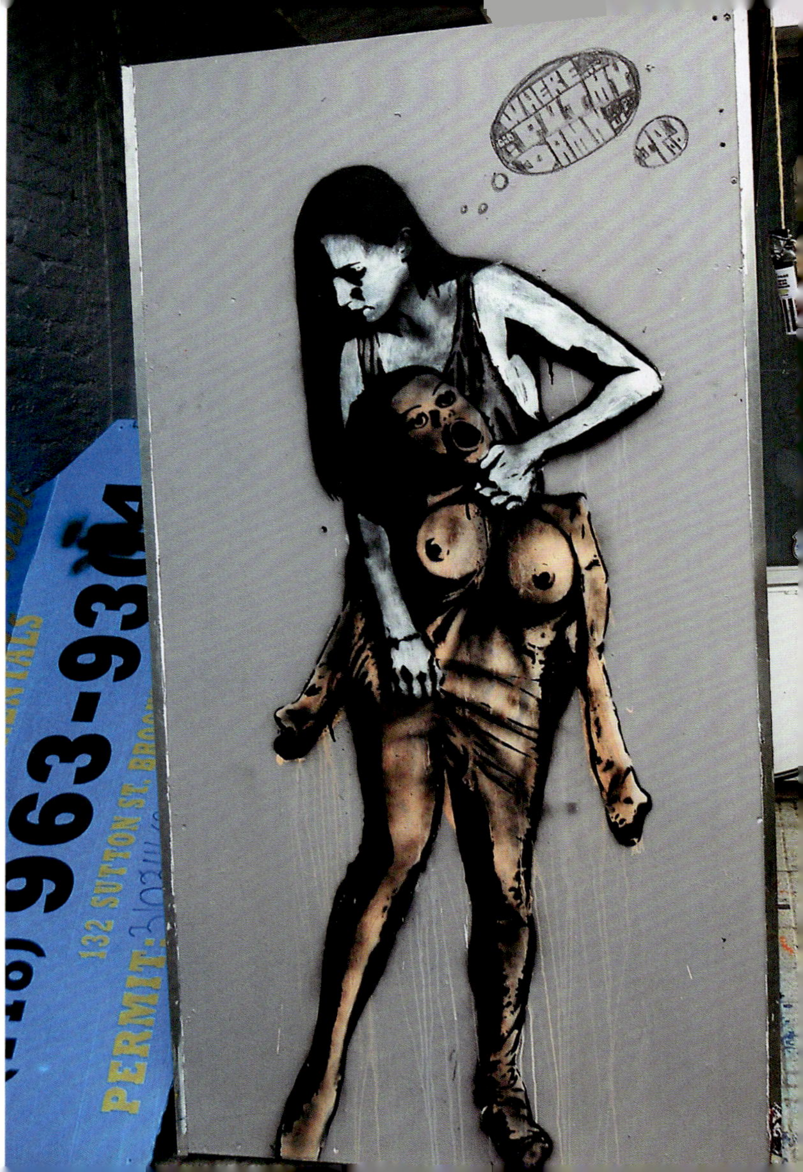
132 SUTTON ST.
PERMIT:

Don 1

The New York City Transit Authority was once made up of three different companies, each privately owned: the IRT, the BMT, and the IND. Most of the great stylemasters yearned for the IRT lines, but every now and then an iconoclast would emerge from the unlikeliest of places—with Don 1 that meant Astoria, Queens, and the BMT line.

Don 1 wrote from 1973 to 1977 while a photography major at the High School of Art and Design [see 167]. In the mid-1970s, when graffiti style was dominated by whole-cars and throw-ups, Don 1 kept doing burners, using a new style called "pipe letters." These were slender letters that spread across a train like a rubber octopus swinging arrows in every direction; his 3-Ds were thick and off to the right or left of his name. When Don 1 really wanted to throw down, he would add a character to his name as the letter "O." The Sicilian stylist formed his own version of the Mafia—the Master Administration for Incredible Art—that Fuzz, Dondi [see 097], and Zephyr [see 363] would revitalize during the 1980s.

Don 1 bombed the trains that he loved, the ones in his own backyard, and so his place in graffiti history remains relatively low-profile; however, when he did venture out to the IRT lines, not only did he hold his own, he eclipsed most of the stylemasters of the day.

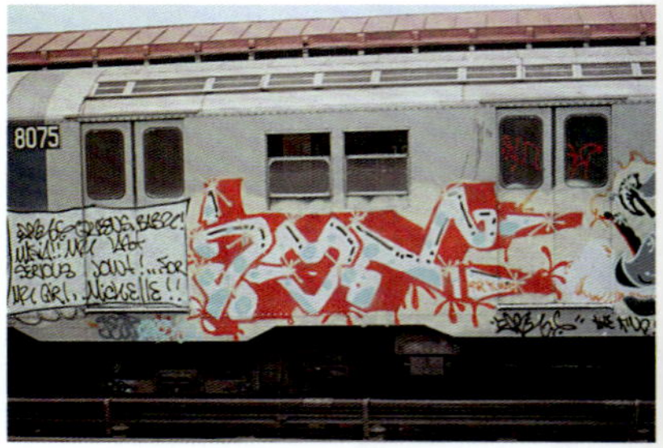

Photographs by Joseph Palletela.
Piece by Don 1 (left), with KO throw-up by Dean BYB (left corner).
New York City, 1976.
Detail: New York City, 1976.

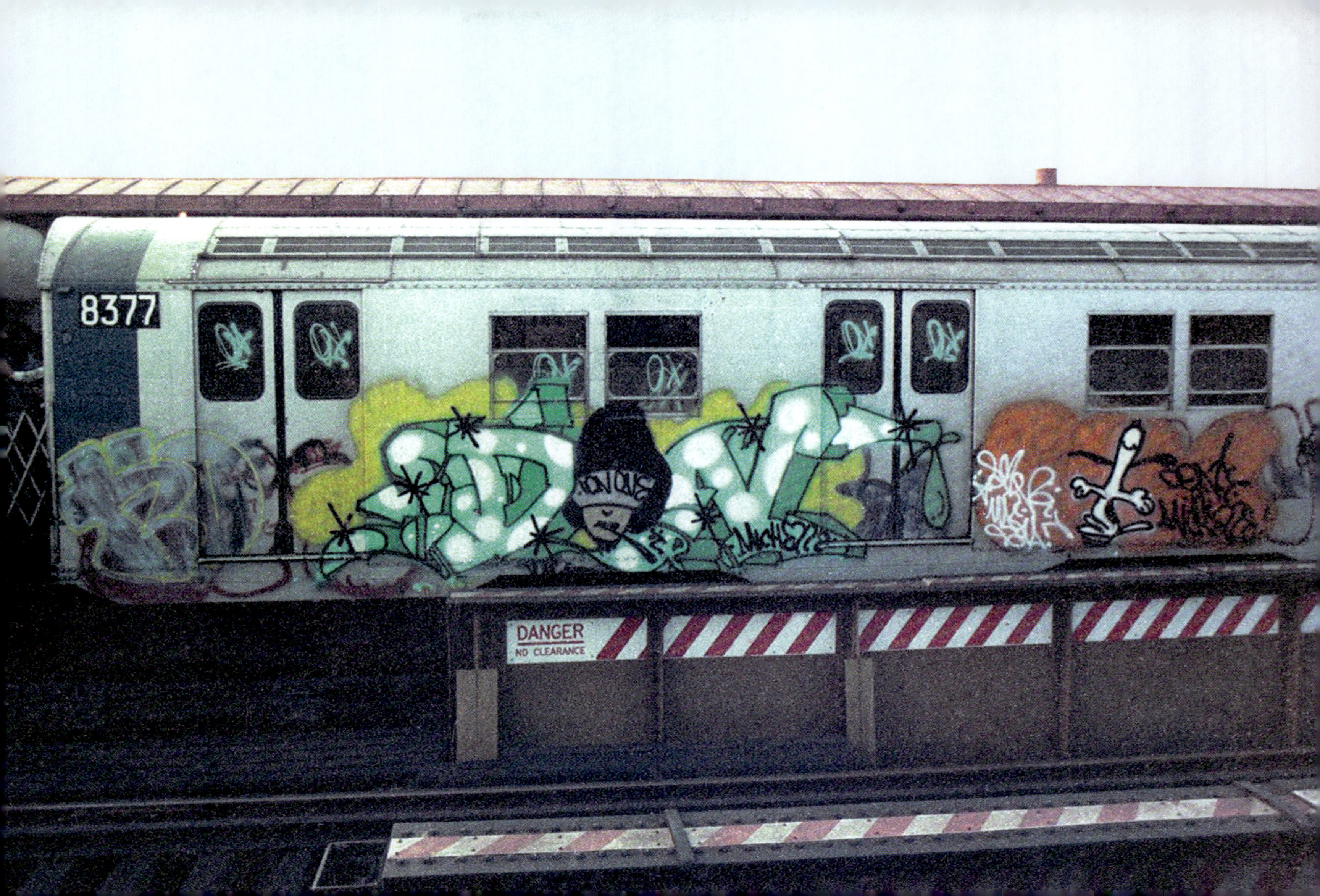
8377
DANGER
NO CLEARANCE

Dondi

Ever-smiling Donald Joseph White was born in East New York, Brooklyn, in 1961. He started writing graffiti in the mid-1970s under the alias Naco, a tag he soon abandoned in favor of the nickname his parents had given him, Dondi. He joined the TOP crew in 1977, and the following year, he formed his own crew, CIA (Crazy Insides Artists), with friends and fellow writers Crash, Doc, Duro, and Rasta (see 270). He invented many graffiti styles and techniques, and while he could paint intricate Wild Style burners that only the most dedicated graffiti enthusiasts could read, Dondi also enjoyed making clear, crisply outlined pieces and tags so his name could spread among the general public as well. In the early 1980s, Dondi appeared in the movies *Style Wars* (see 322) and *Wild Style*; was the first graffiti writer to be given a solo museum exhibition in Germany; and created graphics for the Rock Steady Crew and for Malcolm McClaren's album *Buffalo Gals*. Dondi, one of the friendliest, most popular, and most influential graffiti writers of all time, passed away on October 2, 1998. As he had said prophetically six years earlier, "Now, when I come back, it will be strictly my work speaking for me."

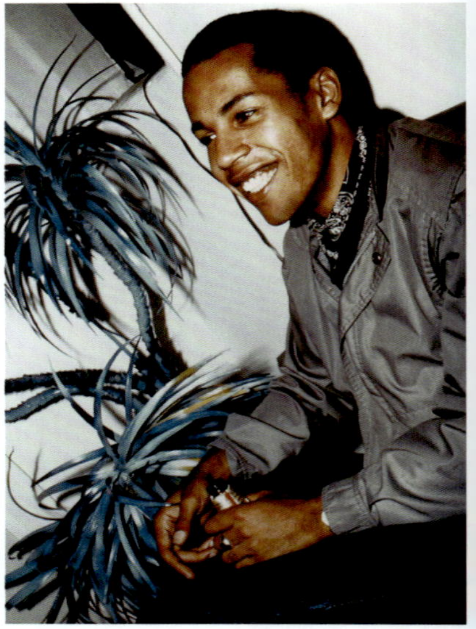

Photograph by Henry Chalfant.
New York City, 1982.
Detail: Photograph by Anita Rosenberg.
The Fun Gallery, New York City, c. 1980.

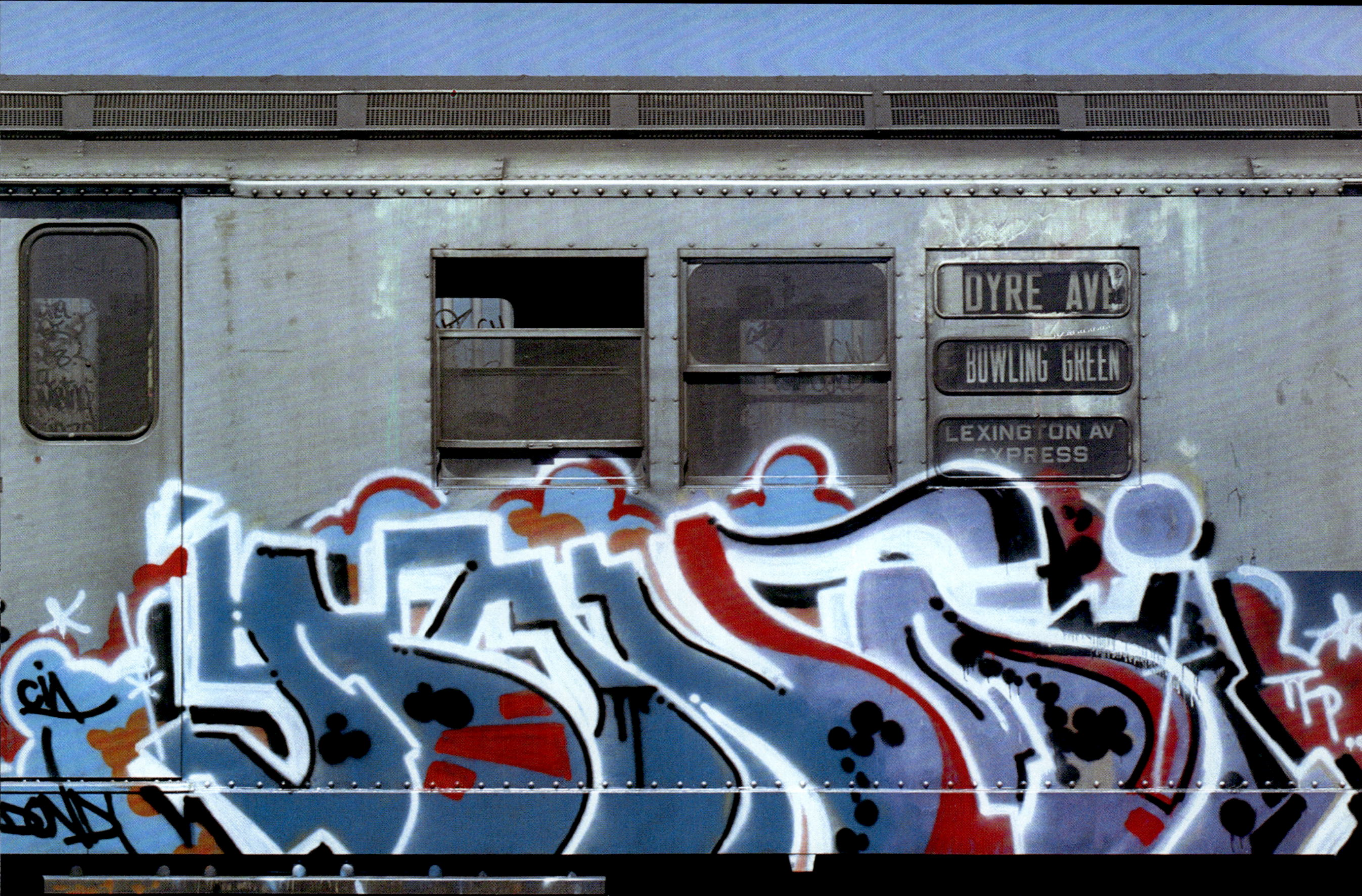
DYRE AVE
BOWLING GREEN
LEXINGTON AV
EXPRESS

Doze Green

A native of New York City, Doze Green was raised on Manhattan's Upper West Side. He started painting graffiti around 1978; one of hip-hop and graffiti's earliest staple characters, he made his way into the infamous break-dance troupe the Rock Steady Crew in the early 1980s.

After attending the High School of Art and Design (see 167) alongside graffiti artists like Lady Pink, Lil Seen, and Mare 139, Doze first exhibited his artwork at a major group show of urban artists at the infamous Fun Gallery (see 140) in 1982. He subsequently appeared in classic cinematic portraits of 1980s culture such as *Style Wars* (see 322), *Wild Style*, and *Flashdance*.

He painted with the second generation of the TC5 crew—The Cool 5—and is credited with popularizing the use of B-boy characters, often drawn in profile and wearing hats, that later became known as "mugs."

In his later years, Doze has moved into a more conceptual realm, taking his fine-art work into an exploration of "fusionistic" styles. Mixing metaphysical imagery with traditional Wild Style elements, Doze creates heady environments laden with earthy colors, and he remains best known for his intricate characters.

Doze has exhibited at the Jonathan LeVine Gallery in New York and internationally, and his paintings can be found in numerous private collections as far away as Japan and Australia. Doze now makes his home in Hawaii, where he paints and works on his farm.

Photograph by Martha Cooper. New York City, 1994.

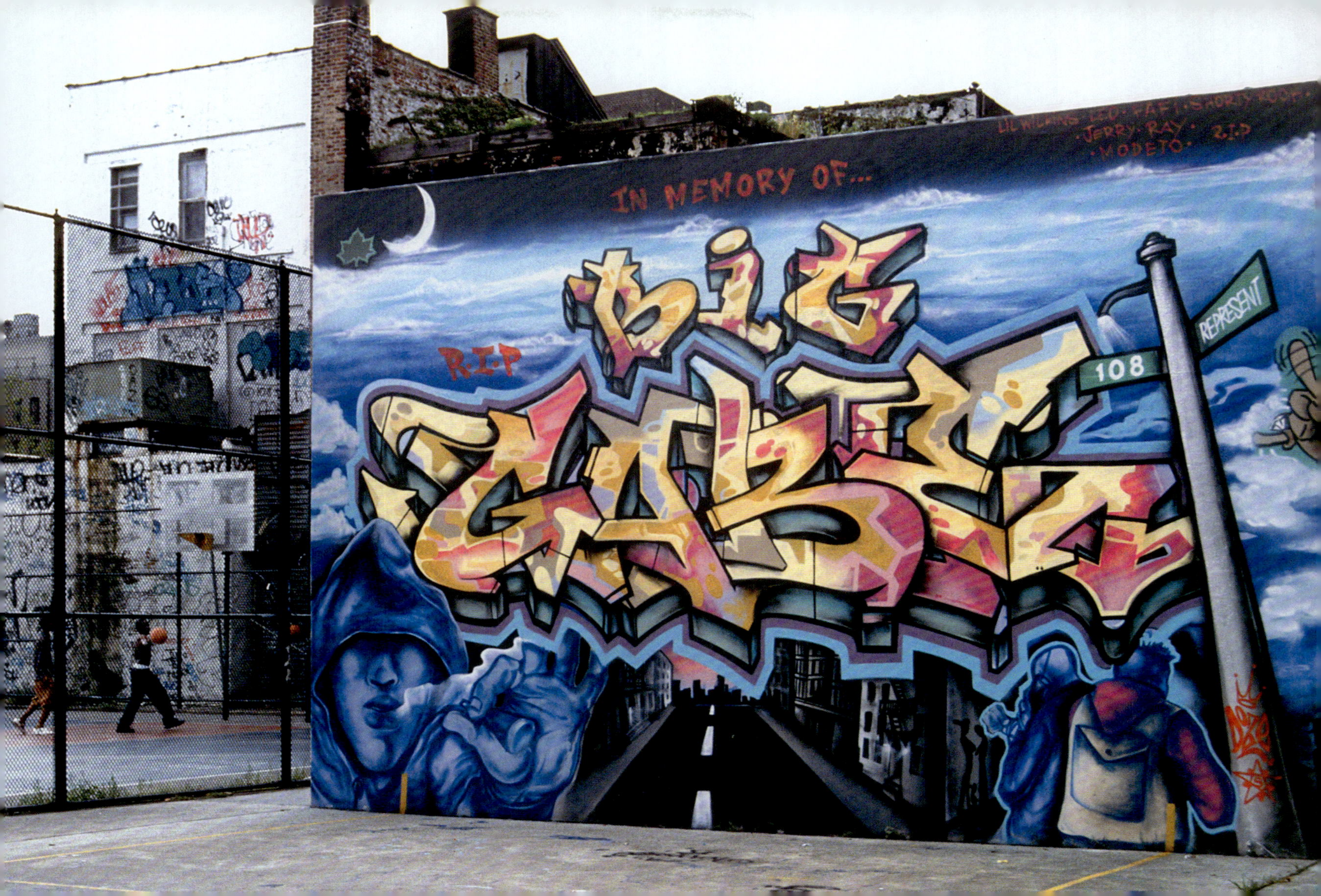
IN MEMORY OF...
R·I·P
·JERRY·RAY·
R.I.P
·MODETO·
108
REPRESENT

Dr. Sex

On May 18, 2005, in Santa Fe, New Mexico, a hypercolor wildlife mural by local artist Federico Vigil, which ran along a one-mile stretch in the city, received a rumored sixty tags bearing the name "Dr. Sex" in one midnight swoop. The damages were estimated at upward of $10,000. Local residents and law enforcement officials were up in arms, and a manhunt began. On May 26, police raided and searched the home of a twenty-five-year-old Santa Fe resident named Karta Khalsa; they confiscated 550 cans of spray paint, numerous photos of Dr. Sex graffiti pieces, and notations on scheduled news broadcasts pertaining to Dr. Sex graffiti. Khalsa was promptly arrested and charged with criminal damage to property.

Dr. Sex had previously made a name for himself in the graffiti world; he was reportedly a member of the Pigs crew and had left extensive tagging and piecework in New York City, New Jersey, Cleveland, and elsewhere in Santa Fe. Clearly, the scale of his antics and the level of risk he was taking had escalated.

Dr. Sex was tried and eventually sentenced to six months of house arrest with ten months of probation thereafter, 160 hours of community service, approximately $6,000 in restitution fines for cleanup costs, and mandatory counseling in anger management.

Throw-ups by Hour (left) and Dr. Sex.
Photograph by Ernie Paneccioli.
Chinatown, New York City, 2007.

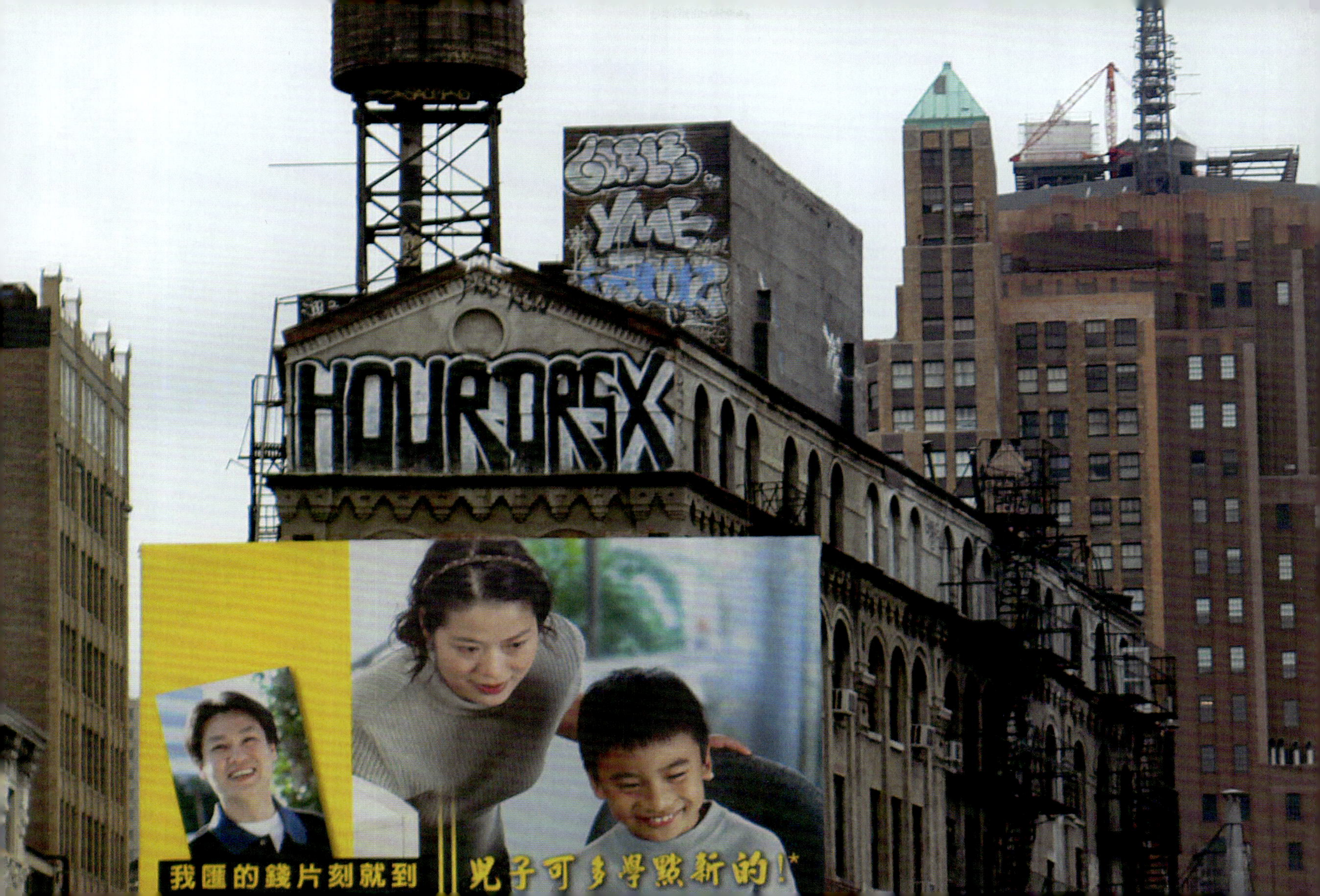
我匯的錢片刻就到
兒子可多學點新的！*

Duster

Duster grew up in a different corner of the same Bronx neighborhood as Seen UA (United Artists). They didn't know each other, but they both knew their way to the #6 yard: Seen, his brother Mad, and their friends began to spot Duster pieces on what they considered to be *their* line. Possessive and territorial, Seen's group decided they'd beat up Duster and boot him off the line when they caught him, but when Duster finally bumped heads with Seen and his cronies, cooler heads prevailed, and Seen brought Duster into the fold. Seen saw potential in Duster, and he gave him some style during his early years, but Duster quickly began to forge his own identity. One of the five original members of United Artists, Duster executed his greatest body of work from 1980 to 1983, mainly on the #6 line. Duster soon evolved into one of the greatest writers of all time, developing a fluidity and mastery of letter connections that was simultaneously seamless and symmetrical. A brilliant color sense and a drug-fueled imagination that produced an army of original characters—including blond-haired B-boys and snarling trains—made his work a perfect target for the lenses of Martha Cooper and Henry Chalfant. Nomadic and adventurous, Duster often ventured to other subway lines, sometimes by himself or, on occasion, with writers as diverse as Dez and Zephyr (see 363).

Duster rode the gallery-scene wave in the early 1980s, selling paintings to renowned art collector Dolores Neumann, as well as participating in early group shows in prestigious galleries. In the mid-1980s, Duster moved to California, where he made a living as a tattoo artist. Duster continues to paint, and in December 2010, he had his first solo show at the London Miles Gallery.

Artwork by Duster; *Dana 123* piece (at right) by Seen. Photograph by Henry Chalfant. New York City, 1984.

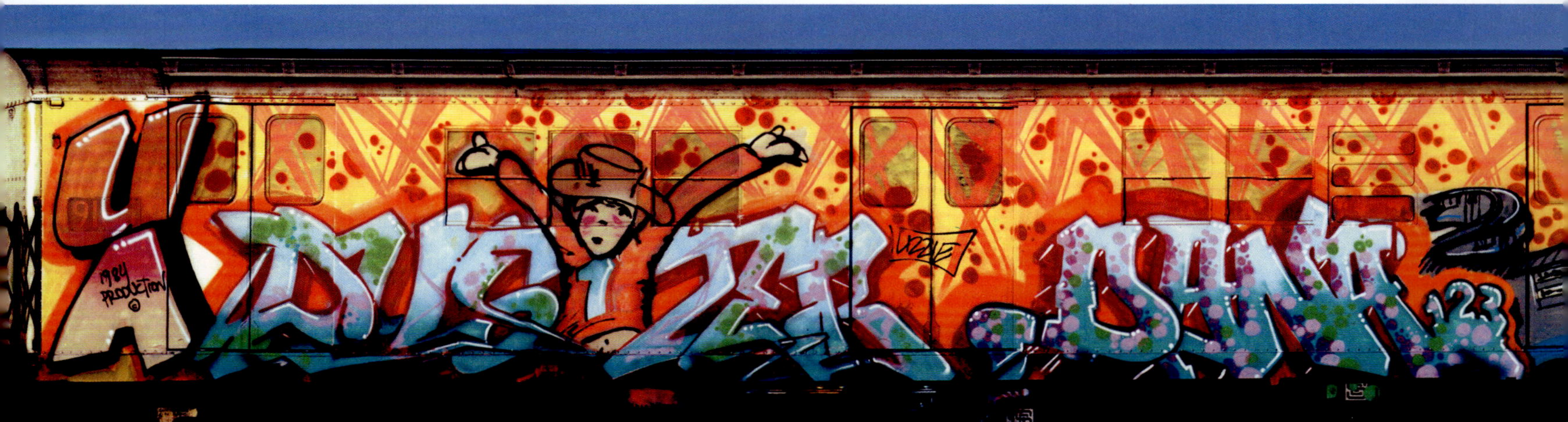
1984
PRODUCTION
©

Earsnot

Earsnot was one of the founding members of the legendary Irak crew; his tags, antics, and attitude have changed the public face of contemporary graffiti. As a featured cast member in the 2008 documentary *Infamy*, Earsnot elaborates on his irresistible appetite for stealing things and goes into great detail about being an openly gay graffiti artist—an extreme rarity. A burly figure, Earsnot stands well over six feet tall and is generally seen with a mouthful of gold teeth. Loud, brash, obnoxious, and notoriously obsessed with proliferating his comical moniker, Earsnot makes it clear that if you are uncomfortable with his sexuality, it makes absolutely no difference to him, and you should keep it to yourself. After severely beating a rival graffiti artist, Earsnot allegedly boasted, "Now go and tell your friends you got y'ass kicked by a homo."

A longtime best friend of artist Dash Snow (see 308), one of Irak's cofounders, as well as photographer Ryan McGinley, Earsnot appears in many images associated with pivotal moments in downtown culture from the first decade of the 2000s, including a Polaroid taken by Snow of McGinley snorting cocaine off Earsnot's erect penis.

Earsnot has avoided any significant participation in the fine-art world, and to this day his tags and Irak stickers can be seen littered around downtown New York.

Photograph by Ray Mock.
New York City, 2010.

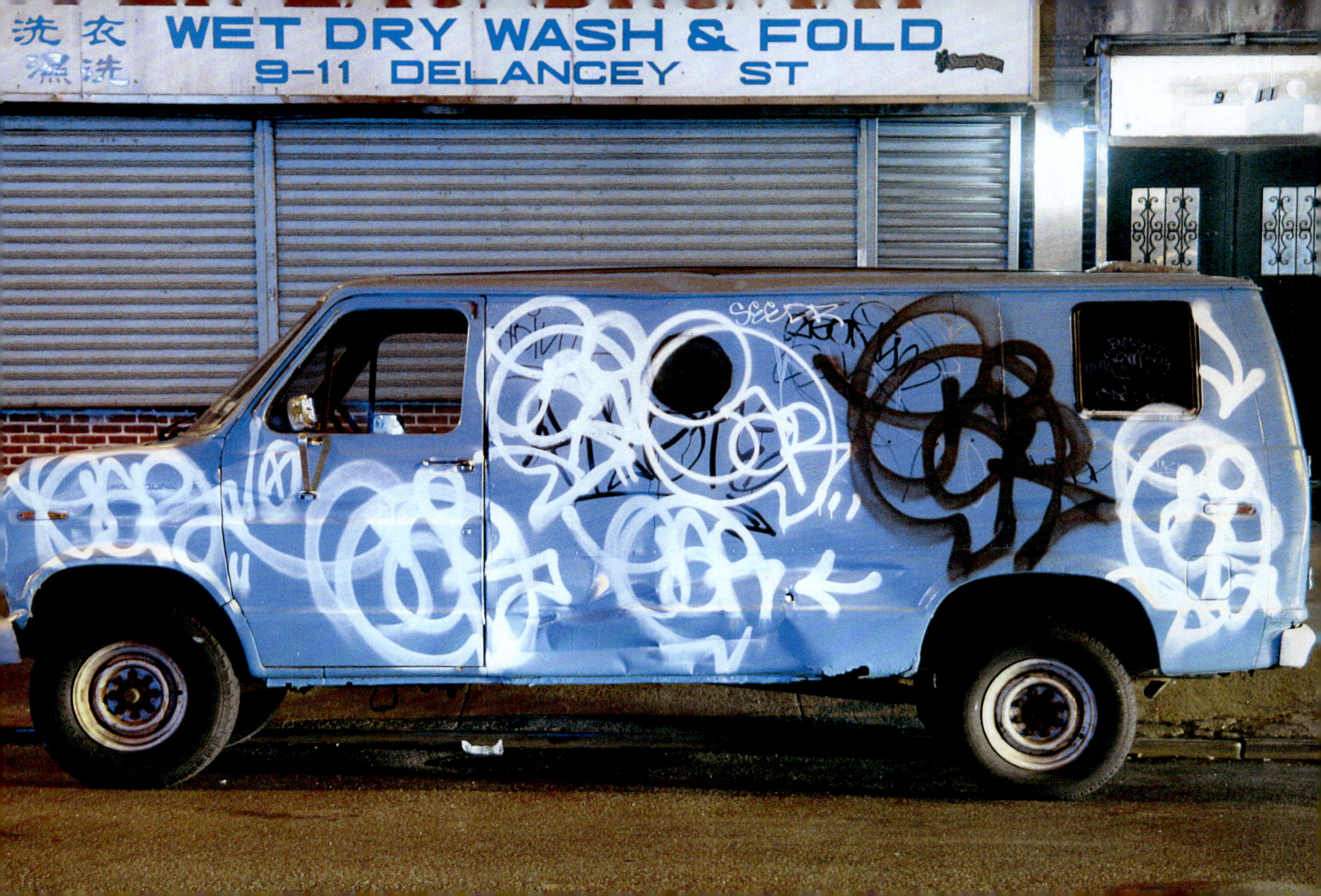
洗衣
濕洗
WET DRY WASH & FOLD
9-11 DELANCEY ST

East Village Wall

At once art and artifact, New York City's East Village Wall is no simple commission, but rather an extended organic expression of a creative community at its zenith. The wall is a testament to heady times when visual artists, musicians, filmmakers, writers, designers, and performers commingled and exchanged ideas. The wall has been legendary in the downtown scene for generations, and the untimely deaths of many its prime participants have only added to its mythic aura.

There is much history and innumerable anecdotes that could be written about the East Village Wall, but what is perhaps most significant is the story of how a modest tenement apartment, in close proximity to the galleries and off-the-map clubs of the East Village, became a sanctuary for a generation of important young artists whose ideas and styles would eventually change the world.

Many have wanted to get up on the wall over the years, but as a curatorial process of aesthetic value and earned respect, few were invited. Such exclusivity has led to its status as a subcultural nexus, where the two most important movements of the late twentieth century—punk rock and hip-hop—met; the East Village Wall is a treasure of immeasurable importance.

Photographs by Rainer Hosch.
New York City, 1981–1997.

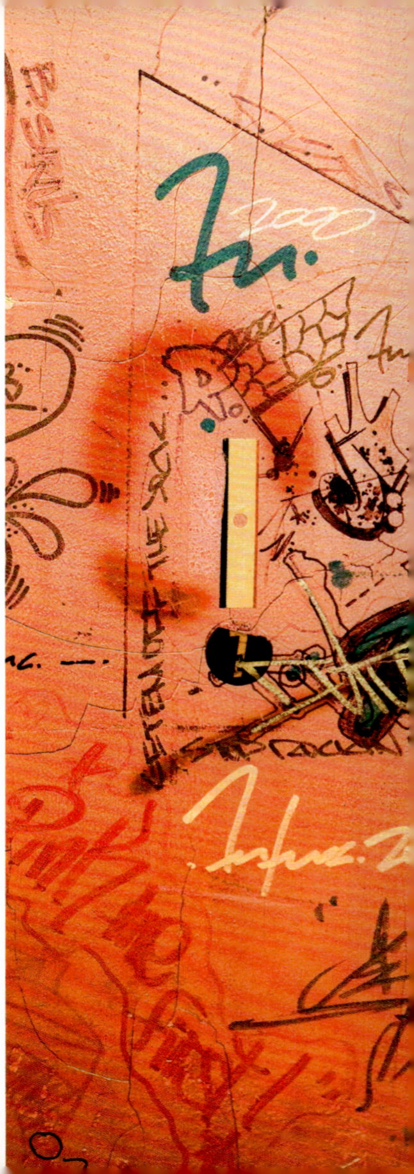

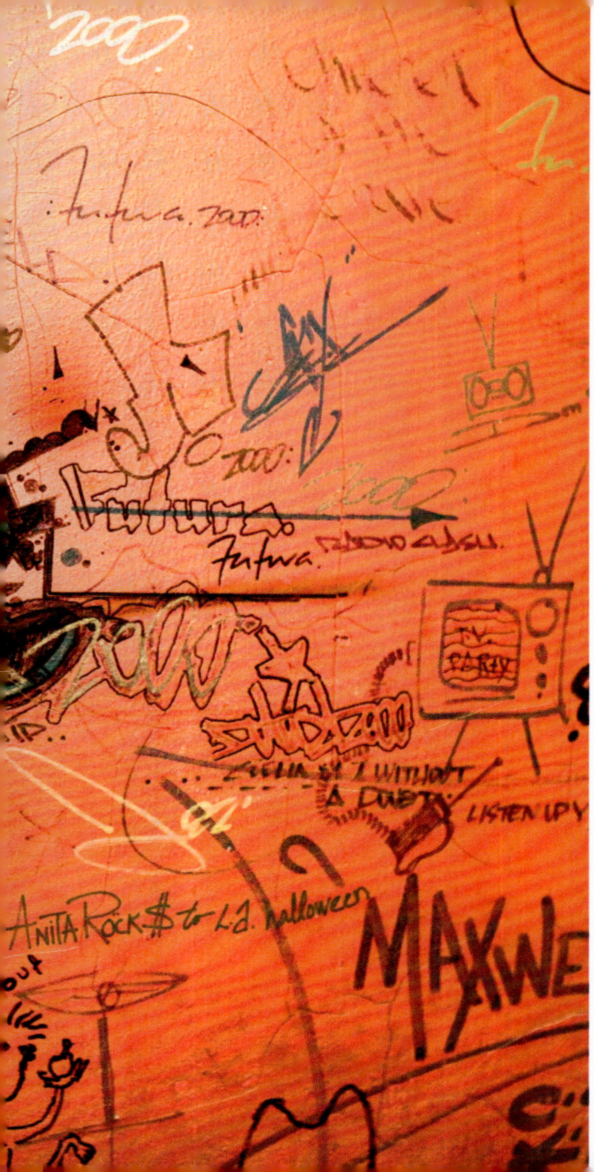

Futura 2000
Futura
LISTEN UP
Anita Rock$ to L.A. halloween
MAXWE

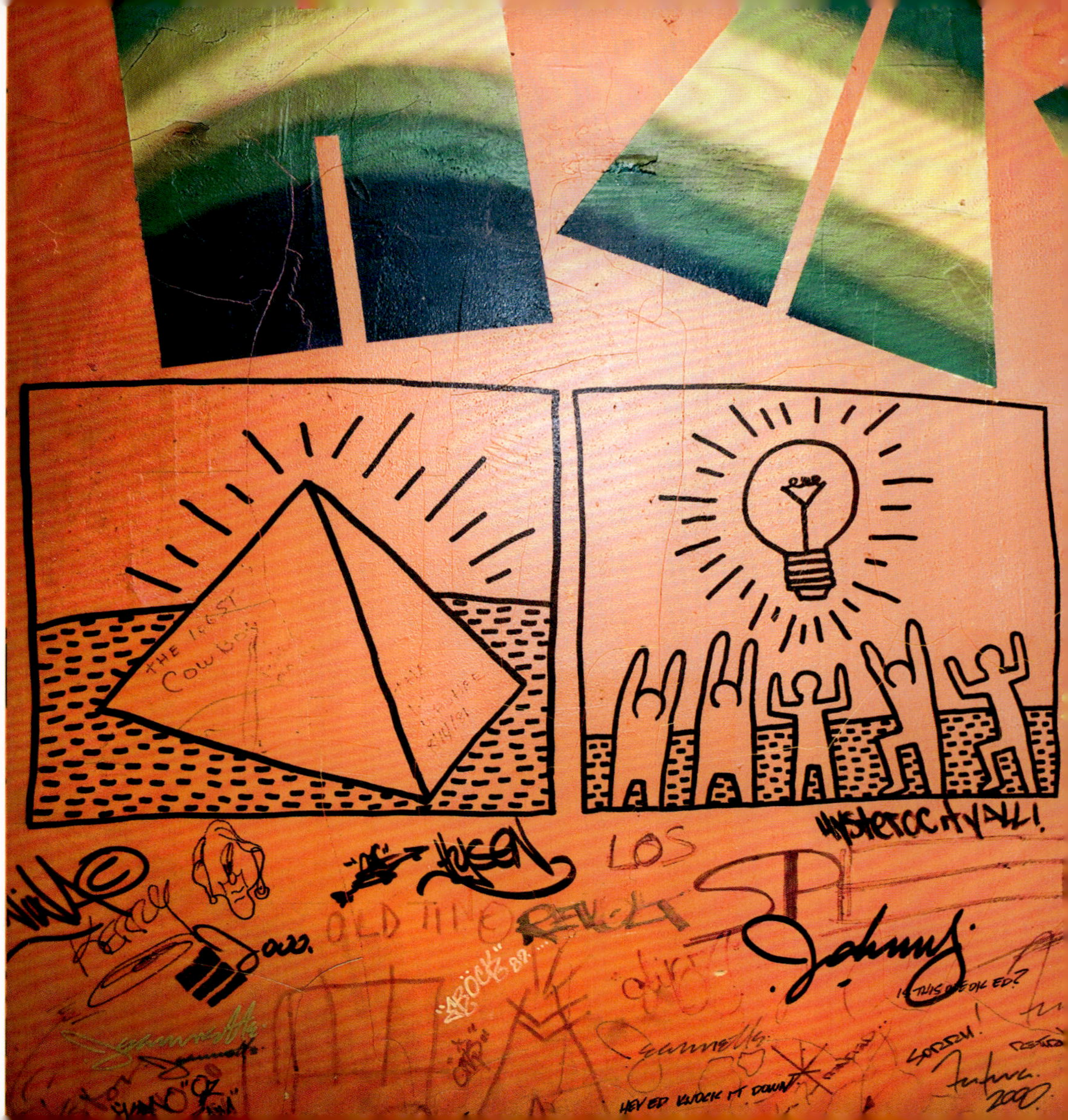

LOS
OLD TIME
Johnny
Futura 2000

Eaz

After a few false starts, Eaz began his real writing career in 1994, while he was growing up in New Jersey. As his painting matured, he hooked up with the FX crew, painting with Ces and Per. It was with FX that he became an artist—and as he learned from them, they certainly gleaned some knowledge as well.

Eaz left the crew at its peak and ventured out on his own. He wanted to paint large solo murals—for better or worse, he wanted his visions to appear on the wall unencumbered. The Eaz murals are often dark, but with highly rendered characters that also reflect his humor. Writers around the world are drawn to his skillfully painted characters and consider them some of the best around, but Eaz isn't hearing it; for Eaz, any art-school kid can do characters. For him, it's all about the letters; if you don't have style, and aren't about advancing style, then you're missing the point of graffiti.

Aware of the vanishing apprenticeship system in graffiti, Eaz set about making a DVD, which he released in 2005, that would serve as a graffiti primer. Kids around the world could learn the trade secrets of big-time writers for $25. He followed the first one with a DVD devoted to style and the art of lettering. Only time will tell whether Eaz the painter or Eaz the filmmaker had, or will have, greater impact on the culture.

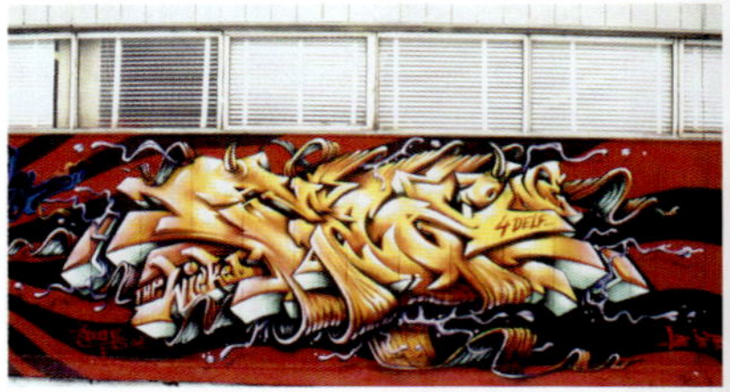

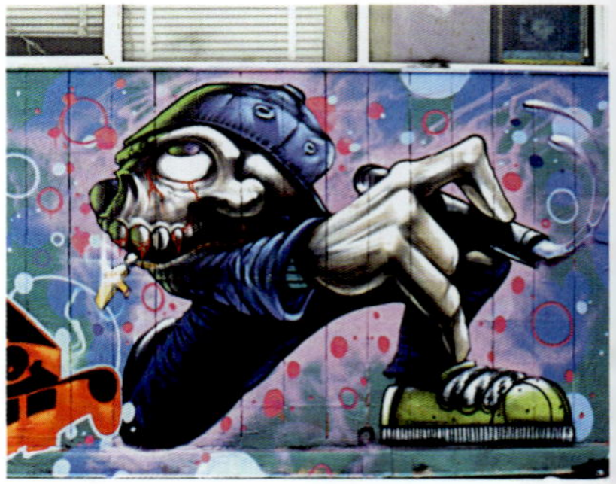

Photograph by Ces One. Bronx, New York, 2007.
Character by Eaz; *Wish* piece by Ces One.
Details: Photographs by Ces One. Bronx, New York.

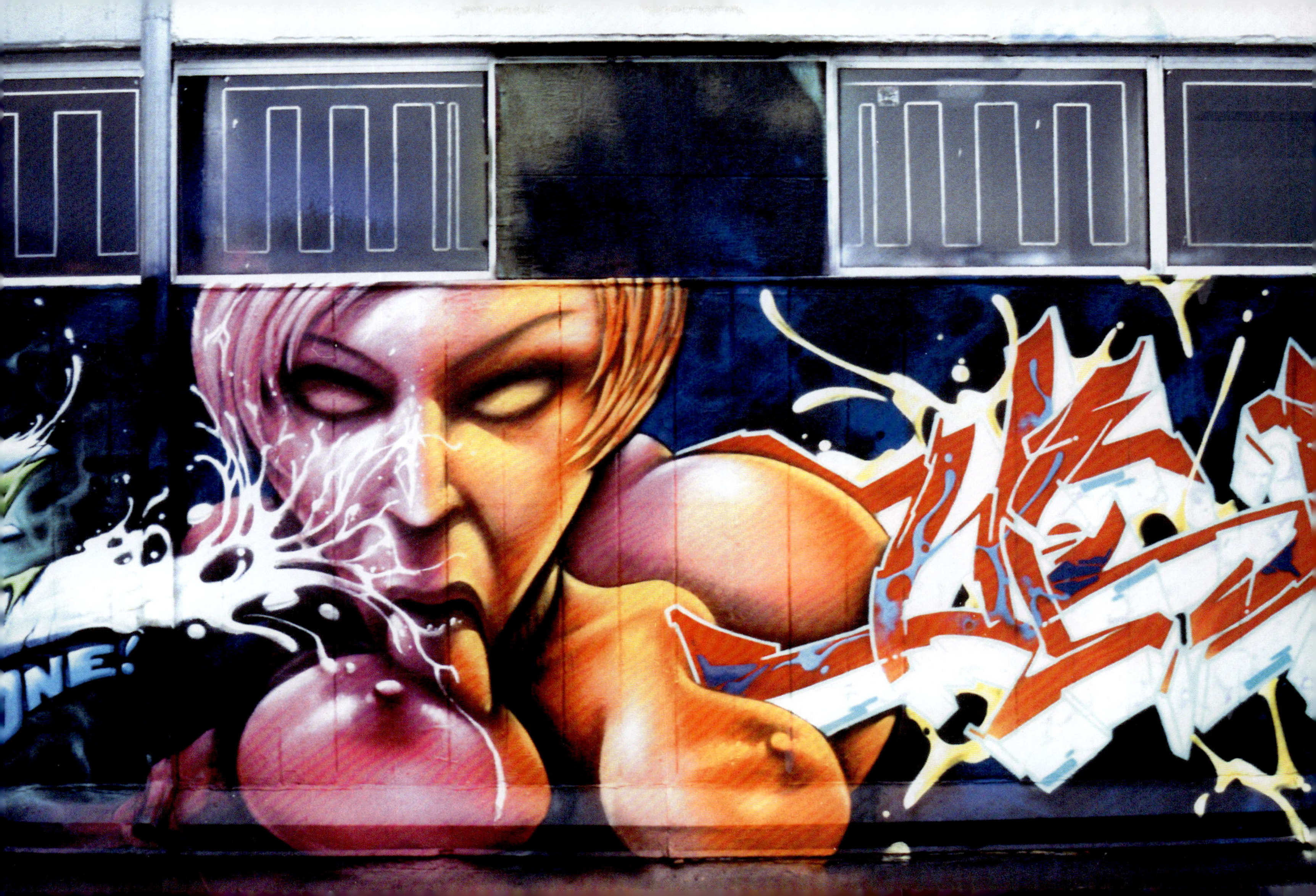
ONE!

Eine

Ben Flynn, better known as Eine, was a prolific graffiti artist before he ever considered the crossover into what is now known as street art, and eventually into commercial art. Born in 1970, Eine took London by storm in the late 1980s and early 1990s, proliferating his pieces and stickers. Eventually, he began to produce custom clothing featuring his lettering, and he moved into an exploration of screen printing.

In the late 1990s and early 2000s, Eine entered into a partnership with then-rising street-art star Banksy [see 024], and he was one of the early partners in a screen-printing outfit called Pictures On Walls [POW], one of the first companies to offer street artists' work in the form of high-quality, limited-edition screen prints.

POW was an instant success, and Eine was inspired by the possibility he saw for limitless growth and financial success in commercial work. So he returned to his graffiti roots, beginning what would become his best-known project to date: his shutter alphabet series.

Later in the decade, Eine painted single, stylized, graphic letters on roll-down storefront gates. Instantly recognizable and visible from blocks away, the pieces shot him to international recognition. Eine soon began showing his alphabet series, in hand-painted and screen-printed form, on the walls of street-art galleries all over the world.

**Photograph by Luna Park.
London, 2009.**

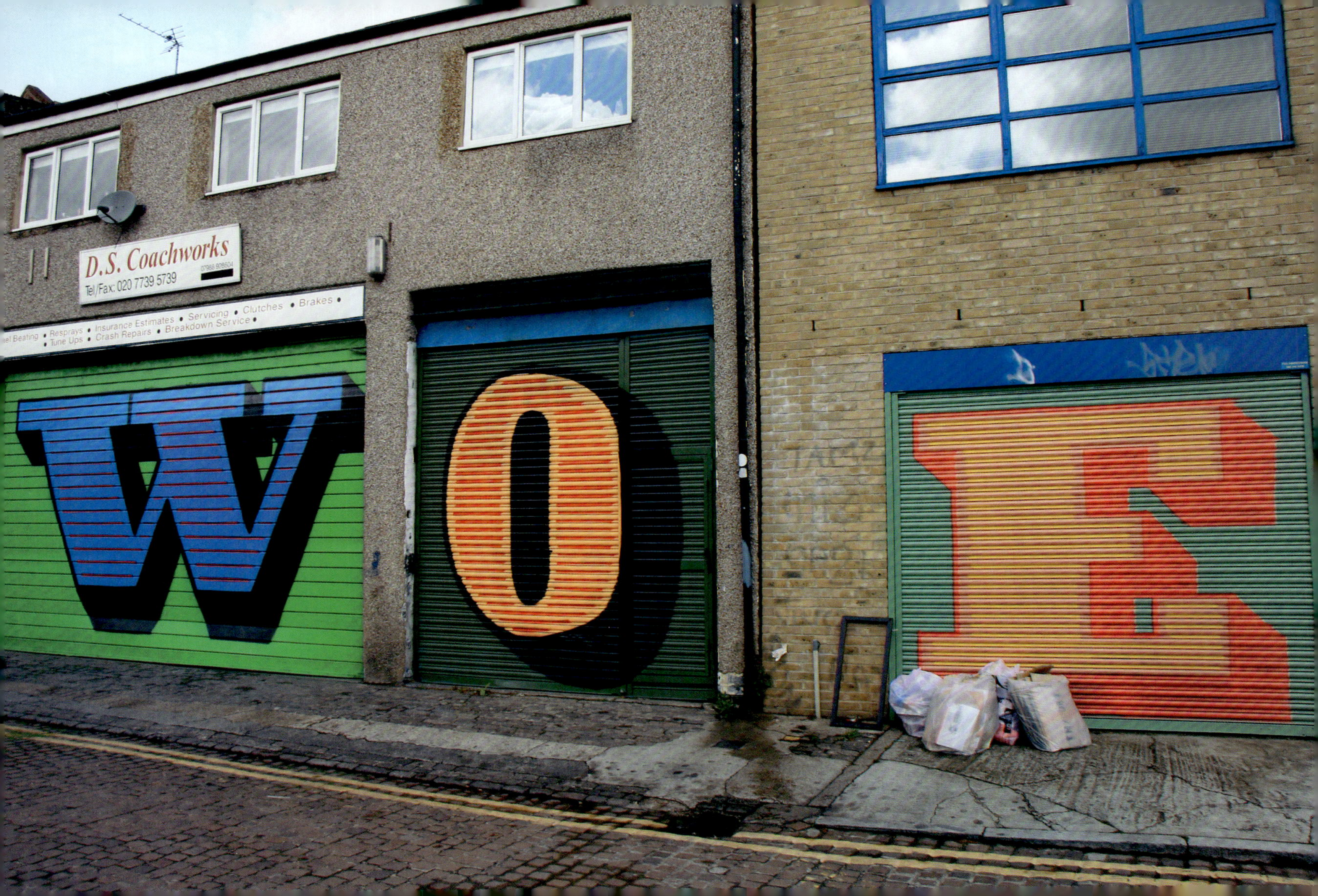
D.S. Coachworks
Tel/Fax: 020 7739 5739
Resprays • Tune Ups • Insurance Estimates • Crash Repairs • Servicing • Breakdown Service • Clutches • Brakes •
W
O

El Bocho

Known for the tape art, posters, cutouts, and tiles that he pastes onto walls in Berlin and Hamburg, El Bocho has been creating art on the streets since 1997. Most keenly identified with his character-based images (particularly Little Lucy, who bullies and massacres cats), he has become one of Germany's most celebrated street artists.

As a member of the collective known as Wallbreakers, El Bocho also takes part in a variety of street-art activities designed to break down walls and barriers and prevent the construction of new ones. In 2009, as part of its "Go Beyond Borders Tape Art Project," CNN commissioned El Bocho to create artwork commemorating the twentieth anniversary of the fall of the Berlin Wall. In executing this project, El Bocho used more than forty thousand yards of tape to re-create scenes that had transpired at the wall.

Although his work is increasingly featured in galleries worldwide, from São Paulo to London, El Bocho is more interested in sharing his art and communicating with those folks who don't visit galleries. The street remains his favorite venue. His recent use of fire hoses to create street art has inspired the design of bags created from fire hoses that are marketed as cutting-edge fashion.

Photographs by Vincent Cornelli.
Berlin, Germany, 2009.

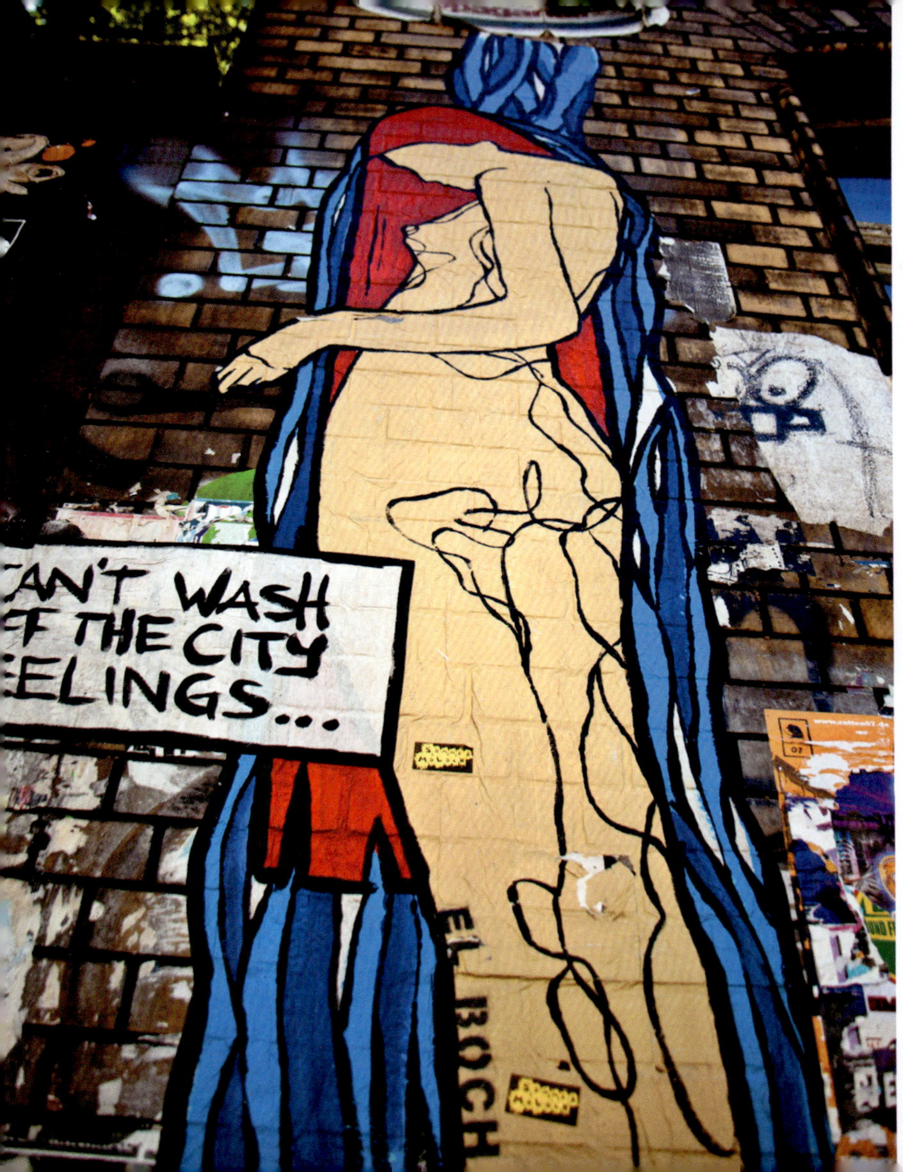
AN'T WASH
F THE CITY
ELINGS...
EL BOCH

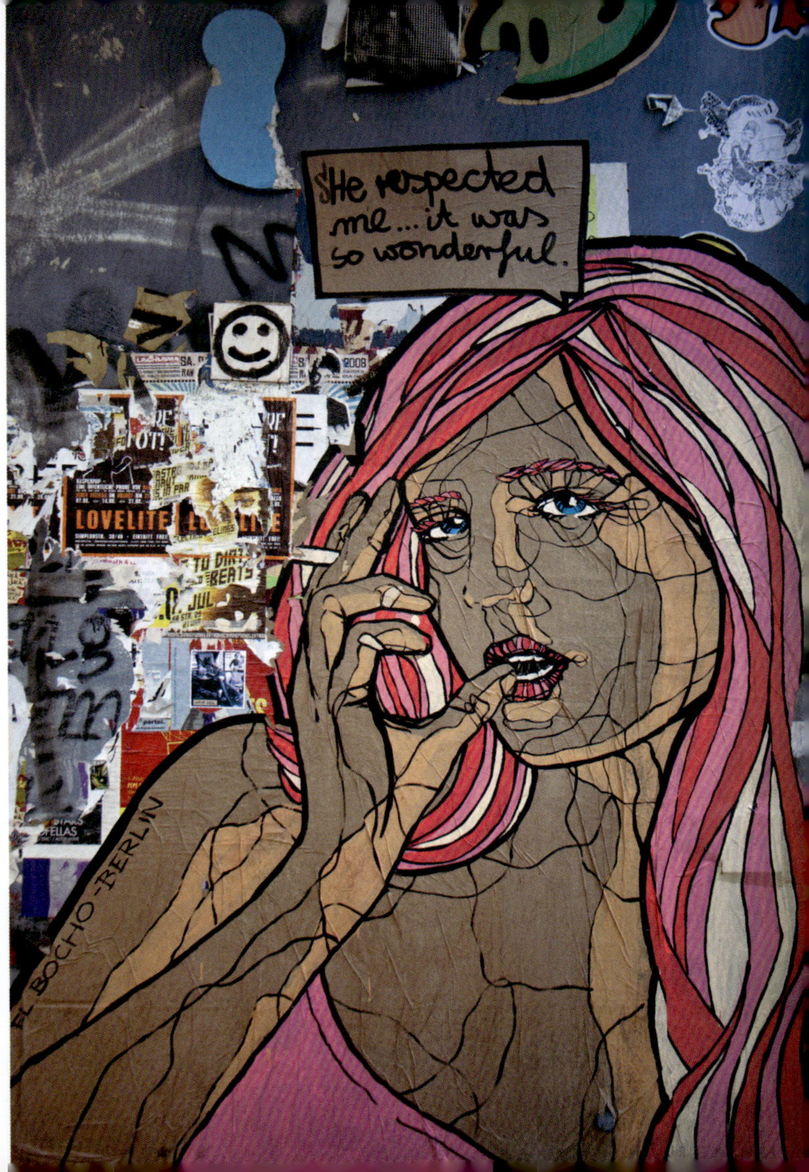
SHe respected me... it was so wonderful.
LOVELITE
EL BOCHO-BERLIN

Elbow Toe

Brian Adam Douglas, aka Elbow Toe, is a Brooklyn street artist who found art first and the street second. He attended art school but made his living as a computer programmer, all the while pining to be a fine artist; he made art in his spare time but had no audience outside of friends and family.

A friend at work gave him a book on the street artist Neck Face (see 239); Douglas's adopted name, Elbow Toe, was a spoof on this, but it stuck. Elbow Toe started out drawing a configuration of an elbow and a toe, but later experimented with several tried-and-true street-art motifs, including the Cost and Revs loose-leaf paper wheatpaste technique.

He wrote sayings with a grease stick. It was his discovery of Swoon's (see 329) exquisite wheatpaste figures that made him realize he could place highly skilled artworks in public spaces.

Elbow Toe's latest works are silky collages that are so stylized they appear to be painted onto the walls on which he places them. His characters are often twisting in unusual movement. The abandoned and decrepit sites he seeks out and the inevitable decaying of his work are designed to evoke complicated feelings of nostalgia.

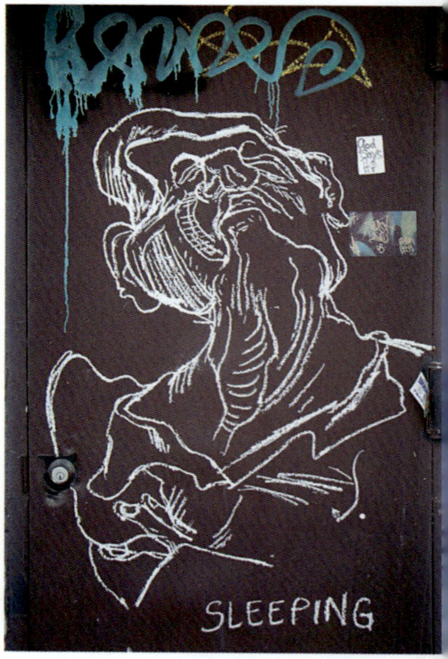

**Photograph by Luna Park.
Brooklyn, New York, 2009.
Detail: Photograph by Vincent Cornelli.
Brooklyn, New York, 2009.**

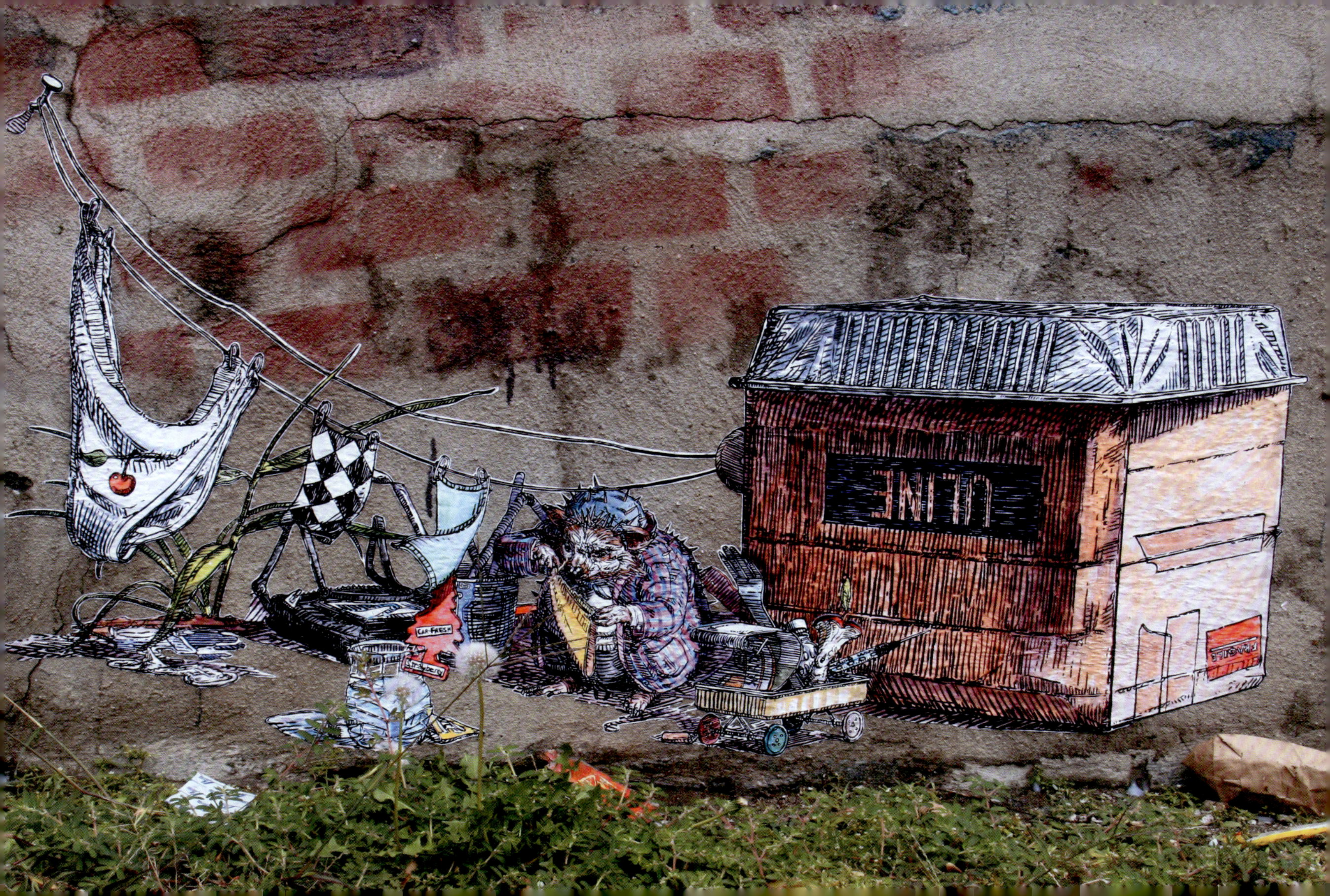

El Celso

In the vast sea of artists emerging from New York City's overpopulated streets, it is easy to lose track of the names that don't lobby for the spotlight. Often, dedication and perseverance are the only means of separating the weekend warriors from the lifers. The artist known as El Celso has shown his tried-and-true dedication to disseminating ephemeral public art, with almost a decade of active duty in the field.

El Celso was one of the founding members of New York's Endless Love Crew, a ragtag gang of street artists who originated the collaborative mash-up style, in which numerous artists layer color, characters, letters, and paintings on top of each other. The ELC was known for hosting invitational painting parties, during which numerous large sheets of paper would be collaborated on at one time, creating mash-up pieces that were later wheatpasted onto the streets.

El Celso, now based in Brooklyn, is known for his simplistic, duotone line-drawing paintings of women with no eyeballs. He continues to create work for the streets and has also made the crossover into exhibiting indoors, at Brooklyn's Factory Fresh and numerous other venues.

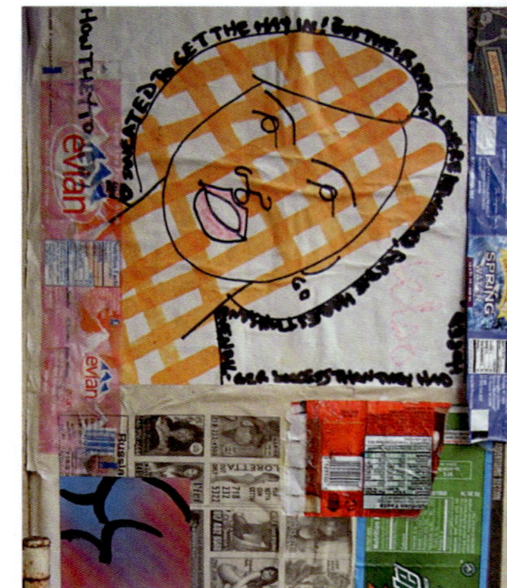

Photographs by Becki Fuller.
Right: New York City, 2007.
Far right: Brooklyn, New York, 2008.
Detail: New York City, 2007.

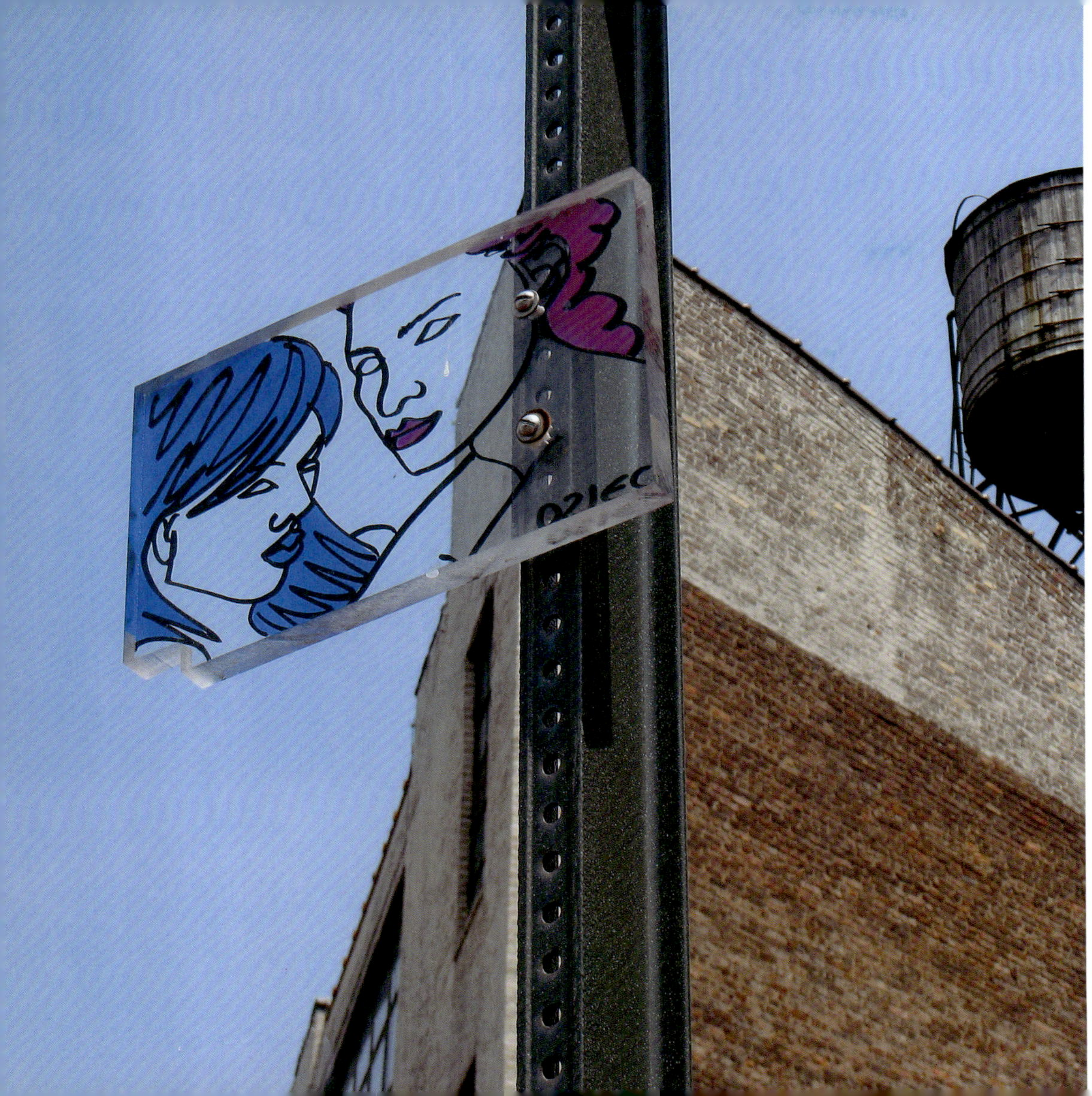

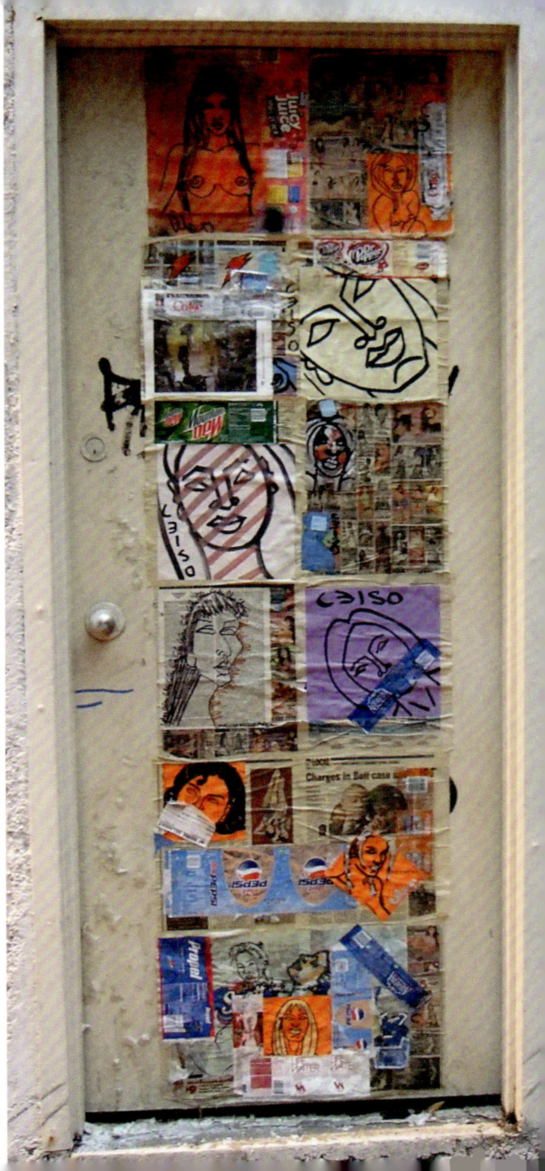

El Gato Chimney

El Gato Chimney started his career on the streets of New York in 1996. An autodidactic artist, he got involved with the local hip-hop scene and took to graffiti at the early age of fifteen. His passion for painting, steampunk culture, and surrealism led him to participate in the street-art culture he saw flourishing around him. With its vivid palette and dreamy landscapes, El Gato's world appears as one where nothing is as it seems—a land of flying tea pots, abandoned carnivals, and a cotton candy smell that seems to melt over them. On canvas or concrete, the universe he creates is layered and detailed.

Inspired by local community art leaders like Microbo and Bo130, El Gato's electric and precise visual language soon earned attention from a continuing list of international galleries and media.

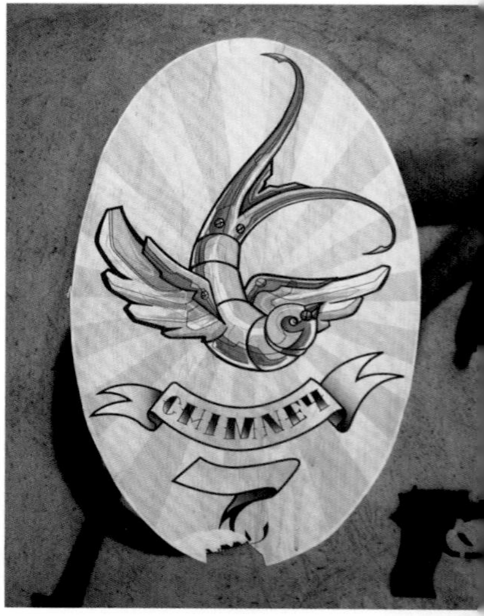

Photographs courtesy of El Gato Chimney.

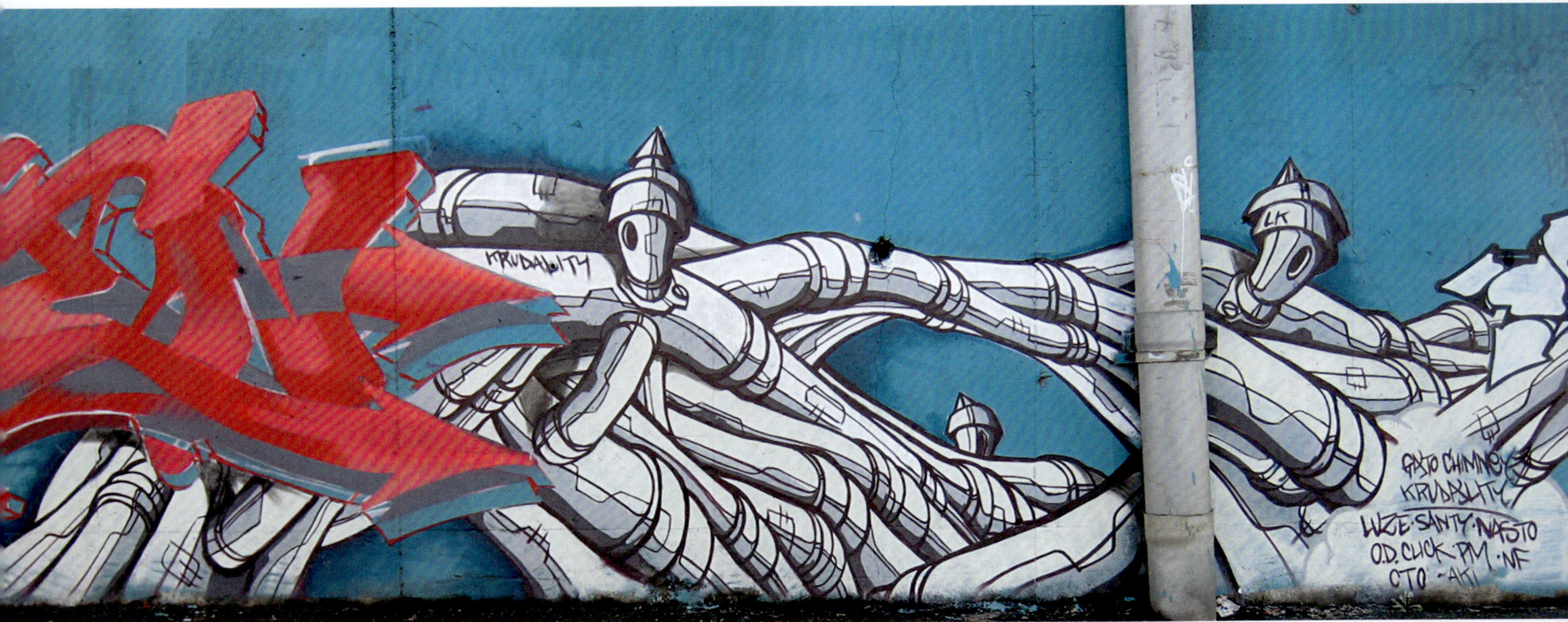
KRUDALITY
GASTO CHIMNEY
KRUDALITY
LUZE·SANTY·NASTO
O.D. CLICK·PM·NF
CTO·AKI

David Ellis

David Ellis (aka Skwerm) was born and raised in Raleigh, North Carolina, in 1971. In 1994, he attended Cooper Union, New York's scholarship-based fine-arts college. One of the most respected names in urban art, David Ellis has become renowned for his intensely prolific outpouring of paintings and mural works, as well as his role as spearhead and founder of the legendary, ephemeral mural collaboration project the Barnstormers (see 025).

Although he is best known for his work with paintbrushes and rollers, Ellis is profoundly inspired by music. Born into a family immersed in musicality, he was influenced by music at a very early age. Ellis has made numerous kinetic sculptures involving music and sound, and he often invites musicians to play while he creates his motion paintings, which can involve painting and repainting a certain object in a public space for several days. He works directly on a wall, generally improvising the painting, with onlookers sharing his process.

Ellis has exhibited internationally, including at Deitch Projects in New York, New Image Art in Los Angeles, and Fifty24SF in San Francisco. He continues his studio practice in Brooklyn, New York.

Photograph by Luna Park.
Grottaglie, Italy, 2009.

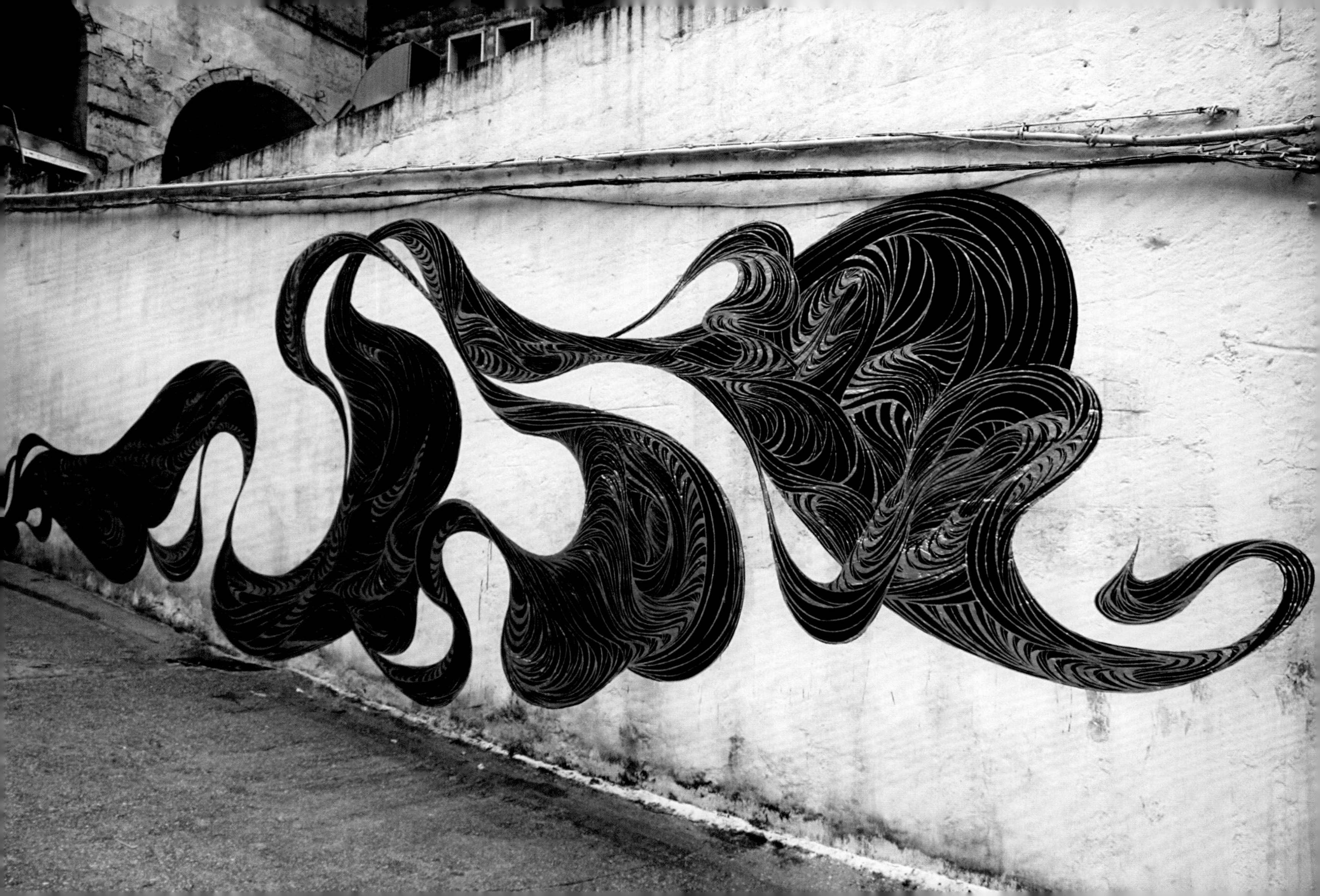

Ellis G.

Ellis Gallagher, aka Ellis G., is best known for his chalk works. Born and raised in New York City, Gallagher was an early participant in graffiti culture, but after an arrest in 1999 and a string of violent incidents (one of which took the life of a writer friend), he abandoned traditional graff. Several years later, feeling somewhat down on his luck, he found himself paying extra attention to his surroundings, especially to the shadows cast by street lamps and everyday city objects. So, in 2005, he began experimenting with a new creative outlet: tracing those very shadows in thick lines of white and colored chalk.

In a practice he called "ocular echoism," Gallagher has been furiously tracing the shadows of everything from bicycles and lampposts to mailboxes and fire hydrants throughout New York City. At Art Basel Miami Beach in 2009, Gallagher was invited to participate in a number of events, and he graced the city's streets with countless shadow tracings.

Since the practice of painting on the streets with chalk is entirely legal, Gallagher is not relegated to working at night by street lamps—he is free to use the sun as a tool as well. He is constrained only by the extremely ephemeral nature of his medium—if it rains, it's gone.

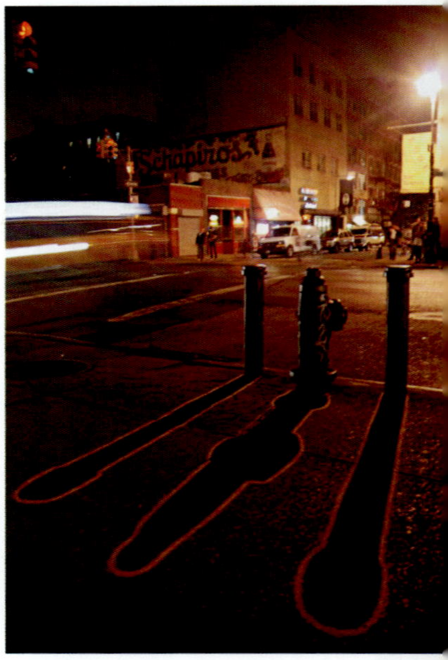

Photographs courtesy of Ellis G.
New York City, 2009

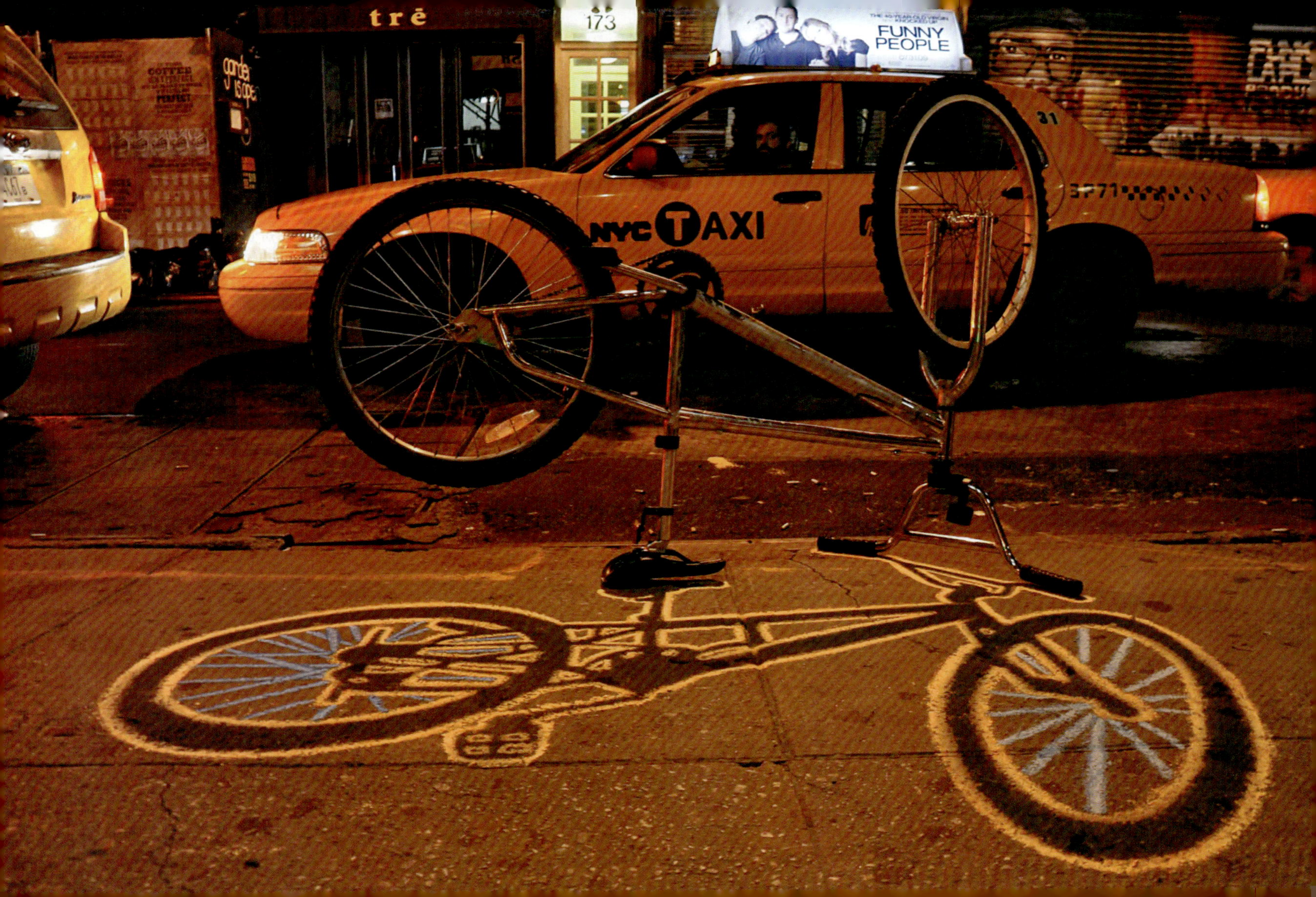
tré
173
FUNNY PEOPLE
31
NYC TAXI

El Mac

A big fan of large-scale works, El Mac burst into prominence on the international urban- and ephemeral-art scenes relatively late in the game. A native of Los Angeles but a current resident of Phoenix, Arizona, Mac considers himself a studious painter, finding inspiration for his work in that of great masters like Caravaggio. Although he never went to art school, he credits constant drawing and painting since childhood for his expansive technical abilities and photorealism skills.

Mac's intricate line work is instantly recognizable, and his ability to create elaborate, completely proportionate intricacies on grand scales has not gone unnoticed. Also heavily inspired by religious imagery, Mac's murals often appear to be a crossover between graffiti and religious iconography.

Within the last two years, Mac has had solo exhibitions in Los Angeles, in San Francisco, and at Art Basel Miami Beach, and he released his first book, *Alianza*, through the San Francisco–based brand Upper Playground. His mural work can be found in Mexico, Sweden, Canada, South Korea, Belgium, and Italy, among other countries.

Mac often collaborates with other artists on his mural work, including, most recently, legendary graffiti artist Retna [see 273] and the Los Angeles–based painter Augustine Kofie [see 198].

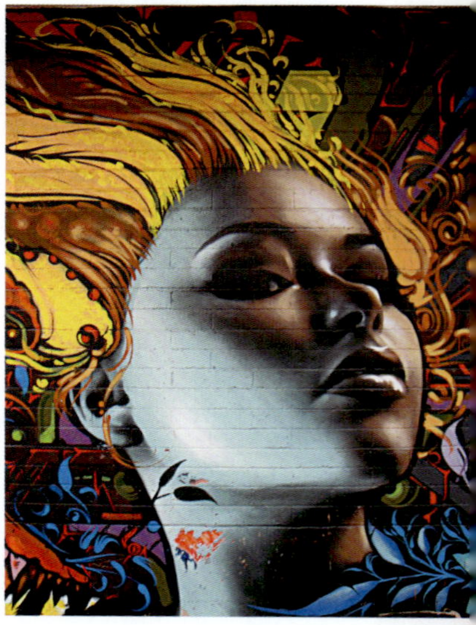

Portrait of Raul "Frame" Gamboa. Photograph courtesy of El Mac. Phoenix, Arizona, 2010. Detail: Collaboration with Reyes. Photograph by Matt Isles. San Francisco, 2006.

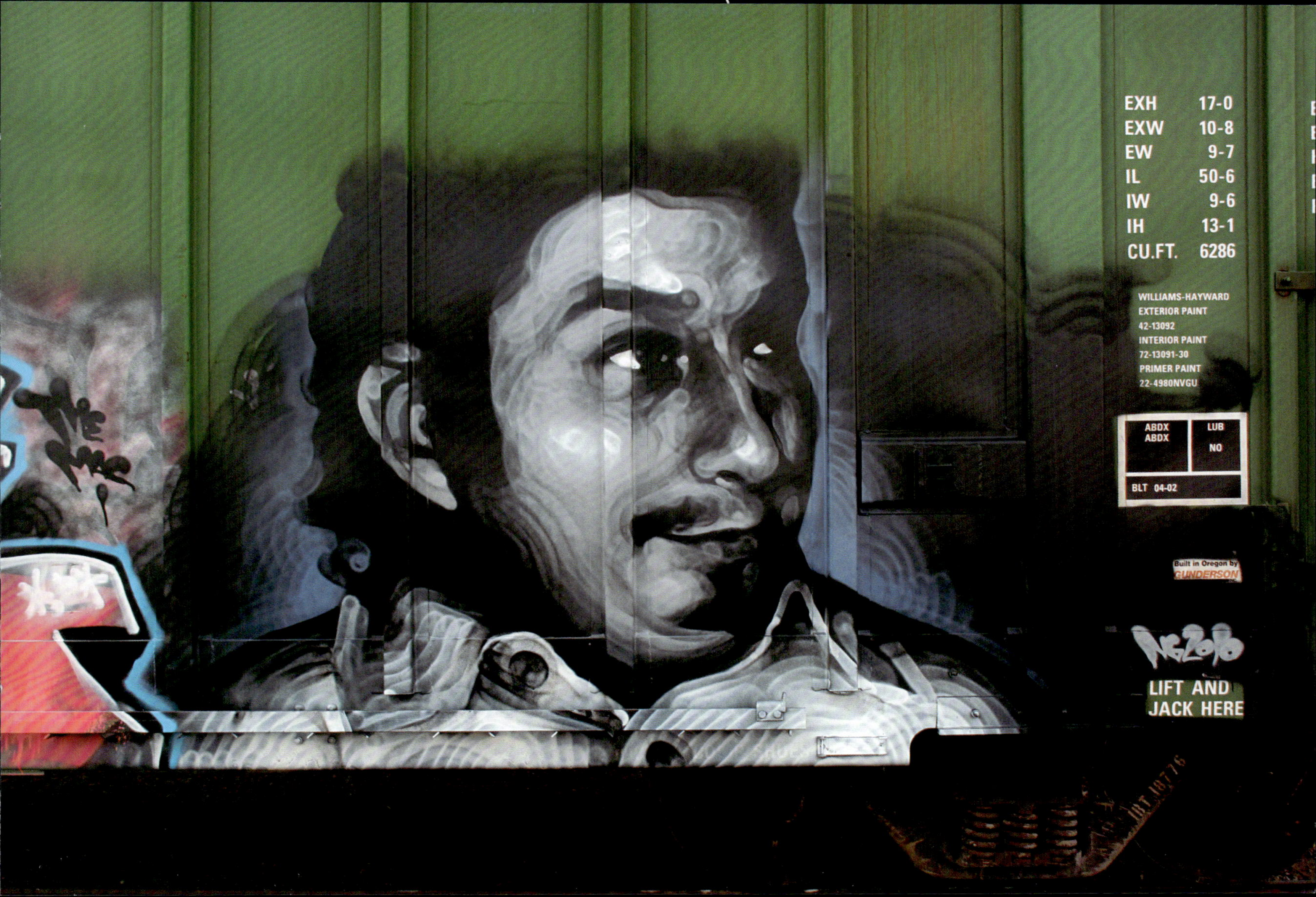
EXH 17-0
EXW 10-8
EW 9-7
IL 50-6
IW 9-6
IH 13-1
CU.FT. 6286
WILLIAMS-HAYWARD
EXTERIOR PAINT
42-13092
INTERIOR PAINT
72-13091-30
PRIMER PAINT
22-4980NVGU
ABDX
ABDX
LUB
NO
BLT 04-02
Built in Oregon by
GUNDERSON
LIFT AND
JACK HERE

Elph

Glasgow's bleak streets are not known for an abundance of enlightening graffiti or street art. But throughout this grim landscape, an artist has continued to put hopeful faces and happy colors in the public's eye. That artist is Elph. Raised in Scotland in the 1970s and 1980s, Elph was hanging out with older kids in 1989 and became a breakdancer and graffiti artist, coming up in the world of lettering. Taking as his moniker a nickname derived from the *Lord of the Rings* trilogy, Elph began putting his Wild Style creations on the streets of Glasgow.

Eventually, his interest moved toward drawing characters. He began to obsessively draw renditions of the hardworking, alcohol-abusing blue-collar men surrounding him, creating a signature style of flat-nosed character that adapted itself to any scenario.

Struggling to survive in a culture that doesn't seem to understand or support the creative process, Elph claims to battle a collective belief that he is wasting his time with his pens and brushes. In his late twenties, impelled by a need to provide, Elph embarked on a career in graphic design and illustration, through which he now supports himself and his family. But the street carries a perennial allure for him: the freedom to do anything he wants. Elph often commutes to cities outside of Scotland, especially London, to paint and exhibit his work.

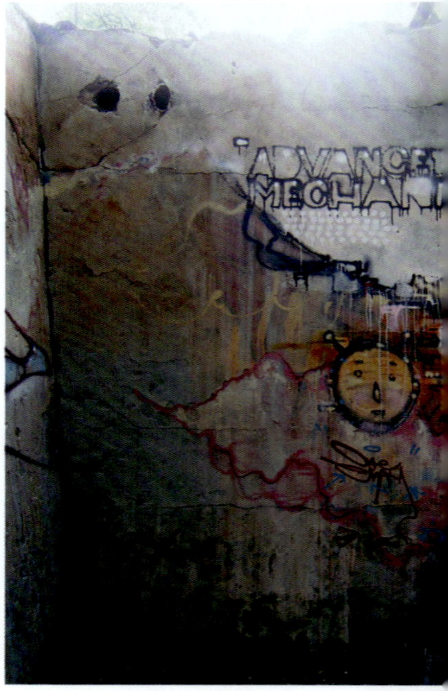

Collaboration with Pure [VK].
Photograph courtesy of Elph. Edinburgh, Scotland, 2010.

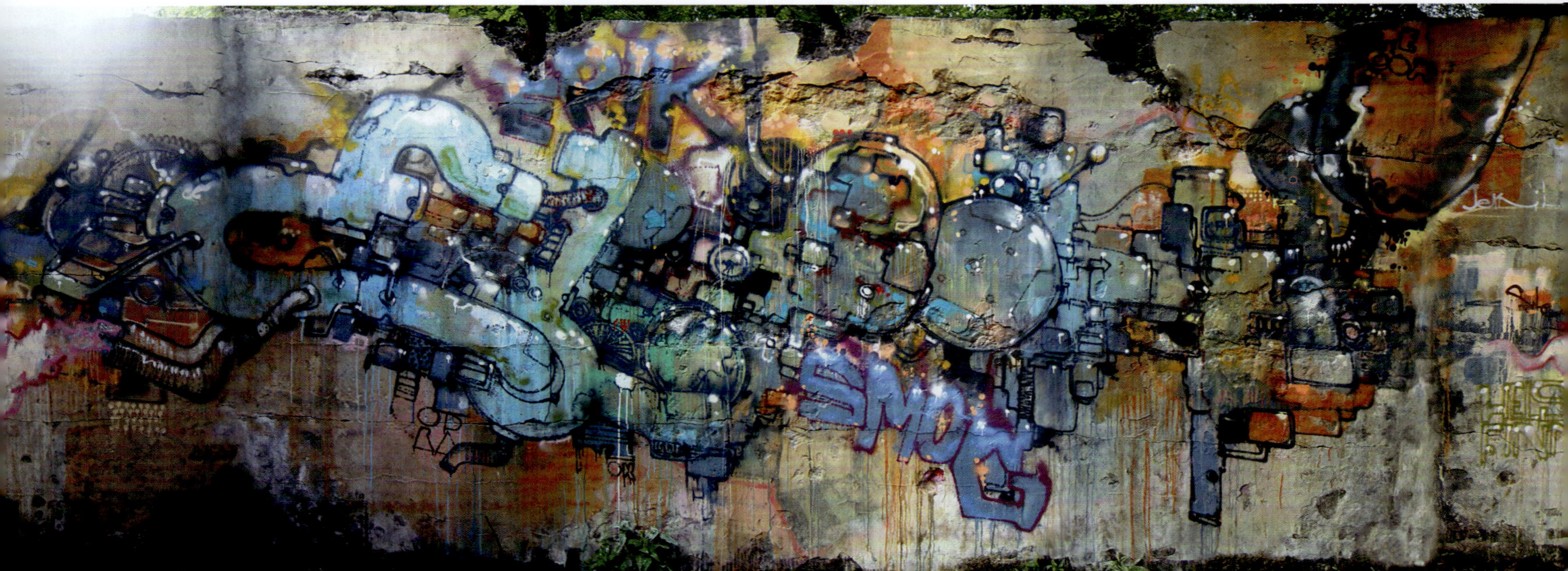
SMOG

Ron English

Being a relative of Bonnie Parker (of Bonnie and Clyde fame) may have sealed this artist's fate as a billboard bandit. In Texas, during his college years, Ron English began affixing his own paintings onto existing billboards. Ron's early billboard works were surreal and psychedelic in nature, but English's approach, like his paintings, has changed dramatically since then. While traditional graffiti artists have used billboards as backdrops for their names, English has instead chosen to use them for delivering his own brand of social commentary.

To date, Ron English has painted over numerous billboards in locations around the globe, and has had more run-ins with the authorities than Bonnie and Clyde. Ron's advice to anyone looking to get involved in this type of culture jamming is to do it in broad daylight. According to English, if you sneak around at night, you look like you're up to no good.

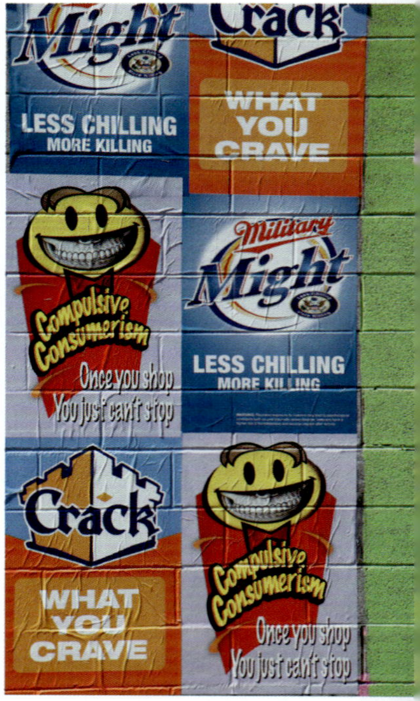

Photographs courtesy of Ron English. Queens, New York, 2010.

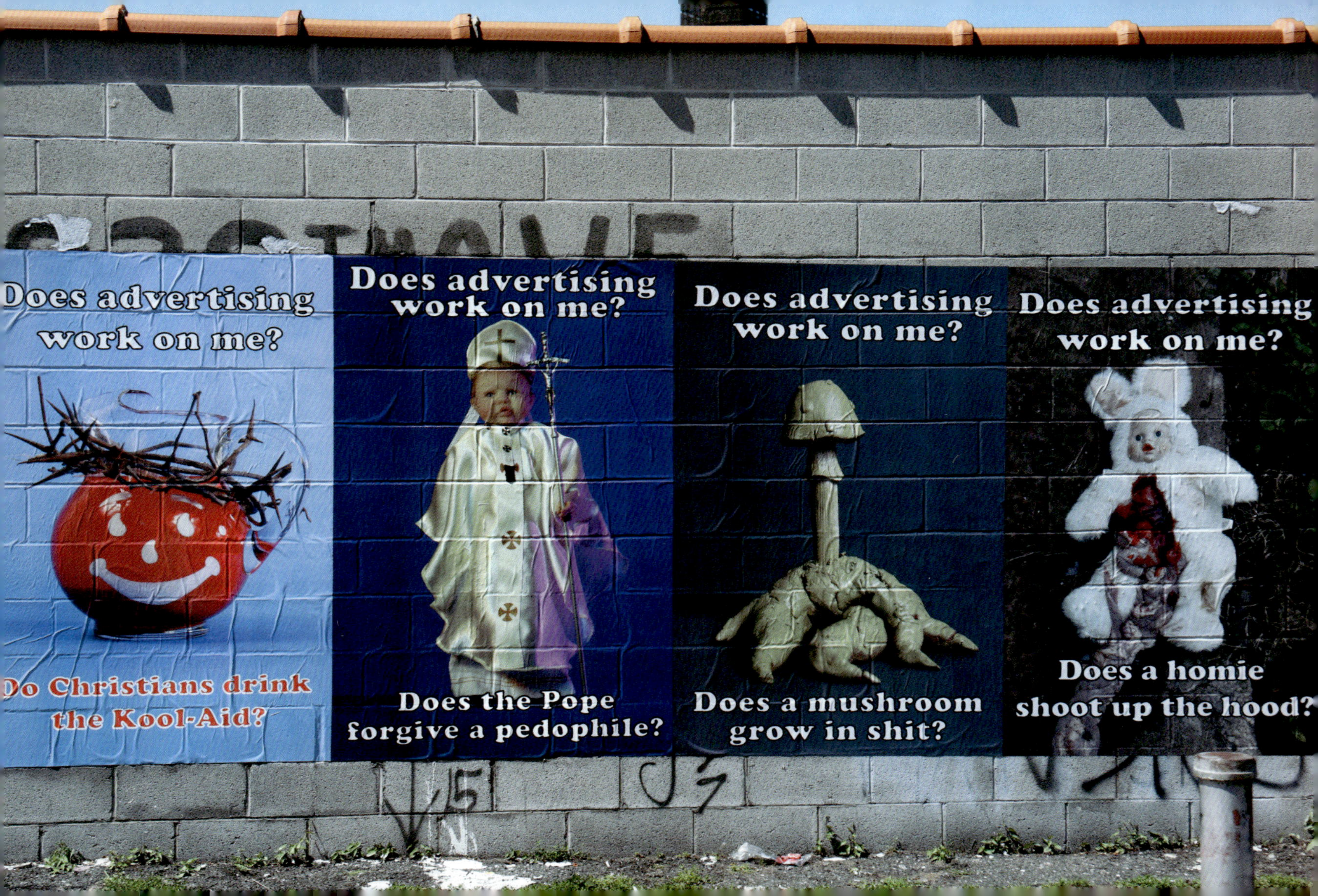
Does advertising
work on me?
Do Christians drink
the Kool-Aid?
Does advertising
work on me?
Does the Pope
forgive a pedophile?
Does advertising
work on me?
Does a mushroom
grow in shit?
Does advertising
work on me?
Does a homie
shoot up the hood?

Escif

Based in Valencia, Spain, Escif began tagging the walls of his native city with markers in 1997. A few years later, he was creating poetic paintings and drawings around concepts aimed at opening his viewers' minds and provoking dialogue. In his own words, he perceives painting as an "exercise in reflection" to be shared by others. Among the many symbols he uses in his compositions are walls. His 2010 solo show in Barcelona, "Against the Wall," reflects his yearning to break down the walls between us and within our own psyches. "I want to see life as a journey of constant investigation where there is no end, as a process of eternal learning in which every step puts the past in doubt," he has stated.

Largely inspired by the places he has visited and the books he has read, he cites Blu [see 040], Herbert Baglioni, San, and Hello Monster as influences. Escif's favorite artists include Pablo Picasso and the Italian artist Mauritzio Cattelan, best known for his satirical sculptures. Escif generally works on his own, but in Valencia he has collaborated with On_ly and other members of XLF, with DOCS, and with Hyuro. Escif sees the settings of his paintings as an essential aspect of his work, and he is always intent on exploring beforehand the places to be used as his canvases.

Escif has also exhibited his work worldwide in galleries such as Luis Adelantado in Valencia and Miami, the Carmichael Gallery in Los Angeles, and Pictures on Walls in London.

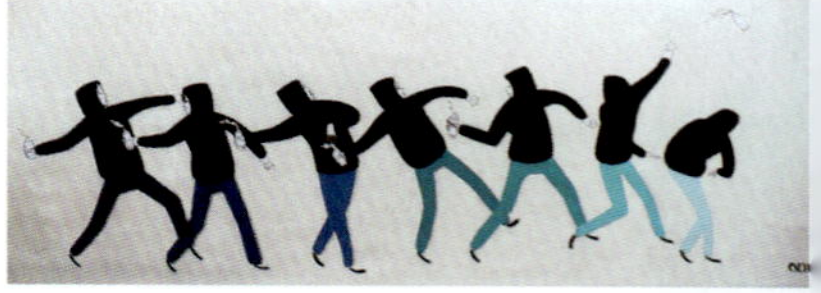

Photographs courtesy of Escif.
Miajadas, Spain, 2010.

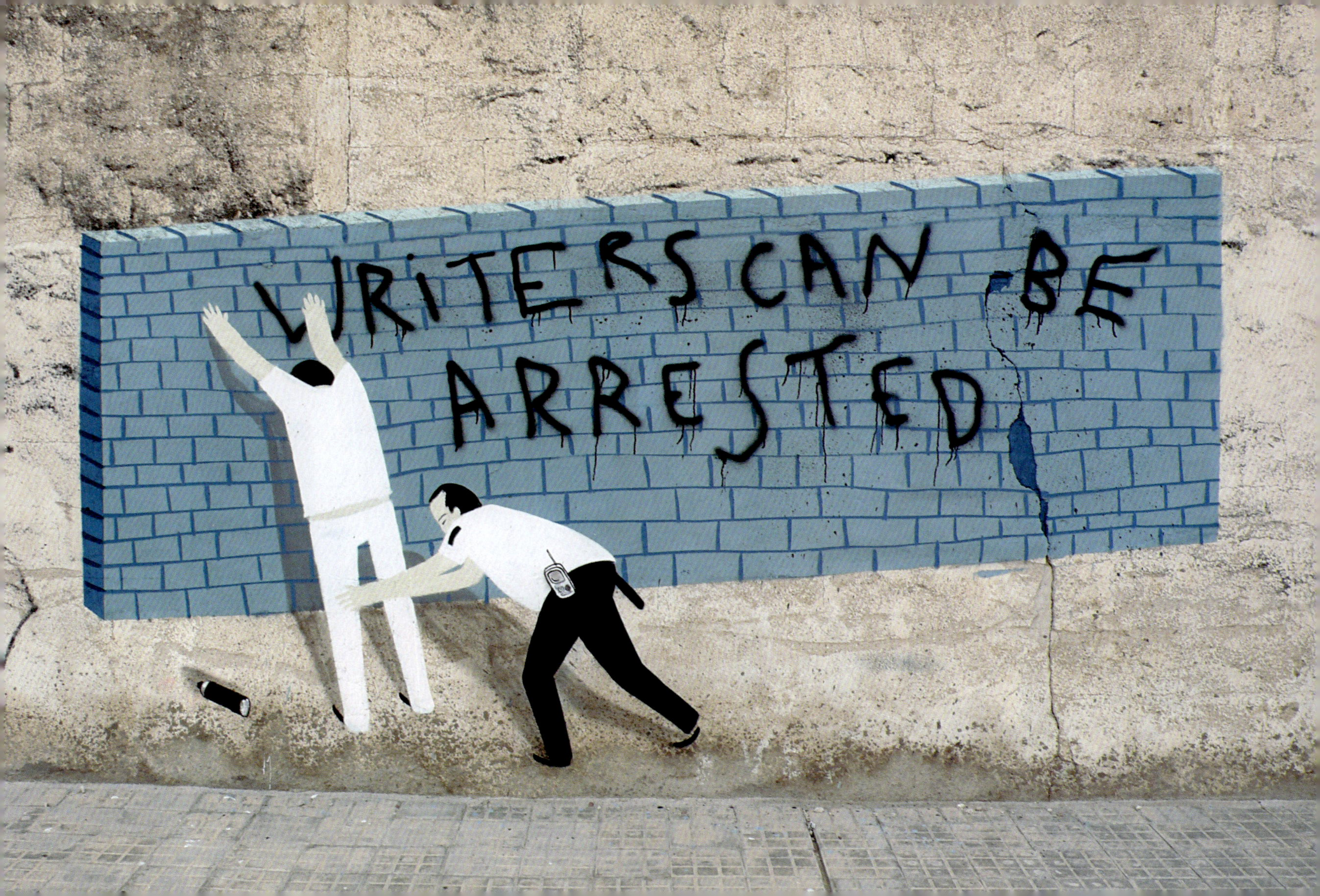
WRITERS CAN BE
ARRESTED

Espo

Before there was Espo at Jeffrey Deitch's influential New York gallery, before there was Steve Powers in the "Beautiful Losers" traveling exhibition, and before there were Espo canvases selling for five figures, there was Stephen J. Powers, born and bred on the gray streets of Philadelphia. It was in Philly that his work, with its signature clever wordplay, first began to crop up, and it was there that Espo first made his mark with his conceptual text pieces.

In 1994, Espo moved to New York where, using the visual language of billboards and sign painting, he brazenly worked in broad daylight, painting storefront gates with legitimate-looking signage, pretending to be from the "Exterior Surface Painting Outreach" to any curious passersby. This sign work, coupled with his prolific graffiti sprees, made a distinct impression on the downtown community, where he began to show his work in galleries.

Espo went on to become a Fulbright scholar in 2007, creating public murals in Dublin and Belfast, and in 2008, he collaborated with renowned public arts organization Creative Time, creating a number of signage works at Coney Island in Brooklyn.

Today, Powers lives in New York with his wife and son and is a full-time studio artist who has exhibited at numerous galleries and museums. He devotes a fair amount of his practice to public art projects, the most recent of which involved a trip home and was titled "Love Letter," an endeavor in which he and a crew of artists painted messages illustrating the ups and downs of relationships on fifty walls throughout Philadelphia.

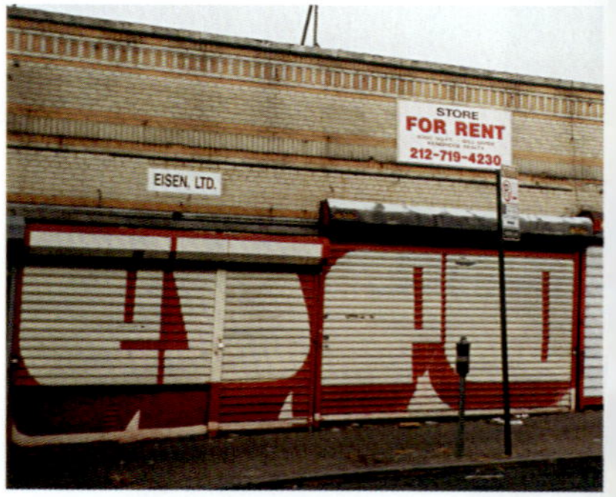

Photographs by Cycle.
San Francisco, c. 1998.
Detail: San Francisco, c. 1999.

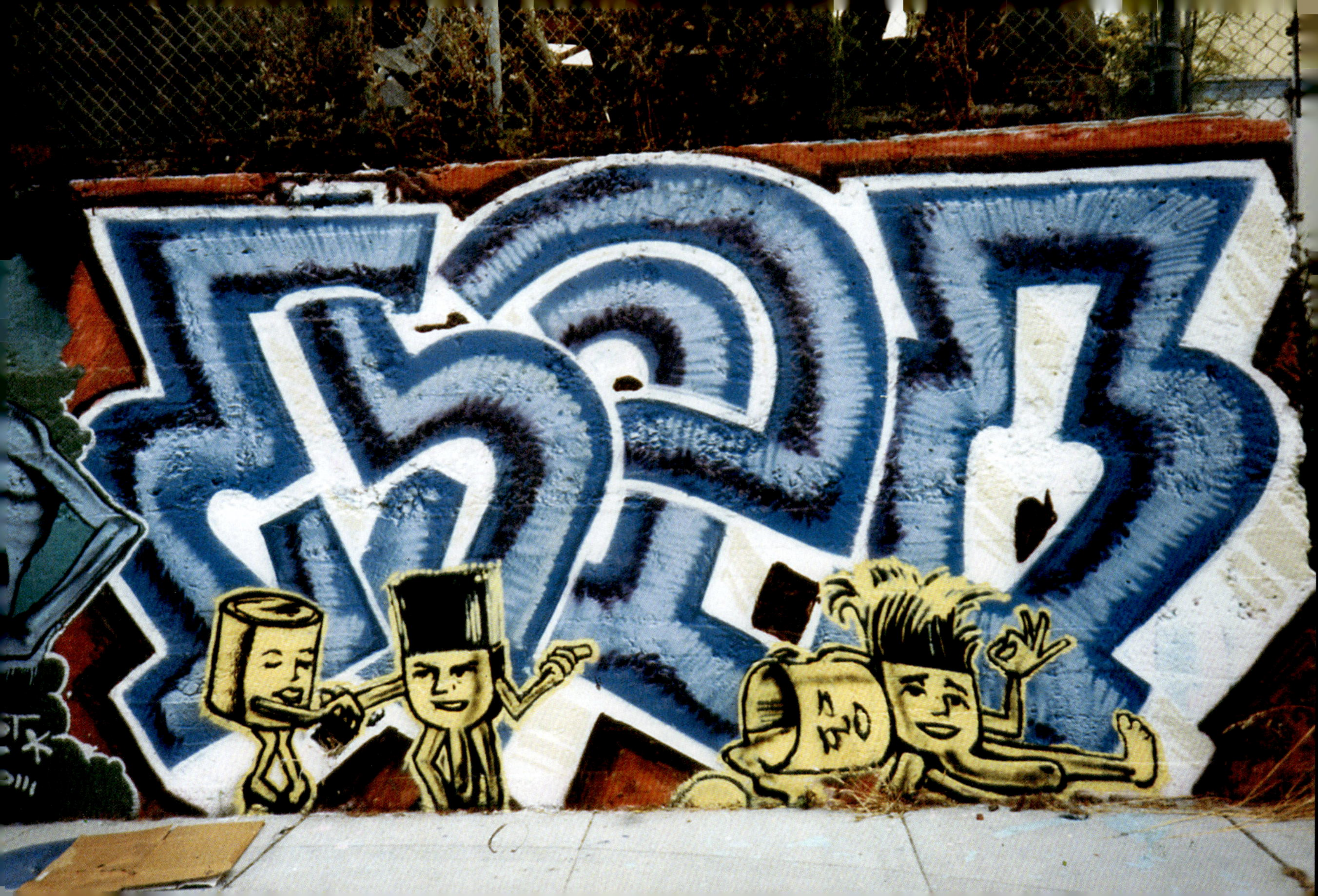

Ethos

The artist known simply as Ethos is, in fact, the Brazilian painter Claudio Ethos. Born in São Paulo in 1982, Ethos now lives in the city of Birigui. At fifteen, he began creating work with aerosol paint and ballpoint pen, which remain his tools of choice.

Although Ethos grew up influenced by Brazilian street-art gods such as Os Gemeos [see 248] and Vitche [see 353], he quickly began to develop his own style, which manifests itself today in a dark amalgam of realistic character work and abstracted fantasy.

Having evolved away from São Paulo's *pixação* [see 257] tradition, Ethos's work lends itself far more to the arm of street art that one might expect to find on a gallery wall. Just as he evidences a command of detail in his ballpoint work, Ethos uses a technique called "threading" to create the same highly detailed effect within his outdoor pieces; he is devoted to replicating the fineness and nuance of his ink-and-pencil drawings when he works in larger scale. With a nod to the surrealists, his subject matter extends into the fantastical, with stretched-out figures and textile patterning used to create atmosphere.

While Ethos is known for his street work, he celebrated the opening of his first show in Birigui in 2005 and has continued to exhibit internationally, most recently in New York City.

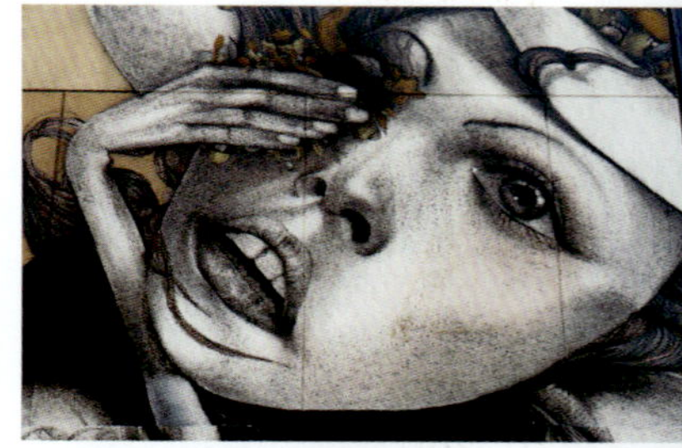

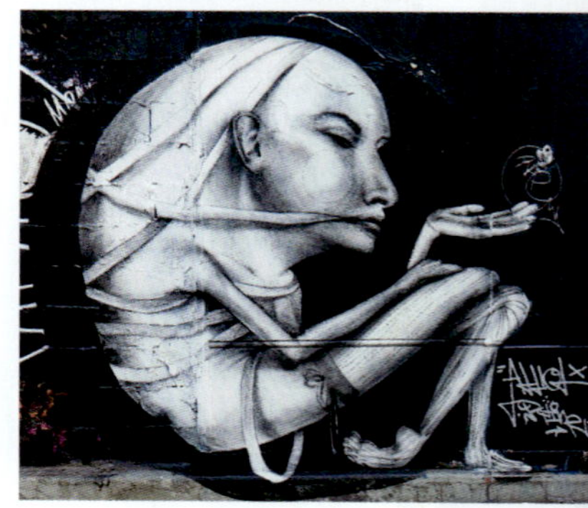

Photographs by Lionel Belluteau. Paris, 2010.

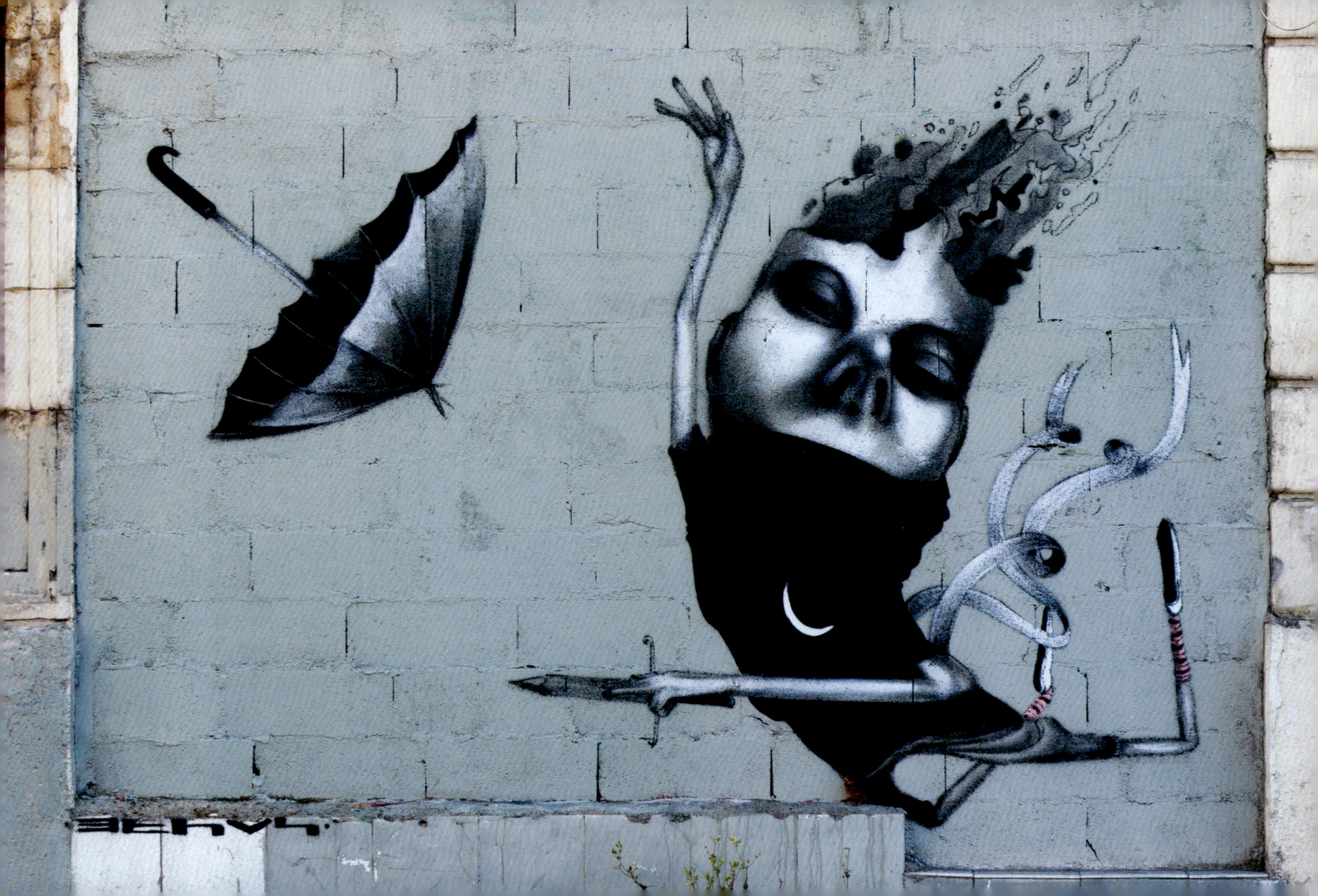

Ewok/MSK

Ewok's earliest memories of graffiti involve trips to Chicago and New York. While he had been aware of graffiti while growing up in Milwaukee, the work he discovered in Chicago and New York was on a different playing field—and he found that field intriguing. Soon after, he and his friend Mber picked up Magnums and started tagging in the late 1980s. In 1991, he did his first piece in his new hometown of Minneapolis.

While watching the anime film *Akira*, Ewok had an epiphany: He decided to break down his letters into their own distinct personalities. Each letter in his name would have emotion, motion, and texture—that was the formula. He became a master of rendering textures, with melting wax and shiny plastic used as mainstays. Some pieces were super crisp, while others took on the look of a tidal wave of psychedelic ooze, as though the piece itself could jump right off the wall.

While developing his new style, he played an important role in the development of the graff magazine *LifeSucksDie*. As the magazine became popular, it required deadlines and became less fun and spontaneous, so Ewok put it behind him. During this time, pictures of his works were finding their way into the hands of MSK writers, who recruited Ewok into the crew without ever meeting him.

As painting—both illegally and on canvas—became his primary focus, Ewok made the move to California to be closer to MSK and the 7th Letter crew [see 022]. He's never looked back.

Photographs courtesy of Ewok.
Top: Miami, 2009.
Bottom left and right: Hollywood, California, 2010.

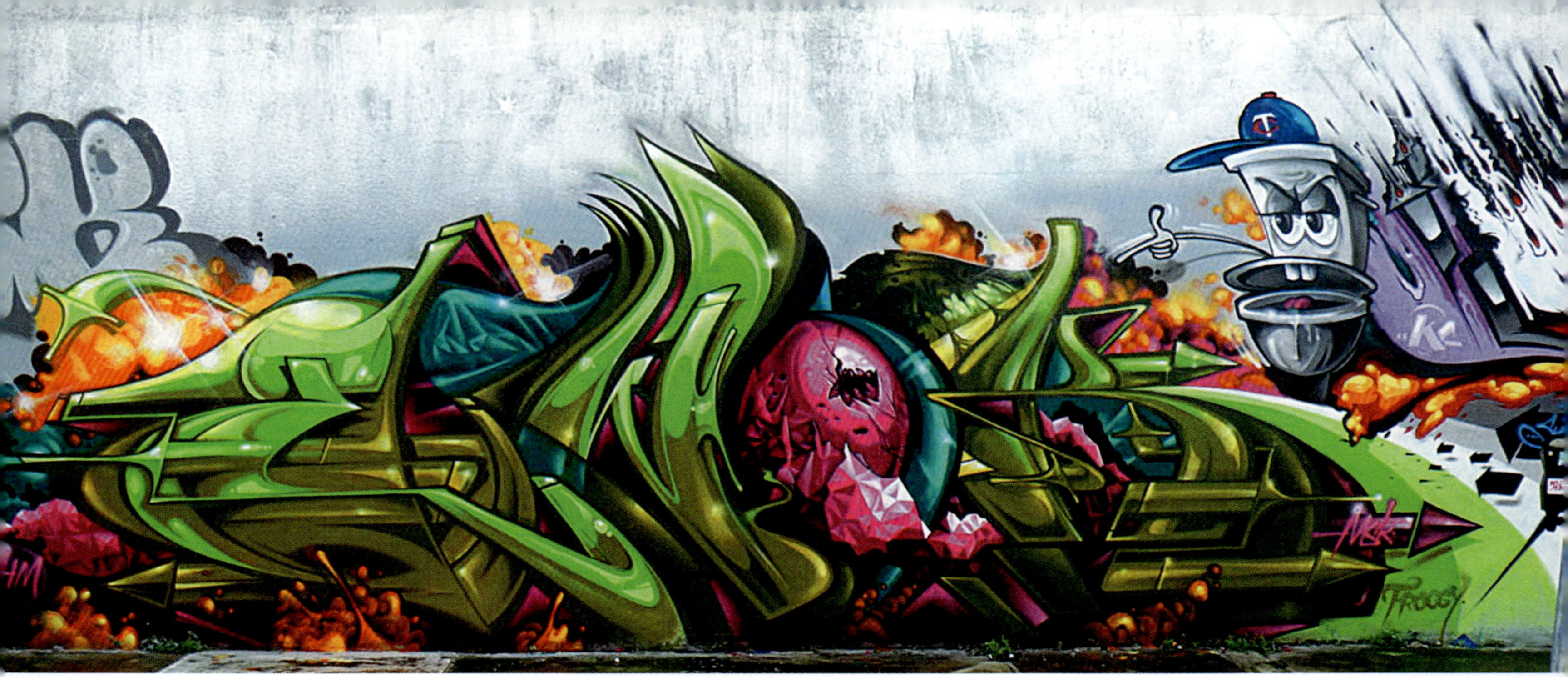

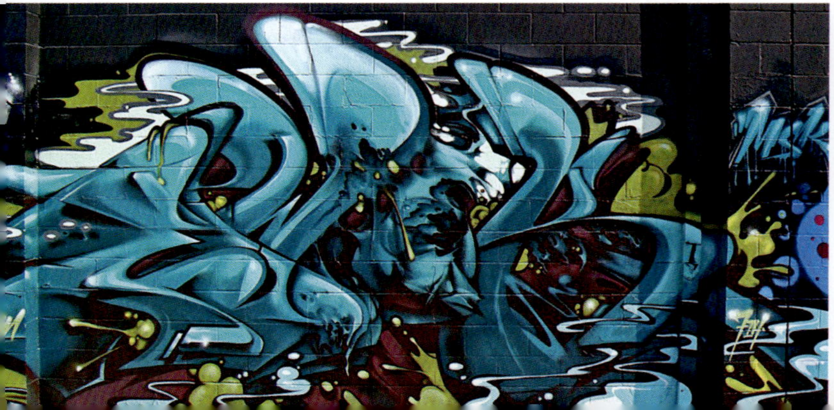

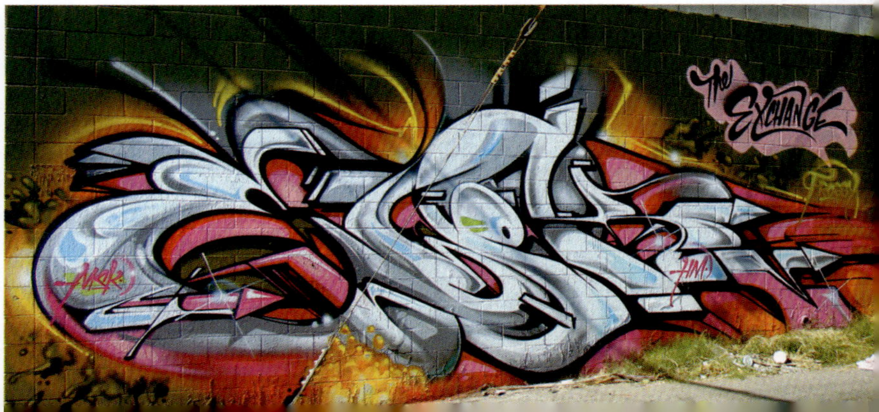
The EXCHANGE

Ex Vandals

In the late 1960s and early '70s, there was a resurgence of street gangs in New York. The time line paralleled the beginnings of the graffiti movement, and some gangs wrote their names throughout the city. In 1971, Dino Nod, a Brooklyn-based writer from Erasmus High School, invited the top writers he knew to a secret meeting at his house. The goal was to form a graffiti gang that would make them all famous. There was one caveat, however: The writers who joined the crew would have to hit up the crew's name first and then add their tag. The crew itself would be the celebrity. Although writers like Scooter and Playboy opted out, most of the others in the room joined up.

They became known as the Ex Vandals, the "Ex" standing for "experienced."

The Ex Vandals were highly methodical in their approach to writing. Dino Nod and his vice president, Wicked Gary, acquired maps of neighborhoods they hadn't hit and covered a new section each week. Before long, the group had blanketed the city with the Ex Vandals logo. They were at their peak in 1972, when Wicked Gary made a trip to the Bronx to make Phase 2 [see 255] the borough president. He soon recruited graffiti superstars like Stay High 149 [see 316], Superkool 223 [see 325], and Snake 131, giving the Ex Vandals a major presence in the three boroughs.

By 1973, other crews had formed, and they had more artistic aspirations. The Ex Vandals gradually disappeared, as the members all began turning eighteen and the fines for writing became stiffer.

Photograph by Flint Genari.
New York City, 1973.

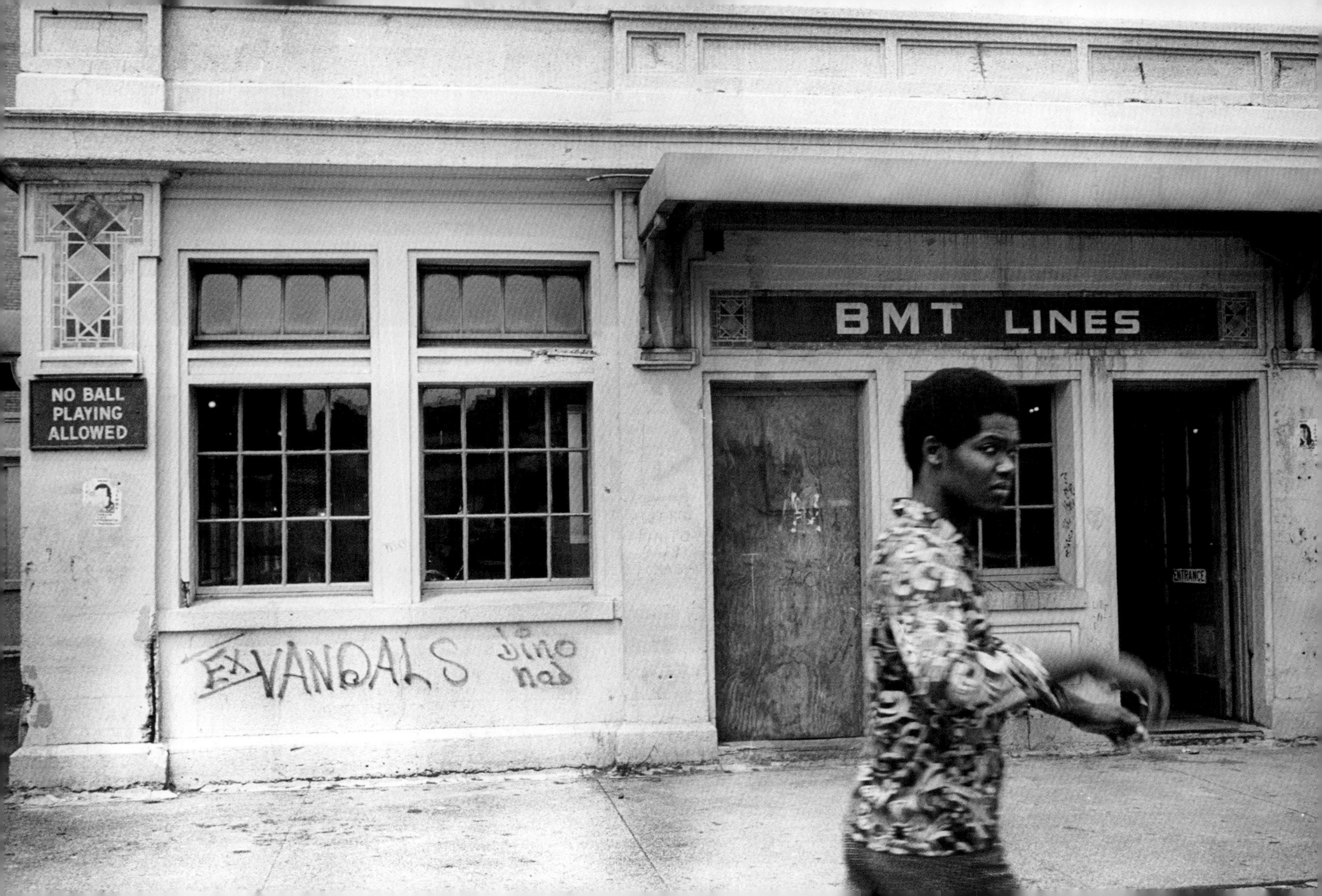
NO BALL
PLAYING
ALLOWED
BMT LINES
EX VANDALS
ENTRANCE

Ezo

Joseph "Ezo" Wippler was born in 1963 and raised in the milieu of traditional Puerto Rican spiritual culture, a sharp contrast to the cynicism of modern American urban life. His family moved to an apartment in Queens in 1971. Before he ever picked up a spray can, Ezo found inspiration in art books. Artists as diverse as Vaughn Bode, Frank Frazetta, Dürer, and Grünewald inspired him to draw, and in 1978 a new world opened up when he entered the doors of the High School of Art and Design [see 167]. It was there that Ezo discovered The Ramones, The Clash, and graffiti.

In 1979, he began to hit the Queens subway lines with the TPA crew, until a famous headline-making bust ended his career in the early 1980s. In 1983, Ezo began exhibiting his work, including a seminal group show at the Sidney Janis Gallery. He continued his art studies, receiving a BFA from the School of Visual Arts in 1989. Ezo has curated shows in galleries, as well as on the streets. He presided over Harlem's Hall of Fame event from 1996 to 2000, bringing in top talent at a time when New York's graffiti scene was on life support. Ezo continues to create art in a variety of mediums, including oils and aerosol. His commercial work has appeared in movies, videos, and magazines. It is rumored that, as of 2011, he continues to bomb.

Photographs by Joseph Wippler.
New York City, 1997.

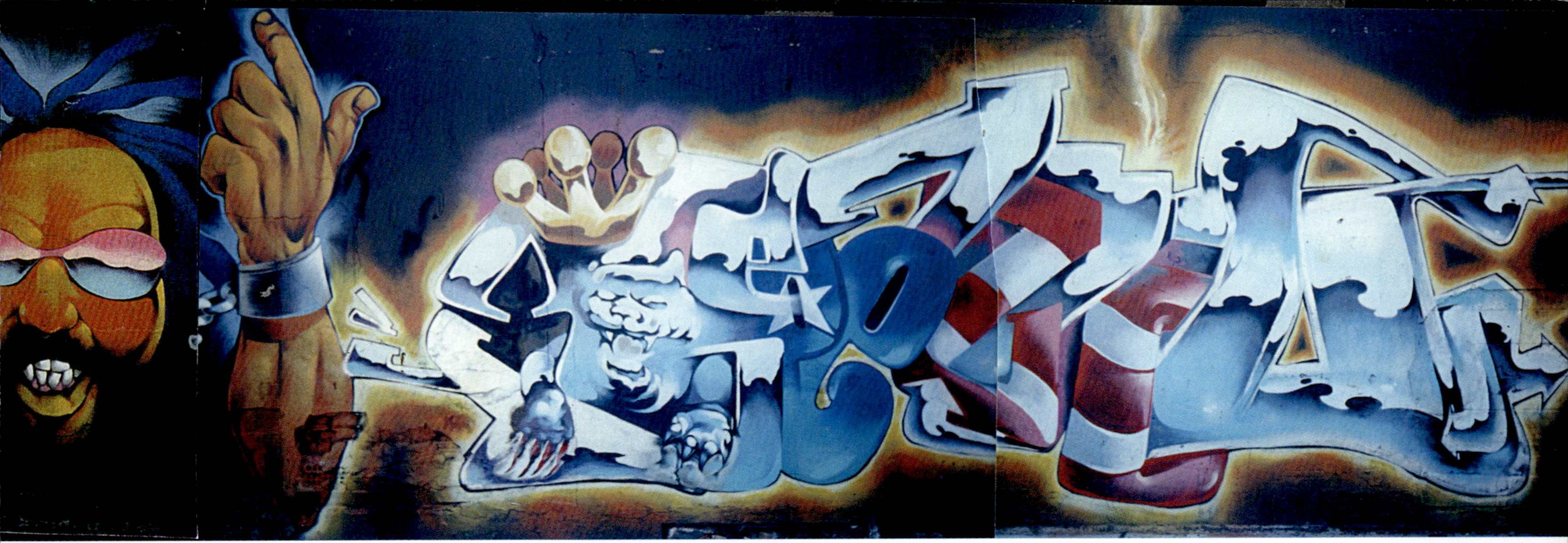

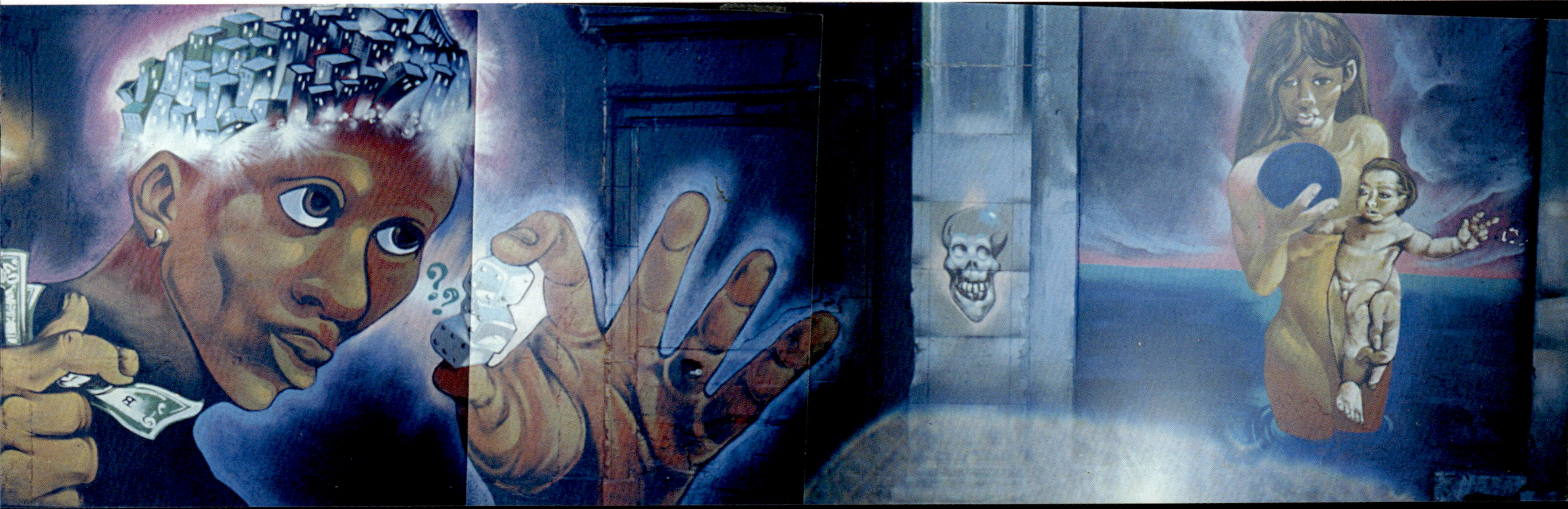

The Fab 5

The Fabulous Five (TF5) had a clear mission statement: paint whole-cars, and lots of them. The crew formed in the mid-1970s, with Slug as the original president; the more prolific members of the group included Lee, Mono, Doc 109, and Slave.

Lee and Slave were the two stars of the group. Lee specialized in whole-car paintings that reflected the post-Watergate paranoia of the 1970s. Lee himself had many fears—among them the end of the world (Stop the Bomb) and being alone in life (The Lovesick Bomber)—and he expressed them all on the trains, many times doing two cars at once. Slave was a window-down stylemaster from the BMT lines in Brooklyn.

Undoubtedly, the greatest moment for the crew was when they pulled off the second and last whole-train done in the history of the movement. (The first had been done a year earlier by Caine 1 [see 054].) This train was done in December 1977 over a two-night span, with most of the work being attributed to Lee. The two Christmas-themed cars at the end of the train ran together untouched until 1980.

Most of the crew had retired by 1977, but Lee and Slave continued, painting their last cars in 1980.

Pieces by Lee Quinones (left) and Slave.
Photograph by Chris "Daze" Ellis.
New York City, 1976.

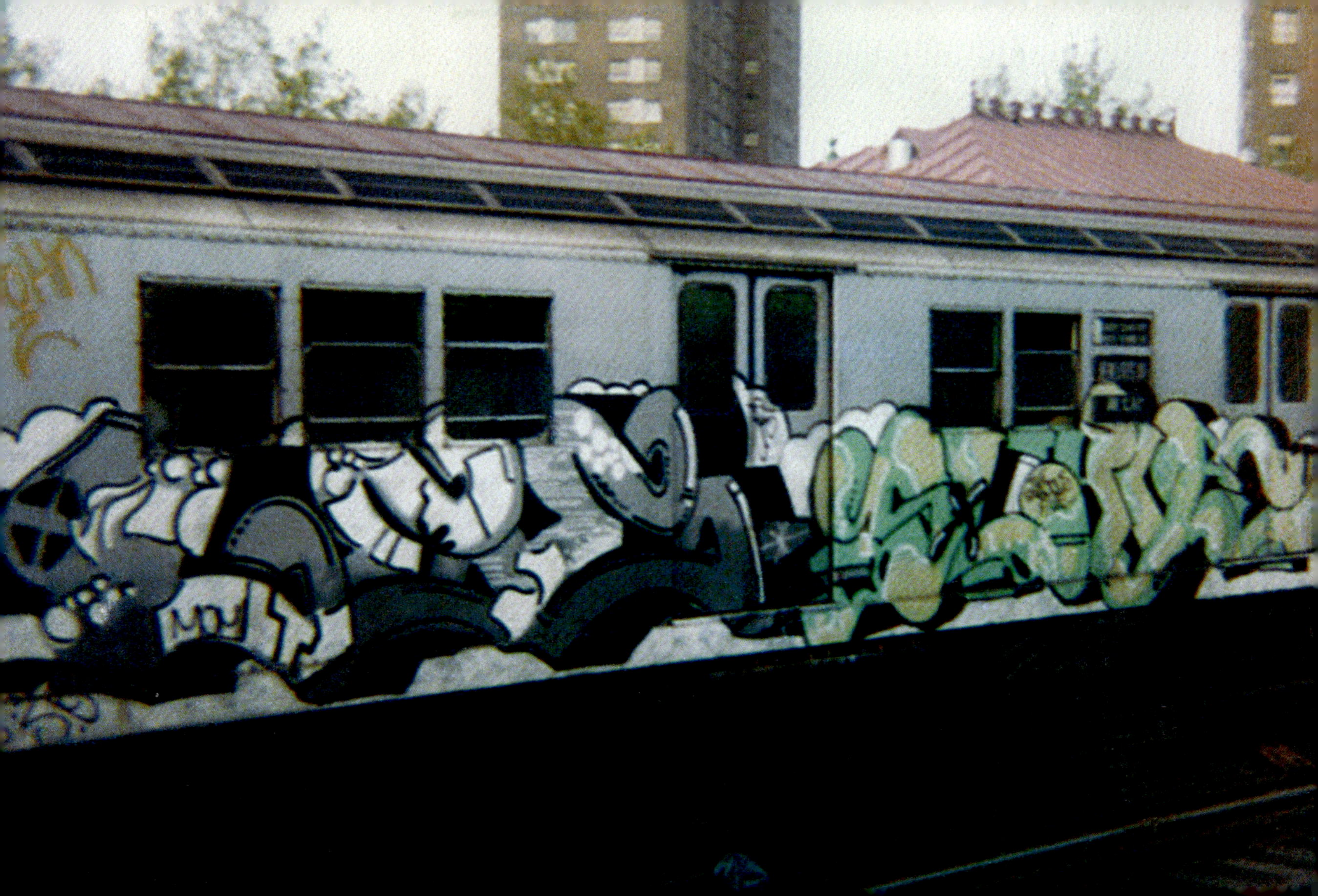

Faber

A pioneer of Peru's expressive street-art scene, Faber began using the streets as his canvas when he was sixteen years old. In the beginning, he made his mark primarily with tags in Lima's bohemian Barranco quarter. A member of Lima's OSK (One Style Krew), he was influenced by his city's emerging graffiti landscape, its vibrant skateboarding scene, and Peruvian popular culture.

Faber's romance with the streets and passion for graffiti spurred his interest in other visual art forms. From 2005 to 2009, he studied fine arts and graphic design at the Universidad Católica del Perú. Along with other art students and painters, he began to create huge murals on wide avenues throughout the capital. But he was drawn most strongly to Lima's impoverished and semi-abandoned neighborhoods, where he felt acutely the striking contrast between the wealthy few and the poor masses.

Injustice and solidarity are among Faber's main concerns. The unease that his city's inequality triggers within him continues to be his primary motivation. Faber's work has evolved into a synthesis of styles in which classical and contemporary art forms pulsate with the rhythm of the streets. "The streets have always been my main source of inspiration," he says. "I now give them back little pieces of my soul as a way to thank them."

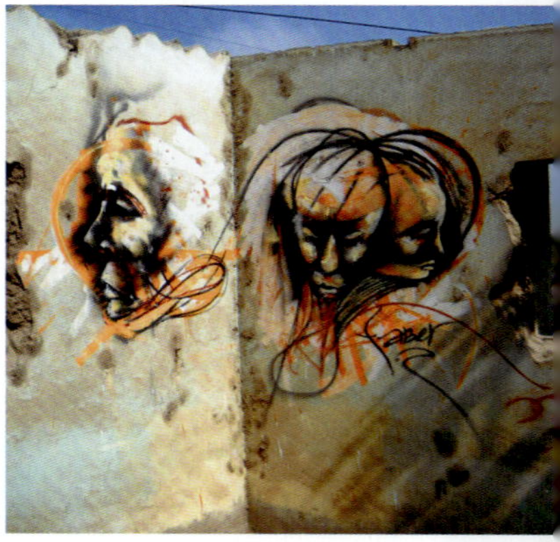

**Photographs courtesy of Faber.
Lima, Peru, 2009.**

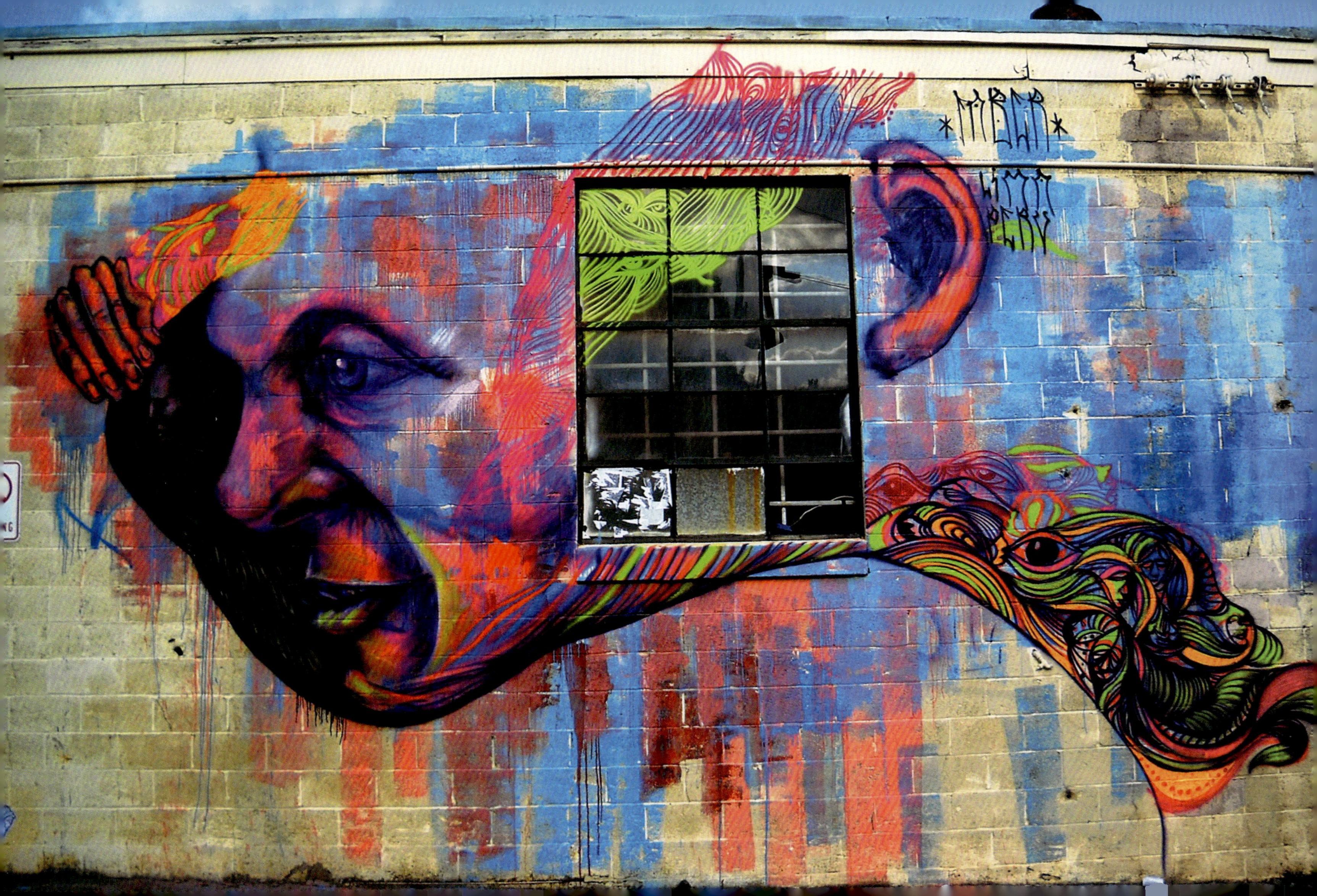

Fafi

A native of Toulouse, the southern French city that is home to several notable female graffiti powerhouses, Fafi began painting in 1994. Her characters evolved from fantastical cartoon images into more stylized, self-reflective images, often crossing the line into a sexualized version of her girls, whom she dubbed Fafinettes. The attractive and accessible nature of her work garnered Fafi widespread recognition, and she began to travel the world, creating street work and, eventually, commercial commissions, using spray paint and acrylic brush paint. Now best known for her commercial work, Fafi has collaborated with mega-brands such as Sony, Adidas, Coca-Cola, M.A.C. cosmetics, and LeSportsac.

Fafi has come under much critical fire for the spirit of her work; she is often accused of objectifying and contributing to a shallow perception of womanhood. Dismissing these criticisms, Fafi claims that her work is empowering to girls everywhere and does not contribute to a negative public perception of them—it simply represents women who want to look sexy. Fafi also paints imaginary characters she calls Hmilos, bloblike creatures who often appear depressed, and a character called Birtak, a former pirate.

Fafi recently became a mother and took up residence in Paris, where she now lives and works on her fine art, graphic design, and commercial art.

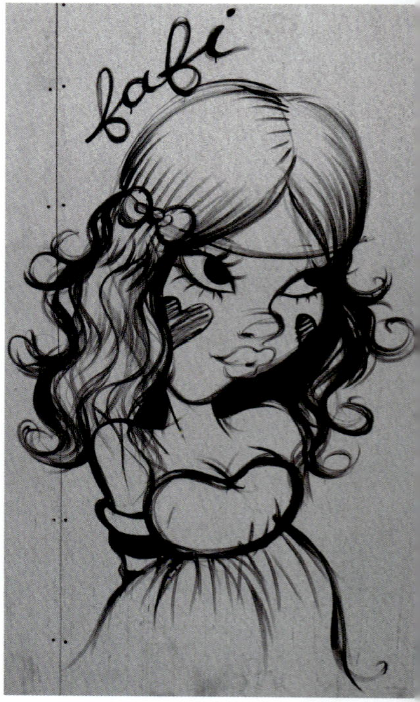

Photographs by Lionel Belluteau.
Right: Paris, 2009.
Right center: Paris, 2006.
Far right: Paris, 2008.
Detail: Paris, 2004.

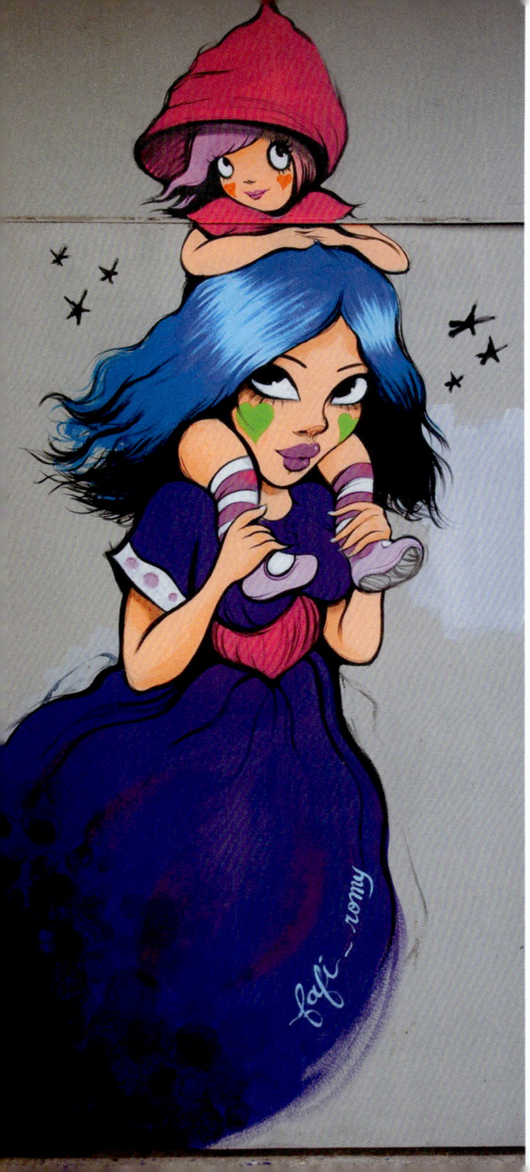
fafi_romy

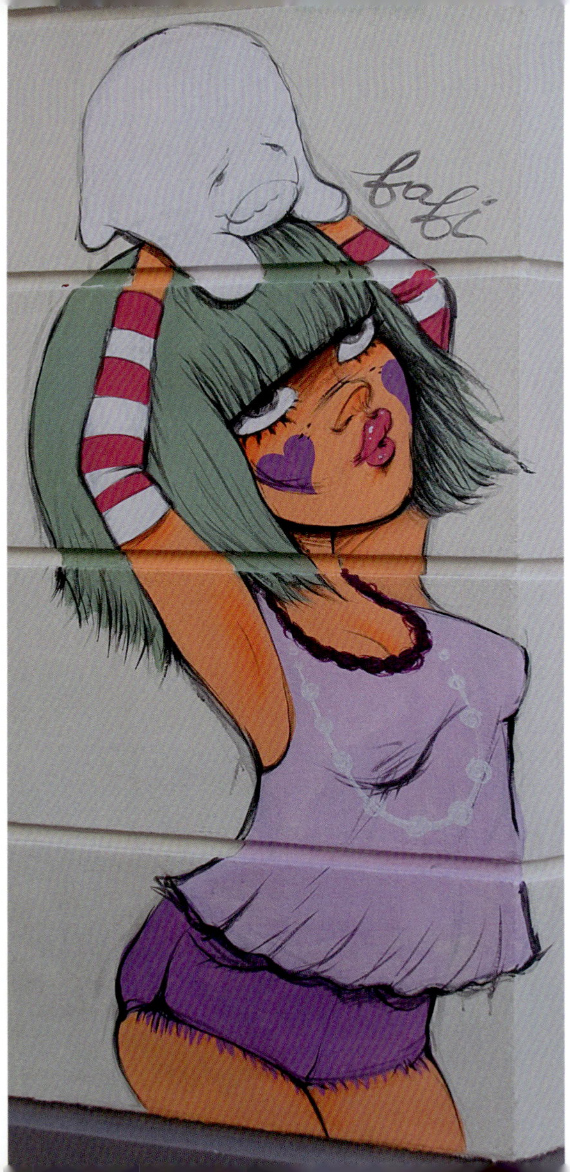
fafi

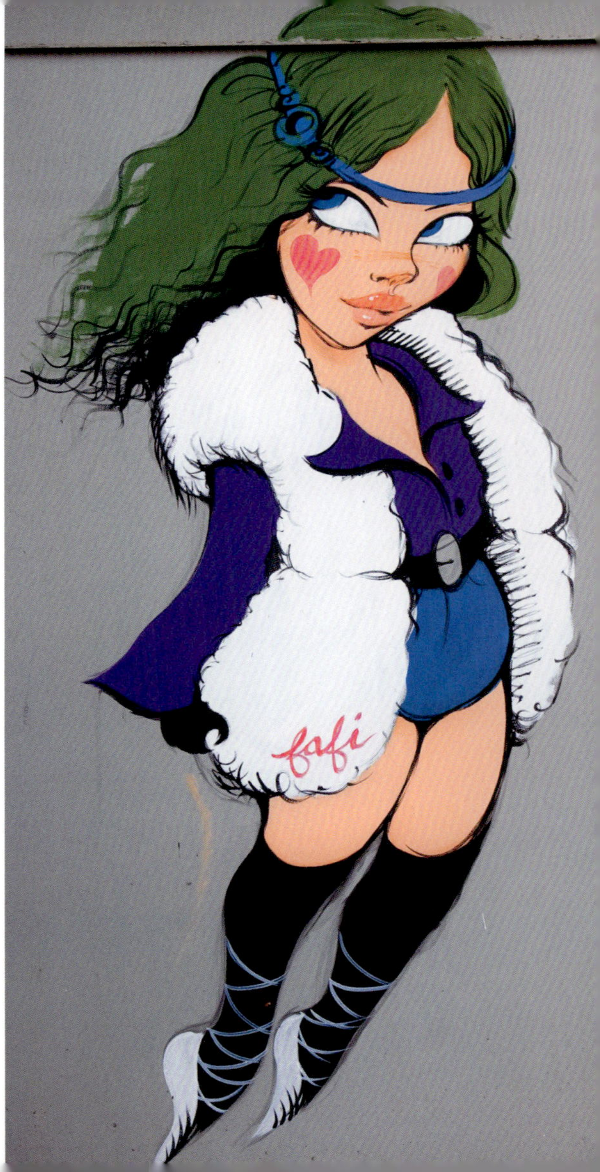
fafi

123

Faile

In the early 1990s, two guys, both named Patrick, met while attending high school in Scottsdale, Arizona. After graduation, Patrick McNeil headed to New York and Patrick Miller was off to Minneapolis. While in Minneapolis, Miller met Aiko Nakagawa [see 009], with whom he created a series of prints that Miller and Nakagawa would later paste up in the streets of New York with McNeil.

Initially, the trio's prints read "A-Life," a notation taken from a childhood sketchbook. Just a month into their street-art careers, the Patricks were both arrested. While behind bars for defacing public property, they found themselves in a real dilemma, both legally and in terms of their street-art identity, as they were now aware of the similarly named A-Life Gallery in lower Manhattan. Not to be discouraged, they mixed up the name's letters and created the anagram Faile. In a 2007 *Fecal Face* interview, McNeil said, "We really liked the idea of it, that you could Faile to succeed. That there was this growth process where you could create the most from what you were given and move forward."

Over the years, they focused less on printmaking and more on the use of paint and stencils. In 2006, Aiko left the trio to pursue her own art interests. In later years, dualism has become a dominant theme in Faile's work, reflecting a stark contrast between good and evil. In 2008, Faile participated in an outdoor exhibit at Tate Modern, securing their fame as street-art pioneers. Despite their enormous success, the Patricks still live humbly in Brooklyn, New York.

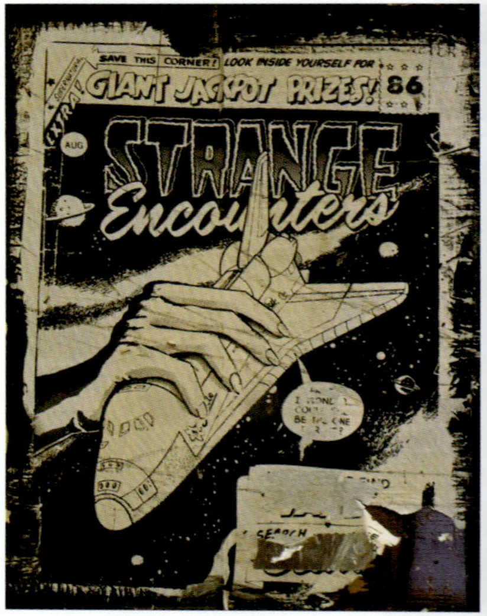

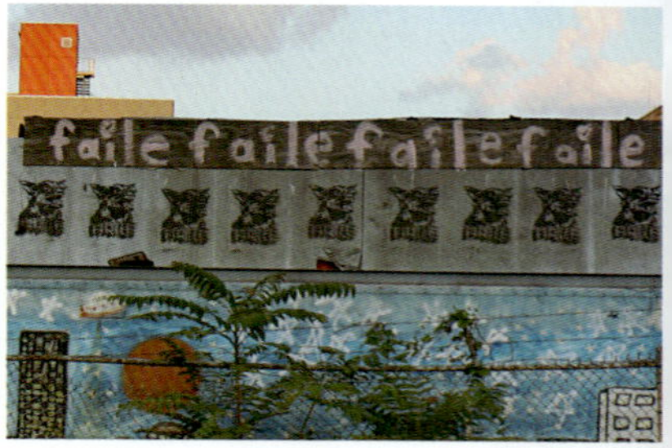

Photograph by Vincent Cornelli. Brooklyn, New York, 2007.
Detail top: Photograph by Vincent Cornelli. Brooklyn, New York, 2009.
Detail bottom: Photograph by Jake Dobkin (streetsy.com). Brooklyn, New York, 2006.

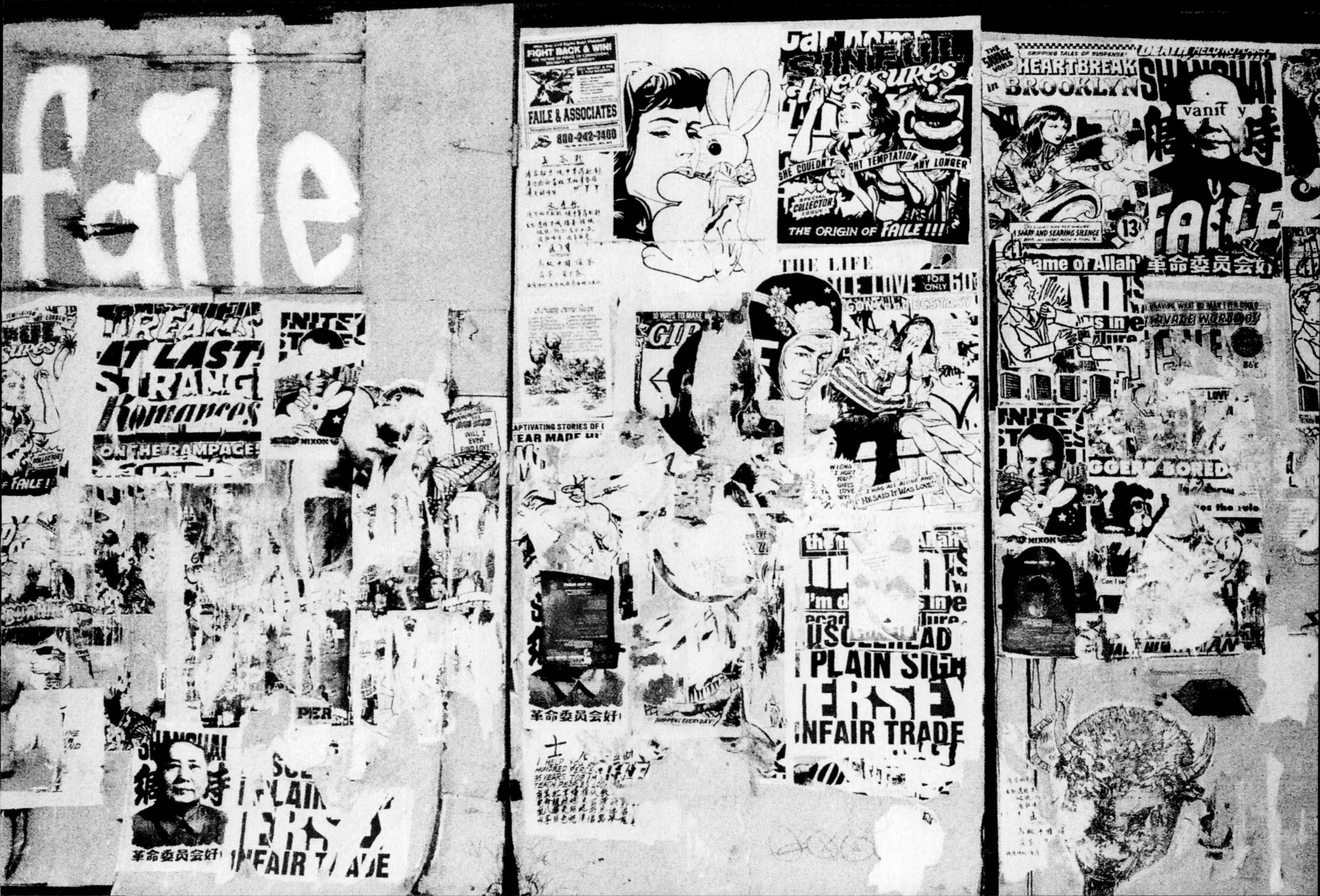
faile
FIGHT BACK & WIN!
FAILE & ASSOCIATES
800-242-7400
THE ORIGIN OF FAILE!!!
SPECIAL COLLECTOR ISSUE
GRIPPING TALES OF SUSPENSE!
HEARTBREAK
in BROOKLYN
vanity
FAILE
A SHARP AND SEARING SILENCE
革命委员会好
THE LIFE
AT LAST
Romances
ON THE RAMPAGE!
NIXON
WILL I EVER FIND LOVE?
I WAS ALL ALONE AND HE SAID IT WAS LOVE!
PLAIN SIGH
INFAIR TRADE

Shepard Fairey

When Barack Obama made history by becoming the first black president of the United States in 2008, most of his supporters around the world touted the same bold, graphic image to show their enthusiasm: a red-and-blue stencil-like image of Obama's face with the word HOPE stamped underneath it. It appeared on stickers, posters, T-shirts, and all manner of campaign paraphernalia, lighting up the Internet like a bottle rocket. This image was designed by one of street art's kingpins, Shepard Fairey.

Fairey has a lot of experience designing imagery—often verging on propaganda—that goes viral. He began his street-art career in the late 1980s, with the now legendary OBEY GIANT campaign, featuring a stenciled image of now-deceased wrestler Andre the Giant. He continued the campaign for more than twenty years, placing hundreds of thousands of stickers, stencils, and massive wheatpasted posters of the OBEY imagery on the walls of major cities around the world. Today, the OBEY GIANT campaign is seen as a cornerstone of street art's evolution, having laid the groundwork for the medium of wheatpasting.

Based in Los Angeles, Fairey is also responsible for the Studio Number One graphic design agency, *Swindle* magazine, Subliminal Projects Gallery, and the Obey clothing brand. The artist still sells signed, limited-edition prints from his website, and he exhibits internationally, including most recently at the Institute of Contemporary Art/Boston.

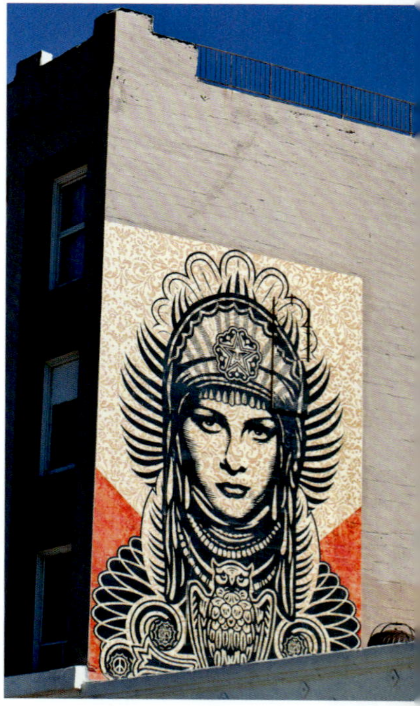

Photograph by Ernie Paniccioli. Brooklyn, New York, 2007.
Detail: Photograph by Vincent Cornelli. Los Angeles, 2010.

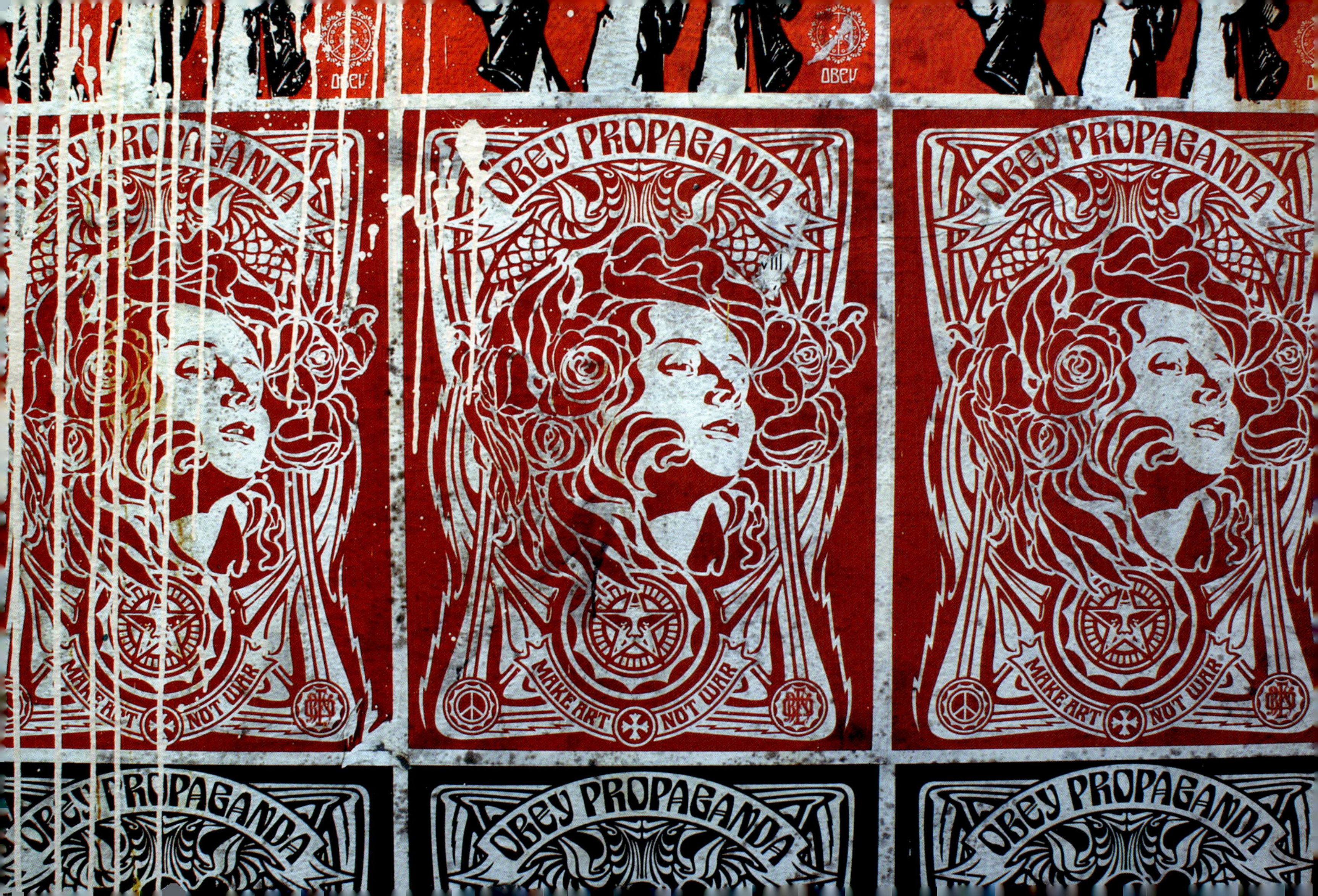
OBEY
OBEY
OBEY PROPAGANDA
MAKE ART
NOT WAR
OBEY PROPAGANDA
MAKE ART
NOT WAR
OBEY PROPAGANDA
MAKE ART
NOT WAR
OBEY PROPAGANDA
OBEY PROPAGANDA
OBEY PROPAGANDA

Faith 47

The graffiti artist known as Faith 47 is a native resident of the embattled city of Cape Town, South Africa. A firsthand witness to the effects of apartheid, Faith's work carries a mixed tone of uplifting optimism and weighted darkness. A blonde, lanky lady, Faith 47 is visually influenced by traditional graffiti lettering, classical character work, and the uniquely unstable social and political landscapes of Cape Town.

After becoming a mother at eighteen, Faith continued to paint on the street, attempting to heighten awareness of injustices within Africa, and she has exhibited her work internationally, including at the Carmichael Gallery in Los Angeles and the ATM Gallery in Berlin. She doesn't shy away from politically provocative work, such as her project "Restless Debt of Third World Beauty," in which she can be seen painting through Africa.

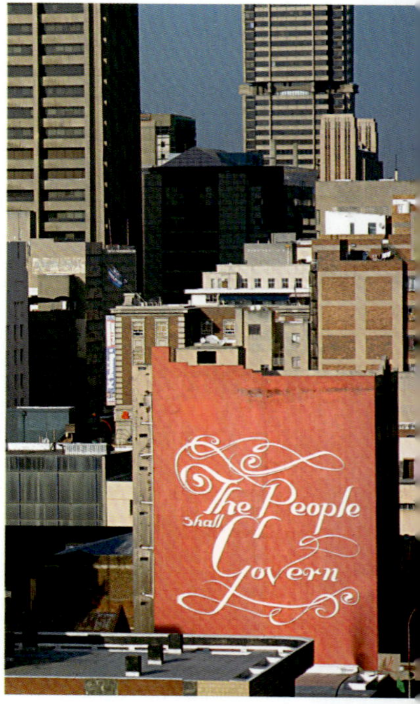

Photograph by Rowan Phybus.
Cape Town, South Africa, 2010.
Detail: Photograph by Rowan Phybus.
Johannesburg, South Africa, 2010.

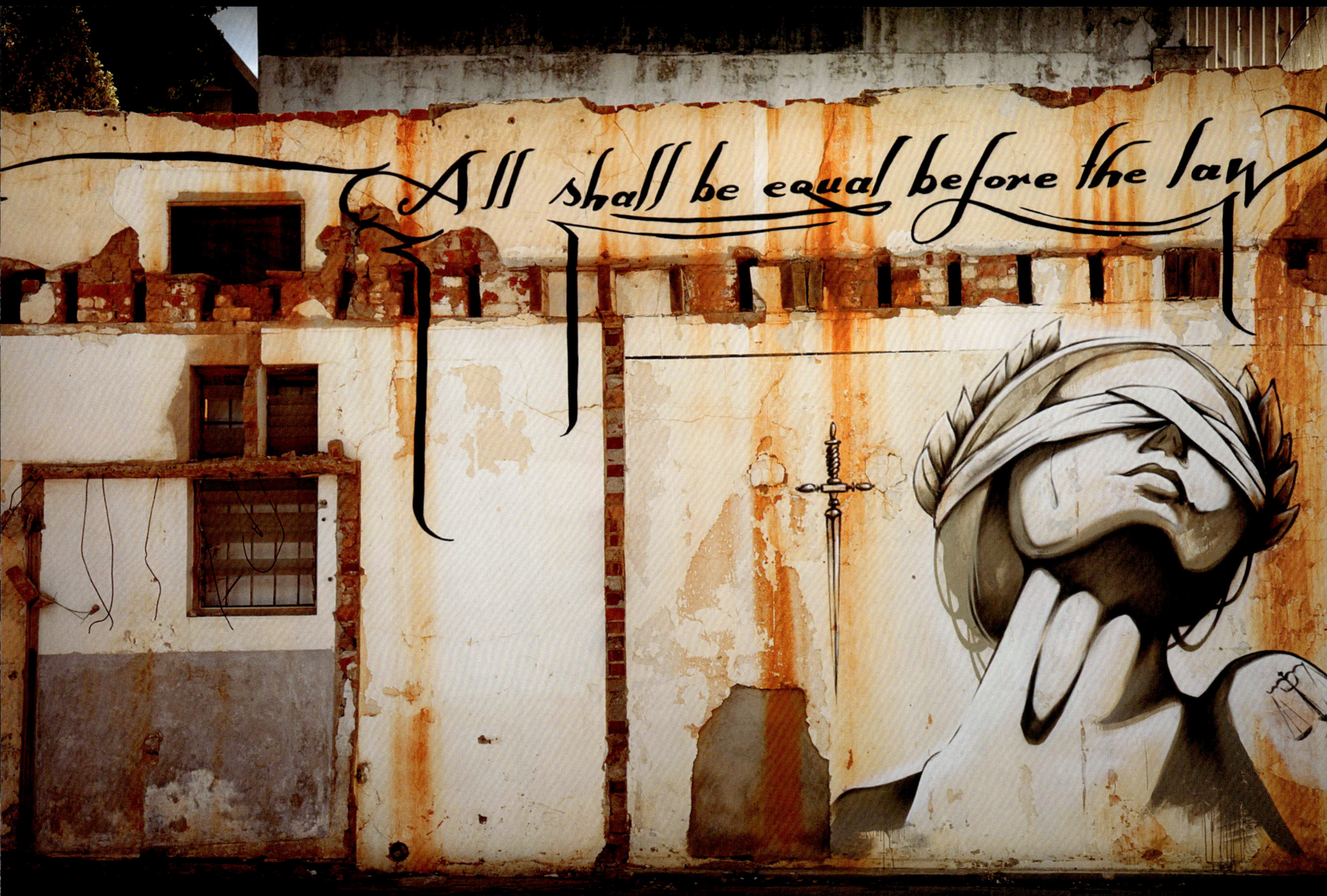
All shall be equal before the law

The Faith of Graffiti

In 1973, photographer Jon Naar roamed the streets and subway platforms of New York City, shooting more than three thousand photos of graffiti in just ten days. Accompanied by the graffiti writers while filming their handiwork, Naar faced constant harassment from intolerant cops, who resented his glorification of vandalism. The book that resulted, *The Faith of Graffiti*, captured graffiti at a time when the baby had just learned how to walk. Tags morphing into the beginnings of pieces gave the world a brief glimpse of what lay ahead.

Norman Mailer, who penned the book's text, interviewed writers of the day with a reverence usually reserved for celebrities. To him, Junior 161 and Cay 161 [see 186] may as well have been Jackson Pollock or Andy Warhol. Mailer characterized the graffiti movement as art, a novel and unpopular stance at the time.

The Faith of Graffiti became the bible for first-generation graffiti writers, many of whom quit before the dawning of a more artistic era. Naar's inclusion of a glossary featuring the names of all whose tags appeared in his tome became a source of pride or jealousy for those included on or left off "the list."

The book has appeared in several incarnations, including a hard- and softcover, a British version titled *Watching My Name Go By*, a French version, and a super-scarce [only 350 exist] signed, limited edition. Finally, a 2009 expanded edition of *The Faith of Graffiti*, with thirty-two additional pages of material, gives a new generation a chance to examine the old.

Photograph by Jon Naar.
New York City, 1973.

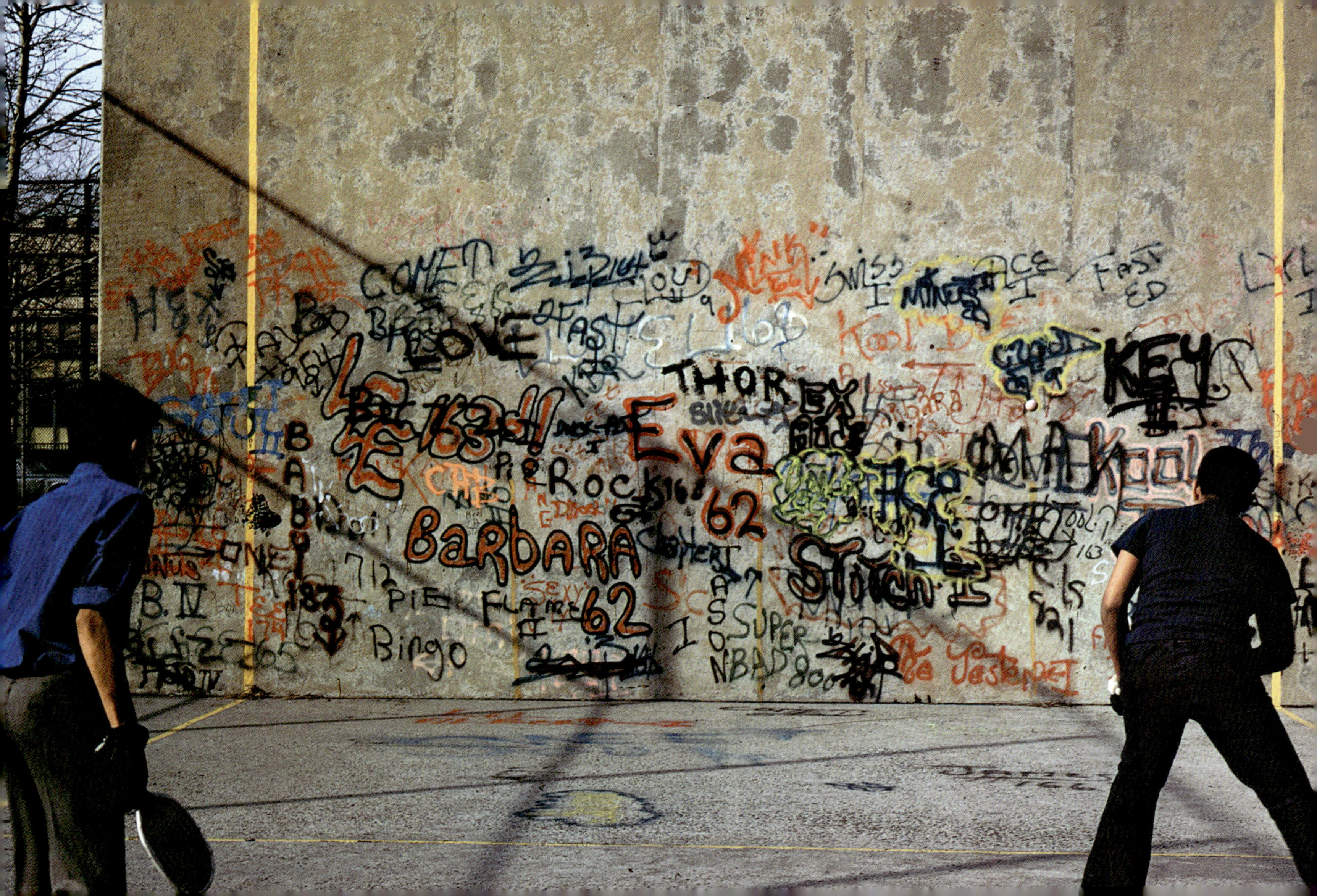
COMET
LOVE
2FAST
FAST ED
KEY
THOR
Eva
62
ROCK
BARBARA
62
Stitch I
Bingo
SUPER
FLAME
PIE

Farm Prod

The Farm Prod crew started to get active on the streets of Brussels in 1999. A double-digit-deep collective of friends, Farm Prod has been one of the few active street-art crews in that European capital over the past decade. Each member shows different influences, styles, and subject matters, which reflect the entangled concerns of a diverse group.

Faces and texts play a large role, and themes from *bandes dessinées* (Franco-Belgian comic strips) are consistently present. While the collective continues to work around Brussels, appearing at various festivals, exhibitions, and events, individual members are now also earning recognition for individual projects in the areas of animation, 3-D, illustration, and music.

In 2010, Farm Prod organized the first Kosmopolite Art Tour to be hosted in Brussels; for this festival, more than fifty international artists came together to color the gray streets of the European capital.

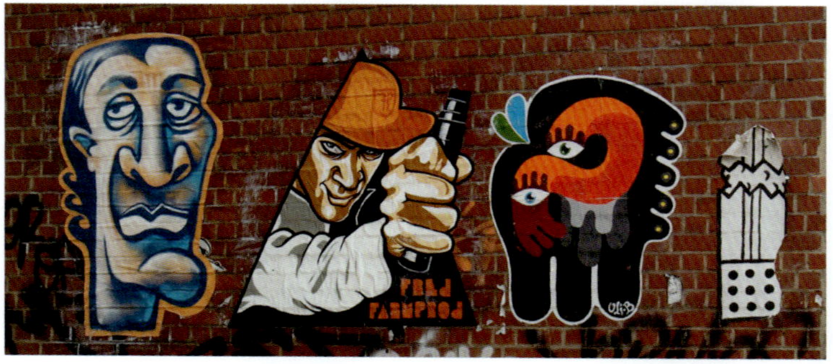

Photographs courtesy of Farm Prod.

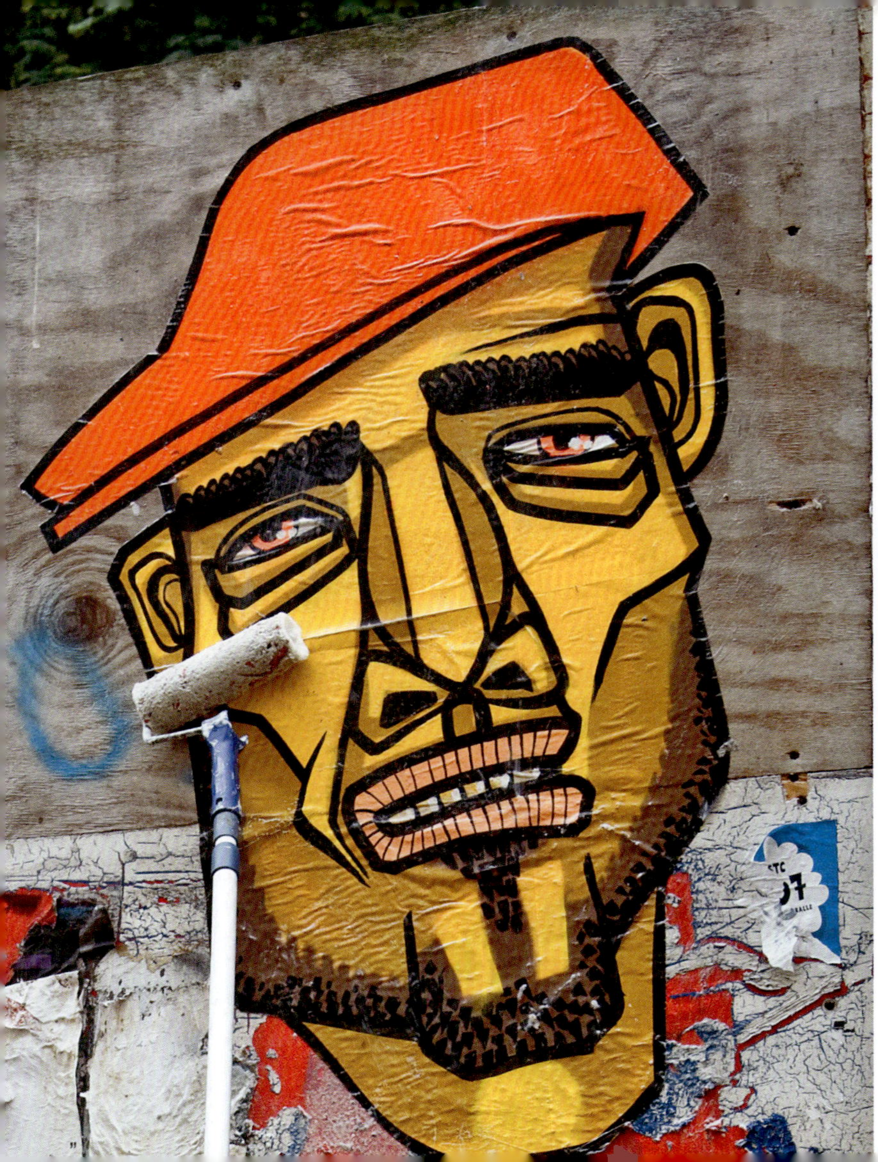

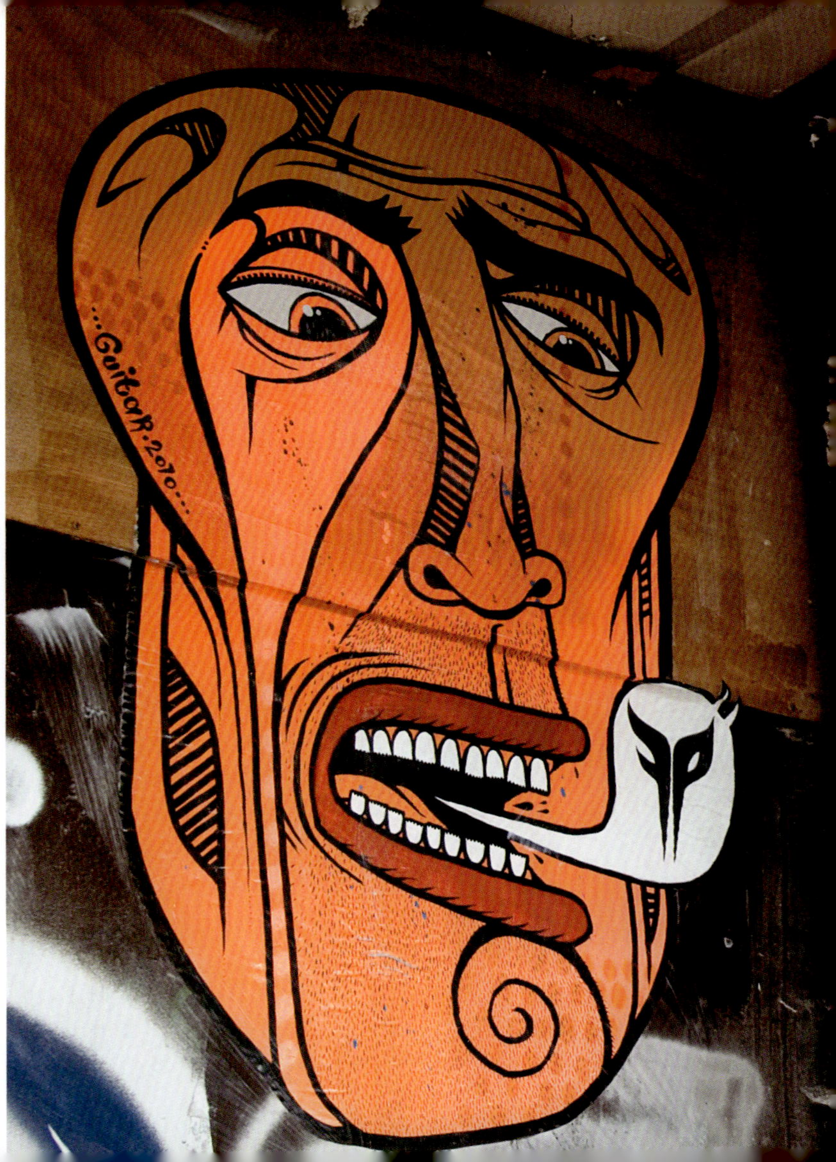
...GuitaR.2010...

fatcaps

Once upon a time, in the early 1970s, unenlightened graffiti writers toiled laboriously to gain recognition, first using markers and then spray paint. Unlike markers, which came in different widths, spray cans came with stock caps that made uniformly thin lines. These standard-issue caps sufficed only until graffiti's evolution demanded bigger and thicker renditions of one's name. Nowadays, foreign paint manufacturers design spray cans using writers' input and produce caps that can render lines small enough to draw a single hair on a character's head and wide enough to paint a whole subway car in minutes.

The discovery of the "fatcap" remains uncredited; some unsung hero transplanted a cap from Jifoam oven cleaner onto a can of Red Devil spray enamel and accomplished two things: first, greater comfort—the finger-friendly Jifoam cap eliminated the painful, nerve-deadening sensation incurred by prolonged stock-cap usage. Secondly, the new cap made the can spray three times as wide, opening the door to bigger and bolder tags and spawning the modern masterpiece. Writers found other caps capable of boosting production on air fresheners and spray starch and cleansers. Once the word spread, writers flocked to the supermarkets, trying to hoard every fatcap in the store. Finally, the affected companies changed their caps to render them incompatible with spray paint.

**Photograph by Martha Cooper.
Baltimore, Maryland, 2010.
Far right, top: Photograph by Brent Kerr.
Brooklyn, New York, 2010.
Far right, bottom: Photograph by PJay One.
New York City, 2009.**

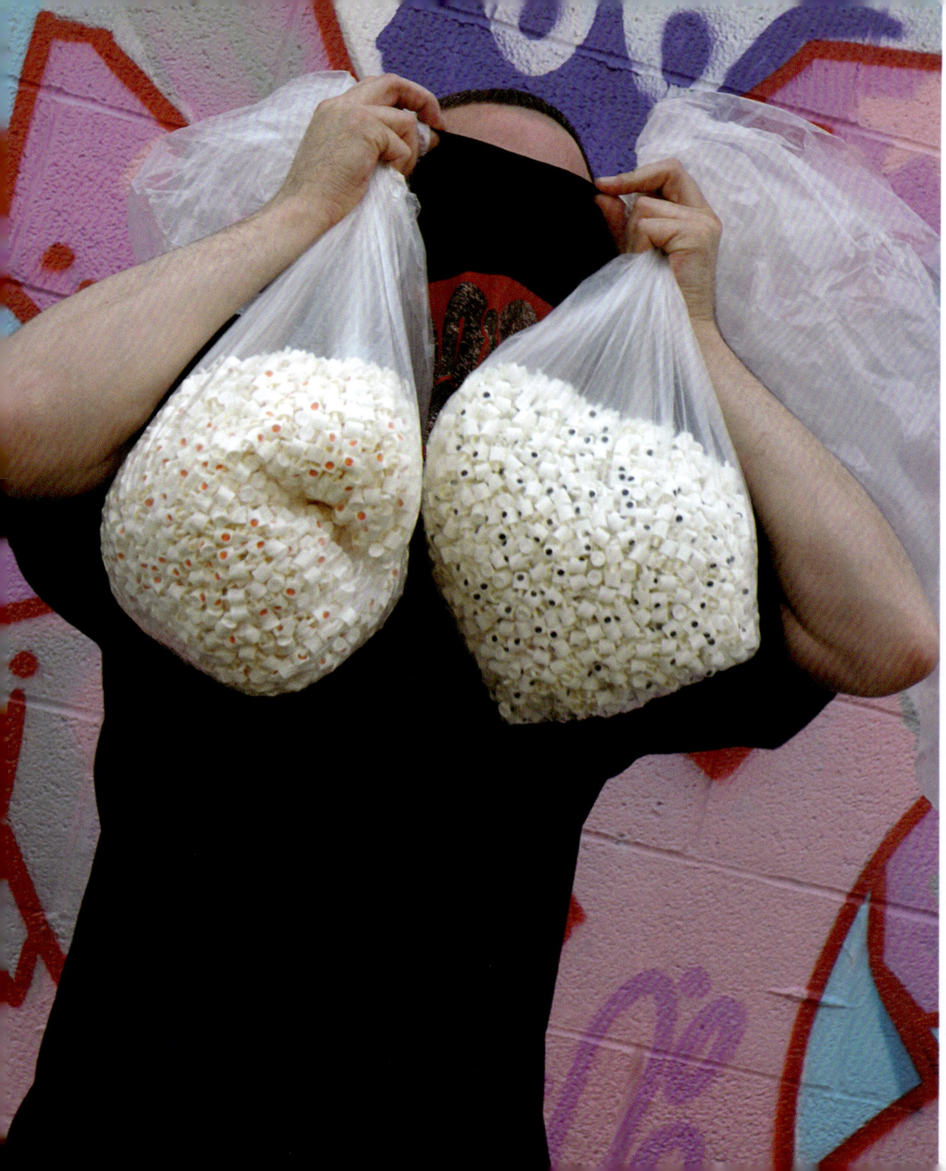

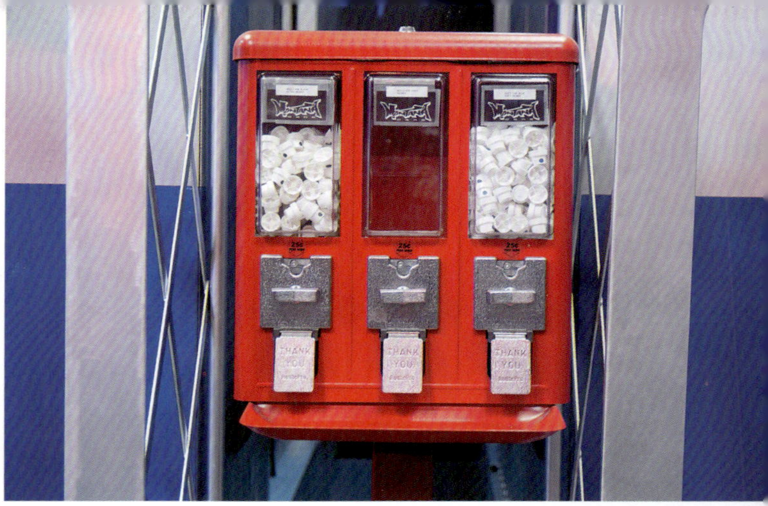
THANK YOU
THANK YOU
THANK YOU

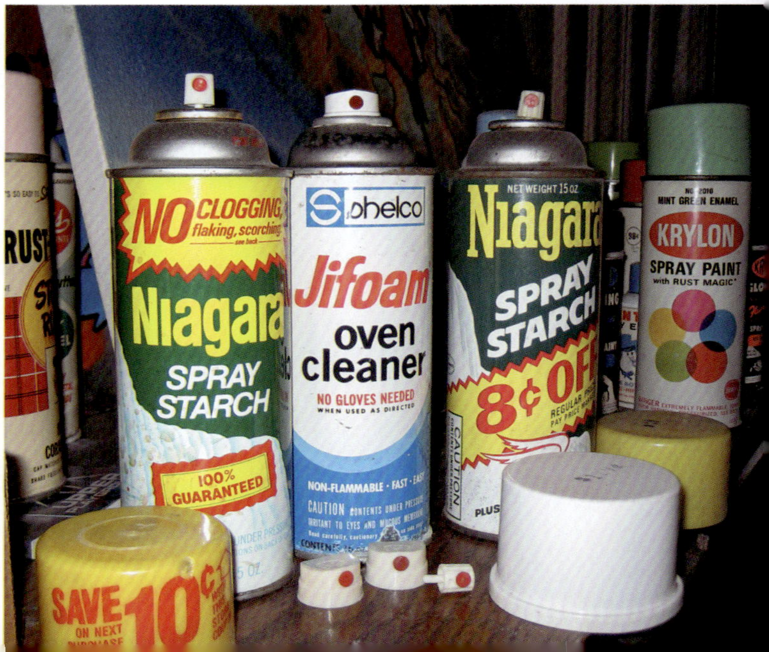
NO CLOGGING, flaking, scorching
Niagara
SPRAY STARCH
100% GUARANTEED
Shelco
Jifoam
oven cleaner
NO GLOVES NEEDED
WHEN USED AS DIRECTED
NON-FLAMMABLE · FAST · EASY
CAUTION
NET WEIGHT 15 OZ
Niagara
SPRAY STARCH
8¢ OFF
CAUTION
MINT GREEN ENAMEL
KRYLON
SPRAY PAINT
with RUST MAGIC
SAVE 10¢
ON NEXT

Faust

Among all the amateur scribbling and indecipherable hieroglyphics that make up the average tagger's landscape, a skilled hand at penmanship is a rarity. New York–based artist Faust is best known for his impeccable calligraphy skills, which draw heavily on a graffiti aesthetic, but also lean toward graphic design in their clean lines and solid blacks.

A longtime graffiti writer and a self-professed traditional lettering purist, Faust grounds his ethos in the idea that a graffiti writer needn't change his style of artwork to be a legitimate fine artist—the letters are enough. In fact, the artist says, one needn't even venture into piecing or working in color to find the art. After many years of bowing to graffiti's rules, Faust decided to buck them; he expanded his tag as his art form, taking it as large as possible, even covering entire rooms with one tag.

Faust continues to work toward a career in fine art, but he also does commercial calligraphy work for hire, collaborating with advertising companies on branding campaigns, as well as with motion-graphics companies. He is perpetually striving to discombobulate notions of what is graffiti and what is fine art. Under his real name, Faust is a prolific oil painter with an active studio practice, but he works hard to keep these two worlds separated.

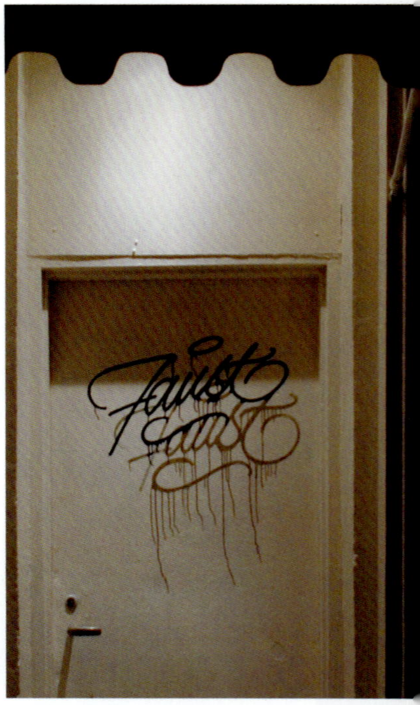

Willoughby Windows Installation.
Photograph by Michael Angeles.
Brooklyn, New York, 2010.
Detail: Photograph courtesy of Faust.
New York City, 2010.

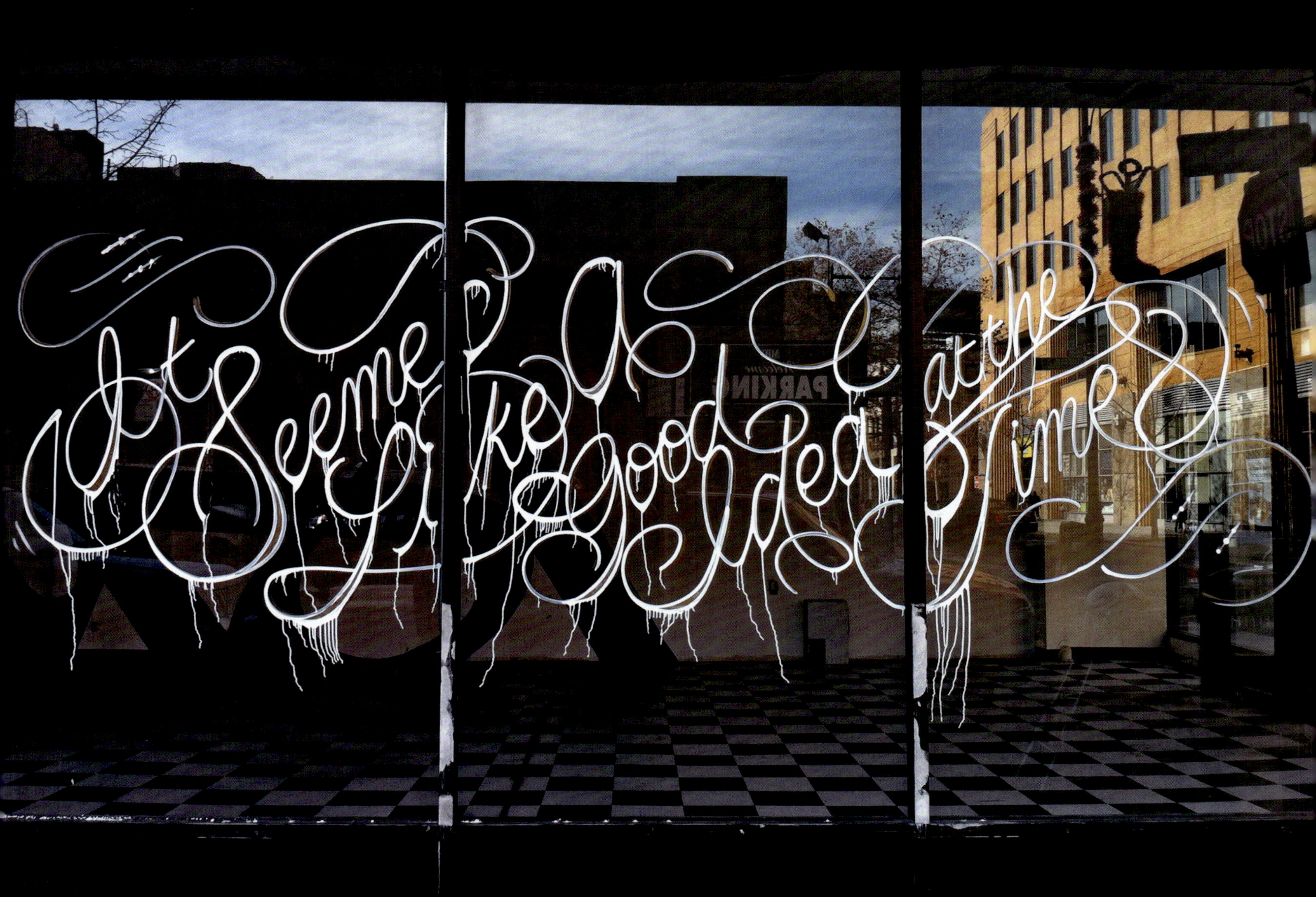
It Seemed Like a Good Idea at the Time

Fauxreel

For the last ten years, artist Dan Bergeron has been making a name for himself under the moniker Fauxreel. The street-art community is well versed in his photo-based pieces: They are hard to miss. Having worked extensively in the field of photography, Fauxreel transforms his images into large-scale black-and-white images, which he wheatpastes onto dilapidated walls in densely populated urban areas around the world. His images are often portraits of everyday people; sometimes his pieces are full-body, but they often consist of massive faces on the sides of buildings. Bergeron states that he is attempting to draw attention to current social and political themes, and that by working in the streets, he hopes to liberate physical spaces, rather than simply reappropriating or contextualizing them.

Based in Toronto, Canada, Bergeron came to prominence within the street-art community around 2005, and he has since taken the fine-art world by storm. He has exhibited at the Royal Ontario Museum, the Royal Art Gallery of Ontario, Show & Tell Gallery in Toronto, and the Luminato Festival, to name a few.

Photograph by Becki Fuller.
Brooklyn, New York, 2008.

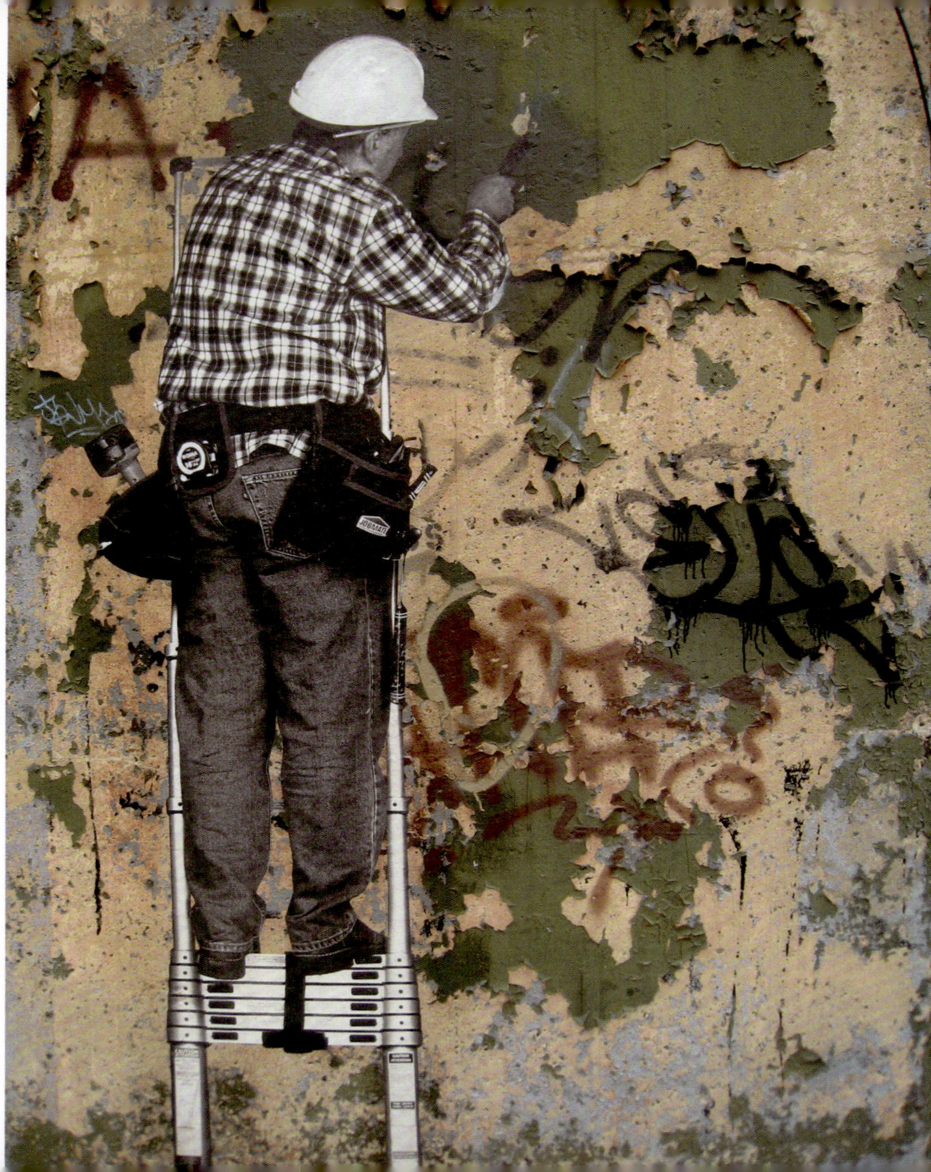

FBA

Style on the trains had been building from 1974 to 1980, culminating in a synthesized dance of color and contrast. The foundation for a piece was usually a blended interior with a series of designs laid on top; the 3-D was generally to the bottom and left of the piece. Few writers strayed from the plan, because it worked—then came FBA, a group of kids who had their own vision of what a piece should look like.

The FBA crew, like so many others, was born in the cafeteria at the High School of Art and Design [see 167]. The name stood for Fast Breaking Art, and some of its early members included Tack, Spade 127, Airborne, and Kaze. They began to throw away elements of style that had been around for ages, including the blend, blood drips, cobblestones, bits, and the ubiquitous left-side/bottom 3-D.

The FBA pieces were done with a one-color fill-in with harsh-edge geometric patterns stamped on top—only then were the outlines done. The 3-Ds were almost always a thick bottom 3-D that helped raise the piece from the train. They bookended the pieces with characters they had created [with a little inspiration from Vaughn Bode]. Their pieces and whole cars ran proudly on the Broadway line from 1979 to 1985.

FBA reshaped style, and the next group of writers coming up would reap the dividends.

**Top: Pieces by Spade 127 [left] and Tack.
Photograph by Henry Chalfant.
New York City, 1982.
Bottom left and right: Canvases by Serve.
Photographs by Adam Reich. New York City, 2007.**

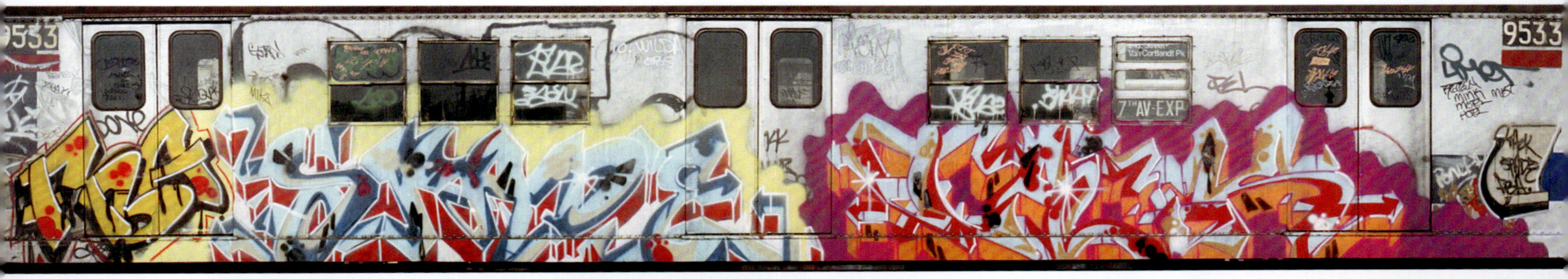
9533
9533
7TH AV-EXP

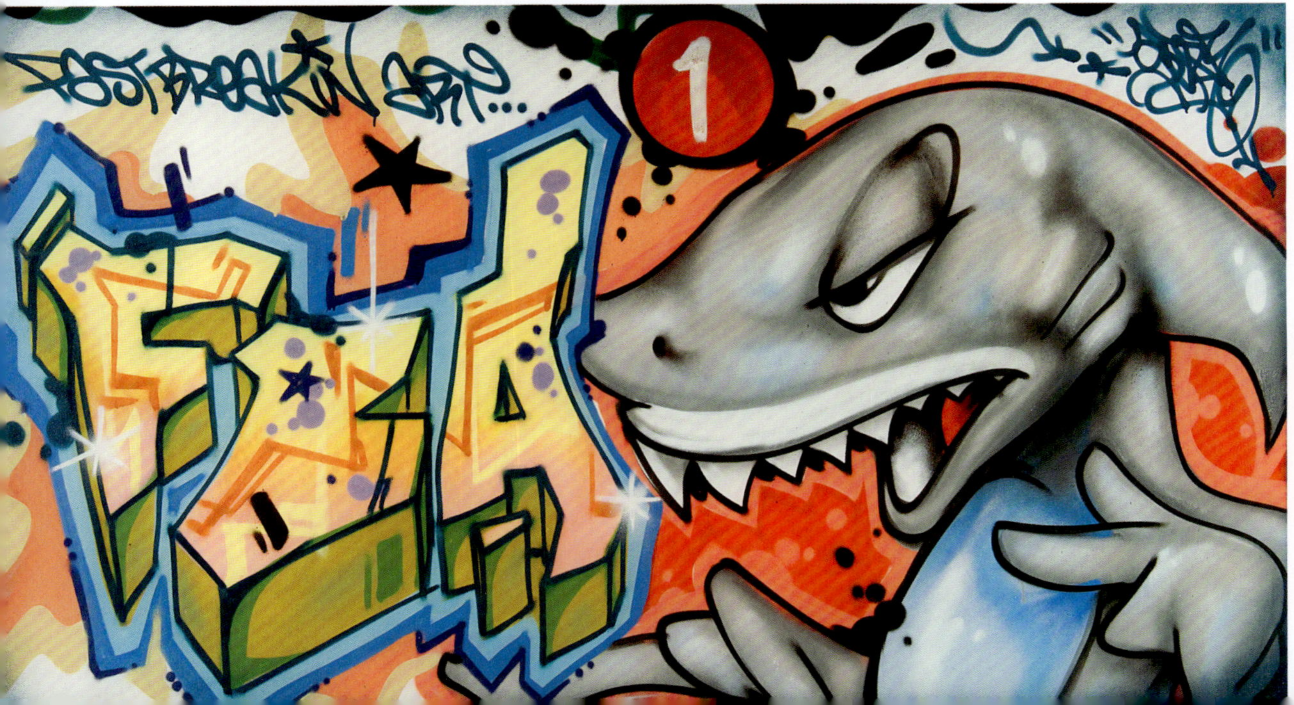

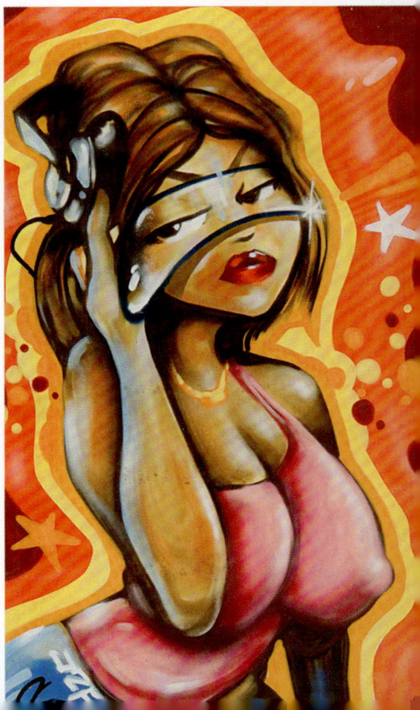

John Fekner

New York City–born John Fekner is an internationally known multimedia artist who has spray-painted hundreds of environmental, social, political, and conceptual works in outdoor locations across North America and Europe. Fekner began practicing street art in the early 1970s. His unsigned messages typically consist of stenciled words, symbols, dates, and icons intended to point out hazardous urban conditions desperately in need of demolition, construction, or reconstruction. Whether his projects remain for years or last only a few hours, this crusading artist's objective is to call attention to squalor and urge city officials, agencies, and individuals to take action to improve our communities. Fekner labels highway overpasses, toxic dumps, and abandoned lots—the outdoor urban environment is his studio; bricks, rocks, crumbling walls, and rusting metal his canvas; recycled cardboard, stencils, found objects, and inexpensive spray paint his materials of choice. Unconcerned with the preciousness or monetary value of traditional art forms, he has abandoned paintbrushes, chisels, charcoal, and other customary artists' tools. Fekner focuses on creating public visual experiences that spark people to enact positive change in their environment. About his salutary artistic goals, Fekner says the job of the street artist is to "act as the eye of the community, for the community."

Top left: *DK*. Woodside, New York, 1981.
Top right: *Toxic*. Maspeth, New York, 1981.
Bottom left: Photograph by Jee Won Shin. Brooklyn, New York, 2010.
Bottom right: *RUA VIDIOT*. Maspeth, New York, 1983.

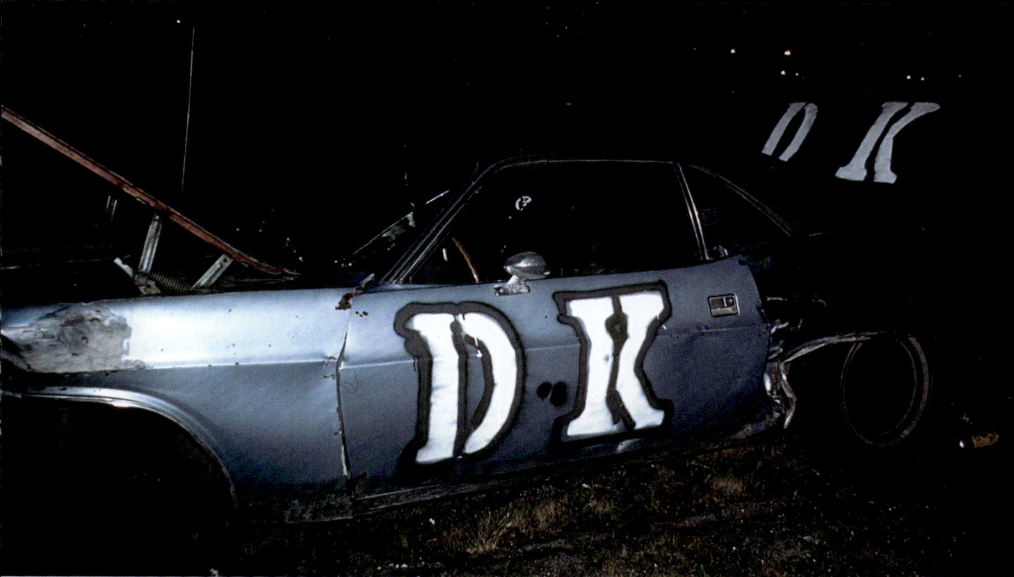
DK
DK

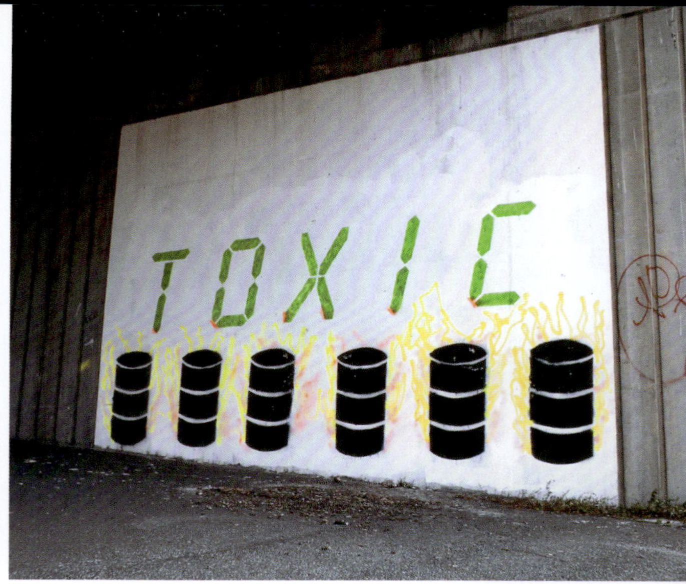
TOXIC

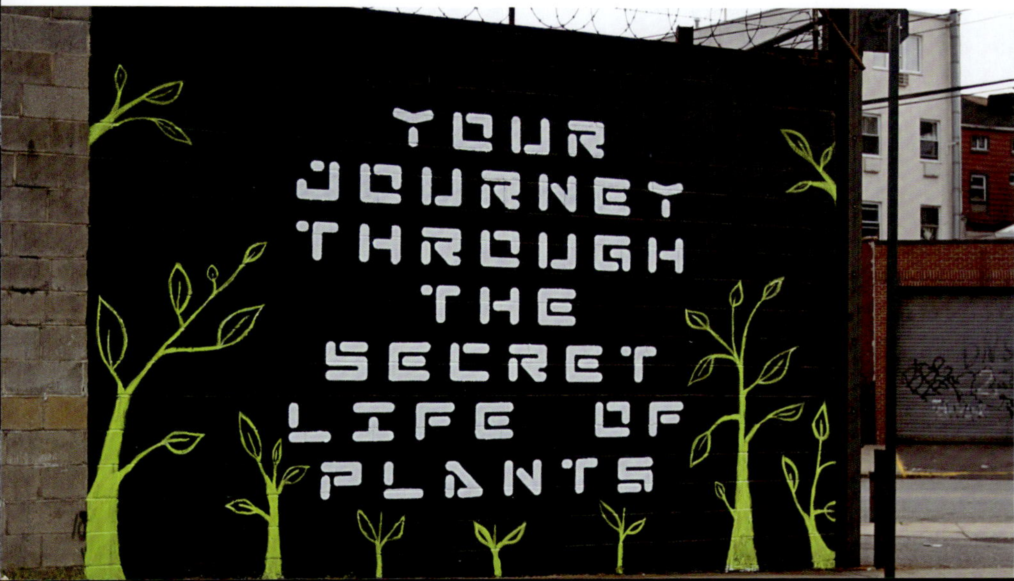
YOUR
JOURNEY
THROUGH
THE
SECRET
LIFE OF
PLANTS

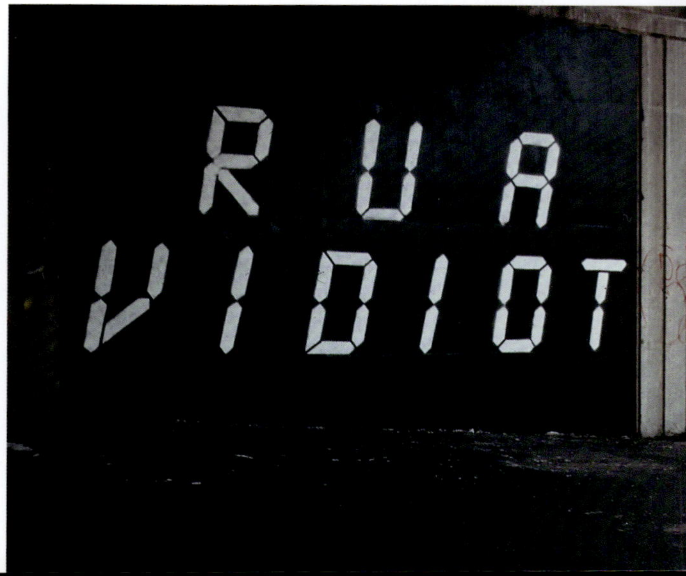
R U A
VIDIOT

fire extinguisher

Sandblasters, razor ribbon, police raids, and constant repainting of public spaces—each has taken its toll on the outlaw artist's arsenal. Desperate times call for desperate measures. Scratchiti and acid-filled markers that burn permanent images on metal and glass offer little creative range, but they do keep the rebellious, vandalistic spirit alive.

In the last few years, vandals have added a new weapon to the mischief menu that makes a six-inch-wide fatcap seem anorexic: the paint-filled fire extinguisher. It may be much harder to conceal, but this bazooka of the graffiti game provides stunning results. There is no bigger bang for the buck in terms of impact; tags that cover a five-story building can be executed in seconds.

One street-savvy entrepreneur is currently trying to cash in by marketing stylized extinguishers.

Artwork by Katsu.
Photograph by Ray Mock.
Brooklyn, New York, 2010.

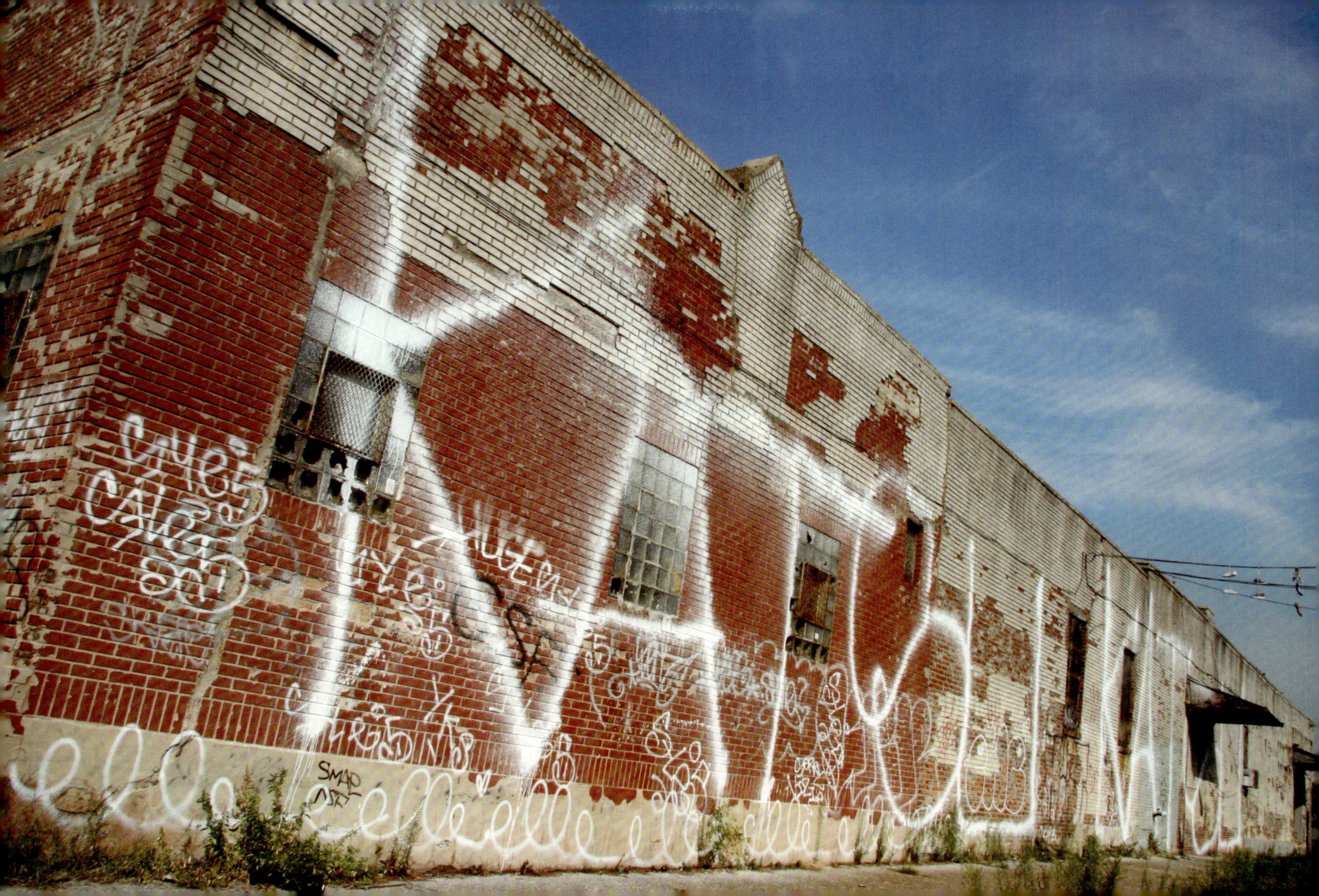

Flint . . .

Flint began writing on the streets of Brooklyn in the early 1970s. He first started hitting train stations as a way to while away the time after visiting his girlfriend. Going back and forth from her apartment to his late at night left him with the time to expand on his tag, and he quickly came up with a series of sayings that went with his name: FLINT . . . FOR THOSE WHO DARE, FLINT . . . FOR LADIES ONLY, and FLINT . . . FOR YOUR EYES ONLY. He soon entered the High School of Art and Design (see 167), where he hooked up with writers from other boroughs, including Tracy 168 (see 340), who would eventually introduce him to LSD Om (see 206), his future writing partner.

From 1974 to 1976, Tracy 168, Flint . . ., and LSD Om hung out a great deal, motion tagging and hitting stations. In 1974, they had formed the Rebels (the name came from an early moniker of the Beatles, a band they both admired). The two writers put down artists they liked; early members included Roger from Queens, Shadow from Brooklyn, Rebel from the Lower East Side, and Hoy 56 from the Bronx.

Though Flint quit in 1976, his legacy lives on the amazing photographs he took of his writing friends.

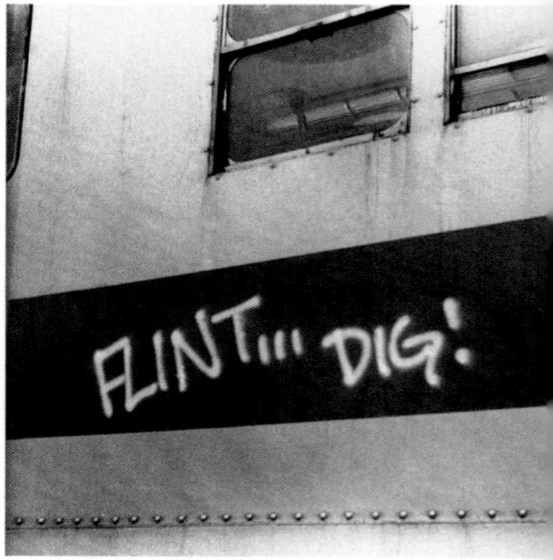

Photographs courtesy of Flint Genari.
New York City, 1974.

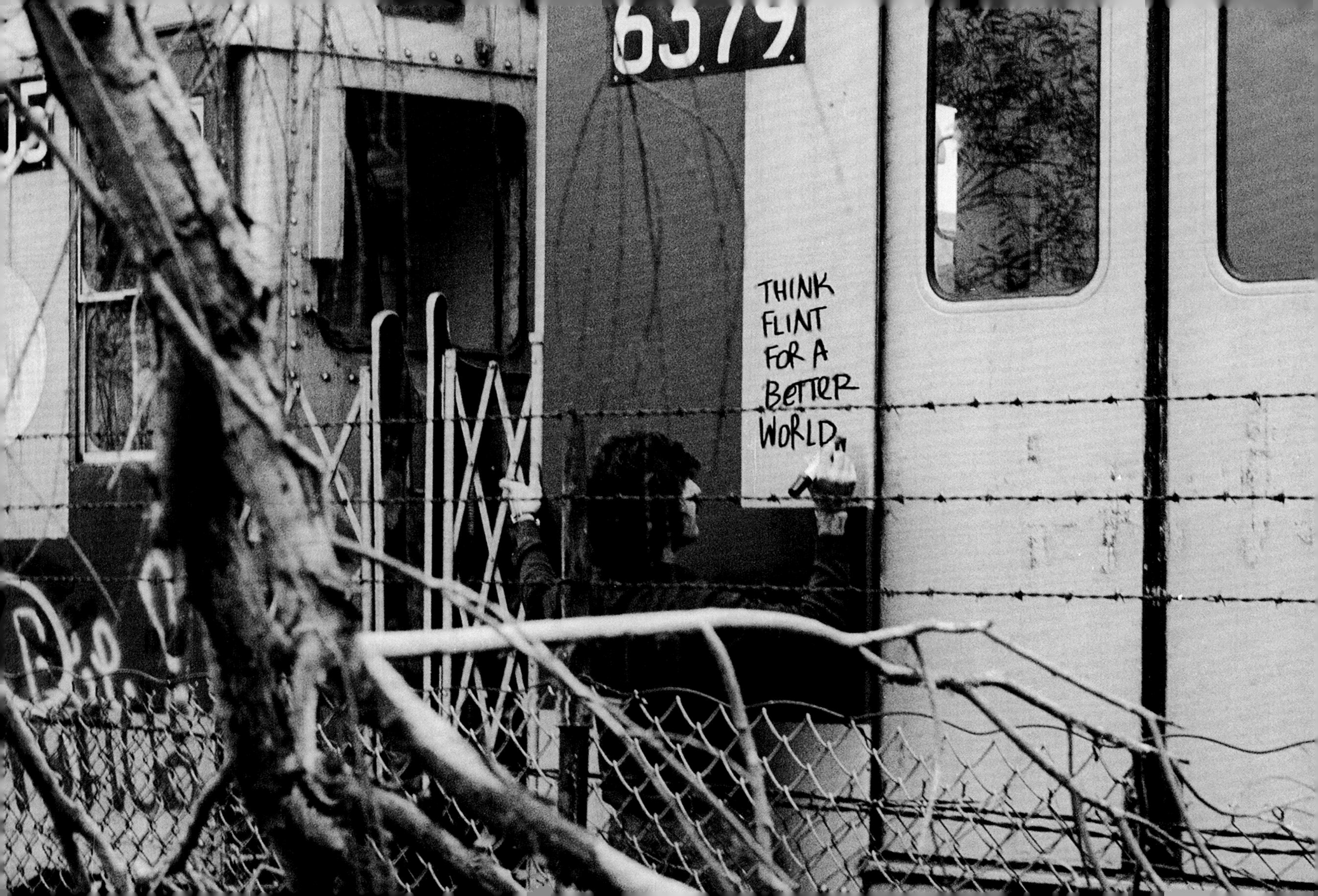
6379
THINK
FLINT
FOR A
BETTER
WORLD

Flint 707

Flint 707 was a Brooklyn writer who began his career on the BMT lines in 1972. He quickly found a much bigger audience on the IRT lines that ran through the Bronx and Manhattan. Like most writers in 1972, he was a tagger; he had a very distinct style with an elongated capital "F" that was copied by other writers.

In 1973, he did two major pieces that helped revolutionize graffiti style. Both pieces were wider versions of his tag; what made them interesting was the incredible 3-D he put on each of them. At that time, one-point perspective was not being taught at graffiti school, and yet, somehow, Flint figured it out.

Flint 707's second piece was perhaps more important, because it was a top-to-bottom that covered half the length of a subway car; the thick 3-D perspective made it seem to jump right off the train. At the time, it was the most sophisticated piece to be executed in the movement, and writers applauded it as it traveled through the boroughs. Within months, other writers responded with their own versions of the 3-D style, and it eventually became part of the toolkit of any advanced writer. Flint 707's pieces could not be overlooked by the fledgling group of writers at UGA [see 346], and they quickly voted him in. After leaving the group in 1973, he gave up hitting trains and switched to painting on canvas.

Pieces by Flint 707 (left) and Devil.
Photograph by Jack Stewart.
New York City, 1973.

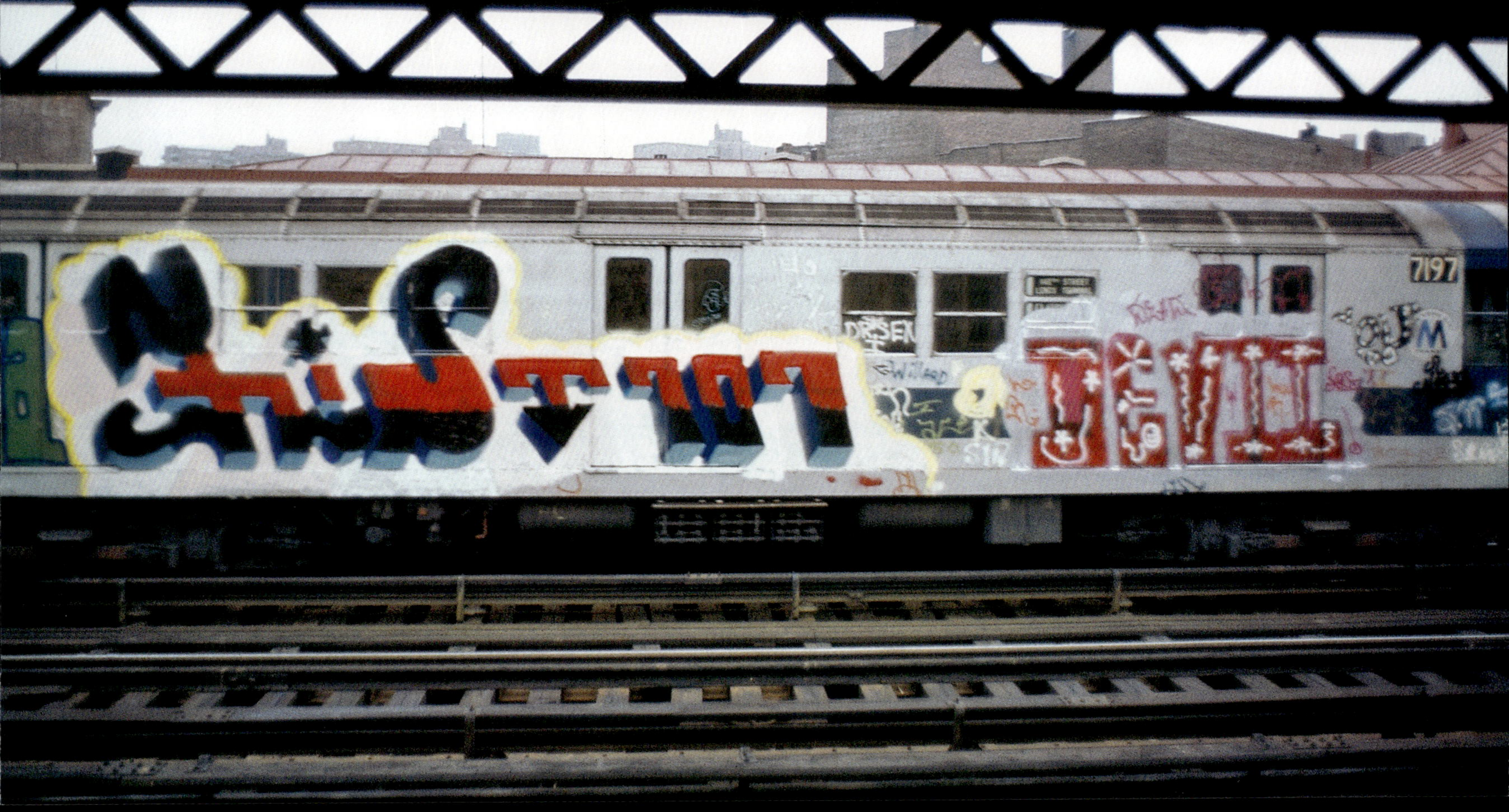
7197

Flying Fortress

As street art gained mainstream popularity in the early 2000s, artists scrambled to capitalize on the work they were gifting to the communities around them. Some waltzed over the line into the fine-art world, some moved into graphic or apparel design, and some took up illustration or screen printing—and a few made an interesting leap into vinyl toys. One of the best-known artists to come from the streets and eventually master the art of the vinyl toy is a German artist who goes by the playful name of Flying Fortress.

Characters, a core element of graffiti art, are beloved by viewers and often begin to take on personalities of their own. In collaboration with toy makers, Flying Fortress soon discovered the exponential niche value of a toy that taps into the buyer's own creativity. This spawned the creation of Teddy Troops, a series of toys designed by Flying Fortress; each toy soldier comes with a base-color body and helmet, and the purchaser is meant to paint his own outfit or design onto the soldier.

A challenge for most street artists was envisioning their characters in 3-D, as opposed to the flat imagery they had previously generated. Flying Fortress leaped this hurdle with ease, transitioning from his graffiti background into a full-fledged commercial business, marketing his Teddy Troops, Fortress books, T-shirts, and—of course—canvases.

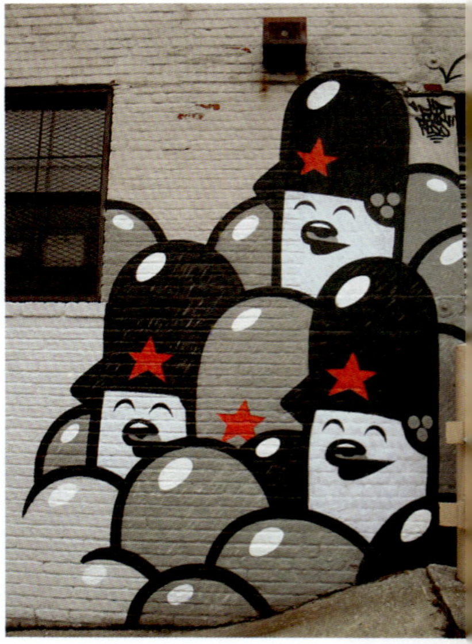

Photographs by Becki Fuller.
New York City, 2009.
Detail: Brooklyn, New York, 2008.

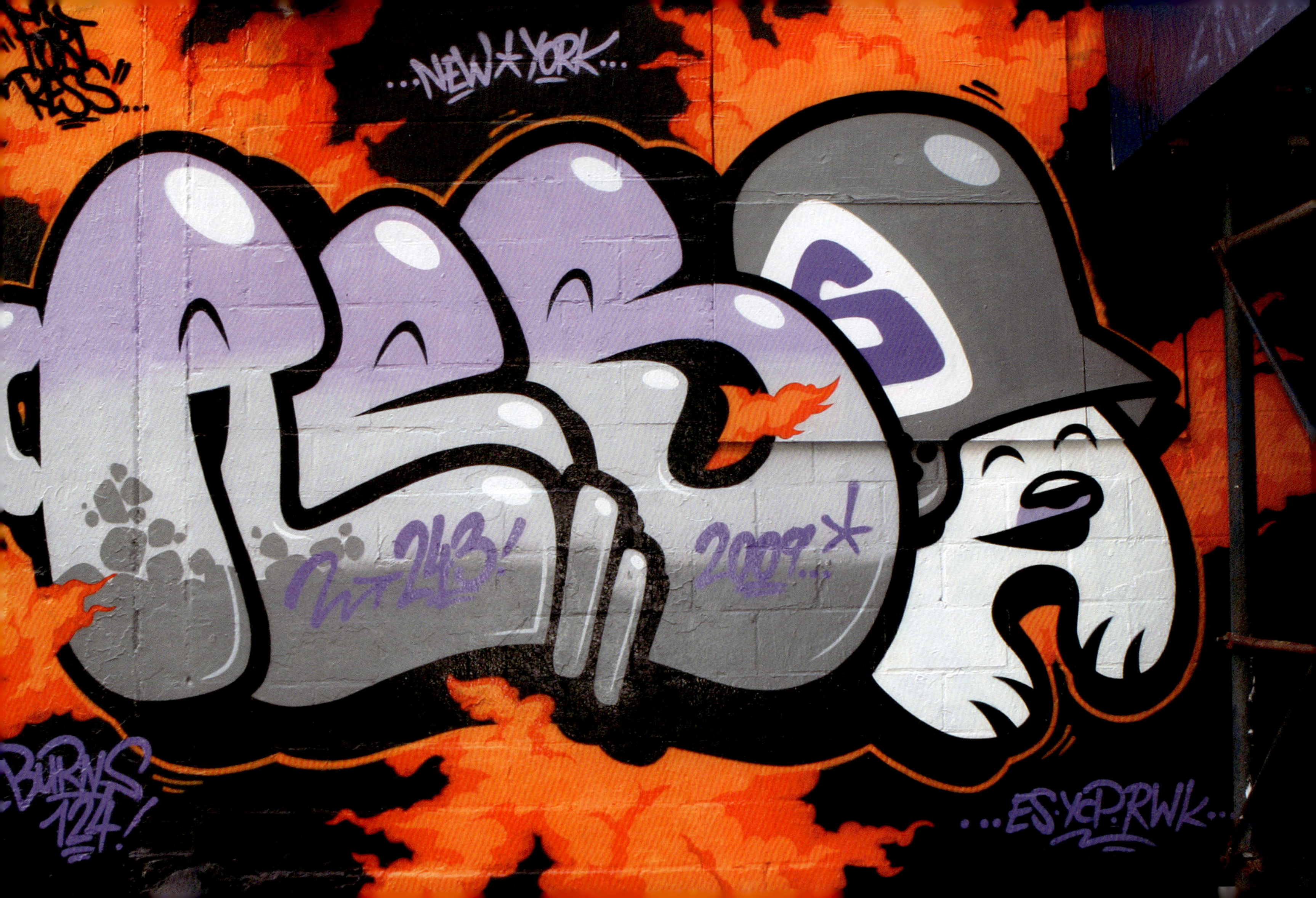
NEW YORK
243!
2009
BURNS 124!
ES·YEP·RWK

forced to buff

In the 1970s and '80s, anti-graffiti cops used to patrol the subway lines. These cops, who often worked in tandem, pursued graffiti writers vigilantly, often attempting to befriend the writers they apprehended in the hopes of converting them into informants. The names of cop teams such as Hickey and Ski, Wasserman and Rodin, and Curley and Ferrari were as familiar to graffiti writers as the names Cliff 159 [see 070], Tracy 168 [see 340], and Phase 2 [see 255]. Some overenthusiastic officers beat writers or spray-painted various parts of their bodies, their brutality no doubt stemming from the frustration they felt knowing that even the most prolific bombers they arrested would just receive a slap on the wrist from the courts.

The most severe penalty a repeat offender could expect in those days—community service—proved to be more reward than punishment. A judge would sentence writers to scrubbing details, resulting in kids from every part of the city being grouped together to clean trains and stations.

A neophyte could wind up spending a day with a stylemaster, and a Brooklyn writer might wind up bombing a yard the following week with a kid from the Bronx he met while scrubbing. Even writers who weren't arrested would come to scrubbing locations just to hang out and meet their heroes. Unfortunately for today's writers, technology and more stringent laws have turned what was once a cat-and-mouse game into all-cat.

Private collection.
New York City, 1985.

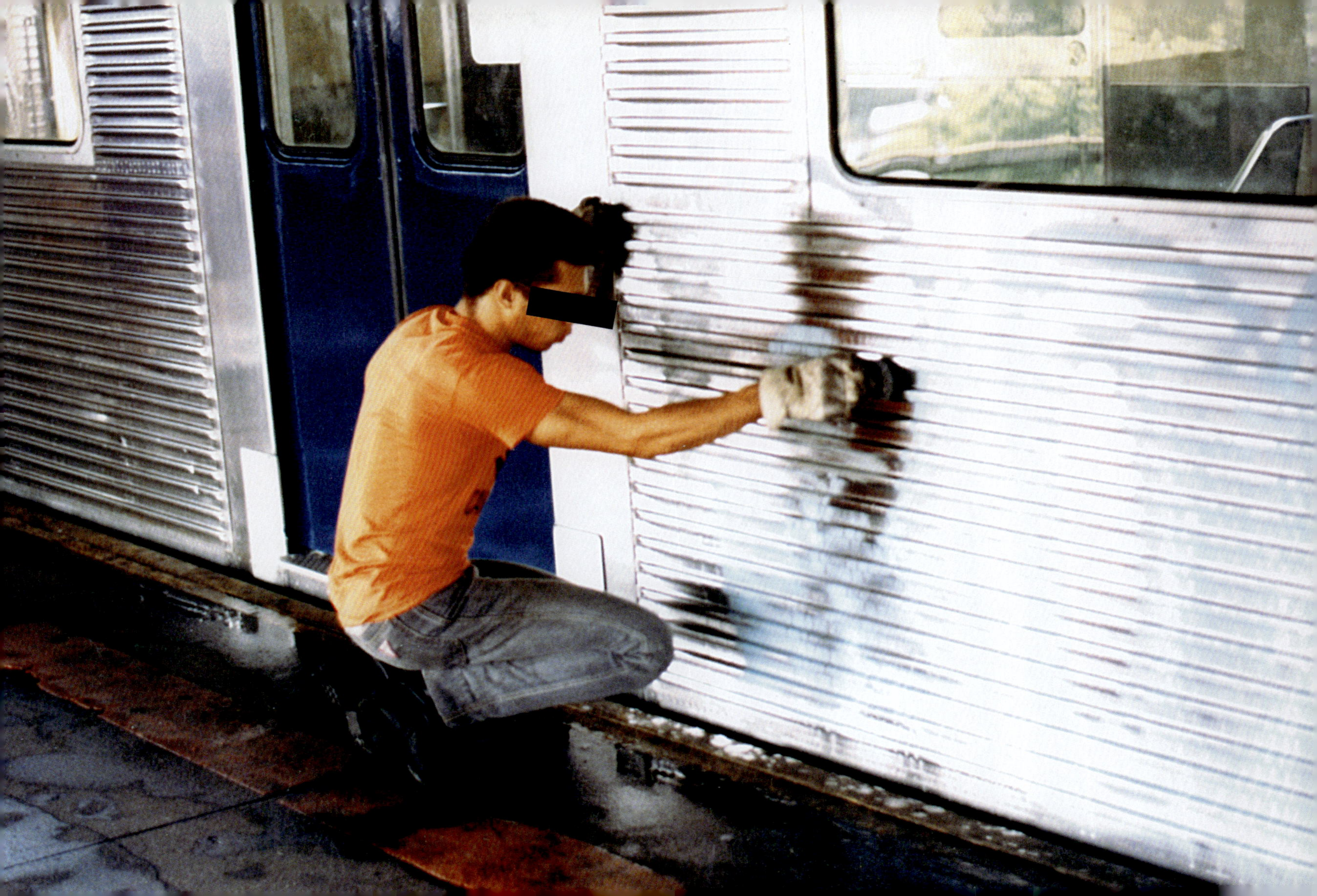

The Freedom Tunnel

In 1979, while painting a blockbuster piece on the side of a #1 train, the artist known as Freedom discovered that he could get tonal qualities from black spray paint. This discovery would enable him to sketch almost anything in spray paint; now, he just needed the right place to do it.

In 1980, Freedom started painting in an abandoned tunnel in Riverside Park. Some of his earliest images were references to times in his childhood when he would spend hours dangling a string with gum on it down into the IRT gratings. On a good day, he could fish out nickels, dimes, and other assorted treasures, such as a Tony Kubek baseball card. The detritus of his 1960s youth became the springboard for his early paintings.

His newer works were done in silver and black and were painted directly under gratings, where light illuminated them. Under one grating would be a soda can; the next one had a Ted Williams baseball card; farther down was a pack of cigarettes. Freedom also enjoyed doing portraits and reinventing major works of art—including Dalí's image of a melting clock, of which Freedom painted four different versions. He collaborated with Smith on an enormous re-creation of Goya's *Third of May 1808* in 1992.

In 1989, when the subway-graffiti movement ended in New York, younger writers found a new place to paint: the tunnel beneath Riverside Park, which would forever be dubbed the "Freedom Tunnel."

Photograph by Martha Cooper. New York City, 1982.

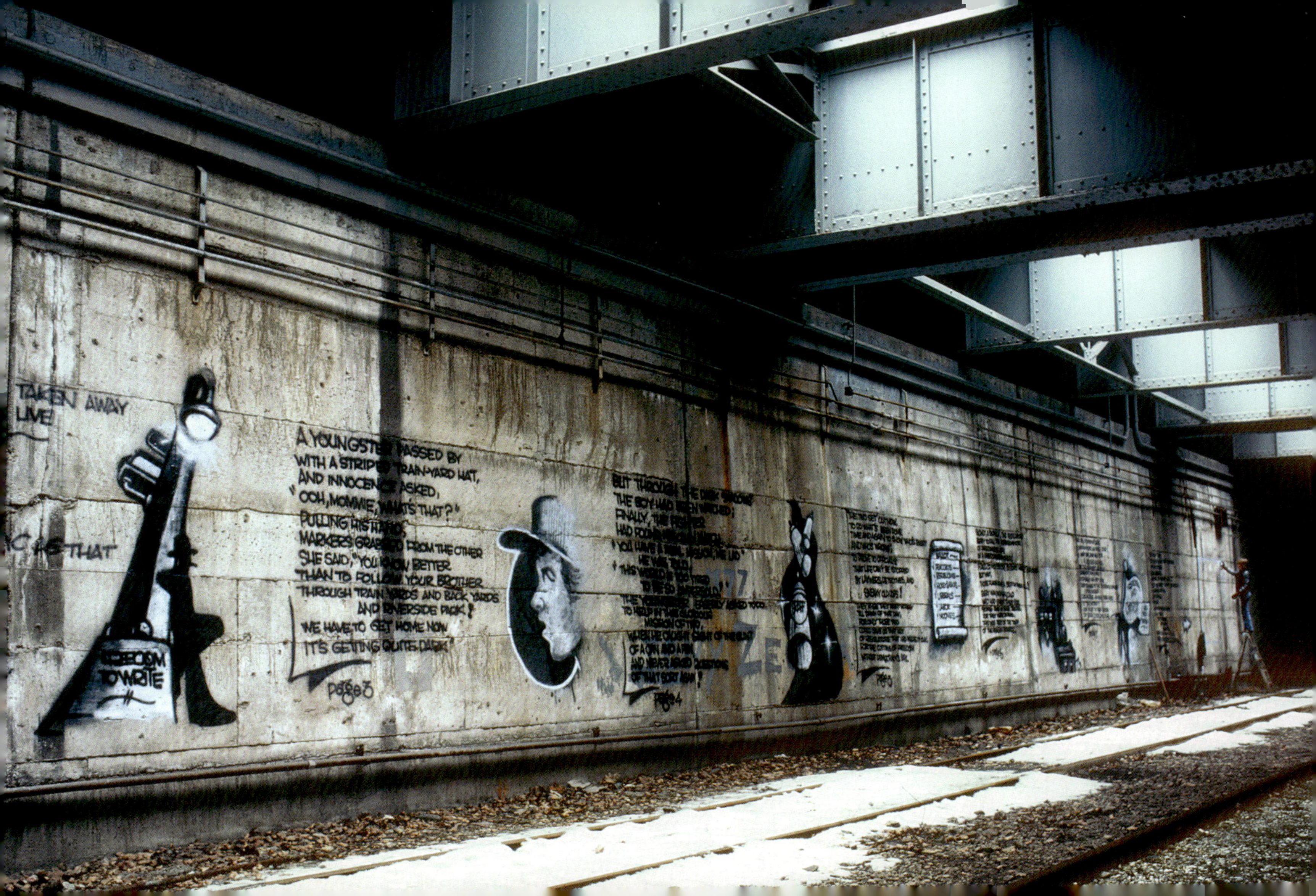
TAKEN AWAY LIVE!
FREEDOM TO WRITE
A YOUNGSTER PASSED BY
WITH A STRIPED TRAIN-YARD HAT,
AND INNOCENCE ASKED,
"OOH, MOMMIE, WHAT'S THAT?"
PULLING HIS HAND,
MARKERS GRABBED FROM THE OTHER
SHE SAID, "YOU KNOW BETTER
THAN TO FOLLOW YOUR BROTHER
THROUGH TRAIN YARDS AND BACK YARDS
AND RIVERSIDE PARK!
WE HAVE TO GET HOME NOW
IT'S GETTING QUITE DARK!"

freights

Although subway painters Tracy 168 [see 340], P'nut 2 [see 259], and Ton 5 painted freights as early as 1974, the widespread proliferation of graffiti on America's railroads didn't begin until the mid-1980s. Freight trains became the preferred medium for a generation that came of age after the New York Transit Authority instituted its clean-train policy in 1989. Although many subway writers felt that freights were inadequate, since the public would no longer see their work, some made the transition as a way to keep painting illegally. Though the freight scene was largely incestuous—writers writing for other writers—it did allow the boundaries to expand from local to national. The Internet provided a means for artists from the West Coast to send East Coast artists pictures of their paintings laid up in places like Chicago or Oakland. A new set of standards was established, and certain freight cars, such as the Tropicanas, became highly sought-after canvases. Unlike work on subway cars, a piece done on a freight could run from coast to coast for years, but the risks could be just as high—freight writers were frequently shot at or pursued by the railroad's version of the Vandal Squad. Also, the dimensions and surfaces of freights make them harder to paint on, and the limitless number of cars in existence makes the dream of being a king a nearly impossible one.

**Piece by Erupto.
Photograph by Ernie Paniccioli.
Sacramento, California, 2006.**

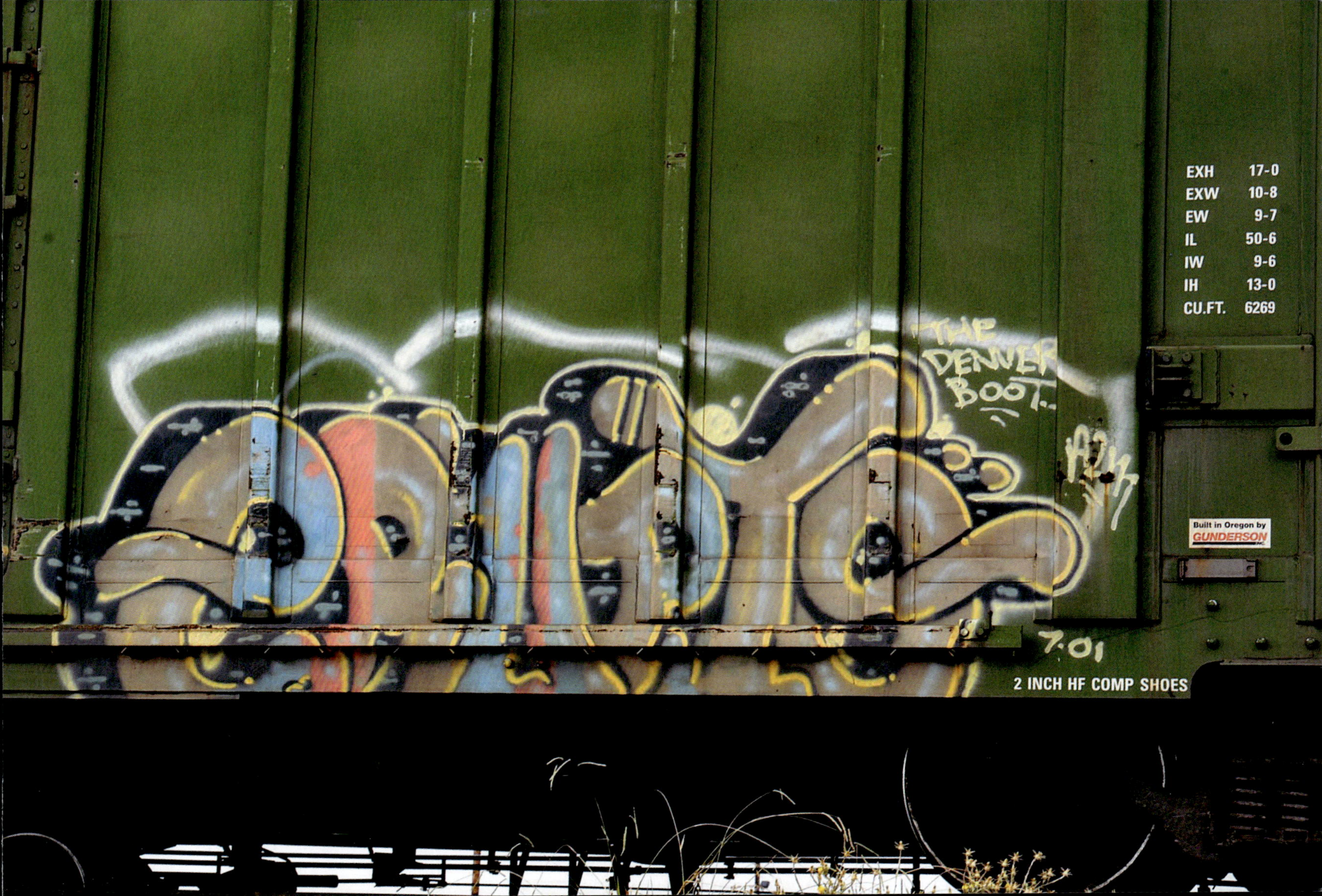
EXH 17-0
EXW 10-8
EW 9-7
IL 50-6
IW 9-6
IH 13-0
CU.FT. 6269
THE DENVER BOOT
Built in Oregon by GUNDERSON
7.01
2 INCH HF COMP SHOES

The Fun Gallery

The Fun Gallery, a small art space in downtown New York founded in 1981 by underground film star Patti Astor, was instrumental in graffiti's crossover from the street to the gallery world. It was one of the first legitimized art spaces to show the works of legendary graffiti artists such as Jean-Michel Basquiat [see 026], Lee Quinones [see 267], Keith Haring [see 160], Zephyr [see 363], Dondi White [see 097], Futura 2000 [see 141], Kenny Scharf [see 291], and Revolt. Through its mixture of graffiti's street cool and Patti Astor's cult-celebrity status, the Fun Gallery served as a vital bridge between the rough street culture of the outer boroughs and Manhattan's uber-hip elite—and also between street writers and wealthy collectors, who recognized and supported them as legitimate artists.

The gallery was home to countless parties and gatherings, and in 1983, Jeffrey Deitch was quoted as calling the Fun Gallery "one of the hottest galleries in the city." The gallery was patronized by seminal figures in the burgeoning graffiti and hip-hop cultures—Fab Five Freddy, filmmaker Charlie Ahearn, photographers Henry Chalfant [see 064] and Maripol, and even pop queen Madonna, who dated Jean-Michel Basquiat.

**Photograph by Martha Cooper.
New York City, 1981.**

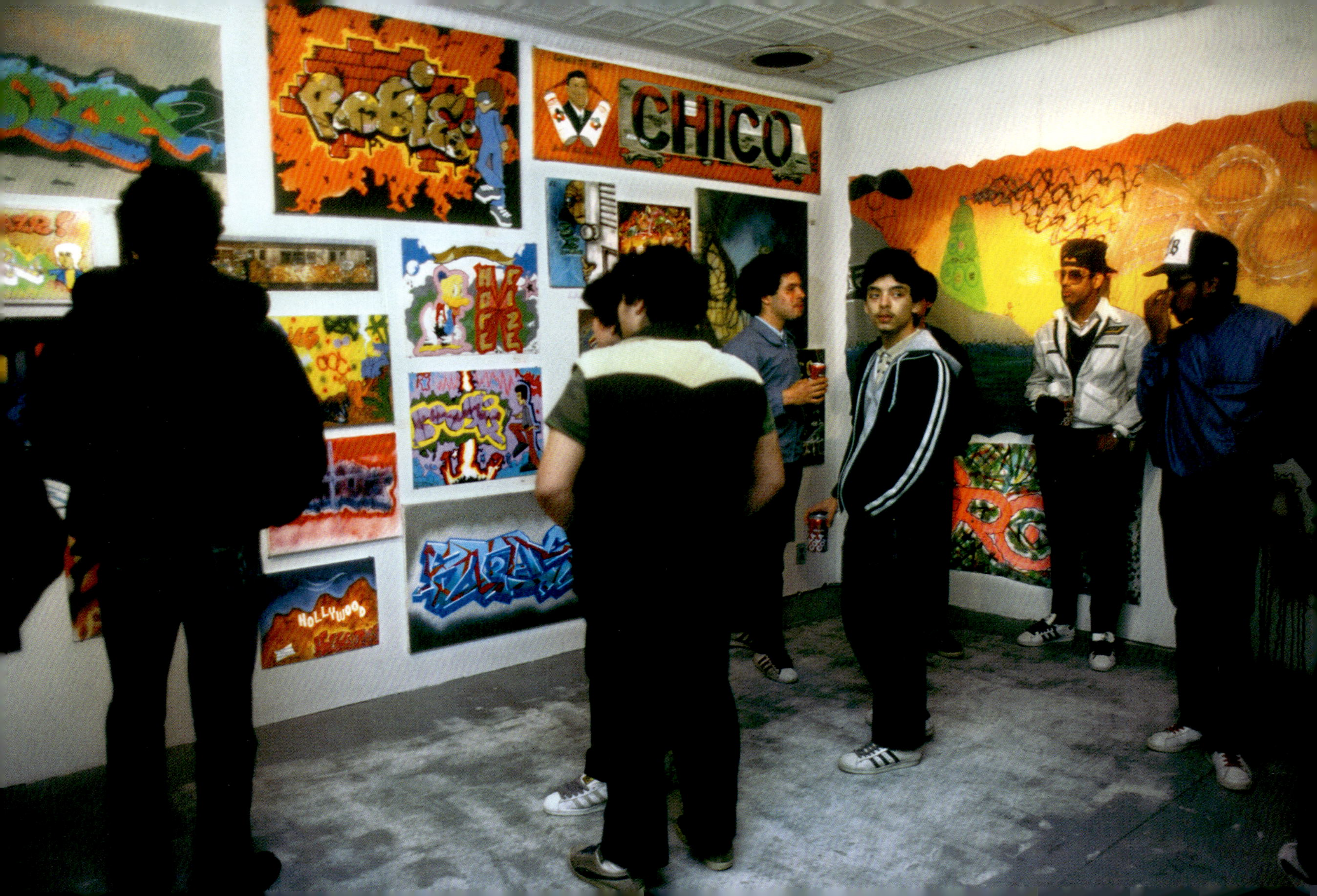
CHICO
HOLLYWOOD

141

Futura 2000

Leonard Hilton McGurr has always been ahead of the times. In 1970, inspired by the typeface Futura and the epic science-fiction film *2001: A Space Odyssey*, the fifteen-year-old New Yorker adopted the tag Futura 2000. He had fallen in love with the ultra-creative street art of Phase 2 [see 255], as well as other graffiti progenitors like AMRL, Flint 707, and Stay High 149 [see 316], and he was determined to become part of the scene. McGurr served in the U.S. Navy from 1974 to 1978, but when he returned to civilian life, he started painting entire subway trains, always preferring solo missions. His unique work earned him space in a 1980 exhibition at Fashion Moda, and in New Museum and Mudd Club shows the next year. By 1982, "Fut" was featured in solo exhibitions at Tony Shafrazi and the Fun Gallery and was tapped to design album covers and stage sets for The Clash. It's been a long time since Futura painted subways, but he remains true to his aesthetic, continuing to create inventive and visually stunning art on everything from broken windows and burnt exhibition invitations to clothing, toys, footwear, and his website, where he has posted new art every day for years. Futura's Kandinsky-esque abstractions look as though he takes a chain saw to the solar system and cuts, carves, and colors his very own cosmos. Whatever he chooses to do in the future, one thing is certain—people will be following.

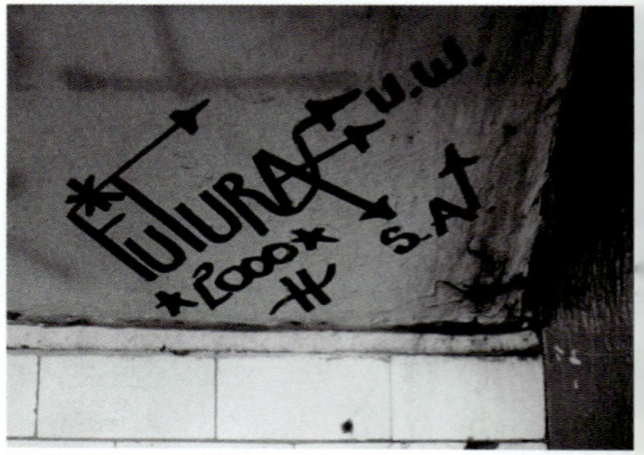

Futura 2000 (left) and Patti Astor.
All artwork by Futura 2000.
Photograph by Anita Rosenberg.
New York City, 1981.
Detail: Photograph by Flint Gennari.
New York City, 1974.

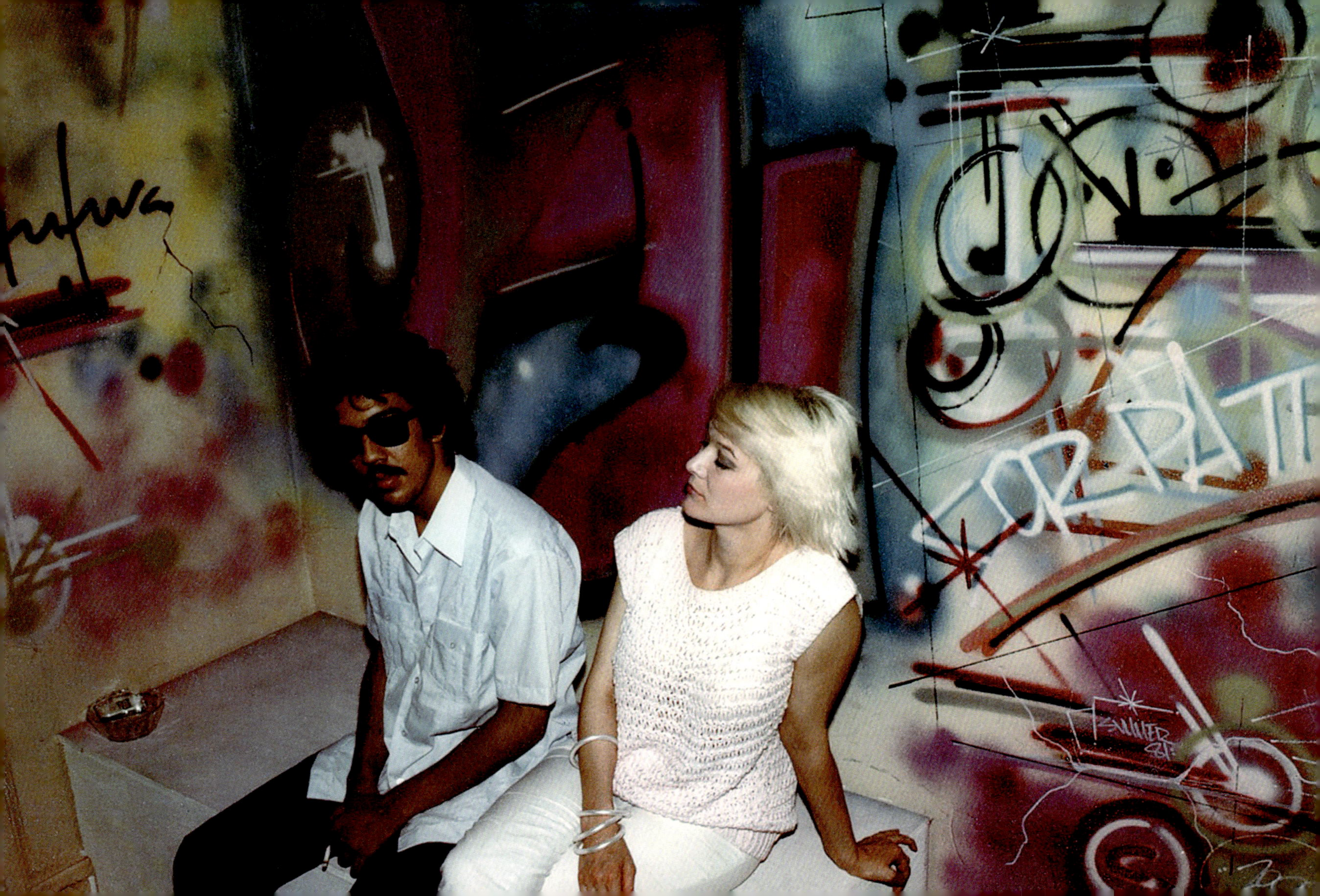

Gaia

The street artist known as Gaia was but a babe when he shot to prominence for his contributions to the streets of New York. A freshman at art school at the time, Gaia began wheatpasting detailed linocuts of animal heads and imagined creatures all around New York in the latter part of the first decade of the 2000s. Just as street art was experiencing a vacuum after its first great boom, New Yorkers accustomed to an abundance of fresh street work weekly were eager to see something new. With many older artists already having made the transition into the gallery world, Gaia, with his prolific outpourings and uniquely recognizable style, was welcomed as a street-art prince, and he became a street-art celebrity via the Internet almost immediately.

His style, which has been referred to as urban-romantic, translated easily onto canvas and an indoor environment, and shortly after his arrival on the streets, he began showing in local galleries such as Ad Hoc Art in Brooklyn and also in Chashama projects. While he finishes art school, Gaia continues to show in the gallery environment.

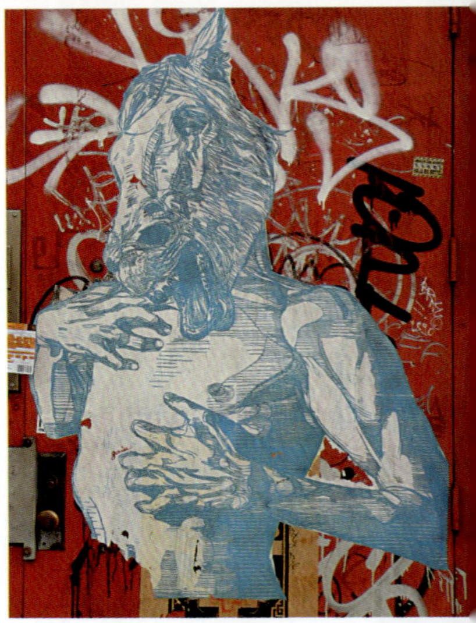

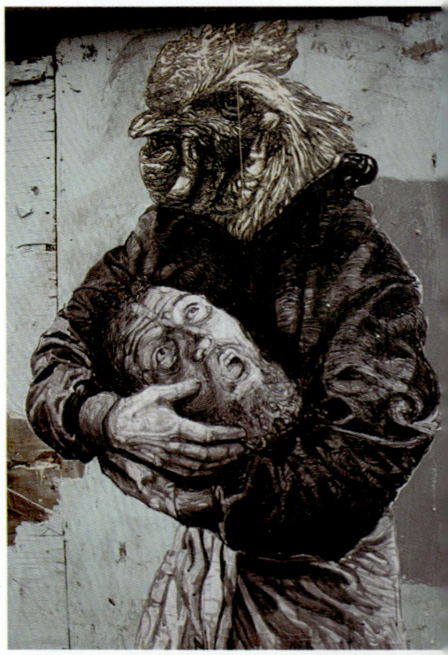

Photograph by Vincent Cornelli.
Brooklyn, New York, 2010.
Detail top: *The Rooster & St. John*.
Photograph courtesy of Gaia. Baltimore, Maryland, 2010.
Detail bottom: Photograph by Vincent Cornelli.
New York City, 2010.

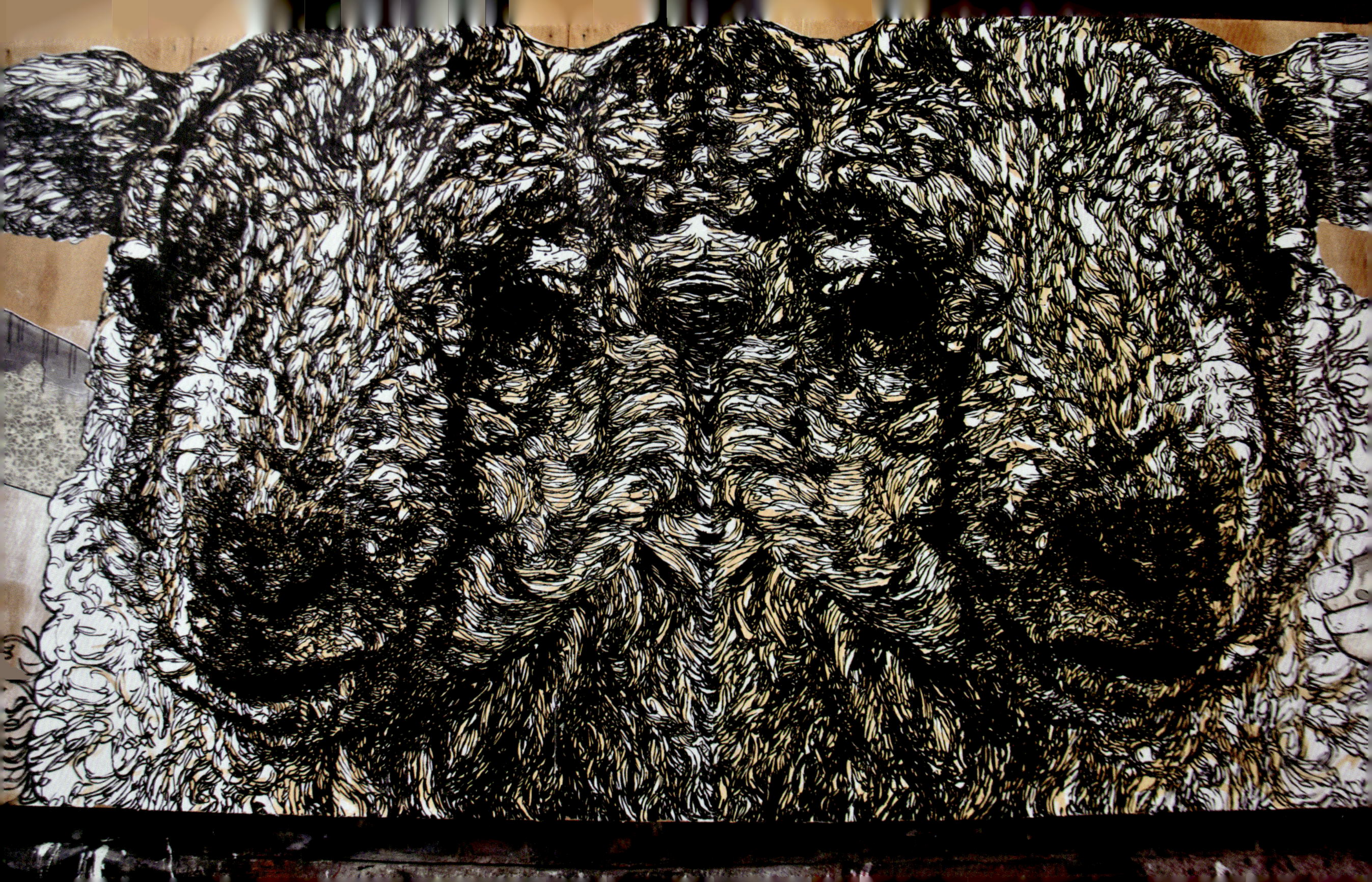

Galo

Within the street-art community, the name Galo conjures a number of things: his infamous long hair and beard, black paint markers, squiggled faces jumbled together in an almost psychedelic array, marijuana, and laughter. Galo is a throwback to a time when Vikings fought battles with spiked sticks, but he wields a stick dripping with black ink instead.

A longtime cohort of Chaz, of the Amsterdam group the London Police, Galo has been a staple member of street art's core scene for well over a decade. When the Wooster Collective's website embraced its first crop of street-art favorites and catapulted them to international Internet fame, the London Police were regularly traveling and painting with Galo, so he became integrated into the culture spawned during that period.

Originally a native of Italy, Galo travels a majority of the year, mounting exhibitions, creating commissions, and painting on the streets. His characters express a very free-form spirit; often free-styled, they consist of numerous black-line drawings with bugged-out eyes and expressive, gaping mouths. Although he exhibits in galleries, Galo's work still retains a very strong note of its graffiti roots, and his work on canvas mimics his street work. Galo continues to paint on the streets to this day.

Photograph by Vincent Cornelli.
Factory Fresh Gallery Wall, Brooklyn, New York, 2009.

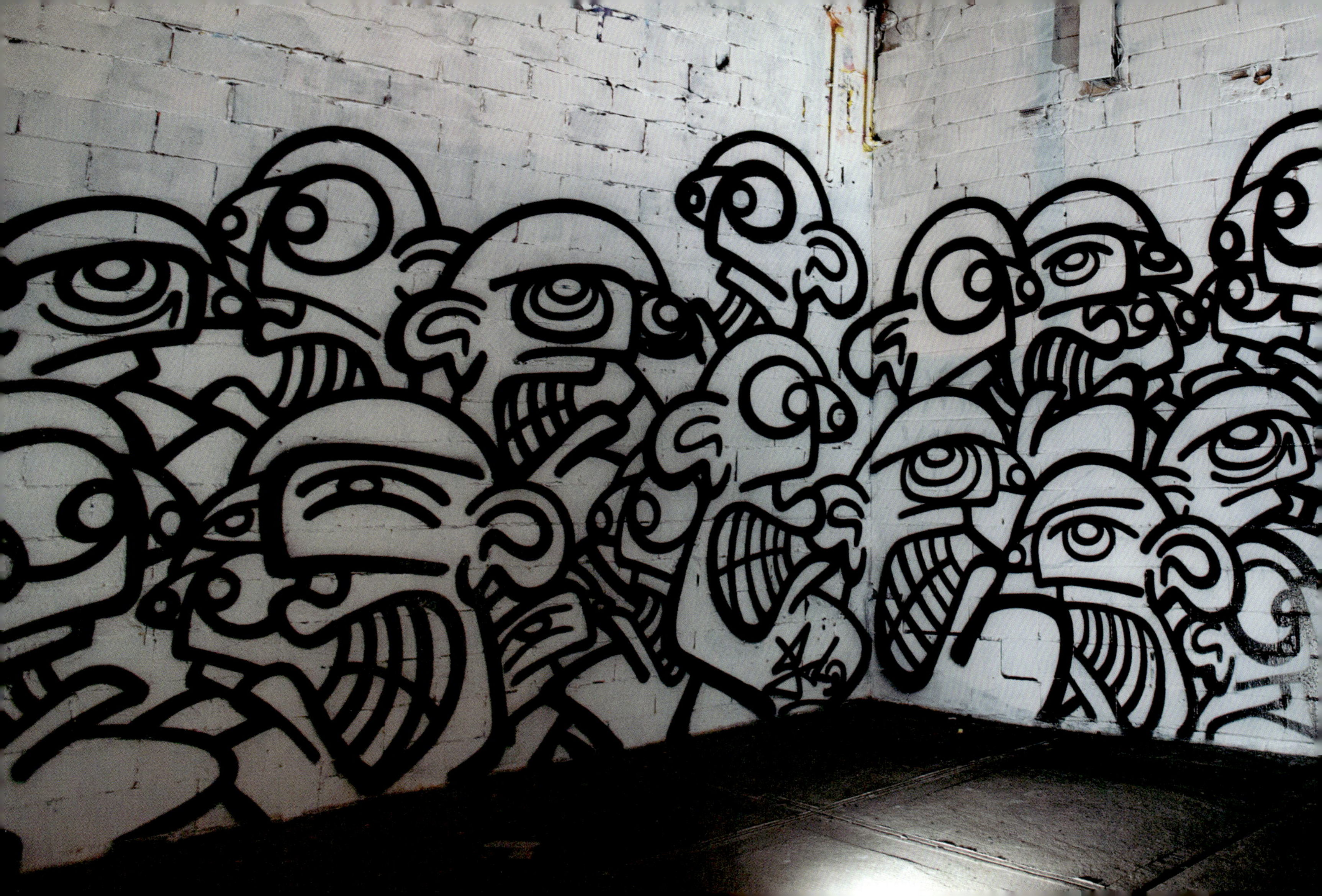

Jorge Rodriguez Gerada

While many street artists are revered for their nontraditional training, some are undeniably technically gifted. Jorge Rodriguez Gerada creates proud, masterful, immense portraits in a hyperrealistic style only achievable through an in-depth grasp of dimension, light, and shadow.

Born in Cuba in 1966, Gerada moved to the United States in 1970, where he was raised. In college, Gerada found his way into several art collectives, painting and drawing among his peers. In the mid-1990s, he teamed up with fellow public artists to alter billboards and create what he refers to as "guerilla performances," which garnered major media attention in and around New York City.

In 2002, Gerada began work on what he calls the "Identity Series," a sequence of massive charcoal portraits of anonymous faces, scaled to the size of the walls of city buildings. He placed these in cities around the world. This project continued for a number of years and earned Gerada international attention.

In 2008, Gerada created a two-and-a-half-acre sand painting of Barack Obama, expressing Gerada's endorsement of him. Gerada is based in both Barcelona and New York City and continues to produce prolific large-scale public works.

Photograph courtesy of Jorge Rodriguez Gerada. 2002.

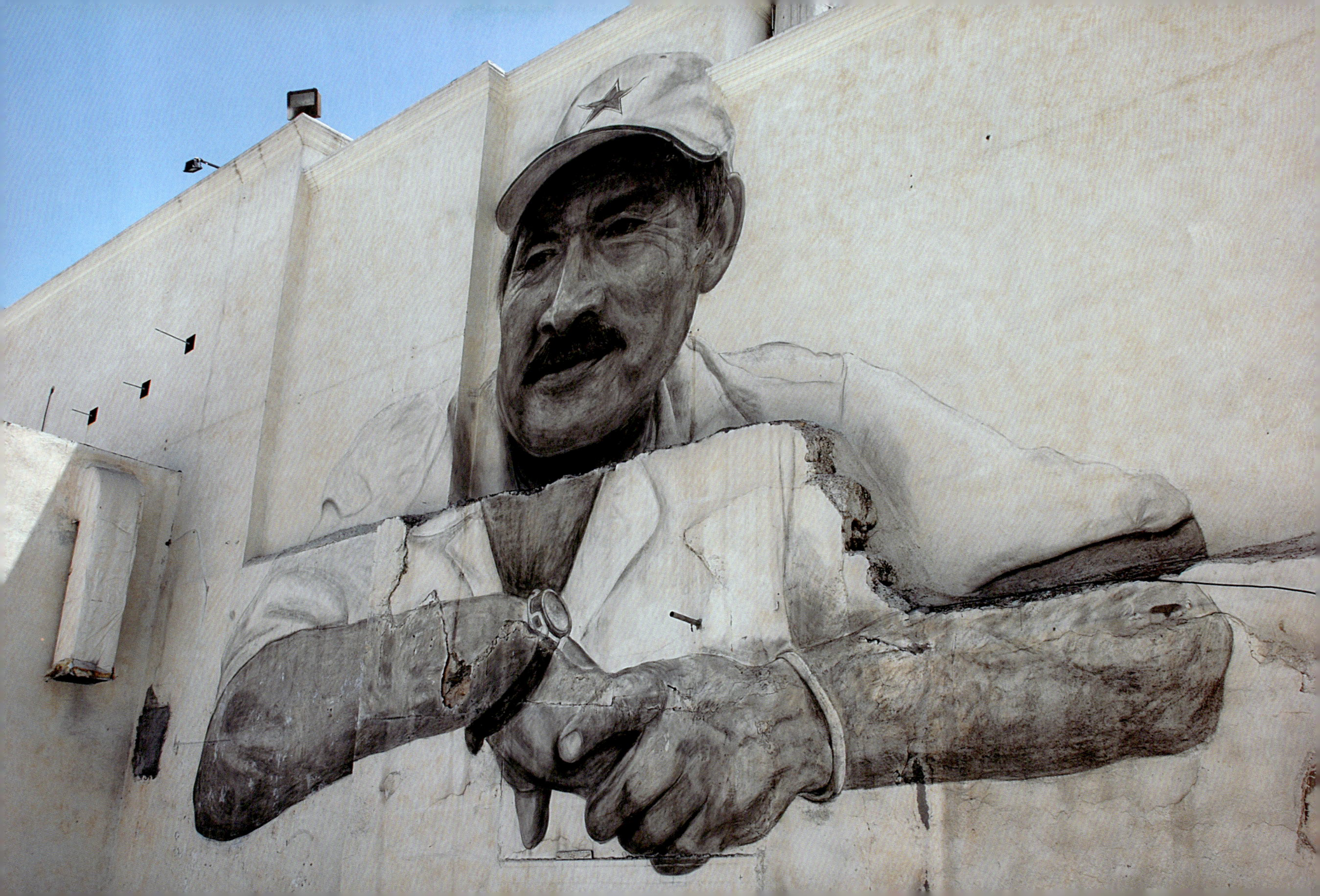

Ghost

As graffiti evolved, the artistic bar was gradually raised to loftier heights, and by the 1980s old dogs had laid the foundation for almost all the new tricks. Most styles relied on newer writers refining the styles of their forefathers, tightening and sanitizing them, but rarely innovating. Ghost changed that.

Ghost first rose to prominence as a bomber in the early 1980s, peppering all subway lines with a barrage of his soon-to-be-iconic GH throw-ups and battling crews and individuals with paint and, when necessary, his fists. Throw-ups soon became his stock and trade, and no station walls or train lines escaped his applied moniker. In 1983 his partner, Lost, founded the RIS [Rockin' In Style] crew. Although the crew was deep, more than any other member's, Ghost's efforts solidified the crew's rep in graffiti history, as he started to concentrate his efforts on piecing. Ghost joined forces with other talented writers, such as Reas, Ven, and Tekay, and he developed a loose, flowing, psychedelic style that synthesized elements of poster artist and underground cartoonist Rick Griffin with letter forms derivative of Mitch 77 [see 227], Duster UA, and Strider. He bombed NYC subways to the end and then some, becoming a major proponent of the clean-train movement in the early 1990s. His name has also been spotted on trains rolling through a slew of European countries.

Ghost's greatest triumphs, however, came *after* the subways, when he overcame his demons and rechanneled his restless energies into his studio art: He now makes his living as a full-time artist. Currently, his work on canvas, which looks like what Picasso might have done if he'd had an angel-dust period, continues to be highly sought after.

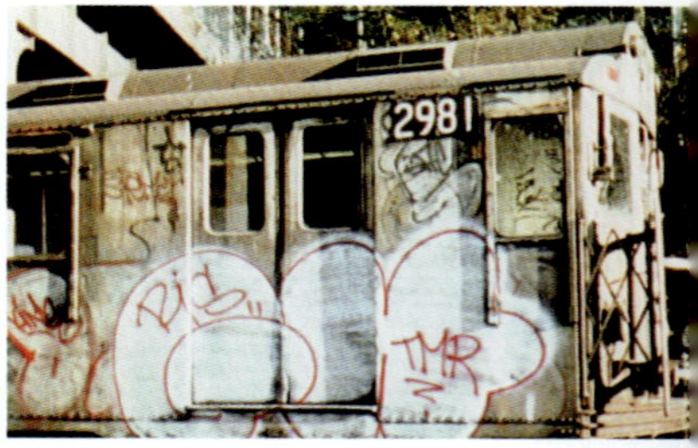

**Private collection.
New York City, 1983.**

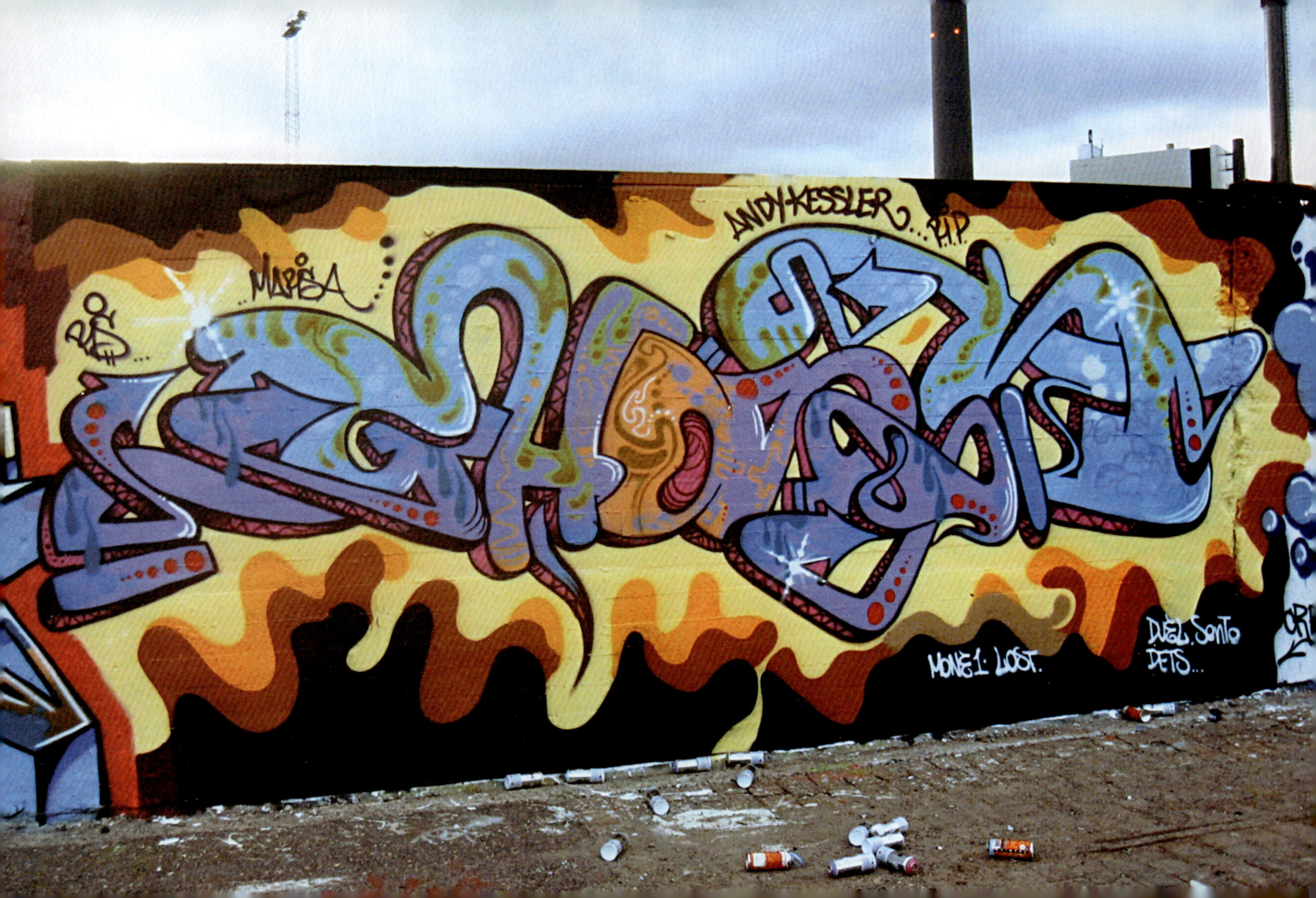
ANDY KESSLER... R.I.P.
MARISA
MONE 1. LOST.
DUEL. SONTO
DETS...

Mike Giant

When you're born color-blind *and* nearsighted, one of the least likely occupations for you is that of a visual artist. Nonetheless, that's precisely the path Mike Giant took. Born in upstate New York, Giant moved to Albuquerque, New Mexico, with his family in 1979, at the age of eight. Once one of the most legendary tattoo artists wielding a gun, Giant has influenced the worlds of graffiti, skin art, and fixed-gear bikes, and he is making a strong, steady move into the fine-art world. Known for his flawless inked drawings featuring solid blacks and whites, Giant's style is highly recognizable, whether on a wall or on skin.

Giant began writing graffiti in 1989 and moved to San Francisco in 1993. It was there that he joined forces with Bay Area legends Barry McGee [see 214], KR [see 199], and Reminisce. In addition to his business endeavors, Giant was still proliferating his ephemeral—and eventually legal—artwork, and in 2002, he traveled to Tokyo to participate in an exhibition with Sam Flores and the artist known as Bigfoot. In 2003, switching gears yet again, Giant opened the now legendary Stay Gold tattoo shop in San Francisco, and in 2005, he went head to head with street-art godfather Shepard Fairey in a show titled "Giant vs. Giant."

Eventually, Giant gave up the grueling art of tattooing to concentrate on fine art and graphic design. He has returned to his roots in Albuquerque, where he now meditates, rides track bikes, and finds it easier to focus in the studio.

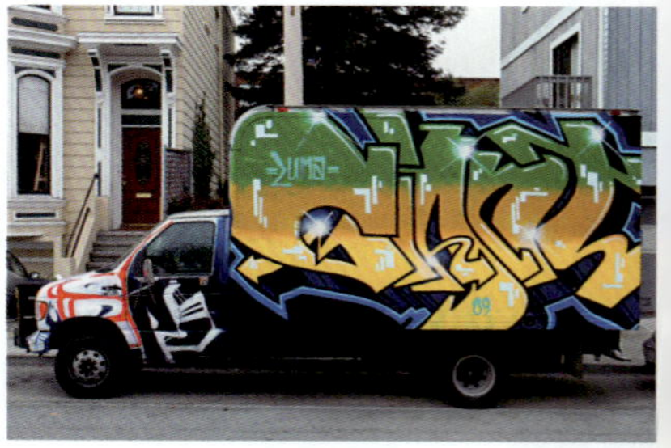

Photographs by Steve Rotman.
San Francisco, 2010.
Detail: San Francisco, 2009.

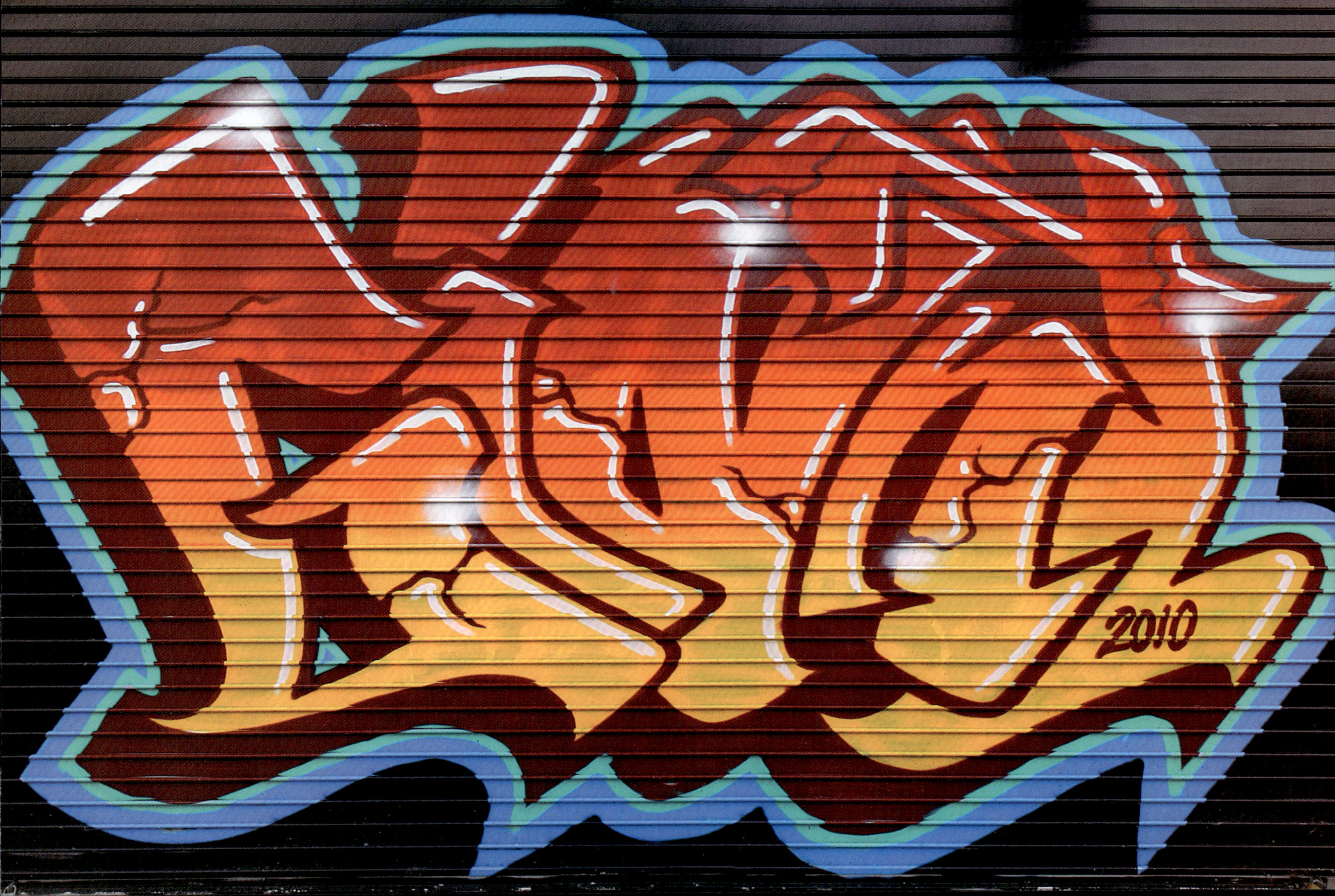
2010

The Go Club

The Go Club gained prominence in the mid-1970s. This West Village-based crew became famous for two things: writing and fighting. On the writing side, their leader was Team, a Renaissance man with a unique tag style who, along with partners Fuse and Max, would blaze a colorful trail on the #1 Broadway line; Rebel, Shadow, Vane, and Aztec blasted the insides of transit with exquisite tag styles. In addition to trains, the Go Club members T.Boy, Poke, Piggy 10, and Mex 10 gave the crew complete dominance over New York City trucks. The Go Club took on any beef that came their way with fervor—a great bunch of guys to write with, but the last people you'd want to cross.

In the late 1970s, the partnership of Team and Fuse would yield several rock-and-roll and drug-themed burners. As their graffiti interests waned, Team, Fuse, and several other members of the crew pursued music, eventually forming a band they appropriately named Urban Blight.

Currently, Team hosts a radio show with another Go Club alumnus, ME 62. Team was an avid painter who never forgot where he came from, and his work can still be found on the walls of streets and galleries alike.

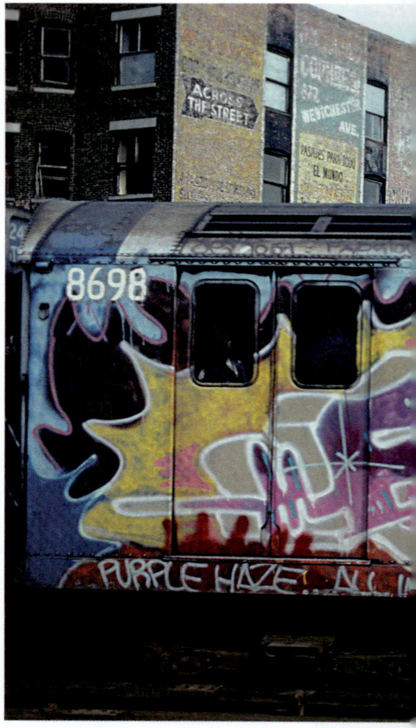

Pieces by Fuse (*Purple Haze* portion of two Jimi Hendrix-themed cars done with team "Stone Free"). Photograph by Jack Stewart. New York City, 1975.

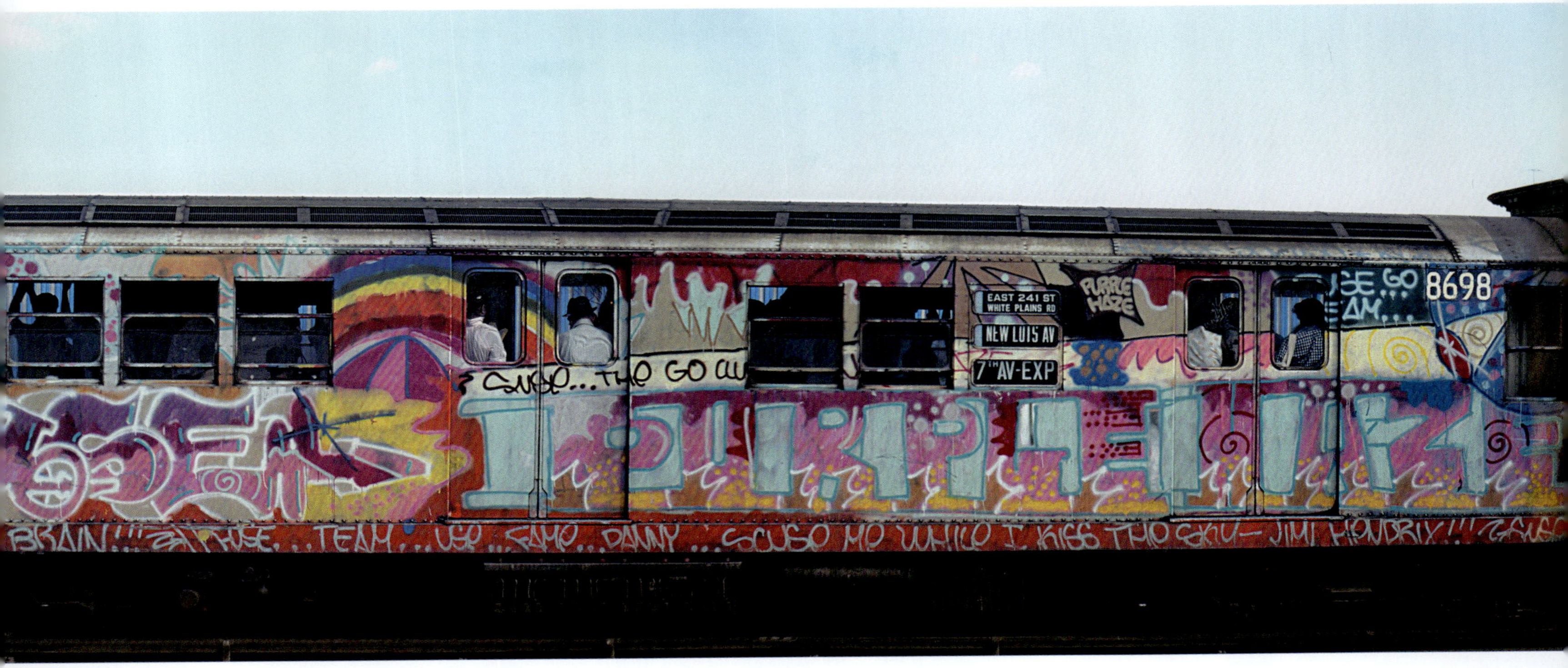
EAST 241 ST
WHITE PLAINS RD
NEW LOTS AV
7TH AV-EXP
8698

Gola

Born in Cesena, Italy, in 1982, Gola is best known for creating playful, colorful landscapes inhabited by genetically modified creatures in revolt against their condition. Admitting that he feels "closer to the animal sphere than the human one," Gola creates these characters to serve as his voice against their unjust treatment. On walls, canvases, and an array of other surfaces, he continually strives to investigate the relationship between humans and other living creatures. Critical of man's tendency to dominate every other species, Gola pays homage to the supernatural powers and mythical lure of these living organisms. Acutely sensitive to the suffering animals experience when they are mistreated, Gola adopted a vegetarian diet when he was sixteen.

Among Gola's inspirations are Eduardo Kac, Tissue Culture & Art, Alexis Rockman, and Karin Andersen, artists known for espousing similar political and ideological views. Gola also credits outsider art and expressionism as influences and attributes his growth as an artist to traveling from one public space to another and working alongside others on the streets. He refers to the streets as an "open-minded world" that continually spurs his creativity.

Gola holds a degree in fine art from the Accademia di Belle Arti di Bologna and has exhibited his work widely in Europe.

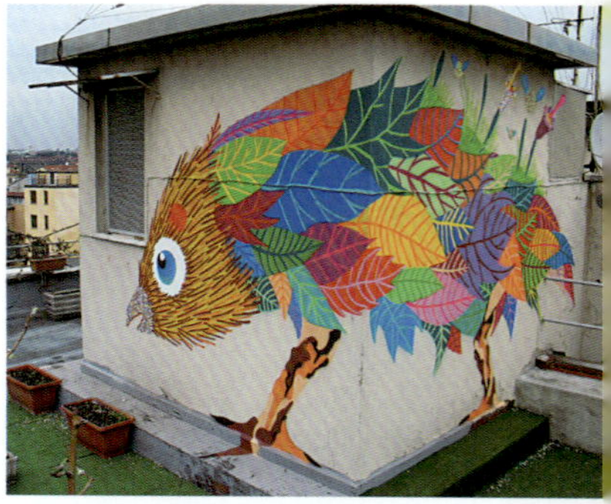

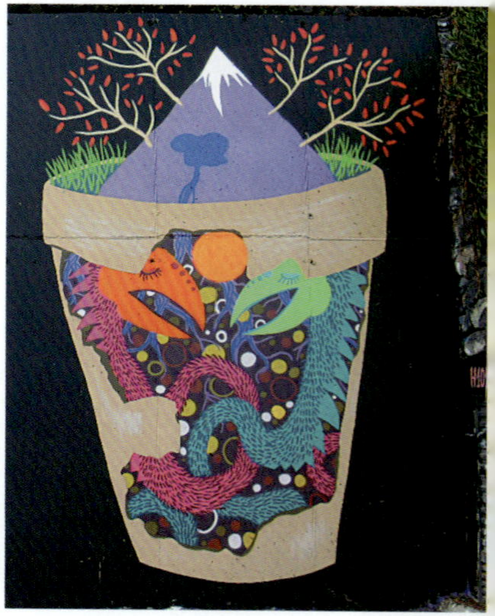

Photographs courtesy of Gola.
Rimini, Italy, 2010.
Detail top: Milan, Italy, 2010.
Detail bottom: Santa Cruz de Tenerife, Spain, 2010.

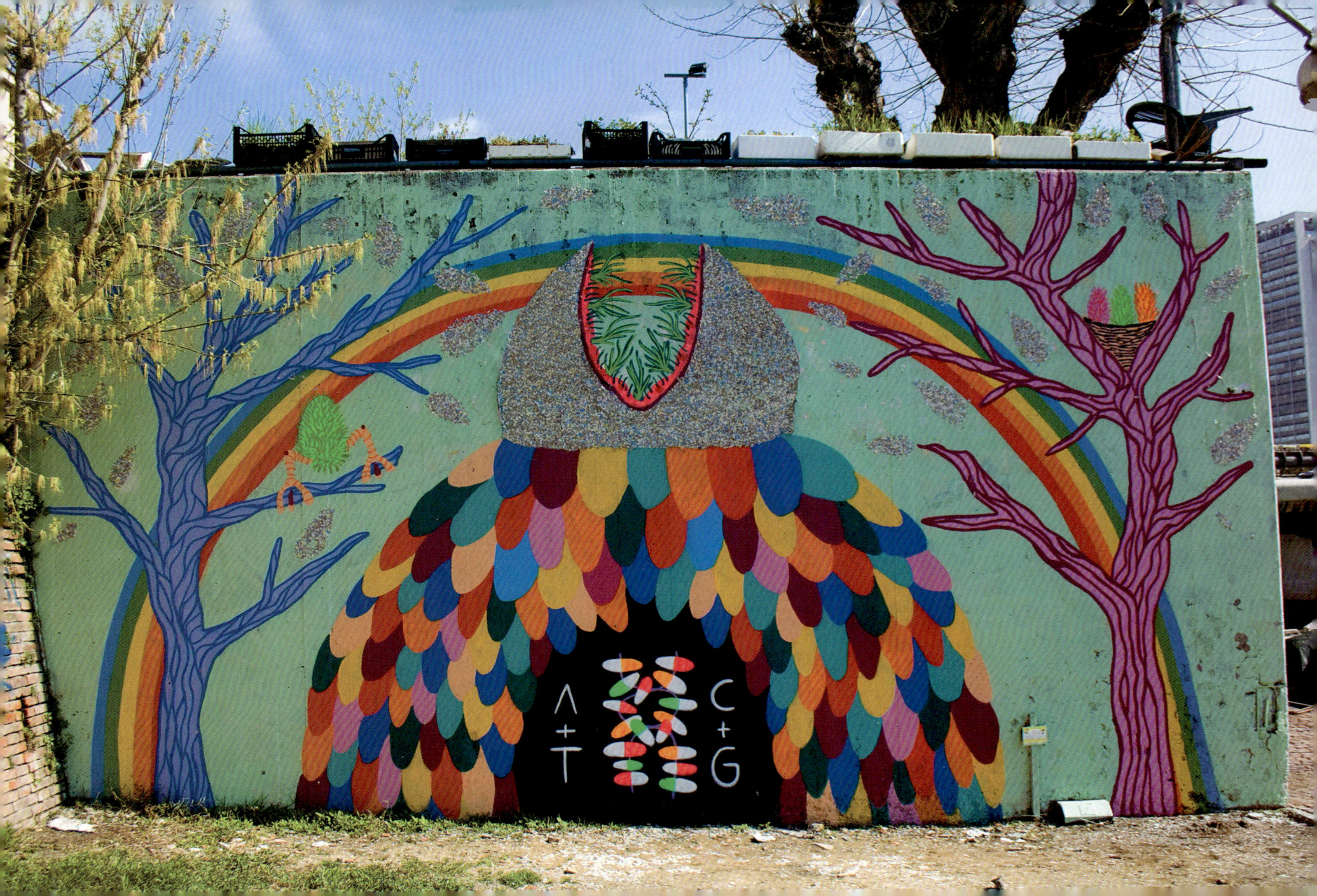
A
+
T
C
+
G

Gore-B

As one of New York City street art's early pioneers, Gore-B is widely credited for the invention of a new method for street-art installation: a painted wood plank secured by screws and bolts inserted through the holes on street-sign poles.

Gore-B is a native of Northern California who transplanted to New York at the beginning of the twenty-first century; he was protective of his identity and largely flew under the radar, but his work inspired innumerable copycats who placed their work on wood and screwed it into signposts. Gore-B's paintings often depicted characters he pulled from vintage catalogs and magazines, couple with snippets of text from technical guides.

Gore-B was also a core figure in the early years of the Orchard Street Art Gallery, which was created by Adam Skewville (see 305) and Pufferella and was New York's first gallery space devoted wholly to street art.

As a longtime member of the loosely organized street-art crew ELC, along-side New York City street-art icons like Infinity Man and Royce Bannon, Gore-B participated in the famed Wooster Collective (see 359) group show at 11 Spring Street (see 001) in 2006, painting an intricate mural of reimagined religious figures. In 2007, Gore-B returned to California to study biology.

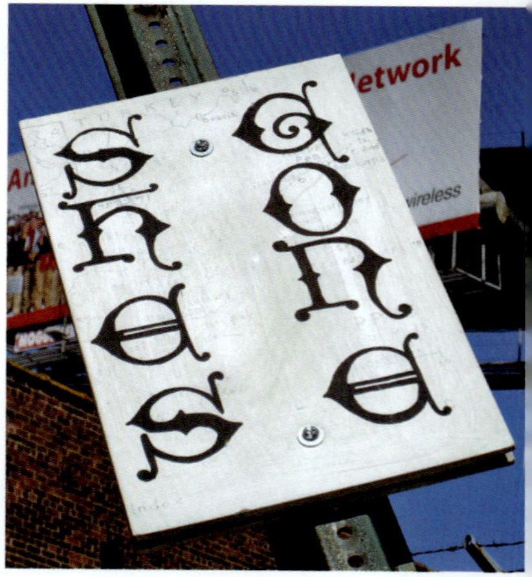

Photograph courtesy of Gore-B.
Coos Bay, Oregon, 2010.
Detail: Photograph by Becki Fuller.
Brooklyn, New York, 2010.

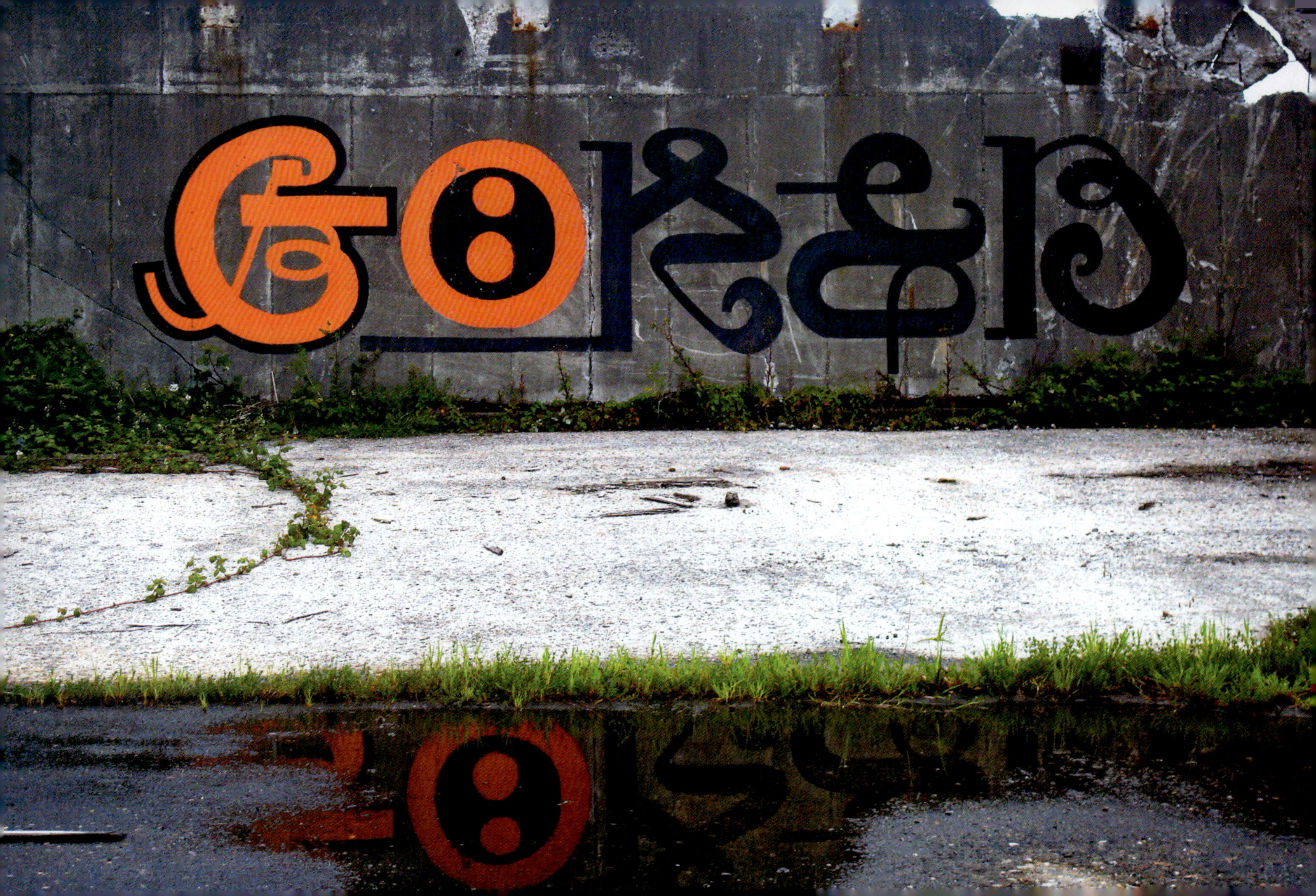

Graffiti 1980 Studio

Sam Esses was the father of a girl whom graffiti writer Zephyr [see 363] knew as a teenager. One night in 1979, Sam was invited to dinner at the home of a gallery owner who had recently started working with the graffiti artist Lee, who had just painted the gallery owner's terrace. He went home and told his daughter about Lee's work. She told him that she knew some graffiti artists, and Sam said he wanted to meet them. When Zephyr got Sam's invitation, he phoned his friend Rasta [see 270], and the two headed over to the posh apartment. They showed Sam photos of their pieces. He loved their stuff and said it needed to be preserved. Sam decided to create a studio where they could paint on canvas. At that time, spring 1980, canvas was new to them; subways were their medium. So with the help of his friend Futura 2000 [see 141], Zephyr organized the Graffiti 1980 Studio.

Prior to that time, a lot of graffiti artists knew one another's work, but hadn't met. Once word of the studio got out, all the great writers of the period began coming by to paint. There were Dondi [see 097] and his boys from way out in Brooklyn, and Seen [see 294] and the UA crew from the opposite end of the city. And after a day of painting canvases at the studio, they'd all go out and paint trains together. Over thirty canvases were painted at the studio, and around the same time many other things started happening. The media became very interested in graffiti, and a lot of new opportunities cropped up. Magazine articles and gallery exhibits were suddenly commonplace. As new opportunities emerged, so did new incentives. The artists found themselves in a world aboveground. In so many ways, the Graffiti 1980 Studio is where the early '80s renaissance began.

Noc 167 [left] and Dondi. Photograph by Martha Cooper. New York City, 1980.

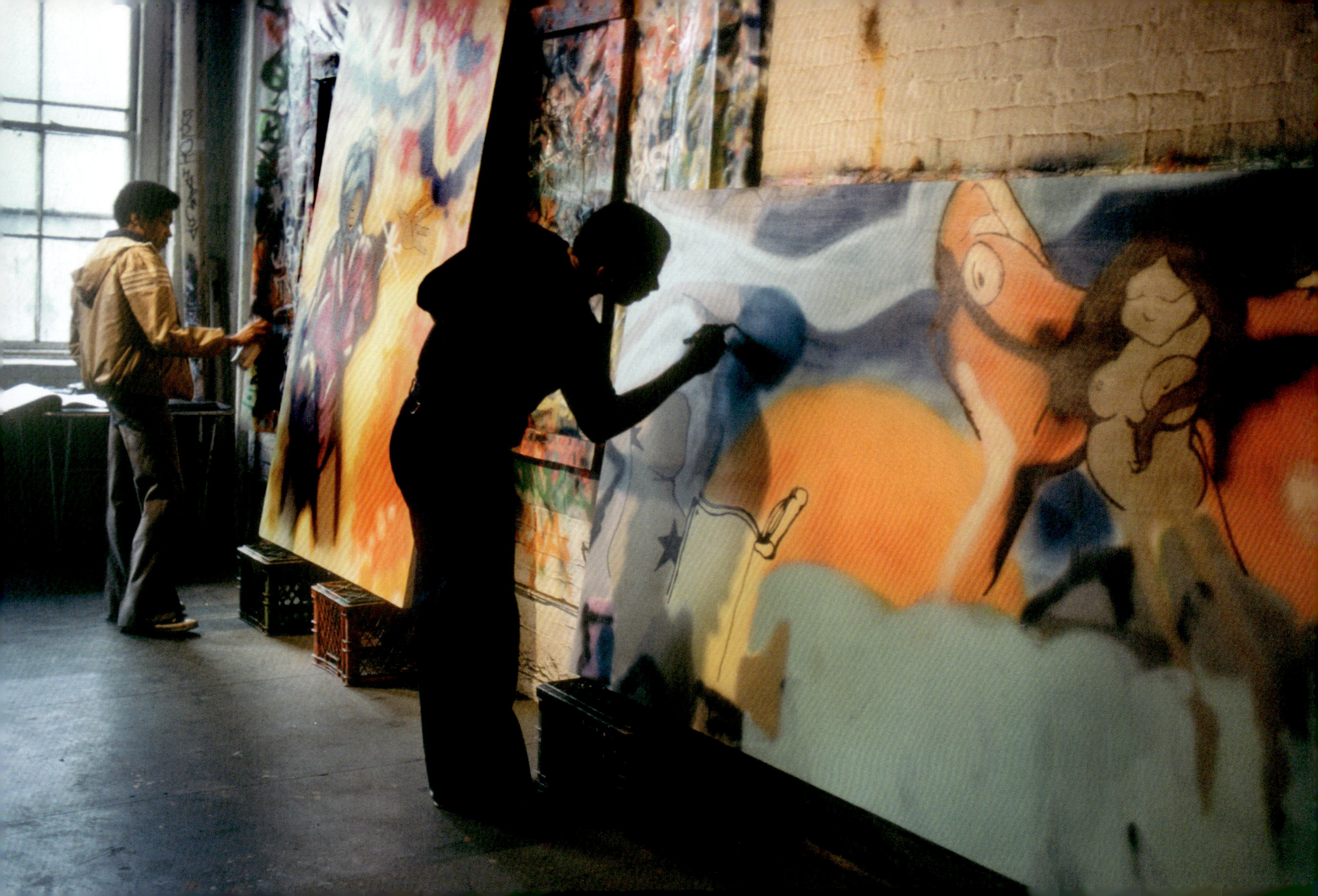

Graffiti Hall of Fame

In 1980, Dez [see 092], along with community activist Ray Rodriguez [aka SR106], Part [see 251], and Vulcan, founded the world-famous Graffiti Hall of Fame, which originated in New York City's Park East High School, where Dez was a student. Later that year, they convinced a public school on the corner of 106th Street and Park Avenue to allow their schoolyard walls to become a proving ground for graffiti's top writers. Once or twice a year, honored invitees culled from an elite talent pool of subway artists came to showcase their skills. Beautiful production walls became the norm and instilled a sense of neighborhood pride. The schoolyard eventually became known as the Graffiti Hall of Fame and has, over the years, been curated by graffiti artists Joey TDS and Ezo [see 114], among others. The schoolyard attracts writers from all over the world and is even a destination on Grand Master Caz's hip-hop bus tour. The lineup of painters changes each year, but a few old-school masters such as Dez, Chain 3 [see 062], Part TDS, and the Tats Cru add profile to the event.

Today, the Graffiti Hall of Fame is anything but, as admission is gained fairly easily, even by artists who are virtually unknown. It's a good way for novices and masters to collaborate and learn from each other while sustaining a now forty-year-old culture.

During years when the streets were raw and battles raged, violence could erupt at the Hall of Fame. Beefs would occur regularly after walls got dissed by rivals. Today, the schoolyard studio has become a photo backdrop for tourists who return home with evidence of their pilgrimage to hallowed ground.

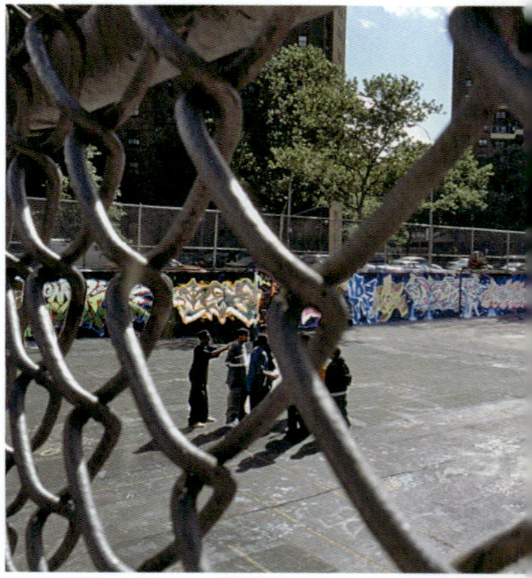

Photographs by Ernie Paniccioli.
Artwork by Dez [left] and Vulcan [right].
New York City, c. 1983.
Detail: New York City, c. 1983.

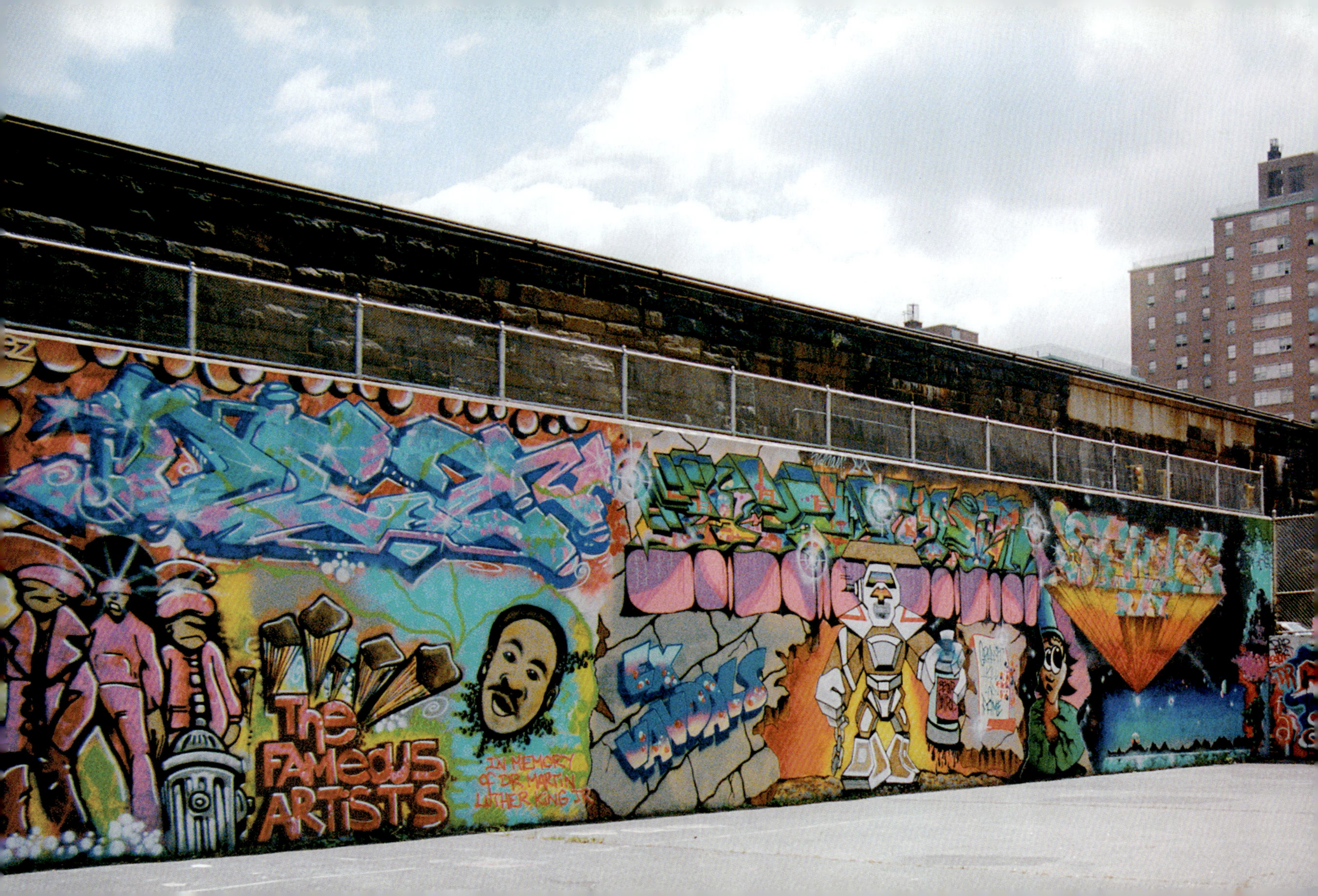
The
FAMEOUS
ARTISTS
IN MEMORY
OF DR. MARTIN
LUTHER KING JR.
EX
VANDALS

Graffiti Never Dies

In 1973, gangs ran wild on the streets of Brooklyn; a few small gangs, including the Hangmen and Kelly Park Boys, combined to form a larger gang—The Satan's Reapers. The Reapers' home base was Kelly Park, located in the Gravesend section of Brooklyn. An elevated train lay-up ran through the middle of Kelly Park, dividing it in two: Big Kelly Park was off-limits and controlled by a local mobster who ran the neighborhood, but Little Kelly Park became the wrong side of the tracks, as The Satan's Reapers claimed it as their own. One of the Reapers, Mr. Ice, a tough-as-nails son of a cop known for a lightning-fast left hand, founded a graffiti crew from within the ranks of this gang and christened it Graffiti Never Dies. The original members, Sgt Bones, his brother Dusty, Lil Bomb, Whiz, Ax, Hash, and their nonwriting confederates, owned the park and the lay-up. Kelly Park became one of the wildest places in the city, with fifty to a hundred people partying there every night and the GND boys using paint they stole four hundred cans at a clip to hit the lay-up. Getting high, listening to music, bombing trains, and the occasional shootout characterized the park's nightlife.

GND members allegedly perfected a way to short out the subway's third rail using steel garbage cans and were accused of blowing up a park house by igniting hundreds of used spray cans inside it. The original crew retired in 1976. Lp136, aka TRIKE/TO, who joined the crew a year or two after its formation, revived it in the '80s, recruiting modern writers such as Joust, Set 3, and Sake. GND's founder, James "Mr. Ice" Donovan, was murdered in the summer of 2010.

Piece by Mr. Ice, with tag by Lil Bomb. Photograph by Jack Stewart. New York City, 1973.

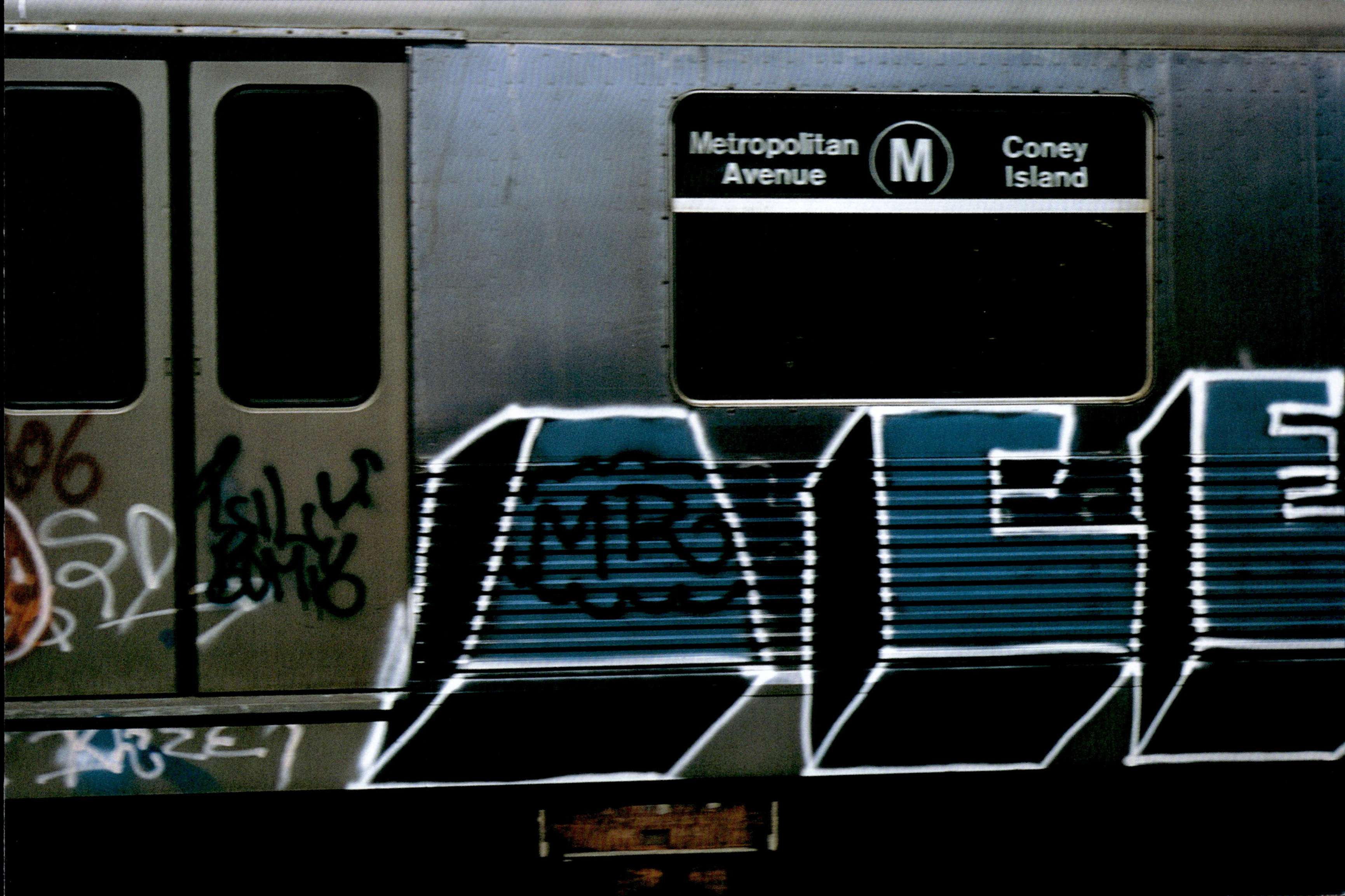
Metropolitan Avenue
M
Coney Island

Graffiti Research Lab

In the first decade of the 2000s, while most street artists functioned within the limitations of static materials [paint, wood, metal, and so forth], Evan Roth and James Powderly, the founders of Graffiti Research Lab [GRL], had the technical savvy to explore an entirely new vernacular: electronic street art. GRL, a brainchild birthed during fellowships with the New York–based arts organization Eyebeam, created a laser pointer that essentially allowed an artist to project a live rendering of the painting of their tag onto whatever surface they chose. GRL was also responsible for the creation of "LED Throwies," electronic lights that can be installed with high-strength glue on public walls in the form of an art piece.

GRL quickly graduated to appearances at international art events, as well as participation in art shows in gallery settings. In 2008, Roth and Powderly joined in the renowned "Street Art" exhibit at London's prestigious Tate Modern.

In the summer of 2008, Powderly traveled to Beijing, China, planning to assist protesters in the use of lasers to project pro-Tibet messages onto the side of a building near Tiananmen Square. Powderly and five other Americans were arrested and held in a Chinese prison for six days. Eventually, Powderly was released, but $2,000 had gone missing from his bank account.

Graffiti Analysis: 2ESAE. **Photograph by Evan Roth. Tudela, Spain, 2010.**

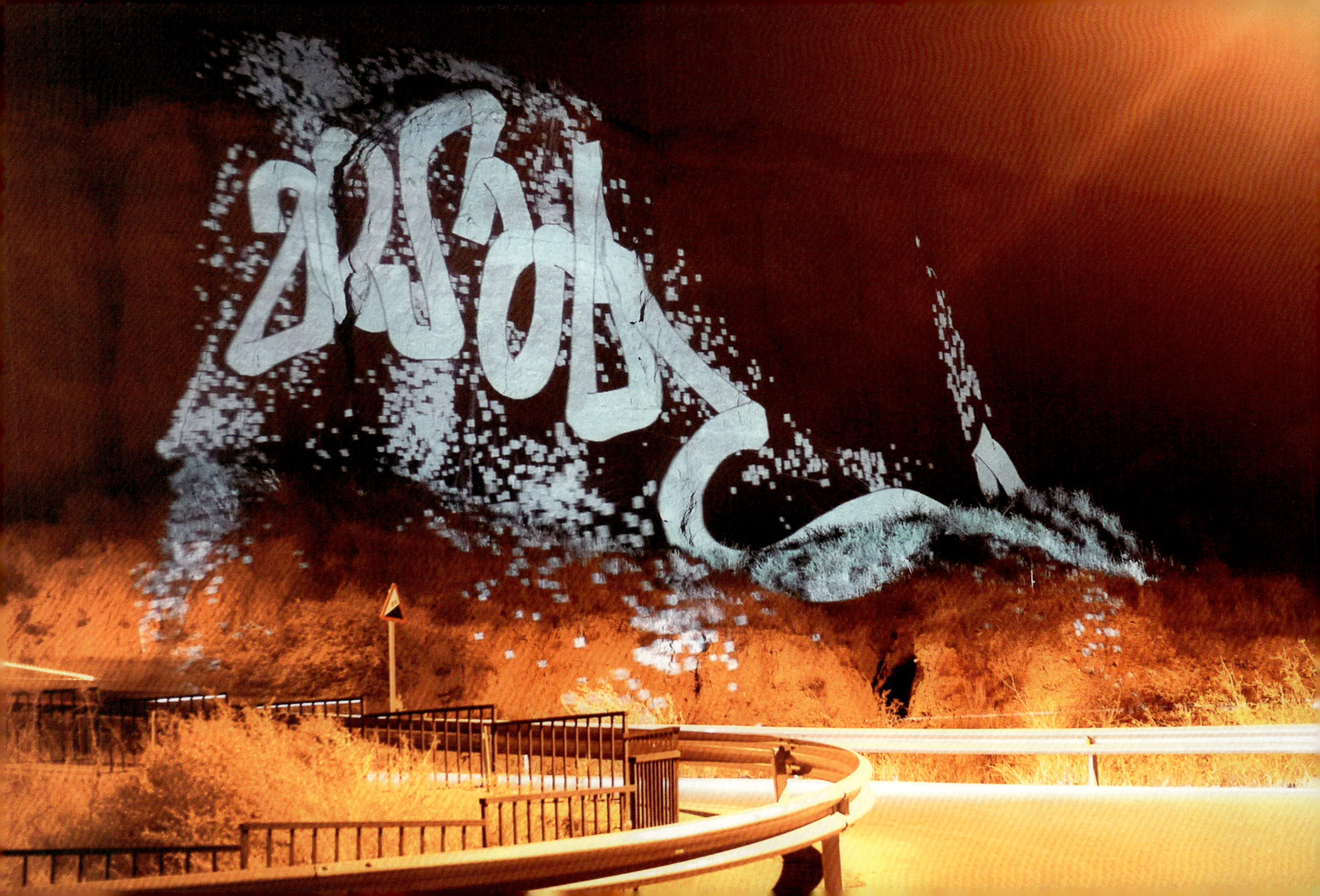

Graphiti Above Ground

In 1980, after a successful show of graffiti canvases at Fashion MODA, John "Crash" Matos decided to help create a new gallery with Joyce Towbin and Mel Neulander. Towbin had a degree in fine art, and Neulander's sole responsibility was to hustle up business, particularly in the commercial area. Neulander was a mercenary and was very up front about it; while this was a turn-on for the writers that signed with him, others found it offensive and looked elsewhere.

The writers who showed consistently at Graphiti Above Ground were Crash, Daze, Freedom, Noc 167, Cey, Tracy 168 [see 340], Iz, Lady Pink, Erni, Wasp 1, and Caine 1 [see 054]. The gallery averaged six shows a year, and the openings were a merging of uptown breakdancers and downtown trendsters.

In 1982 and 1983, the gallery became a hangout for writers who had their blackbooks [see 036] tagged by other graffiti writers, as well as Keith Haring [see 160] and Jean-Michel Basquiat [see 026]. The night before an opening in March 1983, Caine 1 was shot to death [he had recently appeared on television and in newspapers via the gallery, and his work was considered some of the best the group had to offer].

The artists' works matured greatly in the two years the gallery stayed open, and the prices for some canvases were as high as $2,000, with the gallery taking a third. By 1984, Graphiti Above Ground had failed to reach the European audience it desperately needed to stay afloat, and it shut its doors forever.

Mel Neulander [left] and Joyce Towbin.
Photograph by Martha Cooper.
New York City, 1981.

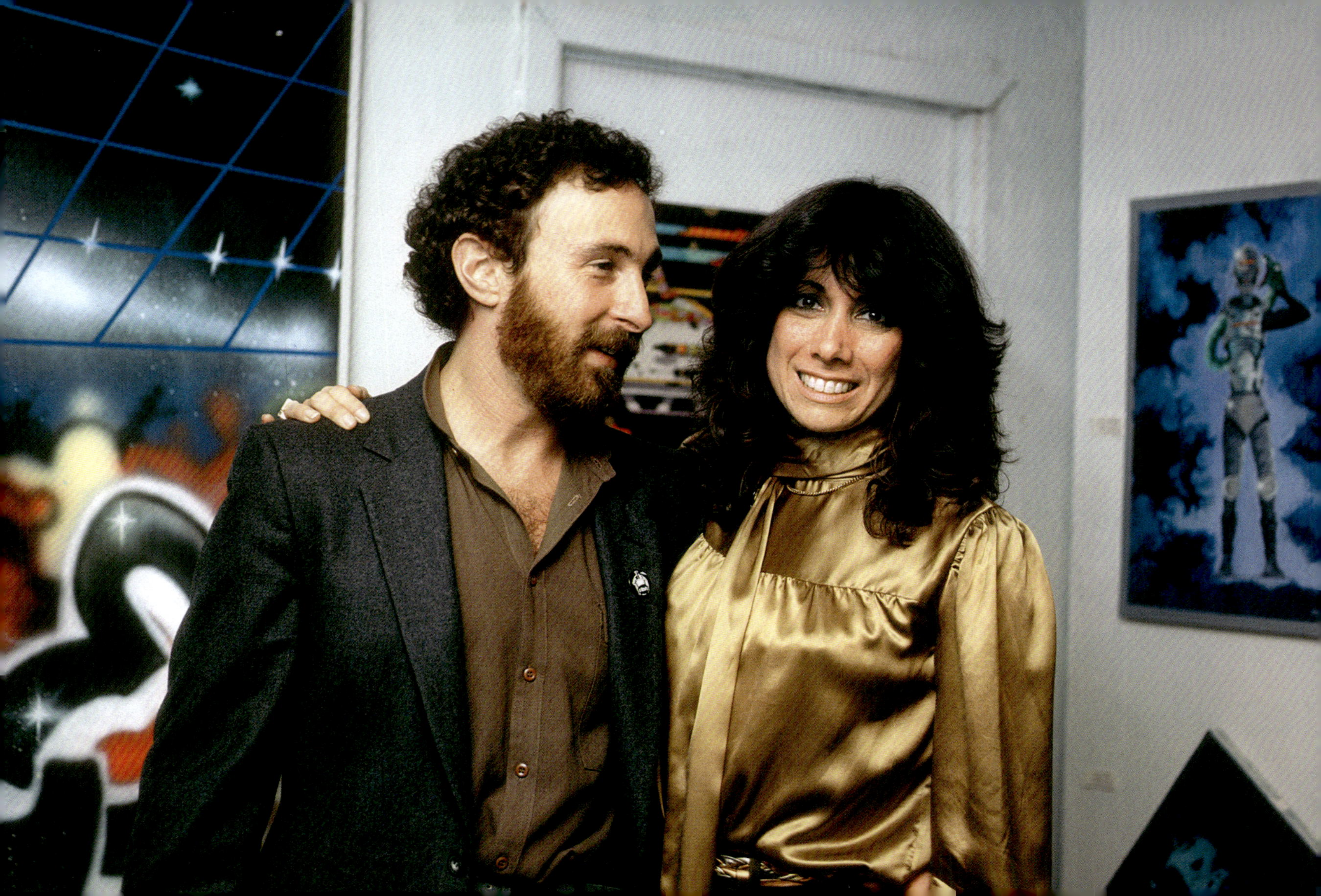

Gualicho

Born in 1977 and raised in the suburbs of Buenos Aires, Argentina, Pablo Harymbat, aka Gualicho, started drawing under his father's guidance when he was five years old. He became interested in graffiti while studying graphic design at the University of Buenos Aires. Within a few years, he was creating vibrant surrealistic pieces that earned acclaim throughout South America and Europe. Following the 2008 release of the landmark book *Graffiti Argentina*, Gualicho—along with fellow Argentine artists Aire, Poeta, Jaz, and Caru—painted with Amose in Paris, and then with El Bocho (see 105) and Loomit (see 205) in Berlin. Gualicho's unique aesthetic fuses elements of Latin American folk art with graffiti culture. With influences ranging from religious icons to comic graphics, Gualicho refers to his work, populated by imaginary—often malevolent—images of plants, animals, and characters as mystical neo-graffiti representing "the expansion and evolution of the Universe and consciousness."

Working with brushes and rollers on the street—instead of the more-typical spray paint—Gualicho prefers to paint in open public spaces. He also creates artwork on paper and on canvases that have made their way into commercial galleries. *Gualicho*, a 192-page book of the artist's distinctive artwork, was released in 2010.

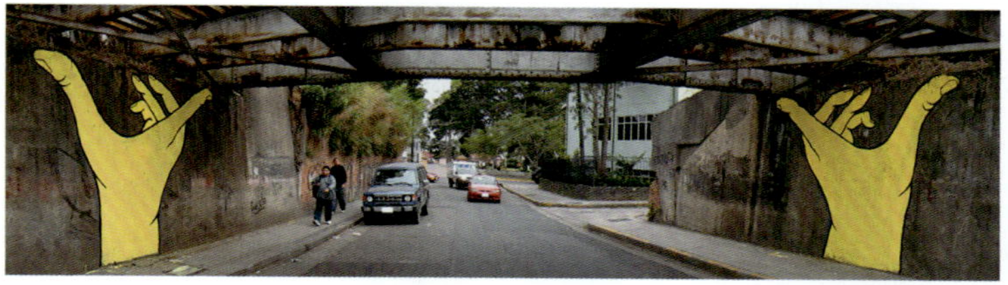

Photographs courtesy of Gualicho.
Buenos Aires, Argentina.
Detail: San José, Costa Rica, 2009.

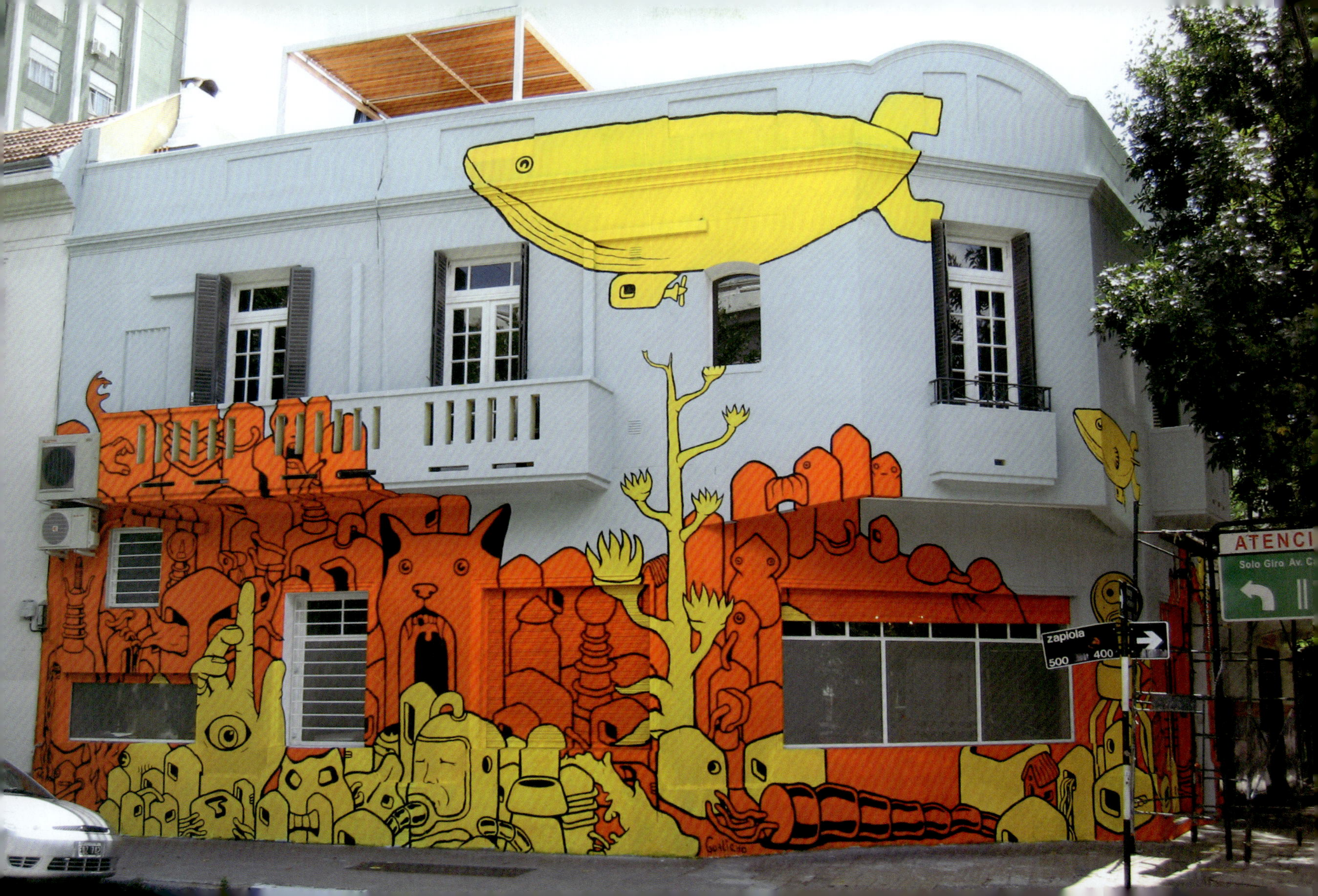
ATENCI
Solo Giro Av. C
zapiola
500 400

Guillaume

Guillaume Desmarets signs his street work Guifar, a name that has been recognizable in public spaces since the turn of the century. His hyperrealistic work is a comic undressing of daily life consisting of bold lines and exaggerated images.

While he earned recognition for works using a spray can, upon finishing school, he began to work in animation and to focus on his studio practice, soon adding wheatpaste to his list of publicly exhibited artworks. He creates one-off pieces, sometimes screened and sometimes hand-painted, pasting them up in frequently visited spots around Brussels. There is a repetition of style and subject matter, but every time it is a fresh communication, and this authenticity helps draw the public deeper into the faces he puts before them. This is not reproducing hundreds of pieces for branding or other forms of propaganda, but rather a citizen sharing his passion in public spaces.

You won't find Guifar's work as easily as some other artists', but when you do find it, you can't help but realize that each of his pieces is an intimate and emotional production.

Photographs courtesy of Guillaume.
Brussels, Belgium, 2009

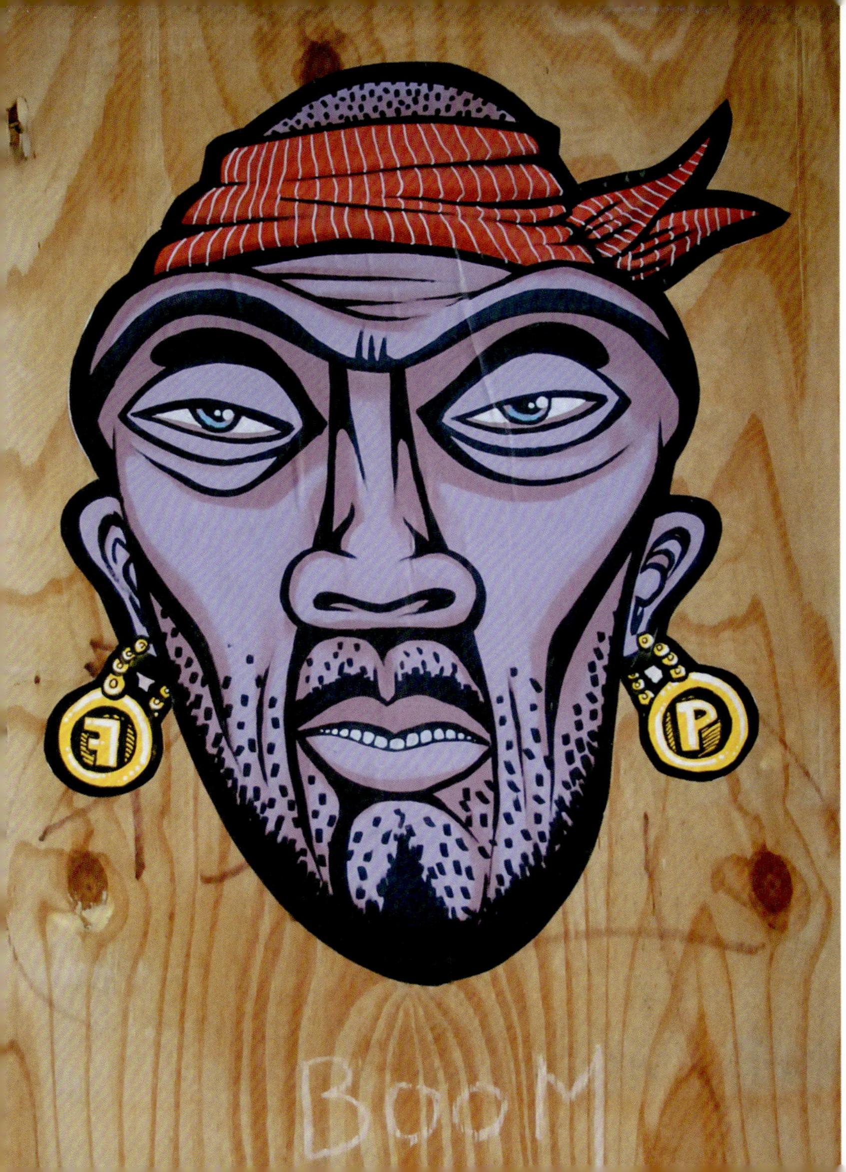
BooM

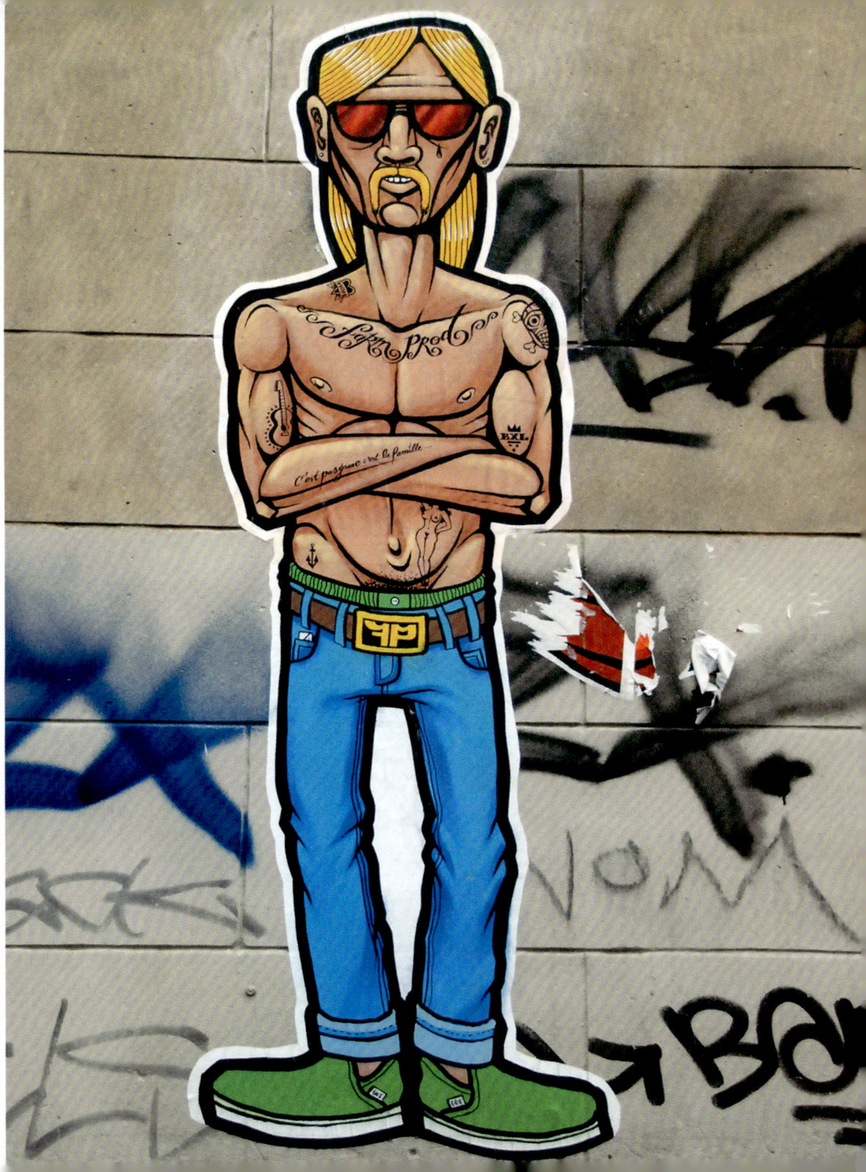

Ha-Ha

Ha-Ha is one of Australia's most legendary street-art monikers. Known for both his stencils and his large-scale rolled letters, Ha-Ha has made a name for himself as an omnipresent artist in and around the city of Melbourne. The New Zealand native did not have classical training in the arts, but took his early inspiration from fellow Australian artists Psalm, Rone [see 284], and Phibs [see 256] in his early years.

Ha-Ha has been known to create roller tags three stories tall, seemingly poking fun at whoever or whatever inhabits the structure he has painted. He creates graphically simplistic two-toned stencils, often in large scale. His most recurring theme is robots, and he has been known to sign his pieces with the numbers 2010, giving his pieces a futuristic nod.

Through an intensely prolific period in the first decade of the 2000s, Ha-Ha earned his reputation as a street-art king within Australia.

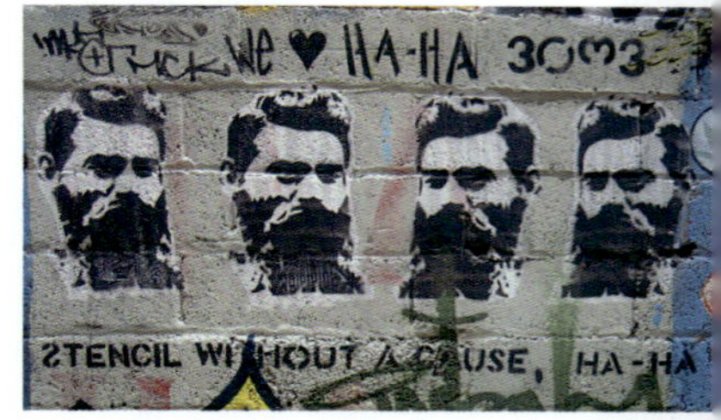

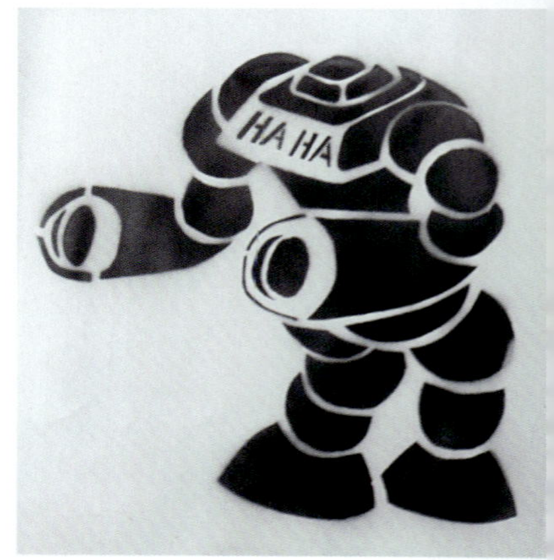

Photographs courtesy of Ha-Ha.
Melbourne, Australia, 2001.
Detail top: Melbourne, Australia, 2002.
Detail bottom: Melbourne, Australia, 2000.

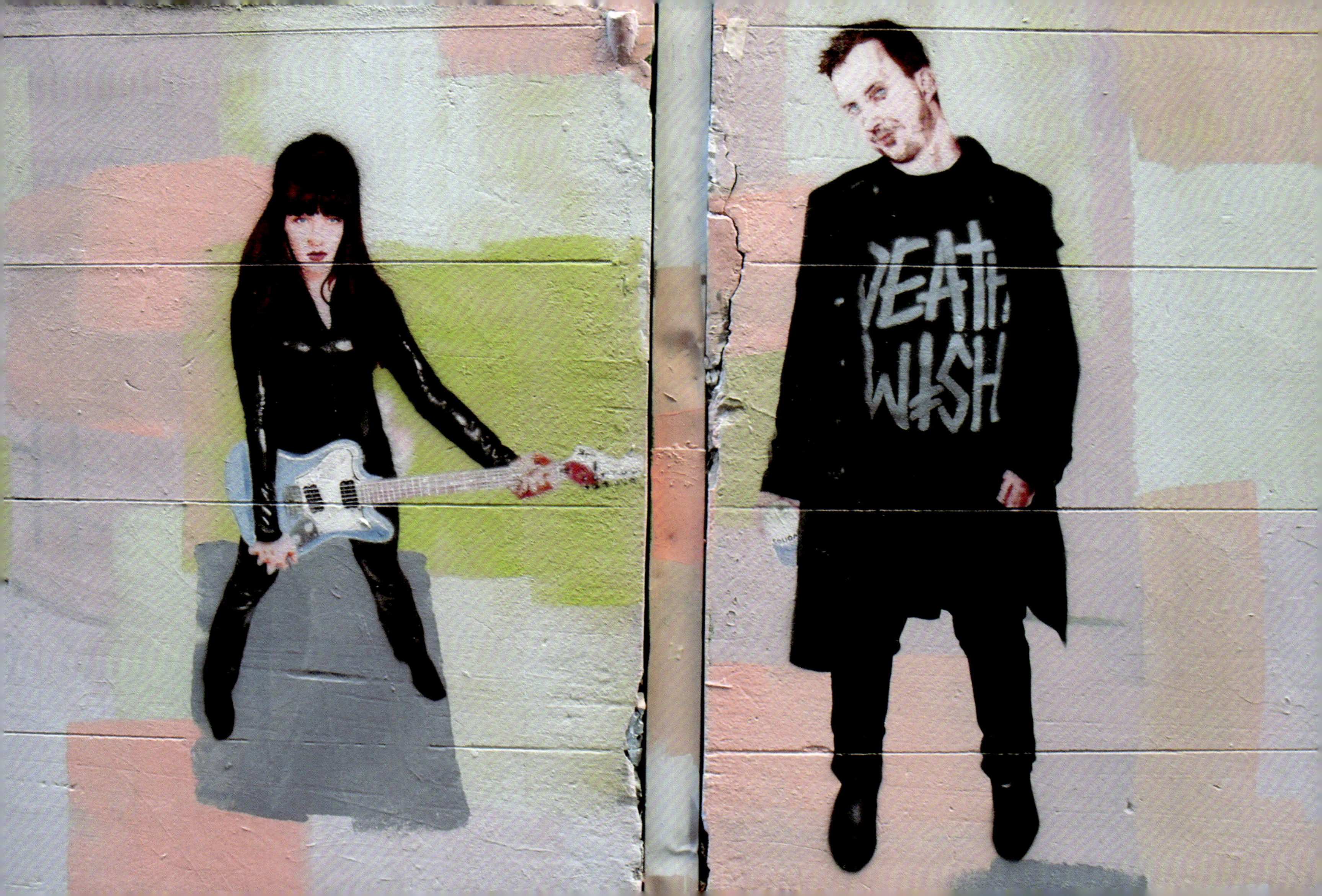

Richard Hambleton

Born in 1954, Richard Hambleton was an early practitioner of public art who gained fame for his 1980s "Shadowman" figures splashed on gritty urban walls around the world. The deliberately sloppy and indistinct figures were usually brushed on walls in splattered black paint. When seen from a distance or at night, the uncannily realistic images often seem to be actual people lurking in the shadows of doorways, jumping off buildings, pissing in alleyways, or lying down to sleep on broken patches of sidewalk. Sometimes only the top third of a person appears, as if crossing in front of a stop sign or climbing onto a bridge from the watery depths below. The Shadowman figures grew out of Hambleton's late-1970s public-art series titled "Mass Murder," wherein he outlined actual bodies in white chalk and then splashed the images with red paint to create the look of crime scenes.

Hambleton's work has twice been chosen for the Venice Biennale (in 1984 and 1988) and is included in important museum collections such as the Museum of Modern Art in New York and the Andy Warhol Museum in Pittsburgh. In early 2010, Hambleton was given a solo exhibition at Giorgio Armani's Teatro in Milan.

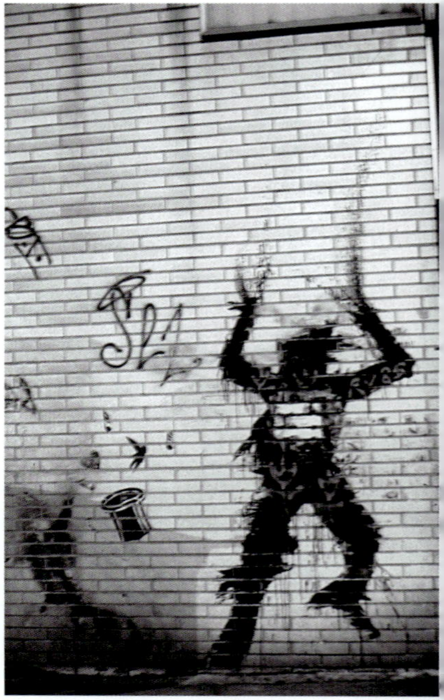

Photographs by Allan Molho.
New York City, 1980.

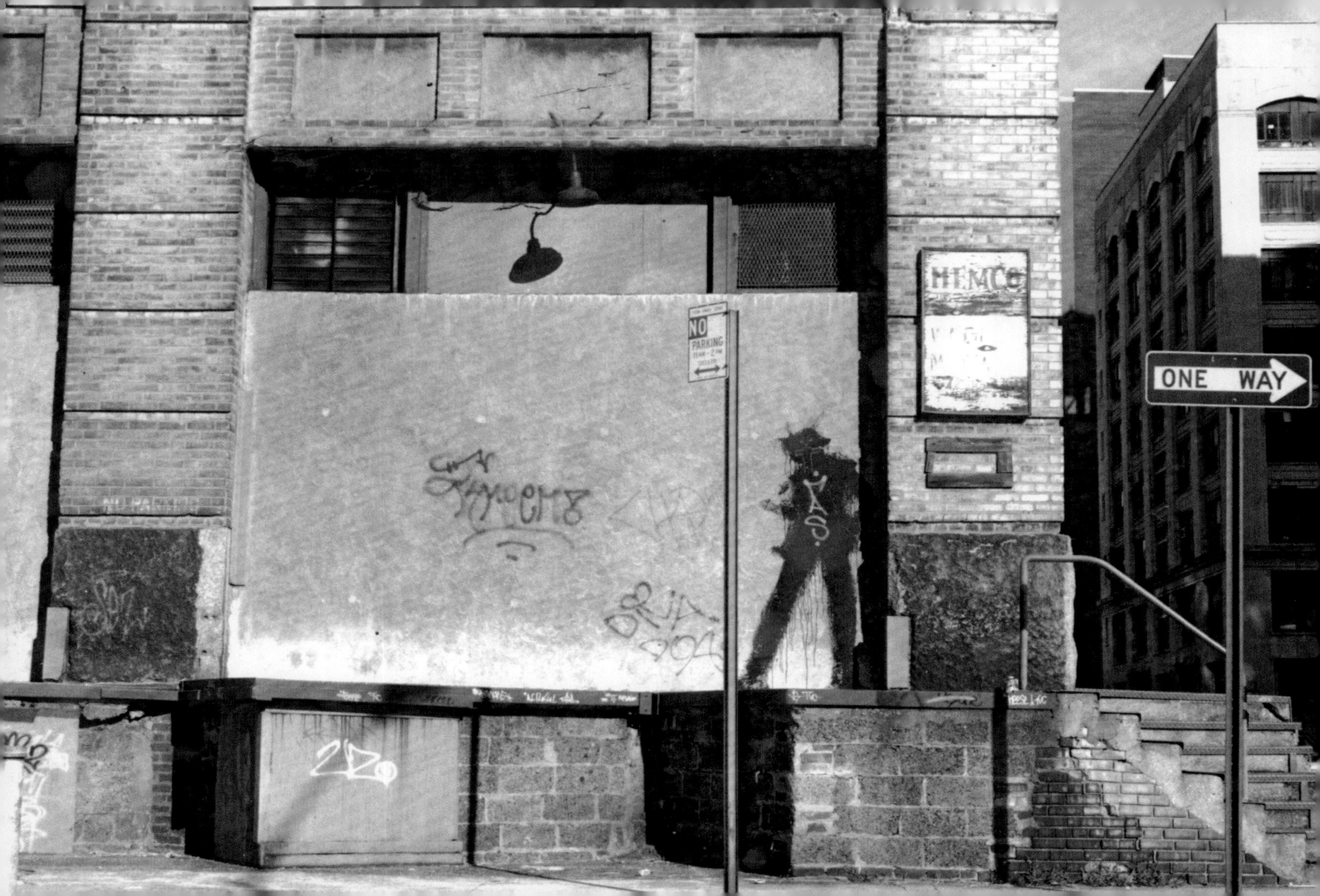
HEMCO
NO
PARKING
ONE WAY

Hargadon

As street art progressed beyond painting, it became a much more inclusive art form, allowing for people with a message to express themselves on the street. As more and more mediums became acceptable within the culture, it became increasingly difficult for some street-art fans to contain their desire to contribute something. One such artist is Boston-based Geoff Hargadon. Previously known for his parody of Christo and Jean Claude's "Gates" installation in Central Park, in which he sold miniaturized versions of their piece, Hargadon took a tongue-in-cheek approach to his first contribution to the graffiti world.

When the international stock market took a nosedive at the end of 2008, signs advertising CASH FOR YOUR HOME began to spring up all around his neighborhood. The fine-art market was in the worst shape it had been in years, and museums were threatening to close because they couldn't meet their budgetary goals. So Hargadon created a slew of signs that read CASH FOR YOUR WARHOL, with a phone number interested parties could call. In a pointed commentary on capitalistic greed and what happens when the economy bottoms out, Hargadon placed hundreds of these signs all over Boston and New York.

**Photograph by Becki Fuller.
Brooklyn, New York, 2010.**

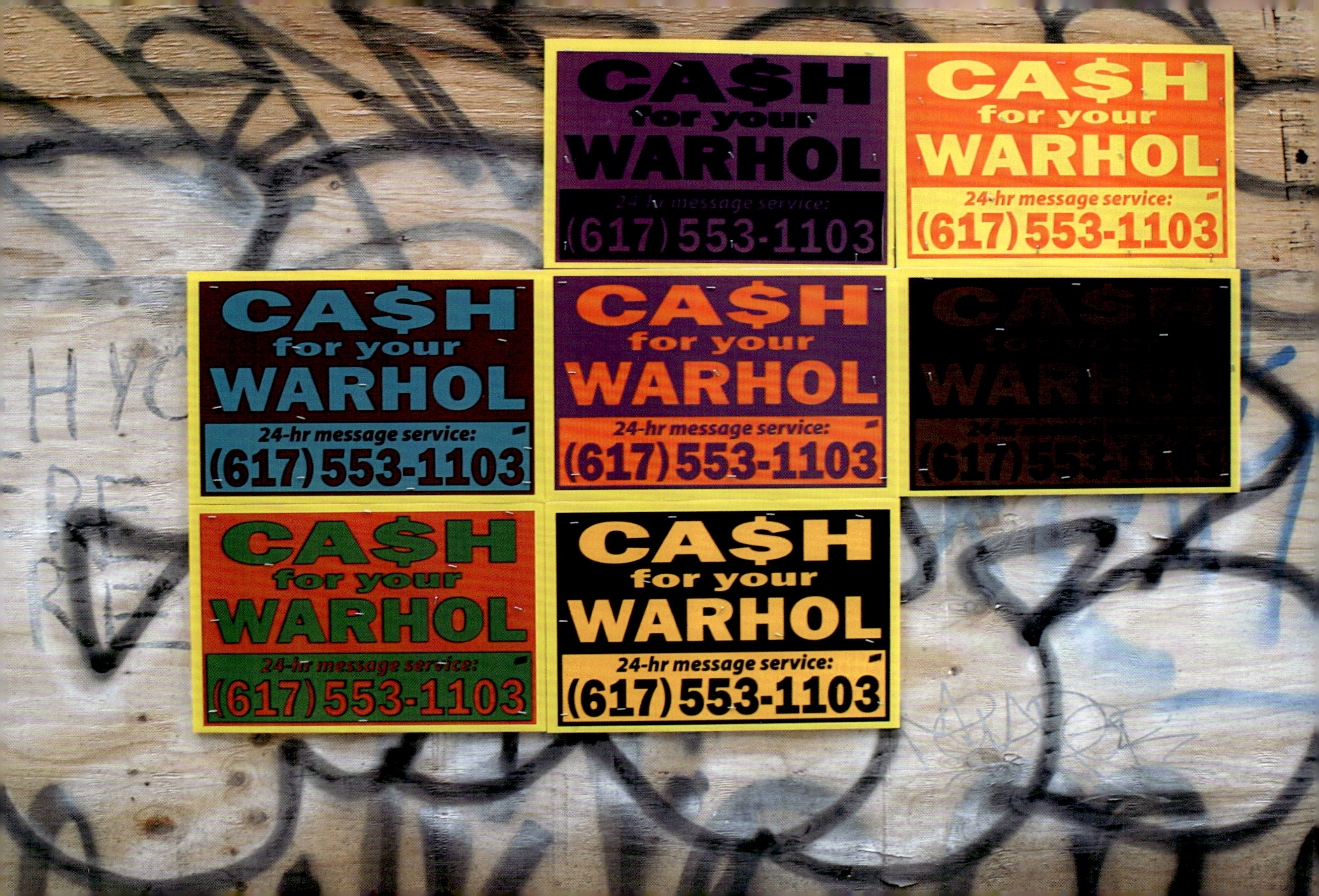
CA$H
for your
WARHOL
24-hr message service:
(617) 553-1103
CA$H
for your
WARHOL
24-hr message service:
(617) 553-1103
CA$H
for your
WARHOL
24-hr message service:
(617) 553-1103
CA$H
for your
WARHOL
24-hr message service:
(617) 553-1103
CA$H
for your
WARHOL
24-hr message service:
(617) 553-1103
CA$H
for your
WARHOL
24-hr message service:
(617) 553-1103

Keith Haring

A child of the late 1950s, Keith Haring developed an early passion for the cartoons of Dr. Seuss and Walt Disney. After completing high school in Pennsylvania, he studied commercial art but lost interest. He moved to New York in 1978, enrolled in the School of Visual Arts, and started hanging out downtown. Swept up in the artistic foment of the time, Haring began to organize and participate in exhibitions and performances at Club 57, The Mudd Club, and elsewhere. In 1980, he noticed that unused subway advertising panels were covered in black matte paper, and his white-chalk drawings thereon soon became so famous that transit police officers often asked for an autograph instead of arresting him.

Haring had his first solo exhibition at Westbeth Painters Space in 1981, and during the next several years he participated in renowned international exhibitions such as Documenta and the São Paolo and Whitney Biennials. Throughout his all-too-brief career, Haring devoted himself to public works with social messages, such as the now famous 1986 "Crack Is Wack" mural on a Harlem handball court. Haring's numerous collaborations include projects with William S. Burroughs, Jenny Holzer, Bill T. Jones, Grace Jones, Timothy Leary, Madonna, Yoko Ono, and Andy Warhol. His powerful lines and direct messages attracted a huge range of fans, and images like his radiant baby and barking dog continue to be universally recognized. Keith Haring died of AIDS-related complications in 1990.

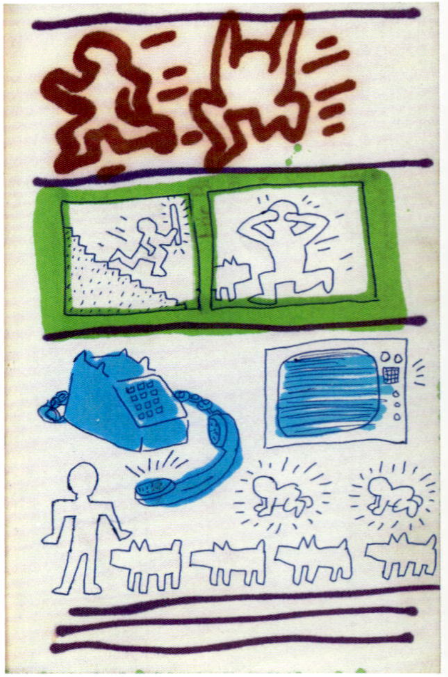

Panel by Keith Haring; tags by Pain the MOB and Hyper (aka Mackie RTW).
Photograph by Doug Evans.
New York City, 1981.
Detail: Private collection.
1981.

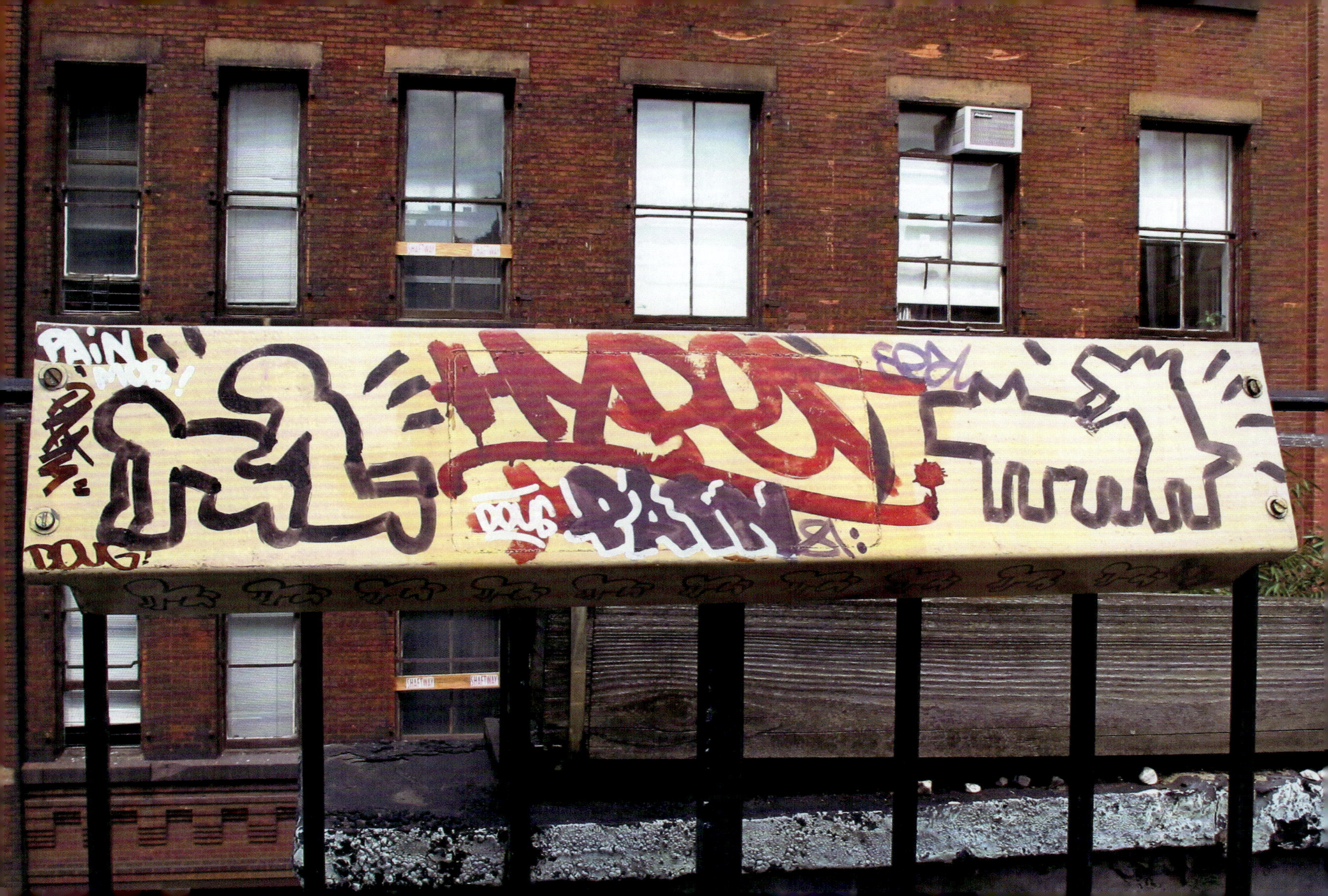
PAIN!
MOB!
DOUG!

Connor Harrington

When Connor Harrington was coming up in the small city of Cork, Ireland, where he was born in 1980, he knew he was going to be an artist. Unable to help himself, he was already drawing at a very young age, and eventually his scribblings on paper led to writing on walls. It was only a matter of time before Harrington would leave Ireland for grander shores, and that he did, migrating to London in his mid-twenties after graduating from art school, where he studied painting and design.

Harrington's unique mixture of intricate oil-painting skill with a strong taste for the graffiti aesthetic creates a bold, hyperreal visual explosion, both on canvas and in his elaborate public mural works. Harrington's paintings are a mash-up of colonial warriors and modern male figures—a meditation on masculinity and vulnerability swathed in bright, graphic colors.

Upon his arrival in London, Harrington approached the owners of StolenSpace Gallery, one of the more respected venues for street-to-fine-art crossovers, and the gallery offered to exhibit his work. Almost immediately, Harrington was picked up by Steve Lazarides, art star-maker and seller of urban art to the rich and famous. who began exhibiting Harrington alongside legends such as Banksy (see 024) and David Choe (see 065). Soon to follow for Harrington was the cover of *Juxtapoz* magazine—and the rest is history.

Right: Photograph by Andy Telling.
Bethlehem, Israel, 2010.
Far right: Photograph courtesy of Connor Harrington.
Grottaglie, Italy, 2009.

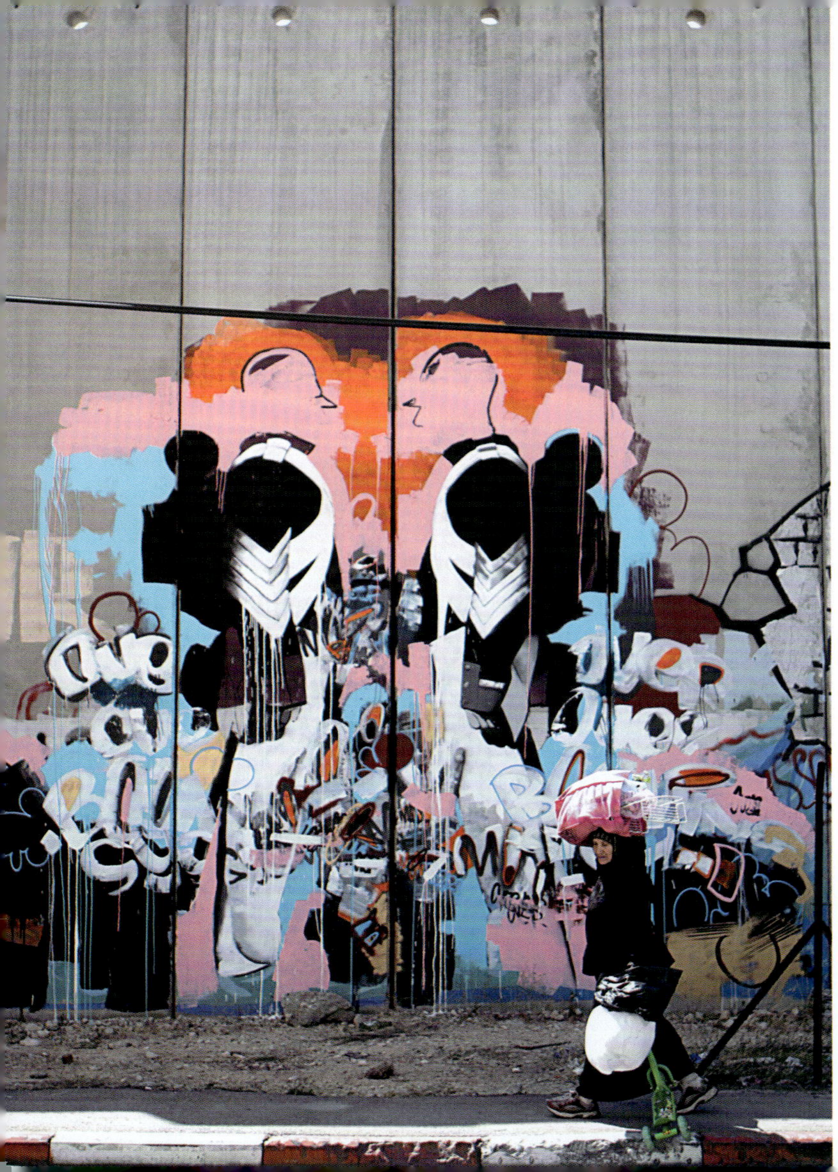
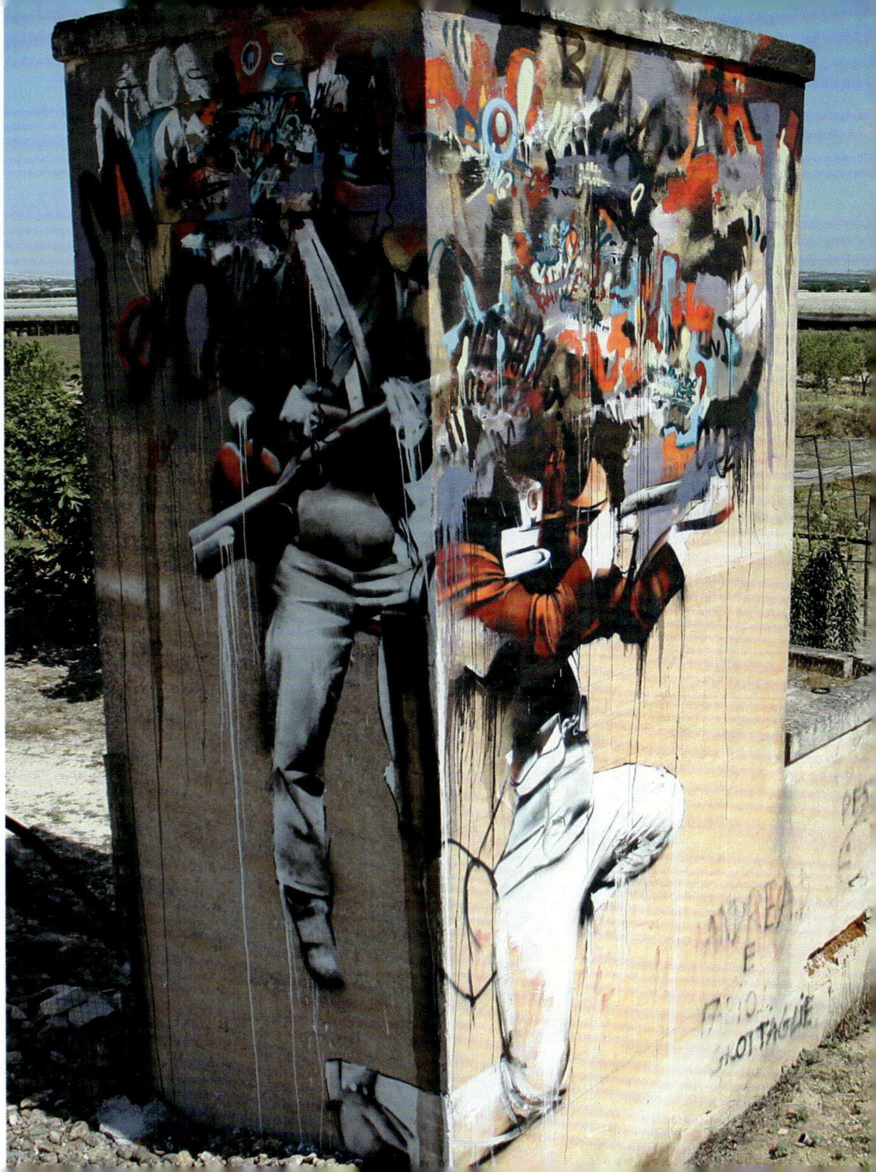

Maya Hayuk

Maya Hayuk's contributions to street art are manifold. Her intricately detailed, almost psychedelic paintings can be found all over the world, but proliferate especially around the Williamsburg section of Brooklyn. She is a first-generation American of Ukrainian descent, which is a great source of pride for her and an influence in her work. In the winter, Hayuk is busy working in her studio on smaller pieces, as well as sculpture, music, and video art. This warmhearted artist has also cultivated a reputation as a catalyst and art patron, housing artists new to the city and curating shows of her friends' work.

Raised in Baltimore, Hayuk began to travel the world extensively as a child, and the exposure to eclectic cultural mixes is readily visible within her work. Hayuk studied performance, sound sculpture, film, ceramics, and religion, but she never had formal training in the two mediums that she would eventually gravitate toward the most: painting and photography.

She is a valued member of the Barnstormers (see 025) artists' collective, and Hayuk continues to paint large-scale murals, as well as exhibiting her work in New York, San Francisco, Brussels, London, and Barcelona, to name a few. Hayuk lives and works in Brooklyn.

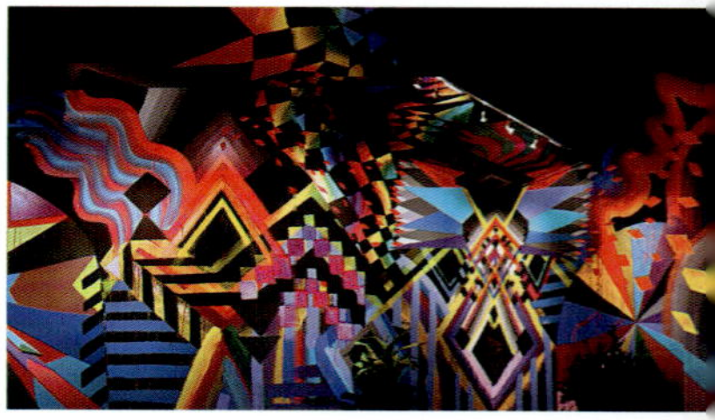

Photographs courtesy of Maya Hayuk.
Top left and right: *Grow House*. Braddock, Pennsylvania, 2008.
Bottom left: *Pilgrim*. Rental Gallery, New York City, 2007.
Bottom right: *For Yay!* Collaboration with Ben Wolf. Scope Art Fair, New York City, 2009.
Detail: *Raising the Sparks*. MIAM Musee, Sete, France, 2007.

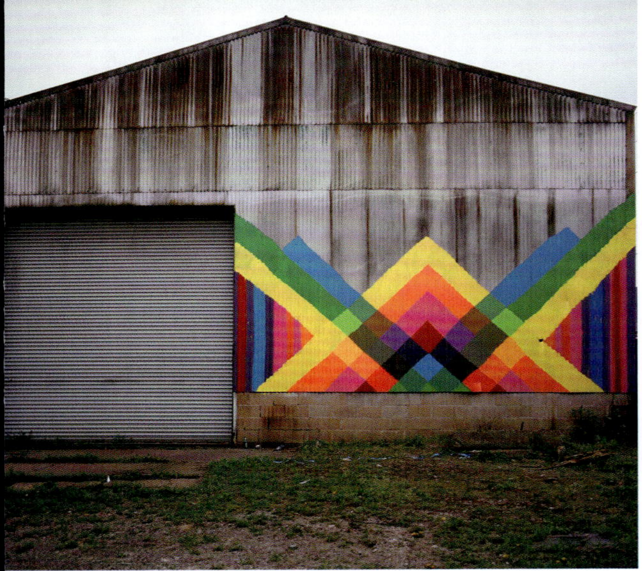
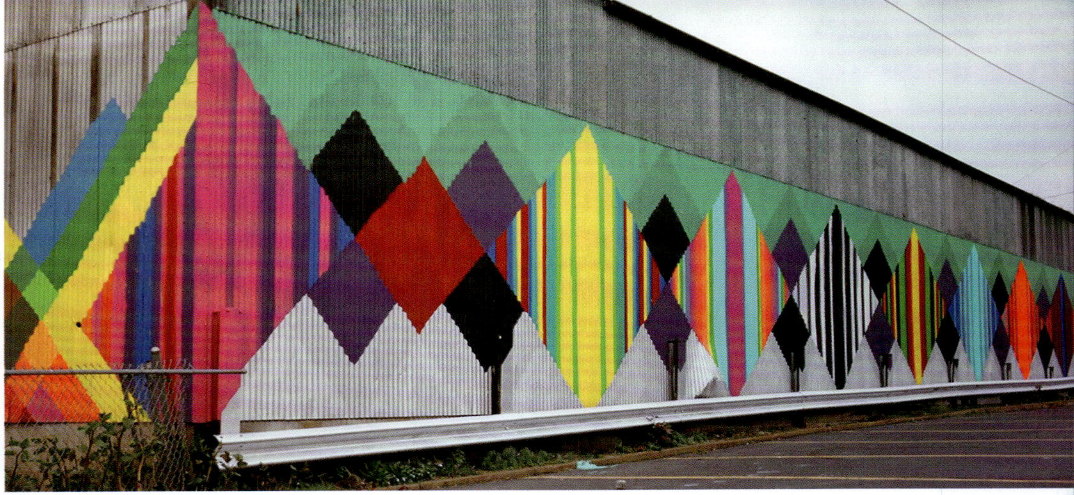
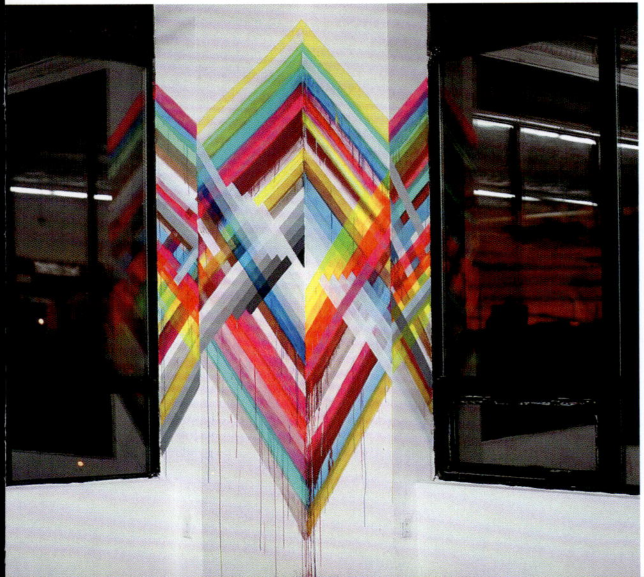
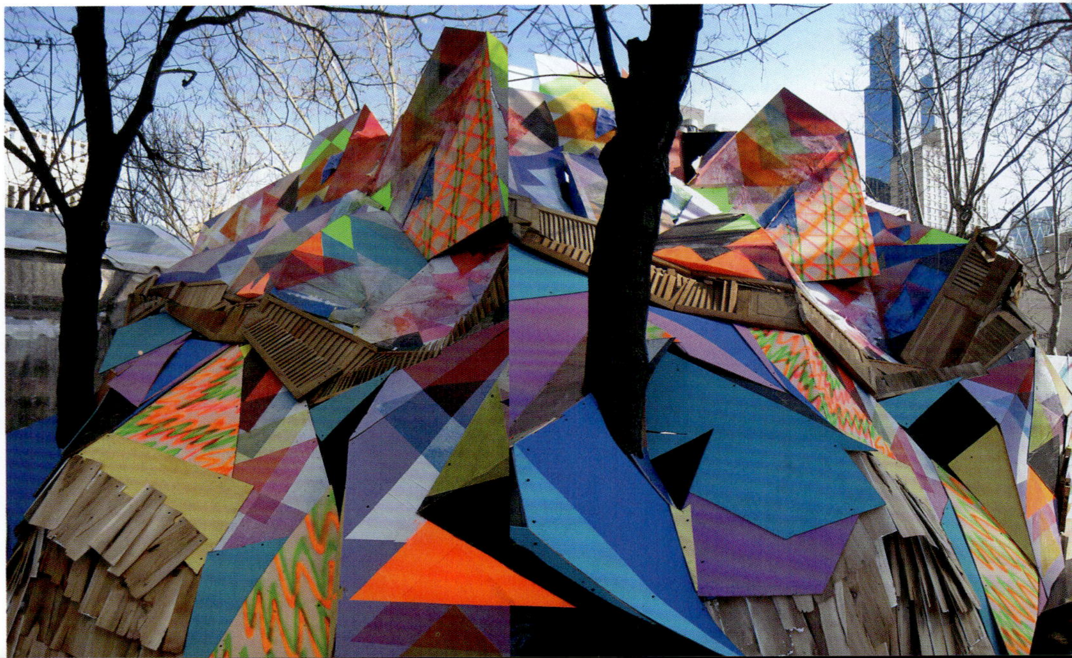

heavens

"Heavens" are the graffiti equivalent of having your name on a Broadway marquis. Water towers, freeway signs, billboards, rooftop overhangs, highway overpasses, and bridges all constitute heavens. The term encompasses a double meaning, as these high, difficult-to-access locations are often very dangerous, and to paint there may lead to death, i.e., "going to heaven." Heavens give maximum exposure and offer a longer shelf life, because cleanup crews simply aren't crazy enough to risk their lives the way writers do.

Risk [see 280] began the trend in California in the early 1980s by hitting the first highway overpass; this was elaborated upon a few years later by Ser and Wisk, who started to hit the backs of freeway signs that stretched over four lanes of traffic. In later years, the AM7 crew made billboards its primary targets. Currently, the Los Angeles-based 7th Letter crew [see 022] has taken the art of billboard bombing to unprecedented levels by matching the colors of existing ads and incorporating them seamlessly into the crew's work, producing an ironic collaboration with the advertiser. Japanese super-artist Murakami loved his altered billboard so much he had it taken down and sent to himself.

On the East Coast, JA One [see 180], the Evel Knievel of street bombing, has been scaling bridges and overpasses for years—and has many broken bones to show for it. Currently, PK and Kid own heaven spots in the New York–New Jersey area. Their names can be seen across the horizon on hard-to-reach water towers, factory rooftops, and rocky cliffs—it seems as if these daredevils shun ground-level vandalism.

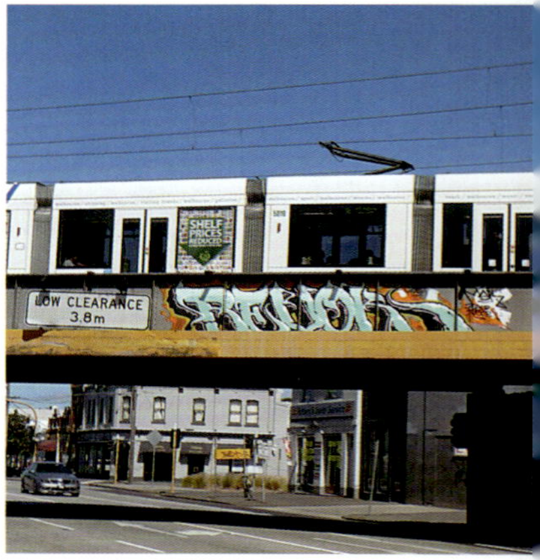

Piece by Sane [left]; tag by Smith. Photograph by Smith. New York City, 1988.
Detail: Piece by Revok. Photograph by Akuze. Australia, 2010.

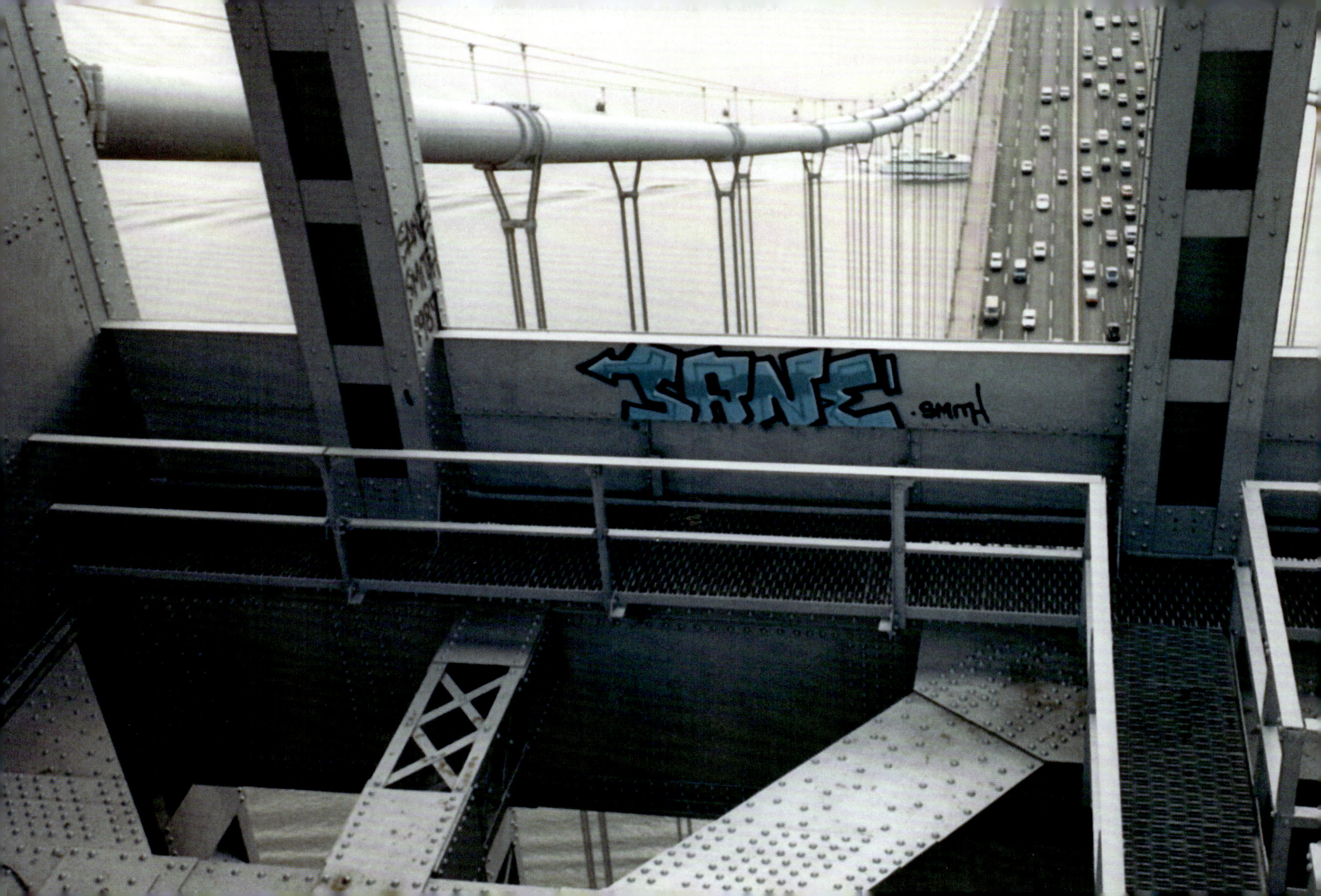

Heavy Artillery

The U.K.-based Heavy Artillery crew was formed out of necessity: Members of a former crew grew tired of going to court for hitting trains but still loved to paint, so Heavy Artillery began in the summer of 2006. These like-minded individuals needed to create a new identity to pursue their love of day painting, but they soon found success, as well—the original lineup of members [Jiroe, Gary, Odisy, Rench, and Aroe [see 018]] gathered so much momentum that expansion became inevitable. They slowly invited artists who shared a common vision—and who were also good friends.

Over the next few years, Heavy Artillery recruited mainland European writers, who added an extra dimension, creating great opportunities for them to be in a lot of places at one time. Original member Aroe sums up the crew's philosophy: "Our main purpose is to try and push the boundaries of accepted graffiti without straying into any street-art bullshit and continuously try to outdo one another."

The crew is loosely affiliated with the L.A.-based MSK crew, taking on projects as a tight-knit unit.

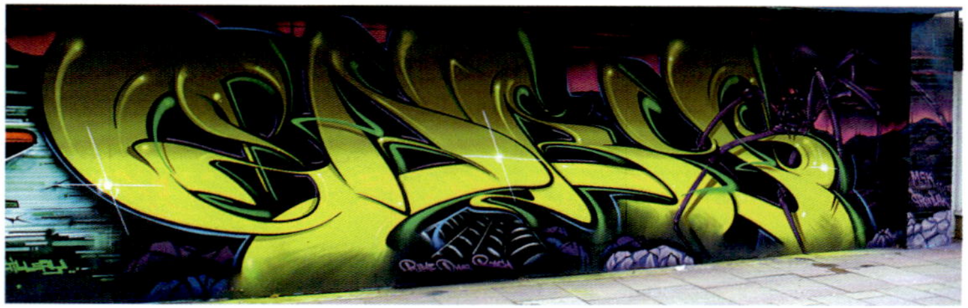

Odissy **by Heavy Artillery.**
Photograph by David Stuart [NoLionsInEngland].
London, 2010.
Detail: Photograph by GaryMSKHA.
Brighton, United Kingdom, 2010.

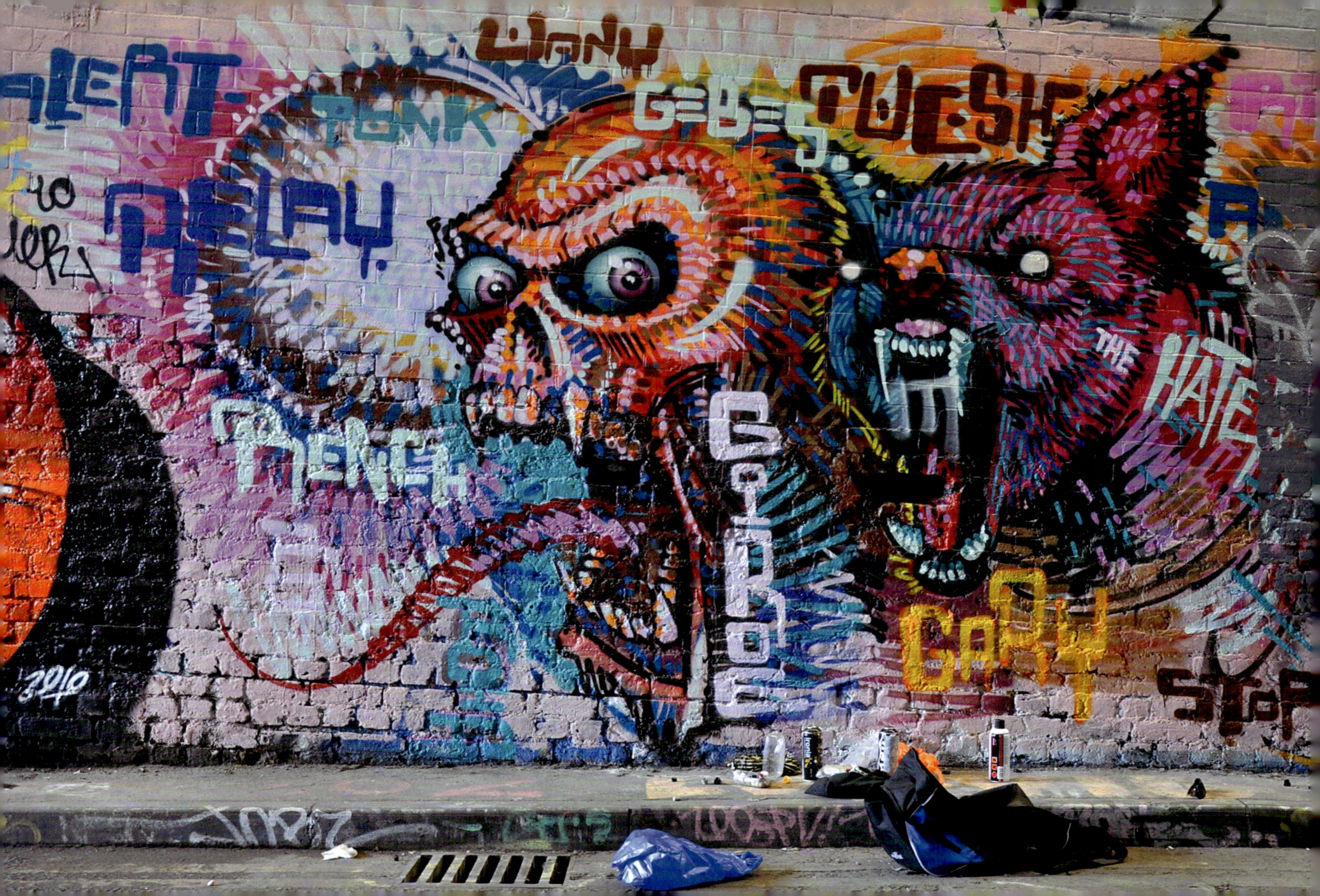
ALERT
RELAY
THE HATE
GARY
2010

Hera

Hera and Akut (formerly known as Herakut) were a powerhouse duo within the German graffiti scene. Akut, a member of the notorious Maclaim (see 209) crew, is one of Europe's best-known hyperrealistic graffiti artists. Hera, hailing from Frankfurt, is a masterful brush painter, with a highly recognizable, sloppy style. Having met at an urban-art festival in Seville, Spain, the artists began collaborating in love and art in 2004. Their work gained recognition on the international urban-art circuit later in the decade.

Hera's obsession with all things hip-hop began at age fourteen, when she started tagging with markers, but she did not begin painting on the street until 2001, when she started college. Though she received classical training as a painter in Germany's rigorous art-school system, her work serves as a rebellious outburst against convention.

Half-German, half-Pakistani, Hera draws her name from the character in Greek mythology, to whom she relates closely. Alienated from her Pakistani roots by that culture's perception of making art as a waste of time, she claims to use painting as a therapeutic release. She has stopped painting on the street in recent years due to an arrest, and she now concentrates on exhibiting her work in galleries internationally, where both her solo work and that of Herakut have met with much success.

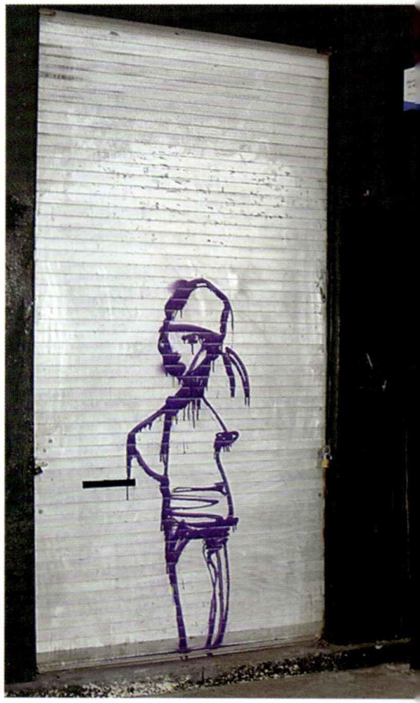

Photographs by David Stuart (NoLionsInEngland).
Shoreditch, London, 2008.
Detail: Shoreditch, London, 2007.

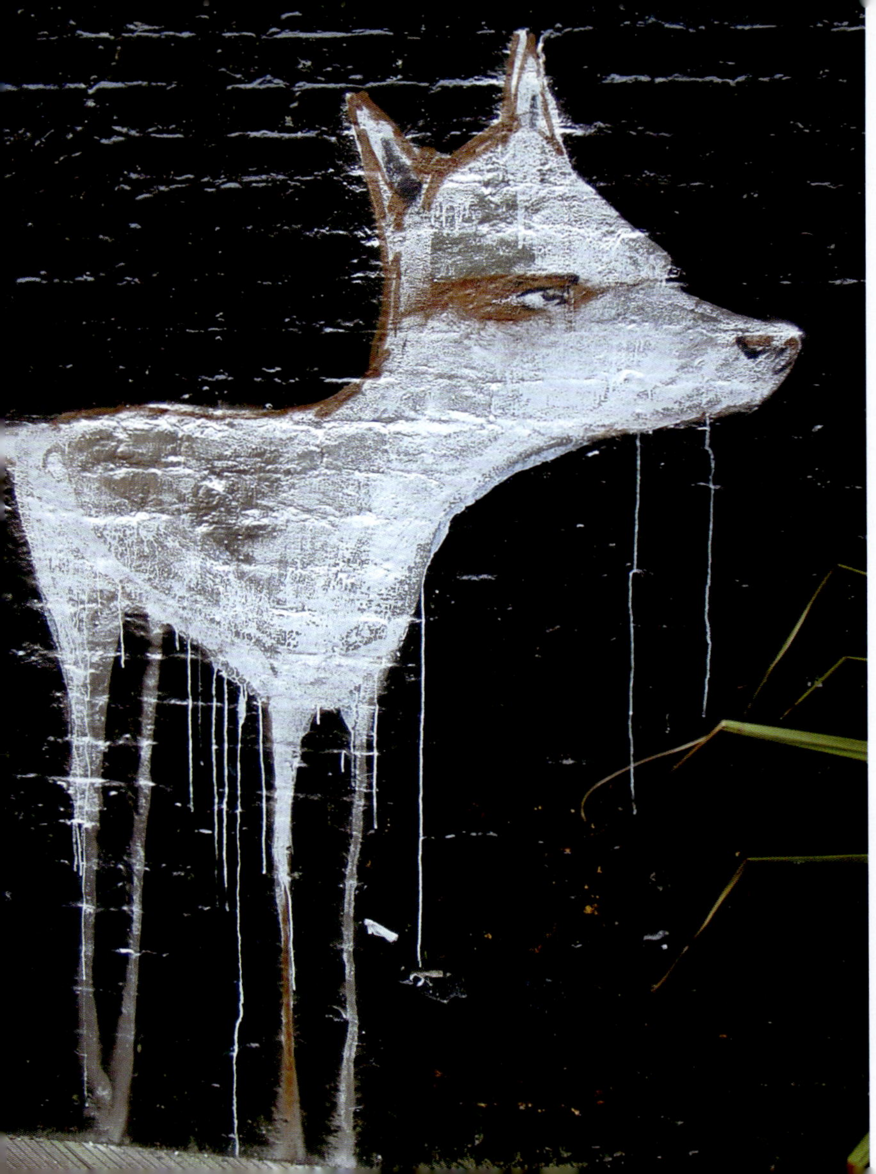

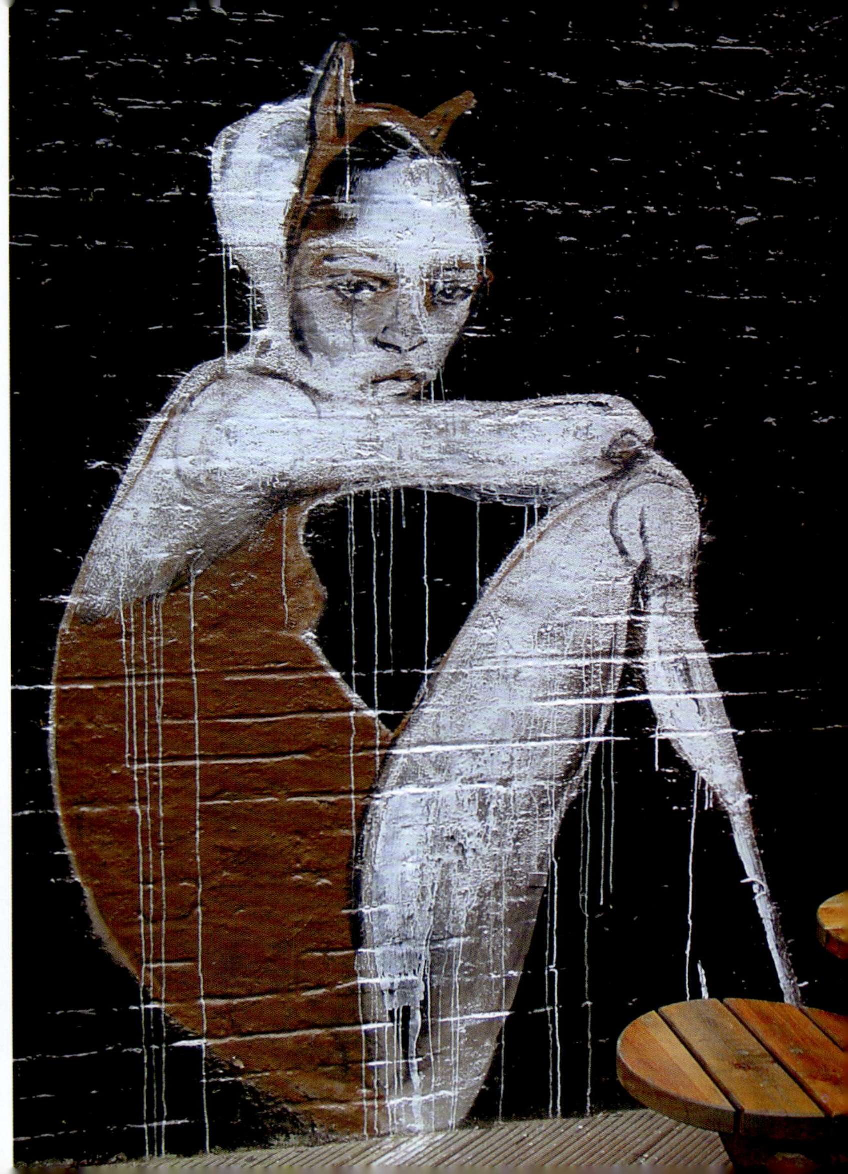

Logan Hicks

When creating a stencil piece, one cuts an image from a sheet of card, or thin plastic, for each different color in the final work, then sprays through each stencil, layering the colors on top of one another. According to Logan Hicks, stenciling suits his personality perfectly, because it is a "real direct, hardworking, no-bullshit kind of approach." He's not kidding. Cutting normal stencils (four or five layers at most) is an exhausting, detail-oriented, muscle-straining process. Hicks's stencils stretch into several dozen layers, leaving him cutting for up to a mind-boggling hundred hours to create his hyperdetailed images.

Originally a screen printer from the streets of Baltimore, Maryland, Hicks took up stenciling over a decade ago. He moved to Los Angeles, where he perfected his craft and began showing in galleries before eventually migrating to New York City.

In November 2009, Hicks created his largest piece to date: a 30-by-8-foot mural piece featuring the face of his infant son, Sailor, on a street in the Williamsburg section of Brooklyn.

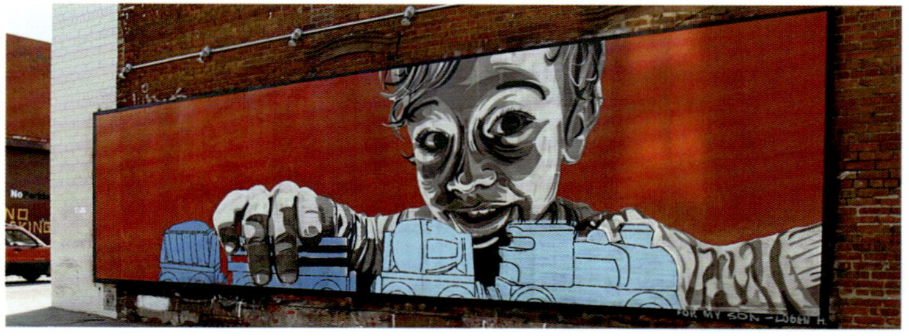

Photographs courtesy of Logan Hicks.
***Self Portrait*. Cans Festival, London, 2008.**
Detail: *Portrait of Sailor Hicks*. Brooklyn, New York, 2010.

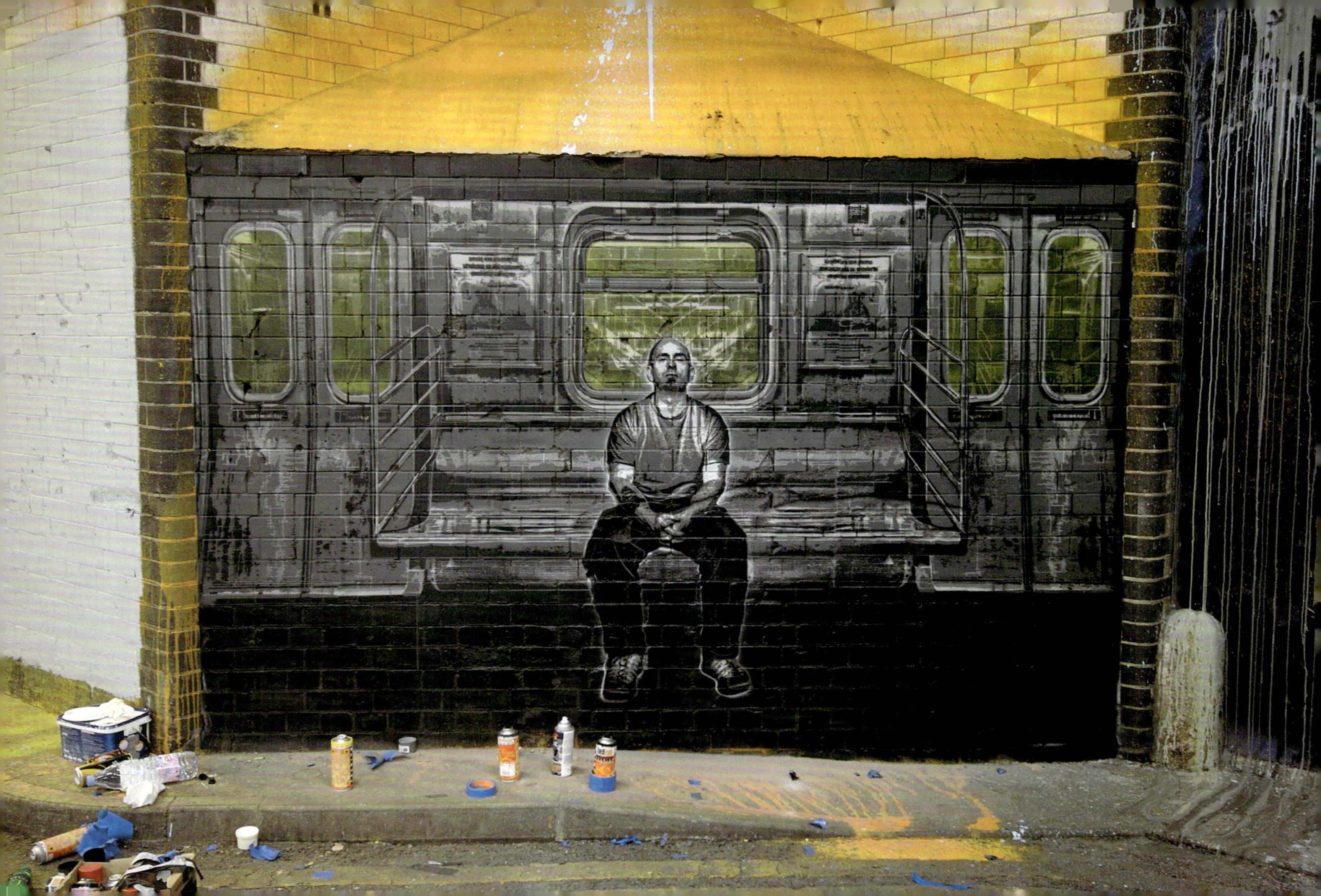

High School of Art and Design

If a true Graffiti Hall of Fame [see 151] were to enshrine its illuminati à la Cooperstown, the High School of Art and Design's alumni could fill their own wing. Wikipedia's entry for the high school cites Chris "Daze" Ellis [see 185] and Sandra "Lady Pink" Fabara as graduates, but the site's abbreviated list is shamefully sparse. Missing from the roster and deserving inclusion are Pistol 1, Sjk 171, Stop 700, Tracy 168 [see 340], Flint . . . [see 134], Steve 61, Earl, Don 1 [see 096], Inca, Chino Malo, Aim 1, Delta 2000, Shadow, Revolt, Defie, Dime 139, Reas, Pure, Lil Seen, Tack, Son 1, Mare 139, Lyndah, Doze Green [see 098], Ezo [see 119], and Bomb 1.

Lunchtime blackbook [see 036] sessions determined the future of transit design. Classes in advanced letter science were given free of charge by style professors. Other bastions of graffiti higher learning include DeWitt Clinton High School in the Bronx and the Music and Art High School in Manhattan—but these were a distant second to Art and Design. Competition raged fiercely, culminating in the first graffiti-related shooting during an art show in 1980—piece and love seeming to be mutually exclusive.

Shadow (far left); Bomb 1 [aka Al Diaz—far right, with glasses).
Photograph by Flint Genari.
New York City, 1975.

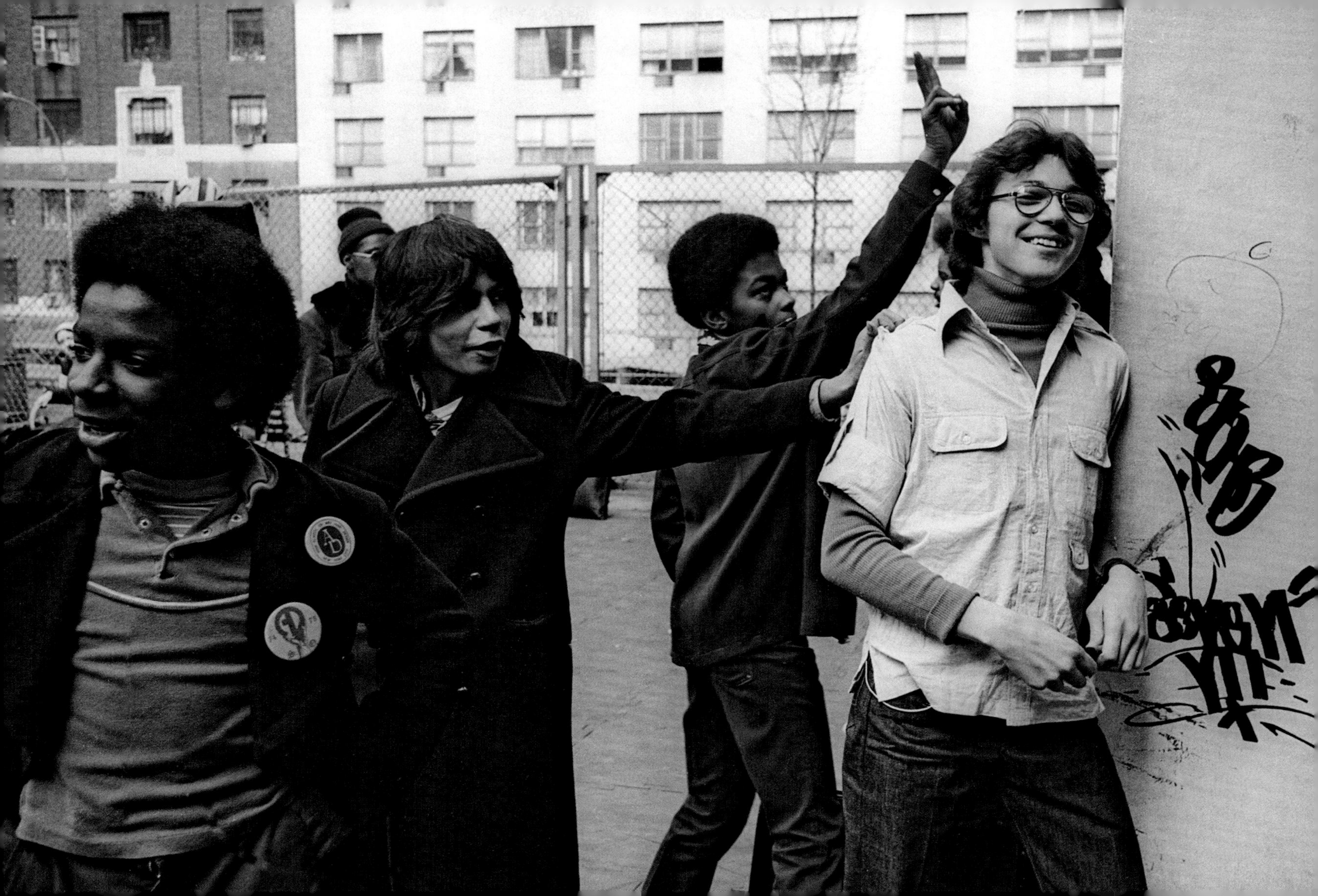

Honet

Born in 1972 and based in Paris, Honet began doing graffiti at age fifteen, on the trains and along the tracks of his native city. Within a few years, his markings, ranging from minimal tags to more intricate pieces, could be found throughout Europe in such cities as Bucharest and Helsinki, and in places as remote as Beijing and Tokyo.

In the 1990s, Honet developed a predilection for painting the walls, floors, and ceilings of such murky places as abandoned aquariums, underground bunkers, and similarly obscure venues. Narrative in style, Honet's distinctive artwork fuses images of a city's architecture, culture, and activities. Reflecting a gothic sensibility, these paintings are often infused with skeletons, monsters, and dead women.

Honet's paintings have been exhibited in galleries worldwide. Though he also has a successful career as a graphic designer, collaborating with such high-profile companies as Prada, Honet defines himself first and foremost as a graffiti artist and still creates huge vibrant pieces on the streets of Paris. If not for graffiti, he maintains, he would not have discovered his talent for art. "I failed everywhere else," he quips.

Together with Krink, Flying Fortress, and SozyOne, in the spring of 2010 Honet was selected to paint part of the landmark 150-foot tower on the Schloßstraße in Steglitz, the center of Berlin.

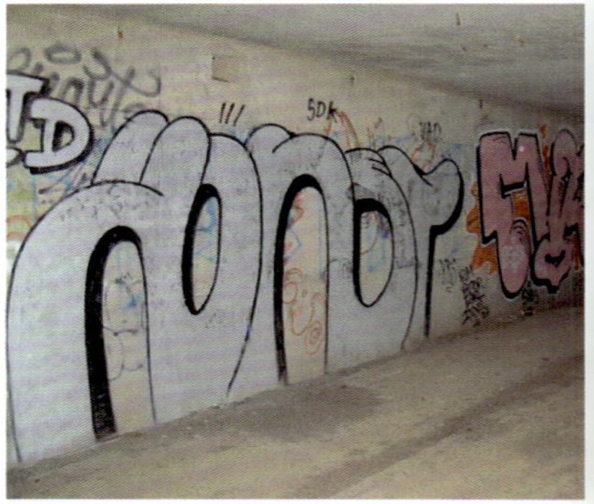

Photograph by Vitostreet.
Paris, 2009.
Detail: Photograph by Angelo Lanza.
Queens, New York, 2010.

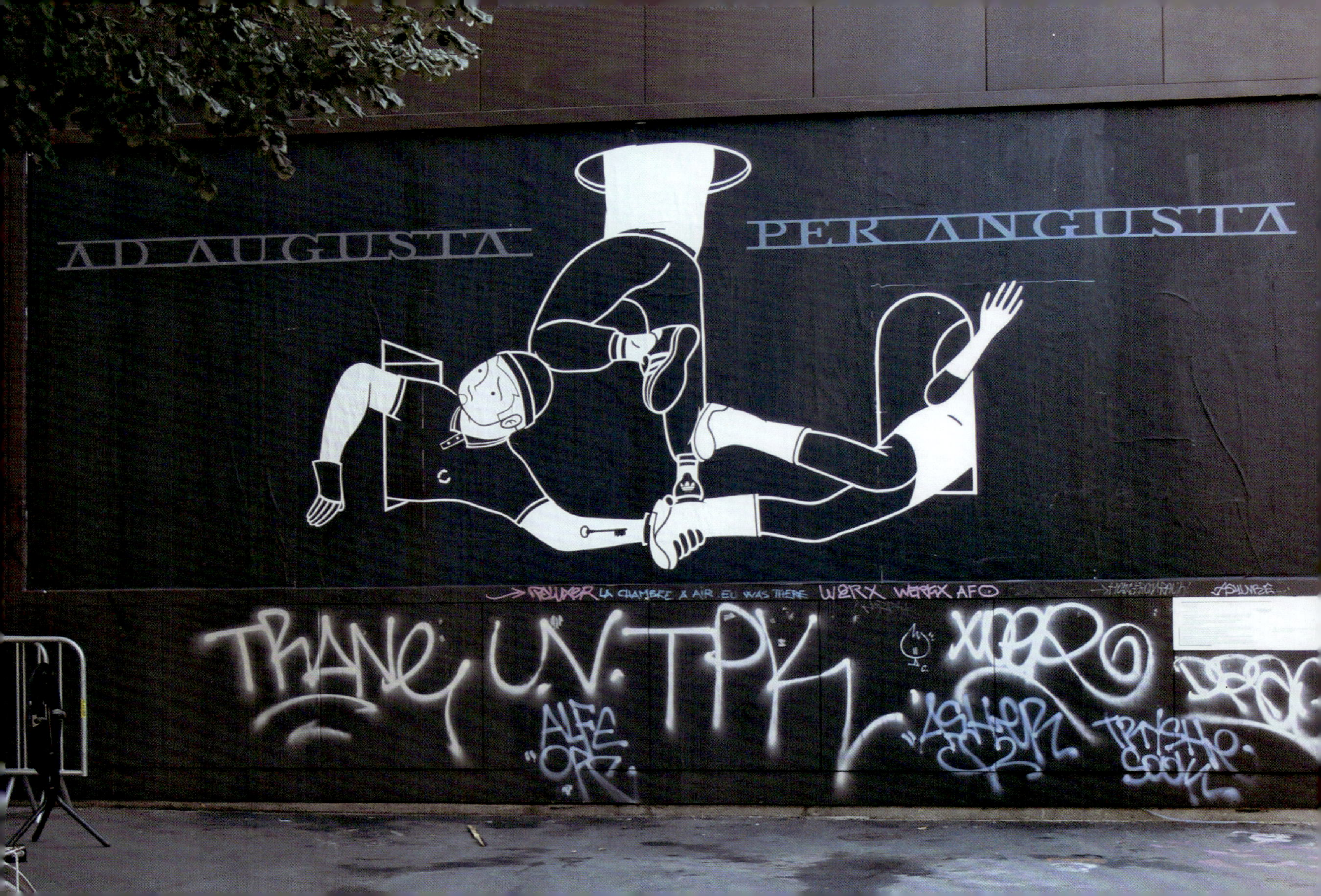
AD AUGUSTA
PER ANGUSTA

How and Nosm

How and Nosm are twin brothers born in Spain and raised in Germany. They started painting in the late 1980s, hitting trains and walls while living in Düsseldorf. In 1997, they had an offer to come to New York and stay for free at the house of a friend; the house happened to be in the South Bronx—home to one of the greatest graffiti crews ever, Tats Cru.

There was no orchestrated plan for the twins to meet with the group and get down with them, yet that's what happened. By the time they went back to Europe, How and Nosm were representing Tats Cru on trains and walls wherever they went. They were able to play with different styles in their travels, and they have their own distinct take on graffiti on trains—trains should be done with a little bit of dirt, like old-school New York graffiti.

How and Nosm have been going strong for over two decades, and unlike their Tats Cru counterparts, they still feel the need to travel the globe and paint in different places. They have been chased by dogs and shot at on several continents, but still they persist, leaving a trail of paintings in their wake. Many of the places How and Nosm have painted in had never seen graffiti until the brothers paid a visit.

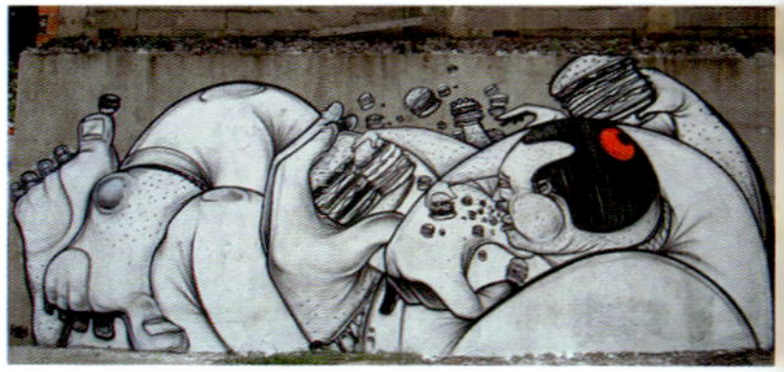

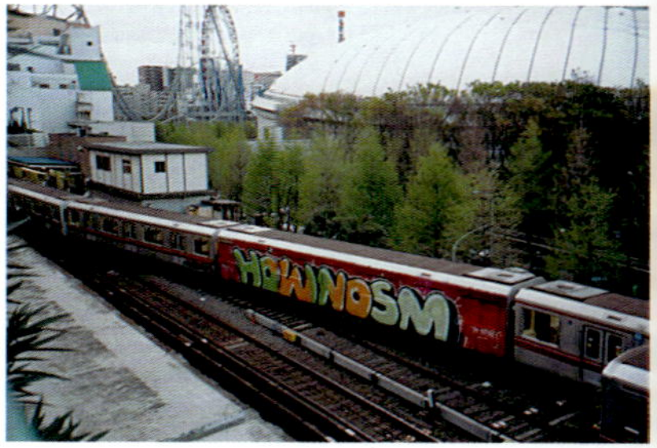

Photograph by Monica LoCascio.
Primary Flight, Miami, Florida, 2010.
Detail photographs by How and Nosm.
Detail top: Rio de Janeiro, Brazil, 2009.
Detail bottom: Korakuen Subway Station, Tokyo, 2006.

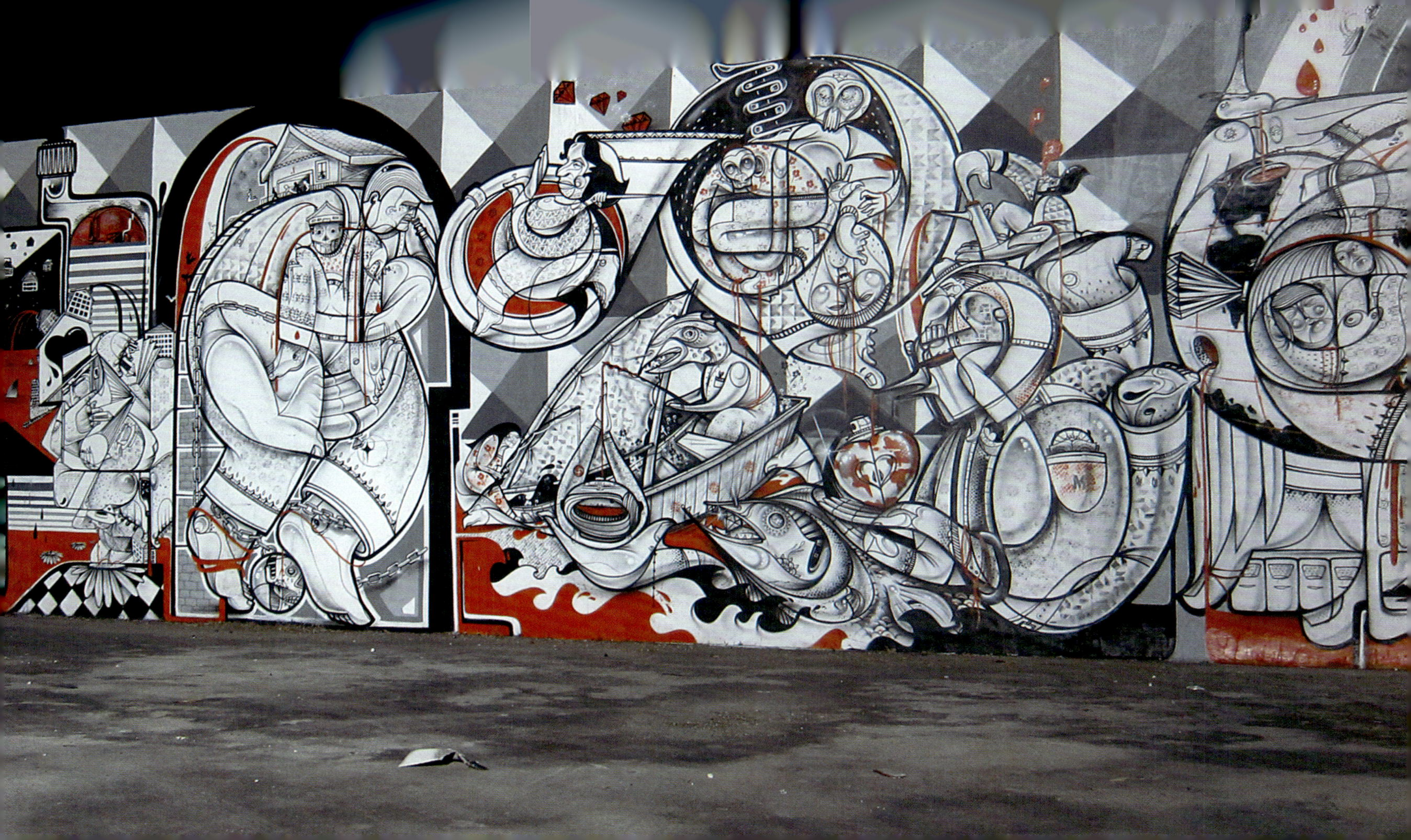

Imminent Disaster

When the first street artists made the crossover into the institutionalized fine-art world, none was more revered than the queen bee of the medium, Callie Curry, better known as Swoon [see 329]. This pint-size hippie came with a band of troops with whom she worked closely on all her projects, and who had cultivated their own unique aesthetic. Some of them were strictly collaborators, while others served as her assistants, working intimately with her on the execution of her massive installations and intricate woodcuts. One of these artists emerged with a voice of her own and made a name for herself on the streets under the moniker Imminent Disaster.

Despite her rather melancholy name, Disaster is an affable Floridian who moved to New York at age seventeen. She graduated from a design program, and she specializes in printmaking. Toward the end of the first decade of the 2000s, with access to the endless resources of a university, she began to dabble in what is known as "culture jamming"—creating artworks and making additions to public objects already in existence (adding words to a sign, for example). Eventually Disaster branched off into her own woodcuts, which she places on the street, and she has also begun to exhibit in galleries.

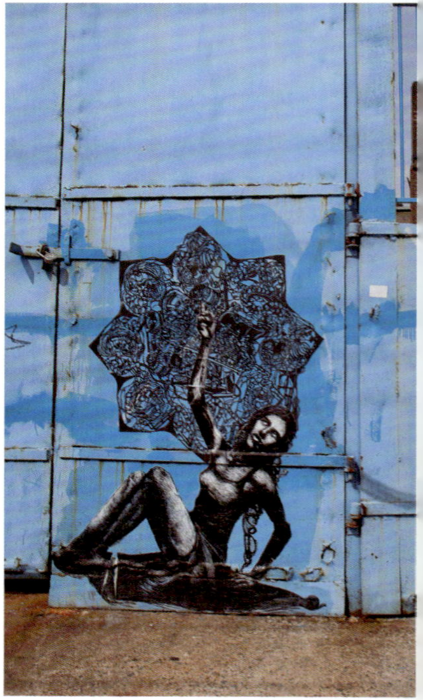

Photograph by Becki Fuller. Brooklyn, New York, 2010. Detail: Photograph by Vincent Cornelli. Brooklyn, New York, 2009.

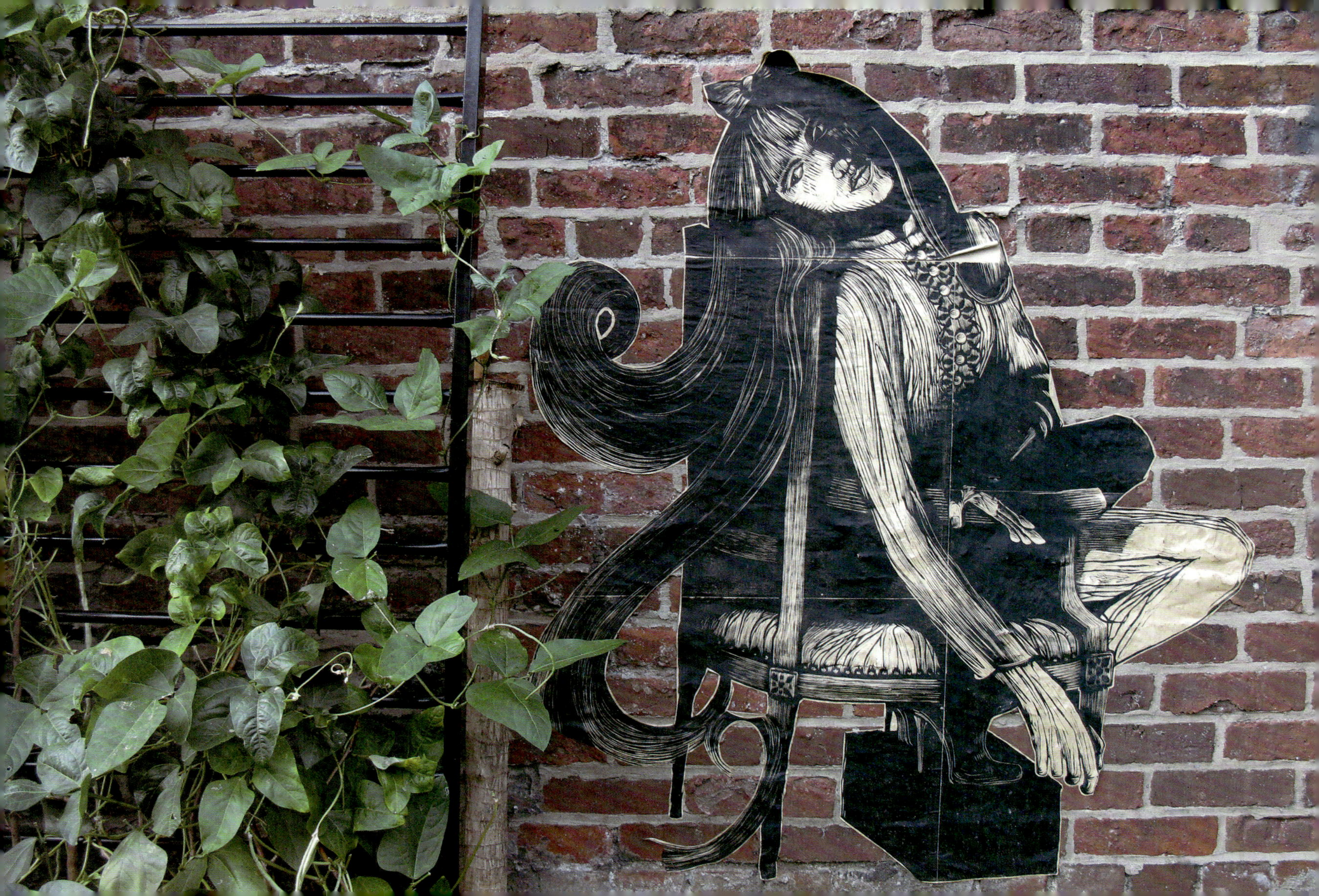

In

Kill 3 was a writer from the Bronx who began writing "In" during the mid-1970s and dramatically changed not only graffiti, but also the way we perceive the urban landscape. A banner year for style in graffiti, 1974 saw groups like Wanted and INDs (see 172) putting in some of the best work ever. It had been a continual push forward since the first pieces were done in 1972, with each piece owing a debt to the ones before it. In was responsible for bringing graffiti back to its urban competition roots.

In the fall of 1974, In started writing his two-letter name on the outside of every train he could find. The interior of the name was filled in so quickly that it left a hazy mist. The writers dubbed it a throw-up. As he began to get noticed, he met Cliff 159 (see 070) at the Writers' Bench (see 362), and as 1975 rolled around, Cliff 159, Tracy 168 (see 340), and In began hitting yards all over the city. Their methodology had Cliff and Tracy going first to do highly stylized pieces; the next night, all three of them would go and do as many throw-ups as possible. In, because of his short name and misty fill-in, could dominate an entire yard in a night, walking far ahead of the other two writers. By the summer of 1975, In was declared king.

As 1976 rolled around, In became a founding member of the TOP crew in Brooklyn. He wrote with them for two years and became famous to a new audience of writers on the BMT and IND lines. He retired in 1977 and remains the only writer in history to ever hold the title "king of all lines."

Photograph by Bryan Mechutan (Uni). New York City, 1975.

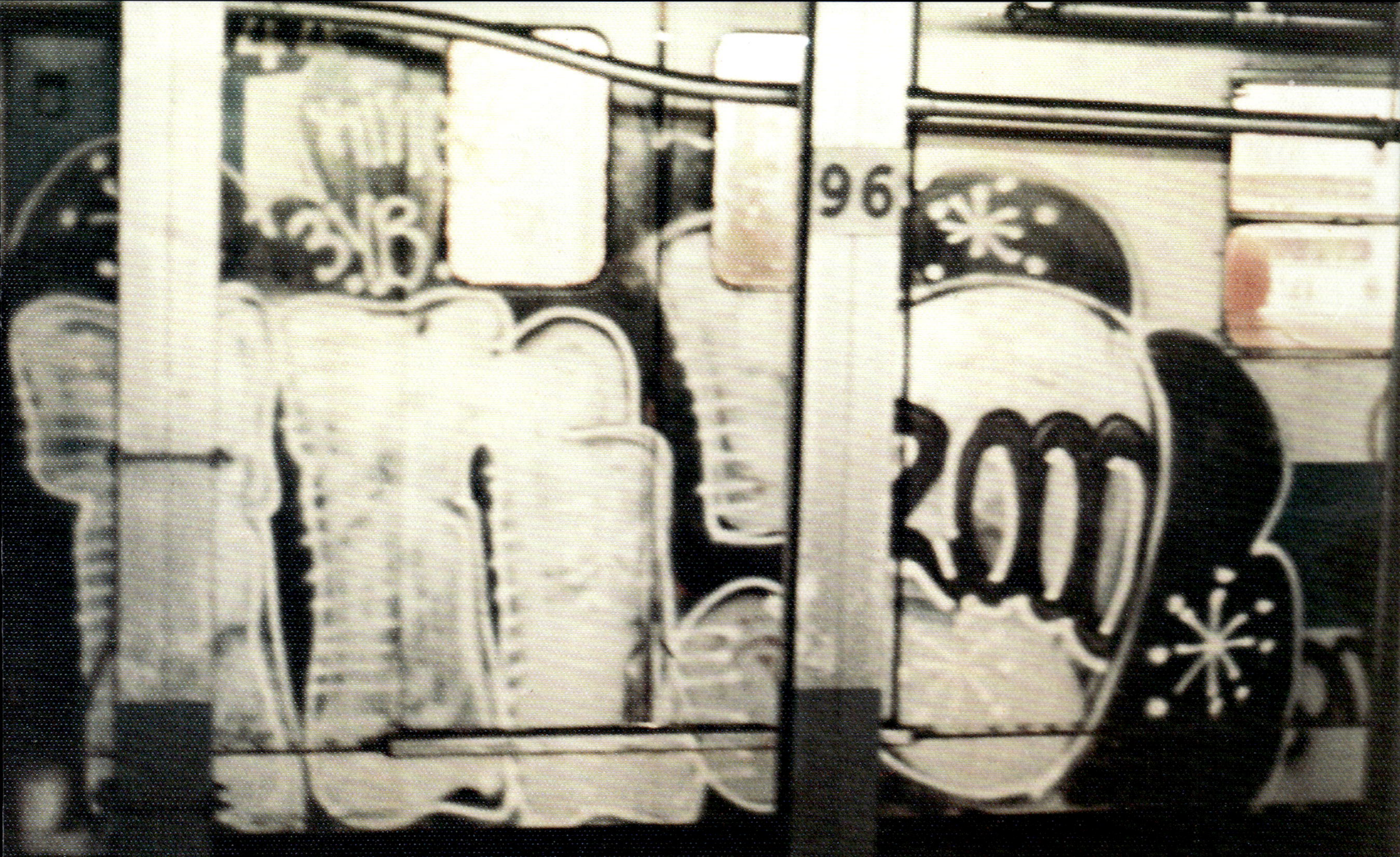

The INDs

In late 1973, a group of Bronx writers, inspired by Brooklyn's Ex Vandals [see 118], decided to create a group of their own and formed The Independents, thus establishing one of the most important crews in graffiti's stylistic development. Phase 2 [see 255] gave outlines to countless writers, who would then practice until they were good enough to put them on the train. Riff 170, Phase 2's greatest disciple, changed the way the letters looked, and then changed his name almost monthly [changing names allowed Riff to master nearly the entire alphabet]. Pel then learned from Riff in a field apprenticeship that would make him one of the nastiest stylists in the game by 1974. Soon, Jive 3, Spencer, Voe 61, Stick 1, P'nut 2, Cliff 159 [see 070], Jester 1, Billy 167 [see 034], Lava 1-2 and Ale 1 [see 011] all joined the INDs family. Restrictive membership policies made The INDs one of the hardest crews to gain acceptance in, and the INDs peaked in 1976. Phase 2 lost interest in subway painting after his good friend Solid 1 was killed by a train that year, and Riff then did his last subway piece, designing the famous whole-car memorial *Riff, Solid, Bot, Don.*

In 1977, the Death Squad [see 086], a group of younger writers inspired by The Independents, grabbed the torch of letter evolution from The INDs, fine-tuning the styles of its predecessors and making them its own. The group appropriated the multi-name approach that Riff popularized, even using some of his former aliases in its productions.

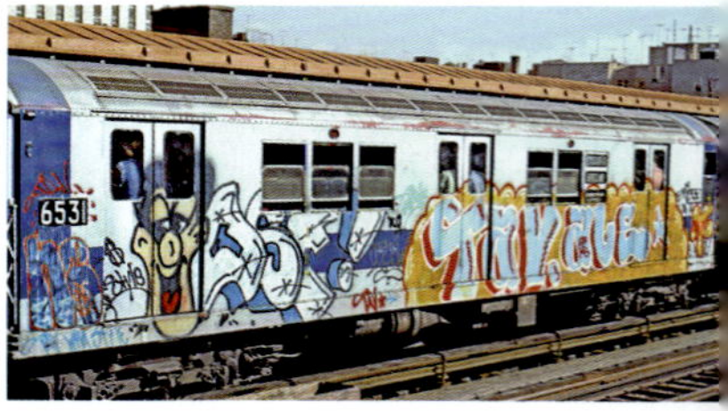

Pieces by Sonny 107 [left] and Checker 170. Photograph by Jack Stewart. New York City, 1975. Detail: Don Martin–inspired character [left] by Cost 170 [aka Palo INDs], with two-man cloud by Tav and Ale 1 INDs. Photograph by Keith Baugh. New York City, 1975.

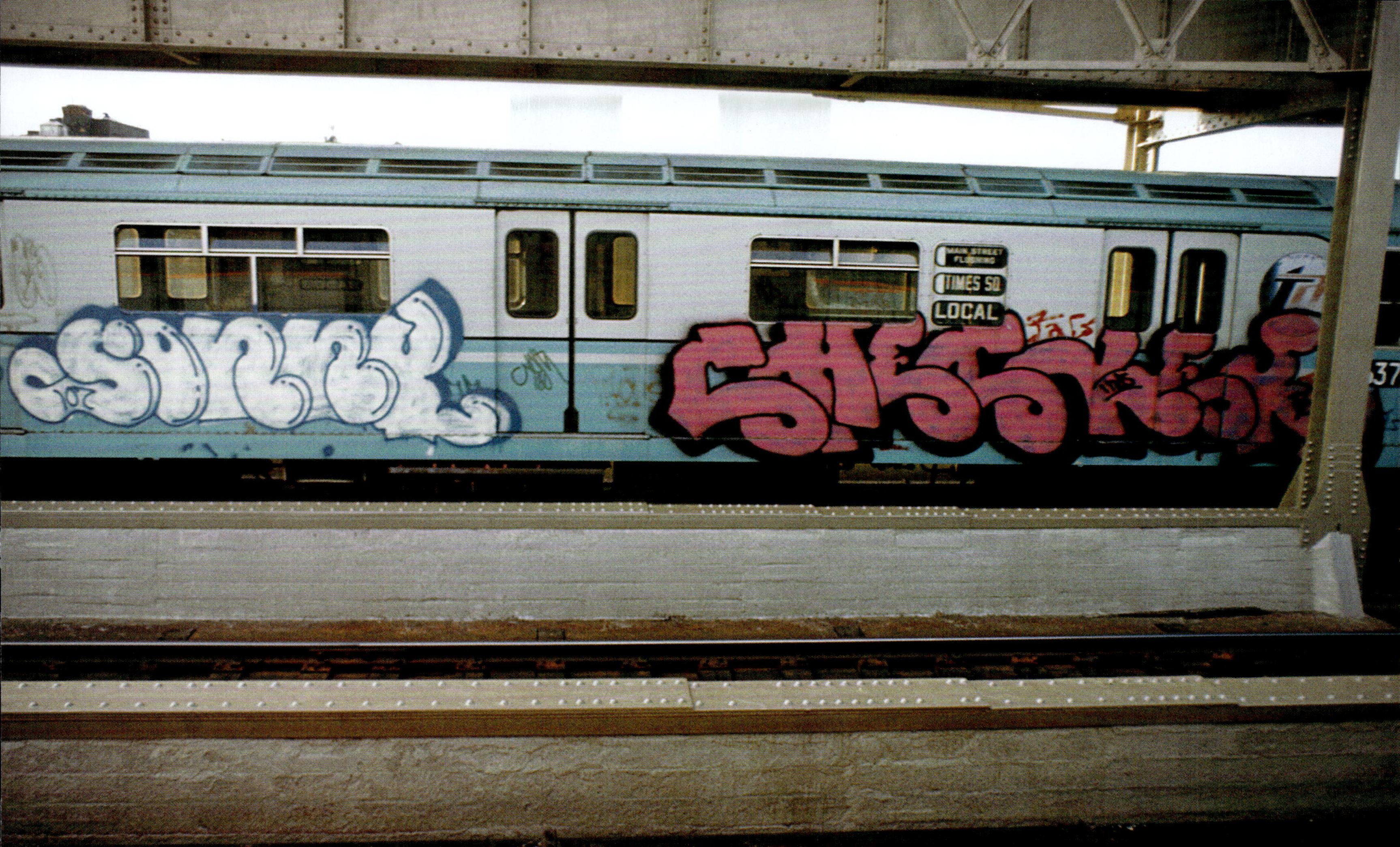
TIMES SQ
LOCAL

Influenza

Influenza (aka Jeroen Jongeleen) lives and works in Paris and Rotterdam. His practice has evolved out of an ongoing engagement with public space, and much of his work is presented in the form of subtle interventions that target advertisements, architectural structures, and city signs. Often he creates imprints of these interventions, viruses left to "engage with the body of the citizenry and disrupt status quo signification." In other cases, he leaves no trace that could place him on the radar, instead seeming to concentrate on the joys of failures, findings, and improvements.

As artworks, these actions speak of opportunities and demonstrate an ongoing relationship between artist and subject, an examination of urban potentiality and pitfalls. It is not simply doing for doing, but doing to discover what can be done and in documenting that process as a work of art, that Jongeleen manages to reveal parts of his act without compromising the magic. What we see in this case is not a conceptual movement, but a personal philosophy being lived. This time there is no violent gesture. There is only the artist's joy as he explores himself in the world.

Photograph courtesy of Influenza.
Amsterdam, The Netherlands, 2008.

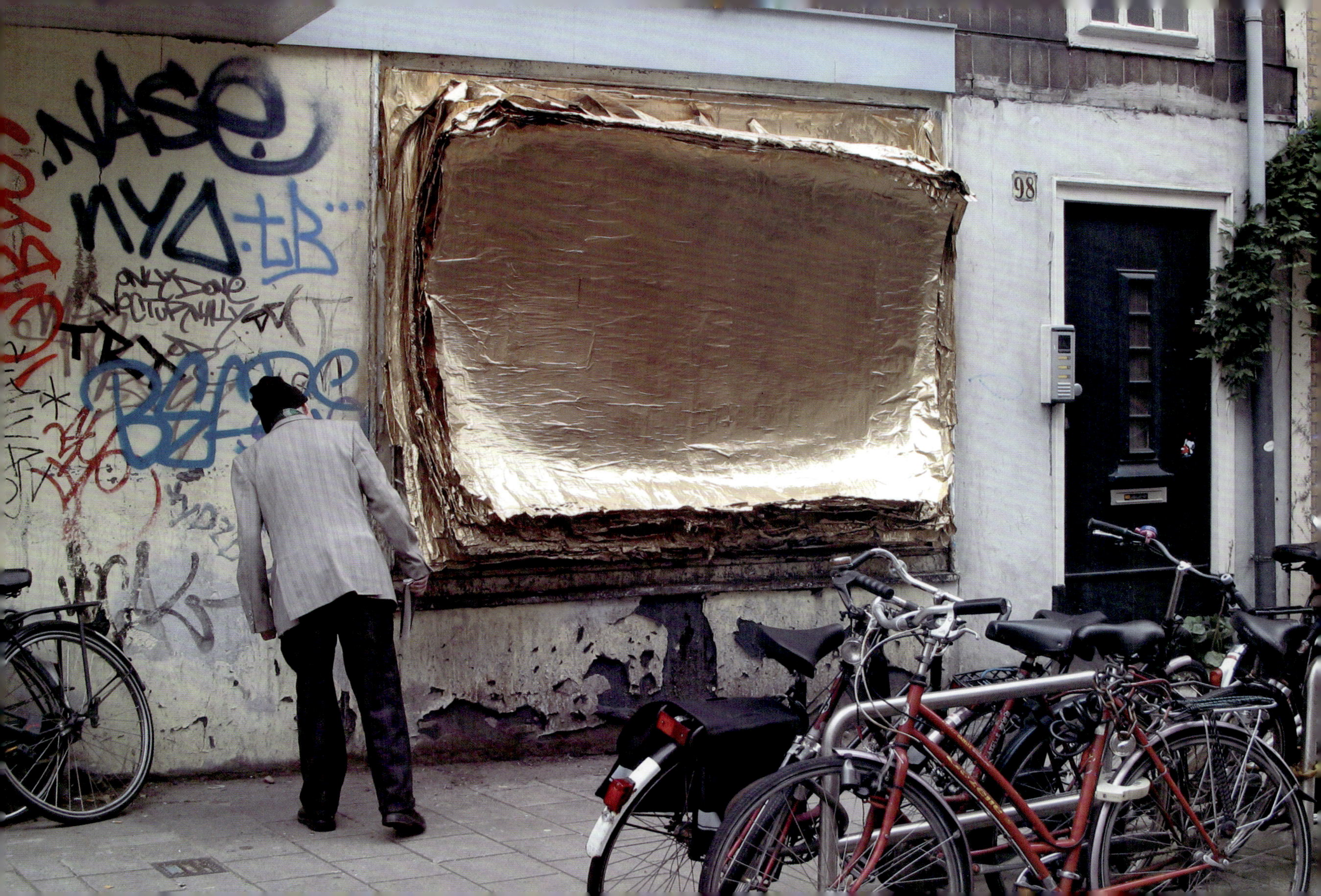
NASE
98

ink

Books may bombard us with images of Lee [see 267], Blade [see 037], and Dondi [see 097] whole-cars, but half the history of graffiti—inside writing—remains largely overlooked: A separate world flourished on the insides of the trains. Kids armed with markers of varying widths filled every inch of virgin space with a rainbow of colors, much to passengers' chagrin.

Of the early inks used for graffiti, Flo-Master reigned supreme. The brand offered a wide array of colors and came in two consistencies, transparent and opaque. Very few stores sold Flo-Master; the ones that did knew its intended purpose and kept it well secured. Garvey's purple ink, used to fill primitive supermarket price-stampers, was a writer's sole alternative. While a handful of writers developed exquisite penmanship to set themselves apart, others used innovation. Stay High 149 [see 316] invented the two-tone Uni-Wide marker and blew away the competition.

High lead content eliminated Flo-Master from the marketplace in the early 1980s, and Marsh filled the void, but Marsh offered a narrower line of colors and no opaque option. The insides became a battlefield during this era, and big, black, drippy tags written over smaller ones ruled the day. Style took a backseat to destruction.

Marsh also soon went out of business, but Krink, an ink invented and marketed by a graffiti writer, took the 1980s aesthetic a step further. Krink still comes in bottles or markers designed to drip and gives tags a molten-lava appearance.

Photograph by Monica LoCascio. Brooklyn, New York, 2010.

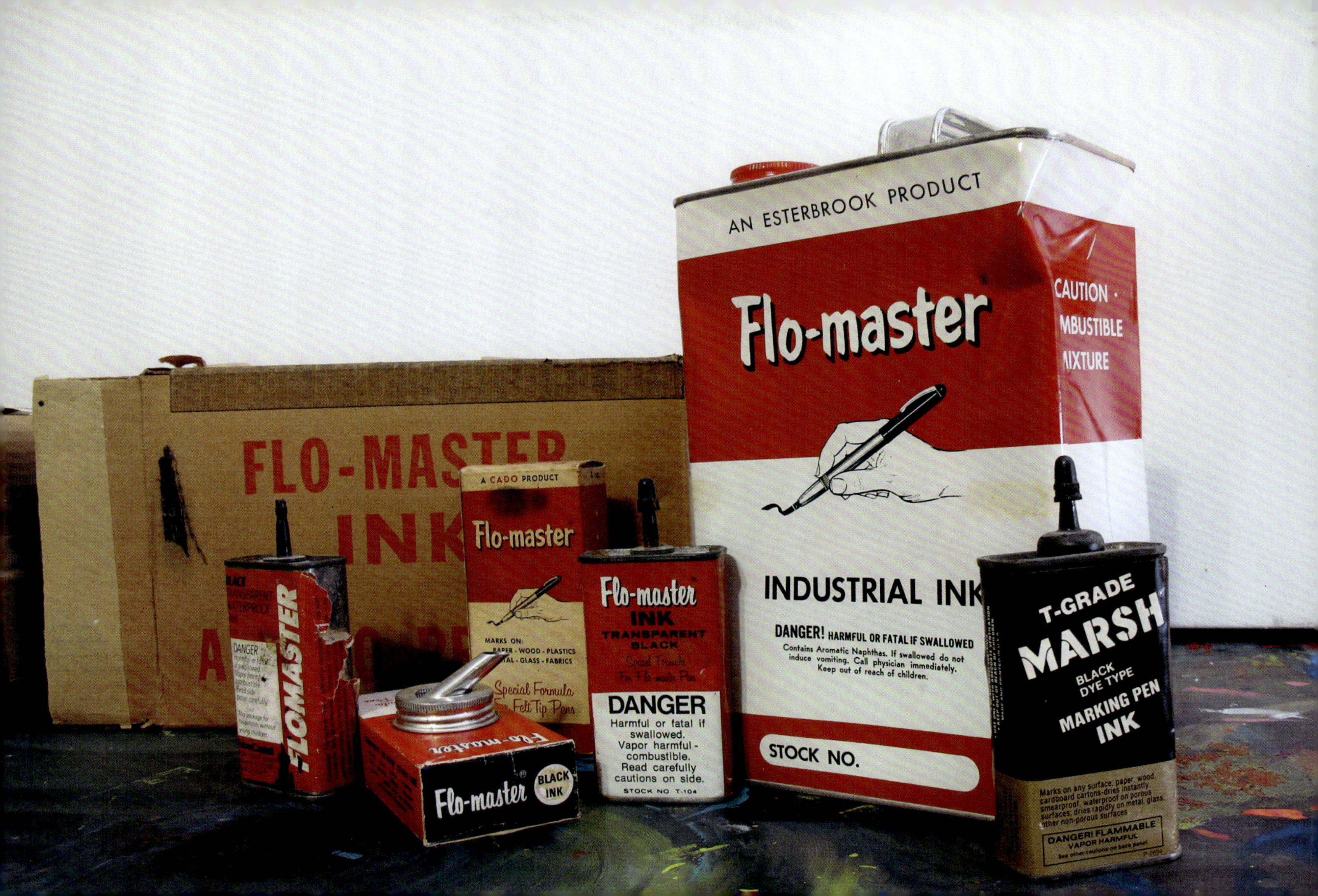
AN ESTERBROOK PRODUCT
Flo-master
CAUTION ·
MBUSTIBLE
IXTURE
INDUSTRIAL INK
DANGER! HARMFUL OR FATAL IF SWALLOWED
Contains Aromatic Naphthas. If swallowed do not induce vomiting. Call physician immediately. Keep out of reach of children.
STOCK NO.
FLO-MASTER
INK
A CADO PRODUCT
Flo-master
MARKS ON:
Special Formula
Flo-master
INK
TRANSPARENT
BLACK
DANGER
Harmful or fatal if swallowed.
Vapor harmful - combustible.
Read carefully cautions on side.
STOCK NO. T-104
FLOMASTER
Flo-master
BLACK INK
T-GRADE
MARSH
BLACK DYE TYPE
MARKING PEN INK
DANGER! FLAMMABLE
VAPOR HARMFUL

Irak

For the last decade and a half, one graffiti crew has remained at the forefront in downtown New York. Virtually owning the lower half of the borough, the Irak crew has become legendary. More than just a graffiti crew, Irak (a reference to "racking," the slang term for stealing) was the first artistic family to such downtown notables as the troubled artist Dash Snow (see 308), the photographer Ryan McGinley, and the pop band The Virgins. Since the 1990s, tags and stickers bearing the Irak moniker have covered downtown areas in New York and Brooklyn, put there by such notable graffiti names as Sacer, Earsnot (see 101), and Semz.

In 2001, Simon Curtis, a member of the Irak crew best known for spraying wiggly spermlike characters all over New York, stole an image from an art show at a gallery in Brooklyn and ran to a car in which Ryan McGinley was awaiting him. The gallery owners gave chase, one of them hanging from the hood of the car. Eventually, McGinley was cleared of charges, but Curtis was slapped with criminal charges, resulting in a one- to three-year sentence.

In 2007, Joey Semz, another integral part of the Irak crew, died suddenly at his parents' home from what appeared to be a heroin overdose, and on July 13, the best-known member of the crew, Dash Snow, followed suit, fatally overdosing in a bathtub at the Lafayette House hotel.

Pieces and tags by Espo, Revs, Sacer (Dash Snow), and Earsnot (left to right); throw-up by Kid (top right). Photograph by Becki Fuller. Brooklyn, New York, c. 2009.

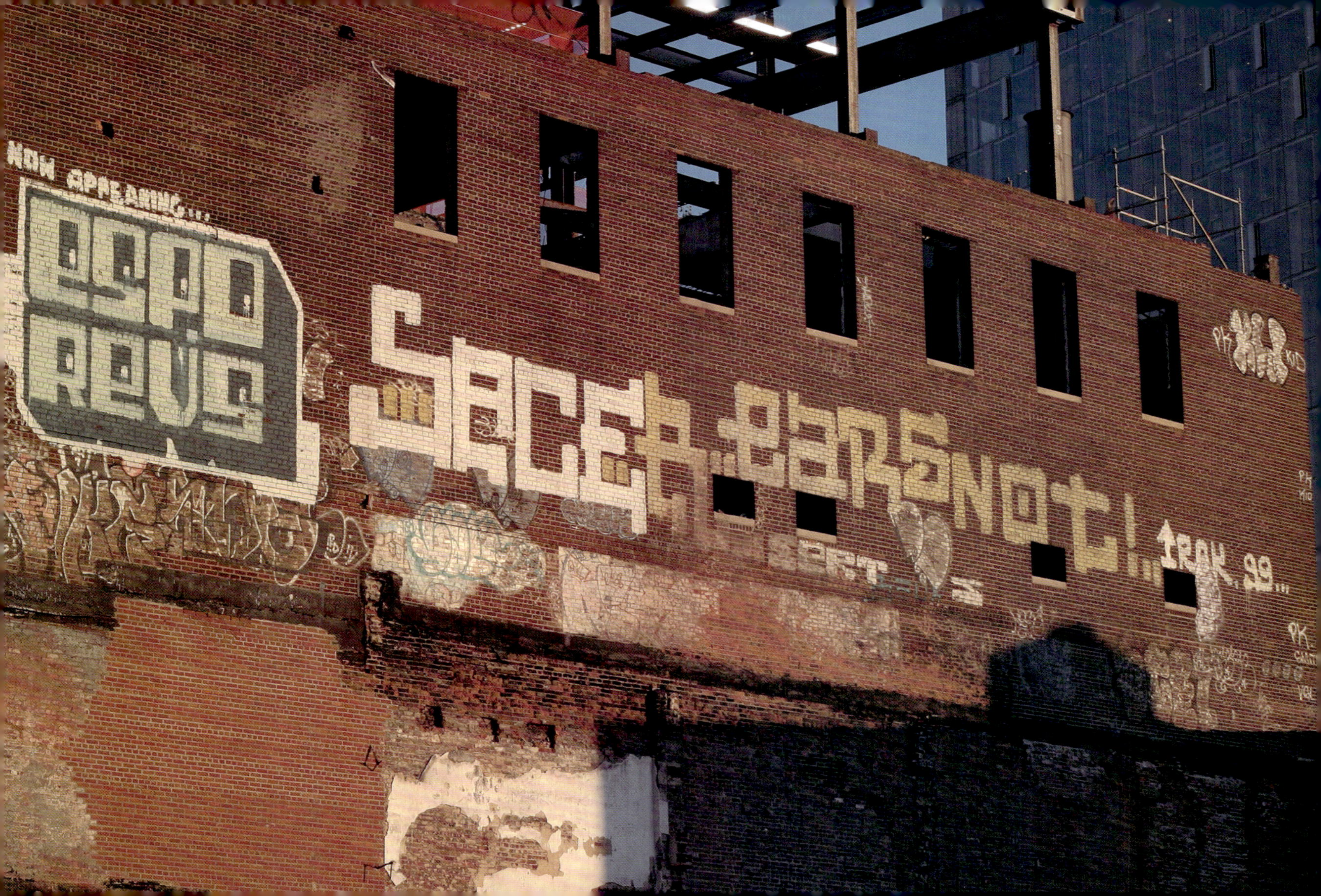
NOW APPEARING...
TRAK. 99...

Ivory

1989 marked the end of graffiti on New York City trains and the beginning of Joshua Ivory's career in writing. A student of graffiti history, he grew up observing the work of the Riverdale-based Masters of Broadway crew and the rolling museum on the #1 line elevation. He started writing in a Bronx schoolyard and had a burning desire to be the best. He met the older, more experienced Brooklyn stylemaster Roler at the Pearl Paint store and decided to become his apprentice. Ivory became a style sponge, not only absorbing what Roler taught him, but also focusing on stylemasters of all eras, especially the subway legends Billy 167 [see 034], FliteTDS, Seen UA, and T.Kid 170 [see 335]. During the 1990s, Ivory joined forces with a new crop of writers that included Tich, Yes 2, and Ces [see 061]. Ivory became a synthesis of all his idols and a stylistic force in his own right. In 2007, Ivory commissioned writers from all eras to paint large canvases, many of which were re-creations of famous pieces from the subways. The resulting collection debuted in the landmark 2008 show "The Legends of Style" at the now defunct Alphabeta Gallery in Brooklyn and resurfaced later that year as the "Style Masters" exhibition at New York University and the *Style Wars* [see 322] benefit at Brooklyn Academy of Music in 2010.

Ivory is also an avid collector of vintage automobiles and rare guitars and has an eye for style in whatever form it comes. Unlike many collectors who buy graffiti art based on who showed next to Haring and Basquiat in the 1980s, Ivory has based his acquisitions on a deep knowledge of who made the greatest impact on the subways. Ivory mastered the art he loved and has become its greatest homegrown patron.

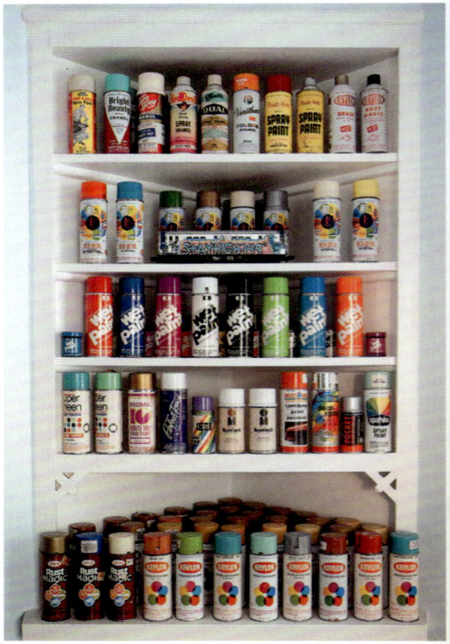

Photographs by Brent Kerr. New York City, 2010.

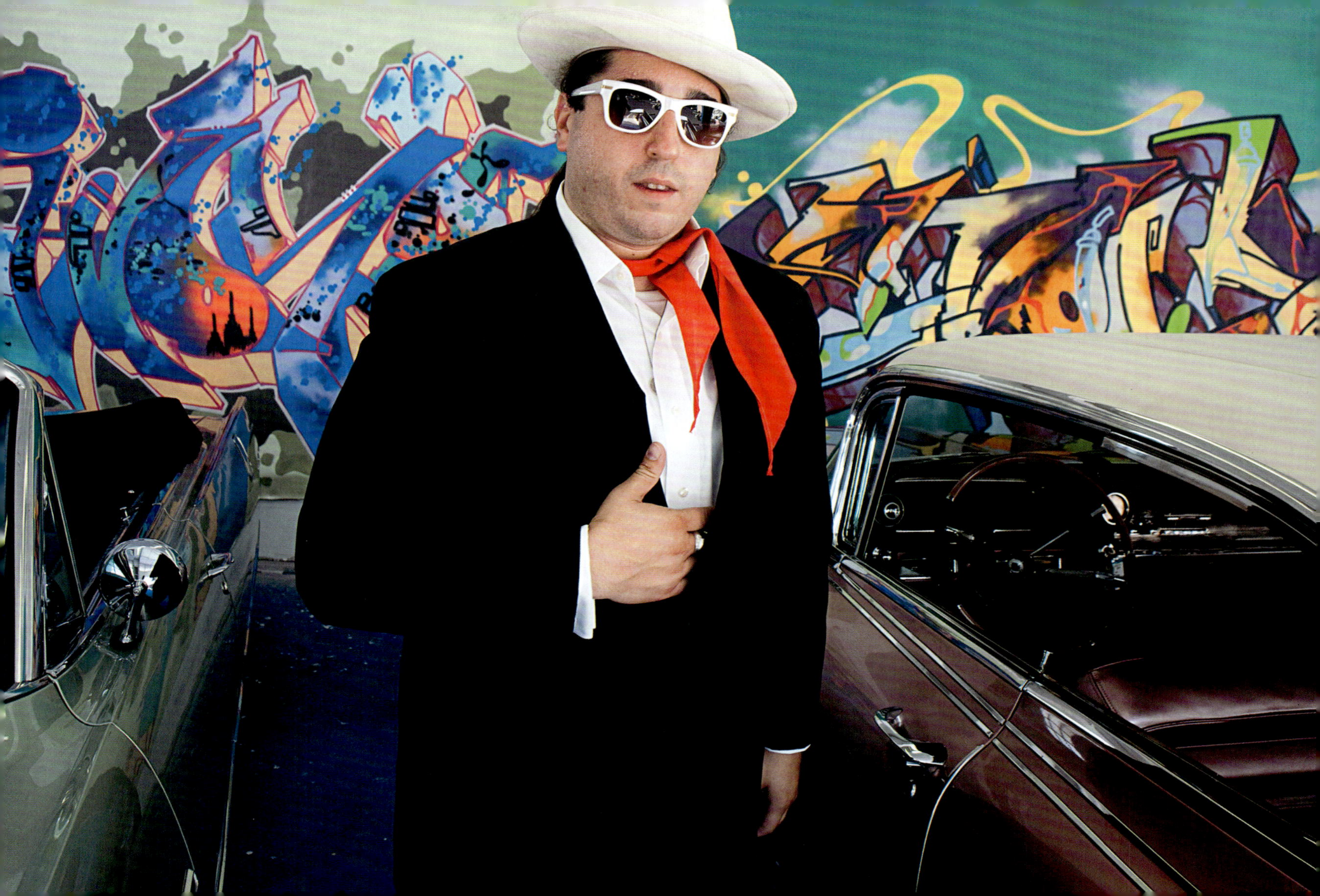

Iz the Wiz

Iz the Wiz was one of the greatest graffiti bombers of all time, with an illegal career that spanned more than two decades. In 1972, he began writing on the buses in Queens, New York, graduating to trains in early 1973. By the mid-'70s, he had built a reputation for himself as Ike 327. In 1975, after being inspired by a poster for the new Broadway musical *The Wiz*, he quickly renamed himself Iz the Wiz.

Inspired by the legendary bomber In, Iz quickly set out to do throw-ups on as many lines as possible, and the two developed a friendly rivalry. Teaming up with Queens writers Vinny and PI made Iz an unstoppable force on the IND and BMT subway lines. As whole-cars became more prevalent, Iz joined an IRT crew called the Master Blasters, and with his partner, Caz, he completed numerous whole-cars. Iz continued to do throw-ups at the same time, bouncing from one line to another like a pinball. In 1980, after seeing the Futura 2000 [see 141] break car, Iz started to use a similar fill-in using two spray cans at once, allowing the aerosol to mist in the air before settling into the piece. He began to show a more artistic side in his work, which led to a gallery career in the early '80s. He continued to paint, even through the clean-car campaign of the late '80s and early '90s.

Iz was perhaps best known to first-generation European writers as the undercover cop in the film *Wild Style* and as himself in the documentary *Style Wars* [see 322]. When he finally quit the trains for good, he was pivotal in the early days of the Phun Factory, where he acted as goodwill ambassador to hundreds of writers around the world. He died in June of 2009, just a few days after his last show at Tuff City Styles in the Bronx—a fitting sendoff for one of graffiti's kings.

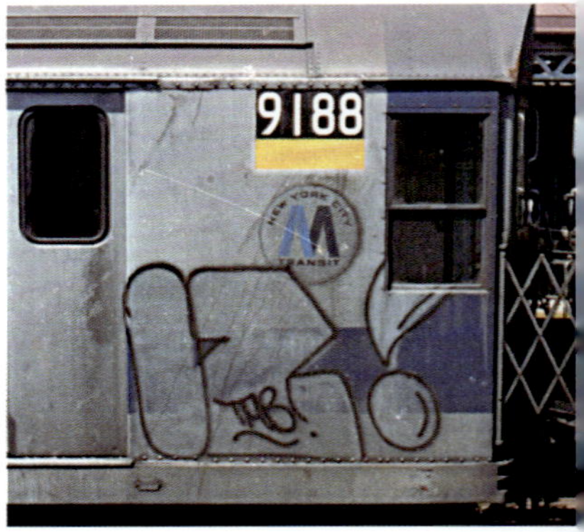

Photograph courtesy of Metal Man Ed, from the collection of Iz the Wiz. New York City, 1979. Detail: Private collection. New York City, 1981.

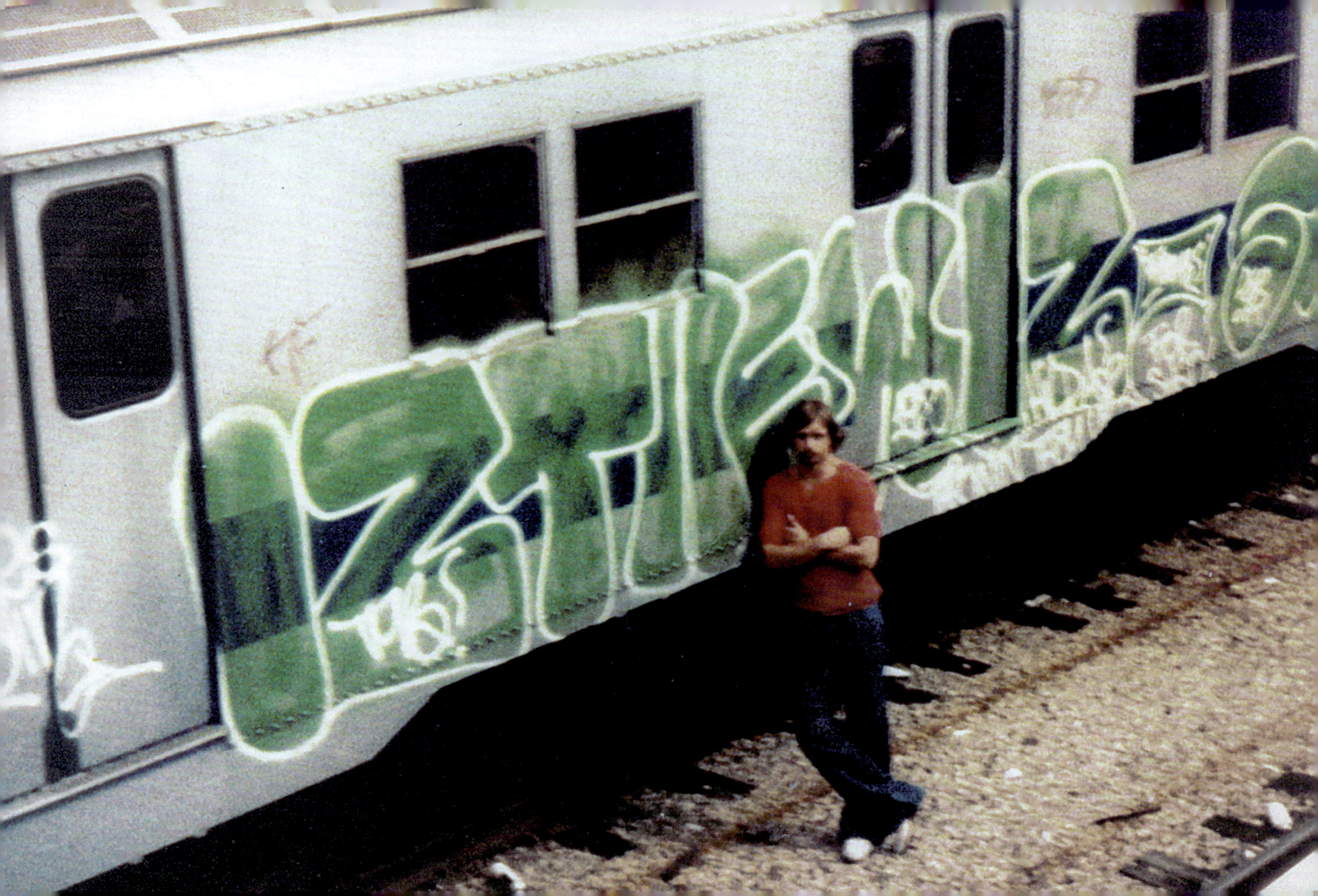

Jace

Réunion island, located in the Indian Ocean off the coast of Madagascar, is hardly world renowned for its artistic exports. Yet one of its small population of 48,000 citizens managed to drag himself out of the sun long enough to develop a unique style of painting and an affinity for presenting it on public property. Jace, an artist native to the area, was inspired by the legendary New York City graffiti book *Subway Art* (see 323) and began painting on walls in 1989. As he was developing his own style, Jace created his most famous character, Gouzou, in 1992.

A mischievous practical joker, Jace uses Gouzou to interact with public property, especially advertisements. Gouzou can often be found painted onto billboards, humorously interacting with an advertisement and often ridiculing its content.

Jace and Gouzou are celebrities on Réunion, but Jace's paintings can also be found in London, Rome, Paris, Bali, Hong Kong, Barcelona, and many other cities. Jace has made the transition into the gallery world, but he regularly returns to the streets, as he feels that is Gouzou's native habitat and his own true home.

Photograph by Jake Dobkin (streetsy.com). Brooklyn, New York, 2008.

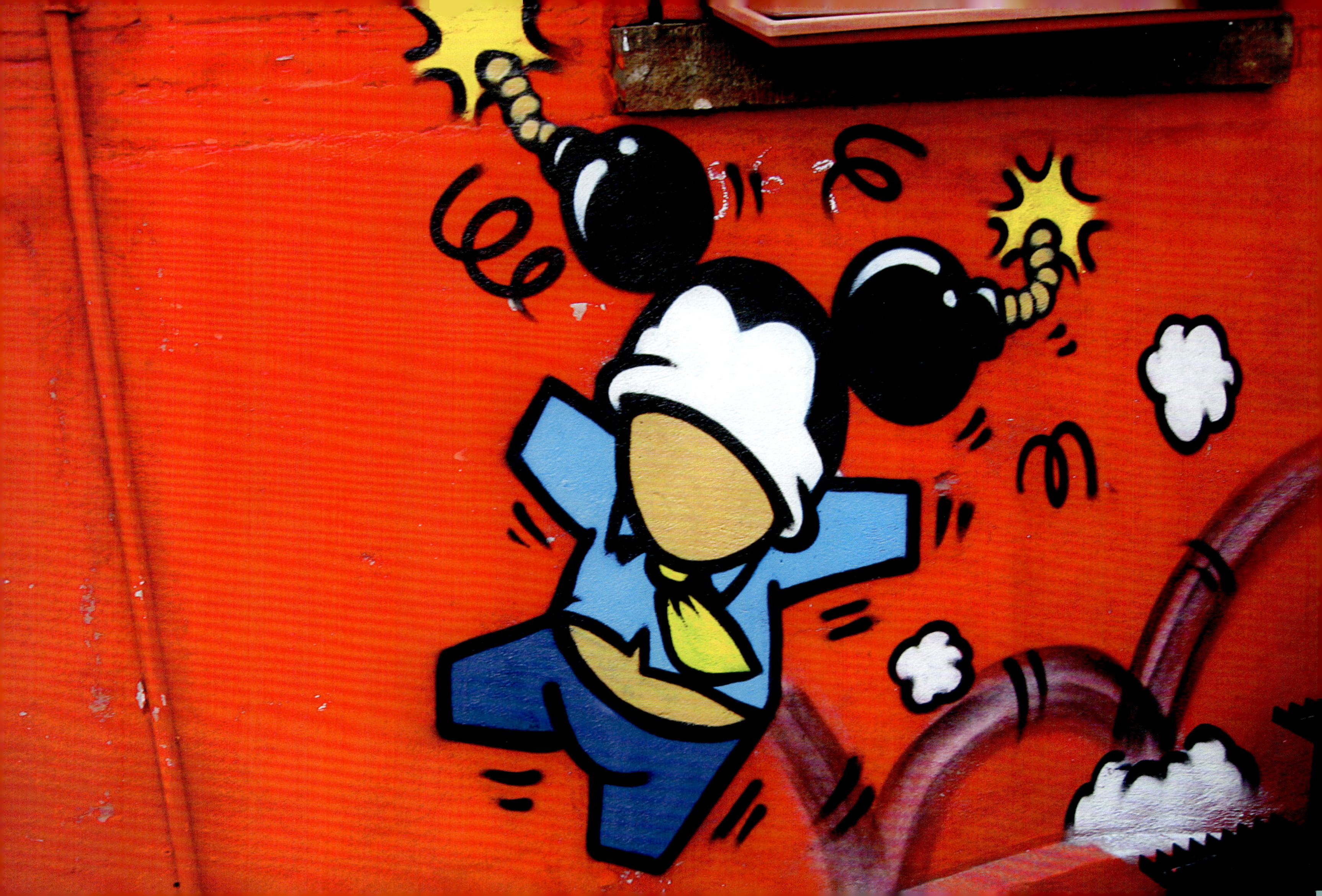

Todd James

A prime example of the myriad ways in which a graffiti artist can make the crossover from the streets to the galleries, Todd James is as much a celebrated fine artist as he is a respected contributor to the legacy of graffiti. Yet another alumnus of the Beautiful Losers school, James is revered for his mural and illustrative work, as well as for his graffiti under his moniker, Reas.

James began painting in the subways of New York as a teenager in the 1980s; he combined comedic and conceptual elements in pieces that included his name cooking in a frying pan and his infamous Eat Shit whole-car with a cartoon turd character. He began creating intricate, large-scale works influenced by comic books, mixing caricature with his graffiti roots. Often painted in flat colors, James's subject matter crosses lines of sexuality and vulgarity that would never be accepted in mainstream publications. His tongue-in-cheek paintings encompass violence, quirky creatures, naked women with bombs as perky breasts, pools of blood, and grim reapers—a psychedelic mishmash of imaginary worlds.

James took part in the seminal Deitch show "Street Market" in 2000, alongside Stephen "Espo" Powers (see 115) and Barry "Twist" McGee (see 214). The show traveled to the Venice Biennale, heralding graffiti's arrival in the fine-art realm, and presenting James, McGee, and Powers as the standard-bearers of the art form.

Today, James exhibits his work internationally, including at the Tate Museum in Liverpool, the Institute of Contemporary Art in Philadelphia, the V1 Gallery in Copenhagen, and the Alleged Gallery in New York.

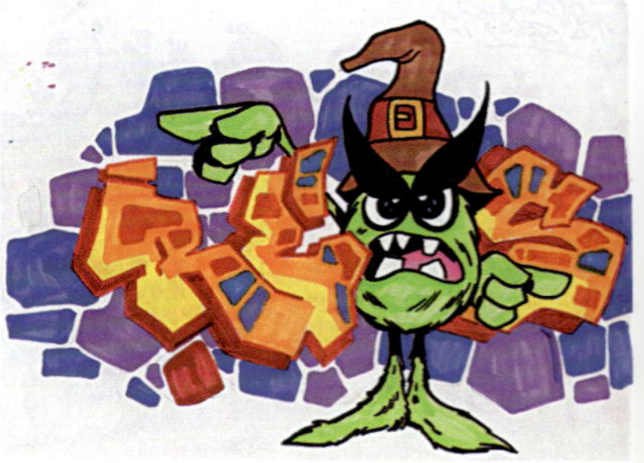

Photographs by Todd James.
New Jersey, 2001.
Detail: New York City, 2007.

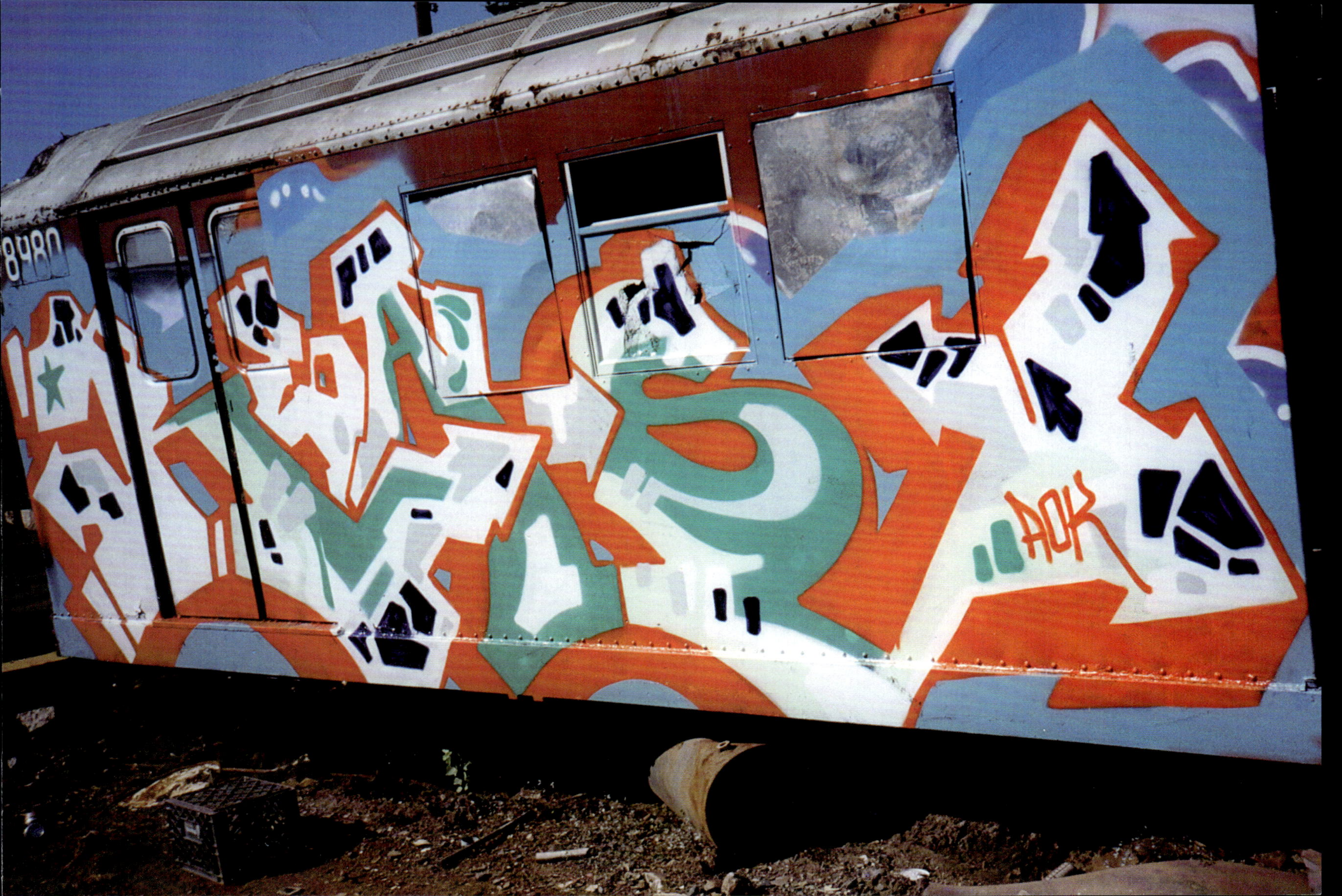
8480
AOK

JA One

JA One has perhaps painted more surfaces in New York than any writer in history over a career that started in 1986 and still rages on. The son of a legendary Hollywood director, he has appeared in a few movies himself, but JA's own life contains more drama than any Tinseltown production his dad ever directed. He commandeers daredevil spots such as bridges and highway overpasses, and other writers have gotten famous simply by going to war with JA (two young Brooklyn writers were in the process of writing over JA's work in a tunnel when they were struck and killed by a train). JA has staked claims in active subway tunnels and rooftops, often tagging up the names of his dead friends, most notably his former best friend Sane.

He is the founder of the XTC crew, and over the years JA has represented other crews such as YKK, RIS, and WKS. His passion has nearly gotten him killed on several occasions. He has fallen from great heights numerous times, and he once received 150 stitches for a head wound from a nightstick following a police chase. He has been viciously sliced up by members of rival crews, but none of it has deterred him. He has continued to plaster throw-ups and tags throughout the boroughs, often singlehandedly keeping graffiti alive during its less active periods—half of the trucks in New York seem to bear his name. After all he's accomplished, JA no longer needs graffiti, but graffiti still needs JA.

Throw-up by JA One; tags by Sane (left) and Left.
Photograph by Cycle.
New York City, 2009.

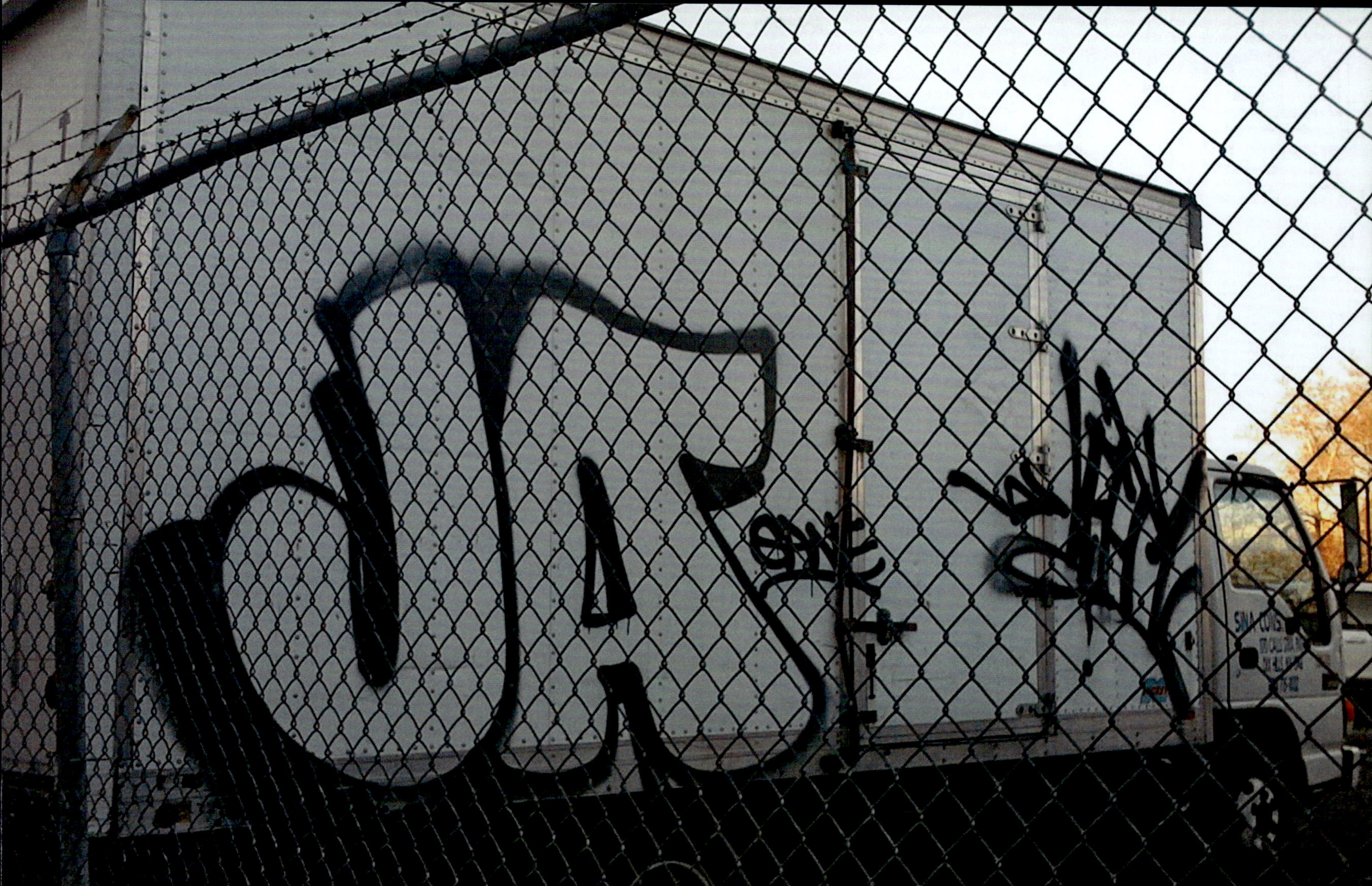

Jeff Aerosol

A legendary stencil artist and gifted musician, Jeff Aerosol was born John Francis Perroy in 1957 in Nantes, a coastal town in western France. While in college, he began creating photo-collages with images culled from comics, popular magazines, album covers, and personal photos. In 1982, while teaching English in Tours, Jeff Aerosol created his first stencil. He recalls that there were few stencils at the time to inspire him, other than the small antinuclear stencils seen in the streets of his hometown.

Once Jeff Aerosol hit the streets with his stencils, he couldn't stop. The sense of rebellion and freedom, tinged with fear, kept him out nights, and he became addicted to the smell of his spray paint and the spell of the city. He saw himself, in fact, as an accomplice to the city, as he spent his days cutting stencils and his nights applying them to the city's surfaces. Jeff Aerosol has since made his mark on walls in dozens of countries and has been invited to exhibit in galleries and expos all over the globe.

Although he has composed stencils inspired by a range of objects and places, he prefers to create portraits. Among his subjects are Bob Dylan, Muddy Waters, Jimi Hendrix, Andy Warhol, Martin Luther King Jr., Charlie Chaplin, Jean-Michel Basquiat, and Jay-Z.

Photographs by Vincent Cornelli.
Brooklyn, New York, 2010.

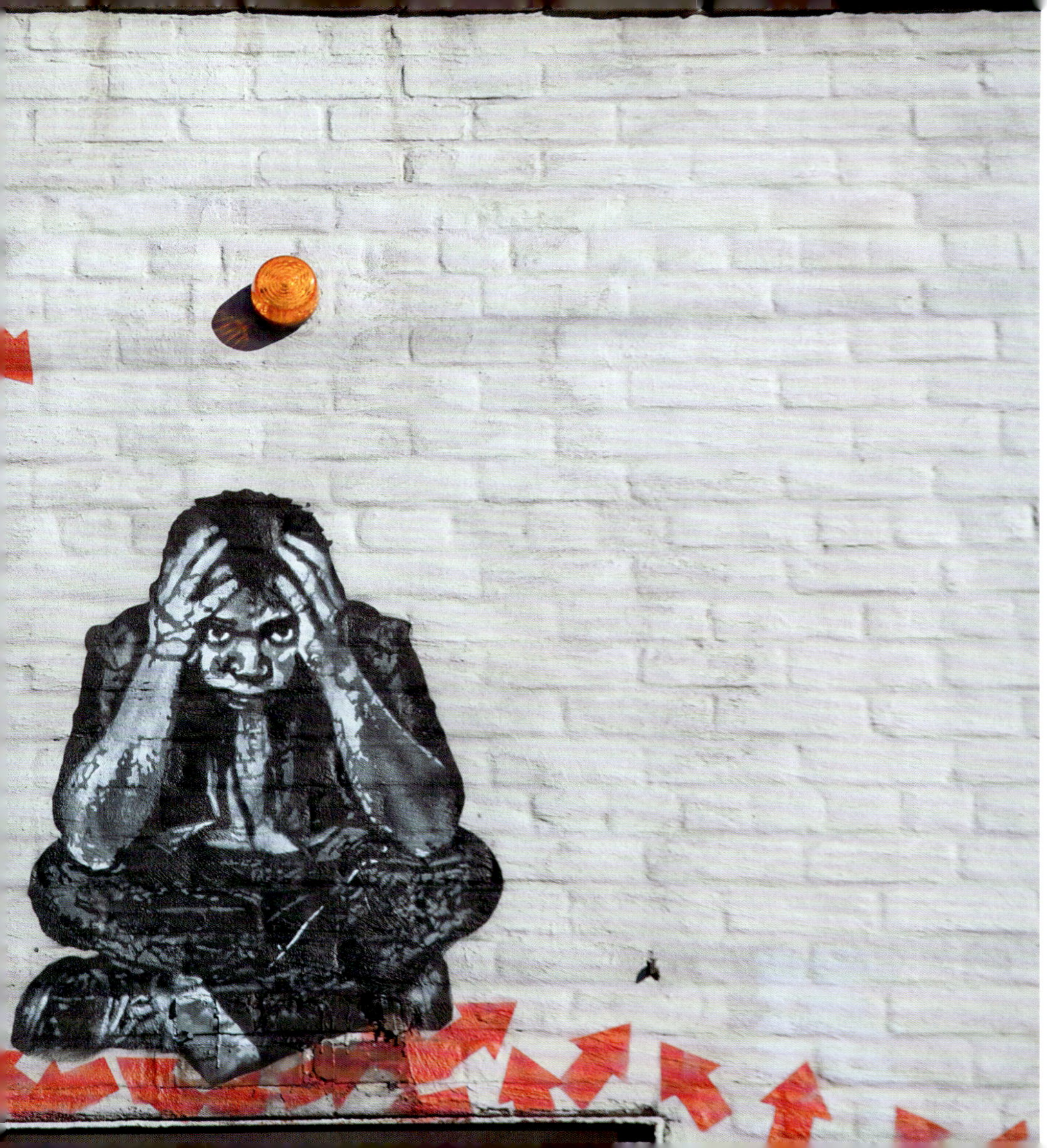

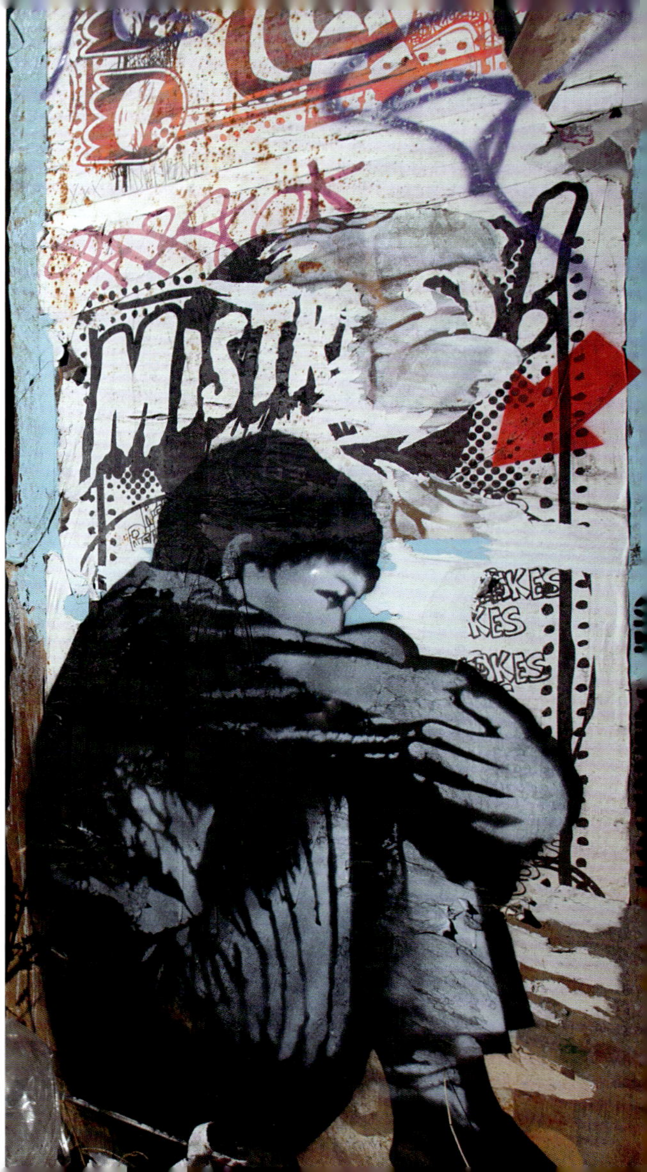

Mark Jenkins

One of the pioneers of street-installation work came to the forefront of the urban art movement in the middle of the first decade of the 2000s. Mark Jenkins created life-size and lifelike sculptures out of transparent packing tape and placed them on the street in strategic, often humorous ways.

Jenkins would often dress his see-through mannequins in human clothing and arrange them in compromising positions, so as to shock passersby. For example, one tape sculpture of a girl sitting on the edge of a rooftop, complete with a blonde wig, caused a huge commotion when pedestrians believed it was a real girl contemplating suicide and began frantically phoning the police. Another of Jenkins's famous street installations is a tape sculpture dressed as a man with his head seemingly embedded in a wall. Numerous photos are available on the Web of pedestrians staring in shock at the highly realistic figure who seems to have smashed his head through the brick.

Jenkins, a native of Virginia, quickly moved from street work to the fine-art world setting, showing his pieces in numerous venues, including the famed Lazarides Galleries, based in London.

Photograph Courtesy of Mark Jenkins.
Lisbon, Portugal, 2007.

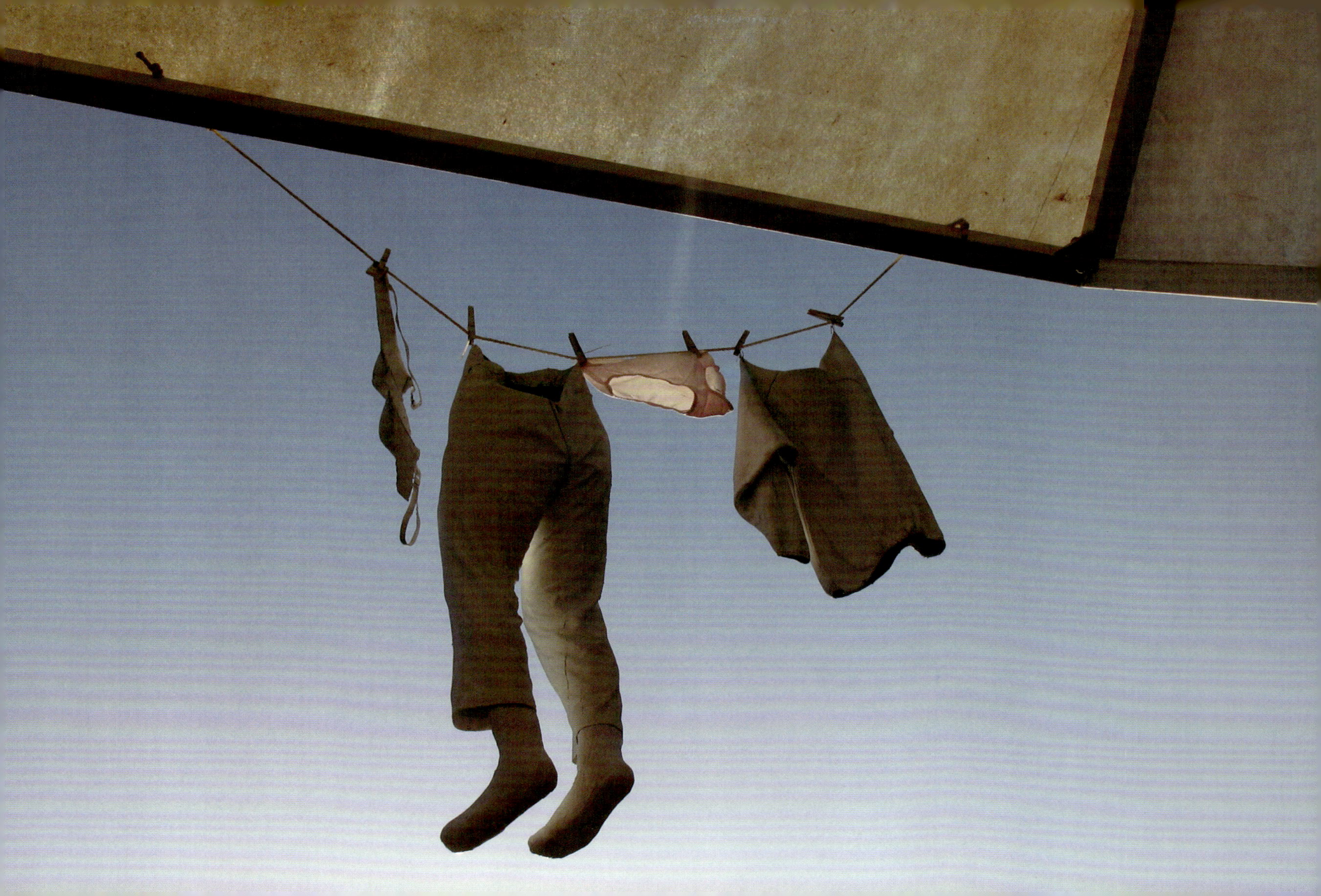

Jester

Jester began writing in 1971, the year he began taking the train to school. Graffiti found him early, he recalls: "I was inspired by Broadway writers. One day . . . on the A train, a bunch of writers came into the car I was in and bombed the shit out of it with spray paint. It was Frank 207, Junior 161, Cay 161 (see 186), Jockey 1-2, Butler 1-2, Jec, and Slick 1. I'll never forget it, and I took my handwriting style from each of those dudes."

Jester developed the most elegant tag style of his day, executing perfectly symmetrical throw-ups by the thousands while simultaneously painting under the names Tint 2, Dye 167, and Sony 2, in addition to his own. Jester moved to Queens in 1976, embracing the two-letter throw-up style popularized by In (see 171). Of this period he says, "There was a couple of reasons why I dropped the *e* from Dye 167. Number one, I was hitting with In, who was so incredibly fast that I was trying to keep up with him. Number two, we used to hit the pull-ins-pull-outs. The trains left so fast that some of my *e*'s never got trimmed, and I was trying to do as many pieces as I could." Jester retired in 1977. He led by example, mastering every aspect of an art form he helped to create.

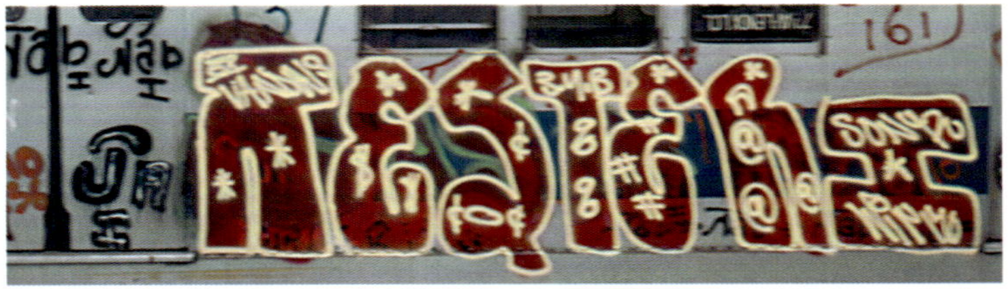

Photographs by Jack Stewart.
Pieces by Jester INDs (left) and Mingo One M.O.G.
New York City, 1974.
Detail: New York City, 1974.

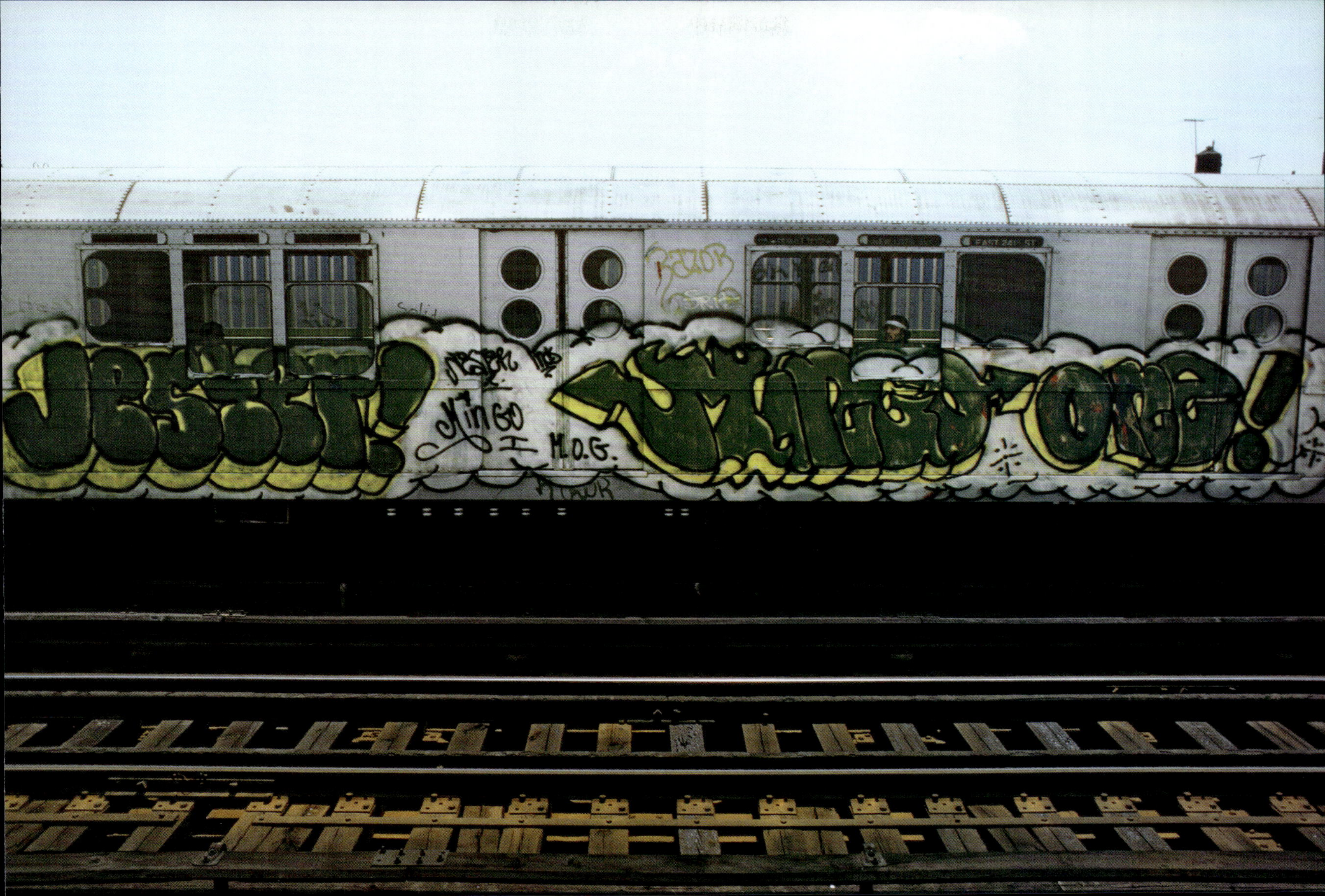

Jon One 156

Born in New York City in the 1960s, John Andrew Perello, aka Jon One 156, grew up in Harlem and started writing graffiti in the early 1980s at the tender age of seventeen. The self-taught artist developed his unique style after studying the techniques of graffiti writers like Ban 2, Mackie, Min One, OE3, Rasta (see 270), and Zephyr (see 363). For Jon One, graffiti art is, first and foremost, about handwriting, and subway trains were his ultimate educational blackboard.

Early in his career, Jon One concentrated on tagging with ink, making markers by stuffing the padding from chalkboard erasers into empty beer bottles refilled with Flo-Master paint, leather dye, stamping ink, and any permanent marking fluid he could get his hands on.

Like many artists from the United States, he has found more respect for his work in Europe and now makes Paris his home. Today, Jon One counts Asian and Arabic calligraphy among his most important influences, but he can never forget his formative years in New York and the many times he exited train yards at night, his arms throbbing from having written hundreds (if not thousands) of tags, a feeling he compares to the satisfaction of "a fat cat raiding a garbage can."

Photograph by Steam 156.
Paris, 1998.

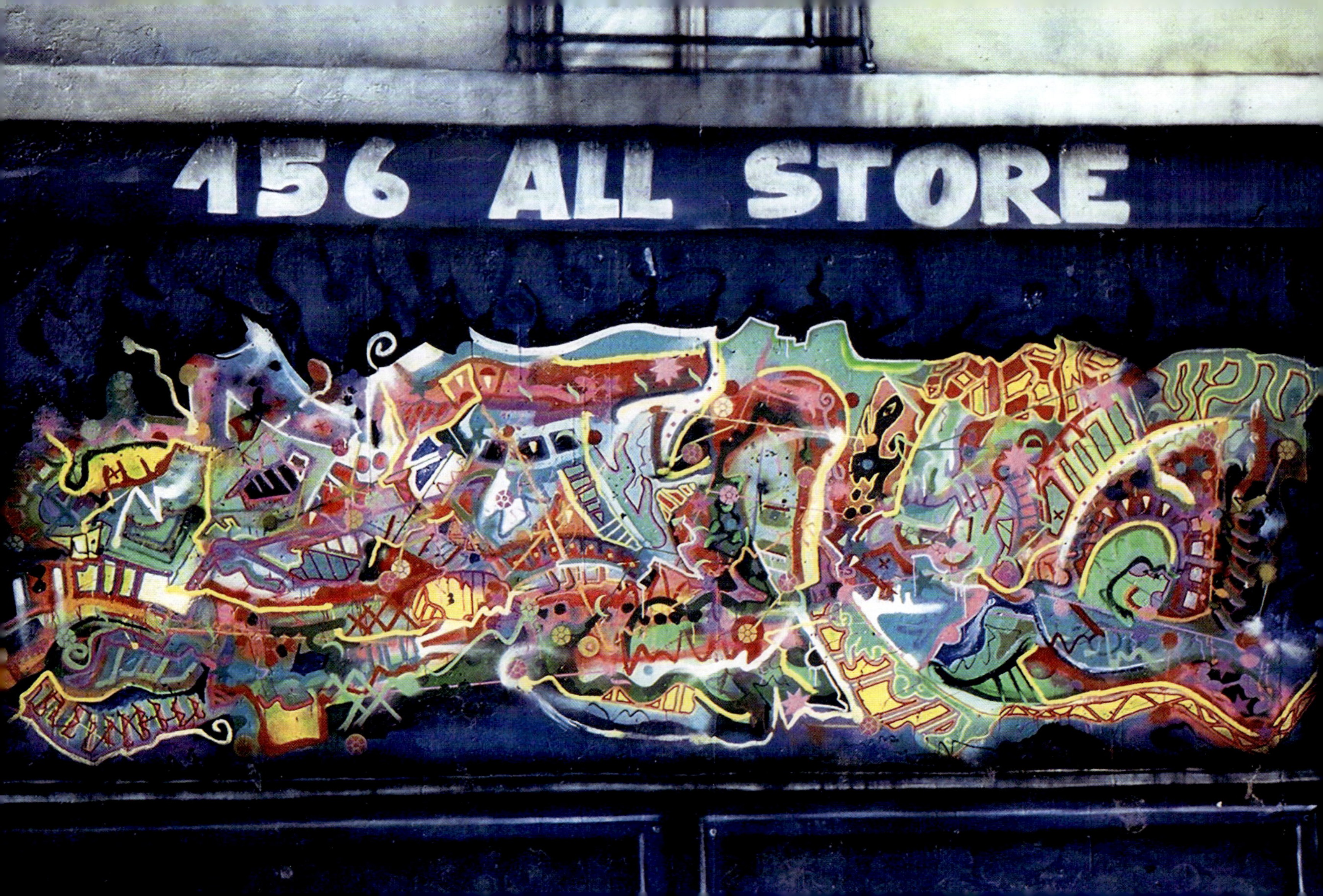
456 ALL STORE

JR

At twenty-five years young, Parisian street artist JR is blowing up heads. He was a graffiti writer for a while, but then became fascinated with photography after finding a camera in the Métro. The camera begat JR's practice of wheatpasting large photos of ordinary people within the neighborhoods where they live. In 2006, his photos of street toughs, titled "Portrait of a Generation" and posted in Paris's bourgeois districts, created much hubbub. When City Hall was wrapped, Christo-style, in colossal versions of the photos, JR had arrived. In Kibera, a small Kenyan village, JR created massive images of the faces of local women. He placed giant photographs of their faces, primarily their eyes, on the tin roofs of their homes, using a waterproof vinyl that served an important utilitarian purpose—it prevented rain from coming in. His smaller, movable work now sells at posh auction houses, but in true Robin Hood fashion, he reinvests his art profits into future projects, and many are planned.

In an effort to give back, JR has funded the building of a community center in a drug-ridden Rio favela, a shantytown that was the site of an earlier project. JR is committed to making art in the poorest parts of the world. "I see them in the media, but I want to see them with my own eyes. You realize when you do go to these places that there is no art. My aim is to show that art can work anywhere."

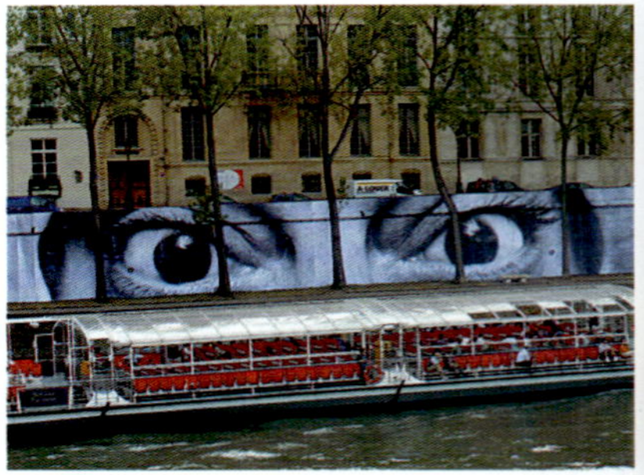

Photograph by Lionel Belluteau. London, 2011.
Detail: Photograph by Eric Marechal. Paris, c. 2010.

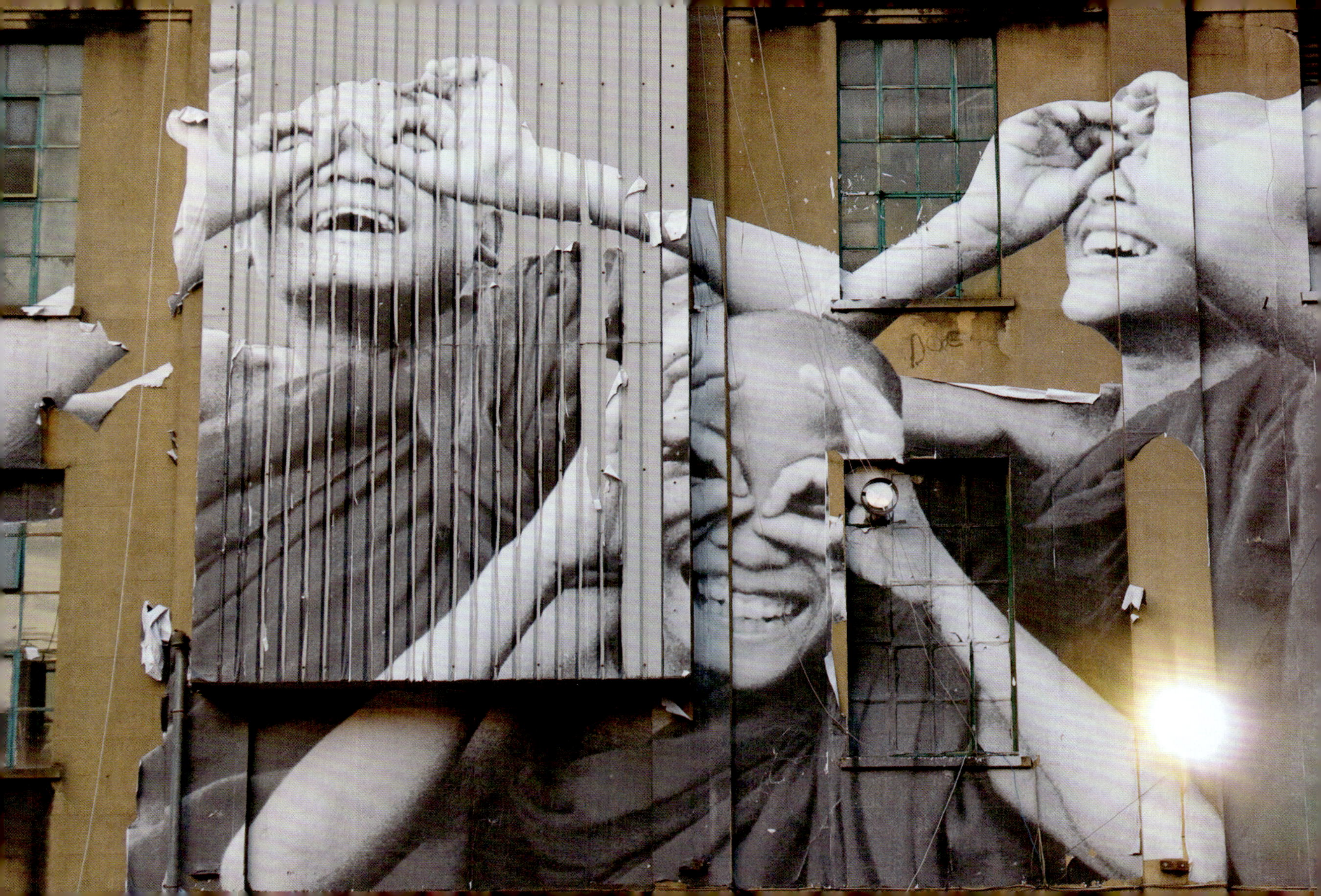

Junior 161 and Cay 161

Junior 161 and Cay 161 were two of the most famous writers of the single-hit period and are historically inseparable. They started writing in Washington Heights in 1970. The two drew inspiration from Taki 183 [see 331], who went to the same high school as Junior. Taki relied on markers, however, while Junior and Cay preferred to use paint. In 1970 and 1971, writers were looking to gain fame from hitting hard-to-reach spots, and Junior and Cay gained a certain notoriety in that area. In one of their most famous exploits, Cay climbed to the top of the winged angel sculpture in Central Park's Bethesda Fountain and tagged her hand with spray paint. Spray-painted exteriors debuted on the Broadway line in late 1971, and Junior and Cay were among the first group of writers ever to hit it. By late 1972, the pair had painted their names on almost every train station in the New York transit system.

When Norman Mailer tracked them down and told their story in *The Faith of Graffiti* [see 126], he cemented their names in popular legend. Cay's writing career came to an end when he crashed a stolen car during a police chase. It took years of rehabilitation to get him back into shape. By the time he recovered, the subculture had evolved, and the era of the single-hit taggers was over.

Photograph by Jon Naar.
New York City, 1972.

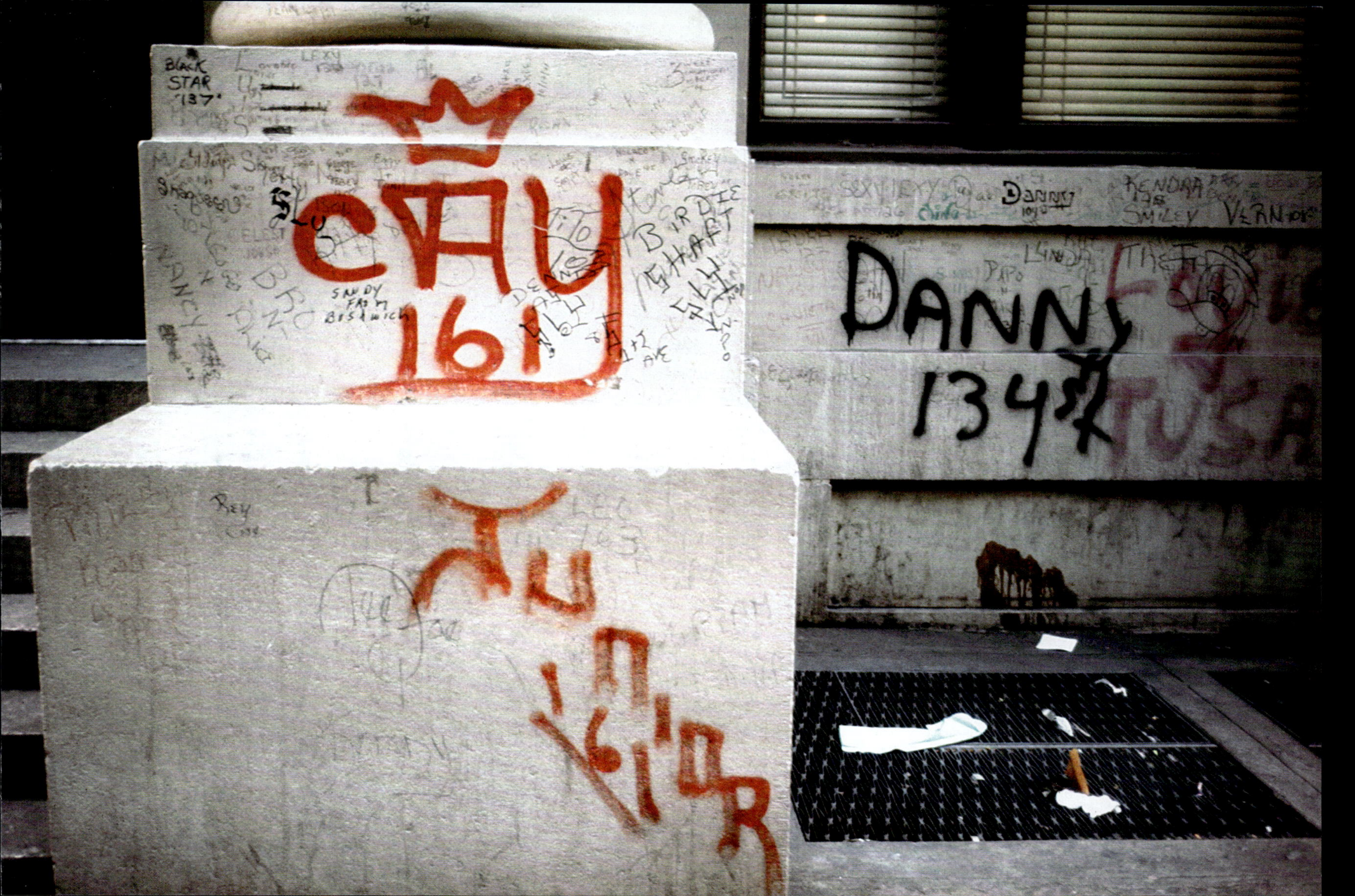
BLACK STAR '137'
CAY 161
DANNY 134

Kami and Sasu

In 1999, artists Kami and Sasu formed a lasting personal and artistic partnership. Kami's strong, wavy lines and Sasu's colorful geometric patterns form a near-perfect union of styles.

In 2000, the couple participated in the infamous Barnstormers (see 025) project, alongside David Ellis (see 109), Swoon (see 329), and numerous others, and they began to concentrate on murals.

Based in Japan, they concentrate on large-scale mural work, as opposed to traditional street art or graffiti, due to the extremely harsh anti-graffiti laws in their home country. Working meticulously by freehand, they have now become known for their extremely large murals, which they proliferate in Japan and internationally. They are considered by many to be the heart of Tokyo's street-art scene.

Since the beginning of their collaboration, Kami and Sasu have referred to their collective project as "Hitotzuki," which means, roughly, the sun and the moon, representing opposing forces that fuse to create a whole element. Hitotzuki exhibit and install their work internationally, everywhere from the Netherlands, to kunst-halles in Germany, to a two-person show at Fifty24SF Gallery in San Francisco.

Kami and Sasu recently welcomed their first son.

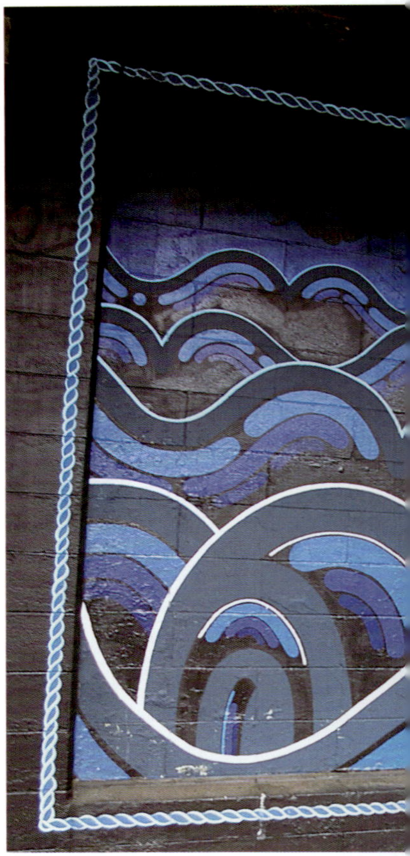

Photographs by Spencer Eakin.
Sakuragi-cho, Yokohama, Japan, 2009.

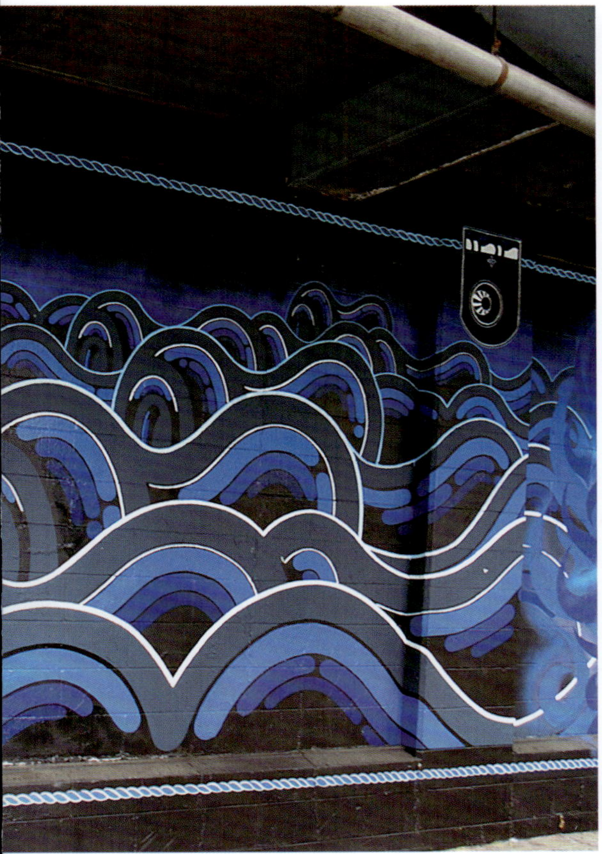
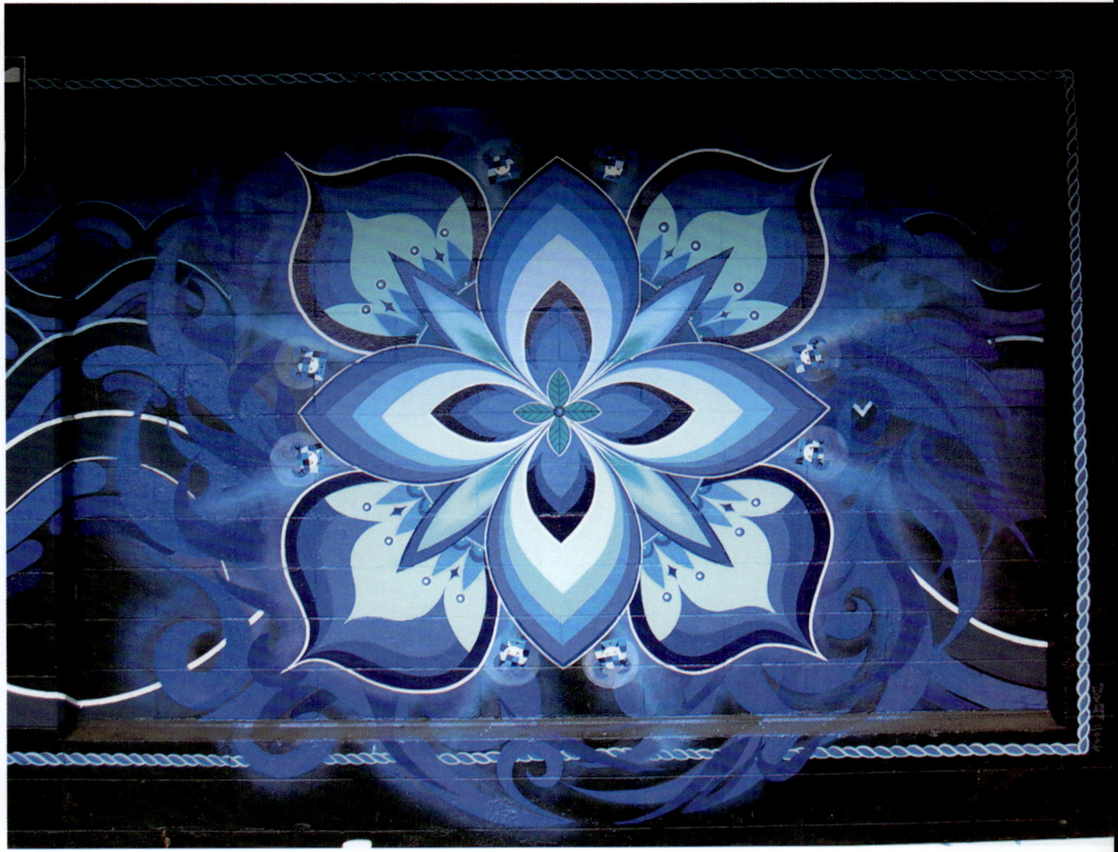

Kaves

Mike "Kaves" McLeer walks the streets of Bay Ridge, Brooklyn, like its unofficial mayor. This tight-knit Italian neighborhood has remained the type of place where everyone knows everyone, and people stick together. That's why it's hard to believe that young Kaves didn't get his legs broken when he began breakdancing, painting his name on the local BMT line, and promoting a Public Enemy show in a club that usually hosted a *Saturday Night Fever*–style crowd.

Graffiti changed Kaves's life. When he was arrested at an early age for "creative vandalism," Kaves decided to quit the trains and concentrate on showing what a spray can could do on the city's walls. He briefly attended the School of Visual Arts in Manhattan, but trying to keep a Renaissance man like Kaves in a classroom proved to be a losing proposition. In no special order, he has founded a band (Lordz of Brooklyn), opened a graffiti store, written and produced a successful autobiographical cable TV show, and shown canvases in galleries. He also currently owns a retro tattoo shop in his neighborhood.

Kaves continues to paint in the streets, where you can recognize his work by the gang of animated mobsters (The Family Mooks) that seem to constantly loiter around his pieces.

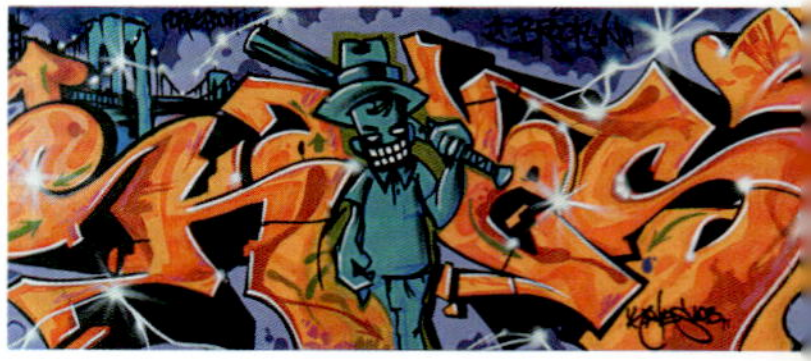

Pieces by Revs (left) and Kaves, with Revs sculpture attached to top of wall. Photograph courtesy of Kaves. New York City, 2009. Detail: Photograph by Adam Reich. 2007.

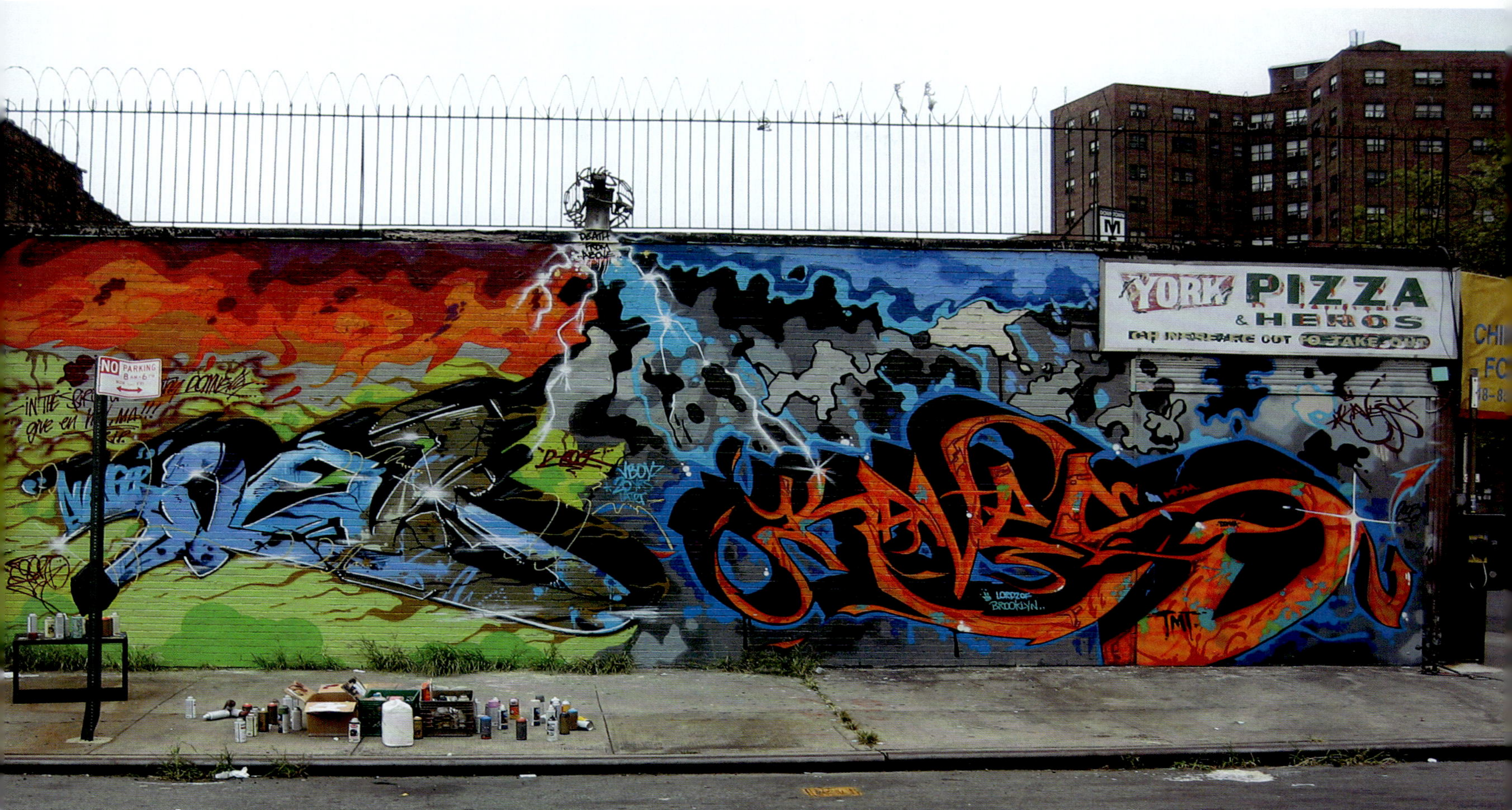
YORK PIZZA
& HEROS
NO PARKING
LORDZ OF BROOKLYN..
TMT

Kaws

Brian Donnelly, "Kaws," was born in Jersey City, New Jersey, in 1974. At an early age, he began noticing the runoff of more prominent graffiti writers in New York City. After graduating from high school, he began studying at the School of Visual Arts in Manhattan, and he quickly gained the respect of many of the more established graffiti writers through his willingness to take risks while still delivering quality products. During this time, he also began to incorporate standard graffiti lettering within existing advertising on billboards, as opposed to the conventional method of simply painting over it. This technique was not widely practiced prior to Kaws.

Later, Kaws began removing fashion advertising found in bus-stop shelters and phone booths with a door key (supplied by the infamous Barry "Twist" McGee [see 214]), replacing them with altered versions he created in the privacy of his studio. In the beginning, Kaws's alterations flew just under the radar and blended well with the increasingly provocative style of fashion advertisements in the late 1990s—sometimes his substitutes went unnoticed for months at a time. Kaws soon developed a strong following, turning these ads into sought-after works of art.

In 2000, Kaws created his breakthrough painting series, "The Kimpsons," which took a jab at the mainstream animated icons in the *The Simpsons*. Almost immediately, Kaws realized the commercial value of his work, and he capitalized on his newfound fame by doing various projects through Bape, based in Tokyo, and Colette, based in Paris. In 2003, he had his now-historic solo show, "Original Fake." *Wonderful World*, a sculpture piece he developed, sold for a staggering $400,000.

Pieces by Zephyr (left) and Kaws. Photograph by Zephyr. New Jersey, c. 1995.

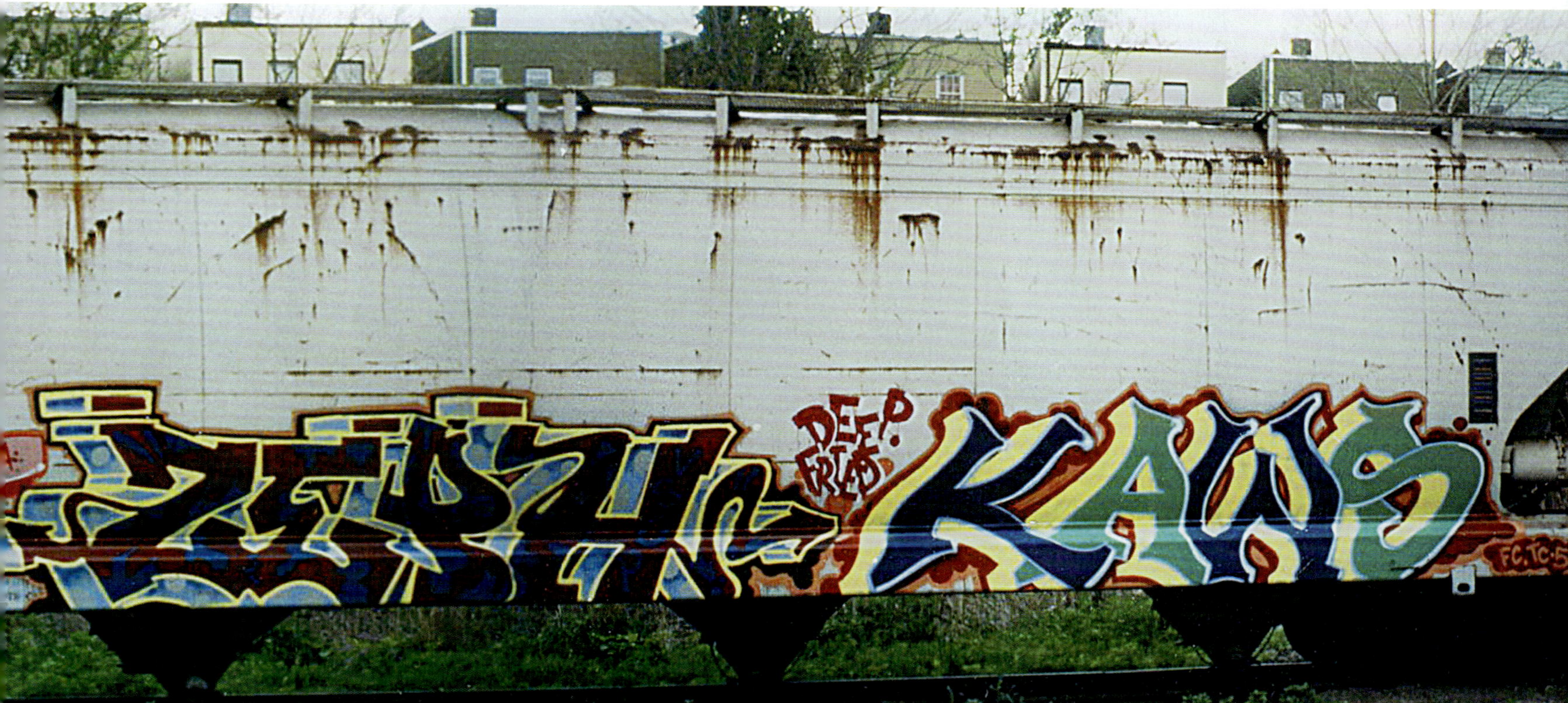
DEEP FRIED
KAWS
FC.TC.5

Kel 139

Kel 139 has played a number of roles in the development of graffiti style. He started that trend in 1978 as an established writer by leaving the showcase IRT lines to paint on the less-prestigious BMT lines with Dondi (see 097) and his new crew, CIA.

In late 1979, Kel 139 had an epiphany. Why not get the best writers available and go to the yards with the goal of doing a ten-car train of window-down burners and whole-cars? He took an existing crew and turned it into the Roc Stars. The core of the group included Crash, Cos 207, Shy 147 and Kel's younger brother, Mare 139. They would hit a tunnel or lay-up, and Crash and Kel would do at least four pieces each before the night was through. Roc Stars became a highly popular group, and Kel became a graffiti star. His reputation as a stylist was unassailable, but his personal reputation took a hit when he aligned himself with The Vamp Squad, a crew that ripped off other writers and citizens.

In 1980, Kel took on a third crew, as he began a partnership with Min. By 1981, Min had reformatted the RTW crew (see 286), taking it away from its style roots and having it go all-city with its throw-ups. When Kel came on board, he gave the crew an even balance of style and throw-ups, incorporating top-to-bottom Wild Style burners with MIN, as well as giving outlines to other crew members. This made Kel 139 a dominant force in three of graffiti's most important crews.

Private collection.
New York City, 1980.

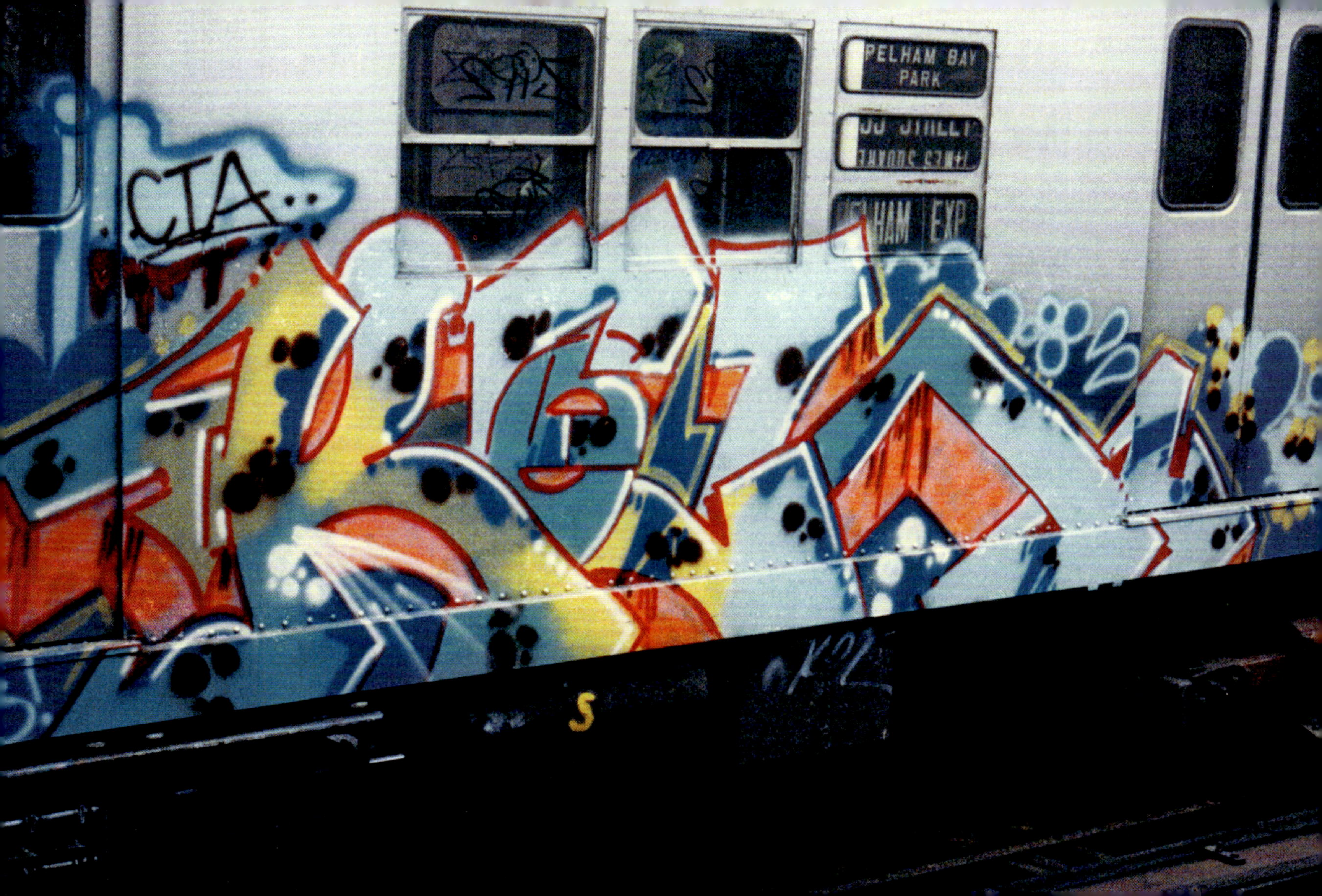
PELHAM BAY
PARK

Kenor

The government of Spain depresses the street artist known as Kenor; it consistently pursues painters who create beautiful, colorful pieces on the streets of Barcelona and paints over their works in gray. The native Spaniard feels that this is the worst crime possible, and that it borders on fascism.

Kenor has been creating his intensely colorful, almost cubistic works on a grand scale and in the public sphere for over a decade, and the streets of his home city are extremely important to him. Well-known in the Spanish graffiti community as well as the international street-art scene, Kenor is a vocal opponent of the exploitation of ephemeral art by industry, as well as the defacement of illegal murals by the law's heavy hand, which he sees as a blasphemous crushing of freedom of expression.

Kenor refers to galleries as "prisons," claiming that the street artist is a slave to his need for a paycheck, and that he works with galleries only to be able to survive. Kenor is unimpressed with street-art superstars and art-world darlings, and consistently threatens to drop off the face of the earth and go paint in the wilderness forever.

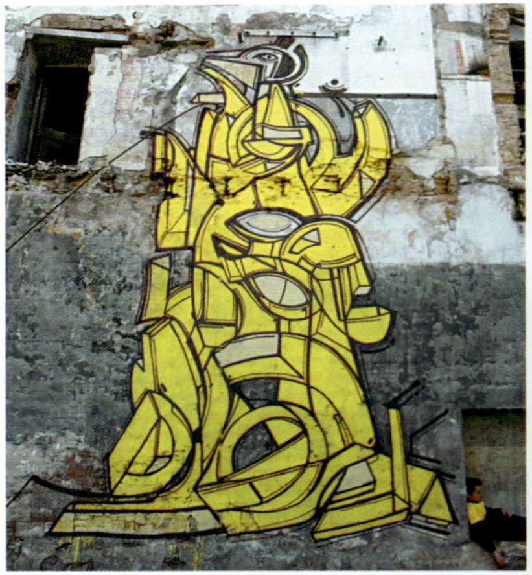

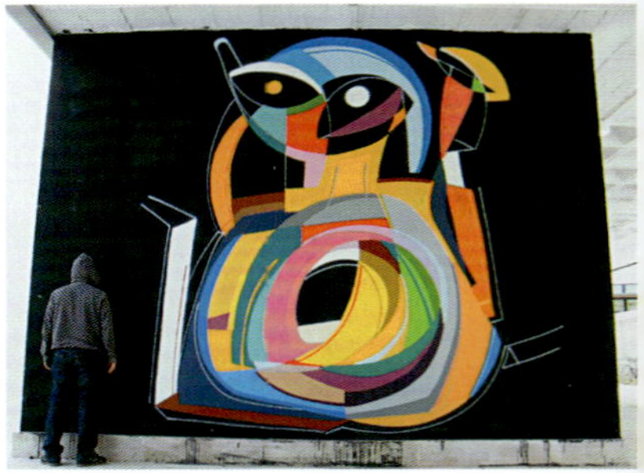

Photographs courtesy of Kenor.
***Besos*. Barcelona, Spain, 2010.**
Detail top: *Poble Nov*. Barcelona, Spain, 2010.
Detail bottom: Valencia, Spain, 2010.

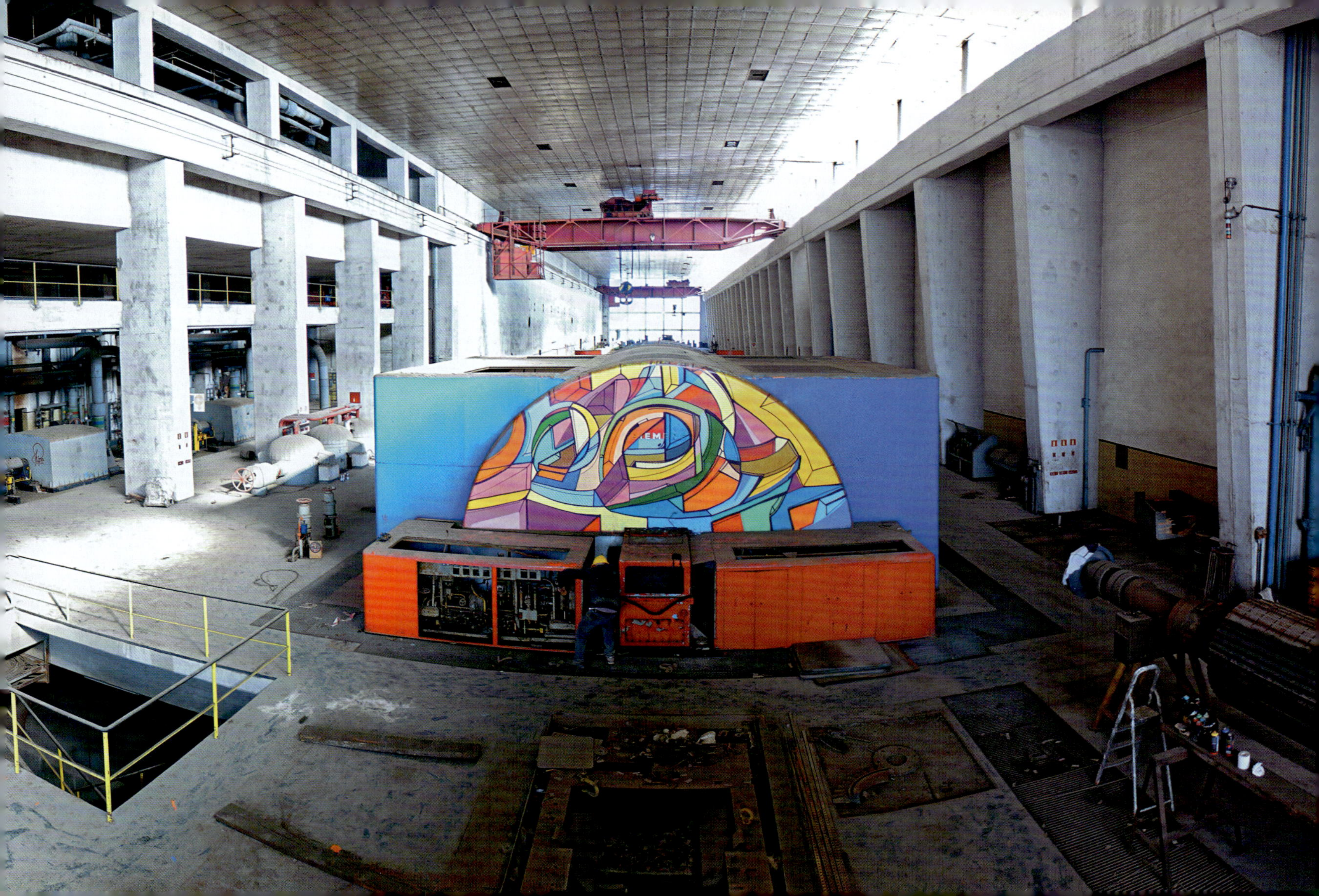

Keramik

The juxtaposition of the eternal with the ephemeral existence of street art led Vienna, Austria, native Thomas Mock to his moniker, Keramik. "Sometimes, all that remains of a past culture are a couple broken fragments of ceramics," he explained in a 2010 interview. With a diverse background that includes formal architectural training, Keramik is known for his "Oneliner" ink tag, resembling a bunnylike creature, and sculptural installations of a wooden "Mr. Horse." After bombing the streets of Vienna for five years with spray can and brush and being credited by some as a major style influence in Austria, Keramik had his first gallery show in 1999.

On the street, Keramik's fanciful animal creatures, brightly colored and accentuated with a bold outline, appear at first to be from a child's cartoon. With more careful inspection, dark undertones of sexual and morbid themes reveal themselves in a way that is both aggressive and cynical. A commentary on cliché stereotypes of graffiti is in much of his outdoor work. Phrases like "Hmm . . . I should stop pickpocket and go into graffiti business, too" are found in the thought bubble of a character next to his tag. A 2010 painting on wood panel is titled "You can't earn money with graffiti." Despite his stance, which nearly ridicules the worth of his own art, Keramik's art has been commissioned internationally. Go figure.

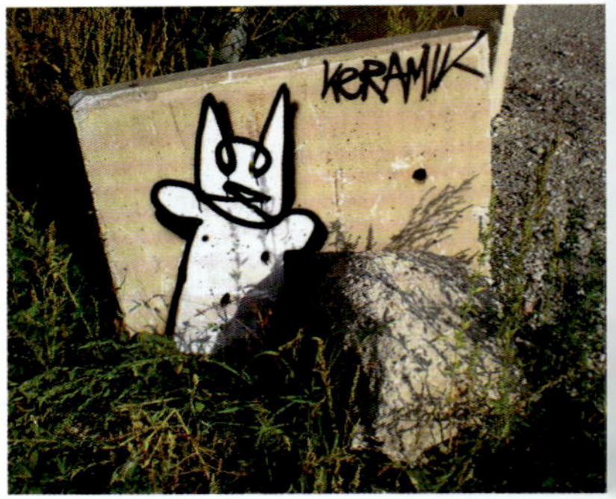

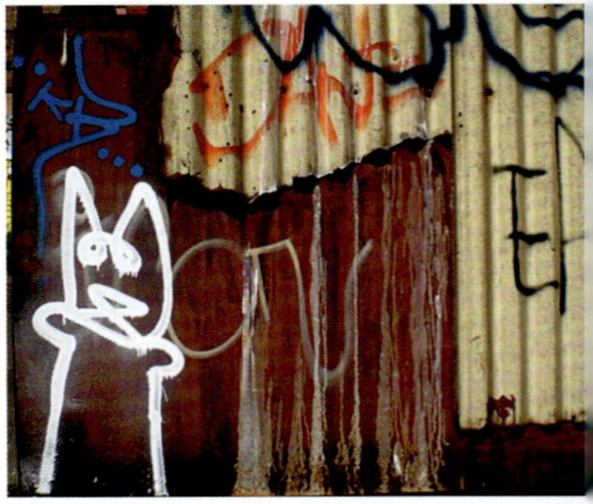

Photographs courtesy of Keramik.
Southern Austria, 2010.
Detail top: Vienna, Austria, 2006.
Detail bottom: Berlin, Germany, 2007.

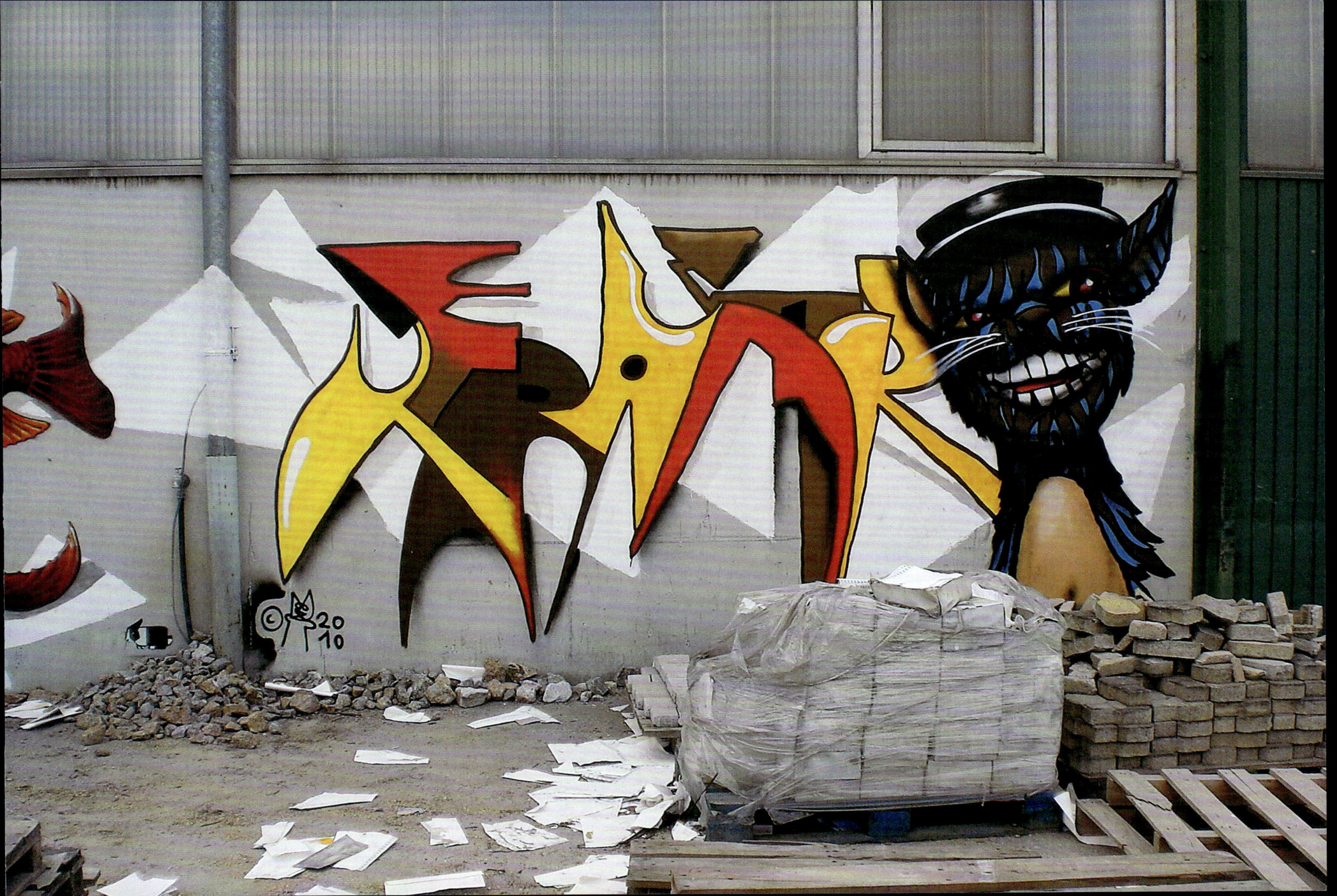
© 2010

Kid Acne

In the early 1990s, a bored teenager began making and trading fanzines in Sheffield, northern England—mainly because there's very little else to do there. This was the start of a blisteringly prolific career for an artist who simply can't stop creating, whatever the medium.

Kid Acne is a respected graffiti writer, illustrator, and rapper, and in more than fifteen years of doing his thing, there isn't much he hasn't experimented with. As well as releasing a few albums, he's written and self-published a hundred-page comic book called *Zebra Face*, designed toys for Kidrobot, and even created custom knitwear.

His street art is fantastic in every sense of the word. Originally based on his brother's childhood drawings, his illustration-style "Warrior Girl" characters have been on walls, T-shirts, prints, and album covers since mid-decade and have become more erotic as time goes by. One can see the influence of the early 1990s work of SheOne and Fire DFM.

It's always tough to predict what Kid Acne will do next, but one thing's for sure: It doesn't look like he'll be slowing down anytime soon.

Photographs by George Macdonald.
Far right: Hackney Wick, London, 2008.
Details: Shoreditch, London, 2008.

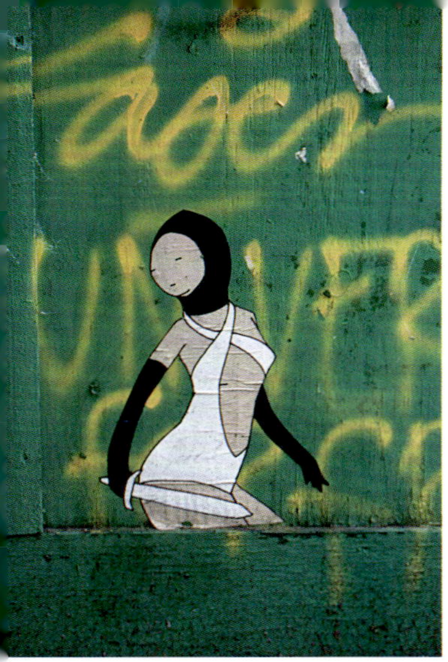

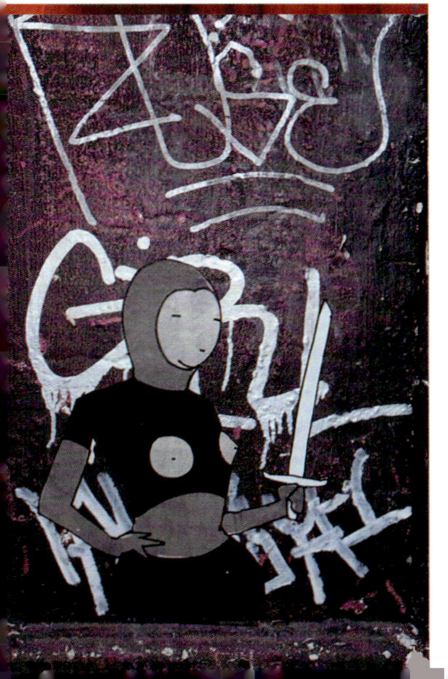

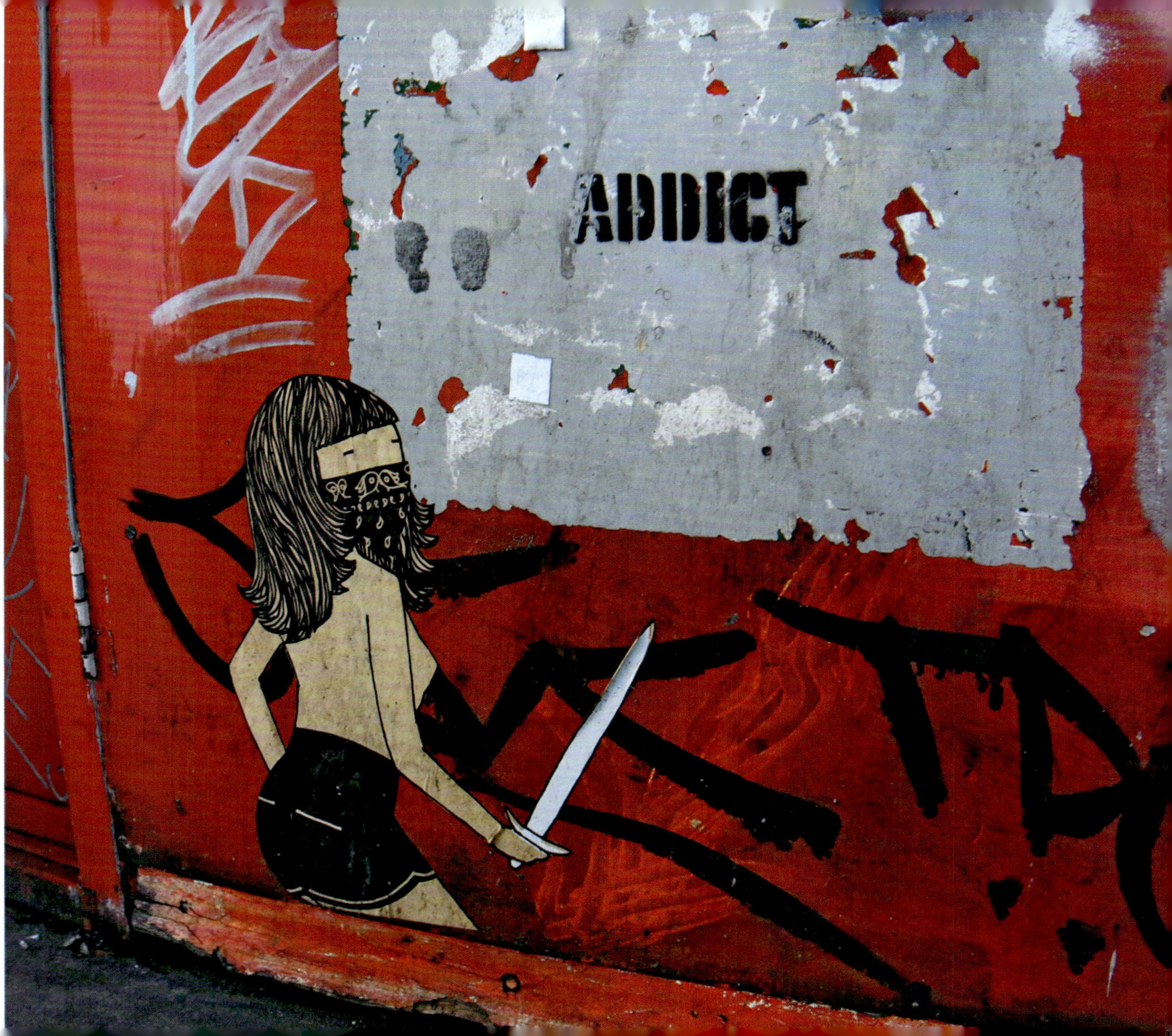
ADDICT

Kingdrips

Kingdrips is a project run by four artists based in Hamburg whose aesthetic influences range from graffiti and urban scenes to design and fine arts. This has led to a wide range of very recognizable imagery. Just as they juggle with different individual styles, they juggle with the boundaries between fine arts and commercially interesting works: In their eyes, it is a smooth transition, as long as commercial interests don't come into conflict with their creative and artistic freedom.

If you visit Hamburg, you're bound to notice stickers, stencils, throw-ups, and large collaborative pieces from this crew. They're playful, fun, and always down for some.

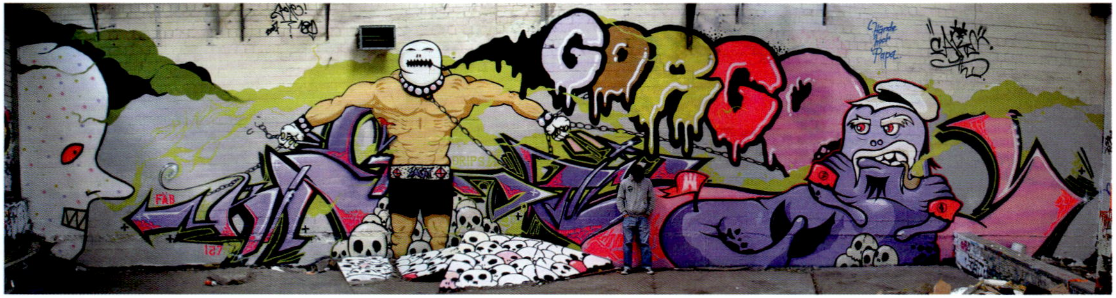

Photographs courtesy of Kingdrips.
***I-Punkt Skateland*. Hamburg, Germany, 2008.**
Detail: Hamburg, Germany, 2008.

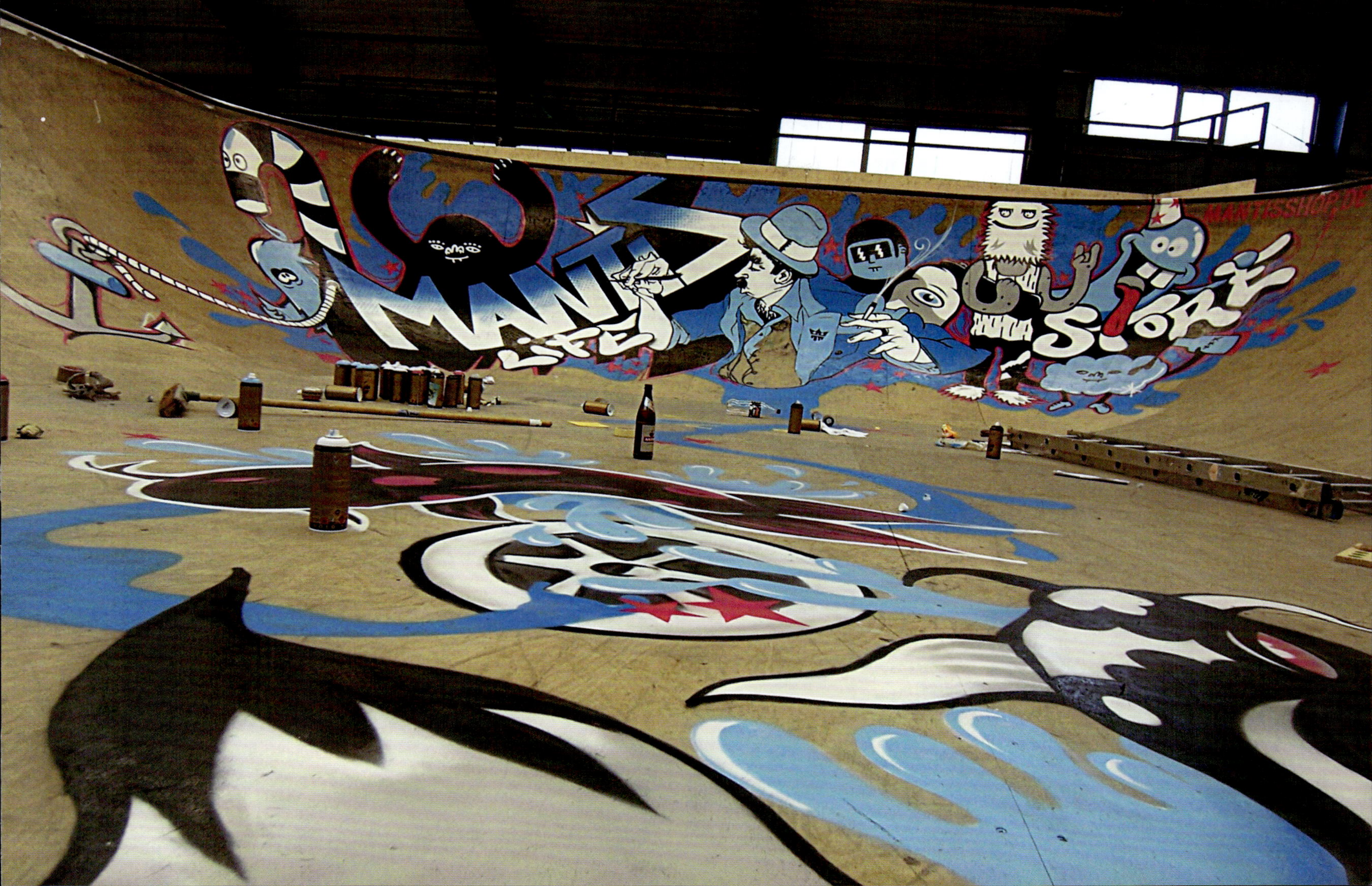
MANTISSHOP.DE

Knitta Please

Graffiti and street art are typically thought of as the byproducts of a surfeit of youthful virility and restlessness, but street-art crew Knitta Please challenges that notion at its core. Made up of several middle-aged people and founded by a grandmother in her seventies, Knitta Please refuses to bend to any stereotype of what a crew should look like.

Founded in 2005 by Magda Sayeg, this mischievous gaggle of tricksters began adorning public objects, such as lampposts, fire hydrants, and even cars, with their hand-knitted works, turning the streets into a gallery of oversize, homemade mittens.

Sayeg asserts that the introduction of the gentle and practical craft of knitting into the harsh realities of city life was her response to the dehumanization of the urban atmosphere, adding a human quality to it that otherwise rarely exists. Based in Austin, Texas, Sayeg led the crew around the United States, making its woven presence known in cities across the country. Knitta Please eventually caught the attention of the blogosphere, and its work has spawned innumerable copycats.

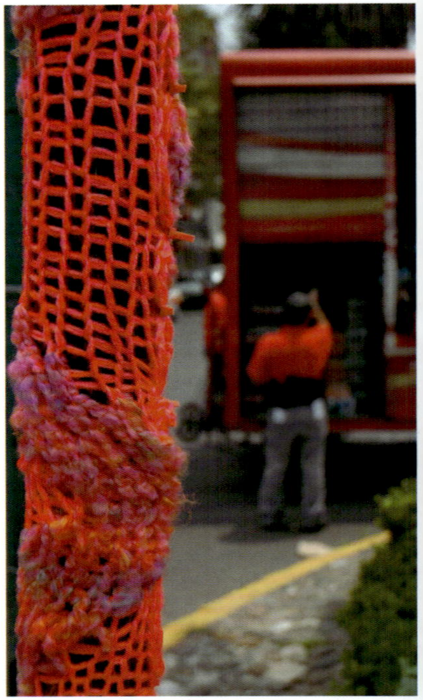

Far right: Photograph by Daniel Fergus.
Sydney, Australia, 2009.
Top right: Photograph by Denise Prince.
Austin, Texas, 2010.
Bottom right: Photograph by Daniel Fergus.
Austin, Texas, 2009.
Detail: Photograph by Daniel Fergus.
Mexico City, Mexico, 2008.

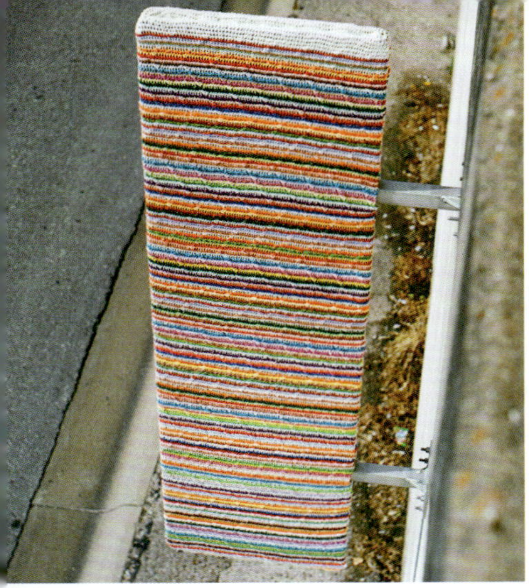

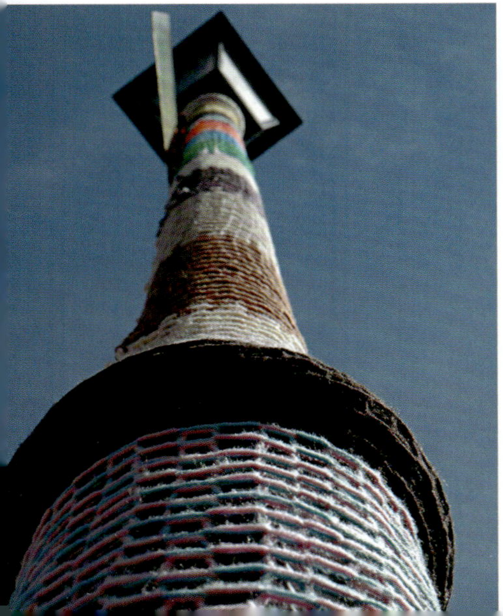

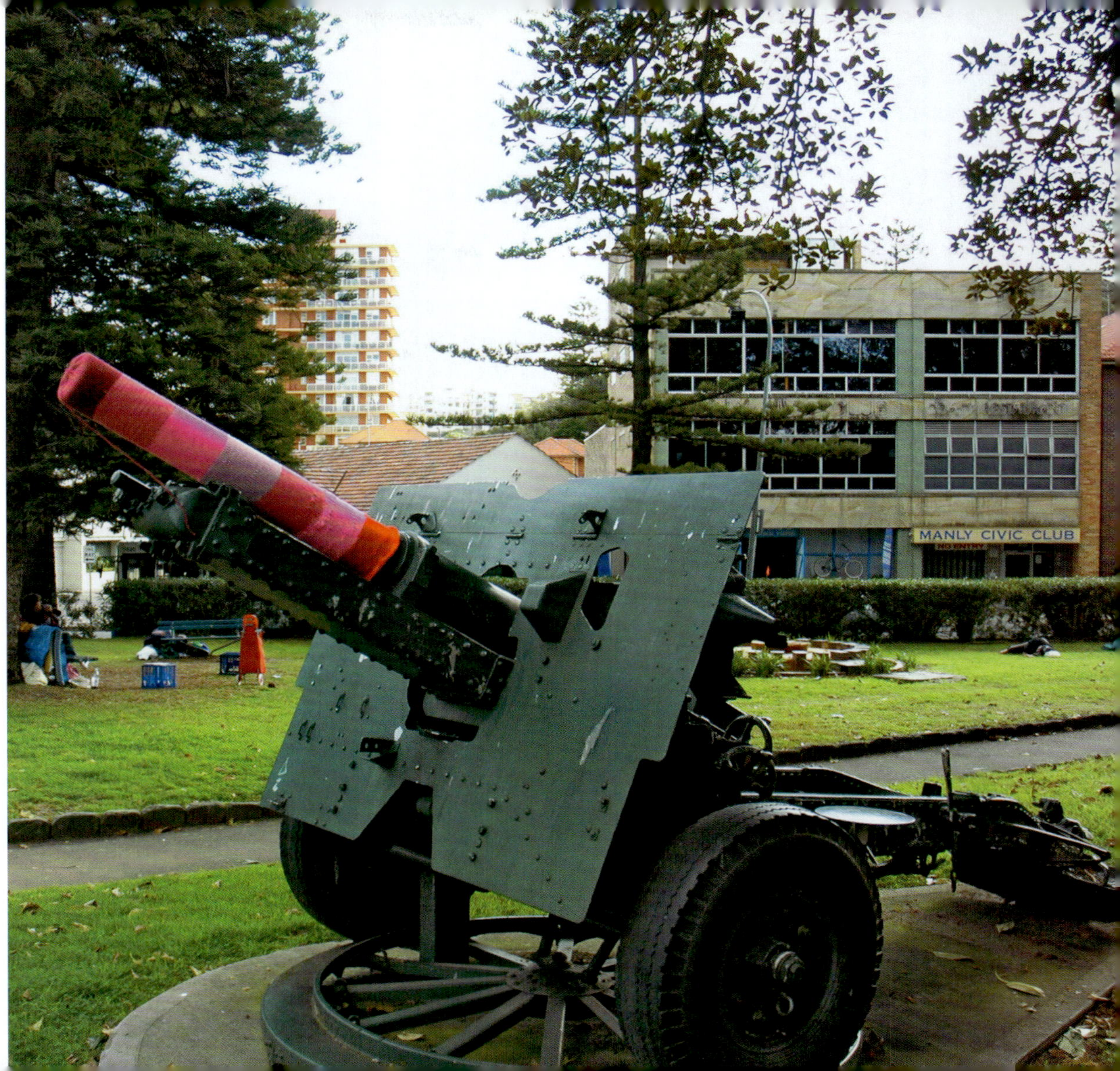
MANLY CIVIC CLUB

Know Hope

Born in 1986 in Southern California to parents who are both artists, Know Hope moved to Israel with his family at age ten. Ten years later, he began pasting the walls and surfaces of Tel Aviv with his forlorn, seemingly wounded, unnamed character, distinguished by a prominent heart. The artist describes this iconic heart as a universal symbol that must be "handled with care and preserved"—like life itself, the heart is in a constant state of flux. And like the young artist, his character, though clearly recognizable, continues to evolve.

Living in a country rife with political tension, Know Hope prefers to avoid direct reference to Israel's unique internal and external struggles, as he is more interested in the universal human condition.

Among his influences, Know Hope cites Chris Johansson, Yoko Ono, Maya Hayuk [see 162], Raymond Pettibon, and the poet Shel Silverstein. Since 2007, his site-specific installations incorporating painted backdrops and cardboard characters have won him international acclaim. Widely exhibited in galleries throughout the world, Know Hope sees his gallery work as thoroughly distinct from what he does on the streets, as both the setting and audience differ so keenly. Yet in both venues his principal object is to provoke dialogue.

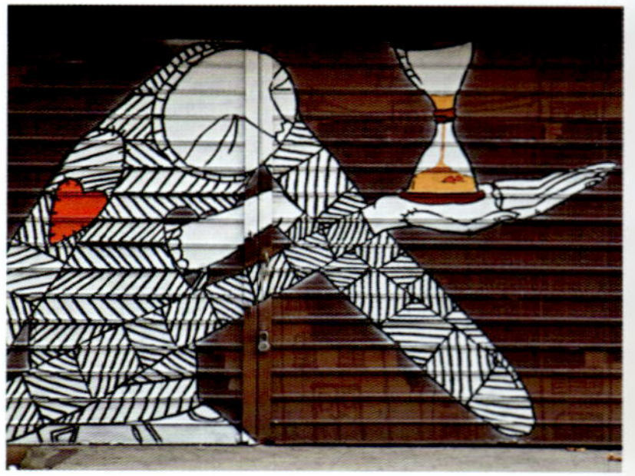

Photograph courtesy of Know Hope.
Tel Aviv, Israel, 2009.
Detail: Photograph by Vincent Cornelli.
Brooklyn, New York, 2009.

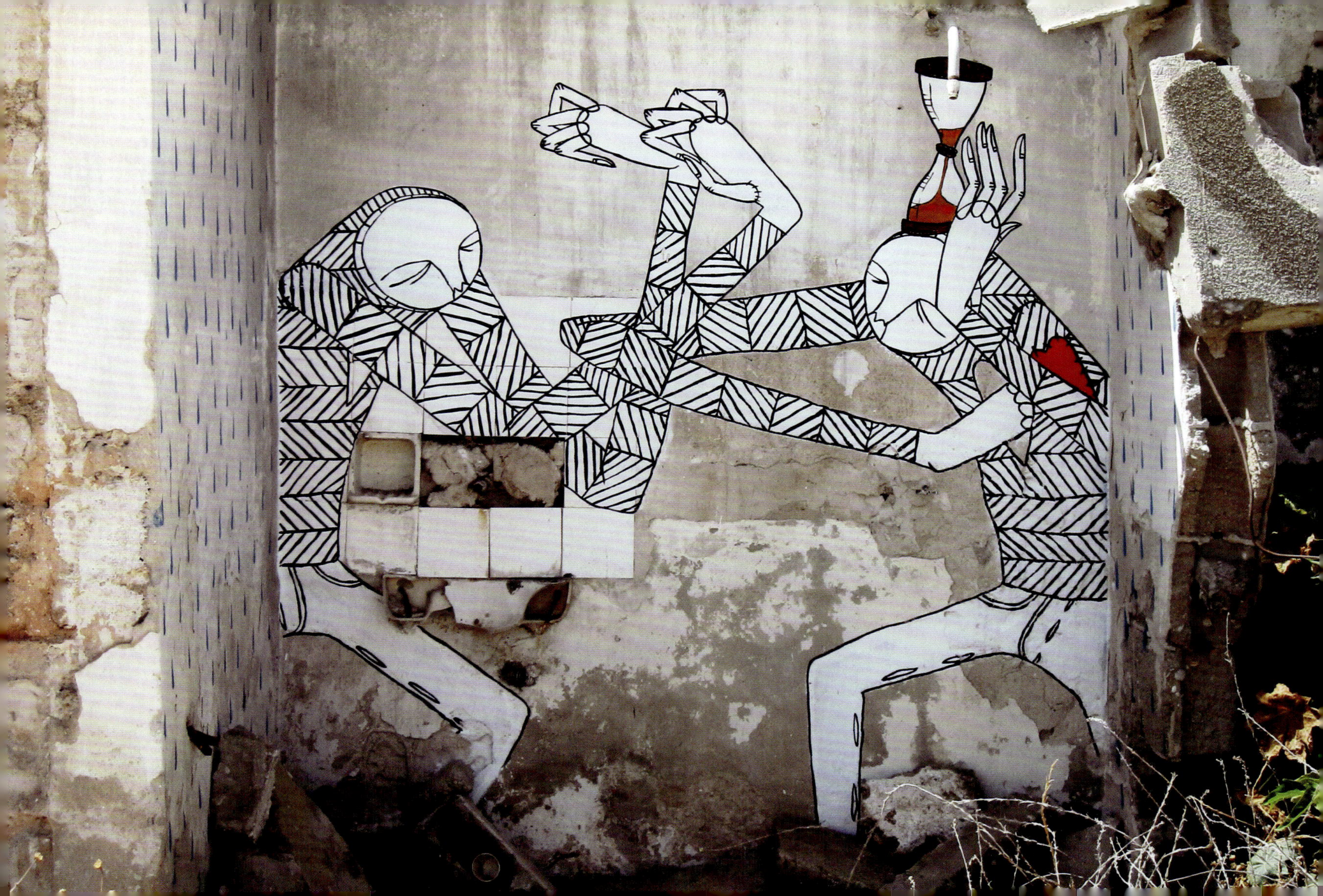

Ed Koch

Graffiti's most vocal nemesis in public office was the three-term mayor of New York City, Edward I. Koch, who served from 1977 to 1988. Amid a hailstorm of controversy over racial tensions and bankruptcy, the Koch administration embarked on an aggressive campaign to clean up the face of New York City, hoping to attract more tourists and businesses. That campaign involved an aggressive attack on the seemingly unstoppable spread of graffiti on the subway system, which was seen as a symbol of anarchy. This initiative involved the installation of high double fences with razor ribbon around all the train yards where artists frequently worked, the use of guard dogs, and eventually, the severity of the crime of graffiti changing from criminal mischief to felony vandalism. Prior to these developments, the city's greatest weapon had been buffing machines that bathed trains in a toxic chemical; this did little more than make a muddy blur of things, merely inspiring writers to accelerate their efforts. In the 1983 documentary *Style Wars* [see 322], "Hizzoner" beams when handed a photo of graffiti artist Spin's DUMP KOCH piece on a #4 train: "That's great. It's the highest praise imaginable, because it means I'm getting to them." By 1989, the transit authority had put an end to subway graffiti. And Koch, a civilian by then, couldn't take the credit.

Frame grab from *Style Wars*.
Image courtesy of Henry Chalfant.
New York City, 1982.

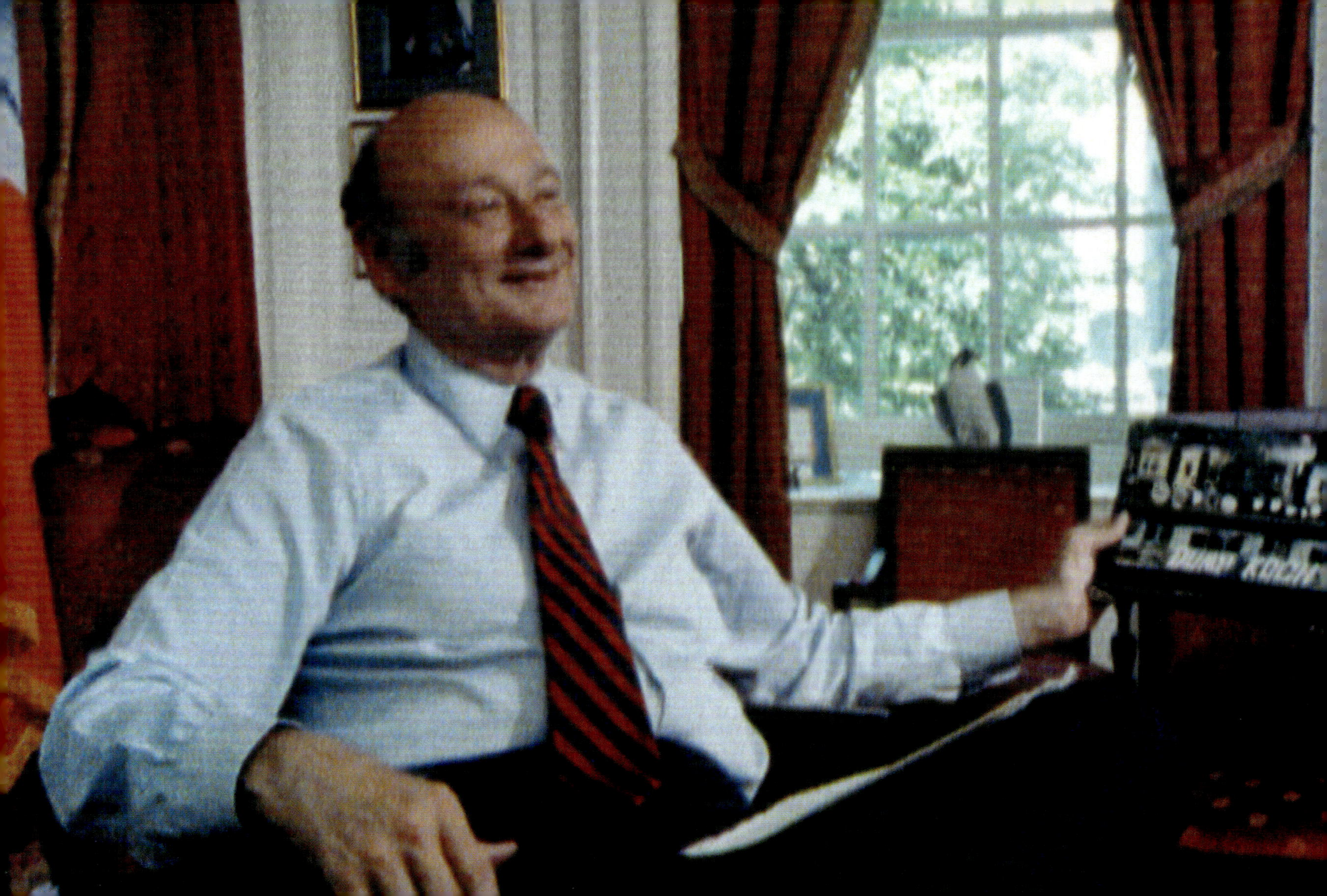

Kofie

An unusually low-key presence, the artist known as Augustine Kofie has been steadily churning out some of the United States' best abstracted structuralist graffiti work for the last decade. Known to be slightly compulsive, Kofie draws on his obsession with perfect angles and fastidious line work, often leaving perfect freehand-drawn circles on public walls instead of a traditional tag. Inspired by building structures and architectural drawings, Kofie's work is reminiscent of intricate blueprints or aerial-view plans for imagined cities.

Born and raised in Los Angeles, Kofie was a member of numerous crews, whetting his appetite for traditional graffiti. He starred in the documentary *Rock Fresh*, in which he is seen churning out painted trucker hats and dabbling in the creation of a clothing line.

In mid-decade, Kofie's worked moved increasingly into the fine-art realm; his canvas and wood pieces began to embrace mixed-media and collage techniques. He has had numerous solo shows in Los Angeles and has exhibited with the Fifty24SF/Upper Playground family, as well as the White Walls Gallery in San Francisco. He has been commissioned for installations and illustrations by clients such as Nike, *Vice*, and Red Bull Records.

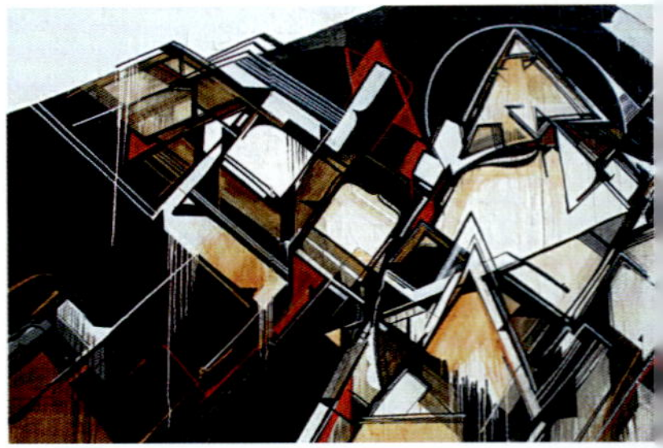

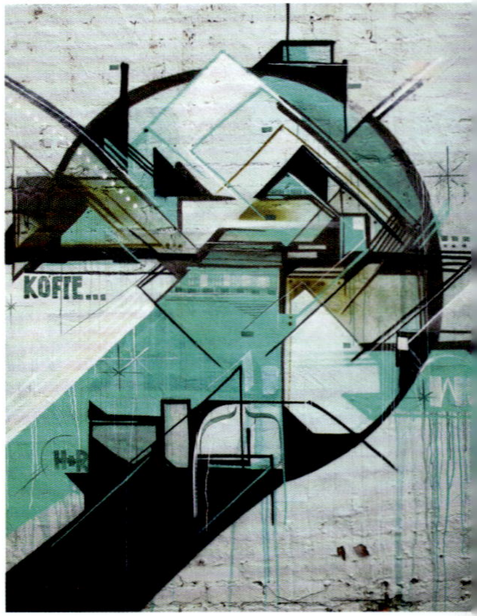

Photographs courtesy of Kofie.
Melbourne, Australia, 2010.
Detail top: Los Angeles, 2008.
Detail bottom: Melbourne, Australia, 2010.

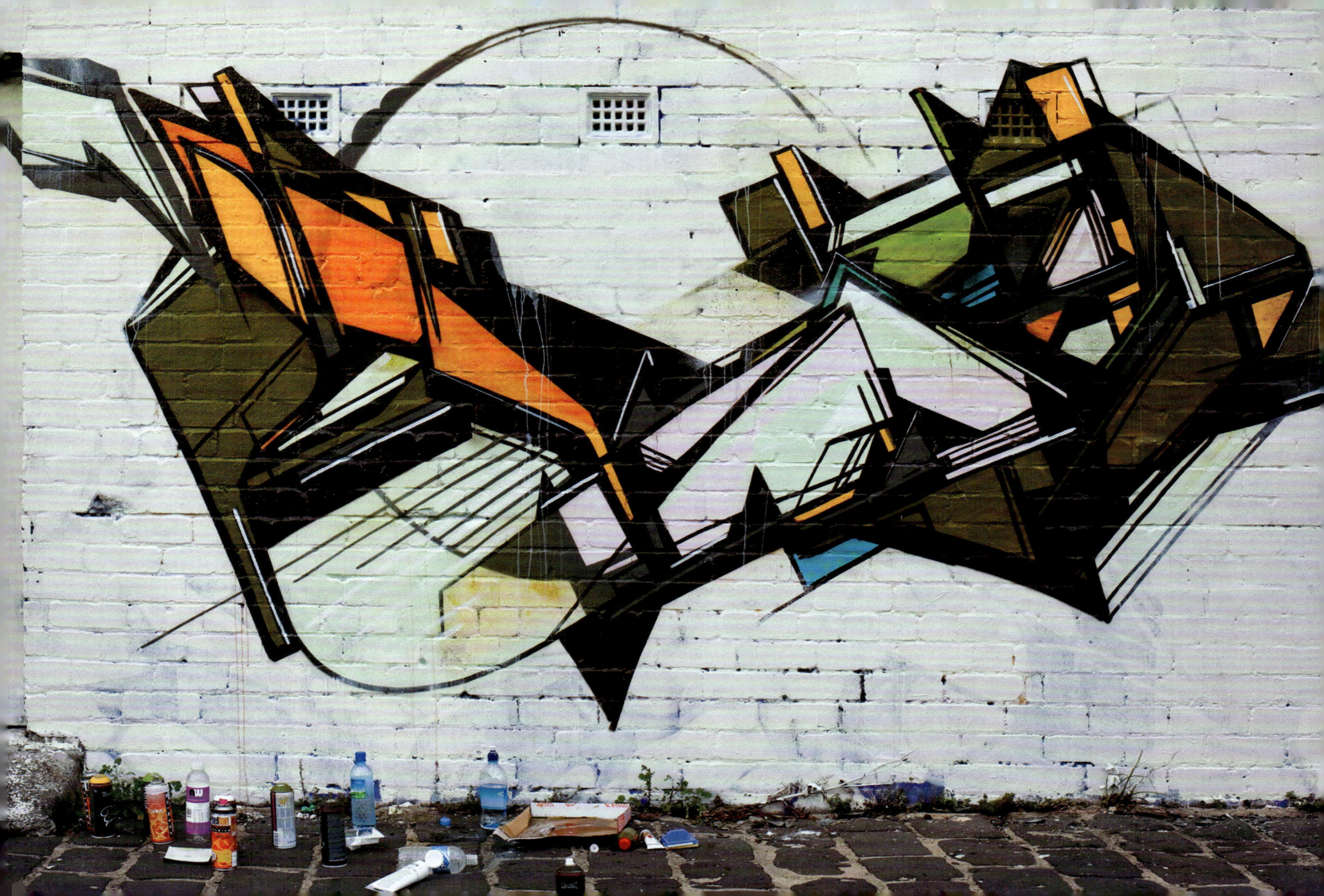

KR

Craig "KR" Costello was raised in Forest Hills, Queens, a doctor's son and the younger of two brothers. His elder sibling, James, wrote as Dash, and KR would often tag along on graffiti missions without really immersing himself in the movement. He started writing in 1989, the year New York's subway movement ended. KR attended art school in San Francisco during the early 1990s and teamed up with artists Barry McGee (see 214), Dug One, and other local legends. KR, more vandal than artist, became known for hitting mailboxes, trucks, and other ink-friendly surfaces with markers so juiced up that the tags they produced oozed like molten lava. A recent caption under a KR interview christened him "The King of Deliberate Drips."

During the mid-1990s, KR began brewing his first batches of homemade inks. After finishing art school, he returned to New York and launched an East Coast drip campaign that spawned a sea of followers. KR bottled his recipe for destruction, marketing his ink commercially; his tireless marketing campaign helped establish Krink as a staple of the modern-day bomber, as well as a tool for legitimate artists. Krink's success enabled KR to expand his product line to markers and even clothing, including sneakers. Viewing himself as more than just an entrepreneur, KR divides his energies between running his Krink business and pursuing his career as a fine artist.

KR's drip-based paintings and installations have found an audience in art galleries across the globe, and in recent interviews, he has referred to graffiti as a part of his past. His work remains divisive; some will find beauty in the technicolor ink that assaults gallery walls, while others will think KR must have emulated Warhol in art school, learning that "Art is anything you can get away with."

Photograph by Jake Dobkin (streetsy.com). New York City, 2007.

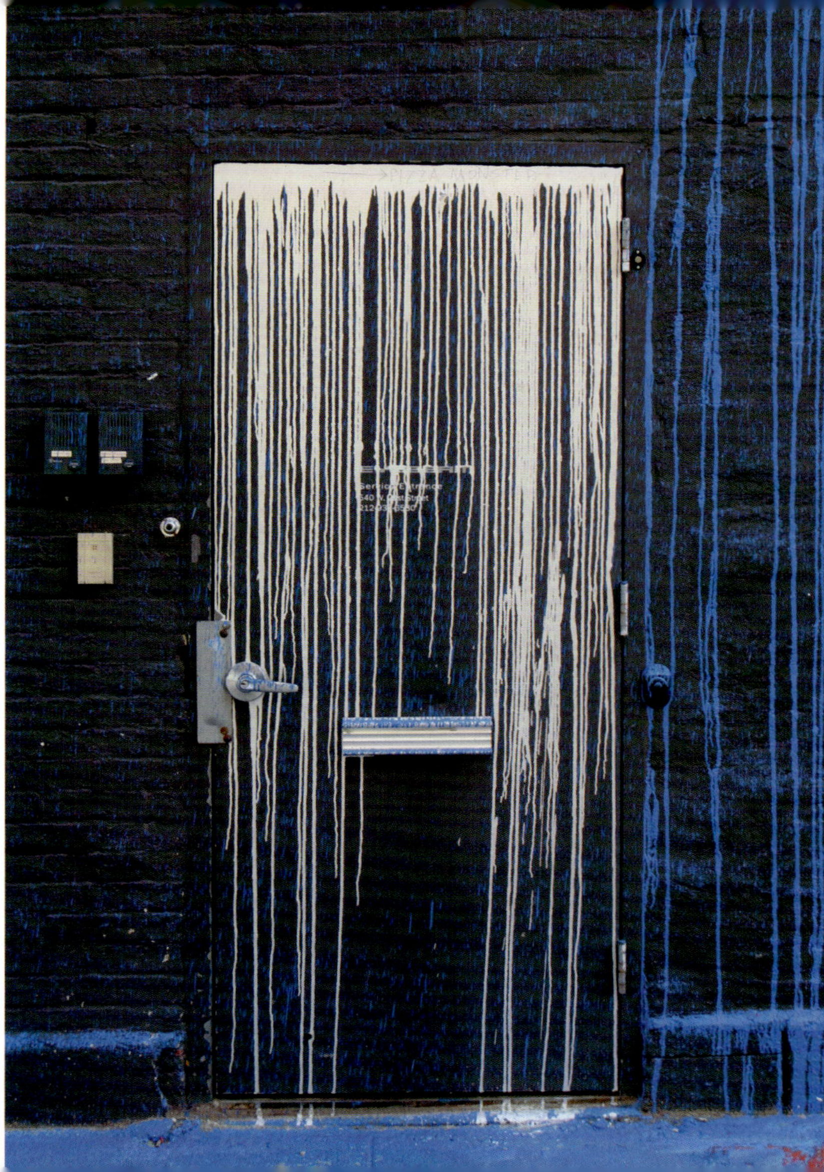

LA 2

In 1980, legendary street-artist-turned-art-star Keith Haring was just beginning to taste fame. His signature style—squiggly lines and two-dimensional stick figures painted in simple black on neon backgrounds—had fully developed, and he was establishing himself as an important commodity in the international art market. That summer, while painting a mural on Houston Street in downtown Manhattan, Haring was approached by a thirteen-year-old graffiti artist named Angel Ortiz. Angel was tagging with the moniker LA 2, and Haring had become fascinated with the signature after seeing it on the streets a few weeks prior to their meeting. The unlikely pair became fast friends, sharing an instant connection and an artistic bond. When Haring discovered Ortiz's age, he took him under his wing and became his mentor. Ortiz eventually traveled the world with Haring, painting alongside him on murals and canvases, adding elements Haring would eventually call instrumental to the development of his style. When Haring died of AIDS-related complications in 1990, Ortiz was left without his mentor and best friend. Without the personal relationship to Haring himself, he became estranged from the Haring estate and was separated from the pieces to which he had contributed. Having only received cash stipends from Haring, there was no structured payment plan for him, so he eventually found himself broke—and having to rebuild his career from the ground up.

Drug problems and jail sidelined Ortiz for several years, but he has recently begun to sell his work, often collaborating with famed artist Mark Kostabi. A lifelong resident of the Lower East Side, LA 2 has shown his work in New York City as recently as 2009.

Patti Astor, with artwork by LA 2 and Keith Haring. Photograph by Martha Cooper. New York City, 1981.

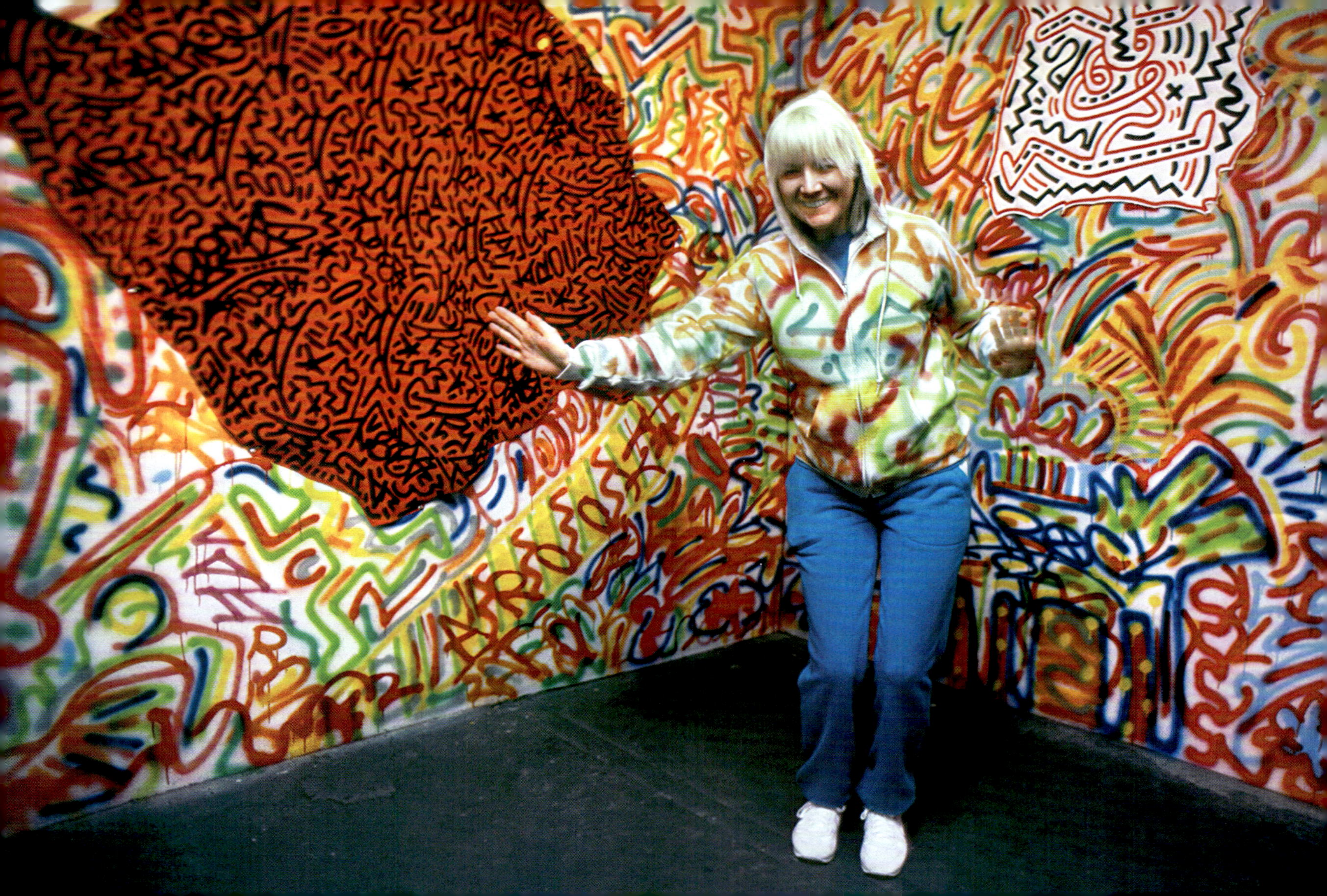

Lady Tribe

Lady Tribe's website credits her as being "The World's Hottest DJ Goddess." Among the many professions and hobbies she lays claim to, graffiti is obviously a powerful draw for Lady Tribe, despite her recent focus on music. According to her bio, Lady Tribe first picked up a Mean Streak marker at the tender age of thirteen and was consumed by an obsession with illegal art that lasted nine years.

Although Lady Tribe alleges that much of her graffiti work was confiscated by "the five-o" (aka the police), she still claims numerous images from her graffiti crews, and also several throw-ups done in and around Los Angeles, California. Lady Tribe has had a notorious career of scaling buildings, hanging from freeway overpasses, and brazenly bombing buses in broad daylight. She currently represents the ubiquitous and much-feared TKO crew, a major bombing force and street presence in Los Angeles.

After "being raided too many times," Lady Tribe has moved on to greener pastures, embarking on careers as both a DJ and a model—she has appeared in several music videos, including 50 Cent's "In Da Club." Lady Tribe prides herself on conquering male-dominated fields, and she is concentrating nowadays on taking the nightclub world by storm.

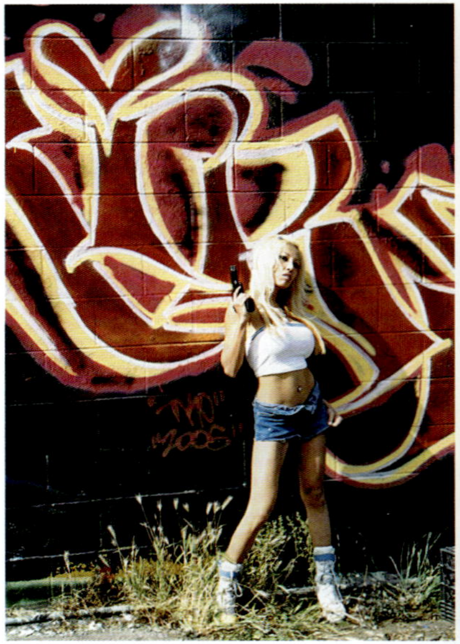

TKO **piece by T.Loks (aka Toomer).**
Photograph courtesy of Lady Tribe.
Detail: Photograph by Ces One.
Los Angeles, 2006.

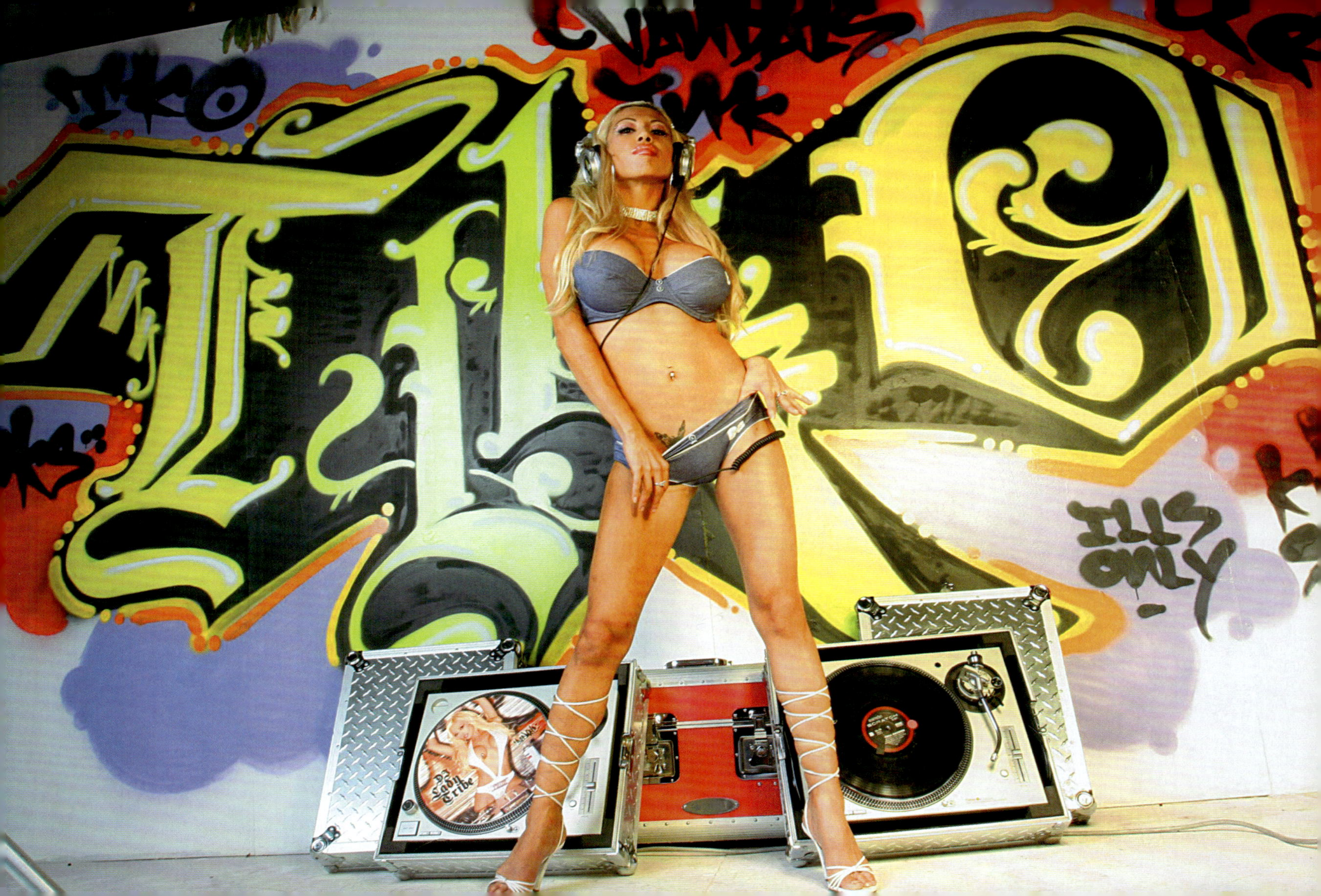
DJ Lady Tribe

Laguna

Laguna began putting his name around the walls of Almagro, a small historic town in the Castilla–La Mancha region of central Spain, around 1995. This sparsely populated region, best known as the homeland of Don Quixote, offered Laguna no connection to the outside graffiti world. Fanzines from other parts of Europe inspired him to paint in the styles of Dare, Toast, Mode 2, and Mast. For the next several years, he painted the walls of his homeland in the fashion of conventional graffiti, but in 2002, Laguna began frequenting other parts of Europe, where strange influences caused him to question the method to his madness.

In 2003, Laguna decided to transition into post-graffiti or street art. No longer interested in identity-based letterforms, he began painting murals that would make any gallerist want to kidnap him and chain him to an easel. The painterly details that go into his work provide reason to stop, stare, and wonder. When asked what motivates him, Laguna says, "I want to leave a part of myself in places and on objects that have been abandoned by their former owners."

Photograph courtesy of Laguna.
Almagro, Spain, 2010.

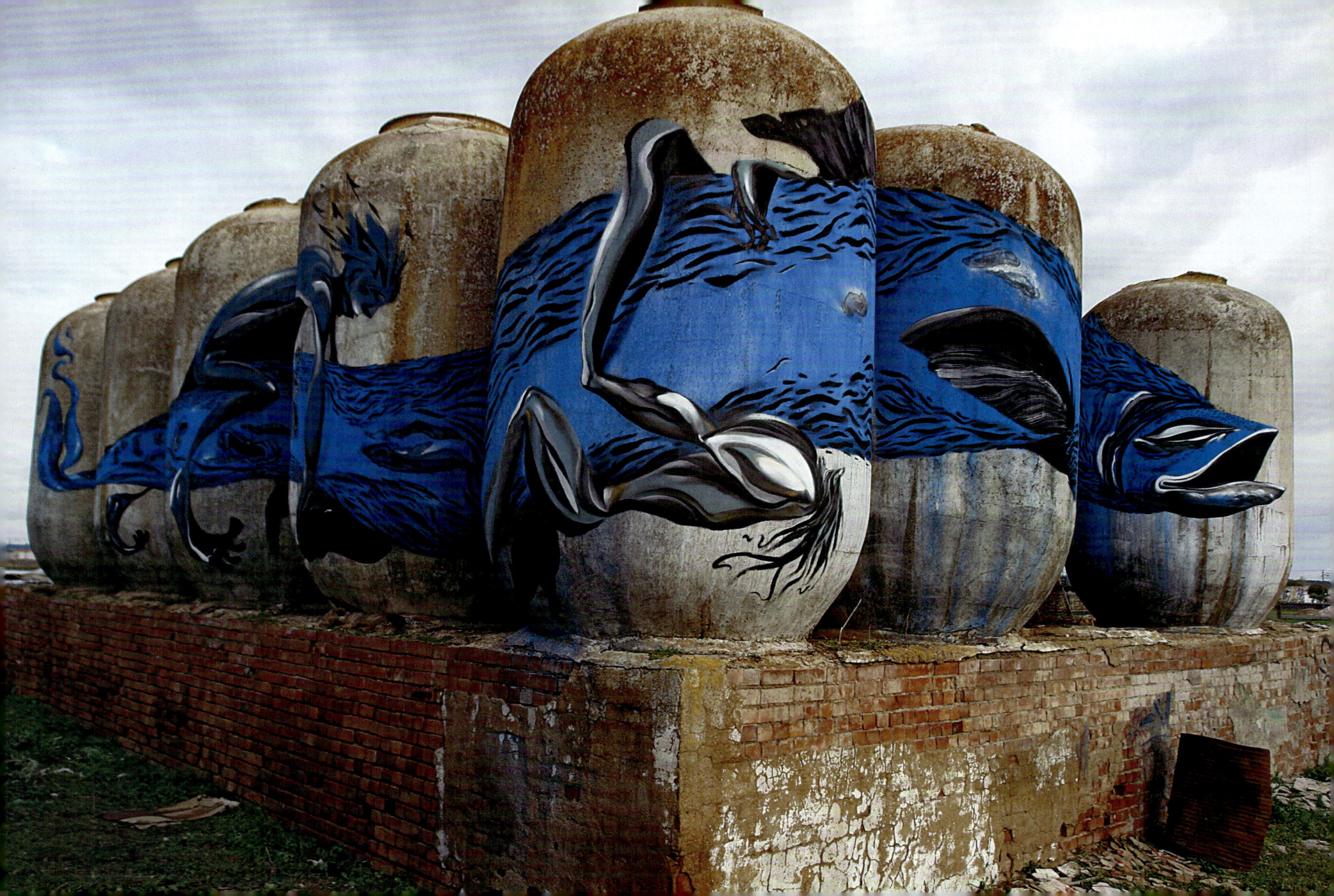

Anthony Lister

Born and raised in Brisbane, Anthony Lister is Australia's best-known public artist, and arguably street art's most notable bad boy, second only to the American hurricane that is David Choe [see 065]. A decorated fine-arts graduate, Lister gained notoriety for his wild, instantly recognizable character style, featuring abstracted faces and a running theme of superheroes. Seamlessly bridging the gap between the street- and fine-art-gallery worlds, he first caught the Australian public eye with a series of works on public electric boxes in the early 2000s. Quickly picked up by the establishment, Lister began exhibiting and selling works on canvas in his early twenties.

Married and a father of two, Lister has traveled the world extensively, painting the streets and exhibiting in New York, Melbourne, London, Los Angeles, and San Francisco, among other cities. His gallery shows have begun to include live performance art, involving costumed sitters dressed as superheroes, often bound to chairs and gagged, writhing uncomfortably or swearing and yelling incoherently. For one installation, in New York, Lister tied live rats to a piece inside a large shipping container for a period of a week.

Lister's Wikipedia entry is not to be trusted. Ever the prankster, he is listed as the son of a wealthy Colombian cocaine dealer and a registered sex offender, neither of which is true.

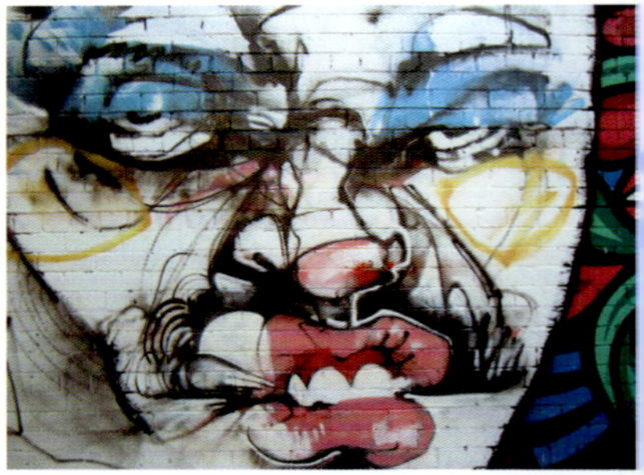

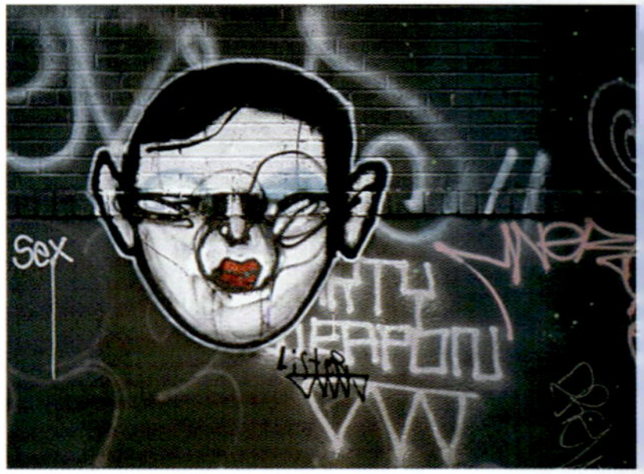

Photograph by Anika Lister. Perth, Australia, 2010.
Detail top: Photograph courtesy of Anthony Lister. Brisbane, Australia, 2010.
Detail bottom: Photograph by iO Tillet-Wright. Brooklyn, New York, 2009.

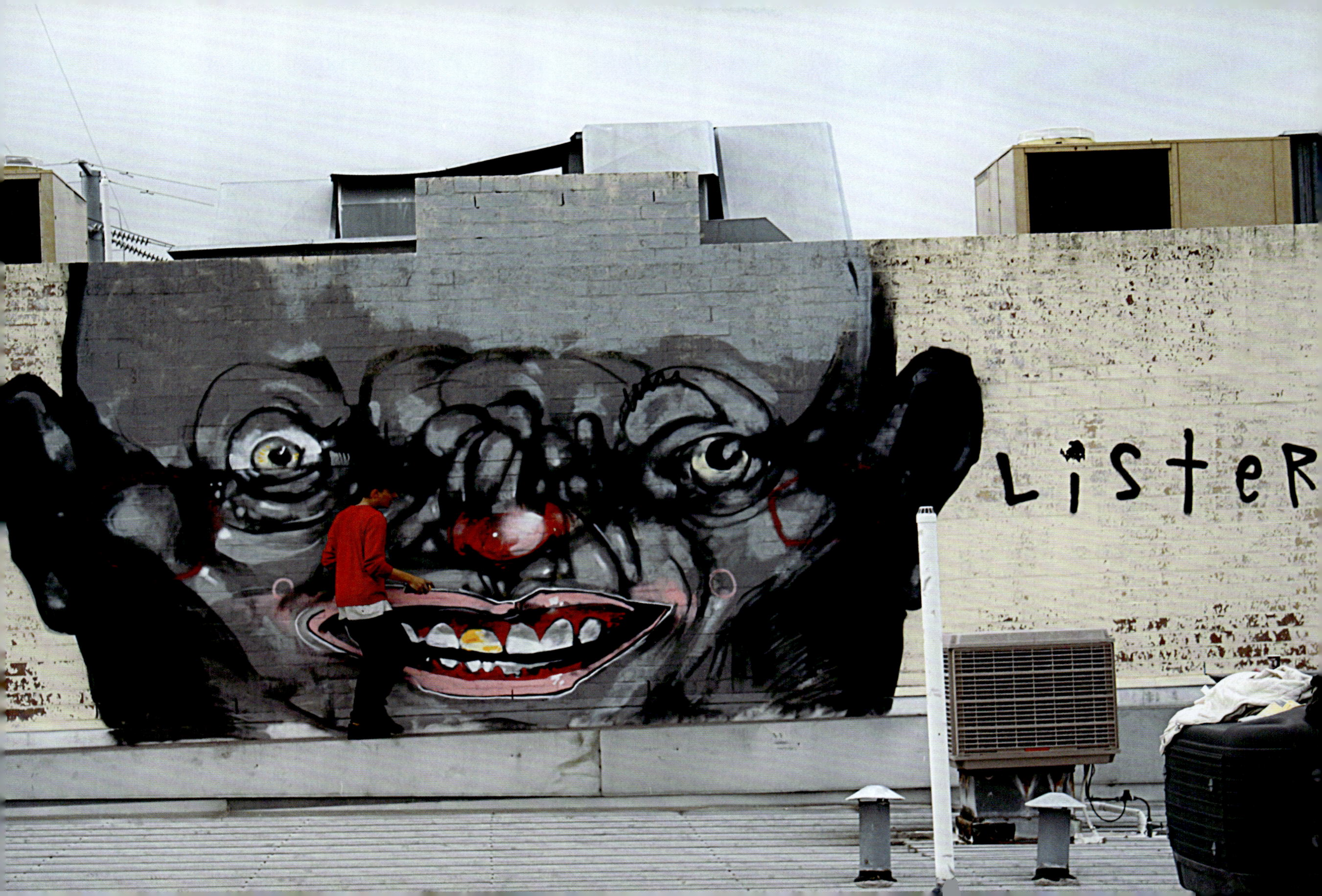
LiSteR

The London Police

Sometime in 1998—so the story goes—a group of British stoners commuted to Amsterdam to beautify its dreary streets. Two founding members, Chaz TLP and Bob Gibson, created what would become the signature style of a new street-art crew called The London Police. Using starkly contrasting rich whites and deep blacks, The London Police developed a species of character called "the lads," rotund little men with gangly legs and perfectly drawn circles for heads; the lads were instantly recognizable and visible from long distances.

In 2002, The London Police took to the road, traveling to thirty-five countries, meeting other artists, and leaving lads on every conceivable surface. Known as one of the Wooster Collective's (see 359) first superstar groups, as well as being one of the most recognizable faces of the early street-art boom, The London Police was heavily influential well into the decade. During this period, the group began exhibiting its work, both on canvases and as installation pieces, in galleries as far-flung as Tokyo, New York, London, Miami, and Barcelona. In 2009, The London Police staged four consecutive exhibitions celebrating ten years of putting work on the streets.

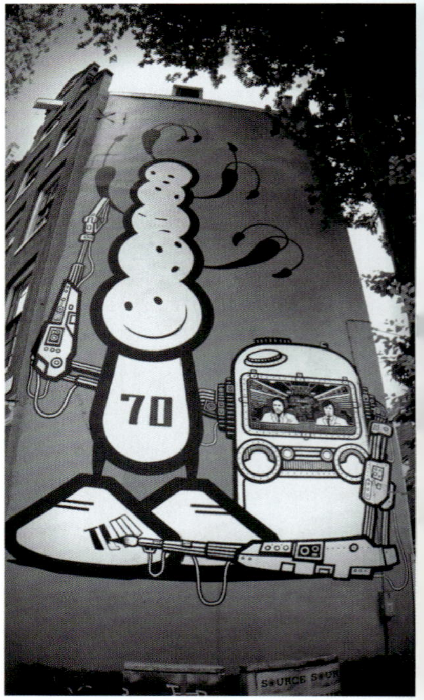

Collaboration with Will Barras and Morcky Troubles. Photograph courtesy of the London Police. Primary Flight, Miami, 2007. Detail: Photograph by George Macdonald. Amsterdam, The Netherlands, 2010.

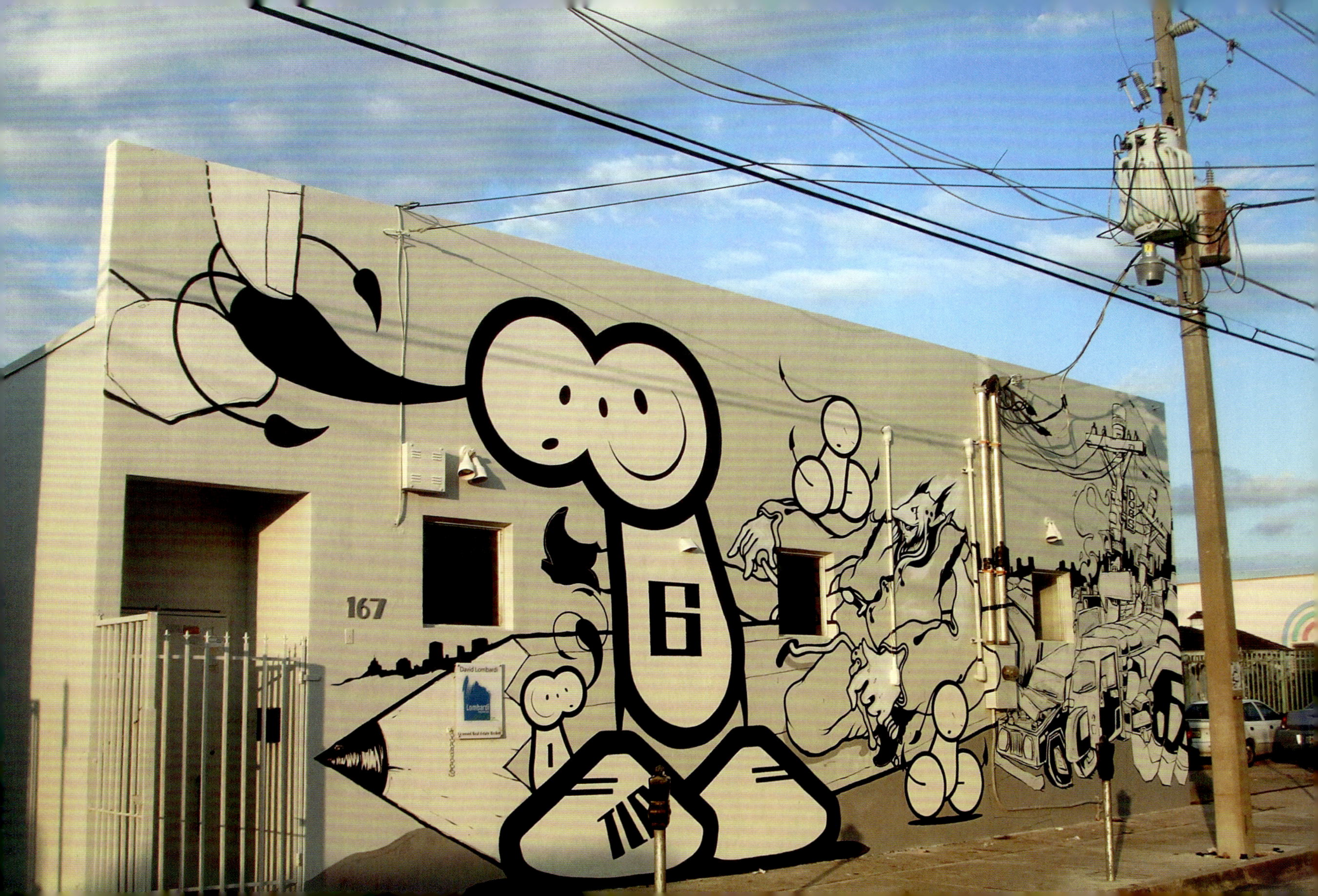
167
David Lombardi
Lombardi

Loomit

Loomit started writing in Munich in 1983, at the very beginning of the European graffiti movement. As he put it, "I was just happy to find people that shared my interests." He painted just about anything that moved and developed a reputation throughout Europe as a top writer.

In 1990, he broke away from other European writers who were still mimicking subway art; he found a way out of that mold by looking at two other famous European writers, Daim [see 083] and Delta [see 089]. Both writers were twisting letters and adding wide 3-Ds to them. Loomit did what all great graffiti artists do: He appropriated the technique and made it his own.

In the 1990s, Loomit made an eleven-month world tour that included the United States, where he wound up at Seen's [see 294] doorstep. The two collaborated on a number of works, and Seen taught Loomit the art of tattooing. Loomit's work developed so rapidly that it seemed to transcend graffiti. He developed a cool, minimalist approach and preferred multiple flat planes of color instead of the aerosol fades of his contemporaries.

In 2003, he received the prestigious Schwaburg Art Award, presented to him by the mayor of Munich, Christian Ude. In the last decade, he's settled in Munich, where he continues to paint.

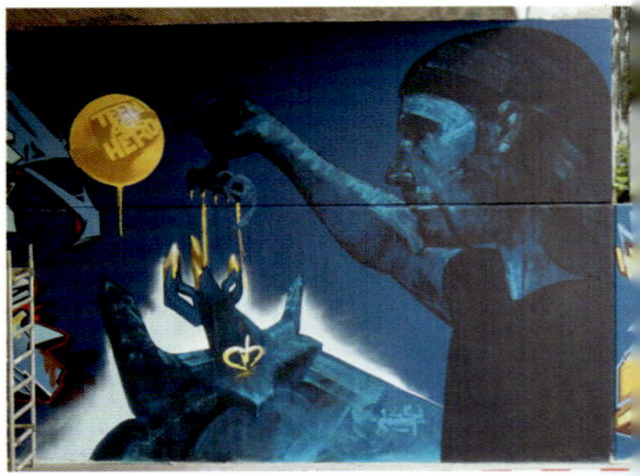

Photographs courtesy of Loomit.
Istanbul, Turkey, 2010.
Detail: Ingolstadt, Germany, 2010.

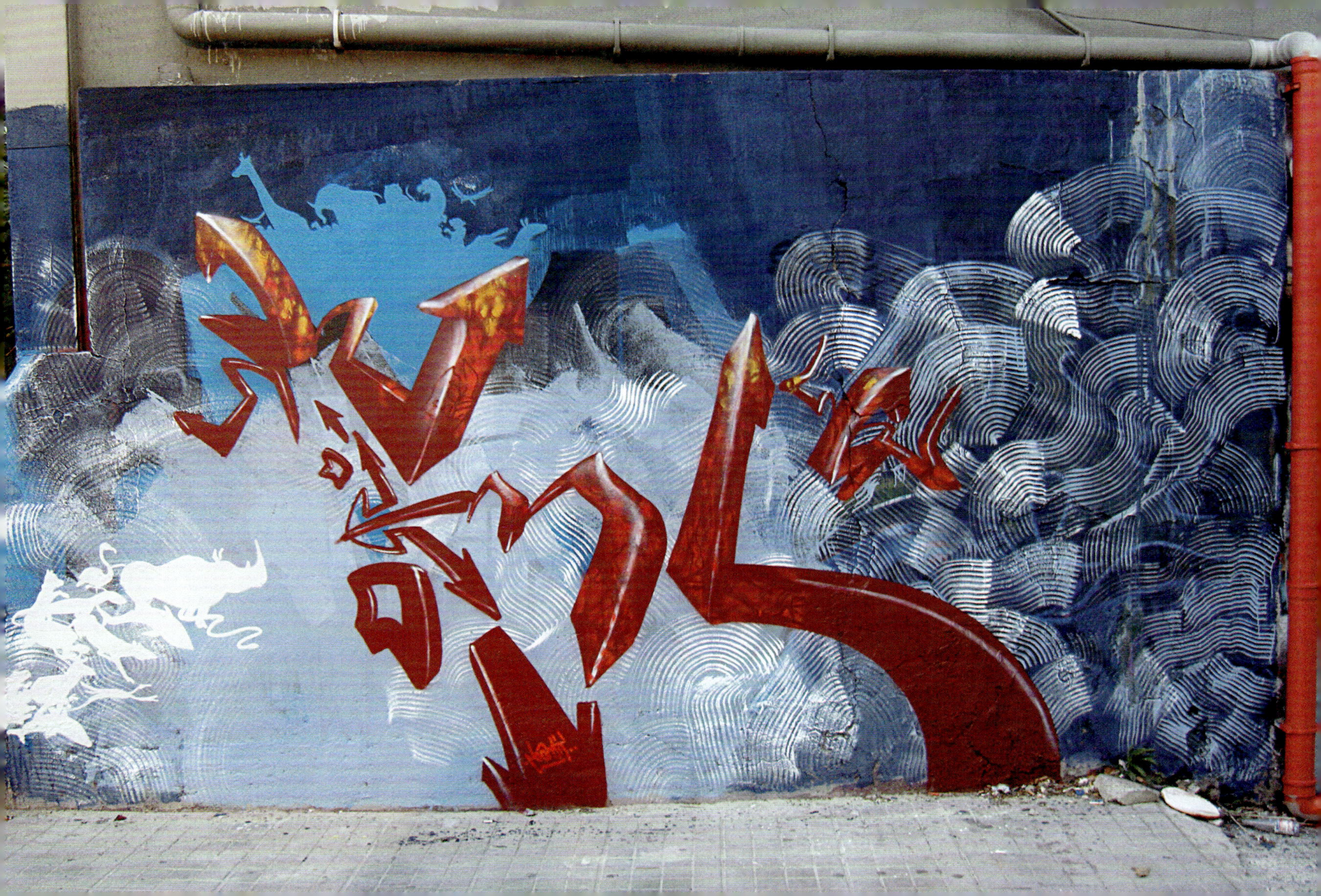

LSD Om

LSD Om began writing graffiti as a young boy growing up on West 86th Street. He was inspired by the political graffiti of the 1960s, including the logo of the SDS, a name he took for himself for a short time. In 1971, his family moved to the Bronx, and he took on the name LSD Om. By 1972, he was imitating the tags of Stay High 149 (see 316) and Deadleg 167, morphing some of their elements into his own psychedelic style.

From 1973 to 1976, he did at least a hundred different pieces, none of which looked the same. LSD appropriated images from underground comics and record covers, and used them as inspiration. In the same three-year time span, he cofounded the writing crew the Rebels; he wanted the Rebels to reflect the diverse culture of writing, and the crew had members of all races. It was a utopian vision that seemed to transcend the complexities of race relations that existed in the graffiti world. For many white writers, running into all-black crews usually meant getting jumped, but somehow LSD seemed to bypass all of this—perhaps because of his age or his great style. His tags were found in some of the most dangerous places in he city, and this just added to his legacy. He quit writing in 1976—and amazingly, some of those tags still stand.

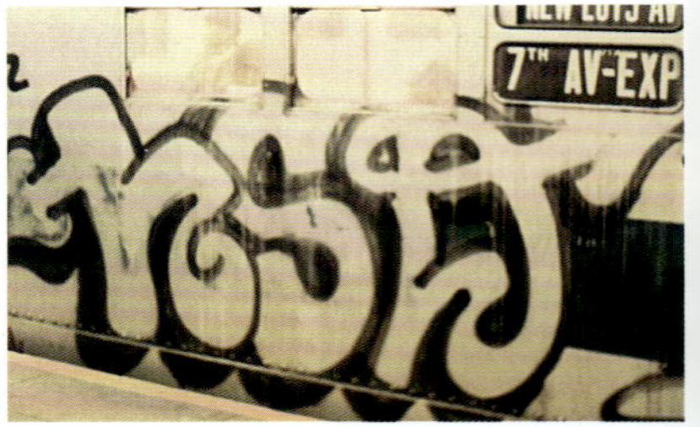

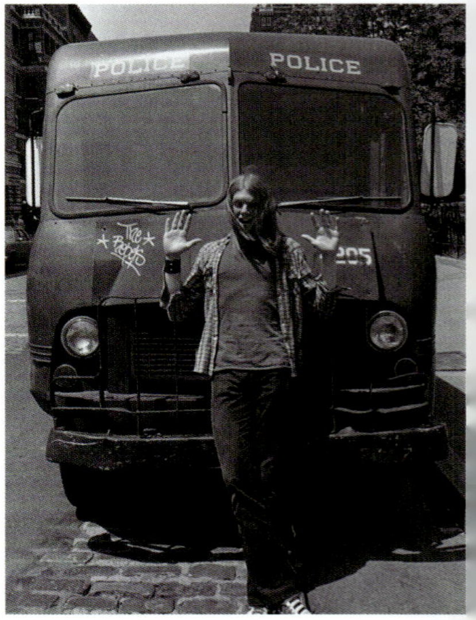

Photograph by Flint Gennari.
New York City, 1975.
Detail top: Photograph by Bryan Mechutan (Uni).
New York City, 1975.
Detail bottom: Photograph by Flint Gennari.
New York City, 1975.

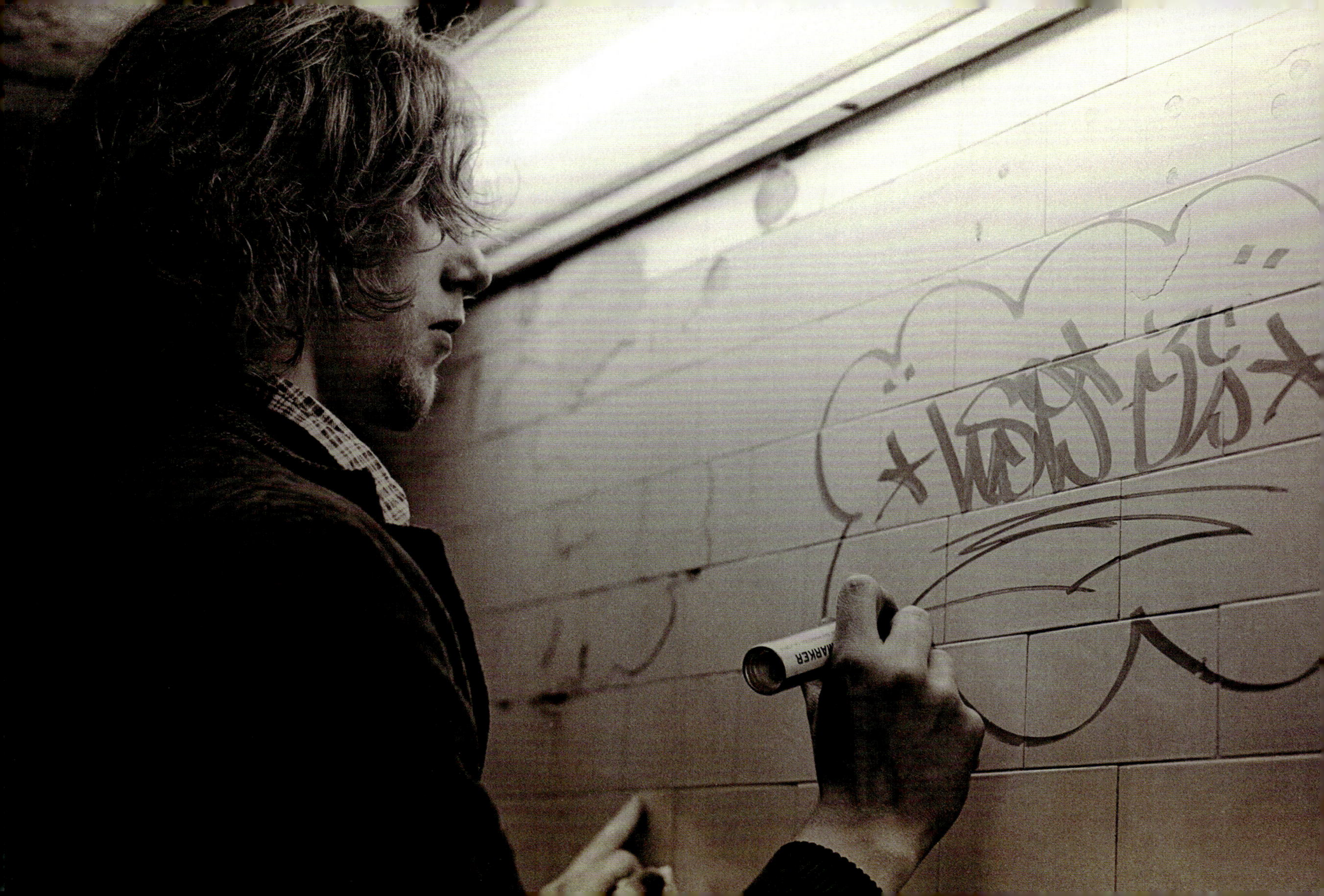

Ludo

Parisian street artist Ludo is probably best known for his 2009 "Nature's Revenge" series—to the point where some people still mistakenly believe that to be his name.

Bunches of grapes with skulls instead of berries, orchids with CCTV cameras emanating from their pistils, Ludo's hybrid vegetal freaks were all done in gray-scale and pasted up with a pea-green wash to emphasize certain areas. His use of computer aided design (CAD) lent a technical, architectural, almost futuristic look to his organic pieces as they lurked on the walls of dark alleyways.

Ludo uses different techniques, with screen printing and paint his preferred choices, but he's also been known to switch to using large printing machines and painting detail over it with acrylic when the scale of the piece demands it, which it often does. Flowers mixed with military weapons may be reminiscent of 1970s antiwar protest imagery, and some read a radically ecological ideology into his work. However, the artist himself insists his message is far simpler: It's about having respect for one's surroundings. A sweetly ironic message for a young rebel still widely considered a vandal by the authorities.

Photographs by George Macdonald.
Right: Bricklane, London, 2009.
Far right: Shoreditch, London, 2009.

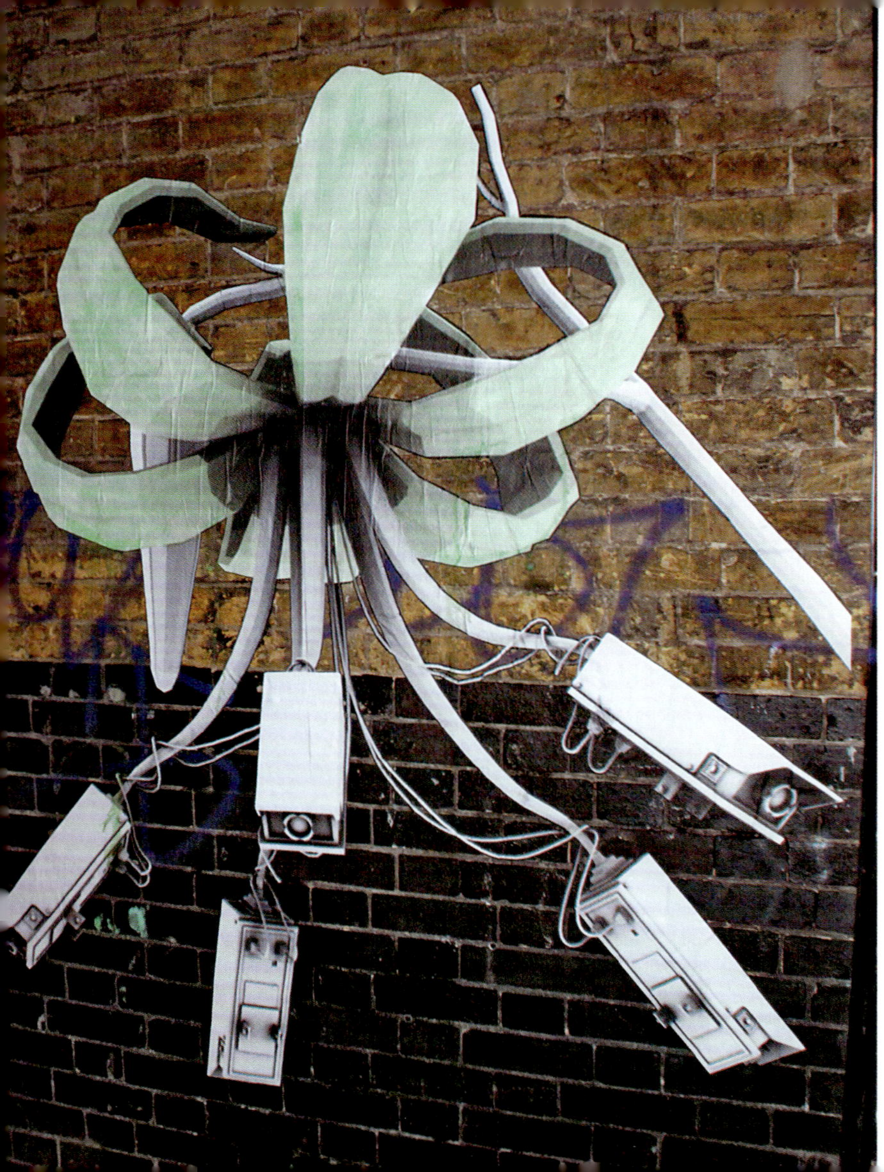

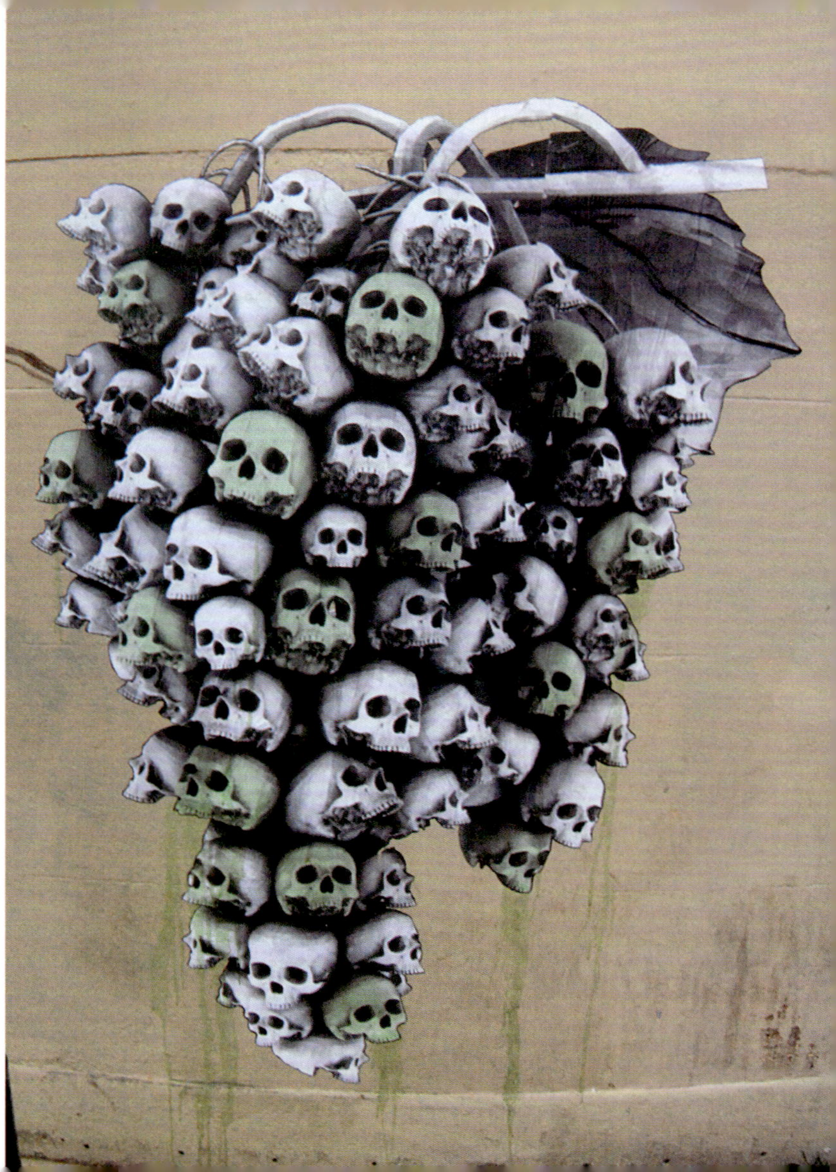

Luz-interruptus

In the endless quest to broaden the scope of what is acceptable street art, a school of technologically inclined artists began experimenting with electronic public art in the first decade of the 2000s. Following in the footsteps of the world-renowned Graffiti Research Lab [see 153], Spain-based crew Luzinterruptus creates large-scale light installations.

In the summer of 2010, as part of the Rizoma Festival, the crew created a quintessential installation called "Floating Presences" in the mountains of La Mancha, in which it placed an army of humanlike figures, with installed lights glowing from within them, in the streams that flowed through the entire town. Eighty figures populated the waters, creating a surreal, supernatural effect.

In another installation, Luzinterruptus installed reading lights in one hundred locations throughout Ljubljana, Slovenia, for the Lighting Guerilla Festival. This project, titled "Private Readings in Public Sites," included the installation of cushions and books in dilapidated, less-frequented areas of the embattled city.

Luzinterruptus continues to travel, creating its light installations and street interventions in conjunction with festivals and galleries across the globe.

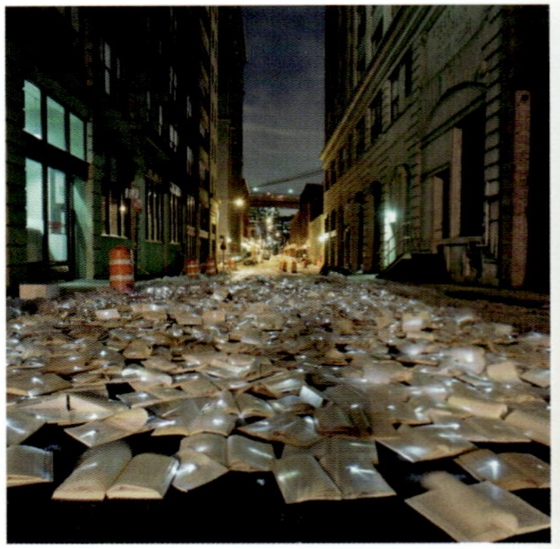

Photographs courtesy of Luzinterruptus.
Molinicos, Spain, 2010.
Detail: Brooklyn, New York, 2010.

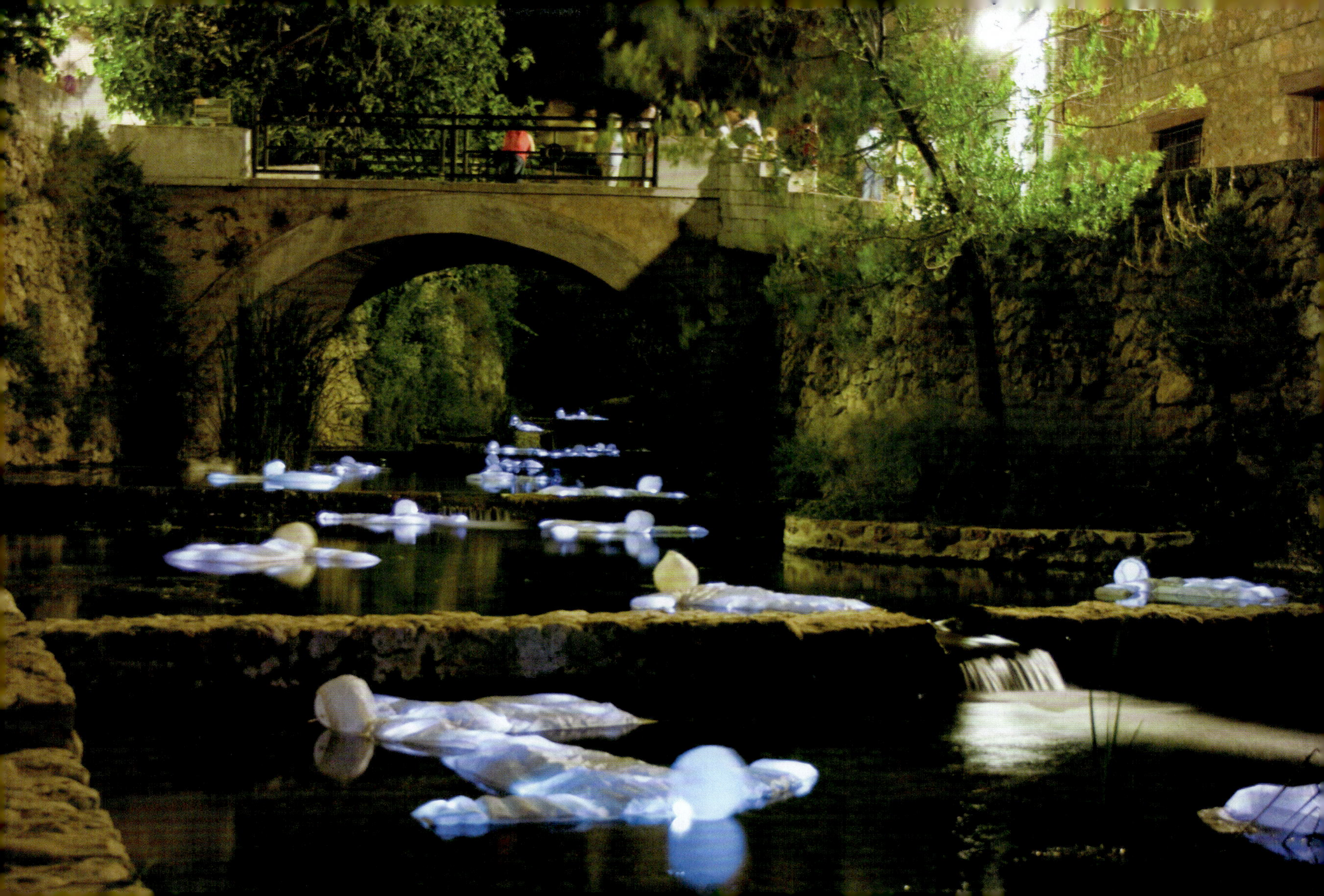

Maclaim

The Maclaim crew hails from Weimar, Germany. Among contemporary spray painters, the crew is elite. The four artists—Akut, Case, Rusk, and Tasso—who founded the Maclaim crew in 2001 have established themselves as international masters of aerosol photorealism. The level of detail in their work is unprecedented, and they have built their formidable reputation by traveling to commercial graffiti jams throughout the world and mesmerizing crowds with large, theme-based works that combine grotesque, erotic, and cultural elements with traditional graffiti lettering.

Apparently, some of the Maclaim artists forgo preliminary sketches and work directly from photographs, reproducing portraits like human cameras. The lettering in Maclaim productions is proficient, but is often overshadowed by the power of their imagery. Purists may wonder if they are truly graffiti artists, or artists who happen to like graffiti. But in the forty years since graffiti's inception, change has been the only constant. Superkool 223 [see 325] would undoubtedly be impressed to see a Maclaim mural of him—painting a train in 1973, at age fifteen—on an Athenian wall in 2009.

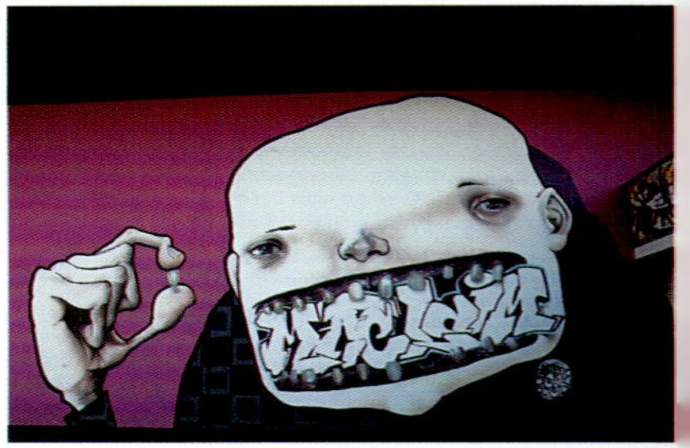

Photographs courtesy of Maclaim.
Splash Festical, Fenopolis, Germany, 2010.
Detail: Vissingen, The Netherlands, 2008.

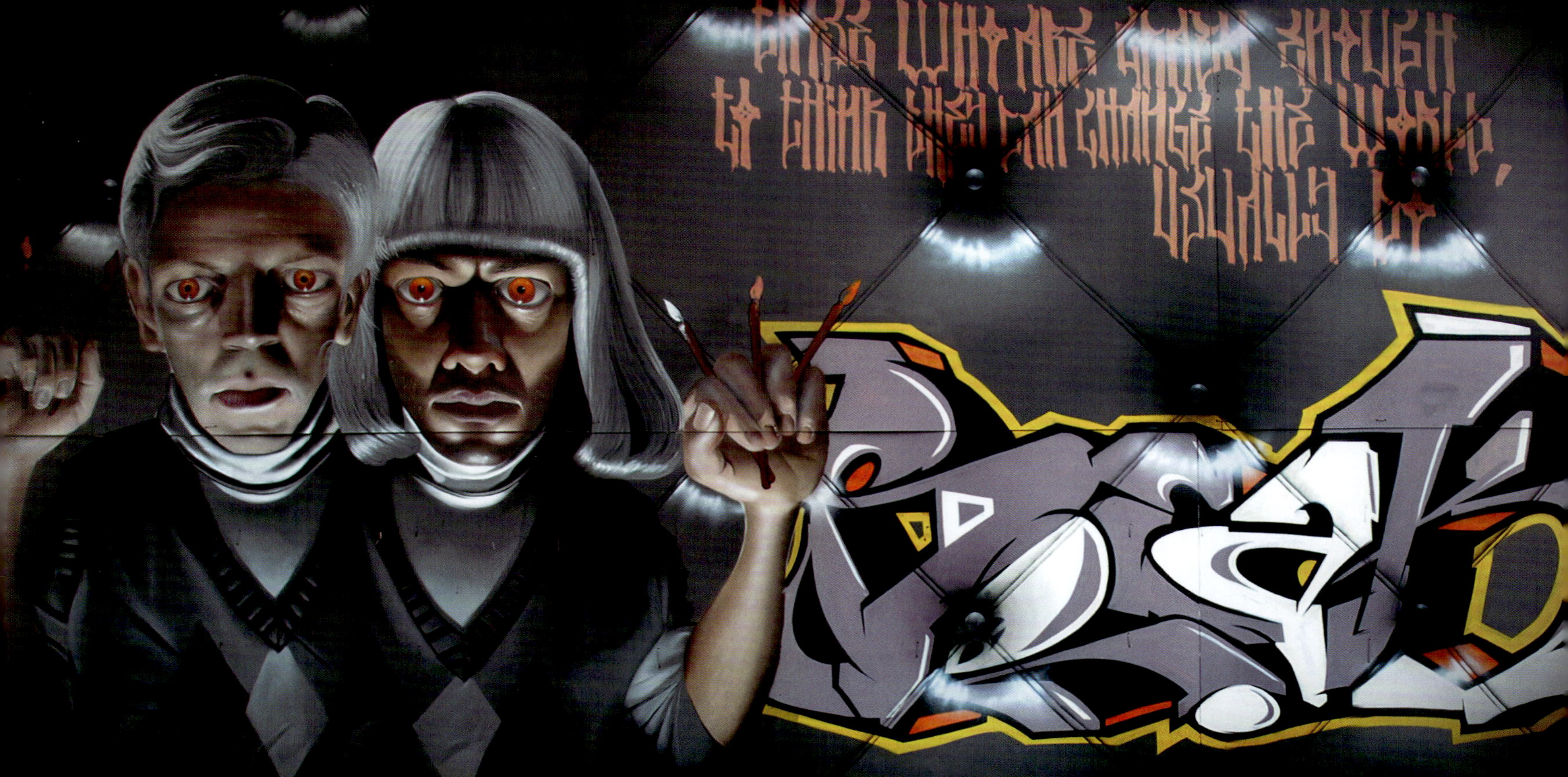

Mad C

Mad C began writing in 1996 after reading the book *Graffiti Art*; though, by her own admission, her career didn't really take off until two years later, when she entered the university in Halle, Germany. It was in Halle that she became part of the graffiti scene and started earning the respect of other writers by participating in numerous collaborative walls.

Mad C has always had a preference for letters, trying out as many styles as possible and inventing many of her own along the way. She often seems to downplay her work on characters, figures that are generally plucked from pop culture and rendered with great alacrity.

Mad C has made a successful leap from murals to the art world and shown in galleries throughout Europe. While her graffiti roots remain strong, she is able to strive for more in a gallery setting—you won't see her name in Wild Style letters on canvas, but it's within this sphere that she now prefers to take risks.

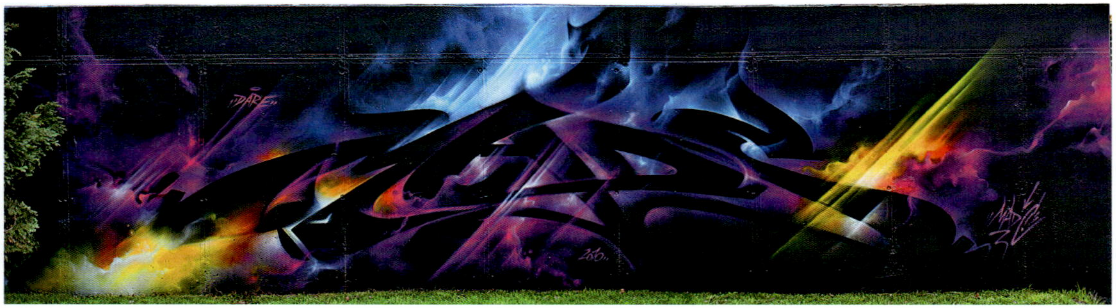

Photographs courtesy of Mad C.
Halle, Germany, 2009.
Detail: Halle, Germany, 2010.

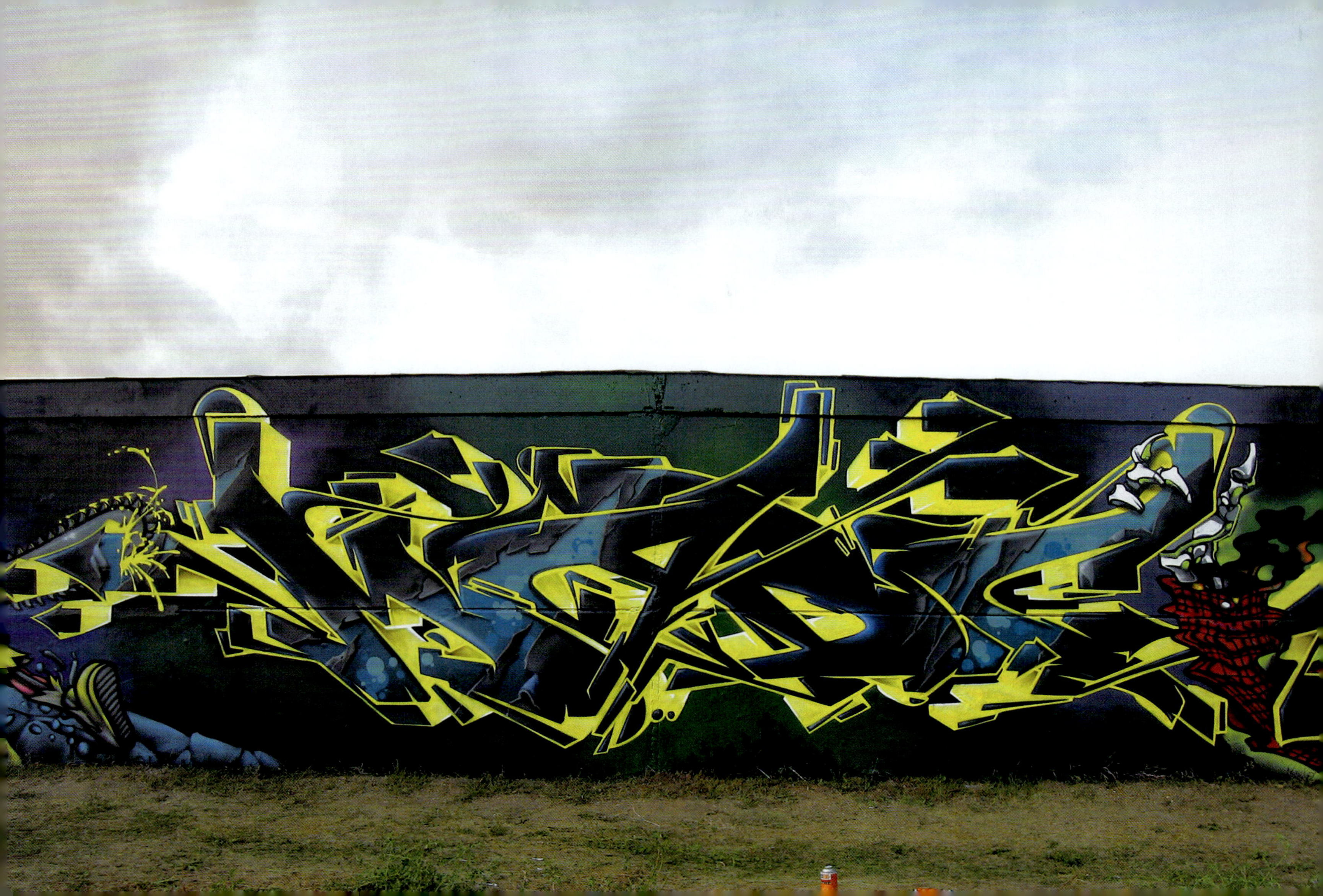

markers

As writers' ranks increased, competition raged, and markers primarily used by art schools in calligraphy classes were discovered and co-opted by a new school of artists. A Pilot was the next step up from the skinny-tipped Dri Mark. You could unscrew the top and flood its felt-filled intestines with Flo-master ink, then stick pins in the tip to widen the nib.

Opaque markers solved the problem of writing on glass, clear plastic, and dark surfaces. The Pentel, a marker filled with milky-white ink, offered writers the ability to fog up the the insides of windows and to decorate mailboxes citywide.

The Mini-Wide, a flat plastic wonder with a ¾-inch flat felt tip, became the greatest marker of all time. Concealable in socks, in underwear, or up your sleeve, the refillable Mini-Wide, when placed in the right hands, rendered the most beautiful tag of any misappropriated implement in history. Its big brother, the Uni-Wide, was basically a 1½-inch version of the Mini; it lacked practicality, as larger spaces and longer names made adequate surfaces harder to find.

DIY types fashioned homemade markers out of empty deodorant dispensers and dismembered blackboard erasers. They produced sloppy tags that dripped uncontrollably and were looked down upon—exactly the aesthetic today's writer strives for.

**Photograph by Monica LoCascio.
New York City, 2010.**

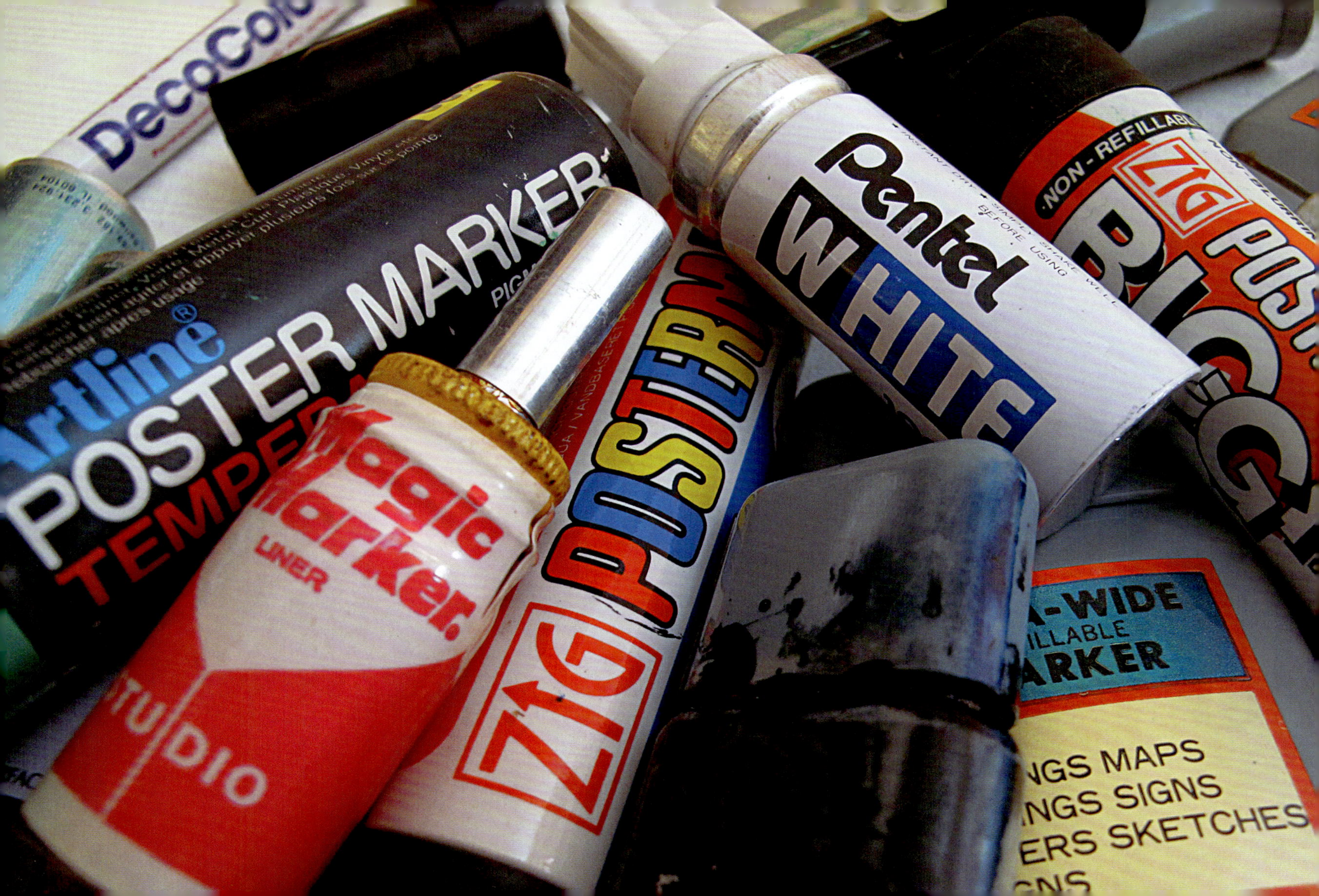

Artline
POSTER MARKER
LINER
STUDIO
ZIG
Pentel
WHITE
BEFORE USING
NON-REFILLABLE
ZIG
WIDE
MAPS
SIGNS
SKETCHES

Mars-1

Born in the rocky mountains of Boulder, Colorado, Mario Martinez, aka Mars-1, relocated with his family at an early age to Fresno, California, where he began to see disturbing images painted on local streets. By the age of thirteen, he was putting up his own paint in his own way, delving deep into the backdrop of his imagination to create what, at the time, was completely foreign to the world of graffiti. Even in his youth, Martinez was heavily influenced and inspired by 1960s-era art: psychedelics, aliens, science fiction, government conspiracies, and other things that defy description.

He chose the name Mars-1 while attending the Academy of Art University in San Francisco during the mid-1990s, and his robotic Mars men soon began popping up on walls all over northern California. He began participating in mural projects around San Francisco, and it was only a matter of time before the world of contemporary art came calling. Mars-1 started showing in San Francisco galleries around the turn of the century. Over the last decade, Mars-1 has gone on to show at many prestigious pop-surrealism and modern-art galleries around the globe, including the now infamous Lineage Gallery in Philadelphia, the Black Market Gallery in San Francisco, and the Jonathan LeVine Gallery in New York. Mars-1 still lives humbly on Haight Street in San Francisco with his wife, Mikas, and their son, Atlas.

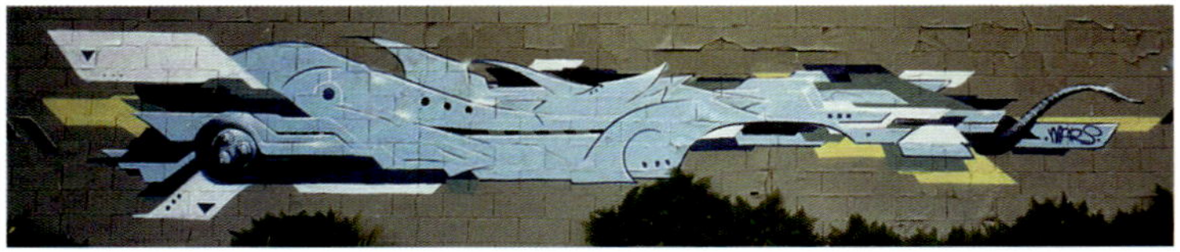

Photograph by Mario Martinez.
Detail: Photograph by Matt Isles.
Oakland, California, 2002.

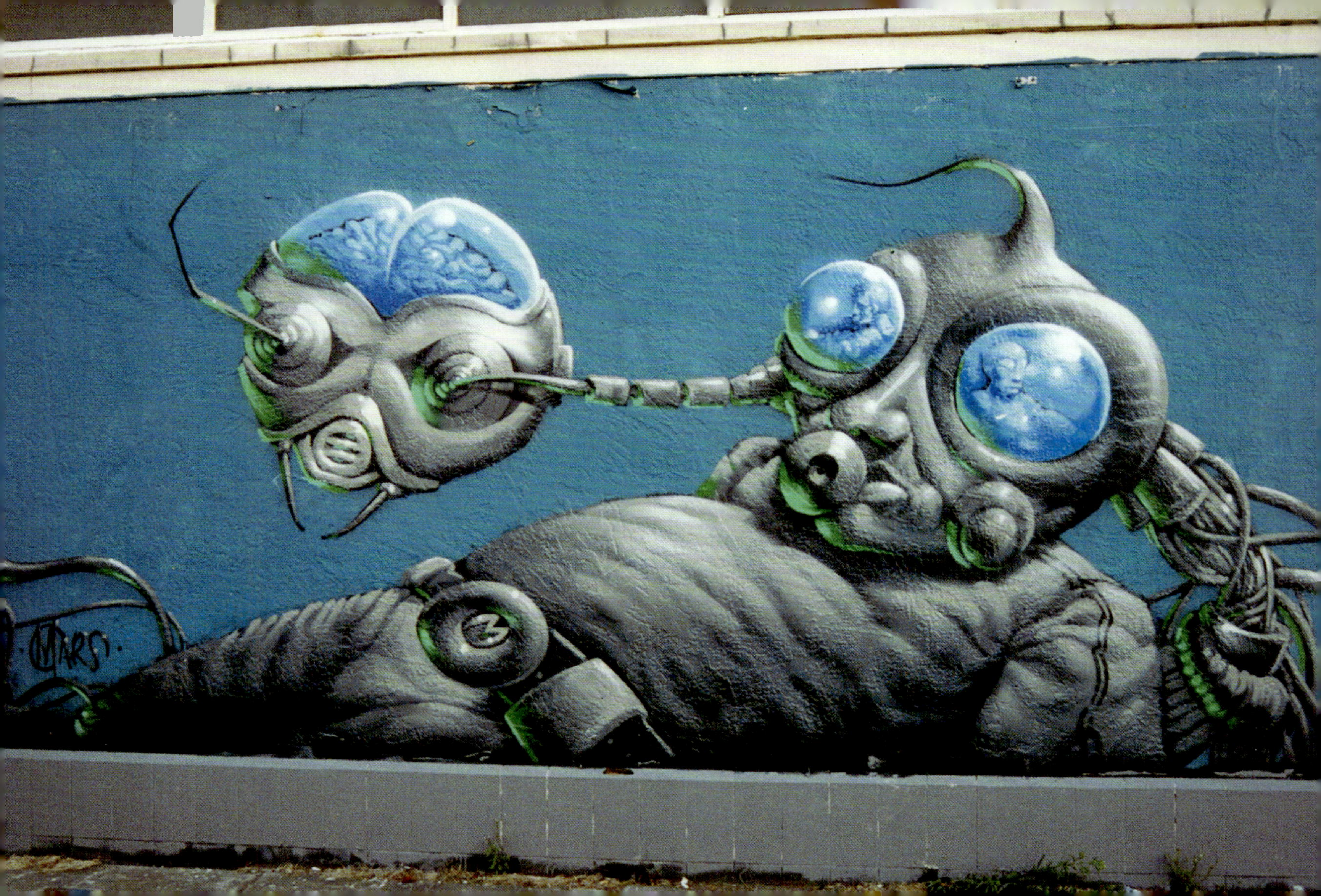
MARS

Pedro Matos

One of the babies of the street-art world is a young Portuguese artist by the name of Pedro Matos. Taking a few pages from the books of Ethos [see 116] and Gaia [see 142], Matos is best known for his intricate, realistic pencil-drawn portraits featuring the worn faces of everyday figures. Matos's detailed faces often pop out of acid-washed backgrounds sprinkled with subtle graffiti tags, giving his work a timeless edge. Matos, who calls Lisbon home, wheatpastes these characters, in large scale, to public walls.

At the tender age of twenty-one, Matos has earned a respect usually reserved for artists several years his senior. A graduate of art college in Lisbon, he creates works of undeniable skill that radiate a humanity typically only present in candid photographs, and that convey an innate grasp of technical skill that exceeds his years.

In 2008, at the age of nineteen, Matos participated in his first show, "Pour Me Some Smoke," at the Carmichael Gallery in Los Angeles, California. Since then, he has exhibited his fine-art work in Spain, Britain, and the United States. Matos also continues to make street-based works.

Photograph by Ribes Sappa
Rome, 2009.

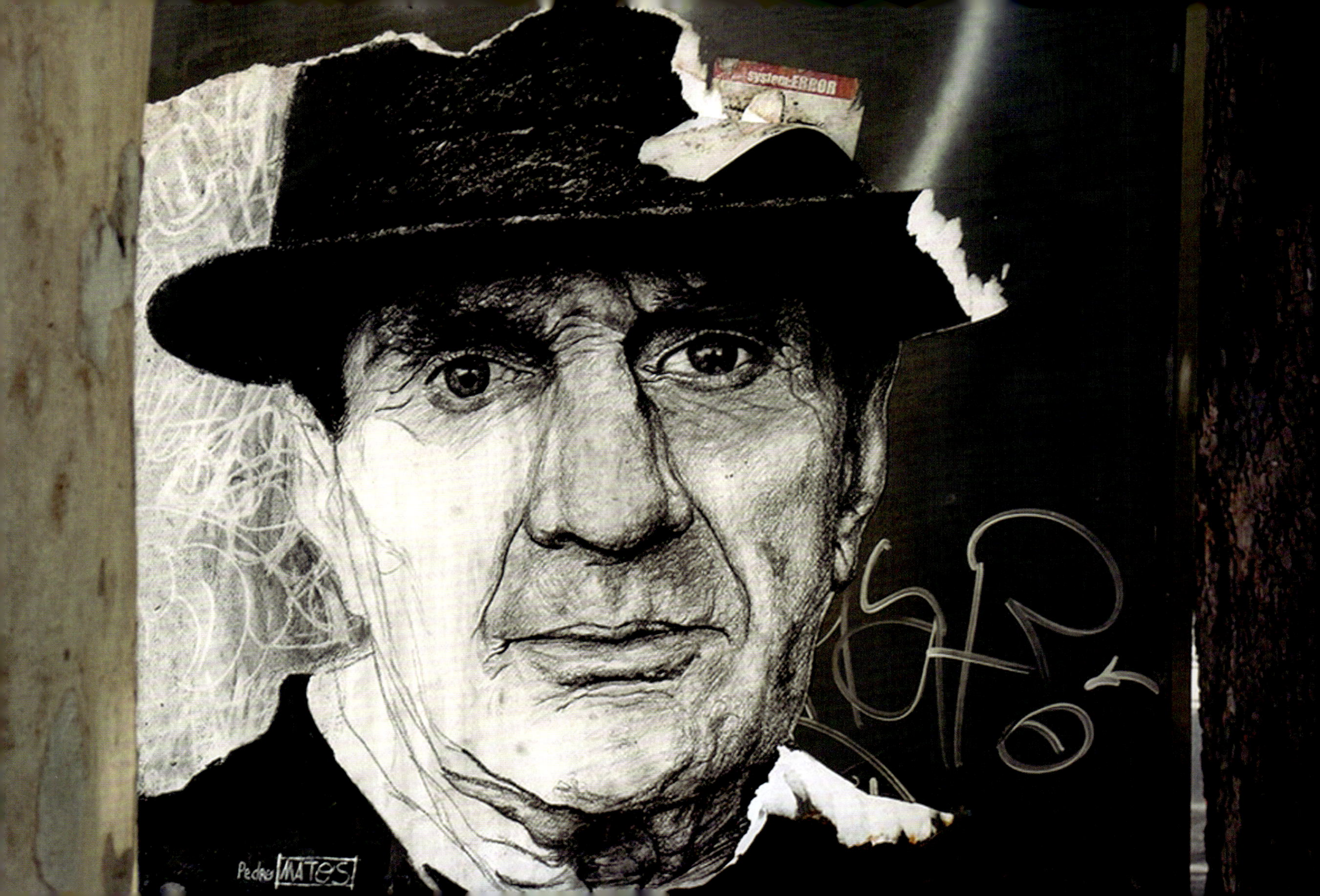
Pedro MATES

Barry McGee

Few artists have achieved such a seamless crossover from graffiti king to art-world prince as Barry McGee. Born and bred in San Francisco and now in his mid-forties, McGee graduated from the San Francisco Art Institute with a degree in painting in 1991. Tagging most often under the name Twist, he made a consistent and prolific name for himself in San Francisco throughout the 1990s, when graffiti experienced a revival. His fluid hand style, intricate caricature work, and social commentary were instantly recognizable, and they soon became emblems of the period. He traveled with Aaron Rose's famous group show, "Beautiful Losers," painting alongside his then-wife Margaret Kilgallen, with whom McGee had a daughter and who died of cancer in 2001. He was also prominently featured in the film accompanying Rose's project.

McGee went on to a flourishing fine-art career, including solo shows at Deitch Projects in New York City, numerous museum shows internationally, and a number of biennial appearances—most notably at the Venice Biennale in 2001, after which his street work started being stolen from walls.

Famous for his reclusiveness, McGee rarely grants interviews or poses for photographs. Despite his powerful influence on the aesthetics of the urban-art world, McGee still lives a secluded life in San Francisco with his daughter, Asha.

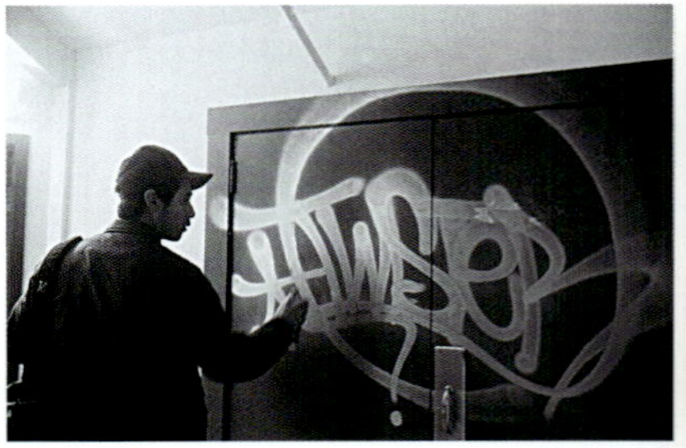

Photograph by Matt Isles.
San Francisco, 2002.
Detail: Photograph by Cheryl Dunn.
San Francisco, 1998.

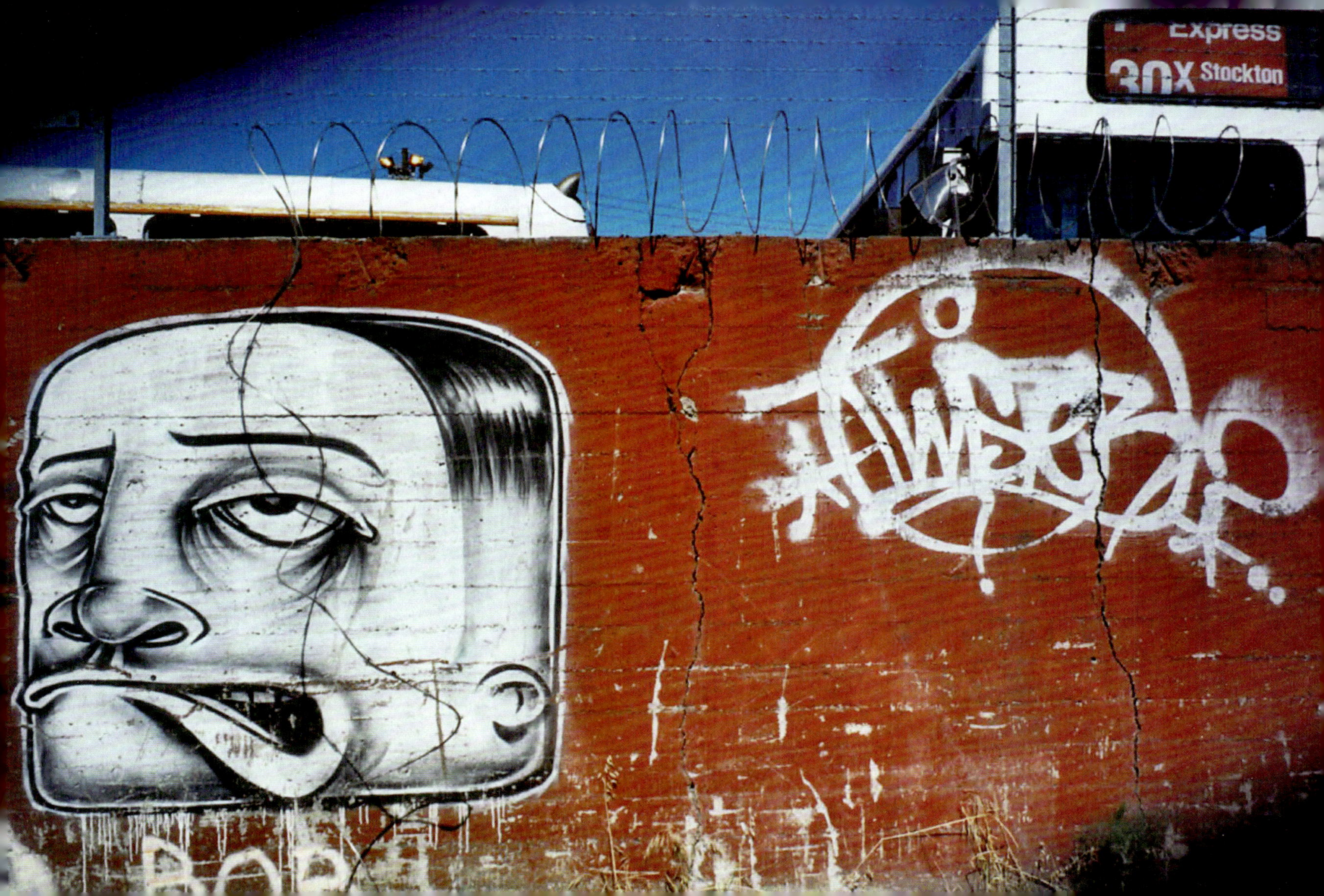
Express
30X Stockton

M-City

Known worldwide as M-City (the title of his remarkable stencil project), Marius Waras was born in 1978 in Gdynia, a seaport town in Poland. A graduate of the department of graphic art at the Academy of Fine Arts in Gdańsk, M-City is Poland's best-known artist working in public spheres.

Always intrigued by industrial spaces and their surroundings, M-City creates large-scale murals inspired by the factories, hydroelectric plants, chimneys, and cranes that dominate his native town. Meticulously crafted, with layers of stencils and seemingly limitless stark black-and-white details, these murals can now be seen throughout the globe. Recent projects include a large-scale three-dimensional sculptural version of an M-City stencil factory. Eager to integrate with his surroundings, M-City prefers to create his work in legal spaces where he can focus on a project for days at a time.

M-City's unique visual language has graced the streets of countless cities, including Warsaw, Berlin, Paris, São Paulo, Budapest, London, Prague, and New York. Along with such notable stencil artists as Hutch and B-Toy, M-City was a special guest at the 2010 Bogotá Stencil Festival. His work has also been featured in both group and solo shows spanning the continents.

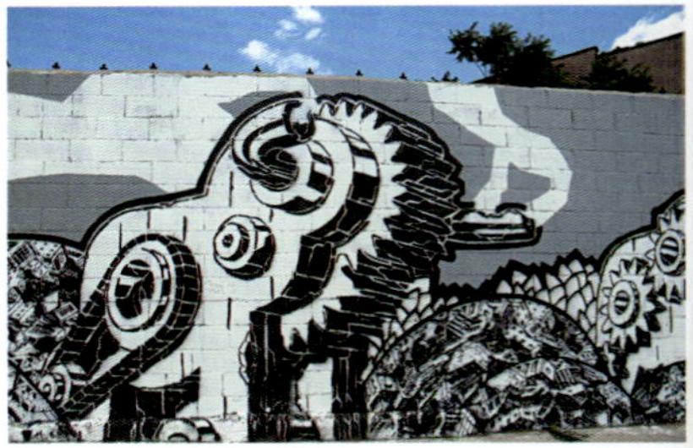

Photograph by Lois Stavsky. Brooklyn, New York, 2010.
Detail: Photograph by Tara Murray. Brooklyn, New York, 2010.

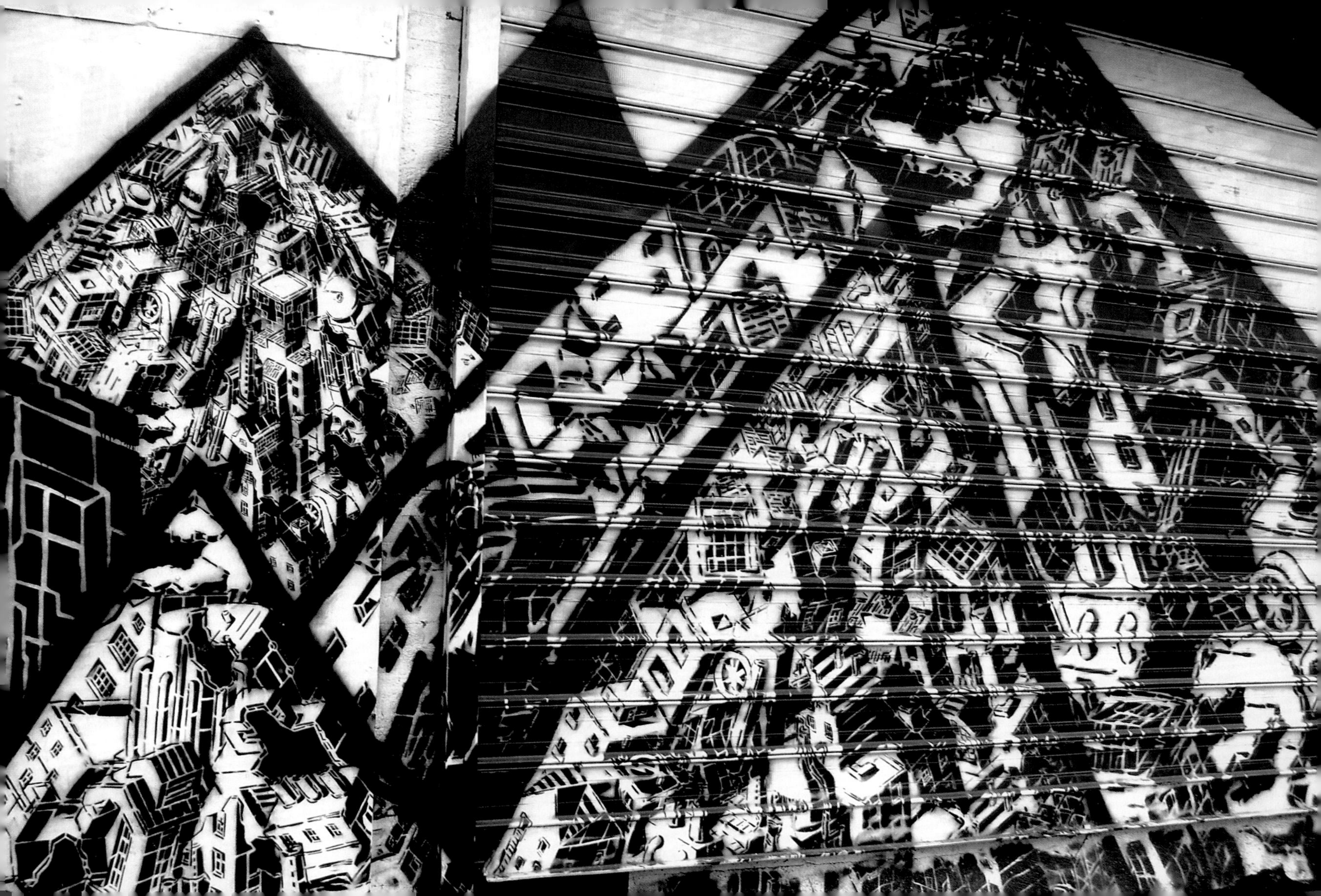

Mear One

Mear One, born Kalen Ockerman in 1971, has been referred to as the Michelangelo of graffiti. A native of Santa Cruz, California, he moved to inner-city Los Angeles at an early age, living on welfare for a time. On his own and in collaboration with the City Bomb Squad and West Coast Artist crews, Mear One has been writing for more than twenty years.

Perceiving art as "a weapon of mass liberation" and graffiti, in particular, as "the voice of the dissatisfied soul," Mear One challenges our assumptions about such concepts as identity, reality, and truth, and spurs us through his art to question our priorities. His name is an acronym for Manifest Energy and Radiate, as he is intent on inspiring people to use their own energies to creatively challenge the status quo. With his deftly crafted surreal images, characterized by vibrant colors and strong narratives, he has achieved international status and is represented in galleries at home and abroad.

Largely self-taught, Mear One cites a range of influences, including the late Skate One, Walt Disney, Salvador Dalí, Alex Grey, Diego Rivera, and Ron English (see 113). Ever evolving, Mear One also works as a graphic designer of clothing, album covers, and political posters.

Photograph by Steam 156. 1989.

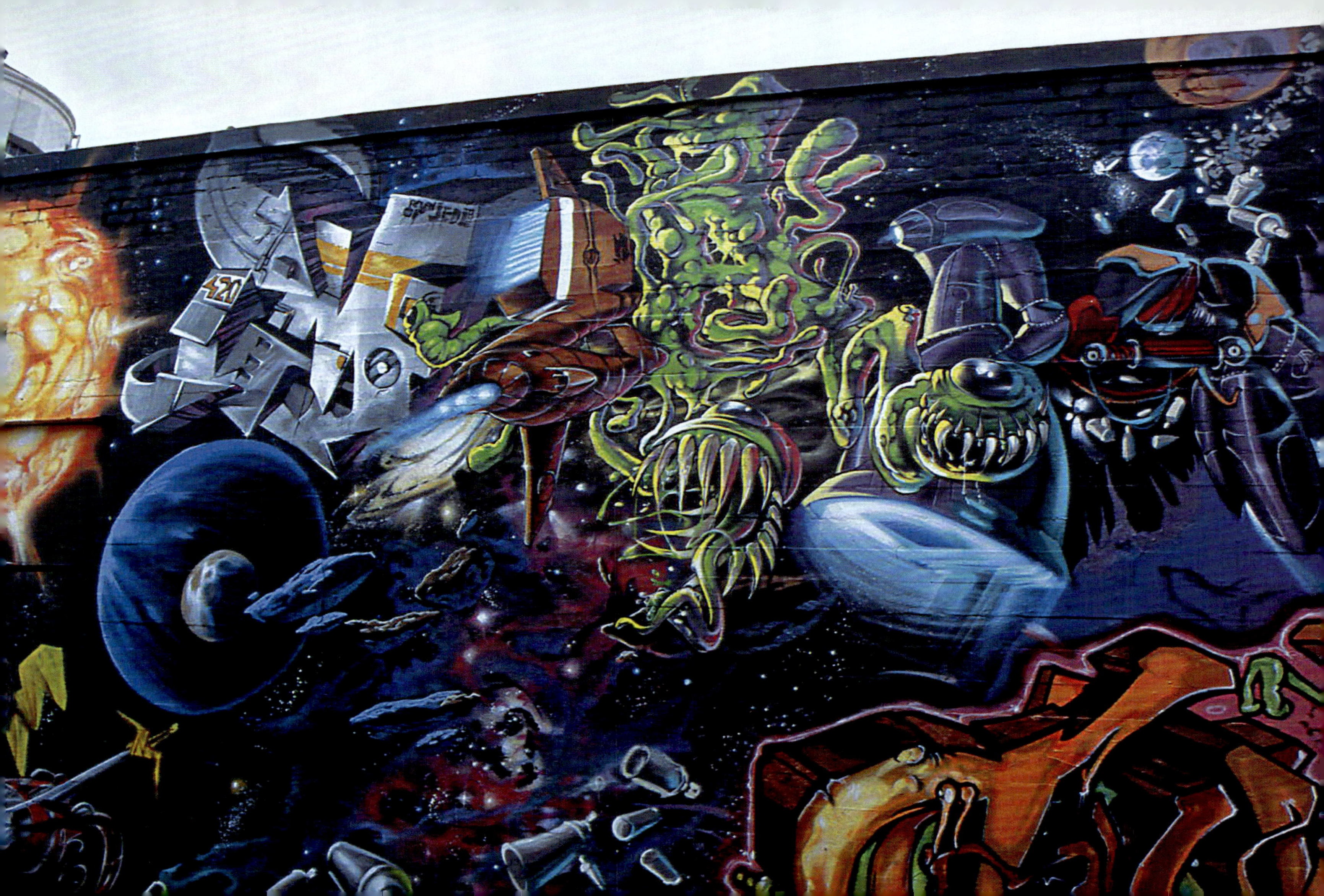
420

memorial walls

Memorial walls make you wonder: Who was that person? How did he die? How old was she? The portraits, and the accompanying written prayers or messages, often tell us little more than the name of the deceased. More often than not, the dates of birth and death inform us that they died too young, and we assume the worst. Have you ever seen a memorial wall with a portrait of an old person?

These walls serve a purpose. They advertise a tragic event to an uninformed public in hope that a collective grief will be easier to bear. Some walls pay tribute to fallen idols: Big Pun, Keith Haring [see 160], Princess Diana, and Michael Jackson have all received aerosol tributes. The September 11 terrorist attacks on New York City provided the impetus for perhaps more memorial walls than any other event in history.

Graffiti writers have long honored their fallen comrades in this fashion. In Oakland, California, the local talent painted a huge wall, each one painting the name "Dream," a friend murdered in a robbery attempt. Recently, the amazingly talented Swiss graffiti artist Dare succumbed to brain cancer. Trains and walls dedicated to his memory appeared on the Internet daily from every country where spray paint is sold. A spray-painted portrait of a young black man named Killa Ben smiles from a wall on a Brooklyn street corner . . . to be continued.

Photograph by Ernie Paniccioli.
New York City, 1996.

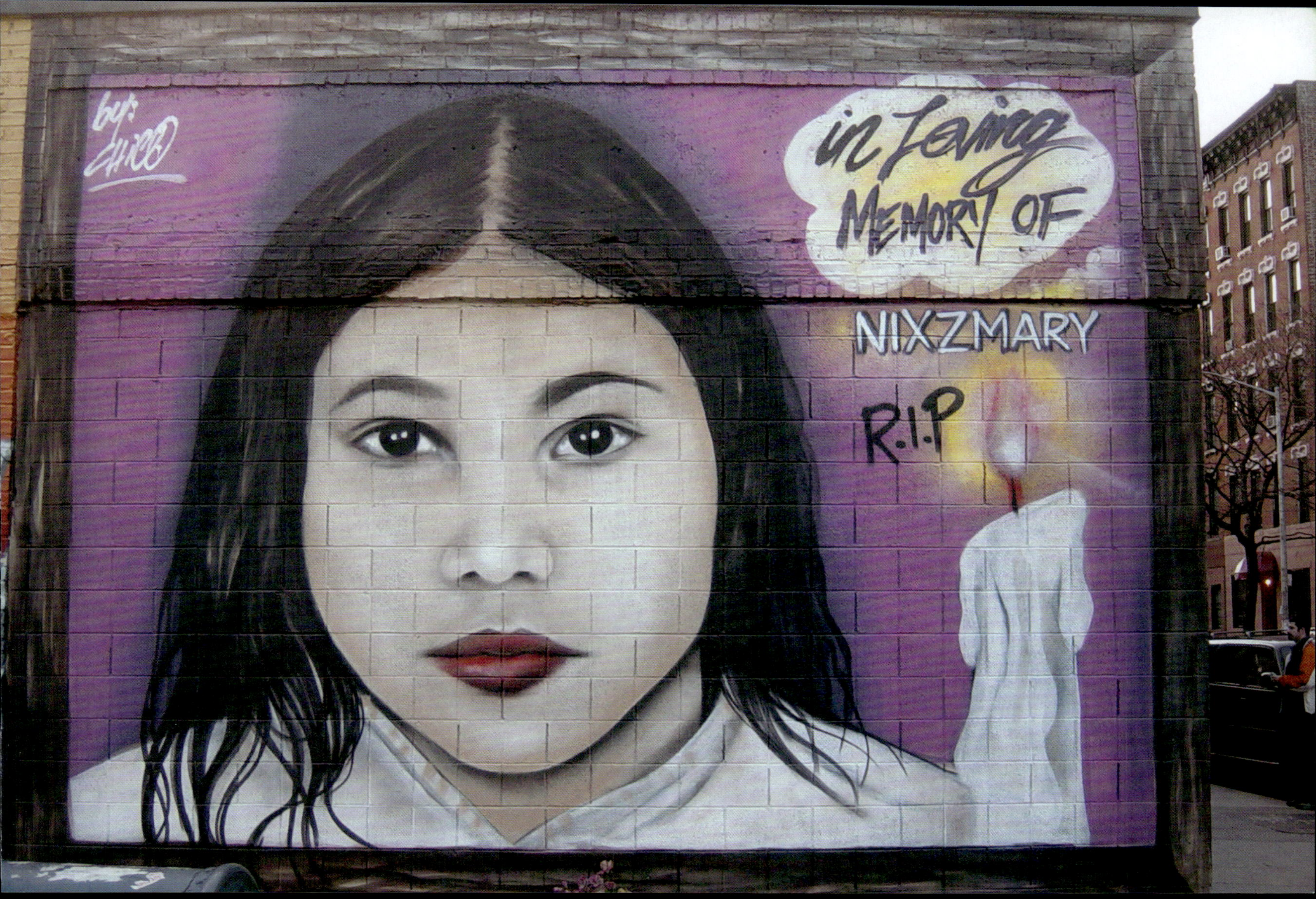
in Loving
MEMORY OF
NIXZMARY
R.I.P

Merda

With bright colors and Wild Style 3-D letters, old-school Australian graffiti artist Jay Rankine, aka Merda, began to make his mark on the walls of Melbourne in the early 1980s. One of the first writers to hit the walls and trains of his city, Merda was inspired by Melbourne's legendary hip-hop-inspired graffiti artist, GS38. Schooled by films like *Beat Street* and *Wild Style* and the book *Subway Art* [see 323], GS38 taught Merda, an art student, how to create outlines and craft letters. They formed the two-man crew the Wild Boyz, and together they hit Melbourne's trains with spray paint for about a year in the mid-1980s.

Merda's impact on Melbourne's graffiti scene was so strong that by the late 1980s, he was garnering international attention in various global graffiti magazines and receiving accolades from such writers as Phase 2 [see 255] for his uniquely intricate letter development. With photos of his work influencing aspiring graffiti artists in Europe, Merda was instrumental in introducing a more advanced 3-D style lettering to the world.

Currently working as a designer and illustrator, Merda creates everything from glow-in-the-dark skate decks to ads for Absolut Vodka. On the website blog.imerda.com, Merda documents his current projects, as well as his earlier involvement in Melbourne's emerging graffiti scene back in the '80s.

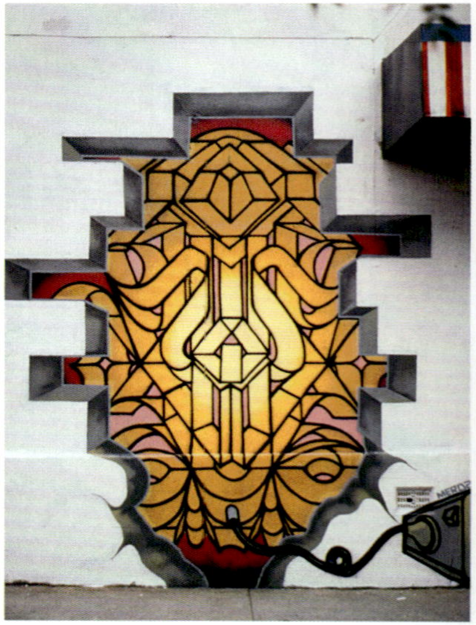

Photographs courtesy of Merda.
***Murda*. South Yana, VIC Australia, 1987.**
Detail: *M*. Greville Street, Praham, VIC Australia, 1989.

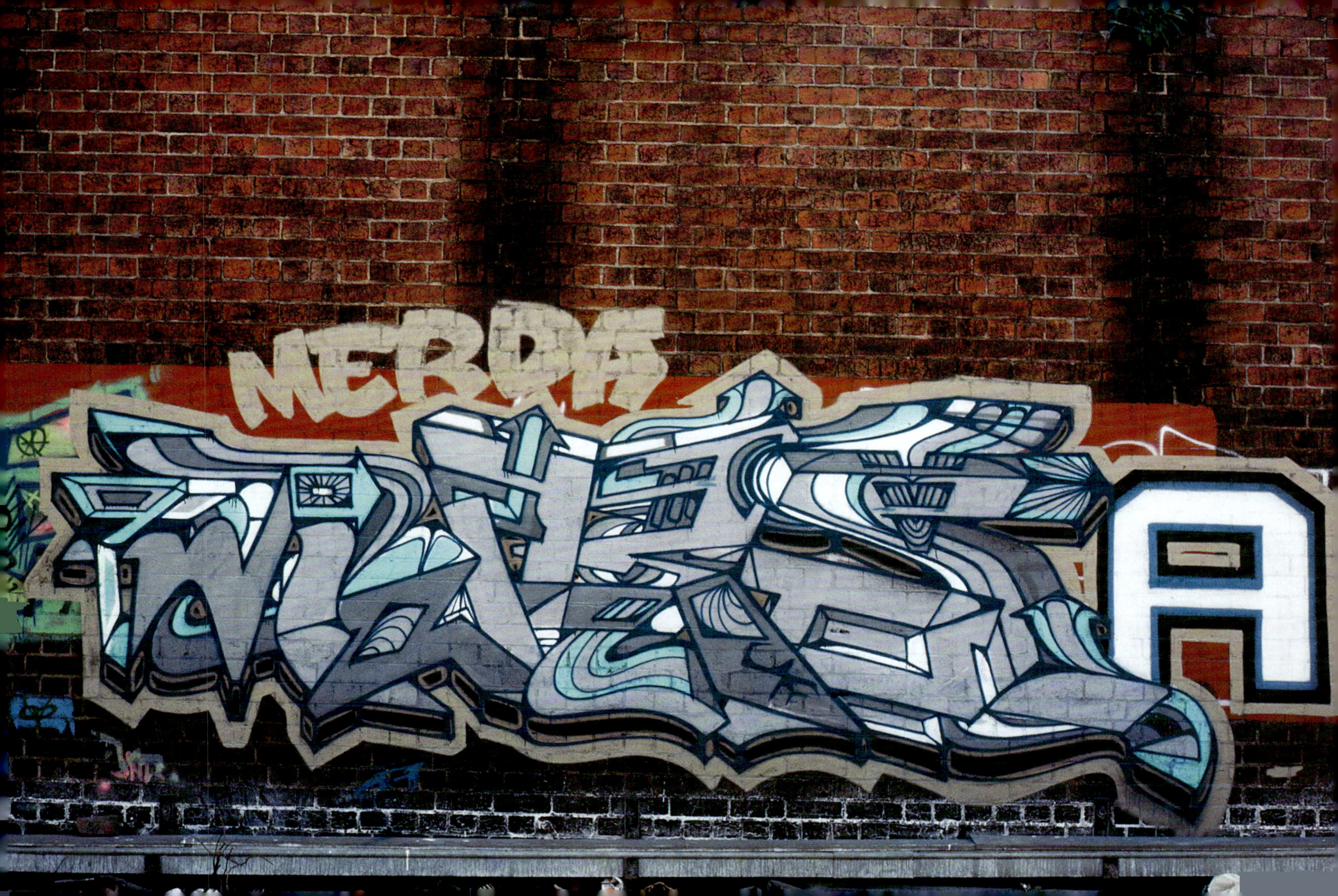
MERDA

Jerome Mesnager

Known for the graceful white ghost figure that haunts Paris's landscape, Jerome Mesnager seeks his city's oldest walls to use as his canvases. "More and more I find debris interesting," he says. "It has color and an atmosphere that carries emotion." His signature ghost has made its way, in fact, to such ancient surfaces as China's Great Wall and Egypt's pyramids. Although Mesnager's ghosts and are often mistaken for stencils, they are drawn freehand. "When I find the right door or wall, everything goes fast," he explains. "I jump against the wall in the pose I want to represent, and I paint very fast. It takes twenty-six seconds."

Born in 1961 in Colmar, France, Mesnager spent his early years in Paris. He attended the École Boulle in Paris for four years, where he studied the art of cabinet-making. In 1982, he spearheaded Zig-Zag, a group of ten artists who took their art into streets and abandoned factories.

Along with Blek le Rat (see 038), Jeff Aerosol (see 181), and Miss Tic (see 225), Mesnager is considered one of the pioneers of French street art. Mesnager's work can now be found in museums, galleries, and commercial venues throughout France. But he prefers painting on the streets, where he is, in his own words, "making art for the people."

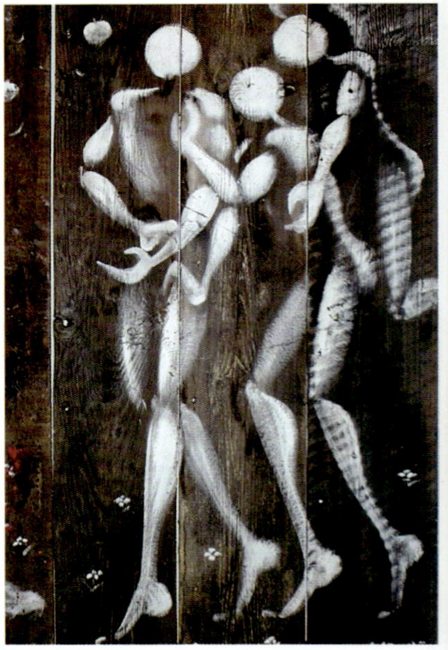

Photographs by Lois Stavsky. Paris, 2009.

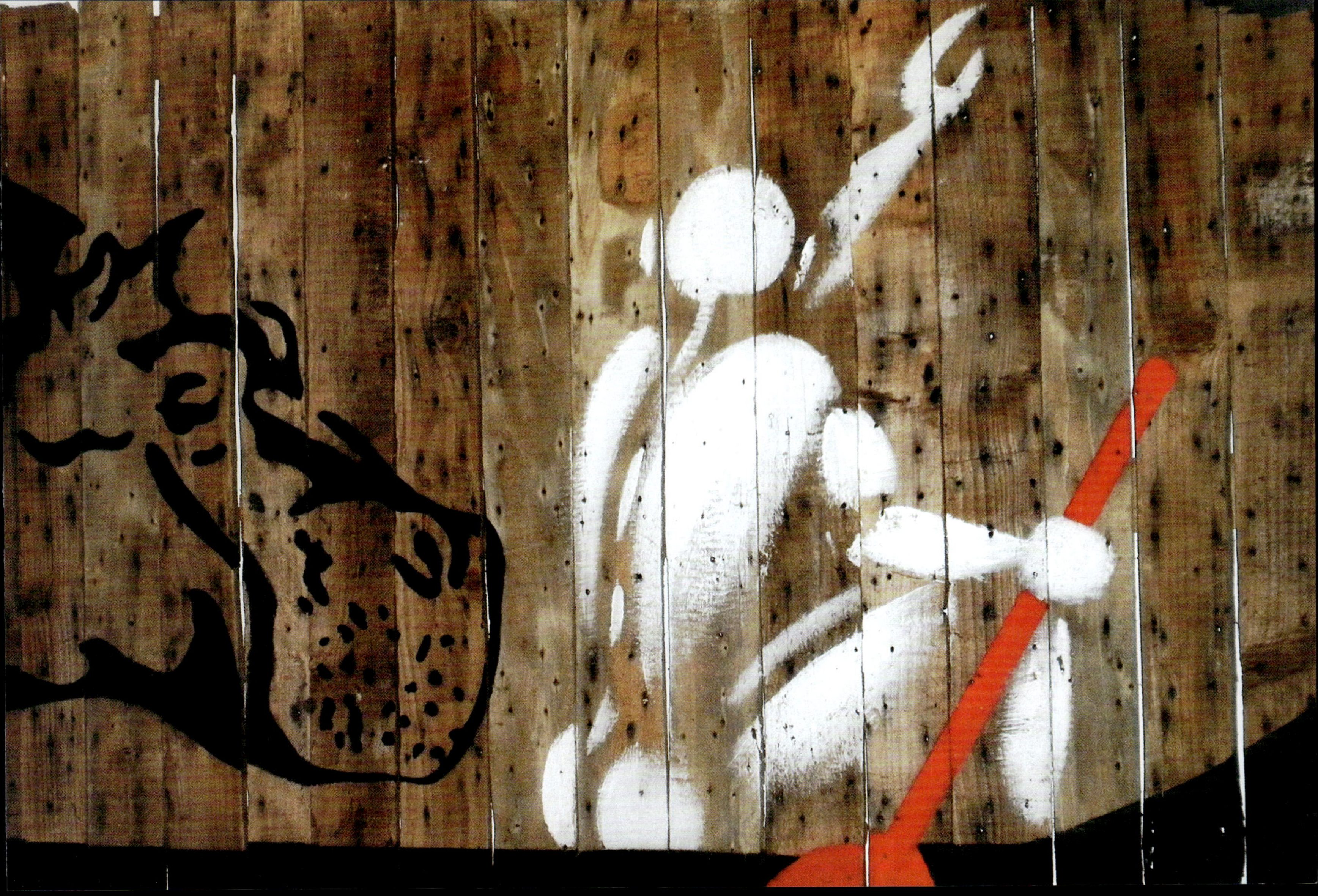

Metal Man Ed

Ed "Metal Man" Walker grew up on the outskirts of San Francisco. He worked for his grandfather's company, which manufactured high-temperature furnaces used in making microchips in Silicon Valley. After watching the documentary *Style Wars* [see 322], Walker decided to follow in the footsteps of his newly discovered aerosol heroes. Beginning in 1986, Metal Man Ed put in a few years painting legal walls in the San Francisco Bay Area while working as a machinist in his father's business. After getting busted painting a legal wall in 1996, he decided to give graffiti a rest.

Eventually, Metal Man Ed began piecing again, until he discovered the work of graffiti-artist-turned-sculptor Carlos "Mare 139" Rodriguez. An arrow on one of Rodriguez's graffiti-inspired metal sculptures pointed Walker in a new direction. He decided to trade in his spray cans for a welder.

After making a couple of sculptures of friends' names, Metal Man Ed, an avid collector of vintage spray paint, decided to make thirty-inch-high mockups of four long-lost Krylon flavors as an homage to the good old days. Walker soon expanded his metal menu to include replicas of New York City subway trains. He has constructed train facades for Marc Ecko and designed subway-car tattoo booths for Tuff City Styles. Metal Man Ed continues to create heavy metal and is currently raising money to fund a book-and-movie project documenting the life and work of his best friend, graffiti icon Iz the Wiz [see 177].

Photograph courtesy of Metal Man Ed. San Francisco, 2009.

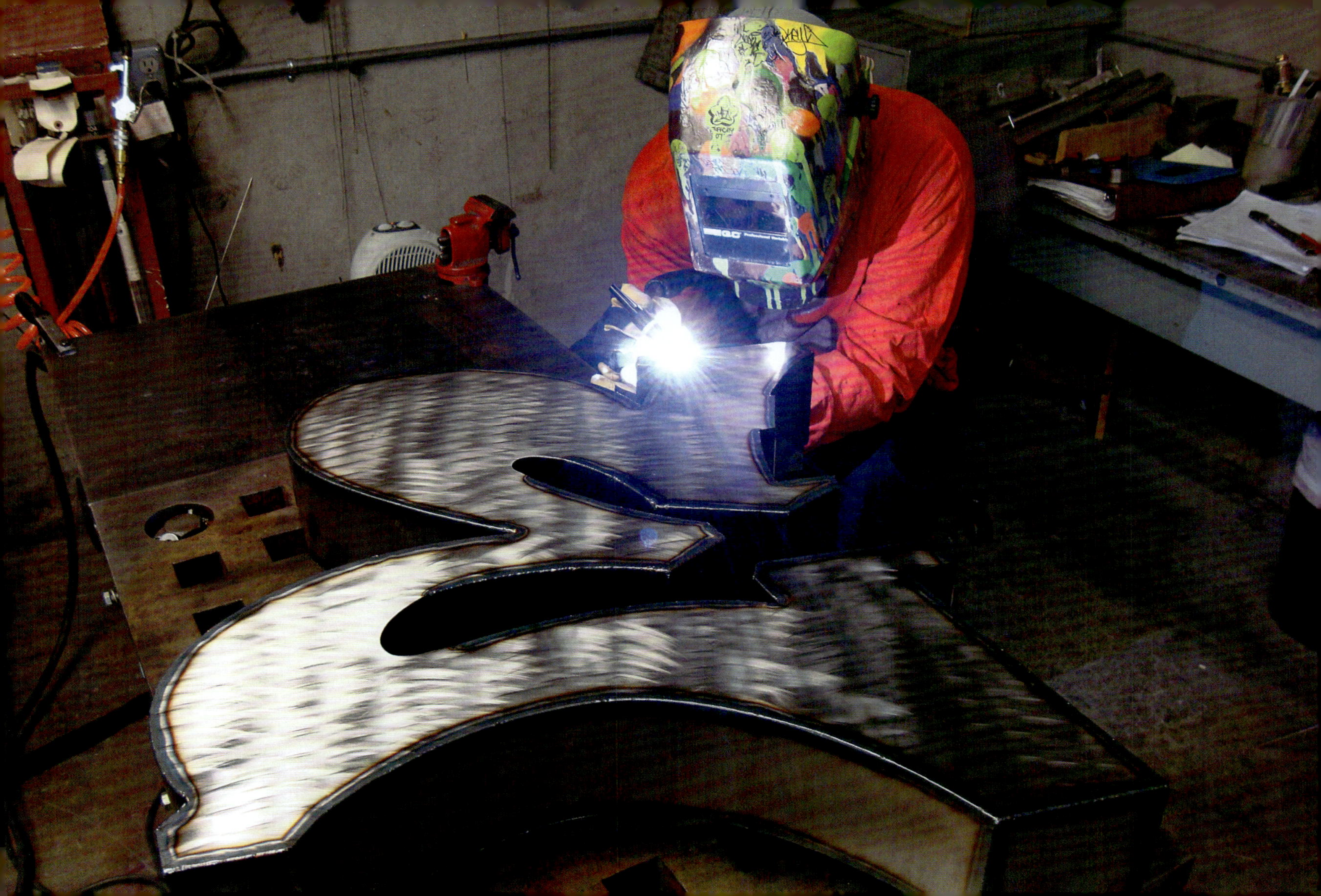

MG Boys

The MG (Mission Graffiti) Boys, formed in 1973 on 198th Street in the East Bronx, started small, but would, along with Wild Style and Wanted, become one of the most important crews in the history of the #4 line. During its peak (the mid- to late '70s) the crew hit the CCs, Ds, #2s, #5s, and too many bus lines to mention.

Hysen and his brother Ise were the first to make their presence felt on the outsides with colorful clouded pieces. Coming up on their heels would be the two most prolific and feared members of the crew, Mark 198 and Kit 17. Their membership gradually expanded to include some of the nastiest stylemasters of their day, such as Nic 707, Billy 167 (see 034), and Padre 2. Additional input from Nine, MS 161, Simon 007, Victor 161, Boots 119, Cuda 181, and MG 1, aka Chicago, made the MG boys unstoppable. Mission Graffiti, a predominately white crew that loved to get high, listen to rock music, and fight, counted a large group of non-graff associates among their ranks, which earned them respect on the #4 line—from the tracks of the elevation down to the streets below.

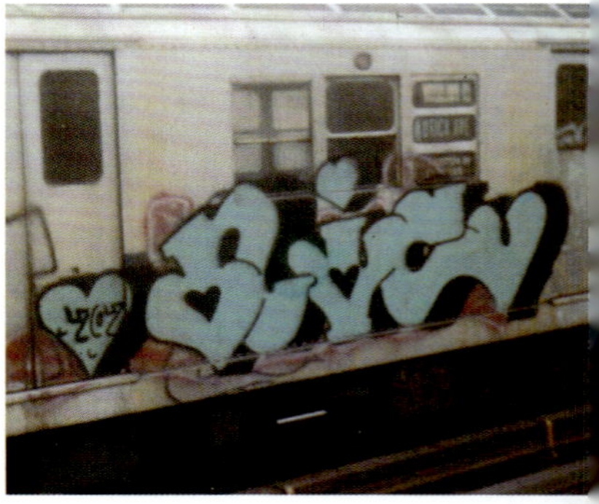

Private collection.
Piece by Mark 198, with tags by Boots 119, Kit 17, and Nine.
Detail: Piece by NIC 707.
New York City, 1975.

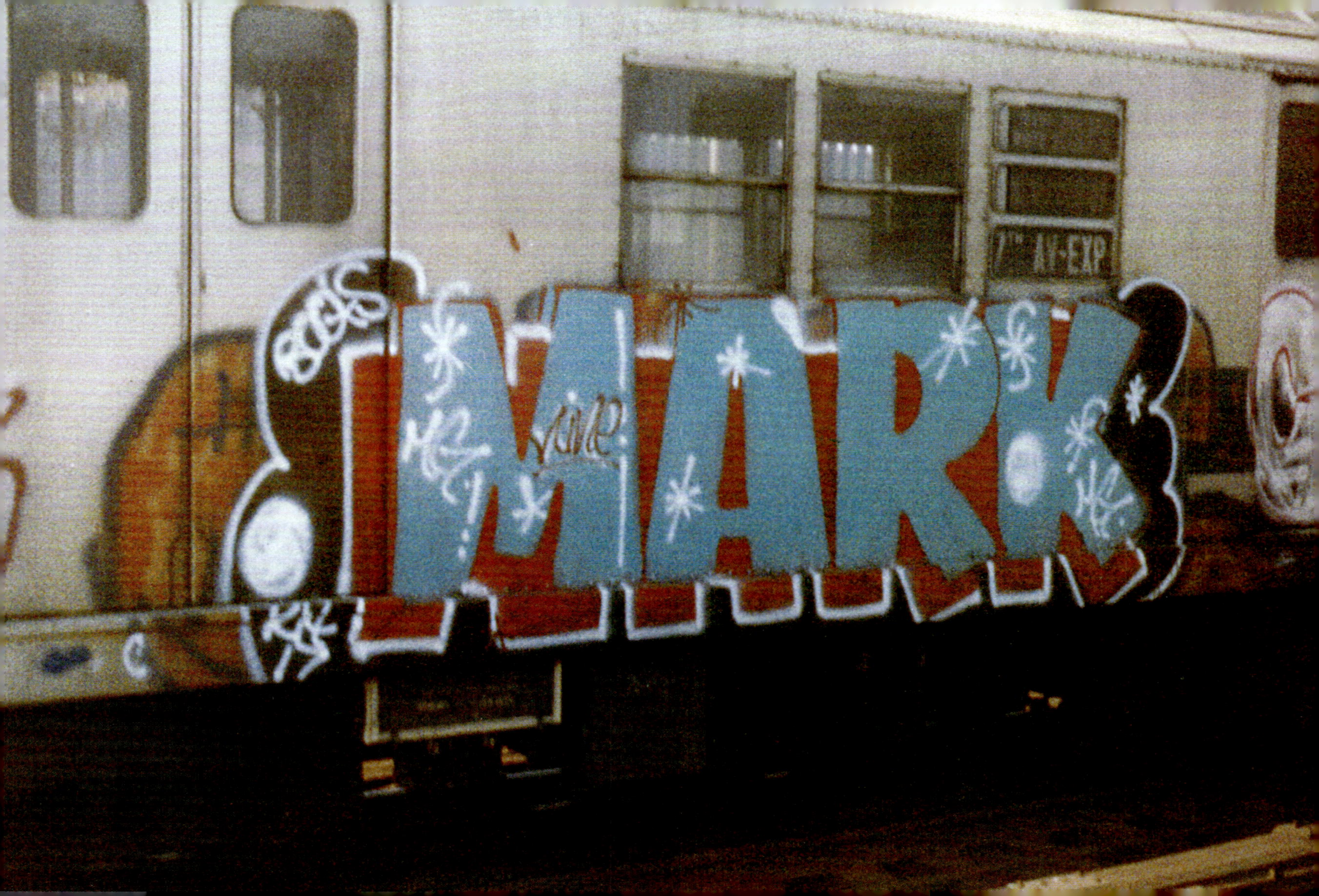
7TH AV-EXP
MARK

Mickey TFP

Mickey was a young girl of fourteen when *Subway Art* [see 323] made its way to the Netherlands. After reading it, she promptly locked herself in her room and did outlines for days. By 1985, she had invented a name for herself and started doing pieces with it, and over the next three years, she would earn the title of all-city king by painting with a New York style in her hometown of Groningen. In a wonderful act of serendipity, the Groninger Museum mounted a graffiti retrospective of New York legends Dondi [see 097], Blade [see 037], Lee, Futura 2000 [see 141], and others. It seemed Mickey wouldn't have to go to New York to meet her heroes—they were coming to her. The writers turned out to be so encouraging that she got an official invitation to come to New York to paint from Iz the Wiz [see 177] himself. Over the next four years, she spent her time between New York and the Netherlands, painting constantly and hitting iconic old-school spots like the New Lots yard in Brooklyn.

She became part of the TFP crew [see 334] when Sento [see 295] recruited her. As the younger TFP members began redefining style, Mickey found herself right in the mix. She abandoned her 1980s New York style and started to stretch her name until it became an abstraction. She received both good and bad reviews for her new works, but for Mickey, playing it safe simply wasn't an option—there was nothing worse than redundancy.

In the late 1990s, Mickey began a new career as a teacher and fine artist.

Photographs courtesy of Mickey TFP.
Top: The Netherlands, 2009.
Bottom left: The Netherlands, 2010.
Bottom right: Bari, Italy, 2008.

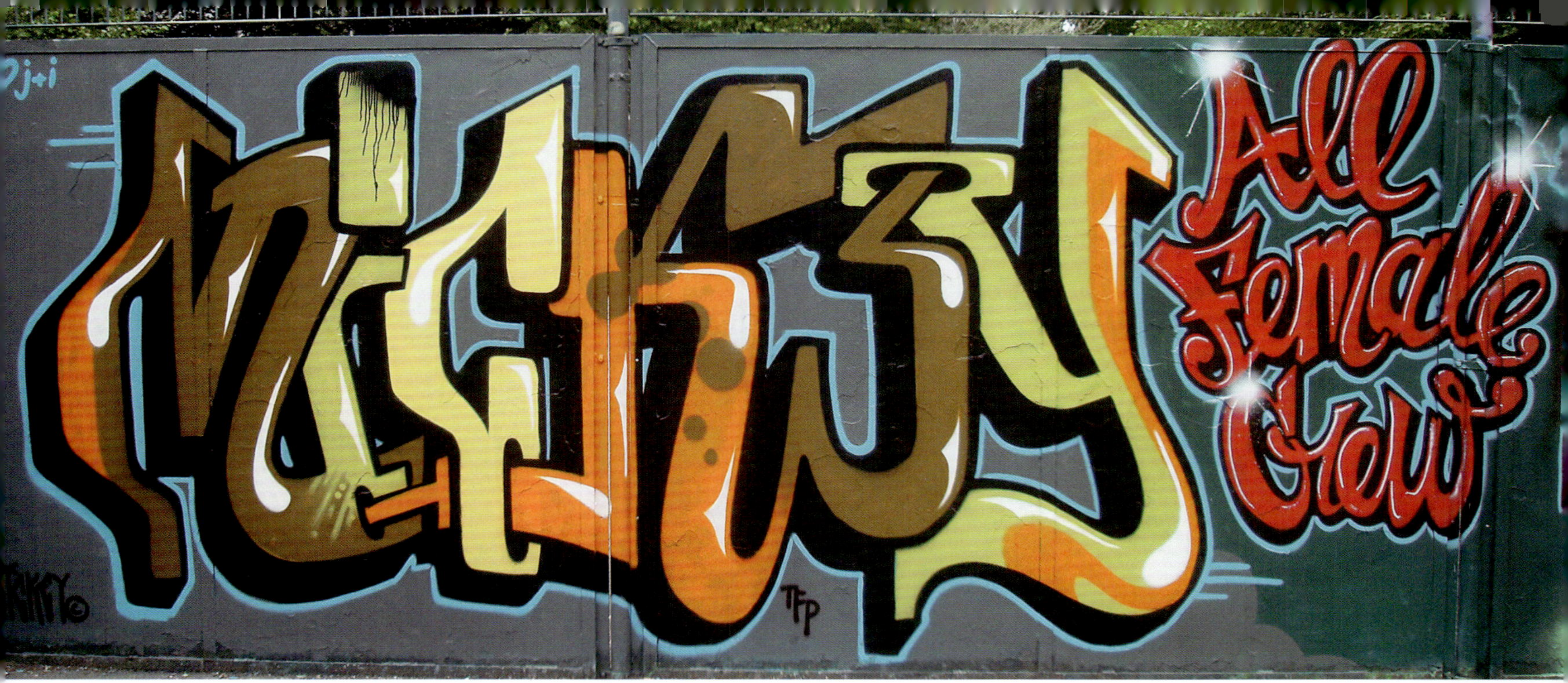
All Female Crew
TFP

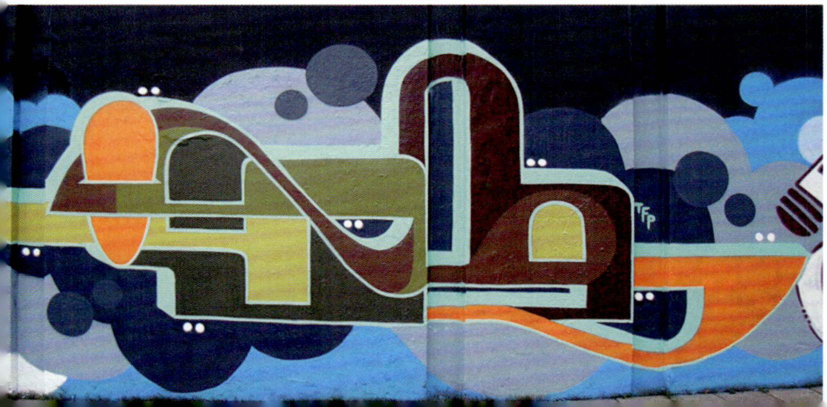

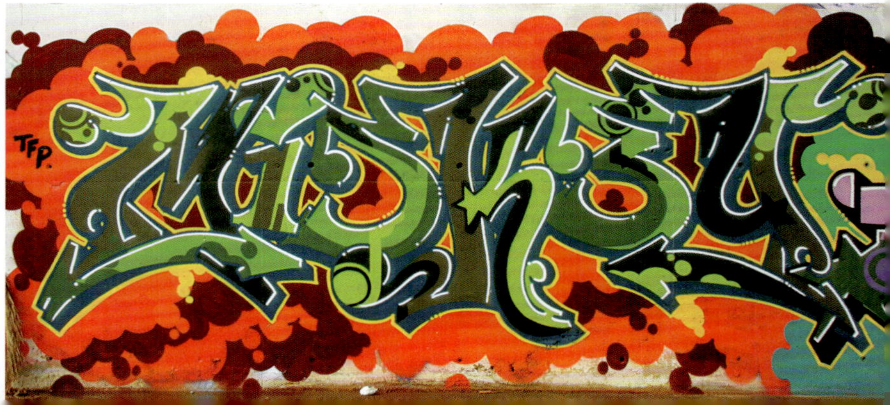
TFP

Min/NE

Min entered the graffiti game in 1977 under the name NE. Looking like Oliver Twist with long hair, he fit right in with the original hippie lineup of RTW [see 286], which included Bilrock, Revolt, Mackie, Rasta [see 270], Crunch, Vandal, and Zephyr [see 363]. Eventually, NE would take over the name Min, which had belonged to fellow crew member Rasta.

When RTW exploded onto Broadway in 1979–1980, NE showed great promise. The #1 train tunnel, RTW's primary base of operations, became a dicey proposition for writers, as crews like TMT and The Ballbusters would often bring violence to the game. Some RTW members simply moved on. Others, such as Min and Bilrock, decided to form new allegiances, forming The Vamp Squad, led by former gang member T.Kid 170 [see 335] and legendary brawler Shock 123. Min's style continued to evolve throughout the early '80s, when he branched out to other lines with the CIA crew. As the cross-out wars raged on the #2s and #5s, Min became a throw-up dynamo, battling Cap and The MPC crew with a barrage of Min and NE throw-ups. After most of CIA retired, Min made his home on the BMT and IND lines, befriending Rich 2, a tough-as-nails Lower East Side writer who became Min's enforcer. Eventually, the mid-'80s version of RTW joined forces with Brooklyn's WOW [Words of Wisdom] crew.

After his graffiti career, ended Min fell on hard times. Substance abuse and prison both took their toll on the former bombing machine. But Min had already established himself as "True Legend"—which, as explained in the movie *Style Wars* [see 322], refers to a king who can master all aspects of graffiti, from insides to whole-cars to top-to-bottoms. He proceeded to do it all.

Photograph by Martha Cooper. New York City, 1983.

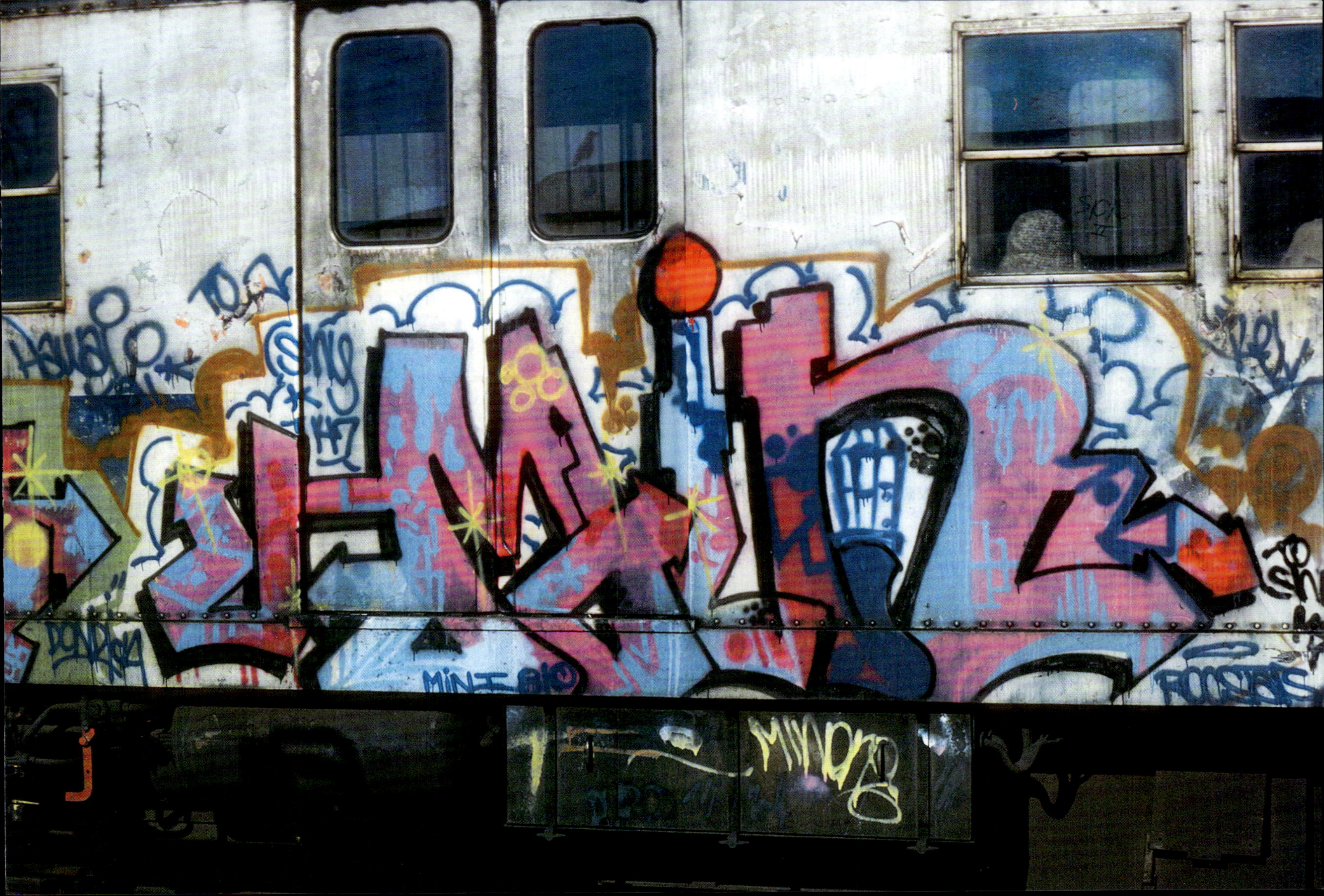

Miss 17

Miss 17 is somewhat of a throwback. In the world of postmillennium graffiti, where legal walls are typically the medium of choice, Miss 17 keeps her work illegal and on the streets—pretty paintings take a backseat to hard-core bombing. One of the hardest-working ladies in the business, Miss 17 has earned a name for herself among the most prolific vandals in New York history. Most often leaving a simple tag or a minimal bubble letter of the number 17, Miss 17 has hit every borough of New York extensively, as well as high-visibility spots in Europe and South America. Miss 17 owns real estate in some of the grimiest parts of New York, impressing her male competitors with her fearlessness.

Committed to maintaining the mysterious aura surrounding her persona, Miss 17 refuses to partake in interviews, gallery exhibitions, or commercial endeavors, either related or unrelated to her work. She did, however, make a small cameo appearance in the movie *Infamy*—but backlit and completely hidden in shadow.

Though she has been a graffiti writer for more than a decade, not much is known about the lady behind the numbers, aside from her fierce devotion to her craft, and the fact that she is a petite woman who resides in New York—or, perhaps, New Jersey.

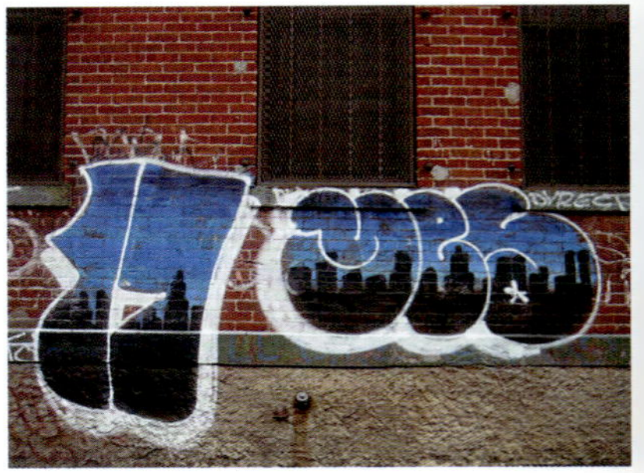

Photograph by Ray Mock.
Berlin, Germany, 2009.
Detail: Artwork by Miss 17 and Yes 2.
Photograph by Becki Fuller.
Brooklyn, New York, 2008.

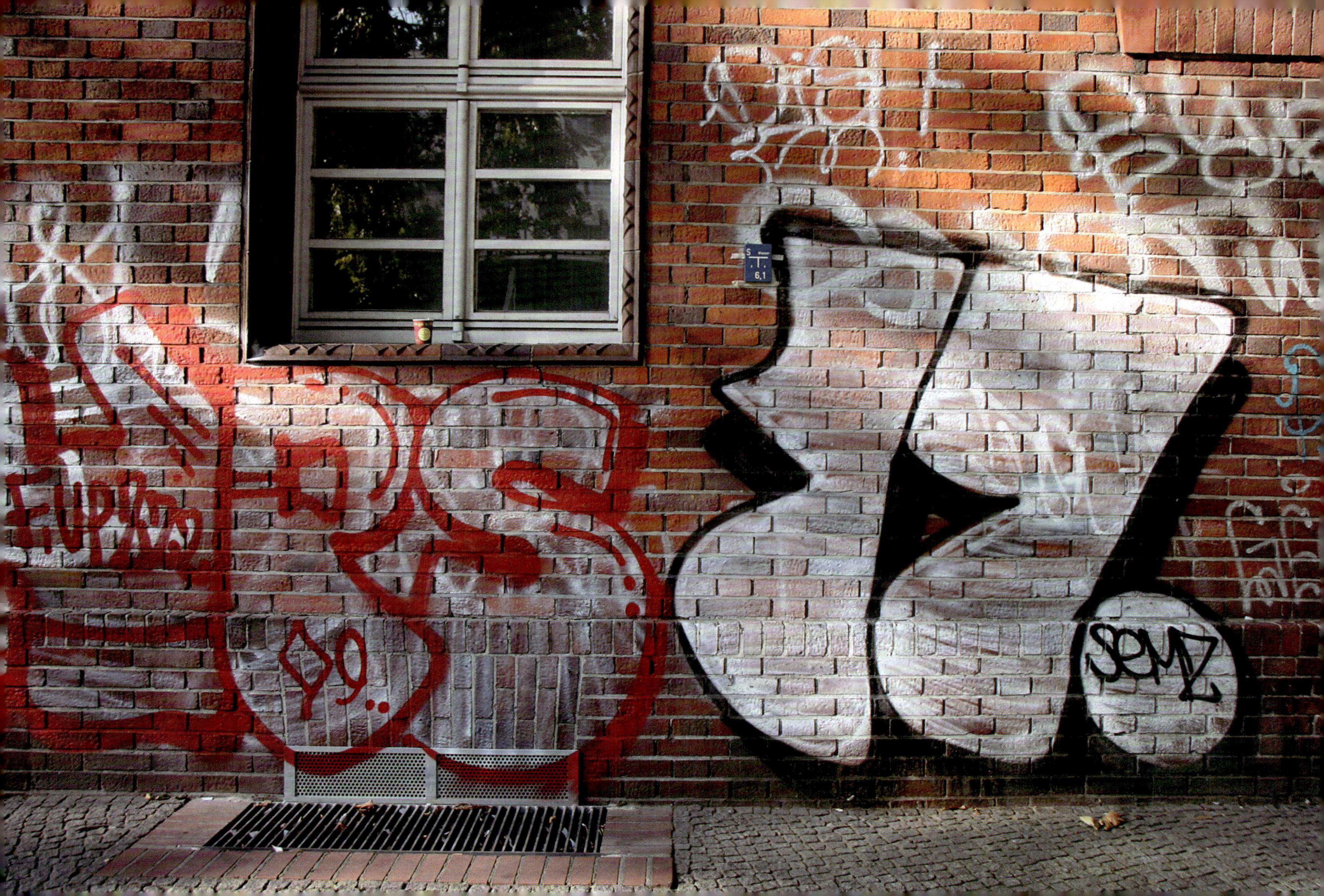
SEMZ

Miss Tic

Born in 1956, Miss Tic is one of the most famed and beloved Parisian stencil artists. Fusing images of stylish Parisian women with clever texts, she imparts witty bits of wisdom to her viewers. Originally a newspaper writer and street performer, she turned to writing on the walls in the mid-1980s following the breakup of her relationship with legendary stencil artist Blek le Rat [see 038].

"The wall is the territory of my poems," she says. "It is my publisher." Often with underlying feminist themes, these poems reflect Miss Tic's talent for wordplay in her clever messages about freedom, love, and the gender roles we so often play. After her arrest in 1998, Miss Tic began seeking permission before spraying a building. "I was condemned as a delinquent," she quips.

In 1986, Miss Tic had her first solo show in Paris at Galerie Epigramme and her first group show at Galerie Agnès B. Since then, her works have been exhibited across the globe. They are in numerous collections and museums, including the Victoria and Albert Museum in London. In 2006, Miss Tic participated in the Venice Biennale. Delighted that street art has experienced such phenomenal growth since she started writing on the walls, she cannot imagine doing anything else.

Photographs by Lois Stavsky. Paris, 2009.

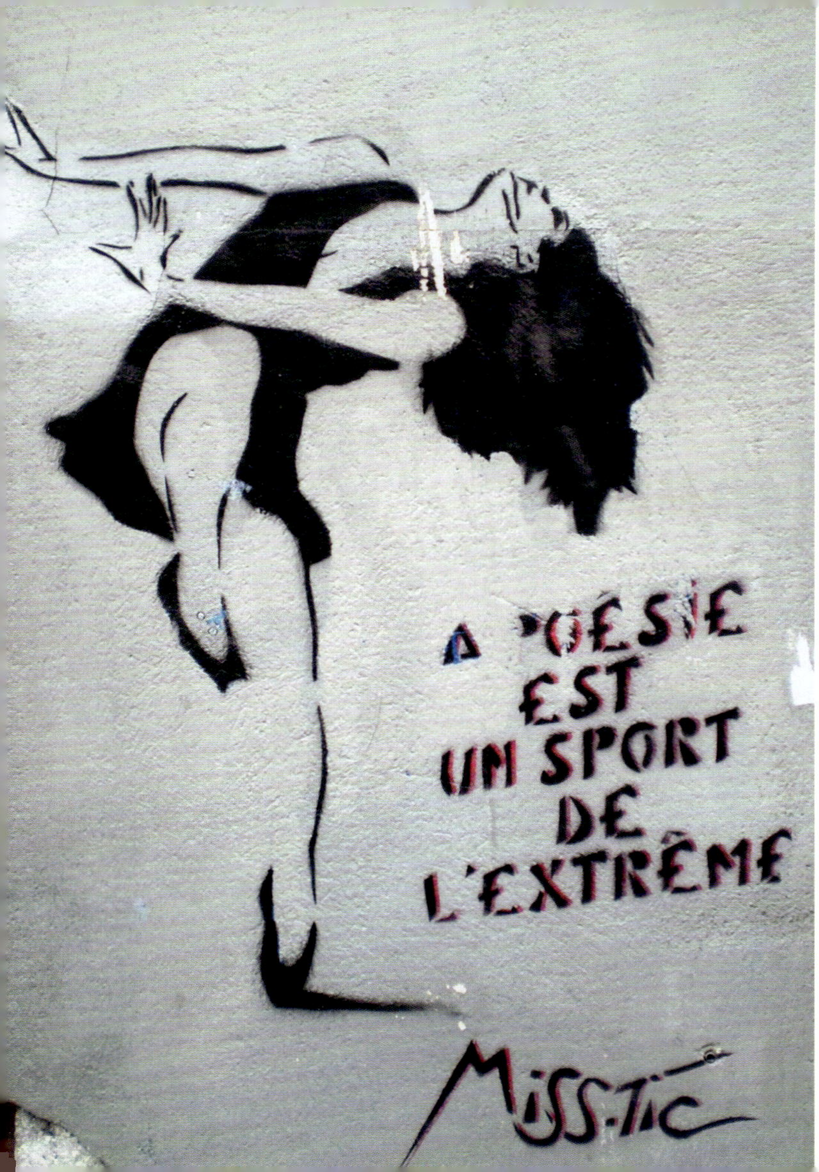
A POESIE
EST
UN SPORT
DE
L'EXTRÊME
MISS-TIC

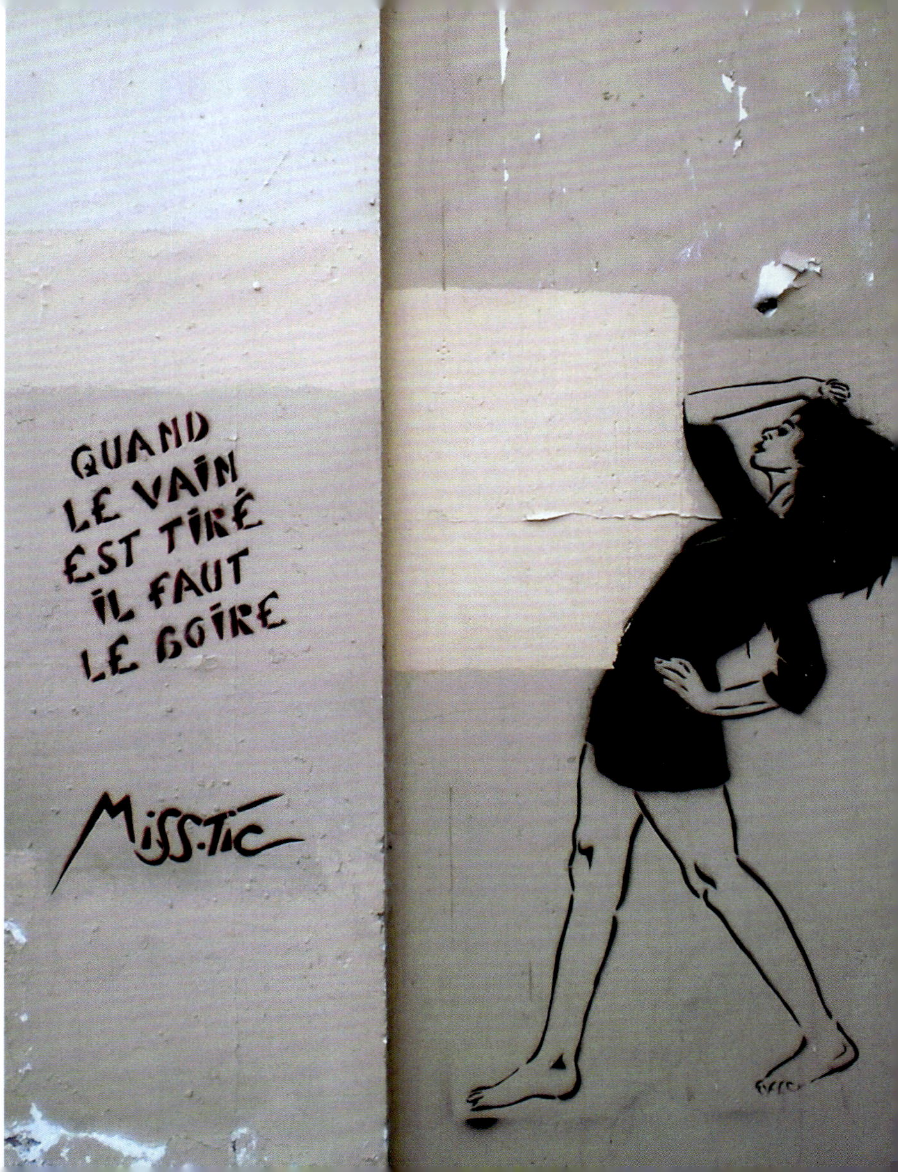
QUAND
LE VAIN
EST TIRÉ
IL FAUT
LE BOIRE
MISS-TIC

Miss Van

Female artists are a rarity in the graffiti and street-art worlds, especially ones who revolutionize the game or invent a specific style, so the French artist known as Miss Van is a welcome breath of fresh paint fumes. Originally hailing from the surprisingly graffiti-friendly southern French city of Toulouse, Miss Van began painting public walls in the early 1990s, at the tender age of eighteen. In 1993, in conjunction with her longtime art partner, Mademoiselle Kat, Miss Van stumbled upon the stylized female character forms she would become known for and inadvertently began what would become a feminine art movement within graffiti culture.

Using latex and acrylic paints, with an old-fashioned brush instead of a can, Miss Van set herself apart from the pack by not only wheatpasting paintings to walls, but actually painting intricate, time-consuming characters directly onto walls around the world. Over time, her work evolved into an army of voluptuous women, with instantly recognizable slanted eyes and an undeniably hypercharged (and perhaps self-referential) sexuality.

Credited with inspiring countless young artists, the painter brushes off invitations to discuss obvious parallels between her work and that of the younger French graffiti artist Fafi (see 122), whom she claims she mentored. Miss Van currently lives in Barcelona, Spain, and exhibits her work internationally, including at the Jonathan LeVine gallery in New York City, and she shies away from invitations to partake in commercial projects.

Photograph by Laundry A.
El Raval, Barcelona, 2009.

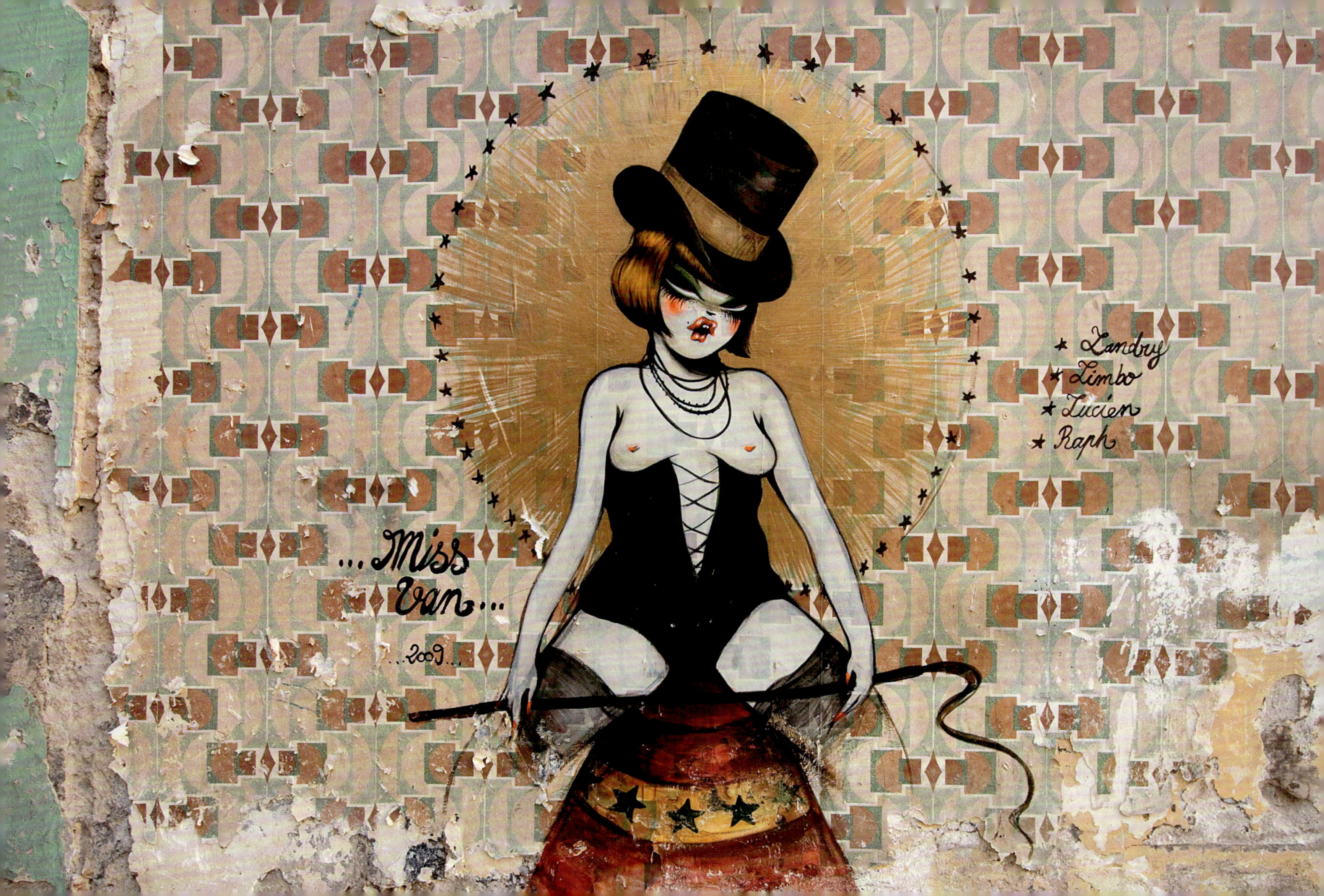

...Miss
Van...
...2009...
★ Landry
★ Limbo
★ Lucien
★ Raph

Mitch 77

Bronx stylemaster Mitch 77 may be the most undercredited writer in graffiti history. His career began around 1977 on the storied #4 line, which had been home to legendary crews like Wild Style, MG Boys, and TCA, and then became the proving ground for this up-and-coming stylemaster, who would reach his peak in the early '80s. Cartoon puppy dogs and a kung-fu hand breaking through a stone wall, combined with perfectly symmetrical whole-cars and Wild Style window-down burners, made Mitch a force to be reckoned with. He also partnered up with Disco/Med 167, PJAY, and Ban 2 during various periods during his career.

One of Mitch 77's most famous pieces was done on a billboard opposite Yankee Stadium. Few spots in graffiti history had greater visual impact than Mitch's "ad," which was impossible for exiting Yankee fans to miss.

Mitch 77 participated in early graffiti art shows such as PS1, but quickly became alienated by art-world politics and posturing. He walked away from graffiti in 1983 and never looked back. Cope 2 [see 074] refers to Mitch 77 as his idol, and there are many graffiti buffs who would concur. Mitch 77 went on to build his life independent of graffiti and continues to lead it that way.

Photographs by Pjay One.
New York City, 1981.

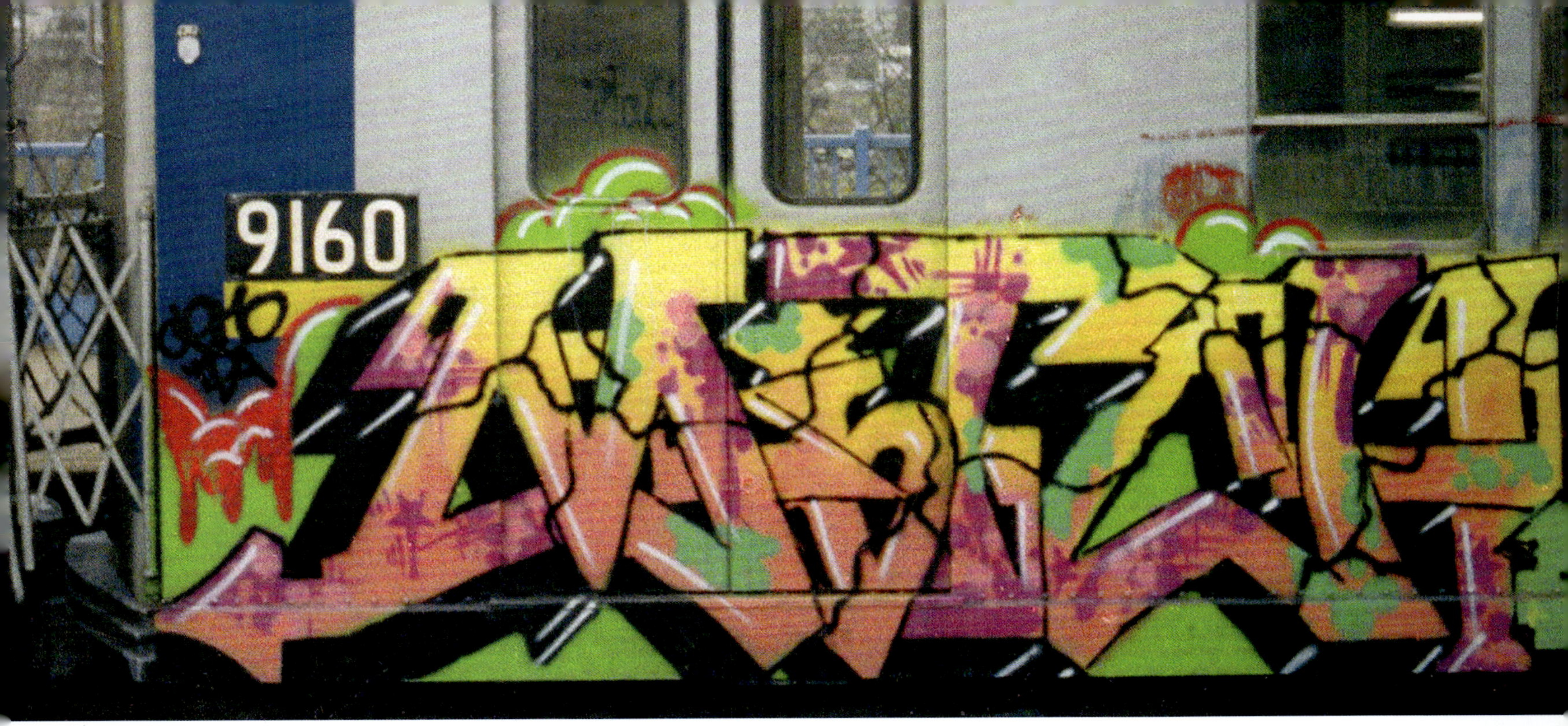
9160

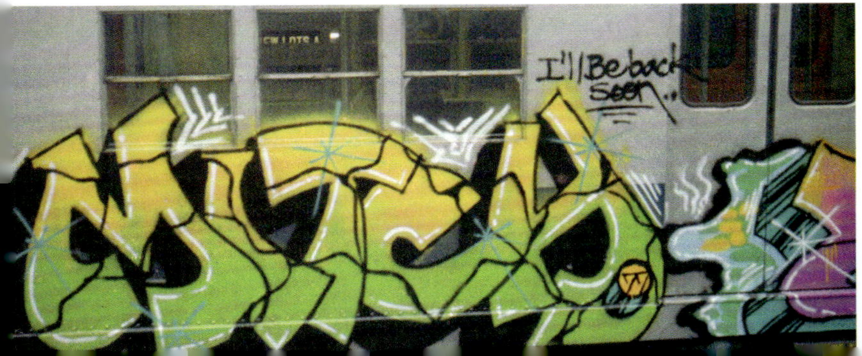
I'll Be back
Soon

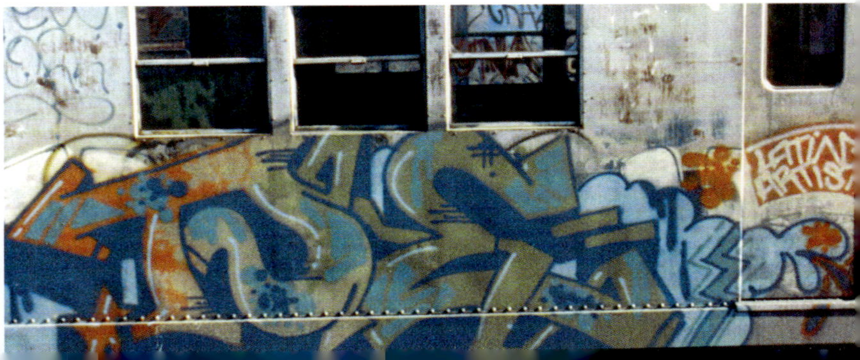

The MOB

The Masters of Broadway, better known by their acronym The MOB, was founded in 1975 by Terror 161 [see 333]. The crew, based in the Riverdale section of the Bronx, was situated in a white middle-class neighborhood with no link to the graffiti world other than being home to the 242nd Street subway yard. The original members of The MOB were Terror 161, Tanx 2, Trail, Cheetah 2, and Neon 2. Later notable additions included Use 2, Anthony 101, Uni, Ammo, and Trex.

Early members of the crew painted almost exclusively on the #1 line and dominated it, inside and out, during intermittent periods from 1975 to 1978. Use 2 took honors as king of the line in 1977 and 1978, and Anthony 101 became a style guru. The MOB faded out in 1978, as most of its members lost interest in graffiti or went on to college.

In 1980, however, MOB alumni Terror 161 and Ammo made a comeback. Over the next four years, the pair left their mark on every IRT line except the #7. By 1984, The MOB had branched out into legitimate businesses—in other words, Terror 161 and Ammo found jobs and retired from writing.

**Tag (left) and *Terror 161* throw-up by Terror 161.
Photograph by Martha Cooper.
New York City, 1981.**

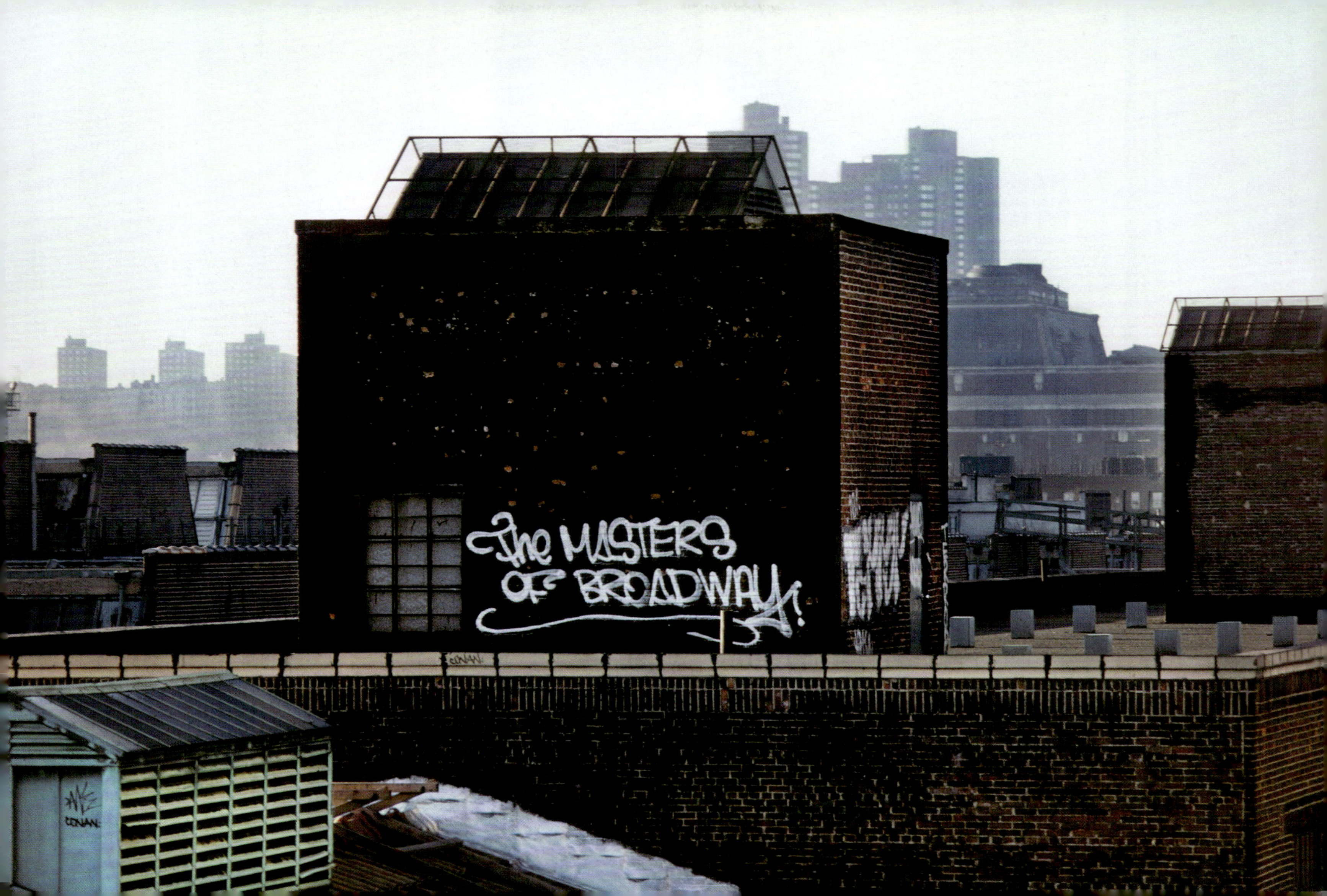
The MASTERS
OF BROADWAY

Mobstr

As his name connotes, British artist Mobstr is involved in what has been deemed illegal activity. In his case, Mobstr explains, this illegal business is "painting walls without permission—not being a member of an organized crime gang." Convinced that public space belongs to all of us, he contends that he has as much right to it as any corporation posting an advertisement. "One is endorsed by money and the other by a creative spirit," he maintains, sensing that most of us would rather look at art on the walls of our city than at advertisements for unnecessary products and services.

Mobstr has earned extensive media attention, as well as acclaim in the street-art world, for the messages he stenciled onto unblemished walls and bricks in his hometown of Newcastle. The purpose of these messages is to engage passersby, as well as to initiate a dialogue with members of the Newcastle City Council, who keep painting over his work. Among these messages are SO MUCH SPACE, SO LITTLE IMAGINATION; COME ON, PAINT ME WHITE AGAIN; and BOOORING.

With his irreverent streak and playful use of words, Mobstr is often compared to Banksy [see 024]. Replicas of his stencil work on canvas have been exhibited at Newcastle's Kitch-en Gallery.

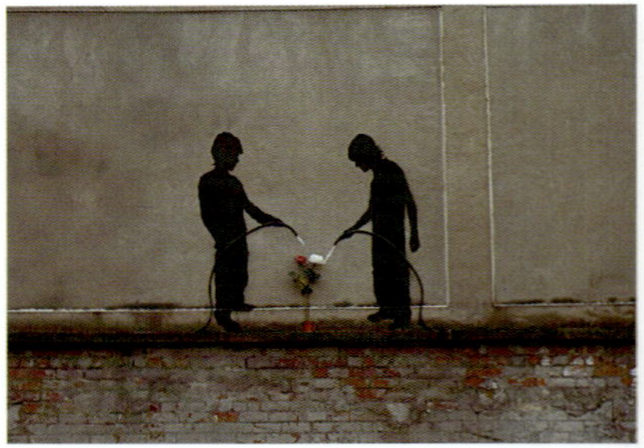

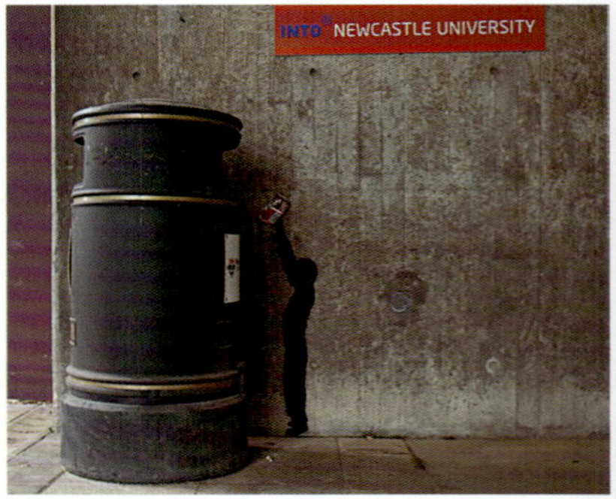

Photographs courtesy of Mobstr.
***Be Humble*. New Castle, United Kingdom, 2010.**
Detail top: *The Urban Garden*. Newcastle, United *Kingdom*, 2008.
Detail bottom: Little. Newcastle, United Kingdom, 2009.

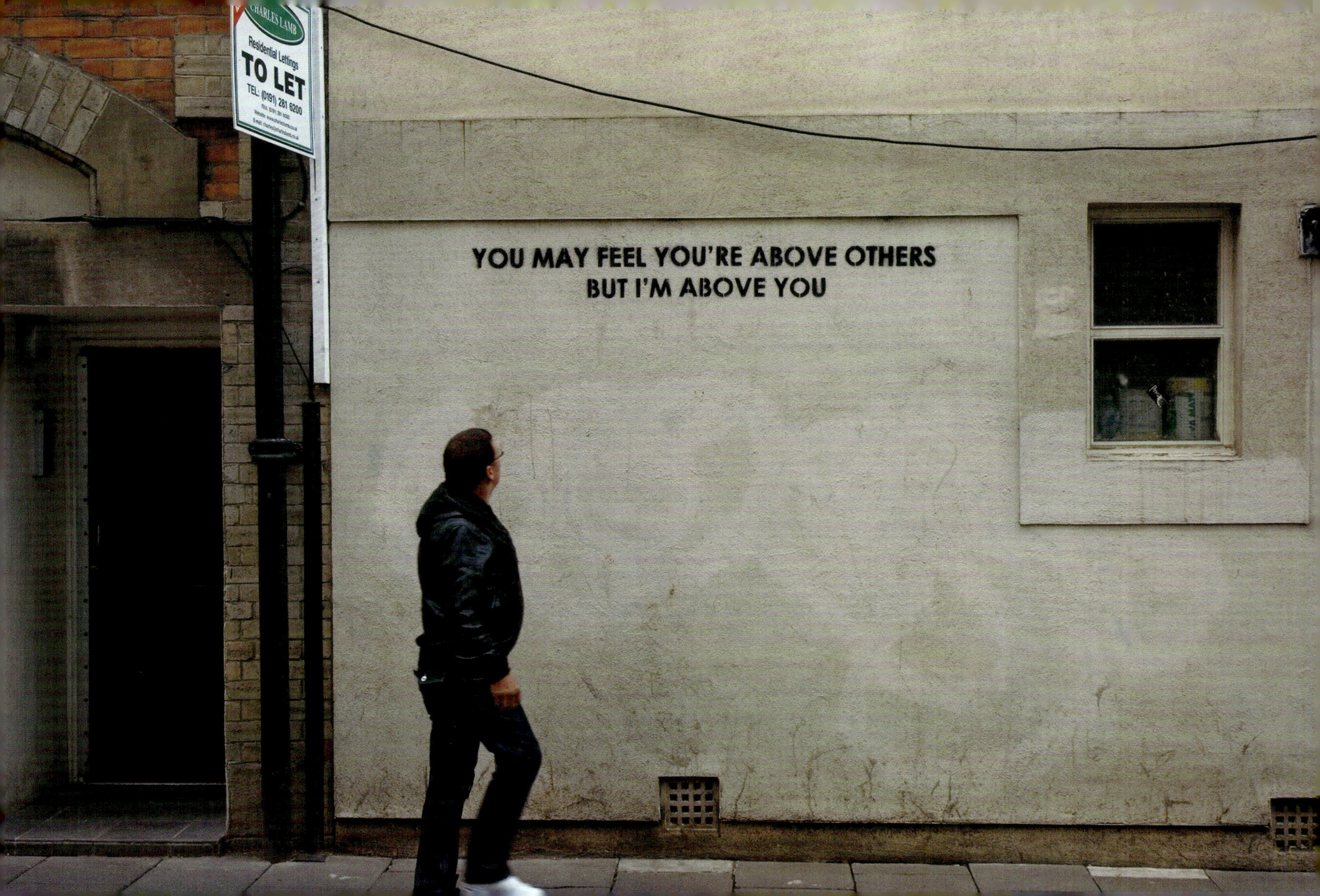
CHARLES LAMB
Residential Lettings
TO LET
TEL: (0191) 281 6200
YOU MAY FEEL YOU'RE ABOVE OTHERS
BUT I'M ABOVE YOU

Lt. Steve Mona

For more than a decade, Lt. Steve Mona was head of the New York Police Department's Anti-Graffiti Task Force, known on the streets as the Vandal Squad. Until his retirement in 2006, Lieutenant Mona managed eight sergeants, more than sixty police officers, and a dozen power-washer trucks capable of removing up to twenty thousand square feet of graffiti per day. Credited with ridding the subway trains of graffiti in the 1990s, the task force has long been plagued by disturbing reports of officers beating offenders and of gross misappropriation of taxpayers' money. The task force has been responsible for more than 2,800 arrests; its strategies include a computer database of vandals' tags and photos of their work, a *Worst of the Worst* book featuring one hundred of the city's most sought-after vandals, and stiff jail sentences. Lieutenant Mona was so despised by citywide graffiti artists that, at the height of tensions in the late 1990s, someone painted the phrase OFFICER MONA HAS AIDS on the Manhattan Bridge.

Always maintaining that the issues are permission and legality, and that police action is not an attack on graffiti as an art form, Lieutenant Mona participated in a forum on graffiti in 2010. Sitting opposite artists Cope 2, Ket, and Ellis Gallagher, Lieutenant Mona defended himself, saying, "The fact is, you guys don't want it to be legal. Without the illegal part of it, you would never be where you are today. When you argued back in the day, it wasn't about better colors or lines, it was about who got more 'ups.'"

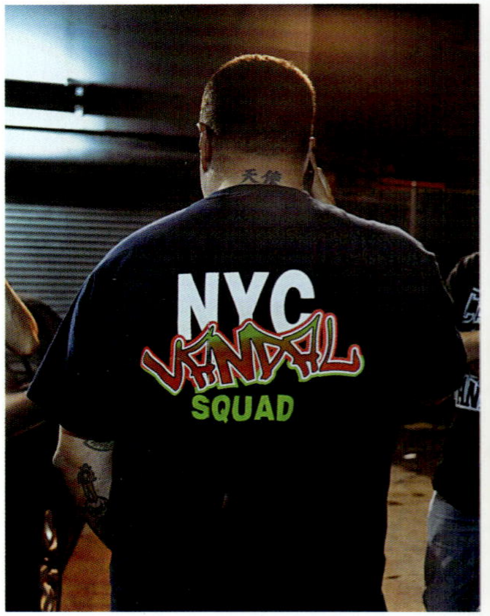

Photographs by Martha Cooper. New York City, 2010.

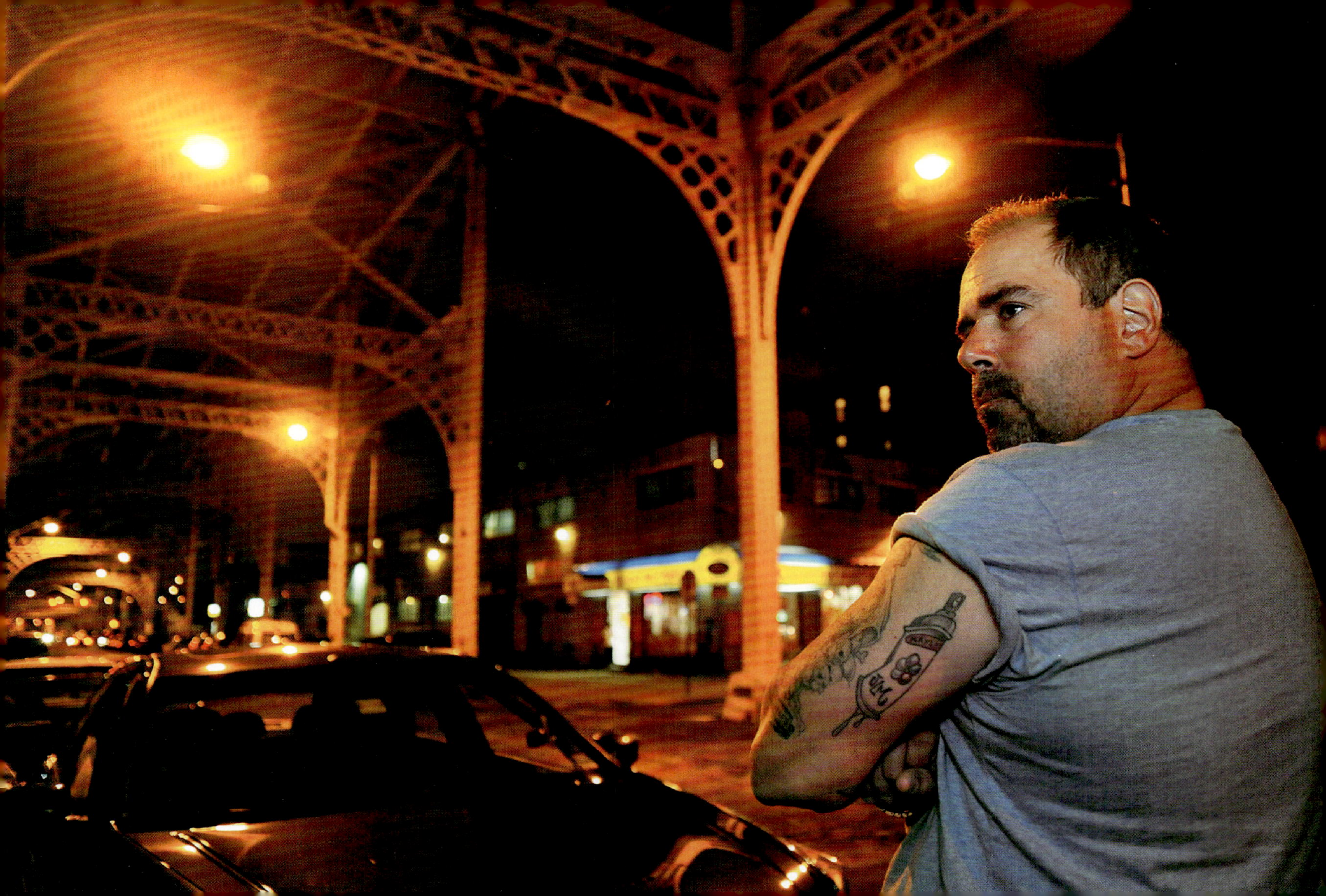

Mone

Mone grew up in Mount Vernon, New York, which shares a border with the Bronx (not far from the last stop on the #2 line). His earliest graffiti recollections date back to 1984, when subway writing first mesmerized him—although he couldn't comprehend it, he felt captivated by it. Timing plays an important part in a writer's career, and when Mone finally grew old enough to hit the subways in 1988, the MTA was just about to close his window of opportunity; unfortunately, the clean-train era and his career as a writer began simultaneously. He hit a few clean subway trains, but could never get pictures of them running. After bombing streets and walls in his neighborhood, Mone found a new medium in 1992: freight trains. (Only a handful of writers painted on them back then, believing that hitting trains that ran away from the public eye was a waste of paint.)

Mone's early influences include unheralded Mount Vernon writers like Rem 311, LM 4, and Westchester stylemaster Vet TMC; his subway influences include Sento (see 295), Reas, and Ghost (see 145).

Today, Mone is still painting, citing the longevity and passion of some of the culture's greatest stylemasters as his motivation. Mone reverently states: "Part (see 251), Chain 3 (see 062), and T.Kid 170 (see 335) started in the 1970s and have remained nasty. Slave TF5 just made a comeback by painting a freight in his fifties. If that's not inspiring, I don't know what is."

Photographs courtesy of Mone.
New York City.

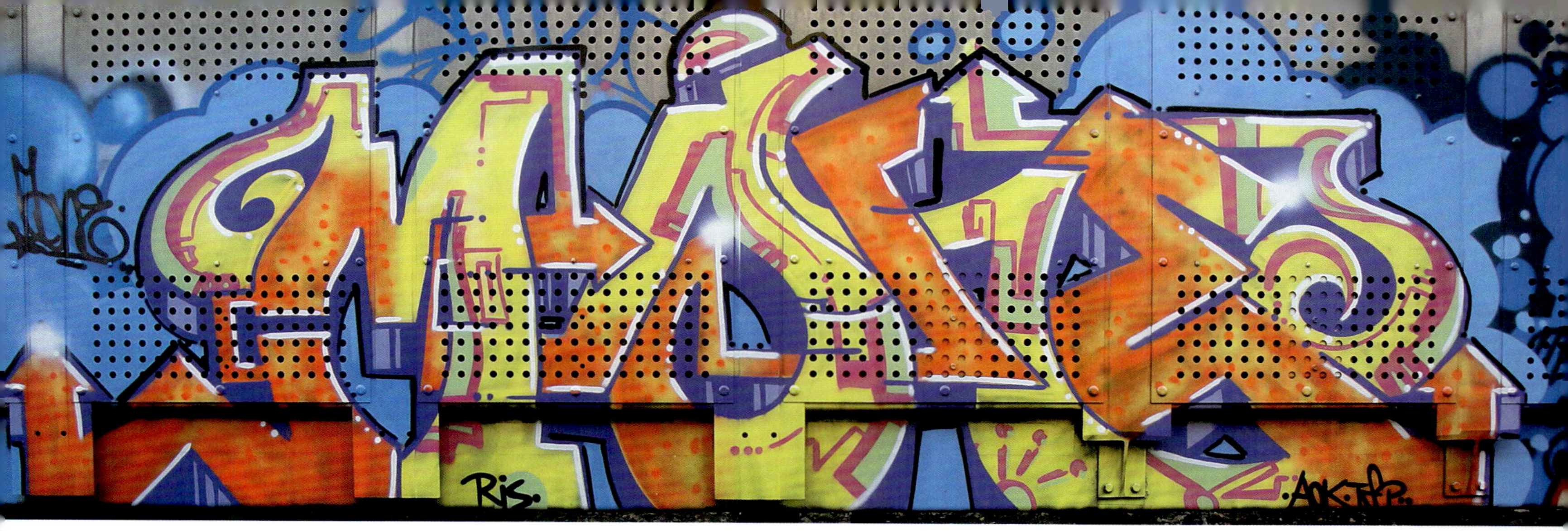
RiS.

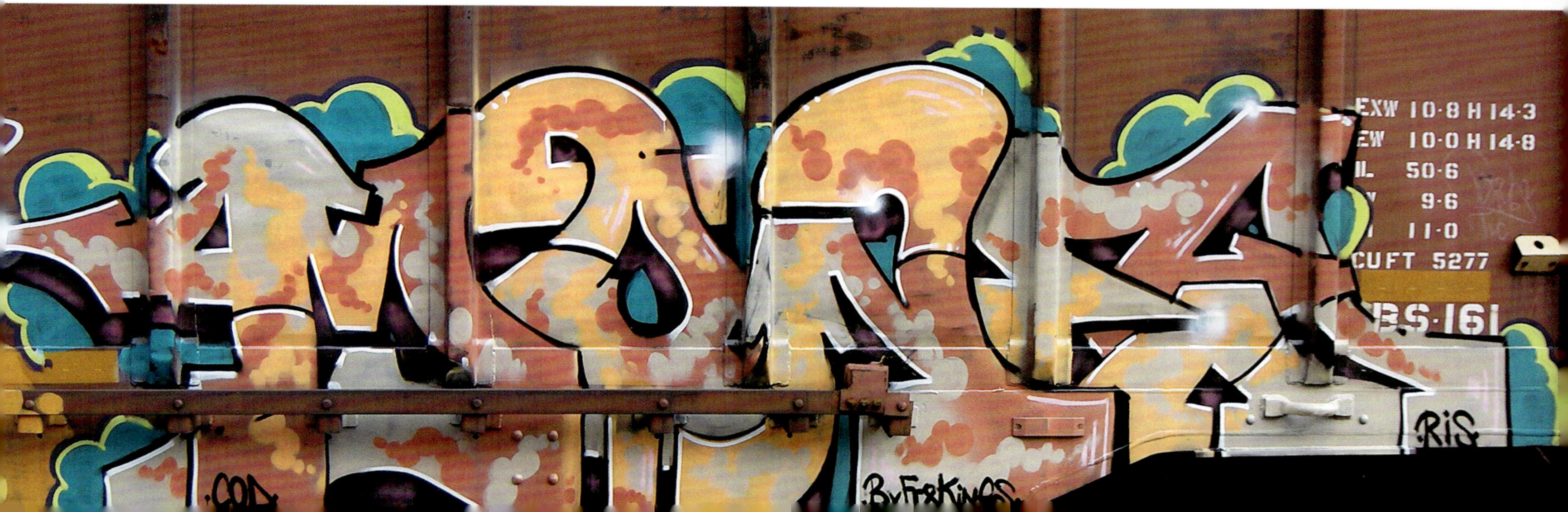
EXW 10-8 H 14-3
CUFT 5277
RiS

monikers

With significantly less human traffic and vastly longer voyages, freight trains are the lonely older brother to city subway cars. However, this does not exempt them from graffiti's mischievous touch. In fact, freight trains have birthed their own unique graffiti culture: a world of what are known as "hobo monikers."

A moniker (the term is taken from the Irish word for "nickname") is most often created on the side of a traveling freight-train car with oil markers, which are weatherproof and extremely hard to remove. Monikers are often depictions of scenes or specific characters. What differentiates hobo monikers from traditional graffiti is a distinctive visual style—often comprised of scribbled lines accompanied by text and marked by a more romantic sensibility, reflecting a lonesome traveler's doodles—but the unique character of moniker culture comes from the people creating it. Entirely separated from hip-hop and its influence on graffiti, freight monikers are often created by vagabond travelers or train workers leaving their marks on trains they have worked or traveled on.

Freight monikers and their somewhat secretive legacy were of profound influence on the groundbreaking "Beautiful Losers" (see 030) artists Barry "Twist" McGee (see 214) and his deceased ex-wife, Margaret Kilgallen.

Photograph by Bill Daniels.
St. Louis, Missouri, 1991.

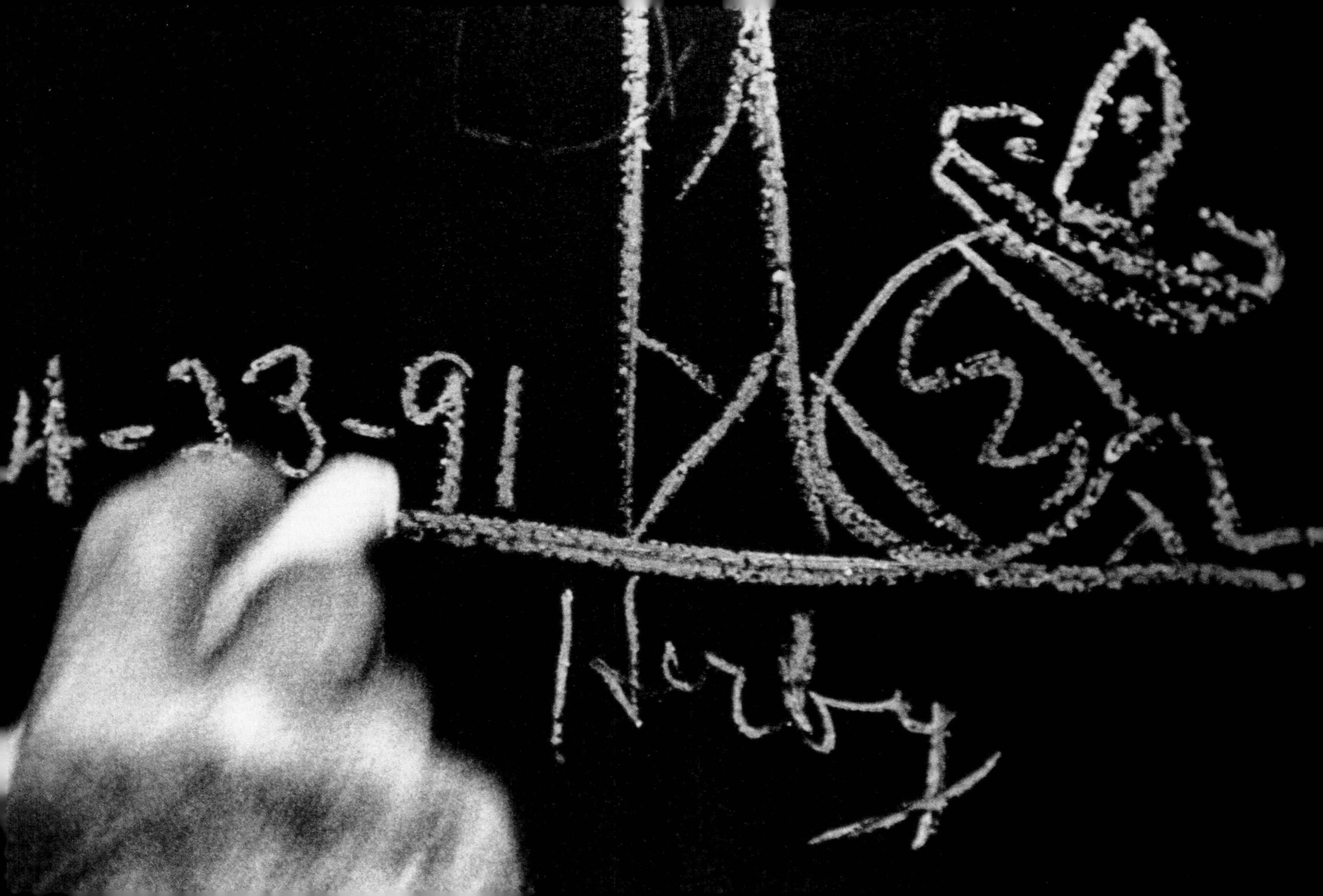
4-13-91

Morcky Troubles

Morcky Troubles knows troubles. He even likes troubles. He approaches them with a smile (at least most of the time). Growing up in Italy, he became interested in graffiti at an early age. Spray cans and large speakers were the core of his social life.

As a young adult, Morcky Troubles went to college, where he earned a degree in physics. Terrified at the idea of a life chained to formulas and equations, he hit the streets and decided to work with lines instead of numbers. He quickly developed a unique, fluid style that earned him attention on the streets, where his art appears as a sort of public sketchbook. If we were able to flip through this book, we'd find open-ended narratives, urban icons, and whimsical spaceships, but nothing that resembles a moral or a message.

Morcky Troubles also formed half of the dynamic duo TwoThings, earning international acclaim for art direction, music videos, and cutting-edge ideas about how to challenge the boundaries of new media. He is one of those artists who genuinely live by the motto "Paint if you have love to share."

Photograph courtesy of Morcky Troubles.
Tirana, Albania, 2010.

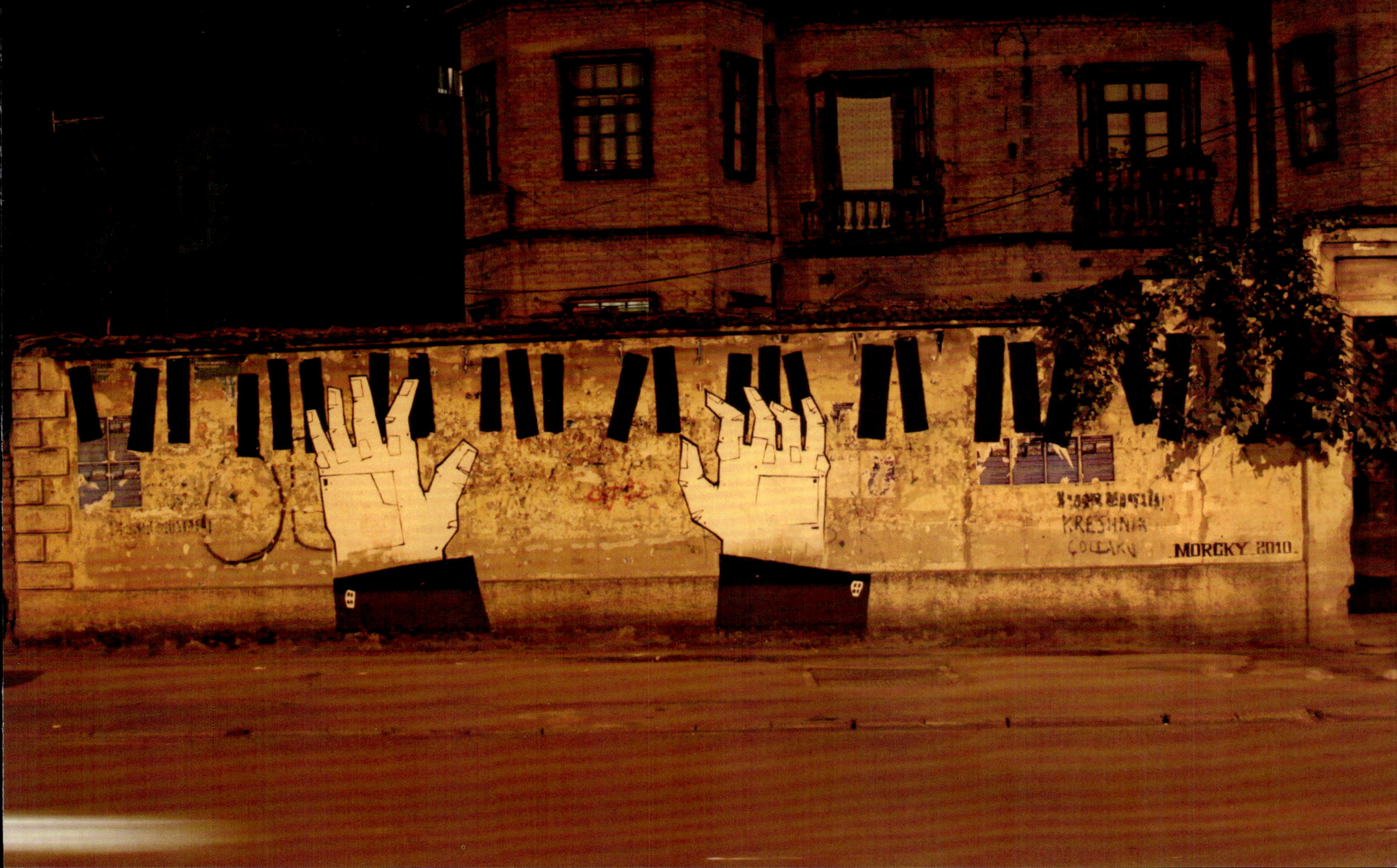
KRESHNIA
ÇOLLAKU
MORCKY 2010.

Moses 147

Moses 147 grew up on the Broadway line in the late 1960s and early 1970s, when it was still a Mecca for graffiti writers. At the time, he lived in a one-room apartment with his grandmother, just two blocks away from the #1 tunnel at 145th Street. In 1972, at the age of fifteen, he took on the name Moses 147, and his younger brother became Patch. They quickly learned the ins and outs of the Broadway lay-ups, hitting the yards at 242nd Street, the #1 tunnel at 137th Street, and the elevated lay-up at 215th Street. By 1973, Moses 147 was ready for more.

He started to do hundreds of pieces almost exclusively on the #1 line, sometimes doing two on one car. While the pieces weren't aesthetically pleasing, they contained a lot of the decorative elements of the day, including polka dots, stars, candy-cane stripes, and background clouds. That summer, Moses moved into a hotel on 94th Street, which gave him the freedom to come and go as he pleased—a rarity for a sixteen-year-old. He was introduced to a new writer named Bone, and they became partners. The friendship came with a rivalry over who could king the line, a title that seemed to change weekly. During this period, Moses 147 developed a stylized piece that he dubbed "wobbly letters," finally inventing a style fit for a king. Having held the title "King of Broadway" for more than a year, Moses retired in 1974.

Photograph by Jack Stewart.
New York City, 1973.

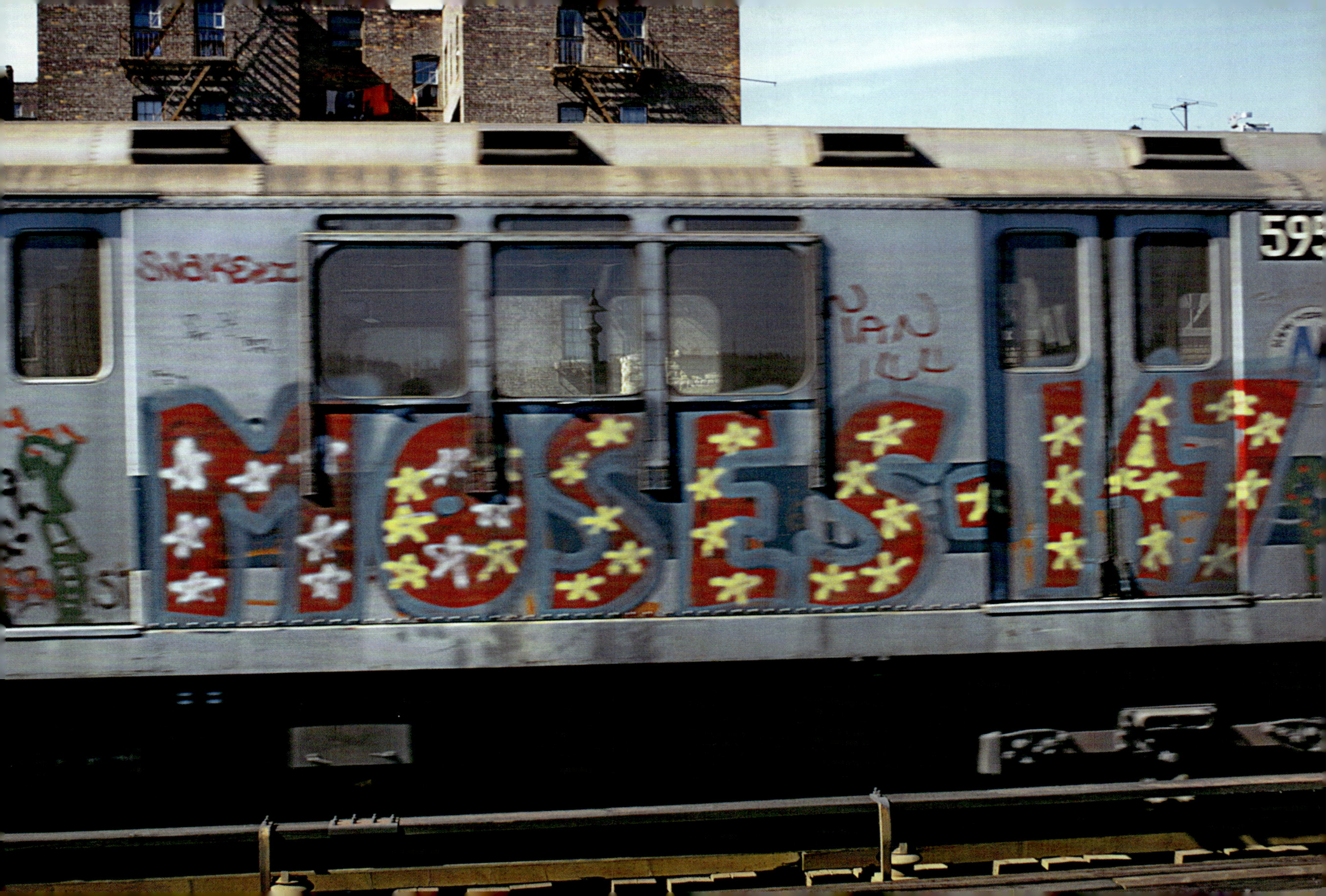

Mr. Brainwash

Thierry Guetta, the subject of British guerilla-art sensation Banksy's [see 024] first film, *Exit Through the Gift Shop*, is either a genius or an idiot savant [or, as many have speculated, a fictional character created by Banksy]. According to the film, Guetta, a former vintage-clothing store owner with a penchant for videotaping everything in his Los Angeles environs, had an epiphany while visiting relatives in France. After discovering that his cousin was leading a secret life as the street artist Space Invader [see 311], Guetta filmed him illegally placing his art on the streets of Paris.

Having found his calling, Guetta returned to Los Angeles and stalked Shepard Fairey [see 124] after meeting him in a Kinko's store. After winning Fairey's confidence, Guetta shadowed him with camera in hand. Guetta spent years filming Fairey, as well as several of the world's most prominent street artists, all the while pining like a starstruck teenager for a chance to meet street-art king Banksy. Guetta's dream came true when Fairey finally introduced him to Banksy, who was in need of a savvy guide to the streets of Los Angeles. Guetta delivered, helping the British stencil superstar to commandeer high-visibility spots throughout the city.

Banksy, convinced Guetta would deliver a brilliant documentary, took him under his wing, allowing him to film all areas of his secretive life [but not his face]. Instead of delivering his long-awaited cinematic masterpiece, Guetta repaid his heroes by stealing their techniques and reinventing himself as a street artist named Mr. Brainwash.

Photograph by Remo Mamerota. Los Angeles, 2008.

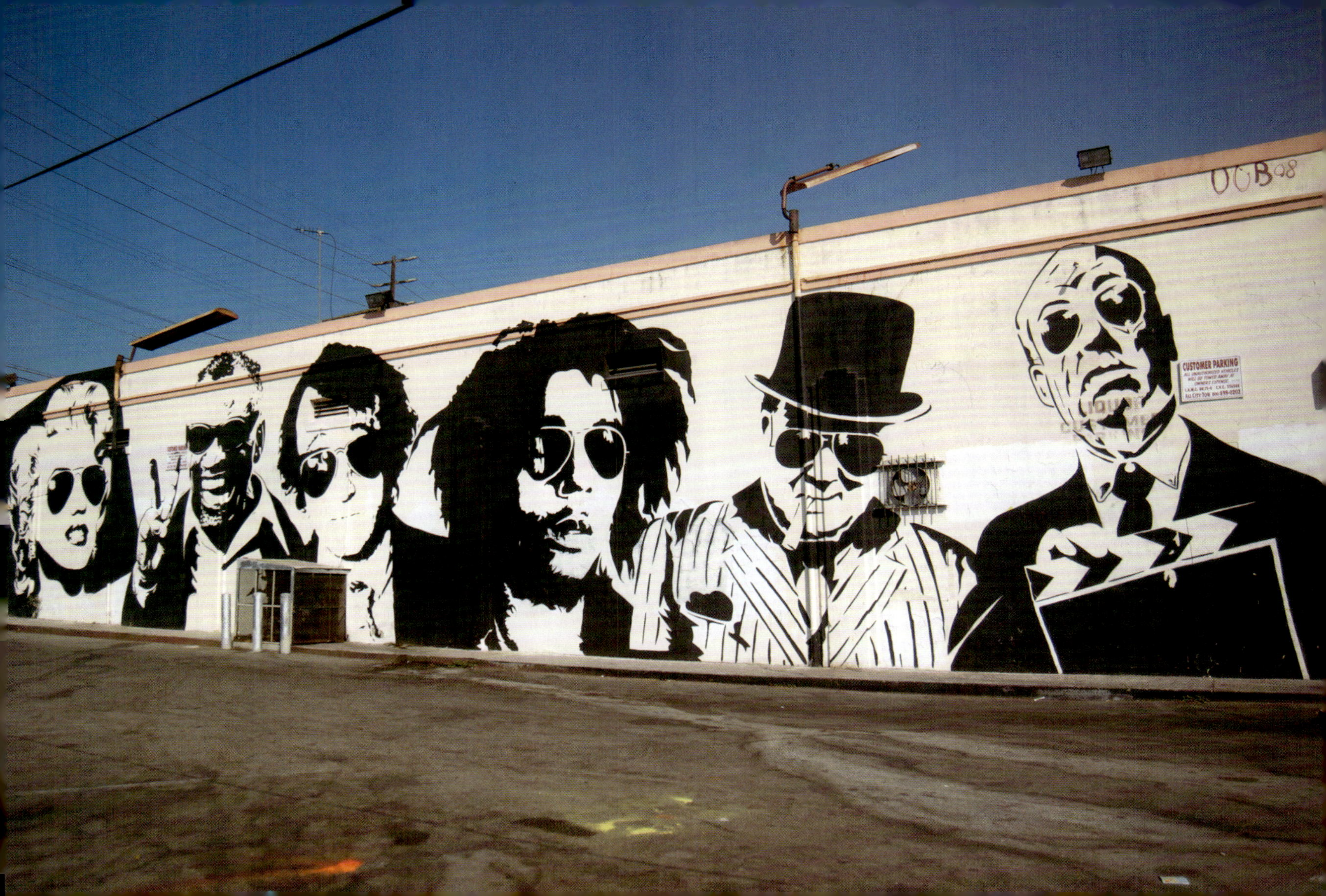
CUSTOMER PARKING

Mr. Gauky

Born in Yorkshire in northern England, Mr. Gauky was an avid doodler from an early age. By age twenty-one, he'd already started to develop his own style when a friend's mother, who was an art teacher, suggested he take an art course. This gave Mr. Gauky the time and encouragement he needed to perfect his character work and fantastically warped style.

While studying studio art, Mr. Gauky started "Free Art Fridays" in Cambridge, during which he would place mini-canvases around town in hard-to-reach locations, photograph and geotag them, and wait to see the results and comments online. This was as close as Gauky ever came to being a street artist; he always considered himself more of an illustrator and never subscribed to graffiti or its related cultures.

Today, Mr. Gauky is famous for his distinctive, wonderfully detailed cartoon characters. His grotesque, distorted freaks with peculiar features, dark noses, hunched backs, and protruding eyeballs have put him on the map as one of the Britain's most exciting and sought-after young artists.

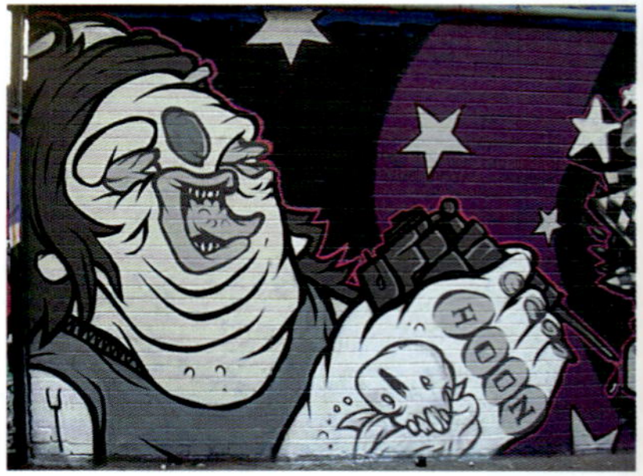

Photographs courtesy of Mr. Gauky.
Dublin, Ireland, 2009.
Detail: *Letherhead*. 2008.

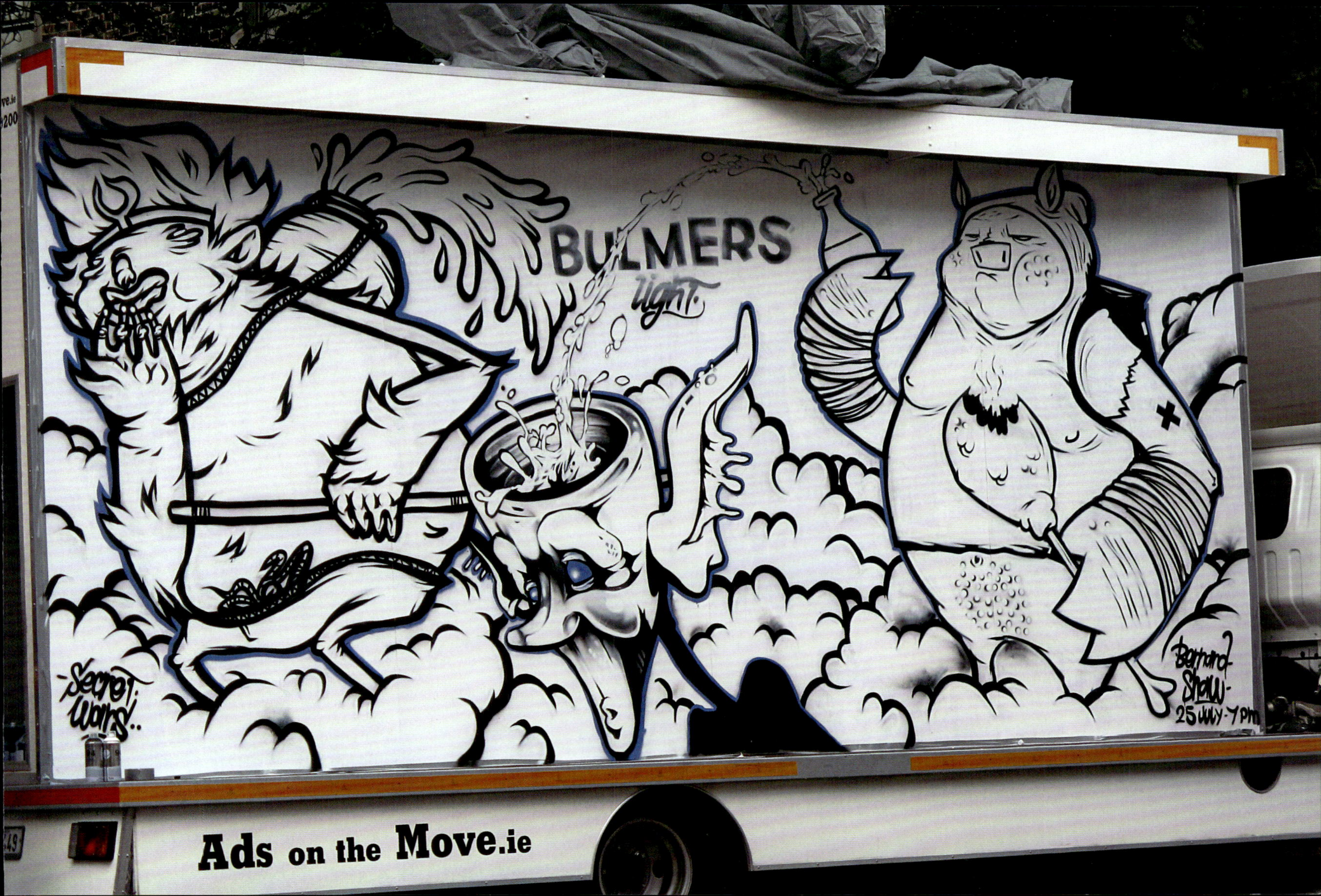
BULMERS
light
Secret Wars..
Bernard Shaw
25 July - 7pm
Ads on the Move.ie

Mystery Train

Ah, the Internet. Bustling with information, misinformation, commerce, conspiracy theories, and double-dealing. And an entirely painted New York City subway train—maybe. It is alleged to have been painted in January 2007, but the backstories that go along with it have no shortage of mystery, as well as a big dose of all the aforementioned.

The complete train says MADE U LOOK, but for us it might as well say MADE U WONDER—wonder, that is, if the paint job really occurred, or if it did, but perhaps only in Photoshop? Painting a subway train ten cars long in 2007 seems implausible, if not downright impossible, and it may well be both. Almost as quickly as photos of this gargantuan feat appeared on the Internet, so too did a website offering to sell a video of the Chicago-based MUL crew accomplishing the deed.

Conspiracy theories abound: The train had never actually been painted, or perhaps the mission was funded by Hasbro as part of a guerilla advertising campaign. After all, the front car did feature Rich Uncle Pennybags (of Monopoly fame). Did Broadway and Park Place suddenly need a little street cred? When the dialogue becomes this confusing, it's perhaps best just to believe that a crew from Chicago rolled the dice, landed on New York, and monopolized the railroad.

Photographs by Mystery Donor.
New York City, 2007.

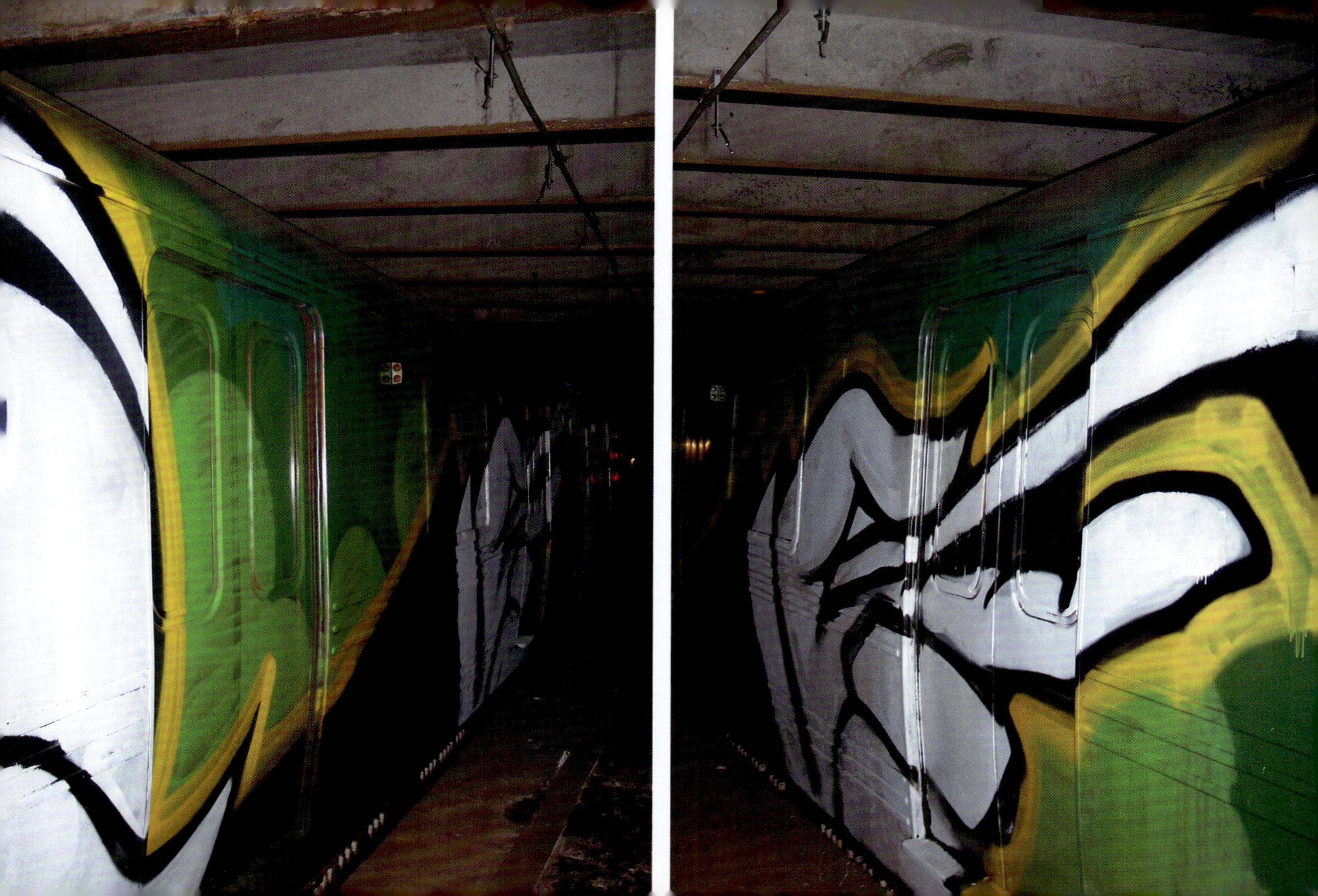

Nada

Of Swiss origin, Nada is a key [and the only international] member of the Los Angeles-based crew All Mighty 7. Founded in 1987, AM7 was one of the first West Coast graffiti groups to paint over entire billboards in the late 1980s and early 1990s, pioneering a Los Angeles tradition that rages on to this day. Known for his ability to create photorealistic imagery with spray cans at any scale, Nada has worked, painting both legally and illegally, in the public realm since 1989.

By traveling the world and painting at innumerable festivals and events, Nada has collaborated with some of the biggest names in graffiti. He made the transition into commercial artwork toward the close of the millennium, and has since been commissioned to paint furniture for legendary designer Phillipe Starcke. Nada founded a graphic design and illustration firm in 2001 and a vinyl-toy design company in 2007. He continues to paint murals on commission and to work on canvas, applying his style to all varieties of mediums.

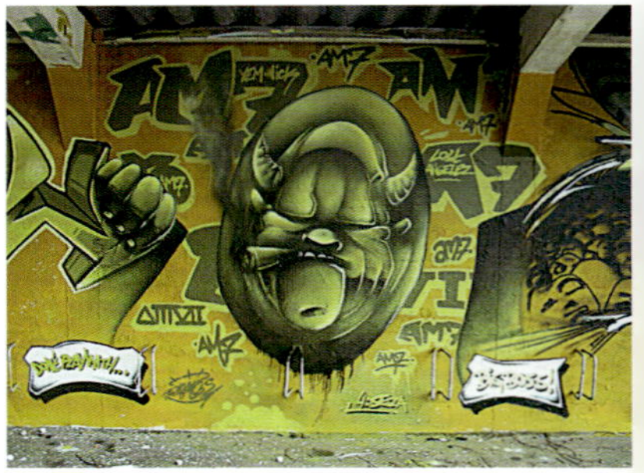

Photographs courtesy of Nada.
Zurich, Switzerland, 2009.
Detail: Martigny, Switzerland, 2008.

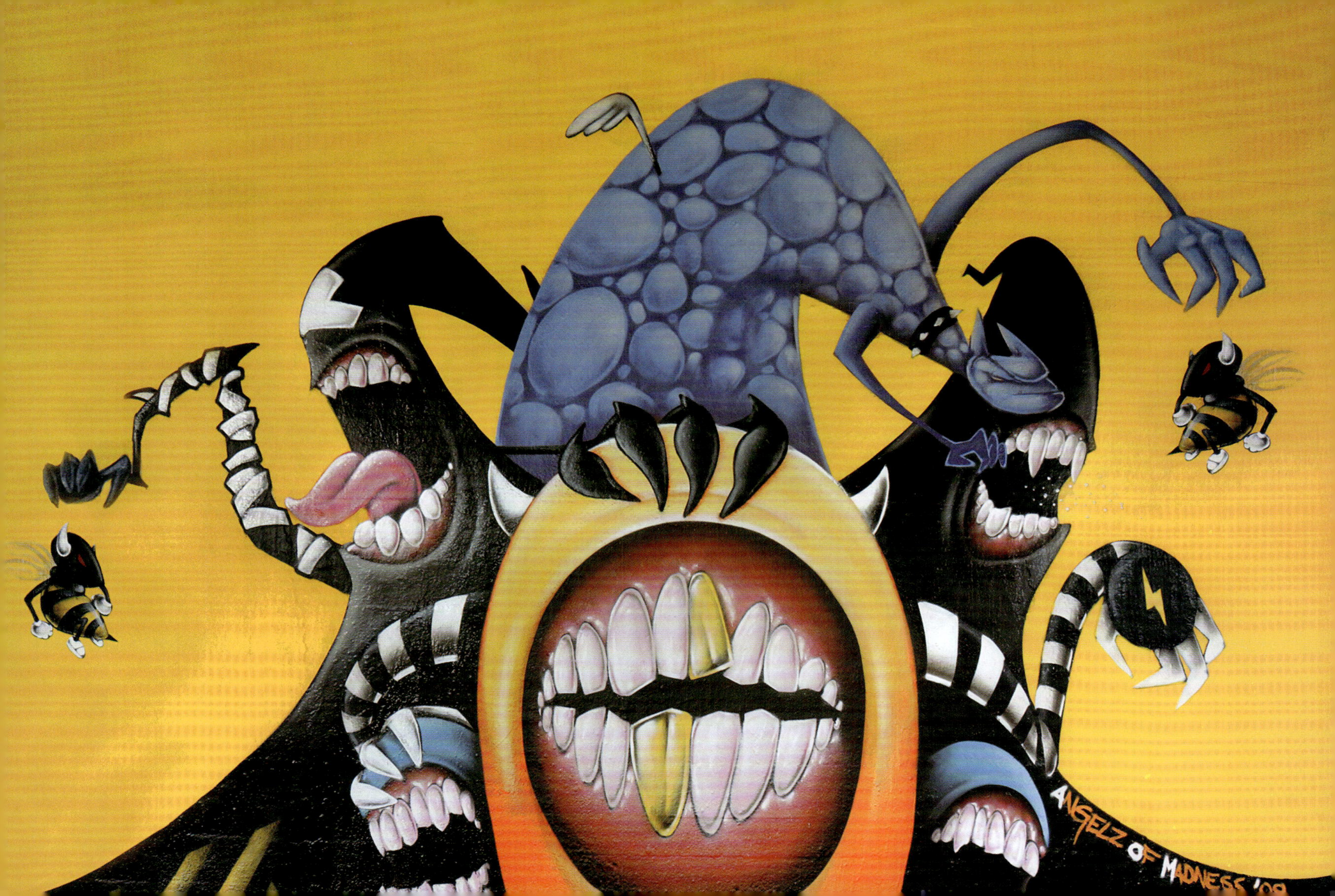
ANGELZ OF MADNESS '08

Neck Face

One of New York's most notorious anonymous street artists is Neck Face. Ominous in moniker and style, Neck Face's stickers and tags first appeared on the streets of Sacramento and San Francisco, California, the state to which the artist is native. Eventually, he moved to New York to study fine arts at the prestigious School of Visual Arts. He dropped out after two years, but his street campaign continued.

Primarily described as scary or monster-centric, Neck Face is as recognizable for his tags as for his signature style of character: bare-fanged imaginary creatures drawn with an oddly unsophisticated, scratchy line style. He gained immense notoriety for a 2005 piece in which he defaced a billboard for the New York shop My Old Lady, transforming it into the comical message MY OLD LADY ♥'S NECK FACE.

Neck Face's work has been included in exhibitions at the New Image Art Gallery in Los Angeles, for which he adapted his style to the indoors; the Luggage Store Gallery in San Francisco; and most recently, the OHWOW Gallery in Miami.

Photograph by Vincent Cornelli. New York City, 2006.

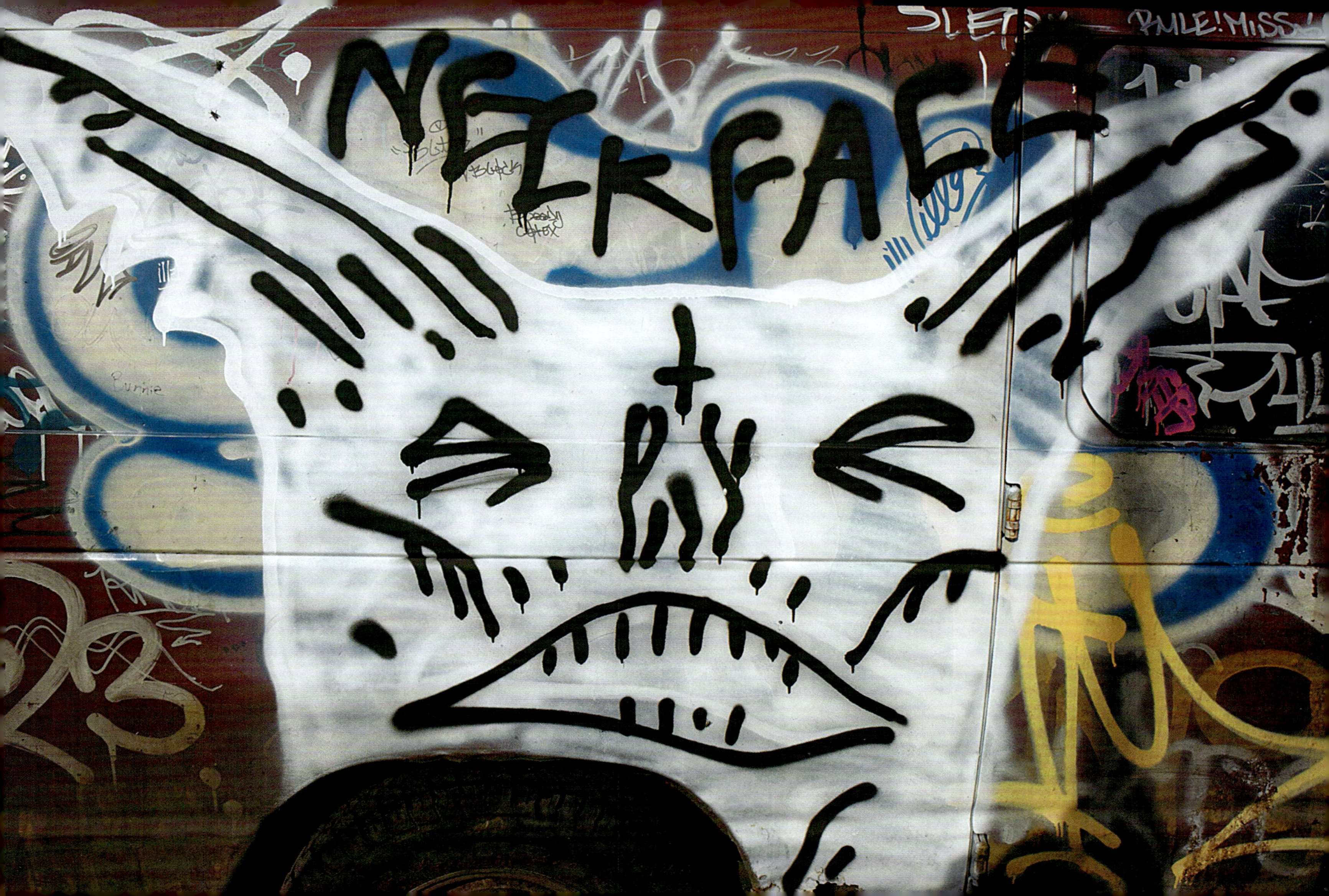

Nina

The Brazilian street artist Nina Pandolfo, known simply as Nina, creates a unique brand of paintings that are simultaneously cute and sweet—with sparkly images of puppies, unicorns, and bug-eyed girls—as well as dark and turbulent. "Menacingly adorable" would be an appropriate description of her work, which she has been creating since the 1980s.

Nina has been painting and drawing since she was a tiny child. Untrained in any classical sense, she dropped out of early art classes because the other students were all boys, and they teased her. In high school, she befriended a number of graffiti artists, including legendary Brazilian graffiti-to-fine-art crossovers Otavio and Gustavo Pandolfo, the twin brothers known as Os Gemeos (see 248). Nina and Os Gemeos formed what would be an enduring bond, and she has painted alongside them for numerous years, eventually marrying Otavio.

Nina has traveled the world, creating large-scale mural works, both in collaboration with her longtime painting partners and as a solo artist. She has also been included in numerous gallery exhibitions from Miami to India, and in several museum shows, including the Örebro Museum in Sweden.

Photograph by Eric Marechal.
São Paulo, Brazil, 2008.

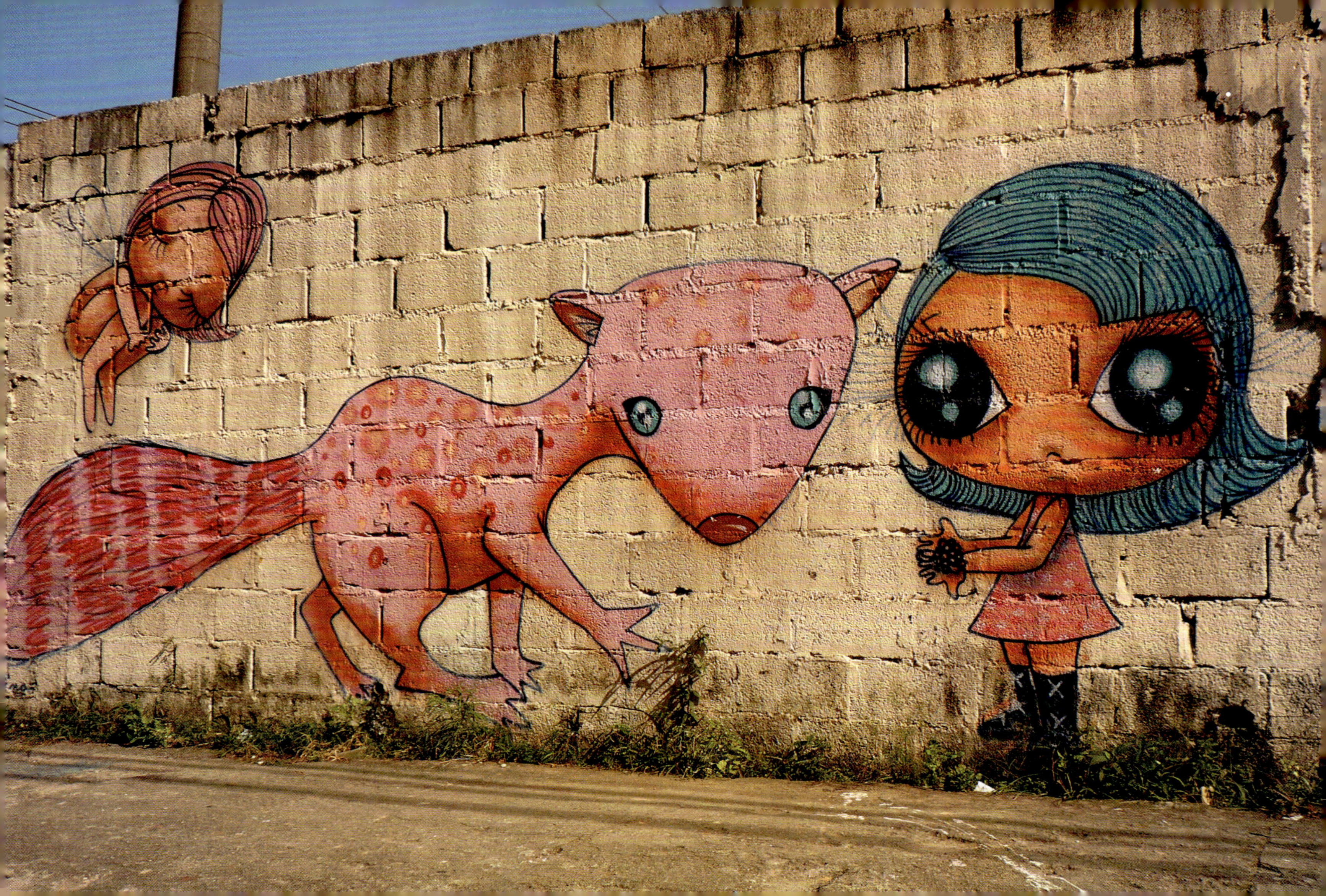

NOGA

Jack Pelsinger had helped Hugo Martinez to form UGA (United Graffiti Artists, see 346); Pelsigner was fascinated with graffiti and the kids who wrote it. In late 1974, he became disillusioned with the Martinez group and its elitism; Pelsinger wanted to form a new art collective that made room for kids of all skill levels. He called the group NOGA, an acronym for Nation of Graffiti Artists, and found an abandoned storefront at 88th Street and Columbus Avenue. Pelsinger swung a deal with the city to rent it for a dollar a month, and soon, the building's exterior wall was painted by the great writers of the day, free of charge.

NOGA membership included a mixture of many local novices, as well as some standout talent. All of them executed highly regarded canvases, although few commercial opportunities existed, as nascent interest in gallery graffiti began to wane by 1975. Some members acted as mentors to younger, less-experienced writers. Most members of the group, particularly the younger ones, found great payoff in the social networking; NOGA became a safe haven where kids could meet, stash stolen paint, and plan future subway missions. NOGA lost its space in 1976 and reinvented itself in the South Bronx, where it continued on and off until 1980.

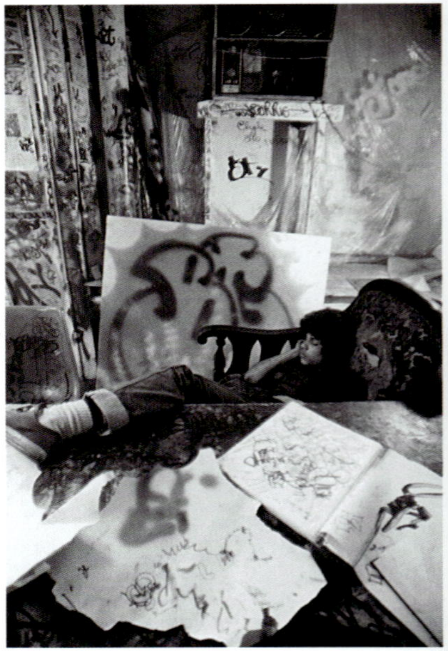

Photographs by Michael Lawrence.
Opie (left, background), with three unknown artists.
Canvases by Blood Tea, Sal 161, and RB1.
New York City, 1975.
Detail: New York City, 1975.

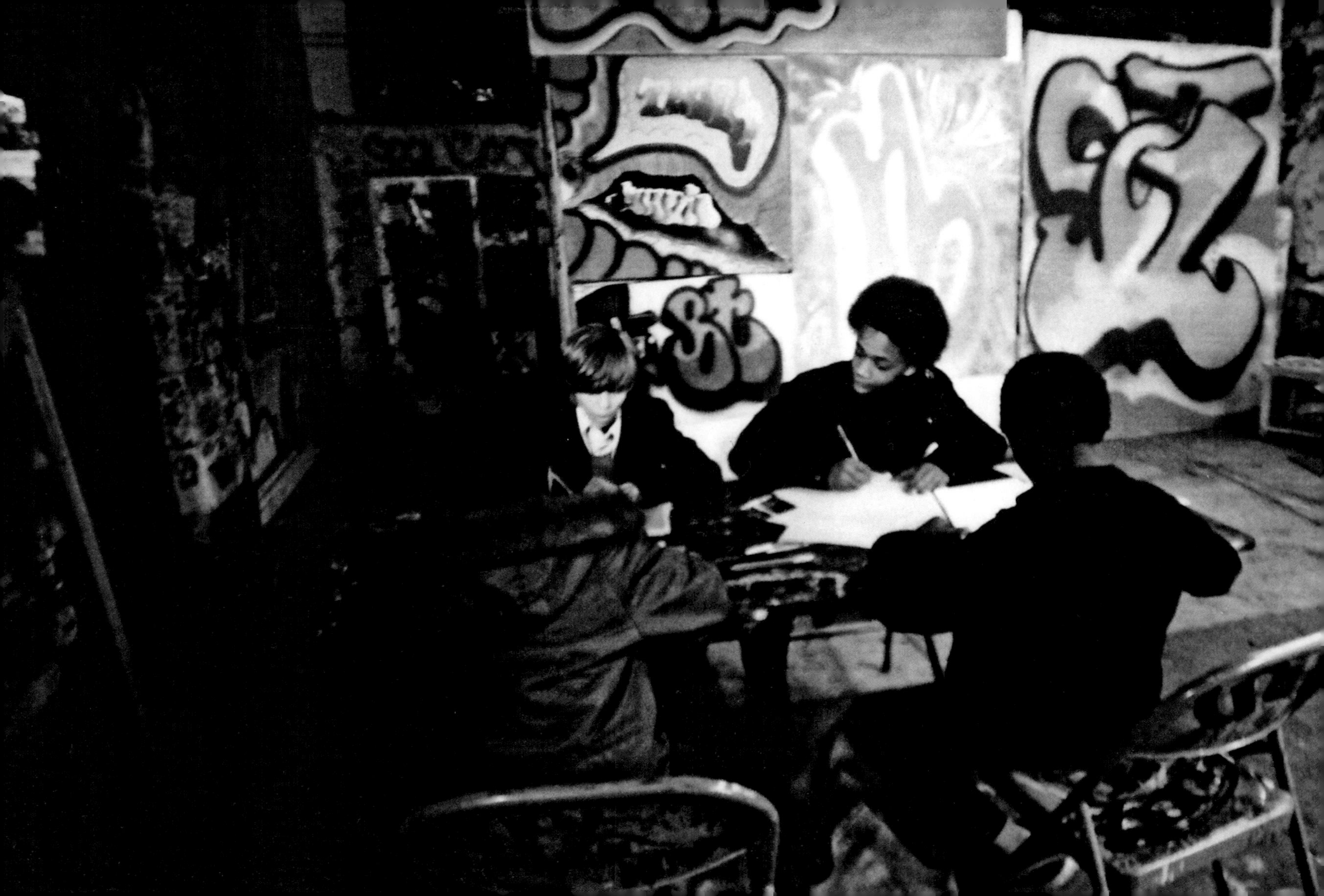

Nomad

One of the best-known names in the Berlin street-art scene, Nomad has been painting walls, hosting gallery shows, and generally, being wildly energetic and zany for more than a decade. Nomad likes to toy with people's notions of what urban art is, or can be, as well as with the boundaries of what people expect from his work. A deeply rebellious spirit, Nomad is increasingly hard to pin down.

Despite the credit awarded him by his community, when he is referred to in interviews as a street artist, he has been known to say, "Street art can kiss my ass." He has expressed open disdain for the hysteria surrounding the culture, and states clearly that he doesn't subscribe to any scene or movement—he is simply a bomber. His mantra is "Stop the thinking, start the doing."

Applying his mischievous and comical instincts to his paintings, Nomad infuses his work with notes of Keith Haring (see 160) and a cartoon culture of poking fun. It is next to impossible to know when Nomad is serious, if ever; he often creates graphic black-line drawings of characters that enter into the fantastical—their heads pop off and become balloons, or their teeth extend the lengths of their bodies.

Nomad has also established a fine-art career for himself, exhibiting internationally, with a base at the Circle Culture Gallery in Berlin.

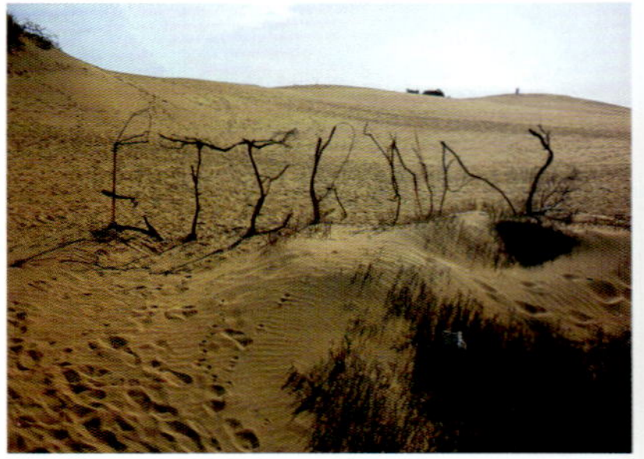

Photographs courtesy of Nomad.
Berlin, Germany, 2009.
Detail: Maspalomas Dunes, Grancanaria, 2010.

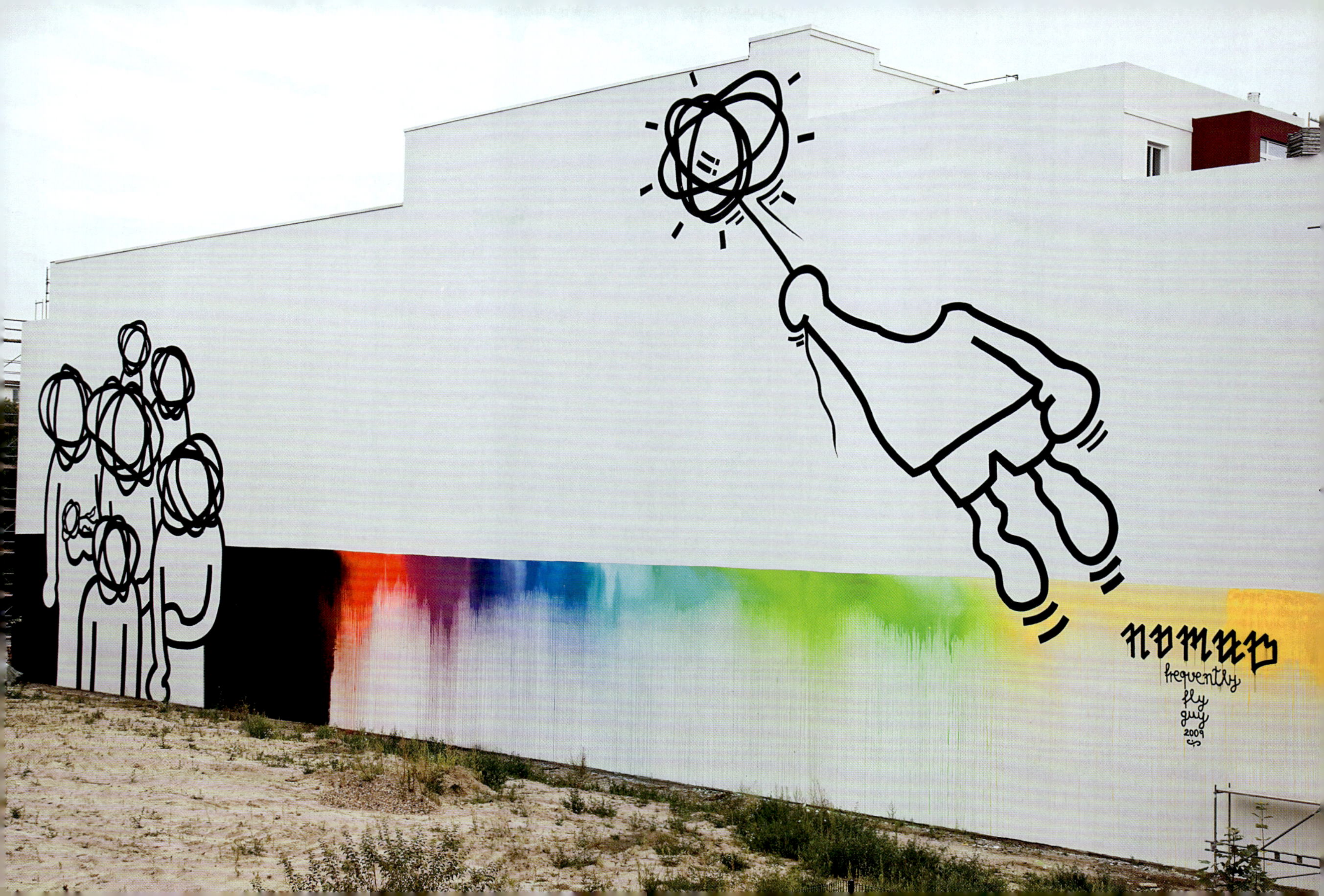
frequently
fly
guy
2009

Nychos

Nychos was raised in the forests of Styria (south of Austria), where he found inspiration in the roughness of nature. From a very early age, he has been interested in comics and cartooning. At age seven, he was profoundly influenced by the film *Watership Down*. Over the years, other films featuring rabbits, such as *Alice in Wonderland* and *Donnie Darko*, have made him consider the links between rabbits, creative destruction, and the breakdown of society. "Rabbits operate outside of our system," says Nychos, "and have no rules to follow. They appear whenever and wherever they want."

And ever since Nychos's entry into the Austrian, and then global, graffiti scene, his rabbits have done just that, with pieces appearing in cities all over the world, including New York, Melbourne, Berlin, and Paris. In 2005, Nychos's obsession with the "white rabbit" led him to create the "RABBIT EYE MOVEMENT!" project—a small but important part of his creative universe.

Nychos has been invited to festivals, graffiti jams, and solo and group exhibitions throughout Europe on the basis of his morbid but highly detailed work. Despite breaking into the gallery scene, Nychos remains active on the streets, whether painting on the Danube canal or abandoned trains. He often collaborates with the worlds' most accomplished painters, making him one of the most noticeable breakout artists from the Austrian scene.

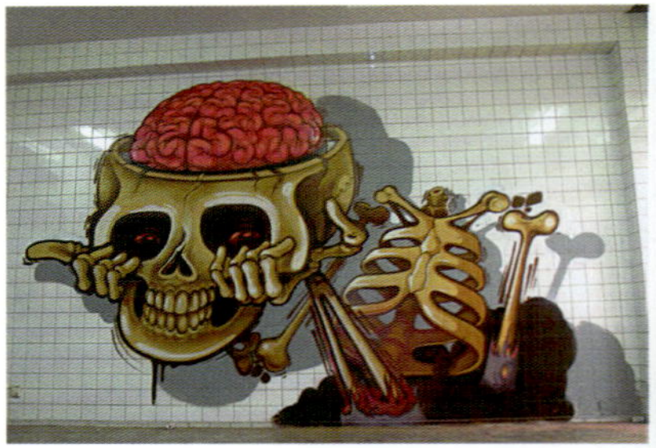

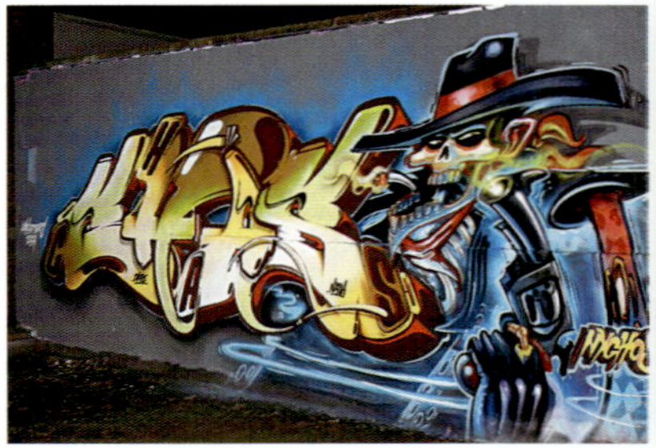

Photographs courtesy of Nychos.
Basel, Switzerland, 2010.
Details: Vienna, Austria, 2010.

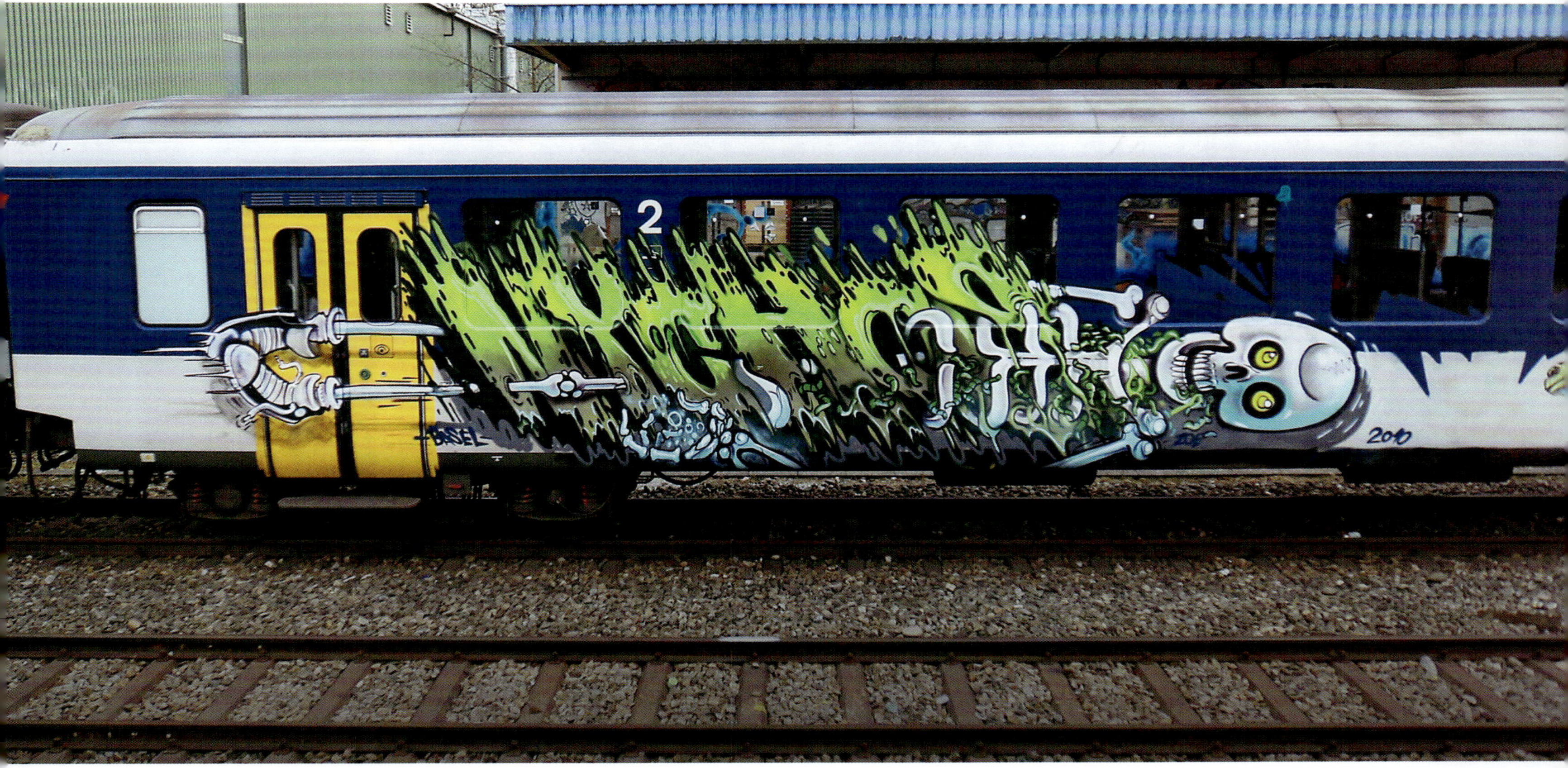
2
BASEL
2010

Odeith

The Portuguese graffiti writer who now goes by the name Odeith has been making his distinctive mark on public walls and spaces since 1996. Originally bombing with the tag Eith, the artist made a deep impression with his highly abstracted lettering work and intricate murals. He created these large-scale pieces mostly in and around Portugal throughout the 1990s and into the early 2000s. In 1999, Odeith opened his own tattoo shop, Estudio Eith, in the Portuguese city of Benfica, which he operated successfully until 2008. He now tattoos on a private-clientele basis. The name Odeith is a hybrid of the Portuguese words for "I hate you," and the artist has been using it since 2004 to avoid confusion with his professional name.

Odeith is also known for his highly detailed mural portraitures, in particular for a stretch of wall in Lisbon known as "Odeith's Hall of Fame"—a collection of massive renderings of faces, mostly those of the destitute and desperate. Odeith claims to come from a rather desperate financial scenario himself, and he uses this as inspiration for his work.

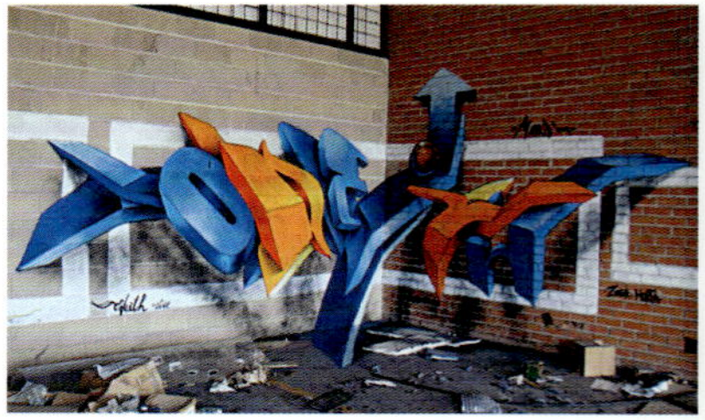

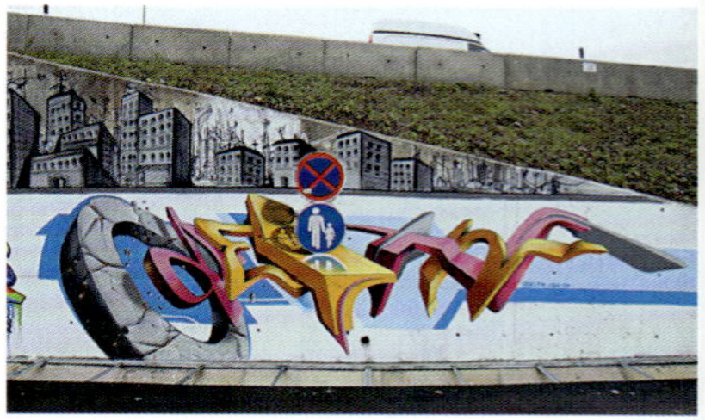

Photographs courtesy of Odeith.
Estoril, Portugal, 2009.
Detail top: Madrid, Spain, 2009.
Detail bottom: Cacem, Portugal, 2010.

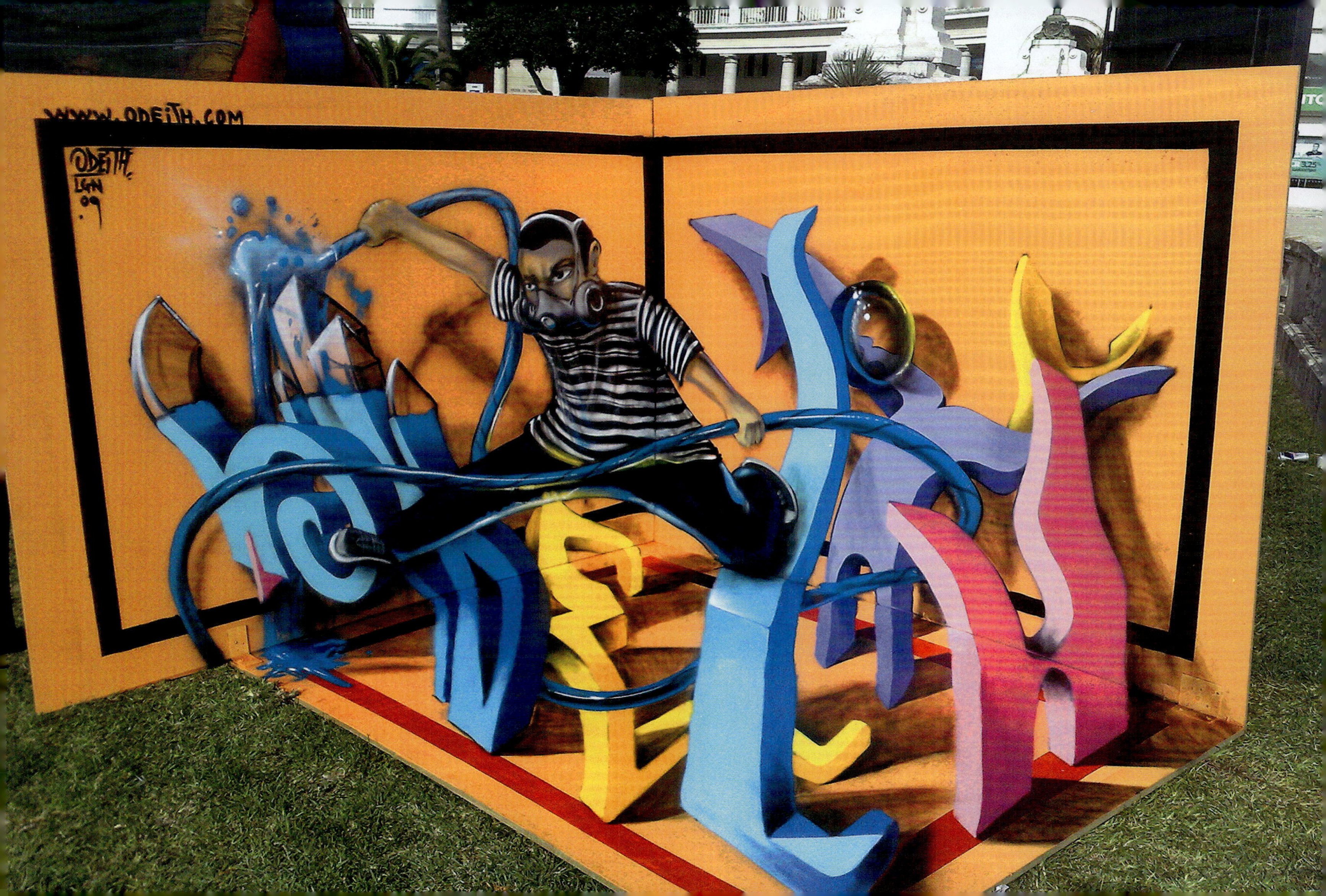
WWW.ODEITH.COM

Okuda

Okuda is Oscar San Miguel Erice, a twenty-eight-year-old Spanish artist. Born in Santander on Spain's northern coast, Okuda began taking graffiti seriously at age sixteen. He moved to Madrid to pursue an art degree and wound up making the city his home. Okuda began as a traditional graffitist, but found the hit-and-run system limiting. Now he paints international wall art, and he is, undeniably, a true master of the form.

Okuda's visual world is populated by open craniums, headless livestock with trees sprouting from their spines, Easter-egg balloons, and minuscule figures in silhouette, often juxtaposed against modern geometric patterns. When lettering appears, it is formed out of cartoon or figurative images that give his name a playful "Where's Waldo?" effect. Okuda's paintings are meticulously rendered in brilliant colors—whimsical dreamscapes that beg for signs reading Best Viewed Under the Influence of Hallucinogens. Although Okuda retains membership in various graffiti art crews, he refers to himself as a "crew of one," and although his website lists an impressive résumé of commercial jobs and gallery shows, his walls in the Bronx confirm that this apple has not fallen far from the tree.

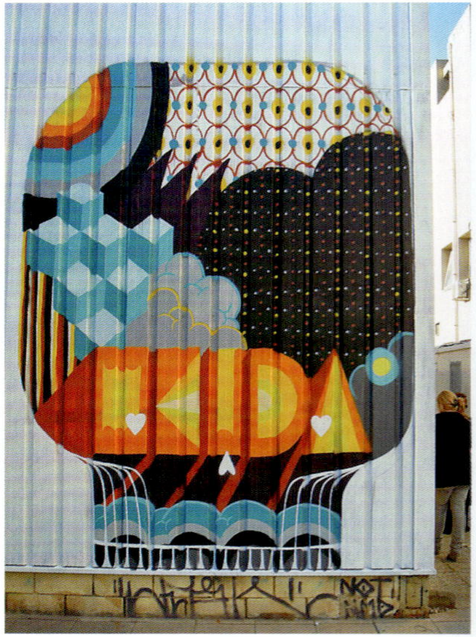

Photographs courtesy of Okuda.
***Natural Revenge*. Valencia, Spain, 2009.**
Detail: *Condemned to Stress*. NYC Showroom Gallery, New York City, 2009.

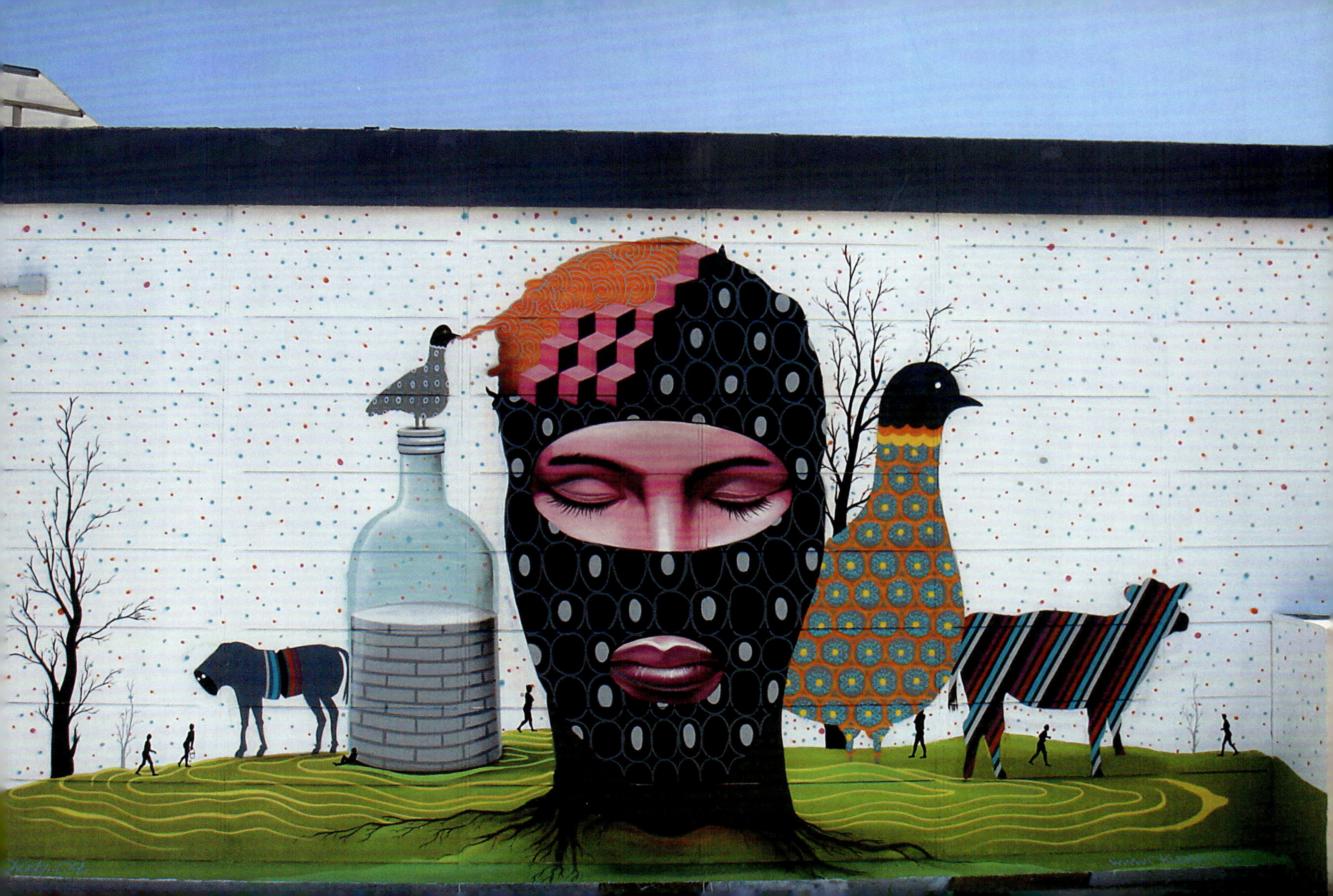

Onesto

Born in São Paulo in 1972, Alex Hornest, aka Onesto, works as a painter, sculptor, and multimedia artist. Playful and often comical, but with an underlying seriousness, Onesto's artwork reflects his deep ties to everyday people, as he celebrates their day-to-day lives in their urban environs. The most widely known of Hornest's seventy-two different writing names, each representing a distinct mode of design, "Onesto" is the one identified with the black-and-white characters that have become his signature (and most beloved) style.

Inspired by the movie *Beat Street* and images of graffiti in magazines and newspapers acquired from abroad, Onesto began painting on the streets of his city in 1992. Along with Os Gemeos and Nina Pandolfo, he was one of the first artists to make a mark on the walls of São Paulo, now renowned as a mecca of street art. A graduate of the Carlos de Campos school, Onesto cites a range of artistic influences, from the Brazilian illustrator Marcelo Grassmann to the English painter Francis Bacon.

Onesto has participated in many exhibits at home and abroad, in spaces ranging from prestigious private galleries to renowned national museums. But true to his democratic belief that graffiti belongs in the public domain, Onesto's favorite venue remains the streets.

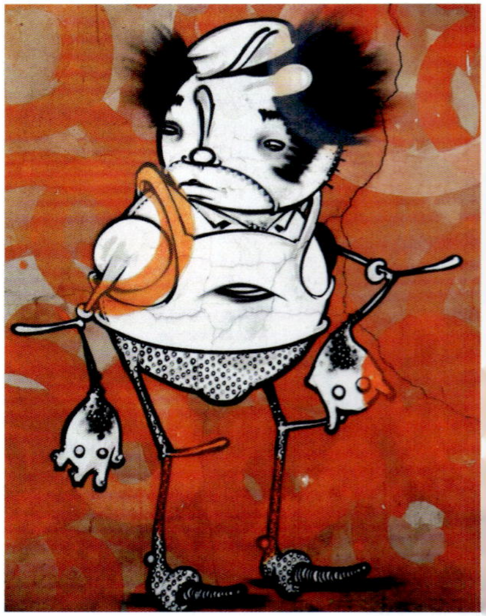

Photographs by Sara Mozeson.
São Paulo, Brazil, 2010.

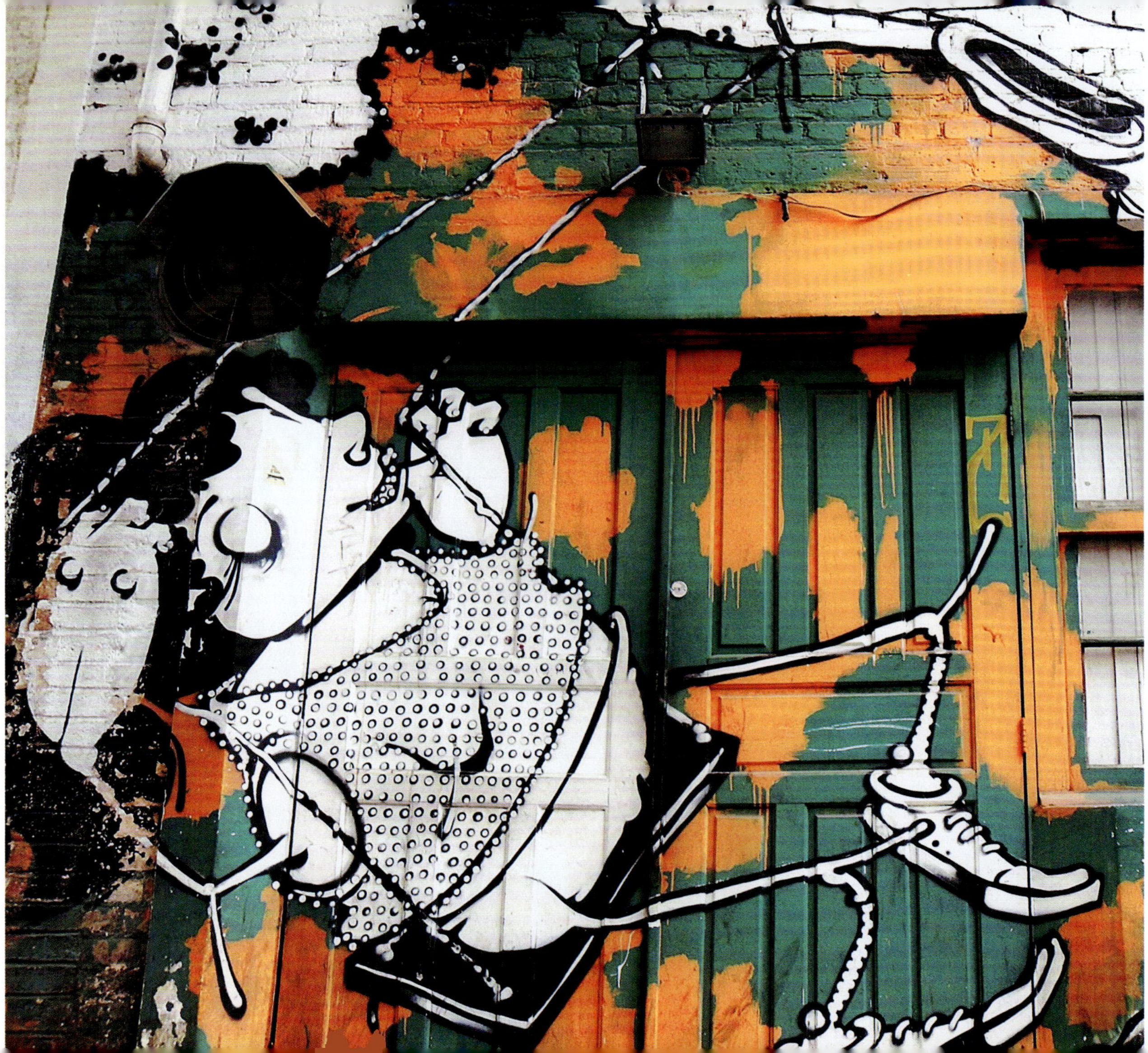

Orticanoodles

Working with multilayered stencils in intricate patterns, Orticanoodles is a crew of innovative artists who fuse elements from both high and low culture. Active on the streets of Europe since 2005, they have earned an international reputation for their first-rate, inventive stencil work. From architectural views and facades of cities to pop objects commenting on the financial crisis and the power of consumerism, their stencils reflect classic Italian traditions, as well as contemporary popular landscapes.

Among their most renowned portraits is a monochrome stencil of Jesus reminiscent of Shepard Fairey's (see 124) André the Giant. This image has achieved iconic status in Europe, where it has become a symbol of Orticanoodles's unorthodox approach to street art.

Originally from Switzerland and now based in Milan, the members of Orticanoodles also work as graphic designers, crediting Fairey as a key inspiration in their sundry styles and techniques. Among their more than fifty exhibitions in fourteen countries is a solo show that took place at the famed Galerie Itinerrance in Paris in 2010, preceded by their highly acclaimed "In Stencil We Trust" exhibition in Milan. They were also among the select group of stencil artists invited by Banksy (see 024) to participate in London's legendary 2008 Cans Festival (see 056).

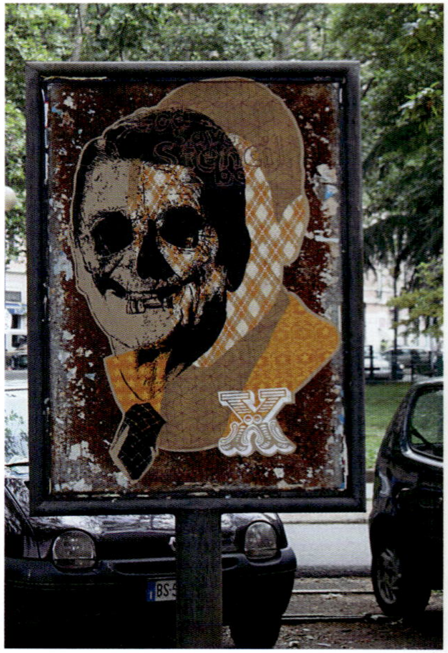

Photographs courtesy of Orticanoodles.
Amsterdam, The Netherlands, 2010.
Detail: Piazzale Susa, Milano, 2010.

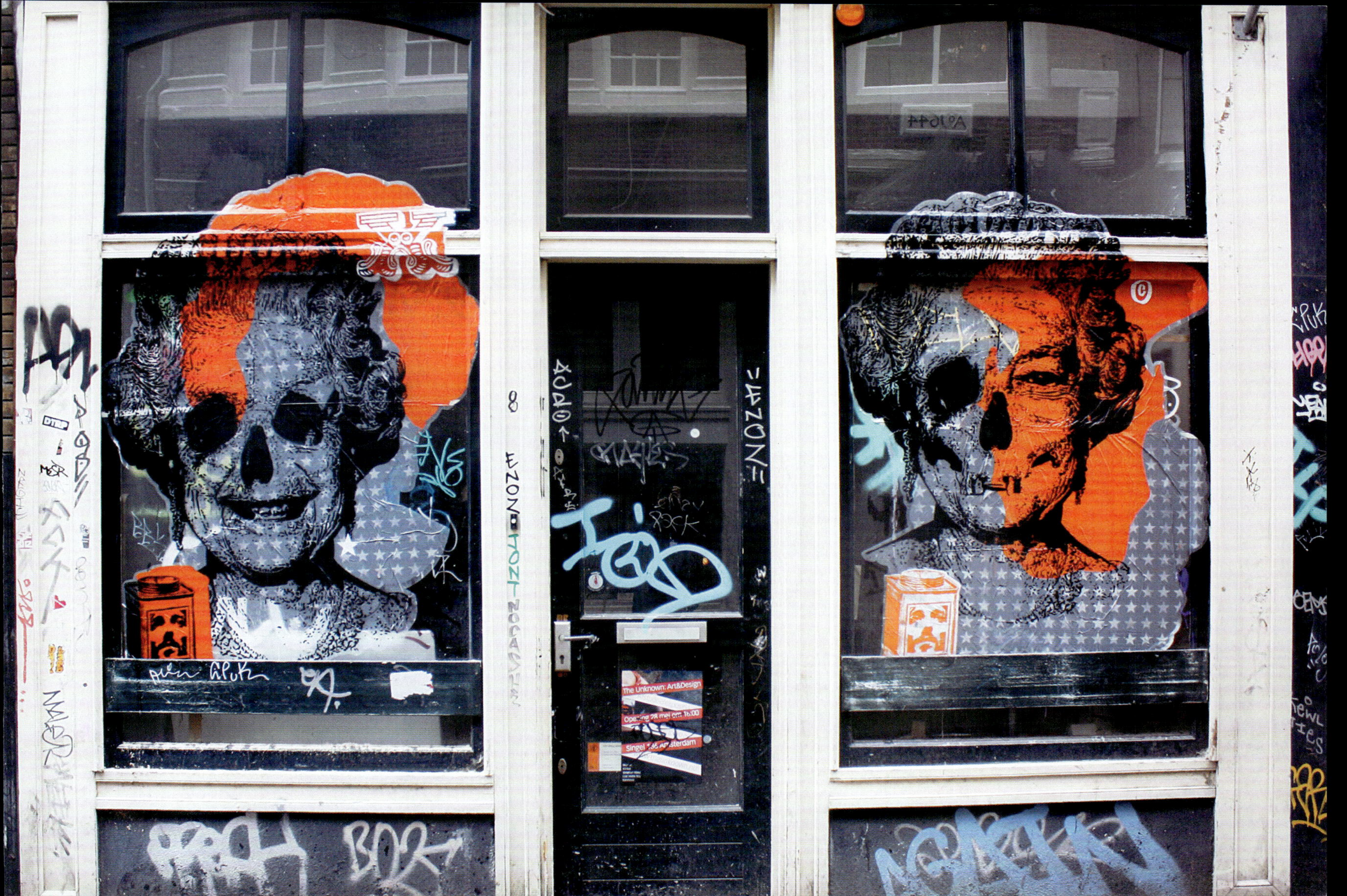
The Unknown: Art&Design

Os Gemeos

Os Gemeos is a Portuguese term meaning "the twins"—in this case a literal moniker, as Os Gemeos are identical twin brothers. Originally from São Paulo, Brazil, Otavio and Gustavo Pandolfo began painting graffiti in 1987, influenced both by traditional graffiti and by São Paulo's native *pixação* [see 257] tagging, a style of graffiti known for its simple, angular lines and cryptic characters. Already influential in Brazil, the twins were exposed to a new world of street art and graffiti when they chanced upon Barry McGee, who was studying in Brazil, in 1993. During the following decade, after several years emulating early New York–style graffiti, they came into what would become their signature look: a mixture of graffiti and murals featuring hyperdetailed caricatures and creatures, often with yellow skin.

In 1997, following an interview featuring their work in *12ozProphet* magazine, the twins were exposed to an international audience. They quickly became super-stars within the street-art world, once websites like woostercollective.com began featuring them early in the next decade.

Uniquely collaborative, the twins don't divide their workload; they create every element together, appearing at times to be almost telepathic in their coordination.

Os Gemeos have exhibited internationally, including a solo show in 2008 at the influential Deitch Projects in New York, and they were also a cameo feature in some of the "Beautiful Losers" exhibition [see 030].

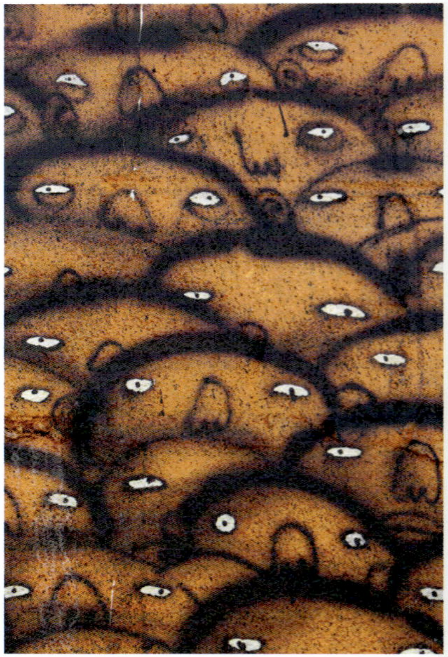

Photographs by Eric Marechal.
São Paulo, Brazil, 2008 [left] and 2009 [right].
Detail: Photograph by Ray Mock.
Brooklyn, New York, 2008.

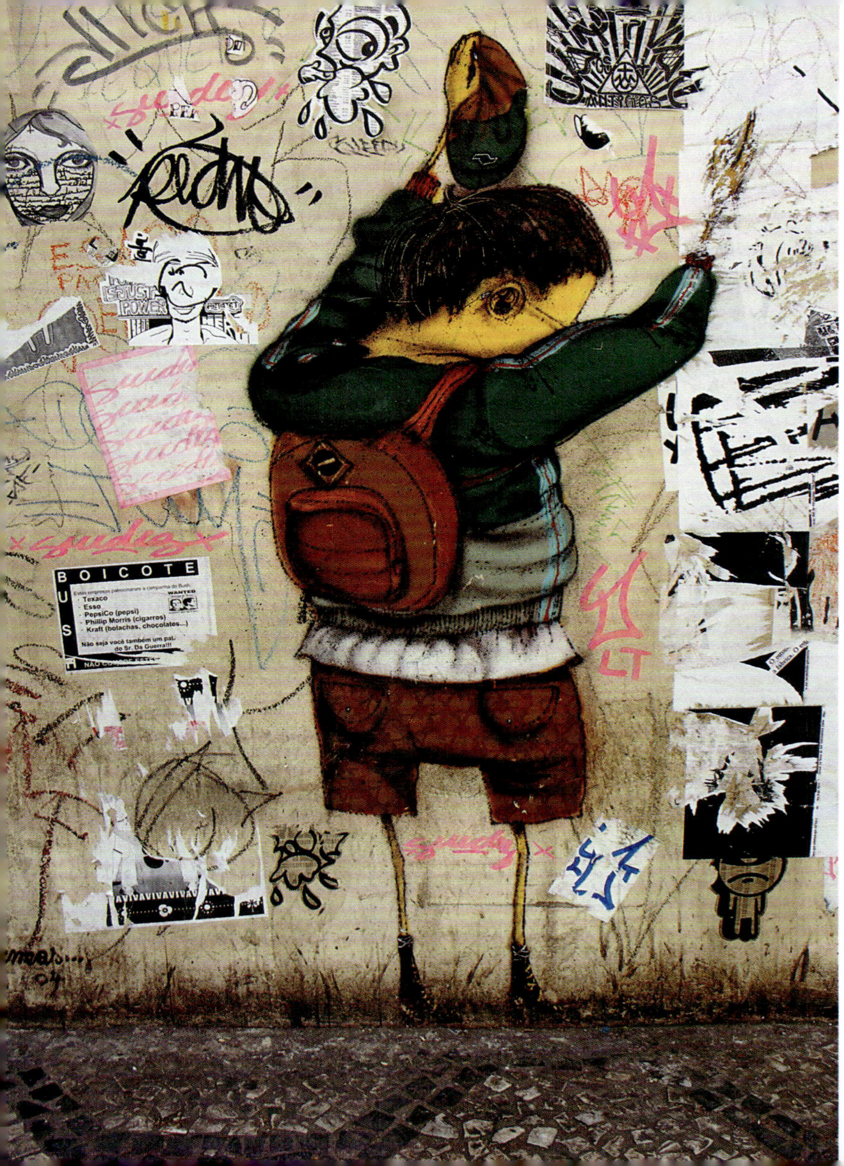
BOICOTE
BUSH
WANTED
- Texaco
- Esso
- PepsiCo (pepsi)
- Phillip Morris (cigarros)
- Kraft (bolachas, chocolates...)
Não seja você também um pai
do Sr. Da Guerra!!!

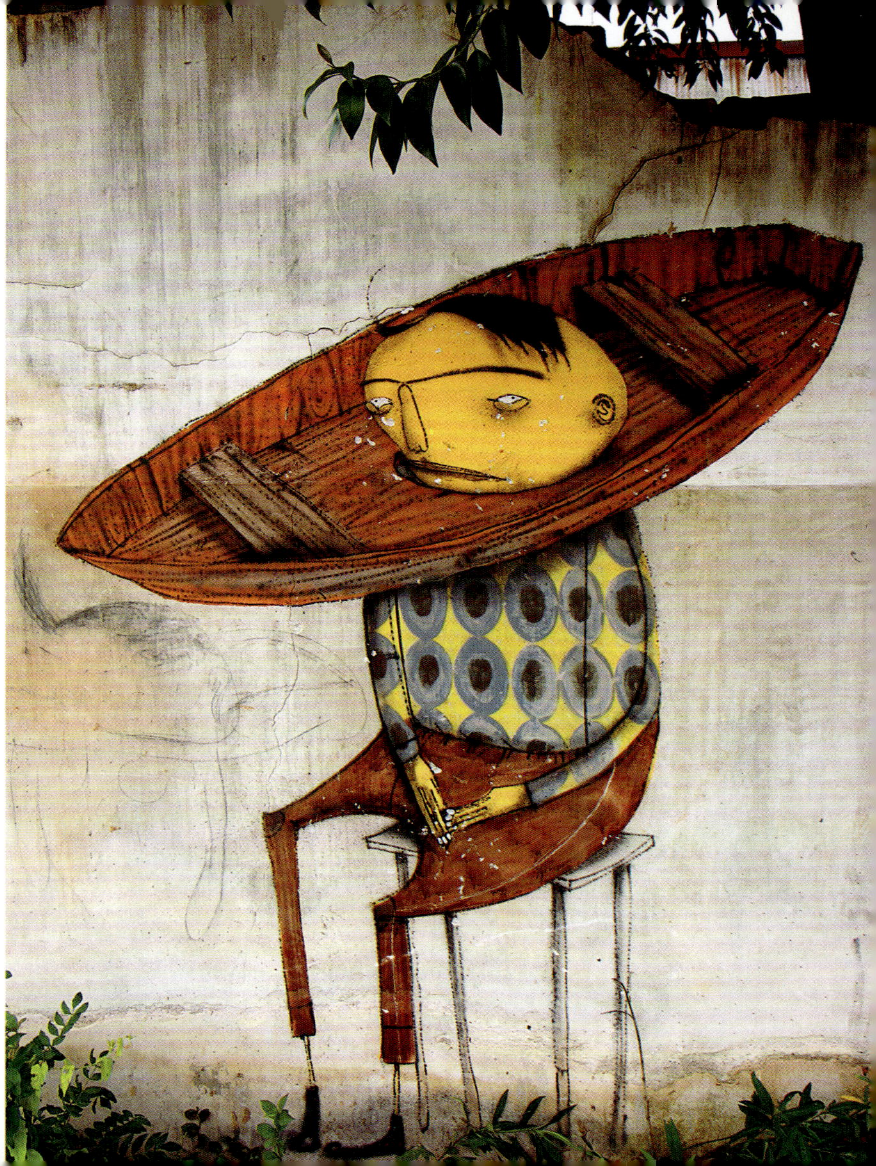

Ovni

Anna Taratiel, aka Ovni, was born in Barcelona, Spain, in 1980. Formally educated in painting and graphic design, she creates stylish landscapes on surfaces ranging from city walls and abandoned factories to stark white paper and canvases. Distinctive in their composition of colors, contours, and forms, they draw on the artist's personal experiences and diverse influences, as she creates an original visual world to share with others.

Complex, spirited, and abstract, Ovni's images, in her own words, are designed to transport her viewers to another place "with different dimensions and perspectives." She particularly enjoys creating installations because they allow her to present her concepts in three dimensions, where beauty and chaos coexist and collide among cardboard boxes and crates. She cites among her influences Spanish architect and designer Antoni Gaudí, renowned for his extraordinary use of color and shape, and she also draws inspiration from children and their fantasies.

Acclaimed as a graphic designer, painter, illustrator, and street artist, Ovni has exhibited her work in galleries worldwide, with solo shows in Lisbon, Milan, and Barcelona. Her distinct artwork, fusing organic and static shapes, has also been widely commissioned for design fairs. Among these was "Dynamic Equilibrium," a site-specific installation for Milan Design Week in 2009.

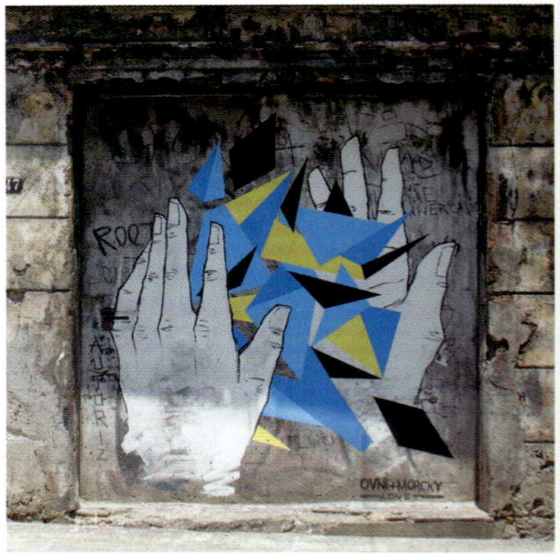

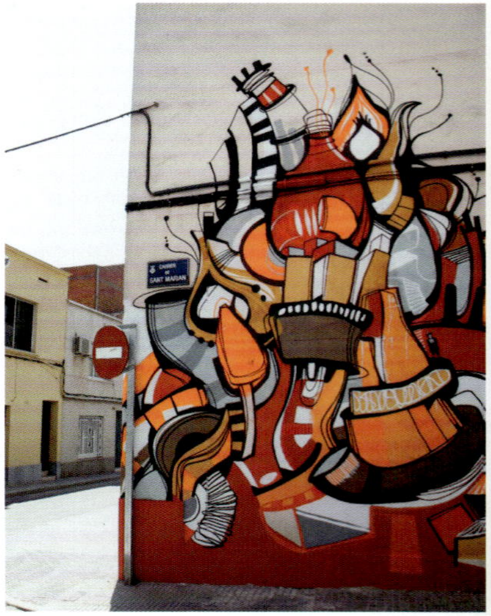

Photographs courtesy of Ovni.
Collaboration with Just. Berlin, Germany, 2007.
Detail top: Collaboration with Morcky Troubles. Brazil, 2009.
Detail bottom: Barcelona, 2008.

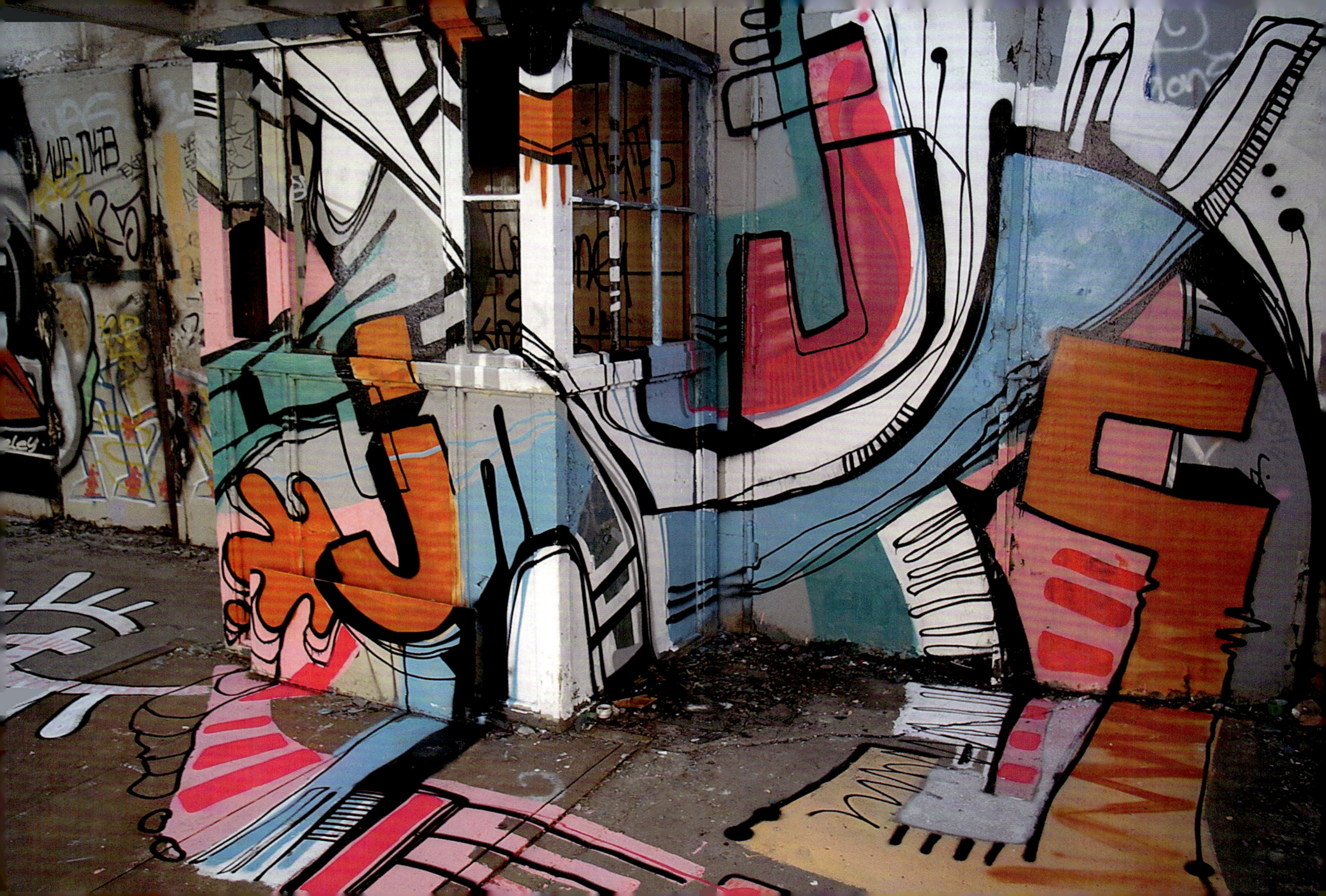

paint

There is no better indicator of graffiti's arrival as a serious art form than the recent improvements to its primary tool, spray paint. Forty years ago, when Taki 183 [see 331] was getting his start, graffiti writers were forced to make do with a limited palette. Hardware-store shelves were dominated by three major brands: Red Devil, Krylon, and Rustoleum, along with countless minor brands of lesser quality. By the late 1980s, with the graffiti movement becoming a global phenomenon, the limitations of the existing paints became an issue.

Traditional spray paint, designed for industrial and hobby applications, lacked the color spectrum and density to satisfy rapidly advancing artistic demands. Germany became the first country to identify and produce spray paint specifically made for a new, quickly expanding market. In the years since, Spain, Italy, and Australia have joined the competitive spray-paint market, often employing international graffiti masters as color consultants, product spokesmen, and field testers.

In the good old days, a can of spray paint cost $2.00 for colors like Lawn Green, Chinese Red, or Leather Brown. Of course, truth be told, most graffiti writers never paid for it. Fast-forward to the present: German designer spray paint costs $8.00 a can, and it is certainly being paid for more often than not these days. For the discriminating sprayer, a limited edition can of Dondi White [see 097], named after the late graffiti master of the same name, will run you about $60.00. That is, if you can find one.

Photograph by Ruedi One.
Montana Paint Factory, Germany, 2009.

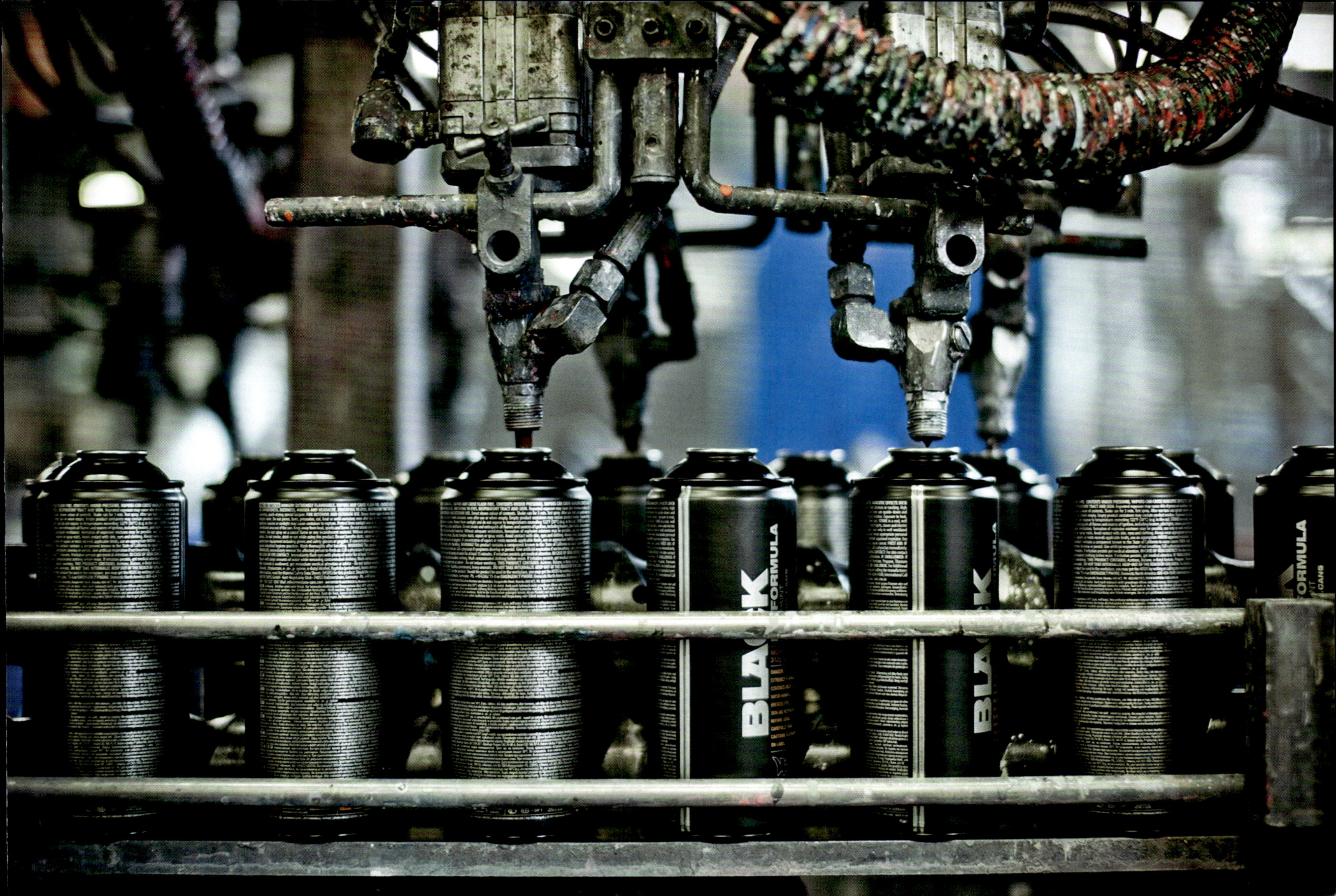
FORMULA

Part

Part grew up in Spanish Harlem during the tumultuous 1960s and started writing on walls in his community in 1973. Late in that year, he made his first visit to the #7 yard in Queens, and by 1974 he had become a fixture on the #6 line, where his style developed quickly. In 1975 and 1976, when writers were no longer putting a premium on style (whole-cars and throw-ups were the new fad), Part continued to expand his vocabulary. The payoff came in the form of an invitation to join the newly formed Death Squad (see 086), a crew that featured only the top stylists. From 1977 to 1979, the Death Squad was untouchable and helped to revive a sagging interest in style on the trains. Part continued to paint trains through 1984, giving him a decade-long portfolio of subway work.

When he left the trains, Part went back to his roots in Spanish Harlem and began painting murals. These pieces showed a newfound maturity that came with not having to look over his shoulder constantly. As graffiti left the trains in 1989 and more writers began doing walls, Part could be found traveling from one site to another, doing two pieces in one day.

As a historical footnote, Part has done stylized pieces illegally almost nonstop for thirty-six years—no other writer can make that claim. In his last visit to Europe, he was one of three New York writers to be asked to paint at the prestigious Cartier Foundation retrospective on graffiti.

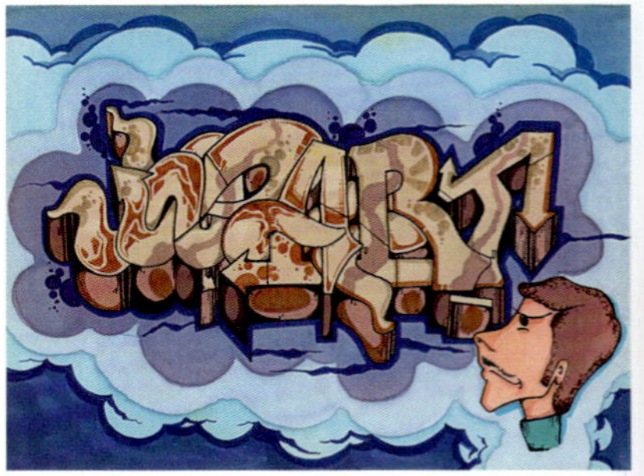

Private collection. 2007.

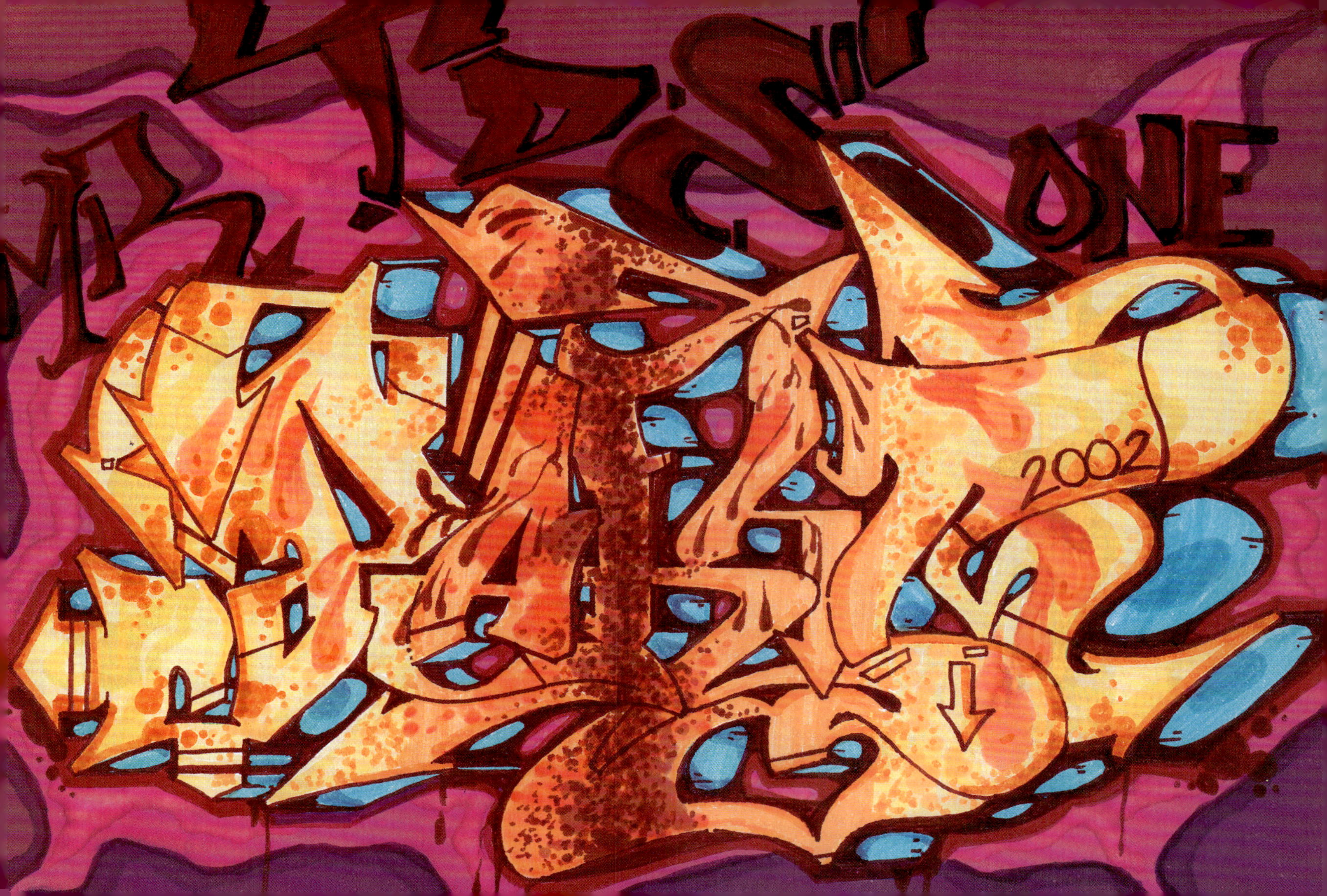
ONE
2002

perm spots

Public artists have been frustrated with the challenges of becoming a permanent fixture in an ephemeral world since their sport commenced. To complicate matters, unsanctioned graffiti and street art have, over the course of the past two decades, become even less tolerated and even more criminalized: Getting caught nowadays can land an artist in the slammer for a couple of years. Painted subway cars are now held back in the station and never hit the public, and freight painters do it simply to impress one another. The work of tunnel bombers lasts forever, but their audience is limited to transit workers and other tunnel bombers. Avenues for trumpeting one's existence to the masses have never been more limited or risky.

Alas, one of the last mainstays of the culture, the perm spot, has now become one of the most popular, and rooftops that can be seen from heavily trafficked roads and streets remain highly coveted. The rule of thumb when anticipating longevity by bombing a perm spot is that the more dangerous and difficult it is to commandeer a location, the less likely that some cleanup crew will paint over it.

LSD Om [see 206], a 1970s subway writer, targeted the spot adjacent to the cornerstones of apartment buildings. His tags survived ten years after the work of his peers vanished. Another writer, Keylo, also got lucky. He painted a rooftop adjoining a building that was subsequently demolished. No stranger to perm spots, he had already made a name for himself on water towers and subway elevations.

Buffing and surveillance technology has curtailed public art, but with the advent of innovations like acid-etch markers, paint-loaded fire extinguishers, and super glue, there is still a mark to be made.

Photograph by Keylo. New York City, 1988.

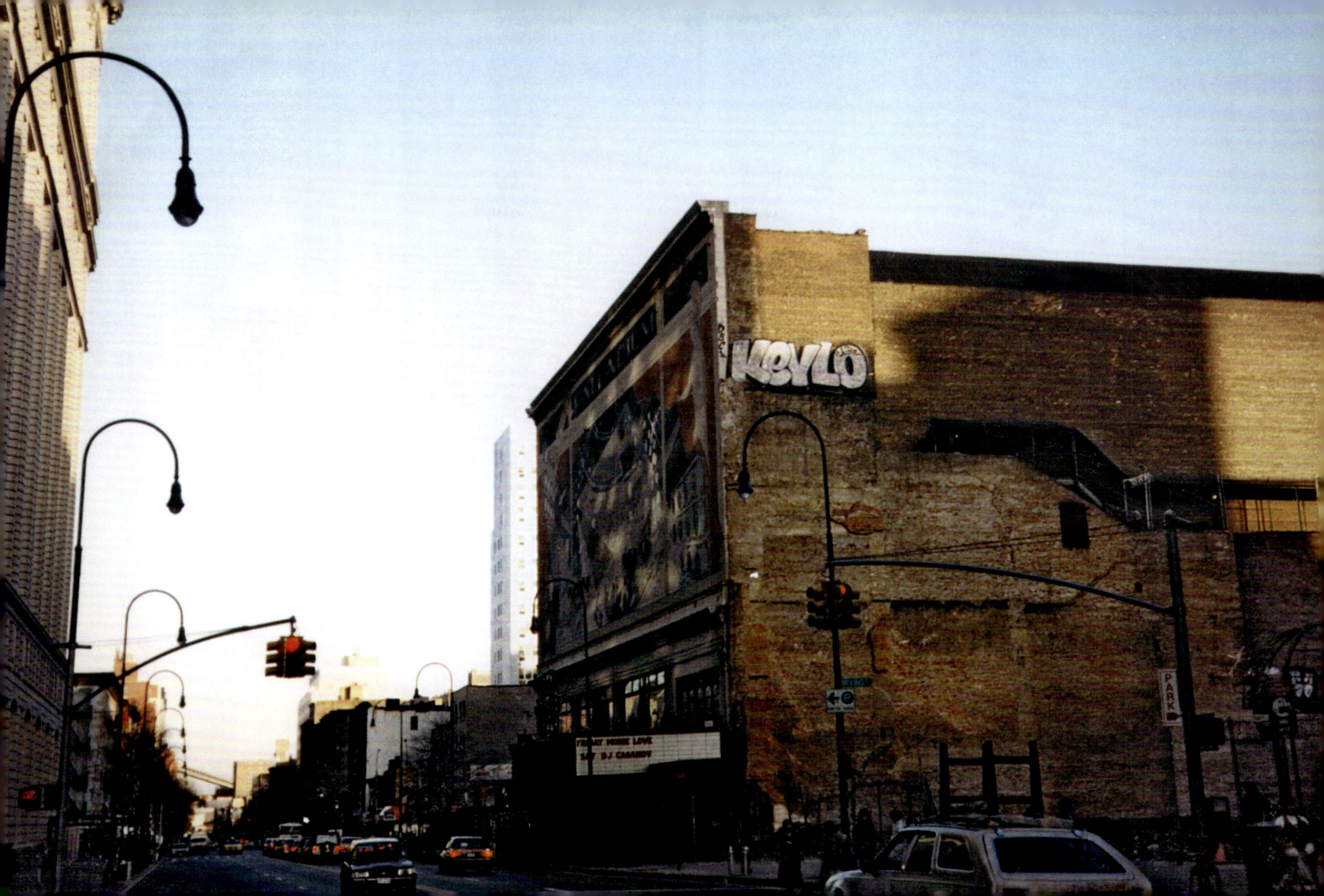
KEVLO
PARK

permission walls

The effective banishment of graffiti from New York City's subway trains, beginning in 1989, left a sea of attention-starved aerosolics homeless. Penalties for hitting trains became stiffer, and all but a few die-hard bombers and European graffiti tourists looked for other avenues to showcase their skills. Thus, by default, the 1990s became the era of the permission wall. Instead of stalking train yards in the wee hours of the night, writers armed with portfolios of their work started approaching property owners in hopes of getting permission to beautify their walls or gates with colorful murals. In New York City, the FX Crew, the TATS CRU, FC, and Cope 2 [see 074] were instrumental in keeping graffiti alive by securing spots to paint and organizing talent from all over the world to join the party.

Without a time limit or fear of arrest, the artistic bar rose to an unprecedented level. As in baseball, where you have a starting pitcher, a short and middle reliever, a setup guy, and a closer, the graffiti game became more specialized. The intricacy of the permission wall required a disparate skill set. Background and character rendering became vital components. These duties were often outsourced to Europeans, who loved collaborating with the American founders of the culture. In the big picture, the city claimed the victory. The permission walls flourished in the poorest neighborhoods, and prime real estate remained unblemished.

Collaboration of Stray, Vents, Askew, Shake, Berst, and Misery.
Photograph courtesy of Askew.
Auckland, New Zealand, 2009.

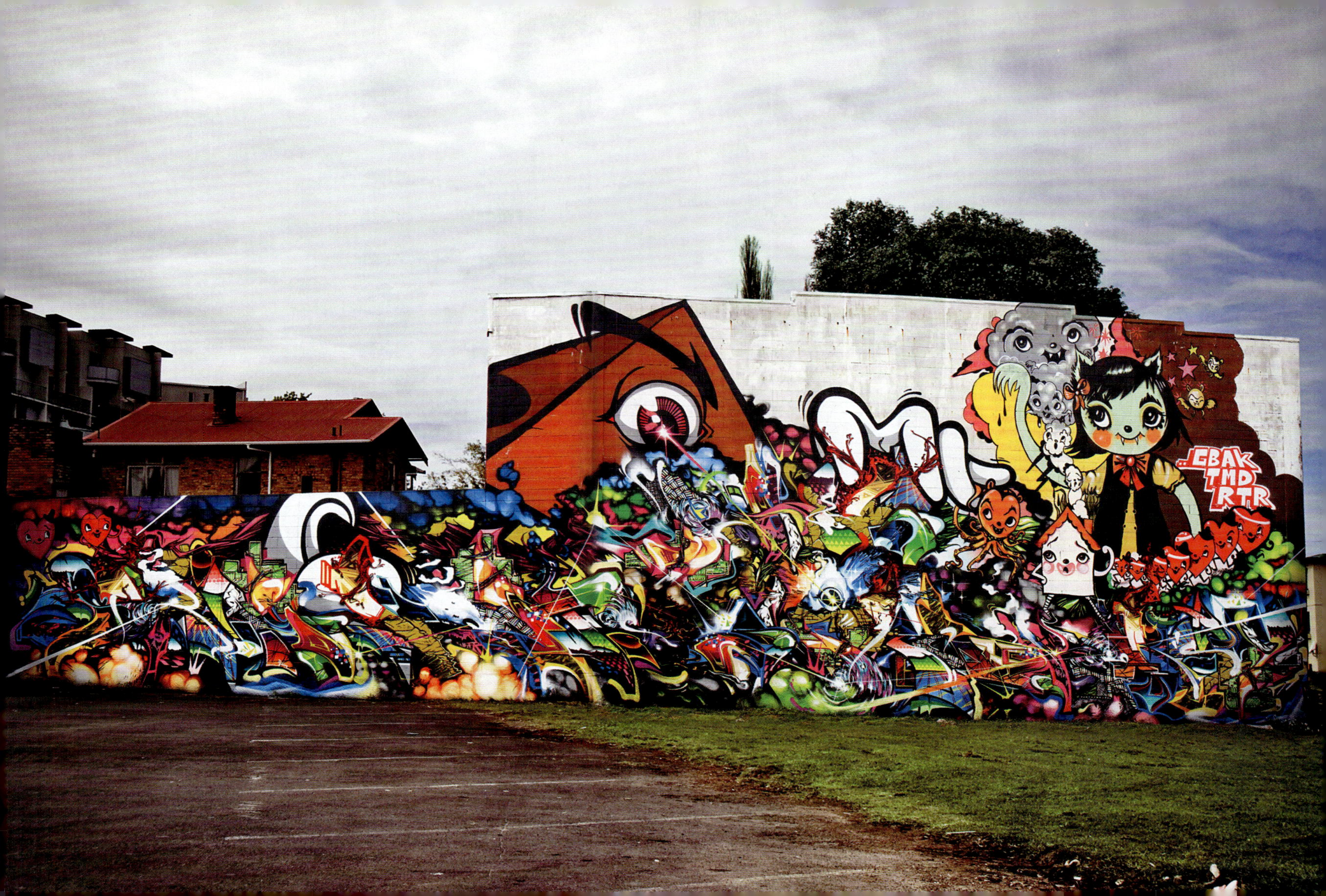
GBAK
TMD
RTR

Pez

Pez [meaning "fish" in Spanish] is a Barcelona-based street artist. A prolific presence on the city's streets since the late 1990s, Pez quickly became a celebrity within Barcelonan street culture. His first tag slowly morphed into the shape of a fish, then eventually evolved into a simple, two-dimensional figure wearing a massive, toothy grin.

Not one to overanalyze his creations, Pez says he doesn't paint to make people think—he paints purely because he enjoys it. A pleasant side effect, however, is that his characters inspire joy in the viewer. Well versed in the graffiti vernacular and mentality, Pez claims a disdain for artists who import a style from other countries and claim it as original work. He also states that "painting on the streets will never be impossible." Though laws may make it increasingly difficult, Pez believes in graffiti's longevity. While some street artists pride themselves on moving away from the negative perceptions of graffiti [as vandalism, destruction, and a form of violence], Pez claims to enjoy the work on the street, no matter what form it takes. Without it, Pez seems to think, the city would be dead.

Entirely without formal training, Pez is known for his consistency and his devotion to public art. He has been invited to exhibit his work internationally, occasionally alongside his close friends and street-art legends, The London Police [see 204].

Photograph by Luna Park.
Brooklyn, New York, 2008.

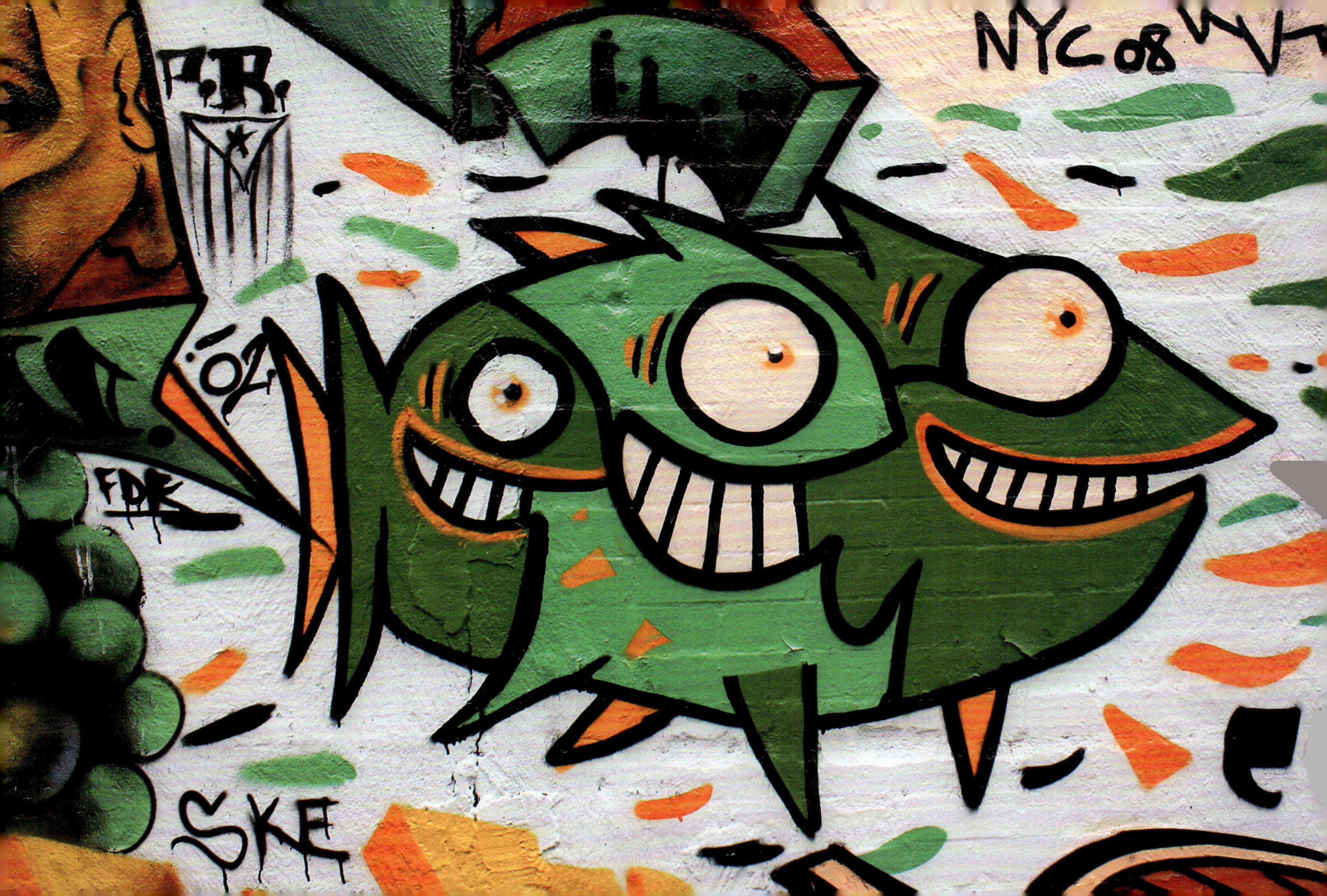
NYC 08
'02
FDR
SKE

Phase 2

One of the first Bronx writers to hit the subways, Phase 2, along with his mentor Lee and a dozen or so contemporaries, followed what was already happening on the Broadway line in Manhattan. Dewitt Clinton High School became a mecca for Bronx writers; Phase 2, Lionel 168, and countless other first-generation writers regularly cut classes there to attack the nearby Bedford Park subway yard during the day.

Phase 2 was a visionary, an innately gifted artist and intellectual. Before anyone else, he saw graffiti as an aerosol art form. He invented bubble letters, liberating writers from the constrictions of stick letters and changing the face of graffiti. He founded the Writer's Bench [see 362] at 149th Street and Grand Concourse. He was also one of the featured artists in Richard Goldstein's cover story on graffiti in *New York* magazine's March 1973 issue. By 1974, his crew, the INDs [see 172], became synonymous with style—membership required a high skill level, and very few made the grade. Phase 2 distinguished himself by creating some of the earliest flyers for the Bronx clubs that gave birth to hip-hop, and he remains one of the most respected voices in aerosol art history, often setting the record straight in print, as well as in live appearances on panels. In the early 1980s, Phase 2 and David Schmidlapp cofounded *International Graffiti Times*, the first graffiti magazine.

Phase 2's futuristic, abstract-style, present-day paintings bear little resemblance to what he once did on the trains, but he has always been about evolution—setting trends, never following them.

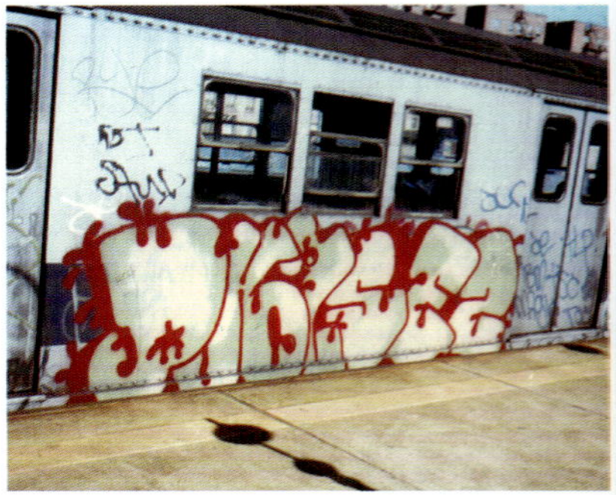

***Pain* piece by Phase 2, with Pain the MOB and Skeme TNT.**
Photograph by Doug Evans.
New York City, 1983.
Detail: Piece by Phase 2.
Private collection.
New York City, 1983.

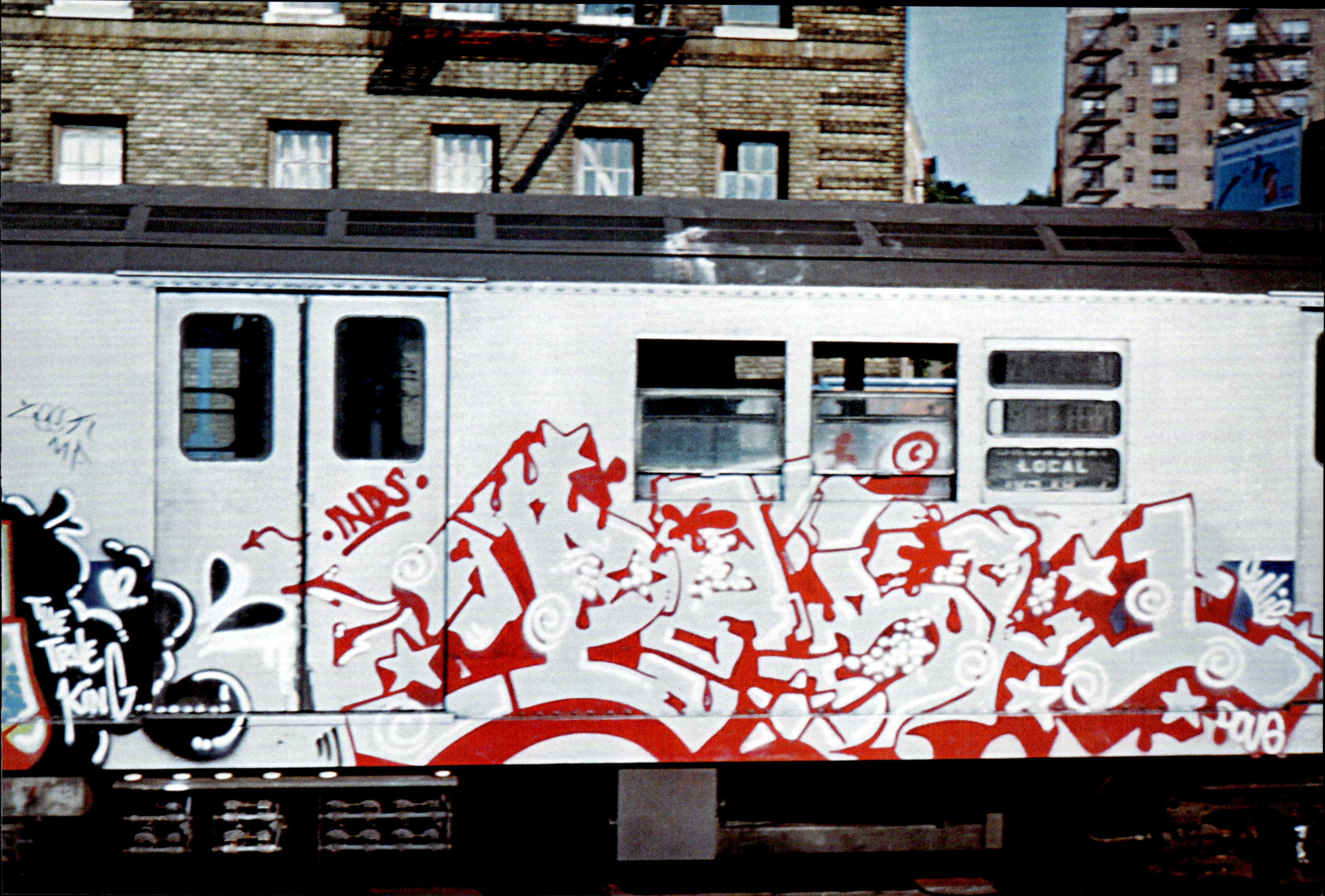
LOCAL
THE TRUE KING

Phibs

Phibs is one of the biggest names in Australian graffiti. Originally from Sydney, Phibs took the more street-art-friendly city of Melbourne by storm in the late 1990s, and he has resided there ever since. Now more than a decade into his career, the artist is a member of the notable Everfresh crew. With a strong background in Wild Style and abstracted traditional graffiti, Phibs is best known for his highly detailed tribal style.

Late in the first decade of the 2000s, Phibs toured Asia with the K-Spray Stencil Art Tour, sponsored by the shoe brand K-Swiss, alongside stencil legend Logan Hicks (see 166). Phibs has since been hired by numerous major brands, including Absolut Vodka, to lend them his signature style. Phibs has expressed an interest in touching as many mediums as possible and has branched into clothing and graphic design, and he has exhibited his work in galleries in and outside of Australia, traveling extensively and creating large-scale mural works in cities as far-flung as Berlin and Tokyo.

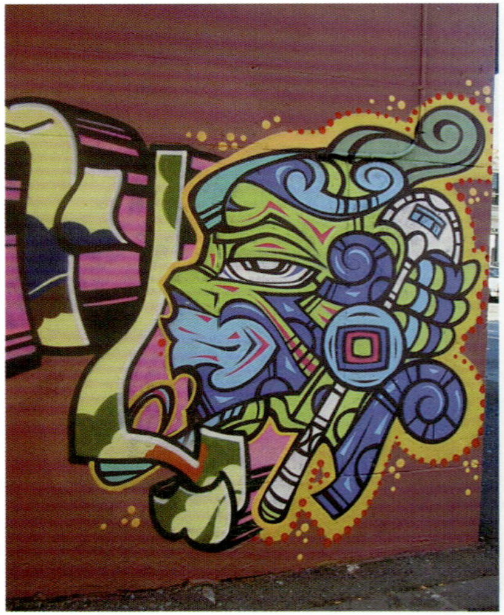

Photographs courtesy of Phibs.
Sydney, Australia, 2009.
Detail: Melbourne, Australia, 2009.

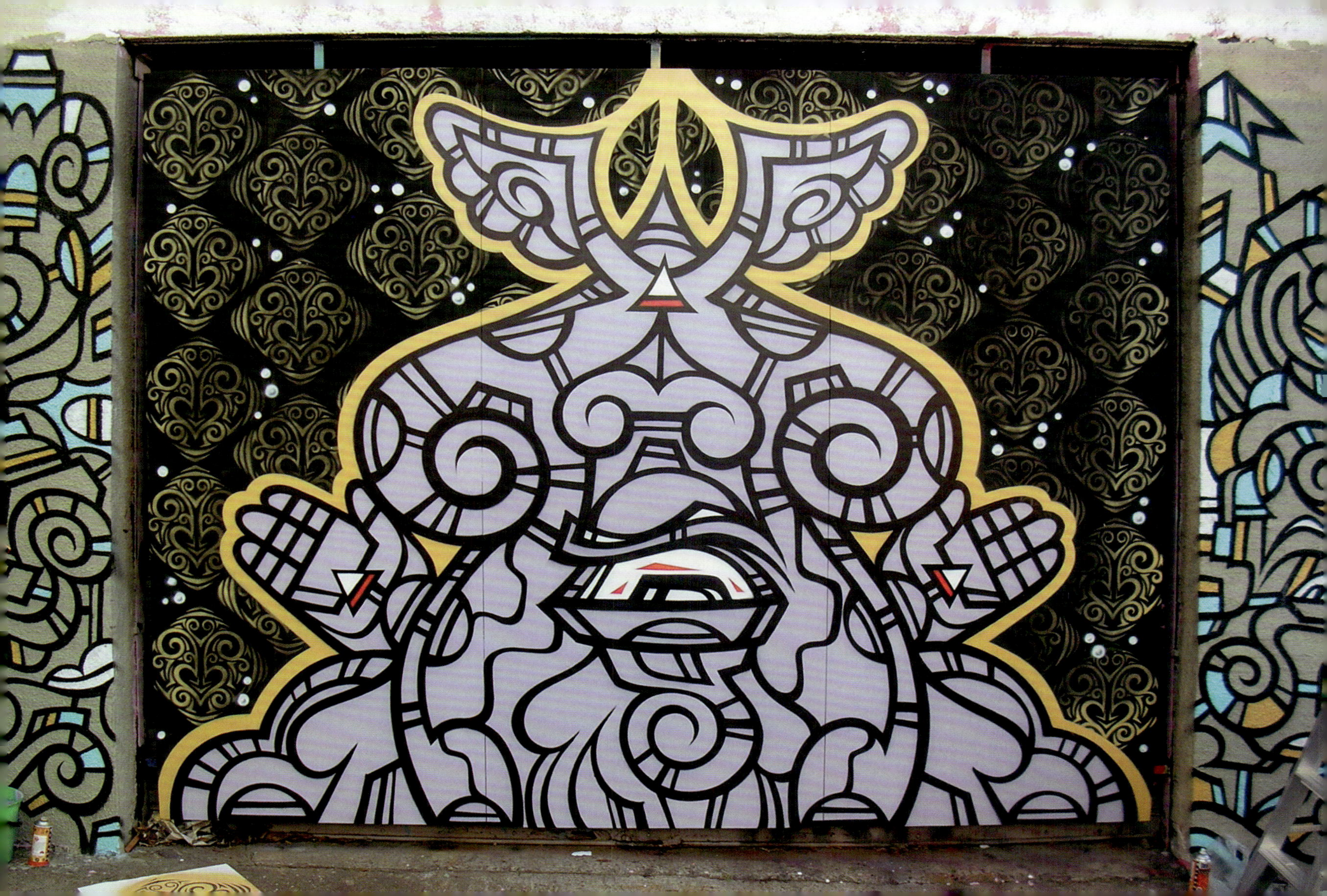

pixação

Pixação is a form of graffiti unique to São Paulo, Brazil's teeming metropolis, the seventh-largest city in the world, and home to some of the planet's tallest buildings. Unusually angular and barely legible, *pixação* borrows from standard tagging culture but awards the most respect for the highest risk-taking. A simple street-level tag is considered chump change, whereas the true gods of *pixação* earn their status by scaling the fronts of buildings with no safety nets or supports, sometimes reaching the top floors of skyscrapers, to leave their pointy marks.

Pixação first appeared in the early 1980s, painted by heavy-metal fans inspired by Viking and barbarian alphabets, as well as by the logos of heavy-metal bands such as Black Sabbath, Slayer, and Iron Maiden. Reminiscent of Egyptian hieroglyphics, *pixação* was created by the impoverished residents of the favelas, Brazil's infamous ghettos, who are treated as "invisibles." Similar to the early work of graffiti artists from the ghettos of New York, *pixação* is a cry for recognition from an ostracized and forgotten caste of people.

Casualties are common among *pixadores* (*pixação* artists), due not only to hazardous drops from extreme heights, but also to attacks from a society eager to punish those responsible for the defacement of São Paulo's facades.

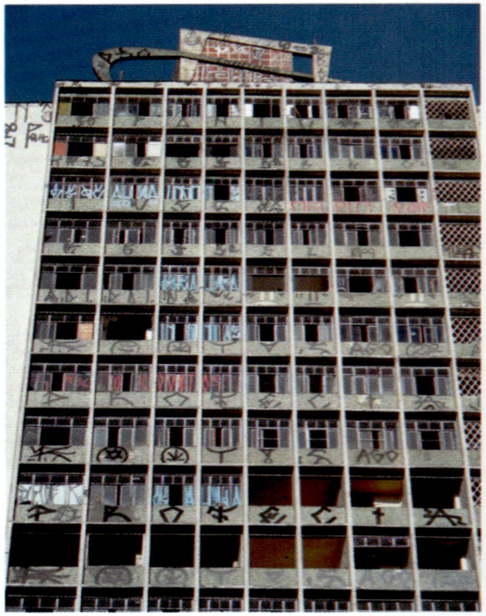

Right: Photograph by Lois Stavsky. São Paulo, Brazil, 2010.
Far right: Photograph by Sara Mozeson. São Paulo,Brazil, 2010.
Detail: Photograph by Sara Mozeson. São Paulo, Brazil, 2010.

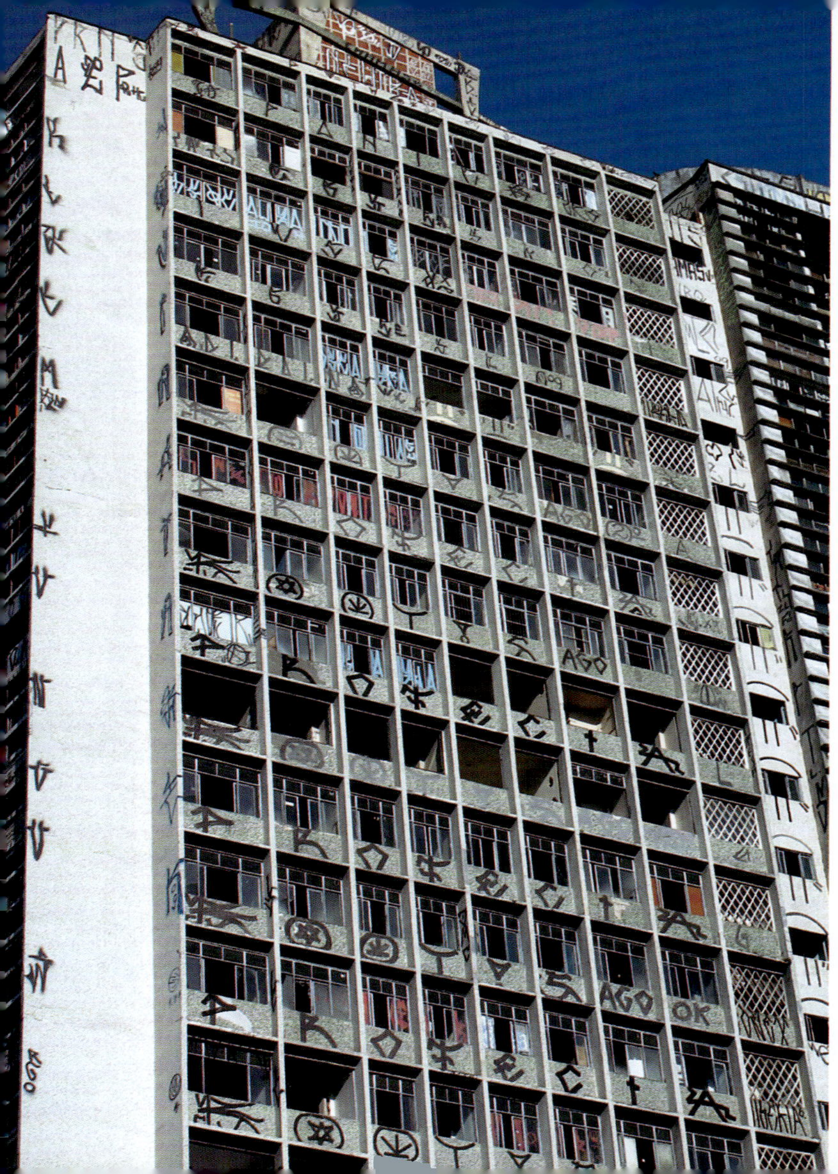

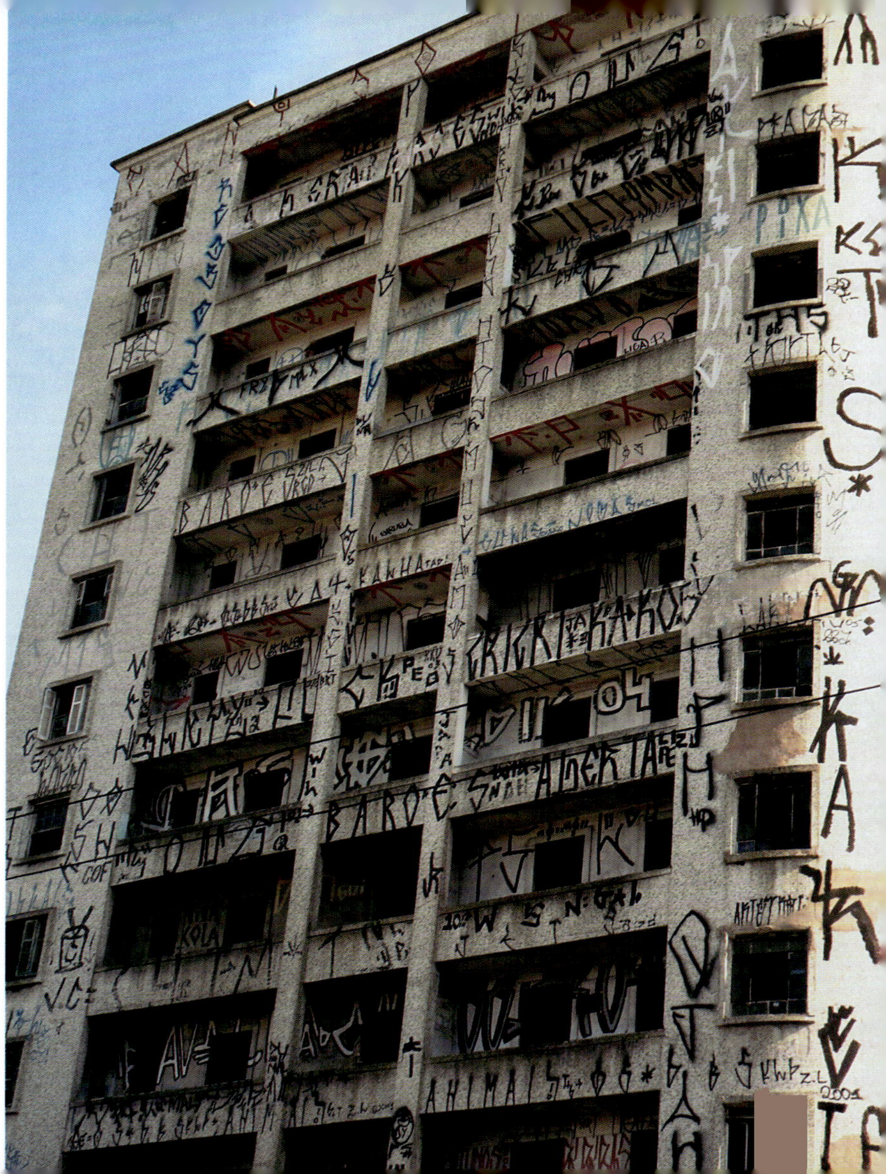

Pjay One

Pjay One made as much noise off the trains as he did on them. One of the five original members of the United Artists crew, Pjay met Seen [see 294], Mad, Duster [see 100], and Sin in 1979, while attending Lehman High School in the Throggs Neck section of the Bronx. He began doing Rider pieces on the #6 line, but was quickly put in his place when Comet [see 071] did a throw-up over some of his work. Eventually, he changed his name to Pjay, using his own initials as his moniker. Although he wrote under other names, including SIR 161, Fame, and Vapor, Pjay was the tune he played the loudest. Of the many whole cars he did, SATAN'S PALACE (featuring a Green Goblin character) and MERRY CHRISTMAS, in Old English lettering (done with then-girlfriend Lyndah), are the most memorable. Not content to be a single-line star, Pjay formed alliances with #4-line stylemaster Mitch 77 [see 227], his partner Med167/Disco, and ink king Ban 2. Few bombed trains harder in the 1980s than these four—and few pursued their enemies more vigilantly. Notable wars with CIA, Cope 2 [see 074], Ghost [see 145], and JA One [see 180] made for some of the best battles in graffiti history. Today, Pjay's collection of vintage spray paint cans remains tops on the planet.

Private collection.
New York City, 1981.

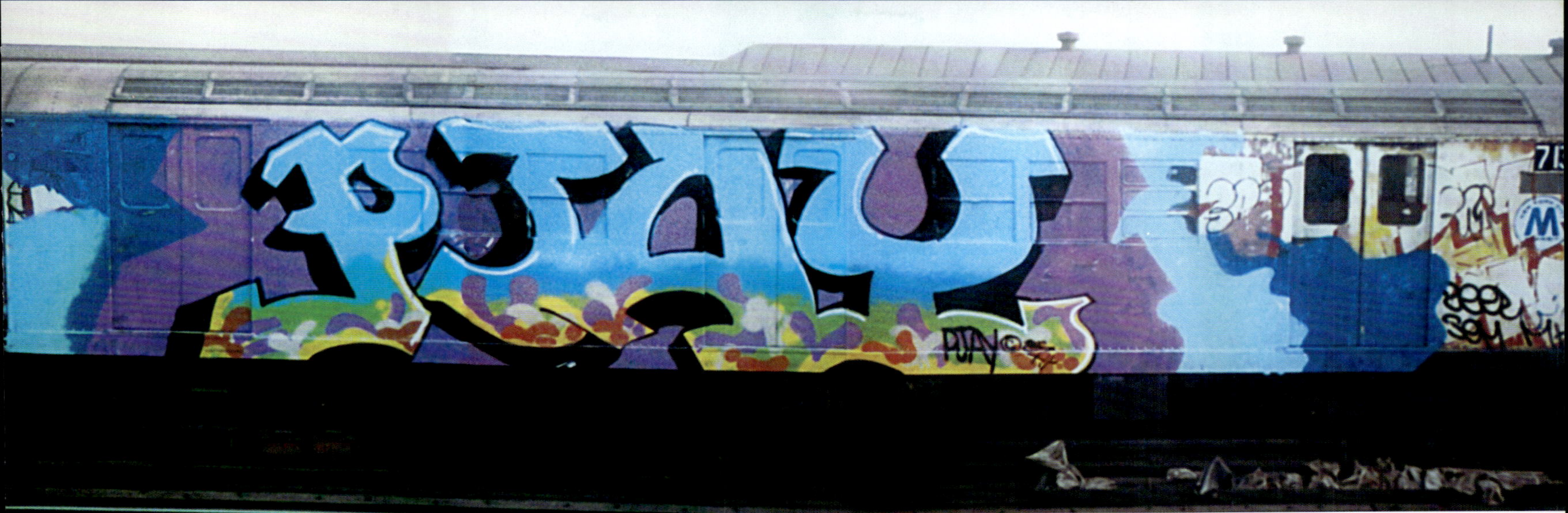

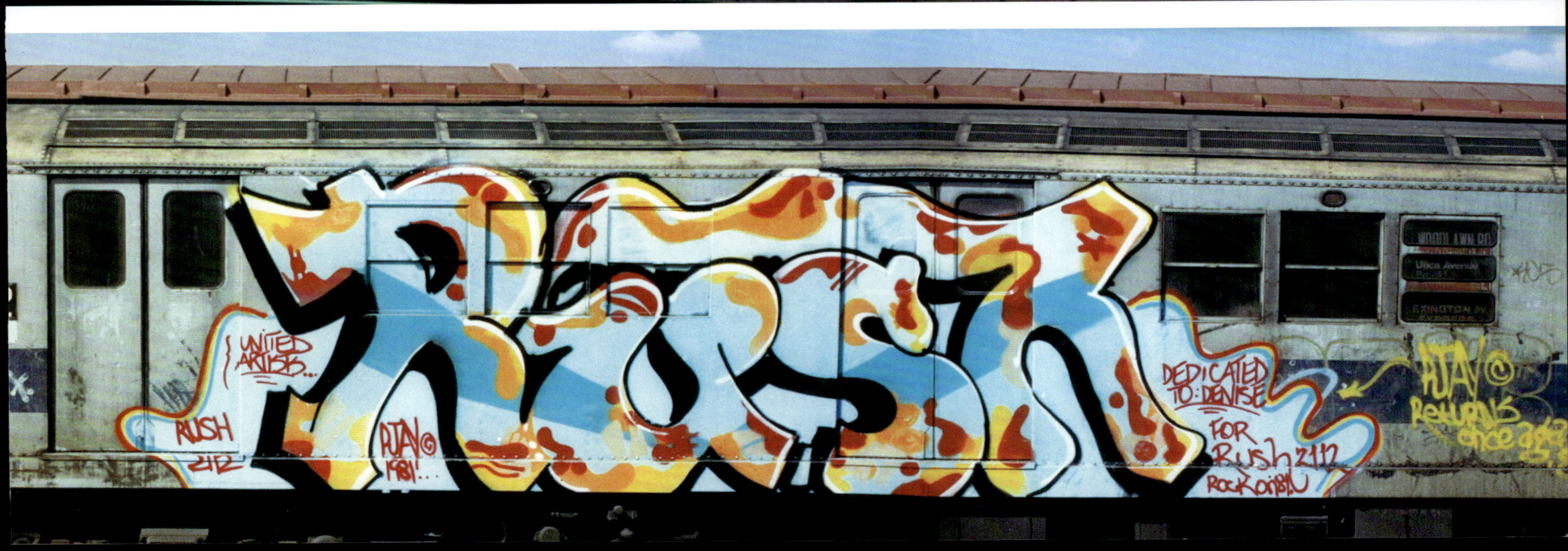
UNITED ARTISTS...
RUSH 2112
PJAY © 1981...
DEDICATED TO: DENISE
FOR Rush 2112
PJAY © Returns once again
Utica Avenue
LEXINGTON AV

259

P'nut 2

P'nut 2 grew up just walking distance from Yankee Stadium and broke into graffiti during the tagging era, around 1971. A few years later, his family moved north to the Bainbridge area of the Bronx, where he adopted the alias P'nut 2. Now living close to the #4 yard, the D yard, the Kingsbridge lay-ups, and the marker-and-ink emporium Cozy's Book Store, P'nut 2 had ample opportunity to immortalize himself. The blond-haired Irish kid had arrived at the right place at the right time.

He fell in with Tracy 168's Wild Style crew (see 340), the INDs (see 172), and the MG Boys (see 221), blanketing the trains inside and out with tags, top-to-bottoms, throw-ups, and burners. Trivia buffs will remember his name rolling by every week during the introduction to the TV show *Welcome Back, Kotter* in 1975.

Historically, he is undercredited due to his partnership with Tracy 168, whose work and reputation overshadowed his, though P'nut 2's character work, outlining ability, and fill-in technique often surpassed that of his higher-profile partner. He remained active on transit lines until 1978, although his name could occasionally be found in streets and on highways after his departure from the subways.

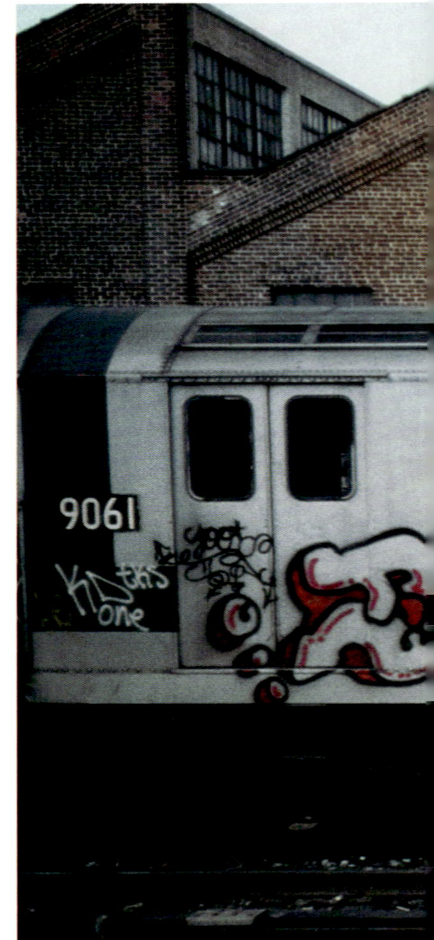

Whole car by Billy 167, P'nut 2, Ton 5, and John 150 (left to right). Photograph by Jack Stewart. New York City, 1975.

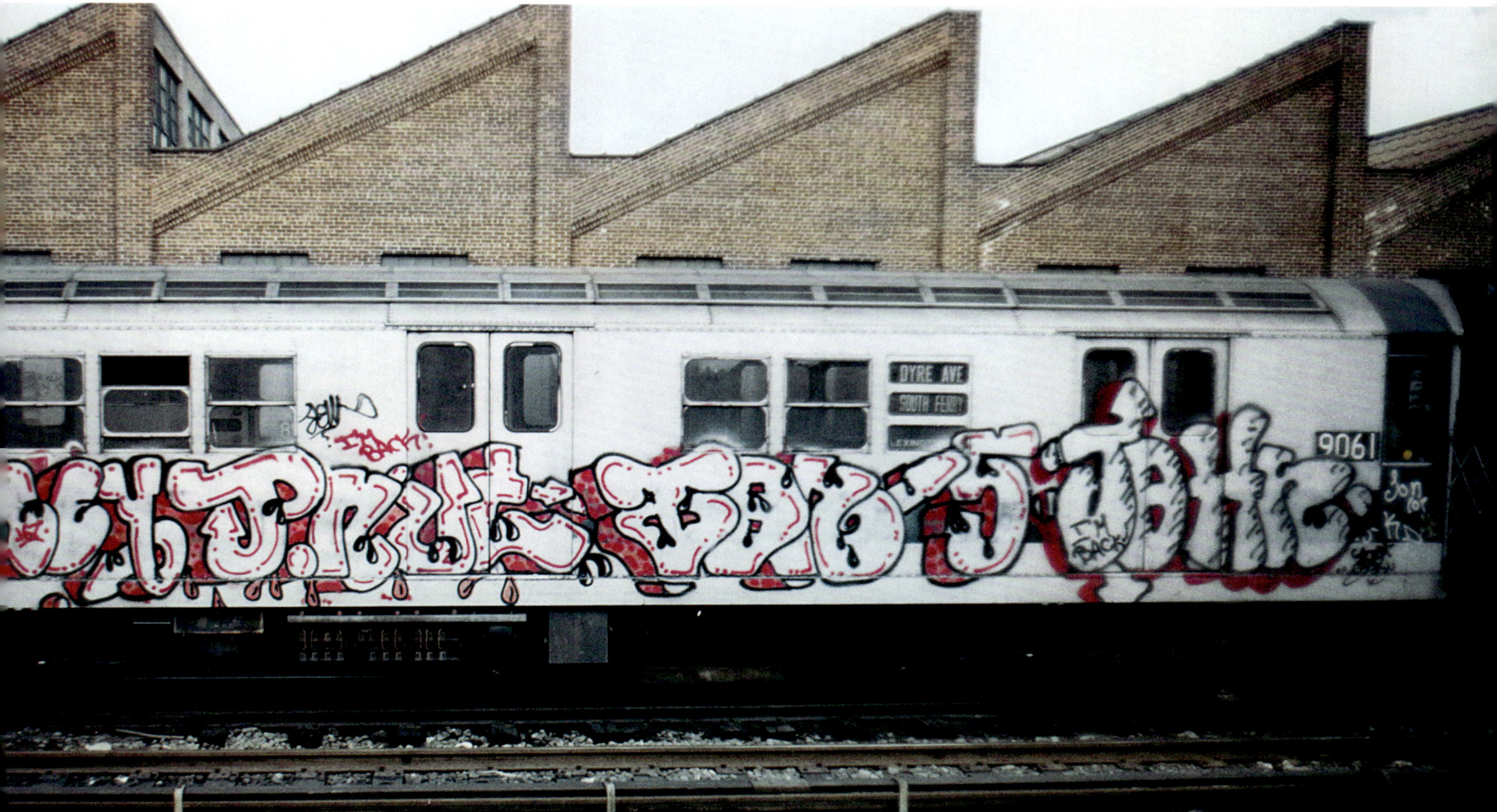
DYRE AVE
SOUTH FERRY
9061

political painters

Long before graffiti and street art became movements, paint was being used on public walls for a more serious purpose: political messages. As far back as records show, graffiti has been used as a means of rallying support, communicating dissent, and expressing political loyalties. In the 1960s, during socialist protests and revolutionary outpourings, leftists made extensive use of graffiti, especially stencils, to communicate with one another, to advertise their disdain for the political regime, and to publicize the locations of rallies.

In 1973 in Brooklyn, the politically conscious subway pioneer Mico painted Hang Nixon on the outside of a train. In the mid-1970s, Lee transformed entire subway cars into illustrated messages. Stop the Bomb, a whole-car featuring a bomb and a mushroom cloud, and the antipolice-themed Open the Pig contained messages that leaped off the trains and into the public consciousness.

During the 2008 presidential election in the United States, street-art ambassador Shepard Fairey's (see 124) now legendary image of Barack Obama became an essential tool in promoting the candidate, and it was widely stenciled, wheatpasted, and stickered on streets across the country to express loyalty.

During the same campaign, an artist took to traveling the country, proliferating his take on the famous Robert Indiana *Love* sculpture, which he had transformed with the word "Vote," to boost voter turnout after the poor turnout in 2004.

Bringing street art back to its most socially relevant roots, the use of graffiti for political purposes is the most commonplace and layman-accessible means of advertising a multitude of standpoints on any issue.

Photograph by Jack Stewart.
New York City, 1973.

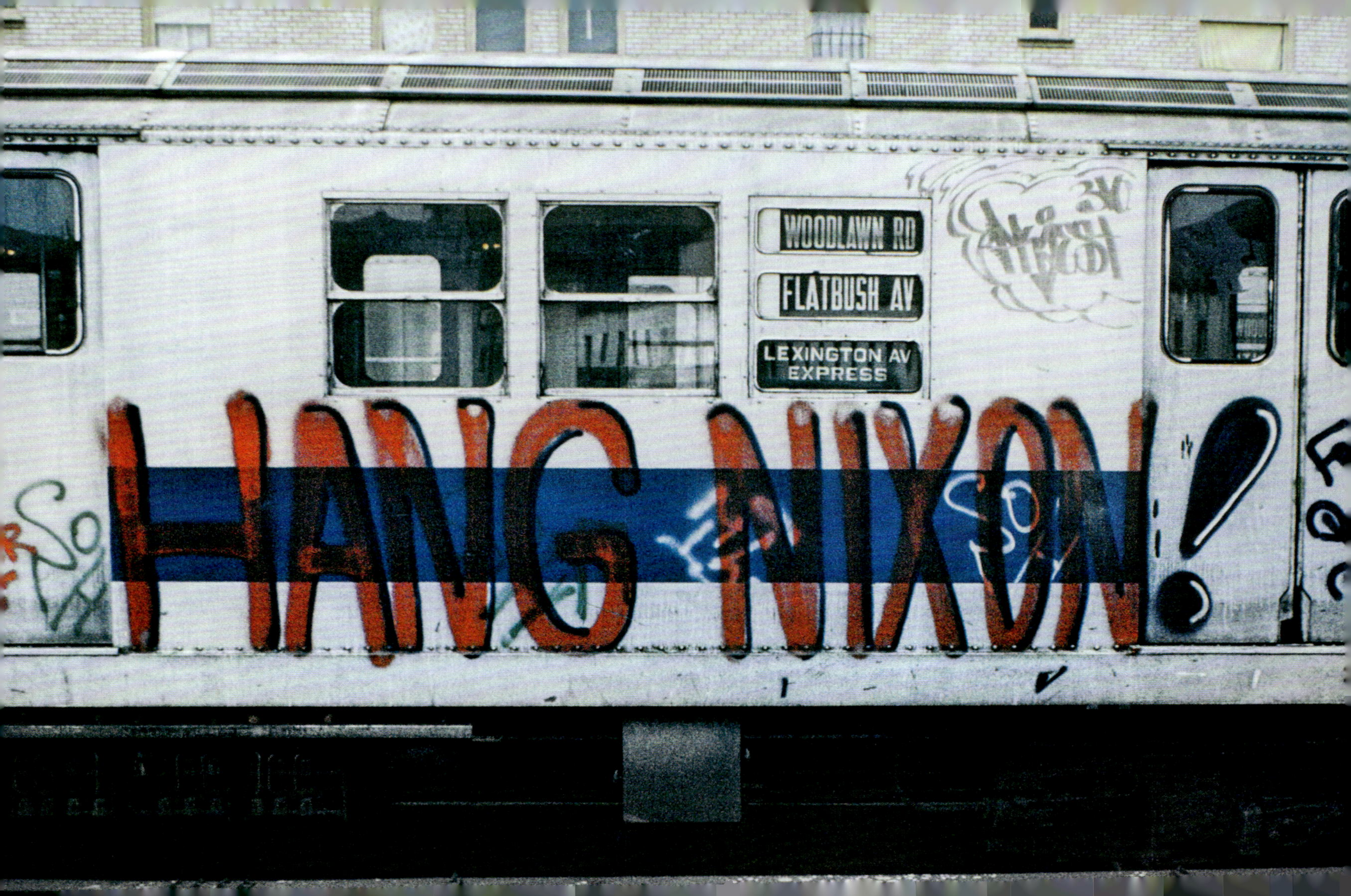
WOODLAWN RD
FLATBUSH AV
LEXINGTON AV EXPRESS
HANG NIXON!

Por El Ojo

The street-art group Por El Ojo: Video sin Cámara (Through the Eye: Video without Camera) was formed in 1989 by Julia Balmaceda, Federico Gonzalez, Daniel Sanjurjo, and Ignacio Sourrouille. All four are related to artists who "disappeared" during Argentina's violent, state-sponsored "Dirty War" of the 1970s and early '80s. In the late 1980s, when Argentina was caught up in the fervor of the return to democracy, Por El Ojo refused to forget those crimes. Further angered by the banality of late-80s artistic and cultural production and the privatization of public space, they launched a series of ironic and acidic public artworks. Undeterred by their inability to afford society's latest technical fetish, the video camera, the group plastered Buenos Aires with images of television screens carrying provocative messages.

In 1994, Por El Ojo was chosen for an exhibition in Manhattan and, surprisingly, the Argentine government gave it a travel grant. Inspired by the teeming SoHo street-art scene, Por El Ojo painted a few illegal murals, but were soon arrested and sent to jail. Ironically, in a place presumably tolerant of free expression, the landlord who insisted on pressing charges had once led his own antiwar activist group, The Fugs.

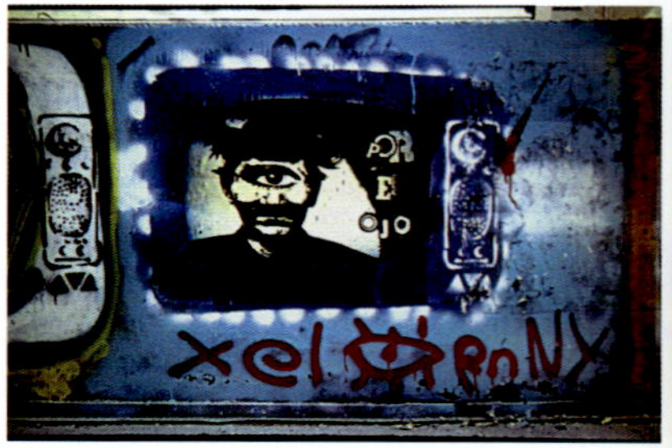

Photographs by Ignacio G.
Mercer Street, SoHo, New York City, 1994.

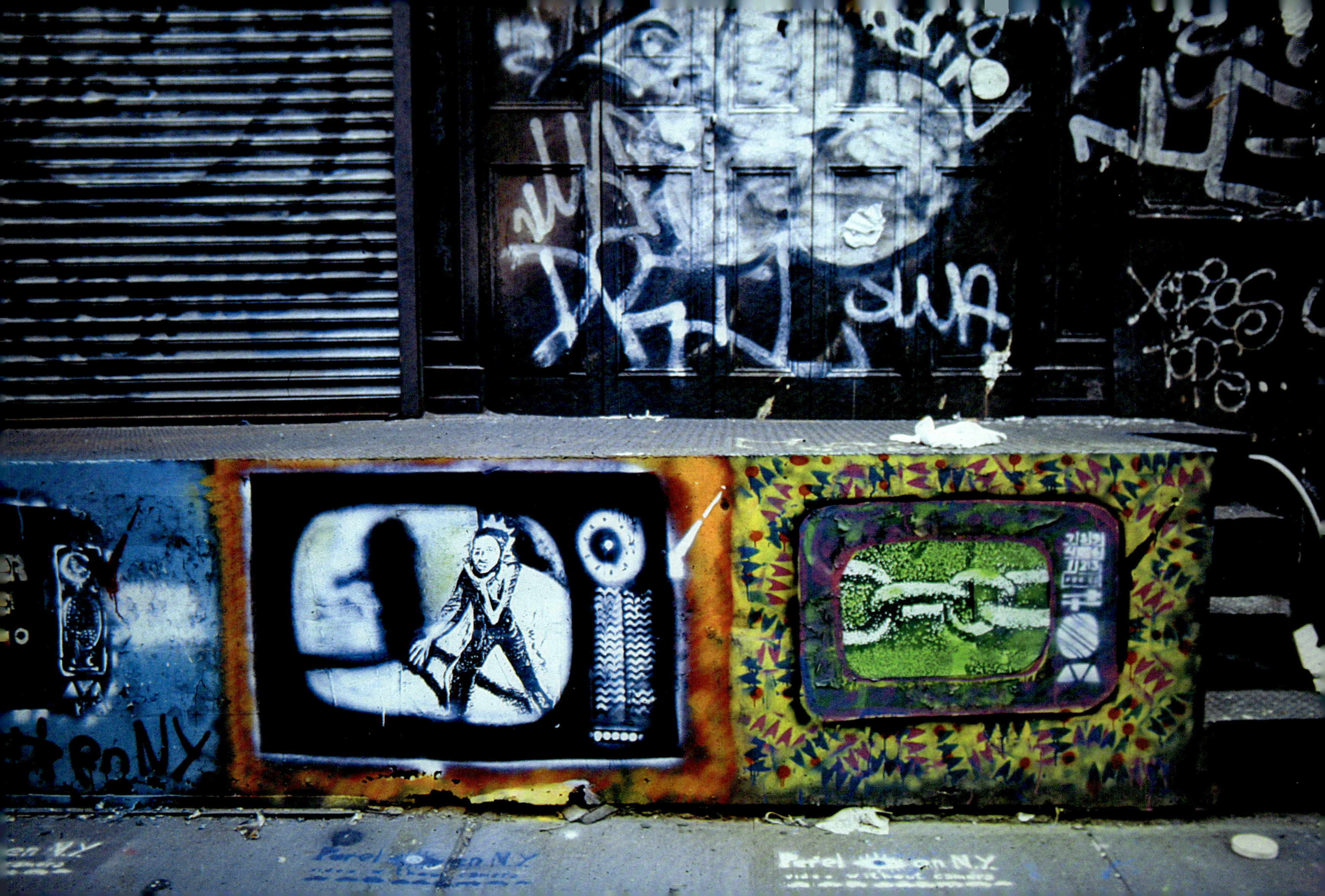

Poster Boy

Many public artists have defended their craft by condemning the offensive images advertisers throw at us daily: the media vs. artists, the haves vs. the have-nots. For years, Ron English [see 113] and the 7th Letter crew [see 022] have been giving media moguls fits by co-opting billboards with their own messages, but a newcomer, Poster Boy, has joined the fight using a new weapon.

Armed with a razor blade, he turns the media on themselves. With no preconceived concept, Poster Boy invades train stations and revives the ancient art of cut-and-paste advertising by slicing bits and pieces from subway posters, transforming them into his own satirical or political messages. An ad for the movie *Iron Man* became Iran=Nam after a little slicing and dicing. Since the ads are all adhesive-backed, Poster Boy needs no glue. He only needs to scope out spots and monitor police activity.

With hundreds of "revised ads" to his credit, he has developed a following. Unfortunately, some members of his following carry badges, and he was arrested at a show. [Police rarely catch anyone in the act anymore.] For creating humorous, thought-provoking imagery from insipid media drudgery, Poster Boy was sentenced to 210 hours of community service. The advertisers remain at large.

Photograph courtesy of Poster Boy.
New York City, 2009

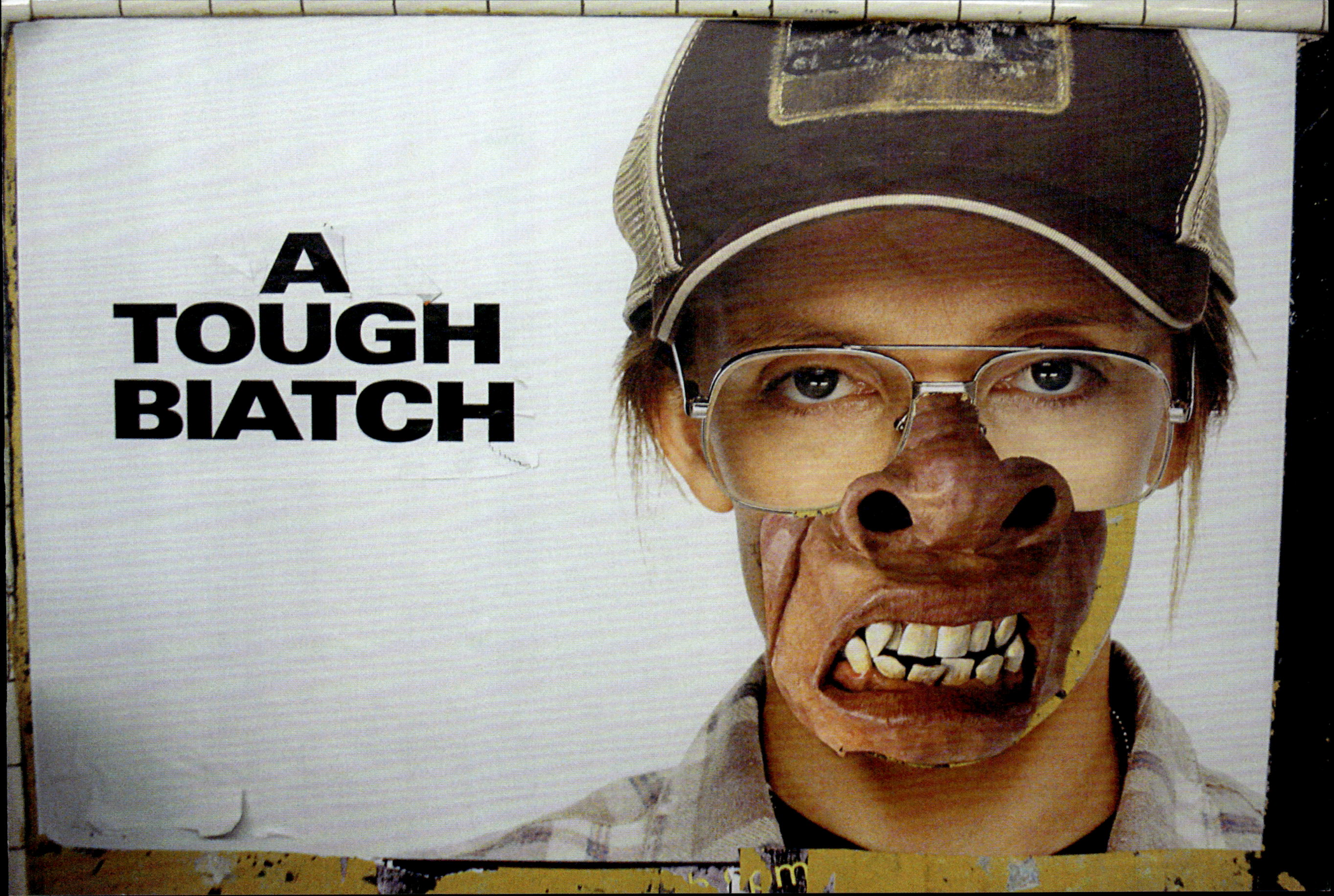
A
TOUGH
BIATCH

Pray

When the question "Who is the most famous graffiti writer of all time?" is asked, the hands-down winner's name would never receive mention. The inventor of scratchiti and message-based graffiti began writing around 1970 and, over the course of three decades, conquered a subculture that barely acknowledged her.

Already elderly when graffiti was young, a homeless woman with a religious message did her preaching by etching onto pay-phone coin boxes, subway vending machines, park benches, and almost any other place one would look. This lady, referred to as Pray by graffiti writers, was as revered as she was ubiquitous. Theories abounded that the Pray etchings—and a plethora of others attributed to her—such as Go to Church, Worship God, and Read Bible had to be the work of many artists.

The graffiti artist Zephyr (see 363) pays tribute to the elusive Pray in an eloquent essay on his website, zephyrgraffiti.com. Though he stalked her over an eight-year period, his only attempt to converse with her caused her to flee without completing her tag.

In 1986, Zephyr encountered Pray reading a newspaper on a bench in Washington Square. Zephyr's companion that day, the photographer Laura Hanafin, snapped the only known photo of the godmother of graffiti. Looking like a greasy nun, she lived her life under a cloak of anonymity. The words she left behind may not have brought anyone closer to God, but she is worshipped by graying graffiti writers who bore witness to the gospel according to graffiti's patron saint.

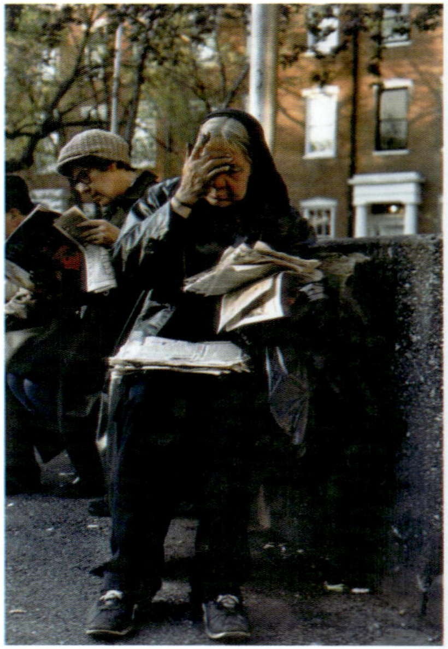

Photograph by Martha Cooper. New York City, 1981.
Detail: Photograph by Laura Hanifin. New York City, 1986.

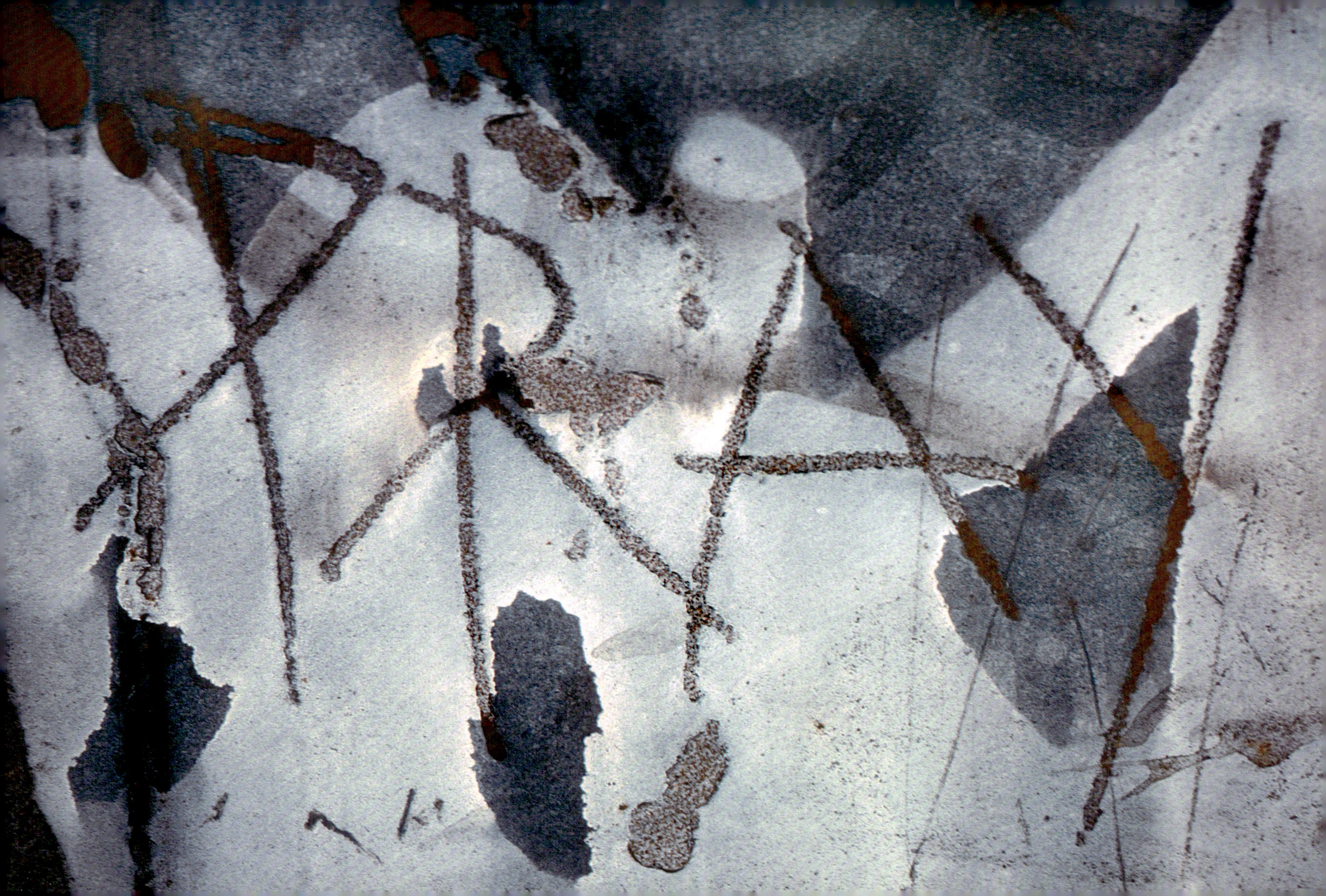

Prune

The French artist known as Prune is obsessively scientific. Her work pertains to chimeras, a hybrid embryo of human and animal, and biochemics far too advanced for the average layman to wrap his head around. Referencing Darwin's theory of natural selection, as well as the evolution of test-tube genetics, Prune wanted to provoke discussion and thought when she developed her hybrid-baby sculpture project. Hoping for an interactive experience, the artist experimented with both resin and ultra-pricey silicone, eventually settling on two series of what she refers to as her hybrid babies: one series in resin to be affixed on public streets, and another series of eight babies fashioned from silicone to be snapped up by collectors. And cause a stir they did.

In mid-decade, Prune mounted several of her hybrid resin children, which look like a mixture of infant and dog, often with leashes attached to their necks, on the grounds outside public establishments such as bakeries and train stations. The startlingly realistic creatures sat naked on the asphalt. Dozens of images of pass-ersby examining them with concern are available.

In 2006, one of Prune's sculptures appeared in the Wooster Collective's (see 359) mammoth retrospective at 11 Spring Street (see 001).

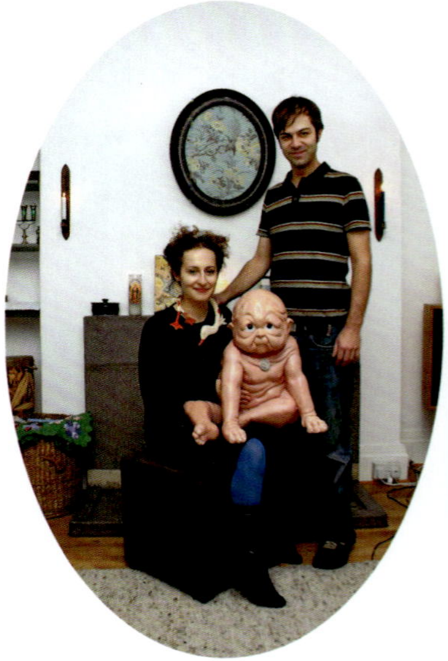

Photographs courtesy of Prune.
***Petshop*. Paris, 2007.**
Detail: *Adoption Family*.
London, 2007

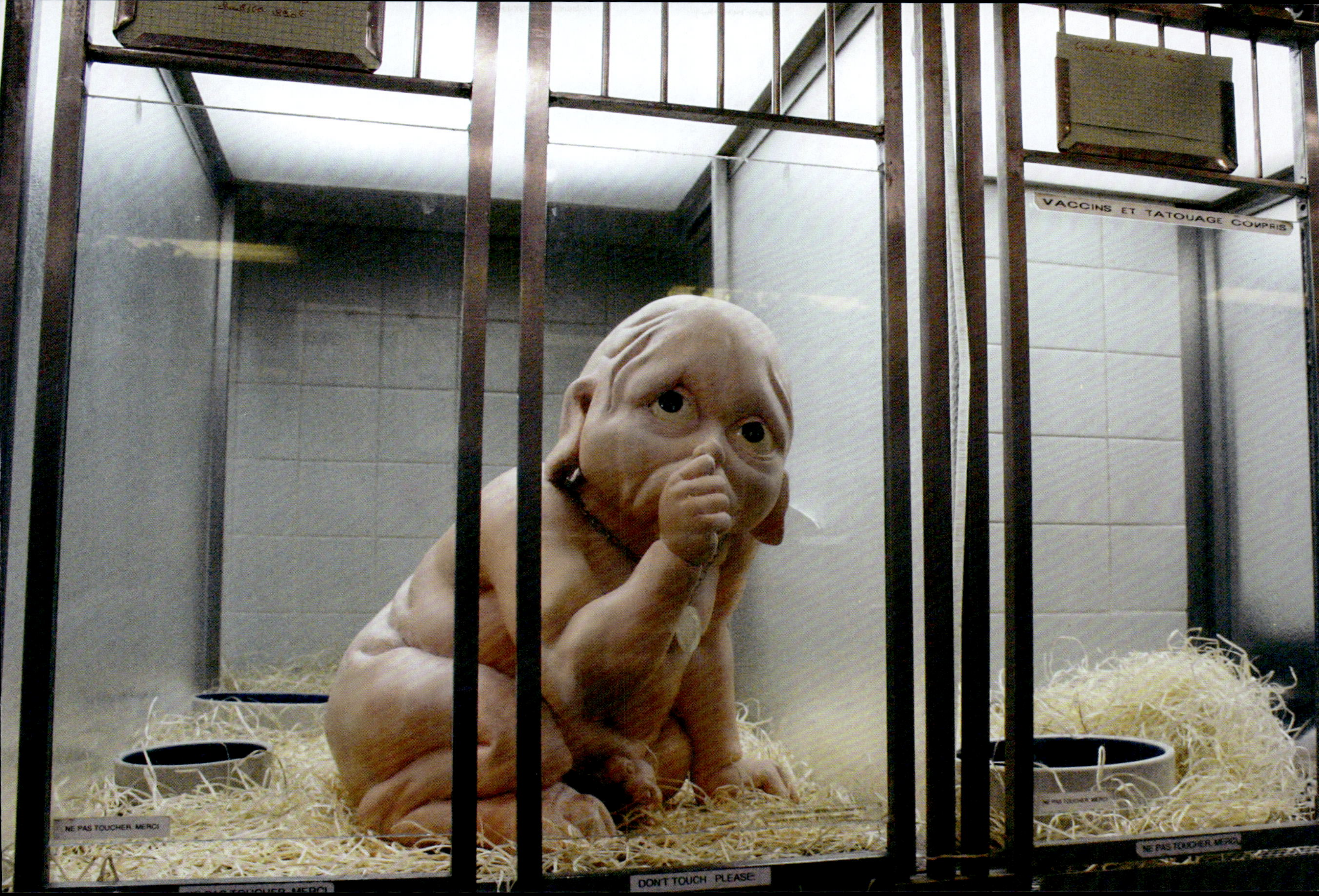
VACCINS ET TATOUAGE COMPRIS
NE PAS TOUCHER. MERCI
DON'T TOUCH PLEASE
NE PAS TOUCHER. MERCI

Puppet

Graffiti arrived in Scandinavia and most of Europe around 1983, when the American print and visual media fell in love with it. So it was in 1983 that a young Puppet began tagging his name on buses in Stockholm, Sweden, never dreaming it would change his life.

His journey began in earnest in 1984, when he decided to take bombing seriously. He honed his skills for the next five years, putting in work on streets, walls, and trains, and experimenting with different names and lettering styles. In 1989, Puppet created DRAGON WALL, one of Sweden's legendary pieces. He has painted in jams all over Europe and painted a wall with Seen in New York City in 1990. Puppet's artistic abilities evolved during the 1990s; he became an art director for ten years before creating his company, Puppet Industries. He has designed logos for Coca-Cola, adidas, MTV, and Nike. But his success has never curtailed his love for outdoor painting, and he continues to rock walls with a new grid-based style, detouring from the graffiti path-most-traveled. Puppet's work places him in rare company as one of the world's best and most innovative artists to wield a can.

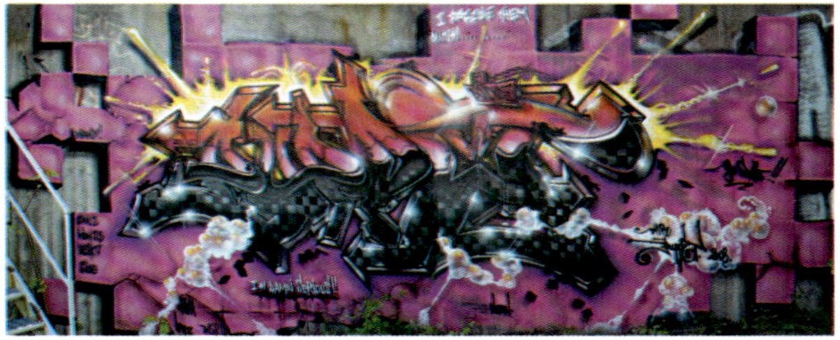

Photographs courtesy of Puppet.
***Gridwalker*. Denmark, 2010.**
Detail: Stockholm, 2008

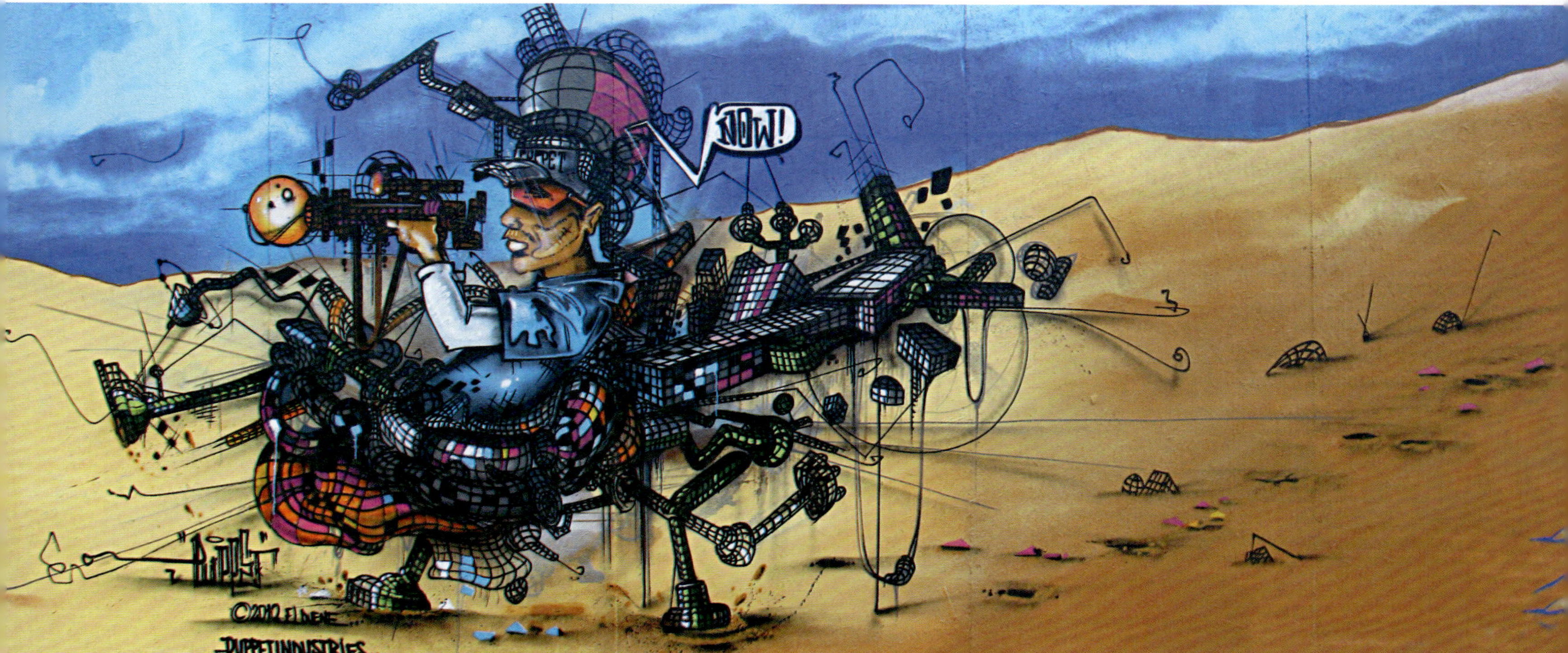
NOW!
©2012 ELDENE...
PUPPETINDUSTRIES...

Quik

Lin "Quik" Felton grew up in Hollis, Queens, before Run-DMC made it famous. He began writing on trains in the early 1970s, rubbing elbows with Queens-based legends of the era. His suburban home lay miles from the nearest subway line, so the young Quik had to travel great distances on the bus to gain access to trains.

In 1979, Quik's reputation transformed when he met Bilrock 161, founder of the Rolling Thunder Writers, and Hughie. Bilrock 161 recruited Quik as a crew member, and the two became best friends. Quik was soon one of the hardest-hitting members of RTW, and from 1979 through the mid-'80s he dominated subway lines on every division of transit, often destroying several different yards in a single night. Quik had a repertoire that included blockbusters, whole-cars, streets, and highways; he was one of the handful of writers who could rightfully lay claim the title "all-city." Regarding his body of work, Quik has described himself as "the best of the worst." What he lacked stylistically, he made up for with ubiquity.

Quik established himself in the art world in the early 1980s and has created a prolific and diverse body of work, often dealing with themes of oppression and dysfunctional romance. He has lived in Europe for more than twenty years and now seeks to dominate museum walls as he once did subway trains.

Top right: Photograph by Henry Chalfant. New York City, c. 1982.
Bottom right: Photograph by Pjay One. New York City, 1981.

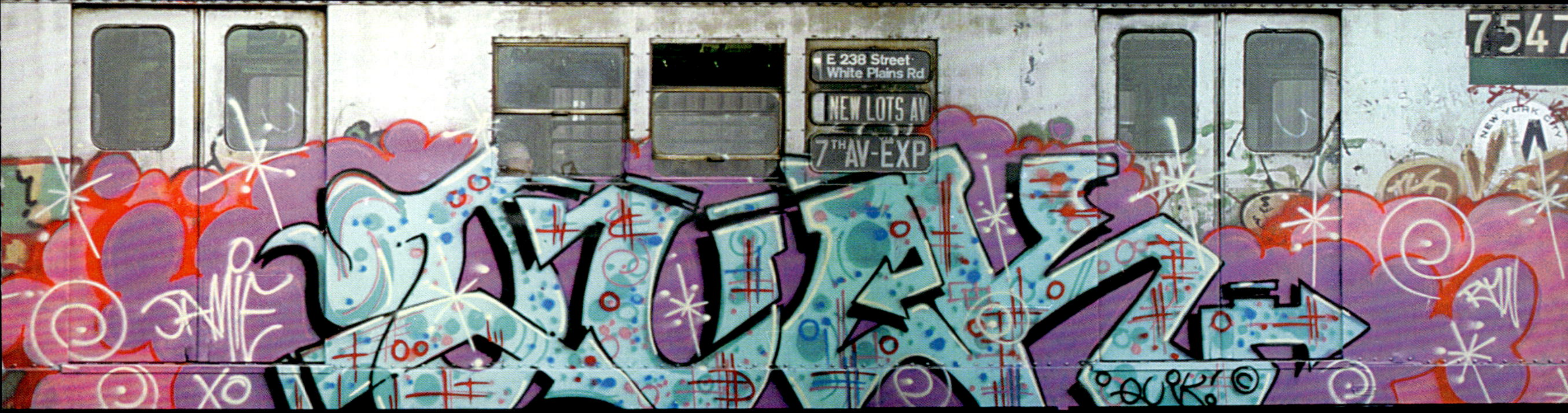
7547
E 238 Street
White Plains Rd
NEW LOTS AV
7TH AV-EXP

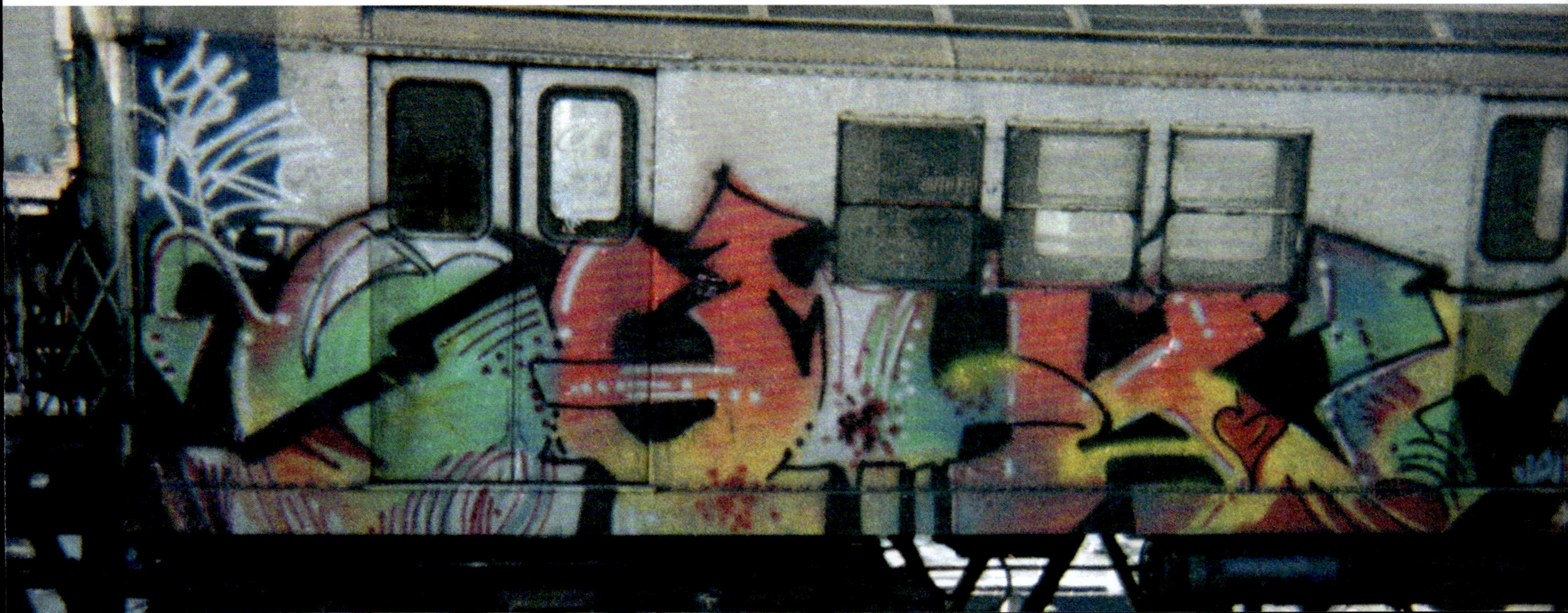

267

Lee Quinones

Lee Quinones began hitting trains in 1974, at a time when style was the driving force of the movement. Lee became proficient so quickly that he moved on to whole-cars by 1975, inspired by writers like Cliff 159 [see 070], Caine 1 [see 054], and Blade [see 037]. While painting trains at the Brooklyn Bridge station, he met Doc and Slug, two of the original members of The Fabulous Five. He was quickly recruited, and the crew dedicated themselves to being whole-car specialists. In 1975, whole-cars primarily featured cartoon characters; they were coloring-book images and easy to paint on a train, but the results were essentially two-dimensional characters originally created by someone else. Lee changed that.

Lee exposed himself as no other writer had in the past. He talked about his fears and did magnificent depictions of them on the sides of trains. He tapped into the pulse of the human condition, which is what an artist is supposed to do. Lee quickly became the best argument the graffiti movement had that it was an art form, not mere vandalism.

Lee painted well over one hundred whole-cars in a career that spanned six years. He's continued to paint on canvas for the last thirty.

Photograph by Ernie Paniccioli.
Worth Street Station, New York City, 1982.

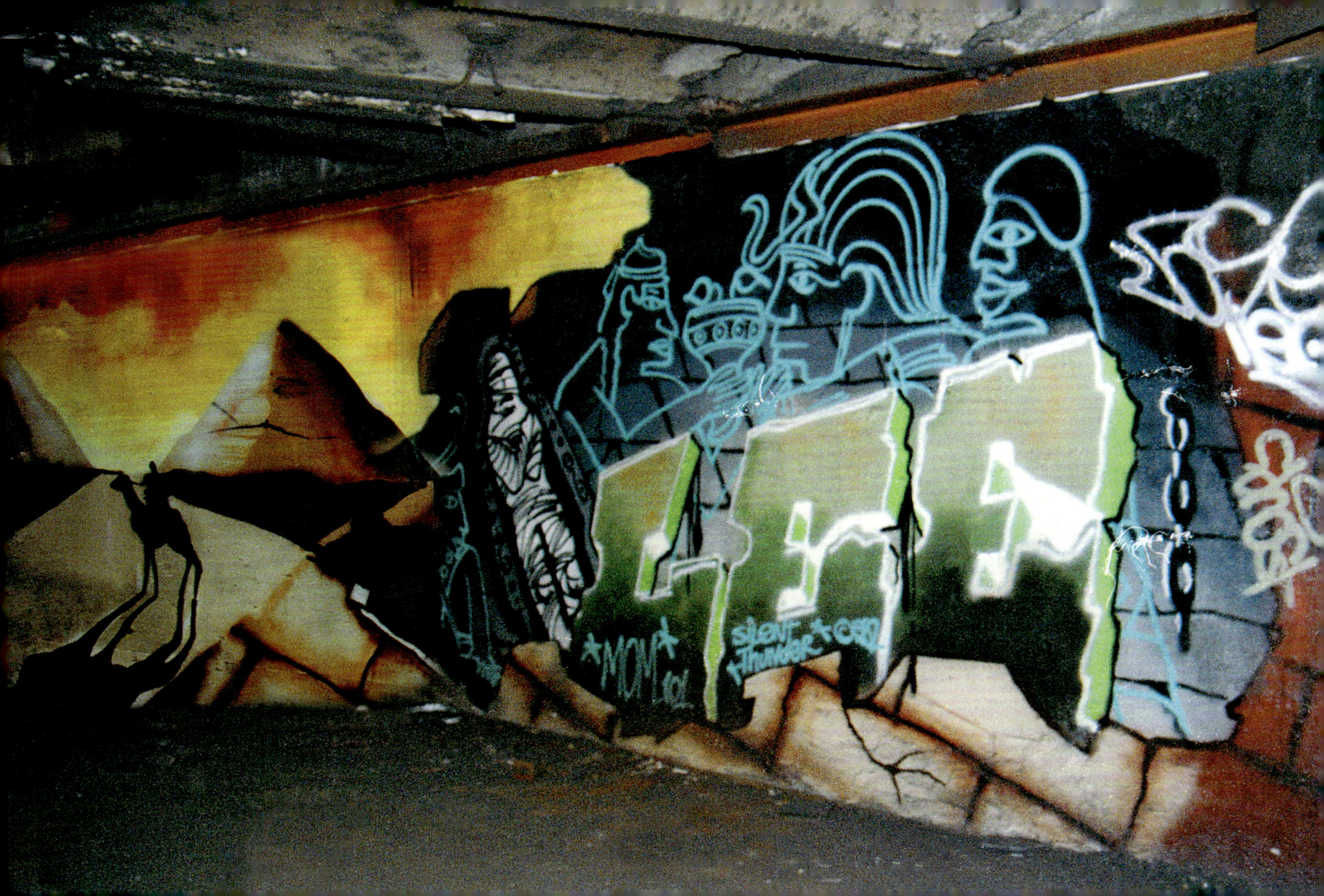

Rabodiga/ Turkesa

Rabodiga hails from the small town of Zaragoza, Spain, located in between Barcelona and Madrid. Her moniker comes from two Spanish words that describe a hyperactive kid. Her parents bought her a set of oil paints when she was seven years old, and she began painting and has never stopped. At sixteen, she attended art school, but found it was too limiting. Feeling she knew more than her teachers, she took to painting in the streets. She never completed her degree, because she constantly moved around—Italy and the UK are among the many places she has called home.

Rabodiga belongs to a segment of the public art world that is hard to categorize. She renders highly detailed portraits, primarily of women, using spray paint as her medium. She often collaborates with traditional letter-based graffiti artists, but her solo work is strictly figurative. However, Rabodiga has a definite idea about where she stands in the culture: "Even though I paint on the street and it's not letter-based stuff, I still consider my characters to be graffiti and not street art. I know that there's a fine line between the two; both employ the same tools [the spray can], but I feel street art is about showing the public your message. My work lies in between art and graffiti, because a lot of times I want to paint because it's fun, or just to hang out with my friends and paint purely for pleasure."

Rabodiga uses her art to fill an emptiness she has felt in her life. Recently, she changed her nom de plume to Turkesa, the Spanish word for her favorite color, turquoise. She paints walls, canvases, and commercial jobs, and is also a graphic designer. Presently, her tiny apartment doubles as her studio—as do the streets.

Collaborations with Saturno.
Photographs courtesy of Rabodiga, c. 2010.

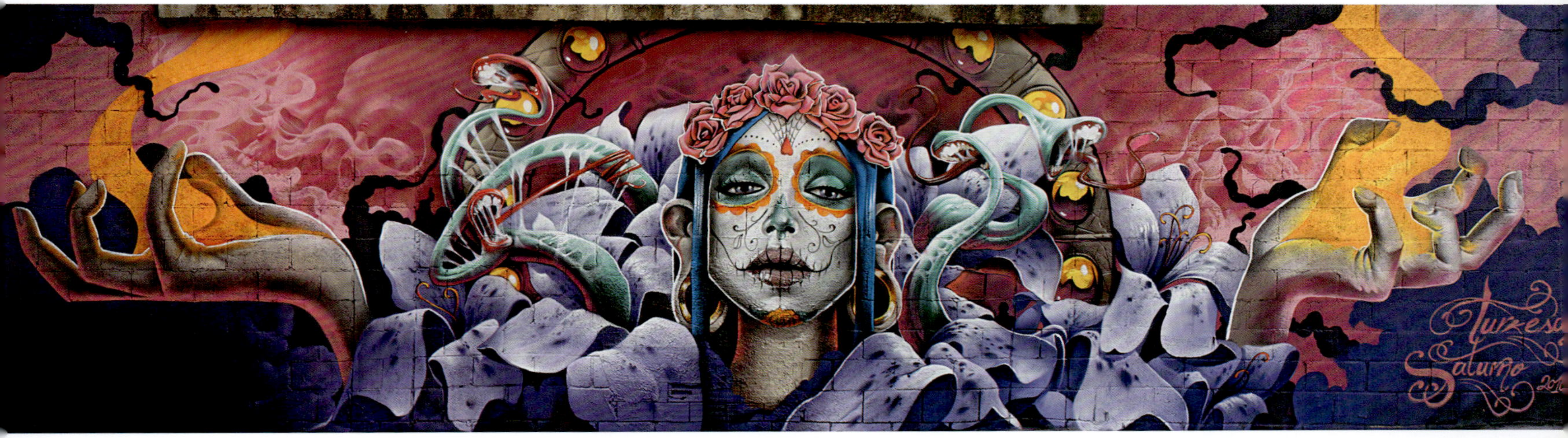

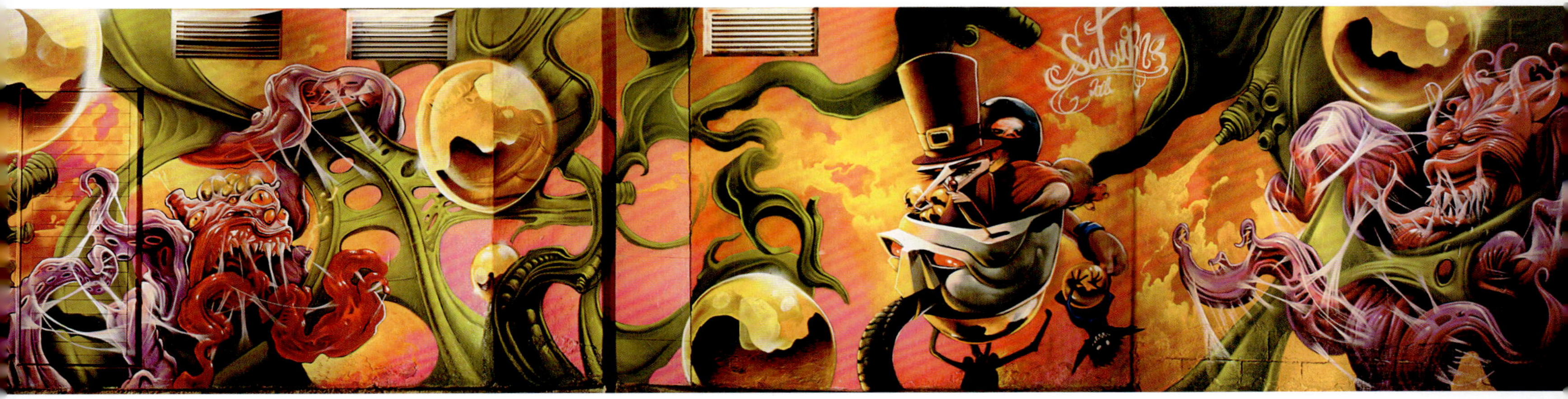

Rammellzee

Rammellzee is one of the most "out-there" characters in graffiti's history. Although Rammellzee barely participated in NYC's subway movement, he greatly influenced the culture when it moved aboveground. He would become a gallery-world staple with his unique rapping stylings, the most famous being Beat Bop (which he performed in the documentary *Style Wars* [see 322]). An early collaborator of graffiti legends like Dondi White (see 097) and Dr. Revolt, Rammellzee first shot to fame when he appeared in the film *Wild Style* in the early 1980s. He was a key figure in the downtown '80s scene, attending events at the Fun Gallery (see 140), and eventually appearing in Jim Jarmusch's 1984 film *Stranger Than Paradise*.

Known for his particularly eccentric personal style—he usually performed in George Clinton-ish garb of his own design—and his extremely conceptual musings, Rammellzee created a school of thought known as "Gothic Futurism," out of which sprang his paintings and other artworks. Gothic Futurism describes a battle between letters, and the constraints placed on them by the traditional, restrictive rules of the alphabet. At one point, he published a treatise on this philosophy titled *Iconic Panzerisms*—several hundred pages of theorizing detailing a plan to revise and redeploy language within society. Rammellzee also created a series of robot letters in which the alphabet is transformed into war machines, such as tanks and other weaponry. Rammellzee often collaborated with musical artists and presented this work in conjunction with his graffiti-based visual art. He lived life hard and fast, throwing caution to the wind. A native of the outer New York borough of Queens, Rammellzee passed away at his home in Far Rockaway, on June 27, 2010. He was forty-nine.

Photograph by Lisa Kahane, c. 1982.

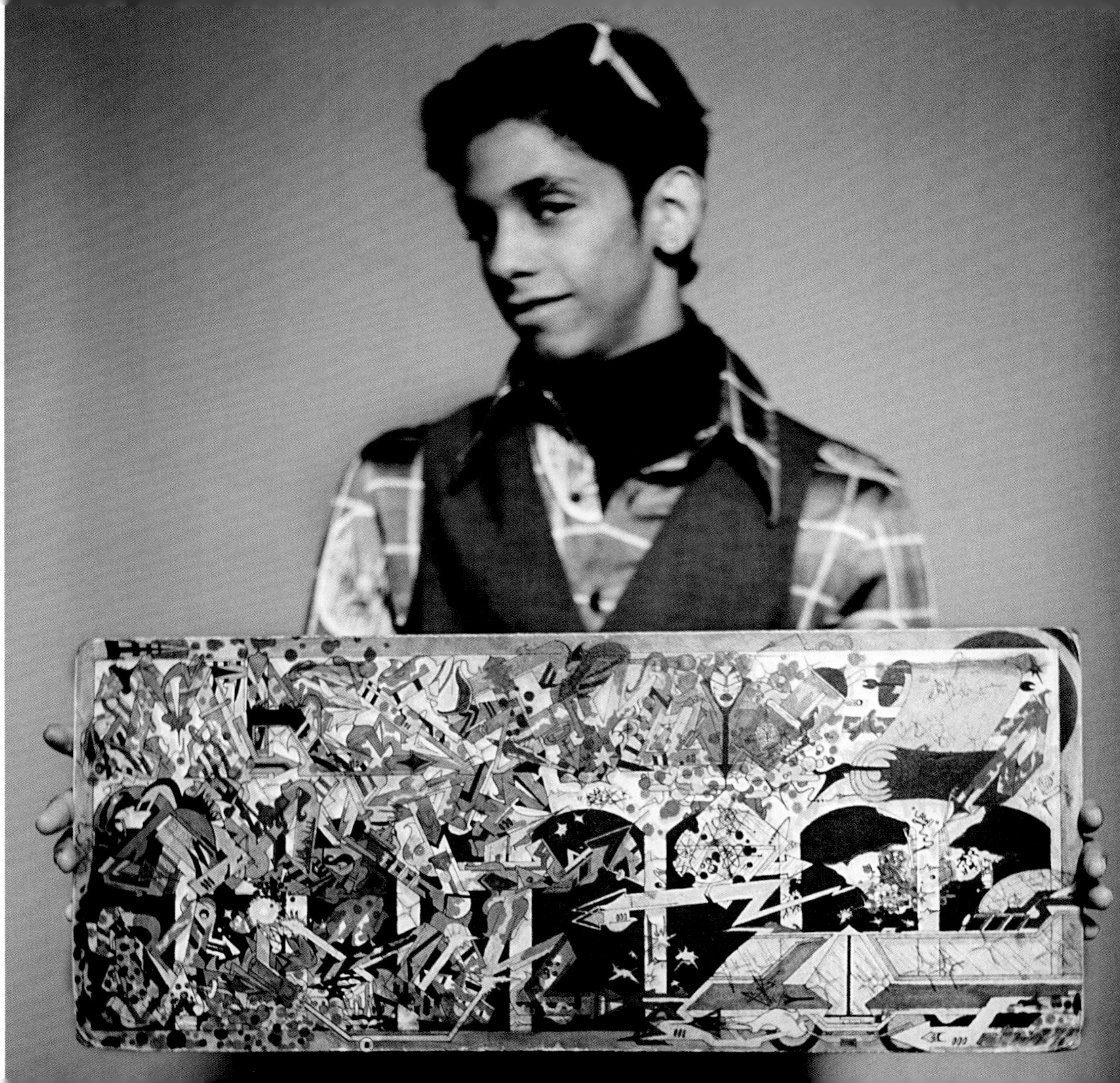

Rasta

Rasta was a young writer from Queens whose major works were done on the #1 line from 1979 to 1982. He was one of a number of young people who hung out at the Bandshell [see 023] in Central Park, along with Zephyr [see 363], Revolt, Min [see 223], and Bilrock. He was there when Bilrock formed the Rolling Thunder Writers [RTW, see 286], and he was one of the first of the group to emerge with a distinct piecing technique, making a quick transition from psychedelic imagery to a harder-edged style. This style allowed Rasta to compete with the best writers of the day, including Dondi [see 097]; the two writers were both perfectionists famous for laboring over pieces for hours.

In 1981, Rasta developed a personal trademark of outlining his pieces with high-gloss white paint that made his pieces appear to jump out from the others. His tag style was also very distinctive and virtually illegible, a series of swirls that somehow held together as a composition, though he also sometimes used a simpler style of tagging for the uninitiated.

Rasta painted during a four-year period when graffiti style had peaked. He not only held his own—on some days he even led the pack.

Piece by Rasta [left]; character by Revolt.
Photograph by Pjay One.
New York City, 1979.

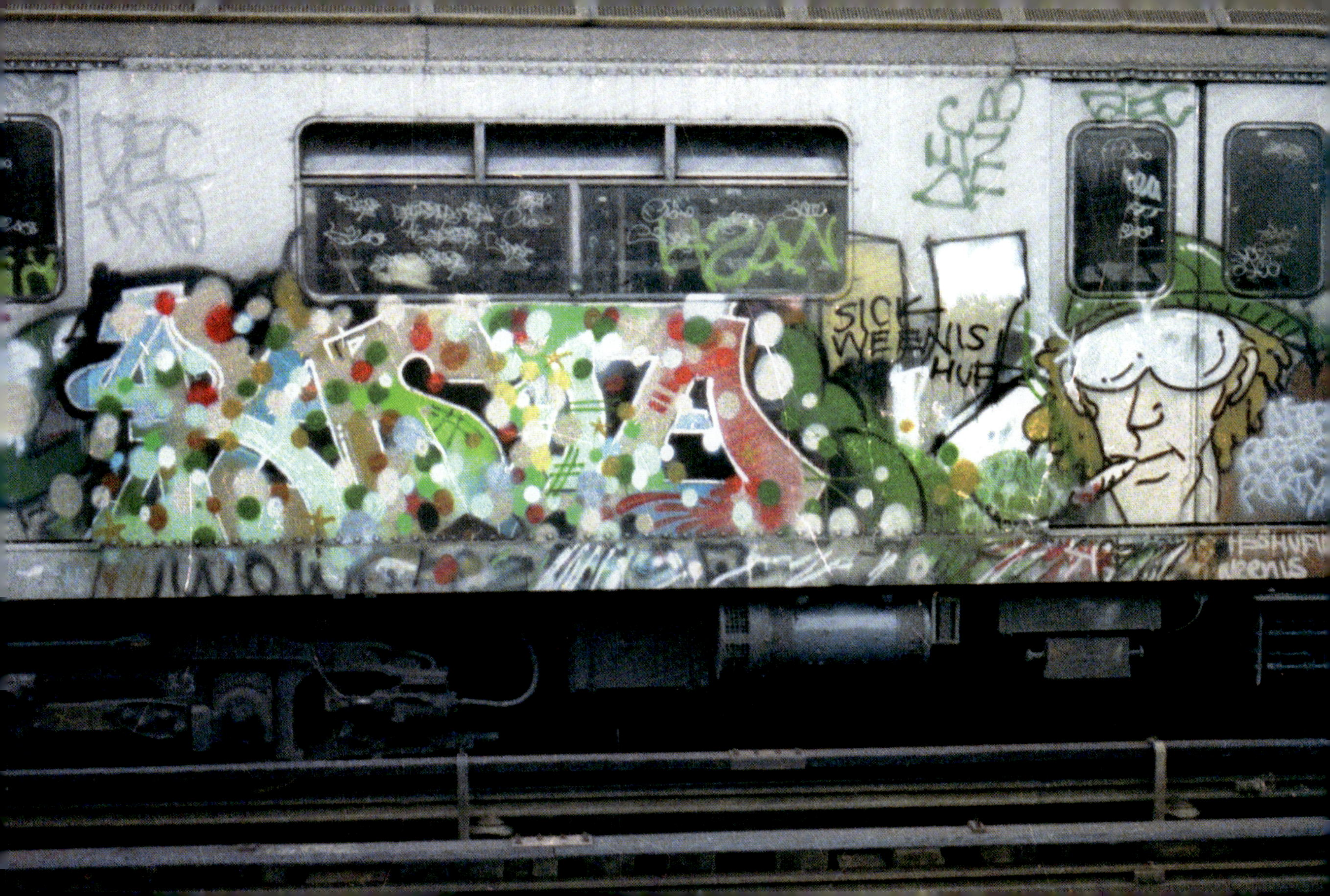
SICK
WEENIS
HUF

red trains

For those who witnessed the birth of subway graffiti in late 1971, red trains have a timeless, romantic appeal. So much of graffiti's DNA can be traced to the crimson carriages: Jack Stewart captured the evolution of graffiti from the signature era to the piecing era against these red backgrounds, and Jon Naar's photograph of the iconic Stay High 149 (see 316) top-to-bottom (on a red train) graces the cover of his *Faith of Graffiti* (see 126) reissue. But by 1974, the red train had gone the way of the dinosaur. Advanced lettering techniques and characters were coming into play, however, and kids happily made their reputations on the good old silver trains with the blue stripe running across them. The writers from the BMT and IND lines dealt with unorthodox-styled trains, from "ding dongs" (named for the doorbell-like sound that rang when the doors opened and closed) to "flats" (trains with perfectly flat tops) to "ridgies" (trains with ridged sides). They all painted their own diverse canvases, forgetting that red trains ever existed.

Then, after more than a decade, a funny thing happened: The MTA reincarnated the red ghosts of graffiti's past. By 1984, a successful graffiti-cleansing system had been implemented by the MTA, and the red trains, which were simply the older IRT variants with a coat of red paint, were brought back into service. Reintroduced as redbirds, they ran relatively graffiti free for most of their service lives, lasting until 2003, when the last eleven cars made their final run on the #7 line. The images of red trains then being dumped by cranes from barges into the icy waters of the northern Atlantic ocean meant nothing to most modern-day New Yorkers—just another severed link to the past, like the demolishing of Yankee Stadium or the closing of CBGBs.

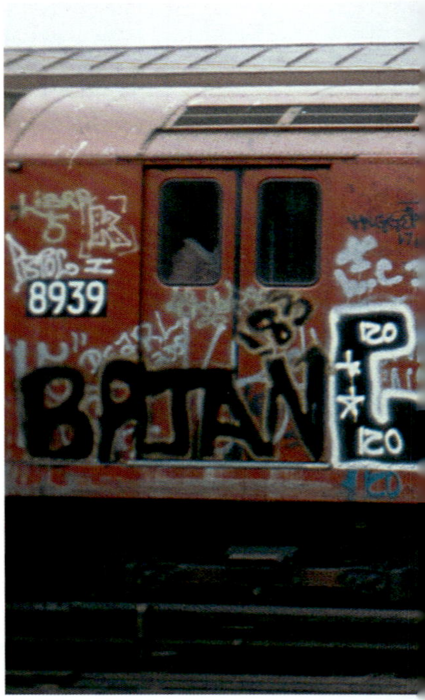

Pieces by Clancy 120 (left and right); assorted tags by Spin, Cool Jeff, Hulk 62, and Cool Fool. Photograph by Jack Stewart. New York City, c. 1972.

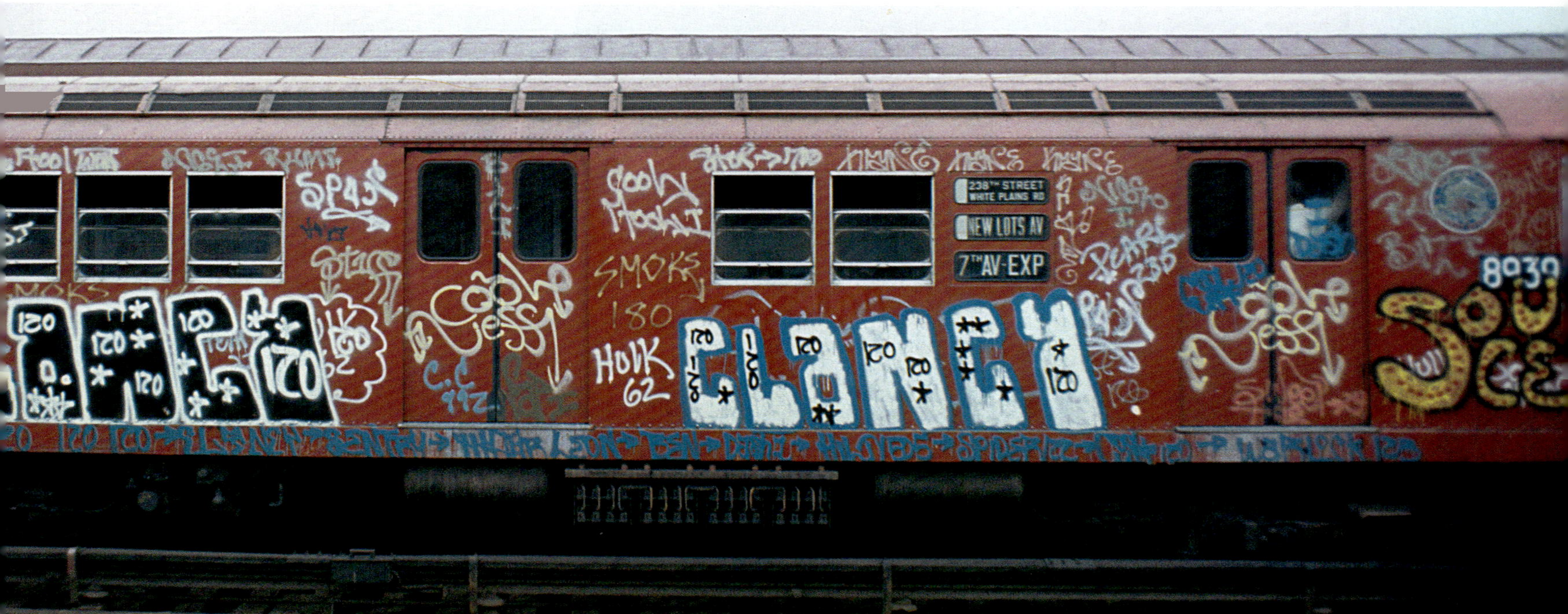
238TH STREET
WHITE PLAINS RD
NEW LOTS AV
7TH AV-EXP

Leon Reid

In the late 1980s and early 1990s, Leon Reid was a teenager living in Ohio, beautifying the streets of Cincinnati with the requisite sophomoric contributions to the growing world of graffiti under the moniker Verbs. In 1995, however, he moved to Brooklyn and began creating two- and three-dimensional sculpture work on the streets that signaled the beginning of a sweeping change in ephemeral art.

Together with his then-partner-in-crime, Brad Downey, Reid would brazenly don a city worker's uniform and take to the streets, removing all manner of public structures, from street signs to telephone booths, taking them back to the studio, transforming them, and reinstalling them on the street—in broad daylight. Suddenly, signposts were kissing or had been welded into giant roses. Taking the art of environmental manipulation to a new level, Reid and Downey completely transformed urban landscapes, creating an important advancement in what was accepted as and expected from street art.

Reid continues to work as a public artist, with commissions completed in South America, the United States, and Europe. His contemporary public work uses much of the humor and wit found in his previous work as a street artist.

Photographs by Ray Mock.
Brooklyn, New York, 2009.

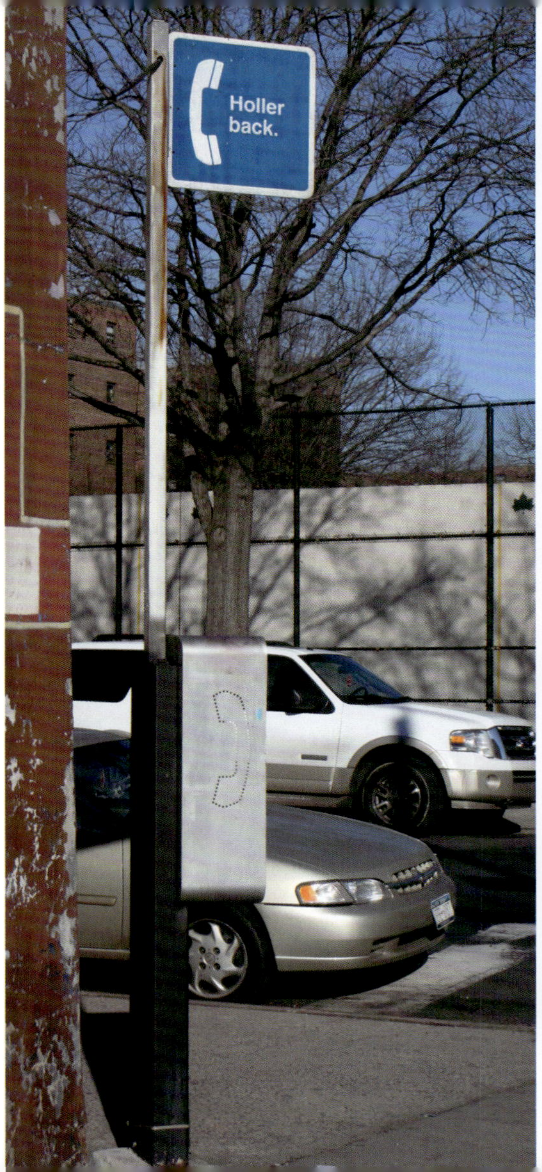
Holler back.

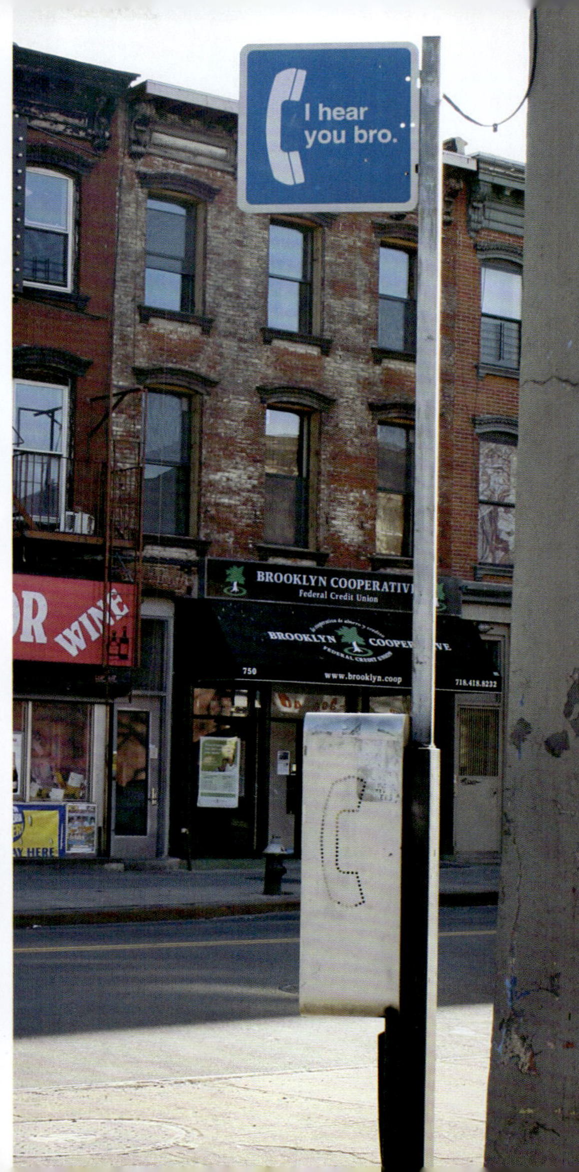
I hear you bro.
Federal Credit Union
WINE
750
www.brooklyn.coop

Retna

A native of Los Angeles, California, and a founding member of the 7th Letter crew (see 022), Retna is credited as one of the most influential artists in the world of urban–fine art crossover. In the mid-1990s, his work began appearing on walls, freeways, and overpasses, and he even turned down an opportunity to attend the Museum of Fine Arts in Boston on a full scholarship, for fear of losing the cred he'd built on the streets. Bred in the expansive city's mural culture, Retna created a unique style of painting, using both brushes and spray paint and creating a crossover between traditional graffiti lettering and the intricate calligraphic handstyles he has become known for in recent years.

Drawing inspiration from Mayan, Egyptian, and Asian motifs, as well as classical calligraphy, Retna began exhibiting his work in a fine-art setting in 2000 with a group show at the 01 Gallery in Los Angeles. He has since made the crossover from street work to both fine art and commercial work, where he is known for "Retnafying" advertisements and for collaborations with musical acts like Metallica and Kylie Minogue. Some of his finest collaborative works paired his calligraphic genius with the flawless portraiture of fellow artist El Mac (see 111).

Retna continues to paint on the street today, creating intricate murals for the likes of the "Primary Flight" exhibition at Art Basel Miami Beach.

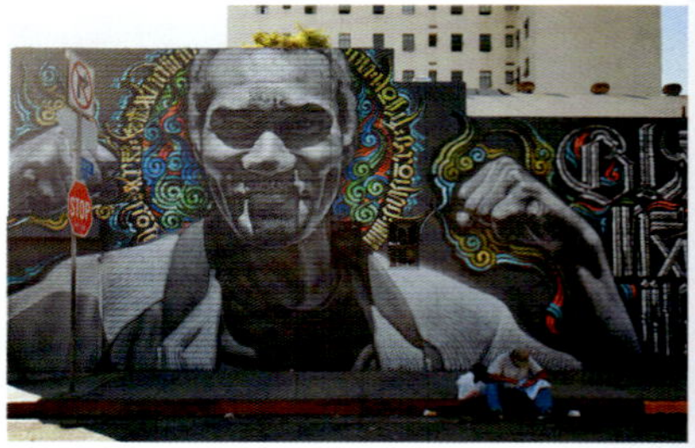

Photograph by Jake Dobkin (streetsy.com). Los Angeles, 2009.
Detail: Artwork by Retna, with El Mac. Photograph by Jake Dobkin (streetsy.com). Los Angeles, 2010.

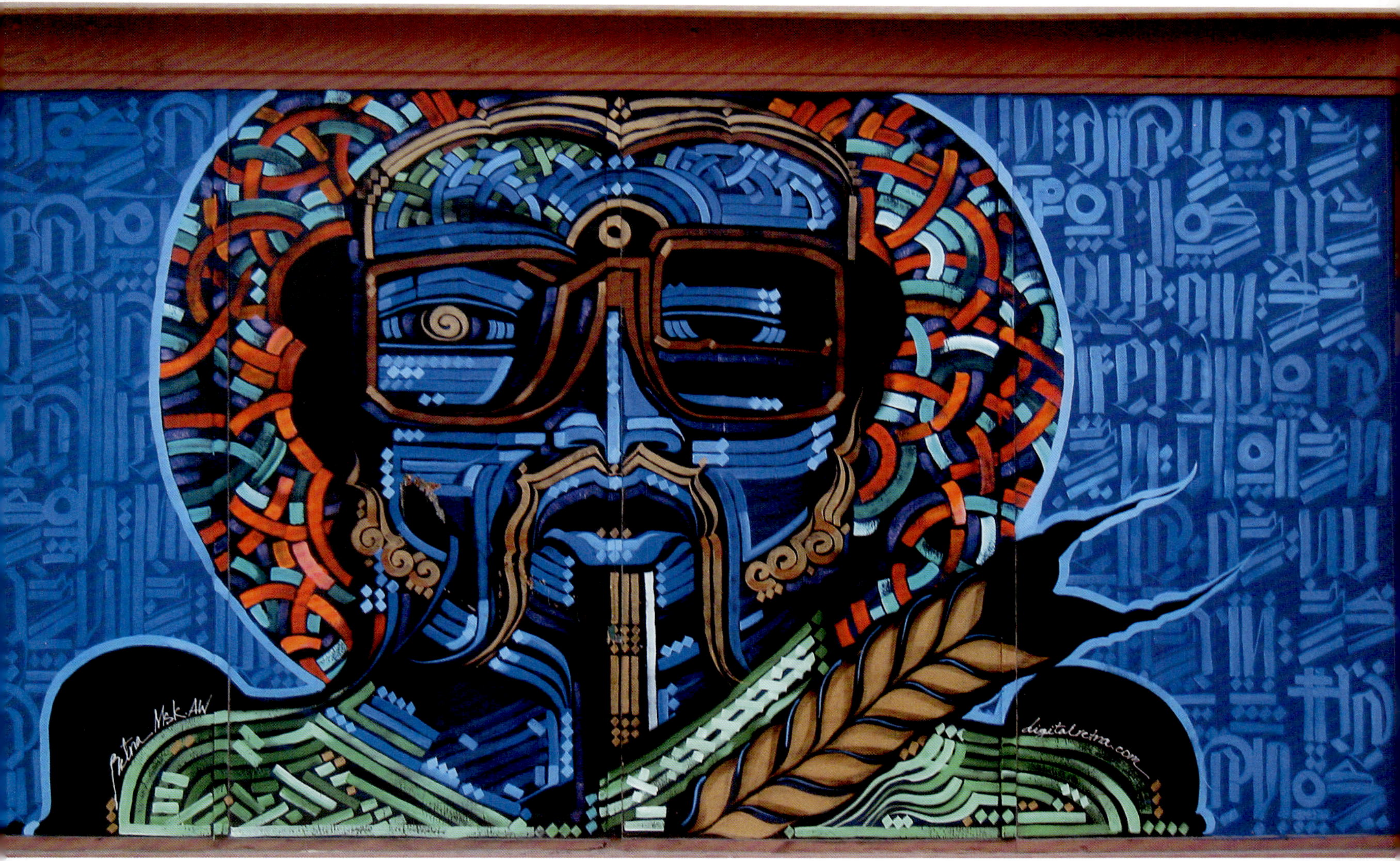
Retna MSK AW
digitalretna.com

Revok

On November 22, 2009, Revok drove to a local graffiti-art supply store, where he was scheduled for a paid appearance. As Revok shook hands with admirers and signed their blackbooks, the LAPD, LA Sheriff's Department, and California Highway Patrol collaborated to secure the building's perimeter and arrest him. After learning of their plans, Revok slipped out the back of the building, successfully eluding a circling helicopter and more than forty officers. Some ten blocks away, he emerged from his hiding spot onto the streets. An intended rendezvous with a friend never happened. Instead, he was spotted by undercover officers in a passing car. Within seconds, Revok found himself facedown on the ground, surrounded by police.

The official police report stated that the arrest, one of his dozens in recent years, was for carrying spray-can nozzles. Ironically, Revok has never been arrested for actually *doing* graffiti; his arrests have more to do with the perception of him as a major threat to the city of Los Angeles than with his possession of a few fatcaps.

Revok started writing in 1991, at the age of thirteen, and advanced rapidly with a crisp MSK style and a bomber's mentality. By his own admission, he says, "When I come to your town, I'm coming to make my presence known."

He remains one of graffiti's rarest creatures: a highly talented and articulate writer who makes a demonized art form look exciting and glamorous. One of the first writers to secure a paid sponsor, Revok has been hired by a slew of companies. He's become the poster-boy for this newly positive public perception of graffiti, and the police have tried to make his life miserable because of it. But the more he's arrested, the higher his profile is raised—and isn't that the object of the game?

Photograph by Steve Rotman. San Francisco, 2007.

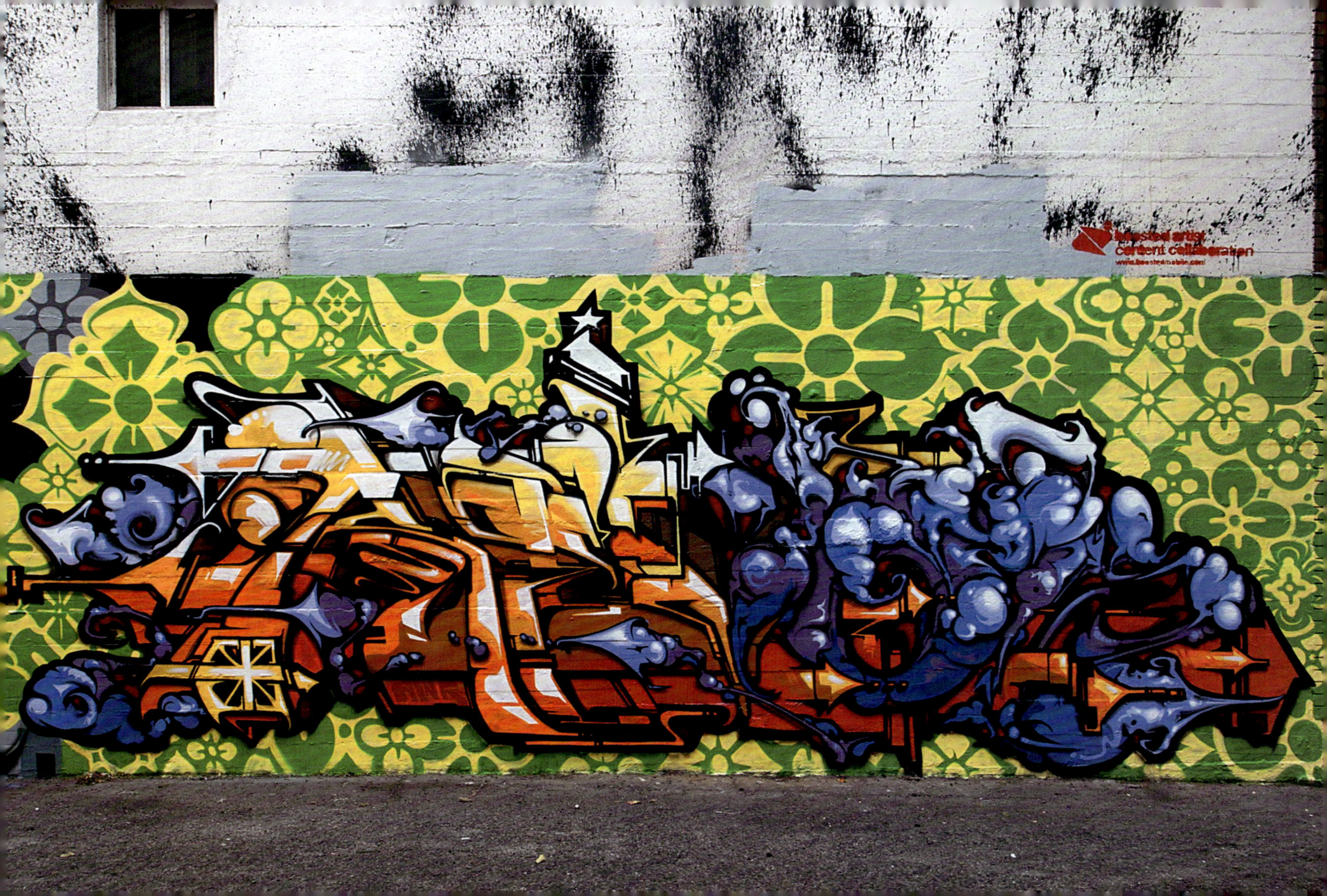
boosted artist
content collaboration
www.boostedmobile.com

Revs

The artist Revs, a metal worker by trade, has used the outside world as his personal canvas for decades. Revs has mastered a myriad of media, but perhaps his most enduring (and endearing) work is his metal sculpture. These extraordinary pieces are welded together in his clandestine studio, and affixed, surreptitiously, to buildings, bridges, and sidewalks—gifts to the people. The sculptures are designed to live outside, ripening as they rust.

Revs began painting in 1983 on the BMT subway trains that ran through his Brooklyn neighborhood. He evolved into a respected artist in the traditional New York graffiti genre, but while other writers changed subway lines to broaden their game during the 1990s, Revs reinvented the game itself. Armed with twelve-inch xeroxed placards, Revs and his partner, Cost, launched a massive postering barrage on New York that lasted for years. Their simple paper messages became more ubiquitous than parking meters.

After Cost's arrest, Revs decided to chill—quite literally—in Alaska. He reemerged a few years later as an underground novelist—again, quite literally. In the bowels of the subway system, he painted one "page" of his autobiography on the wall of each tunnel between subway stations in the system. But the vandal squad gave the book of Revs a surprise ending: They arrested him. Rumor has it Revs received royal treatment from the cops who nabbed him—he served no jail time, despite holding the top spot on the vandal squad's most-wanted list. Apparently, his fans were as diverse as his methods. Revs has said that art is no longer art when money changes hands, and his work has never been for sale.

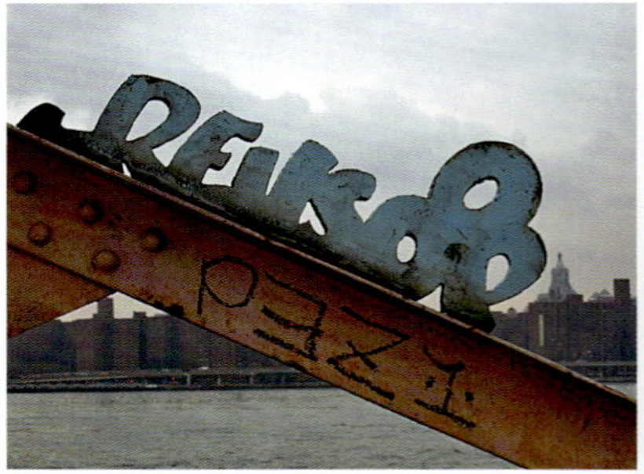

Photographs by Sam Horine. Brooklyn, New York, 2007.

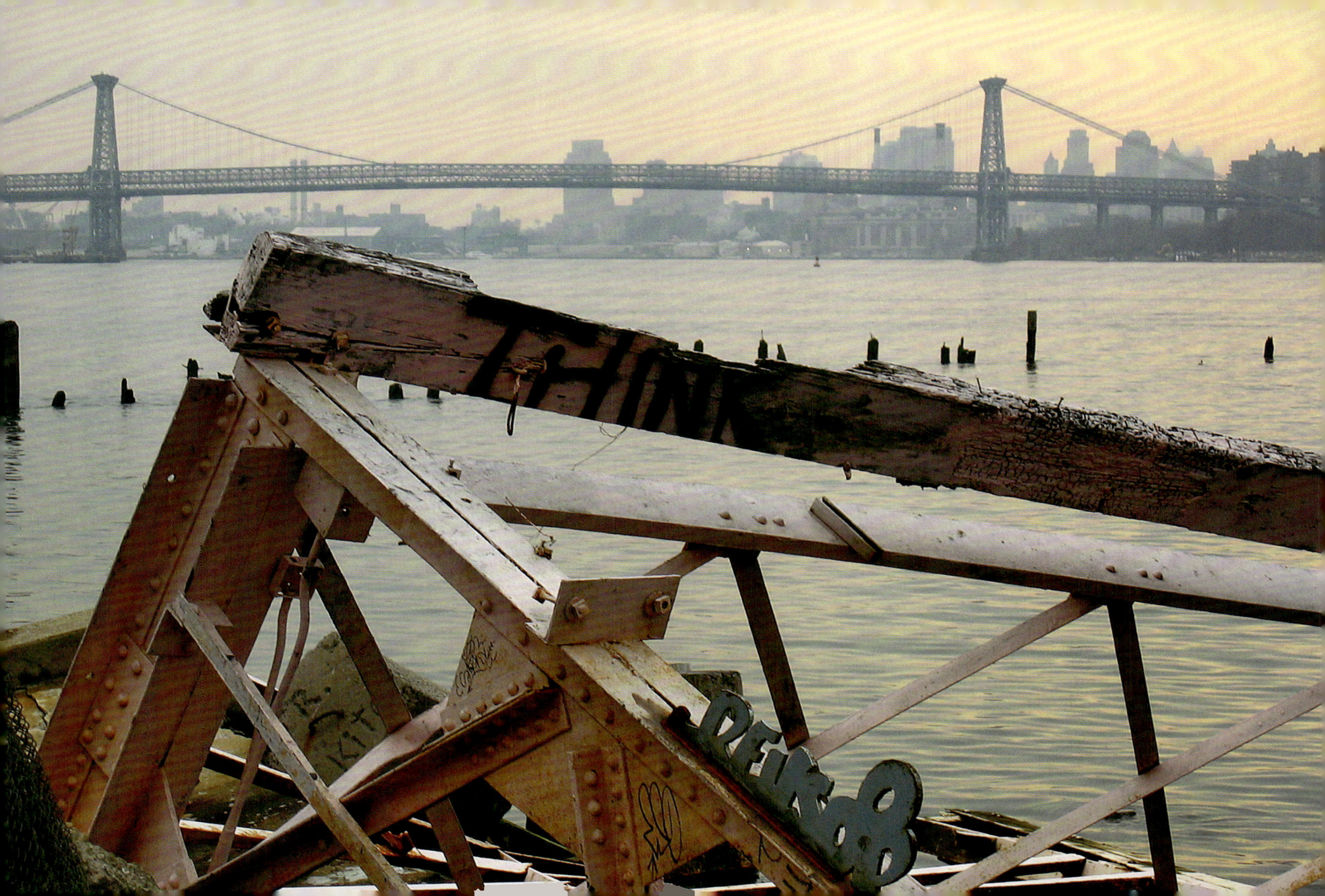
THINK

Victor Reyes

Born in 1978 to a middle-class family in Southern California, Victor Reyes evolved into a West Coast graffiti legend by developing a unique style of lettering that fuses classical Baroque elements with old-school graffiti. Characterized by bold colors and swooping patterns, Reyes's signature has made its way onto hundreds of walls as he painted along with the other members of his crew, AWR/MSK [see 022]. Reyes's work is notably devoid of the bold macho elements that normally dominate the genre.

In 1998, Reyes moved to San Francisco, where he continued painting until 2008, when he decided to challenge himself by crafting something different. The outcome of this venture, which would take two years to complete, was a distinct graffiti alphabet. Reyes entitled it "The Misspelled Project," an allusion to the stereotype that graffiti writers can't spell.

Painted on walls, trucks, rooftops, and fences throughout his neighborhood, the Mission District, Reyes's alphabet has spurred a book, a solo gallery show at E6 Gallery, and recognition in the fine-art world. Reyes anticipates that it will inspire some of the young writers in his neighborhood to hone their craft as well. Self-taught, Reyes also works as a freelance illustrator and graphic designer. Along with such notable graffiti writers as Revok [see 274], Retna [see 273], Saber [see 287], Push, Rime, El Mac [see 111], and Zes, Reyes is a member of the 7th Letter [see 022], a collective of artists with roots in AWR/MSK.

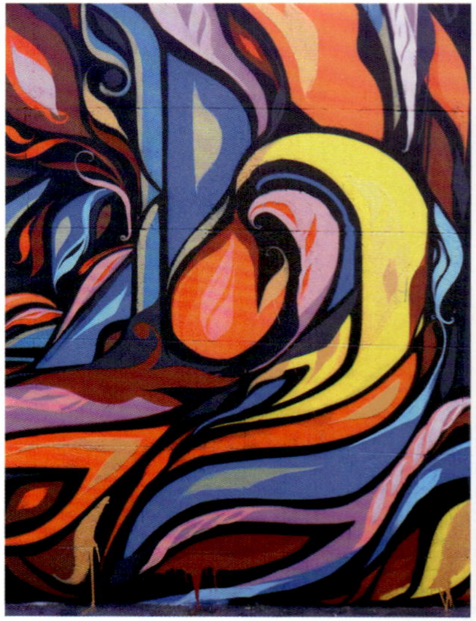

Photographs by Steve Rhodes. San Francisco, 2010.

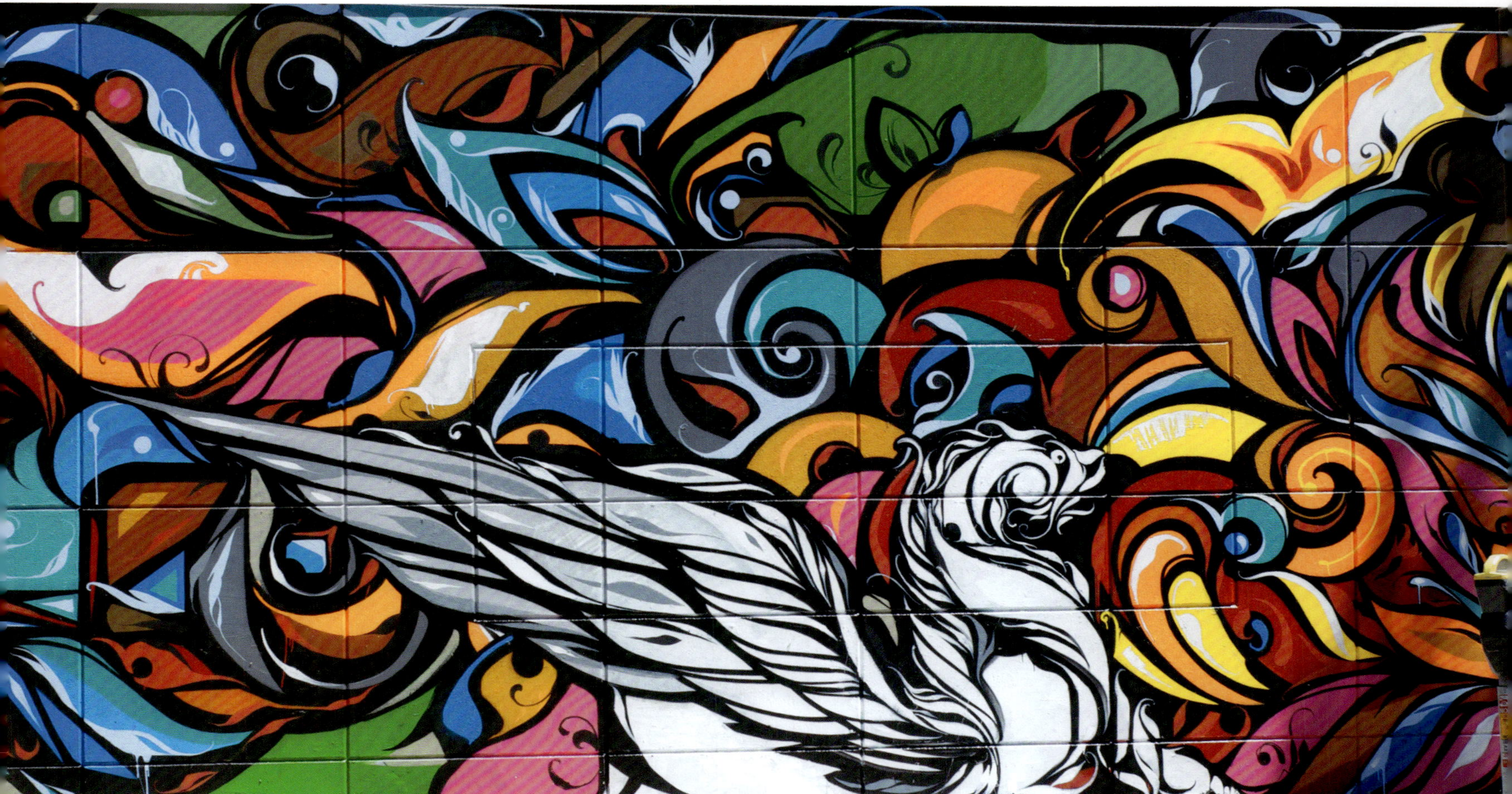

Paul Richard

Late in the first decade of the century, curiously emotional, single-line portraits of men's faces began to appear, the paint seemingly dripped, on sidewalks in Williamsburg, Brooklyn. Every alternate corner along Bedford Avenue was adorned with a face. Heightening the mystery, an elderly couple who sold miscellaneous vintage items on the neighborhood's main drag claimed that they were the artist's managers and attempted to hawk his canvas renditions of the drippy faces for several thousand dollars. Eventually, it was revealed that the artist behind the mischief was none other than Paul Richard, an eccentric but immensely talented artist based in both New York and Boston.

While he is best known in Brooklyn for his drip paintings on sidewalks, Richard also embarked on another prolific street-art campaign, in which he tacked plaques to public objects (fire hydrants, signposts, and the like) that listed the contents of the object in question, attached his name as the artist responsible, and gave an exorbitant estimate of the object's price ($145,000, for example).

Conveying a little of the flavor of Banksy's stunt antics, Richard is also a highly adept oil painter. He uses the medium to create canvases, largely portraiture, which he sells in the international fine-art marketplace. Richard continues to paint on the street as well.

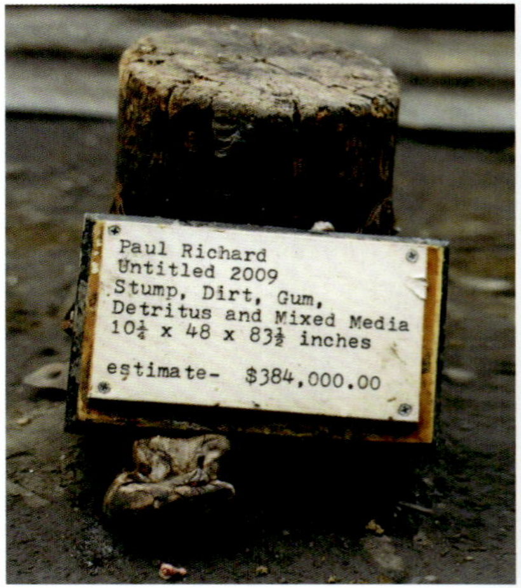

Photographs courtesy of Paul Richard.
Brooklyn, New York, 2010.
Detail: Brooklyn, New York, 2009.

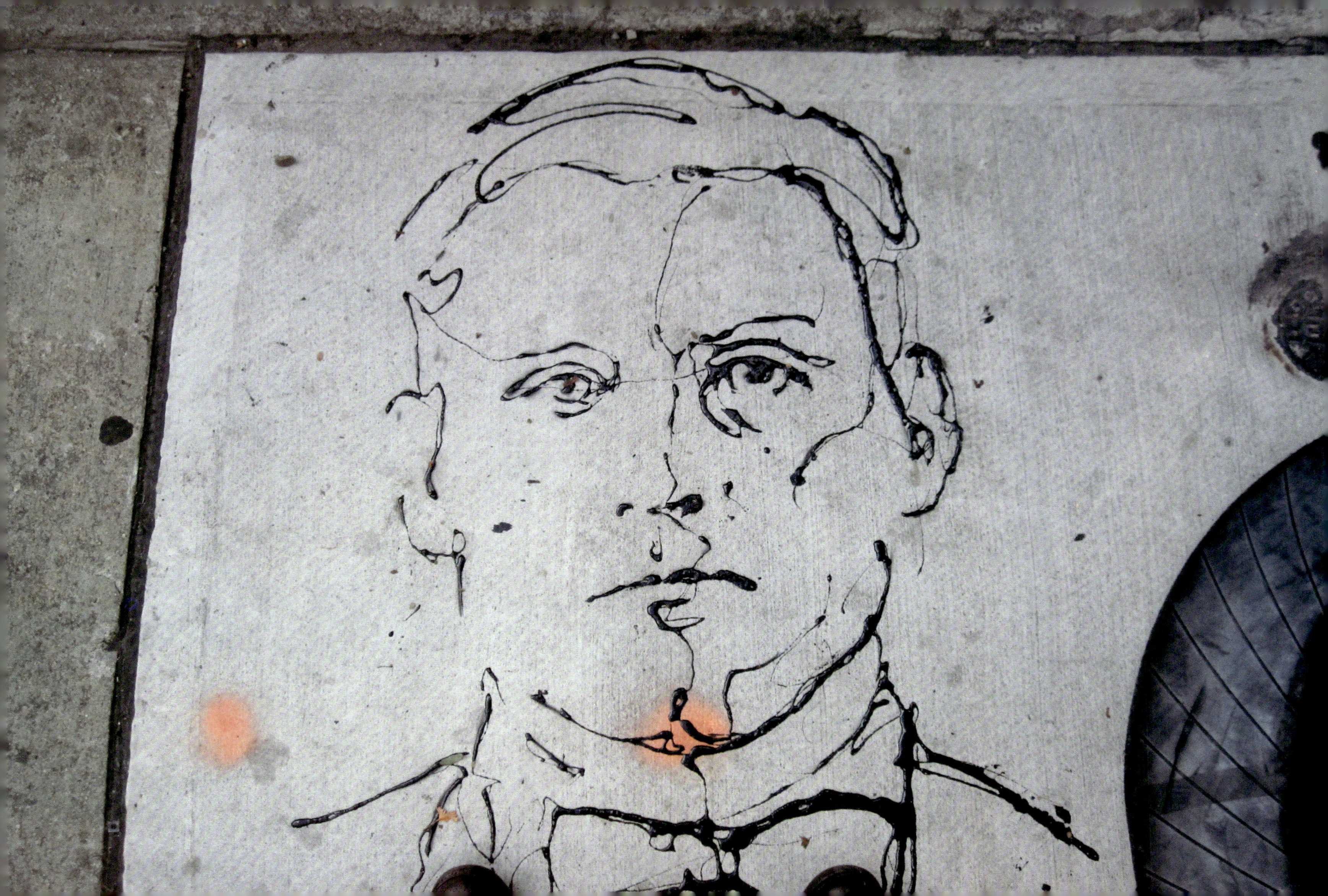

Riff

Riff grew up in the Bronx, just north of Yankee Stadium, in a family of ten children. He met Chris 170 and Bonanza, two brothers who were experienced writers, in 1972 in the neighborhood, and they showed Riff where the lay-ups were. Shortly thereafter, he started hitting the insides of the trains. This was during the signature era, when handwriting counted for everything, so Riff made his tags elegant and ubiquitous, and his work caught the eye of the legendary Phase 2, who would take the younger Riff under his mighty stylistic wing.

By 1973, Riff had become a force to be reckoned with. Signatures blossomed into pieces, and Riff's style progressed light-years ahead of his peers. One name wasn't enough for Riff, who sought complete alphabet domination. He rocked the trains with a multitude of colorful aliases: Worm 161, Mr. 6, Conan, Crunch, Cash, Flip, Real, Peal, Mr. Dirt, Boy 170, 2Bad, As 2, and Dove 2, to name a few of them. Riff is known as the father of mechanical lettering, and he was the inventor of almost as many designs as he had names.

Today, thirty-three years after Riff retired, it is virtually impossible to find a graffiti recipe without one of his ingredients in it.

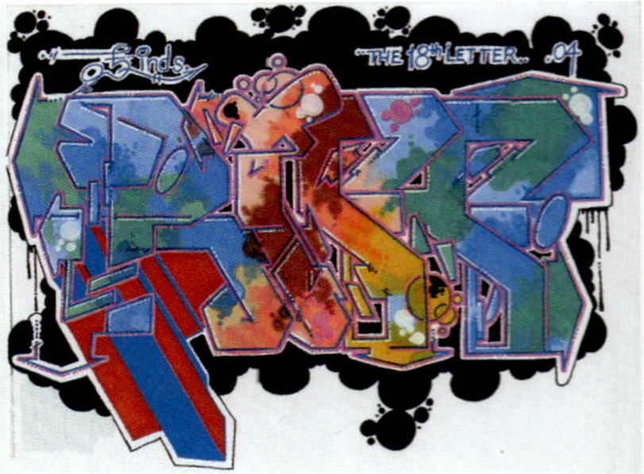

***Flip* piece by Riff 170, with tags by Priest 170, Tracy 168, PJ 104, and RC 162.**
Photograph by Jack Stewart.
New York City, 1974.
Detail: Private collection, 2011.

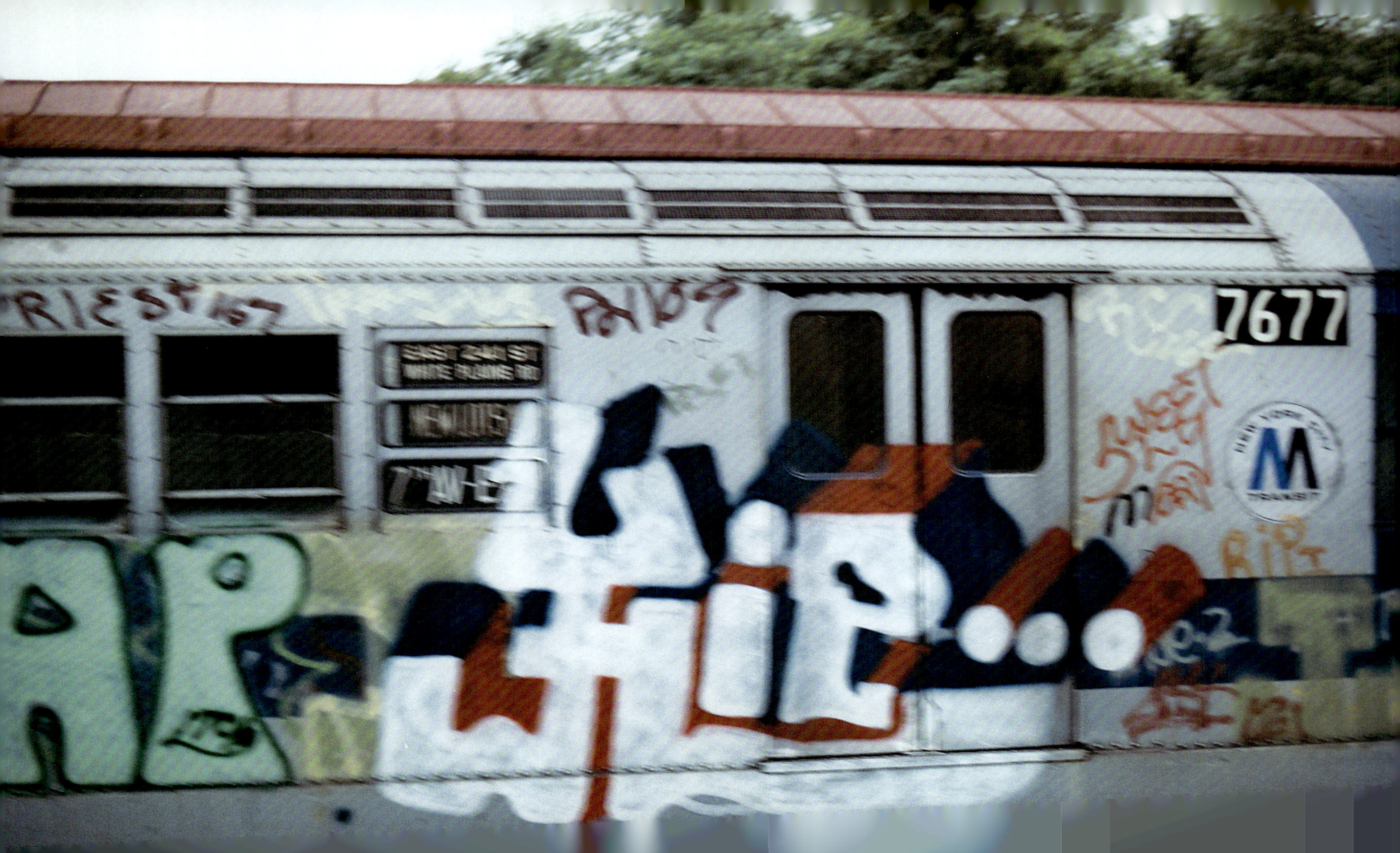
7677
EAST 241 ST
WHITE PLAINS RD

Ripo

Inspired by the calligraphy of classical graffiti, as well as by the linguistic acrobatics in works by the likes of Espo (see 115), Ripo is quickly making a name for himself in the international street-art community with his text-based art. Ripo has created statements and letters on every possible surface, using bold, oversize lettering that is viewable from miles away.

Fluent in Spanish and English, Ripo utilizes his bilingualism to create works in the language native to whatever place he is visiting. A transplanted resident of Barcelona, Spain, who now lives in New York, Ripo has traveled the world extensively, most notably with fellow street artist Above (see 006), with whom he completed a tour of thirteen South and Central American countries, collaborating on innumerable text-based murals along the way.

In 2009, Ripo completed a residency in Vienna, Austria, where he created his most elaborate work to date: Using daily headlines from local newspapers, each day Ripo painted individual murals of ten statements, taped off a sliver of each one to protect it, and then painted over it. Finally, he removed the tape strips from the previously painted canvas to reveal ten strips of full murals, creating one final work that reflected how text influences us every day, as well as the absurdity of everyday life.

He remains one of Barcelona's most prolific ephemeral artists.

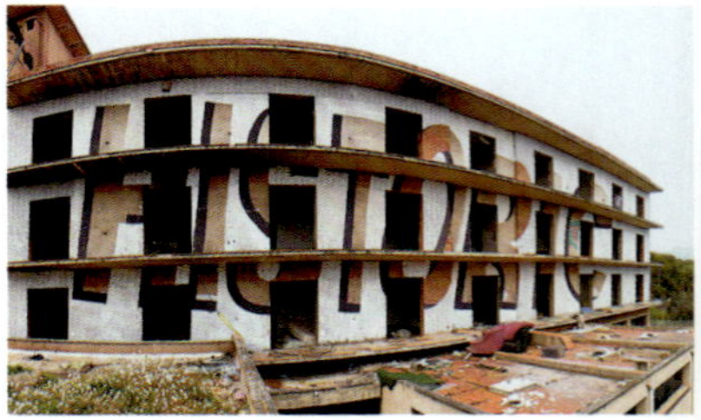

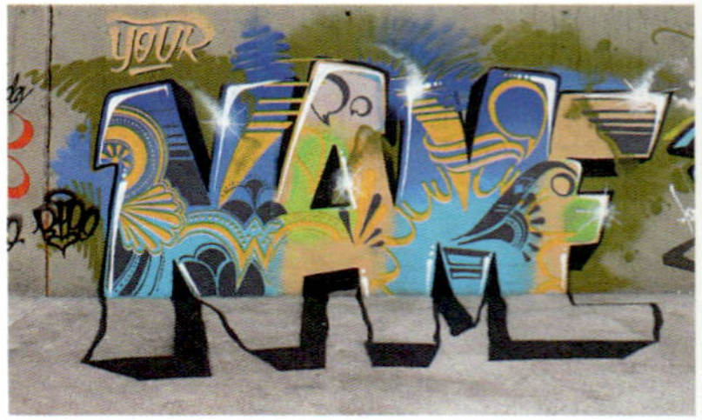

Photographs courtesy of Ripo.
***Casanova*. Barcelona, Spain, 2009.**
Detail top: *Historic*. Barcelona, Spain, 2009.
Detail bottom: *Your Name*. Barcelona, Spain, 2010.

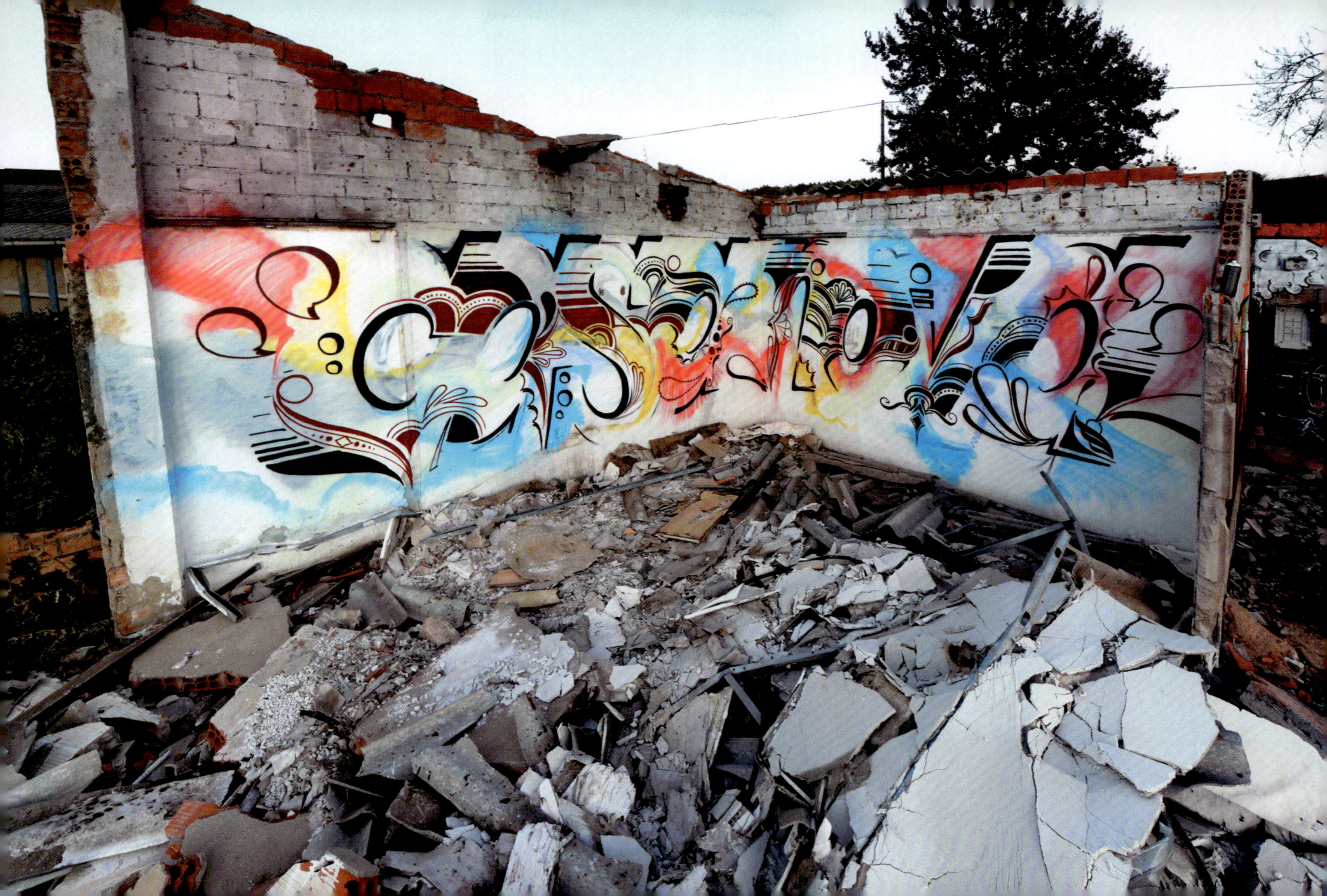

Risk

Kelly Graval, aka Risk, boasts one of the most complete résumés in the graffiti world. His name has been synonymous with Los Angeles graffiti since the early 1980s, when he helped pioneer painting heavens [see 163] and freights. He formed the WCA [West Coast Artists] crew with fellow artist Rival, and the crew saturated Los Angeles with murals, throw-ups, and tags. Risk's artistic evolution won him a high-school scholarship at the Pasadena Art Institute, and he went on to study fine art at USC. He cofounded Third Rail, one of the first graffiti-inspired clothing lines, and soon became an award-winning fashion designer.

Risk's work is characterized by super-clean lettering often paired with tattoo imagery, and his style continues to influence a new generation of talented artists. He is now part of the 7th Letter crew [see 022], one of the most active creative groups in the world. Risk's present collaborators include Abel, Rime, Revok [see 274], Pose, Sever [see 297], Saber [see 287], and Tyke/Witnes [see 345].

A veteran of numerous solo gallery shows, Risk regularly sells his canvases for prices in the five-figure range. Sell out? Hardly. He gives back to the community by teaching free workshops, which he calls "blackbook sessions," in schools throughout California. "Risk-y business" has never interfered with his painting for the love of the game.

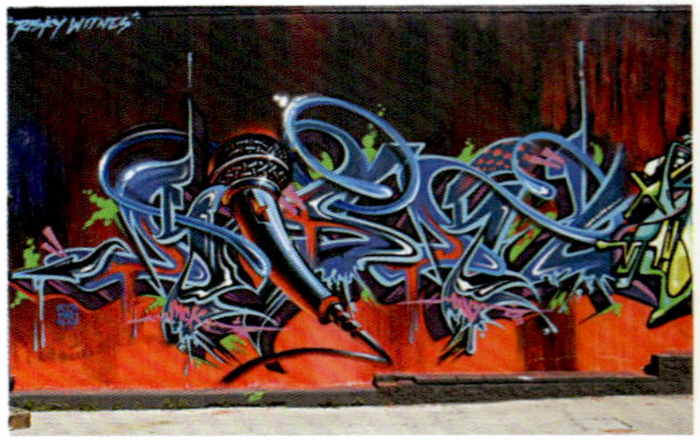

Photographs courtesy of Risk. Los Angeles, 2010.

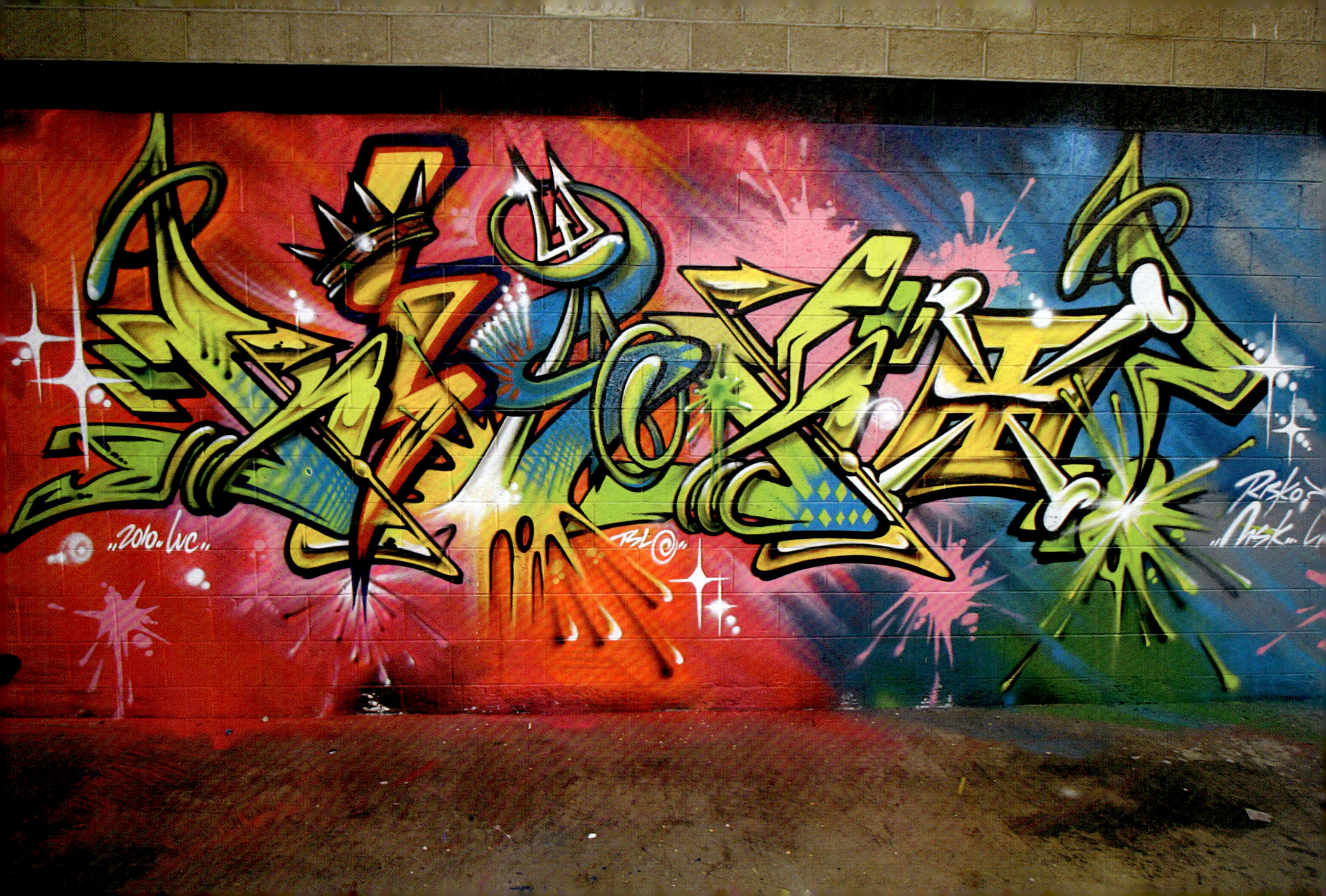

Roa

Young Belgian artist Roa spent years perfecting his style in disused buildings and warehouses on the outskirts of his hometown of Ghent. Today, his iconic giant animals are gracing the busy streets of cosmopolitan cities like Berlin, Paris, and London.

Using a simple illustration style, he spray-paints the oversized beasts freehand in black-and-white, always with macabre undertones. Often taking the form of rats and ravens, these beasts either have an accusatory, beady-eyed stare or they're shown lying dead—decapitated or cut in half. When Roa does use color, it's strictly to highlight gory details, often revealing blood, organs, or circulatory systems using clever tricks of perspective.

In December 2009, Roa's giant rabbit in busy East London caused a real stir with its use of a clever "reveal" mechanism. As viewers walked past it, the wonderfully detailed animal transformed into a morbid cross-section, in which its heart and veins became visible against a black bunny silhouette.

As Roa's work continues to spread, more people will have the chance to experience the devastating simplicity of his work—and learn a bit about the inner workings of small mammals at the same time.

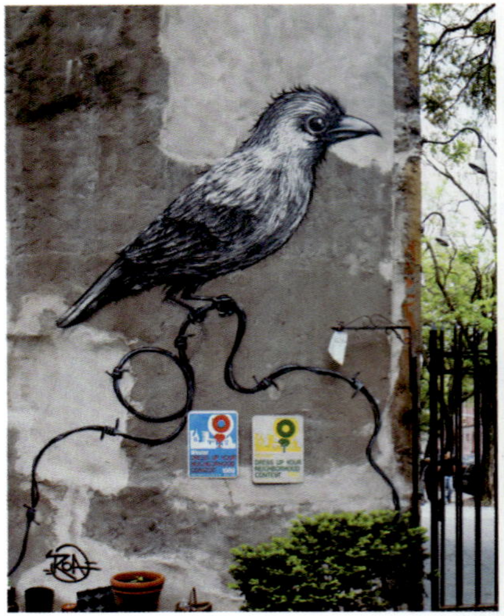

Photographs by Jake Dobkin (streetsy.com).
New York City, 2009.
Detail: Brooklyn, New York, 2009.

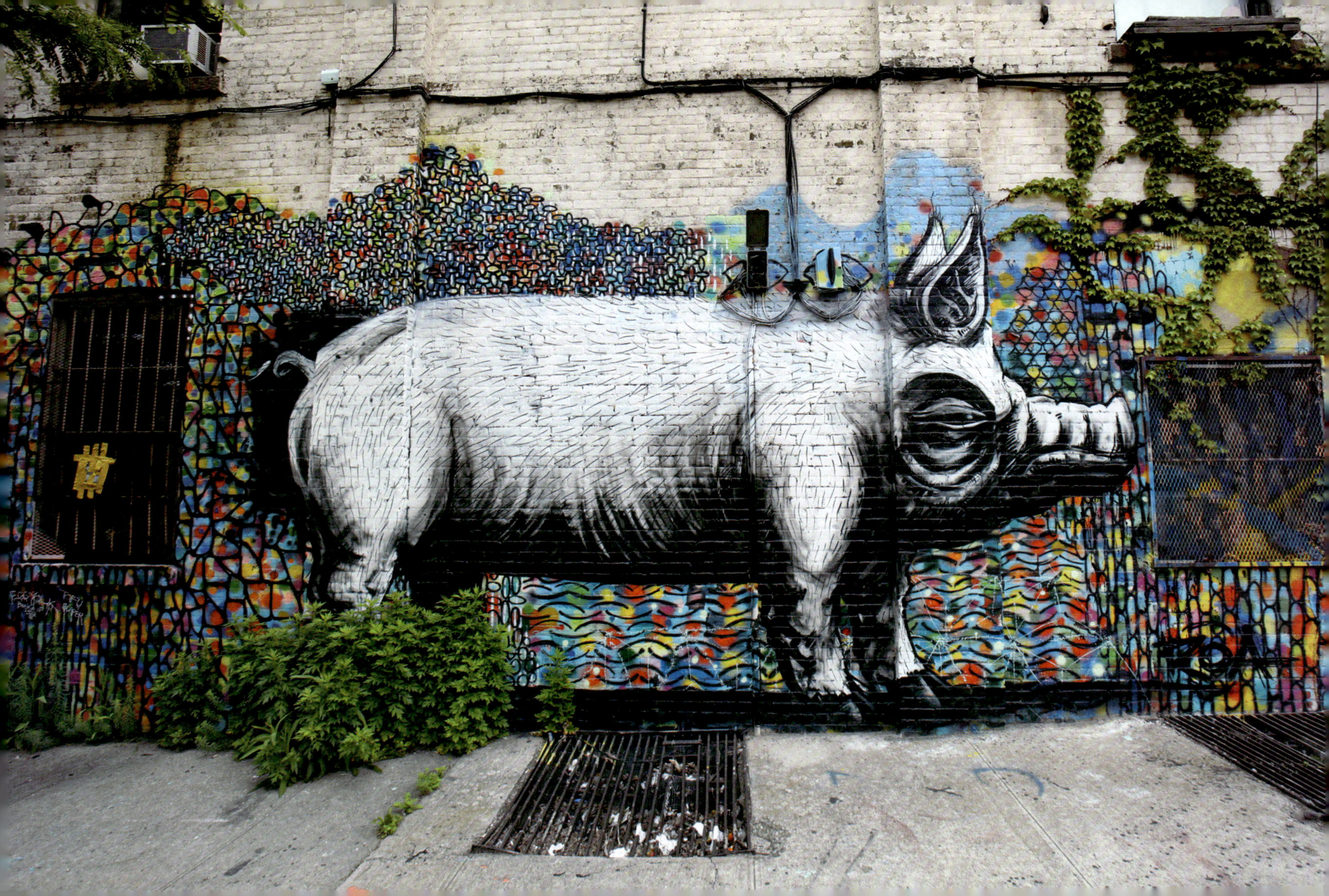

Roadsworth

In the aftermath of the September 11 terrorist attacks, one Canadian artist was struck by a sense that he had nothing to lose. Peter Gibson finally felt ready to put his work on the streets of his hometown of Montreal. He adopted the moniker Roadsworth—a riff on the name of artist Andy Goldsworthy, who had inspired him with his public installation work—and went to work on the city's actual roads.

Employing the white and yellow spray paint used to delineate traffic lanes and public walkways, Roadsworth began to transform these public thoroughfares into everything from ornate wreaths to candelabra to giant footprints. Oftentimes, his work carried a political undertone, such as a commentary on the overuse of cars and the gluttonous wasting of fuels in our culture.

Roadsworth's work made his mark on the city's populace and started heated debate in the media, dividing residents and city officials. In 2004, Roadsworth was arrested and prosecuted to the full extent of the law. Charged with the Canadian equivalent of felony vandalism, Gibson was threatened with a possible $250,000 fine, jail time, and a criminal record. A massive international outpouring of support followed his arrest, and eventually, he was let off with a relatively lenient sentence.

Photographs courtesy of Roadsworth.
Top: *Conveyor Belt*. North Carolina, 2009.
Bottom left: *Blip*. North Carolina, 2003.
Bottom middle: *Dominoes*. North Carolina, 2009.
Bottom right: *Full Asphalt Jacket*. Montreal, Canada, 2003.

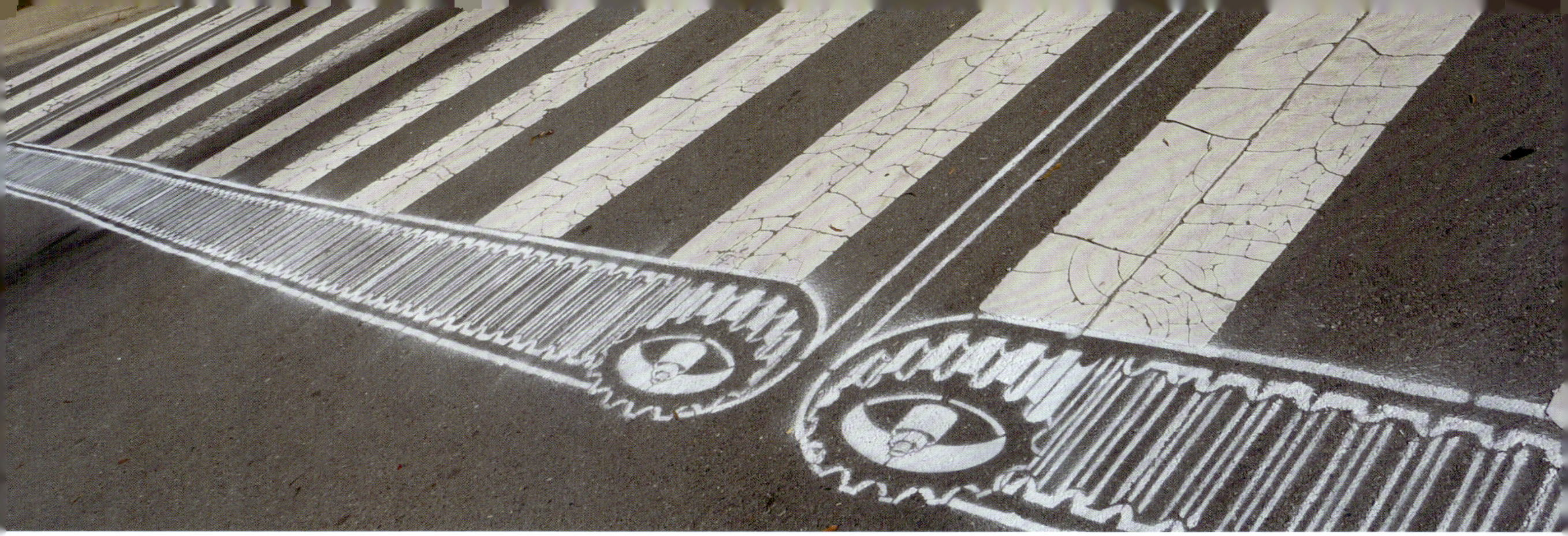

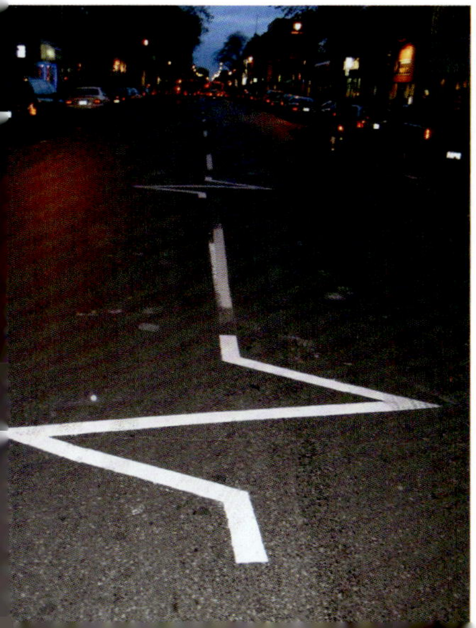

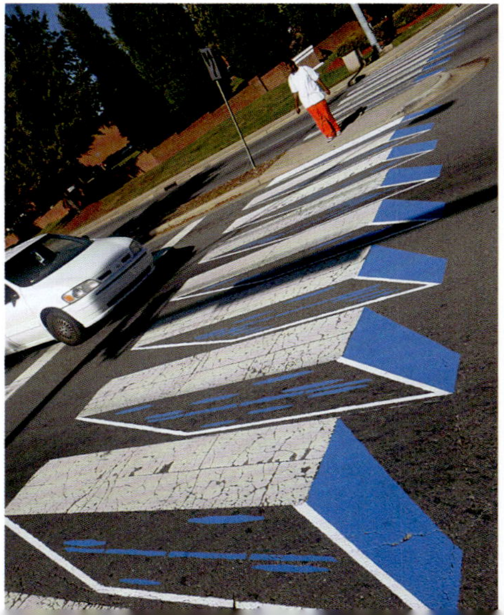

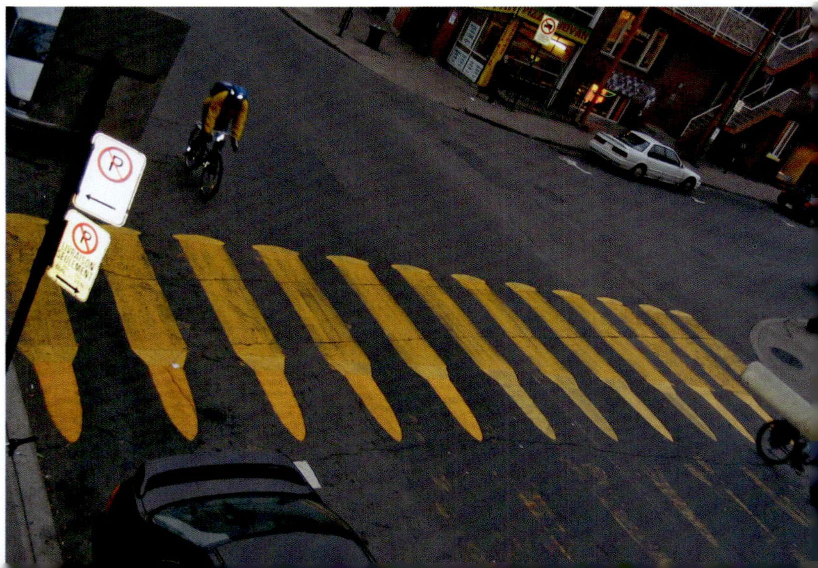

Robots Will Kill

While it began as a website—an attempt to create an online forum for like-minded artists—Robots Will Kill quickly became better known for the paintings and murals created by its member artists. Founded in 2001 by the artist simply known as Chris, the website serves as a gallery of images by up to eight thousand artists. It is also an online shop for stickers and related merchandise, as well as a virtual graffiti encyclopedia, showcasing artists and promoting urban-art culture.

The Robots Will Kill crew, which includes Chris, Veng, and an artist known as kev/psyn, creates uniquely identifiable mural and canvas works that merge the extremely graphic, almost childlike work of Chris with the hypertechnical, surrealistic work of Veng into cultural mishmashes. The crew has changed membership over the decade of its existence, but one fact remains steady: It is based in Staten Island, the oft-forgotten fifth borough of New York City, from whence it organizes events and shows of painted works.

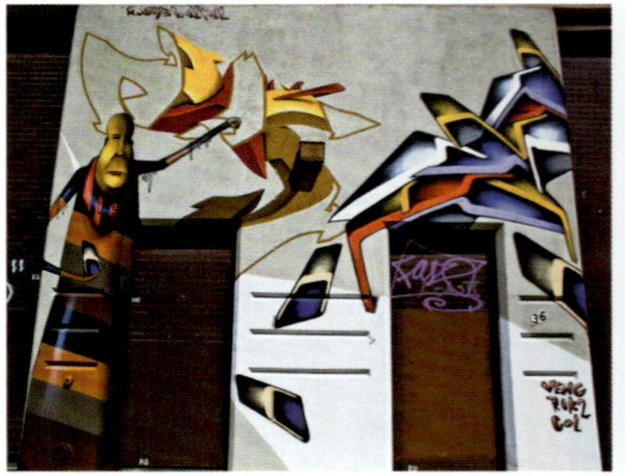

Photograph by Becki Fuller.
Brooklyn, New York, 2008.
Detail: Photograph by Vincent Cornelli.
Brooklyn, New York, 2009.

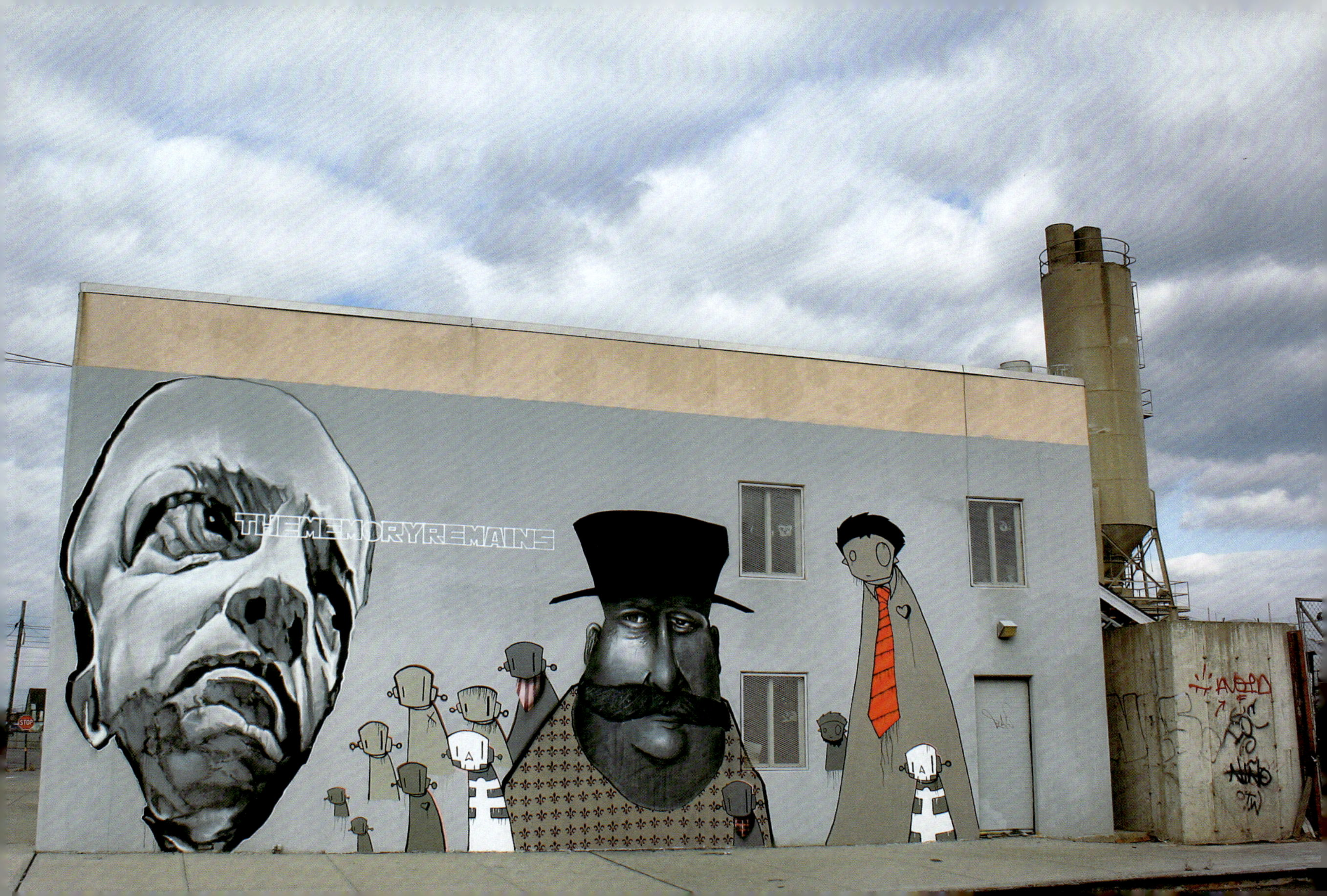
THEMEMORYREMAINS

Rone

Born in 1980, Tyrone "Rone" Wright, like many others, grew up immersed in graffiti and hip-hop culture, though unlike many others fascinated by these movements, he grew up in the small town of Geelong, Australia. At the turn of the century, Rone moved to the more populated city of Melbourne, where he fell in with the skateboard scene and began adorning skate parks with his work.

Using stencils as his medium of choice, Rone has become one of the best-known street artists in Australia, and he has garnered international recognition for his technically adept, haunting pieces. Rone is a founding member of Melbourne's infamous Everfresh crew, alongside fellow Aussie superstars Phibs (see 256) and Reka.

An advocate of placing his work in extremely high-traffic areas, Rone opened himself to intense risk. Although Melbourne was known for being lax on punishment for graffiti, in 2003, Rone and fellow street artist Civilian were busted at an illegal exhibition organized at an abandoned warehouse.

Rone participates in gallery exhibitions, and throughout the popularity boom of stencil graffiti, he shipped his work to be shown internationally. Today, he continues to work on the street, but he is primarily a graphic designer, working out of the Everfresh studios in Melbourne.

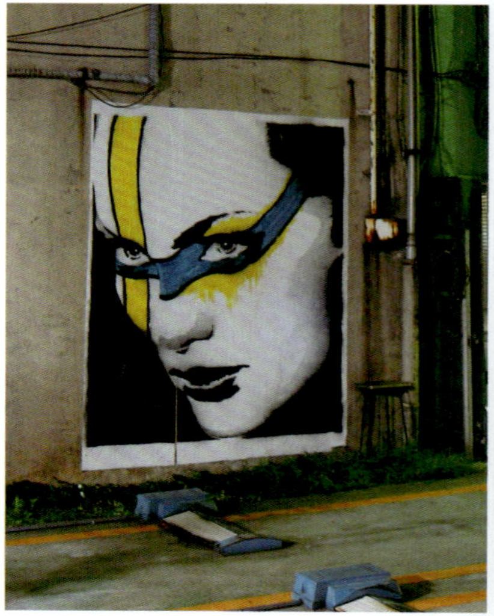

Photographs courtesy of Rone.
Melbourne, Australia, 2009.
Detail: Tokyo, 2007.

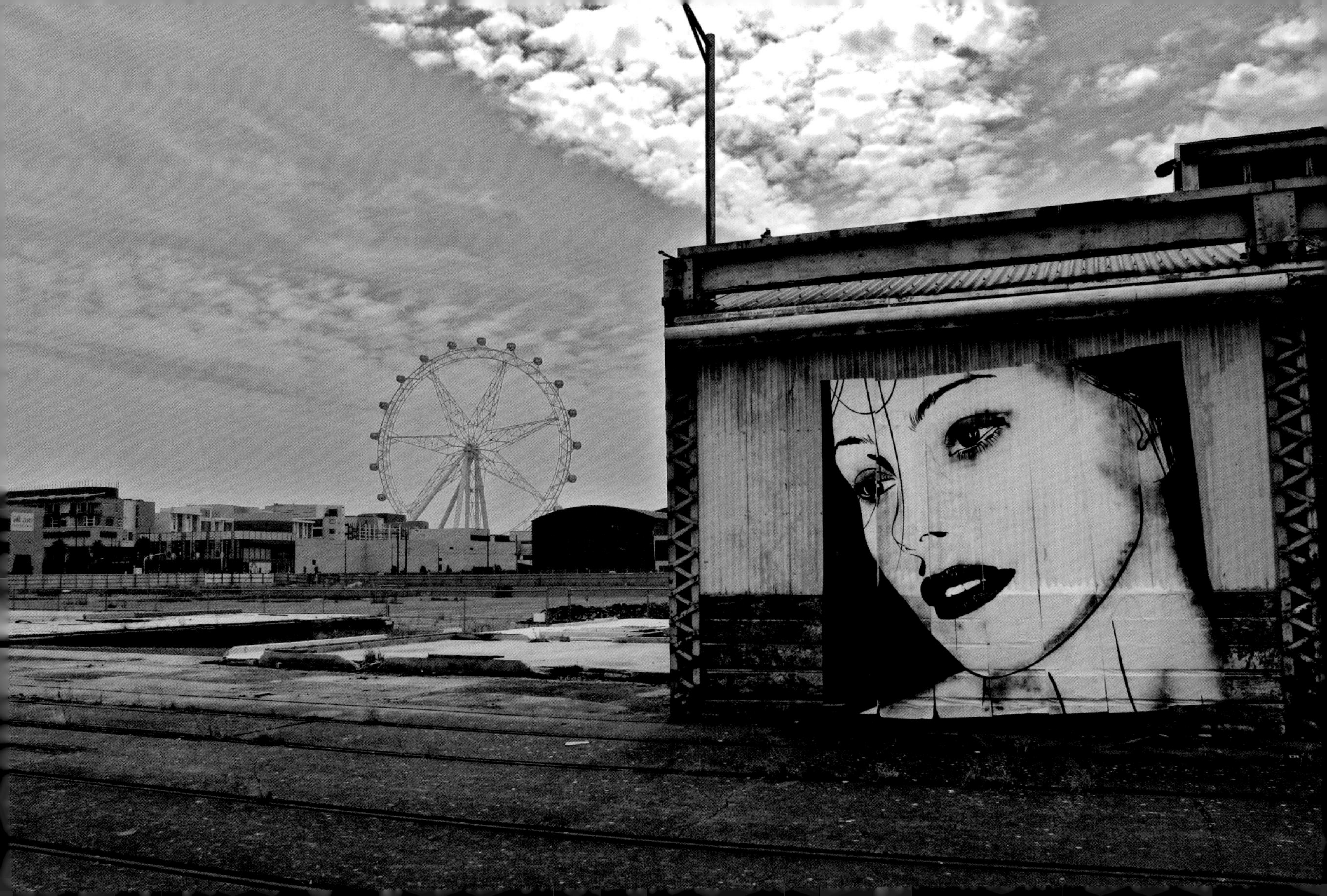

Rookie

Born in Dresden, Rookie studied illustration at the University of Applied Science in Münster, Germany. His interest there was primarily in painting and illustration, and recently he arrived on the scene as one of those shy artists who either really isn't interested in fame—or just doesn't let that hunger appear in his practice.

Rookie is known around Germany for street works of a painterly nature; his striking images quickly earned him a reputation as one of the most interesting up-and-comers in Europe, and in 2010 his work has featured in several indoor shows.

But whether it is client work, a commission, or a piece executed without permission, his paintings and illustrations remain remarkably idiosyncratic, with crisp lines, well-formed doodles, and a palette that reveals a sensitive comprehension of composition and color. Rookie's art is playful, scared, shocked, and sweet, but the most common reaction to one of his works is a simple smile.

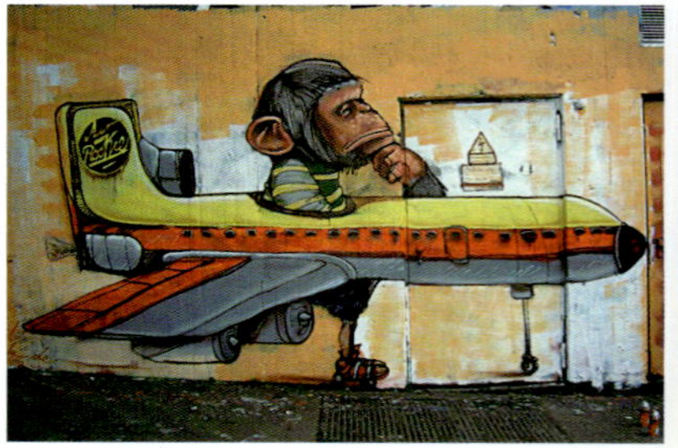

Photographs courtesy of Rookie.

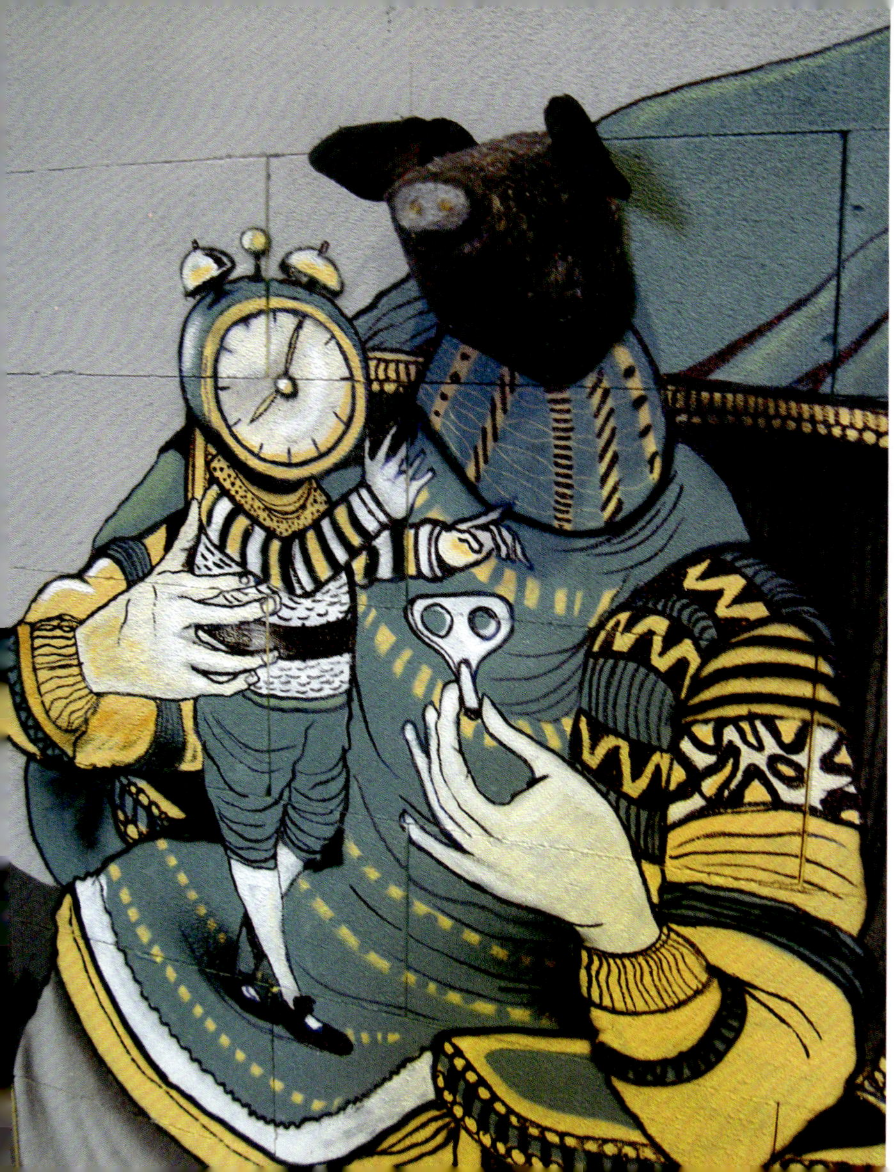

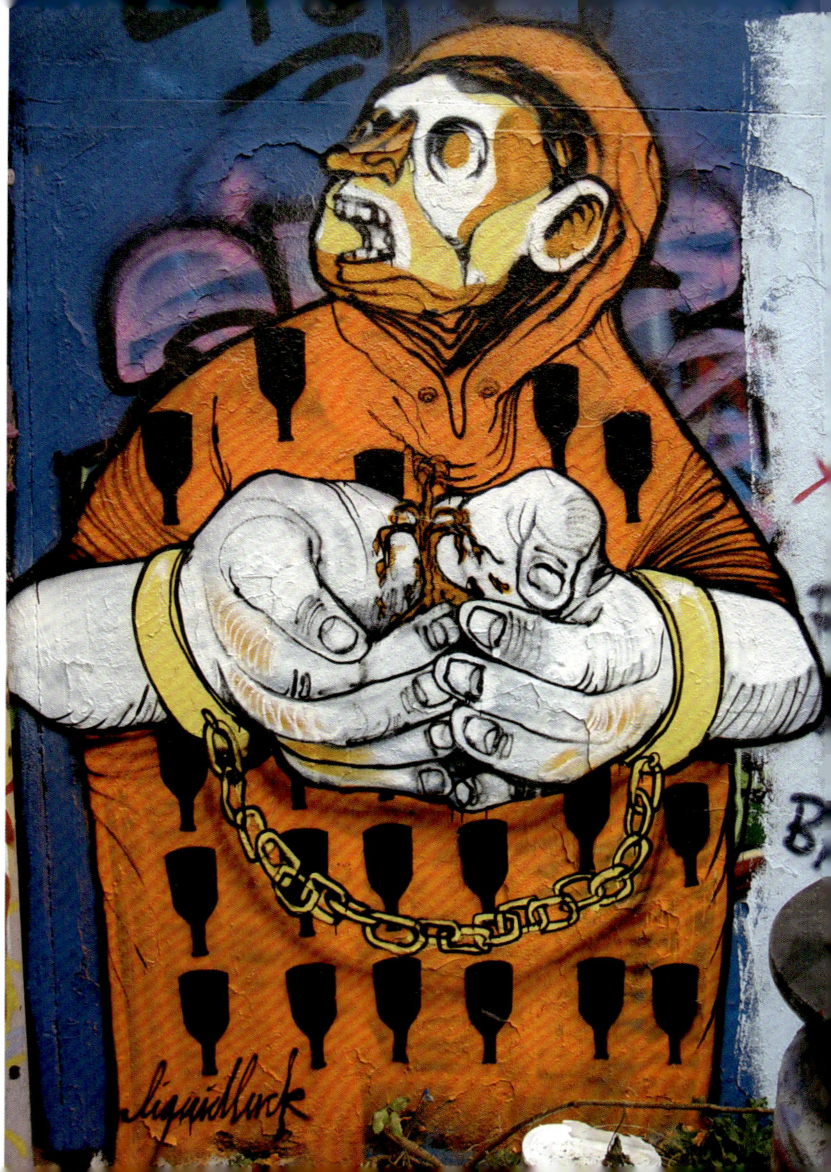

RTW

The Rolling Thunder Writers were founded in 1977 by Bilrock 161, an Upper West Side writer who had been active for several years. The crew drew its influences from older writers who lived in the neighborhood, many of whom had gained fame on the #1 Broadway line and hung out at the Central Park Bandshell (see 023). The Soul Artists (see 310) and the Rebels greatly influenced Bilrock 161, as well as the RTW's original members, who were predominately hippie/skateboarding types. RTW's original lineup included Mackie, Rasta (see 270), Min (see 223), Revolt, Zephyr (see 363), Vandal, and several others.

RTW gained early recognition when Bilrock brought his Bandshell buddies to the #1 tunnel, where they focused on bombing insides. In 1979 and 1980, RTW members began doing psychedelic pieces in wild rainbow colors. Older Upper West Side writers like Se3, Sie 1, Crunch, and War 1 would soon join the team, and RTW took over Broadway, inside and out.

RTW's peaceful nature did not prepare it for the violent climate that characterized the early-'80s graffiti world. In 1980, Min and Bilrock joined forces with members of the Vamp Squad. Writers such as Shock 123, Rin 1, T.Kid 170 (see 335), and Kel 139 (see 190) added a violent presence of their own to the group. Around this time, many of the crew's original members quit or branched out on their own. Min headed the crew from 1982 on, gradually forming alliances with other crews such as CIA, TD, Roc Stars, and Words of Wisdom in order to ensure his own safety and strengthen RTW's stronghold.

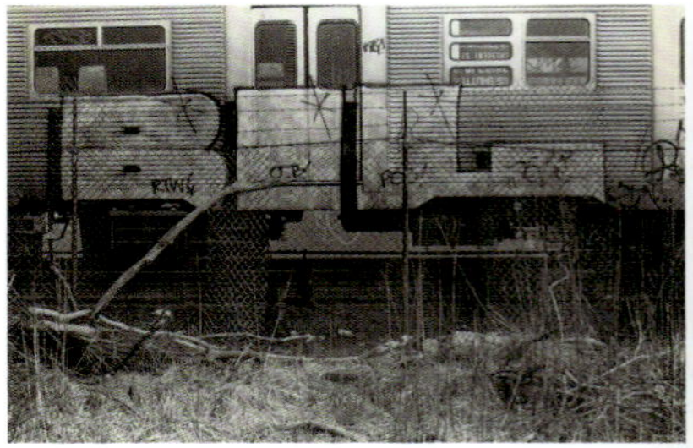

Pieces by Revolt, Rasta, and NE (aka Min; left to right).
Photograph by Pjay One.
New York City, c. 1980.
Detail: Throw-up by Bilrock 161.
Private collection.
New York City, 1980.

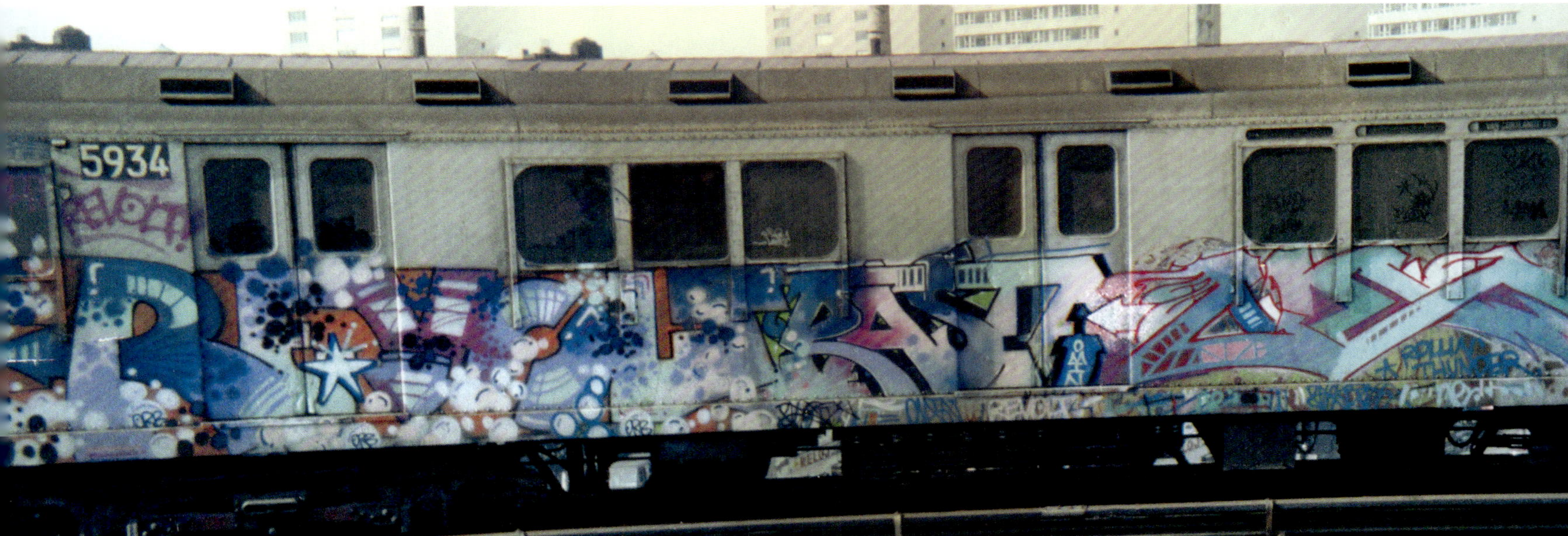
5934

Saber

Born and raised in Glendale, California, a suburb of Los Angeles, Saber discovered the art form of graffiti at the age of thirteen, when his cousins took him to see the spray-painted Belmont tunnel. Since then, he has consistently developed his intricate style, tagging and bombing his way into ephemeral-art stardom. Saber's shining moment came in 1997 when, over the course of thirty-five nights and using ninety-seven gallons of paint, he created the largest graffiti piece to date, on the sloping banks of the Los Angeles River. The piece, nearly the size of a football field, instantly catapulted the artist to legendary status.

In the first decade of the 2000s, Saber was one of the lead characters in Doug Pray's graffiti documentary *Infamy*, in which he relates his feelings of anger and depression, and is famously quoted as saying, "Every single graffiti writer is a manic-depressive, insecure person, because that's the only thing that makes you want to go out and write on somebody's shit."

Somewhat of a rarity in the graffiti world, Saber, is a Renaissance man; his artistic pursuits include painting beautiful landscapes in oils and building wood-and-metal sculptures. He has recently moved into the fine-art realm, exhibiting his work at the White Walls gallery in San Francisco, and in 2007 Gingko press released his monograph, *Saber: Mad Society*.

Photograph by Steve Rotman. San Francisco, 2007.

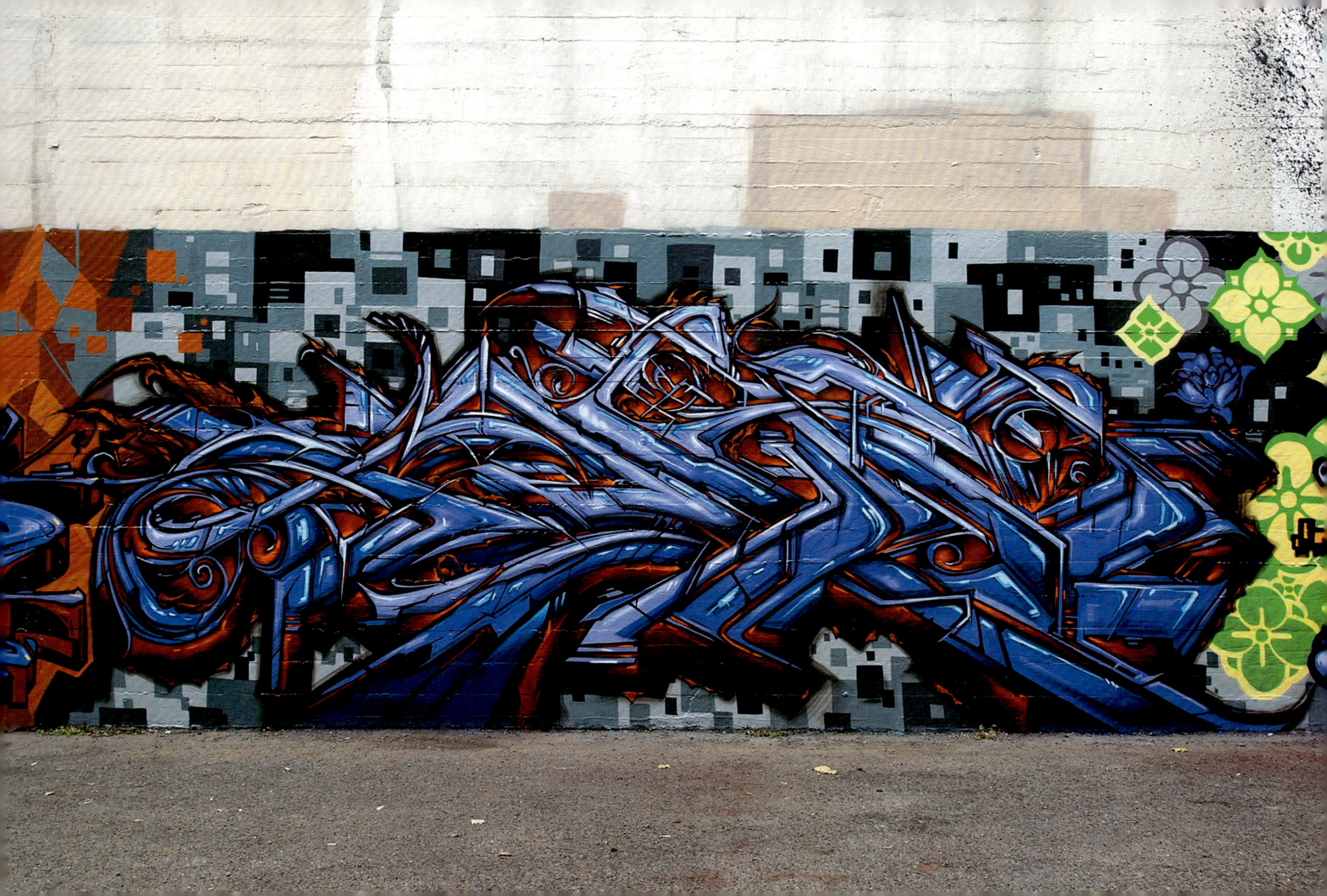

Sachs Project

Jack Stewart [see 318], the legendary graffiti photographer, art professor, and painter, likened graffiti on canvas to a still life. For adrenalized subway artstists, the movement of the train and the fear of arrest resulted in a different aesthetic altogether, but those works, executed on rolling steel, defied preservation. In an effort to help graffiti artists produce and market more permanent works on canvas, UGA and NOGA [see 241] were formed in the 1970s, and GPI and Sam Esses Studio in the 1980s, as organizations that involved people from outside of graffiti culture coordinating studio projects.

Decades later, in 2007, Terror 161 [see 333], a subway writer from the 1970s and 1980s, found inspiration in these efforts and convinced an elite group of writers from all eras to create a series of paintings on wood and canvas. Terror had previously met with German art collector Gunter Sachs, who was then just starting to collect international graffiti art in earnest. Sachs, who had been collecting European graffiti art, needed to purvey a sampling of New York graffiti for a museum show highlighting his own life and art collection at the Museum Der Bildenden Kunste in Leipzig, Germany. The invited artists painted on speculation, hoping that their works would sell, but with no guarantees.

Terror 161 and his business partner, Robert Roth, turned an empty retail space in the South Bronx into a studio over a weekend, providing materials and a crew to stretch finished canvases for hanging. Over six weeks, a lineup of T.Kid 170 [see 335], Part [see 251], Chain 3 [see 062], Serve [see 296], Ces [see 061], Ghost [see 145], Riff 170, and Kaves [see 188] produced more than seventy canvases.

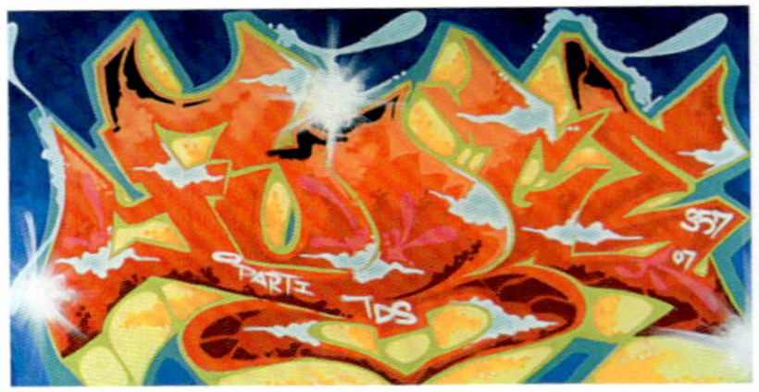

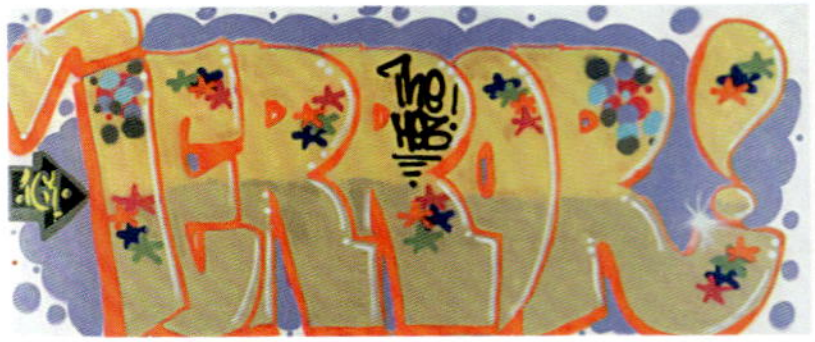

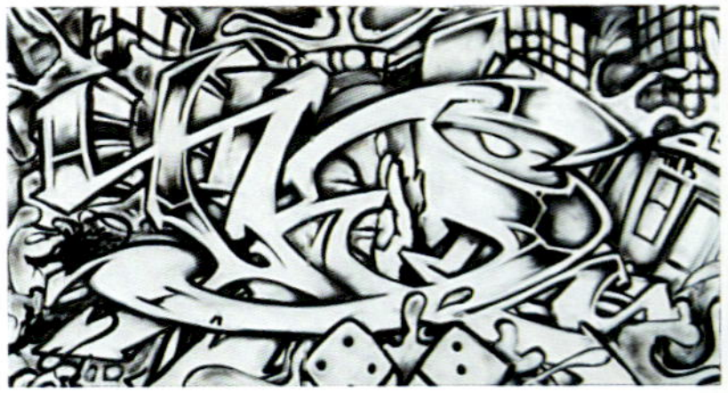

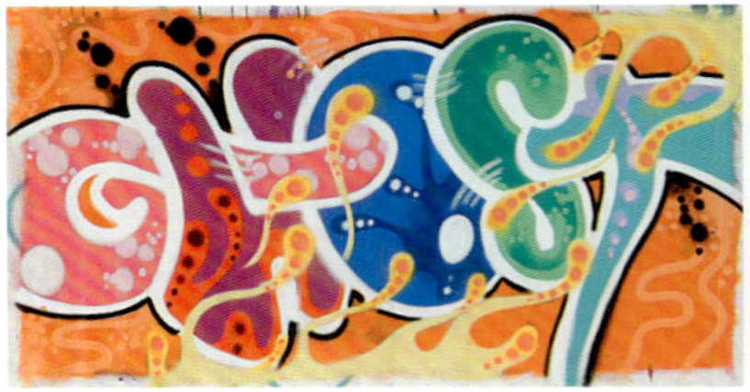

Photographs by Adam Reich. New York City, 2007.

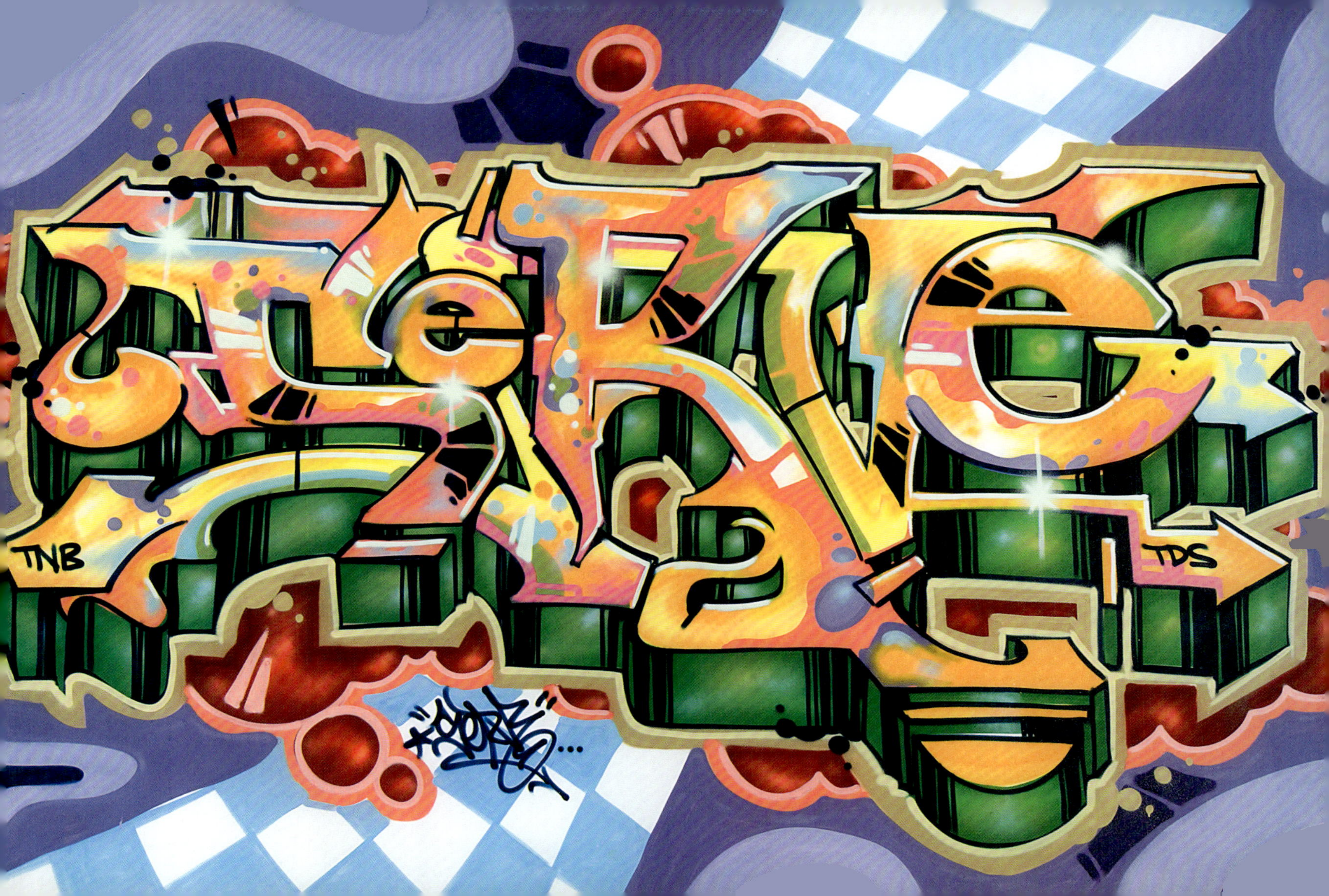
TNB
TDS

Sane and Smith

Two Caucasian youths from Manhattan's Washington Heights neighborhood, the brothers Sane and Smith, participated in the last few years of New York's subway graffiti movement, but their biggest achievements came during the post-train era. Without trains to work on, prime targets became any well-situated wall, rooftop, or bridge.

The idea to paint their names on the Brooklyn Bridge was that of Sane, the younger brother. In a rare interview given more than two decades after the feat, the older brother, Smith, details the plot: "On reflection, painting a monument such as the Brooklyn Bridge was probably a bad idea, since we were unprepared for the consequences. Around that time, we had been painting a couple of the other bridges around New York and thought it would be just another spot. By this time, we had been using bucket paint a lot instead of spray paint, since it was easy to acquire, custom colorable, and so much thicker that the color just boomed. One day, Sane said, 'Yo, I got this spot in mind. I scoped it. It looks easy enough, so let's do it. There's this ladder and a ledge just wide enough. . . .' The next morning, we looked at our handiwork on both sides of the bridge, smiled, and took our photos."

The grafftermath: front-page newspaper coverage and a Sane television interview caught Mayor Koch's [see 197] attention. The brothers—as well as their mother—were slapped with a massive lawsuit by the city of New York. Civil rights attorney Ron Kuby came to their rescue, but the boys, whose real names are David and Roger Smith, were forced into exile in Queens—and now everyone knows both sets of their names.

Photograph courtesy of Smith. New York City, 1987.

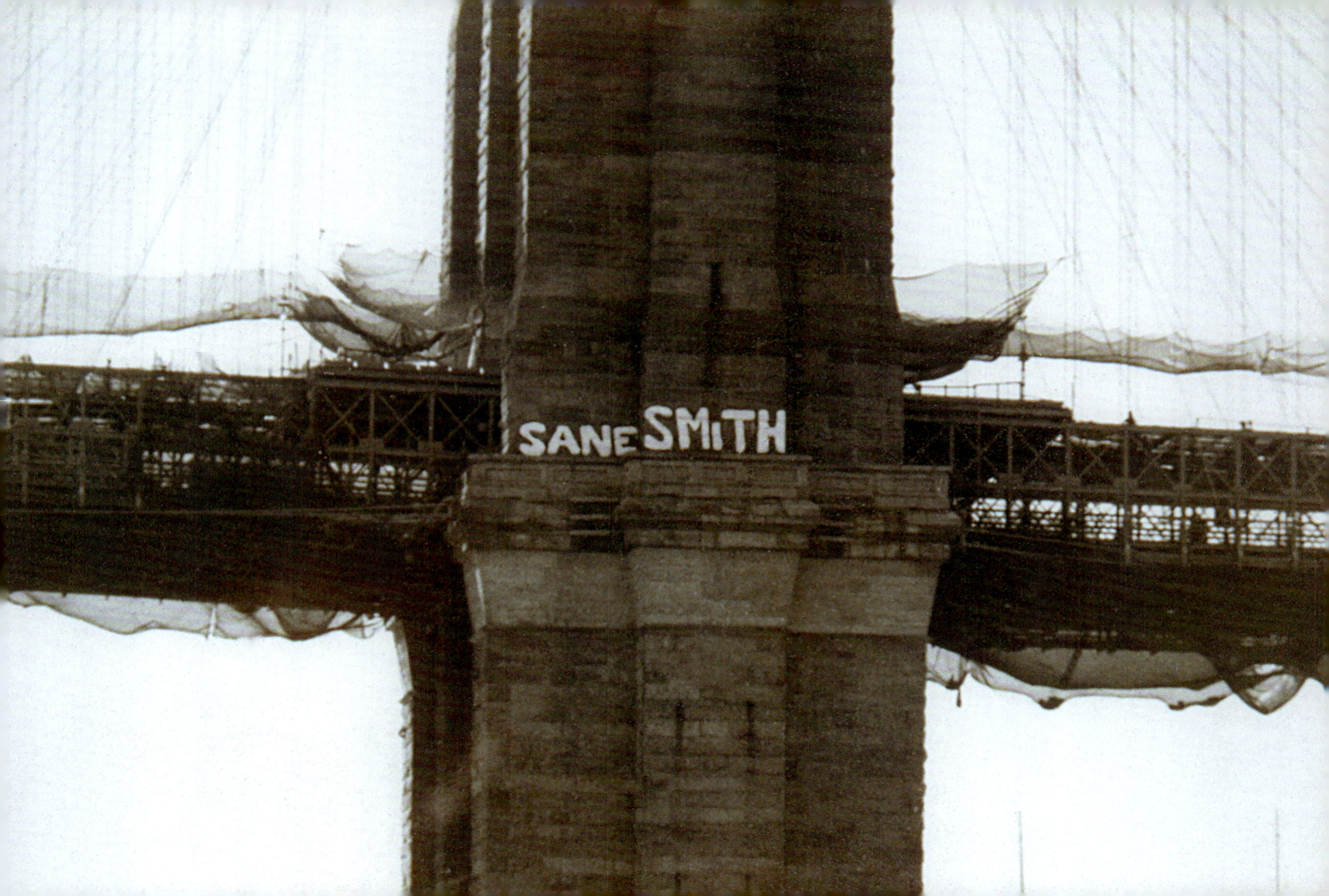
SANE SMITH

Saner

Edgar Flores, aka Saner, is a street artist, born in Mexico City in 1981, whose work reflects the rich culture he grew up in: He randomly paints masks and skulls in barren areas. The placement and patterns of these playful, sometimes ominous figures beckon passersby to imagine their own meanings and create their own stories.

The skulls and masks that proliferate his body of work are influenced by the imagery from the many Day of the Dead festivals he has witnessed. In Mexico, the Day of the Dead is a celebration of departed loved ones, but it is a happy, not morbid, occasion. Re-creating the likenesses of the deceased, however, is taboo in Mexican culture; they can only be depicted in masks.

Saner's art has caught the international art world's eye, and he has been invited to participate in mural collaborations around the globe. He has had solo and group gallery shows and been featured in numerous art magazines. Saner has also earned a few pesos for his graphic design work. No matter where his talents may take him, it is doubtful that he will ever stop painting in the streets, where mystery and rebellion, his secret ingredients, keep the people's gallery a place of ever-changing wonder and inspiration.

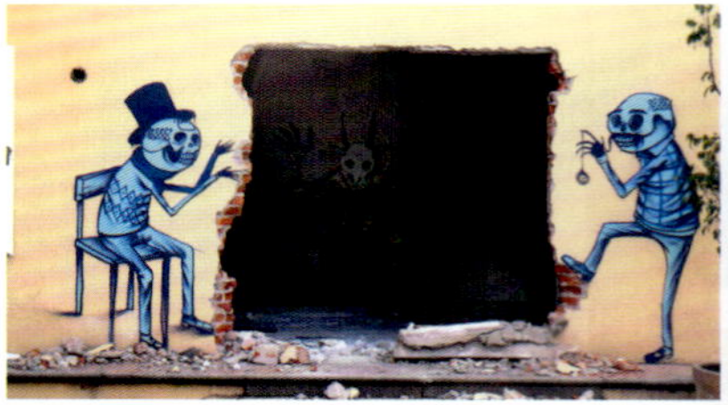

Photographs courtesy of Saner.
Top right: *The Hunters*. Collaboration with Smithe. Mexico, 2010.
Bottom right: *Fighting Cocks*. Collaboration with Smithe. Mexico, 2010.
Detail: *Blue Die*. Photograph by Zurdo. Mexico City, Mexico, 2010.

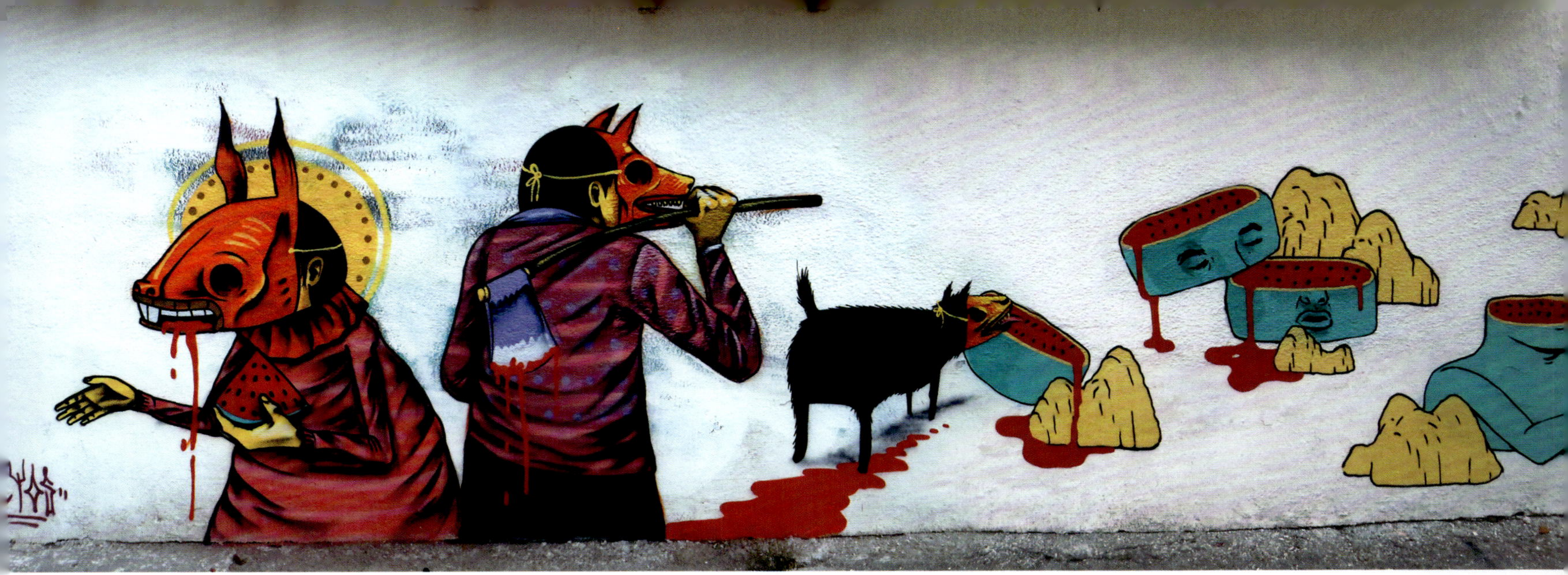

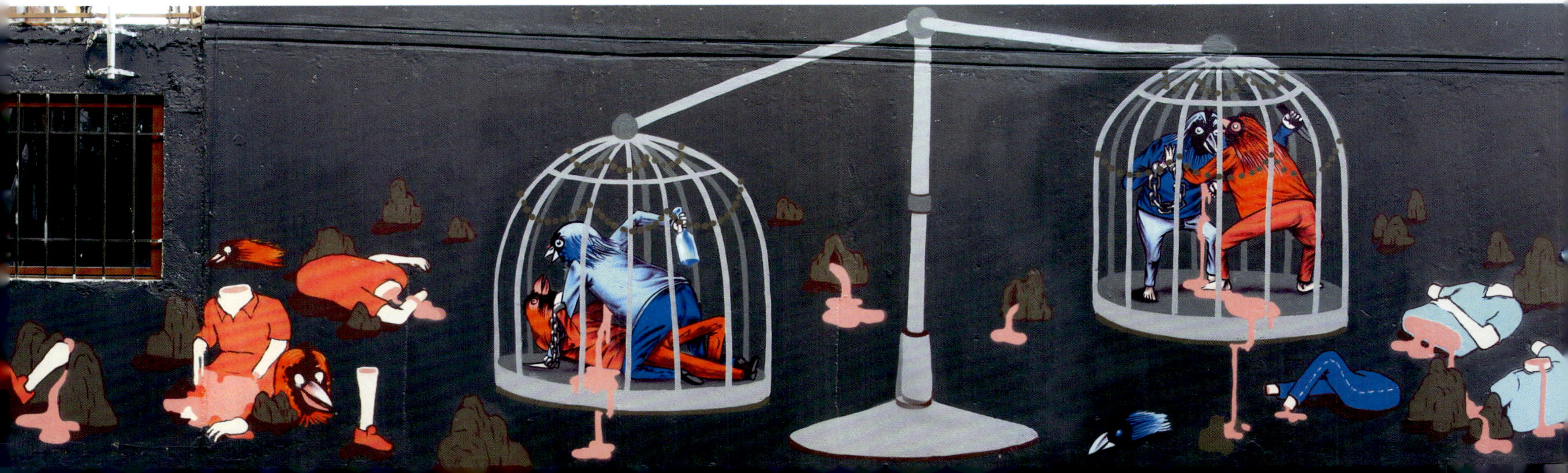

Kenny Scharf

World-renowned multimedia artist Kenny Scharf's paintings, sculptures, site-specific installations, cartoons, and performances have been seen in noted art museums, galleries, and major cultural venues. Born in 1958 in Los Angeles, California, Scharf earned his BFA in 1980 from the School of Visual Arts in New York City. He became a key figure in Manhattan's East Village art scene during the 1980s, when his impressive résumé included shows at the Fun Gallery (1981; see 140), Tony Shafrazi Gallery (1984), and the Whitney Museum of American Art's Biennial (1985). Scharf has also created album covers for the new-wave band The B-52s, designed a room at the popular Manhattan nightclub The Tunnel, and seen his art featured on the cover of the *New York Times Magazine*.

Kenny Scharf was doing mash-ups before the term was invented, and he is still best known for his early paintings depicting imaginary scenes such as the prehistoric cartoon characters Wilma and Fred Flintstone riding in spaceships with George, Jane, Judy, and Elroy from the futuristic Hanna-Barbera cartoon *The Jetsons*. Scharf's work is included in important public collections around the world, and over the years he has made substantial progress in his professional ambition to erase elitist boundaries between fine art and popular culture.

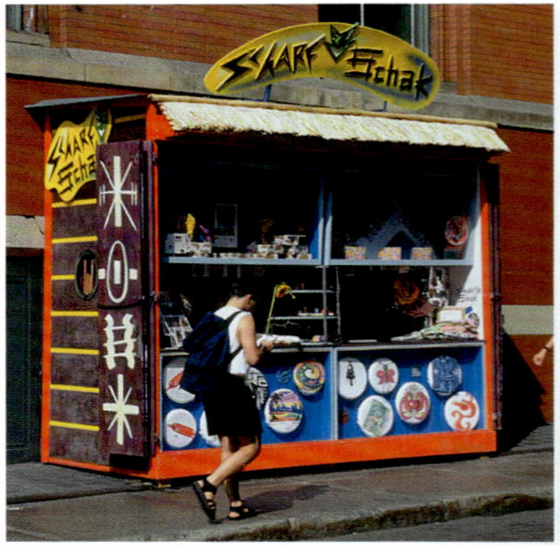

Photographs by Martha Cooper. New York City, 1981.

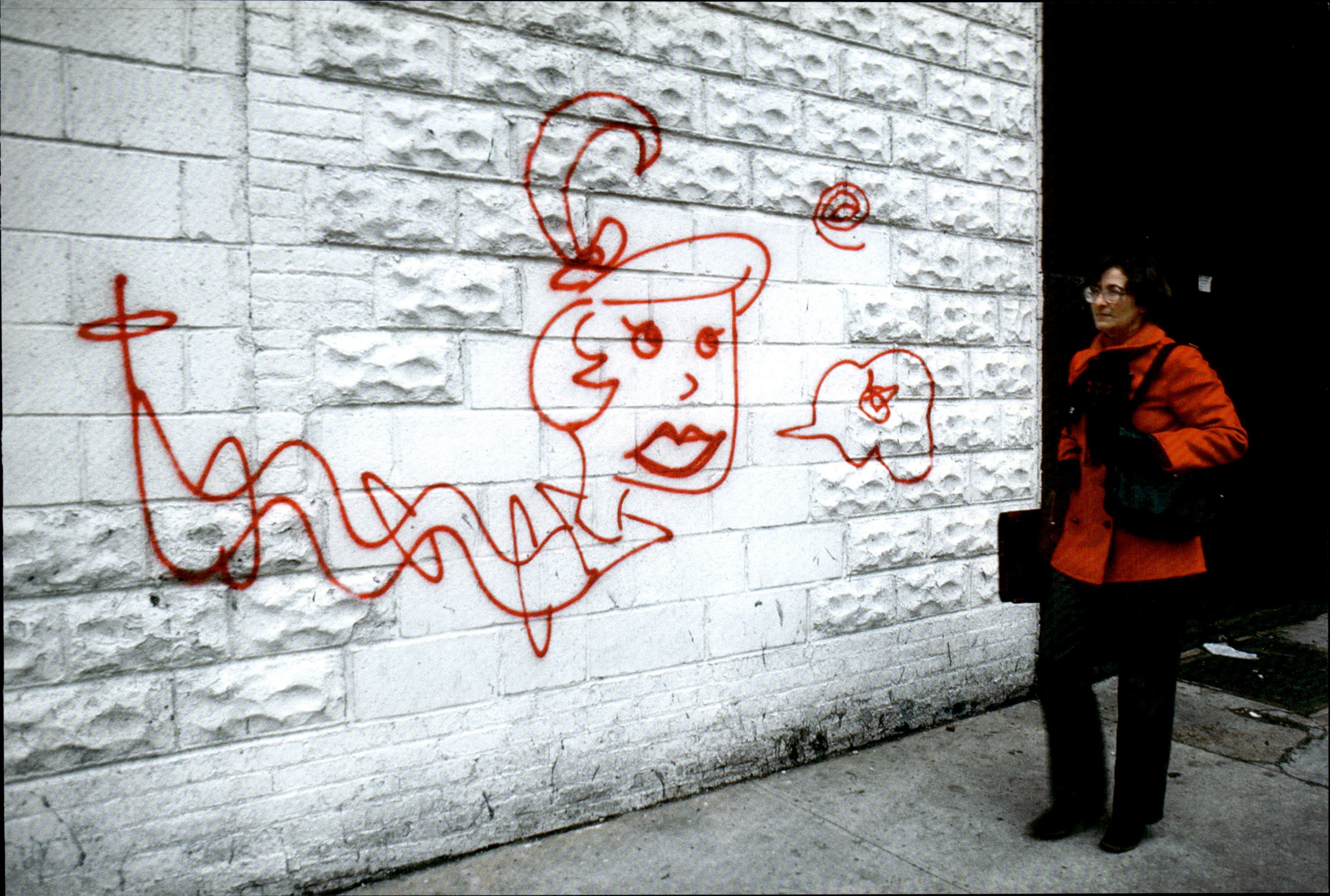

scraps

In 1989, shiny new trains replaced the antiquated carriages of the New York City subway system, which had served as graffiti's canvases for almost two decades. Once removed, the retired subway cars were shipped to train cemeteries, which came to be known by writers as the "scrap yards."

Graffiti writers refusing to heed the transit authority's GAME OVER sign sought solace by painting the corpses of their old, beloved canvases in these scrap yards. The scrap yards were identical in appearance to active train yards, and pictures taken of masterpieces done on the dead trains were sent into magazines and fraudulently passed off as real McCoys. A scrap scene soon developed, complete with robberies, vandal-squad stakeouts, and arrests. Certain writers became kings of scrap, and others would go every weekend and paint over the same train repeatedly, just for the photo op. After a few years, the trains warehoused in the scrap yards were unceremoniously dumped into the ocean along the northern Atlantic coast, officially killing a scene that had already, supposedly, died.

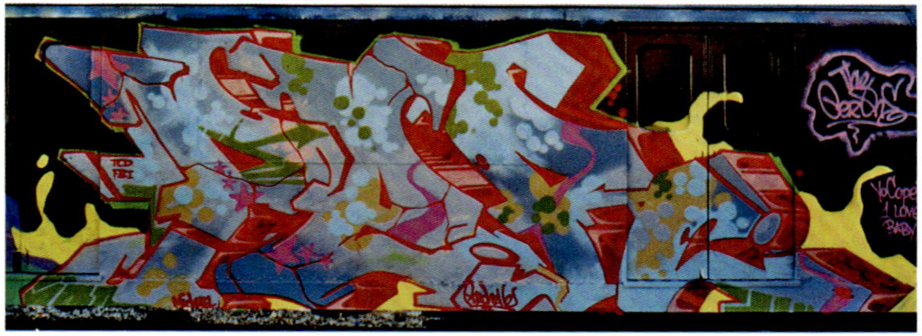

Photographs by Ces One.
Throw-up by Key.
Detail: Piece by Per One FX.
New York City, 1994.

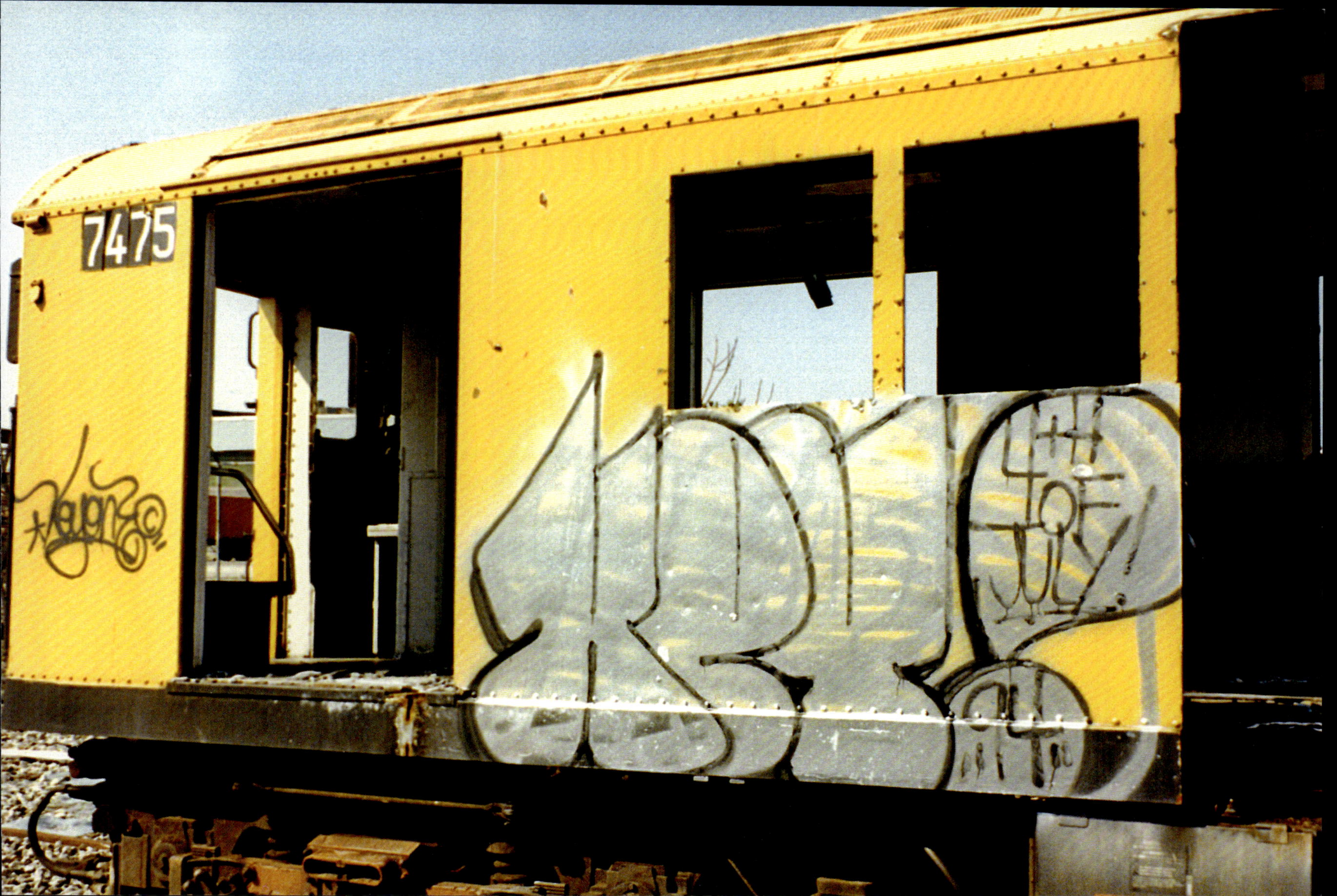
7475
4th OF JULY

scrawl

To Whom It May Concern:

This page is dedicated to the dozens of anonymous artists who have, for decades, filled the walls of New York City with urgent and captivating pronouncements, from terse suggestions to indecipherably complex amalgams of math, philosophy, and politics. The statements come in many languages; are often biblical, sexual, or psychological in nature; and can be impeccably drafted in unique calligraphy or wildly scribbled in unintelligible palimpsests. The creators, reclusive or otherwise, tend to the impassioned and the visceral, often urging their unmet public to do something to right wrongs both personal and universal.

Such unsigned street postings inevitably lead to queries about their makers' states of mind. Some are created by psychologically and socially marginalized homeless people; others are written by people with good jobs and loving families. Why the anonymity? Maybe it's related to feelings of shame. These scrawlers may be alone, or simply *feel* alone. Perhaps they don't dare voice their opinions directly, and the anonymous street postings afford them greater freedom of expression. New York City can be trying at its best, a war zone at its worst. Who's to say who's crazy?

Photographs by Harley Spiller.
New York City, 2008.

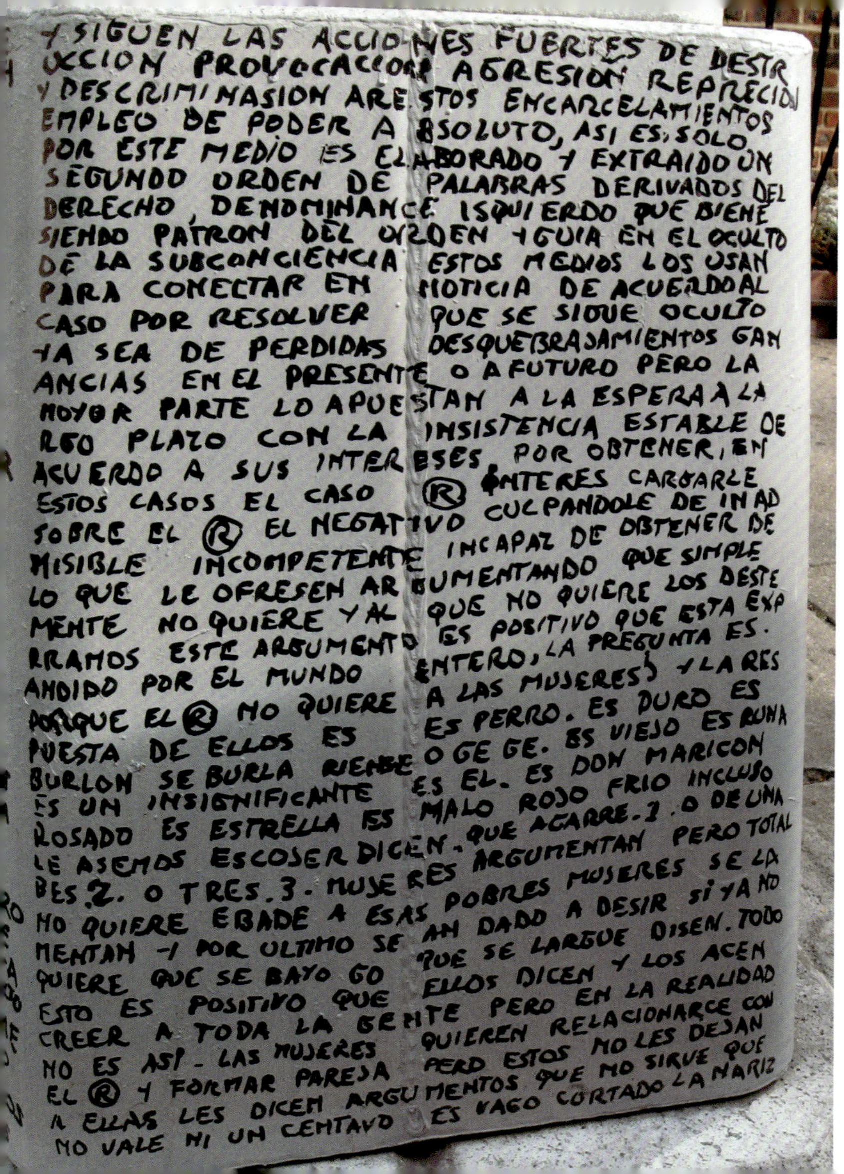
Y SIGUEN LAS ACCIONES FUERTES DE DESTR
UCCION PROVOCACION AGRESIÓN REPRECION
Y DESCRIMINASION ARESTOS ENCARCELAMIENTOS
EMPLEO DE PODER ABSOLUTO, ASI ES. SOLO
POR ESTE MEDIO ES ELABORADO Y EXTRAIDO UN
SEGUNDO ORDEN DE PALABRAS DERIVADOS DEL
DERECHO, DENOMINANCE ISQUIERDO QUE BIENE
SIENDO PATRON DEL ORDEN Y GUIA EN EL OCULTO
DE LA SUBCONCIENCIA ESTOS MEDIOS LOS USAN
PARA CONECTAR EN NOTICIA DE ACUERDO AL
CASO POR RESOLVER QUE SE SIGUE OCULTO
YA SEA DE PERDIDAS DESQUEBRAJAMIENTOS GAN
ANCIAS EN EL PRESENTE O A FUTURO PERO LA
MAYOR PARTE LO APUESTAN A LA ESPERA A LA
RGO PLAZO CON LA INSISTENCIA ESTABLE DE
ACUERDO A SUS INTERESES, POR OBTENER, EN
ESTOS CASOS EL CASO ® INTERES CARGARLE
SOBRE EL ® EL NEGATIVO CULPANDOLE DE INAD
MISIBLE INCOMPETENTE INCAPAZ DE OBTENER DE
LO QUE LE OFRESEN ARGUMENTANDO QUE SIMPLE
MENTE NO QUIERE Y AL QUE NO QUIERE LOS DESTE
RRAMOS ESTE ARGUMENTO ES POSITIVO QUE ESTA EXP
ANDIDO POR EL MUNDO ENTERO, LA PREGUNTA ES.
PORQUE EL ® NO QUIERE A LAS MUSERES? Y LA RES
PUESTA DE ELLOS ES ES PERRO. ES DURO ES
BURLON SE BURLA RIENDE O GE GE. ES VIEJO ES RUINA
ES UN INSIGNIFICANTE ES EL. ES DON MARICON
ROSADO ES ESTRELLA ES MALO ROJO FRIO INCLUSO
LE ASEMOS ESCOSER DICEN. QUE AGARRE. 1. O DE UNA
BES 2. O TRES. 3. MUSERES ARGUMENTAN PERO TOTAL
NO QUIERE EBADE A ESAS POBRES MUSERES SE LA
MENTAN - Y POR ULTIMO SE AN DADO A DESIR SI YA NO
QUIERE QUE SE BAYO GO QUE SE LARGUE DISEN. TODO
ESTO ES POSITIVO QUE ELLOS DICEN Y LOS ACEN
CREER A TODA LA GENTE PERO EN LA REALIDAD
NO ES ASI - LAS MUSERES QUIEREN RELACIONARCE CON
EL ® Y FORMAR PAREJA PERO ESTOS NO LES DEJAN
A ELLAS LES DICEN ARGUMENTOS QUE NO SIRVE QUE
NO VALE NI UN CENTAVO ES VAGO CORTADO LA NARIZ
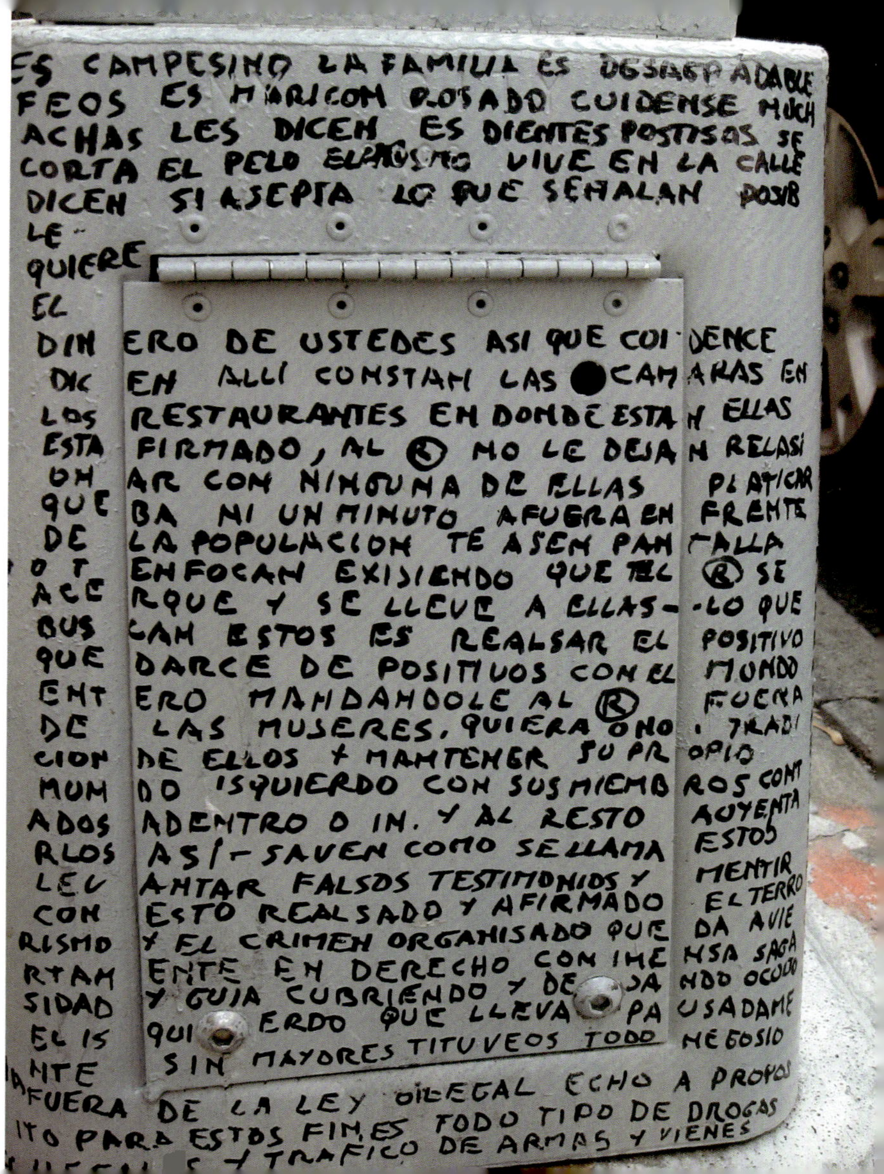
ES CAMPESINO LA FAMILIA ES DESAGRADABLE
FEOS ES MARICON ROSADO CUIDENSE MUCH
ACHAS LES DICEN ES DIENTES POSTISOS SE
CORTA EL PELO ES MISMO VIVE EN LA CALLE
DICEN SI ASEPTA LO QUE SEÑALAN POSIB
LE QUIERE EL
DIN ERO DE USTEDES ASI QUE COINCIDENCE
DIC EN ALLI CONSTAN LAS CAMARAS EN
LOS RESTAURANTES EN DONDE ESTAN ELLAS
ESTA FIRMADO, AL ® NO LE DEJAN RELASI
ON AR CON NINGUNA DE ELLAS PLATICAR
QUE BA NI UN MINUTO AFUERA EN FRENTE
DE LA POPULACION TE ASEN PANTALLA
O T ENFOCAN EXISIENDO QUE EL ® SE
ACE RQUE Y SE LLEVE A ELLAS - LO QUE
BUS CAN ESTOS ES REALSAR EL POSITIVO
QUE DARCE DE POSITIVOS CON EL MUNDO
ENT ERO MANDANDOLE AL ® FUERA
DE LAS MUSERES, QUIERA O NO. TRADI
CION DE ELLOS Y MANTENER SU PROPIO
MUN DO ISQUIERDO CON SUS MIEMBROS CONT
ADOS ADENTRO O IN. Y AL RESTO AVENTA
RLOS ASI - SAVEN COMO SE LLAMA ESTOS
LEV ANTAR FALSOS TESTIMONIOS Y MENTIR
CON ESTO REALSADO Y AFIRMADO EL TERRO
RISMO Y EL CRIMEN ORGANISADO QUE DA AVIE
RTAM ENTE EN DERECHO CON IMENSA SAGA
SIDAD Y GUIA CUBRIENDO Y DE NDO OCULTO
EL IS QUI ERDO QUE LLEVA PAUSADAMENTE
NTE SIN MAYORES TITUVEOS TODO NEGOSIO
AFUERA DE LA LEY ILEGAL ECHO A PROPOS
ITO PARA ESTOS FINES TODO TIPO DE DROGAS
Y TRAFICO DE ARMAS Y VIENES

Seen

Richard Mirando, aka Seen, grew up in the Throgs Neck section of the Bronx, a stone's throw from the #6 line elevation on Westchester Avenue. Artistically gifted from a young age, Mirando began pinstriping at his uncle's auto-body shop at age twelve. His graffiti career began on buses in the mid-1970s and escalated to the trains, where he would reach prominence in 1979 on his home #6 line with the Throgs Neck crew. Seen's most productive years began with the formation of the United Artists; its original lineup included Seen, his brother Mad, Pjay, Dust, and Sin.

An artist who drew perfectly executed characters, often culled from Walt Disney cartoons, *Looney Tunes*, and comic books, in conjunction with letters, ranging from symmetrically perfect block letters to color-infused Wild Styles, Seen not only rendered his own pieces, but often mentored less-experienced peers. After his subway years, Seen entered the tattoo world, replacing trains with skin as his medium. He still owns the eponymous Tattoo Seen shop in his old Bronx neighborhood.

One of the first graffiti artists to enter the gallery world in the 1980s, Seen now resides in Paris, where he owns a studio and is represented by the Opera Gallery. He collects vintage motorcycles, lowbrow art, and his own press clippings.

Private collection.
New York City, 1980.

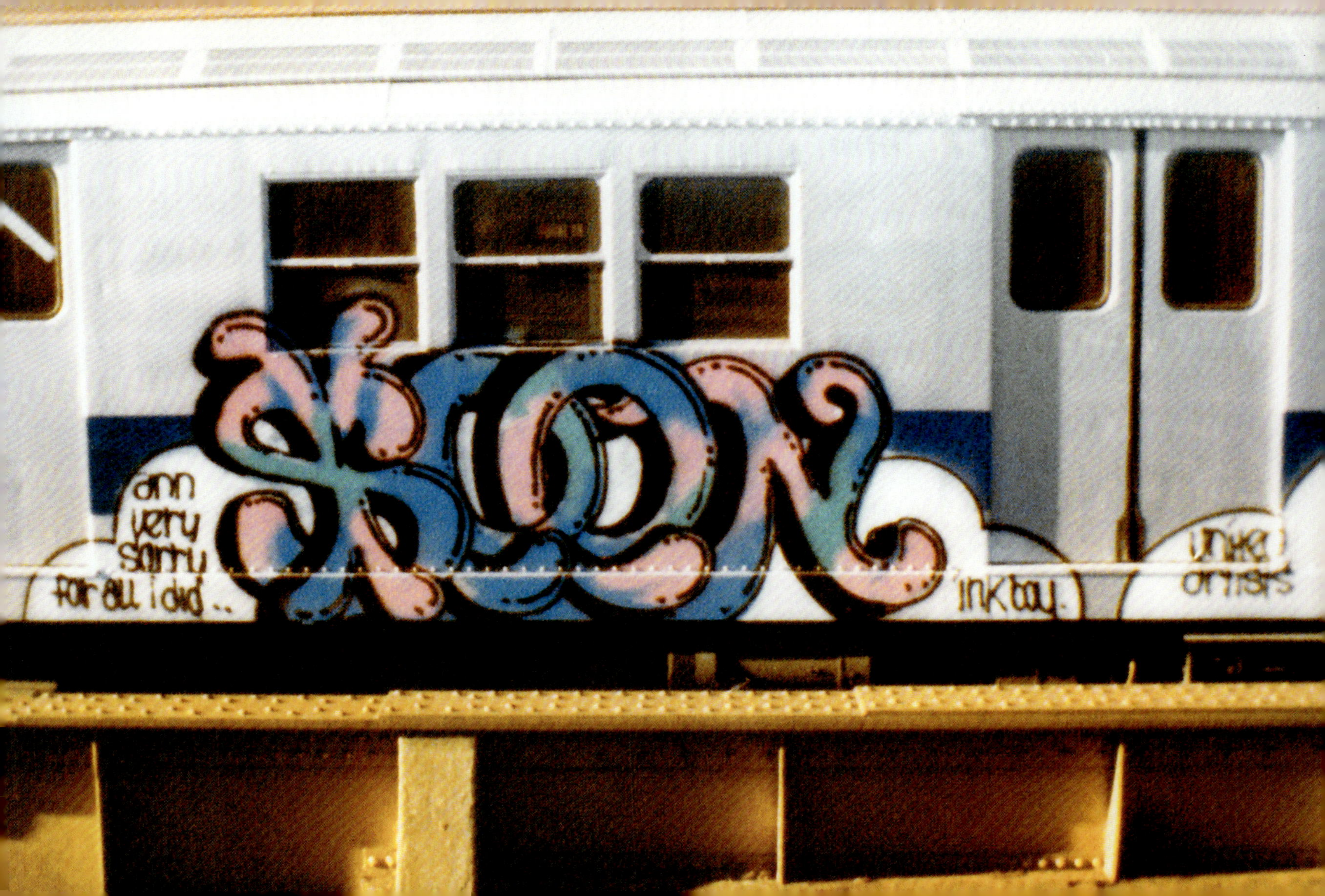
am very sorry for all i did ..

Sento

Sento started writing in 1983, after meeting some of the second-generation TC5 members at the High School of Art and Design (see 167); they gave him entrée to the #1 tunnel, where he started doing his first pieces. He soon abandoned the #1 line, due to the politics there, and in 1986 he formed another partnership with Case 2—it was then that Sento's unique style began to emerge. Nearly three years later, just as the subway era in New York came to a close, some of Sento's more psychedelic works began to appear on trains, and Sento—who seemed to understand the uniqueness of his artistic vision—decided not to stop painting them.

Sento continued to bomb the subway for another decade in New York, all the while playing host to a number of European writers who wanted a shot at a New York train. During that same period of time, he began expanding the scope of his work to walls and freight trains. The walls, because of their infinite size, had a huge impact on his newer works, freeing him up even more. These new paintings featured letters that took on a Rube Goldberg–esque quality, with each letter becoming a unique entity.

Sento's early love for the European writers paid off handsomely in the first years of the new millennium, as he painted his way from country to country, putting down new members in TFP (see 334) with Case 2's blessing. It was one of those rare situations where the second version of a crew actually lived up to the original version. Sento continues to paint worldwide and has no plans to stop.

Private collection.
New York City, 1989.

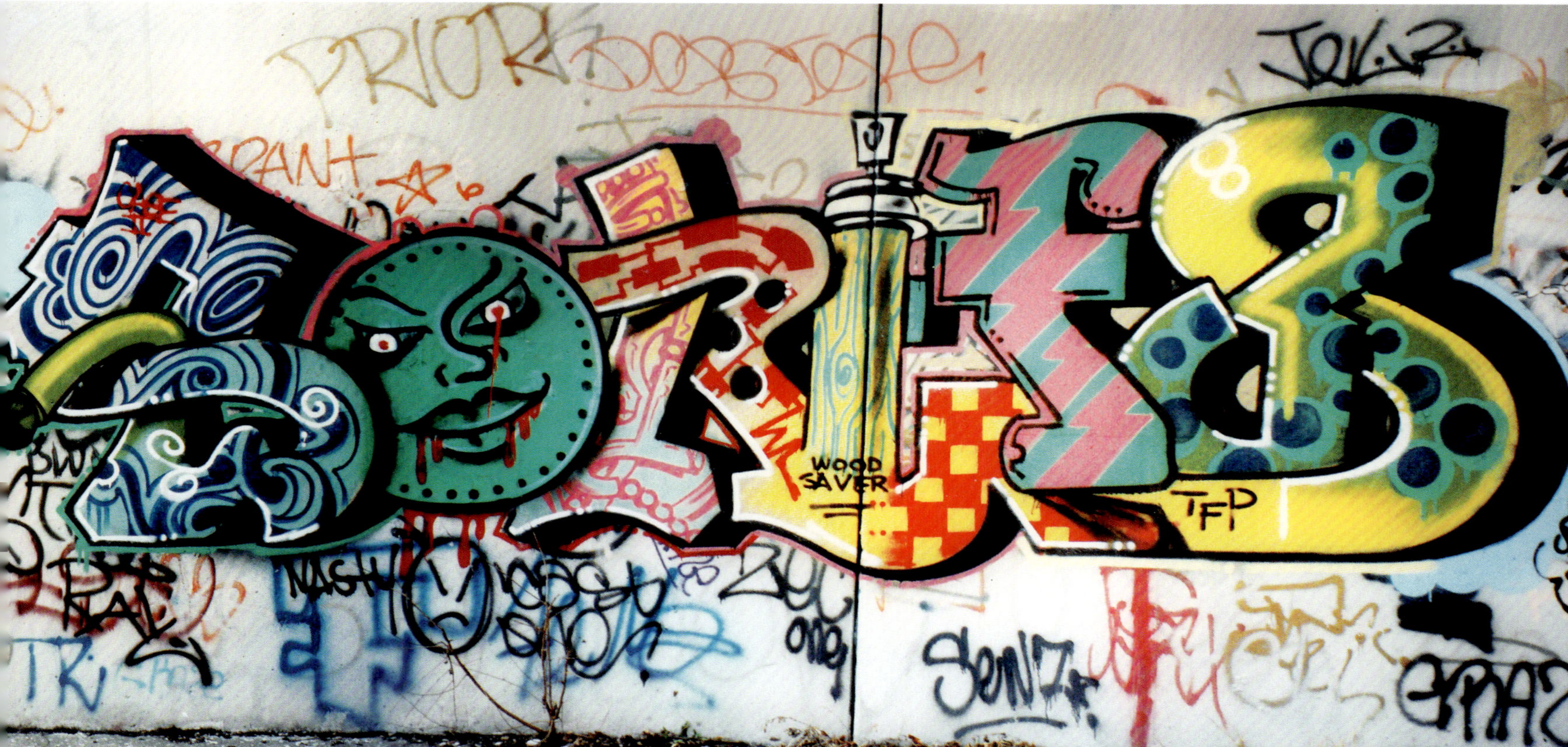
WOOD
SAVER
TFP

Serve

Oddly enough, when Serve began to notice graffiti on trains, it was the characters that caught his eye. Serve studied, and then mastered, the Marvel and DC comics visual lexicon, as well as the characters of Vaughn Bode, which Dondi [see 097] and Kel 139 [see 190] had been using in their train pieces.

In 1979, Serve began to take pictures of graffiti with his Kodak 110 camera. He stayed up late in his room, poring over these photos, copying letter styles of the writers he admired—such as Part [see 251], Chain 3 [see 062], T.Kid 170 [see 335], and Kel 139—in sketchbooks, incorporating their styles into his own.

After an unsuccessful attempt at hitting a CC train in 1982, Serve didn't return to subway writing until 1985, when his friend Jase invited him to the #5 line Baychester lay-up in the Bronx. After a few successful missions at Baychester, Serve went on to paint a half-dozen more cars in the infamous #1 tunnel, where he hooked up with members of TC5, IBM, FC and 156 crews.

Serve's other careers as a hip-hop DJ allowed him to combine his talents: After he retired from train painting, he began drawing album covers and painting club interiors.

Returning to the legal wall-production scene in the early 1990s, Serve established himself as a character wizard, incorporating the influences of Skeme [see 304], Doze, and Tack, while adding his own ingredients.

Serve's magnificent blackbooks, populated by his big-booty girls, B-boys dressed to the nines, and Wild Style burners, have caused people speak his name with reverence in five different languages.

Photograph by Ces One. New York City, 2007.

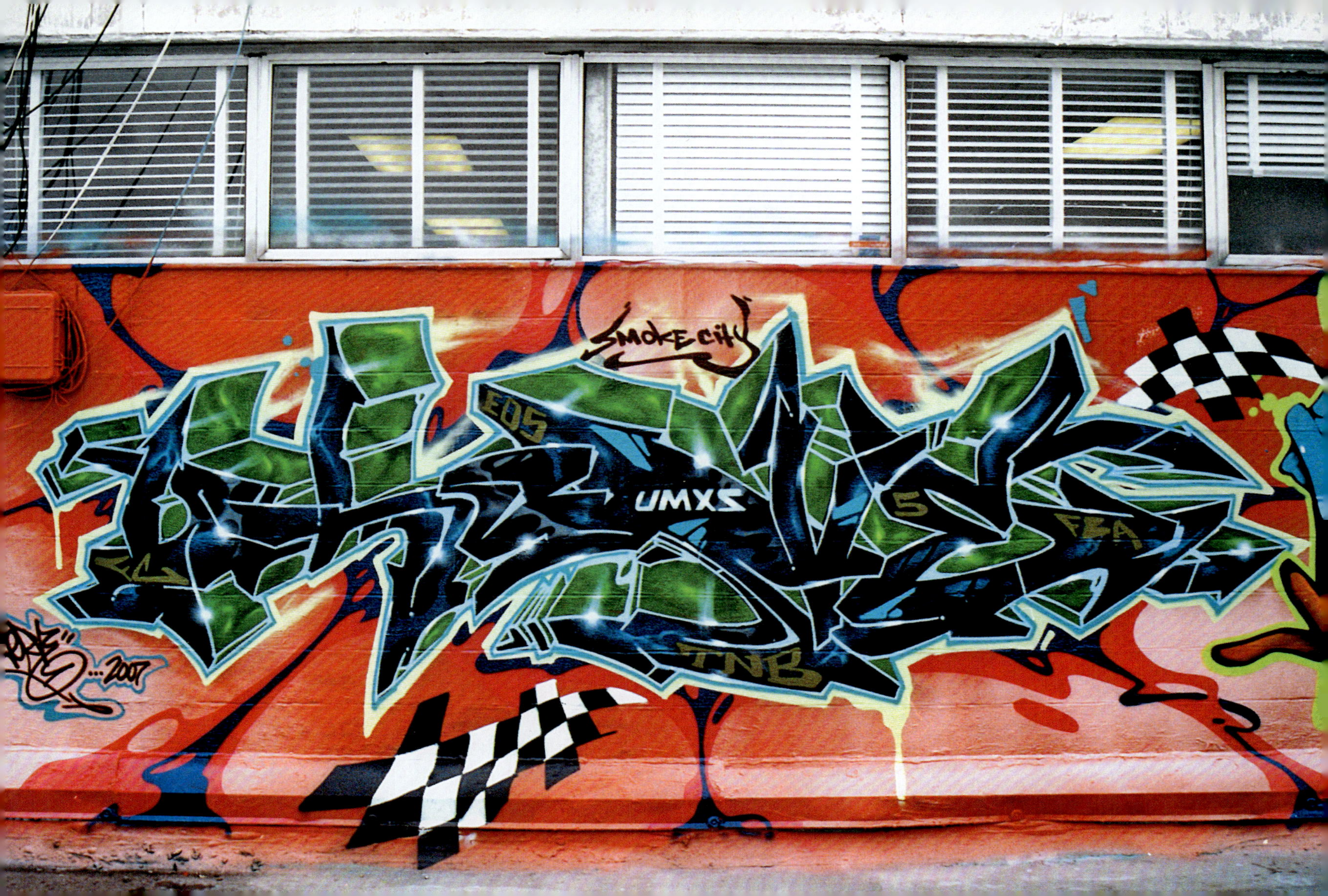
SMOKE CITY
EOS
UMXS
5
FBA
TNB
...2007

Sever

Sever has called a variety of locales home during his thirty-four years, possibly accounting for his varied skill set and the diverse range of styles with which his work has come to be associated. Born in Nashville, Tennessee, in 1976, Sever's earliest influences were subway-art-derived images, which he attempted to emulate at an early age, to varying degrees of success.

Adopting the nickname "Sever" in 1993, he executed some very forgettable first works in his hometown over the next few years. Fully engulfed in graffiti by 1995, Sever began painting alongside fellow teenagers Revok and Beno [RIP], with whom he would relocate to Atlanta prior to the 1996 Olympic Games. Sever began refining his abilities in the heart of the South, producing art both sanctioned and otherwise.

In 1999, Sever would uproot again, this time to the graffiti-friendly streets of the Tenderloin in San Francisco, where his work would continue to evolve, eventually being recognized by the established Los Angeles powerhouse MSK collective. Around this time, he also began creating freelance work and cemented his status as one of the most active outdoor artists in the city, producing new works on a seemingly daily basis. Sever eventually returned to Atlanta in 2001, having become a sought-after graphic artist.

After a brief stint in NYC in 2003, he hopped back to the West Coast in 2004, this time to LA, where he has since become an integral part of the 7th Letter Crew [see 022]. Currently, you can find him producing works, both indoors and out, that range from polished murals to illegible scrawls.

Photograph courtesy of Sever. Atlanta, Georgia, 2009.

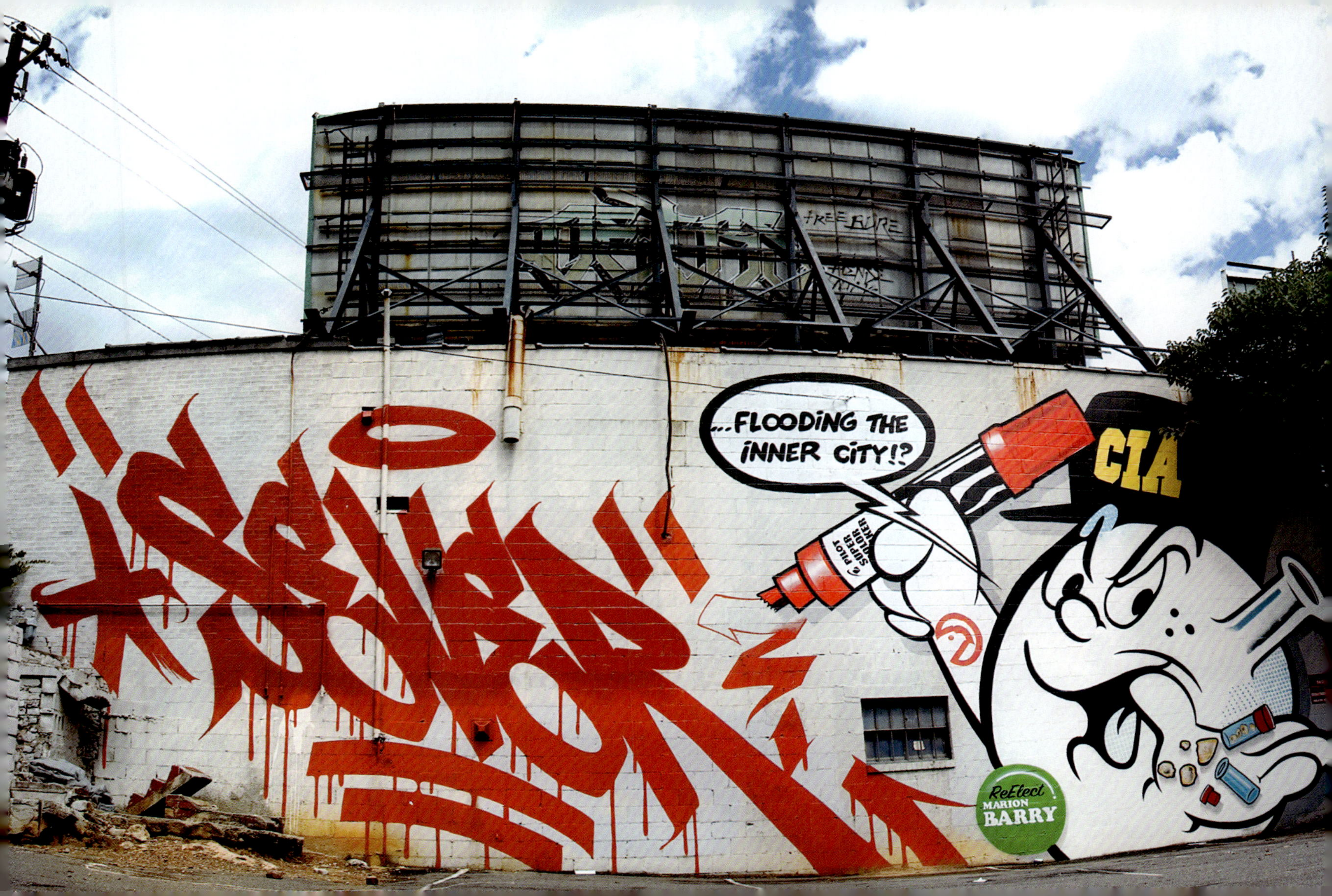
...FLOODING THE INNER CITY!?
CIA
ReElect MARION BARRY

Shiro

Embodying elements of Japanese kitsch, breakdancing culture, and hip-hop style, Shiro's graffiti emerges as a bubbly, brightly colored nod to exuberant self-expression. One of the best-known females in the Japanese street-art world, Shiro has been painting on public walls since 1998.

Drawing heavily on traditional Wild Style graffiti, Shiro is known to paint classic letters, as well as stylized caricatures of busty women. She is influenced by cartoons, and her figures often suggest the bug-eyed ladies of anime and manga. While living in New York at the turn of the twenty-first century, Shiro collaborated with fellow female painter Toofly and contributed to several community-awareness murals. Generally exuding a feel-good spirit, Shiro has claimed as her slogan, "We exist right now, right here."

Currently based in Japan, Shiro has worked as an illustrator, a graphic designer, and a set designer for theater productions, and in her hometown of Shizuoka she has organized several graffiti exhibitions and hip-hop culture events.

With her passion for activism and community organizing, Shiro continues to paint murals on public walls all over the world. She has been featured in numerous art events, as well as gallery exhibitions, internationally.

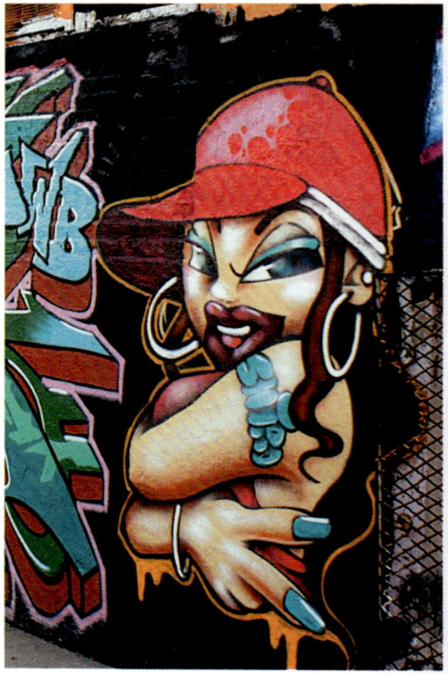

Photograph by Martha Cooper. New York City, 2008. Detail: Photograph by Ernie Paniccioli. New York City, 2007.

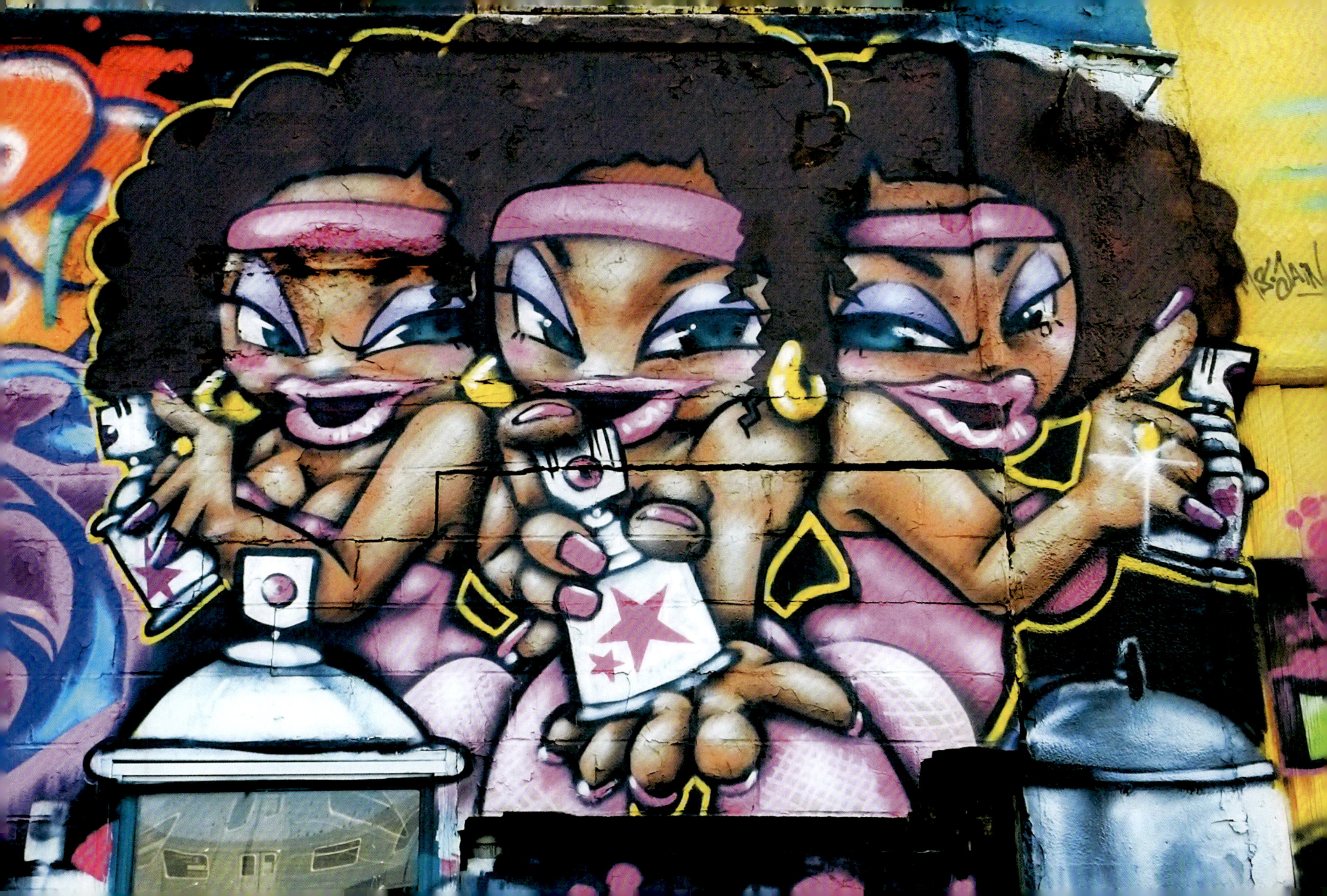

Shok1

In the summer of 1984—at the height of graffiti's international boom and in the middle of hip-hop's most important decade—the street-culture bug bit Shok1 at the tender age of fourteen, and he began obsessively creating. By 1989, he had begun to take his artwork beyond his British hometown and started familiarizing himself with his peers, from Brooklyn to Berlin. The archetypal outsider, Shok1 is entirely self-taught, and in the decades to come, he would go on to produce thousands of letter pieces, characters, large-scale wall pieces, posters, and paintings on canvas. Shok1 has now spent more than twenty-five years proliferating his unique style of extremely detailed and abstracted work.

In 1993, he began commercial collaborations with brands such as Guinness, Tim Westwood, and Molotow, which named a special color of its spray paint after his repeated use of it: "Shok1's Evil Olive."

Shok1 is a mainstay and highly influential figure for the current generation of British graffiti writers.

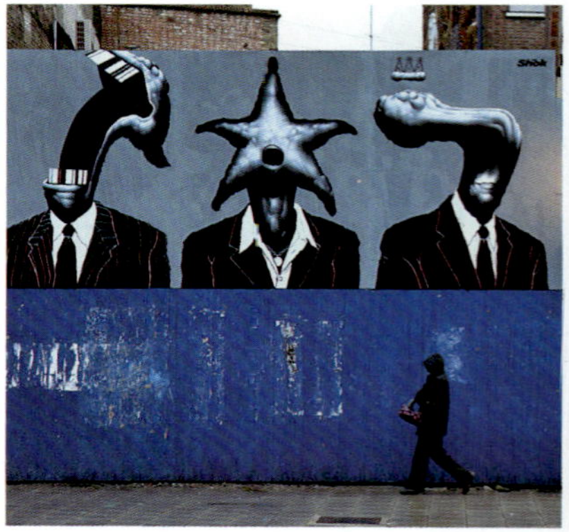

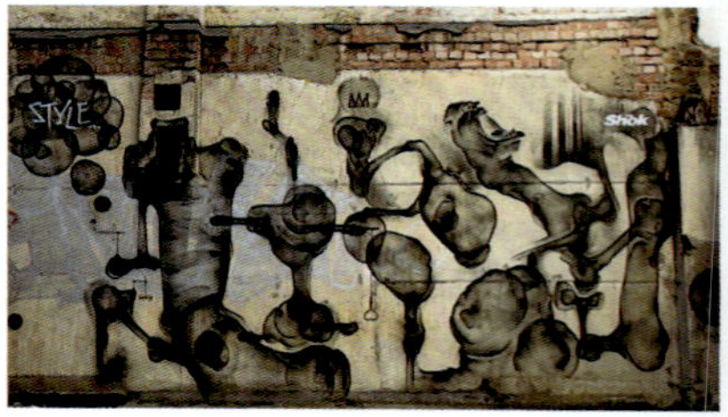

Photographs by Artofthestate.
***Be*. London, 2009.**
Detail top: *Money Fame Power*. London, 2009.
Detail bottom: *Style=Dies*. London, 2009.

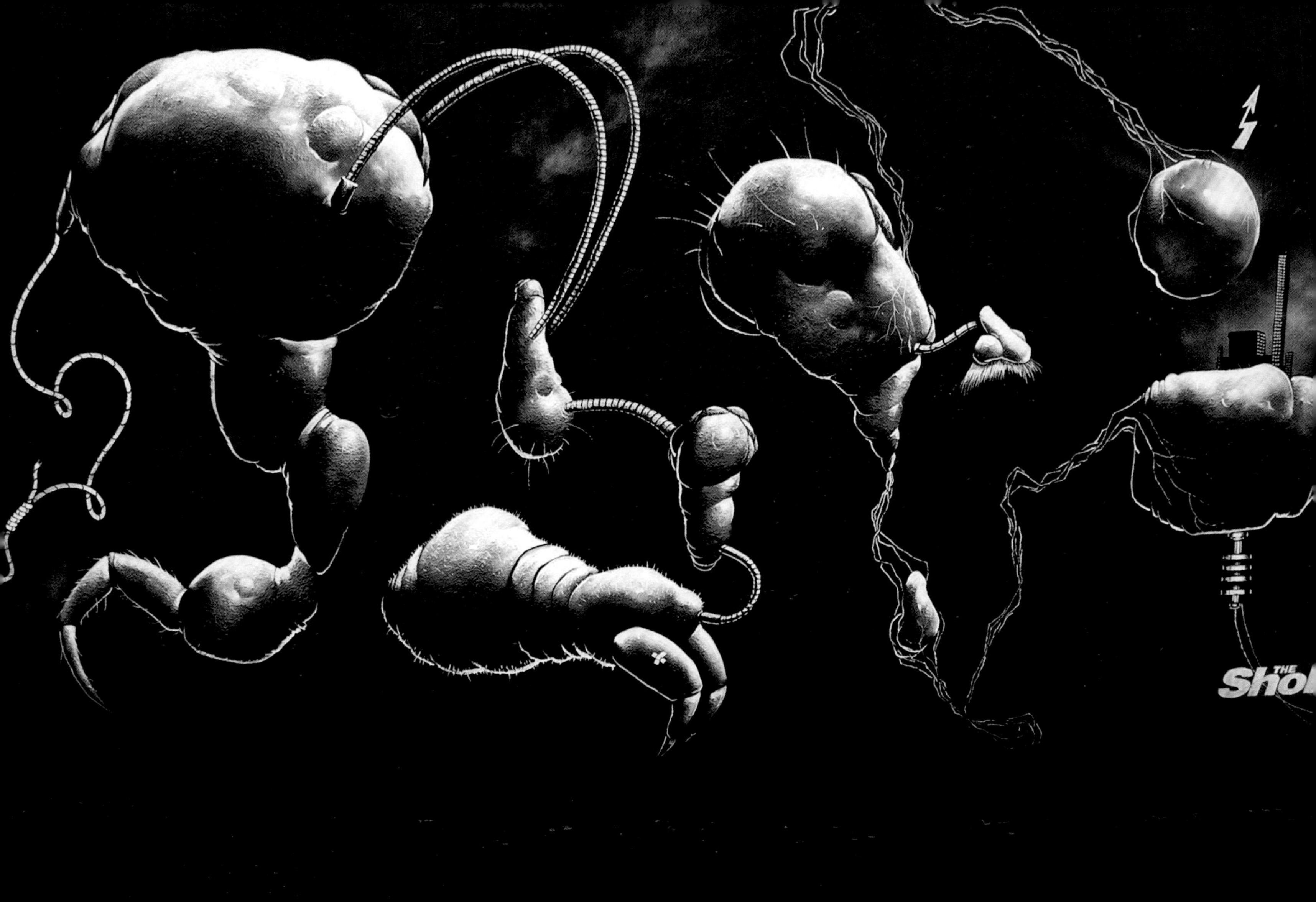

Silver Tips

In a culture where making a quick getaway is a key survival skill, having a ten-letter name defies reason. Perhaps Silver Tips, a small white kid with a big heart and ego to match, found inspiration in the successful, lengthy aliases of Stay High 149 [see 316] and Superkool 223 [see 325], and wanted to follow suit.

Raised in the same East Bronx neighborhood that spawned Comet [see 071] and Ajax [see 010], and that held the precious trains of the #2 and #5 lines, Silver Tips began writing graffiti around 1972. He painted on remote subway lines at first, doing stick-letter pieces that were standard for the era. In 1973, Silver Tips formed a partnership with the immortal Comet. After the fortuitous retirement of the #2 and #5 line king, Hondo, in 1974, the pair staked their own claim to graffiti's most hallowed ground. Comet and Silver Tips, among the earliest inductees of the original Crazy 5 [see 079], unleashed a barrage of throw-ups, top-to-bottoms, and two-man window-down clouds, all of which exemplified bubble-letter perfection.

Perhaps Silver Tips had indeed tried to lift too heavy of a letter load. After all, Comet painted like lightning and only had half the letters. Around 1975, Silver Tips condensed his moniker to S.Tips to cover more ground, and then adopted UPS as a throw-up name. Silver Tips's style soon advanced way ahead of his graffiti contemporaries—his UPS throw-ups were often done with black fill-ins outlined in white that blew away half the color pieces running at the time—but he remains largely overlooked in graffiti's history. However, with the resurgence of 1970s graffiti documentation in several art and photography books, many of his masterpieces will surely resurface as eye candy for a new generation.

Photograph by Jack Stewart. New York City, 1973.

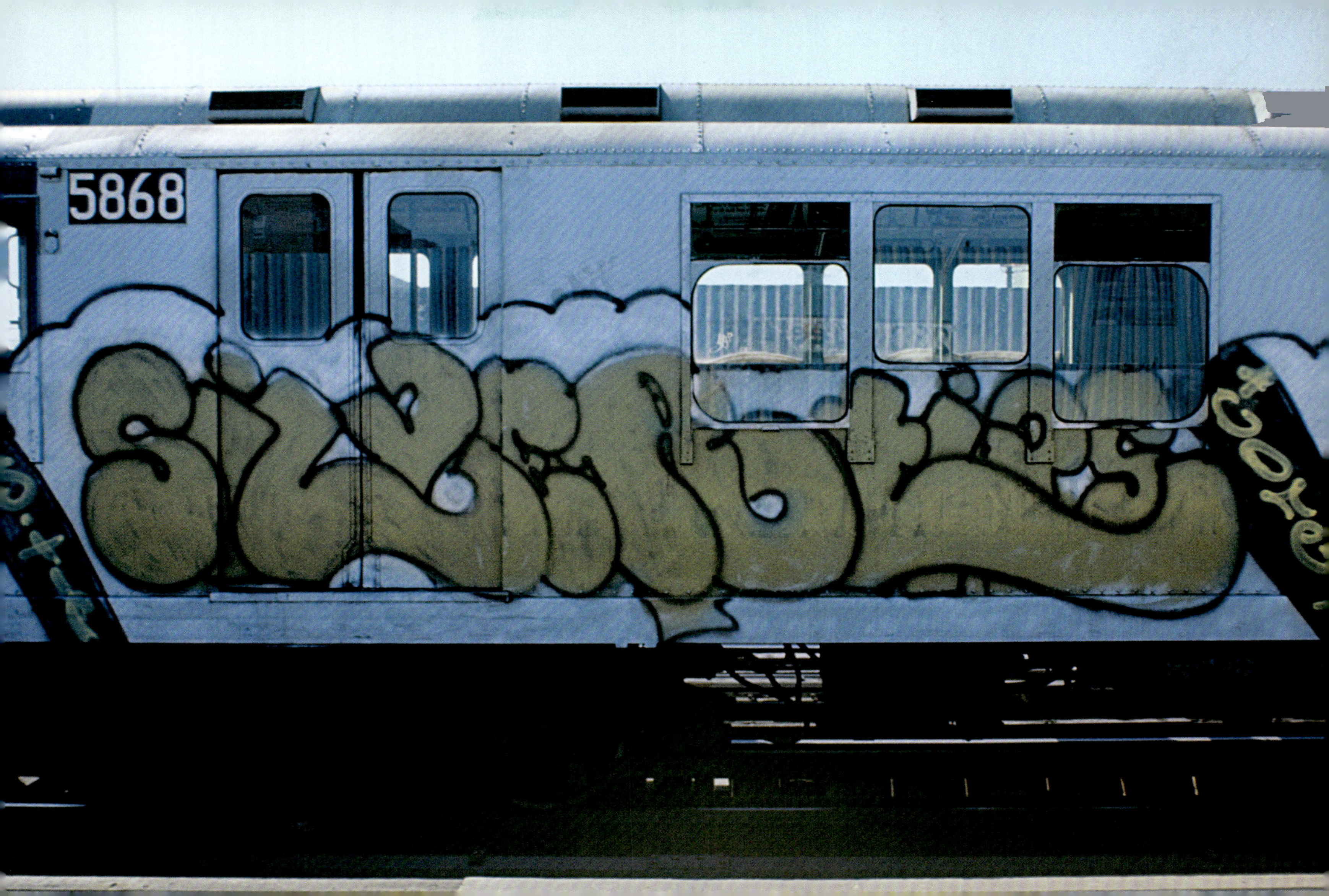
5868

Sinboy

Sinboy grew up in Madrid next to a big wall of fame and remembers watching Suso33 hit the streets on a regular basis (he himself started getting up in 2001). As a kid, he recalls liking what he saw as "regular things," like cartoons, Jedi Knights, comic books, and punk music. The son of travelers, Sinboy graduated high school, moved to Bucharest, spent a year at the Fabrica project in Venice, and then headed over to Brussels.

Sinboy has professed his love for clean graffiti, dirty vandalism, tattoos made with blunt objects, and conceptual art—at least, when it has some production value to it. His work stems from cartoons, tries to say important things, and in his estimation, usually fails because "besides being active and putting your money where your mouth is, what's that important?"

In Romania, Sinboy has become the street-artist's guide, helping dozens of foreign artists learn their way around the streets of Bucharest and put up work in a situation that has been described as wild, wild west. While his self-published zines and comics have earned him international recognition, it is easy to recognize that his sense of humor is always linked to misadventures on the streets.

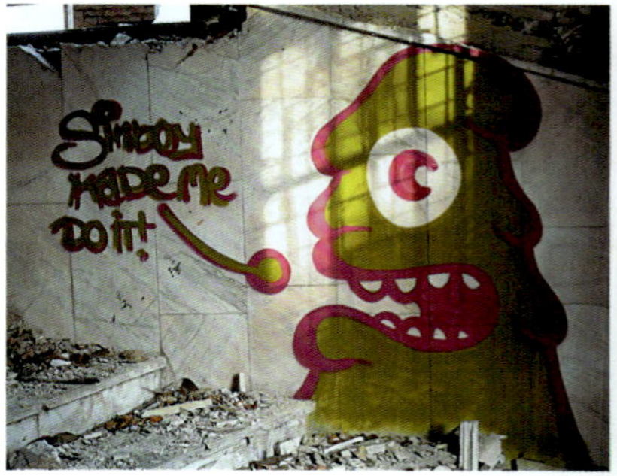

Photographs courtesy of Sinboy.
Collaboration with Saddo.
Bucharest, Romania, 2010.
Detail: Bucharest, Romania, 2007.

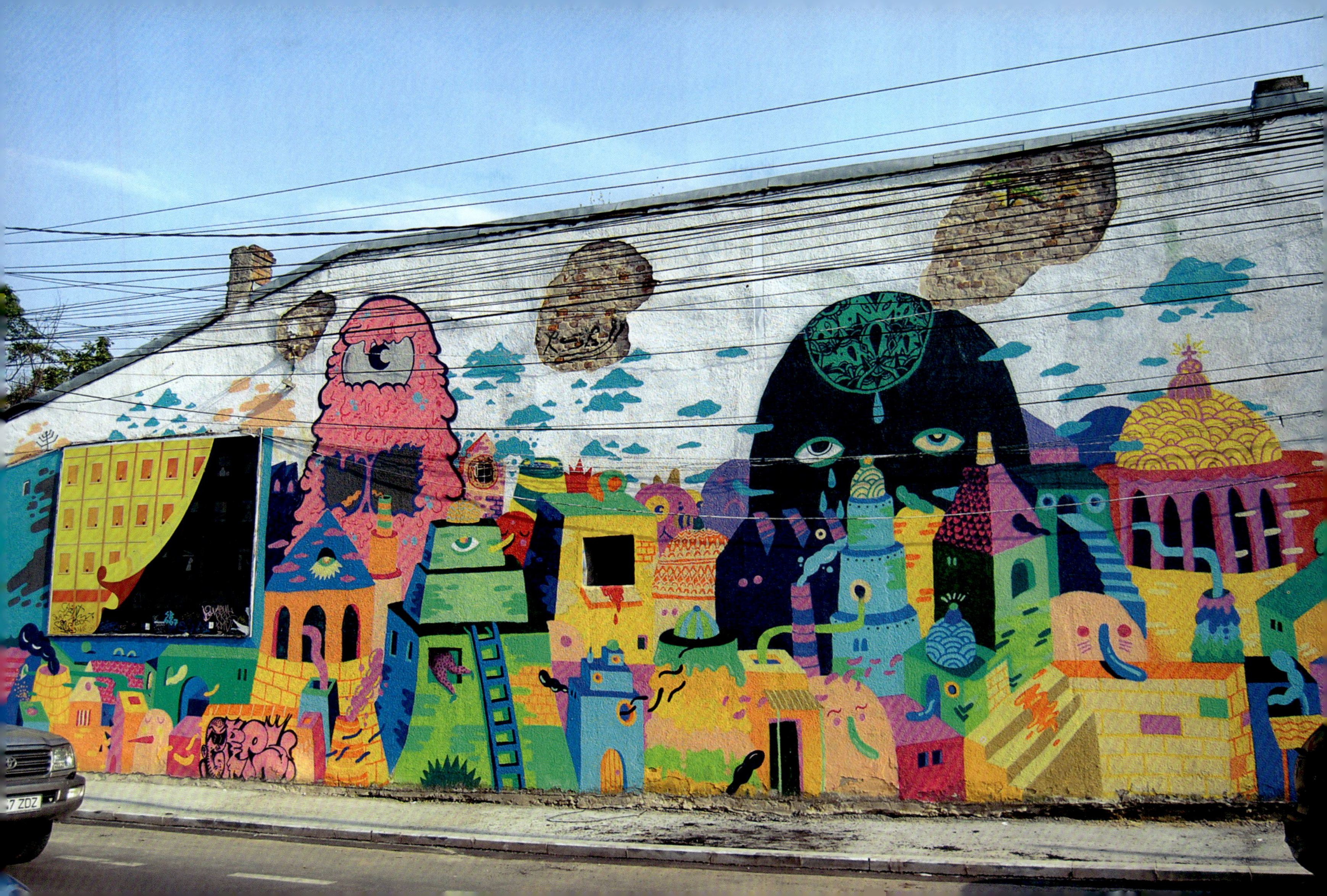

SjocoSjon

Born and raised in Amsterdam, all-round visual artist SjocoSjon has been using the streets since 2006 as an easily accessible playground in which to express himself. "When I have an idea or when something bothers me," he says, "I can draw it and wheatpaste it up the same night. Or pick up a bucket of paint and some brushes. I am very happy that this easy and fun way to express myself exists on such an international level."

The way he laughs with his practice says a lot. He takes the work, but not himself, seriously, as he mashes up layers of influence. His recent show at the Mediamatic (2010) took this a step further, paying tribute to Jerry Springer, spontaneity, and amateurism in art.

Photographs courtesy of SjocoSjon.
Right: Amsterdam, the Netherlands, 2009.
Far right: São Paulo, Brazil, 2010.

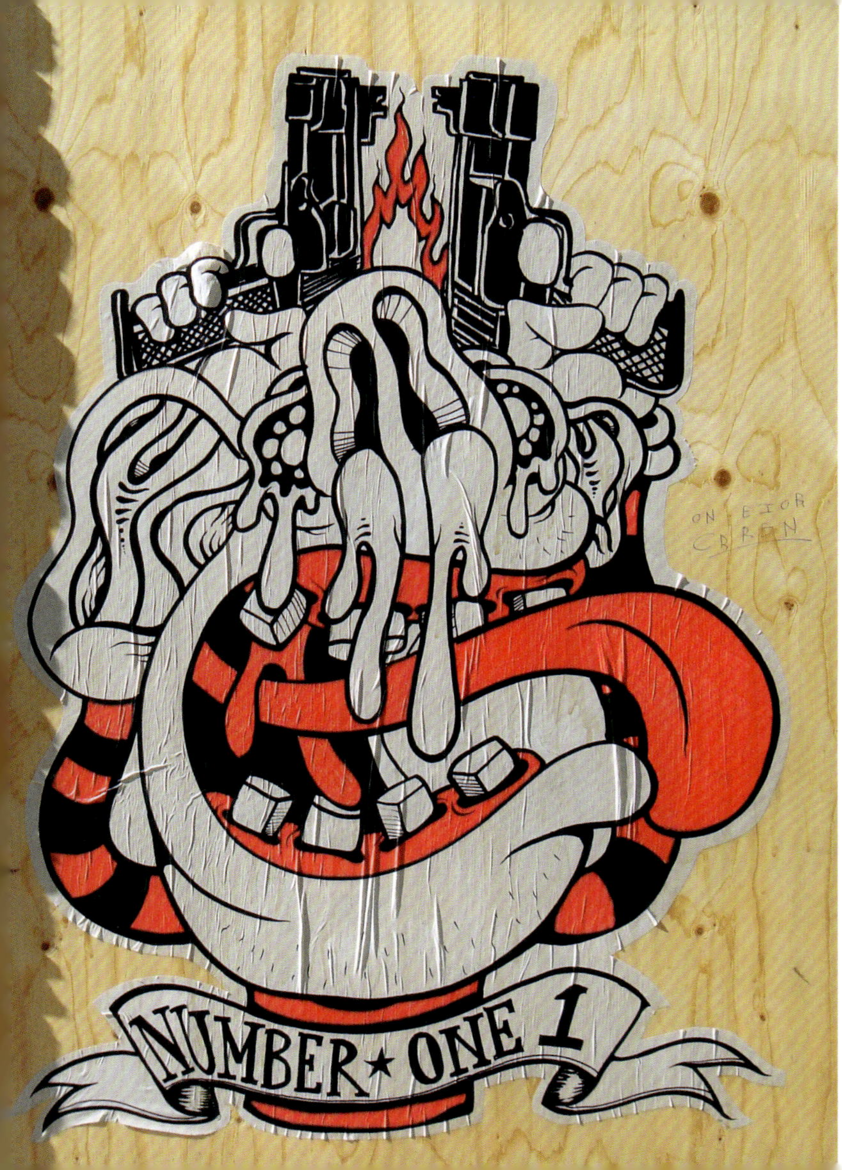
NUMBER ★ ONE 1

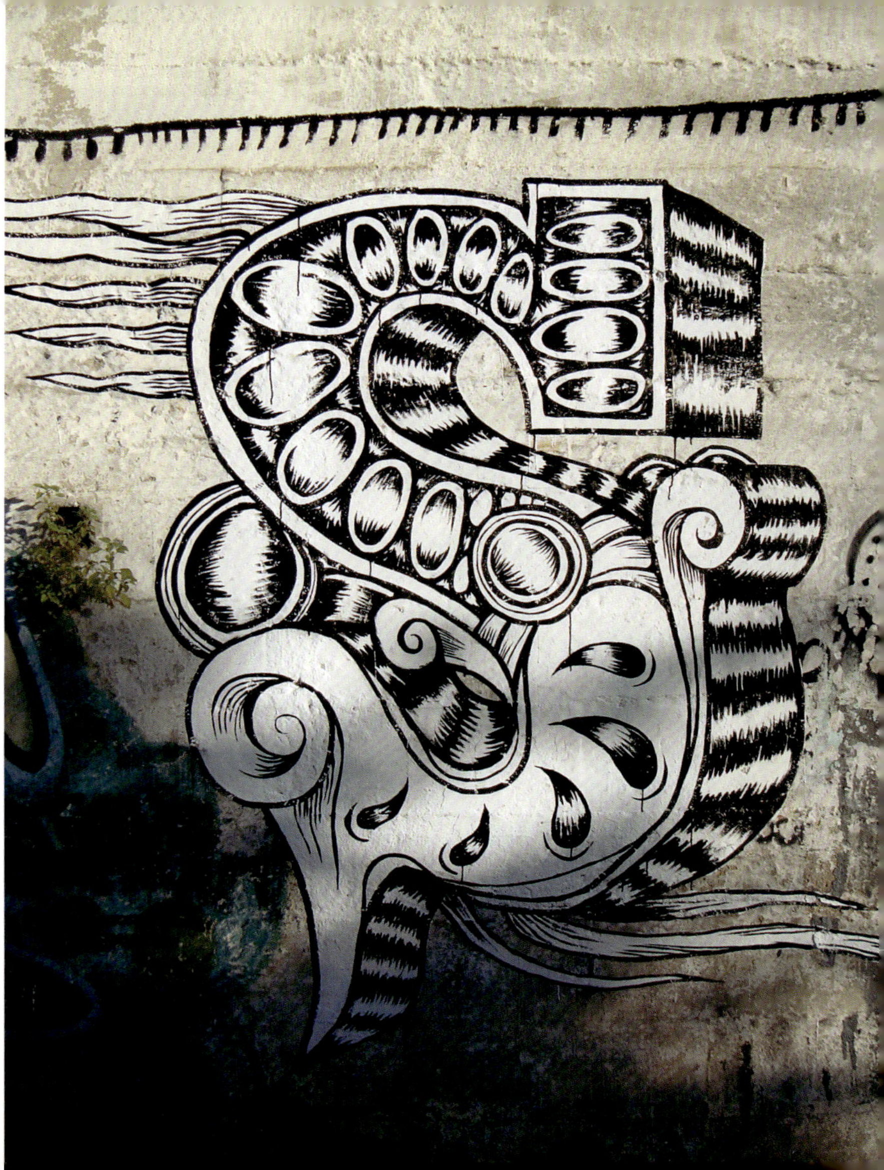

SKE

SKE started writing in Puerto Rico in 1980, just before the graffiti movement expanded beyond the subways of New York and became a worldwide phenomenon. During his early years of writing, he would go from school to school, battling leading graffiti writers and always emerging the victor. In 1985, the tide turned when a writer named Rom moved to his hometown of Carolina. Rom was the complete package, with style to spare.

From 1985 to 1988, SKE, his partner, Soze, and Rom painted together, and SKE's style began to improve. In 1989, Rom disappeared, and the scene in Carolina was dwindling. In 1991, Soze moved to New York, leaving SKE to paint on his own. A quick trip to the Bronx in 1992 brought SKE in contact with the FX crew and TNB, who were impressed with his amazing rendering of figures; by the mid-'90s he was repping both crews.

SKE's New York style eventually gave way to a more contemporary European flair, with plenty of hard-edged planes and backgrounds full of realistically rendered sci-fi imagery rooted in Geiger and Frazetta. He remains one of the best painters on the scene, and with thirty years in the game, he remains the top dog in Puerto Rico.

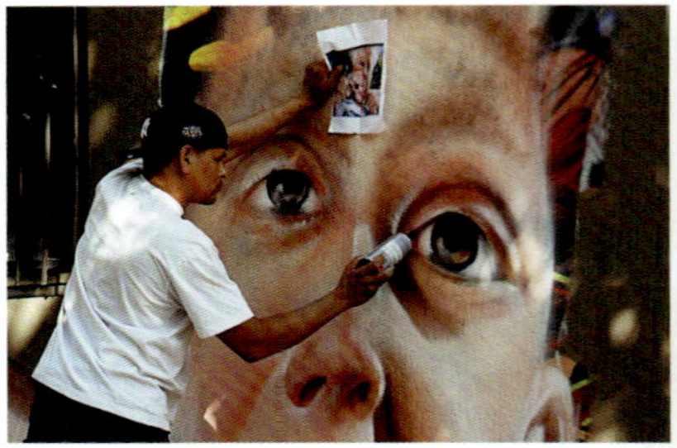

Photographs courtesy of SKE.
Bottom right: Piece by T.Kid 170 (left); character by SKE.

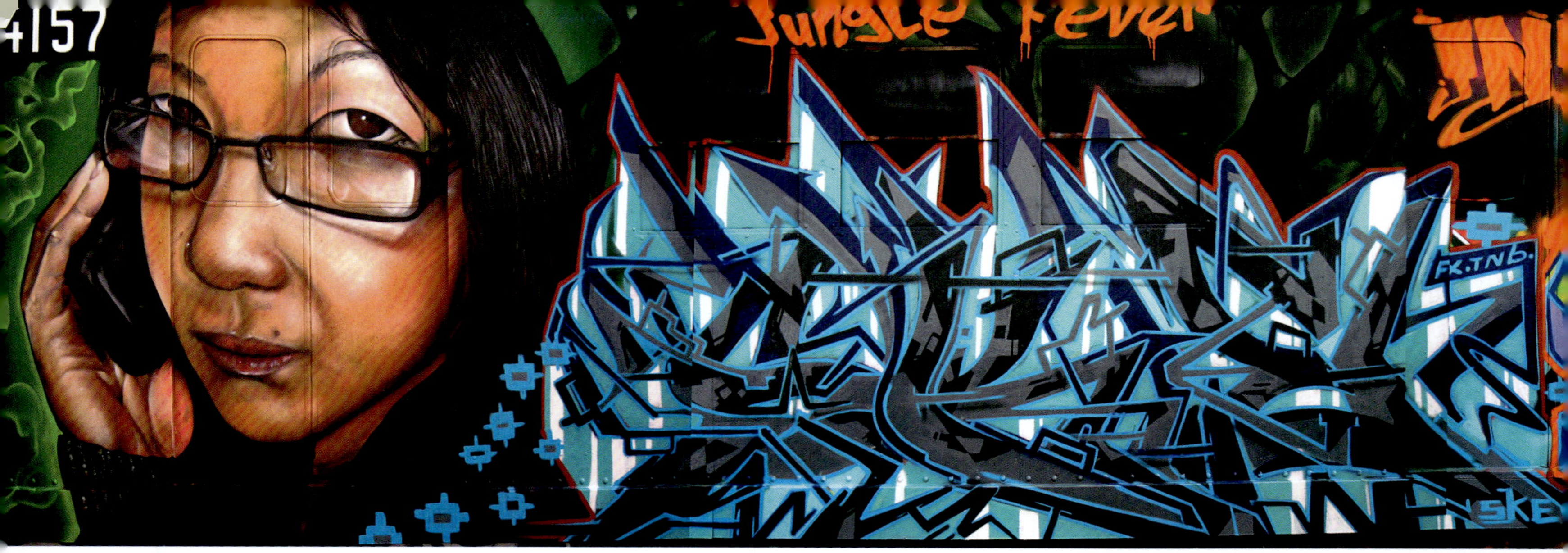
4157
Jungle Fever
FK.TNB.

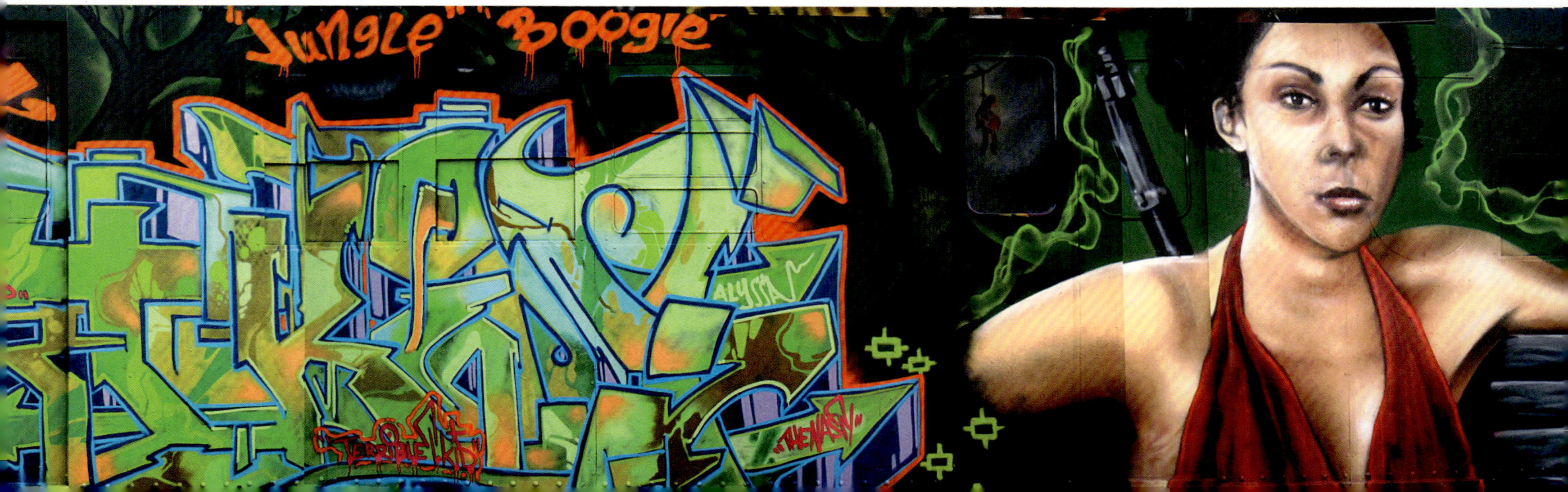
"Jungle" "Boogie"
ALYSSA

Skeme

Skeme's storybook career began in 1981. He attended the High School of Music and Art and, blessed with natural artistic ability, began drawing characters at an early age. Skeme's Harlem apartment bordered on the #3 yard adjacent to the East River. As a neophyte, Skeme approached a writer he met at the yard and showed him some of his character sketches. The writer turned out to be legendary #3 line king Dezzy Dez (DJ Kay Slay), who was impressed with Skeme's talent. They would go on to take over the #3 line and frequented many other lines. Skeme's precise clean letters and original breakdancing characters made his pieces instantly recognizable.

Skeme's mother became the most famous lady in graffiti when she was featured arguing with her then seventeen-year-old son in the documentary *Style Wars* (see 322). Immensely popular and respected, Skeme painted with earlier heavyweights such as Chain 3 (see 062), Tean, Kade 198, and Phase 2 (see 255). Skeme joined the army at the end of 1982 and spent almost thirty years serving his country, but had managed to accomplish in just a year and a half what few graffiti writers could do in a lifetime.

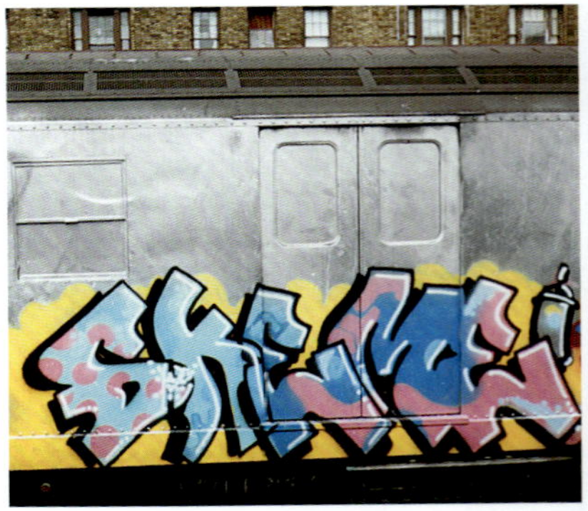

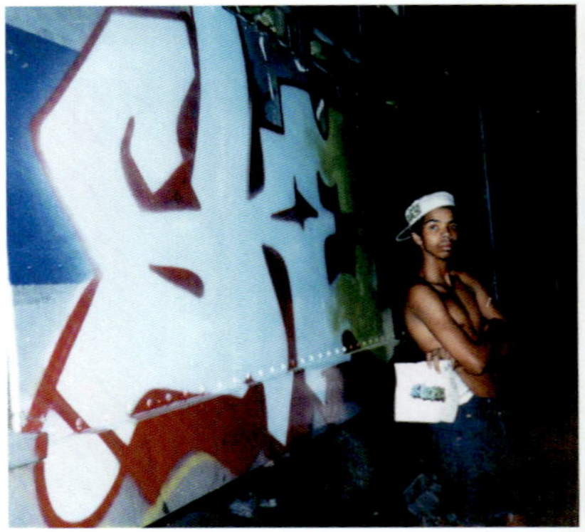

Photographs by Doug Evans. New York City, 1983.

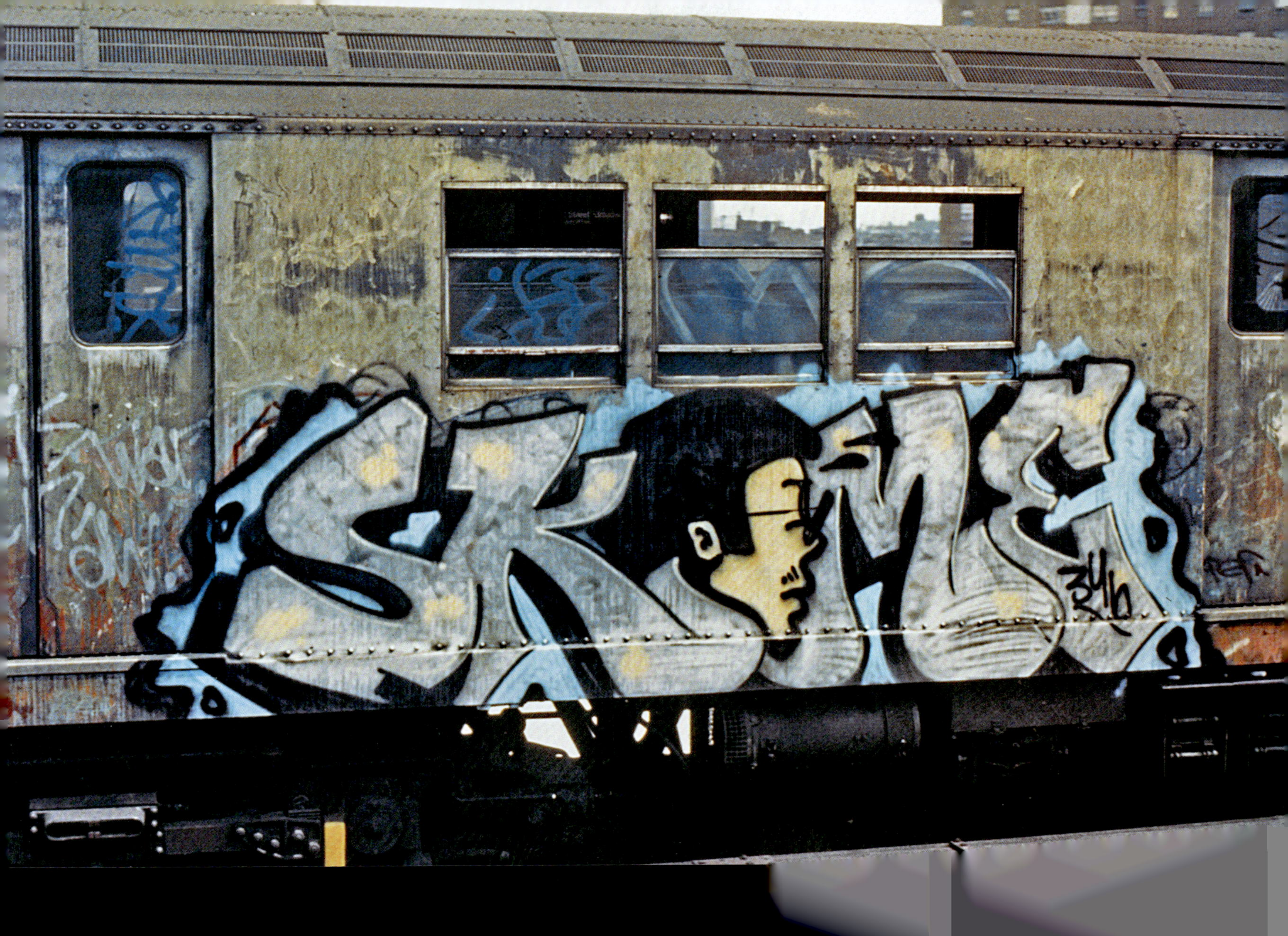

305

Skewville

Alongside other New York street-art superstars in the middle of the first decade of the 2000s, one mischievous presence made itself very recognizable. Common public objects, such as fences and police barricades, were being turned into sculptures, each bearing a signature blocky typeface, that seemed to poke fun at passersby. Infused with a uniquely "stoner" tone, the work included a milk crate with foliage glued to it, seeming to overflow from inside. The words KEEP ON GRASS were screen-printed on the crate as a tongue-in-cheek public sign.

The mischievous work was credited to an artist who called himself Skewville. As it turned out, Skewville was not just one artist, but an irresistibly comical pair of identical twins. Born and raised in Queens, New York, Adam and Drew grew up constructing rocket ships and secret worlds in their backyard. As adults, they opened a business selling glass pipes with witty slogans emblazoned on them, and eventually turned to industrialized street art, breathing a much-needed element of humor into the culture. The twins, under the Skewville moniker, were included in the Wooster Collective's (see 359) legendary 11 Spring Street (see 001) show. Adam went on to open New York City's first street-art-centric venue, the Orchard Street Art Gallery, with his partner, Pufferella, and the twins eventually settled on the still-active Factory Fresh gallery space in Brooklyn.

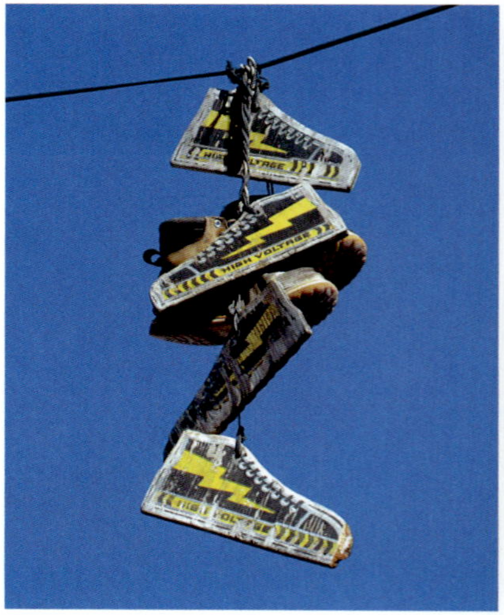

Photographs by Jake Dobkin (streetsy.com). New York City, 2009.

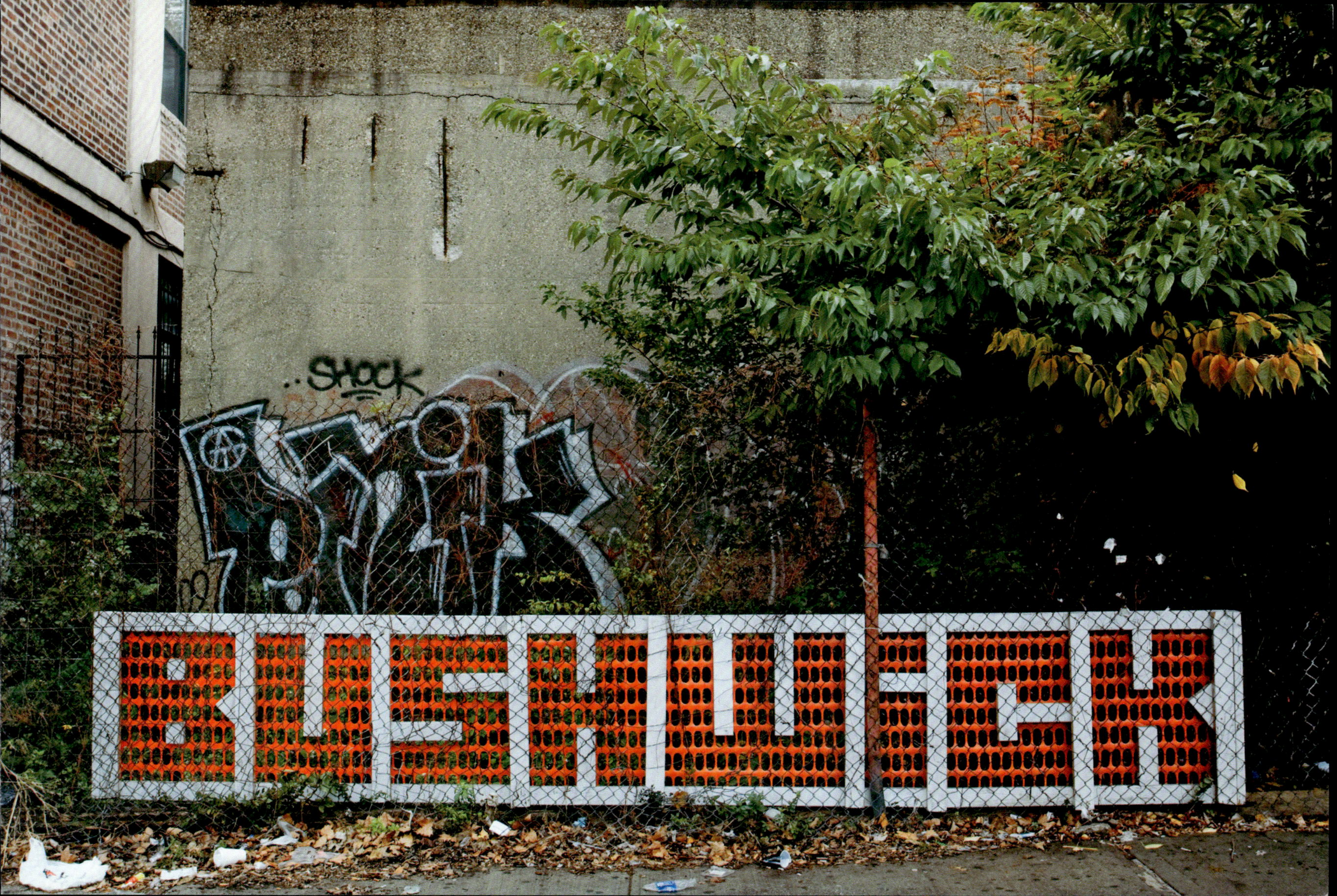
SHOCK
BUSHWICK

Skullphone

Unidentified to date, and pathologically wary of cameras and interviewers, the man behind the iconic Skullphone image remains a mystery. Skullphone is known to carry fake identification and allegedly uses up to three pseudonyms at any given time, never giving his real name at an event or on an art-show flyer.

Based in Southern California, Skullphone has been wheatpasting, stenciling, and stickering his stark image of a skull talking on a cellphone for almost a decade. Skullphone was also responsible for a series of stickers and posters that appeared around New York, advertising a gate-installation service and bearing an 800 number that delivered the caller to a mystifying voice recording. Skullphone moved into billboard liberation and high-stakes installation in 2008, when he hacked ten Clear Channel billboards in Los Angeles and placed his name into the series of ads that flashed on the screens.

A classically trained painter, Skullphone has recently been branching out into oil painting, spearheading a new labor-intensive style of imagery that utilizes the color pixels found in LCD screens to create the deceptive effect of an electronically glowing painting.

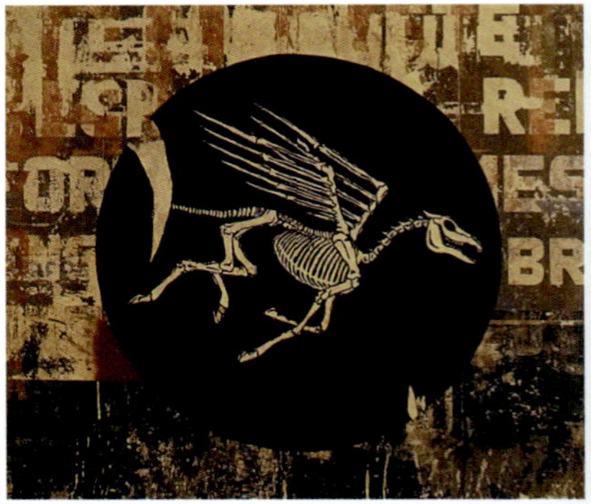

Photographs courtesy of Skullphone. Los Angeles, 2009.

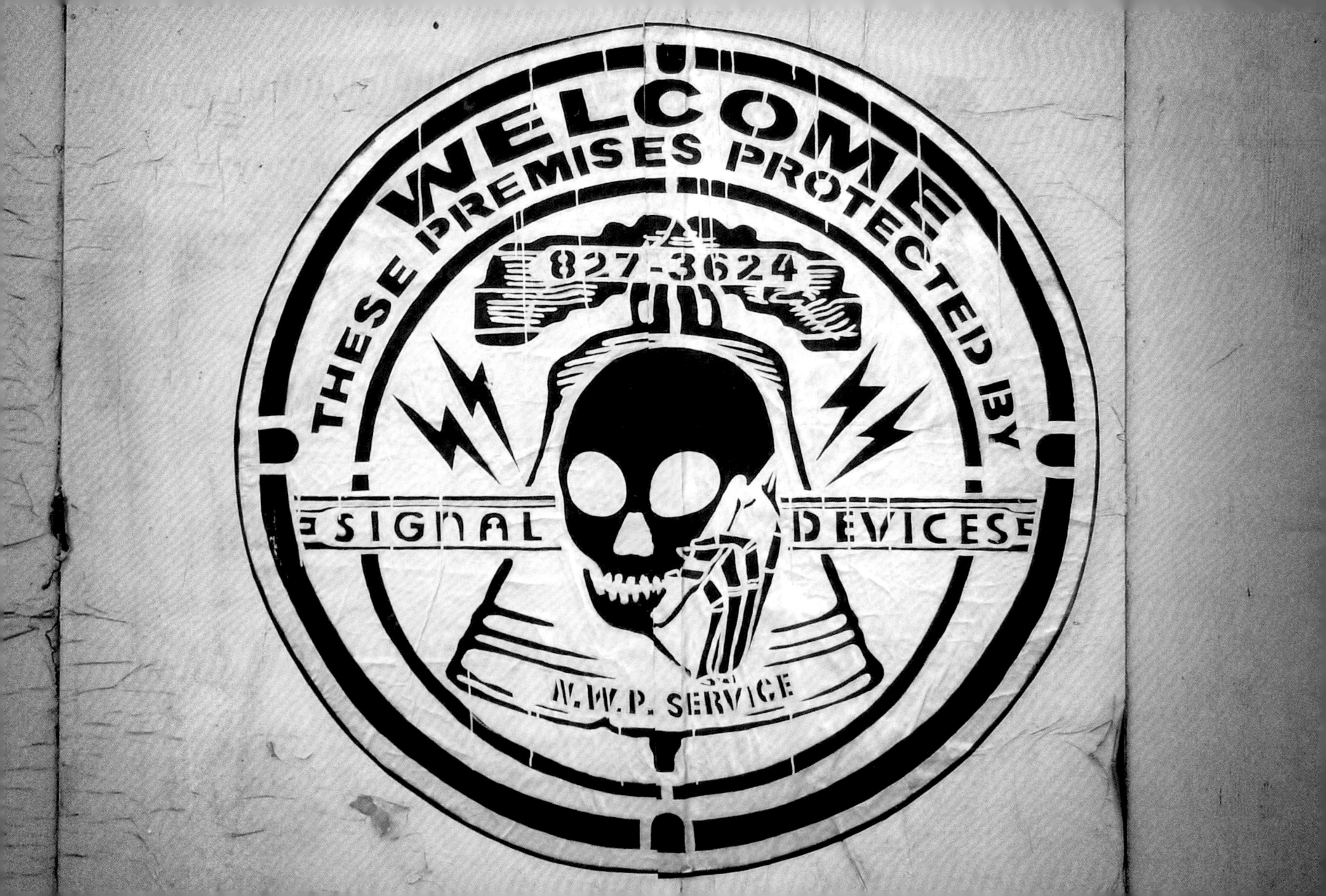
WELCOME
THESE PREMISES PROTECTED BY
827-3624
SIGNAL
DEVICES
N.W.P. SERVICE

Smart

By the mid-1980s, the influence of American graffiti had driven deep into Europe. Taking direct inspiration from across the Atlantic, the first generation of European sprayers used lettering styles that were strictly New York in nature. Before long, European writers began to introduce their own indigenous styles, and today there is a sense of pride among European writers when they bring their own personal flavors to the party. That initial NYC–Europe connection, however, remains undeniably strong.

For Smart, an Italian painter from Florence, Italy, such connections to the NYC graffiti scene are both personal and aesthetic. Smart's work evidences close characteristics of his New York mentors, and of Reas, in particular; Reas is a New York writer, and Smart is a member of his crew, AOK (All Out Kings). The pieces Smart renders solidify the camaraderie with his AOK crewmates, as he not only paints alongside them, but their pieces all share a distinct look.

Is Smart a New York graffiti artist with a fabulous grasp of the Italian tongue, or an Italian graffiti wiz on a stateside visit? Next time Smart hits New York, check his passport.

Photograph courtesy of Smart.
Italy, 2008.

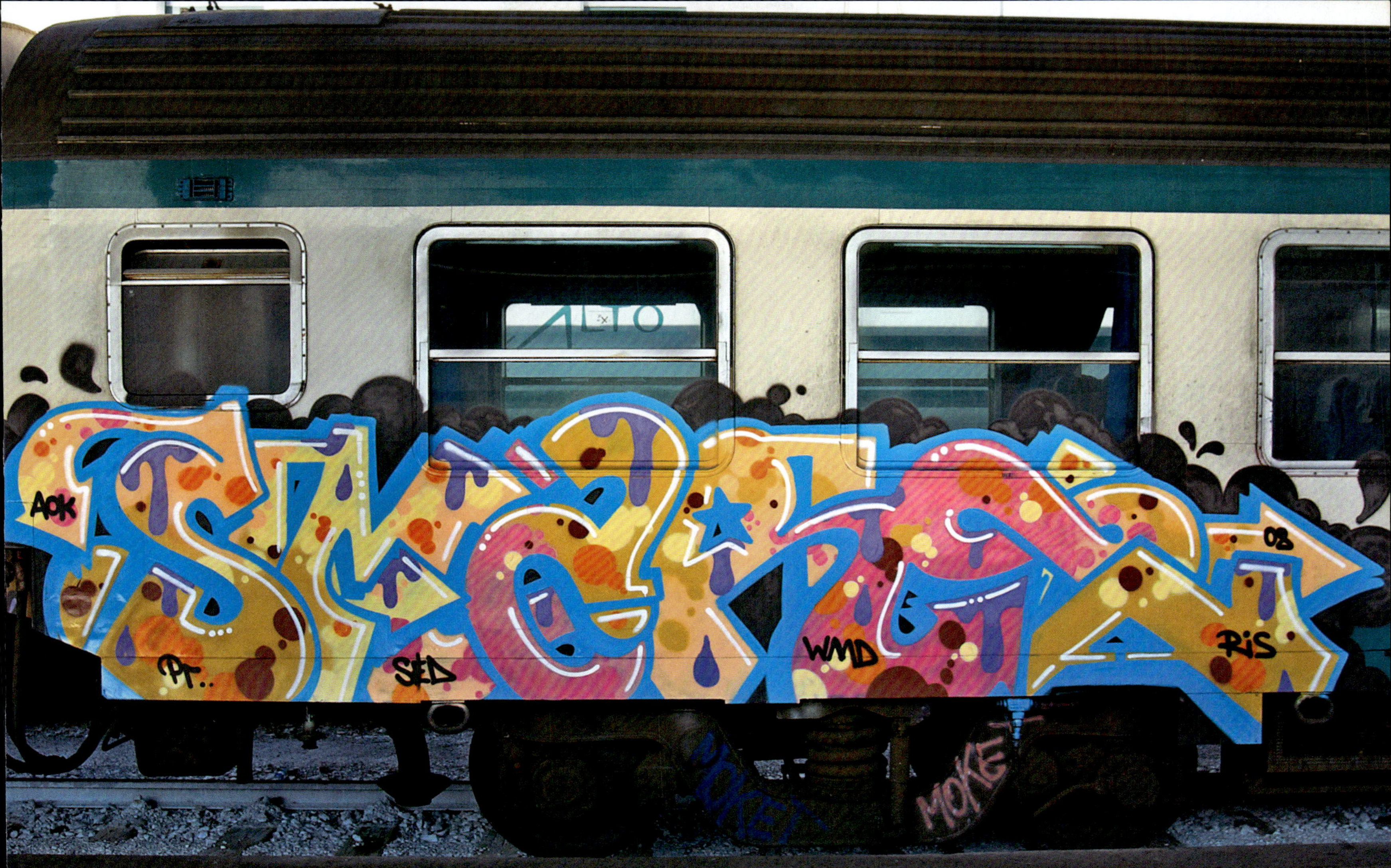
ALTO
AOK
WMD
RiS
08
MOKET
MOKET

Dash Snow

Often called the enfant terrible of the contemporary street-art world, Dash Snow was best known for his wild appearance and raucous, devil-may-care lifestyle. Snow gained early recognition on the streets for his prolific presence under the moniker Sacer, as part of the legendary Irak crew [see 175], and for his collection of Polaroid snapshots documenting his boozing and drugging—including an image of a young Ryan McGinley snorting cocaine off Earsnot's [see 101] erect penis. In his twenties, Snow moved on to a fine-art career, creating collages out of newspapers [sometimes sprinkled with semen] and frequently showcasing his obsession with Saddam Hussein.

After exhibiting his work at museums around the world and fathering a child, Snow decided to clean up his act; he enrolled in an extended rehabilitation program to kick drugs for good. Unfortunately, a relapse proved fatal, and on July 13, 2009, Snow was found submerged in a bathtub in a downtown hotel, lethally overdosed on heroin.

After his death, the *New York Times* published a lengthy article detailing how Snow was the grandson of legendary art benefactor Christophe de Menil and the nephew of Hollywood actress Uma Thurman. The writer mused on the lethal cycle that was created by Snow's lack of control with drugs and his endless access to the means to buy them.

In August 2009, a massive group show was hosted at Deitch Projects Gallery in New York commemorating Dash Snow's life and spirit.

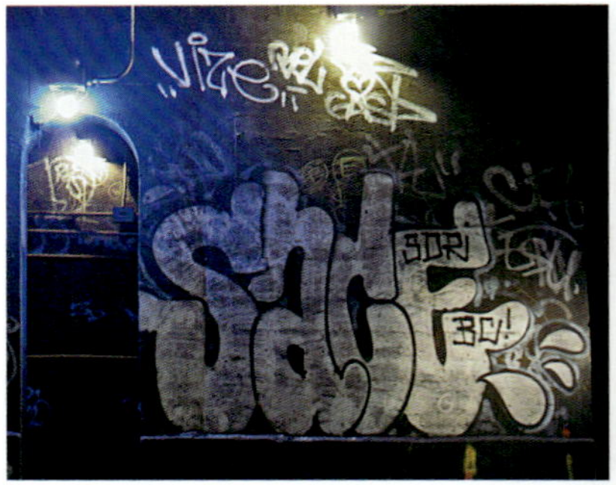

Photograph by Cheryl Dunn. New York City, 2000.
Detail: *Sacer* by Dash Snow. Photograph by Becki Fuller. New York City.

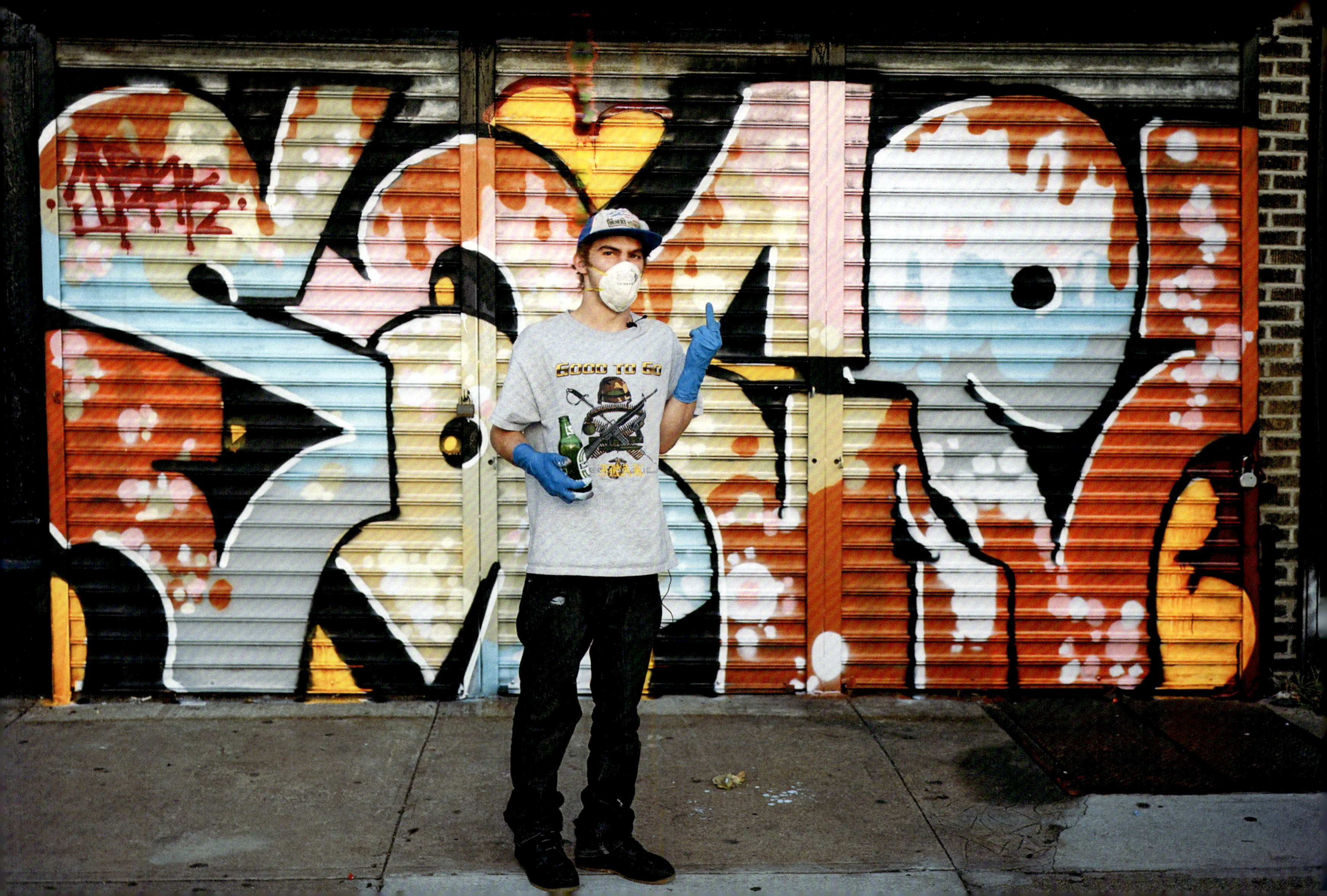
GOOD TO GO

Jeff Soto

Known in the early years of the twenty-first century for his popular, happy-looking robots, California-based Jeff Soto has seen the tone of his work slowly become darker as time has gone on. The shift is plain to see, and the artist attributes it to increased responsibilities in his personal life, not the least of which was the birth of his first daughter.

This is not to say his style has changed completely; Soto's works still contain a certain controlled messiness, a conscious blending of various styles and themes that give texture and depth to his whimsical characters. With time, along with the shift toward greater seriousness, one can also see a sharpening of his impressive eye for detail.

Many of his street pieces are done using a paintbrush rather than aerosol, which worked in his favor in London in early 2009, when police approached as he painted his first illegal piece in almost a decade. After watching him for a minute, they simply walked on, not imagining that such a fine artist could be doing anything unlawful.

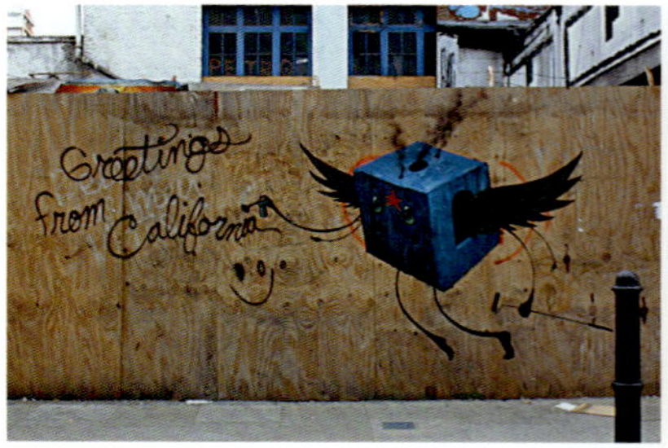

Photograph by Jake Dobkin (streetsy.com), New York City, 2010.
Detail: Photograph courtesy of Jeff Soto. London, 2009.

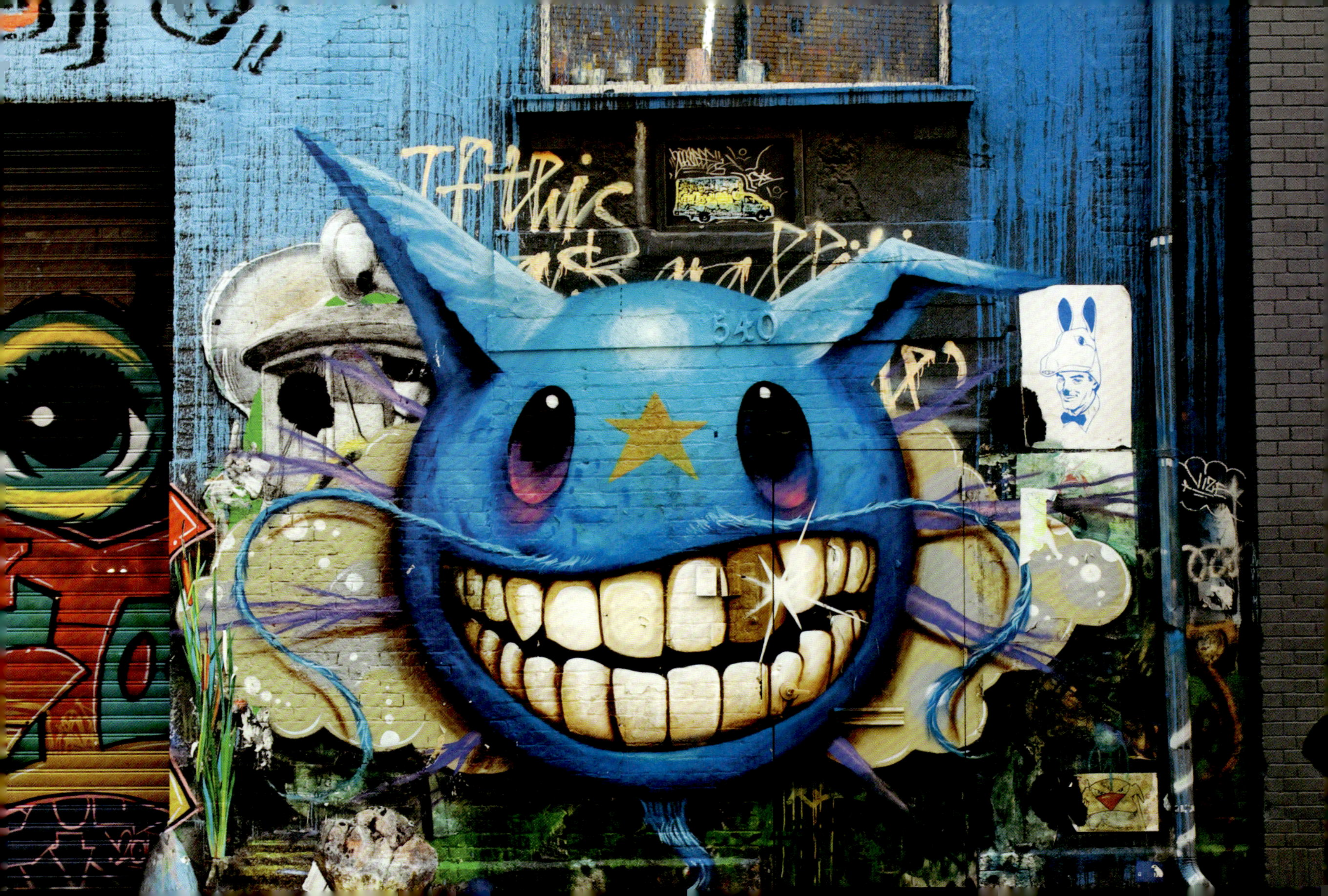
If this
540

Soul Artists

The Soul Artists were created in the locker room of a YMCA in 1972, when three writers—Ali, Futura 2000 [see 141], and Coca 82—decided to tag "SA" after their names, which originally stood for "Strikes Again" but was quickly amended to "Soul Artists." Ali became the president and Futura the vice president; they printed membership cards, and the crew held meetings in Riverside Park.

Ali was not a major bomber; in fact, his philosophy at the time was that one well-placed tag was worth a hundred lesser ones. The crew's name got around after he recruited Moses 147 and B-1, two writers who were battling to be king of the #1 line. Ali collaborated on some highly stylized pieces with Malta and Futura 2000, but Ali was clearly the more charismatic and visionary figure.

In May 1973, a terrible accident nearly took the life of Soul Artists's leader. While he was painting a train in the #1 tunnel with Futura, a spark from the third rail set Ali's paint on fire, burning him severely. Ali recovered, but he was finished with painting trains and from then on stayed on the sidelines, mentoring other writers. Then the crew disbanded.

In 1979, a more mature incarnation of the crew emerged, with Ali, Futura, Zephyr [see 363], and Haze at the forefront. The group received a grant from the government to paint storefront signs on the Upper West Side. It formed a gallery and helped other painters with their first canvases. By 1980, many graffiti artists were co-opted into the art world, not as groups, but as individuals, and this put a permanent end to the Soul Artists.

Photograph by Martha Cooper. New York City, 1980.

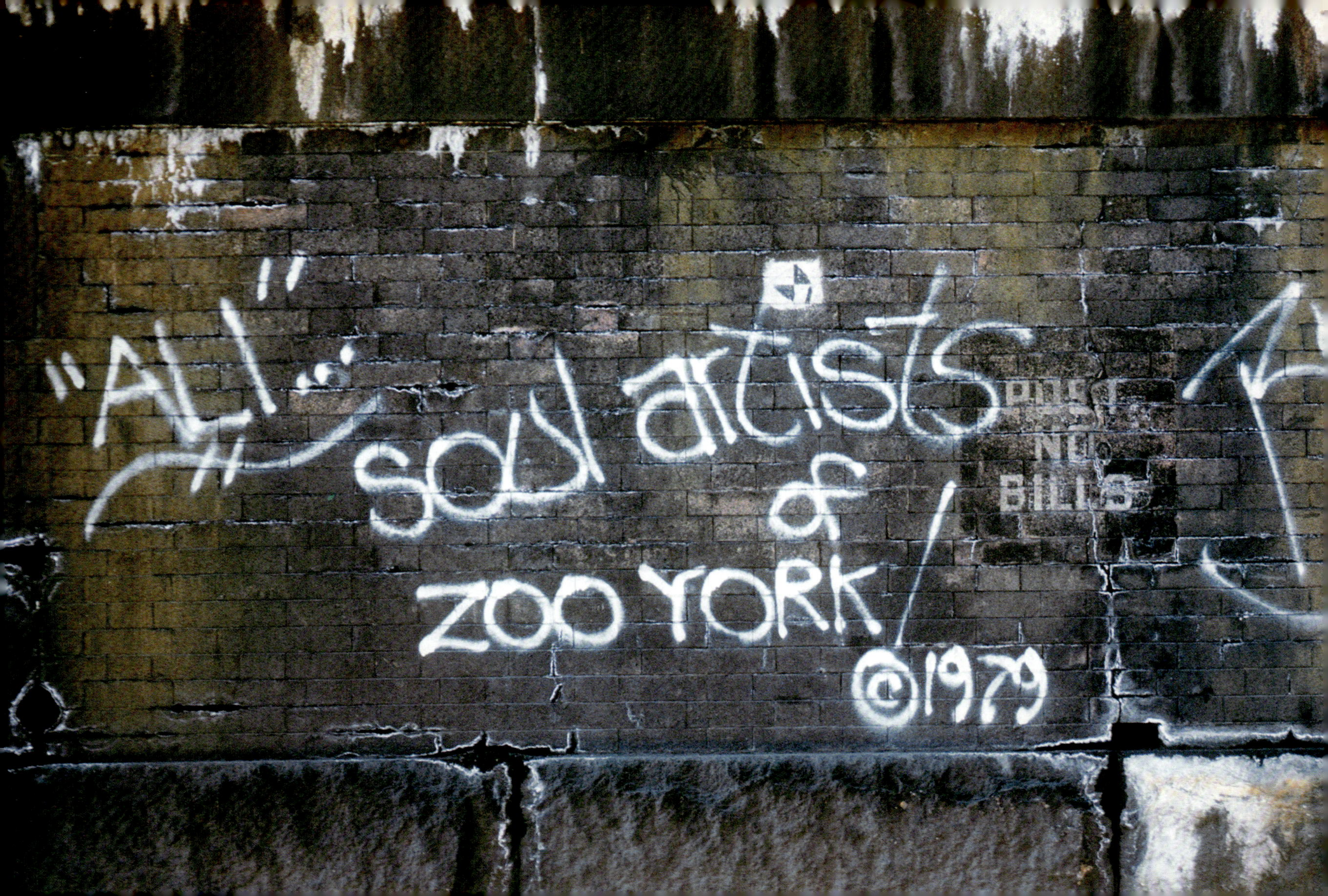
"ALI"
soul artists
of
ZOO YORK
©1979
NO
BILLS

Space Invader

An unlikely superstar among the familiar icons of street art is Space Invader, named after the popular 1970s video game. This French artist, who remains anonymous, began creating mosaics from small, colorful tiles to mimic the video game's highly pixelated alien characters, and in 1998 he began an all-out assault on the streets of Paris. The artist installed the mosaics with heavy-duty construction glue in high-traffic locations, creating mystery and intrigue about the odd little sculptures long before what we now know as street art had hit the mainstream consciousness.

Highly influential in the street-art community, Space Invader is seen as one of the godfathers of modern street art. His anonymity also sets a strong precedent; numerous attempts by the media to reveal his identity have only increased his notoriety. When he appeared in the popular Banksy [see 024] film *Exit Through the Gift Shop*, he was credited as the cousin of Mr. Brainwash [see 235] (the veracity of this claim, however—and that of Mr. Brainwash in general—remains suspect).

Though Paris remains his most targeted city, Space Invader has installed works in more than thirty-five cities internationally, as far-flung as Perth, Bilbão, Tokyo, and Mombasa.

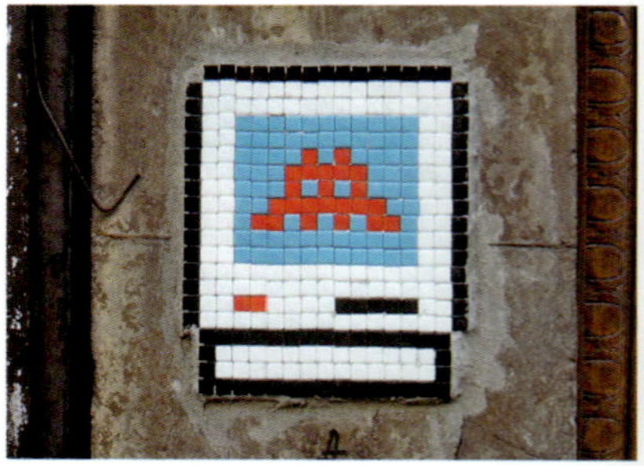

Photograph by Luna Park.
New York City, 2009.
Detail: Photograph by Jake Dobkin (streetsy.com).
New York City, 2009.

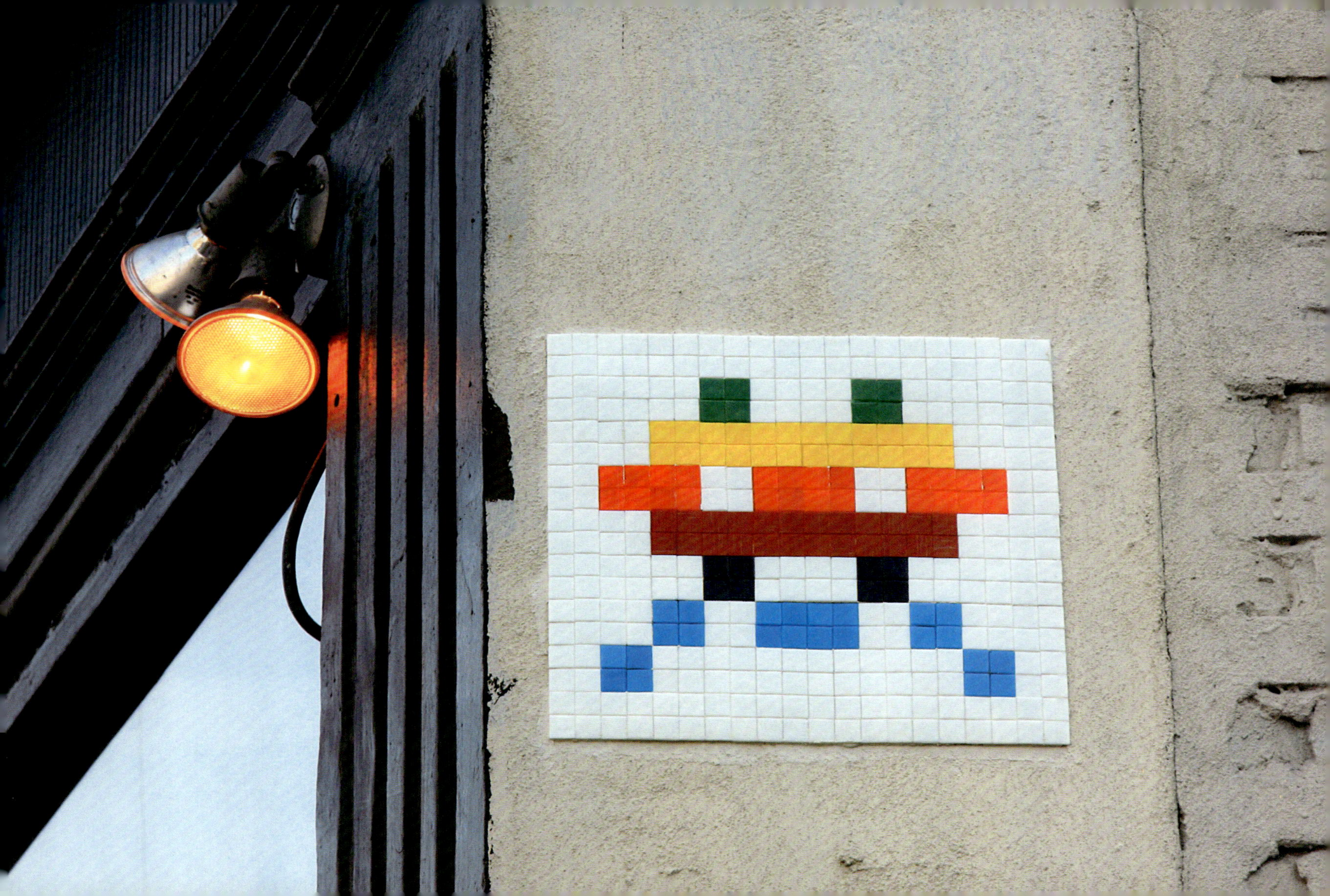

Specter

The Canadian-born artist Specter developed his style through trial by fire, experimenting in the public eye of the streets: After becoming frustrated with art school, Specter went straight out to the walls of the world. Ten years later, he has settled into a highly detailed, often three-dimensional style, developing a body of work that encompasses painting, stencil, and sculpture installation, including a slatted drawbridge that the artist strung between the rooftops of two buildings in Toronto.

Always working alone, Specter claims that each of his pieces is site-specific—assembled, and taken apart in a studio, then later reassmebled on-site. All his pieces, so far, have been illegal, which leaves him working on pieces for weeks that may last only a few hours on public view.

Working with everything from concrete and wood to paints and brushes, Specter employs an unparalleled array of mediums. He maintains that interaction with his environment is his biggest inspiration, and although he is interested in exhibiting his work in galleries, his primary focus is on outdoor public works.

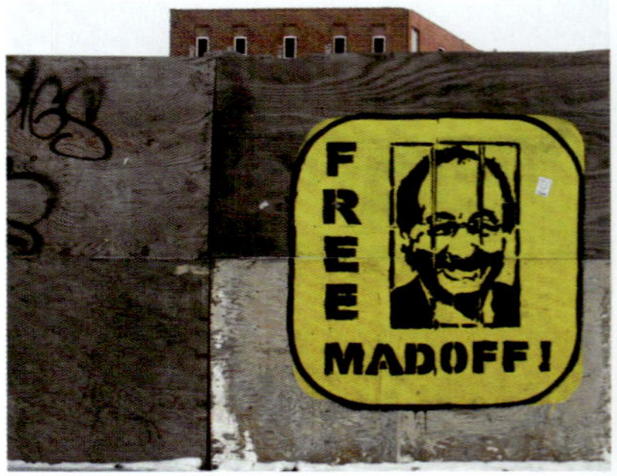

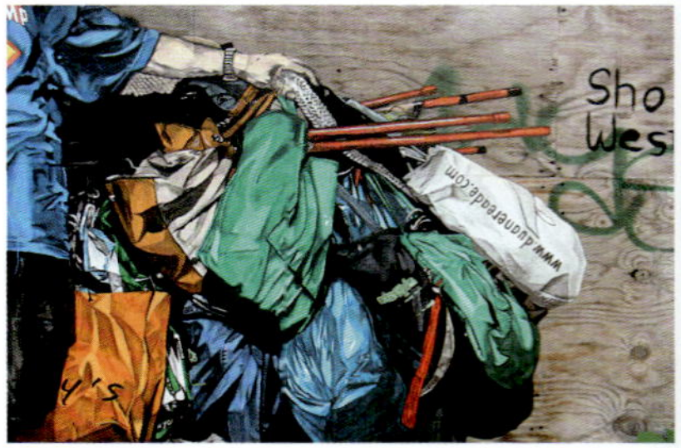

Photographs by Ray Mock.
Brooklyn, New York, 2009.

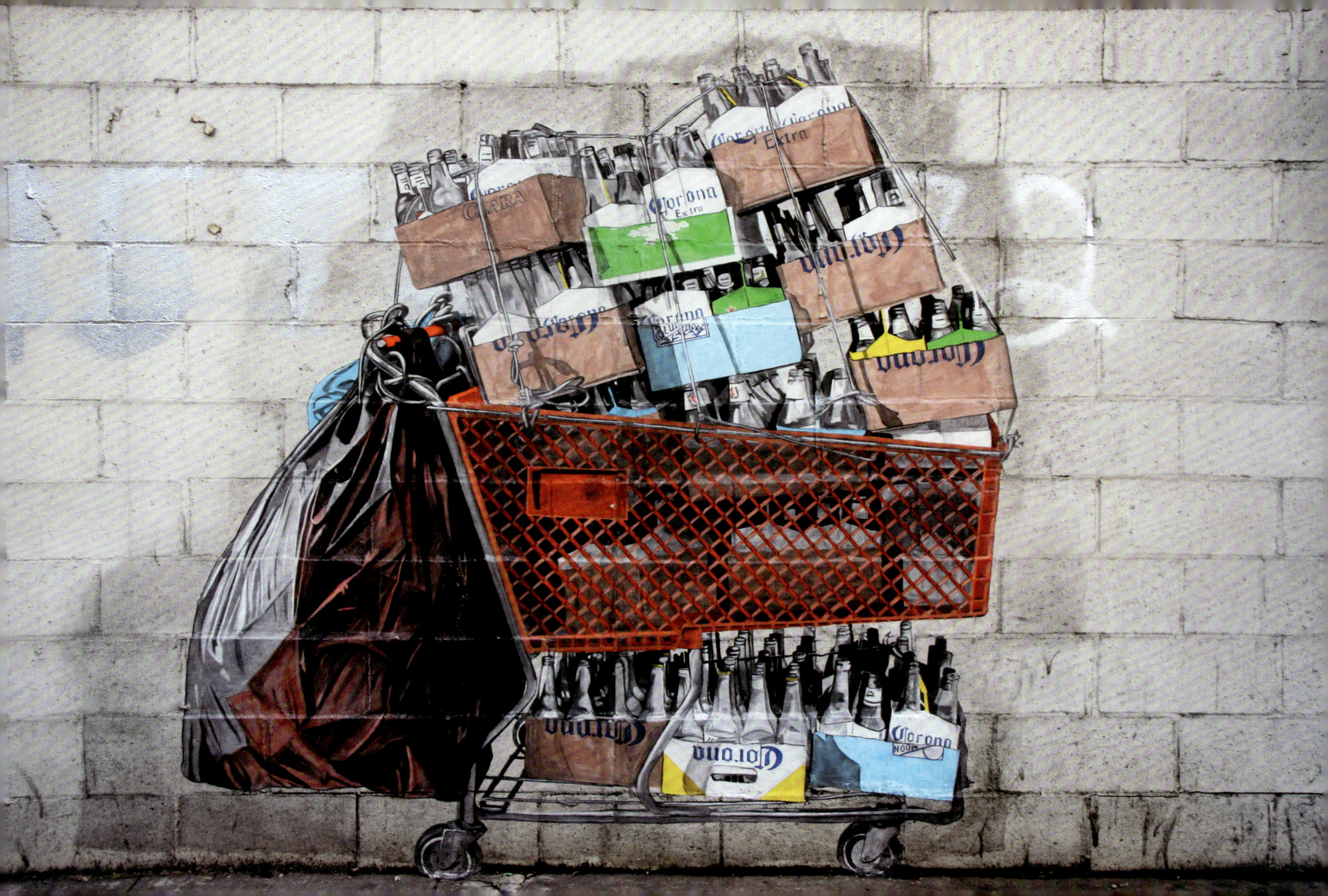
Corona
Extra
Corona
Extra
Corona

The Splasher

In 2006, one man mounted an all-out assault on the wave of public art cropping up in New York by throwing paint over prominent pieces by street-art superstars such as Shepard Fairey [see 124], Swoon [see 329], and WK. This antagonist threw splashes of brightly colored paint across several classic New York wall installations, especially on the Lower East Side, earning himself the nickname "The Splasher."

During the Wooster Collective's [see 359] seminal 2006 exhibition at 11 Spring Street [see 001], The Splasher took things a step further and created a manifesto, which he claimed to have glued to the walls of the building with wheatpaste mixed with glass, in order to make it difficult to remove without injury. In this ranting manifesto, The Splasher decried street art's catering to "the Bourgeoisie" and expressed a deep disdain for street artists taking their work into museums and other institutions. The community, outraged that someone would deface their beloved works of public art, mounted a manhunt for the person responsible, spear-headed by journalists at the popular website gawker.com. Eventually, a mountain of evidence pointed a finger at a young activist named Zac, allegedly a jilted fan of the artist Swoon who felt betrayed when she sold works to the Museum of Modern Art.

In summer 2007, the mystery took on new proportions when one man was arrested and another escaped while trying to set off a stink bomb at a heavily attended Shepard Fairey exhibition. The man arrested, James Cooper, was charged with third-degree arson and reckless endangerment. Days after his arrest, a sixteen-page manifesto was distributed at another Fairey opening, leading to the belief that The Splasher was actually a group of individuals. The case remains unresolved.

Photograph by Jake Dobkin (streetsy.com). Brooklyn, New York, 2007.

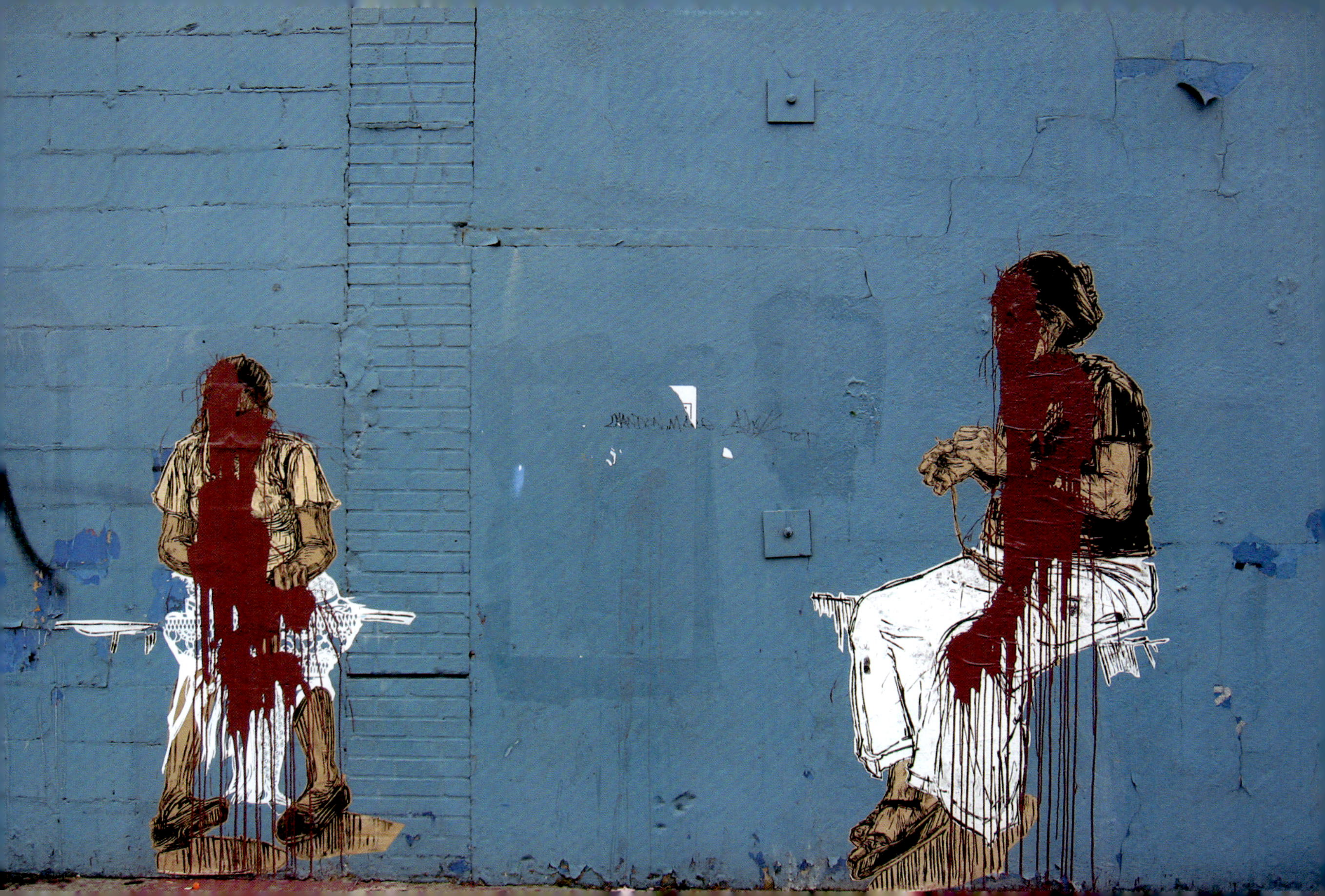

Spok

Spok took his name from Mister Spock on *Star Trek*, began writing in 1989 in Madrid, and quickly established himself as a train painter, hitting subways in many different countries. Over the next decade, he refined his technique to the point of hyperrealism, perhaps more so then any other writer. He could've banged his name out forever and been lumped in with the other great stylists of Europe, but a newer, more mature Spok began to emerge.

Spok's hyperreal paintings, more than those of any other writer in the history of the movement, are now viewed as fine-art murals. His mode is surrealism, and his paintings seem to take random objects and throw them up in the air, leaving to the viewer the challenge (and the fun) of wondering what it all means. There are no letters, nor are there high-gloss shiners or cartoon characters borrowed from pop culture. What is shown on the wall has been carefully composed in Photoshop, but there's always room for improvising on the spot (a graffiti artist's best tool).

If Spok's paintings have misled the viewer into believing that they can truly be called "fine art," then that opens up a whole new kettle of fish. Is Spok really a graffiti artist? Has he been mislabeled by the writing community, as well as the public at large, who seem to embrace his work? The answer is almost irrelevant; it's the dialogue he's opened simply by being himself, and in the end, that may be Spok's greatest legacy.

Photograph by Chris Beckett. London, 2008.

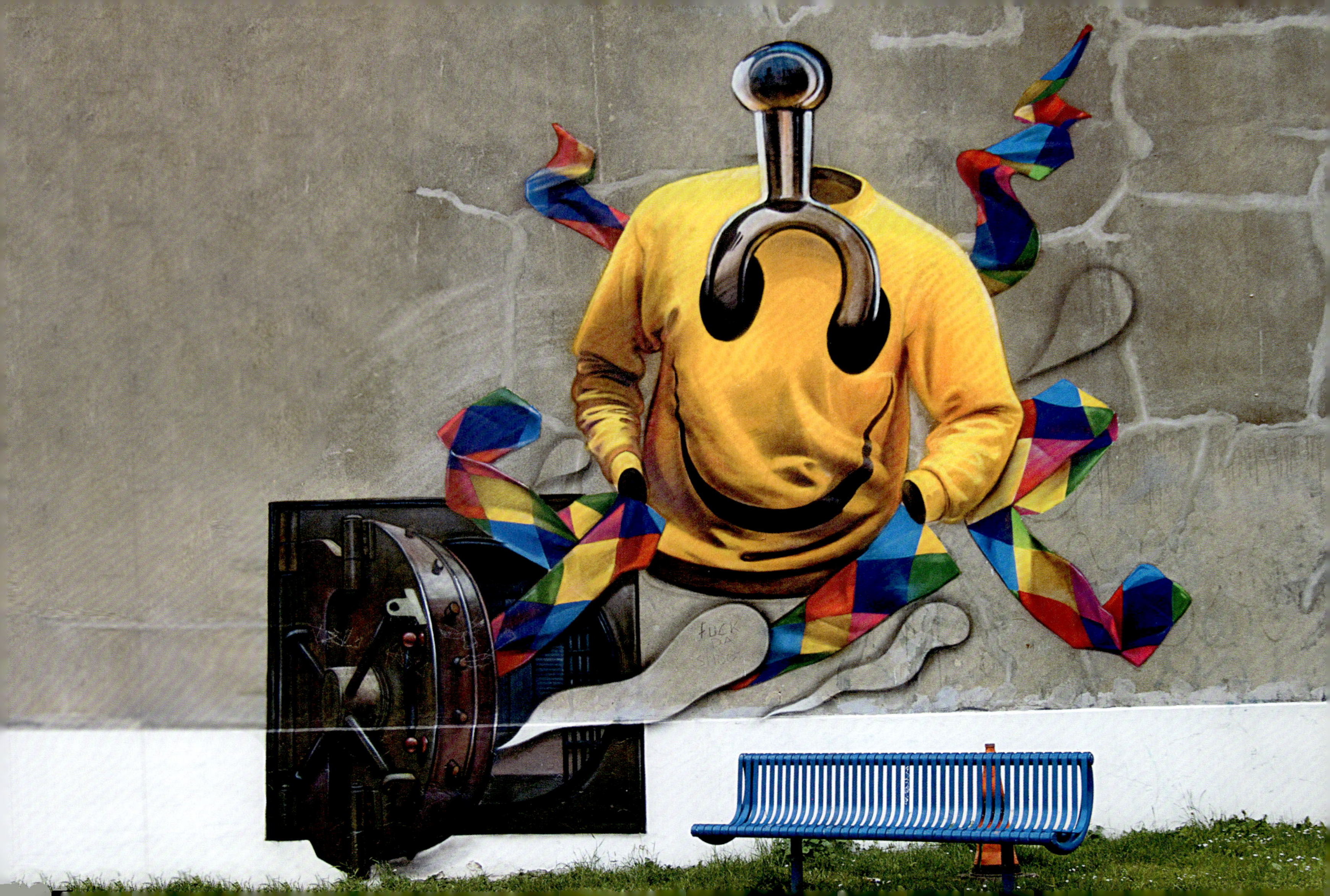

Chris Stain

Strongly motivated by a dissatisfaction with social injustices, Chris Stain creates detailed stencil pieces, both on and off the streets, that depict the world around him. Growing up in the rough-and-tumble streets of Baltimore, Maryland, a notoriously hard-knock city, Stain came face-to-face with vast poverty, racial prejudice, and improperly nurtured children, which gave him a lasting desire to change those things.

A contemporary of artists like Armsrock [see 017] and Logan Hicks [see 166], Stain has been a mainstay in the street-art community since the 1990s. He began painting in the mid-1980s, when he discovered hip-hop and traditional graffiti culture. In 1998, he began using stencils, and in 2000 he was offered his first solo show. Later in that decade, he began wheatpasting his work around New York City with legendary street-art queen Swoon [see 329], at which point he caught the eye of the mainstream. He is now the father of two, lives in Brooklyn with his family, and continues to support himself with his fine-art sales.

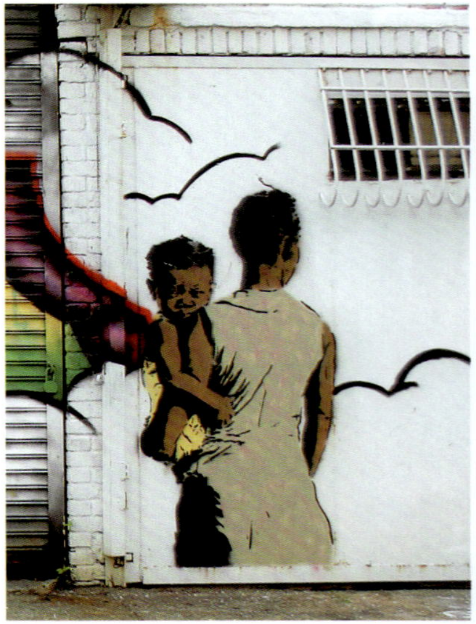

Photographs by Becki Fuller.
Brooklyn, New York, c. 2010.

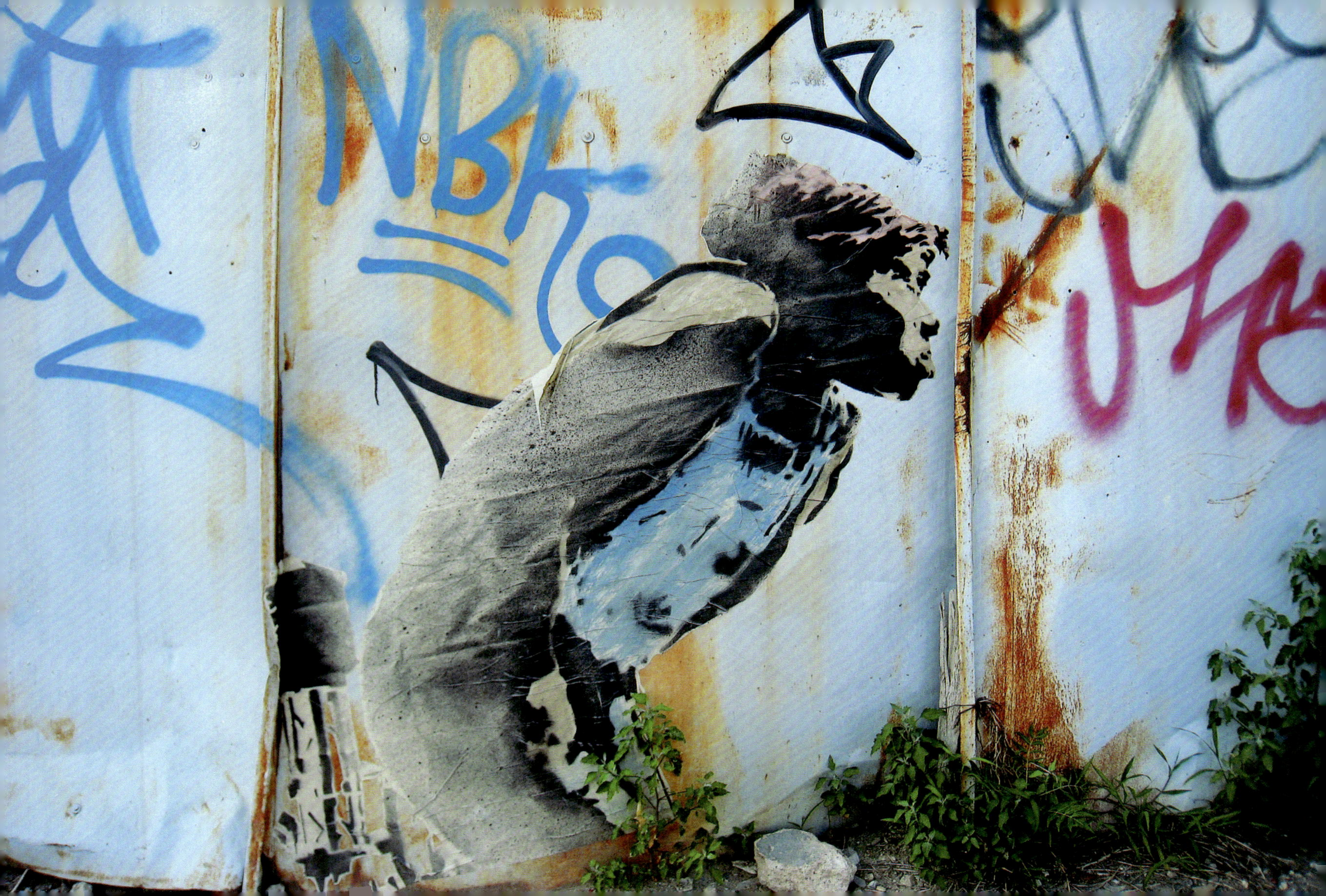

Stay High 149

In graffiti's early days, circa 1970–1973, most writers swore they'd retire after turning sixteen, when the system no longer considered them to be juveniles. But Stay High 149 started writing in 1970 when he was twenty—ancient by the culture's standard. He chose the perfect icon to complement his name: the halo-adorned stick figure from the television show *The Saint*—only Stay High's figure, aka The Smoker, was puffing a joint. With a handwriting that oozed fluidity and perfection, Stay High's tag became the most famous in the culture's history. Different versions of The Smoker appear in the works of today's graffiti and street artists, who are most likely oblivious of its origin.

Stay High, one of the first writers to garner mainstream media attention, found that his newfound celebrity status worked against him; by the end of 1973, Stay High had become *too* famous. Known to the police who despised his celebrity, he decided to change his name. The born-again king lengthened his name to Voice of the Ghetto. He would combine contrasting color inks within one marker tip, the resulting tags trumpeting his existence in rainbow splendor. After 1975, Stay High disappeared, becoming graff's greatest unsolved mystery. He reappeared at an art opening in 2000, and the love he received from the graff world was overwhelming. In 2010, The Smoker turned forty and Stay High, sixty!

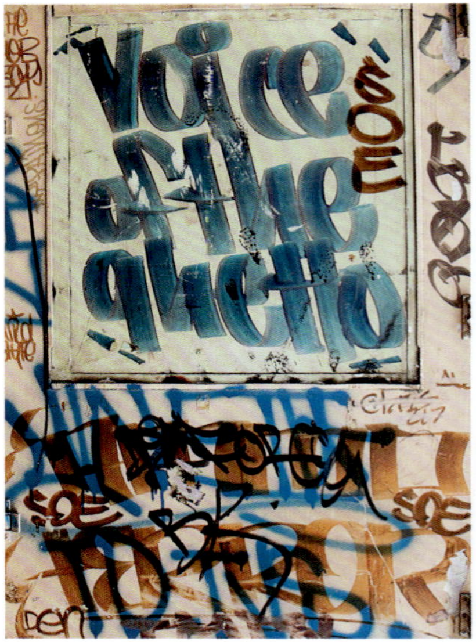

Photograph by Flint Gennari.
New York City, 1975.
Detail: Private collection.
New York City, 2011.

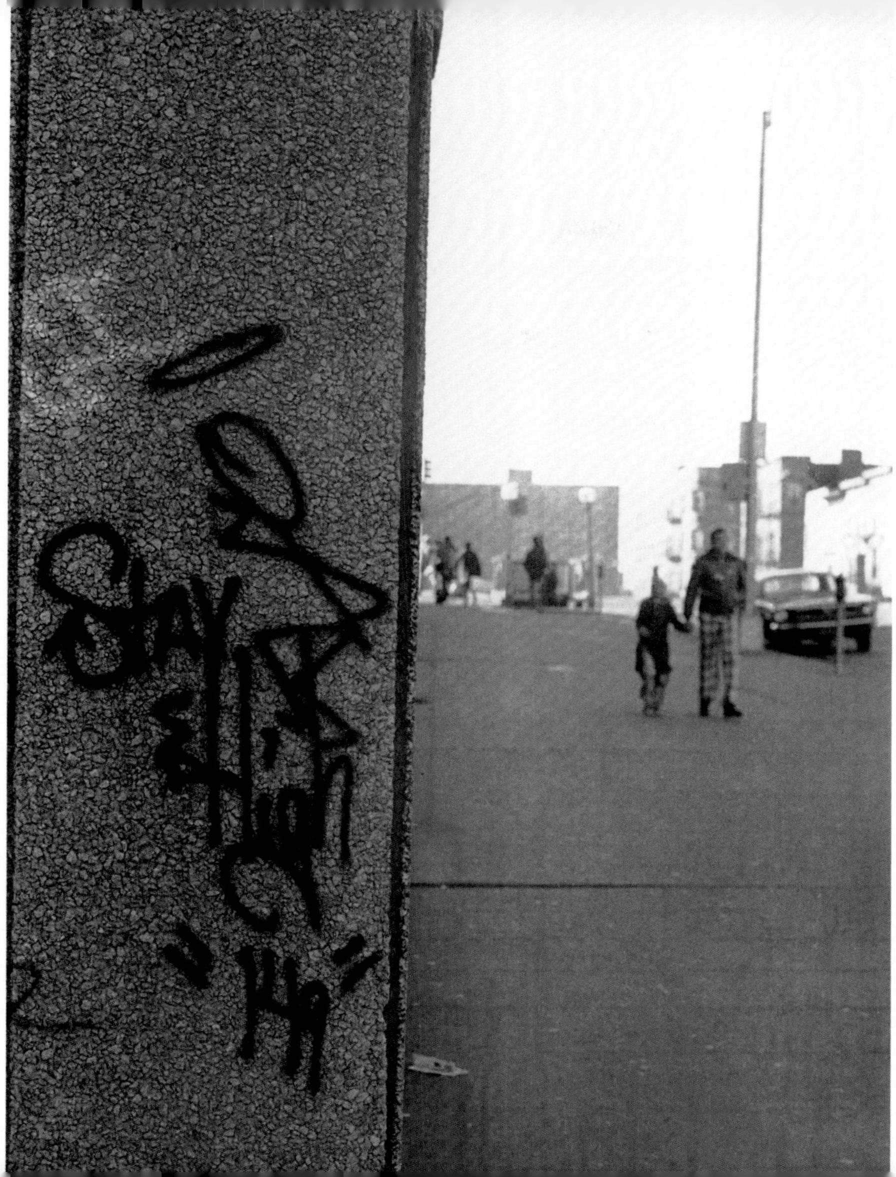
STAY
High
"149"

Sten and Lex

Sten (short for "stencil") and Lex (meaning "law") are two of Europe's most beloved stencil artists. They have been creating art together since 2002, when they met as university students. Working mostly in black-and-white, Sten and Lex create stylish, humorous portraits of popular cultural, religious, and political figures—from van Gogh to the pope to Eisenhower.

Without any formal art background, Sten and Lex devised a unique art form, consisting of a series of stencils with many holes of different sizes that together provide a distinctly photographic image. Also making use of superimposed lines, they print their stencils on lightweight paper that they paste onto the walls of the city. These large pieces have come to be known as "stencil posters." Among their inspirations is the late Italian painter Mimmo Rotella, best known for his works of collage and décollage, and work made from torn advertising posters.

The first artists to be considered stencil-graffiti artists in Italy, they have exhibited their work throughout the world, on city walls, in galleries, and in various other indoor and outdoor venues. They were among the select group of stencil artists invited by Banksy (see 024) to participate in the 2008 Cans Festival (see 056) in London.

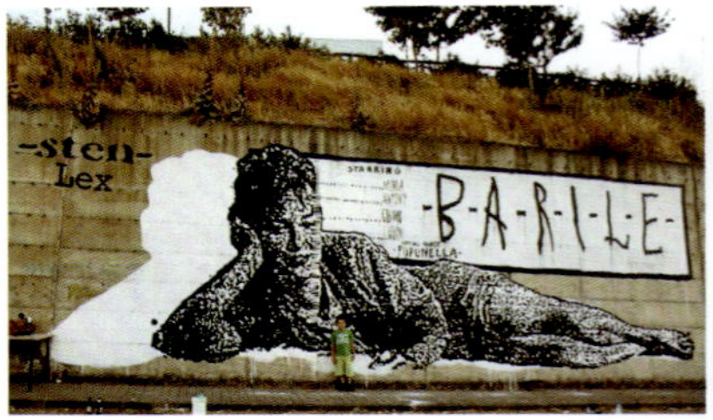

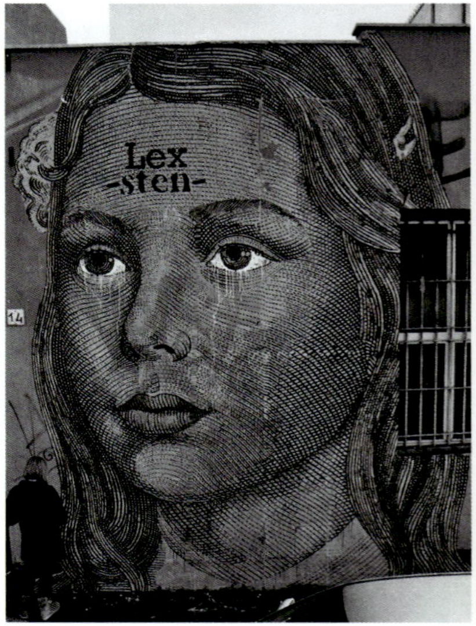

Photographs courtesy of Sten and Lex. Italy, 2009

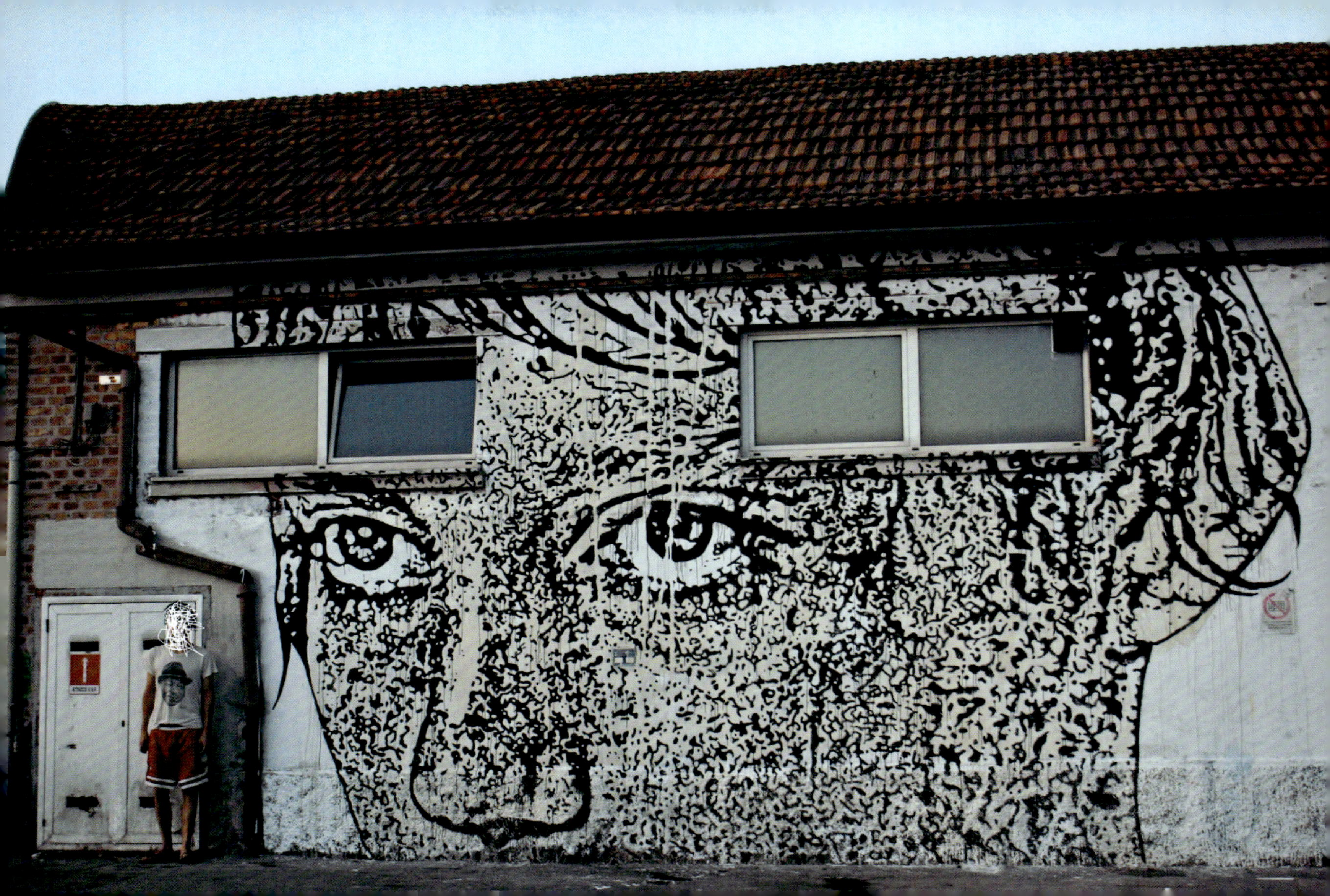

Jack Stewart

In the early 1970s, the artist Jack Stewart roamed the subway stations of the Bronx with a wild bunch of rebellious teenagers who were pioneering a groundbreaking art movement on the insides and outsides of New York City's subway system. Stewart and his 35 mm lens were there to capture a new art form, mass-transit art, where tags quickly evolved into bubble letters, drop shadows, clouds, and cartoon characters. During the course of his travels, Stewart met Bama, Billy 167 [see 034], Blade [see 037], Chi Chi 133, Cliff 159 [see 070], FDT56, Phase 2 [see 255], Taki 183 [see 331], Tracy 168 [see 340], Wasp 1, Wicked Gary, and other legends of the period. He would invite them to his East Village studio, where he would project slides of his photographs, conduct interviews, and lead salon-style critiques of the artists' works. He published approximately 300 of his 2,000 photos as part of his PhD dissertation, "Mass Transit Art: Subway Graffiti," in 1989.

In his dissertation, Stewart's photographs appeared only in black-and-white. Much of his photography, however, can be found in full color in the pages of *Graffiti Kings: New York City Mass Transit Art of the 1970s*, which serves as an invaluable record of the art created between the eras documented in *The Faith of Graffiti* [1974; see 126] and *Subway Art* [1984]. Stewart received a BFA from Yale University, where he studied with Josef Albers and Willem de Kooning. He later served as professor of art at NYU, Columbia University School of the Arts, and Queens College; he was also as chairman of the art departments of both Cooper Union and Indiana State University, as well as vice president and provost of the art department at the Rhode Island School of Design.

Photograph by Martha Cooper. New York City, 2002.

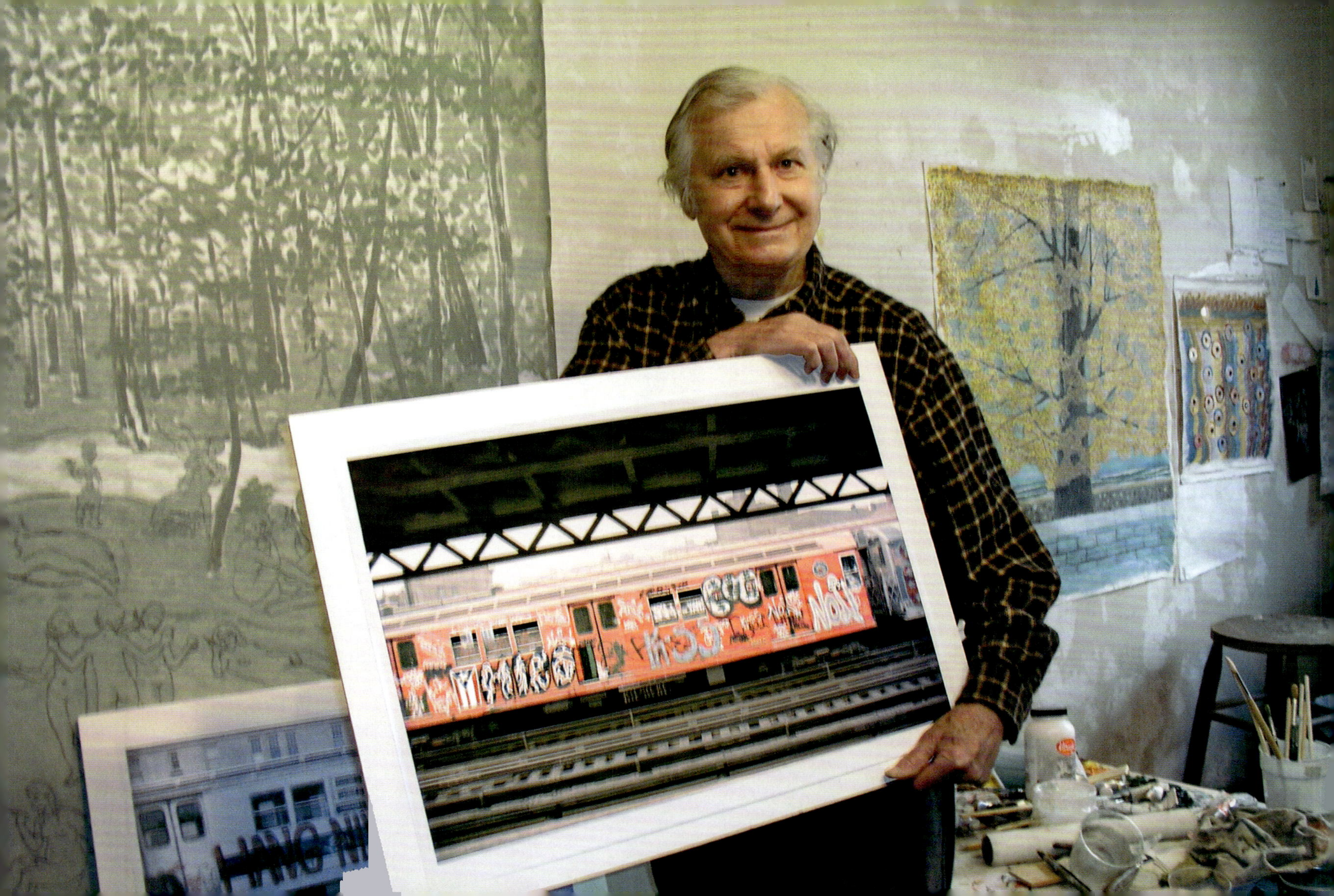

sticker show

The world's first exhibition of graffiti stickers was presented in 1988 by Manhattan's Franklin Furnace gallery. By the early 1980s, many New Yorkers had tired of subway cars covered from top to bottom in spray paint, and the city began implementing ever-stronger anti-graffiti policies. Police surveillance was increased, and train yards were secured with electrified barbed-wire fencing. As an alternative to increasingly dangerous subway spray-painting, some graffiti writers took to tagging commercially produced adhesive labels. This enabled them to take as much time as they wanted to design stickers in private before quickly and safely slapping them up in the public eye.

Over three thousand stickers peeled from the streets of New York—covering topics including music (Bring the Noise), sex (Vin: Suck My Nuts), drugs (Crazy Jose—Crack It Up), fashion (Sportin' Fly Gear), and politics (Dose Ronnie)—drew throngs of graffiti writers and curious fans to the Tribeca museum. Here, they were able to see the earliest stickers by the Talent Rascals and the X-Men; the colorful, fun, and intelligent work of art school–trained writers like Green Cheese Man; and hundreds of "Hello! My Name Is . . ." labels that had been repurposed by the prolific Cost. A new art form was launched, inspiring a *Wall Street Journal* article headlined "One Thing's for Certain: Better in a Museum Than on the Subway."

Photograph by Harley Spiller. New York City, 1988.

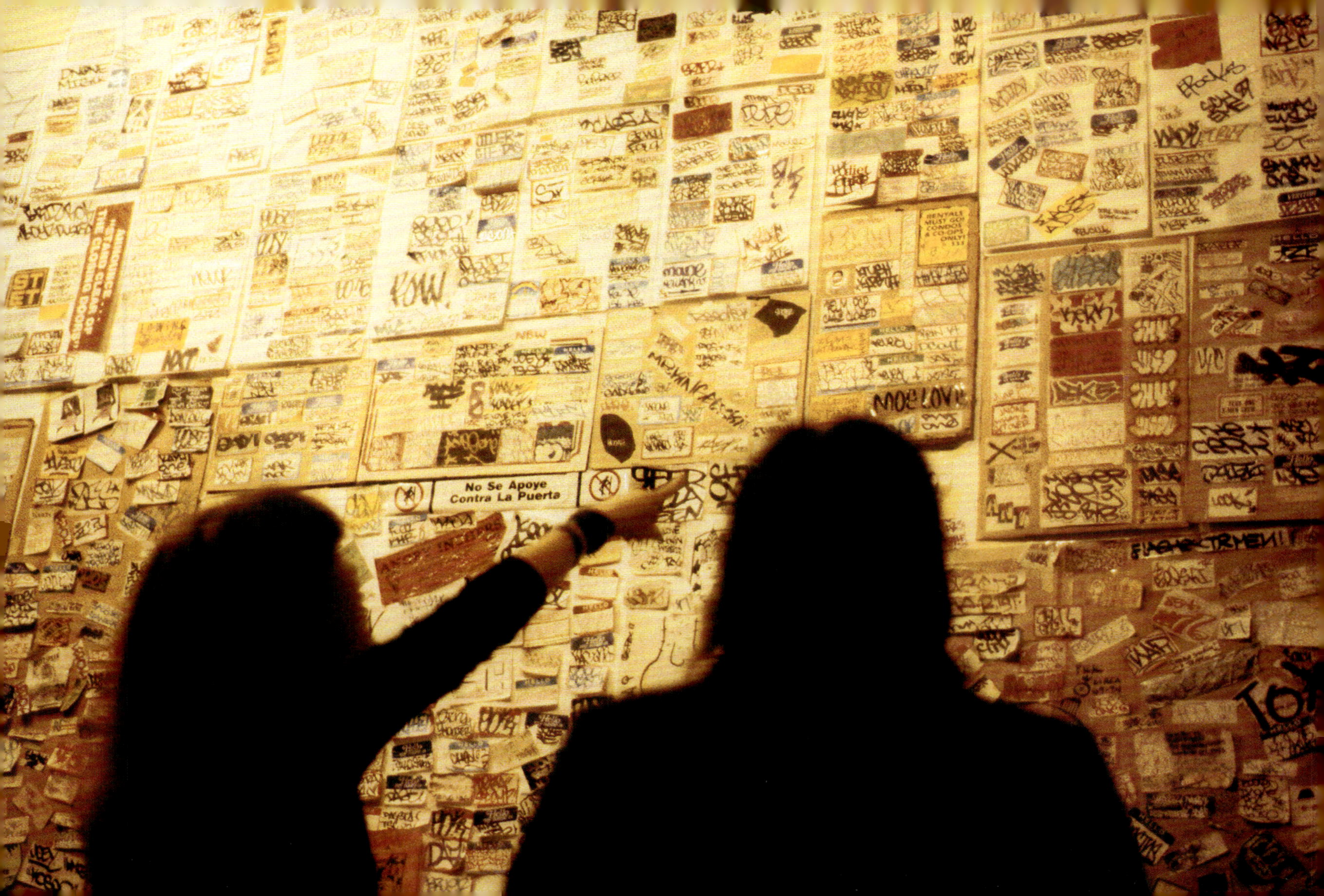
No Se Apoye
Contra La Puerta

320

Stikman

As the movement known as street art exploded in popularity, it became increasingly difficult to call to mind an urban artist who actually remained anonymous. One rare instance was the elusive Banksy [see 024], who engendered hysteria whenever his stencils popped up because no one could pin an identity on him; at one point, national newspapers ran stories when someone claimed a Banksy sighting in Jamaica.

Another rare example of sustained secrecy is the mysterious artist known as Stikman. He caught the eye of many a city dweller at the turn of the new century with his tiny stick-figure men, sometimes crafted from wood and attached to walls and objects, but more often fashioned from brightly colored plastic adhesive of some kind and stuck onto the ground at crosswalks. The stick figures were everywhere in East Coast cities, but despite repeated attempts to locate the artist—including in public forums such as the Wooster Collective [see 359] website—he never revealed himself.

Numerous newspapers and blogs mounted headhunts; they were determined to out Stikman and attributed their curiosity to an abundance of public interest. A few reporters succeeded in reaching a man who claimed responsibility for the Stikman campaign; he refused to offer a real name, choosing to be referred to as "Bob." Bob claimed that he had traveled the East Coast extensively, proliferating the stick figures, and that he was so conscious of the safety of his viewers that he placed his figures close to the curb so pedestrians didn't have to step into the street.

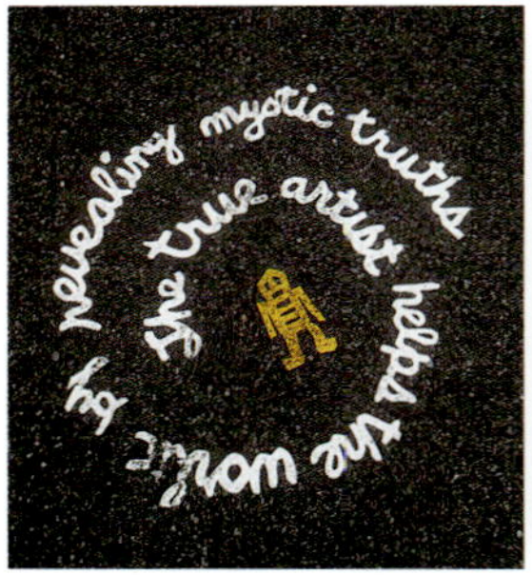

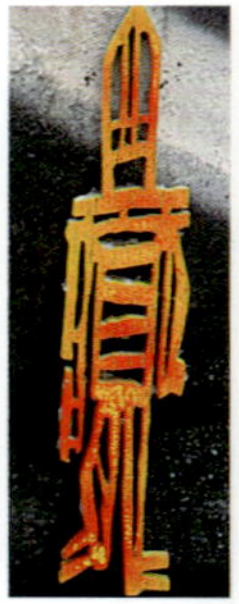

Photograph by Martha Cooper.
New York City, 2010.
Detail left: Photograph by Jake Dobkin [streetsy.com].
New York City, 2009.
Detail right: Photograph by Vincent Cornelli.
New York City, 2007.

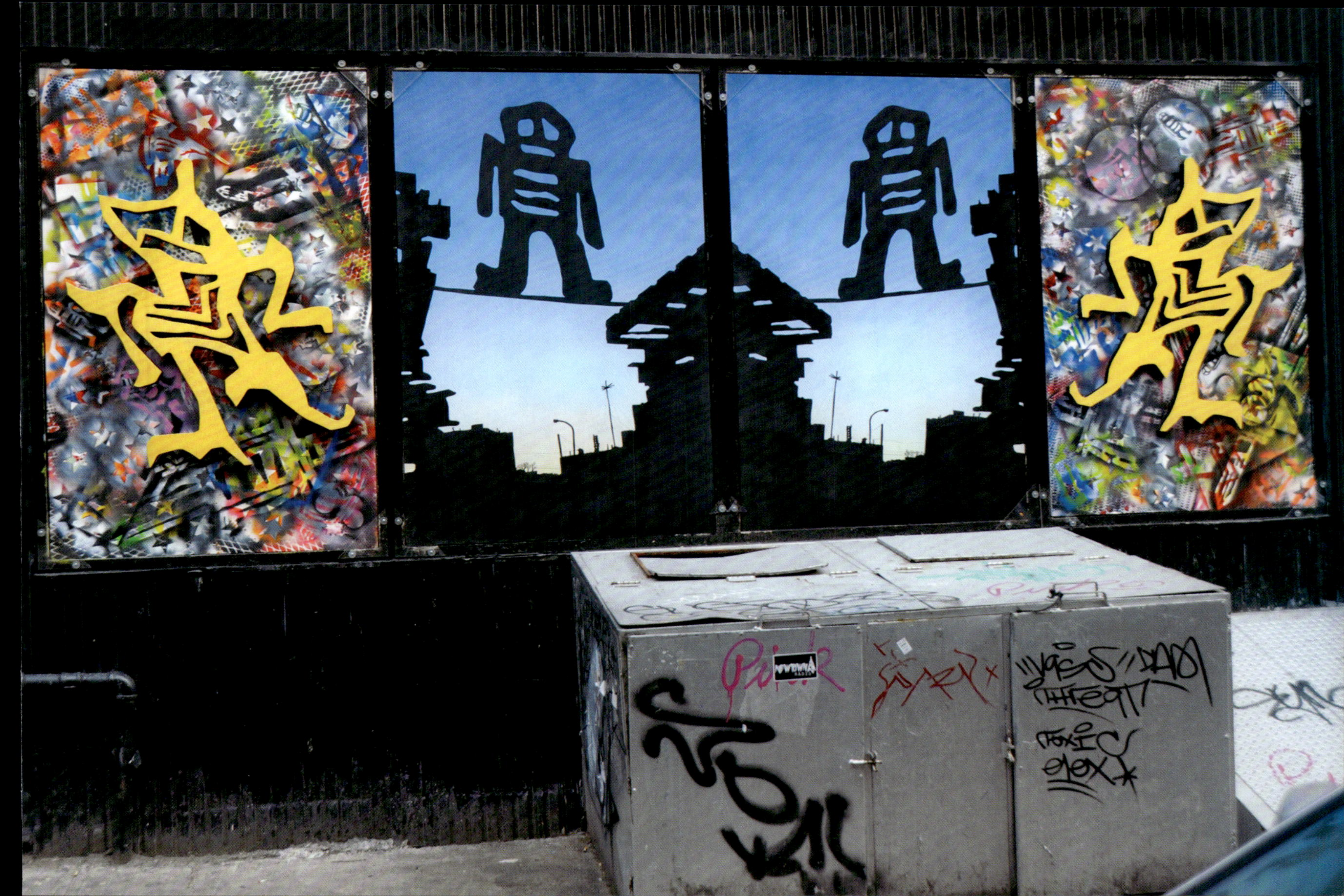

Stinkfish

Born in Mexico City, Stinkfish is now based in Bogotá, Colombia, where he has become a local legend. Characterized by vibrant colors and pulsating rhythms, Stinkfish's stylish murals are informed by pre-Columbian indigenous art, abstract expressionism, and contemporary graffiti.

Whether he's meandering through alleyways or painting on walls, Stinkfish feels most at home on the streets. He loves the diversity of the people he meets and the sense of freedom that the streets stir within him. Their energy spurs him to create images that he enjoys sharing with other passersby. He perceives street art as an antidote to the crass commercial billboards that bombard us daily.

Stinkfish has collaborated with countless artists and has partnered with Bastardilla for many projects and events. Like Bastardilla, he is particularly drawn to the gritty walls of a city's most forbidding streets. He has participated in artists' residence programs in Oaxaca, Mexico City, and Guatemala, and has organized exhibits including "Memoria Canalla," the acclaimed 2009 urban-art retrospective at the Museum of Bogotá. His artwork has been featured in galleries in the United States and in Spain, as well as in Central and South America.

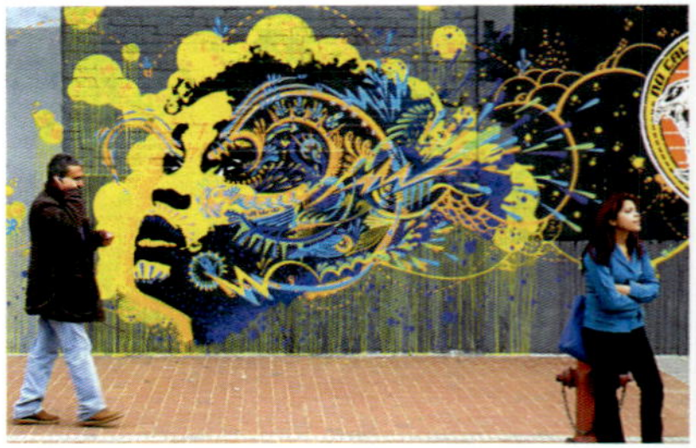

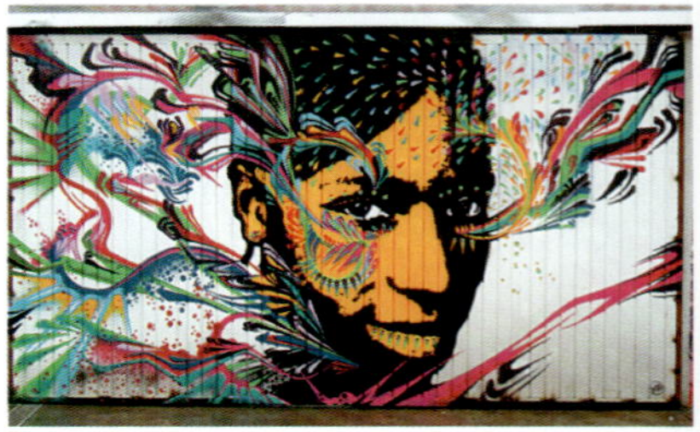

Photographs courtesy of Stinkfish.
Oaxaca, Mexico, 2010.
Detail top: Bogotá, Colombia, 2010.
Detail bottom: Mexico City, Mexico, 2010.

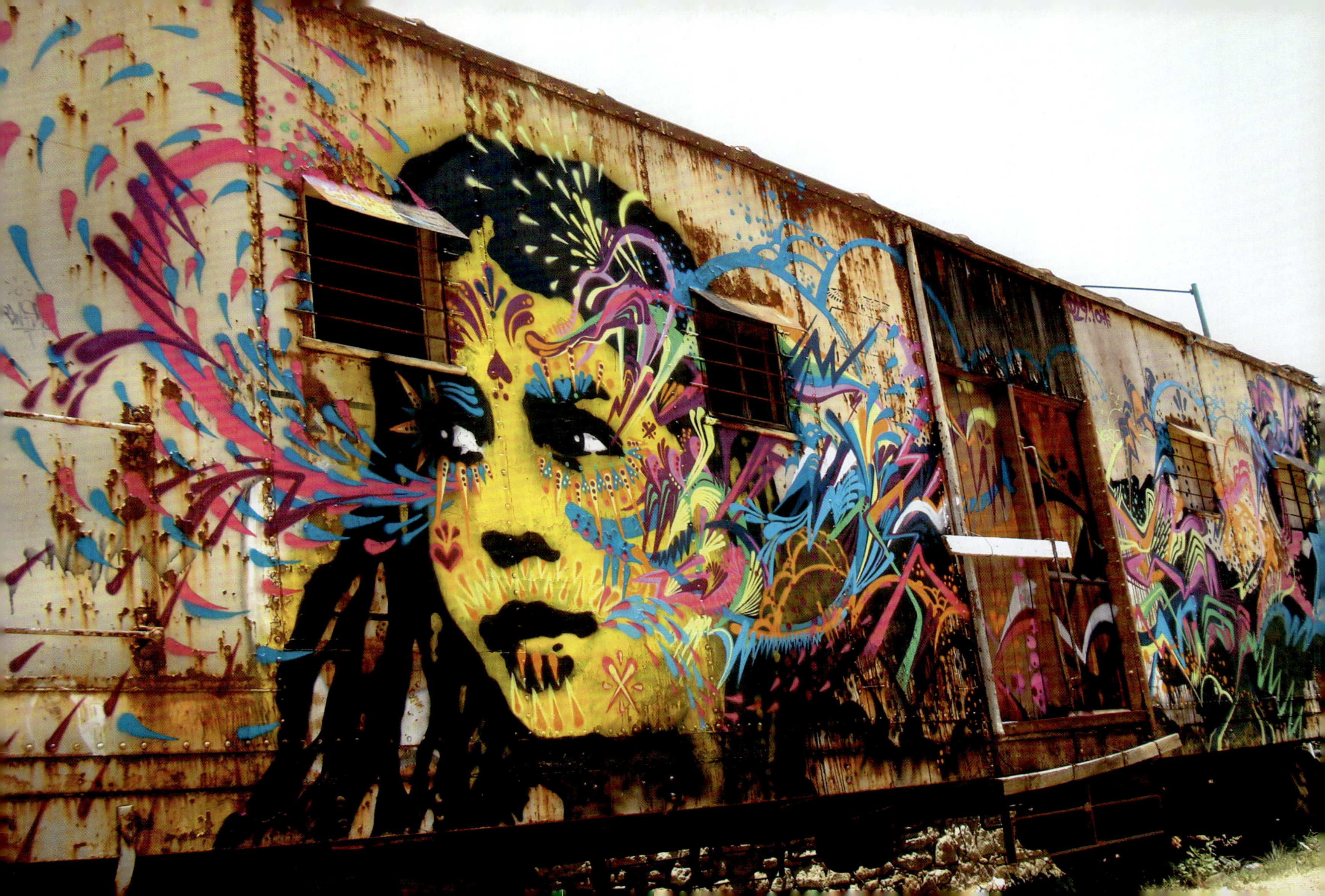

Style Wars

The 1982 film *Style Wars*, directed by Tony Silver and produced by legendary graffiti documentarian Henry Chalfant [see 064], is a seminal record of a pivotal moment in graffiti history. Chalfant had established close ties with many of New York's graffiti artists through photographing their paintings on the city's subways, and the relationships he built with them allowed him unprecedented access to what was, at the time, a largely clandestine world.

While the film also takes a look at breakdancing and rap music, *Style Wars* primarily focuses on the world of graffiti and its now legendary artists, such as Seen [see 294], Dondi [see 097], Zephyr [see 363], Kase 2, and Cap One Da Bronx [see 057]. Memorable footage includes Mayor Ed Koch [see 197] boasting, with an insidious grin, of having installed razor-ribboned fences and guard dogs around train yards. The argument between Skeme [see 304] and his mother over the pros and cons of graffiti became a classic scene, universally identifiable to all writers and their parents. The sequences featuring the Rock Steady Crew battling the Dynamic Rockers to the sounds of the late Rammellzee's [see 269] rapping brought breakdancing to worldwide attention.

Through Silver and Chalfant's film, it became clear for the first time how ethnically diverse the subculture of graffiti actually was. Awarded the Grand Prize for Documentaries at the 1983 Sundance Film Festival, *Style Wars* was one of the first truly intimate glimpses into hip-hop and graffiti culture.

Henry Chalfant [second from left].
Whole car artwork by Seen UA [left] and J.SON.
Photograph by Martha Cooper.
New York City, 1983.

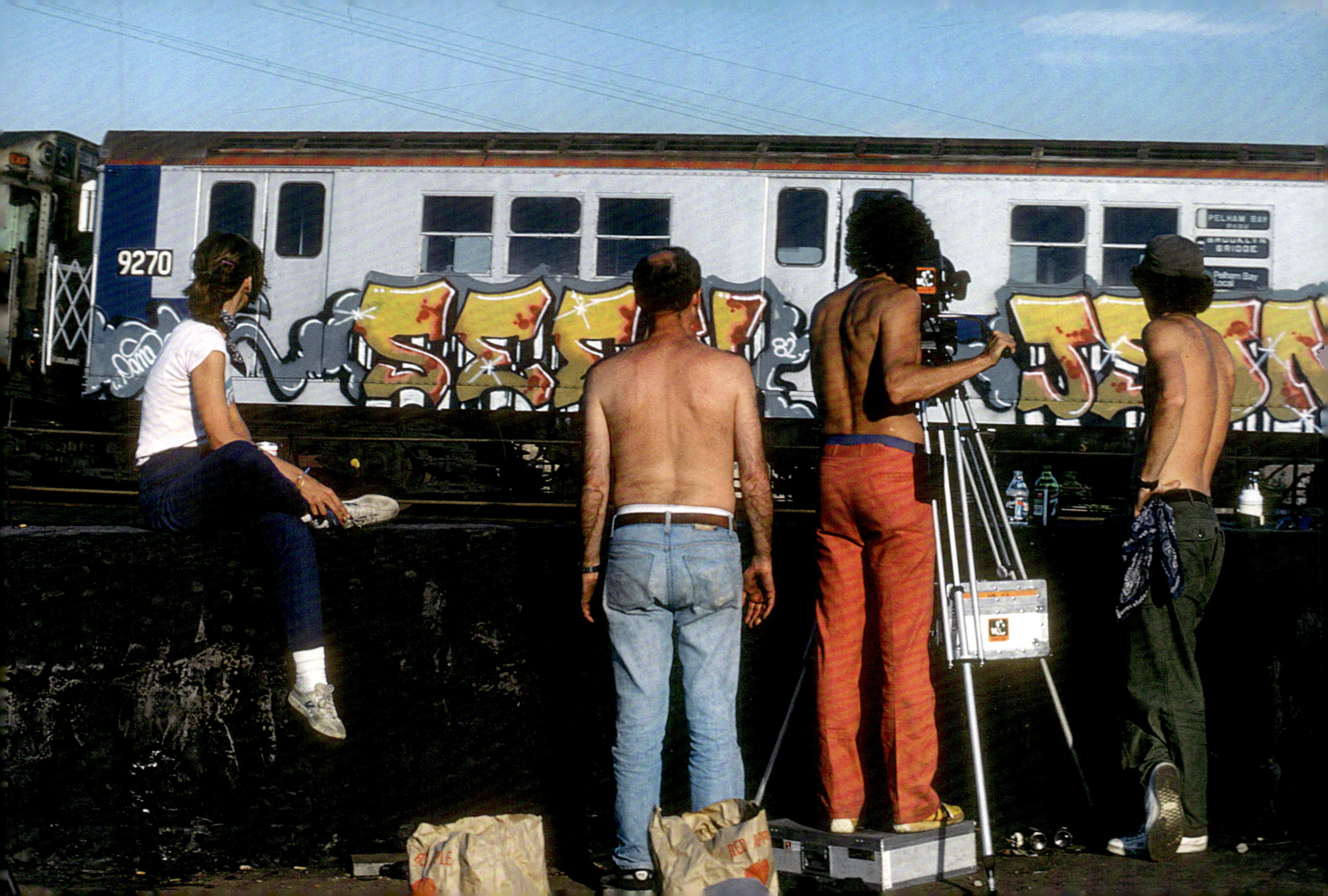
9270
PELHAM BAY
BROOKLYN BRIDGE

Subway Art

In the age before digital photography and the Internet, most graffiti pieces, painstakingly created over many hours, were buffed, gone over, or crossed out before a single pair of eyes had seen them. Artists were often too busy running from the police or putting final touches on a train car before it rolled out of the yard to worry about snapping a photo. So when photographers Henry Chalfant (see 064) and Martha Cooper (see 073) began to capture the colorful pieces exploding out of the city's tunnels, it was a welcome sign of graffiti's cultural significance.

In 1984, the two photographers released a book called *Subway Art*, one of the first comprehensive documents of the extremely influential culture of New York City graffiti. A simple book featuring page after page of full-color imagery, *Subway Art* showed a young Dondi White in action, early Seen pieces, and Lee's epic whole-car messages. *Subway Art* also introduced characters and tag styles that would become standard-bearers for the global spread of the art form. *Subway Art* is often referred to by many graffiti artists as The Bible; this book allowed a worldwide audience to discover and fall in love with graffiti, thus spawning new generations of mass-transit art in formerly uncharted territories.

In 2009, Chalfant and Cooper, who still obsessively document graffiti, released a twenty-fifth-anniversary edition of *Subway Art* to a new audience, twenty years after the last painted subway cars ran through New York City.

Henry Chalfant (left) and Martha Cooper.
Photograph by Akim Walta.
New York City, 2005.

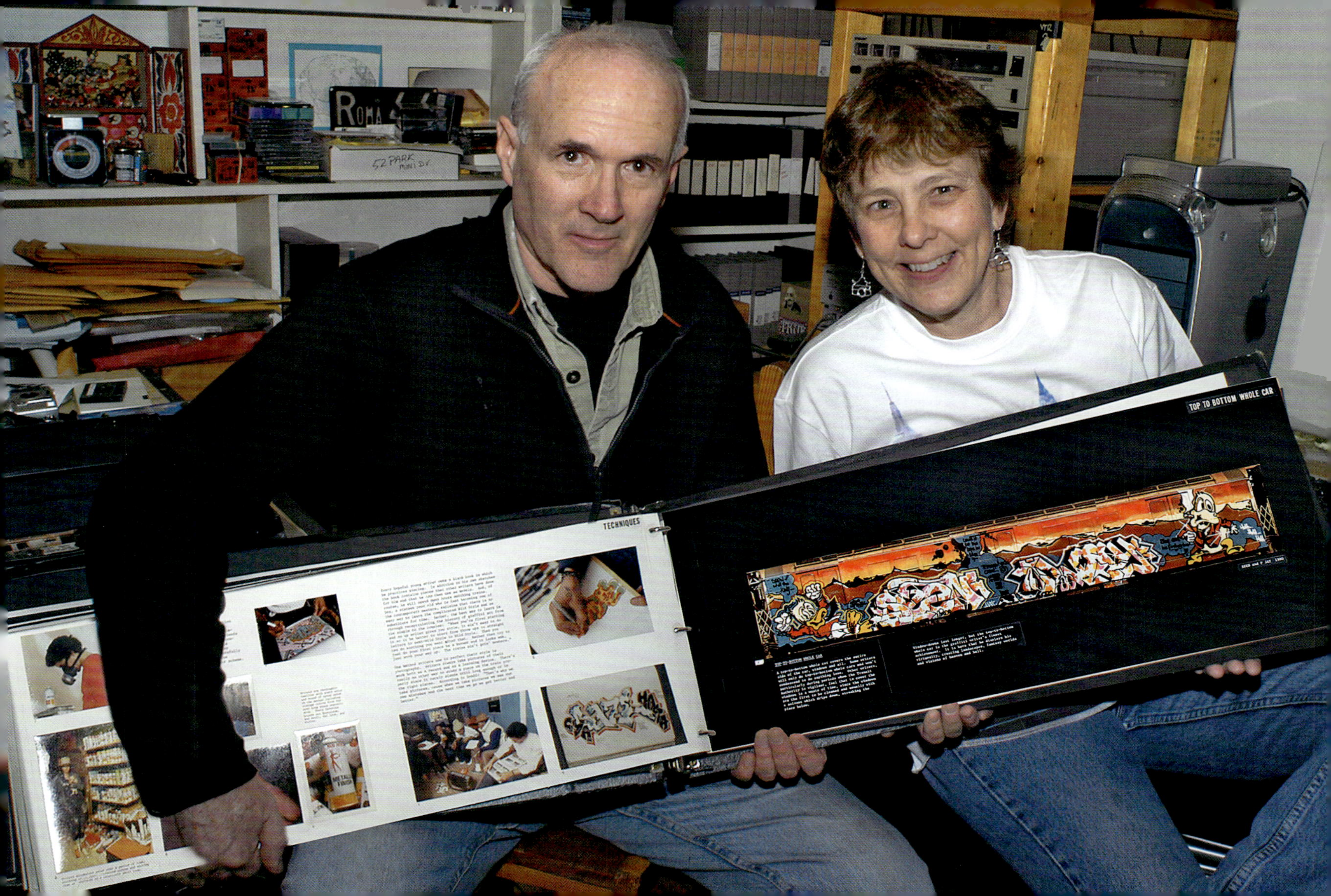
ROMA
52 PARK
TECHNIQUES
TOP TO BOTTOM WHOLE CAR

Supakitch and Koralie

Born in Paris in 1978, the artist known as Supakitch was raised on 1980s and early 1990s hip-hop culture. In 1990, he first dabbled in graffiti, and by 1994 the art form became a mainstay in his life. A unique influence colored his creative style: Japanese design culture, with manga in particular. An avowed capitalist, Supakitch never ascribed to the hard-core street world that rejected commercial art, and he began as an art director for advertising agencies at the tender age of twenty-one.

In the late 1990s, he met fellow street artist and his future wife, Koralie, while painting at a graffiti festival, and she encouraged him to exhibit his work in galleries, a practice he began in 2000. Later in that decade, as the street-art movement began to take hold, Supakitch discovered that he was not alone in his looser definition of what constituted graffiti, and he began to collaborate with other artists who utilized not just spray paint, but also brushes, pens, and collage.

Now the parents of two children, Supakitch and Koralie have founded their own line of clothing called Metroplastique. Supakitch has also dabbled in vinyl-toy design and has done extensive work as a graphic designer. In his fine art, Supakitch has branched into sculpture and installation, and he has exhibited worldwide. Supakitch and Koralie are now based in Brooklyn.

Photographs courtesy of Supakitch and Koralie.
Right: New York City, 2007.
Far right: Rome, Italy, 2008.

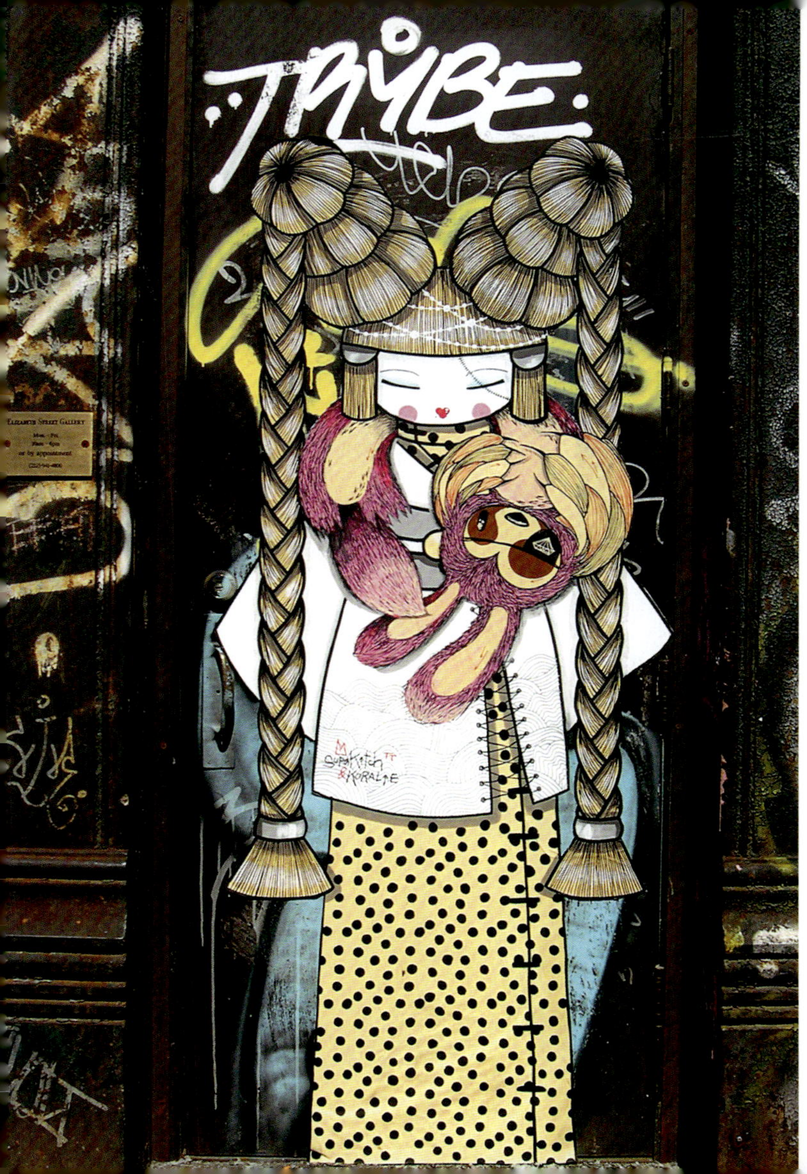

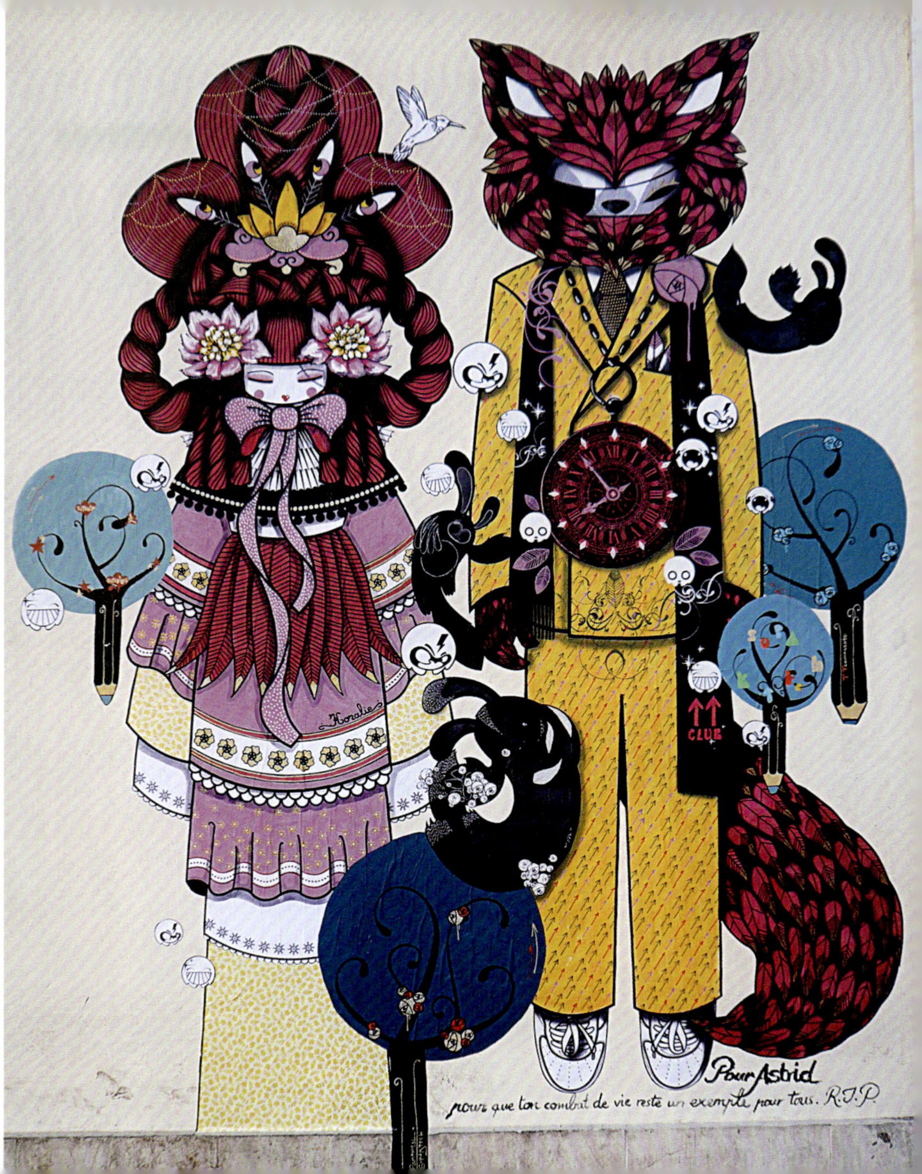
Koralie
Pour Astrid
pour que ton combat de vie reste un exemple pour tous. R.I.P.

Superkool 223

Superkool 223 is one of the earliest writers to emerge from the Bronx scene. He started writing in 1971, tagging the insides of trains for hours a day with his girlfriend acting as a lookout. In 1972, he did a tag with a wide-tipped marker that so intrigued Stay High 149 [see 316] that Stay High went to the tagger's house to find out what it was. Superkool could not have been more accommodating, and he introduced Stay High to the Uni-Wide marker that would become his trademark.

In 1972, two types of pieces began to appear on the sides of trains: signature pieces, in which an artist would outline his name, and stick-letter pieces, which resembled thick straight-letter tags. In another graffiti innovation, Superkool 223 took the nozzle off of a can of industrial cleanser and painted his name as large and bubbly as possible. This was considered a turning point in the movement. The mainstay of graffiti at that point had been the tag, and a lot of writers didn't like where this was headed. What was the point of wasting so much paint on one train when you could get twenty hits from the same can?

As the debate raged, Superkool 223 continued to do his pieces, and his fame grew to legendary proportions, especially as a whole generation of taggers quit writing. By 1973, the tag and the piece had equal relevance; however, it was not enough to just be a tagger—piecing had to be in your arsenal. In an ironic twist, Superkool himself was done in by another innovation; as stylized pieces became the heart and soul of the movement, Superkool's pieces were considered anachronistic, and by 1974 the father of the masterpiece had retired.

Piece by Superkool 223, with original Dr. Sex I tag.
Photograph by Jack Stewart.
New York City, c. 1972.

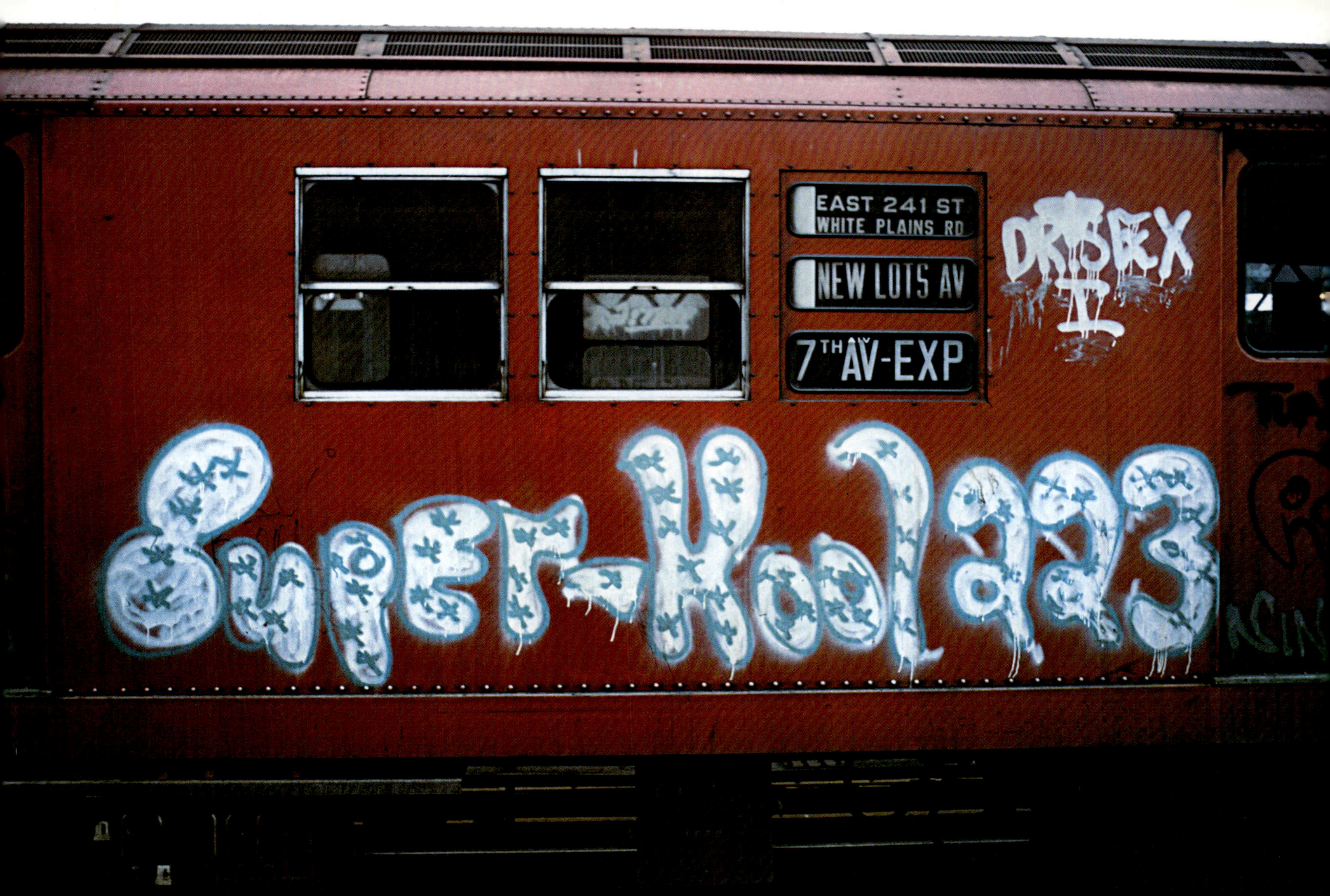
EAST 241 ST
WHITE PLAINS RD
NEW LOTS AV
7TH AV-EXP

Judith Supine

Ever the prankster, the artist known as Judith Supine made waves in the street-art community in the early years of the new millennium, including one stunning bomb of the United States Army recruitment center smack in the middle of New York City's bustling Times Square. In a video posted on the web, Supine is seen nonchalantly approaching the building and wheatpasting his image, which includes a blood-spattered Condoleezza Rice, straight onto the front window, in broad daylight.

Under the moniker he lifted from his own mother, Supine creates intricate collage work. As can be seen in another web video, he Dumpster-dives for his source material, scavenging images from everything from fashion magazines to classical painting catalogs, which he cuts out, pastes together, photocopies, enlarges, and paints in bright colors, creating psychedelic mash-ups of body parts that he then glues to walls.

Supine's largest work to date is a fifty-foot-tall collage hanging from the Manhattan Bridge; the image was of a fluorescent green man with bright pink lips. Photos of the installation of the piece show the artist brazenly dumping it over the side of a walkway at high noon.

Eventually making the inevitable crossover to canvas, Supine is now represented by New Image Art Gallery in Los Angeles and has exhibited internationally.

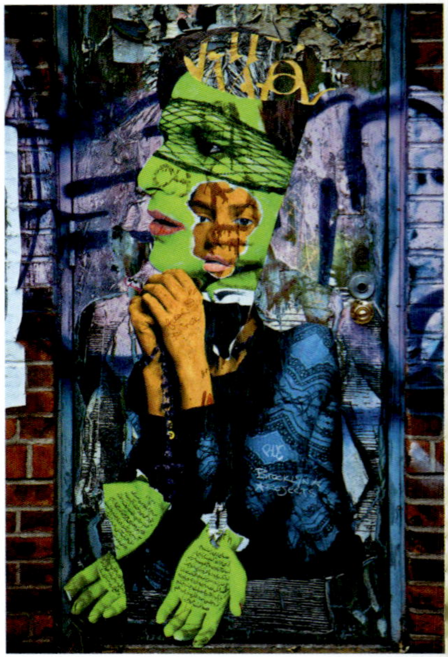

Photograph by Luna Park.
New York City, 2009.
Detail: Photograph by Vincent Cornelli.
Brooklyn, New York, 2007.

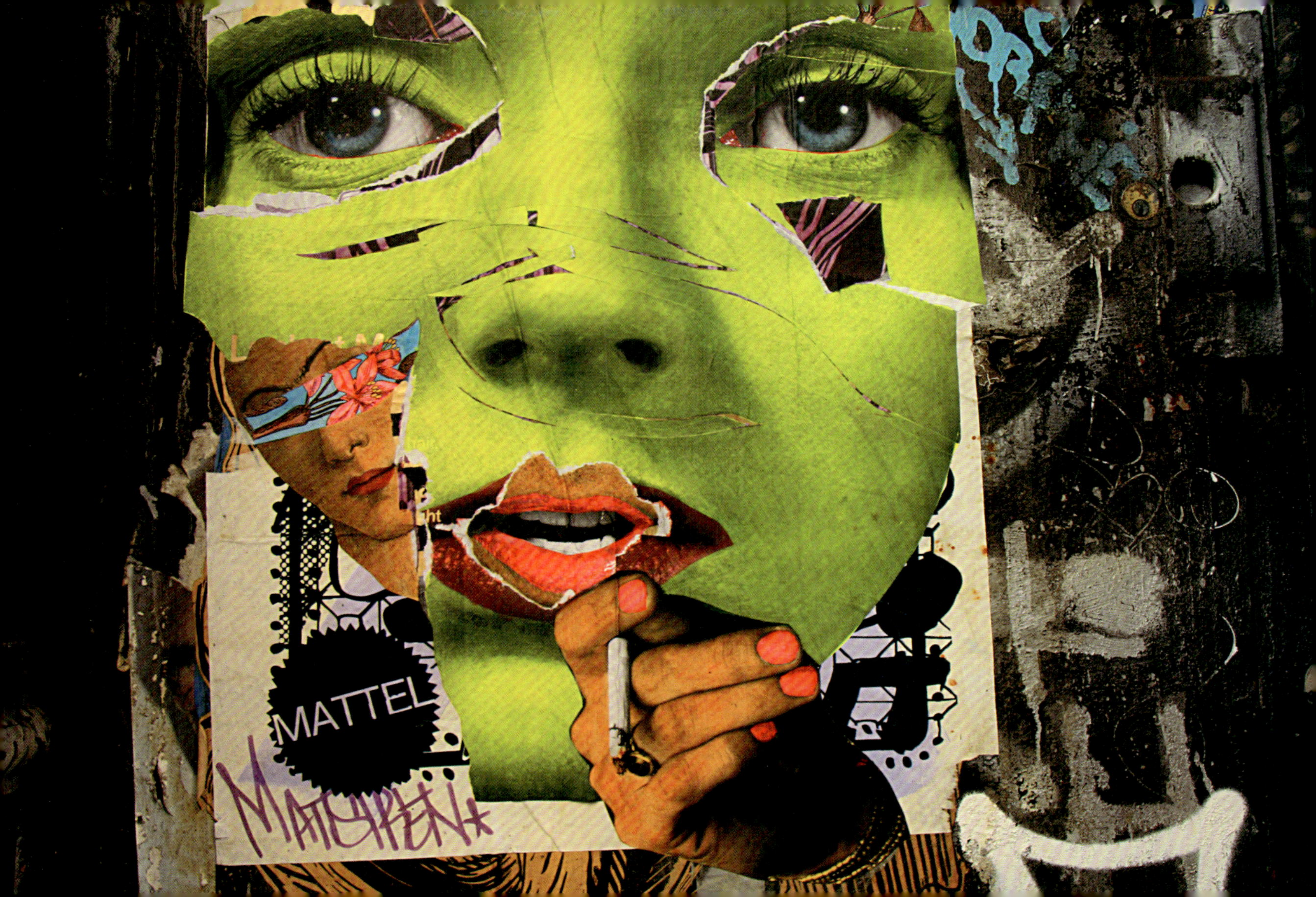
MATTEL

Swanski

Polish artist Swanski's story parallels that of many American artists: His love of skateboarding mixed with his love of art to yield a public art in motion, as well as a lifestyle that informs his creative practice. One of the most prolific artists in Europe, Swanksi has spread his trade on decks, prints, and album sleeves, via his own clothing line, and on walls—wherever he finds them.

His slogan, "Enthusiasm not Escapism," is a direct call to create one's own visual language and share it. The message implies a desire to rewrite the world and tweak the shape of things, and that is something that Swanski has done very well. His distinct illustrative style is recognizable, but his subject matter seems to change shape constantly.

During the past few months, Swanski has collaborated with a series of international stars like James Jarvis, Jeremy Fish, and Will Barras, as his appeal not only takes his vision of Polish life around the world, but entices other artists to come out and taste the pierogies for themselves.

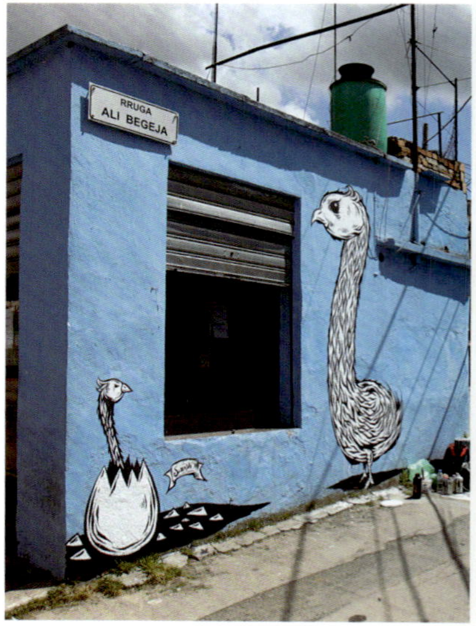

Photographs courtesy of Swanski.
Tirania, Albania, 2010.

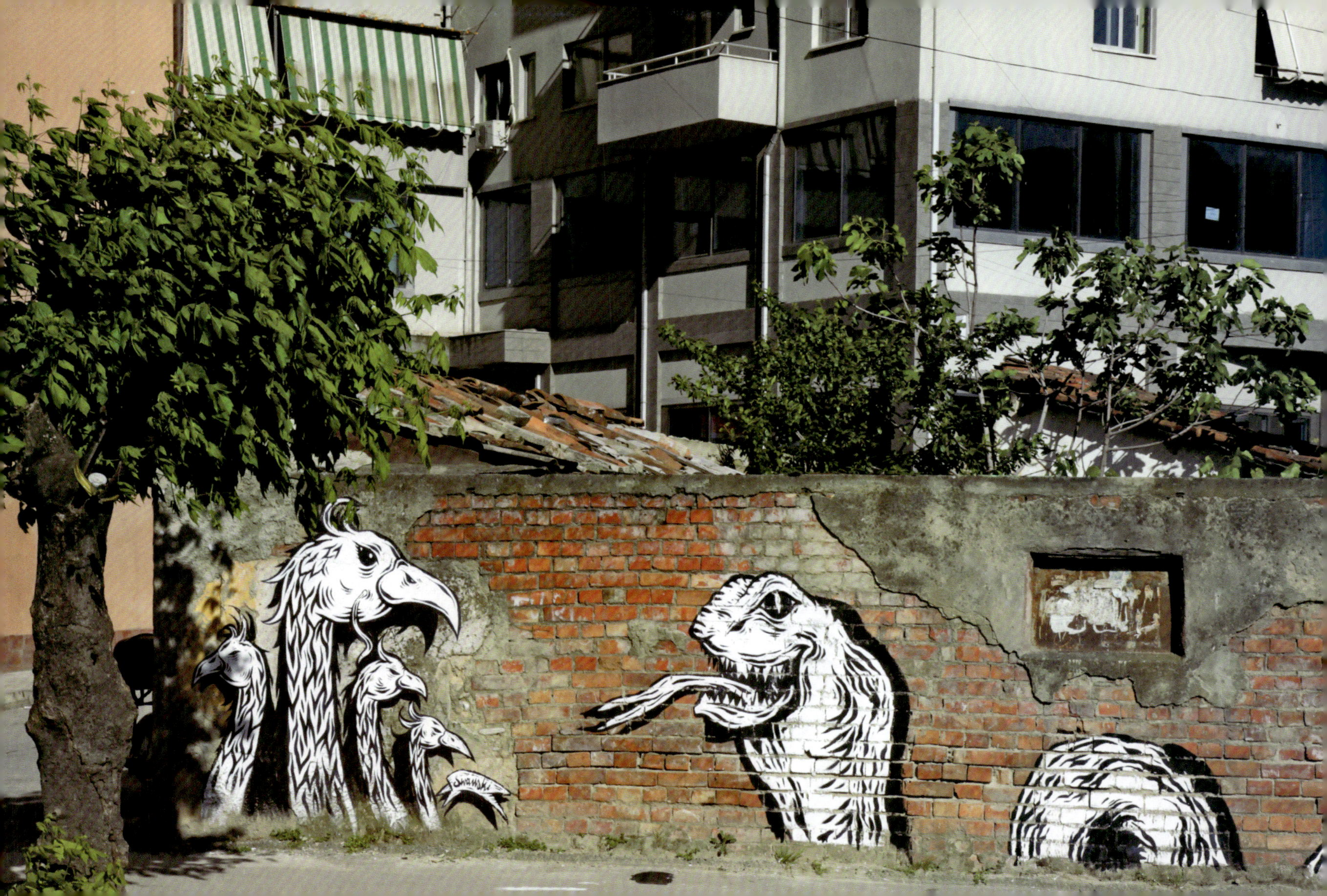

Sweet Toof

The British artist Sweet Toof straddles the fence between painstakingly maintained anonymity and a quest for recognition; similarly, Sweet Toof's work bridges the worlds of street culture and fine art, thanks to his time spent as a student at the Royal Academy Schools in Britain, where his classical training gave him an immense technical facility.

Working in a wide range of mediums, Sweet Toof became known in and around London in the middle of the first decade of the 2000s, mostly for his large-scale paintings and installations, including a giant subway car he painted that sat atop a roof in the eastern part of the city.

A fan of collaboration, Sweet Toof has worked with renowned urban artist Cyclops and Tek33 to create some of his signature works. Sweet Toof continues to paint large-scale murals, create public installations, and travel the world with his cans. He also cultivates his burgeoning fine-art career; his work is seen in galleries internationally.

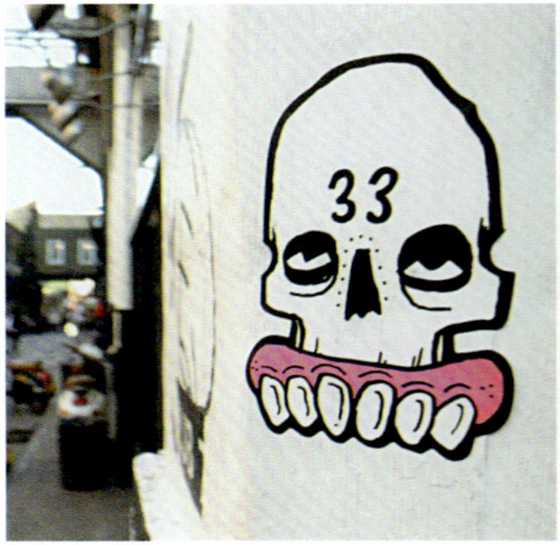

Collaboration with Roa.
Photograph by David Stuart (NoLionsInEngland).
Regents Canal, London, 2010.
Detail: Photograph by George Macdonald.
Brick Lane, London, 2009.

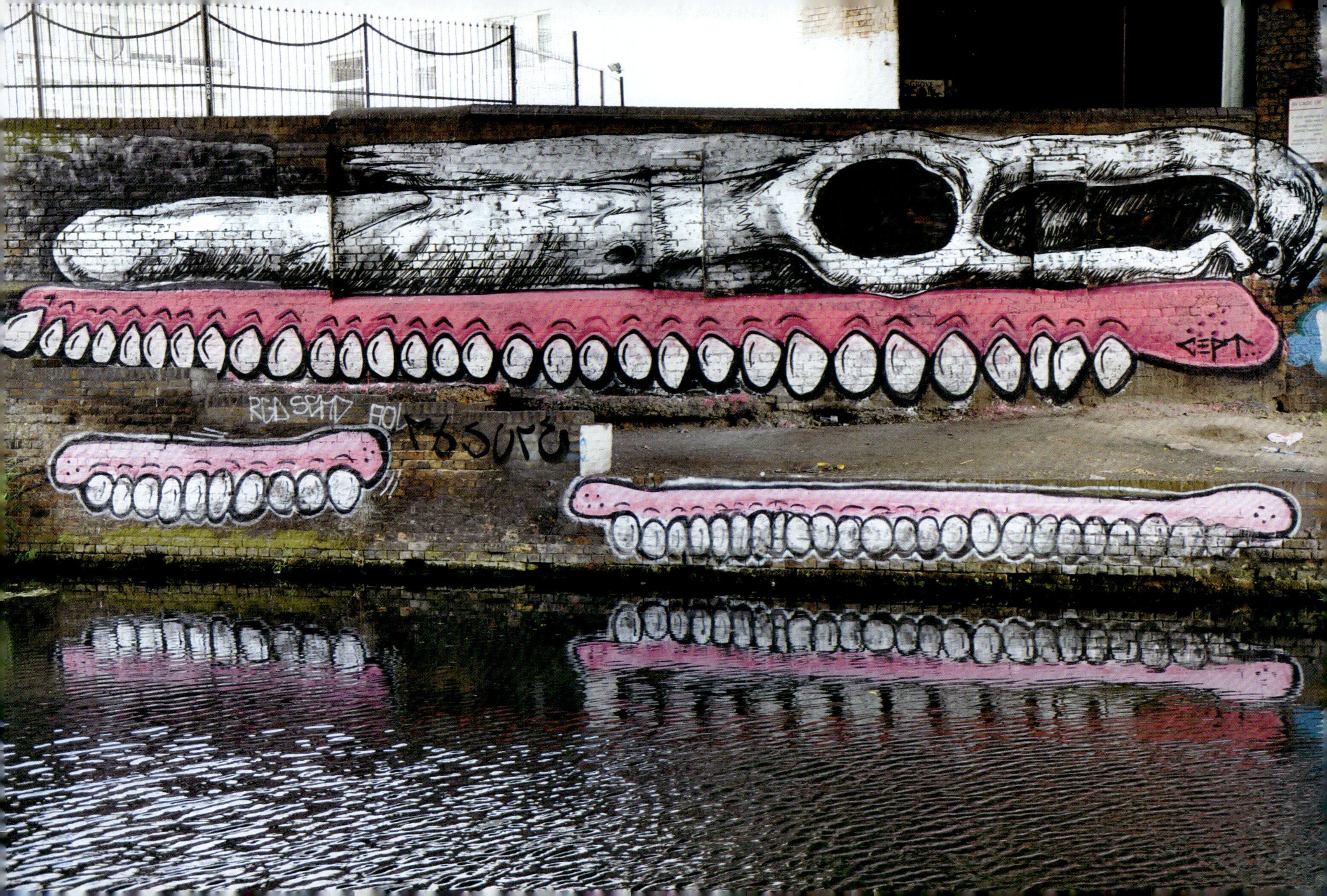

Swoon

When Swoon's work first appeared on the streets of Brooklyn and Manhattan in the late 1990s, the skill of the artist and the intricacy of her life-size woodcuts stopped people in their tracks, forever raising the bar on the quality of street art. When it was revealed that the tender hands making those woodblock prints belonged to a beautiful woman, it left the testosterone-heavy ephemeral-art world swooning. But Caledonia "Callie" Dance Curry, the petite, rambunctious redhead behind it all, prefers running around barefoot in the mud to sitting on her throne as street art's arch demigoddess.

Born and raised on a farm in Florida, Swoon came to New York to attend art school at the Pratt Institute. During her time there, she became fascinated with the idea of reclaiming public spaces for the people and began to put work on the street. Her boyfriend at the time spoke of a dream in which she had been a street artist who went by the moniker "Swoon." She took the name from his dream, and a legend was born.

In 2005, Deitch Projects caught on to her effortless art making and scathing intelligence and offered her a solo show at their downtown space. More than a thousand people turned up, jamming up traffic on Grand Street.

In recent years, Swoon has gravitated toward group projects, commandeering "Miss Rockaway Armada" and "The Swimming Cities of Switchback Sea," two boat-and-raft projects, where dozens of collaborators and friends floated down the Mississippi and Hudson Rivers, performing and creating art projects along the way.

Photograph by Luna Park. Philadelphia, 2010.

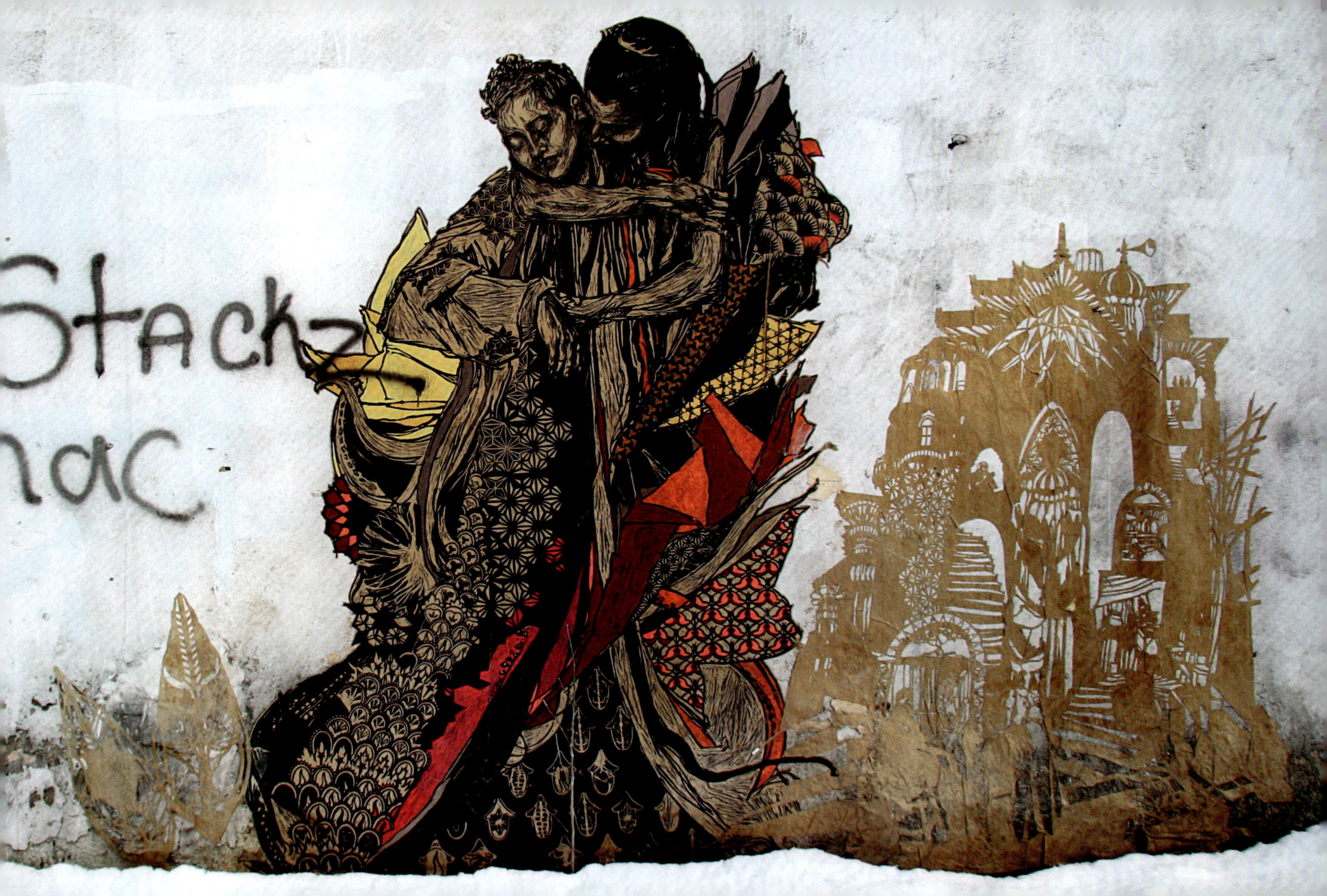
Stachz

Take 5

The #6 line, which runs from the Pelham Bay section of the Bronx down to Manhattan's tip, was shortchanged in graffiti's documentation until the appearance of Seen [see 294], the all-time #6 line king who dominated at the dawn of the '80s. But before Seen's name appeared on trains, another king of the #6 had an amazing run. In 1974 and 1975, Take 5 did the best pieces running on the #6s—and had style for miles.

Other writers on the line sharing space with Take 5 couldn't complete with him. His color schemes, tag style, and characters lit up the #6 trains like nobody's before him ever did. Take 5 and his main partner, Piece 2, raised the stylistic bar to the stratosphere, but in addition to Take 5's exterior dominance, he also saturated the trains' insides with an incredible tag style. Soon, he formed his own crew, the Kools Incorporated, which ruled the #6 along with the Six Boys and the Fantastic Partners and battled with other talented artists who shared space with them, such as Banet, Hornet, Kindo 2, and Love 1.

A hopeless romantic, Take 5 made his girlfriend's name known throughout the graffiti world. "Take 5 n Tina" tags were as ubiquitous on the #6 line as the MTA logo. In 1975, there was a changing of the guard, however, with a lot of writers leaving the scene to pursue girls, work, or more devious ways of making money. Take 5 left a huge mark on the #6 line, as well as graffiti history, and then disappeared.

Photograph by Jack Stewart.
New York City, 1974.

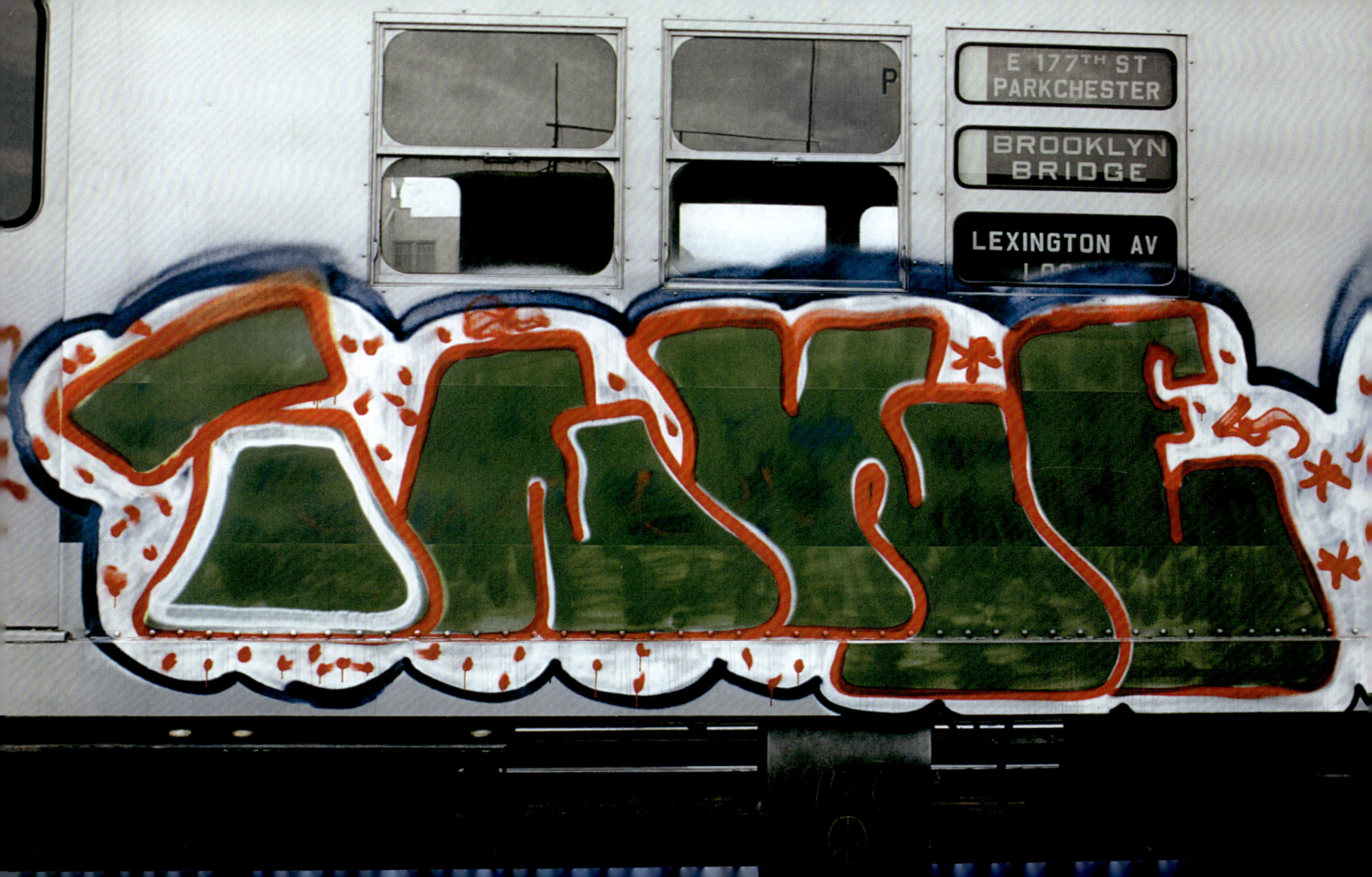

E 177TH ST
PARKCHESTER
BROOKLYN
BRIDGE
LEXINGTON AV

Taki 183

In 1969, a bored young Greek kid named Demetrius started writing his nickname, Taki, followed by his street number, 183, all over his neighborhood in Manhattan. He got the idea from Julio 204, one of the first taggers in New York; Julio 204 predated Taki, but never left Inwood, the neighborhood his gang was based in. Taki 183 became the first citywide writer, starting in Washington Heights and gradually making his way south on the #1 line, as he commuted downtown to high school. In the early 1970s, he took a job as a bike messenger, and soon, throughout the five boroughs, Taki 183 was appearing everywhere.

Eventually, Taki's friends became teammates in his new sport. Seldom given credit were Taki's cohorts, Greg 69, Bronson, and two different kids who wrote under the moniker Phil T. Greek. The diminutive tags, plainly scrawled with a magic marker, were modest by artistic standards, but the scope of Taki's tag, appearing even in unlikely places like Wall Street, was impressive.

On July 21, 1971, the *New York Times* published a brief article on the elusive Taki 183 and a photo of his tag. Youths across the city began emulating him, and the graffiti movement gained momentum. Taki 183 ensured himself a prominent spot in the annals of graffiti; he wasn't the first writer, but he was the first writer with a little bit of press.

Over time, Taki 183 gradually slipped from the scene. Aside from a flashy website for worldwide graffiti enthusiasts to drool over, when he put down his marker, he didn't look back.

Photograph by Jon Naar.
New York City, c. 1971.

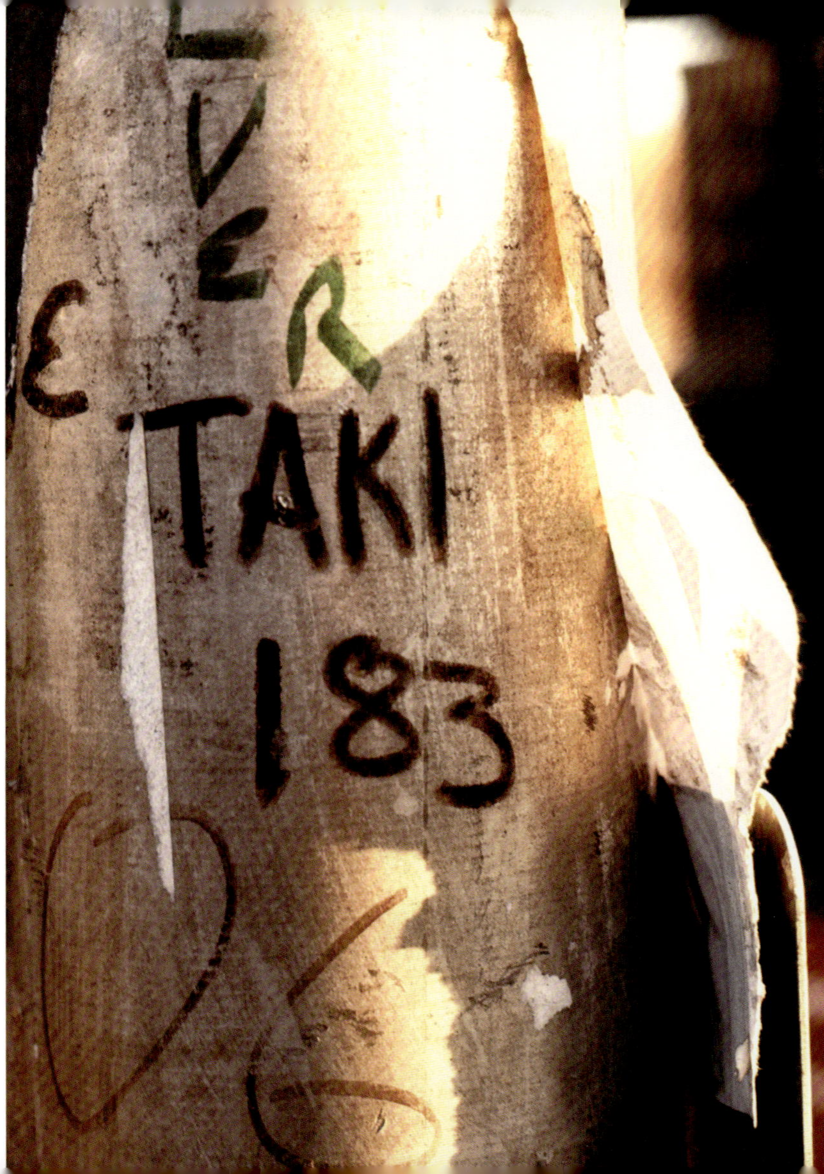
TAKI
183

TED Inc.

The Ebony Dukes, aka TED Inc., started out as a gang in the South Bronx in the late 1960s; as graffiti-covered trains began to fly over the heads of the gang members on the elevated tracks, the gang's leader took note. Staff 161 had always had a certain artistic inclination, but like so many kids from the ghetto, he didn't know what to do with his talent. Now, there was an answer, displayed on the trains in front of him—his future was graffiti, and he brought TED Inc. with him.

Staff 161 possessed some of the most elegant handwriting in graffiti history, and his brother AJ used a heart extending from his name to set himself apart from the pack. In 1973, uptown powerhouse Death crossed out Staff's cannon piece, almost causing a Bronx civil war, but cooler heads prevailed. The prodigious writer Blade has always credited Staff 161 as being the first writer to do conceptual pieces, the most impressive being the "Reaper" car. The train featured a hand coming out of a grave and spray-painting the name Staff, as the Grim Reaper looks on. Staff 161 finished the piece by painting large drops of blood oozing from the top of the car. It was the most well-conceived piece of its day and led to the beginning of the whole-car movement.

Photographs by Jack Stewart.
Top: Piece by Adam 12 (aka AJ 161). New York City, 1975.
Bottom left: Piece by Staff 161. New York City, 1974.
Bottom right: Piece by Staff 161. New York City, 1973.

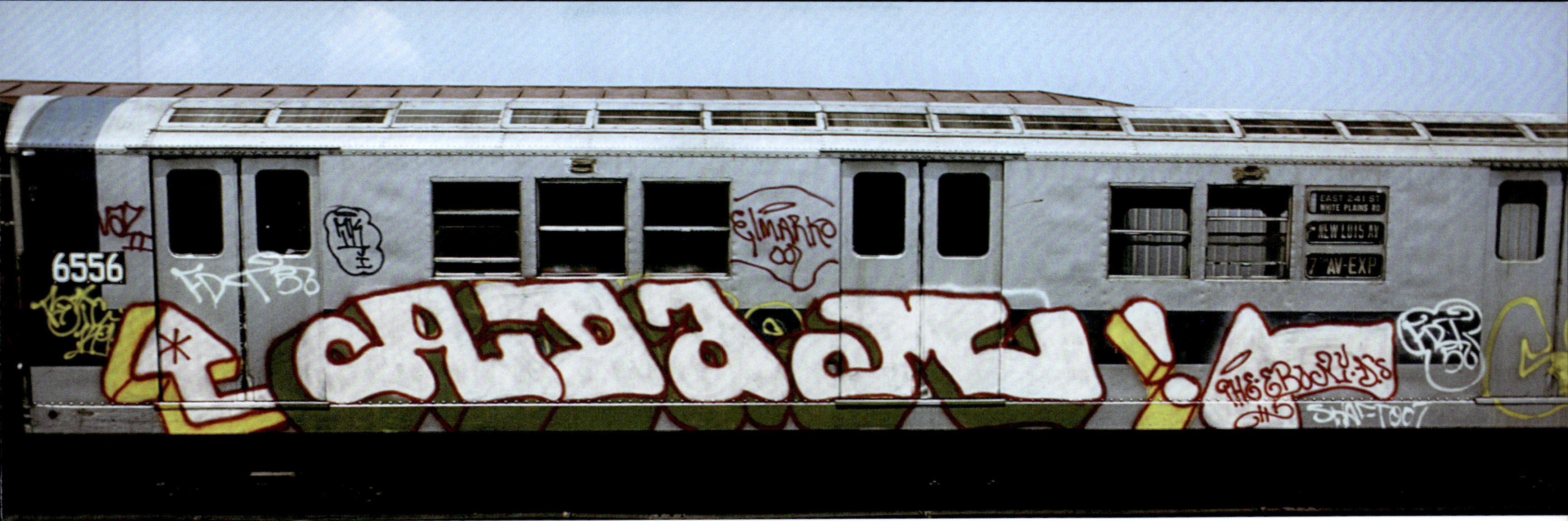
6556
EAST 241 ST
WHITE PLAINS RD
NEW LOTS AV
7 AV-EXP

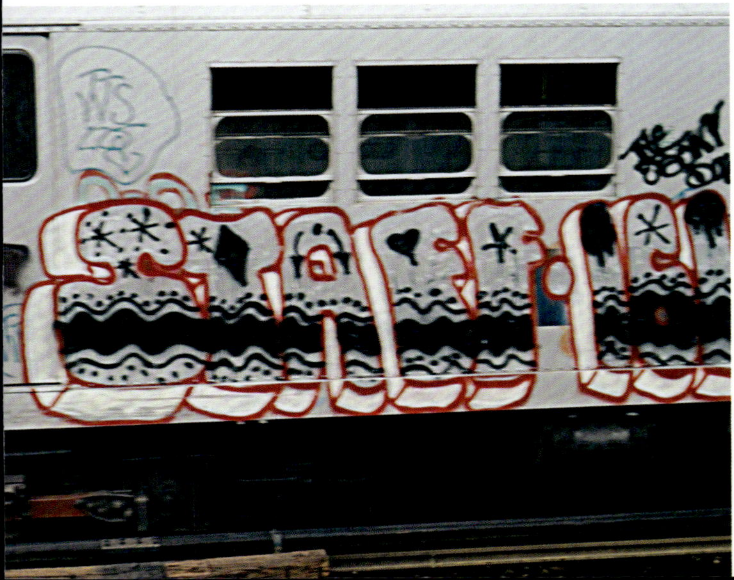

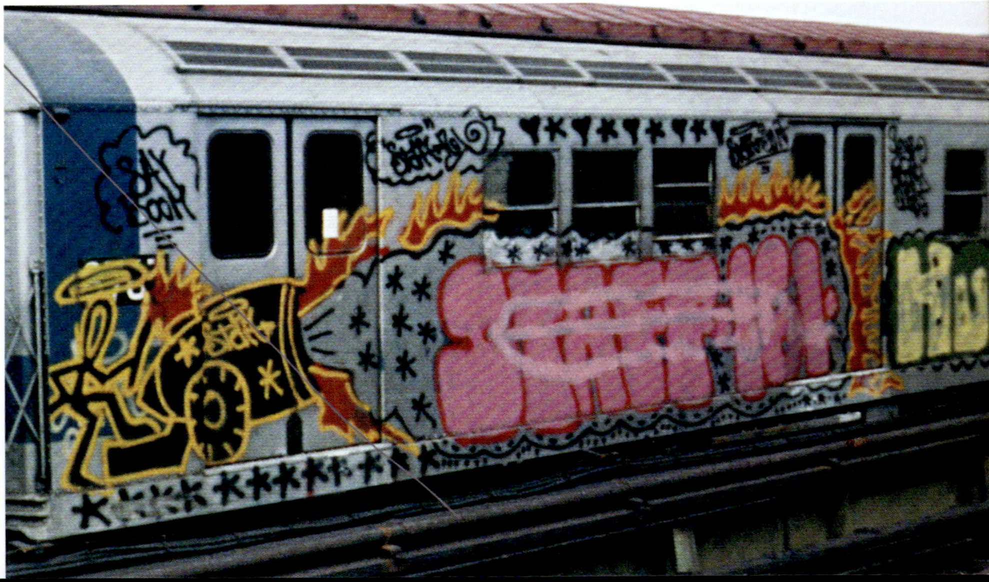

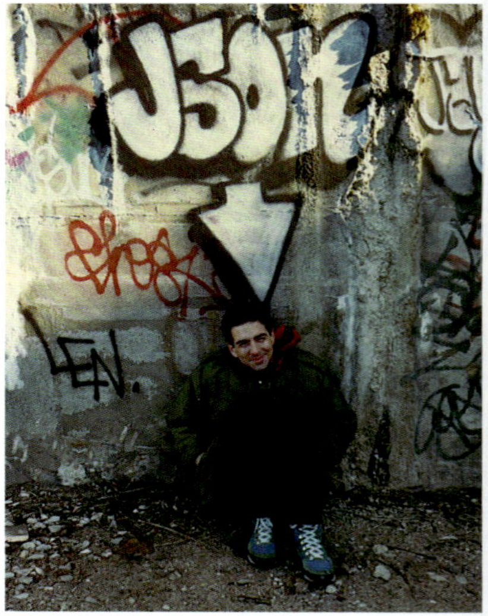

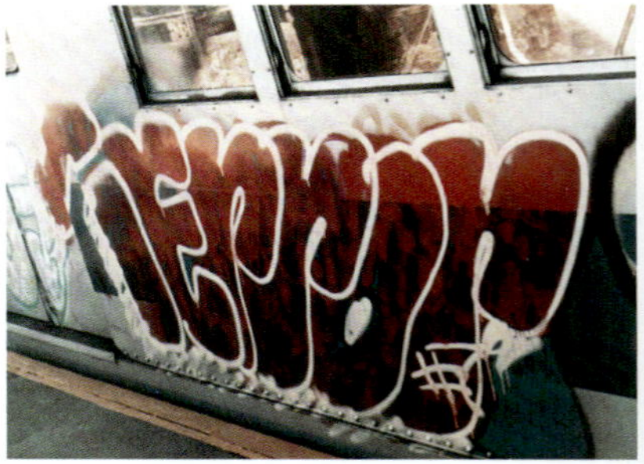

Terror 161

Terror 161 began his career in 1973 under the name Tarantula 235, to which he would add a spider icon. He quickly came to dominate the virgin territory of his neighborhood, the Riverdale section of the Bronx. By 1974, he had developed true style, as well as a new name, Terror 161—an homage to the two great writers Junior 161 and Cay 161 [see 186].

From 1974 to 1977, Terror 161 and his crew, the MOB (Masters of Broadway, see 228), went to the #1 yard—located steps away from their homes—every weekend. Terror started a string of crude pieces that he began numbering, and he hit the insides hard as well. In 1977, he retired with a reputation as a strong blue-collar writer on the #1—but there were a lot of those, and Terror 161 wanted more.

In 1980, he bumped into his old crewmate AMMO. The two old friends got to talking, and before either one of them knew it, they were climbing the fence to the #1 yard with a bag of paint. Terror changed his name to Jayson (J.SON for short), and The MOB was back. The older and wiser duo began to venture onto other lines with writers as diverse as Cap, Seen (see 294), Skeme (see 304), and T.Kid 170 (see 335).

By this time, the once-prestigious #2 and #5 lines had become battlefields. Silver throw-ups had replaced the colorful burners of the past. Not so on the #6 train, an isolated line and safe haven dominated by Seen and the UA crew. From 1982 to 1983, Seen and J.Son teamed up to do some highly memorable cars in the demilitarized zone. Although J.Son retired in 1984, he has remained active in documenting graffiti for more than fifteen years.

Photograph by Smith.
New York City, 1993.
Detail top: Photograph by Bryan "Uni" Mechutan.
New York City, 1974.
Detail bottom: Photograph by Smith.
New York City, 1989.

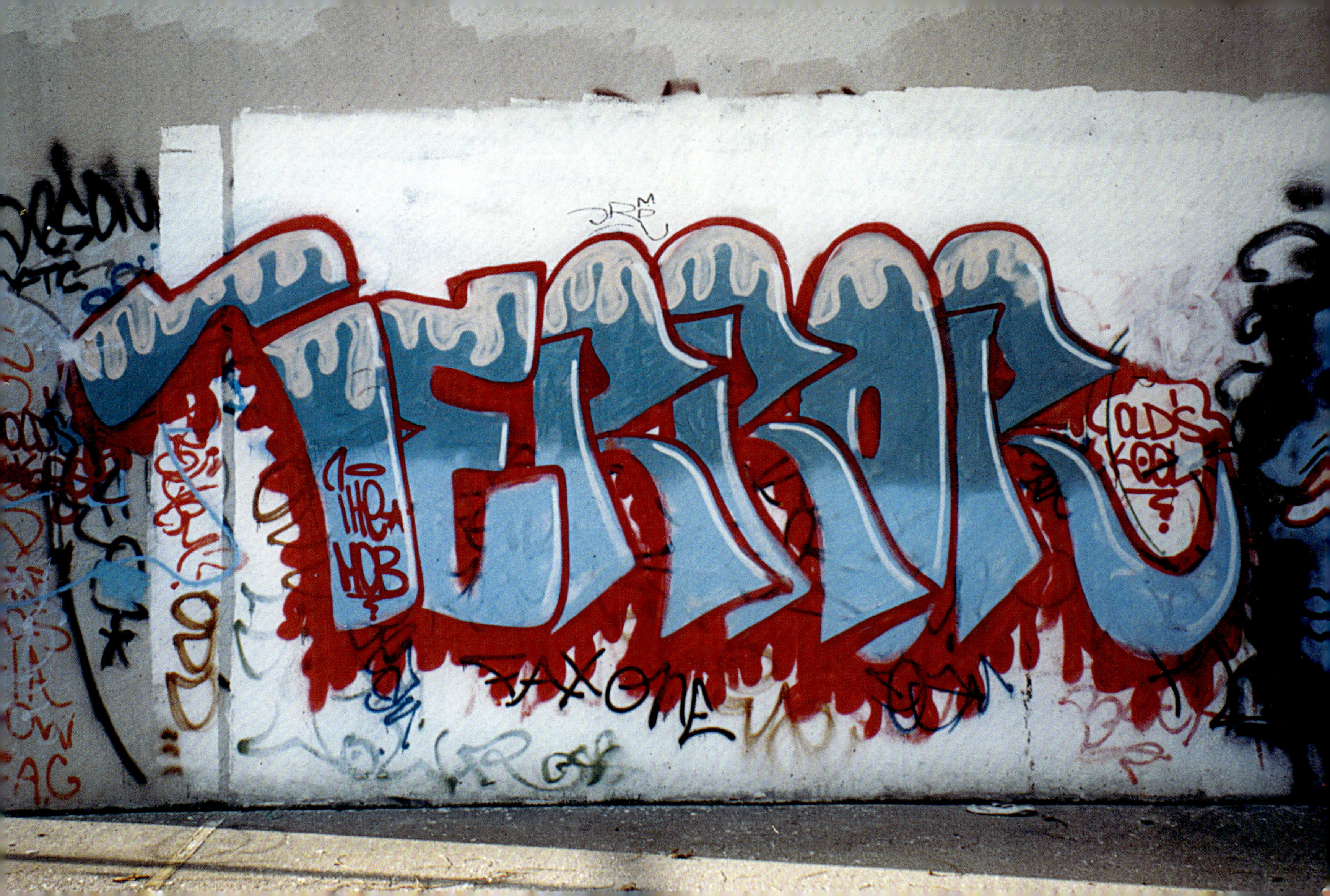

TFP

The Fantastic Partners (TFP) were a group of friends from the north Bronx that included Butch 2, Kase 2, Bot 707, Solid, Hydra, Hash 161, Voe 56, Kindo, Derby, and others. In 1974, Bot seemed to be leading the way for the crew in style, and Butch and Kase pulled out one whole car after another. In 1976, just as some members of the group began to retire, they were dealt a terrible blow when Solid 1, Bot's brother, was dragged by a train and killed. This seemingly ended the run of the first generation.

Kase 2 retired for a while, but then reinvented his career in the late '70s as a stylemaster. Fuzz One had continued to paint and adopted the name Solid One to keep Solid's memory alive. Both writers held a major presence on the IRT lines from 1978 to 1981, marking a resurgence for TFP. In the mid-'80s, Kase put Sento (see 295) in the crew and gave him recruiting power. Sento and Kase put in Pure, Noah, Sane, and Stak, among others, to refill the talent tank.

In 1989, as the subway movement came to an end, the clean-car movement began, and Sento was at the forefront of it. European writers, who had balked at hitting the yards during the 1980s, when graffiti and violence were synonymous, traveled to New York in droves during the clean-car era. They would come to the city for two weeks, do pieces, and then leave, making it tough for transit cops to build a case against them. Sento kept track of the better European writers and put them in TFP; that list included Mickey, Atome, Blue, and Milk. This group cemented the crew's fame internationally and kept it running on European transit lines through the next decade.

Piece by Butch 2.
Photograph by Jack Stewart.
New York City, 1974.

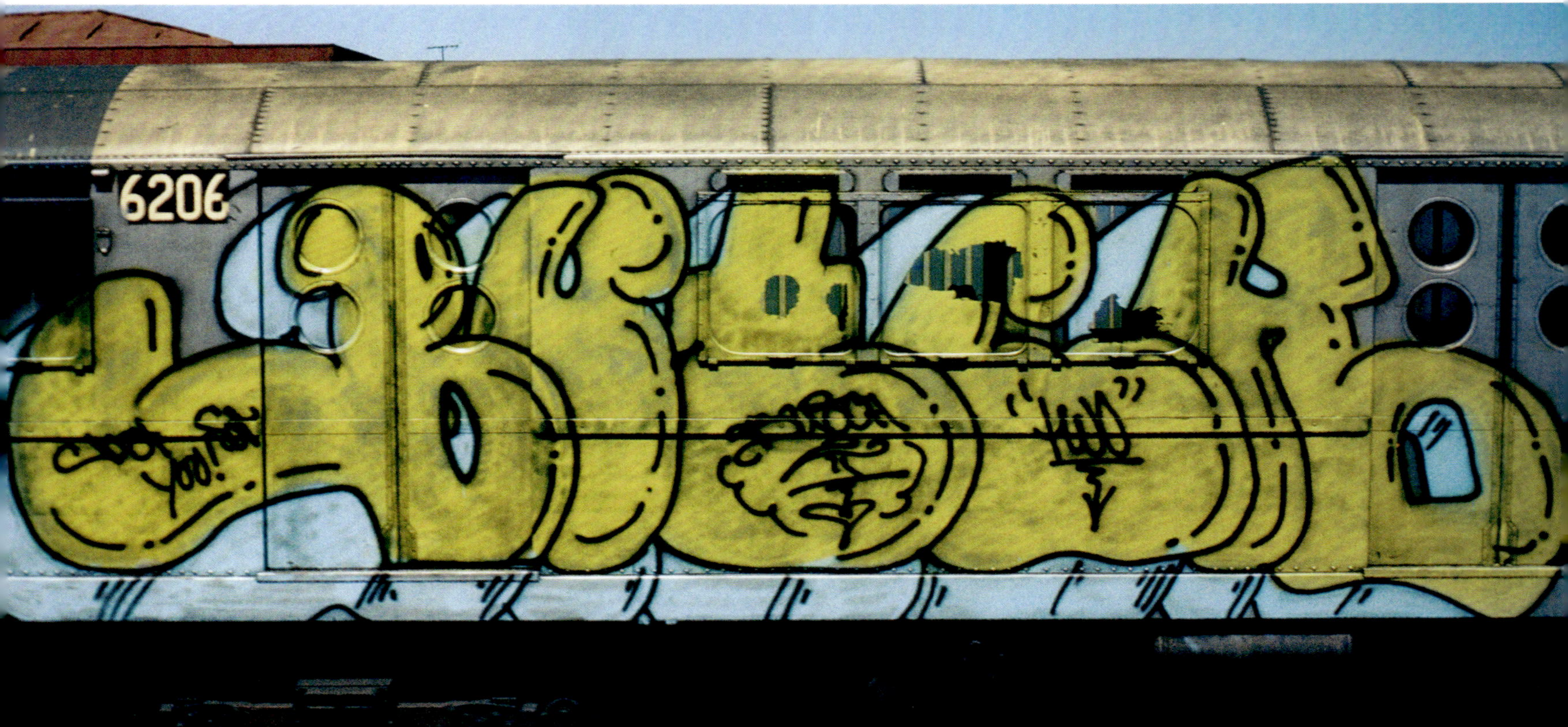
6206

T.Kid 170

Julius Cavero, aka T.Kid 170, left the street-gang life he grew up in after being shot by a rival in a Bronx park. In the mid-'70s, he decided to concentrate on graffiti. Under the tutelage of #4 line stylemaster Padre Dos and Wild Style president Tracy 168 [see 340], T.Kid learned to burn. T.Kid and his first partner, Peser, then invaded the #1 tunnel in 1979; T.Kid found a home in the #1 tunnel and became a frequent visitor.

T.Kid's crew, the Nasty Boys, brought a street-gang mentality to train tunnels and yards, much to the dismay of their future victims, who were beaten and robbed on sight. T.Kid's artistic skills evolved rapidly, and by 1980, he battled the early members of RTW [see 286] for the Broadway style crown. Together with the newly formed crew the Vamp Squad, which included Min [see 223], Kel 139 [see 190], and Rin 1, T.Kid began to go all-city. Like Dondi [see 097], CIA, and Chain 3 [see 062], T.Kid also did outlines for other members of his crew, shaping the look of many beautiful whole-cars. T.Kid, with Boozer, then rocked a slew of whole-cars on the #1 line in 1983, and finished his train career in the Ghost Yard with compadres Bio, Mack Kenn, Cem2, Shame 125, and Raz.

After retiring from the subways in 1985, T.Kid took his act over to Europe and changed the face of graffiti overseas. Today, Cavero still paints walls for love, but canvases to pay the bills.

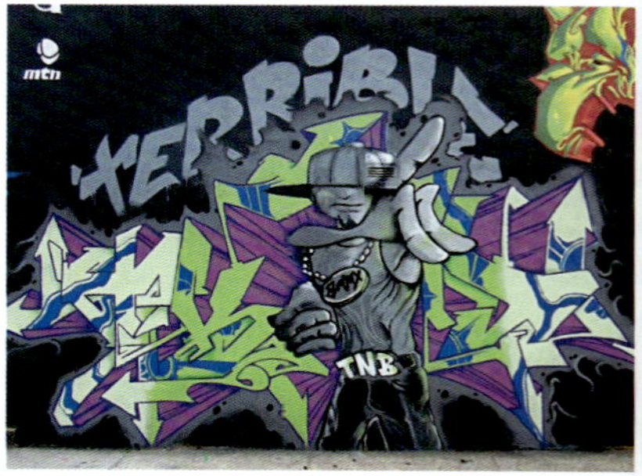

Photograph by Adam Reich.
New York City, 2007.
Detail: Photograph courtesy of T.Kid 170.
New York City, 2009.

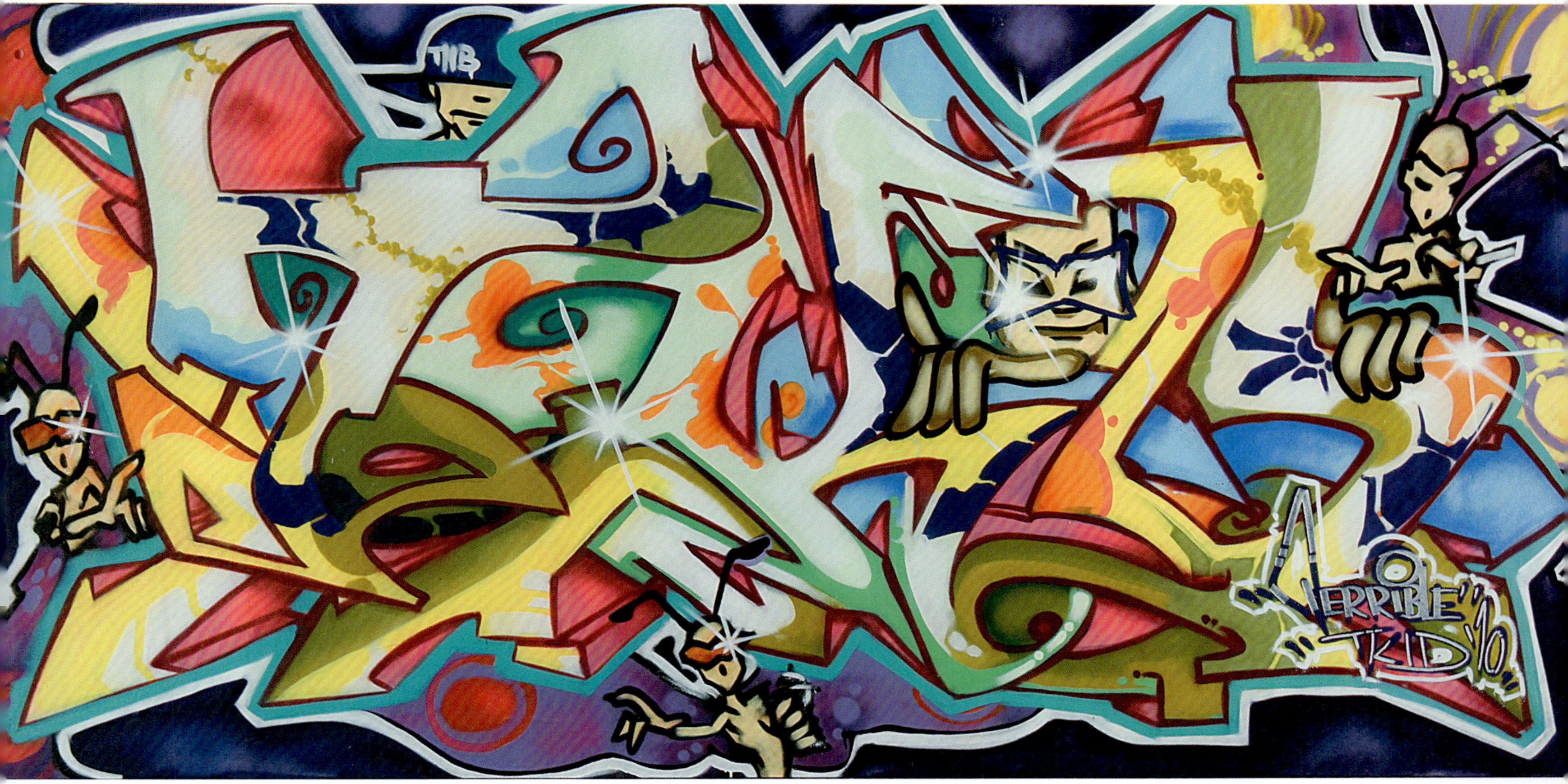
TNB
TRID

Toasters

It was following a typical British house party that a trio of old schoolmates created the Toaster crew. With beer and cider coursing through their veins, they painted an image of a toaster on a wall in the city of Wolverhampton, and this eventually become their trademark. It was 1998, and over the next decade they were to become widely respected and regarded as true street-art pioneers.

Despite adhering loyally to their simple toaster motif, the crew could never be accused of being a one-trick pony. They've constantly pushed boundaries with their variations in style, medium, and scale, as well as some quite brilliant collaboration pieces displayed most recently at their "Trespassers of the World Unite" show in 2009.

They've used their now-famous image of the ubiquitous electrical appliance to remake sandwich-board advertising signs, hijack the 2010 British parliamentary election, and even create a new movement protesting the local authorities' practice of buffing tags and street art with unsightly splotches of ill-matching color. This movement, known as the "buff bluff," is just one of the many ways in which the Toasters continue to revolutionize a movement they have done so much to foster.

Photograph by George Macdonald. Waterloo, London, 2008

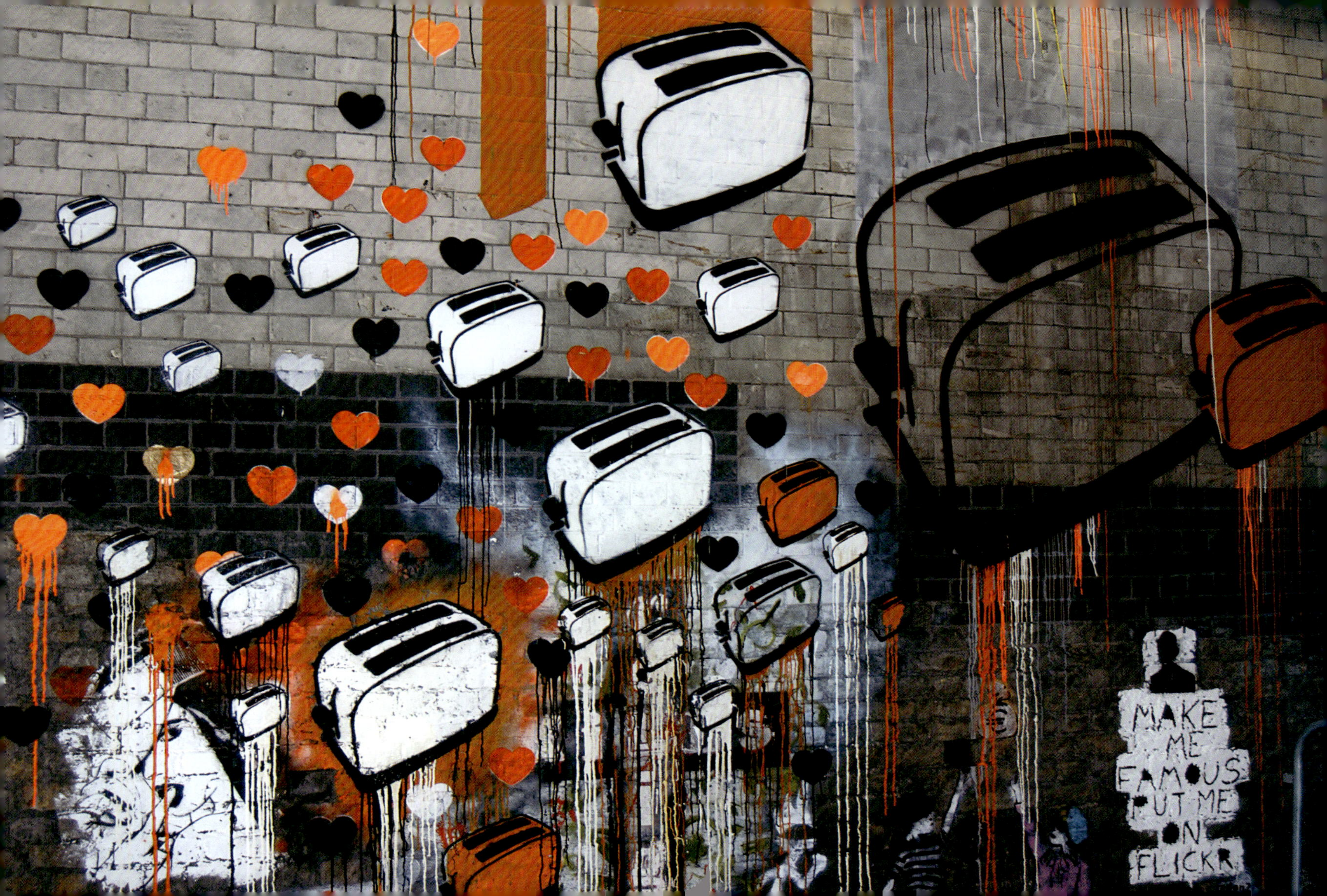
MAKE
ME
FAMOUS
PUT ME
ON
FLICKR

Topcat 126

Topcat 126 had a rather brief career in New York graffiti that ran from 1972 to 1973, but his impact was great. Topcat had moved to the Manhattanville projects from Philadelphia with his parents in the early 1970s. The Philadelphia graffiti movement had already developed its own "Philly style" that featured long, slender letters with platforms at the bottom, and Topcat began running this style in New York in 1972, hitting buses and trains.

Topcat became quite famous on Broadway and had a slew of followers, including T-Rex 131, who became his writing partner. In the two years they wrote together, the alphabet got tighter as the letters became longer, and stars were introduced into some of them. T-Rex's cousin Peso 131 recalls, "Topcat had three lives. He was nice at ball. He dressed fly. He was the first brother to wear a Kangol, and he wrote graffiti." Topcat also covered buses with Cop 5 and Spade 130, often writing with his brother, Blood 126, and another partner, James 2. When UGA [see 346] formed in 1972, Topcat had a chance to meet some of the famed stylists from the Bronx, and by 1973 he had abandoned the long-letter look in his pieces, though his tag style remained pure Philly.

Photograph by Jack Stewart.
New York City, 1973.

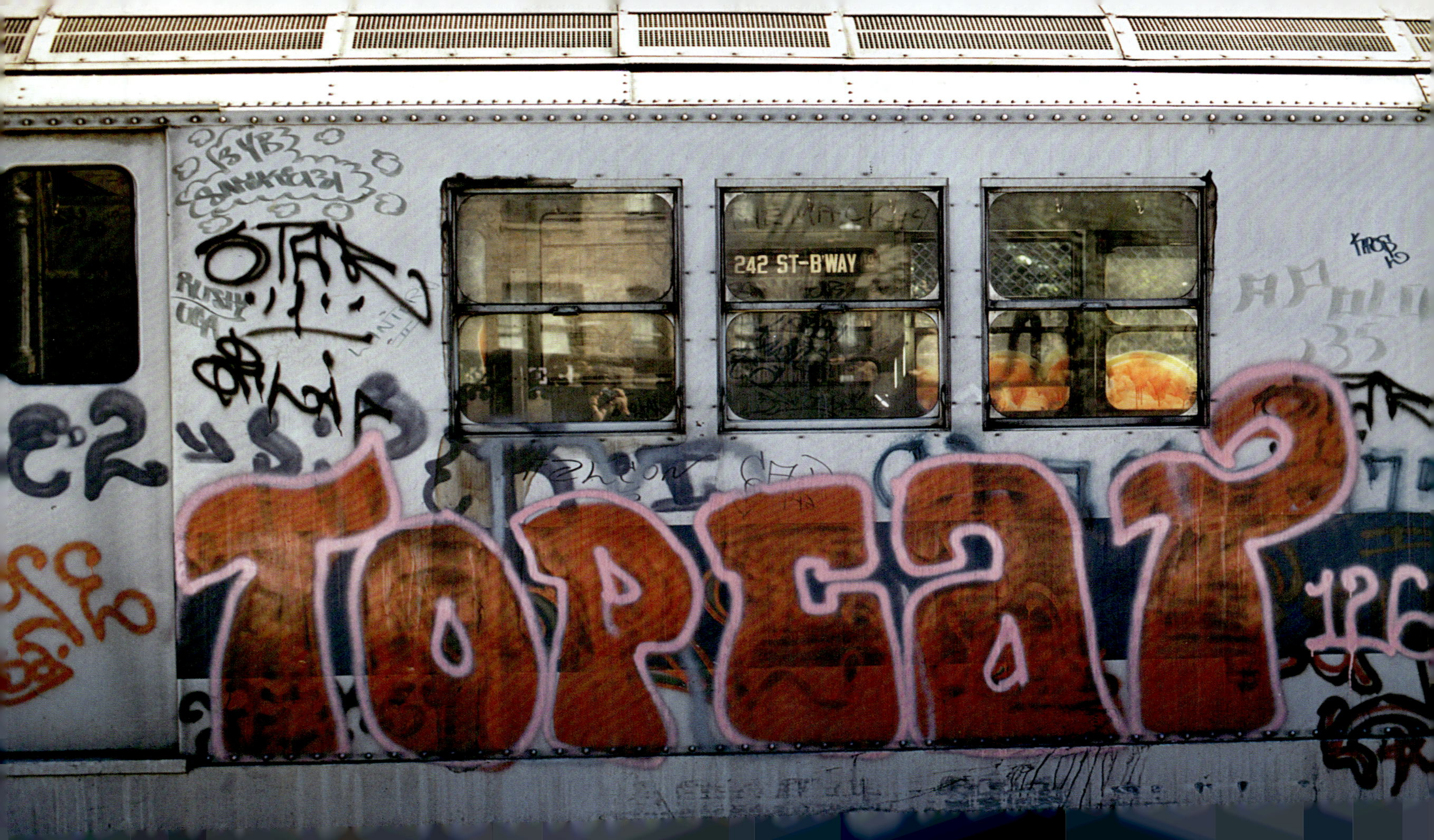
242 ST-B'WAY

Totem

Totem began painting on the walls and tunnels of his Atlanta, Georgia, hometown in the early 1990s. Since then, his signature letters and characters have traveled to lands as distant as the Philippines and New Zealand. His vibrant murals evoke imaginary worlds and reflect his love of animation. His innovative, highly developed 2-D and 3-D stylings against elegantly designed backgrounds have gained him recognition and respect on an international level, while his huge masterpieces continue to grace Atlanta's walls, often covering entire corners.

Countless corporations and companies, such as BlueCross BlueShield, Coca-Cola, Shell Oil, the BBDO advertising agency, Nike, PlayStation and PSP, Xbox, and Red Bull have commissioned his work. He has designed artwork for many music industry celebrities, including Usher, Outkast, and Lil Jon. Totem's work has also been featured in gallery exhibits in New York, Los Angeles, and Japan.

A breakdancing legend as well, Totem began dancing in 1986 and was a member of the competitive Hi-Fi Tribe, before forming Atlanta's legendary crew Burn Unit. For more than a decade, Totem has been giving breakdancing lessons to Atlanta's youth. Among the other many crews this versatile artist represents are Tats Cru, 3A Crew, and TGE.

Photographs courtesy of Totem.
Top: Atlanta, Georgia, 2010.
Bottom: Shanghai, China, 2010.

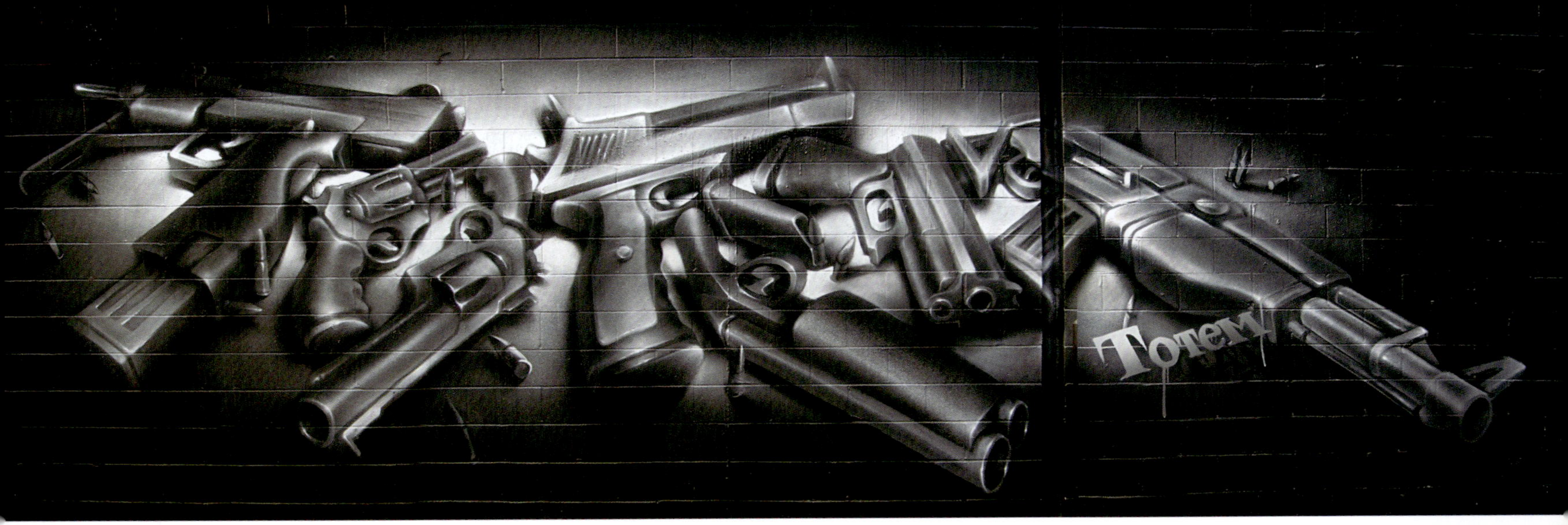
TOTEM

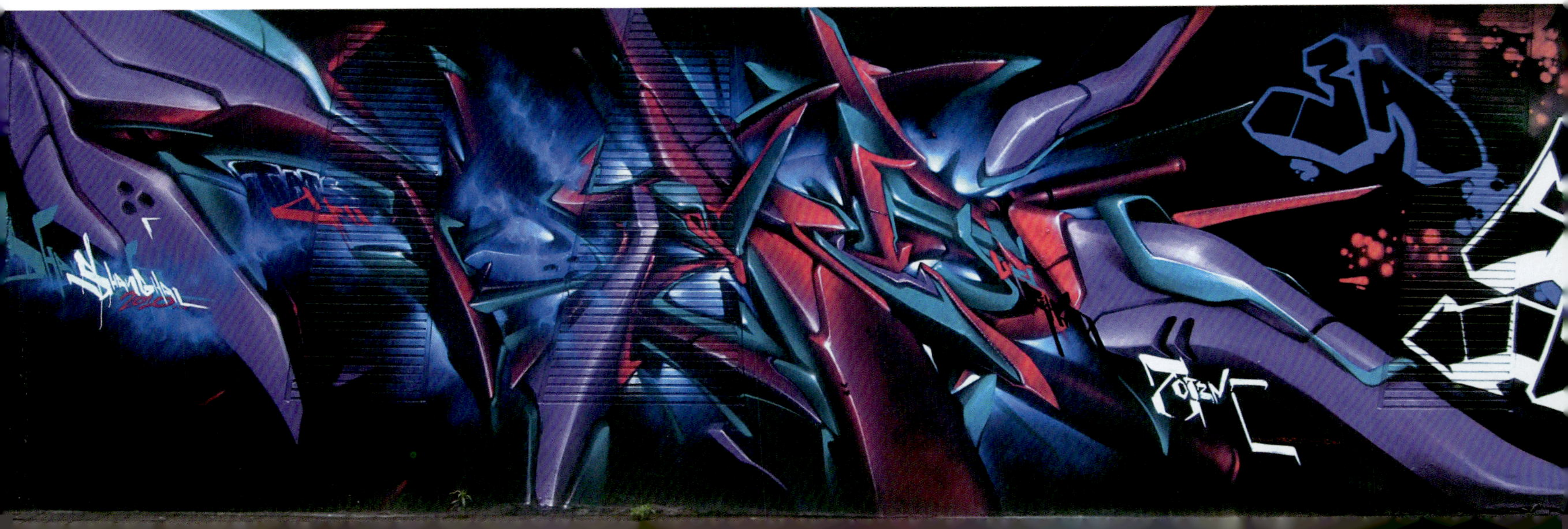
Shanghai

Tower

In the early years of the twenty-first century, one wasn't able walk three feet in Berlin's hip neighborhoods without seeing a sticker bearing the moniker Tower. Every lamppost, street sign, mailbox, and other flat surface was adorned with at least one and up to twenty variations on the colorful tag, always printed or scrawled on some manner of sticky paper or vinyl.

The man behind the sticker spree kept himself shrouded in a cloud of mystery, never revealing his identity and never making any attempt to cross over into the fine-art world. When questioned about his motivations, Tower explained that he "couldn't draw to save his life" and he was "ridiculously fascinated with the alphabet." This fascination, and a mind-boggling talent for innovation and invention, are readily apparent in all of his work; silk-screened, rubber-stamped, letter-pressed, and handwritten, every single one of Tower's stickers is clearly the product of a human hand. With a nod to traditional graffiti, Tower plays with abstractions on the alphabet, turning an image of the Berlin TV tower into an "R," or creating pieces such as his poster series that read TOWER WROTE WORTE, (*Worte* being the German word for "words").

Having handmade hundreds of thousands of stickers to date, Tower is undeniably the sticker king of Berlin, and he is credited with revolutionizing the culture internationally.

Photographs courtesy of Tower.
Berlin, Germany.

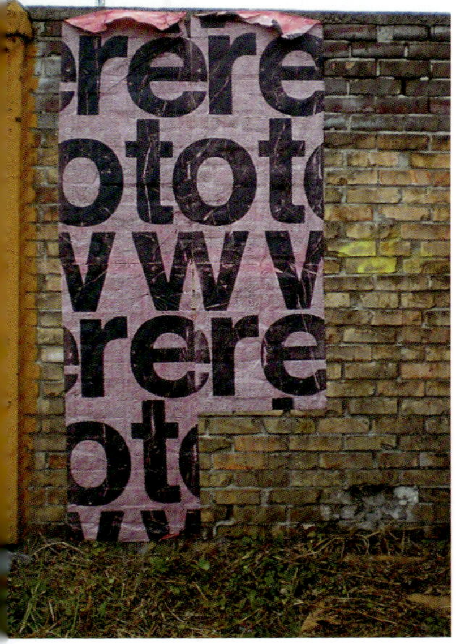

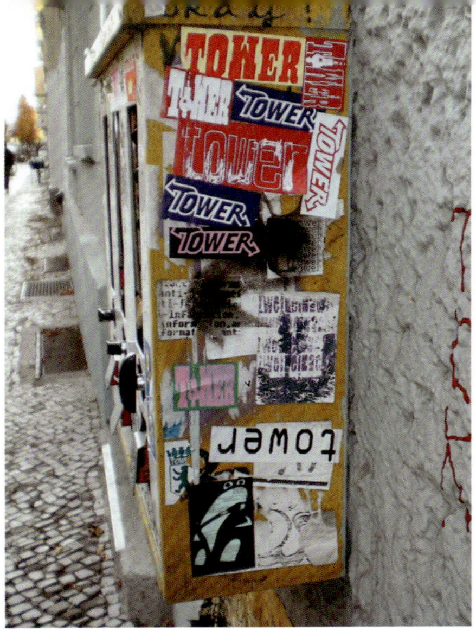
TOWER
TOWER
TOWER
TOWER
TOWER
tower

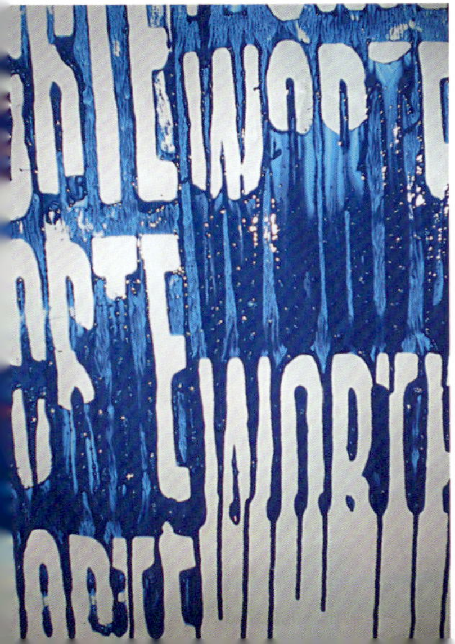

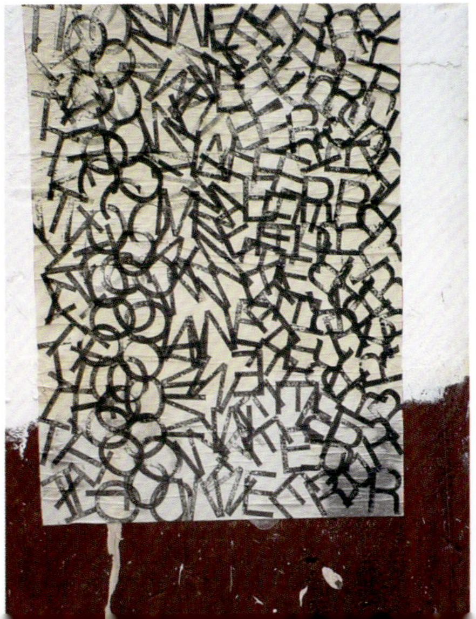

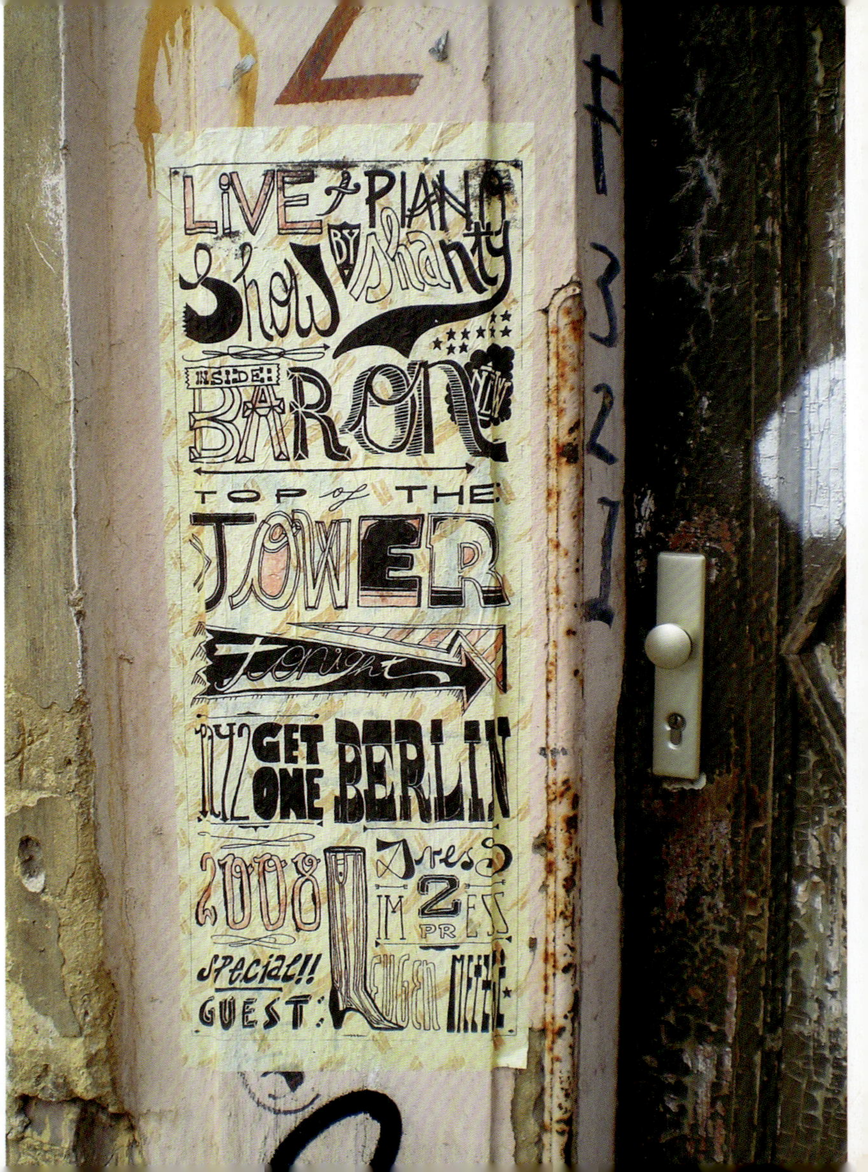
LIVE PIANO
SHOW BY SHANTY
INSIDE BARON
TOP of THE
TOWER
tonight
GET ONE BERLIN
2008
DRESS 2 IMPRESS
special!!
GUEST:

Tracy 168

Growing up in the Bronx in the early 1970s gave Tracy 168 easy access to Bedford Park and the #4 yard, but his horizons stretched way beyond his home turf. His numerous accomplishments include coining the term "Wild Style," the name of his second crew; founding the crew Wanted; and venturing out to the #7 line in Queens with a battalion of Bronx stylemasters to battle Caine 1 [see 054], the king of that line. Tracy's color sense, clean lettering, and ability to render detailed characters made him a top competitor and a stylistic mentor to some of the greatest writers ever.

Tracy stopped painting subways in 1977 [save for a few cameo appearances in the 1980s] and became one of the first to paint commercial murals on businesses across the city. Never the nine-to-five type, Tracy has survived as an independent artist for more than thirty years. " 'Wild Style' is a term I made up to describe the way we lived," says Tracy. Now in his fifties, with a face that shows the signs of a life lived hard and fast, he can be found on the streets of the Bronx, hustling his canvases, holding court, and living life *his* way: Wild Style.

Photograph by Jack Stewart.
New York City, 1974.

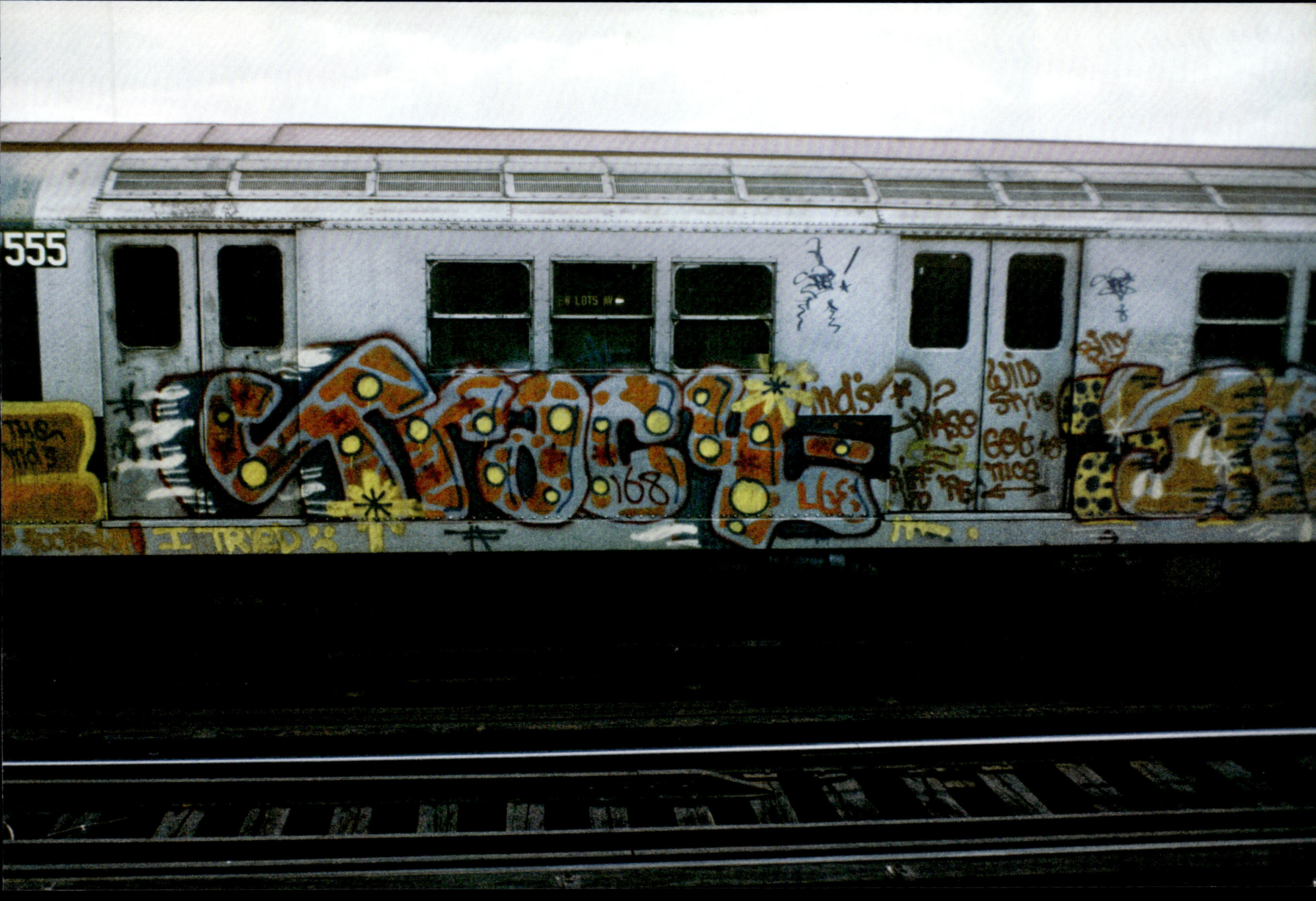
555
I TRIED

train yards and lay-ups

Train yards and lay-ups are as many and diverse as the kids who once used them as studios. High overhead and deep beneath the earth, they store the idle subway cars that once carried the messages of a movement.

Train yards vary in size and character—from small village to burgeoning metropolis. Some yards, such as the Ghost Yard, which borders the East River in upper Manhattan, offered an aquarian escape. The #3 yard, located a few miles down the river at 148th Street in Harlem, offered a stunning view of a lit-up Yankee Stadium across the water. Elevated yards and lay-ups could be perilous, as rotted wooden planks would often collapse underfoot and snag a fleeing writer faster than any pursuing cop could. Underground tunnels, such as Esplanade, Grant, and the #1, held more trains than some yards. Grant, a multilevel lay-up, had a platform that allowed writers to stand at eye level with the trains for easy execution of top-to-bottoms.

Most yards held cars belonging to a specific line, and hard-core bombers intent on gaining citywide attention hit most of them. The Ghost Yard and the Coney Island Yard housed several different lines, allowing one-stop shopping for writers looking to go all-city.

Lay-ups parked on middle tracks of elevations provided the biggest challenge. A writer had to watch out for police, other writers, and oncoming trains. Trains moved quickly, and any slow-moving writer who got spotted on the tracks by a conductor knew that his night was over.

Dime 139 (left) and Flip 1.
Photograph by Flint Genari.
#7 yard, Corona, Queens, New York, 1975.

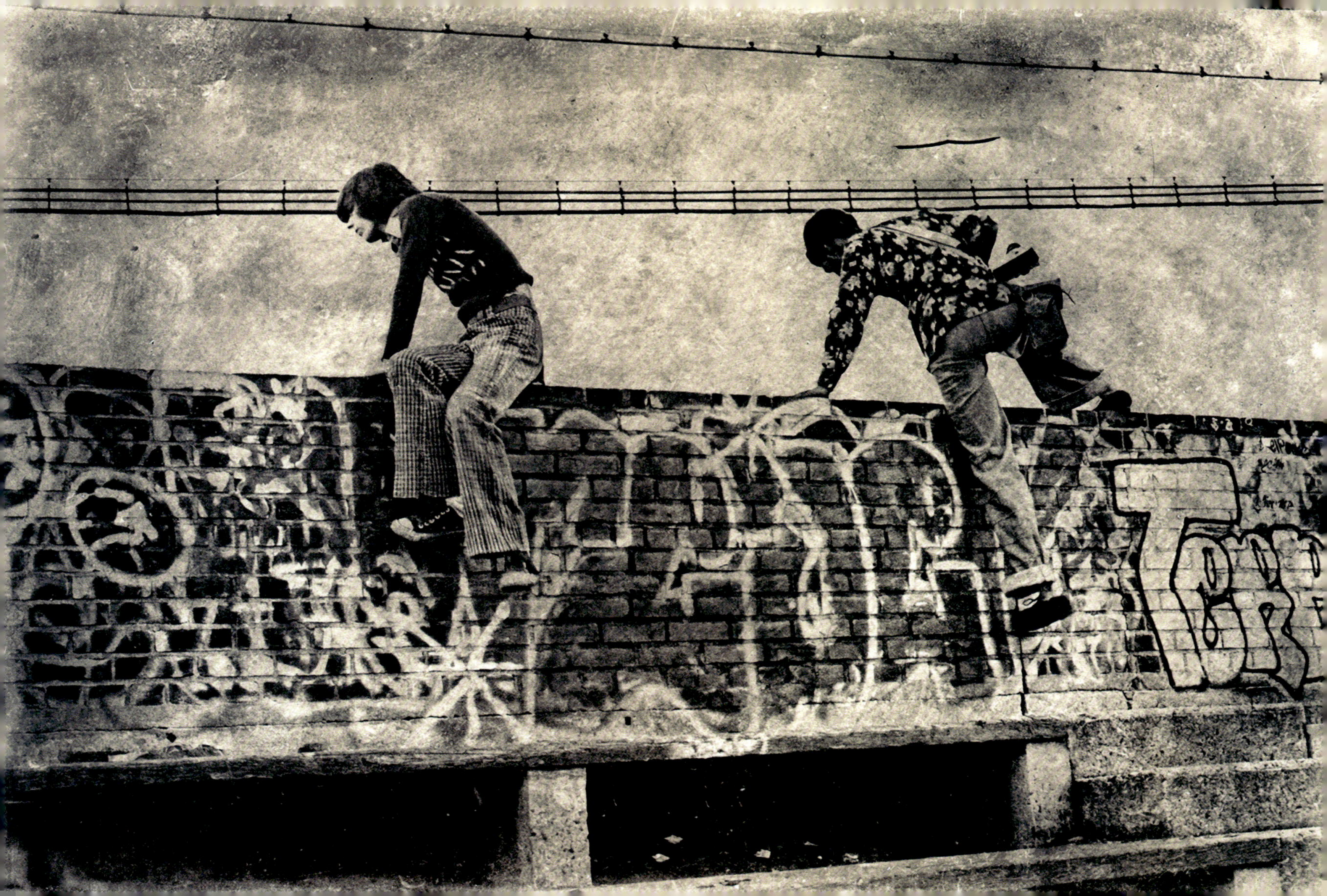

trucks

When graffiti found its way onto moving targets, trucks ranked number three on the hit parade. In 1971, buses became a prime target, as kids carried markers while the buses carried them. In 1972, trains became the Holy Grail. In those days, trucks were just an afterthought, something to use up leftover paint on while returning home, and writers hitting trucks didn't attract much attention.

By the 1990s, however, the culture of painting graffiti on New York subway cars was all but dead. With the instigation of buffing and numerous other removal methods, as well as heightened security measures around overnight yards, the risk involved in painting on trains was far too high. To achieve the same high visibility for their mobile artwork, many artists turned to the next best thing, the vehicular equivalent of a primed, rolling, giant white canvas: the truck.

Trucks are depended upon for their utilitarian service and not their appearance; therefore, they often stay painted for extended periods of time. Driven to the far corners of a city and frequently stalled in traffic, they are visible to all manner of pedestrian, commuter, and passerby, making them a source of free publicity for artists and one of the more desirable graffiti repositories in an inner city. Many writers today still use trucks as rolling permission walls—in the quest to mobilize one's gospel, trucks may be graffiti's final frontier.

**Top: Artwork by Spon GNR.
Photograph by Martha Cooper.
Bottom left: Artwork by UFO and Sadu.
Photograph by Becki Fuller. New York City, 2007.
Bottom center: Piece by NORM.
Photograph by Steve Rotman. San Francisco, 2009.
Bottom right: Artwork by LOST.
Photograph by Steve Rotman. San Francisco, 2010.**

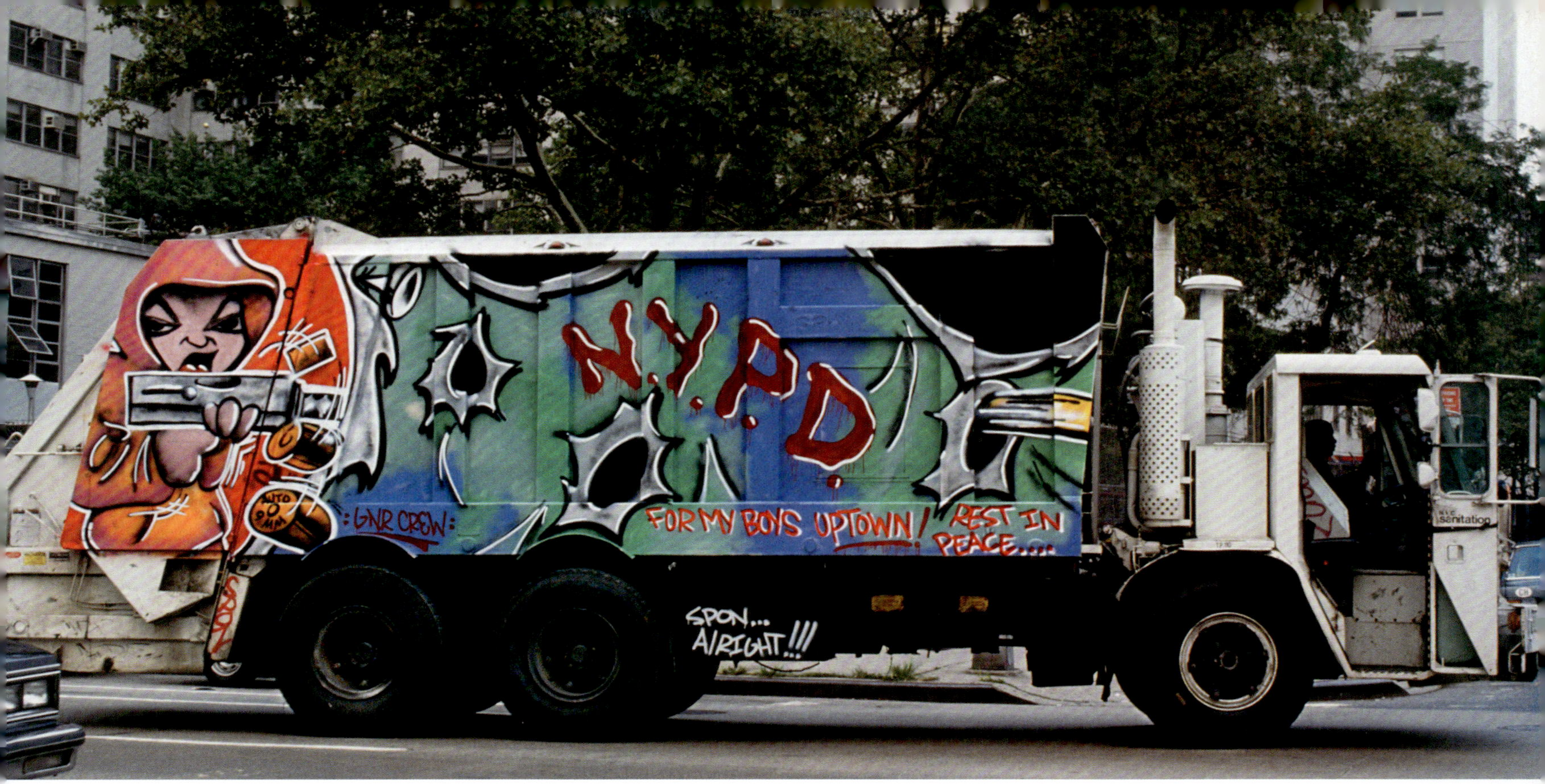
N.Y.P.D
:GNR CREW:
FOR MY BOYS UPTOWN! REST IN PEACE....
SPON... AIRIGHT!!!
sanitation

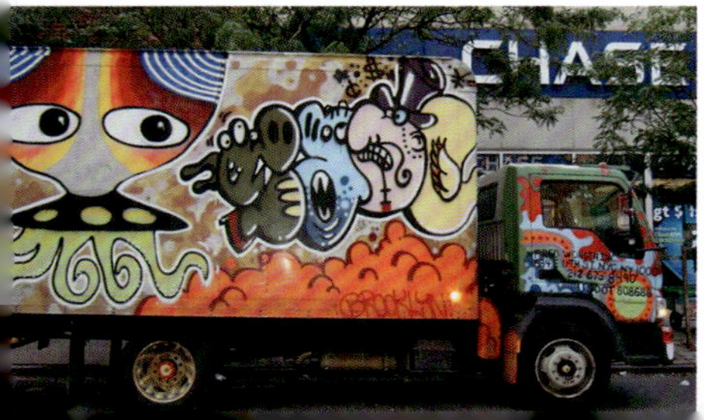
CHASE

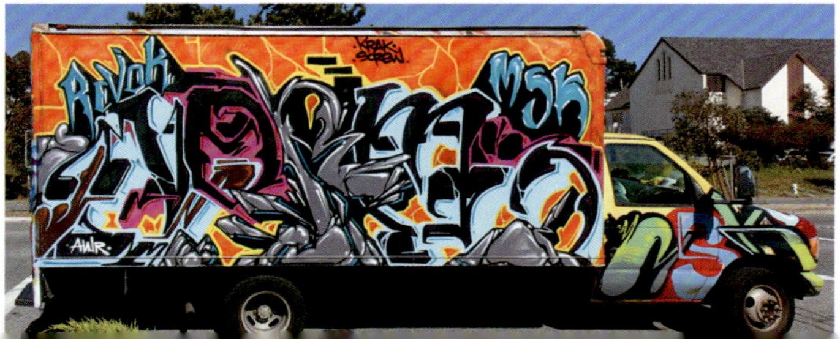

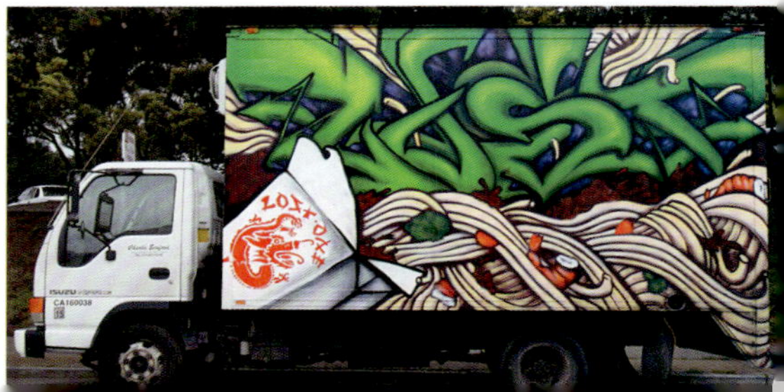

tunnels

After the Metropolitan Transit Authority effectively ended subway graffiti in 1989, many artists moved to higher ground; highways, bridges, and rooftops became the game's top prizes. Freights also drew some interest for those addicted to steel and wheels, but a more elusive type of graffiti emerged: tunnel bombing. A new breed of writer declared the tunnels of the New York subway system as its domain—a vast netherworld with little chance for exposure except to other like-minded bottom-dwellers. Writers had long written their names in the tunnel segments between stations, where trains would park, but making the cavernous catacombs the primary objective? Preposterous.

Smith and JA were among the first to popularize the new sport, and they walked hundreds of miles of track, dodging oncoming trains, to become the first tunnel kings. The lit-up spots along tunnel walls were the most coveted locations, because from the window of a slow-moving train, the graffiti would at least be visible for a few seconds.

Competitions arose and beefs ensued, one culminating tragically when Slick and Soni, two Brooklyn writers trying to write over JA's work in the tunnels, misjudged an oncoming train and were killed on impact. Following the terrorist attacks of September 11, tunnels drew greater police scrutiny, and graffiti activity subsided.

J.SON (left) and Seen.
Photograph by Martha Cooper.
Esplanade Tunnel, New York City, 1982.

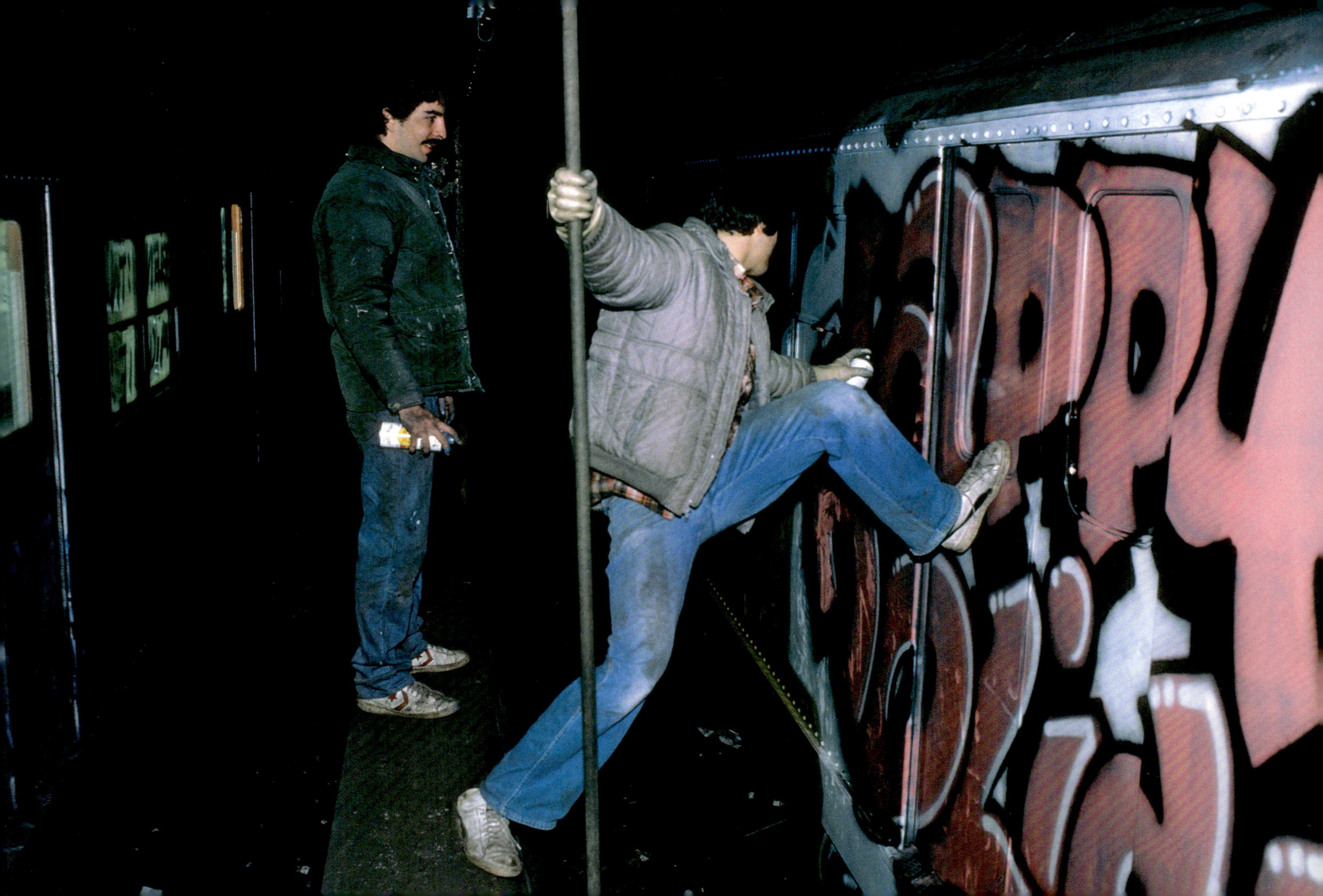

Txtual Healing

In early 2006, mischievous technical wizard Paul Notzold began a project he would eventually title "Txtual Healing." His idea was to create a collection of public projections and performances that encouraged dialogue and interaction with viewers through the use of text messages submitted by audience members. As a play on spontaneity, Notzold would set up giant projectors aimed at the sides of buildings, often with speech bubbles seemingly popping out of windows, and viewers on the street would send in text messages of whatever sort they liked, to be projected onto the buildings. The project created a consummately ephemeral, spur-of-the-moment storytelling experience controlled by the collective viewership, which made for an unpredictable and humorous event.

As the experiment gained notoriety, the technology began to advance as well, eventually branching into a digitalized version of the handwriting styles of various graffiti writers, and even going so far as movies, where the audience texted the dialogue of the actors to trigger the film forward.

Eventually, although he was based in New York, Notzold was approached to collaborate with numerous corporate clients and even the Barack Obama campaign, and he began to travel the world exhibiting the Txtual Healing project.

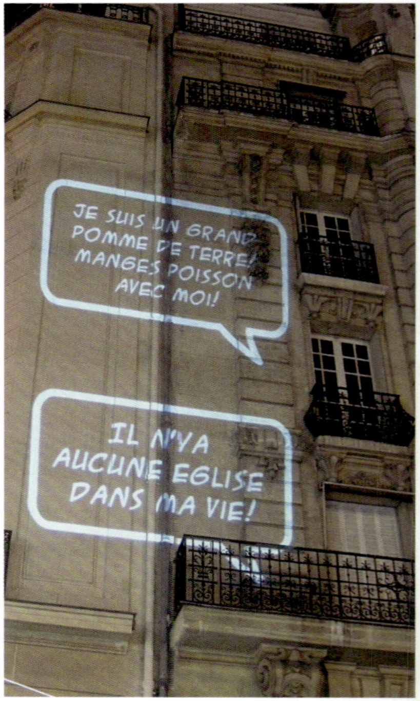

Photographs courtesy of Paul Notzgold.
Top left, top right, and bottom left: Toronto, Canada, 2007.
Bottom right: Brooklyn, New York, 2007.
Detail: Paris, 2008.

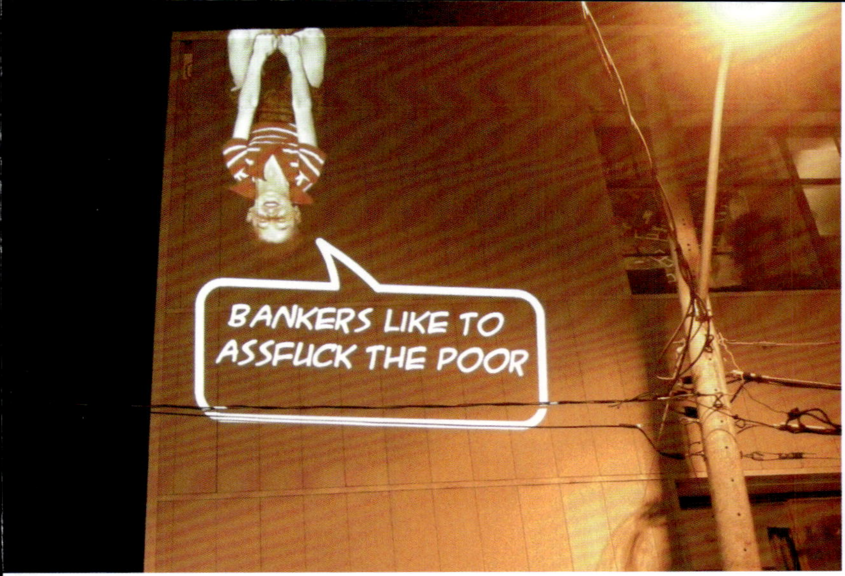
BANKERS LIKE TO ASSFUCK THE POOR

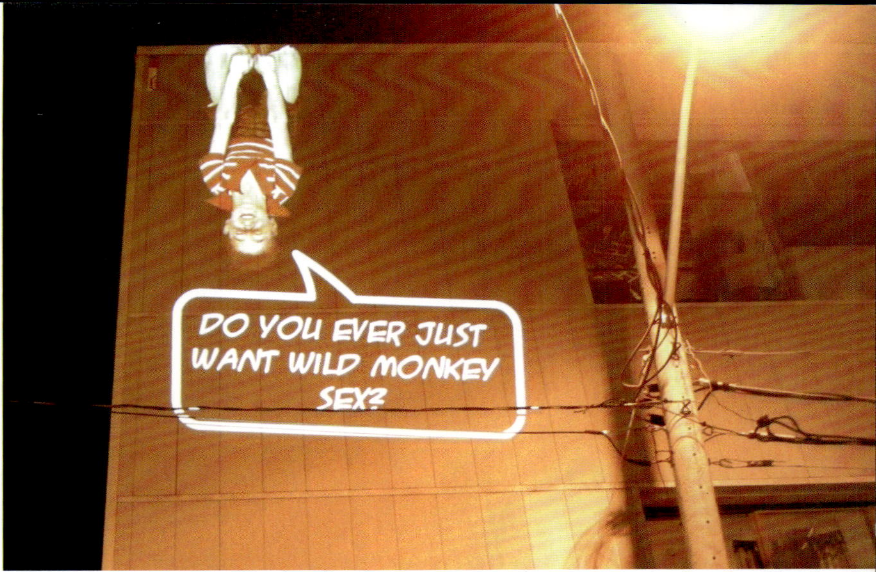
DO YOU EVER JUST WANT WILD MONKEY SEX?

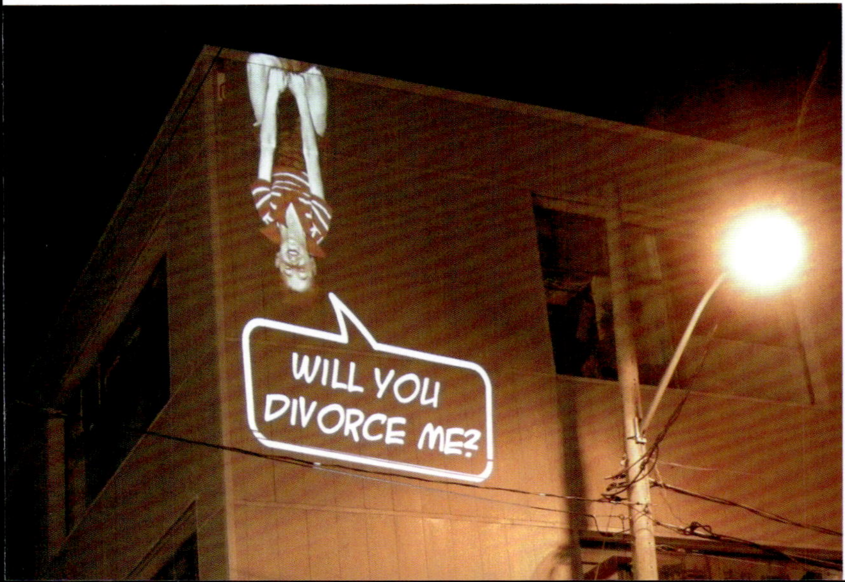
WILL YOU DIVORCE ME?

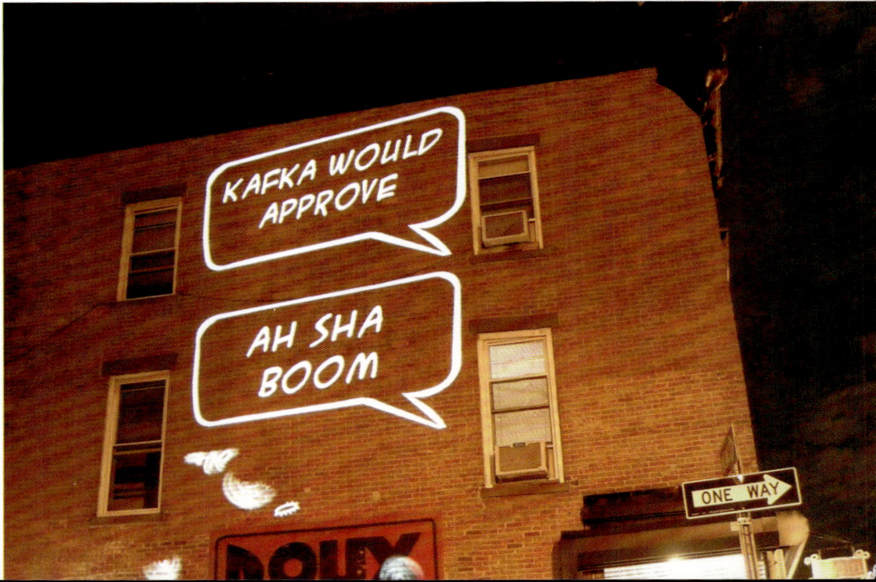
KAFKA WOULD APPROVE
AH SHA BOOM
ONE WAY

Tyke/ Witnes

It's hard to imagine that Tyke, at six foot three, was given his moniker by his older brother's friends for being the runt of the litter back in 1987. Tyke had begun to draw monsters in kindergarten, but never thought about graffiti until his older brother Sumet AWR started writing and let Tyke tag along that same year. A few years later, Tyke met Krush KSN, an early LA stylemaster who taught him a lot about technique, and Tyke soon began to intertwine characters within very complex letterforms, heavy on detail and texture. Greatly influenced by the interlocking mechanical lettering of Case 2, a style known as "computer-rock," Tyke put his own spin on things and developed "organic monster rock."

After a brief hiatus to start a clothing line called EyeWitness, Tyke returned to graffiti with a new name: Witnes. He liked the symmetry of the name and began executing pieces with personalities of their own. Monsters reminiscent of Big Daddy Ed Roth's hotrod creatures—with drooling fangs and eyes popping out of misshapen faces—placed inside twisted, color-changing letters make Witnes pieces instantly recognizable.

Recently, he completed graffiti tours of Amsterdam and Vietnam and completed a project at Le Grand Palais in Paris. He maintains a separate career as a gallery artist and remains a key component of the MSK/AWR/7th Letter crew [see 022]. Revok [see 274], one of LA's—and the world's—top writers, cites Tyke and Krush as the two most significant influences on the development of his personal style.

Photographs courtesy of Tyke. California, 2010.

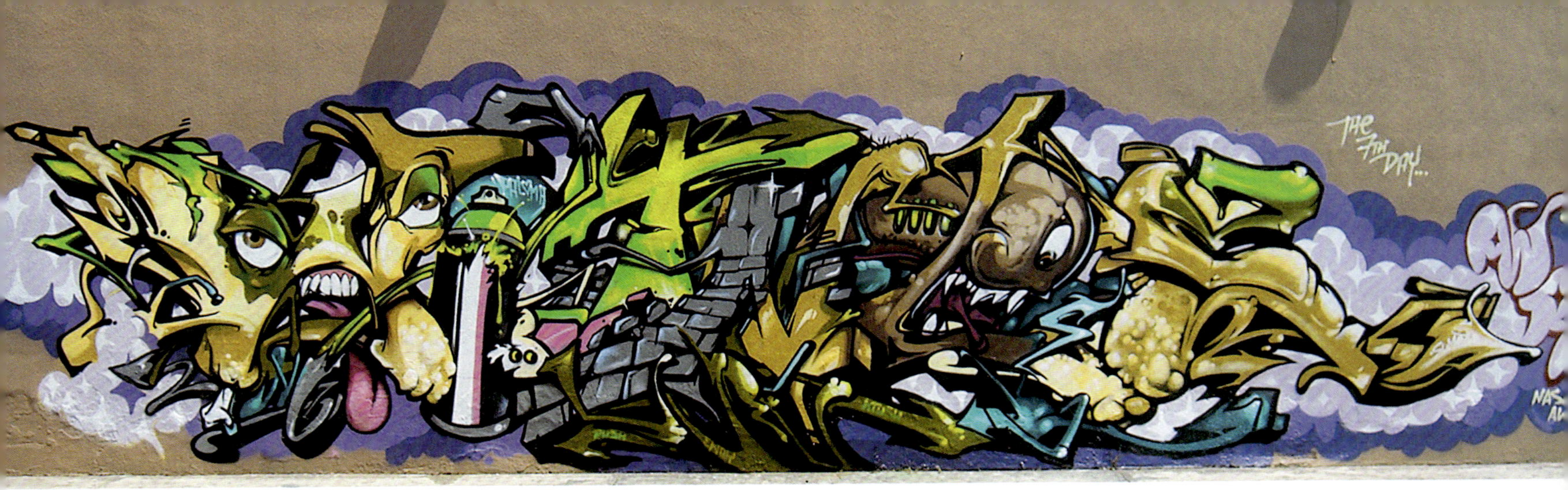
THE 7TH DAY...

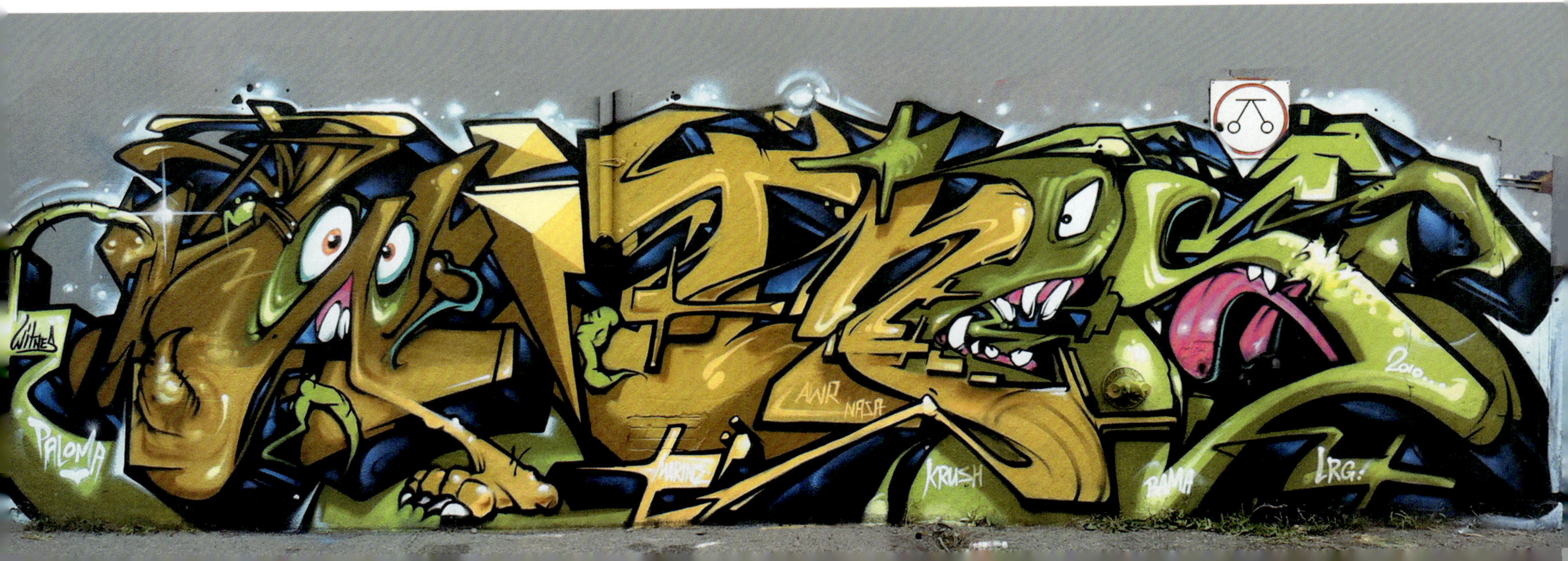
PALOMA
AWR
NASA
KRUSH
BAMA
LRG!
2010...

UGA

In 1972, Hugo Martinez was a PhD candidate at the City College of New York when he decided to immerse himself in the graffiti subculture. He took a tour of the Upper West Side with Henry 161 and met some of the top writers of the day, including Snake 1 and Stitch 1 from Writers Corner 188.

Over the course of the next few months, the writers showed up at Hugo's apartment to draw and paint, and this gave birth to the collective known as UGA, or United Graffiti Artists. The collective featured an initial roster that included Coco 144, Sanke 1, Stitch 1, C.A.T. 87, Sjk 171, Mike 171, Henry 161, and others.

In 1973, the group had achieved two huge milestones: a feature article in *New York* magazine and a collaborative effort with Twyla Tharp called "Deuce Coupe," where the writers appeared on stage, painting.

As writing shifted from the single-hit tags to the masterpiece, Bronx writers like Phase 2 [see 255] and Bama were invited into the group, while Brooklyn was represented by Mico, Flint 707 [see 135], and WG. Manhattan writers with gang ties, like Henry 161 and Mike 171, refused to give ground to the Bronx writers, and a fight broke out, leaving Hugo Martinez and others bloodied. The violent members were asked to leave, and UGA went on to have its greatest success in 1974, with a group show at the Razor gallery in Soho.

Front row, left to right: Lee 163, unknown artist, Coco 144, Mico; back row, left to right: Snake I and two unknown artists. Photograph by Herb Migdal. New York City, 1974.

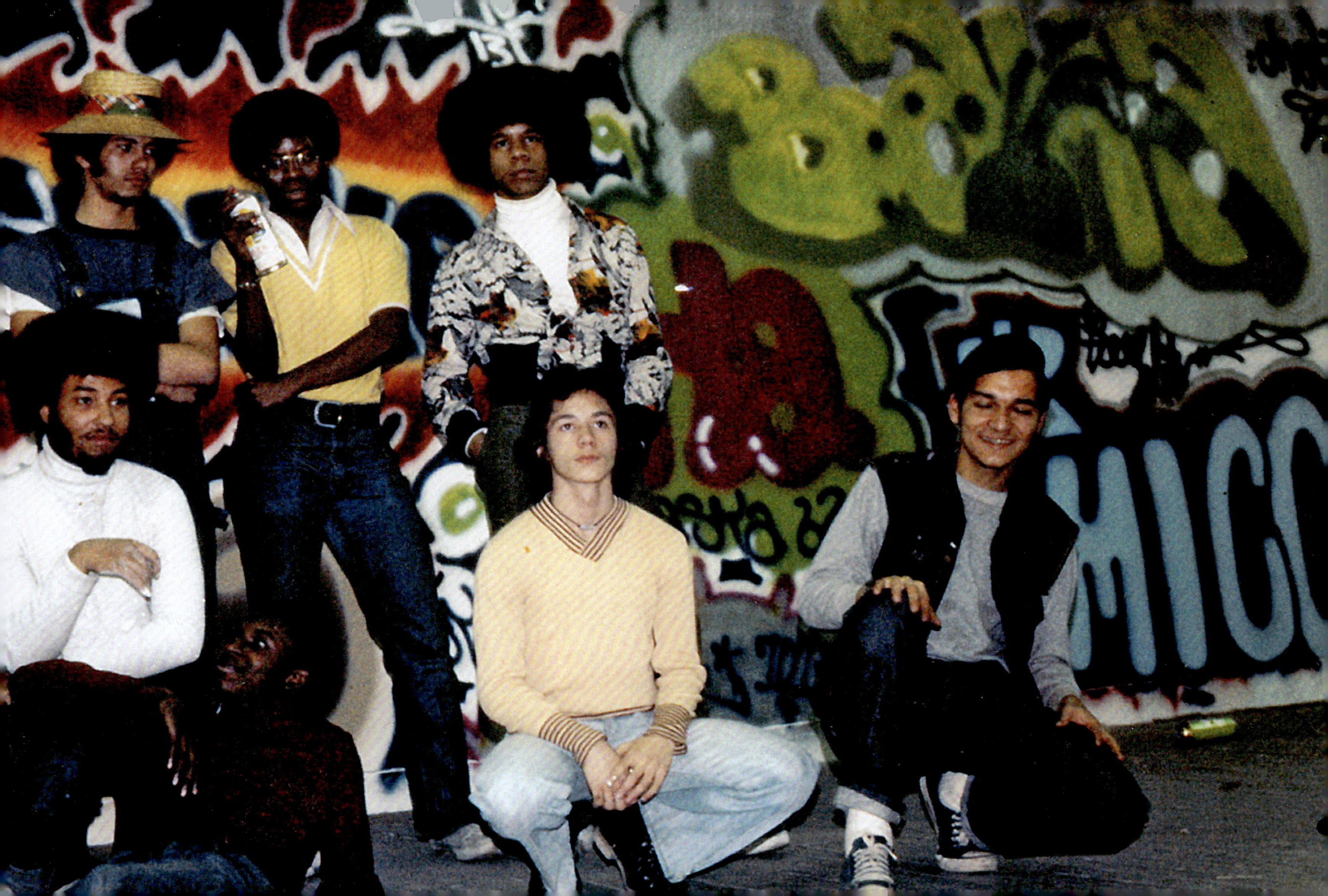

Underbelly Project

Back in the day, in this case almost a century ago, construction companies used to build underground subway tunnels on spec, in the hopes of getting the city's business once the tunnels were complete. One such "free sample" tunnel, constructed but never utilized, has sat for decades, moldy and abandoned, deep beneath the streets of New York City. Recently, this tunnel, known only to a smattering of urban-explorer types, became the unlikely home of an ambitious art project.

In 2009, Workhorse and Pac, the two organizers of the Underbelly Project, saw the tunnel's vast potential. Inviting only their most trusted friends, the curatorial pair brought in one hundred street and graffiti artists to transform the massive blank catacomb into an inaccessible art gallery—a ghost museum. But for what purpose?

Workhorse explains: "There are plenty of other parallel 'causes,' but at the heart of it was to just *have fun*. We felt like it was a shame to have such a massive place under New York City and not do something with it. The other thing is that we were sort of getting tired of the commercialism of everything. People were ripping down doors, cutting walls, and tearing off electrical panels to sell them on eBay—just because some artist did a shitty doodle. We wanted to do something that wouldn't be cut down, something that couldn't be repackaged and sold to some collector. We managed to take a year and a half, work, in a close environment, with some of the most dedicated, focused, and talented artists in the world, and share an experience that most people never get to have. It *was* fun."

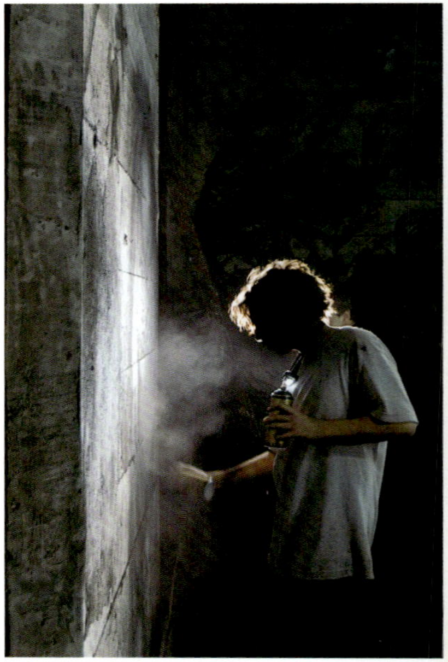

Artwork by [left to right] Dennis McNett, Anthony Lister, Flying Fortress, Ema, Swoon (on pole), WK Interact, Dabs Myla, and Daryl Peirce.
Photographs courtesy of Workhorse.
New York City, 2010.

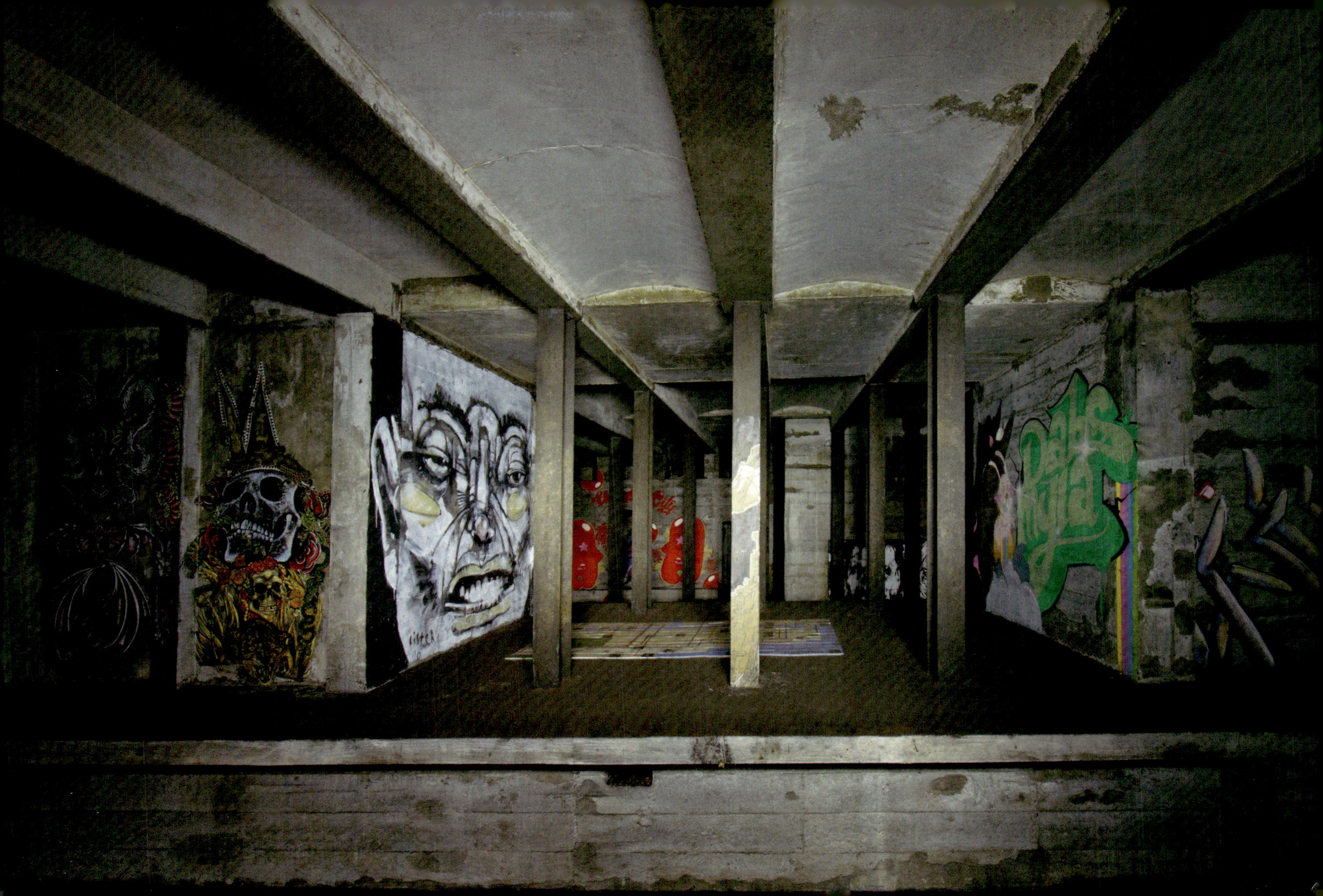

Various and Gould

Various and Gould are a unique pair: boyfriend and girlfriend, longtime life partners and art cohorts.

Gould has been an influential figure in the Berlin street-art scene for more than a decade, founding and maintaining the groundbreaking "Wall Street Journal" project, in which a newspaper was published and wheatpasted to a wall in Berlin's Friedrichshain neighborhood, and viewers could interact with it. Gould became known for artworks wheatpasted all over dilapidated city streets, alongside other Berlin legends like Tower [see 339] and CT'ink [see 080].

Various worked alongside Gould in creating numerous street-art group exhibitions in Berlin, but is perhaps best known for her own project "Paper Girl," a public art installation/intervention piece, during which numerous artists submit as many copies of an artwork as they can [for example, screen-printed or photocopied images], which are then collated, rolled into newspaperlike bundles, and tossed from a passing bicycle to people's doorsteps, much like newspapers would have been delivered in earlier times.

Together, Various and Gould have created numerous street-art projects, and they have also made the transition into the fine-art world, exhibiting their works collaged on wood at New York's Brooklynite Gallery in 2010.

The couple continue to live and work in Berlin.

**Photograph by Luna Park.
Brooklyn, New York, 2010.**

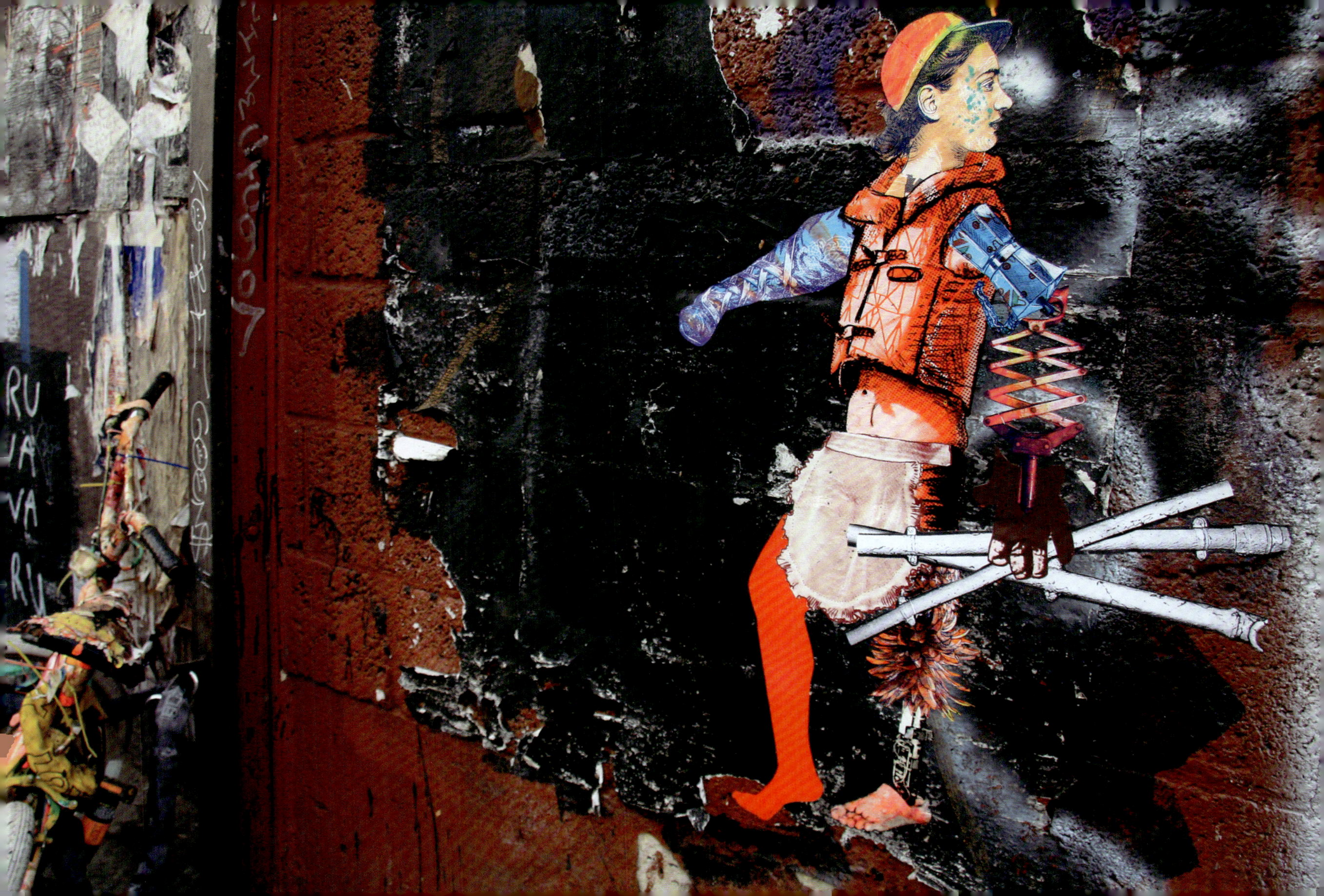

Alexandros Vasmouslakis

Alexandros Vasmouslakis was born in 1980 and grew up in Athens, Greece, where he was well aware of graffiti's place on the map of artistic possibility; graffiti most likely gave Vasmouslakis his first taste of color on a grand scale. Later, having graduated with honors from art school in Athens, Vasmouslakis took to painting massive public works of his own, creating works that covered the full height of an apartment complex.

Quoted as having said that his characters are a break from the "inanity" of Greek culture, Vasmouslakis generally paints people, unique individuals with a highly stylized, almost illustrative quality—girls with bugged-out eyes, men with impossibly skinny legs, torsos bursting into shards of color, and the like.

Although a fine-art career was always Vasmouslakis's intention—he has been exhibiting his work since 1999—his public work is what he is best known for in Greece, and he began to catch the world's eye with appearances on the wildly popular street-art blog, the Wooster Collective (see 359). In 2009, the artist was living and working in Berlin, transforming the urban landscape, and in 2010 he debuted his first U.S. solo show at Lebasse Projects in Los Angeles.

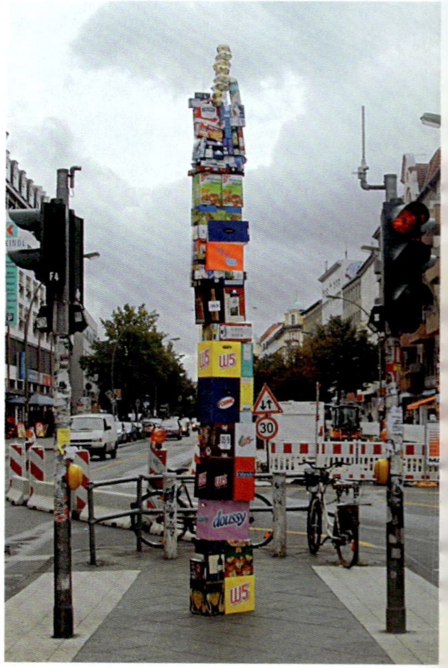

Photographs courtesy of Alexandro Vasmoulakis.
Athens, Greece, 2007.
Detail: Berlin, Germany, 2009.

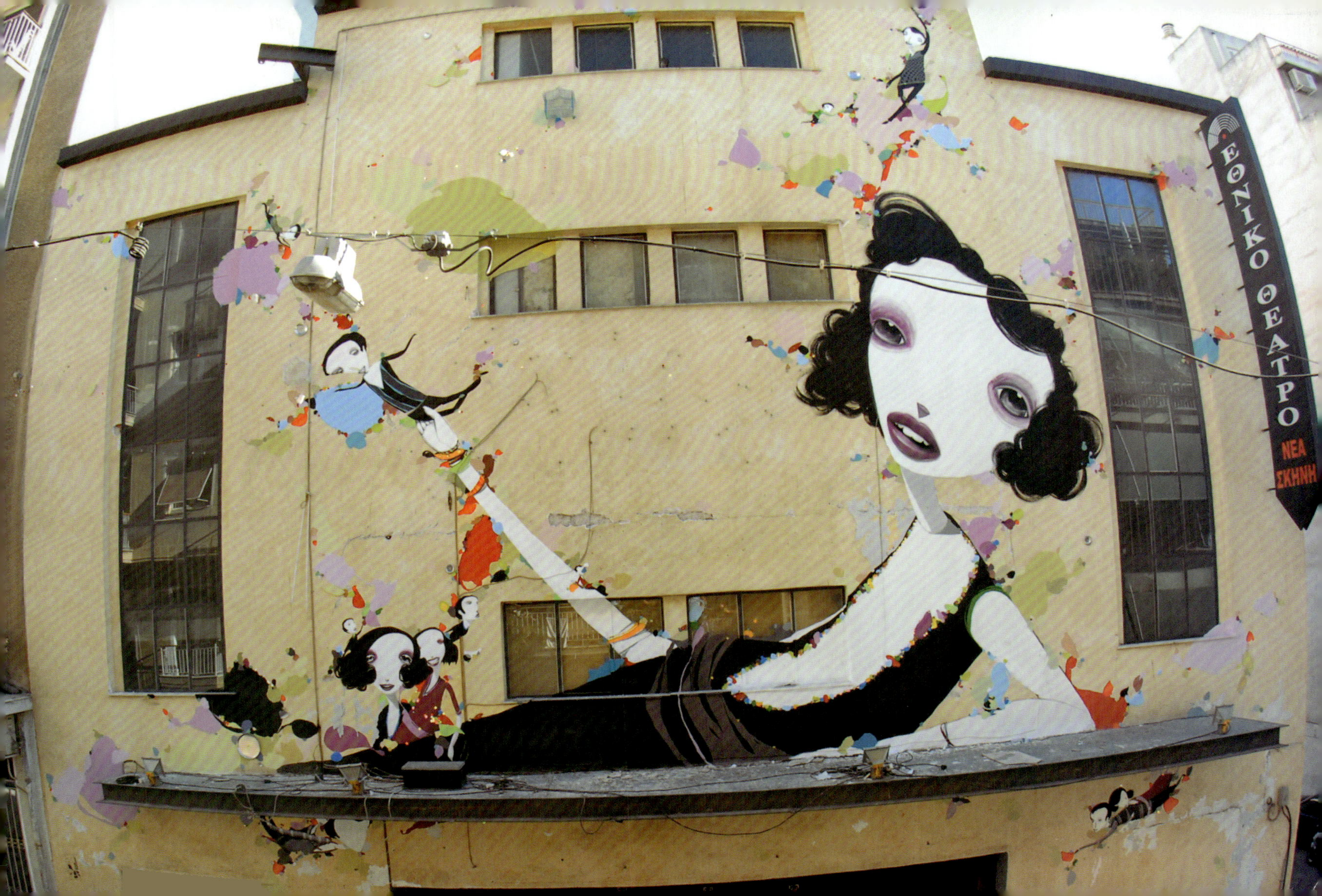
ΕΘΝΙΚΟ ΘΕΑΤΡΟ
ΝΕΑ ΣΚΗΝΗ

Vexta

Vexta is one of Australia's few female stencil artists to have achieved wide recognition. She began stenciling in 2002, soon after moving from Sydney to Melbourne, gaining inspiration from the countless stencils she saw on her adopted city's streets. She was particularly drawn to the notion of sharing art in public spaces, as her primary goal is to connect with others in an expressive manner.

Intent on raising questions, Vexta often employs urban icons and images from popular culture, such as skeletons and skulls, in unorthodox scenarios. "I think the best art should be revolutionary and drive us forward as a society, or make us stop and think," she says. Her latest works utilize three-dimensional found objects and have become increasingly experimental, as she deals with such themes as our relationship to other creatures or time and space.

Vexta has painted in several European cities including London, Paris, and Berlin. In 2010, she was one of several international artists invited to take part in the Bogotá Stencil Festival. Vexta's artwork has found a place in many public and private collections and spaces, including the National Gallery of Australia. Self-taught, she attributes her passion for art to her mother, who supplied her with endless pencils and paper as she was growing up.

**Photographs by Lois Stavsky.
London, 2008.**

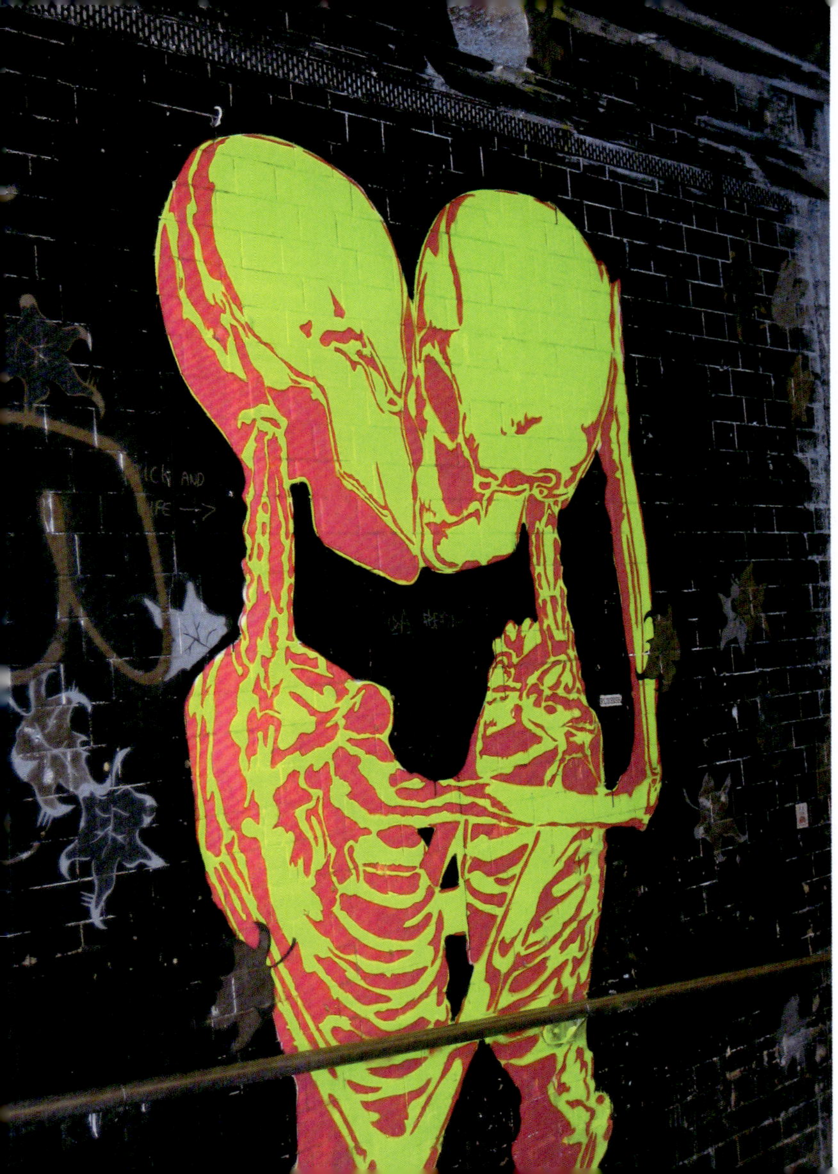

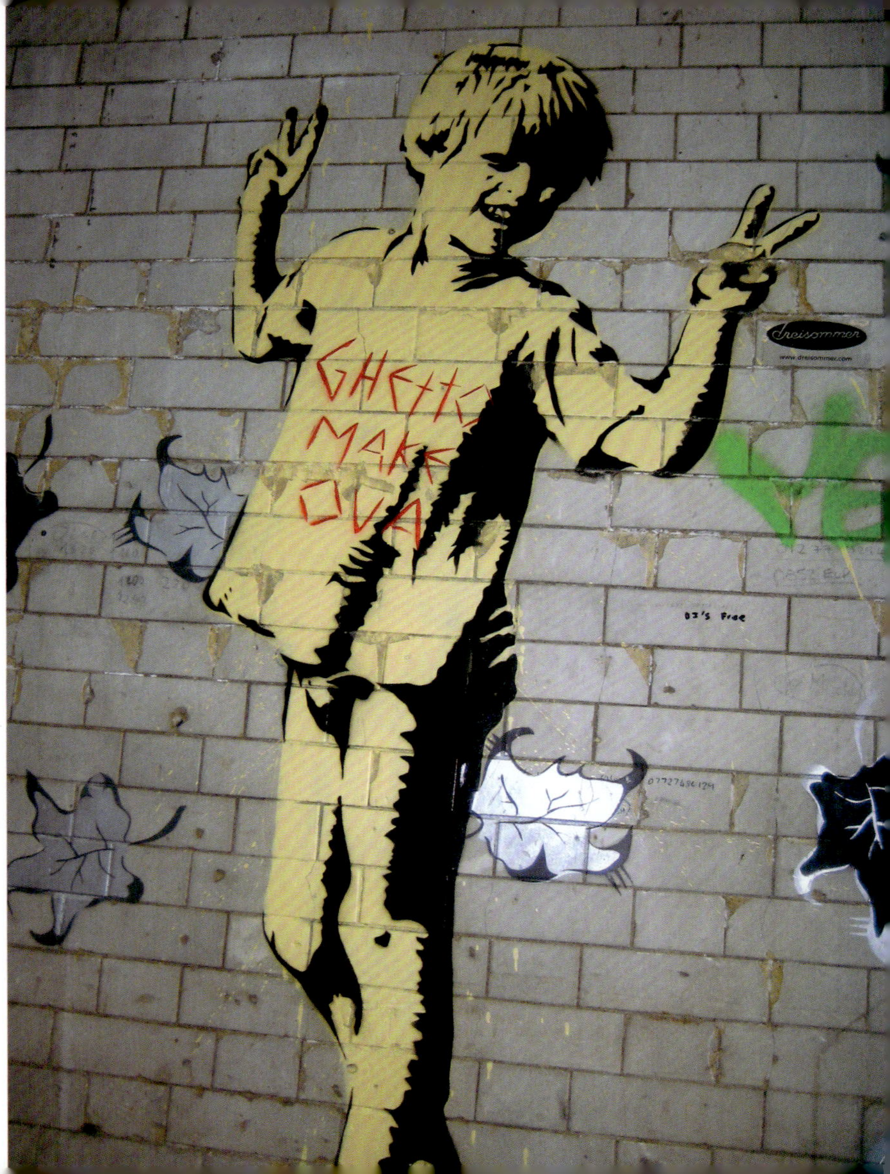
GHetto
MAKE
OVA
dreisommer
www.dreisommer.com
DJ's Free

Vhils

In 2008, gallerist Steve Lazarides came to New York and mounted a show called "The Outsiders." Housed in an abandoned restaurant space on the highly trafficked corner of Houston and Bowery Streets in Manhattan, the show involved a full-scale installation and over a dozen of the highest-profile artists to have emerged from the streets. Works were priced as high as $200,000, and on opening night the line to get in stretched to the corner.

A standout piece in the show was a wall in the basement displaying an intricate and sensitive portrait of a face, painted in a decayed white directly onto the wall. The unique and astonishing thing about the piece was that, instead of simply painting the layer of white onto the surface, the artist had painstakingly cut out the concrete from all the negative area in the piece, making it appear as if the face were jumping off the wall at the viewer. This simple idea—and the extra labor it required—made the artist known as Vhils a star. Shockingly, at the time of "The Outsiders," Vhils, a Portuguese artist by the name of Alexandre Farto, was only twenty-two years old.

Now a resident of London, Vhils went on to sold-out exhibitions with Steve Lazarides at his new flagship gallery on Rathbone Place, as well as countless large-scale public installations internationally. Renowned for his contribution to the furthering of stencil art, Vhils is one of street art's best-known creators.

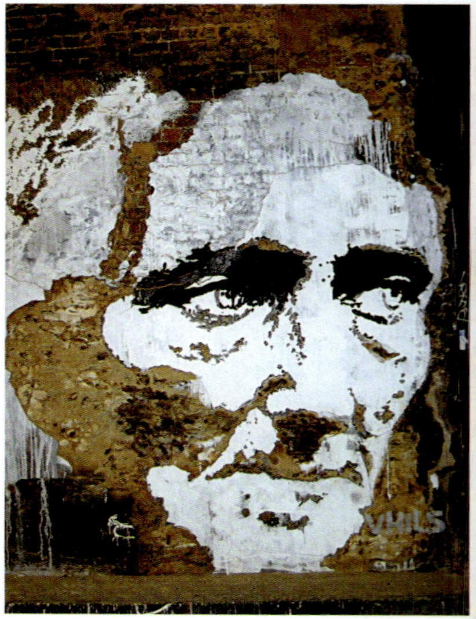

Photographs by Lois Stavsky. London, 2008.

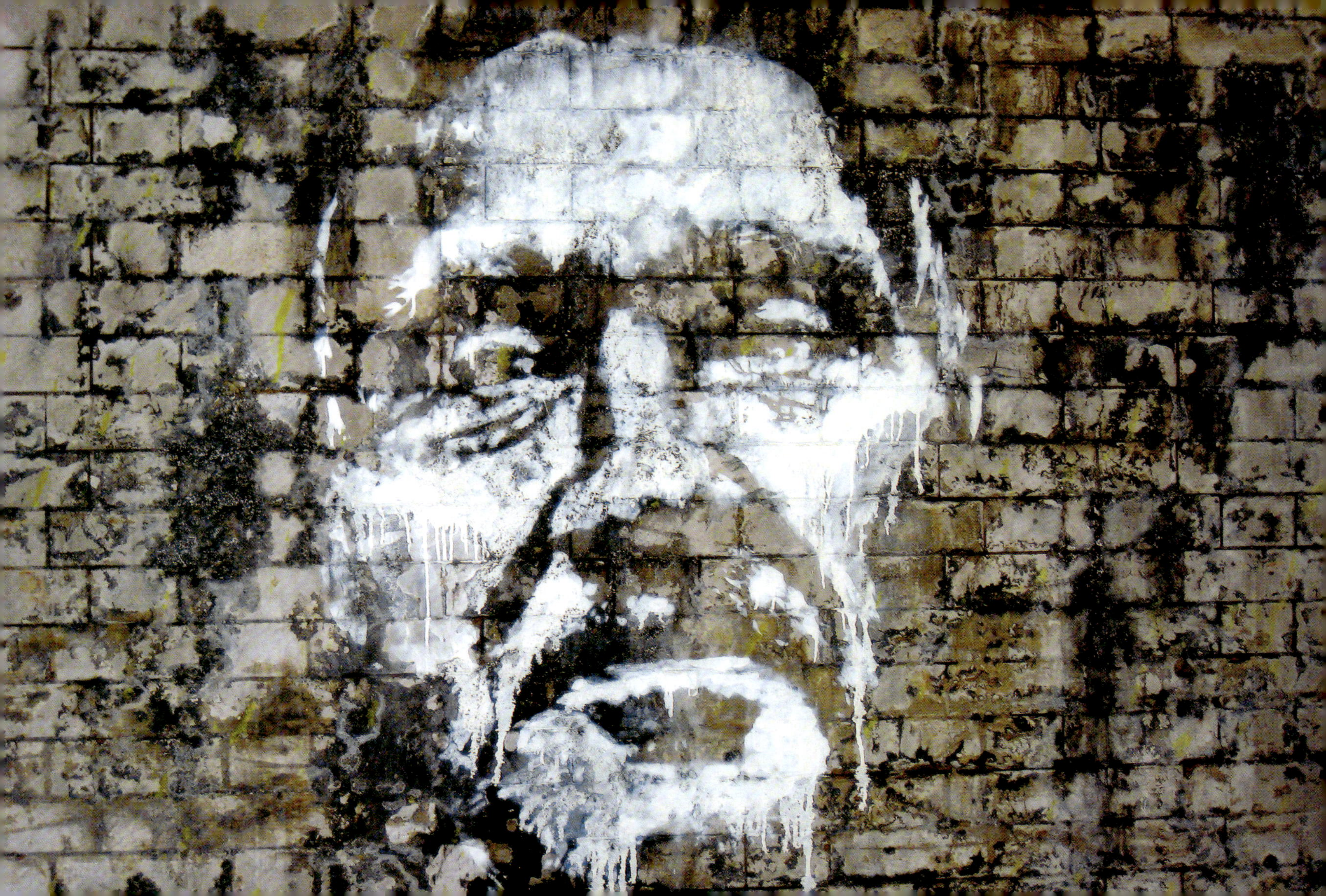

Vinchen

As secretive and elusive as Banksy (see 024) and working in a similarly guarded style, Vinchen remains a mystery. It is assumed the name Vinchen refers to one man, but even that hasn't been confirmed. Unwilling to disclose any particulars about his identity, he reveals himself exclusively through his socially relevant images and sardonic statements. Although he has been known to respond to e-mails, he hasn't granted any interviews to date.

Playful and political, his clever street art takes on such issues as human excess and wastefulness, our misplaced priorities, our abuse of the environment, and our corrupted values. Wall Street's corporate greed, for example, becomes the focus of such stencil works as a forlorn-looking child alongside the words We Put Hedge Fund Interest Before Our Children's.

Like Banksy, Vinchen is a prankster, a master of guerrilla street art. He created posters featuring a revealing image of Paris Hilton with the words: Hilton, Pampered & Privileged. For Over 80 Years the Hilton Name Has Been Synonymous with Elegance and Class. The posters were mounted inside the walls of the Hilton Hotel in Columbus, Ohio, causing quite a stir.

Vinchen remains intent on provoking people to question what they accept as fact.

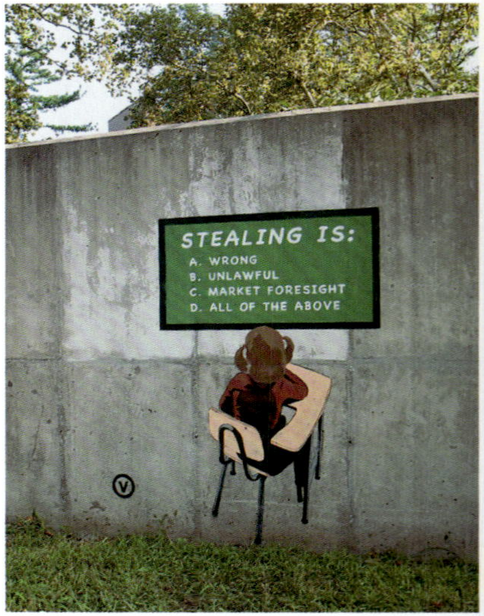

Photographs courtesy of Vinchen. Columbus, Ohio, 2010.

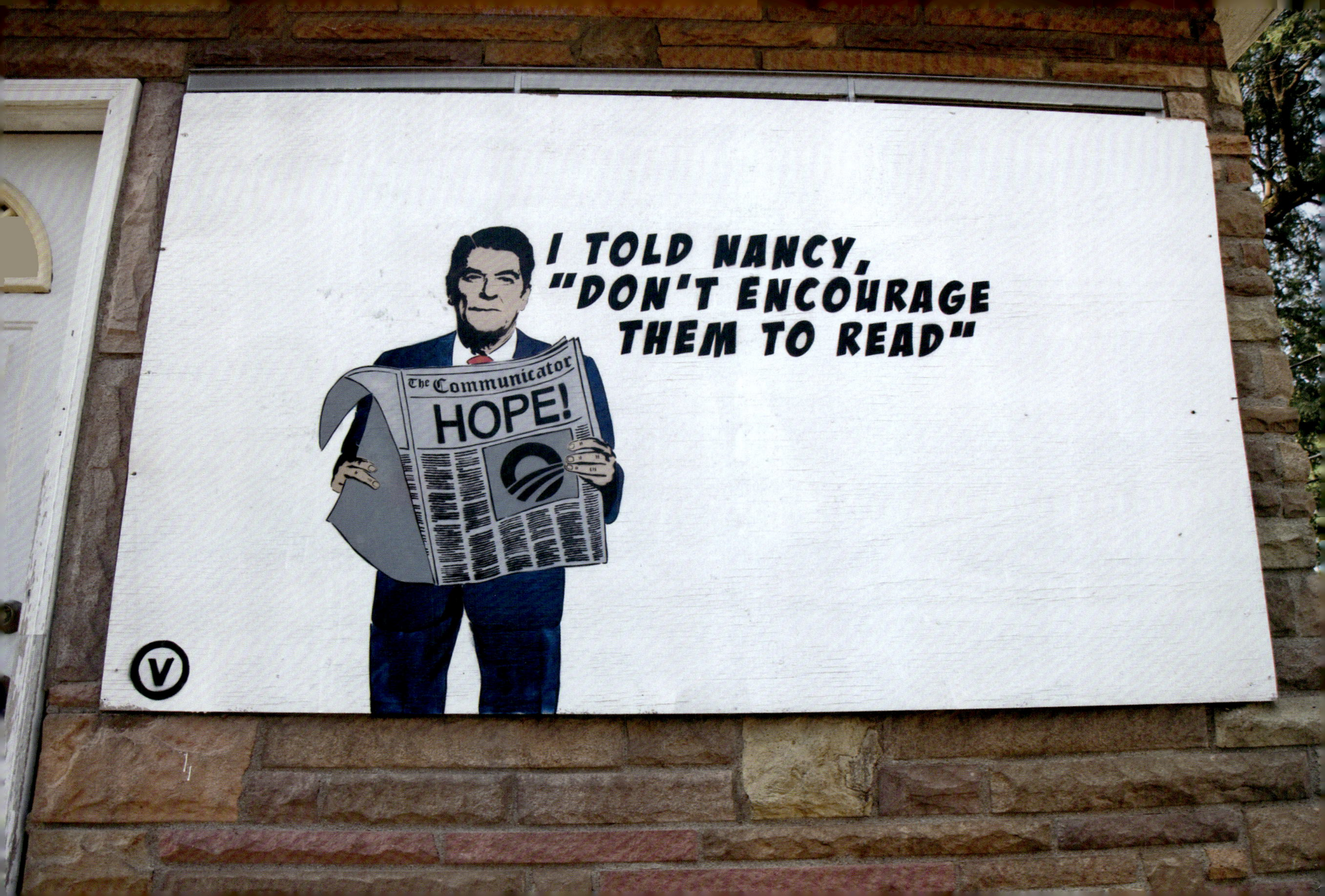
I TOLD NANCY,
"DON'T ENCOURAGE
THEM TO READ"
The Communicator
HOPE!
V

Vitche

Since the 1980s, the artist known as Vitche has been creating public works, beginning, like most young ephemeral artists, with traditional graffiti. Born and raised in São Paulo, Vitche was exposed to *pixação* [see 257] and the coming of New York Wild Style, but developed his own unique voice over decades of prolific painting.

Inspired by the forgotten emotions and natural beauty that big cities swallow, the playful artist's work covers themes from the nautical to the circus, spanning sculpture, photography, and predominantly, painting. In his painted work, Vitche creates intricate, fantastical, lyrical works, often returning to his favorite color combination of red, black, and white.

The artist is quoted as equating art making with the very fabric of being alive, and he defines himself as a political artist, citing thematic threads within his work that connect to a universal social unconscious.

Already a legend among Brazilian urban artists, Vitche has gone on to make the crossover into fine art, having exhibited extensively, including at New York's Jonathan LeVine Gallery, London's StolenSpace, and San Francisco's legendary street art crossover hub, Fifty24SF.

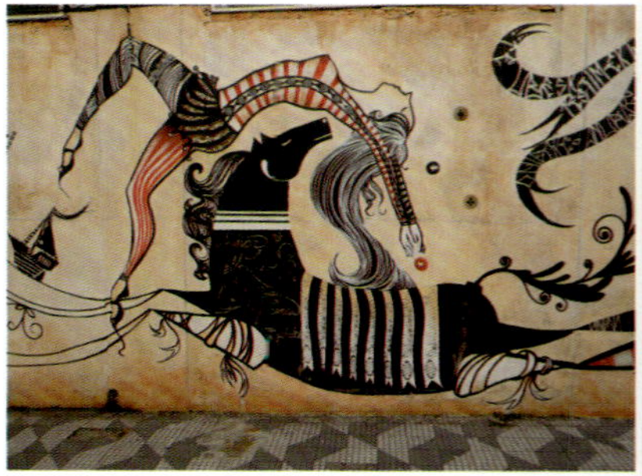

Photographs by Eric Marechal.
São Paulo, Brazil, 2008.

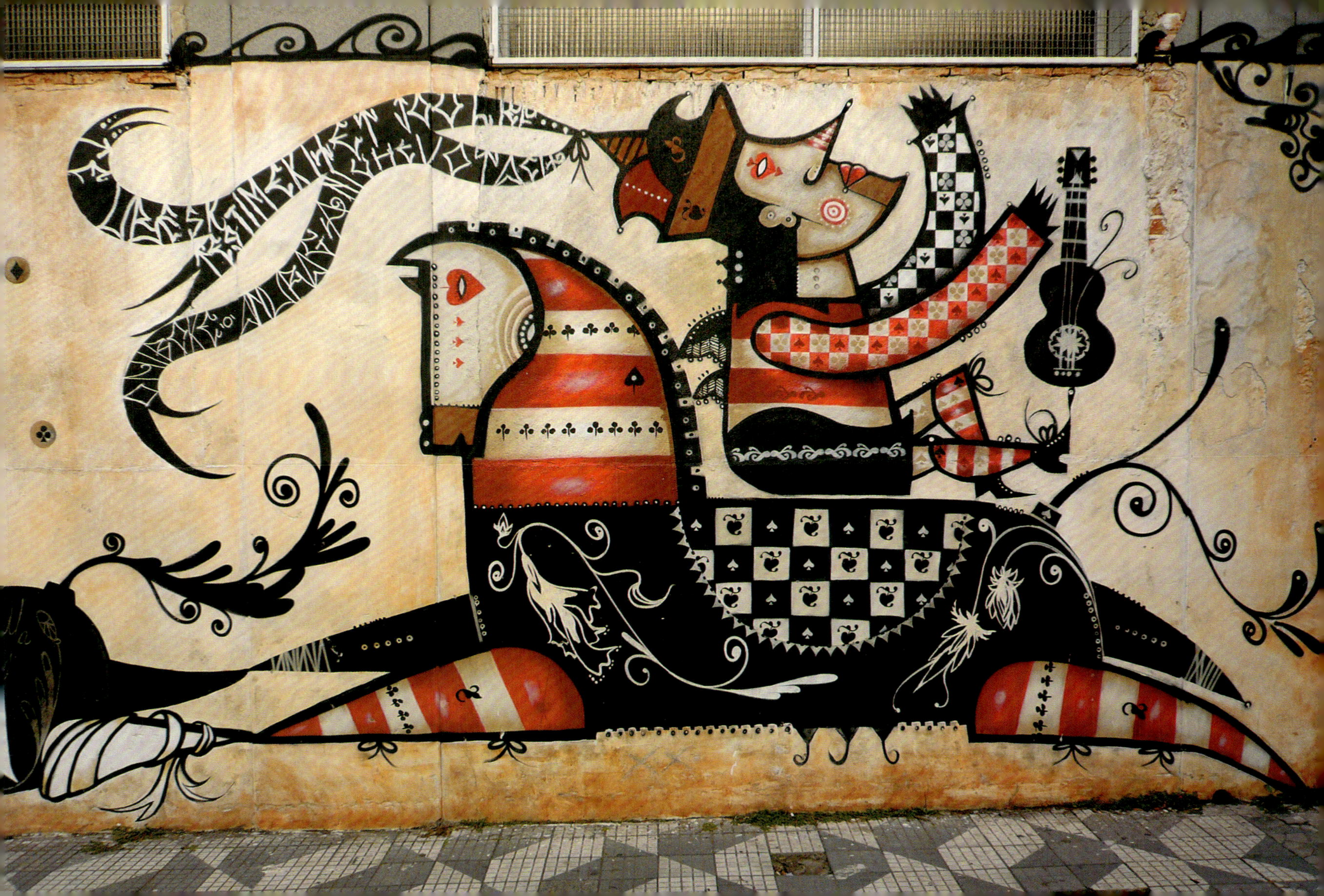

Nick Walker

Born in Bristol, England, in 1969, Nick Walker began to achieve fame within Bristol's underground graffiti scene in the early 1980s. Always finding novel ways to use a spray can, Walker has been deemed a pioneer of England's street-art movement. In 1992, in an effort to impart a vaguely photorealistic look to his artwork, he started to infuse stencils into his spray-paintings. Since then, he has gained an international reputation as an artist who breaks the borders of graffiti, street art, and fine art.

Bristol credits among his influences fellow Bristolian 3-D [aka Massive Attack] and the French illustrator Moebius; his favorite artists include Robert Rauschenberg, Andy Warhol, José Parlá, Shepard Fairey [see 124], Faile [see 123], Mac, and Retna [see 273]. Working also as a set designer and illustrator, Walker has done work for record labels, clothing companies, and major motion pictures, including Stanley Kubrick's *Eyes Wide Shut*. In 2009, his artwork was featured in a Black Eyed Peas music video. Describing his painting as a "form of escapism," Walker strives to lighten his viewers' spirits, as well as his own.

These days, Walker's work, merging stencils, prints, and freehand artwork, is more likely to be found in galleries and museums than on illegal walls. When his 2008 *Life's Too Short* print was released in conjunction with his show at London's Black Rat Press, loyal fans and eager collectors lined up for thirty-six hours prior to the exhibit's opening.

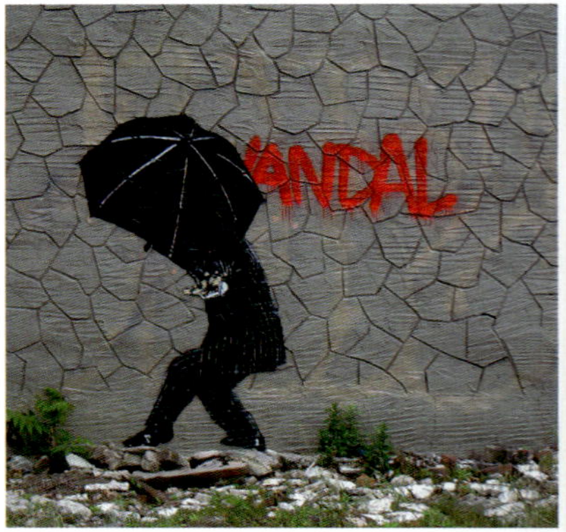

Photograph by Vincent Cornelli. New York City, 2008. Detail: Photograph by Becki Fuller. Brooklyn, New York, 2008.

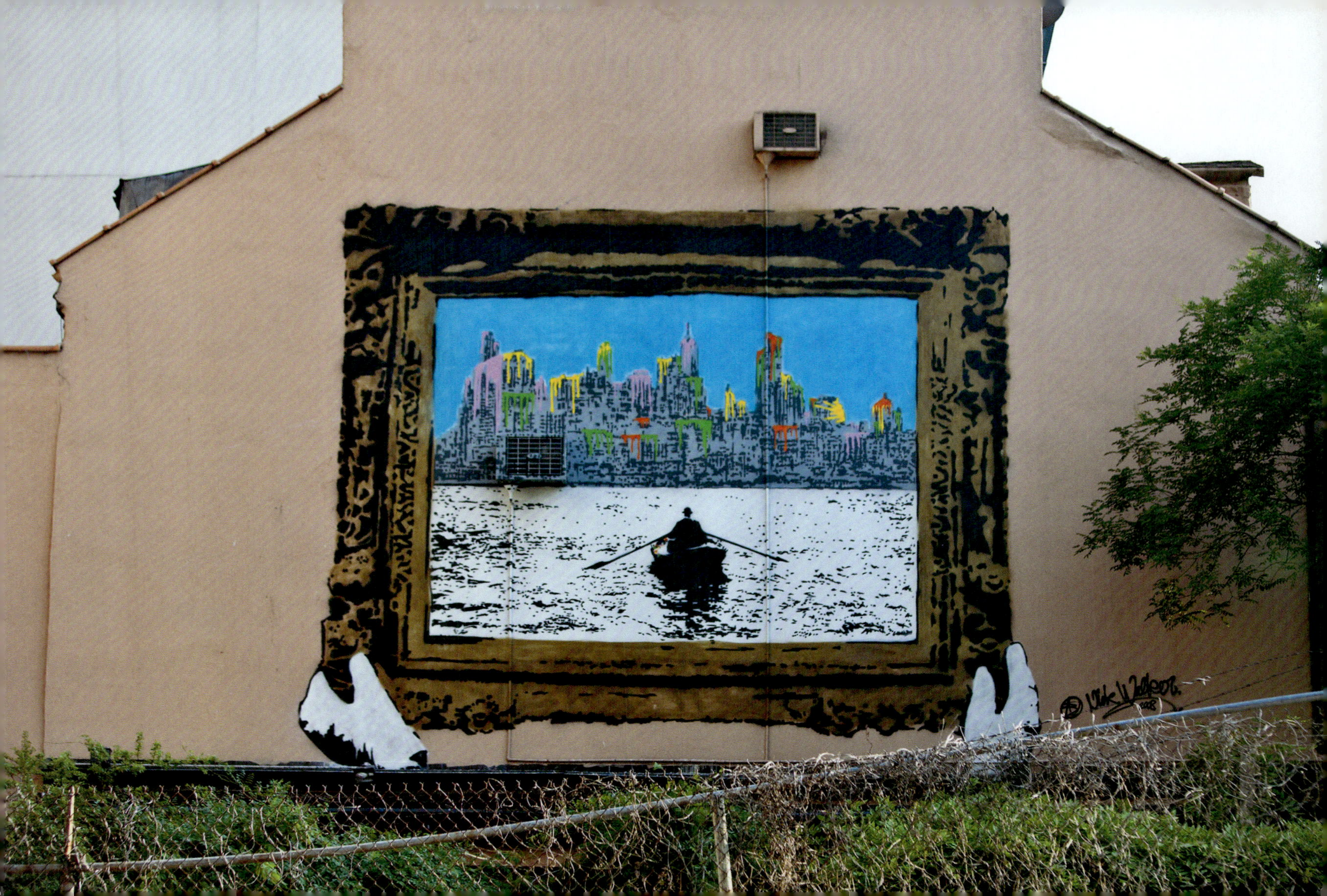

Wany

Andrea Sergio began writing his pseudonym, Wany, on the walls of his hometown of Brindisi, Italy, at age twelve. Innately gifted, Wany won a drawing contest in Puglia at sixteen, which led to his first commercial jobs. In 1996, after graduating from art school, Wany created the hip-hop magazine *Ill Fame*, which became an Italian cult classic.

Since 1998, Wany has wowed audiences at graffiti jams in cities throughout Italy. In 2000, he moved to Bologna, where he took on art-directing responsibilities for Dynit, a publisher of Japanese comics and cartoons. Wany's skills have since earned him a paint sponsorship as a member of the Ironlak team, and he's landed gigs with numerous corporate heavyweights—Nike, Adidas, Coca-Cola, Dolce & Gabbana, Timberland, and Volkswagen, to name a few.

Known for his super-tight character work and innovative concepts, Wany's recent collaborations with the British crew Heavy Artillery (see 164) have earned him worldwide recognition. A fine artist as well, he moved to Milan in 2007 after a major gallery recruited him. Twenty years in the game have inspired Wany to formalize his moniker—no longer a preteen scrawler, he currently bills himself as Mr. Wany.

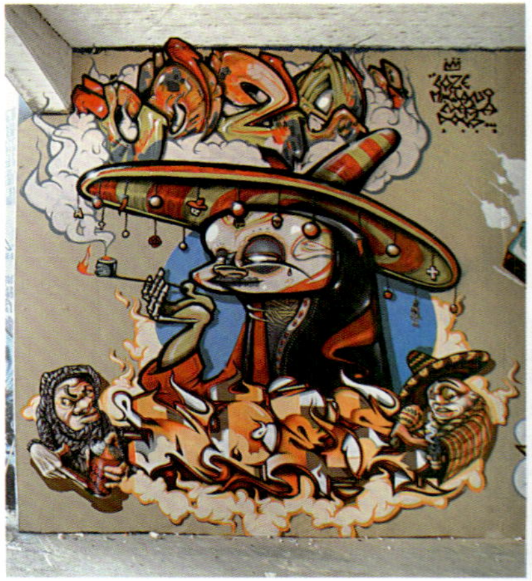

Photographs courtesy of Wany.

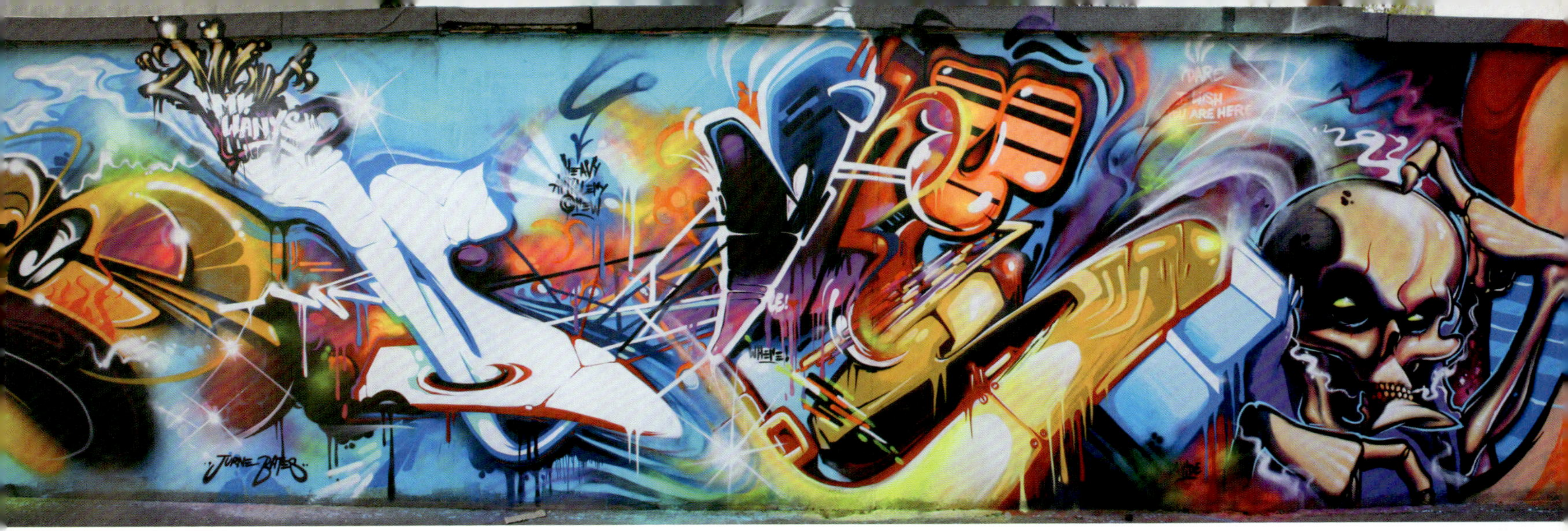

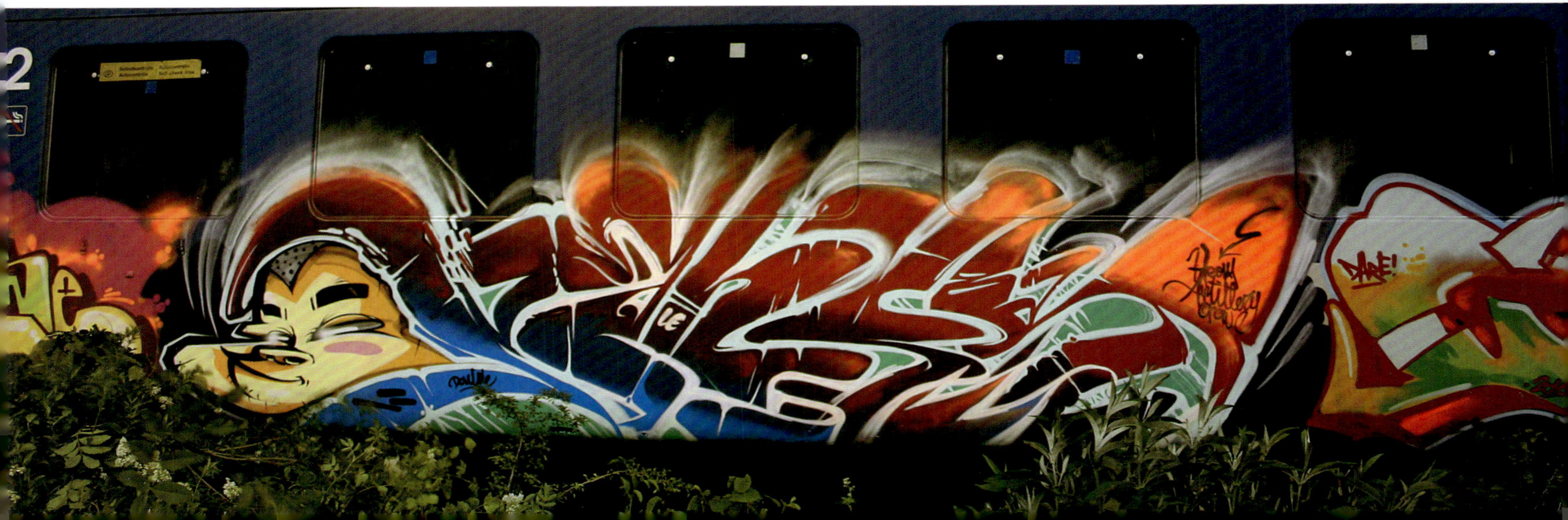

Dan Witz

In the late 1970s, a smattering of photorealistic hummingbird paintings began to flutter across New York City's embattled walls. In stark contrast to the calligraphy-based graffiti culture burgeoning on subway cars, the little birds represented a different aesthetic of art making. They were a calculated labor of love offered to the city, carefully birthed by the skilled hand of an immensely talented craftsman. That hand belonged to painter Dan Witz.

A classically trained oil painter and a graduate of the prestigious Rhode Island School of Design, Witz came to New York in the 1970s. Rebellious in thought and spirit, he has always sought the antithesis of whatever was the popular trend at the time, answering the frenetic, speedy tagging culture with his meditative, time-consuming oil paintings.

Primarily working in series, Witz became widely recognized for his hyperrealistic "hoodies," images of a hooded man, painted in oil before being printed on vinyl decals, that appeared around the newly gentrified Williamsburg neighborhood in the 1990s. Witz continues to put work on the street, although today his primary focus is his studio work, which he still makes in Brooklyn.

Photograph by Luna Park.
Brooklyn, New York, 2010.

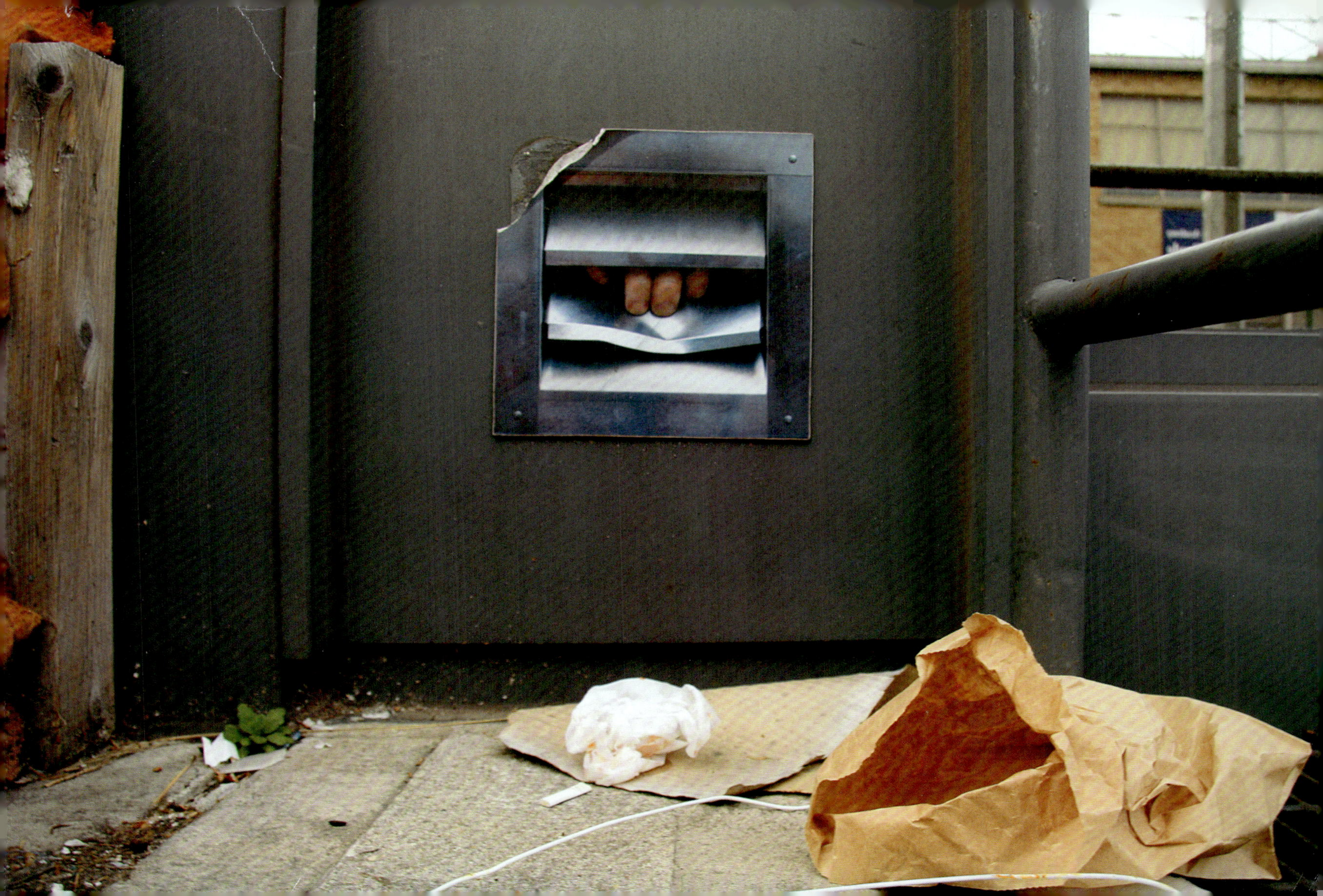

WK Interact

One of street art's early flag bearers was a Frenchman who goes by the unusual moniker WK Interact. Reflecting his obsession with the human body in motion, WK's black-and-white works were a staple of the downtown New York landscape. Featuring the distorted, three-dimensional figures of professional boxers to the chiseled features of supermodels, his prolific monochromatic works were, for countless enthusiasts, primers in New York street art, as well as influential precursors to the international street-art movement of today.

An adoptive New Yorker, WK was born in 1969 in Caen, France. In the 1990s, he immigrated to New York City, where he built his artistic empire and developed his unique technique, which involves photographing, hand drawing, and stretching images by means of a copying machine.

Never one to shy away from commercial work, WK has collaborated with numerous brands, including Adidas, Nike, and BMW, leaving everything from cars to basketballs painted white and splattered with swirly black. He has also exhibited his work internationally; he is represented by the Jonathan LeVine Gallery in New York and Elms Lesters in London.

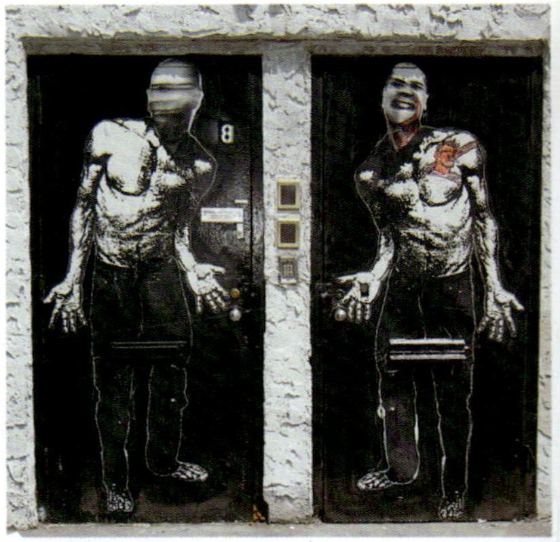

Photographs by Becki Fuller. New York City, 2007.